One Location, Endless Resources

Visit thinkcentral.com

Explore a whole new world of **online learning**. You will find all the components of *Elements of Literature* in one location, including instructional resources, tracked assessments, and tools for planning and instant communication.

Simple Navigation

- Find the right resources in four clicks or less
- View snapshots of
  - ✔ Your calendar
  - ✔ Assignments
  - ✔ Communication with parents and students
  - ✔ Student progress

Easy to use

- Intuitive structure for first-time users
- Advanced options, when and if you want them
- Adjustable features to make your space suit your needs

Use, extend, and customize

- Access pre-loaded course content, including the online textbook, assessments, remediation resources, and standard progress reports quickly and easily
- Add resources from your own files or create new ones
- Modify any resources at any time for your students

Differentiate and remediate

- Assign materials to classes, groups, or individuals for focused instruction
- Handle remediation automatically based on individual student performance
- View reports on student progress anywhere, anytime

HOLT

LITERATURE AND LANGUAGE ARTS

First Course

Kylene Beers
Carol Jago
Deborah Appleman
Leila Christenbury
Sara Kajder
Linda Rief

Senior Program Consultants for English-Language Development

Robin Scarcella
Mabel Rivera
Héctor Rivera

Mastering the California Standards
Reading, Writing, Listening, Speaking

HOLT, RINEHART AND WINSTON

Program Authors

Kylene Beers is the senior program author for *Elements of Literature*. A former middle school teacher, she is now Senior Reading Advisor to Secondary Schools for Teachers College Reading and Writing Project at Columbia University. She is the author of *When Kids Can't Read: What Teachers Can Do* and co-editor (with Linda Rief and Robert E. Probst) of *Adolescent Literacy: Turning Promise into Practice*. The former editor of the National Council of Teachers of English (NCTE) literacy journal *Voices from the Middle*, Dr. Beers assumed the NCTE presidency in 2008. With articles in *English Journal, Journal of Adolescent and Adult Literacy, School Library Journal, Middle Matters,* and *Voices from the Middle,* she speaks both nationally and internationally as a recognized authority on struggling readers. Dr. Beers has served on the review boards of *English Journal, The ALAN Review,* the Special Interest Group on Adolescent Literature of the International Reading Association, and the Assembly on Literature for Adolescents of the NCTE. She is the 2001 recipient of the Richard W. Halley Award given by NCTE for outstanding contributions to middle school literacy.

Carol Jago is a teacher with thirty-two years of experience at Santa Monica High School in California. The author of nine books on education, she continues to share her experiences as a writer and as a speaker at conferences and seminars across the country. Her wide and varied experience in standards assessment and secondary education in general has made her a sought-after speaker. As an author, Ms. Jago also works closely with Heinemann Publishers and with the National Council of Teachers of English. Her long-time association with NCTE led to her June 2007 election to a four-year term on the council's board. During that term she will serve for one year as president of the council. She is also active with the California Association of Teachers of English (CATE) and has edited CATE's scholarly journal *California English* since 1996. Ms. Jago served on the planning committees for the 2009 NAEP Reading Framework and the 2011 NAEP Writing Framework.

Deborah Appleman is professor and chair of educational studies and director of the Summer Writing Program at Carleton College in Northfield, Minnesota. Dr. Appleman's primary research interests include adolescent response to literature, multicultural literature, and the teaching of literary theory in high school. With a team of classroom teachers, she co-edited *Braided Lives,* a multicultural literature anthology. In addition to many articles and book chapters, she is the author of *Critical Encounters in High School English: Teaching Literary Theory to Adolescents* and co-author of *Teaching Literature to Adolescents*. Her most recent book, *Reading for Themselves,* explores the use of extracurricular book clubs to encourage adolescents to read for pleasure. Dr. Appleman was a high school English teacher, working in both urban and suburban schools. She is a frequent national speaker and consultant and continues to work weekly in high schools with students and teachers.

Leila Christenbury is a former high school English teacher and currently professor of English education at Virginia Commonwealth University, Richmond. The former editor of *English Journal,* she is the author of ten books, including *Writing on Demand, Making the Journey,* and *Retracing the Journey: Teaching and Learning in an American High School.* Past president of the National Council of Teachers of English, Dr. Christenbury is also a former member of the steering committee of the National Assessment

Authors and Reviewers

of Educational Progress (NAEP). A recipient of the Rewey Belle Inglis Award for Outstanding Woman in English Teaching, Dr. Christenbury is a frequent speaker on issues of English teaching and learning and has been interviewed and quoted on CNN and in the *New York Times, USA Today, Washington Post, Chicago Tribune,* and *US News & World Report.*

Sara Kajder, author of *Bringing the Outside In: Visual Ways to Engage Reluctant Readers* and *The Tech-Savvy English Classroom,* is an assistant professor at Virginia Polytechnic Institute and State University (Virginia Tech). She has served as co-chair of NCTE's Conference on English Education (CEE) Technology Commission and of the Society for Information Technology and Teacher Education (SITE) English Education Committee. Dr. Kajder is the recipient of the first SITE National Technology Leadership Fellowship in English Education; she is a former English and language arts teacher for high school and middle school.

Linda Rief has been a classroom teacher for twenty-five years. She is author of *The Writer's-Reader's Notebook, Inside the Writer's-Reader's Notebook, Seeking Diversity, 100 Quickwrites,* and *Vision and Voice* as well as the co-editor (with Kylene Beers and Robert E. Probst) of *Adolescent Literacy: Turning Promise into Practice.* Ms. Rief has written numerous chapters and journal articles, and she co-edited the first five years of *Voices from the Middle.* During the summer she teaches graduate courses at the University of New Hampshire and Northeastern University. She is a national and international consultant on adolescent literacy issues.

Program Consultants

Robin Scarcella is a professor at the University of California at Irvine, where she also directs the Program in Academic English/English as a Second Language. She has a Ph.D. in linguistics from the University of Southern California and an M.A. in education/second language acquisition from Stanford University. She has taught all grade levels. She has been active in shaping policies affecting language assessment, instruction, and teacher professional development. In the last four years, she has spoken to over ten thousand teachers and administrators. She has written over thirty scholarly articles that appear in such journals as the *TESOL Quarterly* and *Brain and Language.* Her most recent publication is *Accelerating Academic English: A Focus on the English Learner.*

Mabel Rivera is a research assistant professor at the Texas Institute for Measurement, Evaluation, and Statistics at the University of Houston. Her current research interests include the education of and prevention of reading difficulties in English-language learners. In addition, Dr. Rivera is involved in local and national service activities for preparing school personnel to teach students with special needs.

Héctor H. Rivera is an assistant professor at Southern Methodist University, School of Education and Human Development. Dr. Rivera is also the director of the SMU Professional Development/ESL Supplemental Certification Program for Math

PROGRAM CONSULTANTS continued

and Science Teachers of At-Risk Middle and High School LEP Newcomer Adolescents. This federally funded program develops, delivers, and evaluates professional development for educators who work with at-risk newcomer adolescent students. Dr. Rivera is also collaborating on school reform projects in Guatemala and with the Institute of Arctic Education in Greenland.

 Marilyn Astore is a former teacher, principal, and county office assistant superintendent with over 20 years of classroom experience and over 40 years in the field of education. In her role as chair of both the California Curriculum Commission and its Reading/Language Arts/English Language Development Subject Matter Committees, she worked with other commissioners to advise the California State Board of Education on the adoption of curricular and instructional materials. She has taught teacher education classes at California State University, Sacramento; the University of San Diego; and the University of California, Davis, University Extension. Ms. Astore presents and consults on K–12 reading issues and intervention for older struggling readers.

 Isabel L. Beck is professor of education and senior scientist at the University of Pittsburgh. Dr. Beck has conducted extensive research on vocabulary and comprehension and has published well over one hundred articles and several books, including *Improving Comprehension with Questioning the Author* (with Margaret McKeown) and *Bringing Words to Life: Robust Vocabulary Instruction* (with Margaret McKeown and Linda Kucan). Dr. Beck's numerous national awards include the Oscar S. Causey Award for outstanding research from the National Reading Conference and the William S.

Gray Award from the International Reading Association for lifetime contributions to the field of reading research and practice.

 Margaret G. McKeown is a senior scientist at the University of Pittsburgh's Learning Research and Development Center. Her research in reading comprehension and vocabulary has been published extensively in outlets for both research and practitioner audiences. Recognition of her work includes the International Reading Association's (IRA) Dissertation of the Year Award and a National Academy of Education Spencer Fellowship. Before her career in research, Dr. McKeown taught elementary school.

 Amy Benjamin is a veteran teacher, literacy coach, consultant, and researcher in secondary-level literacy instruction. She has been recognized for excellence in teaching from the New York State English Council, Union College, and Tufts University. Ms. Benjamin is the author of several books about reading comprehension, writing instruction, grammar, and differentiation. Her most recent book (with Tom Oliva) is *Engaging Grammar: Practical Advice for Real Classrooms,* published by the National Council of Teachers of English. Ms. Benjamin has had a long association and leadership role with the NCTE's Assembly for the Teaching of English Grammar (ATEG).

 Sandra Carsten has over thirty-seven years of experience as a teacher and administrator in the Fresno Unified School District. She has been a leader in curriculum, instruction, and professional development and has supervised national grants. As an assistant superintendent for curriculum

Authors and Reviewers

and instruction, she implemented standards-based programs, benchmark assessments, and protocols for monitoring student achievement. In addition, Ms. Carsten served for five years as the director of the Association of California School Administrators.

 Eric Cooper is the president of the National Urban Alliance for Effective Education (NUA) and co-founder of the Urban Partnership for Literacy with the IRA. He currently works with the NCTE to support improvements in urban education and collaborates with the Council of the Great City Schools. In line with his educational mission to support the improvement of education for urban and minority students, Dr. Cooper writes, lectures, and produces educational documentaries and talk shows to provide advocacy for children who live in disadvantaged circumstances.

 Harvey Daniels is a former college professor and classroom teacher, working in urban and suburban Chicago schools. Known for his pioneering work on student book clubs, Dr. Daniels is author and co-author of many books, including *Literature Circles: Voice and Choice in Book Clubs and Reading Groups* and *Best Practice: Today's Standards for Teaching and Learning in America's Schools.*

 Judith L. Irvin taught middle school for several years before entering her career as a university professor. She now teaches courses in curriculum and instructional leadership and literacy at Florida State University. Dr. Irvin's many publications include *Reading and the High School Student: Strategies to Enhance Literacy* and *Integrating Literacy and*

Learning in the Content Area Classroom. Her latest book, *Taking Action: A Leadership Model for Improving Adolescent Literacy,* is the result of a Carnegie-funded project and is published by the Association for Supervision and Curriculum Development.

 Patrick Schwarz is professor of special education and chair of the Diversity in Learning and Development department for National-Louis University, Chicago, Illinois. He is author of *From Disability to Possibility* and *You're Welcome* (co-written with Paula Kluth), texts that have inspired teachers worldwide to reconceptualize inclusion to help all children. Other books co-written with Paula Kluth include *Just Give Him the Whale* and *Inclusion Bootcamp.* Dr. Schwarz also presents and consults worldwide through Creative Culture Consulting.

 Marianne Steverson is currently president and COO of the educational services company known as Smar^{2}tel Learning Links. She has forty-two years of diversified experience in the public school sector and private educational therapy practice. She coordinates the company's in-school professional development for teachers of reading. She also manages the development of new products and methodologies. Her areas of specialization include teaching struggling readers who use African American vernacular English.

Critical Reviewers

Special Consultant
Deborah Keys
Research, Assessment and
    Accountability
Oakland Unified School District
Oakland, California

Laurel Byrd
Hemet USD Professional
    Development Academy
Hemet, California

Jeanne Davenport
Lincoln Middle School
Santa Monica, California

Charlyn Earp
Mesa Verde Middle School
San Diego, California

June Gatewood
Rio Americano High School
Sacramento, California

Gloria Hamilton
Crozier Middle School
Inglewood, California

Marilyn Hoffacker
Foothill Middle School
Walnut Creek, California

Diane Lang
Educational Options Center
Riverside, California

Mary Alice Madden
Lathrop Intermediate School
Santa Ana, California

Laura Smith
Vista Magnet Middle School
Vista, California

Erin Sullivan
University Heights Middle School
Riverside, California

Program Advisors

Joyce Black-Carson
Language Arts Department Chair
Montera Middle School
Oakland, California

Dr. Julie Chan
Director, Literacy Instruction
Newport Mesa Unified
    School District
Costa Mesa, California

Robert Chapman
English Teacher
Eureka High School
Eureka, California

Gabrielle D'Andrea
Instructional Coach
Samuel Jackman Middle School
Sacramento, California

Jeanne Davenport
English Teacher
Lincoln Middle School
Santa Monica, California

Charlyn Earp
Reading Teacher
Mesa Verde Middle School
San Diego, California

Teisha Hase
Reading Coordinator
Oroville High School
Chico, California

Greg Johnson
English Teacher
Liberty High School
Bakersfield, California

Terry Juhl
Principal Director
Twin Ridges Elementary
North San Juan, California

Diana Lester
English Language Development
    Reading Coordinator
Estancia High School
Costa Mesa, California

Joanne Mitchell
President
John Marshall High School
Los Angeles, California

Fern Sheldon
Curriculum Specialist
Rowland Unified School District
Rowland Heights, California

Laura Smith
Assistant Principal
Madison Middle School
Oceanside Vista, California

Robert Valdez
AVID Core 8 Teacher
Pioneer Middle School
Tustin, California

Marsha Zandi
Language Arts Curriculum
    Specialist
Sweetwater Union High School
Chula Vista, California

Authors and Reviewers

California Minimum Course of Study

 The Minimum Course of Study is designed for those teachers whose basic or advanced students can master the *California English-Language Arts Content Standards* without significant reteaching. The Minimum Course of Study covers what students should know and be able to do in each grade. It allows teachers to make efficient use of classroom time while ensuring student competency in mastering the standards.

CHAPTER	SELECTIONS	READING STANDARDS	WRITING, LISTENING, AND SPEAKING STANDARDS
CHAPTER 1 **Plot** **Writing Workshop:** Summary **Listening and Speaking Workshop:** Presenting a Summary	Rikki-tikki-tavi Empress Theodora The Hippodrome	**2.4** Clarify an understanding of texts by creating outlines, logical notes, summaries, or reports. **3.2** Identify events that advance the plot and determine how each event explains past or present action(s).	**Writing** **2.5** Write summaries of reading material. **Listening and Speaking** **2.2** Deliver oral summaries of articles and books.
CHAPTER 2 **Character** **Writing Workshop:** Autobiographical Narrative **Listening and Speaking Workshop:** Presenting an Autobiographical Narrative	The War of the Wall Flea Patrol The Black Death *from* World History: Medieval to Early Modern Times Stopping Plague in Its Tracks Signs	**2.1** Understand and analyze the differences in structure and purpose between various categories of informational materials (e.g., textbooks, newspapers, instructional manual's, signs). **3.3** Analyze characterization as delineated through a character's thoughts, words, speech patterns, and actions; the narrator's description; and the thoughts, words, and actions of other characters.	**Writing** **2.1** Write fictional or autobiographical narratives. **Listening and Speaking** **2.1** Deliver narrative presentations.
CHAPTER 3 **Theme** **Writing Workshop:** Response to Literature **Listening and Speaking Workshop:** Presenting a Response to Literature	User Friendly Annabel Lee Canines to the Rescue	**2.4** Identify and trace the development of an author's argument, point of view, or perspective in text. **3.4** Identify and analyze recurring themes across works (e.g., the value of bravery, loyalty, and friendship; the effects of loneliness).	**Writing** **2.2** Write responses to literature. **Listening and Speaking** **2.3** Deliver research presentations.
CHAPTER 4 **Point of View** **Writing Workshop:** Persuasive Essay **Listening and Speaking Workshop:** Presenting a Persuasive Speech	After Twenty Years Names/Nombres Tilting at Windmills: The Search for Alternative Energy Sources	**2.3** Analyze text that uses the cause-and-effect organizational pattern. **3.5** Contrast points of view (e.g., first and third person, limited and omniscient, subjective and objective) in narrative text and explain how they affect the overall theme of the work.	**Writing** **2.4** Write persuasive compositions. **Listening and Speaking** **2.4** Deliver persuasive presentations.

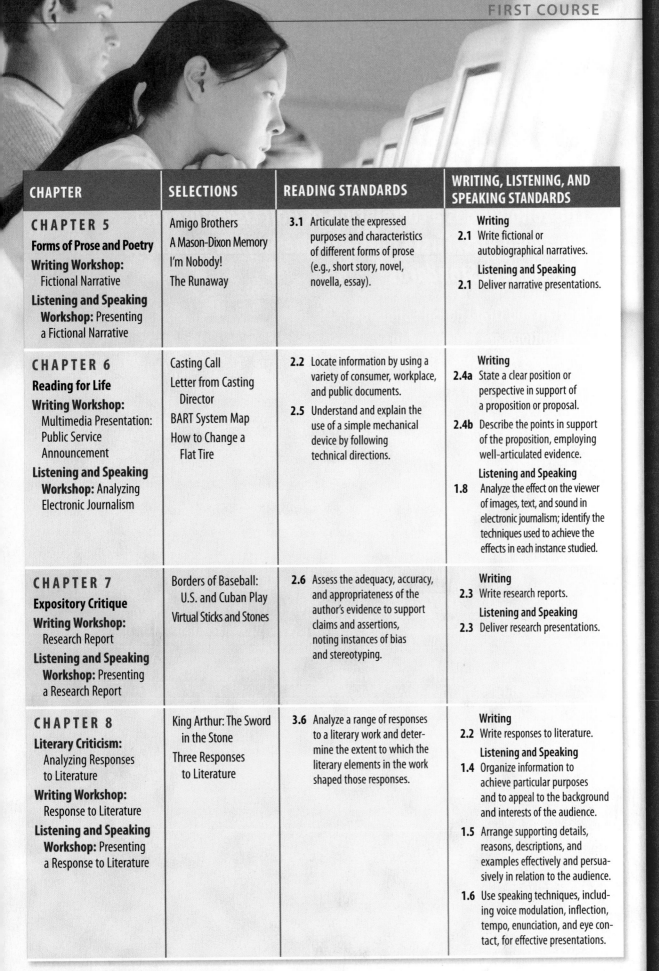

CHAPTER	SELECTIONS	READING STANDARDS	WRITING, LISTENING, AND SPEAKING STANDARDS
CHAPTER 5 **Forms of Prose and Poetry** **Writing Workshop:** Fictional Narrative **Listening and Speaking Workshop:** Presenting a Fictional Narrative	Amigo Brothers A Mason-Dixon Memory I'm Nobody! The Runaway	**3.1** Articulate the expressed purposes and characteristics of different forms of prose (e.g., short story, novel, novella, essay).	**Writing** **2.1** Write fictional or autobiographical narratives. **Listening and Speaking** **2.1** Deliver narrative presentations.
CHAPTER 6 **Reading for Life** **Writing Workshop:** Multimedia Presentation: Public Service Announcement **Listening and Speaking Workshop:** Analyzing Electronic Journalism	Casting Call Letter from Casting Director BART System Map How to Change a Flat Tire	**2.2** Locate information by using a variety of consumer, workplace, and public documents. **2.5** Understand and explain the use of a simple mechanical device by following technical directions.	**Writing** **2.4a** State a clear position or perspective in support of a proposition or proposal. **2.4b** Describe the points in support of the proposition, employing well-articulated evidence. **Listening and Speaking** **1.8** Analyze the effect on the viewer of images, text, and sound in electronic journalism; identify the techniques used to achieve the effects in each instance studied.
CHAPTER 7 **Expository Critique** **Writing Workshop:** Research Report **Listening and Speaking Workshop:** Presenting a Research Report	Borders of Baseball: U.S. and Cuban Play Virtual Sticks and Stones	**2.6** Assess the adequacy, accuracy, and appropriateness of the author's evidence to support claims and assertions, noting instances of bias and stereotyping.	**Writing** **2.3** Write research reports. **Listening and Speaking** **2.3** Deliver research presentations.
CHAPTER 8 **Literary Criticism:** Analyzing Responses to Literature **Writing Workshop:** Response to Literature **Listening and Speaking Workshop:** Presenting a Response to Literature	King Arthur: The Sword in the Stone Three Responses to Literature	**3.6** Analyze a range of responses to a literary work and determine the extent to which the literary elements in the work shaped those responses.	**Writing** **2.2** Write responses to literature. **Listening and Speaking** **1.4** Organize information to achieve particular purposes and to appeal to the background and interests of the audience. **1.5** Arrange supporting details, reasons, descriptions, and examples effectively and persuasively in relation to the audience. **1.6** Use speaking techniques, including voice modulation, inflection, tempo, enunciation, and eye contact, for effective presentations.

California Minimum Course of Study

California Standards Overview

The following is a correlation of *Holt Literature and Language Arts*, First Course, to the *English-Language Arts Content Standards*

Written and Oral English Language Conventions are addressed in *Warriner's Handbook*, First Course.

Holt print resource available

 Holt CD/DVD resource available

 Holt interactive resource available

REVIEW READING STANDARD

Standard	Page
2.4 Clarify an understanding of texts by creating outlines, logical notes, summaries, or reports.	105, 109, 110, 113, 129

READING

Standard	Page
1.1 Identify idioms, analogies, metaphors, and similes in prose and poetry.	263, 278, 305, 366, 387, 406
1.2 Use knowledge of Greek, Latin, and Anglo-Saxon roots and affixes to understand content-area vocabulary.	156, 168, 236, 785
1.3 Clarify word meanings through the use of definition, example, restatement, or contrast.	30, 48, 62, 88, 130, 418, 434, 444, 494, 642
2.1 Understand and analyze the differences in structure and purpose between various categories of informational materials (e.g., textbooks, newspapers, instructional manuals, signs).	201, 204, 205, 210, 211, 216, 217, 235
2.2 Locate information by using a variety of consumer, workplace, and public documents.	367, 649, 651, 655, 657, 663, 665, 669, 671, 677, 695
2.3 Analyze text that uses the cause-and-effect organizational pattern.	469, 473, 474, 477, 493, 751
2.4 Identify and trace the development of an author's argument, point of view, or perspective in text.	337, 343, 344, 347, 365
2.5 Understand and explain the use of a simple mechanical device by following technical directions.	679, 683

RETEACHING OPPORTUNITIES

 Teacher's Edition, Reteaching Lessons

 Universal Access: Holt Interactive Reader, interactive readings

Holt Interactive Reader for English Language Development, interactive adapted readings

Holt Interactive Reader Audio Tutor, audio support for adapted texts in English and Spanish

 Universal Access: Differentiating Instruction, instruction of struggling learners, English learners, and students with special needs; modified lesson plans; and leveled assessment

ThinkCentral Online Remediation, diagnostic tools and individualized tutorials

WordSharp: An Interactive Vocabulary Tutor, practice with academic language

PowerNotes, interactive lesson presentations with activities

Holt Multicultural Reader, interactive readings

Think Central, Student Access, online version of the Student Edition enhanced by audio and video

GrammarNotes, interactive lesson presentations with activities

WritingNotes, interactive lesson presentations with activities

Spelling Lessons and Activities (6–8)

Holt Interactive Spelling (6–8)

READING CONTINUED	
Standard	**Page**
2.6 Assess the adequacy, accuracy, and appropriateness of the author's evidence to support claims and assertions, noting instances of bias and stereotyping.	701, 703, 709, 711, 715, 717, 721, 723, 727, 728, 731, 732, 735, 749
3.1 Articulate the expressed purposes and characteristics of different forms of prose (e.g., short story, novel, novella, essay).	501, 503, 507, 509, 521, 523, 523, 533, 535, 537, 553, 555, 557, 565, 567, 613, 619, 622, 626, 627, 641
3.2 Identify events that advance the plot and determine how each event explains past or present action(s) or foreshadows future action(s).	5, 7, 11, 13, 29, 31, 33, 47, 49, 51, 61, 63, 65, 77, 87, 88, 91, 96, 102, 103, 127
3.3 Analyze characterization as delineated through a character's thoughts, words, speech patterns, and actions; the narrator's description; and the thoughts, words, and actions of other characters.	137, 139, 145, 147, 155, 157, 159, 167, 169, 171, 181, 183, 185, 191, 198, 199, 233
3.4 Identify and analyze recurring themes across works (e.g., the value of bravery, loyalty, and friendship; the effects of loneliness).	243, 245, 251, 253, 262, 263, 265, 277, 279, 281, 285, 287, 293, 295, 297, 304, 305, 307, 323, 334, 335, 363
3.5 Contrast points of view (e.g., first and third person, limited and omniscient, subjective and objective) in narrative text and explain how they affect the overall theme of the work.	373, 375, 379, 381, 387, 389, 391, 405, 407, 409, 417, 419, 421, 433, 435, 437, 443, 445, 447, 457, 463, 466, 467, 491
3.6 Analyze a range of responses to a literary work and determine the extent to which the literary elements in the work shaped those responses.	757, 759, 765, 767, 783, 785, 787, 793, 795, 807, 809, 811, 821, 823, 837

WRITING

Standard	Page
1.1 Create an organizational structure that balances all aspects of the composition and uses effective transitions between sentences to unify important ideas.	117, 223, 351, 479, 481, 687, 739, 827
1.2 Support all statements and claims with anecdotes, descriptions, facts and statistics, and specific examples.	350, 479, 480, 483, 685, 687, 737, 742, 826
1.3 Use strategies of note taking, outlining, and summarizing to impose structure on composition drafts.	115, 222, 350, 630, 687, 738
1.4 Identify topics, ask and evaluate questions, and develop ideas leading to inquiry, investigation, and research.	479, 685, 737
1.5 Give credit for both quoted and paraphrased information in a bibliography by using a consistent and sanctioned format and methodology for citations.	737, 739
1.6 Create documents by using word-processing skills and publishing programs; develop simple databases and spreadsheets to manage information and prepare reports.	635
1.7 Revise writing to improve organization and word choice after checking the logic of the ideas and the precision of the vocabulary.	118, 224, 352, 482, 629, 632, 685, 688, 740, 828

RETEACHING OPPORTUNITIES

Teacher's Edition, Reteaching Lessons

Universal Access: Holt Interactive Reader, interactive readings

Holt Interactive Reader for English Language Development, interactive adapted readings

Holt Interactive Reader Audio Tutor, audio support for adapted texts in English and Spanish

Universal Access: Differentiating Instruction, instruction of struggling learners, English learners, and students with special needs; modified lesson plans; and leveled assessment

ThinkCentral Online Remediation, diagnostic tools and individualized tutorials

WordSharp: An Interactive Vocabulary Tutor, practice with academic language

PowerNotes, interactive lesson presentations with activities

Holt Multicultural Reader, interactive readings

Think Central, Student Access, online version of the Student Edition enhanced by audio and video

GrammarNotes, interactive lesson presentations with activities

WritingNotes, interactive lesson presentations with activities

Spelling Lessons and Activities (6–8)

Holt Interactive Spelling (6–8)

California Standards Overview

WRITING CONTINUED	
Standard	**Page**

2.1 Write fictional or autobiographical narratives:
  a. Develop a standard plot line (having a beginning, conflict, rising action, climax, and denouement) and point of view.
  b. Develop complex major and minor characters and a definite setting.
  c. Use a range of appropriate strategies (e.g., dialogue, suspense, naming of specific narrative action, including movement, gestures, and expressions).
	221, 222, 223, 226, 229, 237, 629, 630, 631, 633, 637, 643

2.2 Write responses to literature:
  a. Develop interpretations exhibiting careful reading, understanding, and insight.
  b. Organize interpretations around several clear ideas, premises, or images from the literary work.
  c. Justify interpretations through sustained use of examples and textual evidence.
	349, 350, 351, 357, 367, 825, 826, 833, 839

2.3 Write research reports:
  a. Pose relevant and tightly drawn questions about the topic.
  b. Convey clear and accurate perspectives on the subject.
  c. Include evidence compiled through the formal research process (e.g., use of a card catalog, *Reader's Guide to Periodical Literature*, a computer catalog, magazines, newspapers, dictionaries).
  d. Document reference sources by means of footnotes and a bibliography.
	737, 738, 739, 742, 745, 751

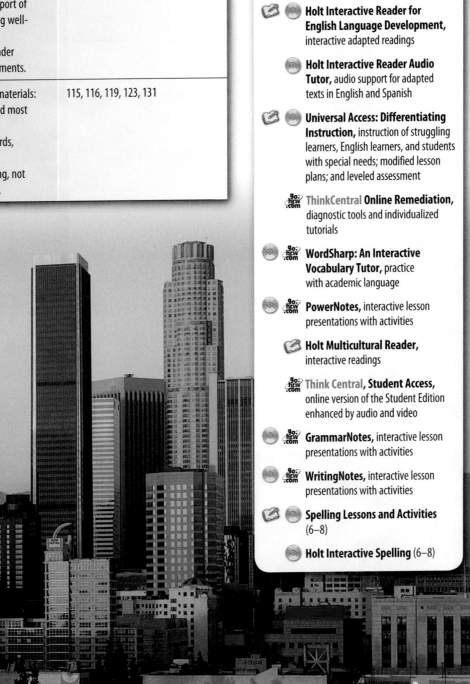

WRITING CONTINUED

Standard	Page

2.4 Write persuasive compositions:
  a. State a clear position or perspective in support of a proposition or proposal.
  b. Describe the points in support of the proposition, employing well-articulated evidence.
  c. Anticipate and address reader concerns and counterarguments.
	479, 480, 487, 495, 685, 689

2.5 Write summaries of reading materials:
  a. Include the main ideas and most significant details.
  b. Use the student's own words, except for quotations.
  c. Reflect underlying meaning, not just the superficial details.
	115, 116, 119, 123, 131

RETEACHING OPPORTUNITIES

- **Teacher's Edition,** Reteaching Lessons
- **Universal Access: Holt Interactive Reader,** interactive readings
- **Holt Interactive Reader for English Language Development,** interactive adapted readings
- **Holt Interactive Reader Audio Tutor,** audio support for adapted texts in English and Spanish
- **Universal Access: Differentiating Instruction,** instruction of struggling learners, English learners, and students with special needs; modified lesson plans; and leveled assessment
- ThinkCentral **Online Remediation,** diagnostic tools and individualized tutorials
- **WordSharp: An Interactive Vocabulary Tutor,** practice with academic language
- **PowerNotes,** interactive lesson presentations with activities
- **Holt Multicultural Reader,** interactive readings
- Think Central, **Student Access,** online version of the Student Edition enhanced by audio and video
- **GrammarNotes,** interactive lesson presentations with activities
- **WritingNotes,** interactive lesson presentations with activities
- **Spelling Lessons and Activities** (6–8)
- **Holt Interactive Spelling** (6–8)

California Standards Overview

Standards Overview continued

LISTENING AND SPEAKING	
Standard	**Page**
1.1 Ask probing questions to elicit information, including evidence to support the speaker's claims and conclusions.	489, 693
1.2 Determine the speaker's attitude toward the subject.	685, 693
1.3 Respond to persuasive messages with questions, challenges, or affirmations.	489
1.4 Organize information to achieve particular purposes and to appeal to the background and interests of the audience.	231, 359, 489, 746, 747, 834, 835
1.5 Arrange supporting details, reasons, descriptions, and examples effectively and persuasively in relation to the audience.	231, 359, 489, 747, 834, 835
1.6 Use speaking techniques, including voice modulation, inflection, tempo, enunciation, and eye contact, for effective presentations.	125, 231, 359, 489, 639, 747, 835
1.7 Provide constructive feedback to speakers concerning the coherence and logic of a speech's content and delivery and its overall impact upon the listener.	489
1.8 Analyze the effect on the viewer of images, text, and sound in electronic journalism; identify the techniques used to achieve the effects in each instance studied.	692, 693

LISTENING AND SPEAKING	
Standard	**Page**

2.1 Deliver narrative presentations:
  a. Establish a context, standard plot line (having a beginning, conflict, rising action, climax, and denouement), and point of view.
  b. Describe complex major and minor characters and a definite setting.
  c. Use a range of appropriate strategies, including dialogue, suspense, and naming of specific narrative action (e.g., movement, gestures, expressions).
	230, 231, 638, 639

2.2 Deliver oral summaries of articles and books:
  a. Include the main ideas of the event or article and the most significant details.
  b. Use the student's own words, except for material quoted from sources.
  c. Convey a comprehensive understanding of sources, not just superficial details.
	124, 125

2.3 Deliver research presentations:
  a. Pose relevant and concise questions about the topic.
  b. Convey clear and accurate perspectives on the subject.
  c. Include evidence generated through the formal research process (e.g., use of a card catalog, *Reader's Guide to Periodical Literature*, computer databases, magazines, newspapers, dictionaries).
  d. Cite reference sources appropriately.
	746, 747

2.4 Deliver persuasive presentations:
  a. State a clear position or perspective in support of an argument or proposal.
  b. Describe the points in support of the argument and employ well-articulated evidence.
	358, 359, 488, 489

RETEACHING OPPORTUNITIES

Teacher's Edition, Reteaching Lessons

Universal Access: Holt Interactive Reader, interactive readings

Holt Interactive Reader for English Language Development, interactive adapted readings

Holt Interactive Reader Audio Tutor, audio support for adapted texts in English and Spanish

Universal Access: Differentiating Instruction, instruction of struggling learners, English learners, and students with special needs; modified lesson plans; and leveled assessment

ThinkCentral Online Remediation, diagnostic tools and individualized tutorials

WordSharp: An Interactive Vocabulary Tutor, practice with academic language

PowerNotes, interactive lesson presentations with activities

Holt Multicultural Reader, interactive readings

Think Central, Student Access, online version of the Student Edition enhanced by audio and video

GrammarNotes, interactive lesson presentations with activities

WritingNotes, interactive lesson presentations with activities

Spelling Lessons and Activities (6–8)

Holt Interactive Spelling (6–8)

California Standards Overview

HOLT

LITERATURE AND LANGUAGE ARTS

Your Road Map *to* **Mastering** *the* California Standards

Holt Literature and Language Arts offers a clear instructional road map for all students, with *on ramps* for strategic, benchmark, and advanced students.

Holt Literature and Language Arts ©2003 was the first English-Language Arts program built exclusively to align with the *Reading-Language Arts Framework for California Public Schools*. Since that time, the achievement of California students using *Holt Literature and Language Arts* ©2003 has been steadily improving. The new *Holt Literature and Language Arts* ©2010 renews its commitment to California students and teachers, with increased emphasis on vocabulary, reading, and writing and a deeper focus on the instructional needs of English learners, students with disabilities, struggling readers, and students who use African American vernacular English. Together, we will continue to work toward mastery of the California Standards for all students.

Organization

Chapters are organized around rigorous content standards, with ample opportunities for practice so that all students can meet or exceed performance standards. There is a focus on helping students make connections between reading and writing and mastering complex standards. Each chapter offers systematic instruction in literary and reading skills and provides a color-coded model to further student understanding of the concepts.

CHAPTER 2

Character

INFORMATIONAL TEXT FOCUS
Structure and Purpose of Informational Materials

California Standards
Here are the Grade 7 standards you will work toward mastering in Chapter 2.

Word Analysis, Fluency, and Systematic Vocabulary Development
1.2 Use knowledge of Greek, Latin, and Anglo-Saxon roots and affixes to understand content-area vocabulary.

Reading Comprehension (Focus on Informational Materials)
2.1 Understand and analyze the differences in structure and purpose between various categories of informational materials (e.g., textbooks, newspapers, instructional manuals, signs).

Literary Response and Analysis
3.3 Analyze characterization as delineated through a character's thoughts, words, speech patterns, and actions; the narrator's description; and the thoughts, words, and actions of other characters.

Writing Applications (Genres and Their Characteristics)
2.1 Write fictional or autobiographical narratives:
a. Develop a standard plot line (having a beginning, conflict, rising action, climax, and denouement) and point of view.
b. Develop complex major and minor characters and a definite setting.
c. Use a range of appropriate strategies (e.g., dialogue; suspense; naming of specific narrative action, including movement, gestures, and expressions).

"Be who you are and say what you feel, because those who matter don't mind and those who mind don't matter."
—**Dr. Seuss (Theodor Seuss Geisel)**

What Do You Think How do other people help you discover something within yourself?

Actors portraying characters from the movie *X-Men: The Last Stand.*

Learn It Online
To understand the role of characterization in novels, visit *NovelWise* at:
go.hrw.com H7-135 Go

134 Chapter 2

Character **135**

LITERARY RESPONSE AND ANALYSIS
Literary Skills Focus
by Linda

What Is Characterization?

Very often, the characters in stories are what keep us reading. We groan when characters make poor choices and cheer when they do the right thing. We love some characters—and love to hate others. We sit on the shoulders of characters and wonder what *we* might do in the situations they face.

Character Traits and Characterization

Character Traits "Patient," "Loyal Friend," "Sneaky." It would be much easier to tell what people were like if everyone wore a T-shirt proclaiming his or her personal qualities. In real life, though, you have to pay attention to various clues in order to figure out a person's **character traits.** The same is true in stories: You gradually discover a character's traits as you read. The process of revealing a character's traits in a story is called **characterization.** Writers use two methods to **delineate,** or carefully describe, their characters.

Direct Characterization Sometimes a writer tells you directly what a character is like: "Luther was the meanest man in town." A statement like this is known as **direct characterization.**

Indirect Characterization Most of the time, writers want you to discover fictional characters just as you learn about people in real life—by observing them and deciding for yourself what they are like. You ask, What do they look like? How do they act? What do they say? How do they say it? How do other people feel about them? When

Elements of Charac

1. **Appearance** Thin immediately from detail about a char

The Russian looke shoes I was wearin that went from m my thigh.

from by D

2. **Actions** The w mad! However, actions reveals

And every time fool question, another spoon was tapping h dangerous wa

Reading Skills Focus
by Kylene

How Do I Analyze Characterization?

Your friend asks, "What's wrong?" and you reply, "Nothing." Your friend *knows* that something is wrong, though. He listened to your answer but also paid attention to your facial expression, connected that to his own experiences, and made an inference—an educated guess. You make inferences as you read by making connections between what the author writes and your own experiences. Making connections helps you read for deeper meaning.

Making Inferences About Characters

To make inferences as you read, use clues in the text and your own knowledge and experiences to make an educated guess. Making inferences about characters will help you analyze what kind of people they are based on how they act, what they say, and how other characters respond to them. You might also make an inference about how a character will resolve a conflict or about what motivates, or causes, a character to behave in a certain way.

Tips for Making Inferences As you read stories in this chapter, look for details that help you make inferences about the characters. To collect evidence, answer questions like these:

- What do I know about the character's appearance, thoughts, words, and actions?
- How do other characters react to the character?
- What does the character learn by the end of the story?

It Says / I Say / And So

You can use an It Says / I Say / And S you make inferences about characte direct characterization by stating the narrator and how boys reacted to girls.

It Says		
Writer's Clues	My Experiences	
Teresa looked at Victor and "smiled sweetly."	Someone who smiles at you usually likes you.	

Remember that an inference is a conc makes sense. You need evidence to sup inferences. That evidence comes from t clues and your own experiences.

Keep in mind that sometimes writer clues that may lead you to draw incorrect sions. That's what makes a story interesting exciting. As you read, keep watching for a then, finding points of connection.

SKILLS IN ACTION **SHORT STORY**
Reading Model

Read with a Purpose Read "Girls" to learn what the narrator, a thirteen-year-old boy, survive the experience of a girl he likes. (This story is told by a first-person narrator wh

Girls

from How Angel Peterson Got His Na by **Gary Paulsen**

Literary Focus
Characterization The writer begins revealing what the characters are like. Here Paulsen uses direct characterization by stating the narrator and other boys reacted to girls.

Reading Focus
Connecting to the Text The boy in this story is close to your age. As you read, relate his thoughts and feelings to your own, finding points of connection.

G irls.
When we were eleven and ever
That is, we could be friends and do pre school and some boys could even talk to t
Not me. I never could. And neither co seemed to have worked out a way to pret there and Wayne swore that it didn't both to girls.
And then we became thirteen.
Everything changed.
Well, not everything. I still couldn't v mortal terror of them, and Orvis was th talked about them all the time, how the f smiled, how they sounded, how they m about us, how Elaine was really cute b and Eileen seemed one day to actually at me. But we couldn't speak to them.
Except that now it became very in speak to them. Before, it didn't seem somehow the only thing that *did* mat

140 Chapter 2

SKILLS IN ACTION
Wrap Up

Reading Standard 3.3 Analyze characterization as delineated through a character's thoughts, words, speech patterns, and actions; the narrator's description, and the thoughts, words, and actions of other characters.

Into Action: Making Inferences
Practice making inferences and analyzing characters. Re-read the end of "Girls." Then, use the chart to make an inference about the narrator's overall impression of his time with Eileen.

It Says	I Say	And So …
Writer's Clues	My Experiences	Inference

Talk About …

1. How realistic is this story? With a partner, evaluate the credibility, or believability, of the characters, especially the narrator. Use story details in your response. Try to use each Academic Vocabulary word listed on the right at least once in your discussion.

Write About …
Answer the following questions about "Girls." For definitions of the underlined Academic Vocabulary words, see the column on the right.

2. What attributes of Eileen's can you infer from her behavior?

3. Identify story details that characterize the narrator's nervousness around girls.

Writing Skills Focus
Think as a Reader/Writer
Paulsen uses description to convey the narrator's appearance and behavior. Imagine a young narrator, male or female, who is confident and friendly when going to the movies on a first date. Write a description that conveys the way this character looks and acts. In this chapter you'll have other opportunities to use the skills, or craft, writers use.

Academic Vocabulary for Chapter 2

Talking and Writing About Character and Characterization

Academic Vocabulary is the language you use to write and talk about literature. Use these words to discuss the stories you read in this chapter. The words are underlined throughout the chapter.

attribute (AT rih byoot) n.: quality or trait of someone or something. *The narrator's most obvious attribute is his awkwardness around girls.*

delineate (dih LIHN ee ayt) v.: describe in detail; portray. *Writers use several means to delineate characters in their stories: the narrator's description; a character's thoughts, words, speech patterns, and actions; and the thoughts, words, and actions of other characters.*

identify (y DEHN tuh fy) v.: recognize and be able to say what someone or something is. *If you identify a character's motivation, you often gain insights into that character's behavior.*

respond (rih SPAHND) v.: say or write something as a reply or answer. *Respond critically to the author's use of indirect characterization.*

Your Turn
Create a chart like this one to list the attributes of key characters in each selection in this chapter.

Selection	Character	Attributes
"Girls"	narrator	shy

Planning Instruction

You need tools that will help you plan for all of the diverse learners in your classroom. **Resources** must be at your fingertips and foster universal access for students. In *Holt Literature and Language Arts*, each chapter begins with a quick overview that identifies the skills that are introduced, applied, and assessed within the chapter. Sections highlighted in yellow offer a suggested minimum course of study to ensure coverage of all standards.

For more customized instruction, additional support and resources are suggested for strategic, benchmark, and advanced students.

Introducing the Skills
identifies the literary, reading, and critical-thinking skills taught in the chapter.

Mastering the Skills provides opportunities for students to demonstrate skills mastery through activities, workshops, reviews, and assessments.

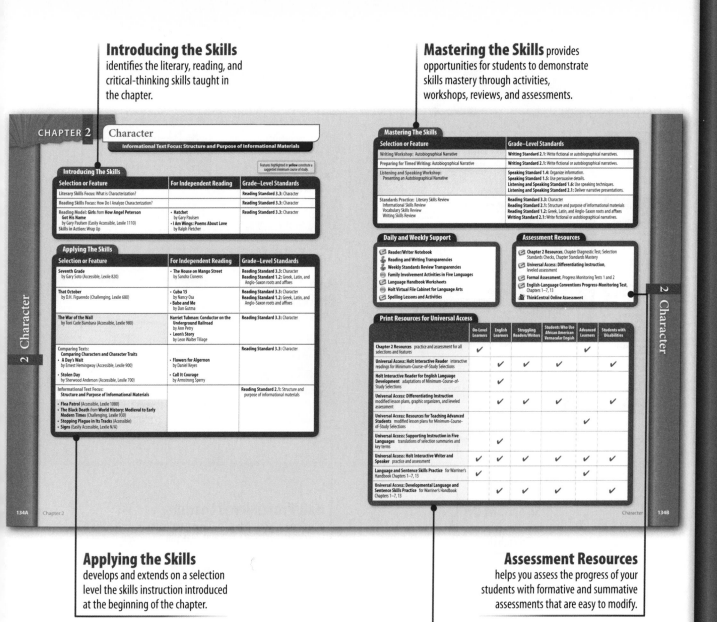

Applying the Skills
develops and extends on a selection level the skills instruction introduced at the beginning of the chapter.

Assessment Resources
helps you assess the progress of your students with formative and summative assessments that are easy to modify.

Print Resources for Universal Access
help you support learning of your diverse learners whether they are struggling readers, English learners, or advanced students.

Planning Instruction

Technology Resources highlights the many digital tools that are available to support you and your students, from research to remediation.

Real Issues, Real Experts introduces authors and consultants such as Kylene Beers, Carol Jago, Isabel Beck, and Robin Scarcella, as well as master teachers who share practical suggestions for meeting the needs of your students.

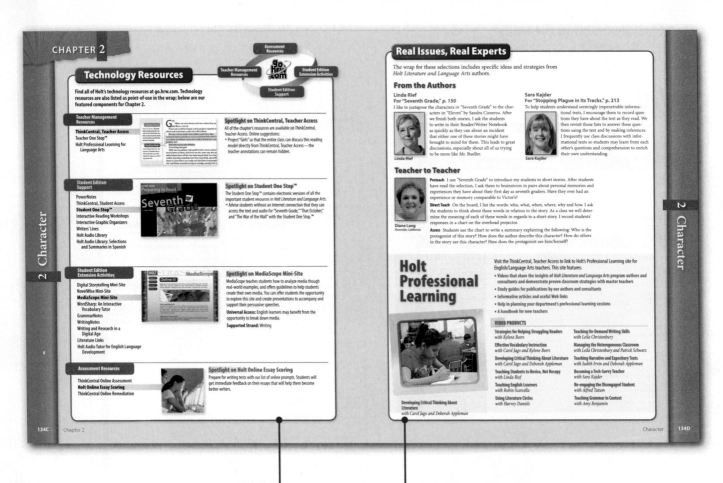

Spotlight On
details key resources
for each chapter.

Holt Professional Learning
offers you opportunities to develop further as a teacher and gives you help with the challenges you face. An online bank of videos and a new-teacher handbook allow you to customize your professional training.

Planning Instruction

A concentrated skills focus helps students master the English-Language Arts content standards while bold visuals and motivating themes engage them. The annotated **Teacher's Edition** makes planning instruction and using supporting resources easier.

California Standards

Word Analysis, Fluency, and Systematic Vocabulary Development

■ **1.2** Use knowledge of Greek, Latin, and Anglo-Saxon roots and affixes to understand content-area vocabulary.

Reading Comprehension (Focus on Informational Materials)

■ **2.1** Understand and analyze the differences in structure and purpose between various categories of informational materials (e.g. textbooks, instructional manuals, signs).

California Standards Overview highlights the standards that will be taught in the chapter.

CHAPTER 2

California Standards
Word Analysis, Fluency, and Systematic Vocabulary Development
■ 1.2 Use knowledge of Greek, Latin, and Anglo-Saxon roots and affixes to understand content-area vocabulary.

Reading Comprehension (Focus on Informational Materials)
■ 2.1 Understand and analyze the differences in structure and purpose between various categories of informational materials (e.g. textbooks, newspapers, instructional manuals, signs).

Literary Response and Analysis
■ 3.3 Analyze characterization as delineated through a character's thoughts, words, speech patterns, and actions; the narrator's description; and the thoughts, words, and actions of other characters.

Writing Applications (Genres and Their Characteristics)
■ 2.1 Write fictional or autobiographical narratives:
a. Develop a standard plot line (having a beginning, conflict, rising action, climax, and denouement) and point of view.
b. Develop complex major and minor characters and a definite setting.
c. Use a range of appropriate strategies (e.g. dialogue; suspense; naming of specific narrative action, including movement, gestures, and expressions).

Analyzing Visuals
Explain to students that the people in this image are characters from the film *X-Men: The Last Stand.* Each of the characters has a superpower that makes him or her unique.

Extension Activity Have students use details from the image to describe the traits that each of these characters might possess. **Possible response:** *Many of the characters have serious or cunning expressions, and they seem very determined. The man in the top left corner has long claws and an expression that makes him look threatening, while the woman in the bottom left looks friendly and less threatening.*

CHAPTER 2

Character

INFORMATIONAL TEXT FOCUS
Structure and Purpose of Informational Materials

California Standards
Here are the Grade 7 standards you will work toward mastering in Chapter 2.

Word Analysis, Fluency, and Systematic Vocabulary Development
1.2 Use knowledge of Greek, Latin, and Anglo-Saxon roots and affixes to understand content-area vocabulary.

Reading Comprehension (Focus on Informational Materials)
2.1 Understand and analyze the differences in structure and purpose between various categories of informational materials (e.g., textbooks, newspapers, instructional manuals, signs).

Literary Response and Analysis
3.3 Analyze characterization as delineated through a character's thoughts, words, speech patterns, and actions; the narrator's description; and the thoughts, words, and actions of other characters.

Writing Applications (Genres and Their Characteristics)
2.1 Write fictional or autobiographical narratives:
a. Develop a standard plot line (having a beginning, conflict, rising action, climax, and denouement) and point of view.
b. Develop complex major and minor characters and a definite setting.
c. Use a range of appropriate strategies (e.g., dialogue; suspense; naming of specific narrative action, including movement, gestures, and expressions).

"Be who you are and say what you feel, because those who matter don't mind and those who mind don't matter."
—Dr. Seuss (Theodor Seuss Geisel)

What Do You Think
How do other people help you discover something within yourself?

Actors portraying characters from the movie *X-Men: The Last Stand.*

Learn It Online
To understand the role of characterization in novels, visit NovelWise at:
go.hrw.com [H7-135] [Go]

Chapter Objectives

■ Students will learn how a writer delineates a character through traits, and how characterization affects plot.

■ Students will also learn how to make inferences while reading, and they will practice making personal connections to a variety of texts.

■ In the Informational Text Focus, students will learn about the structure and purpose of informational materials.

■ At the end of the chapter, students will write an essay supporting a position and present a persuasive speech.

Routines for California Classrooms

For ideas on classroom practices and approaches to grouping, see the discussion of routines on pages T34–T37 of this Teacher's Edition.

What Do You Think?

How do other people help you discover something within yourself?

Read the quotation aloud. Then, ask students to think about how others can help lead them to undiscovered parts of themselves. Ask them to describe times when others have made them feel free to "be who [they] are and say what [they] feel."

Learn It Online
For a multimedia version of the instruction found on this page, use the **PowerNotes** Literary Focus presentation.
go.hrw.com [H7-135] [Go]

Chapter Resources

On Course: Mapping Instruction
Chapter 2 Resources
Warriner's Handbook
• Chapter 3, Parts of Speech Overview
• Chapter 4, Complements
PowerNotes
Teacher One Stop™
Formal Assessment, Progress Monitoring Test 1 and 2

English-Language Conventions Progress-Monitoring Tests
Holt Virtual File Cabinet for Language Arts, grammar, reading, and vocabulary resources
Holt Pronunciation Resources
• Phoneme Sounds and Spellings
• Support for Speakers of African American Vernacular English
ThinkCentral Online Assessment
ThinkCentral Online Remediation

Real Issues, Real Experts: Professional Learning

Spotlight on . . .
Critical Responses to Literature
Works such as "The War of the Wall" and "Seventh Grade" provide students with the opportunity to exercise their critical thinking skills as they respond to the stories' use of characterization and other literary features. To help you access students' responses, consider the suggestions you'll find in this video:

Developing Critical Thinking About Literature, featuring Holt authors Carol

Jago and Deborah Appleman, discusses four methods for eliciting student responses to literature.

The video is accompanied by printable articles, planning materials, and a training guide for supervisors. For these resources and more, visit **Holt Professional Learning for Language Arts** by going to this page in **ThinkCentral, Teacher Access.**

Chapter Resources

helps you quickly find the resources to teach all of your students.

Program Highlights

Building Literacy

Student success requires systematic instruction in vocabulary, reading comprehension, literary response and analysis, and writing. Each chapter and selection develops strong instructional strands in the areas of vocabulary, literature, reading of literature and informational text, and writing.

In **Literary Skills Focus**, new terms are defined and modeled using selected passages from the text. All students need instruction in reading comprehension skills. **Reading Skills Focus**, an instructive essay in student-friendly language by Dr. Kylene Beers, helps you reach struggling and reluctant readers. Graphic organizers make concepts visually clear.

Universal Access offers resources and instructional strategies for all students.

The **Lesson Cycle** clearly delineated in the side wrap of the Teacher's Edition outlines explicit instructions and includes these steps: Preteach, Direct Teach, Check for Understanding, Assess, and Reteach.

Direct Teach provides helpful hints on how to reach your students with demonstrated techniques such as modeling.

Check for Understanding gives your students a quick opportunity for independent practice and you an opportunity for informal assessment.

Support for Reading and Academic Vocabulary

Reading Model provides color-coded highlighting of new literary and reading focus skills in a model text. Side annotations model the skills for students and serve as a built-in tutor.

Wrap Up check students' understanding and provides practice with the concepts introduced on the **Literary Skills Focus** and **Reading Skills Focus** pages of each chapter. **Academic vocabulary** gives students the terms, definitions, and practice with the vocabulary they need to write and talk about literature.

Color-coded highlights
models strategies and skills.

Academic Vocabulary
helps students build their own high-use lexicon of words that cross academic disciplines and are required for academic success.

The **Reading Model** concludes with a Writing Skills Focus to reinforce the reading-writing connection.

Program Highlights

Preparing to Read

Each selection follows a clear instructional pattern to optimize skill development and student comprehension. While the visuals and **What Do You Think?** questions are designed to motivate students, the **Literary**, **Reading**, and **Writing Skills Focus** and **Vocabulary** reinforce the skills introduced at the beginning of the chapter. **Language Coach** gives additional help to those English learners or users of African American vernacular English who may need additional support.

Reader/Writer Notebook
provides students a place to record their thoughts and notes about each selection. This notebook stresses the interdependence of reading and writing.

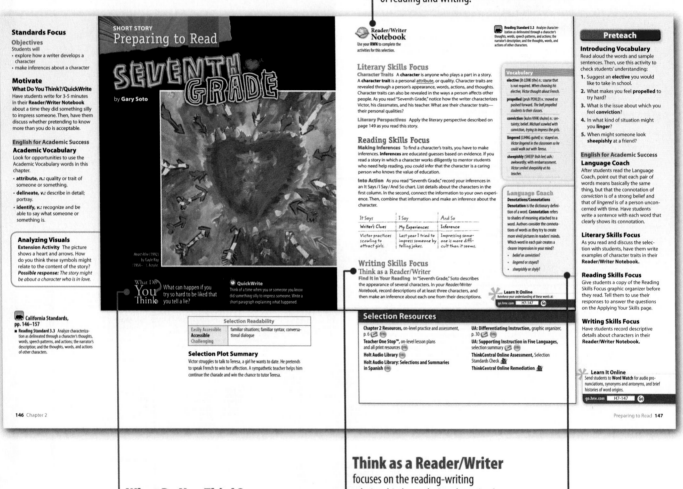

What Do You Think?
provides critical motivation by helping students connect and apply the selection to their lives.

Think as a Reader/Writer
focuses on the reading-writing relationship by exploring the writer's craft in a text and having students apply the technique to their own writing.

Language Coach points out the structure, patterns, and connections of English to assist English learners and users of African American vernacular English, while also reviewing fundamentals for proficient speakers.

Reading the Selection

Students are given the kind of preparation they need to be successful in reading the selection. They first **Meet the Writer** as a person to whom they can relate. **Build Background** provides information needed to understand the selection, while **Preview the Selection** helps set the context of the selection.

Build Background

offers important information about the author, historical context, or cultural influences that pertain to the selection.

Read with a Purpose

helps students make their reading focused and purposeful.

Selection Introduction

More About the Writer
In his youth, **Gary Soto** was not ambitious; in fact, he graduated from high school with a surprisingly low grade point average. After high school, however, he discovered the power of literature. During his second year at Fresno City College, Soto began to come into his own as a writer.

Think About the Writer
Before students answer the question, have them read the Build Background note. Then, ask them to consider how a personal experience can affect what an author writes. Have them discuss how they might use their own experiences in their writing if they were authors.

For Independent Reading
If students want to explore other stories of growing up, particularly in a Mexican-American household, suggest they read *The House on Mango Street** by Sandra Cisneros. This story details the experiences of Esperanza, a young girl growing up in a troubled Hispanic neighborhood in Chicago.

*This title is available in the HRW library.

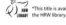
Learn It Online
Writers' Lives offers more information on the life of the author as well as Holt's interactive resources pertaining to the author.
go.hrw.com H7-148 Go

148 Chapter 2

MEET THE WRITER

Learn It Online
Learn more about Soto's life at:
go.hrw.com H7-148 Go

Gary Soto
(1952–   )

"A Name Among *la Gente*"
Gary Soto grew up in a Mexican American family in California, and much of his award-winning fiction and poetry draws on his heritage and his childhood memories. Although his work is vastly popular today, Soto remembers that early on he worked hard to make connections with his readers.

"Unlike most other contemporary poets and writers, I've taken the show on the road and built a name among *la gente*, the people. I have ventured into schools, where I have played baseball and basketball with young people, sung songs, acted in skits, delivered commencement speeches, learned three chords on a Mexican guitar to serenade teachers. . . . From all appearances, my readers care."

Think About the Writer
Why do you think being in touch with his audience is important to Gary Soto?

Universal Access

EL English Learners

English for Academic Success Some students have difficulty understanding certain phrases, particularly idioms. List several difficult phrases from the text and work through each one to make meaning. Some examples include "socked each other in the arm," "watched her on the sly," and "catch her eye."

✔ See the English Language Skill Builder **UA: Differentiating Instruction** for lesson plans and strategies for teaching English learners.

Struggling Readers

Strategic Students Students may have trouble making inferences about character traits Have them work with a partner to identify two details from p. 149. For example, they might note that Victor says it is cool in France, unlike in Fresno. Guide them in a discussion of character traits each detail might suggest; for example, help them infer that Victor dislikes hot weather.

✔ See **UA: Differentiating Instruction** for a graphic organizer to scaffold instruction for teaching struggling readers.

Build Background
Like Victor, the main character in "Seventh Grade," Gary Soto grew up in Fresno, a city in California's San Joaquin Valley with a large Mexican American community. Farmers in this valley grow more than two hundred different types of crops. The valley is one of the nation's leading producers of grapes and raisins.

Preview the Selection
On his first day in the seventh grade, **Victor** tries to impress his classmate **Teresa** by pretending to be someone he isn't.

Read with a Purpose Read this story to see how Victor survives his first day of seventh grade.

SEVENTH GRADE
by **Gary Soto**

On the first day of school, Victor stood in line half an hour before he came to a wobbly card table. He was handed a packet of papers and a computer card on which he listed his one elective, French. He already spoke Spanish and English, but he thought some day he might travel to France, where it was cool; not like Fresno,[1] where summer days reached 110 degrees in the shade. There were rivers in France, and huge churches, and fair-skinned people everywhere, the way there were brown people all around Victor.

Besides, Teresa, a girl he had liked since they were in catechism classes[2] at Saint Theresa's, was taking French, too. With any luck this would be in the same class. Teresa is going to be my girl this year, he promised himself as he left the gym full of students in their new fall clothes. She was cute. And good in math, too, Victor thought as he walked down the hall to his homeroom. He

ran into his friend, Michael Torres, by the water fountain that never turned off.
They shook hands, *raza*-style, and jerked their heads at one another in a *saludo de vato*.[3] "How come you're making a face?" asked Victor.

"I ain't making a face, *ese*. This *is* my face." Michael said his face had changed during the summer. He had read a *GQ* magazine that his older brother had

3. *saludo de vato* (sah LOO doh day BAH toh): Spanish for "homeboy greeting."

1. **Fresno:** town in the San Joaquin Valley, in central California.
2. **catechism** (KAT uh kihz uhm) **classes:** instruction in religious principles.

Ⓐ Read and Discuss What have you learned so far?
Ⓑ Read and Discuss What have you learned about Victor's desire to study French?

Vocabulary elective (ih LEHK tihv) n.: course that is not required.

Literary Perspectives

The following perspective will help you analyze the characters in "Seventh Grade."

Analyzing Credibility When you read a story about everyday people interacting in normal settings, think about whether the characters are **credible**, or believable. Do the characters ring true in the ways they behave? As you read "Seventh Grade," analyze the story—especially its characters—for credibility. Questions in the text will guide you in using this perspective.

Literary Perspectives

Before students read the selection, have them read the **Literary Perspectives** about Analyzing Credibility. Then, ask students to give examples of how a credible, or believable, character might behave in a particular situation. For example, how might a character act who is separated from his or her family in an airport?

Remind students to use the notes and questions at the bottom of the page to help them use the perspective.

Direct Teach

Think About/Talk About
Read with a Purpose Have students read the Read with a Purpose statement. Ask students to discuss what challenges Victor may face on his first day of seventh grade and how he may overcome them.

▶ **Comprehension**

Ⓐ **Read and Discuss**
Possible response: It's the first day of school and a boy named Victor is signing up for French because he thinks he'd like to travel to France someday since it's different from Fresno, California, where he lives.

Ⓑ **Read and Discuss**
Possible response: A girl he's liked since catechism class also is taking French and he's hoping they'll be in the same class.

▶ **Extend the Discussion**
Character Traits What do Victor and Michael's dialogue and actions reveal about them? *Possible response:* They both speak English and Spanish; the way they greet each other reflects their Mexican-American heritage.

Vocabulary: Own the Word
elective: Remind students that an *elective* is not required but chosen. Just as in an *election* (another noun form of the word), you choose your candidate and the candidate is *elected* (past tense verb form). Ask students to name some *electives* they can choose at school.

Seventh Grade 149

Read and Discuss introduces
comprehension questions that you may ask students at critical points in the selection.

Program Highlights

Instructional Support

As you move through a lesson, annotations, such as **Model the Skill**, **Guided Practice: Apply**, and **Comprehension** and **Analysis**, support students by outlining explicit instruction. You will also find additional instructional support for advanced learners, students with disabilities, and students who use African American vernacular English.

Model the Skill

■ Review the concept of **character traits**. Explain that you have a friend who is always late or can never find her car keys. Ask students what character trait would describe your friend's actions and appearance. *[Absent-mindedness]*

■ Tell students that we can also identify traits of characters in a story by observing their words or actions, and by reading their thoughts. Read aloud the second paragraph in the first column, beginning with "He lowered his eyes...." Tell students Victor may be afraid of failing.

■ Then, read aloud the paragraph in which the teacher asks if anyone knows French. Tell students Victor is willing to lie in order to impress a girl. Perhaps he is afraid of failing with the girl, just as he's afraid of failing in math.

Guided Practice: Apply

Have students read to the end of p. 152. Ask them to identify orally Victor's words, actions, and thoughts and identify the character traits these words, actions, and thoughts demonstrate. Record the traits on the board.

Think as a Reader/Writer

Find It in Your Reading Read aloud the paragraph that begins "Great rosebushes...." Point out that the author is describing Victor's physical reaction to being caught pretending to know French. This reaction demonstrates that Victor is easily embarrassed.

Use It in Your Writing Tell students to write two descriptive sentences about a character or person they know that indicates something the subject's personality.

The small, triangle-shaped campus bustled with students talking about their new classes. Everyone was in a sunny mood. Victor hurried to the bag lunch area, where he sat down and opened his math book. He moved his lips as if he were reading, but his mind was somewhere else. He raised his eyes slowly and looked around. No Teresa.

He lowered his eyes, pretending to study, then looked slowly to the left. No Teresa. He turned a page in the book and stared at some math problems that scared him because he knew he would have to do them eventually. He looked to the right. Still no sign of her. He stretched out lazily in an attempt to disguise his snooping.

Then he saw her. She was sitting with a girlfriend under a plum tree. Victor moved to a table near her and daydreamed about taking her to a movie. When the bell sounded, Teresa looked up, and their eyes met. She smiled sweetly and gathered her books. Her next class was French, same as Victor's.

They were among the last students to arrive in class, so all the good desks in the back had already been taken. Victor was forced to sit near the front, a few desks away from Teresa, while Mr. Bueller wrote French words on the chalkboard. The bell rang, and Mr. Bueller wiped his hands, turned to the class, and said, *"Bonjour."*[5]

"Bonjour," braved a few students.

---

5. **bonjour** (bohn ZHOOR): French for "hello" or "good day."

⊙ Literary Focus Character Traits What does the description "smiled sweetly" tell you about Teresa?

"Bonjour," Victor whispered. He wondered if Teresa heard him.

Mr. Bueller said that if the students studied hard, at the end of the year they could go to France and be understood by the populace.

One kid raised his hand and asked, "What's 'populace'?"

"The people, the people of France."

Mr. Bueller asked if anyone knew French. Victor raised his hand, wanting to impress Teresa. The teacher beamed and said, *"Très bien. Parlez-vous français?"*[6]

Victor didn't know what to say. The teacher wet his lips and asked something else in French. The room grew silent. Victor felt all eyes staring at him. He tried to bluff his way out by making noises that sounded French.

"La me vave me con le grandma," he said uncertainly.

Mr. Bueller, wrinkling his face in curiosity, asked him to speak up.

Great rosebushes of red bloomed on Victor's cheeks. A river of nervous sweat ran down his palms. He felt awful. Teresa sat a few desks away, no doubt thinking he was a fool. Without looking at Mr. Bueller, Victor mumbled, "Frenchie oh wewe gee in September."

Mr. Bueller asked Victor to repeat what he said. "Frenchie oh wewe gee in September," Victor repeated.

---

6. **Très bien. Parlez-vous français** (tray bee EHN PAHR lay voo frahn SAY): French for "Very good. Do you speak French?"

⊙ Literary Perspectives Analyzing Credibility How believable is Victor's declaration that he knows how to speak French?

⊙ Read and Discuss How is French class going for Victor?

Los Angeles (2006) by José Ramirez.
Mixed media on canvas.
©Courtesy of the artist.

Analyzing Visuals **Connecting to the Text** What does this image suggest about the story and its main characters?

Think About/Talk About

See Student Edition p. 152 for the questions that relate to the following answers.

▶ **Comprehension**

⊙ Read and Discuss

Possible response: The teacher asked the class if anyone could speak French and Victor raised his hand to impress Teresa. His plan backfired when the teacher asked him to actually speak French.

▶ **Analysis**

⊙ Literary Focus

Possible response: Teresa's smile reveals that she is a kind person; it may also reveal that she likes Victor.

⊙ Literary Perspectives

Possible response: Victor's declaration is not believable because he is desperate to impress Teresa.

▶ **Extend the Discussion**

Character Traits Why do you think Victor tries to bluff by speaking gibberish rather than admitting that he can't speak French? *Possible response:* It is important to him not to look silly in front of Teresa.

Analyzing Visuals

José Ramirez uses art to address contemporary issues facing everyone from Chicanos of his native Los Angeles to young black women.

Connecting to the Text: The image suggests the characters live in a neighborhood on the outskirts of Los Angeles. The figures in the image sit side by side, looking at the city in the distance, perhaps imagining their futures. This suggests the characters, close friends, are introspective and ambitious.

Literary Perspectives

Point out to students that the author has used familiar English words such as "grandma," "Frenchie," and "in September" in Victor's "French" to add humor to the story as well as to help the reader decide if Victor's effort at speaking French is credible.

Universal Access

⊙ English Learners

English for Academic Success Point out the lines "La me vave me con le grandma," and "Frenchie oh wee gee in September" on this page. Clarify that Victor is not speaking French (which is italicized–*Bonjour*) but is simply making up phrases and words that he thinks sound French. In both examples, he ends with a word he knows in English: "grandma" and "September." He is trying to impress Teresa and ends up looking foolish in front of her and the teacher.

⊙ Students Who Use African American Vernacular English

English for Academic Success Some students may have difficulty with the *'s* that indicates singular possessives, such as *Victor's friend*. They may omit the pronunciation of the *'s* in speaking and not use it in writing. Write this sentence on the board: "_____ scowl seems strange to Victor." Ask students how the sentence should begin. Then, ask a volunteer to read the sentence aloud. Have students look for another example of *'s* in the story and practice reading the sentence aloud to a partner.

Literary Perspectives
helps you show students how to approach texts from different angles.

Universal Access
suggests ways to reach all students.

Applying Your Skills

Applying Your Skills completes the learning cycle for each selection. The skills introduced at the beginning of the chapter conclude in a variety of activities that allow you to **Check for Understanding** and give the student an opportunity for **Independent Practice**.

Independent Practice gives students an opportunity to demonstrate the skills they have acquired..

Reading Skills Focus and **Literary Skills Focus** apply key skills practiced in the selection.

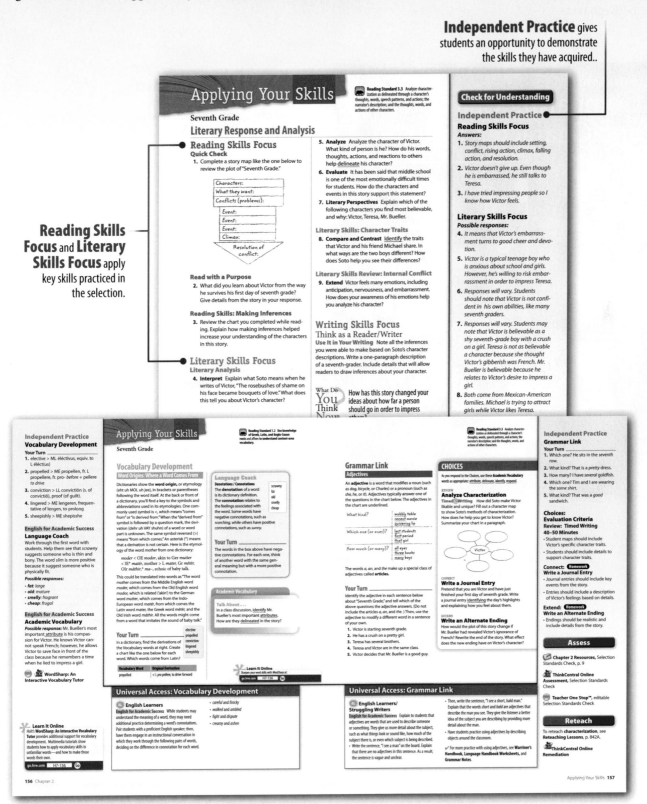

Program Highlights

Comparing Texts

Comparing Texts offers students the opportunity to identify recurring themes across works, analyze the characteristics of different forms of prose, and compare and contrast points of view. Students deepen their understanding of literature and writing by exploring connections between texts.

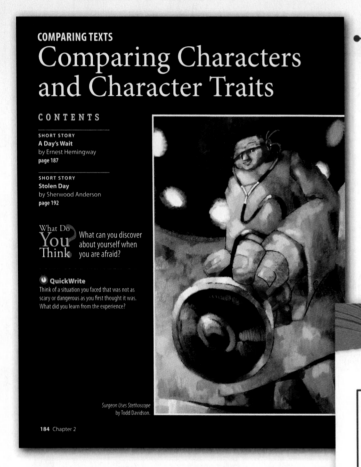

COMPARING TEXTS

Comparing Characters and Character Traits

CONTENTS

SHORT STORY
A Day's Wait
by Ernest Hemingway
page 187

SHORT STORY
Stolen Day
by Sherwood Anderson
page 192

What Do **You** Think — What can you discover about yourself when you are afraid?

QuickWrite
Think of a situation you faced that was not as scary or dangerous as you first thought it was. What did you learn from the experience?

Surgeon Uses Stethoscope
by Todd Davidson.

184 Chapter 2

Comparing Texts continues all the features of the single selections including Literary Skills Focus, Reading Skills Focus, Writing Skills Focus, Vocabulary study, and Language Coach.

Literary Skills Focus and **Reading Skills Focus** stress the similarities and differences among selections.

Preparing to Read

Reading Standard 3.3 Analyze characterization as delineated through a character's thoughts, words, speech patterns and actions; the narrator's description; and the thoughts, words, and actions of other characters.

A Day's Wait / Stolen Day

Literary Skills Focus

Characters and Character Traits How do you get to know the people you meet? They don't carry around signs saying "I am kind" or "I am a mean bully." You have to figure out for yourself what people are like. How do you do it? You notice their appearance. You pay attention to what they do and say. You listen to what others say about them. These clues help you make inferences about their **character traits.**

You do the same things to get to know the characters in a story. What characters say, do, and think; how they are described; what other characters think about them—these are the ways that characters are <u>delineated</u> by writers.

Reading Skills Focus

Comparing and Contrasting Characters The main characters in "A Day's Wait" and "Stolen Day" are both young boys who think they are sick but who behave in different ways. Clues in the text help you understand the boys' character traits. Are they brave or fearful, mean or kind?

Into Action As you read, fill in a chart like this one for each boy. List the story details that suggest each boy's character traits.

Actions	
Words	
Thoughts /Feelings	
Effects on Others	

Writing Skills Focus

Think as a Reader/Writer
Find It in Your Reading As you read "A Day's Wait," note three places where the writer could have revealed a character's thoughts. As you read "Stolen Day," record the narrator's thoughts, and think about what they add to your understanding of him.

Reader/Writer Notebook
Use your **RWN** to complete the activities for these selections.

Vocabulary

A Day's Wait

detached (dih TACHT) *adj.*: not involved emotionally; indifferent. *His reaction to his son's illness was surprisingly detached.*

commenced (kuh MEHNST) *v.*: began. *He did not pay attention when his father commenced reading.*

slack (slak) *adj.*: loose. *Schatz had only a slack hold on his emotions.*

Stolen Day

solemn (SAHL uhm) *adj.*: gloomy; serious. *He wore a solemn expression while explaining that he was sick.*

wriggled (RIHG uhld) *v.*: wiggled; squirmed. *The fish wriggled in his arms as he brought it home.*

Language Coach

Pronouncing mn When you say the word *solemn*, the *n* is silent. This is true of any word that ends in *mn*. When the letters *mn* are in the middle of a word, you hear the sounds of both letters (think of the word *chimney*). With a partner, pronounce the following words: *hymn, remnant, amnesia, condemn.*

Learn It Online
Dig deeper into vocabulary. Use Word Watch to increase your understanding of words at:
go.hrw.com   H7-185 [Go]

Preparing to Read **185**

Informational Focus

The skills used for comprehending informational texts are often different from the ones used for literary texts. A wide variety of expository materials focus on specific reading skills to help students understand the categories of **informational materials** and to assess an author's purpose.

INFORMATIONAL TEXT FOCUS

Structure and Purpose of Informational Materials

CONTENTS

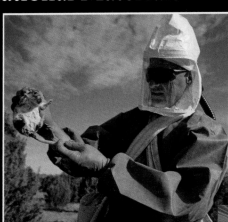

What Do
**You
Think**
How can being well-informed improve—sometimes even save—your life?

🖉 **QuickWrite**
Gaining life skills is part of becoming an independent adult. Why is having knowledge of life's various risks and dangers an important life skill?

200 Chapter 2

Informational Text Focus helps students better understand the categories, structures, and purposes particular to informational texts, such as newspapers, magazine or Web articles, workplace and public documents, and more.

NEWSPAPER ARTICLE
Preparing to Read

🐻 Reading Standard 2.1 Understand and analyze the differences in structure and purpose between various categories of informational materials (e.g., textbooks, newspapers, instructional manuals, signs).

Flea Patrol

Informational Text Focus

Structure and Purpose of a Newspaper Article The **purpose** of a newspaper article is to provide factual information about current events. A good informational article in a newspaper provides detailed answers to the questions *who? what? when? where? why?* and *how?*

Many newspaper articles are structured in what is called an **inverted pyramid** style. (*Inverted* means "upside-down.") The article begins with a **summary lead**, a sentence or paragraph that gives the **main idea** of the story—usually the most important idea or detail in the article. The lead is followed by the less important details of the article. Some articles begin with a lead that grabs your interest in a topic. This type of lead does not summarize but instead describes an interesting situation or fact related to the story. Here are some additional elements in the **structure** of a newspaper article. You will find examples of these elements in "Flea Patrol."

- **Headline:** the catchy, boldface words that tell you the subject of the article
- **Subhead:** the words in smaller type under the headline that add details about the article
- **Byline:** the name of the reporter who wrote the article
- **Dateline:** the location where and the date when the information was reported
- **Lead:** the sentence or paragraph that begins the news article
- **Tone:** the choice of words and point of view that meet the interests of the newspaper's audience. Tone often depends on the subject of the article. Some articles are light and humorous. Others are serious.

Summary lead, or most important information

Important details

Least important details

Vocabulary

transmitted (trans MIHT ihd) *v.:* caused to pass from one thing to another. *Fleas that fed on an infected rats transmitted the plague throughout Europe.*

application (ap luh KAY shuhn) *n.:* act of putting to use. *An application of insecticide kills fleas.*

rural (RUR uhl) *adj.:* of or relating to the countryside. *People living in rural areas are at greater risk of catching the plague.*

Language Coach

Word Roots Many English words have Latin roots and affixes. An **affix** is a word part that is added to a root. The Vocabulary word *transmitted* is made up of the Latin root *mis*, meaning "send," and the word part *trans–*, meaning "across." Identify three things that are transmitted.

Writing Skills Focus prepares students for informational writing.

Writing Skills Focus

Preparing for **Timed** **Writing** As you read this article, record the main idea and important details for use in writing a summary later.

🖊 **Reader/Writer
Notebook**
Use your **RWN** to complete the activities for this selection.

✳ **Learn It Online**
Check out the *PowerNotes* slideshow to get a lesson using words and pictures:
go.hrw.com H7-201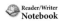

Preparing to Read 201

Program Highlights

Writing Workshop

The instructional strand **Think as a Reader/Writer** culminates in the **Writing Workshop**. Students develop strategies for organizing and focusing their writing. **Preparing for Timed Writing** introduces a writing prompt and strategies students can use to practice and complete a timed-writing assignment.

Scoring Rubric

You can use the rubric below to evaluate your autobiographical narrative from the Writing Workshop or your response to the prompt on the next page.

	Autobiographical Narrative	Organization and Focus	Sentence Structure	Conventions
4	• Is told from a consistent first-person point of view. • Focuses clearly on only one experience. • Clearly and thoughtfully expresses the meaning of the experience.	• Clearly addresses all parts of the writing task. • Demonstrates a clear understanding of purpose and audience. • Maintains a consistent point of view, focus, and organizational structure, including the effective use of transitions. • Includes a clearly presented central idea with relevant facts, details, and/or explanations.	• Includes a variety of sentence types.	• Contains few, if any, errors in the conventions of the English language (grammar, punctuation, capitalization, spelling). These errors do not interfere with the reader's understanding of the writing.
3	• Is told from a consistent first-person point of view. • Focuses mainly on one experience. • Clearly expresses the meaning of the experience.	• Addresses all parts of the writing task. • Demonstrates a general understanding of purpose and audience. • Maintains a mostly consistent point of view, focus, and organizational structure, including the effective use of some transitions. • Presents a central idea with mostly relevant facts, details, and/or explanations.	• Includes a variety of sentence types.	• Contains some errors in the conventions of the English language (grammar, punctuation, capitalization, spelling). These errors do not interfere with the reader's understanding of the writing.
2	• Is told mostly from a first-person point of view, with occasional shifts in point of view. • Focuses mostly on one experience, but contains some extraneous, unrelated information. • Makes only a vague reference to the meaning of the experience.	• Addresses only parts of the writing task. • Demonstrates little understanding of purpose and audience. • Maintains an inconsistent point of view, focus, and/or organizational structure, which may include ineffective or awkward transitions that do not unify important ideas. • Suggests a central idea with limited facts, details, and/or explanations.	• Includes little variety in sentence types.	• Contains several errors in the conventions of the English language (grammar, punctuation, capitalization, spelling). These errors may interfere with the reader's understanding of the writing.
1	• Is told from an inconsistent point of view, with confusing shifts in point of view throughout. • Includes information about several seemingly unrelated experiences. • Provides no insight into the meaning of the experience.	• Addresses only one part of the writing task. • Demonstrates no understanding of purpose and audience. • Lacks a point of view, focus, organizational structure, and transitions that unify important ideas. • Lacks a central idea but may contain marginally related facts, details, and/or explanations.	• Includes no sentence variety.	• Contains serious errors in the conventions of the English language (grammar, punctuation, capitalization, spelling). These errors interfere with the reader's understanding of the writing.

Rubrics set expectations for students and make assessment easier for teachers.

Autobiographical Narrative

Write with a Purpose

Write an autobiographical narrative about a significant experience in your life. Your **purpose** is to tell what happened and to explain to your readers why this experience is meaningful to you. Think about your **audience** as you write, and provide enough information so that they can understand your experience.

Think as a Reader/Writer In this chapter, you have been drawn to powerful themes by the techniques writers have used. Now it is time for you to draw readers into your point of view as you write an autobiographical narrative. Before you begin, take a few minutes to read this passage from Bill Cosby's autobiographical narrative "The Only Girl in the World for Me."

> The first time I saw her, she was crossing the street to the schoolyard and for one golden moment our eyes met. Well, maybe the moment was closer to bronze because she made no response. But at least she had seen me, just about the way that she saw lampposts, hydrants, and manholes. Or ma...

← Notice how the author establishes a definite setting for his first meeting with

---

Preparing for Timed Writing

Autobiographical Narrative

When you respond to an autobiographical narrative prompt, use the models you have read, what you have learned from writing your own autobiographical narrative, the rubric on page 228, and the steps below.

Writing Standard 2.1 Write fictional or **autobiographical narratives: a. Develop a standard plot line** (having a beginning, conflict, rising action, climax, and denouement) and **point of view. b. Develop complex major and minor characters and a definite setting. c. Use a range of appropriate strategies** (e.g., dialogue; suspense; naming of specific narrative action, including movement, gestures, and expressions).

Writing Prompt

Select an important experience in your life and write a narrative about it. Develop a standard plot line with a beginning, middle, and end. Your narrative should have a well-developed setting and characters, and you should use appropriate strategies, such as dialogue, descriptions of characters' actions, and suspense, to move the plot forward. Your narrative should maintain a consistent first-person point of view. The narrative should build to a climax and end with a reflection on why the experience is still meaningful to you.

Study the Prompt

Begin by reading the prompt carefully. Note what is required in your narrative: a standard plot line, a well-developed setting and characters, a consistent point of view, and a final reflection on the meaning of the experience.

Tip: Spend about five minutes studying the prompt.

Plan Your Response

Think of some personal experiences that are important to you. Which of these would you feel comfortable writing about? Once you have settled on your subject,

- write down who was involved, what happened, when it happened, where it happened, why it happened, how it happened, and why it is still meaningful to you
- think about y...

Respond to the Prompt

Using the notes you have just made, draft your narrative. Follow these guidelines:

- In the introduction, use interesting dialogue or a question, statement, or description to grab the reader's attention and set up the main conflict. Create a definite setting.
- In the body, relate events in the order that they occurred. Develop characters using a range of narrative strategies, such as dialogue and descriptions of expressions and gestures.
- In the conclusion, summarize your experience, emphasizing why it is still meaningful.

As you are writing, remember to use words that are best for your audience—not too informal. Write as neatly as you can. If your narrative cannot be read easily, it may not be scored. **Tip:** Spend about twenty minutes writing your draft.

Improve Your Response

Revising Go back over key aspects of the narrative. Did you develop a standard plot line and maintain a consistent point of view? Did you develop characters using appropriate strategies? Did you explain the event's importance to you?

Proofreading Take a few minutes to proofread your narrative to correct errors in grammar, spelling, punctuation, and capitalization. Make sure all your edits are neat, and erase any stray marks.

Checking Your Final Copy Read your narrative one more time to catch any errors you may have missed.

Tip: Save five to ten minutes to improve your paper.

Preparing for Timed Writing gives students practice responding to prompts.

Peer Review

Working with a peer, review your draft. Answer each question in this chart to locate where and how your drafts could be improved. As you discuss your papers, be sure to take notes about your partner's suggestions.

Evaluating and Revising

Read the questions in the left column of the chart, and then use the tips in the middle column to help you make revisions to your essay. The right column suggests techniques you can use to revise your draft.

Autobiographical Narrative: Guidelines for Content and Organization

Evaluation Question	Tip	Revision Technique
1. Does your introduction grab the reader's attention and set the scene? Does it suggest what the main conflict of the plot line will be?	**Underline** the attention-getting opener.	**Add** a memorable quotation, statement, or piece of dialogue to the introduction. **Add** specific details to make the setting more precise.
2. Is the point of view consistent throughout?	**Identify** pronouns (*I, he,* or *she*) that show point of view. **Label** the narrative's point of view, and **circle** any information not given from that point of view.	If any sentences are circled, **delete** them. If necessary, **add** the same information told from the narrator's point of view.
3. Does the narrative include essential background information?	**Put a star** next to details that make clear the context, or background, of the experience.	**Add** information that will help the reader understand the events in your narrative.
4. Are the events in sequential order? Have you developed a standard plot line with rising action, a climax, and a denouement?	**Number** the events in your paper. **Compare** the sequence with the actual order of events.	**Rearrange** any events that are out of order.
5. Do precise details and vocabulary help develop your characters and setting?	**Put check marks** next to specific, precise descriptions. In the margin, note to which senses the details appeal.	**Elaborate** with dialogue or sensory details. **Delete** any unrelated details. **Revise** with more precise vocabulary.
6. Have you described your thoughts and feelings to clarify...	**Put a check mark** under statements of your feelings or thoughts. Put an **excla-**	**Add** any other relevant important thoughts and feelings. **Add** a clear statement...

Evaluating and Revising, the most difficult aspects of writing for many students, are demonstrated by using real student papers.

Standards Review

Standards Review is the culminating activity of the chapter. **Literary**, **Informational**, **Writing**, and **Vocabulary Skills** are reviewed using new texts with a multiple-choice format and writing activities.

Skills are practiced with new reading selections to ensure that students can perform independently.

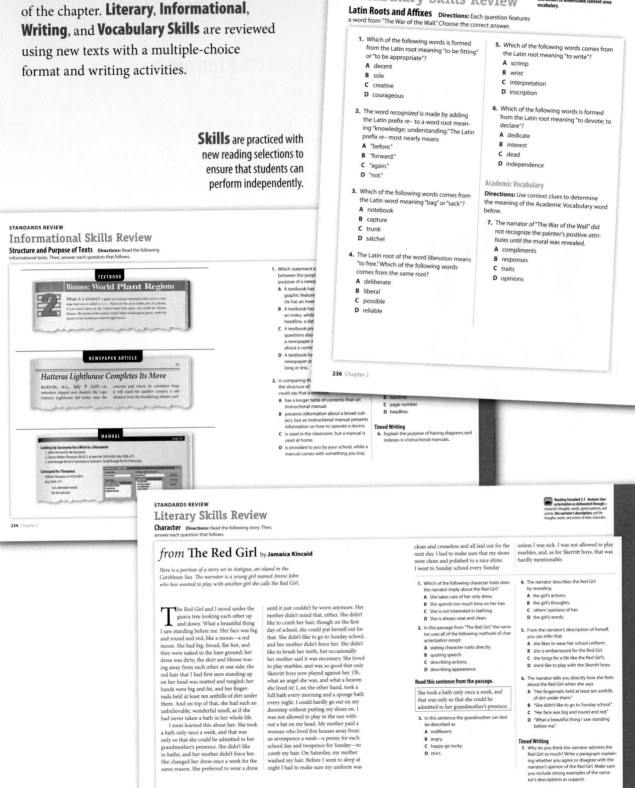

Program Highlights

Program Resources *for* California Classrooms

For the Student

Think Central, Student Access includes the online version of the Student Edition, enhanced by audio, video, hyperlinked vocabulary, and point-of-use links:

- MediaScope
- Digital Storytelling
- NovelWise
- Interactive Graphic Organizers

Student One Stop™ solves the backpack problem. The Student Edition, workbooks, and audio can be found on one CD-ROM.

Reader/Writer Notebook gives students a place to take notes on their reading, on vocabulary, and on writing ideas and assignments.

Lesson Planning

Teacher Edition

Think Central, Teacher Access

Teacher One Stop™ contains everything you need to plan and manage your lessons on one convenient CD-ROM, including

- *Holt OnCourse Planner*
- *ExamView® Assessment Suite*
- *Holt PuzzlePro®*
- *MindPoint® Quiz Show*
- Printable worksheets and more

Chapter Resources (Grades 6–8)

Unit Resources (Grades 9–12)

Holt Professional Learning for Language Arts offers you convenient, on-going support. Resources include

- Professional Learning Videos
- Instructional Strategies
- Training Guides
- Teacher Toolbox
- New Teacher Handbook

PowerNotes®: Instructional Presentations with Motivational Videos (CD-ROM)

GrammarNotes: Effective Grammar for Writing (CD-ROM)

WritingNotes: Process and Strategies for Effective Writing (CD-ROM)

Writing and Research in a Digital Age (CD-ROM)

Lesson Planning continued

Holt Virtual File Cabinet for Language Arts, Expanded Edition

OnCourse: Mapping Instruction provides a planning guide for using *Holt Literature and Language Arts* and *Warriner's Handbook* to ensure standards are covered.

Transition Pacing Guide is a planning calendar to help you move students from an intervention program to the basic program.

Implementation Guide for Administrators

Differentiating Instruction

Universal Access: Holt Interactive Reader

Universal Access: Holt Interactive Writer and Speaker

Universal Access: Differentiating Instruction
- Lesson Plans
- Vocabulary Practice
- Oral and Written Language Practice
- Graphic Organizers
- Leveled Progress and Summative Assessment

Universal Access: Resources for Teaching Advanced Students

Universal Access: Holt Leveled Library is a set of integrated texts and lessons designed to meet the needs of struggling, proficient, and advanced readers.

Universal Access: Supporting Instruction in Five Languages (Grades 6–8)

Universal Access: Supporting Instruction in Spanish (Grades 9–12)

Family Involvement Activities in Five Languages

Holt Pronunciation Resources

Assessment

ExamView Test Generator (on the Teacher One Stop™)

ThinkCentral Online Assessment helps you track progress with customizable reports and deliver effective intruction to all students.

ThinkCentral Online Remediation offers interactive tutorials that coach students towards mastery.

Holt Online Essay Scoring

Formal Assessment: Diagnostic, Progress Monitoring, and Summative Testing

Focus on Standards provides multiple practice opportunities in a consumable student workbook.

Preparing for the SAT and ACT (Grades 11–12)

Skill Building

Holt Six Traits for Writing

WordSharp: An Interactive Vocabulary Tutor
- Skills to Own Words walks students through the steps necessary to determine the meaning of unfamiliar words and provides scaffolded practice opportunities.
- Words You Can Use helps students internalize high-utility vocabulary, including academic language.

Vocabulary Development

Language Handbook Worksheets: Grammar, Usage, and Mechanics

Holt Interactive Spelling (Grades 6–8)

Spelling Lessons and Activities (Grades 6–8)

Program Resources continued

Media

Holt Audio Library provides professional readings of selections in the Student Edition.

Holt Audio Library: Selections and Summaries in Spanish

Analyzing Visuals Transparencies

Reading and Writing Transparencies include

- Proofreading Warm-ups
- Sentence Combining
- Vocabulary
- Critical Reading
- Graphic Organizers
- Daily Writing Instruction

Weekly Standards Review Transparencies provide daily/weekly standards practice.

Warriner's Handbook

Warriner's Handbook features John Warriner's unrivaled approach to grammar, usage, and mechanics to ensure mastery of language skills and conventions. Warriner developed the three-step instructional approach used in the grammar, usage, and mechanics chapter: teach students the rule, show examples of the rule, and provide immediate practice and review to reinforce the skill.

Student Edition

Teacher's Edition

Language and Sentence Skills Practice worksheets provide practice, reinforcement, and extension for *Warriner's Handbook*.

Universal Access: Developmental Language and Sentence Skills supplements *Language and Sentence Skills Practice* by providing additional instruction and practice to students who have not yet mastered key language skills.

ThinkCentral, Student Access offers convenient online access to the Student Edition.

ThinkCentral, Teacher Access provides instructional resources online.

English-Language Conventions Progress-Monitoring Tests

More Reading Choices

African American Literature

Latino Literature

Holt Multicultural Reader

Holt Leveled Library

HRW Library

Houghton Mifflin Harcourt Trade Holt, Rinehart and Winston has partnered with Houghton Mifflin Harcourt Trade to offer you additional reading options. Houghton Mifflin Harcourt Trade publishers provide high-quality, award-winning books for all ages. You will find the latest in current titles as well as beloved classics for your students and a professional library for you. For teaching materials see **www.harcourtbooks.com/ChildrenBooks/ teachertools.asp**

English Language Development (Grades 6–10)

This package provides one hour of daily instruction in addition to that found in the core Teacher's Edition. This instruction is connected to and consistent with the core instruction to foster student achievement in language arts. It features a balance of 1) systematic English-language instruction with strong emphasis on oral language and vocabulary development and 2) focus on language arts standards. The main goals of these materials are to build English proficiency, develop speaking and writing vocabulary for everyday and academic use, and accelerate students' transition to core curricular materials.

Newcomer Guide

- Four-week module
- Survival vocabulary and language (including obtaining necessities, making requests, and understanding instructions)
- Introduction to academic language study

Holt Interactive Reader for English Language Development (with Answer Key) Selections that form the Minimum Course of Study—with adapted text or adapted apparatus to provide additional scaffolding.

Teacher's Edition Daily lessons organized around the following strands: Build Background, Vocabulary Development, Literature and Language Study, Reading & Fluency, Writing Strategies and Applications, and Grammar and Conventions. The lessons are written to maximize student speaking and listening opportunities and to help teachers scaffold instruction for English learners.

Writing & Speaking Handbook Practice opportunities for grammar, speaking, and writing—from short writing assignments to process writing.

Holt Audio Tutor for English Language Development Audio recordings of the Minimum Course of Study selections together with side annotations; Spanish summaries and translations of annotations are also provided.

One location, endless educational resources

ThinkCentral brings *Holt Literature and Language Arts* to a whole new online environment designed to make teaching and learning both simple and powerful. When you log into ThinkCentral you not only find the *Holt Literature and Language Arts* program at your fingertips, but you also discover the management tools and resources that you would expect to find in an online learning management system—from tracked assessment to specialized instruction, from planning day-to-day activities to instant communication. Most important, it's all in one place. There is only one Web location you have to remember, thinkcentral.com, for everything you need to do.

- Browse and search program resources with ease.
- Choose from robust assessment and reporting tools to track student progress.
- Provide individualized remediation for students automatically.
- Save time with calendar-based lesson planning.
- Personalize the look and feel of your homepage.
- Communicate assignments, resources, due dates, and grades to students and parents—all in one place.

For more information, go to thinkcentral.com.

Program Authors

Kylene Beers

from **Kylene Beers,** Senior Reading Advisor
Teachers College Reading and Writing Project
Columbia University, New York, NY

Dear Educator:

Since 2003, *Holt Literature and Language Arts* has set the benchmark for a standards-designed, not just a standards-aligned, language arts program. The achievement of California students has been significant, but there is still work to be done. To help you with that task, we have brought together a remarkable author and consultant team—people with decades of classroom experience, research experience, and expertise in helping students and teachers in diverse classrooms. We believe that in teaching all students we must first teach each student and that each student offers a promise of a better tomorrow.

Through this program, our team shares with you its collective knowledge of what works with struggling readers, English learners, students with disabilities, and those who use African American vernacular English, as well as those sometimes-overlooked populations of basic and advanced students. We contributed our time to this project because we believe that what you do and what you say to students in your classroom makes an incredible difference. We want to help you make that difference with a road map to success.

Now, please let me introduce you to the other members of our team. We are all proud to be your colleagues.

Kylene Beers

MORE ABOUT READING INSTRUCTION...

Beers, K. 2002. *When Kids Can't Read/What Teachers Can Do.* Portsmouth, NH: Heinemann.

Beers, K., R. Probst, and L. Rief, eds. 2007. *Adolescent Literacy: Turning Promise into Practice.* Portsmouth, NH: Heinemann.

Alliance for Excellent Education. 2004. *Reading Next: A Vision for Action & Research in Middle and High School Literacy.* Literacy.

**For more from Kylene Beers...
go to** thinkcentral.com.

Carol Jago

The book you hold now is the result of a collaborative effort of authors, consultants, editors, and classroom teachers who, together, considered the issues in language arts instruction for the twenty-first century.

As you look through the pages, you'll see the influence of Carol Jago, who constantly returned us to the backbone of this series—great literature:

> **"** Words. Words. Words." That's all they are, yet when the words are Shakespeare's they have the power to transport readers. I want students to enjoy contemporary literature for all that it brings to their lives; but I also want them to read the classics so they can see the wine dark sea through Homer's eyes and to reflect on ways that human nature, for better and for worse, remains surprisingly constant through the ages. Great literature is a window to times and places we can never travel except on the page. With Emily Dickinson I believe that there really "is no frigate like a book to take us lands away. **"**

Carol Jago
Teacher, Santa Monica High School, California
Director, California Reading and Literature Project, UCLA
Author, Heinemann Publishers
Board Member, National Council of Teachers of English, Los Angeles, CA

PROGRAM AUTHORS:

Kylene Beers

Carol Jago

Deborah Appleman

Leila Christenbury

Sara Kajder

Linda Rief

Real Issues, Real Experts

MORE ABOUT TEACHING THE CLASSICS...

Jago, C. 2000. *With Rigor for All: Teaching the Classics to Contemporary Students.* Portsmouth: Heinemann.

Calvino, I. 1999. *Why Read the Classics?* New York: Pantheon.

For more from Carol Jago... go to thinkcentral.com.

Deborah Appleman

Deborah Appleman kept us focused on why studying literature is so important. Her vision of literature instruction helped guide the entire project:

> "*Reading literature is one of the few school subjects that is also recreation. How, then, should teachers approach literature in ways that encourage students to both love literature and to learn from it? Although literature remains a powerful site for self-exploration, it is also an opportunity to enter textual worlds far different from one's own experiences. Our job is to teach them the critical tools that help them read closely as well as to interpret broadly.*"

Deborah Appleman
Professor and Chair, Educational Studies
Carlton College, Northfield, MN

MORE ABOUT TEACHING LITERATURE...

Appleman, D. 2000. *Critical Encounters in High School English.* New York: Teachers College Press.

Scholes, R. 2001. *The Crafty Reader.* New Haven: Yale University Press

For more from Deborah Appleman... go to thinkcentral.com.

Leila Christenbury

You'll note teaching tips and powerful instructional strategies that were the direct result of Leila Christenbury's efforts. Leila reminded us that great literature without effective practice of informed teachers means little...

> "*Even though schools are large and busy places with hundreds of students and adults interacting every day, the fact is that most teachers work alone and often feel isolated. Reaching out to other teachers, reading professional literature and going to conferences, finding and using the many resources available can open up classrooms and connect teachers to a world of effective strategies and appropriate support. This connection is crucial; the practices of informed teachers make a critical difference in student achievement.*"

Leila Christenbury
Professor of English Education
Virginia Commonwealth University, Richmond, VA

MORE ABOUT GOOD TEACHING...

Christenbury, L. (2006). *Making the journey: Being and becoming a teacher of English language arts.* 3rd ed. Portsmouth, NH: Heinemann.

Website: read/write/think.org

Journals: *English Journal, Voices from the Middle*

For more from Leila Christenbury... go to thinkcentral.com.

Sara Kajder

The literacy demands of the 21st century are, of course, tied to a world that is increasingly more networked, more wired, more dependent on a wide range of technology. As Sara Kajder constantly pushed us to remember,

> *Equipping our students with 21st-century literacies means, in part, expanding the technology toolset students use as readers and writers. But that shouldn't surprise us because literacy has always been intimately tied to technology. We must teach them how to synthesize a range of texts that appear on a screen at lightning speed and communicate to authentic, global, wired audiences with the explosion of new tools, modes, and media now made readily accessible by Web 2.0.*

Sara Kajder
Assistant Professor
Virginia Polytechnic Institute and State University, Blacksburg, VA

MORE ABOUT TECHNOLOGY…

Kajder, S. 2003. *The Tech-Savvy English Classroom.* Portland, ME: Stenhouse

Alvermann, D. 2007. "Multiliterate Youth in the Time of Scientific Reading Instruction." In *Adolescent Literacy: Turning Promise into Practice* edited by K. Beers, R. Probst, and L. Rief. Portsmouth, NH: Heinemann, pp 19-26.

**For more from Sara Kajder…
go to thinkcentral.com.**

Linda Rief

As much as I'd push us toward reading, Linda Rief would push back showing us time and again that we want students who read as a writer and write as a reader. As Linda put it,

> *Writing, every bit as much as reading, helps our students become literate, articulate, and thoughtful citizens of the world. Reciprocal processes, both require capturing and working out meaning. When students are given opportunities to write about their reading—short, quick responses to questions—What did this reading bring to mind? What questions did it raise? How does this alter or confirm my view of the world?—our classrooms become laboratories of high-level thinking and our students become problem-solvers and producers of ideas. They move from just answering to questioning, just knowing to creating, just consuming to producing.*

Linda Rief
Instructor, University of New Hampshire
Summer Literacy Institute
Teacher, Oyster River Middle School, Durham, NH

MORE ABOUT WRITING…

Rief, L. 2003. *Quickwrites.* NY: Scholastic.

Alliance for Excellent Education. 2007. *Writing Next: Effective Strategies to Improve Writing of Adolescents in Middle and High Schools.*

**For more from Linda Rief…
go to thinkcentral.com.**

Real Issues, Real Experts

Program Consultants

Holt's program consultants come from richly varied areas of educational expertise to ensure that the program meets the disparate needs of your classroom—students who have comprehension problems or are learning English as a second language, who are visual learners, or who are disengaged. These specialists have done the research and provided the best practices to help you do the best for your students.

Comprehension

"Too many students do not leave a text with an understanding of an author's ideas. This shuts them out of rich opportunities to make contact with life lessons and human universals that literature offers, not to mention experience with the exquisite language that express such ideas."

Beck and McKeown developed an approach to comprehension called Questioning the Author that is the basis of the Read and Discuss questions in *Holt Literature and Language Arts*.

Isabel L. Beck
Professor, Department of Instruction and Learning
Senior Researcher, Learning Research and Development Center
University of Pittsburgh, PA

"Questioning the Author has been shown to be successful in supporting students to develop meaning from what they read and a coherent understanding of a text."

Students build comprehension as they read by using the sequenced questions built into *Holt Literature and Language Arts*.

Margaret McKeown
Senior Scientist, Learning Research and Development Center
University of Pittsburgh, PA

Adolescent Literacy

"For many students, the teacher is the individual most responsible for successful lives. Who can deny the power of a teacher who enables students to fall in love with learning? Academic success should be an opportunity for all, not just a gift to some."

Eric Cooper has reviewed both *Holt Literature and Language Arts* and *African American Literature*.

Eric Cooper
President for National Urban Alliance for Effective Education

For more from Real Issues, Real Experts . . . go to thinkcentral.com.

English Language Development/Academic Vocabulary

In many cities and school districts, students who are acquiring English are the fastest growing population. Acquiring academic language, the language that is used in schools, in testing, and in scholarly discourse, is the key to success for these students.

Academic Vocabulary is introduced at the beginning of each chapter and reinforced throughout it so that students can master it.

Robin Scarcella
Director, Program in Academic English/English as a Second Language
University of California, Irvine, CA

English Language Development

Many students enter our classrooms without the basic skills in English that they need to be successful. We want to support teachers in meeting the needs of those students and provide a program with a literary base that is accessible to those students.

English Language Development is a program that helps students who are acquiring English to get the critical skills they need.

Mabel Rivera
Research Assistant Professor, Texas Institute for Measurement,
Evaluation, and Statistics, University of Houston, TX

English Language Development

Teaching is assisting students' performance at the Zone of Proximal Development (Tharp & Gallimore, 1988). This requires an understanding of the means for assisting students during literacy activities that are socio-culturally meaningful. My research is focused on unfolding those socio-cultural components to be used as tools for effective teaching practices.

The English Language Development Program addresses the acquisition of critical English language skills.

Hector Rivera
Assistant Professor, School of Education and Human Development
Southern Methodist University, Dallas, TX

Real Issues, Real Experts

Language-Use Instruction

For years some educators have recognized the need to help African American vernacular English speakers gain proficiency in the use of standard English while still maintaining the undeniable "flavor and richness" of the language spoken at home.

Explicit language-use instruction is embedded throughout *Holt Literature and Language Arts* in lessons called Language Coach and Grammar Links. Notes in the Teacher's Edition extend support to meet the needs of all students.

Marianne Steverson
President and COO, Smar²tel Learning Links,
an educational services company

Differentiated Instruction

When you change the way you look at your students with disabilities, the way those students look to you will change. You will see the possibilities, and in that vision, you will see the power of the inclusion.

Meeting the needs of a wide range of abilities is at the core of *Holt Literature and Language Arts*, with scaffolded instruction for the student and suggestions in the Teacher's Edition for the instructor.

Patrick Schwarz
Professor, Diversity in Learning and Development Department
National Louis University, Chicago, IL

Literature Circles

Over the past decade, reading groups have just about doubled in the United States. For teachers trying to bring literature circles into our schools, these adult book clubs have been our implicit model—our prototype. Adult book clubs are voluntary groups of friends that create a powerful and caring community among us.

The Read On feature of *Holt Literature and Language Arts* and the *Holt Leveled Library* offer opportunities for bringing literature circles into the classroom.

Harvey Daniels
National-Louis University, Chicago, IL

For more from Real Issues, Real Experts . . . go to thinkcentral.com.

Grammar in Context

> *Along with diction and rhetoric, grammar is organic to the crafting of sentences and text. Writers with an awareness of grammar can make informed choices about how word order affects meaning. We can make our students better writers if we teach them to use grammatical knowledge.*

The Grammar Link feature in *Holt Literature and Language Arts* offers students contextual examples drawn from the literature to help them better craft their writing.

Amy Benjamin
President of the Assembly for the Teaching of English Grammar
Consultant for National Council of Teachers
Recipient of Excellence in Teaching Awards from Tufts University
and New York State English Council

Adolescent Literacy

> *Taking Action on Adolescent Literacy is the title of my recently published book. It incorporates my life's work. Motivating students to engage with meaningful reading and writing in content-area classes is the key to their achievement. Improved literacy and learning must be supported by a schoolwide effort to create a literacy-rich environment for students.*

See Judith Irving in the Professional Learning Video Reading Narrative and Expository Text.

Judith Irvin
Professor, Department of Educational Leadership and Policy
Florida State University, Tallahassee, FL

Real Issues, Real Experts

Professional Development Strategies That Work

Inspire yourself and your students with effective classroom teaching strategies

English-language arts teachers are responsible for bringing each lesson to life for their students while following the *Reading/Language Arts Framework for California Public Schools.* Holt has partnered with **Action Learning Systems** to provide professional development that includes engaging opportunities for students to establish and deepen reading comprehension skills, enhance vocabulary and concept development, and analyze the differences in text structure.

Sample Development Strategies from Action Learning Systems

Predicting with Evidence

Predicting requires students to hypothesize about what the author might discuss in the text. To hypothesize successfully, students must recall what they already know about the topic. They then read to confirm or disprove their hypotheses. This process helps students link the new information they will encounter in the reading with the information they already know. Predicting also helps students learn to use the structure of the written word. Predictions are made based on evidence from the text. Teachers model how to generate predictions based on evidence. Students need to be taught to make predictions with textual evidence.

Student Strategies for Predicting

- Access prior knowledge and experience.
- Compare what they already know with what they will learn.
- Pay close attention to whether the text is narrative or expository to see if their predictions are verified.

How to Teach It

PREPARATION

- Use a picture from the selection.

IN CLASS

- Ask, "What do you think this story is going to be about? What is your evidence?"
- Have students study the picture and write their predictions in the **Prediction** column and their evidence in the **Evidence** column.
- Ask students to share predictions and evidence with a partner. Have several share with the class.
- As students read the selection, they will continue to make predictions. Students will modify and confirm their predictions by citing textual evidence.

Budget Vocabulary

Budget Vocabulary is a strategy that provides continuous focus on vocabulary, especially for selections in which knowledge of vocabulary is critical for reading comprehension. The matrix can be used as a prereading activity for literary or expository text. The strategy leads to a deeper understanding of word meaning.

How to Teach It

- For the **Word** section, the teacher provides the words.
- The teacher can give the students the **Definition** or ask them to use their dictionary skills to obtain the formal definition of the word.
- For the **Related Words** section, students will use synonyms, antonyms, or words that are related by content or word structure.
- For the **Sentence** section, the teacher will specify that the sentences should be copied from the selection in which the word is introduced or used. The **Sentence** section can be used as an opportunity for students to create their own sentences to show an understanding of the word's meaning.
- The teacher will have students complete the **Visual** section and create an illustration to show their understanding of the word.

Action *Learning* Systems, Inc.

Action Learning Systems helps schools and districts focus on—and meet—their ultimate goal of increasing student achievement by offering research-based teaching strategies, training and coaching, and intervention programs. Action Learning Systems and Holt, Rinehart and Winston are working in partnership to provide exceptional professional development services to California schools.

You may download blackline masters of these instructional strategies at **www.actionlearningsystems.com**. Just click "Resources."

Writing Instruction in *Holt Literature and Language Arts*

Preparing Your Students for Writing Success

More than ever before, today's students need to know how to write for varied contexts and purposes: for success in academic settings, for personal expression, for interpersonal communication, for emerging digital environments, and for communication in the workplace. In *Holt Literature and Language Arts,* you will find consistent and accessible writing instruction that makes success in writing possible:

- Writing Workshops that follow a writing-process approach to developing standards-based forms of writing

- strategy instruction for responding to on-demand, or timed, writing prompts in Preparing for Timed Writing

- opportunities to observe writer's craft in Think as a Reader/Writer: Find It in Your Reading and to use elements of writer's craft in Think as a Reader/Writer: Use It in Your Writing—exemplifying the reciprocal nature of reading and writing

- professional models in each Writing Workshop to reinforce the Think as a Reader/Writer instructional strand

- in the Writing Workshops, student drafts with accompanying focused revision instruction that make revision tangible and accessible to your students

- standards-specific scoring rubrics that present the attributes of standards-based writing, incorporating the academic language students can use to discuss their own writing or provide feedback to their peers

- Timed Writing activities for writing about informational texts

An Overview of the Writing Process

The Writing Workshops in *Holt Literature and Language Arts* consistently follow a four-part writing process that guides students through the planning and development of a piece of writing.

- **Prewriting** shows students how to plan a piece of writing so that it addresses their purpose and audience. Prewriting includes strategies and graphic organizers for finding and narrowing topics, gathering information and ideas about a topic, organizing ideas and information, thinking about purpose and audience, and writing thesis statements. Prewriting also includes opportunities for peer feedback on what students are planning.

- **Drafting** guides students through organizing and shaping their composition within the structure posed by their purpose and audience. A framework provides an organizational snapshot of the type of writing students are drafting, and a Grammar Link highlights a grammatical concept central to that type of writing.

- **Evaluating and Revising** shows students how to refine and re-visit their drafts, using peer and teacher feedback. Specific, standards-based criteria provide direction for evaluating and revising the form of writing. Targeted revision lessons focus on the analysis of realistic student drafts, followed by students' application of the same revision instruction to their own writing.

- **Proofreading and Publishing** shows students how to proofread, or edit, for language conventions, using peer feedback. Proofreading is supported by an additional Grammar Link that targets common problems. Creative and appropriate publishing suggestions encourage accountability in writing for real audiences. The Writing Workshop concludes with Reflect on Your Writing, a metacognitive activity that guides students to consider what they have learned and what they can apply to other writing situations.

Providing Feedback on Students' Writing

Responding to students' writing in a timely way can be a challenge for even the most seasoned teacher. With multiple classes generating papers, the stacks can begin to mount to the ceiling. In her book *Papers, Papers, Papers* (Portsmouth, NH: Heinemann, 2005), *Holt Literature and Language Arts* author Carol Jago suggests some strategies you can use to provide focused, timely feedback to students:

- **Articulate the criteria for a writing assignment to your students *before* they write.** Then, respond to their papers with those criteria in mind. As you review your students' work, note errors or misunderstandings that crop up frequently across the class's work and target follow-up instruction to address those issues.

- **Link your comments on a current piece of writing to previous pieces students have written.** Point out individual improvements you notice as well as provide support for areas that need improvement. Your students will become aware of their own writing growth because you are commenting on it.

- **Stagger the writing assignments you give to different classes.** In this way, you will receive students' writing in manageable chunks rather than in a tidal wave. You can then budget your time to respond promptly to each class or group of students. This will give you a better chance of providing feedback in a time frame that will have an effect on student writing.

- **Determine which papers you will read.** You will likely have your students do a variety of writing in your classroom, from responses to QuickWrite activities to Choices activities to Writing Workshop compositions. Given the volume, you will find it challenging (if not impossible) to read every word they generate. Decide which writing assignments you will concentrate on to ensure that your students are mastering the writing strategies and applications standards. For example, you may choose to focus on your students' persuasive essays, rather than on their QuickWrite or What Do You Think Now? responses to a text.

- **Give your students an opportunity to provide feedback to each other.** Peer review is a strategy that enables students to see their writing as others see it, while also building accountability for providing responsible and constructive feedback. Peer-review partners or small groups can work together to improve each other's writing by using direct questions, such as, "Do you think I have enough supporting evidence?" or, "Is the title effective?" The Evaluating and Revising Guidelines in the Writing Workshops provide specific criteria for each type of writing. Students can use these guidelines as they work with their peers.

Routines *for* California Classrooms

Good habits pave the path to success. What good habits, or routines, might be put in place in California classrooms to encourage and increase academic success?

Some routines are for classroom management. The teacher who sounds a wind chime or flickers the lights to signal students to quiet down is using a classroom management routine. Other routines—academic routines—help students develop the cognitive habits that encourage academic success. For example, when you use a warm-up, you practice an academic routine in your classroom.

Twelve teacher-created and classroom-tested academic routines follow. You know your students best, so decisions about which routines to utilize and at what times are best left to you. Variations on the routines are included to provide you with options for implementation and instruction. Use the Key Questions that follow to decide on the routines best suited to your students' needs. Note that these routines promote the instructional conversations that lead to academic success for a range of students.

Key Questions

Use the questions in the right-hand column as guides for selecting, implementing, and adapting routines most appropriate for your classroom.

FOR SELECTING A ROUTINE
- Which routine will best enable my students to develop a habit that will help them be successful?
- Will I feel comfortable leading the routine on a regular basis throughout the school year?

FOR IMPLEMENTING A ROUTINE
- How will I model the routine? How often will I need to model the routine? How will the routine change (if at all) as I change instruction from standard to standard?
- What cues will I use to signal to my students that it is time to move into and out of the routine?
- What signs should I watch for in students to signal to me that they have taken ownership of the routine?
- How will I know when a routine is effective for my students?

FOR ADAPTING A ROUTINE
- Which parts of the routine are difficult for my students? Which parts are easy for them?
- How can I alter the procedure to help my students make the routine a habit?
  Hint: To avoid confusion, try not to change too many parts of the routine at once.
- Would adding or substituting a different routine help me move my students closer to academic success?

1 Activating Academic Vocabulary

WHAT IS IT?
Academic Vocabulary is the language successful readers and writers use to communicate their ideas within and across content areas. It is the language of learning and assessment. **Activating Academic Vocabulary** is the teacher's conscious and frequent use of these vocabulary words. The teacher should establish a routine in which students regularly use Academic Vocabulary in writing and speaking about the texts they are reading.

HOW DOES IT WORK?
- Teacher provides a list of Academic Vocabulary terms and definitions. (Each chapter in *Holt Literature and Language Arts* focuses on several Academic Vocabulary words that are emphasized and practiced throughout the chapter.)
- Teacher models the appropriate context and usage of each word in class discussion, instruction, and assessment.
- Students use the Academic Vocabulary words in oral discussion, written responses, and assessments.

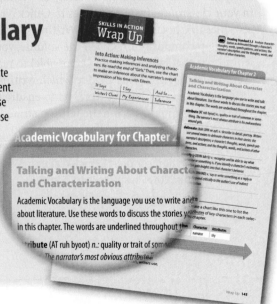

2 Three Before Me

WHAT IS IT?

Three Before Me is a routine that uses a collaborative format to improve editing in student writing.

HOW DOES IT WORK?

- Each student prepares and edits a piece of writing to bring it to final form.
- Each student asks three other students to edit his or her writing before it goes to the teacher. Students can be asked to read for one kind of error at a time or to edit the entire paper.
- Each student writer is responsible for evaluating editing suggestions and making appropriate edits to his or her writing before turning it in to the teacher.

3 Silent Sustained Reading

WHAT IS IT?

Silent Sustained Reading is a routine that extends learning time for all students by promoting independent reading for 30 minutes a day. SSR activates the positive effects of increased reading practice, including improved vocabulary acquisition, expanded background knowledge, better fluency, and contextualized practice of comprehension skills.

HOW DOES IT WORK?

- Teacher establishes a daily routine for a reading requirement of 30 minutes.
- Teacher models choosing a book appropriate for reading level and individual interests.
- Teacher institutes a chart on which students may record title, date, and number of pages read. (The *Reader/Writer Notebook* includes a chart for this purpose.)

HINT: The clock icon accompanying For Independent Reading (with author biographies) and Read On (at the end of a chapter) signals suggestions for students' reading.

VARIATION: The Silent Sustained Reading routine may be required as homework or used in classrooms. Teachers may ask students to record new vocabulary words, respond to questions, and/or provide an oral or written summary of their reading. When reading is assigned for homework, teachers may also require parent or guardian signatures for verfication. Teachers may also use summer reading lists and community resources to further promote this routine.

4 Sticky Note Peer Review

WHAT IS IT?

Sticky Note Peer Review is a partner or small-group activity used to facilitate constructive feedback for student writing, using sticky notes.

HOW DOES IT WORK?

- In pairs or small groups, students provide constructive feedback to their peers.
- As each student in turn reads his or her paper, the other students listen, recording specific feedback on sticky notes.
- Listeners record specific words or phrases that they *liked* and that were *effective* in their classmate's piece of writing.
- On additional sticky notes, listeners record *questions* that they have about the text—especially about the need for additional information.
- On sticky notes, listeners write *suggestions* for the writer.
- It is important for students to keep each purpose separate by writing *positive* comments on one sticky note, *suggestions* on another note, and *questions* on a third note.
- Students initial their sticky notes, giving them to the writer to use for revision.
- The routine is repeated until each student has written constructive feedback for use in revision.

VARIATION: Students may use strips of paper or note cards to record their feedback.

> What a great story. I loved the characters and setting. What a great way to involve the reader.
>
> ML

> More background on the story. Less detail about insignificant facts.
>
> ML

> Why did the ending come right after the plot was revealed?
>
> ML

5 Think-Pair-Share

WHAT IS IT?

Think-Pair-Share is a paired student activity to promote individual accountability and collaborative thinking as preparation for class discussion.

HOW DOES IT WORK?

- Teacher poses a question to the class.
- Students think about the question individually, making notes.
- Each student partners with another student to listen, discuss, and formulate a shared response.
- Teacher calls on each or a selected student to respond to the entire class.

VARIATION: After creating a response, students in a pair may work with another pair to reach consensus before responding.

Routines for California Classrooms

6 Pinwheel Discussion

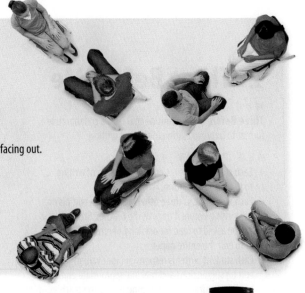

WHAT IS IT?

Pinwheel Discussion is a group format designed to increase participation, accountability, and cooperation within small discussion groups.

HOW DOES IT WORK?

- In groups of eight, four students are seated facing in; four students are seated facing out.
- Students in the inner circle remain stationary throughout the discussion.
- Students in the outer circle move to their right after discussing each question.
- Teacher controls discussion by providing a question for each rotation.

VARIATION: Form groups of fewer than eight members as appropriate, keeping an even number of students. With a group of six, for example, three students would face in and three would face out.

7 Numbered Heads Together

WHAT IS IT?

Numbered Heads Together is a discussion format that increases individual accountability and participation within group discussions.

HOW DOES IT WORK?

- Students form into groups of four and then number off 1 – 2 – 3 – 4 within the group.
- Teacher poses a higher-order discussion question to the group or class.
- Students discuss their responses in their groups.
- Teacher calls a number from 1 to 4. That "numbered" student then responds for the group.

VARIATION: Since classrooms will be comprised of several groups, allow groups to give themselves a name such as "Bobcats" to identify their group. Teacher then calls on Bobcat #4.

HINT: Depending on how effectively a group works together, you may wish to keep the group intact for several weeks before changing its membership.

8 Three-Minute Review

WHAT IS IT?

Three-Minute Review is a routine to enhance individual accountability, active engagement, comprehension, and long-term retention of information.

HOW DOES IT WORK?

- Teacher pauses at any time during reading, lecture, or discussion.
- Teacher directs students to work independently.
- Teacher sets timer for three minutes.
- For three minutes, students re-read material, review class notes, and write clarifying questions.
- Teacher may ask, "What did you notice in your review?" or may solicit clarifying questions from student volunteers. Brief discussion and clarification follow.

VARIATION: Teacher may pose a question to guide the three-minute review period, or may direct students to write clarifying questions to be handed in. Students may also work in pairs or triads.

9 Send a Problem

WHAT IS IT?

Send a Problem is a method for keeping the pace of discussion moving in the classroom by sharing accountability among students. This routine enhances listening skills and participation.

HOW DOES IT WORK?

- Teacher poses a question during discussion and calls on a student to respond.
- Teacher waits up to 11 seconds.
- If student does not have a response, student must call on another student by name to answer the same question.
- The sending student repeats the question as he or she calls on another for assistance.
- Teacher monitors responses and can redirect or ask another question at any time.

VARIATION: If listening is a challenge for some students in your classroom, change the format to have the second student repeat the question before answering. Provide bonus points for every remembered question.

10 Jigsaw with Experts

WHAT IS IT?

Jigsaw with Experts is a collaborative approach to reading especially lengthy or difficult reading assignments.

HOW DOES IT WORK?

- Teacher divides a long or challenging reading assignment into parts—not to exceed six parts.
- Students are either assigned to or count off to match a numbered reading section.
- Students read and take notes on their section of the reading.
- Students get in small groups of three to four classmates who were assigned the same section.

- This group of "experts" discusses their section for a designated period of time, depending on the length and difficulty of the reading.
- Students then form new groups that include one representative for each section of the divided reading.
- Students discuss their respective sections and the whole piece of text for a designated amount of time.

VARIATION: Teacher may then conduct a class discussion and/or assign the entire text to be read by each student. Discussion will provide valuable background knowledge for reading the text as a whole.

11 Double-Entry Journal

WHAT IS IT?

Double-Entry Journal is a routine approach to notetaking during reading. It may be used for either in-class or independent reading. Sometimes called dialectic notetaking, a Double-Entry Journal enhances students' metacognitive skills and increases comprehension of material by having the student conduct a dialogue or conversation with the text. Individual accountability and inquiry are improved. The importance of text evidence becomes apparent in this routine.

HOW DOES IT WORK?

- Students use a notebook or journal for recording Double-Entry Journal notes. This notebook can be spiral or loose-leaf.
- Teacher models the structure of the two-column format. Each page is divided down the middle by drawing a line from top to bottom. The heading on the left side of the page is *Quotes from the Text,* and the heading on the right side is *My Notes.*
- Students record significant, important, or perplexing text passages in the left column.
- Students write their own interpretations, summaries, questions, and restatements in the right column, opposite the quoted material.

VARIATION: Teachers may provide students with a list of stems for use in the right column. Individual students may create a triple-entry journal with another student by exchanging their double-entry journals. Each student draws a line under his or her notes, and passes the journal to a partner who then responds to his or her notes.

12 Reciprocal Teaching

WHAT IS IT?

Reciprocal Teaching is a method of increasing student accountability and collaborative thinking about a specific topic.

HOW DOES IT WORK?

- Teacher presents a brief lecture, facilitates a whole class discussion of a topic, or provides a reading assignment.
- Teacher presents students with a list of generic question stems.
- Students work independently to write three to five questions about the material, using the stems.
- Students do not have to be able to answer the questions they write.

- Students are grouped into learning teams of up to three students.
- Each student offers at least two questions for group discussion without duplicating another student's questions.
- Group reaches consensus on the answer to each question and finds text evidence to support it.

VARIATION: Teachers may allow students from each learning group to share their best question with the entire class. Class discussion may follow. A variety of question stems can be used to practice the instructional standards.

Linguistic Considerations for Instruction in Reading/Language Arts

Research Informing Instruction

In recent years, researchers, linguists, and educators have drawn attention to the relationship of linguistic considerations and instruction in Reading/Language Arts. Of particular interest are the acquisition and/or mastery of standard academic English as a bridge to high levels of student achievement.

- Charity, Scarborough, and Griffin (2004) have found that "higher familiarity with SE [School English] (reproducing SE features more often when imitating) was associated with better reading achievement."

- Labov (2001) and Rickford (1999) have identified phonological and grammatical features of African American vernacular English that relate to the use of formal English in academic settings.

- Scarcella (2003) has used research findings to inform teaching considerations for English learners.

- Francis, M. Rivera, Lesaux, Kieffer, and H. Rivera (2006) have developed research-based recommendations for instruction and academic interventions for English learners.

Drawing from these and other research-based recommendations, Chapter 9 of the *Reading/ Language Arts Framework for California Public Schools*, "Criteria for Evaluating Instructional Materials: Kindergarten Through Grade Eight," specifies that "teacher editions must include the following features" (page 316):

"**19.** The teacher edition clearly references, explains, and provides the location of additional instructional materials and program components designed to provide extra support for students who require it (e.g., English learners, students who use African American vernacular English, struggling readers, and students with disabilities)." (page 317)

"**21.** All suggestions and procedures for meeting the instructional needs of all students are ready to use with minimum modifications to facilitate the program supporting scaffolded instruction for English learners, students with disabilities, struggling readers, and students who use African American vernacular English and providing teachers with guidance on scaffolding instruction." (page 317)

"**22.** The program provides a linguistic, contrastive analysis chart in the teacher edition that shows and explains how new or difficult sounds and features of the English language are taught and reinforced. Comparisons with the five (or more) of the most common languages in California and African American vernacular English will be incorporated as appropriate, accentuating transferable and nontransferable skills." (page 318)

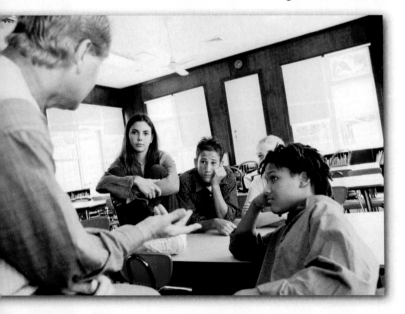

How Does HLLA Address Linguistic Considerations for Instruction?

Educators using the Teacher's Edition of *Holt Literature and Language Arts* (HLLA) may have questions about the instructional support provided for English learners and students who use African American vernacular English, such as the following:

QUESTION: Why does the Teacher's Edition stress the linguistic needs of English learners and of students who use African American vernacular English?

ANSWER: Recent research-based recommendations support instruction in academic or school English (also referred to as formal English) as a pathway to academic success. The Evaluation Criteria of the *Reading/Language Arts Framework* incorporate these research-based recommendations to support teachers in effectively addressing the needs of students in these two groups who may require additional support.

QUESTION: What does this mean for students' home languages?

ANSWER: Instructional support in the Teacher's Edition is aimed at improving students' success in academic settings. At the same time, any instruction must respect students' home languages and cultures. Teachers can guide students to understand the context: that there are differences between the informal English used in conversational or home settings and the formal English used in school or workplace settings. Knowing how and when to use informal or formal English is an important skill for students in school and in the workplace.

QUESTION: How will teachers know when the Teacher's Edition includes linguistic suggestions for instruction?

ANSWER: Teachers will find instructional support for English learners and students who use African American vernacular English in the following locations:

- In the side wrap, the head **English for Academic Success** signals instructional support that focuses on the use of academic vocabulary and language.

- In the bottom wrap, the feature "Universal Access" provides scaffolding for adapting the core lesson to students' instructional needs. Point-of-use references to additional program resources are also included.

- In the side and bottom wrap, the English learner icon **EL** and the AAVE icon **AAVE** signal instruction designed to provide extra support for students who may require it.

- The following pages, T40–T47, present two charts: one, a Linguistic, Contrastive Analysis chart, and two, a chart that identifies phonological and grammatical features of African American vernacular English. These charts can help teachers identify areas of focus for instruction in academic or formal English.

Works Cited

Charity, Anne H., Hollis S. Scarborough, and Darion M. Griffin. "Familiarity with School English in African American Children and Its Relation to Early Reading Achievement." *Child Development 75* (2004): 1340-1356.

Francis, David J., Mabel Rivera, Nonie Lesaux, Michael Kieffer, and Hector Rivera. *Research-Based Recommendations for Instruction and Academic Interventions: Practical Guidelines for the Education of English Language Learners.* Houston: Center on Instruction, 2006.

Labov, William. "Applying Our Knowledge of African American English to the Problem of Raising Reading Levels in Inner-city Schools." *Sociocultural and Historical Contexts of African American English.* Ed. Sonja Lanehart. Philadelphia: Benjamins, 2001. 299-318.

Rickford, John. *African American Vernacular English: Features, Evolution, and Educational Implications.* Oxford: Blackwell, 1999.

Scarcella, Robin. *Accelerating Academic English: A Focus on the English Learner.* Oakland, CA: Regents of the University of California, 2003.

Linguistic Considerations for Instruction

Linguistic, Contrastive Analysis

 EL The Linguistic, Contrastive Analysis chart identifies English sounds and grammatical structures that will or will not pose difficulty for users of languages other than English. Examples of how the sounds transfer or do not transfer from English to students' primary languages are included.

Phonological Features

ENGLISH	SPANISH	VIETNAMESE	CANTONESE OR MANDARIN	
INITIAL CONSONANTS				
/f/ **f**an	Little difficulty.	/b/ **b**an	Little difficulty.	
/v/ **v**an	/b/, /f/ **b**an, **f**an (Note: Spanish has only one sound for /b/ and /v/.)	Little difficulty.	/w/ **w**an	
/th/ **th**ough	Little difficulty.	/d/ **d**oe	/d/ **d**oe (Note: /th/ does not exist.)	
/th/ **th**ink	/d/ **d**ink	/d/, /z/ **d**ink, **z**ink	/d/ **d**ink	
/sh/ **sh**eet	/ch/ **ch**eat (Note: /sh/ does not exist.)	/s/, /ch/ **s**eat, **ch**eat	/s/ **s**eat	
/j/ **j**ar	/h/, /y/ **h**ar, **y**ar	/z/ **z**ar	Little difficulty.	
/y/ **y**es	/j/ **j**es	Little difficulty.	Little difficulty.	
/h/ **h**ouse	The nearest sound to /h/ in Spanish sounds like the *ch* in *Bach*.	Little difficulty.	The nearest sound to /h/ sounds like the *ch* in *Bach*.	
/n/ **n**eed	Little difficulty.	Little difficulty.	/l/ **l**ead	
/r/ **r**ock	/r/ rolled or trilled **R**ock	Little difficulty.	/l/ **l**ock (Note: Many speakers find /l/ and /r/ difficult to distinguish.)	
/s/ **s**tudent	add /e/ before /s/ **es**tudent	Little difficulty.	Little difficulty.	
/z/ **z**oo	/s/ **s**ue (Note: Initial /z/ does not exist.)	Little difficulty.	/s/ **s**ue (Note: /z/ does not exist.)	
/p/, /t/, /k/ **p**ot, **t**ot, **c**ot	/b/, /d/, /g/ **b**ot, **d**ot, **g**ot	Initial /t/ in Vietnamese sounds like /d/: **d**ot.	Little difficulty.	
/b/, /d/, /g/ **b**et, **d**ebt, **g**et	Initial /b/ is sometimes replaced with /v/: **v**et.	Little difficulty.	/p/, /t/, /k/ **p**et, **t**et, **k**et	
MEDIAL CONSONANTS				
/zh/ mea**s**ure	/z/ me**z**ure	Little difficulty.	/z/, /sh/ me**z**ure, mea**sh**ure	
/r/ ho**rr**ible	/rr/ rolled or trilled ho**R**rible	Little difficulty.	/l/ ho**l**ible	

PILIPINO OR TAGALOG	HMONG	KOREAN
/p/ **p**an	/p/ **p**an	/p/ **p**an
Little difficulty.	Little difficulty.	/w/, /b/ **w**an, **b**an
/b/, /f/ **b**ow, **f**oe	/d/ **d**oe	(Note: /th/ does not exist.)
/d/ **d**ink	/d/ **d**ink	/s/ **s**ink
Little difficulty.	Little difficulty.	Little difficulty.
/y/ **y**ar	Little difficulty.	/zh/ as in rou**ge**
Little difficulty.	Little difficulty.	Little difficulty.
Little difficulty.	Little difficulty.	Little difficulty.
Little difficulty.	Little difficulty.	Little difficulty.
Little difficulty.	Little difficulty.	/l/ **l**ock (Note: /r/ does not exist.)
Little difficulty.	Little difficulty.	/sh/ **sh**tudent
/s/ **s**ue	/s/ **s**ue	/j/, /ch/ **ch**oo
/b/, /d/, /g/ **b**ot, **d**ot, **g**ot	Little difficulty.	/p/ may be replaced by /f/: **f**ought.
Little difficulty.	Little difficulty.	/b/ may be replaced by /v/: **v**et.
/z/ me**z**ure	Little difficulty.	/z/, /sh/ me**z**ure, mea**sh**ure
Little difficulty.	Little difficulty.	/l/ ho**l**ible

Linguistic, Contrastive Analysis

ENGLISH	SPANISH	VIETNAMESE	CANTONESE OR MANDARIN	
FINAL CONSONANTS				
/p/, /k/, /t/ ti**p**, si**ck**, si**t**	Little difficulty.	Little difficulty.	Often dropped or replaced with a schwa sound. (Note: there are few final consonants.)	
/s/ after consonant cat**s**, hat**s**	Little difficulty.	Not used in Vietnamese.	Little difficulty.	
/v/ lo**ve**	Usually no difficulty, but may be replaced with /b/ : lu**b**	/b/, /p/ lu**b**, lu**p**	Often deleted.	
/j/ e**dge**	/ch/ e**tch**	Often deleted.	Little difficulty.	
/m/ drea**m**	/n/, /ng/ drea**n**, drea**ng**	Little difficulty.	Little difficulty.	
/ng/ thi**ng**	/n/ thi**n**	Little difficulty.	/n/ thi**n**	
VOWELS				
/ee/ sh**ee**p	Little difficulty.	Little difficulty.	Little difficulty.	
/ih/ l**i**p	/ee/ l**ea**p	/ee/ l**ea**p	Little difficulty.	
/ay/ r**ai**d	Often substitute /e/: r**e**d.	Little difficulty.	Little difficulty.	
/e/ b**e**t	/ay/ b**ai**t	/a/ b**a**t	Vowel sounds might vary as a function of the surrounding consonant sounds.	
/a/ c**a**t	/ah/ c**o**t	/ah/ c**o**t	/a/ does not exist; c**o**t, K**a**te, k**e**t, c**u**t. Learners might nasalize or replace with /ah/: c**o**t, /e/:b**e**t, or /u/: c**u**p. Most frequently substitute /a/ with /eh/.	
/ah/ cl**o**ck	/oh/ cl**oa**k	Little difficulty.	Little difficulty.	
/ah/ **a**bove	Does not exist. Often replaced by another vowel.	Little difficulty.	Does not exist. Often replaced by another vowel.	
/u/ c**u**p	/ah/, /oo/ c**o**p, c**oo**p	Little difficulty.	/ah/ c**o**p	
/oh/ b**oa**t	Little difficulty.	Little difficulty.	Little difficulty.	
/u/ p**u**ll	/oo/ p**oo**l	/oo/ p**oo**l	/oo/ p**oo**l	
/oo/ p**oo**l	Little difficulty.	Little difficulty.	Little difficulty.	

PILIPINO OR TAGALOG	HMONG	KOREAN
Little difficulty.	/b/, /d/, /g/ ti**b**, si**d**, si**g**	Often dropped or replaced with a schwa sound. (Note: there are few final consonants.)
Little difficulty.	Little difficulty.	Little difficulty.
Little difficulty.	Often deleted.	Little difficulty, but may be replaced by /b/: lu**b**.
/eh/ added at end e**dgeh**	Little difficulty.	/eh/ added at end e**dgeh**
Little difficulty.	Little difficulty.	Little difficulty.
/n/ thi**n**	/n/ thi**n**	/n/ thi**n**
Little difficulty.	Little difficulty.	Little difficulty.
/ee/ l**ea**p	Little difficulty.	/ee/ l**ea**p
Little difficulty.	Little difficulty.	/eh/ r**e**d
/ay/ b**ai**t	Little difficulty.	/ee/ b**ea**t
/ah/ c**o**t	/ah/ c**o**t	Little difficulty.
/oh/ cl**oa**k	Little difficulty.	/oh/ cl**oa**k (There are no long-short vowel distinctions in Korean.)
Does not exist. Often replaced by another vowel.	Does not exist. Often replaced by another vowel.	Does not exist. Often replaced by another vowel.
/ah/ c**o**p	Little difficulty.	/ah/ c**o**p
Little difficulty.	/aw/ b**ou**ght	Little difficulty.
/oo/ p**oo**l	Little difficulty.	Little difficulty.
Little difficulty.	Little difficulty.	Little difficulty.

Linguistic, Contrastive Analysis

Grammatical Features

GRAMMAR POINT

	SPANISH	VIETNAMESE	CANTONESE OR MANDARIN	PILIPINO OR TAGALOG	HMONG	KOREAN
VOWELS						
Plural Forms Nouns do not change form to show the plural in the primary language, or plurals are not used in the same way.		✔	✔		✔	✔
Possessive Forms Prepositions are either inferred or are not formed in the same way as English.	✔	✔	✔	✔	✔	✔
The word order in the primary language is different.	✔	✔	✔	✔	✔	✔
Count vs. Noncount Nouns that are count and noncount differ between English and primary language.	✔	✔	✔	✔	✔	✔
ARTICLES						
Articles are lacking, or the distinction between *a* and *the* is not paralleled in the primary language.		✔	✔	✔	✔	✔
Learners sometimes confuse the articles *a/an* with *one* since articles either do not exist in the primary language or serve a different function.		✔			✔	
PRONOUNS						
Gender of Personal Pronouns The third-person pronoun in the primary language is gender-free. The same pronoun is used where English uses masculine, feminine, and neuter pronouns, resulting in confusion of pronoun forms in English.			✔	✔	✔	
Personal Pronoun Forms The same pronoun form is used for *he/him* and *she/her*, and in some primary languages, for *I/me* and *we/us*.			✔		✔	
There is no number agreement in the primary language. In Vietnamese, plurality is never expressed.		✔	✔			
Subject pronouns may be dropped in the primary language, the verb ending supplying information on number and/or gender.	✔					
Direct objects are frequently dropped in the primary language.		✔				
A subordinate clause at the beginning of a sentence does not require a subject in the primary language.		✔	✔			✔
The redundant structure of using pronouns with subject nouns reflects "topic-comment" approach used in the primary language: The speaker mentions a topic and then makes a comment on it.	✔	✔	✔		✔	✔
It is common in the primary language to repeat nouns rather than to use pronouns.		✔	✔			✔
Possessive Forms Speakers tend to omit final *n*, creating confusion between *my* and *mine*.		✔	✔		✔	✔
VERBS						
Subject-Verb Agreement There is no subject-verb agreement in the primary language.		✔	✔	✔	✔	✔
Tense Verb forms do not change to indicate tense, or time is understood from context.		✔	✔	✔	✔	✔
Past Tense Speakers of the primary language have difficulty recognizing that a vowel shift in the middle of the verb, rather than a change in the ending of the verb, is sufficient to produce a change of tense in irregular verbs.	✔	✔	✔		✔	✔
In Negative Statements Helping verbs are not used in negative statements in the primary language.	✔			✔	✔	
Verb Tense The verb form either doesn't exist in the primary language or has a different function. Vietnamese, Hmong, Cantonese, and Mandarin do not use verbs to express time.		✔	✔	✔	✔	✔
Past Continuous In the primary language, the past continuous form can be used in contexts in which English uses the expression *used to* or the simple past.	✔			✔		
Verb as a Noun Unlike English, Cantonese does not require an infinitive marker when using a verb as a noun.			✔			
In Hmong, verbs can be connected without *and* or any other conjunction (serial verbs).					✔	

GRAMMAR POINT	SPANISH	VIETNAMESE	CANTONESE OR MANDARIN	PILIPINO OR TAGALOG	HMONG	KOREAN
VERBS CONTINUED						
Linking Verbs The verb *be* is not required in all sentences. In some primary languages, it is implied in the adjective form. In others, the concept is expressed as a verb.		✔	✔		✔	✔
Passive Voice Passive voice in the primary language does not require a helping verb.		✔	✔			✔
Transitive Verbs vs. Intransitive Verbs Verbs that do and do not take a direct object differ between English and primary language.	✔		✔	✔		
Phrasal Verbs Phrasal verbs do not exist in the primary language. There is often confusion over their meaning in English.	✔					
Have* vs. *Be Some Spanish constructions use *have* where English uses *be*.	✔					
ADJECTIVES						
Word Order Adjectives commonly come after nouns in the primary language.	✔	✔			✔	
Adjectives always come before words they modify in the primary language.			✔			
Comparison Comparative and superlative degrees are usually formed with separate words in the primary language, the equivalent of *more* and *most* in English.	✔				✔	✔
Confusion of *–ing* and *–ed* Forms The speakers of the primary language sometimes confuse these adjective forms, not distinguishing between *an interesting movie* and *an interested viewer,* for example.	✔	✔	✔	✔	✔	✔
ADVERBS						
Adverbs usually come before verbs in the primary language, and this tendency is carried over into English.			✔			
PREPOSITIONS						
English prepositions do not match the prepositions of the primary language precisely.			✔			✔
COMPLEX SENTENCES						
The primary language lacks tense markers so that matching the tenses of two verbs in one sentence correctly can be difficult. Learners may also try to analyze the tense needed in English according to meaning, which in some cases can result in the use of an incorrect tense.		✔	✔	✔	✔	✔
If* vs. *When The primary language has one expression that covers the use of English *if* and *when* for the future.				✔		
SENTENCE STRUCTURE						
The pattern in the primary language is to describe what happens first with later occurrences following. This is not an error in English, but it leads to a lack of sentence variety.			✔			
In Spanish, the phrase with the indirect object can come before the direct object.	✔					
Spanish requires double negatives in many sentence structures.	✔					
QUESTIONS						
The primary language does not use subject-verb inversion in questions.		✔	✔	✔		✔
In the primary language, word order is the same in some questions and statements, depending on the context.			✔	✔	✔	✔
In the primary language, there is no exact counterpart to the *do/did* verb in questions.	✔			✔	✔	✔
Yes/No Questions In the primary language, learners tend to answer yes by repeating the verb in question. They tend to say no by using *not* and repeating the verb.			✔		✔	
Tag Questions The primary language has no exact counterpart to a tag question, forms them differently, or does not add *do/did* to questions.		✔	✔			✔

Linguistic, Contrastive Analysis

Features of African American Vernacular English (AAVE)

 AAVE This chart identifies phonological elements and language structures of formal English that may cause difficulty for some students who use African American vernacular English.

PHONOLOGICAL ELEMENTS	FORMAL ENGLISH EXAMPLE	AAVE EXAMPLE
/th/ as in *though*	voicing /th/ in the middle and end of words: *bro**th**er, brea**the***	voicing /th/ as /v/ in the middle and end of words: *brover, breave*
/th/ as in *think*	voicing /th/ in the middle and end of words: *ba**th**room, dea**th***	voicing /th/ as /f/ in the middle and end of words: *bafroom, deaf*
Initial /th/ as in *this, that, the*	voicing initial /th/: ***th**is, **th**at, **th**e*	voicing /d/ for initial /th/: ***d**is, **d**at, **d**e*
/t/ in contractions	voicing of /t/ in contractions: *it's, don**t***	omitting /t/ in contractions: *i's; don'*
final /g/ as in *thing*	voicing /g/ in /ihng/: *thin**g***	omitting /g/ in /ihng/: *thin'*
/ih/ in /ihng/	voicing /ih/ in /ihng/: *thing, bring, ring*	voicing /ang/ for /ihng/: *th**ang**, br**ang**, r**ang***
/r/ in initial consonant clusters	voicing /r/ in consonant clusters: *throw, through, brought*	omitting /r/ in consonant clusters: *th'ow, th'ough, b'ought*
final consonant clusters	voicing both sounds in final consonant clusters: *te**st**, fi**st**, wi**ld**, fi**nd**, de**sk**, li**ft***	omitting final consonant in final consonant clusters: *tes', fis', wil', fin', des', lif'*
final /r/	voicing /r/ in words with *r*-controlled vowels: *store, door, for*	omitting /r/ in words with *r*- controlled vowels: *sto', do', fo'*
final /l/ after variant vowels	voicing /l/ after variant vowels: *coo**l**, bow**l***	omitting /l/ after variant vowels: *coo', bow'*
/l/ before final /p/, /t/, /k/	voicing /l/ before final /p/, /t/, /k/: *he**l**p, be**l**t, mi**l**k*	omitting /l/ before final /p/, /t/, /k/: *he'p, be't, mi'k*
final /uhl/	voicing final /uhl/: *peop**le**, coup**le**, litt**le***	omitting final /l/ in /uhl/ syllable: *peop/uh/, coup/uh/, litt/uh/*
/ih/ and /eh/ before consonants /m/ and /n/	/ih/ and /eh/ before /m/ and /n/: *h**i**m, h**e**m; p**i**n, p**e**n*	voicing /ih/ for /eh/: *h**i**m for h**e**m; p**i**n for p**e**n*
initial /str/	voicing initial /str/: ***str**eet*	voicing initial /str/ as /skr/: ***skr**eet*
adjacent consonants /sk/	voicing of adjacent consonants: *a**sk***	transposition of adjacent consonants: *a**ks***
syllable emphasis	primary stress on final syllable: *po-LICE*	primary stress on initial syllable: *PO-lice*

LANGUAGE STRUCTURES	FORMAL ENGLISH EXAMPLE	AAVE EXAMPLE
conjugating the verb *to be*	He **is** at school. We **are** young. We **were** playing.	He **be** at school. or He at school. We **is** young. We **was** playing.
use of *be* for habitual action	Her mother **works** hard.	Her mother **be working** hard.
subject-verb agreement	She talks. They look.	She talk. They looks.
use of verb stem as past tense	I **finished.** He **came** down.	I **finish.** He **come** down.
use of past participle form as past tense	I **saw** the book. or I **had seen** the book.	I **seen** the book.
use of *had* to indicate simple past	He **sold** the car.	He **had sold** the car.
past tense verbs with *−ed*	Her cat was **called** Misty.	Her cat was **call** Misty.
use of helping verbs in present tense	She **is** coming. We **are** going.	She coming. We going.
negative constructions	He **won't ever** do that. or He **will never** do that. **Nobody can** do that.	He **won't never** do that. **Can't nobody** do that.
plural nouns	I have **two brothers.** It cost ten **dollars.**	I have **two brother.** It cost ten **dollar.**
irregular plural nouns	This is for the **children.**	This is for the **childrens.**
/s/ in possessives between two nouns	My **dog's** name is Buddy.	My **dog** name is Buddy.
possessive pronoun *mine*	That is **mine.**	That is **mines.**
possessive pronoun *their*	The girls met **their** neighbor.	The girls met **they** neighbor.
/s/ in contractions	**He's** my best friend.	**He** my best friend.
use of articles	**a** ring; **an** apple	**an** ring; **a** apple
inserting *done* in verb forms	He made the team.	He **done** made the team.
double tense marking	We **picked** that day to play.	We **pickted** that day to play.
comparative forms of adjectives	It's **better** than the other one.	It's **more better** than the other one.

Features of African American Vernacular English

Contents in Brief

CHAPTER 1

Plot

"You gain strength, courage, and confidence by every experience in which you really stop to look fear in the face." —**Eleanor Roosevelt**

What Do You Think? How might confronting a difficult situation help you become a stronger person?

California Standards

Word Analysis, Fluency, and Systematic Vocabulary Development
1.3 Clarify word meanings through the use of definition, example, restatement, or contrast.
Reading Comprehension (Focus on Informational Materials)
Gr 6 rev 2.4 Clarify an understanding of texts by creating outlines, logical notes, summaries, or reports.
Literary Response and Analysis
3.2 Identify events that advance the plot and determine how each event explains past or present action(s) or foreshadows future action(s).
Writing Applications (Genres and Their Characteristics)
2.5 Write summaries of reading materials:
  a. Include the main ideas and most significant details.
  b. Use the student's own words, except for quotations.
  c. Reflect underlying meaning, not just the superficial details.

Table of Contents

CHAPTER 2

Character

"Be who you are and say what you feel, because those who matter don't mind and those who mind don't matter."

—**Dr. Seuss (Theodor Seuss Geisel)**

What Do You Think? How do other people help you discover something within yourself?

California Standards

Word Analysis, Fluency, and Systematic Vocabulary Development

1.2 Use knowledge of Greek, Latin, and Anglo-Saxon roots and affixes to understand content-area vocabulary.

Reading Comprehension (Focus on Informational Materials)

2.1 Understand and analyze the differences in structure and purpose between various categories of informational materials (e.g., textbooks, newspapers, instructional manuals, signs).

Literary Response and Analysis

3.3 Analyze characterization as delineated through a character's thoughts, words, speech patterns, and actions; the narrator's description; and the thoughts, words, and actions of other characters.

Writing Applications (Genres and Their Characteristics)

2.1 Write fictional or autobiographical narratives:

  a. Develop a standard plot line (having a beginning, conflict, rising action, climax, and denouement) and point of view.

  b. Develop complex major and minor characters and a definite setting.

  c. Use a range of appropriate strategies (e.g., dialogue; suspense; naming of specific narrative action, including movement, gestures, and expressions).

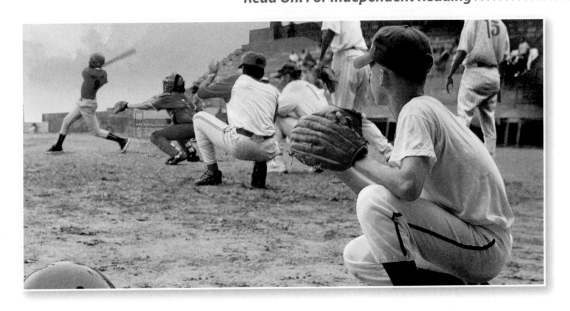
Table of Contents

CHAPTER 3

Theme

"If you live in my heart, you live rent free." —**Irish Proverb**

What Do You Think? What makes us care about certain people? Why do we connect with some people and not with others?

California Standards

Word Analysis, Fluency, and Systematic Vocabulary Development
1.1 Identify idioms, analogies, metaphors, and similes in prose and poetry.
Reading Comprehension (Focus on Informational Materials)
2.4 Identify and trace the development of an author's argument, point of view, or perspective in text.
Literary Response and Analysis
3.4 Identify and analyze recurring themes across works (e.g., the value of bravery, loyalty, and friendship; the effects of loneliness).

Writing Applications (Genres and Their Characteristics)
2.2 Write responses to literature:
   a. Develop interpretations exhibiting careful reading, understanding, and insight.
   b. Organize interpretations around several clear ideas, premises, or images from the literary work.
   c. Justify interpretations through sustained use of examples and textual evidence.

Table of Contents

CHAPTER 4

Point of View

"You cannot control what happens to you, but you can control your attitude toward what happens to you." —Brian Tracy

What Do You Think? How do our attitudes influence the changes and challenges we face in life?

California Standards

Word Analysis, Fluency, and Systematic Vocabulary Development

1.1 Identify idioms, analogies, metaphors, and similes in prose and poetry.

1.3 Clarify word meanings through the use of definition, example, restatement, or contrast.

Reading Comprehension (Focus on Informational Materials)

2.3 Analyze text that uses the cause-and-effect organizational pattern.

Literary Response and Analysis

3.5 Contrast points of view (e.g., first and third person, limited and omniscient, subjective and objective) in narrative text and explain how they affect the overall theme of the work.

Writing Applications (Genres and Their Characteristics)

2.4 Write persuasive compositions:

   a. State a clear position or perspective in support of a proposition or proposal.

   b. Describe the points in support of the proposition, employing well-articulated evidence.

   c. Anticipate and address reader concerns and counterarguments.

Table of Contents

Contents   **A11**

CHAPTER 5

Forms of Prose and Poetry

"Every one of us gets through the tough times because somebody is there, standing in the gap to close it for us." —Oprah Winfrey

What Do You Think? How do you manage through tough times?

California Standards

Word Analysis, Fluency, and Systematic Vocabulary Development
1.3 Clarify word meanings through the use of definition, example, restatement, or contrast.
Literary Response and Analysis
3.1 Articulate the expressed purposes and characteristics of different forms of prose (e.g., short story, novel, novella, essay).
Writing Applications (Genres and Their Characteristics)
2.1 Write fictional or autobiographical narratives:
   a. Develop a standard plot line (having a beginning, conflict, rising action, climax, and denouement) and point of view.
   b. Develop complex major and minor characters and a definite setting.
   c. Use a range of appropriate strategies (e.g., dialogue; suspense; naming of specific narrative action, including movement, gestures, and expressions).

Literary Selections

Comparing Texts

Table of Contents

CHAPTER 6

Reading for Life

"There is an art of reading, as well as an art of thinking, and an art of writing." —Benjamin Disraeli

What Do You Think? How can reading help you to make decisions or solve problems?

California Standards

Reading Comprehension (Focus on Informational Materials)

2.2 Locate information by using a variety of consumer, workplace, and public documents.

2.5 Understand and explain the use of a simple mechanical device by following technical directions.

Writing Applications (Genres and Their Characteristics)

2.4 Write persuasive compositions:

   a. State a clear position or perspective in support of a proposition or proposal.

   b. Describe the points in support of the proposition, employing well-articulated evidence.

   c. Anticipate and address reader concerns and counterarguments.

Table of Contents

TEACHER PLANNING GUIDE
Standards Overview and Resources..... 698A–B
Technology Resources........................ 698C
Real Issues, Real Experts..................... 698D

CHAPTER 7

Expository Critique

"Readers are plentiful; thinkers are rare." —**Harriet Martineau**

What Do You Think? How do you decide whether to believe what you read?

California Standards

Reading Comprehension (Focus on Informational Materials)
2.6 Assess the adequacy, accuracy, and appropriateness of the author's evidence to support claims and assertions, noting instances of bias and stereotyping.

Writing Applications (Genres and Their Characteristics)
2.3 Write research reports:
  a. Pose relevant and tightly drawn questions about the topic.
  b. Convey clear and accurate perspectives on the subject.
  c. Include evidence compiled through the formal research process (e.g., use of a card catalog, *Reader's Guide to Periodical Literature*, a computer catalog, magazines, newspapers, dictionaries).
  d. Document reference sources by means of footnotes and a bibliography.

Informational Selections

Table of Contents

CHAPTER 8

Literary Criticism: Analyzing Responses to Literature

"The hero is one who kindles a great light in the world, who sets up blazing torches in the darks streets of life for men to see by."
—**Felix Adler**

What Do You Think? What truths about life can we learn from tales about great heroes?

California Standards

Word Analysis, Fluency, and Systematic Vocabulary Development
1.2 Use knowledge of Greek, Latin, and Anglo-Saxon roots and affixes to understand content-area vocabulary.
Literary Response and Analysis
3.6 Analyze a range of responses to a literary work and determine the extent to which the literary elements in the work shaped those responses.
Writing Applications (Genres and Their Characteristics)
2.2 Write responses to literature:
  a. Develop interpretations exhibiting careful reading, understanding, and insight.
  b. Organize interpretations around several clear ideas, premises, or images from the literary work.
  c. Justify interpretations through sustained use of examples and textual evidence.

Skills, Standards, and Features

LITERARY SKILLS FOCUS ESSAYS

INFORMATIONAL TEXT FOCUS ESSAYS

READING SKILLS FOCUS ESSAYS

READING MATTERS: STRATEGY LESSONS

LITERARY SKILLS

READING SKILLS FOR LITERARY TEXTS

Table of Contents

SKILLS, STANDARDS, AND FEATURES continued

READING SKILLS FOR INFORMATIONAL TEXTS

VOCABULARY SKILLS
ACADEMIC VOCABULARY

LANGUAGE COACH

VOCABULARY DEVELOPMENT

 ## WORKSHOPS

WRITING WORKSHOPS

PREPARING FOR TIMED WRITING

Table of Contents

SKILLS, WORKSHOPS, AND FEATURES continued

LISTENING AND SPEAKING WORKSHOPS

FEATURES

LITERARY PERSPECTIVES

CROSS CURRICULAR LINKS

GRAMMAR LINKS

STANDARDS REVIEW

Selections by Genre

Table of Contents

SELECTIONS BY GENRE continued

NONFICTION
AUTOBIOGRAPHIES

BIOGRAPHY

ESSAYS

PERSONAL NARRATIVES

SPEECH

INTERVIEW

Table of Contents

SELECTIONS BY GENRE continued

PROFESSIONAL MODELS FOR WRITING
SHORT STORY

PERSONAL NARRATIVE

ARTICLES

REVIEWS

SCRIPT

Table of Contents

English–Language Arts Content Standards
Grade 7

READING

 1.0 Word Analysis, Fluency, and Systematic Vocabulary Development

Students use their knowledge of word origins and word relationships, as well as historical and literary context clues, to determine the meaning of specialized vocabulary and to understand the precise meaning of grade-level-appropriate words.

VOCABULARY AND CONCEPT DEVELOPMENT

1.1 Identify idioms, analogies, metaphors, and similes in prose and poetry. **Chapters 3, 4**

1.2 Use knowledge of Greek, Latin, and Anglo-Saxon roots and affixes to understand content-area vocabulary. **Chapters 2, 8**

1.3 Clarify word meanings through the use of definition, example, restatement, or contrast. **Chapters 1, 4, 5**

 2.0 Reading Comprehension (Focus on Informational Materials)

Students read and understand grade-level-appropriate material. They describe and connect the essential ideas, arguments, and perspectives of the text by using their knowledge of text structure, organization, and purpose. The selections in *Recommended Literature: Kindergarten Through Grade Twelve* illustrate the quality and complexity of the materials to be read by students. In addition, by grade eight, students read one million words annually on their own, including a good representation of grade-level-appropriate narrative and expository text (e.g., classic and contemporary literature, magazines, newspapers, online information). In grade seven, students make substantial progress toward this goal.

STRUCTURAL FEATURES OF INFORMATIONAL MATERIALS

2.1 Understand and analyze the differences in structure and purpose between various categories of informational materials (e.g., textbooks, newspapers, instructional manuals, signs). **Chapter 2**

2.2 Locate information by using a variety of consumer, workplace, and public documents. **Chapter 6**

2.3 Analyze text that uses the cause-and-effect organizational pattern. **Chapter 4**

COMPREHENSION AND ANALYSIS OF GRADE-LEVEL-APPROPRIATE TEXT

2.4 Identify and trace the development of an author's argument, point of view, or perspective in text. **Chapter 3**

2.5 Understand and explain the use of a simple mechanical device by following technical directions. **Chapter 6**

Table of Contents

ENGLISH–LANGUAGE ARTS CONTENT STANDARDS continued

RESEARCH AND TECHNOLOGY

1.4 Identify topics; ask and evaluate questions; and develop ideas leading to inquiry, investigation, and research. **Chapters 6, 7**

1.5 Give credit for both quoted and paraphrased information in a bibliography by using a consistent and sanctioned format and methodology for citations. **Chapter 7**

1.6 Create documents by using word-processing skills and publishing programs; develop simple databases and spreadsheets to manage information and prepare reports. **Chapter 7**

EVALUATION AND REVISION

1.7 Revise writing to improve organization and word choice after checking the logic of the ideas and the precision of the vocabulary. **Chapters 5, 6**

 2.0 Writing Applications (Genres and Their Characteristics)

Students write narrative, expository, persuasive, and descriptive texts of at least 500 to 700 words in each genre. The writing demonstrates a command of standard American English and the research, organizational, and drafting strategies outlined in Writing Standard 1.0.

Using the writing strategies of grade seven outlined in Writing Standard 1.0, students:

2.1 Write fictional or autobiographical narratives:
a. Develop a standard plot line (having a beginning, conflict, rising action, climax, and denouement) and point of view.
b. Develop complex major and minor characters and a definite setting.
c. Use a range of appropriate strategies (e.g., dialogue; suspense; naming of specific narrative action, including movement, gestures, and expressions). **Chapters 2, 5**

2.2 Write responses to literature:
a. Develop interpretations exhibiting careful reading, understanding, and insight.
b. Organize interpretations around several clear ideas, premises, or images from the literary work.
c. Justify interpretations through sustained use of examples and textual evidence. **Chapters 3, 8**

2.3 Write research reports:
a. Pose relevant and tightly drawn questions about the topic.
b. Convey clear and accurate perspectives on the subject.
c. Include evidence compiled through the formal research process (e.g., use of a card catalog, *Reader's Guide to Periodical Literature,* a computer catalog, magazines, newspapers, dictionaries).
d. Document reference sources by means of footnotes and a bibliography. **Chapter 7**

2.4 Write persuasive compositions:

a. State a clear position or perspective in support of a proposition or proposal.

b. Describe the points in support of the proposition, employing well-articulated evidence.

c. Anticipate and address reader concerns and counterarguments. **Chapters 4, 6**

2.5 Write summaries of reading materials:

a. Include the main ideas and most significant details.

b. Use the student's own words, except for quotations.

c. Reflect underlying meaning, not just the superficial details. **Chapters 1, 7**

WRITTEN AND ORAL ENGLISH-LANGUAGE CONVENTIONS

The standards for written and oral English-language conventions have been placed between those for writing and for listening and speaking because these conventions are essential to both sets of skills.

 1.0 Written and Oral English-Language Conventions

Students write and speak with a command of standard English conventions appropriate to the grade level.

SENTENCE STRUCTURE

1.1 Place modifiers properly and use the active voice. *Warriner's Handbook* First Course **Chapters 9, 11**

GRAMMAR

1.2 Identify and use infinitives and participles and make clear references between pronouns and antecedents. *Warriner's Handbook* First Course **Chapters 5, 10**

1.3 Identify all parts of speech and types and structure of sentences. *Warriner's Handbook* First Course **Chapters 1, 2, 3**

1.4 Demonstrate the mechanics of writing (e.g., quotation marks, commas at end of dependent clauses) and appropriate English usage (e.g., pronoun reference). *Warriner's Handbook* First Course **Chapters 8, 9, 10, 11, 12, 13, 14, 15, 16, 17**

PUNCTUATION

1.5 Identify hyphens, dashes, brackets, and semicolons and use them correctly. *Warriner's Handbook* First Course **Chapter 15**

CAPITALIZATION

1.6 Use correct capitalization. *Warriner's Handbook* First Course **Chapter 13**

SPELLING

1.7 Spell derivatives correctly by applying the spellings of bases and affixes. *Warriner's Handbook* First Course **Chapter 16**

Table of Contents

ENGLISH–LANGUAGE ARTS CONTENT STANDARDS continued

LISTENING AND SPEAKING

 1.0 Listening and Speaking Strategies

Deliver focused, coherent presentations that convey ideas clearly and relate to the background and interests of the audience. Students evaluate the content of oral communication.

COMPREHENSION

1.1 Ask probing questions to elicit information, including evidence to support the speaker's claims and conclusions. **Chapters 4, 7**

1.2 Determine the speaker's attitude toward the subject. **Chapters 4, 7**

1.3 Respond to persuasive messages with questions, challenges, or affirmations. **Chapter 4**

ORGANIZATION AND DELIVERY OF ORAL COMMUNICATION

1.4 Organize information to achieve particular purposes and to appeal to the background and interests of the audience. **Chapters 2, 3, 7, 8**

1.5 Arrange supporting details, reasons, descriptions, and examples effectively and persuasively in relation to the audience. **Chapters 2, 3, 4, 8**

1.6 Use speaking techniques, including voice modulation, inflection, tempo, enunciation, and eye contact, for effective presentations.
Chapters 2, 3, 4, 7, 8

ANALYSIS AND EVALUATION OF ORAL AND MEDIA COMMUNICATIONS

1.7 Provide constructive feedback to speakers concerning the coherence and logic of a speech's content and delivery and its overall impact upon the listener. **Chapter 8**

1.8 Analyze the effect on the viewer of images, text, and sound in electronic journalism; identify the techniques used to achieve the effects in each instance studied. **Chapter 6**

 2.0 Speaking Applications (Genres and Their Characteristics)

Students deliver well-organized formal presentations employing traditional rhetorical strategies (e.g., narration, exposition, persuasion, description). Student speaking demonstrates a command of standard American English and the organizational and delivery strategies outlined in Listening and Speaking Standard 1.0.

Using the speaking strategies of grade seven outlined in Listening and Speaking Standard 1.0, students:

2.1 Deliver narrative presentations:
  a. Establish a context, standard plot line (having a beginning, conflict, rising action, climax, and denouement), and point of view.
  b. Describe complex major and minor characters and a definite setting.
  c. Use a range of appropriate strategies, including dialogue, suspense, and naming of specific narrative action (e.g., movement, gestures, expressions). **Chapters 2, 5**

2.2 Deliver oral summaries of articles and books:

a. Include the main ideas of the event or article and the most significant details.

b. Use the student's own words, except for material quoted from sources.

c. Convey a comprehensive understanding of sources, not just superficial details.
Chapter 1

2.3 Deliver research presentations:

a. Pose relevant and concise questions about the topic.

b. Convey clear and accurate perspectives on the subject.

c. Include evidence generated through the formal research process (e.g., use of a card catalog, *Reader's Guide to Periodical Literature,* computer databases, magazines, newspapers, dictionaries).

d. Cite reference sources appropriately.
Chapter 7

2.4 Deliver persuasive presentations:

a. State a clear position or perspective in support of an argument or proposal.

b. Describe the points in support of the argument and employ well-articulated evidence.
Chapters 3, 4

Table of Contents

Why Be a Reader/Writer?

by **Kylene Beers**

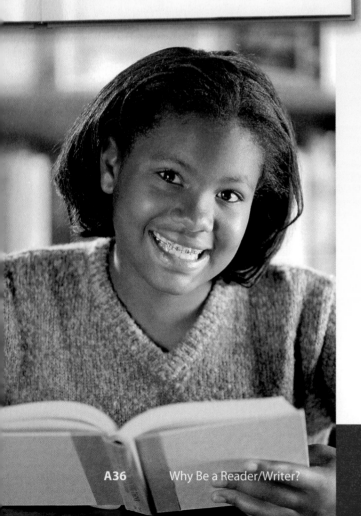

You've heard this story before, haven't you?

Once upon a time there were three bears— Mama Bear, Papa Bear, and Baby Bear.

Goldilocks "visits" the Bear home while the family is out. She destroys their place while searching for the food, chair, and bed that are *just right* for her. When the Bear family returns, Goldie runs off without even an "I'm-so-sorry" apology.

The Bears are left to clean up everything— end of story.

What Is the Message?

Isn't this an odd story to tell young children? Is it trying to teach them that

- children can be more trouble than bears?
- we must lock the door when we leave the house?
- sometimes people might do things they know are wrong?

The message I like most is that we are all searching for the things that are *just right* for us. While I don't like the way Goldilocks went about getting what she wanted, I do understand her need to find the food, the chair, and the bed that were *just right*.

Goldilocks wanted things that fit her needs. Interestingly, as she grows and changes, those needs will change. She'll outgrow the *just right* chair, and the *too big* chair will fit *just right*.

The *Just Right* Reading / Writing Experience

When you read and write, you're often looking for the *just right* experience that fits your needs. *Holt Literature and Language Arts* gives you many opportunities to find out how a book is *just right* for you.

Using the Standards to Set the Standard

Sometimes we need lessons to help us accomplish all the things a skilled reader can do. This book is designed to help you master the skills you need to be a strong reader *and* writer. The California standards are your tour guide. They will lead you through this book, helping you learn the literacy skills you'll need for this year, for your remaining years in school, and for all your life as a member of society.

Everyone who worked on this book—the people who chose the reading selections, the people who wrote the activities, the people who chose the artwork—continually asked themselves, "How do we create a book that not only meets the California standards but also *sets* the standard when it comes to helping students become readers and writers?" We think that, as you read through this book, you'll find that we answered that question by providing you with

- interesting selections to read
- powerful models to help you learn to write
- many opportunities to practice new skills
- specific information about each standard—so that you will always know what is expected of you
- the kinds of topics and art that middle-schoolers have told us interest them

In this book, then, you'll get practice in all kinds of language skills.

- You will read a variety of material, from ads to odes, from stories to Web pages.
- You will learn better ways to speak, listen, and write.
- You will understand more, sound better, and be more confident about what you know and understand.

There are many reasons to be a skillful reader and an effective writer—good grades, passing tests, getting into college. The best reason—the *just right* reason—has to do with reading and writing to discover more about yourself and the world you live in.

So, let what you read and write this year act as a *mirror* that shows you more about yourself or a *window* that shows you worlds beyond where you live.

Whichever you do, you'll be discovering the reason that is *just right* for you.

Kylene Beers

Senior Author
Holt Literature and Language Arts

How to Use Your Textbook

 Getting to know a new textbook is like getting to know a new video game. In each case, you have to figure out how the game or book is structured, as well as understand its rules. If you understand the structure of your book, you can be successful from the start.

Chapter Opener

What is the focus of each chapter, or section of the book? What does the image suggest about what the chapter will cover? On the right, you'll see a bold heading that says "Plot and Setting" or "Character." These are the **literary skills** you will study in the chapter. Also in bold type is the **Informational Text Focus** for the chapter. These are the skills you use to read informational texts such as a newspaper or Web site. Keep the **What Do You Think?** question in mind as you go through the chapter. Your answers may even surprise you.

Literary Skills Focus

Like a set of rules or a map, the **Literary Skills Focus** shows you how literary elements work in stories and poems, helping you navigate through selections more easily. The Literary Skills Focus will help you get to your destination— understanding and enjoying the selections.

Reading Skills Focus

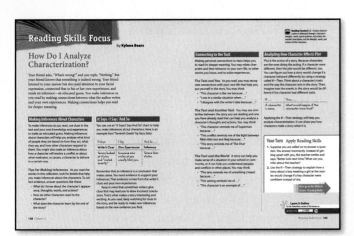

Your mind is working all the time as you read, even if you're not aware of it. Still, all readers, even very good ones, sometimes don't understand what they've read. **Reading Skills Focus** gives you the skills to help you improve your reading.

Reading Model

You tend to do things more quickly and easily if you have a model to follow. The **Reading Model** enhances your learning by demonstrating the literary and reading skills that you will practice in the chapter.

Wrap Up

Think of **Wrap Up** as a bridge that gives you a chance to practice the skills on which the chapter will focus. It also introduces you to the **Academic Vocabulary** you will study in the chapter: the language of school, business, and standardized tests. To be successful in school, you'll need to understand and use academic language.

How to Use Your Textbook

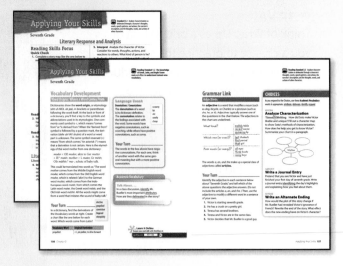

Literary Selection Pages
Preparing to Read

If you have ever done something complicated, you know that things go more smoothly with some preparation. It is the same with reading. The **Preparing to Read** page gives you a boost by presenting the literary, reading, and writing skills you will learn about and use as you read the selection. The list of **Vocabulary** words gives the words you need to know for reading both the selection and beyond the selection. **Language Coach** explains the inner workings of English—like looking at the inside of a clock.

Selection
Meet the Writer

Meet the Writer gives you all kinds of interesting facts about the authors who wrote the selections in this book. **Build Background** provides information you sometimes need when a selection deals with unfamiliar times, places, and situations. **Preview the Selection** presents the selection's main character and hints at what is to come. **Read with a Purpose** helps you set a goal for your reading. It helps you answer the question, "What is the point of this selection?"

Applying Your Skills

If you have a special talent or hobby, you know that you have to practice to master it. In **Applying Your Skills,** you will apply the reading, literary, vocabulary, and language skills from the Preparing to Read page that you practiced as you read the selection. This gives you a chance to check on how you are mastering these skills.

Comparing Texts

You probably compare people, places, and things all the time, such as a favorite singer's new songs with her previous album. In **Comparing Texts,** you will compare different works—sometimes by the same author, sometimes by different authors—that have something in common.

Informational Text Focus

When you read a Web site or follow a technical manual, you are reading informational text. The skills you use in this type of reading are different from the ones you use for literary text. **Informational Text Focus** helps you gain the skills that will enable you to be a more successful reader in daily life and on standardized tests.

Standards Review

Do you dread test-taking time? Do you struggle over reading the passage and then choosing the correct answer? **Standards Review** can reduce your "guesses" and give you the practice you need to feel more confident during testing.

Writing Workshop

Does a blank piece of paper send shivers up your spine? **The Writing Workshop** will help you tackle the page. It takes you step-by-step through developing an effective piece of writing. Models, annotations, graphic organizers, and charts take the "What now?" out of writing for different purposes and audiences.

Preparing for Timed Writing

What is your idea of a nightmare? Maybe it is trying to respond to a writing prompt. **Preparing for Timed Writing** helps you practice for on-demand, or timed, writing so that you can realize your dreams of success.

Informational Text Focus: Note Taking, Outlining, and Summarizing

Features highlighted in **yellow** constitute a suggested minimum course of study.

Introducing The Skills

Selection or Feature	For Independent Reading	Grade–Level Standards
Literary Skills Focus: What is Plot?		**Reading Standard 3.2:** Plot
Reading Skills Focus: How Do I Explain Past, Present, and Future Actions?		**Reading Standard 3.2:** Plot
Reading Model: The Dinner Party by Mona Gardner (Easily Accessible, Lexile 990) **Skills in Action:** Wrap Up	• **Hang a Thousand Trees with Ribbons: the Story of Phillis Wheatley** by Ann Rinaldi	**Reading Standard 3.2:** Plot

Applying The Skills

Selection or Feature	For Independent Reading	Grade–Level Standards
Rikki-tikki-tavi by Rudyard Kipling (Accessible, Lexile 1060)	• **The Jungle Book** by Rudyard Kipling • **Beauty of the Beast: Poems from the Animal Kingdom** by Jack Prelutsky	**Reading Standard 3.2:** Plot **Reading Standard 1.3:** Clarify word meanings
Three Skeleton Key by George G. Toudouze (Challenging, Lexile 1190)	• **The True Confessions of Charlotte Doyle** by Avi • **Shipwreck at the Bottom of the World: The Extraordinary True Story of Shackleton and the Endurance** by Jennifer Armstrong	**Reading Standard 3.2:** Plot **Reading Standard 1.3:** Clarify word meanings
The Dive by René Saldaña, Jr. (Accessible, Lexile 750)	• **Esperanza Rising** by Pam Munoz Ryan • **Runs with Horses** by Brian Burks	**Reading Standard 3.2:** Plot **Reading Standard 1.3:** Clarify word meanings
The Monsters Are Due on Maple Street by Rod Serling (Accessible, Lexile N/A)	• **Running Out of Time** by Margaret Peterson Haddix • **Parasite Pig** by William Sleator	**Reading Standard 3.2:** Plot **Reading Standard 1.3:** Clarify word meanings
Comparing Texts: Plots in Science Fiction Stories • **Zoo** by Edward D. Hoch (Accessible, Lexile 1190) • **He—y, Come on Ou—t!** by Shinichi Hoshi (Challenging, Lexile 890)	• **Tomorrowland: Ten Stories about the Future** compiled by Michael Cart • **A Wrinkle in Time** by Madeleine L'Engle	**Reading Standard 3.2:** Plot
Informational Text Focus: Note Taking, Outlining, and Summarizing • **Empress Theodora** (Challenging, Lexile 1140) • **The Hippodrome** (Accessible, Lexile 1090)		**Reading Standard 2.4:** Create outlines, notes, and summaries

Mastering The Skills

Selection or Feature	Grade–Level Standards
Writing Workshop: Summary	**Writing Standard 2.5:** Write summaries.
Preparing for Timed Writing: Summary	**Writing Standard 2.5:** Write summaries.
Listening and Speaking Workshop: Presenting an Oral Narrative	**Listening and Speaking Standard 2.2:** Deliver oral summaries.
Standards Review: Literary Skills Review Informational Skills Review Vocabulary Skills Review Writing Skills Review	**Reading Standard 3.2:** Plot **Reading Standard 2.4:** Create outlines, notes, and summaries. **Reading Standard 1.3:** Clarify word meanings. **Writing Standard 2.5:** Write summaries.

Daily and Weekly Support

- **Reader/Writer Notebook**
- **Reading and Writing Transparencies**
- **Weekly Standards Review Transparencies**
- **Family Involvement Activities in Five Languages**
- **Language Handbook Worksheets**
- **Holt Virtual File Cabinet for Language Arts**
- **Spelling Lessons and Activities**

Assessment Resources

- **Chapter 1 Resources**, Diagnostic Test; Selection Standards Check, Chapter Standards Mastery
- **Universal Access: Differentiating Instruction**, leveled assessment
- **Formal Assessment**, Entry-Level Test
- **English-Language Conventions Progress-Monitoring Test**, Chapters 1–3, 13
- **ThinkCentral Online Assessment**

Print Resources for Universal Access

	On-Level Learners	English Learners	Struggling Readers/Writers	Students Who Use African American Vernacular English	Advanced Learners	Students with Disabilities
Chapter 1 Resources practice and assessment for all selections and features	✔				✔	
Universal Access: Holt Interactive Reader interactive readings for Minimum-Course-of-Study Selections		✔	✔	✔		✔
Holt Interactive Reader for English Language Development adaptations of Minimum-Course-of-Study Selections		✔				
Universal Access: Differentiating Instruction modified lesson plans, graphic organizers, and leveled assessment		✔	✔	✔		✔
Universal Access: Resources for Teaching Advanced Students modified lesson plans for Minimum-Course-of-Study Selections					✔	
Universal Access: Supporting Instruction in Five Languages translations of selection summaries and key terms		✔				
Universal Access: Holt Interactive Writer and Speaker practice and assessment	✔	✔	✔	✔	✔	✔
Language and Sentence Skills Practice for Warriner's Handbook Chapters 1–3, 13	✔				✔	
Universal Access: Developmental Language and Sentence Skills Practice for Warriner's Handbook Chapters 1–3, 13		✔	✔	✔		✔

Technology Resources

Assessment Resources

Teacher Management Resources

Student Edition Extension Activities

Student Edition Support

Find all of Holt's technology resources at go.hrw.com. Technology resources are also listed at point of use in the wrap; below are our featured components for Chapter 1.

Teacher Management Resources

ThinkCentral, Teacher Access
Teacher One Stop™
Holt Professional Learning for Language Arts

Spotlight on ThinkCentral, Teacher Access

All of the chapter's resources are available on ThinkCentral, Teacher Access. Online suggestions:
- Suggest students use the interactive Venn diagram when comparing and contrasting "Rikki-tikki-tavi" and "Three Skeleton Key."
- Play the audio recording of "The Dive" so students can hear the Spanish words pronounced correctly.

Student Edition Support

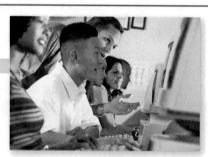

PowerNotes
ThinkCentral, Student Access
Student One Stop™
Interactive Reading Workshops
Interactive Graphic Organizers
Writers' Lives
Holt Audio Library
Holt Audio Library: Selections and Summaries in Spanish

Spotlight on ThinkCentral, Student Access

ThinkCentral, Student Access offers the print book in an online format, and more!
- Encourage English learners to take advantage of the vocabulary help provided at point of use throughout "Rikki-tikki-tavi," "Three Skeleton Key," and "The Dive."
- Spanish speakers can also access the Spanish summaries of the stories to help them with comprehension.

Student Edition Extension Activities

Digital Storytelling Mini-Site
NovelWise Mini-Site
MediaScope Mini-Site
WordSharp: An Interactive Vocabulary Tutor
GrammarNotes
WritingNotes
Writing and Research in a Digital Age
Literature Links
Holt Audio Tutor for English Language Development

Spotlight on NovelWise

Explore science fiction further through the NovelWise mini-site genres section.

Universal Access: Advanced students may appreciate an opportunity to explore this genre and to find science fiction novels.

Supported strands: Literature, Reading

Assessment Resources

5. When a writer uses a **first-person narrator**, the story —
- ○ A does not contain dialogue between the characters
- → ○ B is told by one of the characters
- ○ C does not contain a main character
- ○ D has only one character

Correct Answer: B

7.1.5
point of view

ThinkCentral Online Assessment
Holt Online Essay Scoring
ThinkCentral Online Remediation

Spotlight on ThinkCentral Online Assessment

Find the Chapter 1 Diagnostic Test and Chapter Standards Mastery here, correlated to standards covered in this chapter. The individualized diagnostic reporting will let you see the concepts in this chapter for which each student will need extra help.

The wrap for these selections includes specific ideas and strategies from *Holt Literature and Language Arts* authors.

From the Author

For "Rikki-Tikki-Tavi," p. 16

You can use this story to help your students become more familiar with important literary elements, such as plot, symbol, protagonist, and antagonist. In addition, because animals function as main characters, you can also discuss how authors use literary techniques such as personification. The story of Rikki-tikki-tavi is a story of bravery and loyalty. The little mongoose musters the courage to confront his natural enemy because of the gratitude he feels to the human family he has befriended. Even though he is a mongoose, Rikki-tikki-tavi represents admirable qualities to which human beings can also aspire.

Linda Rief

Teacher to Teacher

Preteach I introduce plot by presenting a plot-structure graphic organizer. Students then read a familiar story, perhaps "The Three Bears." I model "plotting the plot" with the class. We discuss the change in Goldilocks as the plot unfolds: She vowed to never again go to the house of the three bears.

Direct Teach We then read a text selection, for example, "The Dinner Party," and students "plot the plot." We then have a class discussion and record findings on the board or use software to create the graphic organizer on an LCD projector. With "The Dinner Party," there could be discussion about imagery, mood, and point of view. There could also be debate regarding the American's internal and external conflict. In this story, character development is very important to plot development.

MaryAlice Madden
Santa Ana, California

Assess Students write a well organized essay in which they explain what the characters are feeling, and how their actions affect the plot. They should include literary devices and evidence from the story to support ideas.

Holt Professional Learning

Visit ThinkCentral, Teacher Access to link to Holt's Professional Learning site for English/Language Arts teachers. This site features:

- Videos that share the insights of *Holt Literature and Language Arts* program authors and consultants and demonstrate proven classroom strategies with master teachers
- Study guides for publications by our authors and consultants
- Informative articles and useful Web links
- Help in planning your department's professional learning sessions
- A handbook for new teachers

Effective Vocabulary Instruction
with Carol Jago and Kylene Beers

VIDEO PRODUCTS

Strategies for Helping Struggling Readers
with Kylene Beers

Effective Vocabulary Instruction
with Carol Jago and Kylene Beers

Developing Critical Thinking About Literature
with Carol Jago and Deborah Appleman

Teaching Students to Revise, Not Recopy
with Linda Rief

Teaching English Learners
with Robin Scarcella

Using Literature Circles
with Harvey Daniels

Teaching On-Demand Writing Skills
with Leila Christenbury

Managing the Heterogeneous Classroom
with Leila Christenbury and Patrick Schwarz

Teaching Narrative and Expository Texts
with Judith Irvin and Deborah Appleman

Becoming a Tech-Savvy Teacher
with Sara Kajder

Re-engaging the Disengaged Student
with Alfred Tatum

Teaching Grammar in Context
with Amy Benjamin

Woman in Boat Looking at Whale
by Christopher Zacharow.

Analyzing Visuals

Tell students that the artist who created this image, **Christopher Zacharow**, was born in Poland and currently teaches art at New York's Pratt Institute.

Extension Activity Ask students to describe a story that this painting could be telling. What details from the painting suggest this story? ***Possible response:*** *The girl is looking curiously at the whale, who seems to be looking back at her. They look like they're interested in each other. This painting might be telling a story about an unexpected friendship between a girl who is stranded in a small boat and a whale who rescues her.*

Chapter Resources

On Course: Mapping Instruction

Chapter 1 Resources

Warriner's Handbook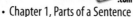
  • Chapter 1, Parts of a Sentence
  • Chapter 2, Parts of Speech Overview

PowerNotes

Teacher One Stop™

Holt Pronunciation Resources
  • Phoneme Sounds and Spellings
  • Support for Speakers of African American Vernacular English

Formal Assessment, Progress Monitoring Test 1

Holt Virtual File Cabinet for Language Arts, grammar, reading, and vocabulary resources

English-Language Conventions Progress-Monitoring Tests

ThinkCentral Online Assessment

ThinkCentral Online Remediation

CHAPTER 1

Plot

INFORMATIONAL TEXT FOCUS
Note Taking, Outlining, and Summarizing

 California Standards
Here are the Grade 7 standards you will work toward mastering in Chapter 1.

Word Analysis, Fluency, and Systematic Vocabulary Development
1.3 Clarify word meanings through the use of definition, example, restatement, or contrast.

Reading Comprehension (Focus on Informational Materials)
Grade 6 Review
2.4 Clarify an understanding of texts by creating outlines, logical notes, summaries, or reports.

Literary Response and Analysis
3.2 Identify events that advance the plot and determine how each event explains past or present action(s) or foreshadows future action(s).

Writing Applications (Genres and Their Characteristics)
2.5 Write summaries of reading materials:
 a. Include the main ideas and most significant details.
 b. Use the student's own words, except for quotations.
 c. Reflect underlying meaning, not just the superficial details.

" You gain strength, courage, and confidence by every experience in which you really stop to look fear in the face."

—Eleanor Roosevelt

 What Do **You** Think

How might confronting a difficult situation help you become a stronger person?

Learn It Online
Learn about plot in novels online at *NovelWise*:

go.hrw.com | H7-3 | **Go**

Chapter Objectives
- Students will read a variety of short stories, exploring the mechanics of plot.
- Students will also learn how to predict future events in a story through clues given by the author, how to visualize descriptions from stories, how authors use suspense to keep a reader's interest, and how to summarize a story's key information.
- In the Informational Text Focus, students will learn how taking notes, outlining, and summarizing help readers better understand the selection.
- At the end of the chapter, students will have the opportunity to share their own unique perspectives by writing and presenting a short story.

Routines for California Classrooms
For ideas on classroom practices and approaches to grouping, see the discussion of routines on pages T34–T37 of this Teacher's Edition.

What Do You Think?
How might confronting a difficult situation help you become a stronger person?
Read the quotation aloud. Then, ask students to think of a time when they or someone they know faced a fear. Have students discuss how facing and conquering these difficulties helped them become stronger and more confident.

Real Issues, Real Experts: Professional Learning

Spotlight on . . .
Effective Vocabulary Instruction
Works such as "Rikki-tikki-tavi" and "Three Skeleton Key" contain unfamiliar words and complex syntax that students may find challenging. To help students become more comfortable with the vocabulary in these selections, consider the suggestions you'll find in this video:

In *Effective Vocabulary Instruction*, Holt authors **Carol Jago** and **Kylene Beers** discuss vocabulary development in three ways: preteaching selection vocabulary, teaching academic vocabulary, and teaching students skills to acquire new vocabulary independently.

This video is accompanied by printable articles, planning materials, and a training guide for supervisors. For these resources and more, visit **Holt Professional Learning for Language Arts** by going to this page in ThinkCentral, Teacher Access.

 Learn It Online
NovelWise includes instruction on choosing, reading, and analyzing novels; it also contains a catalogue of book summaries, study guides, teaching guides, and PowerPoint presentations.

go.hrw.com | H7-3 | **Go**

Literary Skills Focus

by **Linda Rief**

Literary Skills Focus

Objectives

Students will

- understand plot
- understand conflict
- understand suspense and foreshadowing

Preteach

Build Background Ask students to share what they already know about plot. How have they encountered this term and elements in previous readings? Ask volunteers to describe the plots of texts they are familiar with.

Direct Teach

Plot

- Explain the metaphor of the plot being a story's skeleton: Just as our bones give our bodies shape and support, a story's plot gives it a unique structure and holds it together.

- Tell students that characters in a story may face multiple internal and external conflicts, often related to each other. For example, a character might win first place in the talent show and learn to have faith in her talents at the same time.

What Is Plot?

You've heard the expression "the plot thickens." Like cooks who add delicious ingredients to soup or salsa, authors use intriguing tools to make their stories more compelling: suspense that keeps us on the edge of our seats, foreshadowing that gives us clues to future events, and complicated plots with twists and turns. Authors thicken the plot—the story's events—so that we can taste, or experience, the story's various ingredients more fully.

> SHORT STORY
>
> "Once upon a time, they lived happily ever after."

Plot

Plot The **plot** is the story's skeleton. It is a series of related events, each one growing out of another. Most plots consist of four parts.

1. **Basic situation** In the beginning of a plot, you meet the main characters and find out what they want. You also discover the central conflict that **advances** the story, or moves it forward.

   A **conflict** is a struggle between opposing characters, forces, or emotions. There are two main kinds of conflict: external and internal. An **external conflict** involves one character's struggle with another character or with an outside force or event (a bear, a plane crash, a tornado, or an icy path).

   > Rikki-tikki had never met a live cobra before. . . . He knew that all a grown mongoose's business in life was to fight and eat snakes.
   >
   > from "Rikki-tikki-tavi"
   > by Rudyard Kipling

An **internal conflict** takes place within a character's mind, such as a struggle of conscience:

> She saw herself three years later, marching for graduation, everyone taking photos, smiling, everyone happy, except she wouldn't be because she'd remember having cheated that time back in the ninth grade.
>
> from "The Dive"
> by René Saldaña, Jr.

2. **Series of events** As the plot advances, one or more of the characters struggles to work out, or resolve, the conflict. A series of events called **complications** develops. Each complication is a "roadblock" that forces the main character to struggle more in order to get what he or she wants. These complications, which arise from past events introduced earlier in the plot, often hint at the character's future actions.

> Just then the wind rose and the *Cornelius de Witt* changed course, leaned to port, and headed straight for us once more.
>
> from "Three Skeleton Key"
> by George G. Toudouze

Resources

Chapter 1 Resources, Literary Focus Skill Builder, p. 3

PowerNotes, interactive lesson presentation with activities

Teacher One Stop™, on-level lesson plans and all print resources

Universal Access

EL English Learners/Struggling Readers
English for Academic Success To help students learn the academic terms in the Literary Focus, write the definitions for each of the following plot elements on index cards or a transparency without identifying the element.

- **basic situation**—introduction of the main characters and what they want
- **conflict**—struggle between opposing characters, forces, or emotions

Reading Standard 3.2 Identify events that advance the plot and determine how each event explains past or present action(s) or foreshadows future action(s).

3. **Climax** The **climax**, the most suspenseful part of the story, is the point at which the outcome of the conflict is decided.

> Rikki-tikki shook some of the dust out of his fur and sneezed. "It is all over," he said. "The widow will never come out again."
>
> from "Rikki-tikki-tavi"
> by Rudyard Kipling

4. **Resolution** The **resolution** is the last part of the story, when loose ends are tied up.

> Melly could smell the sweetness of the flowers and herbs wafting from across the street. She smiled, closed her eyes, and slept.
>
> from "The Dive"
> by René Saldaña, Jr.

Two Other Important Elements of Plot

Suspense A critical element in fiction and drama is **suspense**, the anxious curiosity that makes us continue reading in order to find out what is going to happen next. Suspense reaches its height just before the climax of a story, but it usually starts building as soon as the conflict becomes apparent. Various complications that advance the plot help to further build the suspense throughout a story.

> Teddy shouted to the house: "Oh, look here! Our mongoose is killing a snake," and Rikki-tikki heard a scream from Teddy's mother.
>
> from "Rikki-tikki-tavi"
> by Rudyard Kipling

Foreshadowing Sometimes suspense is increased by hints or clues about future events. The writer's use of such hints or clues is called **foreshadowing**. For example, a character about to dive into the ocean may hear someone remark that sharks were once sighted near shore. As you read, you suspect the sharks will appear again—and you feel that tingle of fear and excitement that keeps you turning the pages.

> Three Skeleton Key . . . earned its name from the story of three convicts who, escaping from Cayenne in a stolen dugout canoe, were wrecked on the rock during the night, managed to escape the sea, but eventually died of hunger and thirst.
>
> from "Three Skeleton Key"
> by George G. Toudouze

Your Turn Analyze Plot

1. What is the difference between an internal conflict and an external conflict?

2. Look at the excerpts from "Rikki-tikki-tavi" on these pages. What event might these passages foreshadow?

3. Think about a movie, television show, or story you know well. Test your knowledge of its plot by recording the main events of the story.

Learn It Online
To understand the role of literary elements in novels, visit *NovelWise* at:

go.hrw.com | H7-5 | Go

Two Other Important Elements of Plot

- Give students an example of a suspenseful situation, such as waiting to find out whether or not you've gotten a role in a play or a spot on a sports team.

- Then, have students discuss suspenseful events in their lives or examples of suspense that they've encountered in books, movies, or television shows.

Check for Understanding

Your Turn

Possible responses:

1. *An internal conflict occurs in a character's mind, while an external conflict takes place between a character and another person, an animal, or nature.*

2. *These details foreshadow that Rikki-tikki-tavi will fight a snake.*

3. *In Song of the Trees, a developer takes a family's trees by force but is stopped when the father returns to fight for his family's land.*

Reteach

To reteach plot, see **Reteaching Lessons**, p. 842A.

ThinkCentral Online Remediation

- **external conflict**—character's struggle with another character or force
- **internal conflict**—character's struggle within his or her mind
- **complications**—things that make it harder for characters to solve the problem
- **climax**—point at which the problem is solved
- **resolution**—end of the story

Display the definitions one at a time to the class, reading aloud the definition and identifying the plot element it describes. Then, scramble the definitions and have students attempt to identify the plot element described in each.

Advanced Learners

Extension Have students work in pairs to develop a plot and setting for a short story on a topic of their choice, including at least one internal or external conflict for their main character.

Learn It Online
The **NovelWise** mini site includes instruction on choosing, reading, and analyzing novels; it also contains a catalogue of book summaries, study guides, teaching guides, and PowerPoint presentations.

go.hrw.com | H7-5 | Go

Objectives

Students will
- make predictions from a text
- understand how to summarize
- describe mental images that text descriptions evoke
- visualize textual details

Preteach

Build Skills Give students an example of an everyday situation, and ask them to guess what might happen next. You might say, "Juliet was sure she was going to win the school talent show with her amazing singing. On the day of the show, she woke up with a sore throat. What do you think happened next?"

Direct Teach

Making Predictions

Explain that if someone were asked to guess which of two strangers would win a contest without knowing any details, the person would have to make a random guess. If asked to guess which of two friends would win a foot race, the person could use what they know, such as the knowledge that one contestant is on the track team, to make an educated guess or prediction. Tell students to look for events or details that foreshadow what is to come when making predictions.

California Standards, pp. 6–7

■ **Reading Standard 3.2** Identify events that advance the plot and determine how each event explains past or present action(s) or foreshadows future action(s).

Reading Skills Focus

by **Kylene Beers**

How Do I Explain Past, Present, and Future Actions?

The following reading skills will help you think about what might happen next in a plot while you also think about what has already occurred. Predicting means looking at the clues the author gives you to point you in the right direction. Visualizing helps you imagine places, events, and characters. Summarizing helps you keep track of important events in the story's plot.

Making Predictions

To **make predictions,** you must make educated guesses about **future actions**—what will happen next in a story. Predictions are not random guesses. For instance, when you predict the outcome of a sports event, you probably base your prediction on the team's record of wins and losses.

Clues for Predicting When you read, you should base your predictions on:
- clues the writer includes that **foreshadow,** or hint at, future actions
- your knowledge of how people or animals behave in certain situations
- questions you ask yourself as you read

Visualizing

Every story is about characters who live in a particular time and place. Writers fill their stories with details about characters, settings, and actions that make people and places come alive. When you **visualize,** you form mental images of the details in a story. Visualizing helps you to see actions and events as you focus on specific plot elements.

Tips for Visualizing Use the following tips for visualizing text:
- Take note of sensory details that describe how something looks, feels, smells, tastes, or sounds.
- Write notes about key events or draw sketches of the setting and what is happening in it.
- Read aloud. Hearing the words will help you create mental images and clarify plot events.

A Model for Visualizing What images do you *see* as you read this paragraph?

When they were discovered, nothing remained but three heaps of bones, picked clean by the birds. The story was that the three skeletons, gleaming with phosphorescent light, danced over the small rock, screaming . . . .

from "Three Skeleton Key" by George G. Toudouze

← What do you see as you read about the discovery of the dead convicts?

← How about the dancing skeletons?

← Notice the strong verbs and adjectives, which will help paint pictures in your mind.

Resources

Chapter 1 Resources, Reading Focus Skill Builder, p. 4

PowerNotes, interactive lesson presentation with activities

Teacher One Stop™, on-level lesson plans and all print resources

Universal Access

English Learners/Struggling Readers

English for Academic Success Help students learn the academic terms in the Reading Skills Focus by identifying key parts of each word.
- Write the words *prediction, visualize,* and *summarize* on the board.
- Underline the word *predict* in *prediction*. Explain that when you predict something, you make a guess about something that might happen in the future. Therefore, a *prediction* is a description of a possible future event.

Summarizing a Short Story

Some events in short stories are more important than others. When you **summarize** a text, you highlight the most important information in your own words. For a short story you would include the main characters and major plot events. A summary of a text is much shorter than the original.

Summary Sheet: What to Include in a Summary Use a Summary Sheet like the one below to organize the most important information about any of the short stories in this chapter.

Sample Summary Here is the beginning of a summary of "Amigo Brothers" from Chapter 5:

> Seventeen-year-old best friends Antonio and Felix both dream of becoming a boxing champion. They train together until they find out they will fight one another in a match. They pledge to fight to win and then agree not to meet until the big night, a week away. Then the boys fight for three rounds. In the end, . . . (Read the story to find out!)

Time-Order Words for a Summary

Because the **sequence**, or order of events, is an important part of writing a summary, be sure to use time-order words and phrases, such as *first, second, next, then, until, after, later, eventually, finally,* and *in the end.* Which of these words and phrases are used in the sample summary at left?

Your Turn Apply Reading Skills

1. When you make predictions, how can you avoid making random guesses?
2. Read the following passage from "The Dinner Party," a story you will find on the following page. Which details in the passage help you visualize the setting and the characters? What kind of actions are shown here—past, present, or future actions?

> They are seated with their guests—army officers and government attachés and their wives, and a visiting American naturalist—in their spacious dining room, which has a bare marble floor, open rafters, and wide glass doors opening onto a veranda.

Now go to the Skills in Action: Reading Model

Learn It Online
Take another look at summarizing with the interactive reading workshops:
go.hrw.com   H7-7   **Go**

Visualizing

■ As students read the excerpt from "Three Skeleton Key" on p. 6, have them write down words that describe sight, sound, smell, taste, or touch.

■ Then, ask volunteers to share their lists. Record students' words in a "word cloud" on the board, and have students discuss whether or not the words in the word cloud create a mental image of the passage.

Summarizing

■ Draw and label a summary sheet like the one shown on p. 7 on the board. Then, use it to create a brief summary of a familiar text.

■ Have students volunteer the story's title and author, main characters, conflict, plot complications, climax, and resolution. Record students' responses in your summary sheet.

Check for Understanding

Your Turn _____

Possible responses:

1. *Predictions based on your prior knowledge or on clues that the writer provides will be more accurate than random guesses.*

2. *The details of the "spacious dining room," "bare marble floor," "open rafters," and "wide glass doors opening onto a veranda" help me visualize the setting. These are present actions.*

- Underline the word *visual* in *visualize*. Explain that something that is *visual* is something you can see. Remind students that *visual* is also related to the word *vision*. If you can *visualize* something, you can create an image of it in your mind. It's almost as if you can see it in front of you.

- Underline the word *sum* in *summarize*. Explain that in math, *sum* is another word for *total*. When you *summarize* a story, you tell what happened at the beginning, the middle, and the end. In other words, you give a short description of the total story, not just one or two parts.

Advanced Learners

Acceleration Arrange students into groups of three. Provide each group with a generic setting, such as a school, a backyard, a ballpark, or a city street. Have students brainstorm words to describe what someone might see, hear, smell, touch, or taste in this setting. Have each group read aloud their word lists to the class while the class tries to visualize the setting based on the words the group chose.

Learn It Online
Reading Workshops are interactive versions of real-world informational text. Students exercise their reading skills by responding to online polls and answering questions in an engaging format.
go.hrw.com   H7-7   **Go**

Reading Model

Objectives

Students will

- understand how plot and setting function in a short story
- make predictions about, visualize, and summarize story events

Preteach

Read with a Purpose Direct students to read the Read with a Purpose statement. Have students read the first page of "The Dinner Party" and note the colonel's prediction. Tell them to use what they have read so far to make their own educated prediction—do they think the colonel will be proven wrong? Why or why not? Have them respond in their **Reader/Writer Notebook.**

Direct Teach

Model the Skill

Use the Reading Model to demonstrate the application of the Literary and Reading skills in a short selection. As you or students read the model aloud, stop to discuss the side annotations and highlighting, which are aids to comprehension and analysis.

▶ Literary Focus

Plot What characters are introduced in the first paragraph? ***Possible response:*** *A colonial official, his wife, an American naturalist, and other army officers and their wives.*

▶ Reading Focus

Visualizing How do you picture the dining room? ***Possible response:*** *It is huge, fancy, and well-decorated, with a large table full of guests.*

▶ Literary Focus

Plot What details in the fourth paragraph build on the foreshadowing of the crisis? ***Possible response:*** *The hostess stares ahead; her muscles contract.*

Read with a Purpose Read the following short story to discover if a colonel's predictions about women's behavior come true.

The Dinner Party

by **Mona Gardner**

Literary Focus

Plot The author immediately presents the **basic situation,** telling us where the story takes place and what event is occurring.

Reading Focus

Visualizing Notice the sensory details the writer uses to describe the dining room. Words such as *spacious* and *marble* help you create a mental picture of the setting.

Literary Focus

Plot The dinner party discussion **foreshadows** future actions. The colonel's statement hints that this discussion may lead to a future event in which the people in the room may have to react to a crisis and a woman may play a central role.

The country is India. A colonial official and his wife are giving a large dinner party. They are seated with their guests—army officers and government attachés[1] and their wives, and a visiting American naturalist[2]—in their spacious dining room, which has a bare marble floor, open rafters, and wide glass doors opening onto a veranda.

A spirited discussion springs up between a young girl who insists that women have outgrown the jumping-on-a-chair-at-the-sight-of-a-mouse era and a colonel who says that they haven't.

"A woman's unfailing reaction in any crisis," the colonel says, "is to scream. While a man may feel like it, he has that ounce more of nerve control than a woman has. That last ounce is what counts."

The American does not join in the argument but watches the other guests. As he looks, he sees a strange expression come over the face of the hostess. She is staring straight ahead, her muscles contracting slightly. With a slight gesture she summons the Indian boy standing behind her chair and whispers to him. The boy's eyes widen; he quickly leaves the room.

1. **attachés:** (at uh SHAYZ): diplomatic officials.
2. **naturalist:** one who studies nature by observing animals and plants.

🐻 **California Standards, pp. 8–11**

- **Reading Standard 3.2** Identify events that advance the plot and determine how each event explains past or present action(s) or foreshadows future action(s).

Selection Readability	
Easily Accessible Accessible Challenging	background information; familiar language; chronological order

Selection Plot Summary

In India, several people attend a party, where a colonel argues that women will always scream and panic in a crisis, while men have more control. When a cobra appears in the house, a brave woman quietly demonstrates control over her fears.

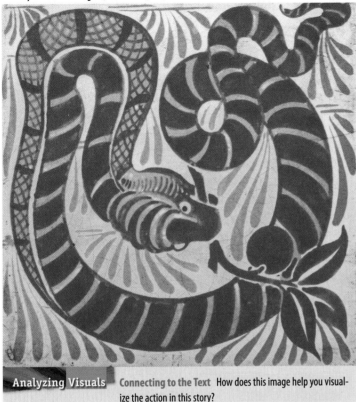

Cobra by William De Morgan (1839–1917). Ceramic.

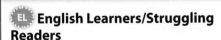
Analyzing Visuals **Connecting to the Text** How does this image help you visualize the action in this story?

Of the guests, none except the American notices this nor sees the boy place a bowl of milk on the veranda just outside the open doors.

The American comes to with a start. In India, milk in a bowl means only one thing—bait for a snake. He realizes there must be a cobra in the room. He looks up at the rafters—the likeliest place—but they are bare. Three corners of the room are empty, and in the fourth the servants are waiting to serve the next course. There is only one place left—under the table.

His first impulse is to jump back and warn the others, but he knows the commotion would frighten the cobra into striking. He speaks quickly, the tone of his voice so arresting that it sobers everyone.

Reading Focus

Summarizing A **summary** of the story would include the fact that the American realizes there's a snake in the room. It would not mention that he looks up at the rafters—that is not a main event in the **plot.**

Literary Focus

Plot The American's actions in the present can be traced back to his earlier observation of the expressions on the faces of the hostess and the boy and to his prior knowledge of what a bowl of milk might mean.

Model the Skill

▶ **Reading Focus**

Summarizing What information on p. 9 would most likely *not* be included in a summary of this story? *Possible response:* details about where the servants are standing

▶ **Literary Focus**

Plot How does the writer build suspense in the last paragraph on p. 9? *Possible response: The reader is waiting for the naturalist's silence to be broken. When the American speaks, he speaks quickly in an arresting tone.*

Analyzing Visuals

William De Morgan, born in 1839, was a true Renaissance man. While most famous for his ceramics, like the one at left, he was also a novelist, knowledgeable chemist, and designer of pottery kilns.

Connecting to the Text: The image helps me visualize the cobra described in the story.

Universal Access: Vocabulary

EL **English Learners/Struggling Readers**

English for Academic Success To help students understand the selection, introduce them to the following vocabulary words:

- **colonel**—a military officer. *The colonel had just arrived home from the war.*
- **veranda**—a porch or balcony. *The boy placed the milk outside on the veranda.*
- **contracting**—becoming tighter. *The woman's muscles began contracting when she saw the snake.*
- **impulse**—reaction or urge. *When the man saw the snake, he had the impulse to jump back.*

Then, give students this statement that explains how the words relate to the meaning of the selection:

At a dinner party, a colonel declares that women don't have as much control over their emotions as men do. When the hostess feels a snake on her foot, her muscles begin contracting as she resists the impulse to scream. At the end of the story, the snake is lured out to the veranda with a bowl of milk.

Model the Skill

▶ Literary Focus

Plot Why is this the story's climax?
Possible response: The conflict between the cobra and the guests is resolved.

▶ Literary Focus

Plot What details earlier in the story hint at the fact that the cobra was crawling on Mrs. Wynnes's foot?
Possible response: On p. 8, a strange expression comes over Mrs. Wynnes's face, and her muscles contract. This suggests nervousness and fear.

Check for Understanding

Read with a Purpose Ask students how the colonel's prediction was proved true or untrue. *Possible response: The colonel's predictions did not work out as expected because Mrs. Wynnes proved to be extraordinarily calm. This was not surprising because many people would disagree with the colonel's original prediction.*

More About the Writer

Mona Gardner wrote extensively on some of the themes found in "The Dinner Party," particularly the difficulties faced by women in male-dominated societies.

Think About the Writer

Have students discuss which details in the story strike them as true to life. You might ask, "Do the story's events seem like they could happen to a real person?"

 For Independent Reading

If students are interested in reading another story about a courageous woman, recommend *Hang a Thousand Trees with Ribbons: The Story of Phillis Wheatley,* Ann Rinaldi's story of America's first published black poet.

"I want to know just what control everyone at this table has. I will count to three hundred—that's five minutes—and not one of you is to move a muscle. Those who move will forfeit[3] fifty rupees.[4] Ready!"

> **Literary Focus**
>
> **Plot** The **climax** of the story occurs when the cobra comes into view.

The twenty people sit like stone images while he counts. He is saying "... two hundred and eighty ..." when, out of the corner of his eye, he sees the cobra emerge and make for the bowl of milk. Screams ring out as he jumps to slam the veranda doors safely shut.

"You were right, Colonel!" the host exclaims. "A man has just shown us an example of perfect control."

> **Literary Focus**
>
> **Plot** Mrs. Wynnes's response to the American's question explains her past actions.

"Just a minute," the American says, turning to his hostess. "Mrs. Wynnes, how did you know that cobra was in the room?"

A faint smile lights up the woman's face as she replies: "Because it was crawling across my foot."

---

3. **forfeit:** (FAWR fiht): give up as a penalty.
4. **rupees:** (roo PEEZ): Indian monetary units.

Read with a Purpose How do the colonel's predictions apply to the story's outcome? In what ways were you surprised by the ending?

MEET THE WRITER

Mona Gardner
(1900–1981)

A Familiar Setting
Many of Mona Gardner's books and stories are set in Near or East Asia. She wrote several books, including *Middle Heaven,* which is about Japan; *Hong Kong;* and *The Shanghai Item.* "The Dinner Party" is a classic story that has appeared in many anthologies since it was first published in *The Saturday Review of Literature* in January 1942.

Think About the Writer Explain whether or not you think Mona Gardner based "The Dinner Party" on personal experience.

Resources

Chapter 1 Resources, p. 5
UA: Differentiating Instruction, Selection and Academic Vocabulary Skill Builder, p. 20
Teacher One Stop™, on-level lesson plans and all print resources
WordSharp: An Interactive Vocabulary Tutor, more practice with academic language

Academic Vocabulary

Writing About Short Stories
English for Academic Success Write the following questions on the board. Tell students these are the kinds of questions on standardized tests.
Discuss the meaning of the words, then have students use "The Dinner Party" to answer the questions.
• How do the American's observations **advance** the plot? Support your answer with details from the text. ***Possible response:*** *If the American had not recognized the signs of a cobra's presence, and alerted the reader to the snake in the room, the story would not have an evident conflict or rising action.*

Reading Standard 3.2 Identify events that advance the plot and determine how each event explains past or present action(s) or foreshadows future action(s).

Into Action: Plot Summary

Practice your summarizing skills by writing a summary of "The Dinner Party." Start by completing a Summary Sheet like the one below. Then, write a short summary based on your notes.

Title and Author
↓
Main Characters
↓
Conflict
↓
Plot Complications
1.
2.
(Add on as many as you need.)
↓
The Climax
↓
The Resolution

Talk About . . .

1. With a partner, identify the events that <u>advance</u> the plot of "The Dinner Party." Which events <u>explain</u> past or present actions, and which foreshadow future events? Try to use the Academic Vocabulary words listed at right in your discussion.

Write About . . .

2. What do you think was the most <u>significant</u> event in "The Dinner Party"? Support your answer with details from the story.

3. List the ways in which the American and Mrs. Wynnes are <u>similar</u>.

Writing Skills Focus
Think as a Reader/Writer

In Chapter 1, you'll read short stories with suspenseful plots. The Writing Skills Focus activities on the Preparing to Read pages will guide you to understand how each writer creates these plots. On the Applying Your Skills pages, you'll practice this aspect of the writer's craft in your own writing.

Academic Vocabulary for Chapter 1

Talking and Writing About Short Stories

Academic Vocabulary is the language you use to write and talk about literature. Use these words to discuss the texts you read in this chapter. The words are underlined in the chapter.

advance (ad VANS) *v.:* move forward. *Important events advance the plot, keeping the story interesting and suspenseful.*

explain (ehk SPLAYN) *v.:* give reasons for; make understandable. *Events in a story work together to explain past, present, or future actions.*

significant (sihg NIHF uh kuhnt) *adj.:* important. *A plot summary should include only significant details.*

similar (SIHM uh luhr) *adj.:* almost the same. *Sometimes characters in a story show similar characteristics.*

Your Turn

Copy the words from the Academic Vocabulary list into your *Reader/Writer Notebook.* Use all four words in a paragraph that summarizes your response to "The Dinner Party." Write the summary in your notebook.

Guided Practice: Apply
Into Action: Plot Summary

Some students may wish to summarize "The Dinner Party" verbally by explaining the plot to a partner. Remind students to focus on main events and leave out minor details.

Talk About...

1. Model for students how to incorporate the Academic Vocabulary words into a conversation. You might say, "When Mrs. Wynnes' look of surprise <u>advances</u> the plot by foreshadowing that something is wrong. This <u>explains</u> the conflict: that a cobra is in the house."

Write About...
Possible responses:

2. *Mrs. Wynnes's reaction to the cobra is the most <u>significant</u> event because it proves the colonel wrong.*

3. *They both deal with crises in a <u>similar</u> fashion: quietly and calmly.*

Writing Skills Focus

The Think as a Reader/Writer activities in the chapter focus on the reading-writing relationship. Use the activities to help students explore the writer's craft in a text and to practice this aspect of craft in their own writing.

Independent Practice

Chapter 1 Resources, pp. 3–5

UA: Differentiating Instruction, Selection and Academic Vocabulary Skill Builder, p. 20

California Standards, p. 11

■ **Reading Standard 3.2** Identify events that advance the plot and determine how each event explains past or present action(s) or foreshadows future action(s).

• **Explain** why the colonel's beliefs about women were not accurate. ***Possible response:*** *The colonel thought that women would scream and panic if they found themselves in danger, but Mrs. Wynnes kept completely calm when she felt the cobra.*

• Is the setting of "The Dinner Party" **similar** to or different from your own home? Explain. ***Possible response:*** *The fancy house in which the story is set is different from my home. I live in an apartment in the United States, not a fancy house in India.*

• In the story, why was the bowl of milk **significant** to the American? ***Possible response:*** *The narrator explains that in India, bowls of milk are used as snake bait. When the American saw the bowl of milk, he immediately realized that there must be a snake in the house.*

Standards Focus

Objectives
Students will
• explore how conflict affects plot
• summarize key story information

Motivate
What Do You Think?/QuickWrite
Use the QuickWrite to have students reflect on bullying. Then, have them describe in their **Reader/Writer Notebook** appropriate responses to bullies and their actions.

English for Academic Success
Academic Vocabulary
Look for opportunities to use the Academic Vocabulary words in this chapter.

• **significant, *adj.:*** important

• **advance, *v.:*** move forward

• **explain, *v.:*** give reasons for; make understandable

• **similar, *adj.:*** almost the same

Analyzing Visuals
Use ThinkCentral, Teacher Access to project this image for viewing.

Extension Activity Have students describe the animal in this photo.
Possible responses: *It looks small, curious, and harmless. It is not menacing.*

Preparing to Read

Rikki-tikki-tavi

by **Rudyard Kipling**

What Do **You** Think

If you were facing a bully, would you fight, run away, or try to negotiate?

QuickWrite
What situations have you heard or read about in which someone had to face a bully? Describe the situation and the way each of the individuals acted and reacted.

California Standards,
pp. 12–31

■ **Reading Standard 3.2** Identify events that advance the plot and determine how each event explains past or present action(s) or foreshadows future action(s).

Selection Readability	
Easily Accessible **Accessible** Challenging	simple dialogue; chronological order; familiar genre

Selection Plot Summary
"Rikki-tikki-tavi" tells the story of a pet mongoose named Rikki-tikki-tavi who lives with a British family in India. The mongoose defeats a pair of cobras that threaten the lives of Rikki's adopted family members.

Reader/Writer Notebook

Use your **RWN** to complete the activities for this selection.

Reading Standard 3.2 Identify events that advance the plot and determine how each event explains past or present action(s) or foreshadows future action(s).

Literary Skills Focus

Conflict All stories are built on some kind of **conflict.** A conflict often results when a character wants something very badly but has a difficult time getting it. Conflict may involve a physical battle—or even simply a battle of wills—between two opposing forces. Think of the stories you see in movies and on TV: You can find a conflict in every one of them. Conflict is worked out in the series of related events called **plot.** In most stories, the characters' past, present, and future actions grow out of, and can be explained by, the central conflict.

Reading Skills Focus

Summarizing Restating the **main ideas,** or <u>significant</u> events, in a text is called **summarizing.** A summary of a text is much shorter than the original text. To summarize a narrative, you must include the main characters, main events, conflicts, and resolutions.

Into Action As you read this story, fill in a Story Map like this one so that you can keep track of the major events that <u>advance</u> the plot. You will use your completed map to write a summary.

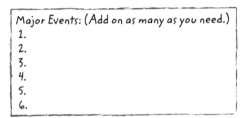

Major Events: (Add on as many as you need.)
1.
2.
3.
4.
5.
6.

Writing Skills Focus

Think as a Reader/Writer

Find It in Your Reading As you read this story, pay attention to the way Rudyard Kipling portrays the snakes Nag and Nagaina. In your *Reader/Writer Notebook,* write down at least ten words or phrases Kipling uses to describe the cobras and their actions.

Vocabulary

immensely (ih MEHNS lee) *adv.:* enormously. *Rikki is immensely brave.*

cowered (KOW uhrd) *v.:* crouched and trembled in fear. *Darzee, who is not brave, cowered before the snakes.*

valiant (VAL yuhnt) *adj.:* brave and determined. *Rikki is a valiant hero.*

consolation (KAHN suh LAY shuhn) *n.:* comfort. *Rikki's consolation comes from protecting Teddy and his parents.*

Rikki-tikki-tavi

↓

is **immensely** brave

↓

cowered before no one

↓

is a **valiant** hero

↓

feels **consolation** when protecting his family

Language Coach

Word Roots The Latin word *consolari* means "to offer comfort." The word *consolation* comes from this Latin word and is made up of a root word (*console*) and a suffix (*–ation*). The root word *console* is a verb. What part of speech does the word become after the suffix is added?

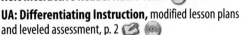

Learn It Online
For a preview of this story, see the video introduction on:

go.hrw.com   H7-13   **Go**

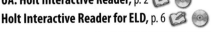

Introducing Vocabulary

Read aloud the Vocabulary words and sample sentences. Then, have students complete each sentence with the correct Vocabulary word.

1. Joe was _____ happy on his birthday. [*immensely*]
2. The scared cat _____ during the storm. [*cowered*]
3. The soldier's _____ actions inspired. [*valiant*]
4. The coach's pep talk gave _____ to the disappointed team. [*consolation*]

English for Academic Success

Language Coach

Point out that some smaller words cannot be found by simply removing letters from the larger word, as is the case in *cowered* and *cower.* Sometimes, letters must be added, such as adding -e to create *console* from *consolation.* [*noun*]

Literary Skills Focus

As you read, ask students to keep a list of the various conflicts by writing Rikki vs. Nag, Nag vs. the family, and so on. Discuss how each conflict advances the plot.

Reading Skills Focus

Give students a copy of the Reading Skills Focus graphic organizer before they read. (See **Chapter 1 Resources.**) Tell them to use their responses to answer the questions on the Applying Your Skills page.

Writing Skills Focus

Have students record details describing the cobras in their **Reader/ Writer Notebook.** Students can use their notes to complete the Writing Skills Focus activity.

Learn It Online
The **PowerNotes** presentation for this lesson includes a short video that introduces the selection. The video is also available on the online version of this page.

go.hrw.com   H7-13   **Go**

MEET THE WRITER

✳ Learn It Online
Get more on the author's life at:
go.hrw.com H7-14 Go

Selection Introduction

More About the Writer

In his childhood, **Rudyard Kipling**'s literary inspirations were numerous and varied. Growing up in Bombay, India, he was read Indian nursery rhymes by his nanny. When he was sent to boarding school in England, he took comfort in the books his parents sent him, including titles like *Robinson Crusoe*.

Think About the Writer

Before students answer the question, work with them to discuss the importance of a short story's setting. Then, discuss Rudyard Kipling's biography with them. What was the significance of India in his life and works?

 For Independent Reading

- If students are interested in reading more works by Rudyard Kipling, they might enjoy *The Jungle Book (The Whole Story)*. It is the story of Mowgli, a boy who is raised by wolves and befriends many jungle creatures.

- If students are interested in reading about remarkable animals, recommend *Beauty of the Beast: Poems from the Animal Kingdom*, Jack Prelutsky's collection of poems for animal lovers.

Rudyard Kipling
(1865–1936)

Nobel Prize WINNER

On His Own
Rudyard Kipling was born in India, but when he was just six years old, his parents shipped him and his sister off to a boardinghouse in England.

Return to India
When Kipling was seventeen, he returned to India and took a job as an editor with an English-language newspaper. He was fascinated by the lives of British colonials in India and the vivid contrast they made with the Indian people they ruled. Soon the paper was printing Kipling's poems and tales about what he saw. Readers begged for more, and Kipling's fame grew. Over the next half century he wrote dozens of books. In 1907, he was awarded the Nobel Prize in Literature. When Kipling was very young, this is what he discovered about books:

"[Books] were among the most important affairs in the world. . . . One could take a pen and set down what one thought, and . . . nobody accused him of 'showing off' by doing so."

Think About the Writer
Why do you think Rudyard Kipling set many of his stories in India?

Build Background

This story takes place in India many years ago, when the British ruled that huge country. The family in this story lives in a cantonment (kan TAHN muhnt), which is a kind of army base. The father is in the British army.

Preview the Selection

Rikki-tikki-tavi is a mongoose who is rescued after a flood by a little boy named **Teddy** and his parents. This story is about the conflict that develops between Rikki and the deadly snakes **Nag** and **Nagaina** as Rikki strives to protect his new family.

Universal Access

 English Learners
Explain to students that this selection is about a struggle between two animals that are natural enemies: mongooses and snakes. Note that the main characters are animals who behave like humans, and the conflict takes place over one hundred years ago in an environment populated by many types of animals.

✔ See **UA: Differentiating Instruction** for lesson plans and strategies for teaching English learners.

Struggling Readers
Benchmark Students Tell students that summarizing is retelling the most important points in a text in their own words. Explain that when readers summarize, they use only the most important details to retell the story. Tell students that sometimes, as in "Rikki-tikki-tavi," the first sentence of a story may contain a brief summary. In this case, the first sentence states that the story is about a "great war" fought by the mongoose Rikki-tikki-tavi. This is not the only important point in the story, so readers should read to find more details,

Learn It Online
Writers' Lives offers more information on the life of the author as well as Holt's interactive resources pertaining to the author.

go.hrw.com H7-14 Go

Rikki-tikki-tavi

by **Rudyard Kipling**

This is the story of the great war that Rikki-tikki-tavi fought single-handed, through the bathrooms of the big bungalow[1] in Segowlee cantonment.[2] Darzee, the tailorbird, helped him, and Chuchundra, the muskrat, who never comes out into the middle of the floor but always creeps round by the wall, gave him advice; but Rikki-tikki did the real fighting.

He was a mongoose, rather like a little cat in his fur and his tail but quite like a weasel in his head and his habits. His eyes and the end of his restless nose were pink; he could scratch himself anywhere he pleased with any leg, front or back, that he chose to use; he could fluff up his tail till it looked like a bottlebrush, and his war cry as he scuttled through the long grass was *Rikk-tikk-tikki-tikki-tchk!* **A**

One day, a high summer flood washed him out of the burrow where he lived with his father and mother and carried him, kicking and clucking, down a roadside ditch. He found a little wisp of grass floating there and clung to it till he lost his senses. When he revived, he was lying in the hot sun in the middle of a garden path, very draggled[3] indeed, and a small boy was saying: "Here's a dead mongoose. Let's have a funeral."

"No," said his mother; "let's take him in and dry him. Perhaps he isn't really dead."

They took him into the house, and a big man picked him up between his finger and thumb and said he was not dead but half choked; so they wrapped him in cotton wool and warmed him over a little fire, and he opened his eyes and sneezed.

"Now," said the big man (he was an Englishman who had just moved into the bungalow), "don't frighten him, and we'll see what he'll do." **B**

It is the hardest thing in the world to frighten a mongoose, because he is eaten up from nose to tail with curiosity. The motto of all the mongoose family is "Run and find

---

1. **bungalow:** in India, a low, one-storied house, named after a type of house found in Bengal, a region of South Asia.
2. **Segowlee** (see GOW lee) **cantonment:** British army post in Segowlee (now Segauli), India.

---

3. **draggled:** wet and muddy, as if from being dragged around.

A Read and Discuss   What has the author told you about Rikki-tikki so far?

B Reading Focus Summarizing   What has happened between Rikki-tikki and the family?

---

like the characters in this war, where it takes place, and how it ends. Walk students through summarizing on a smaller scale using a paragraph from the first page.

Have students read "Rikki-tikki-tavi" in interactive format in **UA: Holt Interactive Reader.** The interactive version provides additional instruction, practice, and assessment of the skills taught in the Student Edition.

Advanced Learners

Acceleration   As students read, have them periodically pause and discuss with a partner the reasons Rikki-tikki-tavi is facing a conflict. What are the aims of each side? Would it be possible for this conflict to be resolved in some way other than a "war"?

✔ See **UA: Resources for Teaching Advanced Students** for lesson plans and strategies for teaching advanced learners.

Students with Disabilities

✔ See **UA: Differentiating Instruction** for lesson plans and strategies for teaching students with disabilities.

Model the Skill

- Provide students with copies of the Reading Skills Focus graphic organizer (See **Chapter 1 Resources**), or have them use their own paper to **summarize** major events.

- Model for students adding additional details to the graphic organizer. Point out that one of the major events of the story is Rikki-tikki-tavi's near-drowning and rescue by the English family. Add "Rikki-tikki-tavi is washed away by a storm and rescued by a family" to your organizer.

> Major Events
> 1. Rikki-tikki is washed away by a storm and rescued by a family.
> 2.

Guided Practice: Apply

Read/Talk/Write Have students read pp. 16–17 in pairs. As a class, evaluate each event on these pages and determine which are major story events to be tracked in the graphic organizers. Have students note these events in their individual organizers.

---

out," and Rikki-tikki was a true mongoose. He looked at the cotton wool, decided that it was not good to eat, ran all round the table, sat up and put his fur in order, scratched himself, and jumped on the small boy's shoulder.

"Don't be frightened, Teddy," said his father. "That's his way of making friends."

"Ouch! He's tickling under my chin," said Teddy.

Rikki-tikki looked down between the boy's collar and neck, snuffed at his ear, and climbed down to the floor, where he sat rubbing his nose.

"Good gracious," said Teddy's mother, "and that's a wild creature! I suppose he's so tame because we've been kind to him."

"All mongooses are like that," said her husband. "If Teddy doesn't pick him up by the tail or try to put him in a cage, he'll run in and out of the house all day long. Let's give him something to eat."

They gave him a little piece of raw meat. Rikki-tikki liked it immensely, and when it was finished, he went out into the veranda[4] and sat in the sunshine and fluffed up his fur to make it dry to the roots. Then he felt better.

"There are more things to find out about in this house," he said to himself, "than all

---

4. **veranda** (vuh RAN duh): open porch that is covered by a roof and runs along the outside of a building.

C **Literary Focus** Conflict How are things looking for Rikki-tikki? What future conflict is hinted at by these words?

my family could find out in all their lives. I shall certainly stay and find out."

He spent all that day roaming over the house. He nearly drowned himself in the bathtubs, put his nose into the ink on a writing table, and burnt it on the end of the big man's cigar, for he climbed up in the big man's lap to see how writing was done. At nightfall he ran into Teddy's nursery to watch how kerosene lamps were lighted, and when Teddy went to bed, Rikki-tikki climbed up too; but he was a restless companion, because he had to get up and attend to every noise all through the night and find out what made it. Teddy's mother and father came in, the last thing, to look at their boy, and Rikki-tikki was awake on the pillow. "I don't like that," said Teddy's mother; "he may bite the child." "He'll do no such thing," said the father. "Teddy's safer with that little beast than if he had a bloodhound to watch him. If a snake came into the nursery now—"

But Teddy's mother wouldn't think of anything so awful.

Early in the morning, Rikki-tikki came to early breakfast in the veranda riding on Teddy's shoulder, and they gave him banana and some boiled egg; and he sat on all their laps one after the other, because every well-brought-up mongoose always hopes to be a house mongoose someday and have rooms to run about in; and Rikki-tikki's mother

> "If a snake came into the nursery now—"

Vocabulary **immensely** (ih MEHNS lee) *adv.*: enormously.

Real Issues, Real Experts

*Holt author **Deborah Appleman** offers strategies for helping students identify literary elements and techniques.*

The authors and editors of this text have tried to compile a collection of stories and poems that combine contemporary works with old favorites. This classic story by Rudyard Kipling is one of our favorites, and we are certain your students will remember and cherish it for a very long time.

For centuries, storytellers have used the animal world

to help us understand certain fundamental aspects of human nature. That's exactly what Rudyard Kipling does in this compelling story about a confrontation between a mongoose and a snake. This is also a classic story about the confrontation between good and evil, with the snake functioning as the classic symbol of evil.

Because of its straightforward structure, you can use this story to help your students become more familiar with important literary elements, such as plot, symbol, protagonist, and antagonist. In addition, because

Connecting to the Text How does the house in this picture compare to the house you visualize when reading the story?

(she used to live in the General's house at Segowlee) had carefully told Rikki what to do if ever he came across white men. **D**

Then Rikki-tikki went out into the garden to see what was to be seen. It was a large garden, only half cultivated, with bushes, as big as summerhouses, of Marshal Niel roses; lime and orange trees; clumps of bamboos; and thickets of high grass. Rikki-tikki licked his lips. "This is a splendid hunting ground," he said, and his tail grew bottlebrushy at the thought of it, and he scuttled up and down the garden, snuffing here and there till he heard very sorrowful voices in a thorn bush. It was Darzee, the tailorbird, and his wife. They had made a beautiful nest by pulling two big leaves together and stitching them up the edges with fibers and had filled the hollow with cotton and downy fluff. The nest swayed to and fro as they sat on the rim and cried.

"What is the matter?" asked Rikki-tikki.

"We are very miserable," said Darzee. "One of our babies fell out of the nest yesterday and Nag ate him."

"H'm!" said Rikki-tikki, "that is very sad —but I am a stranger here. Who is Nag?"

Darzee and his wife only cowered down in the nest without answering, for from the thick grass at the foot of the bush there came a low hiss—a horrid, cold sound that made Rikki-tikki jump back two clear feet. Then inch by inch out of the grass rose up the head and spread hood of Nag, the big black cobra, and he was five feet long from tongue to tail. When he had lifted one third

D [Read and Discuss] What have you learned about the relationship between Rikki-tikki and his new family?

Vocabulary **cowered** (KOW uhrd) *v.:* crouched and trembled in fear.

---

animals function as main characters, you can also discuss how authors use literary techniques such as personification.

The story of Rikki-tikki-tavi is a story of bravery and loyalty. The little mongoose musters the courage to confront his natural enemy because of the gratitude he feels to the human family he has befriended. Even though he is a mongoose, Rikki-tikki-tavi represents admirable qualities to which human beings can also aspire.

Analyzing Visuals
Connecting to the Text: *It is larger than the house I visualized, but it is surrounded by trees and bushes, which is similar to the image I had in my mind.*

Think About/Talk About

▶ ### Comprehension
D **Read and Discuss**
Possible response: Teddy and Rikki-tikki-tavi are becoming closer, as Rikki-tikki-tavi sleeps with Teddy, and comes to breakfast riding on his shoulders. The mom, however, is apprehensive about their relationship, as she is afraid Rikki-tikki-tavi will harm Teddy.

▶ ### Analysis
C **Literary Focus**
Possible response: He is being well taken care of by this new family. The father's words foreshadow that a snake might come into the nursery and Rikki-tikki-tavi will have to protect the family.

▶ ### Extend the Discussion
Conflict In the first full paragraph of column 2 on p. 16, Teddy's parents ominously mention snakes. How might this foreshadow the conflict of the story? *Possible response: Rikki-tikki-tavi may find himself having to defend his human friends against snakes. Teddy's father even mentions that Teddy would be safer with the mongoose than with a bloodhound.*

Vocabulary: Own the Word
- **immensely:** Ask students to list two things that would make them *immensely* happy. *Possible responses: straight As in school, a trip to an amusement park*

- **cowered:** Demonstrate someone who is *cowering*. Ask one or two students to demonstrate.

Model the Skill

- Explain to students that English words are often formed by adding prefixes or suffixes to **root words.** Being able to identify root words can help readers figure out the meanings of words they do not know.

- Write *fledgling* on the board. Explain that *fledgling* is made up of a root word, *fledge,* and a suffix, *-ling.* Write *fledge* and *-ling* on the board. Explain that *fledge* is a verb that means to grow feathers and prepare to fly, and *-ling* is a suffix that means "little one," as in *duckling,* which means "little duck." Point out that when this word and suffix come together, they form *fledgling,* which is a little bird that is just growing its feathers. *Fledgling* is a noun created from a verb and a suffix.

Guided Practice: Apply

Turn and Talk Have students pair up with a classmate to identify the root word or affix, and parts of speech for *disconnect.* Tell students to check their answers with another pair or a dictionary.

Think as a Reader/Writer

Find It in Your Reading Point out that in paragraph 3 of column 2, Nagaina sneaks up on Rikki-tikki-tavi instead of challenging him directly. This reveals the nature of the snakes by suggesting that the cobras do not "fight fair."

Use It in Your Writing Have students write two sentences that describe participants in a conflict in which one participant uses unfair tactics on the other.

---

of himself clear of the ground, he stayed balancing to and fro exactly as a dandelion tuft balances in the wind, and he looked at Rikki-tikki with the wicked snake's eyes that never change their expression, whatever the snake may be thinking of.

"Who is Nag," said he. "*I* am Nag. The great God Brahm[5] put his mark upon all our people, when the first cobra spread his hood to keep the sun off Brahm as he slept. Look, and be afraid!"

He spread out his hood more than ever, and Rikki-tikki saw the spectacle mark on the back of it that looks exactly like the eye part of a hook-and-eye fastening. He was afraid for the minute; but it is impossible for a mongoose to stay frightened for any length of time, and though Rikki-tikki had never met a live cobra before, his mother had fed him on dead ones, and he knew that all a grown mongoose's business in life was to fight and eat snakes. Nag knew that too, and at the bottom of his cold heart, he was afraid. **E**

"Well," said Rikki-tikki, and his tail began to fluff up again, "marks or no marks, do you think it is right for you to eat fledglings out of a nest?"

Nag was thinking to himself and watching the least little movement in the grass behind Rikki-tikki. He knew that mongooses in the garden meant death sooner or later for him and his family, but he wanted to get Rikki-tikki off his guard. So he dropped his head a little and put it on one side.

---

5. **Brahm** (brahm): in the Hindu religion, the creator.

E **Literary Focus** Conflict What possible conflict makes Nag fear Rikki-tikki?

"Let us talk," he said. "You eat eggs. Why should not I eat birds?"

"Behind you! Look behind you!" sang Darzee.

Rikki-tikki knew better than to waste time in staring. He jumped up in the air as high as he could go, and just under him whizzed by the head of Nagaina, Nag's wicked wife. She had crept up behind him as he was talking, to make an end of him; and he heard her savage hiss as the stroke missed. He came down almost across her back, and if he had been an old mongoose, he would have known that then was the time to break her back with one bite; but he was afraid of the terrible lashing return stroke of the cobra. He bit, indeed, but did not bite long enough, and he jumped clear of the whisking tail, leaving Nagaina torn and angry. **F**

"Wicked, wicked Darzee!" said Nag, lashing up as high as he could reach toward the nest in the thorn bush; but Darzee had built it out of reach of snakes, and it only swayed to and fro.

Rikki-tikki felt his eyes growing red and hot (when a mongoose's eyes grow red, he is angry), and he sat back on his tail and hind legs like a little kangaroo, and looked all round him, and chattered with rage. But Nag and Nagaina had disappeared into the grass.

When a snake misses its stroke, it never says anything or gives any sign of what it means to do next. Rikki-tikki did not care to follow them, for he did not feel sure that

---

F **Reading Focus** Summarizing What has happened in this paragraph?

Universal Access

Struggling Readers

- Ask students to create a chart on a piece of paper with four columns: *Somebody, Wanted, But, So.*

- Have students write the name a character in the story under the column labeled *Somebody.* Under *Wanted,* tell students to write the goal the character wanted to achieve. Under *But,* ask students to explain why the character had trouble reaching this goal. Under *So,* have students describe what happened as a result.

- Model by writing "Nag" under the first column.

Explain that Nag wanted to take over the garden, but this clashed with Rikki-tikki-tavi's desire to protect the family, so the snake and mongoose went to war.

- Have students fill out the chart for Rikki-tikki-tavi.

For more information on the Somebody Wanted But So strategy, see ThinkCentral, Teacher Access.

AAVE **Students Who Use African-American Vernacular English**

English for Academic Success Students may have difficulty forming the past tenses of regular verbs.

he could manage two snakes at once. So he trotted off to the gravel path near the house and sat down to think. It was a serious matter for him. If you read the old books of natural history, you will find they say that when the mongoose fights the snake and happens to get bitten, he runs off and eats some herb that cures him. That is not true. The victory is only a matter of quickness of eye and quickness of foot—snake's blow against the mongoose's jump—and as no eye can follow the motion of a snake's head when it strikes, this makes things much

more wonderful than any magic herb. Rikki-tikki knew he was a young mongoose, and it made him all the more pleased to think that he had managed to escape a blow from behind. It gave him confidence in himself, and when Teddy came running down the path, Rikki-tikki was ready to be petted. But just as Teddy was stooping, something wriggled a little in the dust and a tiny voice said: "Be careful. I am Death!" It was Karait, the dusty brown snakeling that lies for choice on the dusty earth; and his bite is as dangerous as the cobra's. But he is

SCIENCE LINK

The Unusual and Deadly Cobra

Snakes are believed to have been on earth for 95 million years. There are now about 2,700 species—populations of <u>similar</u> organisms that breed only among themselves—of snakes. The cobra, native to South Asia, Australia, and Africa, is one of these species. A king cobra, the longest of the poisonous snakes, can grow to some eighteen feet in length.

A cobra has loose folds of skin on its neck that expand into that famous hood. A cobra spreads its hood by spreading its neck ribs, much as you would open an umbrella. The cobra then looks bigger and more frightening. Even if its hood is not spread, a cobra is *always* dangerous.

Unlike your jaw, which opens and closes by means of a set of interlocking bones, a cobra's jawbones can disconnect. The top jaw can open almost flat against the cobra's forehead, while the bottom jaw drops almost straight down, enabling a cobra to spread its jaws like a pair of entry doors. That's how a cobra can swallow prey larger than the snake's own head!

Ask Yourself

What images in the text above help you visualize the way a cobra's neck and jaw work? How does this information help you visualize events in the story?

Explain that in formal English, past tenses of regular verbs are formed by adding the ending -*ed* to the infinitive. Point out *wanted, jumped, chattered, disappeared* at the bottom of column 2 on p. 18. Write *wanted* and *to want* on the board. Explain that *to want* is the infinitive, and *wanted* is the past tense of the verb. Cross out or erase *to,* and add -*ed* to want. Say the word aloud with students. Write *to jump, to chatter,* and *to disappear* on the board, and have volunteers come up to the board to practice forming the past tenses.

Science Link

Ask Yourself _____
Possible response: The image of the top jaw of the cobra opening flat and the bottom jaw dropping down "like a pair of entry doors" helps me see how a cobra can open his jaws wide enough to kill a small animal or a small child.

▶ Comprehension

F Reading Focus
Possible response: Rikki-tikki-tavi avoids Nagaina's bite and retaliates.

Follow up How does this connect to what we just talked about?

Possible response: Nag and his wife knew that Rikki-tikki-tavi would eventually try to kill them, so they were ready for a fight.

▶ Analysis

E Literary Focus
Possible response: Nag knows that mongooses are very good at fighting and eating snakes. He fears that Rikki-tikki will try to kill him.

▶ Extend the Discussion

Making Predictions At the end of p. 19, Rikki-tikki-tavi gains new confidence in himself. What impact do you predict his confidence will have on his future actions? *Possible response: This confidence could give him strength for future fights, but it could hurt him if he becomes overly confident and lets down his guard.*

Conflict How do the wants of Rikki-tikki-tavi put him in conflict with the cobras? *Possible response: Rikki-tikki-tavi wants to protect his new family and his other new friends, such as Darzee. The cobras want to dominate the garden, which may involve harming Rikki-tikki-tavi's family and friends. Each will get in the way of the other's wants.*

Model the Skill

- Explain that all plots are advanced by **conflicts,** in which characters try to fulfill their wants and needs but must overcome obstacles to get the outcome they desire.

- Explain that the conflict between Rikki-tikki-tavi and the snakes starts as a result of Nag's wanting to get rid of Rikki-tikki-tavi because mongooses kill snakes. On p.146, the author establishes that Nag wants to get rid of Rikki-tikki-tavi, but the obstacle he faces is Rikki-tikki-tavi surviving and being quicker than he expected. At the end of p. 149, Nag is trying to get into the house, and it sounds as though he wants to kill Rikki-tikki-tavi's family. He thinks that if he kills the family, Rikki-tikki-tavi will leave. He has met with one obstacle to getting what he wants—for Rikki-tikki-tavi to leave—so he is trying another tactic to achieve his goal.

Guided Practice: Apply

Think/Pair/Share Ask students how Rikki-tikki-tavi will react to Nag's intention to kill the people, knowing what we do about mongooses and Rikki-tikki-tavi's love for his adopted family. Have students share their thoughts with a partner. Then, discuss as a class how students think Rikki-tikki-tavi's wants will clash with Nag's wants and deepen the story conflict.

so small that nobody thinks of him, and so he does the more harm to people. **G**

Rikki-tikki's eyes grew red again, and he danced up to Karait with the peculiar rocking, swaying motion that he had inherited from his family. It looks very funny, but it is so perfectly balanced a gait[6] that you can fly off from it at any angle you please; and in dealing with snakes this is an advantage. If Rikki-tikki had only known, he was doing a much more dangerous thing than fighting Nag, for Karait is so small and can turn so quickly that unless Rikki bit him close to the back of the head, he would get the return stroke in his eye or his lip. But Rikki did not know; his eyes were all red, and he rocked back and forth, looking for a good place to hold. Karait struck out, Rikki jumped sideways and tried to run in, but the wicked little dusty gray head lashed within a fraction of his shoulder, and he had to jump over the body, and the head followed his heels close.

Teddy shouted to the house: "Oh, look here! Our mongoose is killing a snake," and Rikki-tikki heard a scream from Teddy's mother. His father ran out with a stick, but by the time he came up, Karait had

> He remembered that a full meal makes a slow mongoose, and if he wanted all his strength and quickness ready, he must keep himself thin.

lunged out once too far, and Rikki-tikki had sprung, jumped on the snake's back, dropped his head far between his forelegs, bitten as high up the back as he could get hold, and rolled away. That bite paralyzed Karait, and Rikki-tikki was just going to eat him up from the tail, after the custom of his family at dinner, when he remembered that a full meal makes a slow mongoose, and if he wanted all his strength and quickness ready, he must keep himself thin. He went away for a dust bath under the castor-oil bushes, while Teddy's father beat the dead Karait. "What is the use of that?" thought Rikki-tikki; "I have settled it all"; and then Teddy's mother picked him up from the dust and hugged him, crying that he had saved Teddy from death, and Teddy's father said that he was a providence,[7] and Teddy looked on with big, scared eyes. Rikki-tikki was rather amused at all the fuss, which, of course, he did not understand. Teddy's mother might just as well have petted Teddy for playing in the dust. Rikki was thoroughly enjoying himself. **H**

That night at dinner, walking to and fro among the wineglasses on the table,

---

6. **gait** (gayt): the way someone walks or runs.

7. **providence** (PRAHV uh duhns): favor or gift from God or nature.

G | Read and Discuss | What does Rikki-tikki learn from his encounter with Nagaina?

H | Reading Focus | Summarizing What happens between Rikki-tikki and Karait? How does this event <u>advance</u> the plot?

Cross-Curricular Connection

SOCIAL STUDIES: The British in India
Explain to students that Teddy and his family are British colonists living in late nineteenth century India.

- The British presence began in the early 1600s with the English East India Company, which sought the vast resources offered by the Indian subcontinent.
- Throughout the 18th century the French and British fought for dominance in India. By the middle of the century, the British had achieved supremacy.
- The British government soon controlled the bulk of India, either by placing territory under the direct control of London or through alliances with local rulers.
- English law and customs became rigidly enforced in the mid-19th century while the practice of local customs was looked down upon. Although the British implemented wide-ranging reforms and improved the infrastructure of the country, many native Indians resented the new system.

he might have stuffed himself three times over with nice things; but he remembered Nag and Nagaina, and though it was very pleasant to be patted and petted by Teddy's mother and to sit on Teddy's shoulder, his eyes would get red from time to time, and he would go off into his long war cry of *Rikk-tikk-tikki-tikki-tchk!*

Teddy carried him off to bed and insisted on Rikki-tikki's sleeping under his chin. Rikki-tikki was too well bred to bite or scratch, but as soon as Teddy was asleep, he went off for his nightly walk round the house, and in the dark he ran up against Chuchundra, the muskrat, creeping round by the wall. Chuchundra is a brokenhearted little beast. He whimpers and cheeps all night, trying to make up his mind to run into the middle of the room; but he never gets there.

"Don't kill me," said Chuchundra, almost weeping. "Rikki-tikki, don't kill me!"

"Do you think a snake killer kills muskrats?" said Rikki-tikki scornfully.

"Those who kill snakes get killed by snakes," said Chuchundra, more sorrowfully than ever. "And how am I to be sure that Nag won't mistake me for you some dark night?"

"There's not the least danger," said Rikki-tikki, "but Nag is in the garden, and I know you don't go there."

"My cousin Chua, the rat, told me—" said Chuchundra, and then he stopped.

"Told you what?"

"H'sh! Nag is everywhere, Rikki-tikki. You should have talked to Chua in the garden."

ⓘ Reading Focus Summarizing What has Rikki-tikki just learned?

"I didn't—so you must tell me. Quick, Chuchundra, or I'll bite you!"

Chuchundra sat down and cried till the tears rolled off his whiskers. "I am a very poor man," he sobbed. "I never had spirit enough to run out into the middle of the room. H'sh! I mustn't tell you anything. Can't you *hear*, Rikki-tikki?"

Rikki-tikki listened. The house was as still as still, but he thought he could just catch the faintest *scratch-scratch* in the world—a noise as faint as that of a wasp walking on a windowpane—the dry scratch of a snake's scales on brickwork.

"That's Nag or Nagaina," he said to himself, "and he is crawling into the bathroom sluice.[8] You're right, Chuchundra; I should have talked to Chua." **ⓘ**

He stole off to Teddy's bathroom, but there was nothing there, and then to Teddy's mother's bathroom. At the bottom of the smooth plaster wall there was a brick pulled out to make a sluice for the bathwater, and as Rikki-tikki stole in by the masonry[9] curb where the bath is put, he heard Nag and Nagaina whispering together outside in the moonlight.

"When the house is emptied of people," said Nagaina to her husband, "*he* will have

---

8. **sluice** (sloos): drain.
9. **masonry** (MAY suhn ree): structure built of stone or brick.

• The Sepoy rebellion of 1857 was the most serious revolt against British rule. Although it was unsuccessful, it frightened the British authorities. The result was even tighter control by Britain.
• Demands for Indian independence grew steadily throughout the early decades of the 20th century. Following the end of World War II, Britain decided to leave many of its former colonies. India gained its independence on August 15, 1947.

HSS Analysis Skills: HR1

Model the Skill

- Tell students that **vivid verbs** make a piece of writing stronger by enhancing a reader's mental picture of the action taking place.

- Direct students to p. 22, starting at point J, when Rikki-tikki-tavi overhears Nag and Nagaina's plotting. Point out the phrase "tingled all over with rage." Tell students that *tingle* means feeling prickly or stung by something, which helps show how angry Rikki-tikki-tavi is. He is so furious that he feels the anger deeply throughout his body. If the writer had simply said Rikki-tikki-tavi got mad, a reader might not understand how this event affected him or how much he loves his family.

Guided Practice: Apply

Ask students what sort of action they imagine *cartwhipped,* in paragraph 1 on p. 23, to be. Have students work in pairs to explain why *cartwhipped* is a strong, vivid replacement for *moved* or *struggled.*

---

to go away, and then the garden will be our own again. Go in quietly, and remember that the big man who killed Karait is the first one to bite. Then come out and tell me, and we will hunt for Rikki-tikki together."

"But are you sure that there is anything to be gained by killing the people?" said Nag.

"Everything. When there were no people in the bungalow, did we have any mongoose in the garden? So long as the bungalow is empty, we are king and queen of the garden; and remember that as soon as our eggs in the melon bed hatch (as they may tomorrow), our children will need room and quiet."

"I had not thought of that," said Nag. "I will go, but there is no need that we should hunt for Rikki-tikki afterward. I will kill the big man and his wife, and the child if I can, and come away quietly. Then the bungalow will be empty, and Rikki-tikki will go."

Rikki-tikki tingled all over with rage and hatred at this, and then Nag's head came through the sluice, and his five feet of cold body followed it. Angry as he was, Rikki-tikki was very frightened as he saw the size of the big cobra. Nag coiled himself up, raised his head, and looked into the bathroom in the dark, and Rikki could see his eyes glitter.

"Now, if I kill him here, Nagaina will know; and if I fight him on the open floor,

the odds are in his favor. What am I to do?" said Rikki-tikki-tavi.

Nag waved to and fro, and then Rikki-tikki heard him drinking from the biggest water jar that was used to fill the bath. "That is good," said the snake. "Now, when Karait was killed, the big man had a stick. He may have that stick still, but when he comes in to bathe in the morning, he will not have a stick. I shall wait here till he comes. Nagaina—do you hear me?—I shall wait here in the cool till daytime." **K**

There was no answer from outside, so Rikki-tikki knew Nagaina had gone away. Nag coiled himself down, coil by coil, round the bulge at the bottom of the water jar, and Rikki-tikki stayed still as death. After an hour he began to move, muscle by muscle, toward the jar. Nag was asleep, and Rikki-tikki looked at his big back, wondering which would be the best place for a good hold. "If I don't break his back at the first jump," said Rikki, "he can still fight; and if he fights—O Rikki!" He looked at the thickness of the neck below the hood, but that was too much for him; and a bite near the tail would only make Nag savage.

"It must be the head," he said at last, "the head above the hood; and when I am once there, I must not let go." **L**

Then he jumped. The head was lying a little clear of the water jar, under the curve of it; and as his teeth met, Rikki braced his back against the bulge of the

---

J | Read and Discuss | What are Nag and Nagaina doing?

K | Reading Focus | Summarizing | What is Nag's plan?

L | Reading Focus | Summarizing | What is Rikki-tikki's plan?

Universal Access

EL English Learners

Help students visualize the scene in the second column on p. 22 by summarizing the important details. You might say: "Nag has wrapped himself around the bottom of the water jar the family uses to fill the bathtub. Nag will attack Teddy's father in the morning when the man comes to take a bath."

Struggling Readers

Strategic Students Remind students that a conflict can occur between a character and an impersonal force (such as nature) as well as between two or more characters. This is known as an external conflict. Conflicts can also be internal, occurring in a character's mind.

- Point out that in addition to Rikki-tikki-tavi's conflicts with the snakes, he experiences a conflict with nature as a flood washes him down a ditch. He experiences internal conflicts as he struggles to decide his course red earthenware to hold down the head. This gave him just one second's purchase,[10] and he made the most of it. Then he was battered to and fro as a rat is shaken by a dog—to and fro on the floor, up and down, and round in great circles, but his eyes were red and he held on as the body cartwhipped over the floor, upsetting the tin dipper and the soap dish and the flesh brush, and banged against the tin side of the bath. As he held, he closed his jaws tighter and tighter, for he made sure[11] he would be banged to death, and for the honor of his family, he preferred to be found with his teeth locked. He was dizzy, aching, and felt shaken to pieces, when something went off like a thunderclap just behind him; a hot wind knocked him senseless and red fire singed his fur. The big man had been wakened by the noise and had fired both barrels of a shotgun into Nag just behind the hood.

Rikki-tikki held on with his eyes shut, for now he was quite sure he was dead; but the head did not move, and the big man picked him up and said: "It's the mongoose again, Alice; the little chap has saved *our* lives now." Then Teddy's mother came in with a very white face and saw what was left of Nag, and Rikki-tikki dragged himself to Teddy's bedroom and spent half the rest of the night shaking himself tenderly to find out whether he really was broken into forty pieces, as he fancied.

When morning came, he was very stiff but well pleased with his doings. "Now

---

10. **purchase:** firm hold.
11. **made sure:** here, felt sure.

M **Literary Focus** Conflict What is happening here? Why is the father's action significant? How does it advance the plot?

I have Nagaina to settle with, and she will be worse than five Nags, and there's no knowing when the eggs she spoke of will hatch. Goodness! I must go and see Darzee," he said.

Without waiting for breakfast, Rikki-tikki ran to the thorn bush, where Darzee was singing a song of triumph at the top of his voice. The news of Nag's death was all over the garden, for the sweeper had thrown the body on the rubbish heap.

"Oh, you stupid tuft of feathers!" said Rikki-tikki angrily. "Is this the time to sing?"

"Nag is dead—is dead—is dead!" sang Darzee. "The valiant Rikki-tikki caught him by the head and held fast. The big man brought the bang-stick, and Nag fell in two pieces! He will never eat my babies again."

"All that's true enough, but where's Nagaina?" said Rikki-tikki, looking carefully round him.

"Nagaina came to the bathroom sluice and called for Nag," Darzee went on, "and Nag came out on the end of a stick—the sweeper picked him up on the end of a stick and threw him upon the rubbish heap. Let us sing about the great, the red-eyed Rikki-tikki!" and Darzee filled his throat and sang.

"If I could get up to your nest, I'd roll your babies out!" said Rikki-tikki. "You don't know when to do the right thing at the right time. You're safe enough in your nest there, but it's war for me down here. Stop singing a minute, Darzee."

"For the great, beautiful Rikki-tikki's sake I will stop," said Darzee. "What is it,

---

Vocabulary **valiant** (VAL yuhnt) *adj.:* brave and determined.

---

of action and to find the courage to protect the house and garden from the cobras.

- Point out Rikki-tikki's dialogue with himself in paragraphs 3 and 4 of column 2 on p. 22. Model the internal and external conflict he is facing here. Explain that Rikki-tikki is thinking about the best way to defeat Nag, but he is also scared of what will happen to him if he loses to Nag. Rikki-tikki must not only physically defeat Nag, but he must also overcome his own fears.

Benchmark Students Have students pause in their reading at the end of column 1, p. 22, to guide them in summarizing the story so far. Divide students into seven groups, and assign each group to review one of the preceding story pages (pp. 15–21). Ask each group to identify what characters appear on their page, what locations they visit, and what they do. Have the groups share their findings, pausing after each group to guide students in identifying key events or developments evident from the findings. Model noting the important events or developments in a graphic organizer.

Think About/Talk About

▶ Comprehension

J Read and Discuss

Possible response: They are planning to kill the family, so that Rikki-tikki-tavi will leave. Then, they will have the garden to themselves again.

K Reading Focus

Possible response: Nag's plan is to kill Teddy's father when he goes into the bathroom to bathe in the morning, as the father will probably be unarmed and not expecting an attack.

L Reading Focus

Possible response: Rikki-tikki-tavi's plan is to kill Nag by biting his head and not letting go until the snake is dead.

▶ Analysis

M Literary Focus

Possible response: Rikki-tikki and Nag are fighting. Rikki-tikki-tavi bit Nag on the head, and Nag is trying to shake him off. The father is the one who actually kills Nag with a shotgun. This eliminates one of the cobras who is threatening the family.

▶ Extend the Discussion

Conflict In paragraphs 2–4 of column 1 on p. 22, Nagaina believes that the war with Rikki-tikki-tavi will be over when the humans are killed. Considering Rikki-tikki-tavi's personality, would the conflict really be over if there were nobody left to protect? Explain. *Possible response:* Rikki-tikki-tavi would probably continue the fight and try to avenge the deaths of anyone he was unable to protect. He views this conflict as a matter of honor and would only stop following his own death or the deaths of his enemies.

Vocabulary: Own the Word

valiant: *Valiant* means "brave" or "courageous;" an antonym is *fearful*. Use both words in a sentence. The *valiant* hero was ready for battle, but the fearful villain ran away from him.

Model the Skill

- Explain that **conflicts** change and develop throughout a story, therby advancing plot. Situations change, and characters' needs and wants change accordingly.

- Remind students that Rikki-tikki-tavi has just fought to keep Nag from killing Teddy's father, and Teddy's father shot Nag to death during the fight. Though Nag's threat to kill the family is no longer in the way of Rikki-tikki-tavi's desire to protect the family, a new conflict is brewing. Point out that Nag is dead, but Nagaina, who also wanted Rikki-tikki-tavi dead and whose husband has just been killed, is still alive. By the end of p. 23, Darzee has let everyone know that Rikki-tikki-tavi attacked Nag and Teddy's father killed him. Nag's wants may no longer be important, but Nagaina's wants will come into conflict with Rikki-tikki-tavi's. She will want revenge against him and the family, and he will still try to protect the people he loves.

Guided Practice: Apply

Read/Talk/Write Have students read pp. 24–25 independently. Then, have them discuss in groups of three how Rikki-tikki-tavi and Nagaina seek on these pages to get what they want, and what obstacles each puts in the other's way. Have students briefly describe the new conflict in their **Reader/Writer Notebook**.

O Killer of the terrible Nag?"

"Where is Nagaina, for the third time?"

"On the rubbish heap by the stables, mourning for Nag. Great is Rikki-tikki with the white teeth."

"Bother[12] my white teeth! Have you ever heard where she keeps her eggs?"

"In the melon bed, on the end nearest the wall, where the sun strikes nearly all day. She hid them there weeks ago."

"And you never thought it worthwhile to tell me? The end nearest the wall, you said?"

"Rikki-tikki, you are not going to eat her eggs?"

"Not eat exactly; no. Darzee, if you have a grain of sense, you will fly off to the stables and pretend that your wing is broken and let Nagaina chase you away to this bush. I must get to the melon bed, and if I went there now, she'd see me."

Darzee was a featherbrained little fellow who could never hold more than one idea at a time in his head, and just

---

12. **bother:** here, never mind.

N [Read and Discuss] Why does Rikki-tikki want Darzee to pretend his wing is broken?

---

because he knew that Nagaina's children were born in eggs like his own, he didn't think at first that it was fair to kill them. But his wife was a sensible bird, and she knew that cobra's eggs meant young cobras later on; so she flew off from the nest and left Darzee to keep the babies warm and continue his song about the death of Nag. Darzee was very like a man in some ways.

She fluttered in front of Nagaina by the rubbish heap and cried out, "Oh, my wing is broken! The boy in the house threw a stone at me and broke it." Then she fluttered more desperately than ever. **O**

Nagaina lifted up her head and hissed, "You warned Rikki-tikki when I would have killed him. Indeed and truly, you've chosen a bad place to be lame in." And she moved toward Darzee's wife, slipping along over the dust.

"The boy broke it with a stone!" shrieked Darzee's wife.

"Well! It may be some consolation to you when you're dead to know that I shall settle accounts with the boy. My husband lies on the rubbish heap this morning, but before night the boy in the house will lie very still. What is the use of running away? I am sure to catch you. Little fool, look at me!"

Darzee's wife knew better than to do *that*, for a bird who looks at a snake's eyes gets so frightened that she cannot move. Darzee's wife fluttered on, piping

---

O [Read and Discuss] Darzee is supposed to have the broken wing. Why, then, is his wife pretending to have one?

Vocabulary **consolation** (KAHN suh LAY shuhn) *n.*: comfort.

Word-Attack Skills Mini-Lesson

Silent *t* and *b*

English for Academic Success

- Have students locate the words *dust* and *rustle* in the story. Point out that the word *rustle* begins with the word *rust*, so it's logical to think that the beginning of *rustle* would sound like *rust* and rhyme with *dust*. Explain that in this case, the *t* is silent.

- Use the following word pairs to show that *-le* after the consonant blend *st* always has the effect of making the *t* silent: *cast/castle nest/nestle grist/gristle whist/whistle*

- Warn students that *-le* is tricky and doesn't always behave in the same way—that is, it doesn't always make letters silent.

- Then, explore with students the effect of *-le* on another consonant blend: *mb*. When a word ends with *mb*, the *b* is always silent: *crumb*, *plumb*, and *limb*. But when *mb* is followed by *-le*, the *b* is not silent.

- Compare the words *crumb* and *crumble*. The sound of *b* is heard in words ending with *-mble*: *stumble*, *nimble*, and *tremble*.

sorrowfully and never leaving the ground, and Nagaina quickened her pace.

Rikki-tikki heard them going up the path from the stables, and he raced for the end of the melon patch near the wall. There, in the warm litter above the melons, very cunningly hidden, he found twenty-five eggs about the size of a bantam's[13] eggs but with whitish skins instead of shells.

"I was not a day too soon," he said, for he could see the baby cobras curled up inside the skin, and he knew that the minute they were hatched, they could each kill a man or a mongoose. He bit off the tops of the eggs as fast as he could, taking care to crush the young cobras, and turned over the litter from time to time to see whether he had missed any. At last there were only three eggs left, and Rikki-tikki began to chuckle to himself, when he heard Darzee's wife screaming:

"Rikki-tikki, I led Nagaina toward the house, and she has gone into the veranda, and—oh, come quickly—she means killing!" **P**

Rikki-tikki smashed two eggs, and tumbled backward down the melon bed with the third egg in his mouth, and scuttled to the veranda as hard as he could put foot to the

> "Rikki-tikki, I led Nagaina toward the house, and she has gone into the veranda, and —oh, come quickly— she means killing!"

ground. Teddy and his mother and father were there at early breakfast, but Rikki-tikki saw that they were not eating anything. They sat stone still, and their faces were white. Nagaina was coiled up on the matting by Teddy's chair, within easy striking distance of Teddy's bare leg, and she was swaying to and fro, singing a song of triumph.

"Son of the big man that killed Nag," she hissed, "stay still. I am not ready yet. Wait a little. Keep very still, all you three! If you move, I strike, and if you do not move, I strike. Oh, foolish people, who killed my Nag!"

Teddy's eyes were fixed on his father, and all his father could do was to whisper, "Sit still, Teddy. You mustn't move. Teddy, keep still."

Then Rikki-tikki came up and cried: "Turn round, Nagaina; turn and fight!"

"All in good time," said she, without moving her eyes. "I will settle my account with *you* presently. Look at your friends, Rikki-tikki. They are still and white. They are afraid. They dare not move, and if you come a step nearer, I strike."

"Look at your eggs," said Rikki-tikki, "in the melon bed near the wall. Go and look, Nagaina!"

The big snake turned half round and saw the egg on the veranda. "Ah-h! Give it to me," she said.

13. **bantam's:** small chicken's.

P | Read and Discuss | How are things looking for the family? What is Rikki-tikki doing?

Activity Write the following sentences on the board. Ask a volunteer to pronounce the words and explain why each underlined word sounds the way it does.
1. The eggs are nestled in the shade.
2. Darzee trembles as he whistles.
3. Nag's victims are struck dumb with terror.
4. Rikki's home is his castle.
5. If you hear a rustle, don't move a limb.

✔ For additional instruction and strategies, see **ThinkCentral, Teacher Access**.

Think About/Talk About

▶ **Comprehension**

N **Read and Discuss**
Possible response: Rikki-tikki-tavi wants Darzee to distract Nagaina so he can go to her nest.

O **Read and Discuss**
Possible response: Darzee wasn't smart and didn't want Rikki-tikki-tavi to kill the eggs. Darzee's wife is smarter and realizes that the eggs will be threats in the future.

P **Read and Discuss**
Possible response: Things are looking grim for the family, because Nagaina is in a position to kill them. Rikki-tikki-tavi is in the melon bed destroying Nagaina's eggs, and Darzee's wife tells him that Nagaina is headed toward the family's house. They are now in danger.

▶ **Extend the Discussion**

Characterization In column 2 of p. 25, Nagaina taunts the family. What do her comments reveal about her motivation? How does this reflect the way she now views the conflict?
Possible response: Nagaina refers to Teddy as "son of the big man that killed Nag" and later says, "Oh, foolish people, who killed my Nag!" This shows that she is deeply upset by the death of her husband and is looking for revenge. The conflict is now deeply personal.

Conflict Why does Rikki-tikki-tavi bring the egg to the veranda with him? *Possible response:* Rikki-tikki-tavi is using the egg to bargain with Nagaina. He hopes that she will be so concerned with saving her only remaining egg that she will let the family go.

Vocabulary: Own the Word
consolation: Tell students that *consolation* comes from the Latin word parts *solari*, which means "to soothe," and *con*, which means "with." When you give someone *consolation*, you give them comfort.

Tell students that Nagaina's death resolved the **conflict** between Rikki-tikki-tavi and the snakes. The last snake is now dead and the threat to the inhabitants of the bungalow has been removed. The killing of the snakes has eliminated their wants. Rikki-tikki-tavi has fulfilled his wish to protect his family by killing the snakes.

Guided Practice: Apply

Review the key developments in the conflict between Rikki-tikki-tavi and the snakes. Ask students which of these events resolve part of the conflict, and which of them intensify it, and how. Also discuss the ways in which plot depends on conflict to advance. When posing these questions to the class, you may wish to use the Send a Problem discussion format. Have students continue the discussion until they have successfully determined whether each event resolves or intensifies the story's conflict.

Rikki-tikki put his paws one on each side of the egg, and his eyes were blood-red. "What price for a snake's egg? For a young cobra? For a young king cobra? For the last—the very last of the brood? The ants are eating all the others down by the melon bed."

Nagaina spun clear round, forgetting everything for the sake of the one egg; and Rikki-tikki saw Teddy's father shoot out a big hand, catch Teddy by the shoulder, and drag him across the little table with the teacups, safe and out of reach of Nagaina.

"Tricked! Tricked! Tricked! *Rikk-tck-tck!*" chuckled Rikki-tikki. "The boy is safe, and it was I—I—I—that caught Nag by the hood last night in the bathroom." Then he began to jump up and down, all four feet together, his head close to the floor. "He threw me to and fro, but he could not shake me off. He was dead before the big man blew him in two. I did it! *Rikki-tikki-tck-tck!* Come then, Nagaina. Come and fight with me. You shall not be a widow long." **Q**

Nagaina saw that she had lost her chance of killing Teddy, and the egg lay between Rikki-tikki's paws. "Give me the egg, Rikki-tikki. Give me the last of my eggs, and I will go away and never come back," she said, lowering her hood. **R**

"Yes, you will go away, and you will never come back; for you will go to the

> "Come then, Nagaina. Come and fight with me. You shall not be a widow long."

rubbish heap with Nag. Fight, widow! The big man has gone for his gun! Fight!"

Rikki-tikki was bounding all round Nagaina, keeping just out of reach of her stroke, his little eyes like hot coals. Nagaina gathered herself together and flung out at him. Rikki-tikki jumped up and backwards. Again and again and again she struck, and each time her head came with a whack on the matting of the veranda and she gathered herself together like a watch spring. Then Rikki-tikki danced in a circle to get behind her, and Nagaina spun round to keep her head to his head, so that the rustle of her tail on the matting sounded like dry leaves blown along by the wind.

He had forgotten the egg. It still lay on the veranda, and Nagaina came nearer and nearer to it, till at last, while Rikki-tikki was drawing breath, she caught it in her mouth, turned to the veranda steps, and flew like an arrow down the path, with Rikki-tikki behind her. When the cobra runs for her life, she goes like a whiplash flicked across a horse's neck. Rikki-tikki knew that he must catch her or all the trouble would begin again. She headed straight for the long grass by the thorn bush, and as he was running, Rikki-tikki heard Darzee still singing his foolish little song of triumph. But Darzee's wife was wiser. She flew off her nest as Nagaina came along and flapped

Q Literary Focus **Conflict** What is happening between Nagaina and Rikki-tikki? How does this advance the plot?

R Read and Discuss What do you learn about Nagaina here?

Developing Oral Fluency

"Rikki-tikki-tavi" is an exciting story with many interesting characters. Have students work on tone and expression while reading aloud. This will allow students to better understand the emotions of the characters.

Small-Group Activity Put students into groups of three and direct their attention to the dialogue between Rikki-tikki-tavi and Nagaina in the first column of p. 26.

- Model the use of expression and tone while reading dialogue. Explain that at the bottom of column 1 on p. 26, Nagaina is pleading with Rikki-tikki-tavi to

spare her egg. Nagaina's dialogue should have a sad, fearful tone to reflect her desperate situation.

- Then, have groups of students read the first column of p. 26 aloud. Two students should read the roles of Rikki-tikki-tavi and Nagaina, while a fluent student should read the narrative lines in each paragraph.

- After reading, have students discuss the story's conflict from the point of view of their character.

✔ See the Oral Language Skill Builder in **UA: Differentiating Instruction**.

her wings about Nagaina's head. If Darzee had helped, they might have turned her, but Nagaina only lowered her hood and went on. Still, the instant's delay brought Rikki-tikki up to her, and as she plunged into the rat hole where she and Nag used to live, his little white teeth were clenched on her tail and he went down with her—and very few mongooses, however wise and old they may be, care to follow a cobra into its hole. It was dark in the hole, and Rikki-tikki never knew when it might open out and give Nagaina room to turn and strike at him. He held on savagely and stuck out his feet to act as brakes on the dark slope of the hot, moist earth. Then the grass by the mouth of the hole stopped waving, and Darzee said: "It is all over with Rikki-tikki! We must sing his death song. Valiant Rikki-tikki is dead! For Nagaina will surely kill him underground."

So he sang a very mournful song that he made up on the spur of the minute,

and just as he got to the most touching part, the grass quivered again, and Rikki-tikki, covered with dirt, dragged himself out of the hole leg by leg, licking his whiskers. Darzee stopped with a little shout. Rikki-tikki shook some of the dust out of his fur and sneezed. "It is all over," he said. "The widow will never come out again." And the red ants that live between the grass stems heard him and began to troop down one after another to see if he had spoken the truth. **S**

Rikki-tikki curled himself up in the grass and slept where he was—slept and slept till it was late in the afternoon, for he had done a hard day's work.

"Now," he said, when he awoke, "I will go back to the house. Tell the Coppersmith, Darzee, and he will tell the garden that Nagaina is dead."

The Coppersmith is a bird who makes a noise exactly like the beating of a little hammer on a copper pot; and the reason he is

S Literary Focus Conflict What happens when Rikki-tikki fights Nagaina?

Reaching Reluctant Readers

Help students respond to "Rikki-tikki-tavi" by relating the text to their everyday lives.

- Have students revisit the conflict between Rikki-tikki-tavi and the snakes. Point out that animals in the real world resolve disputes with physical confrontations. These are often the only problem-solving tools animals have, because they cannot use speech as humans do.

- Tell students that there are many peaceful methods of negotiating conflicts between people and groups, such as mediation, a formal discussion in which a person outside of the situation brings about a settlement.

- Have students discuss different methods of conflict resolution that they are familiar with. Then, have them work in small groups to practice using these strategies to resolve situations from everyday life, such as an argument between siblings over who gets the computer next. When students finish their scenarios, ask them to relate the conflicts they negotiated to the conflicts in the stories. What were the wants and needs that came into conflict? How did they address these wants and needs but still resolve the conflict? Discuss as a class.

▶ Comprehension

T Read and Discuss

Possible response: Darzee's chant describes how Rikki-tikki-tavi saved the lives of many creatures by killing the snakes.

▶ Extend the Discussion

Theme In the last paragraph, it says that Rikki-tikki-tavi "did not grow too proud." What lesson does this story teach about pride? ***Possible response:*** *It is good to have pride in your accomplishments, but it can lead to disaster if it turns to arrogance. The snakes thought they were more powerful than a mongoose and it led to their downfall.*

Monitor Students' Comprehension

Guide the class in answering these comprehension questions.

1. How does Rikki-tikki-tavi come to live with the family? [*Teddy and his mother rescue him after a flood.*]

2. Why do Nag and Nagaina want to get rid of Rikki-tikki-tavi? [*Mongooses kill snakes, so Rikki is a threat to them. He is also preventing the snakes from taking over the garden.*]

---

always making it is because he is the town crier to every Indian garden and tells all the news to everybody who cares to listen. As Rikki-tikki went up the path, he heard his "attention" notes like a tiny dinner gong and then the steady "*Ding-dong-tock!* Nag is dead—*dong!* Nagaina is dead! *Ding-dong-tock!*" That set all the birds in the garden singing and the frogs croaking, for Nag and Nagaina used to eat frogs as well as little birds.

When Rikki got to the house, Teddy and Teddy's mother (she looked very white still, for she had been fainting) and Teddy's father came out and almost cried over him; and that night he ate all that was given him till he could eat no more and went to bed on Teddy's shoulder, where Teddy's mother saw him when she came to look late at night.

"He saved our lives and Teddy's life," she said to her husband. "Just think, he saved all our lives."

Rikki-tikki woke up with a jump, for the mongooses are light sleepers.

"Oh, it's you," said he. "What are you bothering for? All the cobras are dead; and if they weren't, I'm here."

Rikki-tikki had a right to be proud of himself, but he did not grow too proud, and he kept that garden as a mongoose should keep it, with tooth and jump and spring and bite, till never a cobra dared show its head inside the walls.

T Read and Discuss How does Darzee's chant celebrate past events?

Darzee's Chant

Sung in honor of Rikki-tikki-tavi

Singer and tailor am I—
  Doubled the joys that I know—
Proud of my lilt[14] to the sky,
  Proud of the house that I sew.
Over and under, so weave I my music—
  so weave I the house that I sew.

Sing to your fledglings[15] again,
  Mother, O lift up your head!
Evil that plagued us is slain,
  Death in the garden lies dead.
Terror that hid in the roses is impotent
  —flung on the dunghill and dead!

Who has delivered us, who?
  Tell me his nest and his name.
Rikki, the valiant, the true,
  Tikki, with eyeballs of flame—
Rikk-tikki-tikki, the ivory-fanged, the
  hunter with eyeballs of flame!

Give him the Thanks of the Birds,
  Bowing with tail-feathers spread,
Praise him with nightingale words
  Nay, I will praise him instead.
Hear! I will sing you the praise of the
  bottle-tailed Rikki with eyeballs of red!

(*Here Rikki-tikki interrupted, so the rest of the song is lost.*) **T**

14. **lilt:** song.
15. **fledglings** (FLEHJ lihngz): baby birds.

![bear] **California Standards, pp. 29–31**

■ **Reading Standard 1.3** Clarify word meanings through the use of definition, example, restatement, or contrast.

■ **Reading Standard 3.2** Identify events that advance the plot and determine how each event explains past or present action(s) or foreshadows future action(s).

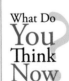 **Reading Standard 3.2** Identify events that advance the plot and determine how each event explains past or present action(s) or foreshadows future action(s).

Rikki-tikki-tavi

Literary Response and Analysis

Reading Skills Focus
Quick Check

1. What does Rikki-tikki do to protect himself and his family?

2. Rikki-tikki fights alone, but he gets a little help from his friends. How do they help him?

Read with a Purpose

3. Use examples from the text to show whether Rikki-tikki handles each threat with cunning or with force.

Reading Skills: Summarizing

4. Review your Story Map. Does it include the most significant events? Now expand and revise your Story Map as shown below. Include the characters, setting, and major events that advance the story's plot.

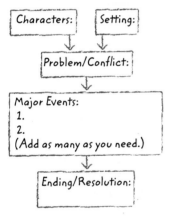

Literary Skills Focus
Literary Analysis

5. **Analyze** What events change the family's views of Rikki-tikki throughout the story?

6. **Interpret** Explain how Rikki-tikki's first fight with Nagaina influenced the outcome of his later fight with Karait.

Literary Skills: Conflict

7. **Analyze** Describe three **conflicts** that Rikki-tikki faces, and explain how each conflict advances the plot. Which conflict is his greatest challenge? What past events led to this conflict?

Literary Skills Review: Setting

8. **Analyze** Could the main events of this story take place in a different setting, or is this setting crucial to the plot? Which plot elements depend on the story being set in India?

Writing Skills Focus
Think as a Reader/Writer

Use It in Your Writing Review the descriptions of Nag and Nagaina you noted. Find words and phrases that make the snakes seem evil. Is Kipling being unfair? Are the snakes just doing what snakes do naturally? Discuss your evaluation of the way Kipling handles his snake characters.

What Do **You Think** Now? In what ways were Rikki-tikki's conflicts similar to or different from conflicts you have faced? Think back to what you said before you read the story.

Reading Skills Focus
Answers:

1. *He fights cobras that want to kill him and his family.*

2. *Darzee, his wife, and Chuchundra share information with Rikki-tikki-tavi. Teddy's father helps to kill Nag.*

3. *He destroys the cobras with cunning, by distracting or sneaking up on them, and with force by biting as hard as he can until they are dead.*

4. *Characters: Rikki-tikki-tavi, Teddy, family, Nag, Nagaina, Darzee, wife; Setting: India; Conflict: Rikki-tikki vs. cobras; Major Events: Teddy's family takes in Rikki-tikki-tavi, the cobras plan to kill him, Rikki-tikki kills Nag, Nagaina threatens him, Rikki-tikki kills her; Resolution: Rikki-tikki-tavi saves his family.*

Literary Skills Focus
Possible responses:

5. *Teddy's mother is afraid of Rikki-tikki-tavi at first, but ends up grateful to him after he saves the family.*

6. *After fighting Nagaina, Rikki-tikki-tavi became more confident and learned the best way to kill a snake. This helped him defeat Karait.*

7. *Rikki-tikki-tavi has conflicts with Karait, Nag, and Nagaina. Fighting Nagaina is hardest because she is determined to get revenge for Nag, but Rikki-tikki-tavi kills her. The past event of killing Nag led to the conflict with Nagaina.*

8. *The story must take place near the forest, where many animals live. The story features animals such as the cobra, that are found in India but not in other parts of the world.*

What Do You Think Now?

Ask students to use their own experiences to consider if Rikki-tikki-tavi's situation is different from that of humans dealing with bullies. Do human bullies present the same threat as the snakes? Would it have been possible to negotiate with either the snakes or human bullies?

Universal Access

Struggling Writers

Some students may need additional scaffolding to complete the Writing Skills Focus activity. Help them evaluate the fairness of the portrayal of Nag and Nagaina. Have students choose one of the two snakes and describe in a paragraph the character traits and behaviors of the snake throughout the story. Have students fill out a semantic web to help them describe their chosen character.

Independent Practice

Vocabulary Development

Your Turn

1. *small*
2. *meek*
3. *frightened*

English for Academic Success

Language Coach

Tell students that countless words and word parts in the English language originally came from Latin, the language of ancient Rome. Becoming familiar with more commonly used Latin words and word parts, such as the prefix *dis-*, can help them more easily decode unfamiliar words. Most dictionary entries will also indicate whether a word has Latin roots.

Answers: *Valere* is the root of *valiant*; *immensus* is the root of *immensely*; *curiosus* is the root of *curious*; *terribilus* is the root of *terrible*; and *serius* is the root of *serious*.

English for Academic Success

Academic Vocabulary

Possible response: Kipling's descriptions of the cobras seem accurate based on what I know about cobras and what I read in the Science Link. He puts <u>significant</u> *effort into describing them because they are major story characters and their behaviors, wants, and needs contribute greatly to the suspense of the story.*

 WordSharp: An Interactive Vocabulary Tutor

 Learn It Online
Word Watch provides audio pronunciations of words, plus synonyms and antonyms, the word used in a sentence, and a brief history of word origins.

go.hrw.com   H7-30   Go

Applying Your Skills

Rikki-tikki-tavi

Vocabulary Development
Clarifying Word Meanings: Contrast

Sometimes you can clarify the meaning of an unfamiliar word by looking for **contrast** clues. A writer who uses contrast will show how a word is unlike another word. For example, you can get a clear idea of what a splendid garden is if you see it contrasted with a dark, narrow hole in the ground.

"The *splendid* garden glowed with roses and great clumps of waving grasses, unlike the *dreary* hole where cobras live."

As you read, watch for these words and phrases, which signal contrast: *although, but, yet, still, unlike, not, in contrast, instead,* and *however.*

Your Turn

Fill in the blanks in the following sentences with words or phrases that contrast with the boldface word. You may find it helpful to make a cluster diagram of the word and its opposites before you write, like the one below for *cowered* and *cowering.*

| immensely |
| cowered |
| valiant |
| consolation |

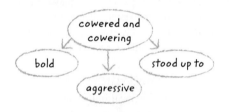

1. The cobras were **immensely** powerful, while the power of Darzee and the other garden creatures was _____.

2. Rikki-tikki was certainly **valiant,** but Chuchundra, the little muskrat, was _____.

3. Rikki-tikki's protection of the house provided **consolation** for the family, though they were _____ when the cobra threatened Teddy.

Language Coach

Word Roots Other words from the story also have Latin roots. Look at these words and their meanings. Then, match them with their roots.

| curiosity |
| serious |
| valiant |
| terrible |
| immensely |

Latin Word	Meaning
valere	be strong
immensus	cannot be measured
curiosus	interested, nosy
terribilus	frightening, awful
serius	solemn

Academic Vocabulary

Talk About . . .

Re-read your notes on the way Kipling describes the cobras. Then, with a partner, <u>explain</u> whether you feel his descriptions are accurate. Consider why he puts <u>significant</u> effort into describing the cobras this way. What do his descriptions add to the story?

 Learn It Online
Explore the Vocabulary words with Word Watch:
go.hrw.com   H7-30   Go

Universal Access: Vocabulary Development

EL English Learners

English for Academic Success Provide students with more practice using and identifying contrast clues.

- Have students brainstorm pairs of opposites: *good/bad, light/dark, clean/dirty, old/new.* Explain that opposite pairs may signal contrast clues.

- Model using opposites and signal words to identify contrast clues for *illuminated* in the following sentence: "The illuminated living room shone in contrast to the kitchen, which seemed never to have emerged

from night." You might say: I know that nights are dark. If there is an opposite, it would be light. The author's use of "in contrast" suggests that there is an opposite pair, so *illuminated* means light or lit up.

- Have students identify contrast clues for *cacophony* in "Park Avenue usually fell silent as the sun went down, but tonight, the street rattled with the cacophony of a block party."

✔ For more practice with using contrast clues, see **Language Handbook Worksheets.**

Grammar Link
Common and Proper Nouns

A **noun** is a word used to name a person, a place, a thing, or an idea.

PERSONS Teddy, Englishman

PLACES India, Segowlee, bathroom, bungalow

THINGS wall, collar, wineglasses

IDEAS friendship, death, victory

A **common noun** is a general name for a person, place, thing, or idea. A **proper noun** is a particular person, place, or thing.

Common	Proper
boy	Teddy
mongoose	Rikki-tikki-tavi
country	India

Your Turn

In the sentences that follow, underline the common nouns and circle the proper nouns.

1. Rikki-tikki was a young mongoose who lived in a big bungalow.
2. Teddy called out to his mother.
3. The Englishman picked up Rikki-tikki between his finger and thumb.
4. The black cobra, Nag, was five feet long from tongue to tail.

Writing Applications Write about your relationship with a favorite pet. Underline the common nouns, and circle the proper nouns.

CHOICES

As you respond to the Choices, use these **Academic Vocabulary** words as appropriate: <u>advance</u>, <u>explain</u>, <u>significant</u>, <u>similar</u>.

REVIEW
Write a Plot Summary

Write a summary of "Rikki-tikki-tavi" by referring to your story map (page 13). Be sure to include the characters, setting, conflicts, <u>significant</u> events that <u>advance</u> the plot, and resolution.

CONNECT
Compare and Contrast Characters

Timed ⌐Writing In a three-paragraph essay, compare and contrast the characters Rikki-tikki and Nag. Organize the essay in the way that works best. You might want to compare their physical appearances in the first paragraph and their personalities in the second. Use the third paragraph to summarize your main points.

EXTEND
Create a Fact Sheet

Create an accurate fact sheet that will inform zoo visitors about cobras. Read "The Unusual and Deadly Cobra" on page 19, and conduct further research. Before you begin your research, decide on the questions you would like to answer. Here are some possibilities:

- How many kinds of cobras exist?
- Where do cobras live, and what do they eat?
- How dangerous are cobras?

Learn It Online
Research more elements of the story using the Internet links at:
go.hrw.com | H7-31 | **Go**

Independent Practice
Grammar Link

1. *P: Rikki-tikki; C: mongoose, bungalow*
2. *P: Teddy; C: mother*
3. *P: Englishman, Rikki-tikki; C: finger, thumb*
4. *P: Nag; C: feet, tongue, tail, cobra*

Choices: Evaluation Criteria

Review: Homework
Write a Plot Summary

- The summary includes the story's characters, setting, conflicts, major events, and resolution.
- The summary is organized.

Connect: Timed Writing 40–50 minutes

- The essay compare and contrasts Rikki-tikki-tavi and Nag.
- The essay ends with a summary of the main points.

Extend: Homework
Create a Fact Sheet
The fact sheet creatively provides detailed information about cobras.

Assess

✎ **Chapter 1 Resources,** Selection Standards Check, p. 9

ThinkCentral Online Assessment, Selection Standards Check

◎ **Teacher One Stop™,** editable Selection Standards Check

Reteach

ThinkCentral Online Remediation

✳ **Learn It Online**
Literature Links directs students to prescreened Web sites offering more information related to a selection.

go.hrw.com | H7-31 | **Go**

Universal Access: Grammar Link

Struggling Readers
English for Academic Success Explain to students that the words *officer, school, book,* and *love* are all nouns. These four words are also all common nouns, meaning they are used in everyday speech to describe nonspecific people, places, objects, or ideas. In contrast, Officer Simmons, The Carter School, *Catcher in the Rye,* and the Monroe Doctrine are all proper nouns, meaning they are terms used to describe specific people, places, objects, or ideas, and require capitalization. Write the following words on the board. Have students work in pairs to determine the correct capitalization for the following words: *jupiter, pencil, independence, abraham lincoln, computer, the chicago art museum, novella.*

Responses: *Jupiter, pencil, independence, Abraham Lincoln, computer, the Chicago Art Museum, novella.*

✔ For more practice with common and proper nouns, see **Language Handbook Worksheets, Grammar Notes,** and **Warriner's Handbook.**

Standards Focus

Objectives
Students will
- identify and analyze suspense and foreshadowing
- make and evaluate predictions

Motivate

What Do You Think?/QuickWrite
Ask students to list a few scary situations and explain what makes them scary. Have students discuss features that are common to most scary settings they have seen or read about. Then, have students list details that make a situation frightening in their **Reader/Writer Notebook.**

English for Academic Success

Academic Vocabulary
Look for opportunities to use the Academic Vocabulary words in this chapter.

- **significant, *adj.:*** important

- **advance, *v.:*** move forward

- **explain, *v.:*** give reasons for; make understandable

- **similar, *adj.:*** almost the same

Analyzing Visuals
Extension Activity Describe a situation in which you would expect to see this rat. *Possible response: I'd expect to see it in an old, rickety, haunted house at midnight.*

 California Standards, pp. 32–49

- **Reading Standard 3.2** Identify events that advance the plot and determine how each event explains past or present action(s) or foreshadows future action(s).

Three Skeleton Key

by **George G. Toudouze**

What Do You Think What kinds of dangerous situations make a horror story scary?

QuickWrite If you were writing a horror story, what detai[ls] you use to create a scary situation? Freewrite ideas.

Selection Readability	
Easily Accessible	complex syntax; difficult vocabulary
Accessible	
Challenging	

Selection Plot Summary
Three lighthouse keepers on an isolated island off the coast of So[uth] America find themselves trapped by man-eating rats. The story r[ecounts] the men's fight for survival against creatures that will stop at not[hing to] devour them.

Reader/Writer Notebook

Use your **RWN** to complete the activities for this selection.

Literary Skills Focus

Suspense and Foreshadowing "My most terrifying experience?" With this opening the writer of "Three Skeleton Key" captures our interest. We immediately want to know about that terrifying experience. This feeling of anxious curiosity is called **suspense.**

Writers often add to the suspense in a story by including hints about what might happen later in the story. This use of clues for added effect is called **foreshadowing.** One example of foreshadowing might be in a story's title. Make a guess about what the title of this story might foreshadow.

Reading Skills Focus

Making Predictions Part of the fun of following any story is guessing what future actions will develop from events at each stage of the story. This process of wondering about and guessing what might happen next is called **making predictions.**

Into Action Make predictions by looking for clues that foreshadow future actions. By paying attention to such clues, you can guess possible outcomes. Of course, you will continue to revise predictions as you read and make new ones as new events develop. Use the following Prediction Chart to record this process.

Page	Foreshadowing Clue	My Prediction
p. 35	"The story was that the three skeletons . . . danced over the small rock, screaming."	Something bad will happen at this lighthouse.
p. 36	"The waters about our island swarmed with huge sharks."	

Writing Skills Focus

Think as a Reader/Writer

Find It in Your Reading As you read this short story, identify and list events that <u>advance</u> the plot. Then, <u>explain</u> how these critical events help build the story's terror and suspense.

Vocabulary

treacherously (TREHCH uhr uhs lee) *adv.:* deceptively; unreliably. *The wet rocks were treacherously smooth.*

maneuver (muh NOO vuhr) *v.:* move or manipulate skillfully. *Sailing vessels can't maneuver as easily as steamers.*

hordes (hawrdz) *n.:* densely packed crowds. *The rats swam ashore in hordes.*

receding (rih SEED ihng) *v.* used as *adj.:* moving back. *At first the ship came toward us, but then it drifted off in the receding waters.*

edible (EHD uh buhl) *adj.:* fit to be eaten. *The rats thought the men were edible.*

Language Coach

Word Origins The word *maneuver* comes from the Latin phrase *manu operare,* which means "to work by hand." Words that come from other languages often change in meaning over time. Read the definition of the word *maneuver* again. Brainstorm with a partner how you think the meanings of *maneuver* and *manu operare* are related. What do you think *maneuver* originally meant? Why do you think its meaning has changed or broadened over time?

 Learn It Online

Hear a professional actor read this story. Visit the selection online at:

go.hrw.com   H7-33   **Go**

More About the Writer

George Toudouze was also the author of a play that later became the film *Wolves*. It shows how criminals in an outlaw camp come to be more like wolves than humans.

Think About the Writer

Explain to students that "Three Skeleton Key" is set in a lighthouse on an island in the Atlantic Ocean. Ask students to discuss what an author might need to know in order to write a convincing, credible story about events that take place on or near the sea.

 For Independent Reading

■ Students who enjoy stories of sailors or of people in desperate situations might like *The True Confessions of Charlotte Doyle*. In this award-winning mystery by Avi, a young girl faces murder and adventure aboard a ship bound for New England.

■ If students are interested in stories of adventure at sea, they might enjoy *Shipwreck at the Bottom of the World: The Extraordinary True Story of Shackleton and the Endurance* by Jennifer Armstrong, which documents the true story of a 1914 Antarctic expedition gone awry and the brave crew's struggle to survive.

George G. Toudouze
(1847–1904)

Man of Many Interests

George G. Toudouze was born in France and grew up to develop many literary interests—he was a playwright, an essayist, and an illustrator. He also had a great interest in the sea and worked on a history of the French navy. "Three Skeleton Key" was first published in *Esquire,* a magazine that was once famous for its macho adventure stories.

Great Storyteller

One critic says of Toudouze's storytelling style, "It has the impact of a powerful man at the fair who, for the fun of it, takes the hammer and at one blow sends the machine to the top, rings the bell, and walks off."

Think About the Writer How do you think George Toudouze's knowledge of the sea helped him in the writing of this story?

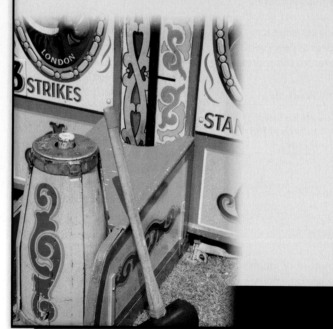

Build Background

The title of this story is the name of a key, or low-lying island, off the coast of French Guiana (gee AH nuh), in South America. At the time the story was written, French Guiana was a colony of France. Cayenne (ky EHN), the capital, was the site of one of the prisons that France maintained there until 1945. Lighthouses, such as the one in this story, are used to guide ships, to alert sailors that land is near, and to point out dangerous rocks and reefs.

Preview the Selection

The **narrator** of the story gives a first-person account of his most terrifying experience. It happened when he was a lighthouse keeper, along with two other men, named **Itchoua** and **Le Gleo,** on a tiny island twenty miles from the mainland of South America.

Universal Access

 English Learners

To help students understand how to make predictions, divide the word *predict* into its parts: *pre–* and *–dict*. Remind students that as a prefix, *pre–* means "before." Tell them that *–dict* comes from the Latin word *dicere*, meaning "to speak." Together, *pre–* and *–dict* mean "to say before." Explain that when you predict what will happen in a story, you are saying what you think before you have finished reading; in other words, you are using what you know to think ahead about what might happen.

Struggling Readers

Tell students that predictions are guesses about what will happen in a story based on what you know from the story and from your own experiences. To demonstrate this for students, you might say, "When I read the first paragraph of 'Three Skeleton Key,' I am struck by the first sentence. The use of *my* tells me that the story is told by a narrator about his or her own life. In this case, it is about the most terrifying experience the narrator ever had. Right away, I can predict that something frightening will happen to the narrator in this story."

Three Skeleton Key

by **George G. Toudouze**

My most terrifying experience? Well, one does have a few in thirty-five years of service in the Lights, although it's mostly monotonous, routine work—keeping the light in order, making out the reports.

When I was a young man, not very long in the service, there was an opening in a lighthouse newly built off the coast of Guiana, on a small rock twenty miles or so from the mainland. The pay was high, so in order to reach the sum I had set out to save before I married, I volunteered for service in the new light.

Three Skeleton Key, the small rock on which the light stood, bore a bad reputation. It earned its name from the story of the three convicts who, escaping from Cayenne in a stolen dugout canoe, were wrecked on the rock during the night, managed to escape the sea, but eventually died of hunger and thirst. When they were discovered, nothing remained but three heaps of bones, picked clean by the birds. The story was that the three skeletons, gleaming with phosphorescent[1] light, danced over the small rock, screaming. . . . **Ⓐ**

But there are many such stories and I did not give the warnings of the old-timers at the *Île-de-Seine* a second thought. I signed up, boarded ship, and in a month I was installed at the light.

Picture a gray, tapering cylinder, welded to the solid black rock by iron rods and concrete, rising from a small island twenty-odd miles from land. It lay in the midst of the sea, this island, a small, bare piece of stone, about one hundred fifty feet long, perhaps forty wide. Small, barely large enough for a man to walk about and stretch his legs at low tide.

This is an advantage one doesn't find in all lights, however, for some of them rise sheer from the waves, with no room for one to move save within the light itself. Still, on our island, one must be careful, for the rocks were treacherously smooth.

---

1. **phosphorescent** (fahs fuh REHS uhnt): glowing.

Ⓐ **Reading Focus** Making Predictions Based on such details as screaming and dancing skeletons, what kind of story do you predict this will be?

Vocabulary **treacherously** (TREHCH uhr uhs lee) *adv.*: deceptively; unreliably.

Model the Skill

- Provide students with copies of the Reading Skills Focus graphic organizer (See **Chapter 1 Resources**), or have them use their own paper to recreate the **making predictions** graphic organizer in their textbook.

- Model for students making predictions using the Reading Focus graphic organizer. Read aloud the second foreshadowing clue in the chart on p. 33. Tell students that the fact that the sharks are huge and swimming around the island suggests that they have an important part to play in the story. Point out that sharks are dangerous. From the text clue and this knowledge of sharks, a reader might predict that the sharks will put the men in danger during the story.

Page	Foreshadowing Clue
p.35	"The story was that the three skeletons... danced over the small rock, screaming."
p.36	"The waters about our island swarmed with huge sharks."

Page	My Prediction
p.35	Something bad will happen at this lighthouse.
p.36	The sharks will threaten the men.

Guided Practice: Apply

Tell students that the sudden appearance of a ship that sails toward the lighthouse instead of away from it on a dark, gloomy night is a foreshadowing clue. Ask what prediction they might make from this clue. Have students write their responses in their organizers.

One misstep and down you would fall into the sea—not that the risk of drowning was so great, but the waters about our island swarmed with huge sharks, who kept an eternal patrol around the base of the light. **B**

Still, it was a nice life there. We had enough provisions to last for months, in the event that the sea should become too rough for the supply ship to reach us on schedule. During the day we would work about the light, cleaning the rooms, polishing the metalwork and the lens and reflector of the light itself, and at night we would sit on the gallery and watch our light, a twenty-thousand-candlepower lantern, swinging its strong white bar of light over the sea from the top of its hundred-twenty-foot tower. Some days, when the air would be very clear, we could see the land, a thread-like line to the west. To the east, north, and south stretched the ocean. Landsmen, perhaps, would soon have tired of that kind of life, perched on a small island off the coast of South America for eighteen weeks until one's turn for leave ashore came around. But we liked it there, my two fellow tenders and myself—so much so that for twenty-two months on end, with the exception of shore leaves, I was greatly satisfied with the life on Three Skeleton Key.

I had just returned from my leave at the end of June, that is to say, midwinter in that latitude, and had settled down to the routine with my two fellow keepers, a Breton[2] by the name of Le Gleo and the head keeper, Itchoua, a Basque[3] some dozen years or so older than either of us. **C**

Eight days went by as usual; then on the ninth night after my return, Itchoua, who was on night duty, called Le Gleo and me, sleeping in our rooms in the middle of the tower, at two in the morning. We rose immediately and, climbing the thirty or so steps that led to the gallery, stood beside our chief.

Itchoua pointed, and following his finger, we saw a big three-master, with all sail set, heading straight for the light. A queer course, for the vessel must have seen us; our light lit her with the glare of day each time it passed over her.

Now, ships were a rare sight in our waters, for our light was a warning of treacherous reefs, barely hidden under the surface and running far out to sea. Consequently we were always given a wide berth, especially by sailing vessels, which cannot maneuver as readily as steamers.

No wonder that we were surprised at seeing this three-master heading dead for us in the gloom of early morning. I had immediately recognized her lines, for she stood out plainly, even at the distance of a mile, when our light shone on her.

---

2. **Breton** (BREHT uhn): person from Brittany, a region of northern France.
3. **Basque** (bask): person from the Pyrenees, a mountain range in France and Spain.

B **Literary Focus** Suspense How is this lighthouse setting significant in the story?

C **Literary Focus** Foreshadowing First you read the past event of the three convicts dying at Three Skeleton Key. What do you learn about the three lighthouse keepers and their present actions?

Vocabulary **maneuver** (muh NOO vuhr) *v.:* move or manipulate skillfully.

Word-Attack Skills Mini-Lesson

Vowel Spellings

English for Academic Success

Remind students of the mnemonic: *When two vowels go a-walking, the first one does the talking.* This mnemonic pertains to two-vowel spellings of long vowel sounds: *ai* for long *a; ea* for long *e; oa* for long *o.* Ask students to locate words in "Three Skeleton Key" that illustrate the mnemonic. Examples include *mainland, remained, heaps, unceasingly, boats,* and *approach.*

Explain that sometimes when two vowels appear together in a word, each vowel has its own sound. Usually this occurs in longer, multisyllabic words, but there are examples in short words, too, such as *liar* and *neon.* Write these two words from the selection on the board: *defiance, nauseating.* Pronounce them, and point out the vowel pair in each word that stands for two distinct vowel sounds: *ia* in *defiance* and *ea* in *nauseating.*

Activity Write these sentences on the chalkboard. Have volunteers read each sentence and underline the

Analyzing Visuals Connecting to the Text How does the sight of a strange ship (such as the one in this image) <u>advance</u> the plot? How might this event foreshadow future actions?

Le Seducteur (The Seductor)
by Rene Magritte (1898–1967)
Oil on canvas.

She was a beautiful ship of some four thousand tons, a fast sailer that had carried cargoes to every part of the world, plowing the seas unceasingly. By her lines she was identified as Dutch built, which was understandable, as Paramaribo and Dutch Guiana are very close to Cayenne.

Watching her sailing dead for us, a white wave boiling under her bows, Le Gleo cried out:

"What's wrong with her crew? Are they all drunk or insane? Can't they see us?" **D**

Itchoua nodded soberly and looked at us sharply as he remarked: "See us? No doubt—if there *is* a crew aboard!"

D Read and Discuss Why do the ship's movements cause Le Gleo to cry out in alarm?

word that has two vowels in sequence representing two vowel sounds.
1. The men toiled in a heroic effort to turn back the invading rats. [*heroic*]
2. The rat's eyes gleamed diabolically. [*diabolically*]
3. Fear and disgust worked together to create panic. [*create*]
4. The tension mounted in the interior of the lighthouse. [*interior*]
5. A maniacal scream cut the air. [*maniacal*]

Analyzing Visuals
The Belgian surrealist painter **René Magritte** (1898-1967) is sometimes described as a "magical realist" because of his seamless, eerie melding of the ordinary and the bizarre.

Connecting to the Text: The sight of the ship foreshadows that the narrator will come into contact with whomever—or whatever—is on the ship.

Comprehension
D Read and Discuss
Possible response: The ship is sailing straight for the lighthouse.

Analysis
B Literary Focus
Possible responses: There are scary stories about the place; it is far from other people.

C Literary Focus
Possible response: The three lighthouse keepers are the narrator, Le Gleo, and Itchoua. They have been working at the lighthouse for several weeks.

Extend the Discussion
Paraphrasing Read the last two paragraphs on p. 36. Then, explain in your own words why the narrator and his fellow keepers were surprised to see a sailing ship heading toward them. *Possible response: The water around the lighthouse is particularly dangerous for sailing ships because it's full of reefs that the ships might crash into, so the ships usually avoid that area if they can. This ship, however, seems to be ignoring the water's dangers.*

Foreshadowing In the last line of p. 37, Itchoua suggests there might not be a crew on board the mystery ship. What does this suggestion foreshadow about the nature of the ship? *Possible response: It suggests that something eerie or sinister may be aboard this ship.*

Vocabulary: Own the Word
maneuver: Ask students: what might make it more difficult to *maneuver* your bicycle? *Possible response: The bicycle could be stuck in mud, or weighed down with something.*

- Tell students that writers use **suspense** to keep their readers interested in the story. Suspense can involve excitement, such as waiting to find out the outcome of a talent contest, or fear, such as wondering what the character will find if she opens the door.

- Read aloud the second-to-last paragraph on p. 39. Explain that this paragraph creates fear and suspense not by what it says, but by what it leads the reader to believe. The author does not say that rats ate the ship's crew, but he gives only two effects of the rats' attacking the crew: driving them from the ship or eating them alive. He then eliminates the possibility that the crew escaped by pointing out that the lifeboats are still on the ship. Knowing that the crew was eaten by the rats gives readers a sense of curious dread about what the rats will do to the lighthouse keepers.

Guided Practice: Apply

Read-Think-Write Have students read pp. 38–39 and identify another example of the writer's use of suspense. Have students think and then write briefly about what details create suspense and the emotions these details generate in the reader.

"What do you mean, chief?" Le Gleo had started, turned to the Basque. "Are you saying that she's the *Flying Dutchman*?"[4] **E**

His sudden fright had been so evident that the older man laughed:

"No, old man, that's not what I meant. If I say that no one's aboard, I mean she's a derelict."[5]

Then we understood her queer behavior. Itchoua was right. For some reason, believing her doomed, her crew had abandoned her. Then she had righted herself and sailed on, wandering with the wind.

The three of us grew tense as the ship seemed about to crash on one of our numerous reefs, but she suddenly lurched with some change of the wind, the yards[6] swung around, and the derelict came clumsily about and sailed dead away from us.

In the light of our lantern she seemed so sound, so strong, that Itchoua exclaimed impatiently:

"But why the devil was she abandoned? Nothing is smashed, no sign of fire—and she doesn't sail as if she were taking water."

Le Gleo waved to the departing ship:

"Bon voyage!" he smiled at Itchoua and went on. "She's leaving us, chief, and now we'll never know what—"

"No, she's not!" cried the Basque. "Look! She's turning!"

---

4. **Flying Dutchman:** fabled Dutch ghost ship whose captain is said to be condemned to sail the seas until Judgment Day. Seeing the *Flying Dutchman* is supposed to bring bad luck.
5. **derelict** (DEHR uh lihkt): here, abandoned ship.
6. **yards:** in nautical terms, rods fastened across the masts to support the sails.

E Read and Discuss What has happened?

As if obeying his words, the derelict three-master stopped, came about, and headed for us once more. And for the next four hours the vessel played around us—zigzagging, coming about, stopping, then suddenly lurching forward. No doubt some freak of current and wind, of which our island was the center, kept her near us.

Then suddenly the tropic dawn broke, the sun rose, and it was day, and the ship was plainly visible as she sailed past us. Our light extinguished, we returned to the gallery with our glasses[7] and inspected her.

The three of us focused our glasses on her poop[8] and saw, standing out sharply, black letters on the white background of a life ring, the stenciled name *"Cornelius de Witt,* Rotterdam."

We had read her lines correctly: She was Dutch. Just then the wind rose and the *Cornelius de Witt* changed course, leaned to port, and headed straight for us once more. But this time she was so close that we knew she would not turn in time. **F**

"Thunder!" cried Le Gleo, his Breton soul aching at seeing a fine ship doomed to smash upon a reef, "she's going to pile up! She's gone!"

I shook my head:

"Yes, and a shame to see that beautiful ship wreck herself. And we're helpless."

There was nothing we could do but watch. A ship sailing with all sail spread, creaming the sea with her forefoot as she

---

7. **glasses:** here, binoculars.
8. **poop:** in nautical terms, the stern (back) deck of a ship.

F Read and Discuss What is happening to the ship now? What future event might occur as a result of this event?

Cross-Curricular Connection

SCIENCE: Ship Rats

Explain to students that black rats, also called ship rats, are often found on ships, which is how they have spread all over the world. Then, provide them with the following information:

- Ship rats probably brought a disease called the Black Death to Europe, where it killed about one-third of the people there.
- Today, ship rats are common in warm areas around North and South America. Usually they are found anywhere near a significant human presence.

- The rats can be about eight inches long. They will eat either fruit or meat, and usually try to find food at night. The rats often fight with each other.
- Ship rats can often be found in coastal cities with ports, where they are the target of health officials attempting to control the spread of rabies and other infectious diseases. Ship rats typically live for just under two years.

runs before the wind, is one of the most beautiful sights in the world—but this time I could feel the tears stinging in my eyes as I saw this fine ship headed for her doom.

All this time our glasses were riveted on her and we suddenly cried out together:

"The rats!" **Ⓖ**

Now we knew why this ship, in perfect condition, was sailing without her crew aboard. They had been driven out by the rats. Not those poor specimens of rats you see ashore, barely reaching the length of one foot from their trembling noses to the tip of their skinny tails, wretched creatures that dodge and hide at the mere sound of a footfall.

No, these were ships' rats, huge, wise creatures, born on the sea, sailing all over the world on ships, transferring to other, larger ships as they multiply. There is as much difference between the rats of the land and these maritime rats as between a fishing smack⁹ and an armored cruiser.

The rats of the sea are fierce, bold animals. Large, strong, and intelligent, clannish and seawise, able to put the best of mariners to shame with their knowledge of the sea, their uncanny ability to foretell the weather.

> No, these were ships' rats, huge, wise creatures, born on the sea, sailing all over the world on ships.

And they are brave, these rats, and vengeful. If you so much as harm one, his sharp cry will bring hordes of his fellows to swarm over you, tear you, and not cease until your flesh has been stripped from the bones.

The ones on this ship, the rats of Holland, are the worst, superior to other rats of the sea as their brethren are to the land rats. There is a well-known tale about these animals.

A Dutch captain, thinking to protect his cargo, brought aboard his ship not cats but two terriers, dogs trained in the hunting, fighting, and killing of vicious rats. By the time the ship, sailing from Rotterdam, had passed the Ostend light, the dogs were gone and never seen again. In twenty-four hours they had been overwhelmed, killed, and eaten by the rats. **Ⓗ**

At times, when the cargo does not suffice, the rats attack the crew, either driving them from the ship or eating them alive. And studying the *Cornelius de Witt*, I turned sick, for her small boats were all in place. She had not been abandoned.

Over her bridge, on her deck, in the rigging, on every visible spot, the ship was a writhing mass—a starving army coming toward us aboard a vessel gone mad!

---

9. **smack:** here, small sailboat.

Ⓖ **Reading Focus** Making Predictions How does the three men's realization here advance the plot?

Ⓗ **Literary Focus** Foreshadowing How does this anecdote, or brief story of past actions, about the dogs and the rats hint at future actions in the story?

Vocabulary **hordes** (hawrdz) *n.*: densely packed crowds.

▶ **Comprehension**

Ⓔ Read and Discuss
Possible response: There's a ship heading straight for the lighthouse. Le Gleo is worried that it might be the *Flying Dutchman, a harbinger of doom.*

Ⓕ Read and Discuss
Possible response: Because the crew was chased away by the rats, there is no one to manage the ship so it moves by wind and currents. It will crash into the reef near the lighthouse.

Ⓖ Reading Focus
Possible response: The men have discovered that the ship is filled with rats, which killed the crew. The men will come into conflict with these rats.

▶ **Analysis**

Ⓗ Literary Focus
Possible response: The anecdote shows that these rats can attack and kill creatures that are bigger than they are. It suggests that the keepers are in danger of being attacked by the rats.

▶ **Extend the Discussion**

Conflict What external conflicts does the author develop on p. 38? Explain. *Possible response:* The men are in conflict with nature, because it could potentially cause a ship to wreck on their island, and they may be in conflict with the supernatural, as there seems to be something eerie and unnatural about the ship.

Vocabulary: Own the Word

hordes: Remind students that *hordes* are densely packed crowds. Say, "The warmup band drew a crowd, but the headline act brought such *hordes* of people that it was impossible to move around." Ask students to create a pair of related statements that show how a *horde* is denser than a crowd.

Universal Access

Ⓐ Students Who Use African American Vernacular English

English for Academic Success Students may struggle with formal English use of negatives. Explain that in formal English, only one negative term, such as *not* or *no*, is used per negative expression. Point out, on p. 38, Itchoua's use of negatives: "*nothing* is smashed, *no* sign of fire, she *doesn't* sail." He describes three things, and uses three negatives, one for each description. Have students work in pairs to create formal English expressions including negatives in the following sentences: *We had homework, He lets everybody borrow his books, She likes all kinds of music.*

Struggling Readers

Benchmark Students Have students read pp. 38–39 in pairs, pausing at point F to review what they have read and predict what will happen in the next short section. Have volunteers share their predictions. Discuss with students ways they formed their predictions, and provide additional strategies. Then, have students work collaboratively to predict what will happen next in the story.

Model the Skill

■ Explain to students that **pronouns** are words that can stand in the place of other, usually proper, nouns. They contribute to a sentence by simplifying the syntax for fluency of reading.

■ Review with students some common prounouns: *I, you, me, we, they, him, her*. Direct students to the sentence, "To them we were..." in column 2 of p. 40. Point out that the pronoun *them* stands in for the rats and that *we* stands in for the three lighthouse keepers. Have students identify other pronouns on the page. Ask students what the prounouns stand in for, and how they know.

Guided Practice: Apply

Divide students into groups of four, and have each group identify as many pronouns as they can on pp. 40–41.

Think as a Reader/Writer

Find It in Your Reading Point out that the writer builds suspense and advance plot when he describes the men as "sealed alive" and "prisoners" in the tower.

Use It in Your Writing Have students use this sentence frame to build suspense and potentially advance a plot: "And there we were, _____, prisoners of _____."

Our island was a small spot in that immense stretch of sea. The ship could have grazed us or passed to port or starboard with its ravening[10] cargo—but no, she came for us at full speed, as if she were leading the regatta at a race, and impaled herself on a sharp point of rock.

There was a dull shock as her bottom stove in, then a horrible crackling as the three masts went overboard at once, as if cut down with one blow of some gigantic sickle. A sighing groan came as the water rushed into the ship; then she split in two and sank like a stone.

But the rats did not drown. Not these fellows! As much at home in the sea as any fish, they formed ranks in the water, heads lifted, tails stretched out, paws paddling. And half of them, those from the forepart

---

10. **ravening** (RAV uh nihng): greedily searching for animals to kill for food. A more common related word is *ravenous* (RAV uh nuhs), meaning "mad with hunger."

---

of the ship, sprang along the masts and onto the rocks in the instant before she sank. Before we had time even to move, nothing remained of the three-master save some pieces of wreckage floating on the surface and an army of rats covering the rocks left bare by the receding tide.

Thousands of heads rose, felt the wind, and we were scented, seen! To them we were fresh meat, after possible weeks of starving. There came a scream, composed of innumerable screams, sharper than the howl of a saw attacking a bar of iron, and in the one motion, every rat leaped to attack the tower!

We barely had time to leap back, close the door leading onto the gallery, descend the stairs, and shut every window tightly. Luckily the door at the base of the light, which we never could have reached in time, was of bronze set in granite and was tightly closed.

The horrible band, in no measurable time, had swarmed up and over the tower as if it had been a tree, piled on the embrasures[11] of the windows, scraped at the glass with thousands of claws, covered the lighthouse with a furry mantle, and reached the top of the tower, filling the gallery and piling atop the lantern.

Their teeth grated as they pressed against the glass of the lantern room, where they could plainly see us, though they could

---

11. **embrasures** (ehm BRAY zhuhrz): slanted openings.

---

❶ **Read and Discuss** What does the narrator want you to understand?

Vocabulary **receding** (rih SEED ihng) *v.* used as *adj.*: moving back.

Universal Access

EL English Learners

• Explain to students that a writer may use punctuation and sentence structure to create suspense.

• Point out the sentence "Thousands of heads rose, felt the wind, and we were scented, seen!" Note that it contains four separate actions. By putting these actions together in one sentence instead of separating them into four, the writer shows that they happened very quickly. This creates suspense by showing how quickly the attack started and making the reader wonder how the men will escape.

• Direct students to the end of the sentence. Explain that the exclamation point adds emphasis. This makes the situation more dramatic and desperate, which makes the reader anxious to see how it will be resolved.

• Have students make notes as they read on any words, sentences, or punctuation that helps build suspense.

not reach us. A few millimeters of glass, luckily very strong, separated our faces from their gleaming, beady eyes, their sharp claws and teeth. Their odor filled the tower, poisoned our lungs, and rasped our nostrils with a pestilential, nauseating smell. And there we were, sealed alive in our own light, prisoners of a horde of starving rats.

That first night, the tension was so great that we could not sleep. Every moment, we felt that some opening had been made, some window given way, and that our horrible besiegers were pouring through the breach. The rising tide, chasing those of the rats which had stayed on the bare rocks, increased the numbers clinging to the walls, piled on the balcony—so much so that clusters of rats clinging to one another hung from the lantern and the gallery.

With the coming of darkness we lit the light and the turning beam completely maddened the beasts. As the light turned, it successively blinded thousands of rats crowded against the glass, while the dark side of the lantern room gleamed with thousands of points of light, burning like the eyes of jungle beasts in the night.

All the while we could hear the enraged scraping of claws against the stone and glass, while the chorus of cries was so loud that we had to shout to hear one another. From time to time, some of the rats fought among themselves and a dark cluster would detach itself, falling into the sea like a ripe fruit from a tree. Then we would see phosphorescent streaks as triangular fins slashed the water—sharks, permanent guardians of our rock, feasting on our jailers.

The next day we were calmer and amused ourselves teasing the rats, placing our faces against the glass which separated us. They could not fathom the invisible barrier which separated them from us, and we laughed as we watched them leaping against the heavy glass. **J**

But the day after that, we realized how serious our position was. The air was foul; even the heavy smell of oil within our stronghold could not dominate the fetid odor of the beasts massed around us. And there was no way of admitting fresh air without also admitting the rats.

The morning of the fourth day, at early dawn, I saw the wooden framework of my window, eaten away from the outside, sagging inwards. I called my comrades and the three of us fastened a sheet of tin in the opening, sealing it tightly. When we had completed that task, Itchoua turned to us and said dully:

"Well—the supply boat came thirteen days ago, and she won't be back for twenty-nine." He pointed at the white metal plate sealing the opening through the granite. "If that gives way"—he shrugged—"they can change the name of this place to Six Skeleton Key." **K**

The next six days and seven nights, our only distraction was watching the rats whose holds were insecure fall a hundred and twenty feet into the maws of the sharks—but they were so many that we could not see any diminution in their numbers.

J Read and Discuss How are the men doing?

K Reading Focus Making Predictions Do you think Itchoua's prediction will prove accurate? Why or why not?

Think About/Talk About

▶ **Comprehension**

I Read and Discuss

Possible response: The rats are attacking the tower, and the lighthouse keepers seem to be in real danger. As long as they are sealed inside the lighthouse, though, the rats probably won't be able to get in.

J Read and Discuss

Possible response: The men have separated themselves from the rats with the glass of the lantern room.

K Reading Focus

Possible response: I don't think Itchoua's prediction will be entirely accurate. I think Itchoua and Le Gleo will be killed, but the narrator must survive because he is telling the story.

▶ **Extend the Discussion**

Imagery In paragraph 1 on p. 41, what sensory images does the narrator use in order to vividly convey the horror of the situation? *Possible response:* The description of the rats' odor as "pestilential" and "nauseating" appeals to the sense of smell, and words like "grated" and "scraped" help the reader imagine what the rats sounded like as they swarmed over the tower.

Suspense Pause after reading paragraph 3 on p. 40. What has the author said about the sea rats that makes the shipwreck suspenseful? Explain. *Possible response:* The author said the rats are unusually strong and used to the ocean, so the reader is anxiously waiting to find out whether the rats might actually survive the shipwreck.

Vocabulary: Own the Word

receding: *Receding* means "moving back." An antonym of this word is *approaching*. Have students write a sentence using both words. *Possible response:* Though the rainstorm seemed to be receding, the weather reporter said another shower was approaching from the west.

Struggling Readers
- To help students identify suspense in the story, guide them through a close reading of p. 40.
- Have a volunteer read paragraph 2 aloud. You might say, "We know that this ship is full of man-eating rats, and it is now crashing into the reef by Three Skeleton Key. As a reader, I feel anxious for the men because we do not know whether the rats will drown or come ashore and attack the men. This situation is suspenseful because I am anxious about what will happen next."

- Continue having volunteers read paragraphs aloud, pausing after each to discuss as a class what makes the reader feel anxious about what is to come.

Advanced Learners

Extension Ask students to discuss with a partner how mental and psychological terror can be more terrifying to a character in a story than an actual physical threat.

Students with Disabilities

Have students work as a group to identify words and phrases that make the reader feel anxious.

- Explain to students that readers **evaluate predictions** as they read to see if what they expected to happen actually did happen.

- Remind students of the prediction made using the foreshadowing clue of the frightening story of the convicts who died on the rock. From that clue came the prediction that something bad would happen to the lighthouse keepers on this island. Point out that something bad has happened: The island is overrun by man-eating rats and the lighthouse keepers are trapped. Thus, the prediction was accurate. If nothing bad had happened by this point, readers might wish to change their predictions based on the events in the story so far.

Guided Practice: Apply

Have students work in pairs to evaluate one prediction that each partner made. Remind students that there is no "right" or "wrong" answer for a prediction—it is a matter of whether the events came to pass as the reader expected.

Thinking to calm ourselves and pass the time, we attempted to count them, but we soon gave up. They moved incessantly, never still. Then we tried identifying them, naming them.

One of them, larger than the others, who seemed to lead them in their rushes against the glass separating us, we named "Nero";[12] and there were several others whom we had learned to distinguish through various peculiarities.

---

12. **Nero** (NIHR oh): emperor of Rome (A.D. 54–68) known for his cruelty.

L **Read and Discuss** Why does the narrator describe the situation as a "living nightmare"?

But the thought of our bones joining those of the convicts was always in the back of our minds. And the gloom of our prison fed these thoughts, for the interior of the light was almost completely dark, as we had had to seal every window in the same fashion as mine, and the only space that still admitted daylight was the glassed-in lantern room at the very top of the tower.

Then Le Gleo became morose and had nightmares in which he would see the three skeletons dancing around him, gleaming coldly, seeking to grasp him. His maniacal, raving descriptions were so vivid that Itchoua and I began seeing them also.

It was a living nightmare, the raging cries of the rats as they swarmed over the light, mad with hunger; the sickening, strangling odor of their bodies— **L**

True, there is a way of signaling from lighthouses. But to reach the mast on which to hang the signal, we would have to go out on the gallery where the rats were.

There was only one thing left to do. After debating all of the ninth day, we decided not to light the lantern that night. This is the greatest breach of our service, never committed as long as the tenders of the light are alive; for the light is something sacred, warning ships of danger in the night. Either the light gleams a quarter-hour after sundown, or no one is left alive to light it. **M**

Well, that night, Three Skeleton Light was dark, and all the men were alive. At the risk of causing ships to crash on our reefs, we left it unlit, for we were worn out—going mad!

M **Reading Focus** Making Predictions Why do you think the men decide not to light the lantern? To what future action might this decision lead?

Developing Oral Fluency

Small-Group Activity Have students practice reading with expression by performing "Three Skeleton Key" as a radio play.

- Tell students that "Three Skeleton Key" was made into a radio program in 1950. Explain that they are going to perform part of the story in the style of a radio program.

- Put students in small groups with students of varying ability levels. Assign each group one spread to perform. Have each group plan expressive dialogue and narration, and, if they wish, sound effects for the events on their pages. For example, tapping on desks may simulate the sound of the rats attempting to enter the lighthouse.

- The groups should rehearse, taking turns reading paragraphs with expression and providing sound effects.

At two in the morning, while Itchoua was dozing in his room, the sheet of metal sealing his window gave way. The chief had just time enough to leap to his feet and cry for help, the rats swarming over him.

But Le Gleo and I, who had been watching from the lantern room, got to him immediately, and the three of us battled with the horde of maddened rats which flowed through the gaping window. They bit, we struck them down with our knives—and retreated.

We locked the door of the room on them, but before we had time to bind our wounds, the door was eaten through and gave way, and we retreated up the stairs, fighting off the rats that leaped on us from the knee-deep swarm.

I do not remember, to this day, how we ever managed to escape. All I can remember is wading through them up the stairs, striking them off as they swarmed over us; and then we found ourselves, bleeding from innumerable bites, our clothes shredded, sprawled across the trapdoor in the floor of the lantern room—without food or drink. Luckily, the trapdoor was metal, set into the granite with iron bolts.

The rats occupied the entire light beneath us, and on the floor of our retreat lay some twenty of their fellows, who had gotten in with us before the trapdoor closed and whom we had killed with our knives. Below us, in the tower, we could hear the screams of the rats as they devoured everything **edible** that they found. Those on the outside squealed in reply and writhed in a

Vocabulary edible (EHD uh buhl) *adj.:* fit to be eaten.

* Have each group perform its part of the radio program for one of the other groups. Listeners should close their eyes and imagine the scene.
* Tape record each group's performance and play it back to them. Ask them to critique the performance and discuss places where the group's reading was particularly expressive, and where more expression could have been added.

✔ See **UA: Differentiating Instruction** for practice passages for developing oral fluency.

HISTORY LINK

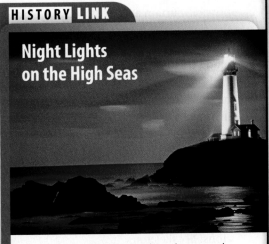

Night Lights on the High Seas

For centuries, lighthouses have been used to alert sailors that land is near, to point out dangerous rocks and reefs, and to cast a bright light into the night to guide ships on their way. Seafarers have relied on these structures since the days of ancient Egypt. The lighthouse built in 300 B.C. on Pharos, an island near Alexandria, was regarded as one of the Seven Wonders of the World.

Lighthouses help guide ships at night by giving off an intense beam of light that flashes every few seconds. Until the eighteenth century the source of light was an oak-log fire. Then coal fires were used for many years, until electricity became common in the early twentieth century. Some modern lighthouses also send out radio signals to help ships find their way in foggy weather.

Even in their modern form, lighthouses still serve their ancient purpose as a guiding light, a flashing speck of civilization in the dark, lonely waters of the night.

Ask Yourself

How are the rats' actions in the story endangering people other than the lighthouse keepers?

History Link
Ask Yourself
Possible response: The rats are preventing the lighthouse keepers from lighting the light and warning ships of the dangerous reefs, which puts the lives of those sailors in danger from shipwrecks.

 HSS Analysis Skills: REP 5

Think About/Talk About

▶ **Comprehension**

Ⓛ **Read and Discuss**
Possible response: There is no fresh air, Le Gleo is raving, the rats are eating through the wood, and the boat won't return for a month.

Ⓜ **Reading Focus**
Possible response: Leaving the light unlit is unacceptable in the world of lighthouse keepers; it only happens when the keepers have died and there's no one left alive to light it. If they leave the light dark, people will realize something is wrong and investigate.

▶ **Extend the Discussion**

Making Judgments In the paragraph on p. 42 that ends at point M, the lighthouse keepers decide not to light the lantern, even though this decision could put ships in danger. Do you think the men made the right decision? Explain. *Possible response: Yes, I think that the keepers' decision is acceptable under the circumstances. Even though it's never good to put other people in danger, the keepers are likely to die unless they take this course of action.*

Suspense Reread paragraphs 1–4 on p. 43. How does the narrator's description create suspense? *Possible response: The narrator describes a fast and furious attack by the starving rats and it is unclear until paragraph 5 that the men will escape this alive.*

Vocabulary: Own the Word
edible: Items considered *edible* to humans include grains, meat, fish, and vegetables. We can change the word to its opposite by adding the prefix (in) to create the word *inedible*. Items inedible to humans include the wood of the ship and the lighthouse. The fact that the rats eat inedible objects adds to the story's horror.

- Tell students that the English language includes words that come directly or distantly from many other languages, including Latin, Greek, German, and French. **Word origins** tell us where words come from.

- Point out the word *vacantly* in the first full paragraph on p. 44. Tell students that the word *vacant* comes from *vacare*, which is a Latin verb that means "empty." The dictionary says that when used to describe a person's expression, *vacantly* means "emptied of feeling or thought." *Vacare* relates to the word *vacantly* because both words involve emptiness.

Guided Practice: Apply

Point out the word *comrades* in the eighth full paragraph on p. 44. Provide students with the following definition and origin for the word: it is from *camarade*, a Middle French word that meant "companion or roommate," and the dictionary definition is "a person one associates with." Ask students what the word origin and the modern definition have in common. How do they think *camarade* became *comrade* as it is used today?

---

horrible curtain as they stared at us through the glass of the lantern room. **N**

Itchoua sat up and stared silently at his blood trickling from the wounds on his limbs and body and running in thin streams on the floor around him. Le Gleo, who was in as bad a state (and so was I, for that matter), stared at the chief and me vacantly, started as his gaze swung to the multitude of rats against the glass, then suddenly began laughing horribly:

"Hee! Hee! The Three Skeletons! Hee! Hee! The Three Skeletons are now *six* skeletons! *Six* skeletons!"

He threw his head back and howled, his eyes glazed, a trickle of saliva running from the corners of his mouth and thinning the blood flowing over his chest. I shouted to him to shut up, but he did not hear me, so I did the only thing I could to quiet him—I swung the back of my hand across his face.

The howling stopped suddenly, and his eyes swung around the room; then he bowed his head and began weeping softly, like a child.

Our darkened light had been noticed from the mainland, and as dawn was breaking, the patrol was there to investigate the failure of our light. Looking through my binoculars, I could see the horrified expression on the faces of the officers and crew when, the daylight strengthening, they saw the light completely covered by a seething mass of rats. They thought, as I afterwards found out, that we had been eaten alive.

But the rats had also seen the ship or had scented the crew. As the ship drew nearer, a solid phalanx[13] left the light, plunged into the water, and swimming out, attempted to board her. They would have succeeded, as the ship was hove to;[14] but the engineer connected his steam to a hose on the deck and scalded the head of the attacking column, which slowed them up long enough for the ship to get under way and leave the rats behind. **O**

Then the sharks took part. Belly up, mouths gaping, they arrived in swarms and scooped up the rats, sweeping through them like a sickle through wheat. That was one day that sharks really served a useful purpose.

The remaining rats turned tail, swam to the shore, and emerged dripping. As they neared the light, their comrades greeted them with shrill cries, with what sounded like a derisive note predominating. They answered angrily and mingled with their fellows. From the several tussles that broke out, it seemed as if they resented being ridiculed for their failure to capture the ship.

But all this did nothing to get us out of our jail. The small ship could not approach but steamed around the light at a safe distance, and the tower must have seemed fantastic, some weird, many-mouthed beast hurling defiance at them.

Finally, seeing the rats running in and out of the tower through the door and the windows, those on the ship decided that we had perished and were about to leave when

---

13. **phalanx** (FAY langks): closely packed group. A phalanx is an ancient military formation, and the word still has warlike connotations.
14. **hove to:** stopped by being turned into the wind.

N **Read and Discuss** What can you identify about the situation now?

O **Reading Focus** Making Predictions **Explain** what the patrol boat is doing. What future action might result from this?

Universal Access

Struggling Readers

Have students work in pairs to connect foreshadowing from the story to subsequent story events.

1. Assign one partner to review his or her notes in conjunction with the first few pages of the story to identify at least four examples of foreshadowing.

2. Assign the other partner to review and briefly summarize the story events beginning with the rats' arrival on Three Skeleton Key.

3. When both partners have finished their respective tasks, have them compare lists to identify examples

of foreshadowing that relate to specific events later in the story, such as the connection between the tale of the three convicts and the three lighthouse keepers, all of whom faced starvation.

4. Have partners jot down an explanation of how each instance of foreshadowing connects to the later event, such as similarity of character and setting.

5. Have each pair share one of their foreshadowing connections with the class.

Analyzing Visuals Connecting to the Text How does this photograph help you connect to the events in the story?

Itchoua, regaining his senses, thought of using the light as a signal. He lit it and, using a plank placed and withdrawn before the beam to form the dots and dashes, quickly sent out our story to those on the vessel. **P**

Our reply came quickly. When they understood our position—how we could not get rid of the rats, Le Gleo's mind going fast, Itchoua and myself covered with bites, cornered in the lantern room without food or water—they had a signalman send us their reply.

His arms swinging like those of a windmill, he quickly spelled out:

"Don't give up, hang on a little longer! We'll get you out of this!" **Q**

Then she turned and steamed at top speed for the coast, leaving us little reassured.

She was back at noon, accompanied by the supply ship, two small coast guard boats, and the fireboat—a small squadron. At twelve-thirty the battle was on.

After a short reconnaissance,[15] the fireboat picked her way slowly through the reefs until she was close to us, then turned her powerful jet of water on the rats. The heavy stream tore the rats from their places and hurled them screaming into the water, where the sharks gulped them down. But for

---

15. **reconnaissance** (rih KAHN uh suhns): scouting for information.

P Read and Discuss How does Itchoua keep the patrol boat from leaving?

Q Reading Focus Making Predictions Explain why you think the patrol boat crew will—or will not—be able to rescue the men.

Think About/Talk About

▶ Comprehension

N Read and Discuss

Possible response: It's even more desperate. The rats ate through the wooden window frames and the door. The men have fought them off and fled to the lantern room with no provisions.

O Read and Discuss

Possible response: The boat has spotted rats covering the lighthouse and moved closer. This means the men might be rescued in the future.

P Read and Discuss

Possible response: He uses the light to signal to the patrol boat that the men are still alive but trapped.

Q Reading Focus

Possible response: I predict that they will be able to rescue the men because they can go and get the help and supplies they need to defeat the rats.

▶ Extend the Discussion

Suspense How does the appearance of the patrol boat in paragraph 6 of p. 44 bring new suspense to the story? Explain your answer. *Possible response:* The patrol boat brings new suspense to the story because it offers the men a chance at being rescued, but they have to let the boat know they're alive, and the boat crew has to get past the man-eating rats. The suspense comes from wondering how these tasks will be accomplished.

Analyzing Visuals

Connecting to the Text: The image helps me connect to the story by giving me an idea of what the swarm of hungry rats might look like, and how much danger the men are in.

▶ Comprehension

® Read and Discuss

Possible response: The patrol boat and four other ships tried to blast the rats away with massive hoses. When that didn't work, they lured the rats onto a barge full of meat and blew it up.

▶ Extend the Discussion

Suspense How does the departing flotilla add to the story's suspense? *Possible response: The men must spend another night in their "prison," suffering from fevers and insanity which they may not survive.*

Character What does the narrator's discussion of Three Skeleton Key in the final two paragraphs of the story reveal about his character? *Possible response: Unlike Le Gleo, the narrator hasn't been particularly affected by the rats' attack. Despite his horrible memories of Three Skeleton Key, he still loves the place and doesn't understand why other people might not want to return there.*

Monitor Students' Comprehension

Guide the class in answering these comprehension questions.

1. What happened to the crew of the Dutch ship that is wrecked near Three Skeleton Key? [*They were killed on the ship by incredibly fierce, vicious sea rats.*]

2. What obstacles must the men overcome to survive the rats? [*They face hunger, thirst, physical danger, and psychological terror.*]

3. What effect does the terror of the rats have on Itchoua and Le Gleo? [*Itchoua dies; Le Gleo goes to an insane asylum.*]

---

every ten that were dislodged, seven swam ashore, and the stream could do nothing to the rats within the tower. Furthermore, some of them, instead of returning to the rocks, boarded the fireboat, and the men were forced to battle them hand to hand. They were true rats of Holland, fearing no man, fighting for the right to live!

Nightfall came, and it was as if nothing had been done; the rats were still in possession. One of the patrol boats stayed by the island; the rest of the flotilla departed for the coast. We had to spend another night in our prison. Le Gleo was sitting on the floor, babbling about skeletons, and as I turned to Itchoua, he fell unconscious from his wounds. I was in no better shape and could feel my blood flaming with fever.

Somehow the night dragged by, and the next afternoon I saw a tug, accompanied by the fireboat, come from the mainland with a huge barge in tow. Through my glasses, I saw that the barge was filled with meat.

Risking the treacherous reefs, the tug dragged the barge as close to the island as possible. To the last rat, our besiegers deserted the rock, swam out, and boarded the barge reeking with the scent of freshly cut meat. The tug dragged the barge about a mile from shore, where the fireboat

> Nightfall came, and it was as if nothing had been done; the rats were still in possession.

drenched the barge with gasoline. A well-placed incendiary shell from the patrol boat set her on fire.

The barge was covered with flames immediately, and the rats took to the water in swarms, but the patrol boat bombarded them with shrapnel from a safe distance, and the sharks finished off the survivors. ®

A whaleboat from the patrol boat took us off the island and left three men to replace us.

By nightfall we were in the hospital in Cayenne. What became of my friends?

Well, Le Gleo's mind had cracked and he was raving mad. They sent him back to France and locked him up in an asylum, the poor devil! Itchoua died within a week; a rat's bite is dangerous in that hot, humid climate, and infection sets in rapidly.

As for me—when they fumigated the light and repaired the damage done by the rats, I resumed my service there. Why not? No reason why such an incident should keep me from finishing out my service there, is there?

Besides—I told you I liked the place—to be truthful, I've never had a post as pleasant as that one, and when my time came to leave it forever, I tell you that I almost wept as Three Skeleton Key disappeared below the horizon.

® **Read and Discuss** | What was the patrol boat's strategy?

🐻 **California Standards, pp. 47–49**

■ **Reading Standard 1.3** Clarify word meanings through the use of definition, example, restatement, or contrast.

■ **Reading Standard 3.2** Identify events that advance the plot and determine how each event explains past or present action(s) or foreshadows future action(s).

Applying Your Skills

Check for Understanding

Three Skeleton Key

Literary Response and Analysis

Reading Skills Focus
Quick Check

1. To review the story, imagine that you are the narrator. Write a journal entry about the day you leave Three Skeleton Key forever.

Read with a Purpose

2. Explain whether you think the men could have escaped without help.

Reading Skills: Making Predictions

3. Review your Prediction Chart. Add a column in which you identify whether your prediction was correct (*Yes*) or not correct (*No*). On what did you base your predictions? Which outcomes surprised you most, and why?

Page	Foreshadowing Clue	My Prediction	Yes / No
p. 35	"The story was that the three skeletons . . . danced over the small rock, screaming."	Something bad will happen at this lighthouse.	Yes
p. 36	"The waters about our island swarmed with huge sharks."	The sharks will attack and kill one of the men.	No

Literary Skills Focus
Literary Analysis

4. **Connect** The three lighthouse keepers each respond differently to the invasion. With which character (if any) did you identify?

5. **Evaluate** What do you think was the scariest part of the story? Explain.

Literary Skills: Suspense and Foreshadowing

6. **Analyze** Early in the story the narrator explains how Three Skeleton Key got its name. How does this past event **foreshadow**—or hint at—the future actions that the lighthouse keepers will have to take?

7. **Evaluate** On the fourth day of the invasion, a wooden window frame in the lighthouse sags inward. How does this incident increase **suspense** and advance the plot?

8. **Analyze** Discuss the roles that **suspense** and **foreshadowing** play in this story and their overall effects.

Literary Skills Review: Setting

9. **Analyze** Why is a lonely, forsaken island a perfect setting for a horror story? How would this story be different if it occurred in a less isolated place?

Writing Skills Focus
Think as a Reader/Writer

Use It in Your Writing Write a brief outline of plot events for another suspenseful story. Make sure each event advances the plot and explains either a past, present, or future action in the story.

What Do **You Think Now**

What dangerous situations are caused by nature? Why are threats from nature so often featured in horror stories?

What Do You Think Now?

Ask students to discuss elements of nature that might be frightening or dangerous to humans. Have students explain how these elements of nature are often used in horror movies or novels.

Independent Practice
Reading Skills Focus
Answers:

1. *Today, I have finally left the terror of Three Skeleton Key behind me. I am sad to leave the lighthouse, but I'm grateful to be alive after my terrible battle against the vicious rats.*

2. *No, because they did not have a boat or food, and they were hurt.*

3. *I was surprised that Le Gleo went mad because I expected him to be eaten by the rats.*

Literary Skills Focus
Possible responses:

4. *I identified most closely with the narrator because I'm usually able to stay calm in a crisis, just like the narrator did when Three Skeleton Key was attacked by the rats.*

5. *I thought the scariest part of the story was when the rats first appeared because I didn't know what they would do.*

6. *Three convicts died of starvation on Three Skeleton Key, and their ghosts supposedly haunt it. This story foreshadows the story's events by suggesting that Three Skeleton Key is a dangerous place that's cut off from the outside world.*

7. *It creates suspense because it indicates that the rats are getting closer to the people.*

8. *Suspense and foreshadowing create a sense of dread and a dark tone throughout the story.*

9. *The fact that the characters are in a lonely, isolated place with no people or supplies to help them adds to the danger they face. If they were in a more populated place, the story would not be as scary.*

Independent Practice
Vocabulary Development
Your Turn _____
1. *receding*
2. *maneuver*
3. *treacherously*
4. *hordes*
5. *edible*

English for Academic Success
Language Coach
To help students determine the meanings of the words listed in the Your Turn activity, use each word in a sample sentence, such as, "I wrote eight pages of my <u>manuscript</u> today." Discuss with students how each word's definition relates to the idea of "working by hand."

Possible responses:

1. *My dad's car has a <u>manual</u> transmission.*
2. *I had to <u>manipulate</u> the dials and levers on the washing machine when I did my laundry.*
3. *Factories <u>manufacture</u> many of the things we use every day.*
4. *Protecting the environment benefits all <u>humanity</u>.*
5. *The author sent a <u>manuscript</u> to his publisher.*

English for Academic Success
Academic Vocabulary
Possible response: *These events had a <u>significant</u> impact on the narrator because he remembers them in detail and calls the episode the most frightening experience of his life. He might have learned that you can't take life for granted and that clever thinking can solve even the worst problems.*

 Learn It Online
Holt's **WordSharp: An Interactive Vocabulary Tutor** provides additional support for vocabulary development. Multimedia tutorials show students how to apply vocabulary skills to unfamiliar words—and how to make those words their own.

`go.hrw.com` `H7-48` **Go**

Applying Your Skills

Three Skeleton Key

Vocabulary Development
Clarifying Word Meanings: Examples

Sometimes you can figure out the meaning of an unfamiliar word by finding other words or phrases that provide an example of what the word means. What words in this sentence give you an idea of what *staples* are?

> The lighthouse keepers were running very low on necessary staples, such as flour, sugar, and salt.

Certain words and phrases often indicate that an example is being used: *for example, for instance, like, such as, in this case,* and *as if.*

Your Turn _____
Fill in each blank below with the Vocabulary word that is <u>explained</u> by the examples in the sentence.

treacherously
maneuver
hordes
receding
edible

1. As he got older, Martin found that his memory was _____ as if it were the ocean when the tide goes out.
2. I had to _____ around the piles of building materials scattered on the floor as if I were a gymnast.
3. He was polite to his associate, but behind her back, he dealt with her as _____ as a murderer would.
4. _____ of mosquitoes started biting us. There must have been hundreds of them!
5. We were lucky to find _____ provisions, such as rice, beans, and even some salsa, in the cabin.

Language Coach
Word Origins You've already learned that the word *maneuver* comes from Latin words meaning "to work by hand." What other words might be in the same word family as *maneuver*?

Look at the words listed below. Read each word, and think about its meaning. If you're not sure of the word's meaning, look it up in a dictionary. Then, use each word in a sentence.

manual
manipulate
manufacture
humanity
manuscript

Academic Vocabulary

Talk About . . .
In a small group discussion, <u>explain</u> why you think this experience was <u>significant</u> for the narrator. Then, brainstorm a list of lessons about life he might have gained from his experience. Present your ideas to the class.

 Learn It Online
Learn how to clarify word meanings with *WordSharp:*

`go.hrw.com` `H7-48` **Go**

Universal Access: Vocabulary Development

EL English Learners/ Struggling Readers

English for Academic Success Students may understand the literal definitions of the Academic Vocabulary words, but have difficulty integrating them into writing or conversation. Pair English learners with fluent speakers and have them discuss the following topics, using the Academic Vocabulary words as often as possible. Consider having fluent speakers offer their opinions first, so that English learners can hear the words used in actual speech.

- Explain how you would tell a friend how to do an activity you enjoy.
- Describe a significant experience from your life, and explain what made it significant.
- Discuss how a discovery advances a field, such as science.

✔ See the Vocabulary Skill Builder in **UA: Differentiating Instruction.**

Grammar Link
Making Pronouns Clear

You know to whom you're referring when you use *he, she,* or *they,* but your readers may not be sure. A pronoun should refer clearly to its antecedent (the noun or pronoun to which a pronoun refers). Unclear, or ambiguous, pronoun references occur when a pronoun can refer to two or more ante-cedents. One way to clarify your meaning in such cases is to replace the pronoun with a specific noun.

UNCLEAR The old-timers warned me about sharks and the three convicts. **Their** skeletons had been picked clean by the birds.

CLEAR The old-timers warned me about sharks and the three convicts. **The convicts'** skeletons had been picked clean by the birds.

CLEAR The old-timers warned me about sharks and the three **unfortunate convicts,** whose skeletons had been picked clean by the birds.

Your Turn

Rewrite the following sentences, correcting each unclear pronoun reference.

1. My two fellow keepers were named Le Gleo and Itchoua. He was the head keeper.
2. The three of us had named the head rat Nero. I was scared as they ate at the window frame.
3. Le Gleo, Itchoua, and I were in the hospital by nightfall. Sadly, he had gone raving mad.

Writing Applications Exchange a sample of your writing with a partner. Read through each other's work, looking for unclear pronoun refer-ences. Point out where your partner has provided clear pronoun references as well.

CHOICES

As you respond to the Choices, use these **Academic Vocabulary** words as appropriate: <u>advance</u>, <u>explain</u>, <u>significant</u>, <u>similar</u>.

REVIEW
Write an Essay

Timed⏳Writing Stories are made up of a series of events that <u>advance</u> the plot and keep you guessing about future actions. The author of "Three Skeleton Key" incorporates crucial infor-mation, such as details about setting, to fore-shadow terrible events to come and increase the suspense. In a paragraph, <u>explain</u> which events in the story <u>advance</u> the plot and show how past and present actions foreshadow future actions.

CONNECT
Write an Opinion Essay

The writer Isaac Asimov once said, "When I was a lad . . . I found myself fearfully attracted to stories that scared me." Do you, in a <u>similar</u> way, enjoy tales of terror like "Three Skeleton Key"? Write a paragraph <u>explaining</u> why or why not.

EXTEND
Write a Job Description

Partner Work With a partner, design a job listing for the position of lighthouse keeper at Three Skeleton Key. Describe the personal character-istics and skills necessary for the job, and also describe the work environment, duties, and pay.

Learn It Online
Examine this story in-depth using the Internet links at:

go.hrw.com   H7-49   Go

Independent Practice
Grammar Link

1. *My two fellow keepers were Le Gleo and Itchoua, the head keeper.*
2. *The three of us had named the head rat Nero. I was scared as he ate at the window frame.*
3. *Le Gleo, Itchoua, and I were in the hospital by nightfall. Sadly, Le Gleo had gone raving mad.*

Choices: Evaluation Criteria
Review: Timed Writing 40–50 minutes
The essay discusses events that advance the plot and explains how they foreshadow future events.

Connect: **Homework**
Write an Opinion Essay
The essay tells whether the student enjoys scary stories, and why.

Extend: **Homework**
Write a Job Description
The listing describes qualifications and conditions of the job based on story details.

Assess

📝 **Chapter 1 Resources,** Selection Standards Check, p. 15

🖥 **ThinkCentral Online Assessment,** Selection Standards Check

💿 **Teacher One Stop™,** editable Selection Standards Check

Reteach

🖥 **ThinkCentral Online Remediation**

Universal Access: Grammar Link

Remind students that many writers use pronouns so they do not have to repeat names within a sentence, which makes writing sound less fluent and natural. If used care-lessly, though, pronouns can make the sentences unclear. Explain that one way to check whether a pronoun refer-ence is clear is to replace the pronoun with what you think is its antecedent. If the sentence does not make sense with the proposed antecedent, or if you have difficulty identify-ing the antecedent, the reference will need to be revised.

✔ For more practice with using pronouns, see the **Language Handbook Worksheets, Grammar Notes,** and **Warriner's Handbook.**

Learn It Online
Literature Links direct students to prescreened Web sites offering more information related to a selection.

go.hrw.com   H7-49   Go

Standards Focus

Objectives

Students will
- identify internal and external conflicts
- visualize the images

Motivate

What Do You Think?/QuickWrite

Use the QuickWrite to have students reflect on dangerous experiences they have had to face. Then, have students use their **Reader/Writer Notebook** to explain why danger appeals to people.

English for Academic Success

Academic Vocabulary

Look for opportunities to use the Academic Vocabulary words in the chapter.

- **significant, *adj*.:** important
- **advance, *v*.:** move forward
- **explain, *v*.:** give reasons for; make understandable
- **similar, *adj*.:** almost the same

Analyzing Visuals

Extension Activity Have students use clues from the image to visualize the setting in which this jump takes place. ***Possible response:** The boys are jumping off an old wooden dock into a lake around sunset.*

![California Standards icon] **California Standards, pp. 50–63**

- **Reading Standard 3.2** Identify events that advance the plot and determine how each event explains past or present action(s) or foreshadows future action(s).

Preparing to Read
The Dive
by René Saldaña, Jr.

What Do You Think? Why do you think people are tempted to take dangerous risks?

QuickWrite If a friend asked you for advice about doing some[thing] dangerous, what would you tell him or her? Why[?]

Selection Readability	
Easily Accessible **Accessible** Challenging	experiences familiar to students; convers[ational] dialogue

Selection Plot Summary

Melly debates whether to join the local rite of passage of diving f[rom] a high bridge. A meaningful story from Melly's grandmother hel[ps her] decide that she doesn't need to prove anything by diving.

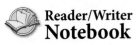

Reader/Writer Notebook

Use your **RWN** to complete the activities for this selection.

Literary Skills Focus

Plot and Conflict An **external conflict** occurs when a character struggles with something *outside* himself or herself, such as another character or a dangerous setting. **Internal conflict,** on the other hand, is a struggle *within* the character's own heart or mind. A story's plot <u>advances</u> toward the **resolution** of the central conflicts, when the problems are solved and the story is wrapped up. In "The Dive," you'll encounter a character facing both an external conflict (with her father) and an internal conflict (over a decision). As you read, notice how past events, which are told to the main character, affect the resolution of these conflicts.

Literary Perspectives Apply the literary perspective described on page 53 as you read this story.

Reading Skills Focus

Visualizing: Pictures in Your Mind When writers describe characters and events, they create sensory **images,** or pictures drawn with words. When you form a mental image from the details of a story, you are **visualizing.** As you read "The Dive," try to visualize, or picture in your mind, the events of the plot as they unfold.

Into Action Descriptive details about characters' appearances can help you imagine how the characters look, and vivid verbs can help you visualize the characters' actions. As you read, use a chart like this one to record details about each character and what he or she does in the story.

Character
Melly:
Mamá Tochi:
Papi:

Writing Skills Focus

Think as a Reader/Writer

Find It in Your Reading As you read, make a list of five sensory details that help you visualize the events of the plot.

Vocabulary

crinkling (KRIHNG klihng) *v.:* wrinkling. *Melly imagined her great-grandfather crinkling his brow in anger.*

stubble (STUHB uhl) *n.:* short, bristly growth. *The stubble on Mr. Otero's cheek was scratchy and gray.*

caressed (kah REHST) *v.:* touched gently. *Melly caressed her cheek where her father had touched it.*

wafting (WAHFT ihng) *v.:* floating in the wind. *We smelled the sweet scent of flowers wafting from the garden.*

Vocabulary word	appeals to sense of
crinkling	sight, hearing
stubble	touch, sight
caressed	touch
wafting	sight, smell

Language Coach

Definitions Sometimes, writers give clues about a word's meaning by placing a definition nearby:

The smell of the flowers came wafting toward Melly as it floated on the afternoon's gentle breeze.

What words give you clues to the meaning of the word *wafting*?

※ **Learn It Online**
Enrich your vocabulary with Word Watch:

go.hrw.com | H7-51 | **Go**

Preteach

Introducing Vocabulary

Read aloud the Vocabulary words and sample sentences. Then, ask students to choose the best synonym for each Vocabulary word.

1. **crinkling** (squeezing, wrinkling, cracking) [*wrinkling*]
2. **stubble** (bristles, chin, scratch) [*bristles*]
3. **caressed** (tickled, touched, stroked) [*stroked*]
4. **wafting** (falling, floating, smelling) [*floating*]

English for Academic Success

Language Coach

Tell students that definitions do not always take the structure of "*clothing* means 'garments you wear.'" Authors may provide definitions in the form of alternate ways of saying what the word means. [*floating, on the breeze, smell*]

Literary Skills Focus

As you read, ask students to think about how an external conflict in the story leads to an internal conflict. Discuss how they work together to <u>advance</u> the plot.

Reading Skills Focus

Give students a copy of the Reading Skills Focus graphic organizer before they read. (See **Chapter 1 Resources.**) Have them use their responses to answer questions on the Applying Your Skills page.

Writing Skills Focus

Have students record sensory details in their **Reader/Writer Notebook.** Students may use their notes to complete the Writing Skills Focus activity.

※ **Learn It Online**
Send students to **Word Watch** for audio pronunciations, synonyms and antonyms, and brief histories of word origins.

go.hrw.com | H7-51 | **Go**

Selection Introduction

More About the Writer

René Saldaña's stories vary in tone from playful to serious, and they feature very different settings and plots. Often, though, Saldaña focuses on realistic teenaged characters learning life lessons.

Think About the Writer

Remind students that there are different ways of being inspired by someone. Perhaps they are inspired by a friend or family member who supports them. They may also be inspired by someone they've never met, like a celebrity who sets a good example.

 For Independent Reading

- For students interested in stories featuring Mexican characters, suggest Pam Munoz Ryan's *Esperanza Rising*, a story about a girl's immigration from Mexico to California in the 1930s.

- Students who want to read another story about a rite of passage might enjoy *Runs with Horses* by Brian Burks. In this novel, an Apache warrior seeks his passage into manhood.

René Saldaña, Jr.
(1968–   )

Feeling Inspired

René Saldaña was inspired to become a writer by his grandfather, who was a first-rate storyteller. Saldaña was also motivated by his students when he taught middle school and high school. He told them about the beginnings of his book *The Jumping Tree,* and as they wrote alongside him in class, he was inspired to continue his story. He has since written *Finding Our Way: Stories* and published more of his work in anthologies and magazines.

A Proud Texan

René Saldaña, Jr., was born and has spent most of his life in Texas. As a writer, Saldaña focuses on Chicano life and the importance of Mexican Americans' creating their own identities. Saldaña now teaches at Texas Tech. He lives with his wife, Tina, their sons, Lukas and Mikah, and their cat, ISBN (ISBN is the International Standard Book Number, found on a book's back cover and used to identify a book), in Edinburg, Texas.

"We can become anything and anyone we want to become with hard work, focus, and dedication."

Think About the Writer Saldaña and his students have inspired one another to do better work. Who inspires you?

Build Background

In Mexican American culture, female elders like Mamá Tochi often share their wisdom by telling *cuentos,* or stories, that serve as "life lessons." In this story one of them involves a game of bingo—*Lotería*—in which the tokens are cards bearing such colorful images as El Cantarito (the little pitcher) and La Rosa (the rose). This selection includes other Spanish words and phrases. See if you can figure out their meanings from the context of the story.

Preview the Selection

Melly is fishing with her **father** when she sees something that rouses her curiosity—and brings her into conflict with her father. Melly then seeks advice from her grandmother, **Mamá Tochi.**

The Dive

by **René Saldaña, Jr.**

Look at them, Papi," said Melly to her father.

Mr. Otero cast his line into the water again and looked up and to his right. "Tan locos, mi'ja. It's a crazy thing to do."

From upriver, Melly and her father could see five or six boys fixing to jump from Jensen's Bridge. They pounded their chests, inched their way to the edge, then dove in all at once, some headfirst, others feet first, and one balled up. The boys disappeared underwater, leaving behind them different-sized splashes, then Melly heard the echoes of their jumping screams a full second or two after they'd gone under. By then, they were shooting up out of the water, their arms raised in the air. They'd done it. Most of the boys in Three Oaks had to dive from the bridge at one time or other to prove themselves real men. Today was their day. **Ⓐ**

Melly saw the boys crawl from the river and turn over on their backs, stretched out like lizards sunning themselves on the bank. Reeling in her line, she thought, So what if they can dive off the bridge! I could do it too if I wanted. Who said it was just for the guys to do? **Ⓑ**

"You'll do nothing of the kind," said Mr. Otero.

"Huh?"

"You said you could dive too if you wanted?"

"I didn't say anything. You must be hearing things."

He smiled. "Just like your mother. Talking your thoughts aloud." He reached

Literary Perspectives

The following perspective will help you think about the plot of this story.

Analyzing an Author's Techniques One way to understand a story is to pay close attention to the specific literary techniques the author uses. In "The Dive," René Saldaña, Jr., makes extensive use of **dialogue**—conversations between characters—in both English and Spanish. As you read, think about where he injects dialogue and how he uses it to <u>advance</u> the plot. Also pay attention to his choice of words, such as the symbolism of the title. As you read, respond to the notes and questions in the text, which will guide you in using the perspective.

Ⓐ Read and Discuss What is going on?

Ⓑ Literary Focus Conflict How does seeing the boys dive create an internal conflict within Melly?

Literary Perspectives

Use the Literary Perspectives feature to differentiate the literature for a variety of students.

Have students preview the story by reading only the dialogue. Ask them to discuss in pairs what information the dialogue alone provides about what is going on in the story. Then, have students read the whole selection. When they finish, ask them to reflect on how the author used the extensive dialogue to tell the story.

Then, have students explore the story's thematic elements by identifying what the bridge, the boys' dive, the bingo game, and Mamá Tochi's garden mean in the story beyond their literal meanings. Have students choose one of these symbols and explain why it is a critical tool used by the author to communicate meaning to the reader. Students may wish to present their explanations in the form of a well-written essay, an oral presentation, or a contribution to a small-group discussion.

Model the Skill

- Provide students with copies of the Reading Skills Focus graphic organizer (See **Chapter 1 Resources**), or have them use their own paper to recreate the **visualizing** graphic organizer in their textbook.

- Model for students using the graphic organizer to visualize characters in the story. Read aloud the paragraph that starts on p. 53 and ends on p. 54. Explain that the writer says that Papi touches Melly's cheek with a rough hand. Knowing that Papi has rough hands contributes to a reader's visualization of him. Write "rough hands" on the chart on Papi's line.

Character's name:
Melly:
Mamá Tochi:
Papi: rough hands

Guided Practice: Apply

Listen/Think/Write Read aloud the first full paragraph of p. 54. Have students think about what they read and identify a detail that can help them visualize Melly. Have them write this detail in their graphic organizers.

over and touched his rough hand to her cheek.

Melly blushed. She stood and set her rod on a rock, then stretched. She held her face and wondered if it was red from the sun. Red from her father's touch?

All along she'd actually been talking. She'd heard the same thing from her tías, from Mamá Tochi, and from her sister, Becky. "Your mom literally spoke her mind," the aunts all told her.

"You're so much like your mother," Mr. Otero told her, casting again.

"She probably would've jumped," she said.

"Probably so, but I said you won't do it. ¿M'entiendes?"

"Yes, sir. I understand. No jumping from the bridge." She looked downriver, then set her sight on the bridge. Her face was warm, and she imagined her mother jumping from the bridge, her long black hair in a ponytail, or all loose and curly; her mother slicing into the water, then exploding out, all smiles and laughter. Beautiful.

"What?"

"What what?"

"Never mind. Just like your mother." **E**

That evening, Melly went to visit her grandmother, Mamá Tochi, down the street from where Melly lived with her father and her sister, who'd only recently left for college.

C [Read and Discuss] What have you learned about Melly now?

D [Reading Focus] **Visualizing** What details in this paragraph help you visualize the scene?

E [Literary Perspectives] **Analyzing Author's Techniques** Think of other ways the author could have introduced the story. What significant information do you learn from the use of dialogue?

July Afternoon
(1993) by Anne Belov.

Universal Access

EL English Learners

Have students close their eyes and listen as you or a fluent English speaker read the first four paragraphs of the story aloud. Then, ask students to think about the mental images they formed of the setting. Students may wish to draw pictures of their visualizations or make lists of single words or short phrases that describe their mental images. Then, have students read p. 54 in pairs and add to their pictures of the setting.

Struggling Readers

Explain to students that visualizing, or creating a mental picture of, people, places, and events in a story helps them better understand what they are reading about. Add that writers often include words that tell readers about the sights, sounds, smells, or even tastes of the setting; readers have to use the words and phrases to imagine what is being described. Encourage students to sketch or draw images of particularly descriptive passages to aid their comprehension.

Analyzing Visuals **Connecting to the Text** How does this image help you visualize what Mamá Tochi's garden is like? (See page 56.)

Think About/Talk About
See page 54 of the Student Edition for questions relating to these answers.

 Comprehension

C Read and Discuss
Possible response: Melly thinks she's brave enough to handle jumping.

D Reading Focus
Possible response: The paragraph tells us that Melly's face is flushed red, that there are rocks along the river bank, and that the sun is shining.

 Analysis

E Literary Perpectives
Possible response: The author could have introduced the story by only using description. The dialogue shows readers that Melly is like her mother: headstrong and bold.

 Extend the Discussion

Drawing Conclusions From the way that Melly's relatives talk about her mother in paragraphs 2 and 3, what can you conclude about Melly's mother? *Possible response: It sounds like Melly's mom has died or gone away. Melly's aunts and her father seem to miss her mother very much, and they say that Melly is a lot like her.*

Analyzing Visuals
Setting is well represented in the paintings of **Anne Belov,** who emphasizes place and time in her artwork. Her work includes landscapes, such as the garden in summer on this page, and still-life images, such as flowers in a vase, sometimes blending the two elements into the same painting.

Connecting to the Text: This image shows a variety of beautiful plants and flowers that are similar to the description of Mamá Tochi's garden.

Advanced Learners
Extension Have students select four or five phrases from pp. 53-54 that help them visualize the setting at the beginning of "The Dive".
- Ask students to create a "found poem" by arranging these phrases in an order and style that makes sense to them. Students may supplement their found poems with figurative language and vivid imagery.
- Have volunteers read their work aloud, and ask students to discuss the mental images that their classmates' poems create.

Students with Disabilities
Pair students with stronger readers and have them read p. 54 together. Then, have students underline three phrases that describe what the scene is like for one of the five senses.

Model the Skill

- Tell students that a **preposition** is a part of speech used to show relationships between words in a sentence. A preposition and its object, and any modifiers in between, make a prepositional phrase. In a sentence, a preposition will refer to a noun or pronoun, or to the verb.

- Read the sentence "Melly sat under the orange tree." Ask students to identify the preposition (*under*) and its object (*orange tree*). Next, ask students what the prepositional phrase tells us (*where Melly sat*). Tell students this prepositional phrase refers to the verb *sat*.

- Read the sentence "Today you kids have all these fancy cafés in your fancy bookstores where you go and study with all your friends." Point out that the prepositional phrase "in your fancy bookstores" tells where the kids "have" their fancy cafés. Also explain that the prepositional phrase "with all your friends" tells who the kids "go and study" with.

Guided Practice: Apply

Have students skim the story and identify one sentence each that contains a prepositional phrase.

Think as a Reader/Writer

Find It in Your Reading Point out that the third paragraph uses sensory images of sight, touch, taste, and smell to describe the garden.

Use It in Your Writing Have students write several phrases with details of a familiar outdoor setting, appealing to at least two of the senses.

Mamá Tochi had lived on her own ever since Melly's grandfather died five years ago. When Mamá Tochi's children all moved and married, each begged her to come live with them, but she refused. She said, "For decades I took care of both your father and myself when you left the house for work and school, and before that I took care of the six of you, from dirty diapers to broken hearts, so what makes you think I need to be looked after?"

Mr. Otero, Melly's dad, was the only one to pull up stakes and move to be closer to Mamá Tochi when Papá 'Tero died. Moving was easy for him. His own wife had died a year before his father's passing, and he once confessed to Mamá Tochi, "With Aurelia gone, I don't know that I can do right by our two girls." **F**

Melly knocked at her grandmother's and walked in. It was early evening, so she knew that Mamá Tochi would be out in her backyard garden with her babies: the herbs that ran up along the house; then the rosales, four bushes of them, red, yellow, white, and pink, big as trees almost; countless wildflower patches; and Melly's favorite, the esperanza bushes, the yellow bells soft on her cheeks. The backyard smelled like honey tasted. **G**

She went out the screen door and said, "Mamá Tochi. Where are you?" Melly could hear the water splashing, but couldn't quite make out her grandmother.

"Aquí, mi'jita. I'm over here." Mamá Tochi was hidden behind the esperanza bush, watering it with her pail. She'd set the hose at the base of one of the rosales. "You don't even have to tell me why you're here. You want to jump from that crazy bridge." **H**

Sometimes Melly thought her grandmother could read minds, see into the future, even talk to the dead. Melly couldn't figure out why she came over for advice. She never got anything but cuentos from Mamá Tochi, stories that somehow served as life lessons. That time Melly had had the chance to cheat on her end-of-term exam her ninth-grade year, Mamá Tochi said, "I remember a time I was calling bingo. Playing that night was my worst enemy, Perla. I kept an eye all night on her four cards, praying a secret prayer that she'd lose every time. On one of her cards I could see all she needed was El Gallo. Without knowing why, I pulled a card from the middle of the deck instead of the top. I pulled La Chalupa, and Manuela won. I was afraid to even look at the top card. I collected all the others and shuffled them real fast. What if it had been El Gallo? I wasn't able to look in Perla's eyes for two weeks and a half, that's how guilty I felt."

Lessons to be learned that time? You do it, you'll get caught. You'll feel worse if you don't get caught.

"It won't be cheating, really, Mamá Tochi. The teacher's already said chances of me passing are slim. There's stuff on the test we've never studied even."

F [Read and Discuss] What is going on?

G [Reading Focus] Visualizing From these details about the garden, what can you guess about past events that Melly has experienced with her grandmother?

H [Literary Focus] Plot and Conflict How does Mamá Tochi know what Melly wants to do? How have past events created tension between Melly and Mamá Tochi?

Developing Oral Fluency

Give students practice in reading for accuracy in both dialogue and description by having them read p. 56 with a partner. Point out that the page contains both dialogue and descriptive phrases. Help students learn to transition between the two types of text with minimal interruption or errors.

Paired activity Put students into pairs and direct them to p. 56.

- First, model effective reading skills by reading the first three full paragraphs on the page for students. Dem-

onstrate switching between dialogue and description smoothly and naturally.

- Then, have students work in pairs to practice reading. Have students alternate reading each paragraph aloud.

- As one student reads a paragraph aloud, the other student should follow along silently and check for errors.

- If a student struggles with any words or phrases, his or her partner should provide assistance.

Mamá Tochi sat on the porch swing and said, "You're a big girl. You'll know what to do."

That night, Melly considered what her grandmother had said. She saw herself three years later, marching for graduation, everyone taking photos, everyone smiling, everyone happy, except she wouldn't be because she'd remember having cheated that time back in the ninth grade. She didn't sleep at all that night. The next day, even before the exam was handed out, two boys and one girl were called out of class. Earlier in the week, they had asked Melly if she wanted a look at the test. They'd found it in one of the teacher's desks and ran off a copy. The morning of the test, she told them, "No thanks. I'll just try my best. I'll fail on my own terms, you know." Then they got busted, and Melly passed the test by two points. "A pass is a pass," said Mamá Tochi. That's just what Melly's mom used to say. **I**

Tonight, Melly said, "What d'you mean? I'm here to visit with my favorite Mamá Tochi."

"Don't give me that. Your papi's already called. He's worried you're gonna jump and get tangled up in the weeds at the bottom of the river and drown."

Melly said, "Ah, Papi knows there's no weeds down there. And besides, no one's ever drowned at the bridge before."

Mamá Tochi put down the pail, turned

> "You don't even have to tell me why you're here. You want to jump from that crazy bridge."

off the hose, then said, "Sit down. I'll bring coffee."

Melly sat under the orange tree. Papá 'Tero had built the table and chairs years ago. He also had carved each of his children's and grandchildren's names and dates of birth into the tabletop in a great big circle. At the center were his name and Mamá Tochi's: Servando Otero and Rosario Garcia de Otero, their dates of birth, and the date of their wedding. Melly traced Mamá Tochi's name. **J**

"I put two spoons of sugar and a little milk in yours, just like you drink it," said Mamá Tochi.

"Gracias," said Melly. "It's not that high of a jump—ten, fifteen feet at most."

"That's not high. About two of my rosebushes, right." Mamá Tochi looked up where the top of the invisible bush would be.

"I mean, if the guys can do it—Aren't you the one always saying, 'You can do anything and everything you set your heart to'?"

"You're right, mi'jita. Anything is possible. How's your coffee?"

"Good, thank you, Mamá Tochi."

"Mi'jita, have I ever told you that my mother never let me drink coffee? It was a grown-up thing to do. I didn't take my first drink of it until I was twenty-one."

Melly knew there was a reason Mamá

I **Literary Focus** Internal Conflict Describe the internal conflict Melly faces in the preceding paragraphs. How does Mamá Tochi help Melly resolve that conflict?

J **Reading Focus** Visualizing What details in this paragraph help you picture past events?

Think About/Talk About

▶ **Comprehension**

F **Read and Discuss**

Possible response: Melly, her father, and her sister moved to be close to their grandmother after their grandfather died.

G **Reading Focus**

Possible response: Melly sees the garden as familiar and comfortable. She has probably enjoyed the time she has spent with her grandmother there.

J **Reading Focus**

Possible response: The paragraph explains that Papá 'Tero carved the names of family members and significant events into the tabletop.

▶ **Analysis**

H **Literary Focus**

Possible response: Mamá Tochi has probably given Melly advice before, so she knows how Melly thinks. Mamá Tochi seems to consider Melly's ideas to be silly.

I **Literary Focus**

Possible response: Melly faces a conflict of whether or not to cheat on the school exam. Mamá Tochi tells her a story about cheating at bingo and feeling guilty about it. This convinces Melly not to cheat.

▶ **Extend the Discussion**

Setting Reread paragraph 3 on p. 56. How does the description of the garden establish the tone of Melly's conversation with Mamá Tochi? *Possible response: It sets up a beautiful, comforting, familiar atmosphere, which suggests that Melly's talk with her grandmother will be comforting and helpful.*

- Remind students that **conflicts** advance the plot of a story and ultimately end in the **resolution** of said conflict. Writers often conclude plot events as they bring the conflict to its resolution.

- Point out that on p. 59, Mamá Tochi ends the conversation with Melly by telling her it is late and her father will worry if she is not home soon. The *cuento* has been told, the discussion is over, and now Melly is left to resolve on her own her internal conflict over whether to jump from the bridge. Explain that the end of the conversation is also a signal from the writer that the plot and conflict are advancing towards resolution. Readers should stay alert for the final resolution and how the characters' problems are solved.

Guided Practice: Apply

Before going on to p. 60, have students review the last paragraph of p. 59. Based on the last portion of the conversation, ask students to discuss what they think the resolution of Melly's conflicts will be.

Tochi was telling her this. She just had to figure it out. She had to pay attention, then sleep on it, and if she hadn't figured it out by after school tomorrow, she'd have to come visit a second time, get another story, then try to figure out two lessons instead of one. **K**

"I'd gotten my first job as a seamstress," Mamá Tochi continued. "My first paycheck, I told my mother, 'First thing I'll buy is a cup of coffee at Martin's Café.' My mother said, 'Then you'll buy for us all.' And so I did, a cup of coffee and a piece of sweet bread for everyone, all thirteen of us. I spent every peso I'd made, and I didn't sleep all night. But I loved the taste so much I haven't stopped, even when Dr. Neely told me I should. What does he know?"

She sat across the table from Melly and sipped her coffee.

Melly thought she'd figured out the lesson: that she should dive, and then she wouldn't be able to stop. She'd be as old as Mamá Tochi and diving would still be in her blood, and one day she'd jump from a bridge too high for such a frail woman and break every bone in her body and drown. But she'd be doing what she loved. **L**

"This is some good coffee," Mamá Tochi said.

"Sure is. Good bread, too."

"Twenty-one, can you believe it? Today you kids have all these fancy cafés in your fancy bookstores where you go and study with all your friends. What was that drink you bought me once? Iced café mocha? Why ruin a good cup of coffee with chocolate syrup? Why ruin it by pouring it into a paper cup? Not like in the old days. A little crema, a pinch of sugar, and steaming hot in a clay jar."

It only seemed like Mamá Tochi had finished telling her story. Melly knew better, so she leaned back, ready for more. She knew she hadn't figured out her grandmother's riddle yet.

"Nowadays, you babies grow up too fast. You're women before you're girls. You never get to be girls, some of you. It's not a bad thing, the way the world is today. You have to know more sooner, and be able to survive it. In my day, all I had to worry about was drinking my first cup of coffee, my first job, and hoping my family would choose the right man for me. They did that back then, you know, chose your husband. My father tried to find the man for me, and—well, let's just say, I was ahead of my time when I told my father I would not marry Marcos Antonio Velasquez. Papá told me, '¿Y tu, quien te crées?'[1] I was twenty-three then, and getting too old to be playing this game, my father said. But I—I had to take a stand sometime. After all," she said, and laughed. Melly imagined Mamá Tochi's young face laughing, her wrinkles somehow gone. "After all, I was a woman now. I was drinking coffee at Martin's every Friday afternoon on my way home. But I didn't smoke like some of

---

1. **¿Y tu, quien te crées?:** Spanish for "And you, who do you think you are?"

K **Literary Perspectives** **Analyzing Author's Techniques** How does the author use the dialogue between Melly and Mamá Tochi to draw you further into the story?

L **Read and Discuss** What does Melly's interpretation of Mamá Tochi's story tell you?

Reaching Reluctant Readers

Giving Advice

Students may have their own ideas of what Mamá Tochi should tell Melly to do. Discuss what Mamá Tochi is really saying with her story and whether students agree with her.

- Have students come up with their own advice for Melly. Ask students, "If your best friend asked you whether or not he or she should dive from the bridge, what would you tell your friend? Why?" As students think of advice, encourage them to include anecdotes from their lives or the lives of people they know.

- Have students deliver their advice orally to a small group. After each group member's advice, have students in the group discuss the anecdotes and how they relate to the story.

- When all group members have shared their advice for Melly, have students come to a consensus about the best strategy for giving Melly advice. Then, ask them to compare this strategy with the strategy that Mamá Tochi uses in the story.

Private collection.

Lady With Hibiscus
(21st century)
by Hilary Simon.
Colored inks on silk.

the others. I tried that once, but once was all I needed. I didn't like the taste. Coffee, now there's taste. Tobacco? Take it or leave it. Better leave it." She sipped some more, then said, "Mi'jita, it's getting late. You better go home before your papi calls looking for you." **M**

Melly stood and helped her with the cups and plate of bread. She hooked the screen door shut. She didn't close the inside door. Mamá Tochi always said she wanted

to smell her flowers. "And what's there in this house to steal? I wish someone would come and take that television. It's just something else I have to dust." Melly knew Mamá Tochi was teasing. She liked to watch her Mexican soaps.

"Dive if you want, mi'jita. I know you can make it. You won't drown. You're strong like all those boys, and smarter. So if you feel you have to, then go ahead, jump from that bridge. It'll make you feel better."

M **Literary Focus** **Plot** What does this story from the past tell you about Mamá Tochi? What advice do you think Mamá Tochi will give Melly?

▶ Analysis

Literary Perspectives

Possible response: At the end of the story, the author flashes back to Melly's dialogue with her dad toward the beginning of the story. These snippets of dialogue frame the story and remind us of the importance of Melly's relationships with her family members.

O Literary Focus

Possible response: Melly listened to Mamá Tochi's advice about growing up and decided not to dive. Her decision shows that she is thoughtful and mature.

Monitor Students' Comprehension

Guide the class in answering these comprehension questions.

1. What does Melly want at the beginning of the story? [*She wants to jump from Jensen's Bridge just like the boys in the neighborhood do.*]

2. Why does Melly choose not to jump from the bridge? [*She realizes that there are other ways to prove she's grown up.*]

Vocabulary: Own the Word

- **crinkling:** Demonstrate what *crinkling* one's face looks like. Ask a volunteer from the class to demonstrate.

- **stubble:** Remind students that *stubble* is short, bristly growth of hair. Ask students what might cause someone to have *stubble*. **Possible response:** *The person has not shaved.*

- **caressed:** Explain to students that *caress* is derived from the Latin word *carus,* which means "dear." Ask students how caress relates to the word "dear." **Possible response:** *When you caress something, you touch it as if it is dear to you.*

- **wafting:** Remind students that *wafting* often refers to sounds or smells. On a beach, the smell of the sea might *waft* through the air. At a festival or a fair, live music might *waft* around the area.

Melly hugged her grandmother tight, then said, "Buenas noches, Mamá Tochi."

"Buenas."

Melly was happy. She'd gotten her grandmother's permission. Now her father couldn't say anything about it. Melly woke to someone revving a car engine down the street. She'd gone to sleep thinking about her grandmother standing up to her own father, looking him in the eye: "I will not marry that boy. I don't love him." Melly imagined her great-grandfather stomping his foot, crinkling his face, pointing at his daughter, and not able to say a word to her. That's how angry Melly imagined him to be, so angry he was speechless. Then later, as the young Mamá Tochi was falling asleep, Melly pictured her great-grandfather bursting into the bedroom to say, "No daughter of mine—I shouldn't have let you drink coffee." And that would be it. He'd slam the door shut, and Rosario wouldn't have to marry Marcos Antonio Velasquez.

Instead she married Servando Otero, a handsome man till the end of his days. Melly remembered how his unshaven face had scratched at her cheeks when he held her tight to him. Like her own father's face tickled her cheeks now when he didn't shave

on weekends. Earlier, at the river, she had noticed more gray in her father's stubble. She'd reached over and rubbed his face. He'd touched her cheek. She laughed and said, "I hope my face isn't as hard as yours."

He shook his head. "Not in a million years. Your face is like your mom's. Soft. Very much a woman's face."

Melly caressed her cheek. Like mom, she thought.

"Yep, so much like her. Don't get me wrong. You're hard as nails inside. Tough, and thick-headed, too." He cast his rod again and said, "Just like your mom." **N**

That's when she saw the boys jumping.

In bed, she felt her cheek where her father had touched it. She knew she wouldn't jump. She didn't have to. She was already grown. Had a woman's face. Had nothing to prove to anybody. Tomorrow, if she wanted to, she could tell her father, "I'm diving no matter what you say." But she wouldn't. She was already drinking coffee, like her Mamá Tochi.

Melly turned onto her side. The window was open, and a cool breeze blew in. Melly could smell the sweetness of the flowers and herbs wafting from across the street. She smiled, closed her eyes, and slept. **O**

> "Dive if you want, mi'jita. I know you can make it."

 Literary Perspectives Analyzing Author's Techniques How does the author use dialogue to connect the beginning and end of the story?

O **Literary Focus** Internal Conflict How has Melly resolved her internal conflict? What does the way Melly solved her problem show you about her?

Vocabulary **crinkling** (KRIHNG klihng) *v.:* wrinkling.
stubble (STUHB uhl) *n.:* short, bristly growth.
caressed (kah REHST) *v.:* touched gently.
wafting (WAHFT ihng) *v.:* floating in the wind.

🐻 California Standards, pp. 61–63

■ **Reading Standard 1.3** Clarify word meanings through the use of definition, example, restatement, or contrast.

■ **Reading Standard 3.2** Identify events that advance the plot and determine how each event explains past or present action(s) or foreshadows future action(s).

Applying Your Skills

Reading Standard 3.2 Identify events that advance the plot and determine how each event **explains** past or present action(s) or foreshadows future **action(s)**.

The Dive
Literary Response and Analysis

Reading Skills Focus
Quick Check

1. Why does Melly visit Mamá Tochi?
2. What decision does Melly reach at the end of the story?

Read with a Purpose

3. What does the dive mean to Melly? What makes her realize that she doesn't need to dive?

Reading Skills: Visualizing

4. As you read "The Dive," you recorded details that helped you **visualize** the characters and their actions. Use the details in your chart to write a brief description of a memorable scene from the story.

Characters' Actions in "The Dive"

Melly: Watched the boys dive; . . .

Mamá Tochi:

Papi:

Literary Skills Focus
Literary Analysis

5. **Interpret** Why do you think Melly's grandmother gives her advice in the form of a story? Why do you think she doesn't simply say, "Don't jump"?
6. **Draw Conclusions** Talk about the way Mamá Tochi passes down life lessons to Melly. Why does this system work for both of them?
7. **Analyze** What does Melly learn about herself in the course of the story?

Literary Skills: Plot and Conflict

8. **Interpret** Which is more <u>significant</u> to the plot of the story: Melly's **external conflict** with her father or her **internal conflict**—the inner feelings with which she struggles? Why?
9. **Analyze** How does Melly's visit to Mamá Tochi's house <u>advance</u> the plot, leading to the resolution of the conflicts?
10. **Literary Perspectives** What might the act of diving symbolize in this story? How does the author make it clear that the dive is a symbol?

Literary Skills Review: Setting

11. **Analyze** What do the descriptions of her house and garden add to your understanding of Mamá Tochi? <u>Explain</u>.

Writing Skills Focus
Think as a Reader/Writer
Use It in Your Writing Look at the description of the boys jumping from the bridge at the beginning of the story. What sensory images does the author use to describe the action? Compare those images with the ones he uses to describe Mamá Tochi's house and what happens there. Then, describe two important events from your life. Use sensory details and vivid, precise verbs—*exclaimed* instead of *said,* for example—to help your reader visualize your actions. How are the two events you described <u>similar</u> and different?

 What Do You Think Now

What advice would you have given Melly? Look back at your Quickwrite notes for ideas.

What Do You Think Now?
Have small groups of students reread their QuickWrite notes and work together to decide whether their initial advice might apply to Melly's situation. Have them adjust their advice as necessary to apply to Melly's situation.

Check for Understanding

Independent Practice
Reading Skills Focus
Answers:

1. *She visits Mamá Tochi to get advice on whether or not she should dive.*
2. *Melly decides not to dive because she does not need to do it to prove herself.*
3. *Melly wants to dive to prove she is grown up and tough, but she learns that she's already proven those things.*
4. *Mamá Tochi and Melly sit near the beautiful garden and drink coffee. Mamá Tochi tells a thoughtful story from her childhood as Melly listens with interest.*

Literary Skills Focus
Possible responses:

5. *She wants to show Melly why it is important to make her own choices.*
6. *Mamá Tochi gives advice by telling stories, so she shares it in a form interesting to Melly, rather than giving her a lecture. Mamá Tochi benefits by getting to share her memories.*
7. *Melly learns that she only has to prove things to herself.*
8. *Melly's internal conflict is more important because the story focuses on her decision.*
9. *During Melly's visit, Mamá Tochi gives her advice about what to do. This leads Melly to decide not to jump off the bridge.*
10. *The author uses the dive to symbolize Melly's official transition into adulthood.*
11. *Her yard is full of flowers, suggesting her love for the natural world around her.*

Independent Practice

Vocabulary Development

Your Turn _____

1. *crinkling*; smile lines

2. *caressed*; brushed, gently

3. *stubble*; short and scratchy

4. *wafting*; smell, on the breeze

English for Academic Success

Language Coach

Tell students that writers provide definitions for some unfamiliar words in their stories by surrounding the unfamiliar word with descriptors or words that might appear in the dictionary definition of the original word.

Possible response: *The phrases "short gray hairs" and "his face" define the word* stubble.

English for Academic Success

Academic Vocabulary

Possible response: *When my neighbors and I organized a food and clothing drive for the local homeless shelter, I felt a <u>significant</u> impact from the experience. I was proud to be part of a group of people who cared so much about those in need, and it was rewarding to give the people at the shelter my help and friendship.*

Applying Your Skills

The Dive

Vocabulary Development

Clarifying Word Meanings: Restatement

When you read the Spanish words and phrases in the story, you were probably able to figure out their meanings because Saldaña put the English meanings either directly afterward or in the next sentence. (For example, "Tan locos, mi'ja. It's a crazy thing to do.") When you encounter unfamiliar English words in your reading, you may also find a restatement in the nearby words or sentences. In the passage below, for example, the meaning of *hurricane* is <u>explained</u> by the phrase *powerful tropical storm*.

The **hurricane** hit the U.S. mainland at about midnight. This **powerful tropical storm** battered coastal towns for more than twelve hours before the winds began to die down.

Your Turn _____

Complete each of the following sentences with the Vocabulary words at the right. Then, write down the restatement clues that helped you complete the sentence.

| crinkling |
| stubble |
| caressed |
| wafting |

1. My father was _____ his face; the smile lines showed that he was proud of me.

2. Grandma _____ my soft skin as she brushed it gently with her fingers.

3. When Dad doesn't shave, his _____ grows in short and scratchy.

4. The smell of the herbs from the garden were _____ through the house on the breeze.

Language Coach

Definitions Writers often help readers understand the meaning of a word by providing a definition of the word within a sentence.

If you come across an unfamiliar word as you're reading, look for clues around the word to help you define it.

The sentence below contains a boldface Vocabulary word as well as a definition of that word. What words define *stubble* in the sentence below?

The **stubble** on her father's chin was now made up of short gray hairs that tickled when he put his face next to hers.

Academic Vocabulary

Write About . . .

Think about a time when an event in your community had a <u>significant</u> impact on you. Was it a unique event or one that occurred frequently? Record your impressions of the event, and <u>explain</u> why it was important to you.

Universal Access: Vocabulary Development

EL English Learners/ Struggling Writers

English for Academic Success Point out to students that the use of restatement and definitions within sentences is an extremely helpful way writers assist readers with meaning. Because sentences or groups of sentences containing restatement and definitions

contain many words, students can be active readers by asking themselves: What is the connection between the vocabulary word and other words in the sentence? Are they the same part of speech? Can I substitute the restatement or definition for the vocabulary word?

✔ See the Vocabulary Skill Builder in **UA: Differentiating Instruction.**

Reading Standard 3.2 Identify events that advance the plot and determine how each event explains past or present action(s) or foreshadows future action(s).

Grammar Link
Pronoun-Antecedent Agreement

A pronoun usually refers to a noun or another pronoun, called its **antecedent.** Whenever you use a pronoun, make sure it agrees with its antecedent in number and gender. Doing this is usually easy, except when you use certain pronouns as antecedents.

Use a singular pronoun to refer to *each, either, neither, one, everyone, everybody, no one, anyone, someone,* or *somebody.*

> The boys were proud after jumping off the bridge; **everyone** raised **his** arms triumphantly.

Everyone is singular, so you use the singular pronoun *his.* You use *his* (rather than *her*) because *everyone* refers to the boys (masculine gender) who jumped.

> **Nobody** would want **his** or **her** daughter to jump off a bridge.

Nobody is singular, so you use the singular pronouns *his* and *her.* You need both *his* and *her* because the gender of *nobody* can be either masculine or feminine.

Your Turn

Act as an editor: Correct the use of antecedents in the following paragraph about "The Dive." Rewrite the sentences if you wish.

Anyone who loves their grandparents will enjoy reading "The Dive." When somebody must make a difficult decision, they should ask an older relative for advice. No one should have to make tough decisions on his own.

CHOICES

As you respond to the Choices, use these **Academic Vocabulary** words as appropriate: <u>advance</u>, <u>explain</u>, <u>significant</u>, <u>similar</u>.

REVIEW
Compare Plots
Timed ⌐Writing The plot of "The Dive" is driven by an internal conflict—Melly's feelings about diving off the bridge. The plots of "Rikki-tikki-tavi" and "Three Skeleton Key," on the other hand, are <u>advanced</u> by external conflicts. Which kind of story do you prefer—one driven by internal or external conflicts? Why? Support your response with evidence from the texts.

CONNECT
Collect Story Ideas
Group Discussion Melly deals with a number of internal conflicts in "The Dive." What other internal conflicts might make a good story? Form a group, and discuss some conflicts around which you might build an interesting story.

EXTEND
Tell a *Cuento*
TechFocus In "The Dive," Mamá Tochi shares wisdom through *cuentos,* retellings of her experiences that teach lessons. Think of an experience you had that taught you something <u>significant</u>. Then, tell the experience to someone else as a *cuento.* Be sure to include the lesson you learned and <u>explain</u> why it was important. You may want to record your *cuento* and play it for the class.

Learn It Online
Make your *cuento* a multimedia exeperience. Try digital storytelling at:

go.hrw.com H7-63 **Go**

Independent Practice
Grammar Link
Anyone who loves his or her grandparents will enjoy reading "The Dive." When somebody must make a difficult decision, he or she should ask an older relative for advice. No one should have to make tough decisions on his or her own.

Choices:
Evaluation Criteria
Review: Timed Writing
40–50 Minutes
The essay explains which type of conflict the student prefers and is supported with examples from both texts.

Connect: ⟨Homework⟩
Collect Story Ideas
The list includes several examples of internal conflicts and explains how they could be used in a story.

Extend: ⟨Homework⟩
Tell a *Cuento*
The *cuento* tells about a real-life experience and shares a lesson.

Assess

Chapter 1 Resources, Selection Standards Check, p. 21

ThinkCentral Online Assessment, Selection Standards Check

Teacher One Stop™, editable Selection Standards Check

Reteach

ThinkCentral Online Remediation

Learn It Online
If students need help adding multimedia features to their projects, send them to the **MediaScope** mini-site, where students can work through an interactive tutorial on creating multimedia.

go.hrw.com H7-63 **Go**

Universal Access: Grammar Link

Explain to students that *each, either, neither, one, everyone, everybody, no one, anyone, someone,* and *somebody* belong to a special category of pronouns that may themselves be used as antecedents. The pronouns students are likely most familiar with are those that follow antecedents, such as *he, she, we,* and *they.* Because the special category of pronouns do not clearly identify gender and number, they have to follow different rules than pronouns such as *he, she,* and *we.* If there is a reference in another portion of the sentence or paragraph to who *everyone* or *each* is, that reference will determine which regular pronoun should be used, based on gender and number. If there is no such reference, all the special category pronouns take a singular pronoun of each gender, as the reference is to one person but that person may belong to either gender.

✔ For more practice with pronoun-antecedent agreement, see **Language Handbook Worksheets, Grammar Notes,** and **Warriner's Handbook**.

Objectives

Students will

- understand plot complications
- make predictions

Motivate

What Do You Think?/QuickWrite

Ask volunteers to describe a time in their lives, or in a story they have read or seen, when fear affected people's judgment. Then, have students use their **Reader/Writer Notebook** to write about the impact of snap judgments based on fear.

English for Academic Success

Academic Vocabulary

Look for opportunities to use the Academic Vocabulary words in this chapter.

- **advance, v.:** move forward
- **explain, v.:** give reasons for; make understandable
- **significant, adj.:** important
- **similar, adj.:** almost the same

Analyzing Visuals

Extension Activity Ask students to describe the setting shown in the image. *Possible response: It looks like a pleasant, quiet suburban town with lots of trees.*

California Standards, pp. 64–89

■ **Reading Standard 3.2** Identify events that advance the plot and determine how each event explains past or present action(s) or foreshadows future action(s).

TELEPLAY

Preparing to Read

The MONSTERS Are Due on Maple Street

by **Rod Serling**

What Do You Think What more often causes confusion in dangerous situations: fear or facts?

QuickWrite

People often make snap judgments in life. Write about a time you or someone else jumped to an incorrect conclusion. What was the mistake? Was it corrected, and if so, how?

Selection Readability	
Easily Accessible **Accessible** **Challenging**	historical context; chronological order; conversational dialogue

Selection Plot Summary

Neighbors in a small town react to a mysterious power outage by panicking and turning on each other.

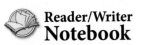
Reader/Writer Notebook

Use your **RWN** to complete the activities for this selection.

Literary Skills Focus

Plot Complications **Complications** in stories make it hard for characters to get what they want. Complications usually develop as the characters take steps to resolve their problems or accomplish their goals. (Complications are events such as a storm breaking out just as climbers are nearing the summit of a mountain.) Complications usually add conflict to a story and advance the plot, making it more complex. Our suspense and tension about how the story will finally end increase as the complications build.

TechFocus As you read, think about how you might create a multimedia presentation based on or inspired by *The Monsters Are Due on Maple Street.*

Reading Skills Focus

Making Predictions Authors often leave clues that suggest what will happen next in a story. If you pay attention to these clues, you may be able to predict what plot complications will emerge—and how the characters ultimately will handle them.

Into Action As you read, try to predict what will happen as the plot <u>advances</u>. Whenever you are prompted to make a prediction—or whenever one occurs to you—list your prediction in a chart. Also note the clue or clues that led you to the prediction.

Clue	My Prediction
Maple Street residents think they see a meteor but don't hear it crash.	It might not be a meteor at all.

Writing Skills Focus

Think as a Reader/Writer

Find It in Your Writing As you read, note the author's use of authentic dialogue. Much of the conversation includes questions ("What was that?") or answers ("Too close for my money. Much too close.") in the form of fragments. Think about how this form of dialogue makes you eager to find out what will happen next.

Vocabulary

transfixed (trans FIHKST) *v.* used as *adj.*: very still, as if nailed to the spot. *The neighbors stood transfixed, staring at the sky.*

intimidated (ihn TIHM uh day tihd) *v.* used as *adj.*: frightened, as by threats or violence. *The Goodmans, intimidated by the angry crowd, began to defend themselves.*

defiant (dih FY uhnt) *adj.*: boldly resisting authority. *Those who speak out against the opinions of an angry crowd are defiant and courageous.*

idiosyncrasy (ihd ee uh SIHNG kruh see) *n.*: peculiarity. *All people have an idiosyncrasy that makes them a little different.*

menace (MEHN ihs) *n.*: danger; threat. *They believed there was a menace to their safety.*

converging (kuhn VUR jihng) *v.* used as *adj.*: coming together. *The crowd converging on the porch frightened the Goodmans.*

Language Coach

Prefixes The prefix *con–* means "with" or "together." How would knowing the meaning of this prefix help you figure out the meaning of the Vocabulary word *converging*?

 Learn It Online

For a preview of this teleplay, see the video introduction on:

go.hrw.com | H7-65 | **Go**

Selection Resources

Chapter 1 Resources, on-level practice and assessment, p. 24

PowerNotes, interactive lesson presentation with activities

Teacher One Stop™, on-level lesson plans and all print resources

Holt Audio Library

Holt Audio Library: Selections and Summaries in Spanish

Holt Interactive Reader for ELD, p. 14

UA: Supporting Instruction in Five Languages, selection summary

ThinkCentral Online Assessment, Selection Standards Check

ThinkCentral Online Remediation

Preteach

Introducing Vocabulary

Read aloud the Vocabulary words and sample sentences. Then, have students work in pairs to compose one sentence for each word.

Possible responses:
- *I was **transfixed** by the movie.*
- *The bully **intimidated** the child.*
- *Rebellious people are **defiant**.*
- *Being able to wiggle one's ears is an **idiosyncrasy**.*
- *The dog was a **menace** to the cats.*
- *Fans were **converging** on the singer.*

English for Academic Success

Language Coach

Explain that *verge* means to move in a particular direction. Adding the prefix *con-* makes the word *converge*, which means to move or come together.

Literary Skills Focus

As you read and discuss the story, have students explain the relationship between conflicts and complications and observe how they work together to advance the plot.

Reading Skills Focus

Give students a copy of the Reading Skills Focus graphic organizer before they read. (See **Chapter 1 Resources.**) Tell them to use their responses to answer the questions on the Applying Your Skills page.

Writing Skills Focus

Have students note examples of authentic dialogue in their **Reader/ Writer Notebook.** Students can use their notes to complete the Writing Skills Focus activity.

 Learn It Online

The **PowerNotes** presentation for this lesson includes a short video that introduces the selection. The video is also available on the online version of this page.

go.hrw.com | H7-65 | **Go**

Learn It Online
Get more on the author's life at:
go.hrw.com H7-66 Go

Selection Introduction

More About the Writer

Early in **Rod Serling**'s career, he wrote scripts for realistic live dramas about serious issues, such as racism, ruthless business people and union organizing. Television networks regularly censored his work. In the late 1950's, Serling turned to science fiction, as it allowed him to address society's problems without being censored.

Think About the Writer

Discuss ways in which science fiction can differ from realistic fiction (non-human characters, supernatural events, a futuristic or outer space setting). Remind students that science fiction has certain elements in common with realistic fiction. Both types of stories include characters who encounter problems as well as some kind of resolution.

For Independent Reading

- Students who are interested in science fiction may enjoy *Running Out of Time* by Margaret Peterson Haddix. In this novel, thirteen-year-old Jessie discovers that her family is part of a secret science experiment.

- If students enjoy humorous stories, suggest *Parasite Pig*, William Sleator's science fiction novel that combines aliens and humor with strong character development and an appealing plot.

Learn It Online
The enhanced author biography offers more information on the life of the author as well as Holt's interactive resources pertaining to the author.

go.hrw.com H7-66 Go

MEET THE WRITER

Rod Serling
(1924–1975)

Man from Another Dimension

How does a fledgling writer with a less-than-dreamy job get from Cincinnati, Ohio, to New York City and then to Hollywood? If you're Rod Serling, you and your wife decide one day that the time has come to reach for your dream!

In the early 1950s, Rod Serling eagerly arrived in New York and found himself a job writing for television, a newly popular invention at the time. He first wrote for a live half-hour drama called *Lux Video Theatre*. From there he went on to create and produce the hit television show *The Twilight Zone*.

The Twilight Zone

In the fifth-dimensional world of the Twilight Zone, Serling made his beliefs known. *The Monsters Are Due on Maple Street* was written at a time when Americans were concerned about the spread of communism in the United States. There was a great deal of suspicion and finger-pointing, and Serling used this teleplay to voice perhaps his most enduring and urgent theme, namely:

"There is nothing in the dark that isn't there when the lights are on."

Think About the Writer — Why do you think Rod Serling chose to express his concerns using the science fiction genre?

Build Background

From its 1959 debut through its more than 150 subsequent episodes, *The Twilight Zone* thrilled and captivated millions of television viewers. Rebroadcasts still run today. As Rod Serling, the show's creator, would eerily alert viewers at the beginning of every episode, things in *The Twilight Zone* are not always what they seem. Ordinary people face extraordinary situations in *The Twilight Zone*, where familiar rules no longer apply.

Preview the Selection

In this teleplay, you will meet the residents of Maple Street, including **Steve Brand** and **his wife,** fourteen-year-old **Tommy** and his mother **Sally, Les Goodman,** and **Charlie.** Each of these people has a very different reaction to a mysterious power outage on Maple Street, and their reactions drive the story's action.

Universal Access

English Learners

Point out to students that the setting of the play is "Maple Street, U.S.A.," which is an unusual way to reference a setting in a literary work. Tell students that Maple Street is one of the most common names for a street because of the prevalence of the trees. Then ask students to predict why the author would specify his setting in this way. What does that suggest to us about the plot we are about to read?

Struggling Readers

Benchmark Students The setting "Maple Street, U.S.A" is an unusual way to identify the location, but it is one way the author lets us know that the actions we will read about could happen anywhere. When authors use that kind of setting, their observations about life are described as universal. As you read, ask yourself if the actions in this plot could happen on your street. Think about what Serling is saying about people everywhere.

The MONSTERS
Are Due on Maple Street

by **Rod Serling**

Teleplay Terms

Scripts written for television or the movies are different from scripts written for the stage. A **teleplay** is a script written for TV; a **screenplay** is a script written for movies. Both kinds of scripts may contain these camera directions:

fade in: the picture's gradual appearance on the screen.

pan: a swiveling movement of the camera, from one side to the other.

fade to black: the gradual disappearance of the picture until all that remains is a black screen.

cut to: a sudden change from one scene or character to another.

outside shot: a camera shot of an exterior.

long shot: a camera shot from far off.

close-up: a camera shot that is very close to its subject.

opening shot: the first scene of the production.

dissolve: the blending of a new scene with a scene that is fading out.

Characters
Narrator

Figure One
Figure Two

Residents of Maple Street
Steve Brand
Mrs. Brand
Don Martin
Pete Van Horn
Charlie
Charlie's wife
Tommy
Sally, Tommy's mother
Les Goodman
Mrs. Goodman
Woman Next Door
Woman One
Man One
Man Two

Direct Teach

Think About/Talk About

Read with a Purpose Have students read the Read with a Purpose statement. Point out that the play focuses on a group of neighbors. Ask students to predict the kinds of conflicts that may arise in this play.

▶ **Extend the Discussion**

Making Predictions Read the teleplay terms on page 67. How might this teleplay utilize these camera directions to enhance or create suspense within the story? *Possible response: A "cut to" in the middle of an intense scene could create suspense because the audience will have to wait to see how it is resolved.*

Speculating Read the list of characters on page 67. Who or what might "Figure One" and "Figure Two" be, and what role might they play in the story? *Possible response: They might just be people or animals who are seen from afar, or they might be the actual monsters mentioned in the title. Because they are listed first in the character list, I think they will be important. in the story. They might invade Maple Street.*

Advanced Learners
Extension Remind students that Rod Serling wrote *The Monsters Are Due on Maple Street* during a time of great paranoia about communism in America. Explain that the author's purpose for writing this teleplay is closely linked to the time period in which he was writing. As students read, have them identify details that refer, either explicitly or implicitly, to communism and McCarthyism. then, ask students to think about whether the teleplay's message and purpose is confined to the world of the 1950s or is more universally relevant.

Students with Disabilities
Invite students to read *The Monsters Are Due on Maple Street* in interactive format in the **Holt Interactive Reader for ELD** and to use the sidenotes as aids to understanding the selection. The interactive version provides additional instruction, practice, and assessment of the skills taught in the Student Edition.

Model the Skill

- To help students make predictions, provide them with copies of the Reading Skills Focus graphic organizer. (See **Chapter 1 Resources**.)

- Tell students that readers benefit from making predictions as they read because it helps them stay engaged in the text. Readers use details included by the author to suggest what happens next, their own knowledge, and current story events to make predictions.

- Point out that the story starts with a flash of light and a loud roar over Maple Street. Then, the narrator explains on p. 69, that "Maple Street [is] in the last calm and reflective moments…before the monsters came!" This immediately catches the readers' attention, causing them to wonder as to what kind of monsters will come to Maple Street, and what is going to happen. This text is a detail provided by the author that suggests what will happen next. Explain to students that from this detail, you will make the prediction "aliens will invade." Write the clue (or detail) and prediction in the chart.

Guided Practice: Apply

- Have students study pp. 68–69 and identify other examples of foreshadowing. Have them explain what effect these examples have on the reader.

- Have students predict what future actions will occur based on the foreshadowing.

Clues	My Predictions
before the monsters came	aliens will invade

ACT ONE

Fade in on a shot of the night sky. The various nebulae and planets stand out in sharp, sparkling relief. As the camera begins a slow pan across the heavens, we hear the narrator offscreen.

Narrator's Voice. There is a fifth dimension beyond that which is known to man. It is a dimension as vast as space and as timeless as infinity. It is the middle ground between light and shadow—between science and superstition. And it lies between the pit of man's fears and the summit of his knowledge. This is the dimension of imagination. It is an area which we call The Twilight Zone. Ⓐ

[The camera pans down past the horizon, stopping on a sign which reads "Maple Street." Then it moves on to the street below. It is daytime. We see a quiet, tree-lined street, typical of small-town America. People sit and swing on gliders on their front porches, chatting across from house to house. STEVE BRAND *polishes his car, while his neighbor,* DON MARTIN, *leans against the fender watching him. A Good Humor man on a bicycle stops to sell some ice cream to a couple of kids. Two women gossip on a front lawn. Another man waters his lawn.]*

Maple Street, U.S.A., late summer. A tree-lined little world of front-porch gliders, hopscotch, the laughter of children, and the bell of an ice-cream vendor.

[The camera moves back to the Good Humor man and the two boys who are standing alongside him, buying ice cream.]

Ⓐ **Read and Discuss** What is the narrator sharing with you?

Reaching Reluctant Readers

Point out to students that while *The Monsters Are Due on Maple Street* is a science fiction teleplay, it addresses common social concerns that students may have thought about or experienced, such as group dynamics, distrust, and exclusion.

- As students read the selection, have them identify points at which the characters jump to conclusions, treat others unfairly, or are caught up in the emotions of other group members. Ask students to consider whether or not they can relate to the characters' actions and reactions at these points.

- Then, help students connect to the selection by having them discuss with a partner times in which they were made to feel unwelcome in a group setting or unfairly accused of something. They may also discuss examples of instances in which they treated someone unfairly or jumped to conclusions.

- Have students use information from their discussions and from the teleplay to think of reasons why people might be afraid of the unknown or of people who are different. What can people do to ease these fears?

At the sound of the roar and the flash of light, it will be precisely 6:43 P.M. on Maple Street.

[*One of the boys,* TOMMY, *looks up to listen to a tremendous screeching roar from overhead. A flash of light plays on the boys' faces. It moves down the street, past lawns and porches and rooftops, and disappears. People leave their porches or stop what they're doing to stare up at the sky.* STEVE BRAND *stops polishing his car and stands* transfixed, *staring upward. He looks at* DON MARTIN, *his neighbor from across the street.*] **B**

Steve. What was that? A meteor?
Don (*nods*). That's what it looked like. I didn't hear any crash, though, did you?
Steve (*shakes his head*). Nope. I didn't hear anything except a roar.

Mrs. Brand (*from her porch*). Steve? What was that?
Steve (*raising his voice and looking toward porch*). Guess it was a meteor, honey. Came awful close, didn't it?
Mrs. Brand. Too close for my money! Much too close.

[*People stand on their porches, watching and talking in low tones.*] **C**

Narrator's Voice. Maple Street. 6:44 P.M., on a late September evening. (*A pause*) Maple Street in the last calm and reflective moments . . . before the monsters came!

[*The camera pans across the porches again. A man is screwing in a lightbulb on a front porch. He gets down off the stool and flicks*

B **Reading Focus** Making Predictions What do you think the roar and the flash of light will turn out to be? On what do you base your prediction?

C **Read and Discuss** What do the stage directions lead you to think about the roaring sound and flashing light?

Vocabulary **transfixed** (trans FIHKST) *v.* used as *adj.:* very still, as if nailed to the spot.

Universal Access

Struggling Readers
Strategic Students Point out that there are two sources of information in the play that help readers understand the action and advancement of the plot. On p. 69, we see both the stage directions, which are in italics and brackets, and the Narrator's Voice. The stage directions provide valuable information about the characters and their actions and motivation. It is important to read the stage directions each time they appear. The narrator has lines that are spoken aloud, but he does not engage in dialogue with the

characters. He acts as a commentator on the action and gives the reader information.

Students with Disabilities
If possible, obtain a video copy of *The Monsters Are Due on Maple Street* for students to watch for assistance in understanding the teleplay as a story with dialogue and action. If unable to obtain such a recording, allow extra time for students to read the play, and assist them in creating visuals, such as illustrations, storyboards, or manipulatives that help them visualize the characters, setting, and action.

Think About/Talk About

▶ **Comprehension**

A Read and Discuss
Possible response: The narrator is telling us that there is a fifth dimension, the imagination, that is beyond man's knowledge.

B Reading Focus
Possible response: I think it will turn out to be an airplane. There are not many other things that could fly overhead and make a loud noise.

C Read and Discuss
Possible response: The stage directions imply that something dangerous might be happening. The neighbors seem to be troubled by the roaring sound and flashing light, which they assume to have been a meteor.

▶ **Extend the Discussion**

Symbolism In column 2 of page 68, the narrator describes "Maple Street, U.S.A." as a "tree-lined little world" of its own. What might Maple Street stand for? *Possible response: It might represent any typical community in the United States.*

Making Predictions What do the narrator's words in the first column on page 68 lead you to predict about the teleplay? *Possible response: Such words as* fifth dimension, space, between science and superstition, imagination, *and* Twilight Zone *hint at science fiction or fantasy.*

Vocabulary: Own the Word
transfixed: Ask students: Have you ever been *transfixed* by something? If so, explain what event occurred that led to this. *Possible response: I saw a magician perform and was transfixed in amazement.*

■ Tell students that **prefixes** are affixes added to base words to modify their meaning. Knowing the common English prefixes will enhance students' ability to decode and understand unfamiliar words.

■ Point out the word *reaction* on the top of p. 71. Explain that *reaction* is made up of a prefix, *re-*, and a base word, *action*. The prefix *re-* means "again" or "back." The word *action* describes a movement made or act performed by a living being. Put together, they form the word *reaction*, meaning "action taken in response to something." Point out that the prefix *re-* is logical in this instance because it describes an action that goes "back" to the original action taken.

Guided Practice: Apply

Have students review the first few pages of the story independently to identify other words with prefixes. Ask students to break their chosen word down into base word and affix, explaining the meaning of each and how they combine to form a new meaning.

---

the switch, only to find that nothing happens. Another man is working on an electric power mower. He plugs in the plug and flicks the switch of the power mower, off and on, but nothing happens. Through the window of a front porch we see a woman at a telephone, pushing her finger back and forth on the dial hook. Her voice is indistinct and distant, but intelligible and repetitive.*]

Woman Next Door. Operator, operator, something's wrong on the phone, operator!

[*MRS. BRAND comes out on the porch and calls to STEVE.*]

Mrs. Brand (*calling*). Steve, the power's off. I had the soup on the stove, and the stove just stopped working.

Woman Next Door. Same thing over here. I can't get anybody on the phone either. The phone seems to be dead.

[*The camera looks down on the street. Small, mildly disturbed voices creep up from below.*]

Voices.
Electricity's off.
Phone won't work.
Can't get a thing on the radio.
My power mower won't move, won't work at all.
Radio's gone dead.

[*PETE VAN HORN, a tall, thin man, is standing in front of his house.*]

Van Horn. I'll cut through the backyard. . . . See if the power's still on on Floral Street. I'll be right back.

[*He walks past the side of his house and disappears into the backyard. We see the hammer on his hip as he walks. The camera pans down slowly until we're looking at ten or eleven people standing around the street and overflowing to the curb and sidewalk. In the background is STEVE BRAND's car.*]

Steve. Doesn't make sense. Why should the power go off all of a sudden, and the phone line?

Don. Maybe some sort of an electrical storm or something.

Charlie. That don't seem likely. Sky's just as blue as anything. Not a cloud. No lightning. No thunder. No nothing. How could it be a storm?

Woman One. I can't get a thing on the radio. Not even the portable.

[*The people again murmur softly in wonderment and question.*]

Charlie. Well, why don't you go downtown and check with the police, though they'll probably think we're crazy or something. A little power failure and right away we get all flustered and everything.

Steve. It isn't just the power failure, Charlie. If it was, we'd still be able to get a broadcast on the portable.

Cross-Curricular Connection

HISTORY: The Cold War and Communism

Explain to students that the selection takes place during the Cold War.

- The United States and the Soviet Union fought on the same side in World War II, but neither government trusted the other. When the war ended in 1945, the US feared its wartime ally because the Soviet Union had a communist government while the United States had a democratic government.

- The US and the Soviet Union began what is called the Cold War in the late 1940s. Neither nation attacked the other directly, but each government built nuclear weapons and threatened to destroy the other nation. The American public lived in fear of nuclear attack.

- In 1950, a senator named Joseph McCarthy began publicly accusing government workers and then entertainers of being Communists. People lost their jobs. Some were jailed. Already frightened of nuclear war, ordinary people began to suspect neighbors and coworkers of being Communists.

[*There's a murmur of reaction to this.* STEVE *looks from face to face and then over to his car.*]

I'll run downtown. We'll get this all straightened out.

[STEVE *walks over to the car, gets in it, and turns the key. Through the open car door we see the crowd watching him from the other side.* STEVE *starts the engine. It turns over sluggishly and then just stops dead. He tries it again, and this time he can't even get it to turn over. Then, very slowly and reflectively, he turns the key back to "off" and slowly gets out of the car. Everyone stares at* STEVE. *He stands for a moment by the car, then walks toward the group.*]

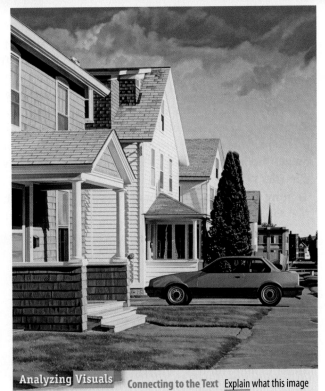

Analyzing Visuals
Connecting to the Text Explain what this image suggests about Maple Street.

I don't understand it. It was working fine before. . . .

Don. Out of gas?
Steve (*shakes his head*). I just had it filled up.
Woman One. What's it mean?
Charlie. It's just as if . . . as if everything had stopped. . . . (*Then he turns toward* STEVE) We'd better walk downtown.

[*Another murmur of assent at this.*]

Steve. The two of us can go, Charlie. (*He turns to look back at the car.*) It couldn't be the meteor. A meteor couldn't do this.

[*He and* CHARLIE *exchange a look, then they start to walk away from the group. We see* TOMMY, *a serious-faced fourteen-year-old in spectacles, standing a few feet away from the group. He is halfway between them and the two men, who start to walk down the sidewalk.*]

Tommy. Mr. Brand . . . you better not!
Steve. Why not?

Reading Focus Making Predictions Will Steve be able to go downtown? Why or why not?

Read and Discuss What has happened?

• In 1954, the nation realized that Senator McCarthy's accusations were false. He was sharply criticized for his actions, but many lives had already been destroyed.

 HSS Analysis Skills: HR 1, 2

Analyzing Visuals
Connecting to the Text: The image suggests that Maple Street is a quiet suburban neighborhood.

Think About/Talk About

▶ **Comprehension**
Ⓓ **Reading Focus**
Possible response: I don't think Steve will be able to go downtown. That would solve the problem too easily and would ruin the suspense of the story.

Ⓔ **Read and Discuss**
Possible response: All the neighbors are discovering and talking about their lack of electricity. It's strange that even phones, cars, and portable radios are not working.

▶ **Extend the Discussion**
Plot On p. 70, we are told four times that the phones don't work and twice that the radios are out. How might these problems contribute to the story's plot? *Possible response: The phone is the best way to call for help, and the radio is a way to get news. If the phones and radios are out, the neighbors are cut off from the rest of the world.*

Author's Purpose The stage directions at the top of the second column of p. 70 describe "ten or eleven people standing around the street and overflowing to the curb and sidewalk." What might be the author's purpose in including these directions? *Possible response: The description of the crowds of worried people increases the reader's suspense as he or she takes in the neighborhood's collective reaction to the power outage.*

- Remind students to fill in their Reading Skills Focus graphic organizer with their **predictions** as they read.

- In a Think Aloud format, say: This scene with Tommy adds an element of mystery and fear to the people on Maple Street because he uses the word "them" as he thinks about what caused the power outage. I predict that his words will add to the panic because "them" suggests a monster or unknown force.

Guided Practice: Apply

Have students fill in their graphic organizers with a prediction about what Charlie and Steve will find in town.

Tommy. They don't want you to.

[STEVE *and* CHARLIE *exchange a grin, and* STEVE *looks back toward the boy.*]

Steve. Who doesn't want us to?
Tommy (*jerks his head in the general direction of the distant horizon*). Them!
Steve. Them?
Charlie. Who are them?
Tommy (*very intently*). Whoever was in that thing that came by overhead.

[STEVE *knits his brows for a moment, cocking his head questioningly. His voice is intense.*]

Steve. What?
Tommy. Whoever was in the thing that came over. I don't think they want us to leave here.

[STEVE *leaves* CHARLIE *and walks over to the boy. He kneels down in front of him. He forces his voice to remain gentle. He reaches out and holds the boy.*]

Steve. What do you mean? What are you talking about?
Tommy. They don't want us to leave. That's why they shut everything off.
Steve. What makes you say that? Whatever gave you that idea?
Woman One (*from the crowd*). Now isn't that the craziest thing you ever heard?
Tommy (*persistently but a little intimidated by the crowd*). It's always that way, in every story I ever read about a ship landing from outer space. **F**
Woman One (*to the boy's mother,* SALLY, *who stands on the fringe of the crowd*). From outer space, yet! Sally, you better get that boy of yours up to bed. He's been reading too many comic books or seeing too many movies or something.
Sally. Tommy, come over here and stop that kind of talk.
Steve. Go ahead, Tommy. We'll be right back. And you'll see. That wasn't any ship or anything like it. That was just a . . . a meteor or something. Likely as not— (*He turns to the group, now trying to weight his words with an optimism he obviously doesn't feel but is desperately trying to instill in himself, as well as the others.*) No doubt it did have something to do with all this power failure and the rest of it. Meteors can do some crazy things. Like sunspots.
Don (*picking up the cue*). Sure. That's the kind of thing—like sunspots. They raise Cain with radio reception all over the world. And this thing being so close— why, there's no telling the sort of stuff it can do. (*He wets his lips and smiles nervously.*) Go ahead, Charlie. You and Steve go into town and see if that isn't what's causing it all.

> "That wasn't any ship or anything like it. That was just a . . . a meteor or something."

F Read and Discuss What does this show you about Tommy?

Vocabulary **intimidated** (ihn TIHM uh day tihd) *v.* used as *adj.:* frightened, as by threats or violence.

Developing Oral Fluency

Use the exchange between Tommy and the adult neighbors to give students practice in reading with expression. Explain to students that in this scene, Tommy is frightened and upset, but at first the adults are amused by him. Fluent readers try to express each character's emotions in their voice as they read that character's lines of dialogue.

Small-group activity Put students into groups of five, making sure that there is at least one fluent reader in each group.

- Model reading a few lines of dialogue from the scene in which Tommy reveals his alien theory, making sure to emphasize expression as you read. For example, the line "They don't want us to leave" should be read with a fearful voice. Begin with the first line on p. 72.

- Next, have each group read the scene aloud. Have a fluent student in each group play the role of Tommy. Each of the remaining students in the group may choose to read the role of Steve, Charlie/Don, Woman One, or Sally.

[STEVE *and* CHARLIE *walk away from the group again, down the sidewalk. The people watch silently.* TOMMY *stares at them, biting his lips, and finally calls out again.*]

Tommy. Mr. Brand!

[*The two men stop again.* TOMMY *takes a step toward them.*]

Tommy. Mr. Brand . . . please don't leave here.

[STEVE *and* CHARLIE *stop once again and turn toward the boy. There's a murmur in the crowd, a murmur of irritation and concern as if the boy were bringing up fears that shouldn't be brought up; words that carried with them a strange kind of validity that came without logic, but nonetheless registered and had meaning and effect.* TOMMY *is partly frightened and partly* defiant.]

You might not even be able to get to town. It was that way in the story. Nobody could leave. Nobody except—
Steve. Except who?
Tommy. Except the people they'd sent down ahead of them. They looked just like humans. And it wasn't until the ship landed that—

[*The boy suddenly stops again, conscious of the parents staring at him and of the sudden hush of the crowd.*]   **G**

Sally (*in a whisper, sensing the antagonism of the crowd*). Tommy, please, son . . . honey, don't talk that way—
Man One. That kid shouldn't talk that way . . . and we shouldn't stand here listening to him. Why, this is the craziest thing I ever heard of. The kid tells us a comic book plot, and here we stand listening—

[STEVE *walks toward the camera and stops by the boy.*]

Steve. Go ahead, Tommy. What kind of story was this? What about the people that they sent out ahead?
Tommy. That was the way they prepared things for the landing. They sent four people. A mother and a father and two kids who looked just like humans . . . but they weren't.   **H**

[*There's another silence as* STEVE *looks toward the crowd and then toward* TOMMY. *He wears a tight grin.*]

Steve. Well, I guess what we'd better do then is to run a check on the neighborhood and see which ones of us are really human.

[*There's laughter at this, but it's a laughter that comes from a desperate attempt to lighten the atmosphere.* CHARLIE *laughs nervously, slightly forced. The people look at one another in the middle of their laughter.*]

G **Literary Focus** Plot Complications What is stopping Steve and Charlie from going downtown?

H **Read and Discuss** What is on Tommy's mind?

Vocabulary **defiant** (dih FY uhnt) *adj.:* boldly resisting authority.

- Encourage students to think about the emotions their character might be feeling during this scene, and remind students to let those emotions guide their expression as they read. Remind students that the stage directions in parentheses can be a helpful guide to the characters' emotions and movement.

  ✔ See **UA: Differentiating Instruction** for practice passages for developing oral fluency.

Think About/Talk About

▶ **Comprehension**
F **Read and Discuss**
Possible response: Tommy's idea seems foolish and juvenile.

H **Read and Discuss**
Possible response: Because of the story that Tommy knows, he insists that Steve not leave. The only people who can leave, according to Tommy, are those emissaries who look like humans and have been sent ahead.

▶ **Analysis**
G **Literary Focus**
Possible response: They do not leave because they are scared of the possible consequences. Tommy implies that if they are able to leave, they must be aliens, and if they are human, something bad will happen to them.

▶ **Extend the Discussion**
Motivation The teleplay directions in the second column of page 72 say that Steve is "trying to weight his words with an optimism he obviously doesn't feel but is desperately trying to instill in himself, as well as the others." What made Steve lose his optimism? Why does he want to appear optimistic? *Possible response: The effects of the flashing light are impossible to explain. Part of him believes Tommy's alien idea, but the idea of alien invasion is so terrifying that he can't stand to think about it. He wants to be optimistic so the rest of the neighbors will, too.*

Vocabulary: Own the Word

- **intimidated:** Have students explain whether or not they would want to be *intimidated*, and why. *Possible response: I would not want to be intimidated, because I would feel threatened by something.*

- **defiant:** The connotation of *defiant* is that a person is resisting authority. Ask students: What actions suggest that Tommy is *defiant*? *Possible response: He continues to talk about the aliens, even though the townspeople think it is nonsense.*

Model the Skill

- Tell students that **plot complications** are obstacles that interfere with characters' abilities to resolve a conflict. Complications add suspense and tension to a plot, making the story more interesting for readers.

- Have a volunteer restate what has happened in the story so far: A strange object flew over Maple Street, the power is out, cars won't start, and one of the neighborhood kids suggested that aliens are to blame. Then, point out that, on p. 74, one family's car starts by itself when no one else's will start at all. The fear and concern on Maple Street is now complicated by suspicion. The residents of the street believe that the starting car sets this family apart from the rest of the neighborhood, and accusations begin to fly.

Guided Practice: Apply

Have students study the neighbors' reactions to Les Goodman's car starting. Use a **Pinwheel Discussion** (p. T28) to have students consider what appears to be happening to the residents of Maple Street and how their behavior will be affected by this new suspicion about the Goodmans.

Think as a Reader/Writer

Find It in Your Reading Point out the use of questions and sentence fragments in the exchange between Charlie and Don on p. 74, column 2. Note how these two devices contribute to the tension of the scene as well as the authenticity of the dialogue.

Use It in Your Writing Have students use questions and sentence fragments as they write three or four brief lines of dialogue about a tense situation.

Charlie. There must be somethin' better to do than stand around makin' bum jokes about it. (*Rubs his jaw nervously*) I wonder if Floral Street's got the same deal we got. (*He looks past the houses.*) Where is Pete Van Horn anyway? Didn't he get back yet?

[*Suddenly there's the sound of a car's engine starting to turn over. We look across the street toward the driveway of* LES GOODMAN'S *house. He's at the wheel trying to start the car.*]

Sally. Can you get it started, Les?

[LES GOODMAN *gets out of the car, shaking his head.*]

Goodman. No dice.

[*He walks toward the group. He stops suddenly as behind him, inexplicably and with a noise that inserts itself into the silence, the car engine starts up all by itself.* GOODMAN *whirls around to stare toward it. The car idles roughly, smoke coming from the exhaust, the frame shaking gently.* GOODMAN'S *eyes go wide, and he runs over to his car. The people stare toward the car.*]

Man One. He got the car started somehow. He got his car started!

[*The camera pans along the faces of the people as they stare, somehow caught up by this revelation and somehow, illogically, wildly, frightened.*]

❶ **Literary Focus** **Plot Complications** What has the group decided about Goodman? What future actions might this complication foreshadow? Support your answer with evidence.

Woman One. How come his car just up and started like that?
Sally. All by itself. He wasn't anywhere near it. It started all by itself.

[DON *approaches the group. He stops a few feet away to look toward* GOODMAN'S *car, and then back toward the group.*]

Don. And he never did come out to look at that thing that flew overhead. He wasn't even interested. (*He turns to the faces in the group, his face taut and serious.*) Why? Why didn't he come out with the rest of us to look?
Charlie. He always was an oddball. Him and his whole family. Real oddball.
Don. What do you say we ask him? ❶

[*The group suddenly starts toward the house. In this brief fraction of a moment they take the first step toward a metamorphosis from a group into a mob. They begin to head purposefully across the street toward the house at the end.* STEVE *stands in front of them. For a moment their fear almost turns their walk into a wild stampede, but* STEVE'S *voice, loud, incisive, and commanding, makes them stop.*]

Steve. Wait a minute . . . wait a minute! Let's not be a mob!

[*The people stop as a group, seem to pause for a moment, and then much more quietly and slowly start to walk across the street.* GOODMAN *stands there alone, facing the people.*]

Goodman. I just don't understand it. I tried to start it and it wouldn't start. You saw me. All of you saw me.

[*And now, just as suddenly as the engine started, it stops. There's a long silence that is gradually intruded upon by the frightened murmuring of the people.*]

I don't understand. I swear . . . I don't understand. What's happening?
Don. Maybe you better tell us. Nothing's working on this street. Nothing. No lights, no power, no radio. (*And then meaningfully*) Nothing except one car—yours! **J**

[*The people pick this up. Now their murmuring becomes a loud chant, filling the air with accusations and demands for action. Two of the men pass* DON *and head toward* GOODMAN, *who backs away, backing into his car. He is now at bay.*]

Goodman. Wait a minute now. You keep your distance—all of you. So I've got a car that starts by itself—well, that's a freak thing, I admit it. But does that make me some kind of criminal or something? I don't know why the car works—it just does!

J Literary Focus **Plot Complications** Why is Don speaking to Goodman like this? How is the crowd's confrontation of Goodman a significant plot complication?

[*This stops the crowd momentarily, and now* GOODMAN, *still backing away, goes toward his front porch. He goes up the steps and then stops to stand facing the mob.* STEVE *comes through the crowd.*]

Steve (*quietly*). We're all on a monster kick, Les. Seems that the general impression holds that maybe one family isn't what we think they are. Monsters from outer space or something. Different than us. Fifth columnists[1] from the vast beyond. (*He chuckles.*)

---

1. **fifth columnists:** people who aid an enemy from within their own country.

Think About/Talk About

▶ **Analysis**

❶ Literary Focus
Possible response: They have decided that he must be behind the mysterious things that are happening in town. This might foreshadow the group trying to take him into custody. They approach him menacingly.

J Literary Focus
Possible response: Don is accusing Goodman of being an alien because his car has power. The crowd's confrontation could signal violence.

▶ **Extend the Discussion**

Plot What complication develops in the first column of p. 74? How might this development affect the story?
Possible response: Les Goodman's car starts by itself. The neighbors might suspect that Les is behind the mysterious things that are happening in town.

Making Judgments What do you think of the crowd's treatment of Goodman on p. 75? *Possible response: The neighbors are being unfair to him, and they're letting their fears get in the way of their judgment. They shouldn't gang up on him until they have more evidence that he's dangerous.*

to respond to predictions, comments, questions, and connections with their own ideas.
• Have partners switch roles and continue the activity by reading p. 75.

go.hrw.com For more information about the **Say Something strategy**, see this page in ThinkCentral, Teacher Access.

Think About/Talk About

▶ Comprehension

Ⓚ Reading Focus

Possible response: *Goodman will probably think Steve's comments are ridiculous.*

Ⓛ Read and Discuss

Possible response: *The neighbors' fear is being turned against Mr. Goodman, and their behavior might cause something terrifying to happen.*

▶ Extend the Discussion

Making Judgments Note Steve's interjection in the first column. How do you feel about the way he is handling the situation? *Possible response: I admire him for trying to calm the crowd down and persuade them to leave Mr. Goodman alone. His behavior seems calm and rational.*

Mood Describe the mood at the end of Act One, as the neighbors gang up on Goodman. *Possible response: The mood becomes tense and fearful as the neighbors fling accusations at Mr. Goodman and he warns them about what they are starting.*

Monitor Students' Comprehension

Guide the class in answering these comprehension questions.

1. What strange event happens at the beginning of the teleplay? [*A screeching roar is heard while a flash of light passes above the neighborhood.*]

2. Where does Mr. Van Horn go after the incident? [*He goes to Floral Street to see if that street also has a power outage.*]

3. Where does Tommy get the idea that the light, sound, and power outage might be caused by aliens? [*He gets it from a story he read.*]

You know anybody that might fit that description around here on Maple Street? **Ⓚ**

Goodman. What is this, a gag or something? This a practical joke or something?

[*The spotlight on his porch suddenly goes out. There's a murmur from the group.*]

Now, I suppose that's supposed to incriminate me! The light goes on and off. That really does it, doesn't it? (*He looks around the faces of the people.*) I just don't understand this—(*He wets his lips, looking from face to face.*) Look, you all know me. We've lived here five years. Right in this house. We're no different than any of the rest of you! We're no different at all. Really . . . this whole thing is just . . . just weird—

Woman One. Well, if that's the case, Les Goodman, explain why— (*She stops suddenly, clamping her mouth shut.*)

Goodman (*softly*). Explain what?
Steve (*interjecting*). Look, let's forget this—
Charlie (*overlapping him*). Go ahead, let her talk. What about it? Explain what?
Woman One (*a little reluctantly*). Well . . . sometimes I go to bed late at night. A couple of times . . . a couple of times

I'd come out on the porch and I'd see Mr. Goodman here in the wee hours of the morning standing out in front of his house . . . looking up at the sky. (*She looks around the circle of faces.*) That's right. Looking up at the sky as if . . . as if he were waiting for something. (*A pause*) As if he were looking for something.

[*There's a murmur of reaction from the crowd again. As* GOODMAN *starts toward them, they back away, frightened.*]

> "That's right. Looking up at the sky as if . . . as if he were waiting for something."

Goodman. You know really . . . this is for laughs. You know what I'm guilty of? (*He laughs.*) I'm guilty of insomnia. Now what's the penalty for insomnia? (*At this point the laugh, the humor, leaves his voice.*) Did you hear what I said? I said it was insomnia. (*A pause as he looks around, then shouts.*) I said it was insomnia! You fools. You scared, frightened rabbits, you. You're sick people, do you know that? You're sick people—all of you! And you don't even know what you're starting because let me tell you . . . let me tell you—this thing you're starting—that should frighten you. As God is my witness . . . you're letting something begin here that's a nightmare! **Ⓛ**

[*Fade to black.*]

Ⓚ **Reading Focus** **Making Predictions** How do you think Goodman will react to Steve's questioning?

Ⓛ **Read and Discuss** What message is the author bringing up here?

 California Standards, p. 77

■ **Reading Standard 3.2** Identify events that advance the plot and determine how each event explains past or present action(s) or foreshadows future action(s).

Applying Your Skills

Reading Standard 3.2 Identify events that advance the plot and determine how each event explains past or present action(s) or foreshadows future action(s).

The Monsters Are Due on Maple Street, Act One

Literary Response and Analysis

Reading Skills Focus
Quick Check

1. What steps do the residents initially take to figure out the cause of the power failure?

2. What is Tommy's theory about the power failure?

Read with a Purpose

3. What do you know about the power failure so far? What do you think might have caused it?

Reading Skills: Making Predictions

4. Review the predictions you recorded in your chart for Act One. Add a column to the chart, and indicate with a check mark for *yes* and a minus sign for *no* whether each prediction was correct. If it's still too early to tell, leave the third column blank for that prediction.

Clue	My Prediction	Yes/No
Maple Street residents think they see a meteor but don't hear it crash.	It might not be a meteor at all.	

Literary Skills Focus
Literary Analysis

5. **Interpret** What is the group's reaction when Les Goodman's car starts? What conclusion does the group draw?

6. **Interpret** At the end of Act One, Les Goodman warns the residents that they are starting something that should frighten them, and he goes on to call it a "nightmare." What could he mean by this?

7. **Analyze** A *scapegoat* is someone whom people blame for their troubles. How has Les Goodman become a scapegoat?

8. **Evaluate** What is the difference between a crowd and a mob? (Think about the connotations—the feelings and ideas associated with a word—of *mob*.)

Literary Skills: Plot Complications

9. **Extend** Describe the way the Maple Street residents are behaving, and explain whether their actions are making their situation more or less difficult. To what future actions in Act Two might their behavior lead?

Literary Skills Review: Character

10. **Evaluate** Which significant character behaves most reasonably in Act One? What effect does this character have on the plot? Give examples to support your answer.

Writing Skills Focus
Think as a Reader/Writer
Use It in Your Writing Use what you have noted about questions and fragments in this teleplay to write several lines of authentic dialogue that could go with this play or another story you have read. Be sure your language conveys a tense situation and the need to communicate quickly.

What Do **You** **Think** **Now?** Explain whether the group is acting on fear or facts. Support your explanation with details from the teleplay.

Universal Access

Struggling Writers
Some students may need additional scaffolding to complete the Writing Skills Focus activity. Have students brainstorm tense situations in which people would need to communicate quickly. After they have finished, write their suggestions on the board. Allow students to choose one of these situations as the subject of their dialogue.

Assess

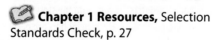 **Chapter 1 Resources,** Selection Standards Check, p. 27

 ThinkCentral Online Assessment, Selection Standards Check

Teacher One Stop™, editable Selection Standards Check

Check for Understanding

Independent Practice
Reading Skills Focus
Answers:

1. *They try to listen to news on radios and use the telephone.*

2. *He believes aliens are invading.*

3. *The failure affects things that are plugged in and battery-operated things like radios and cars. It makes things turn on and off by themselves. It might have been caused by a meteor.*

4. *I predicted that monsters would attack Maple Street. So far, there have not been any monsters, although the townspeople may be the real "monsters."*

Literary Skills Focus
Possible responses:

5. *The crowd is terrified when Goodman's car starts. The neighbors infer that he is behind the power outage.*

6. *Goodman might mean that the crowd is becoming dangerous because of their fear and that they may turn on each other.*

7. *He hasn't done anything wrong, but the crowd is inspecting his behavior, looking for anything that makes him different, and then using those differences to accuse him of wrongdoing.*

8. *A crowd is a large group of people. A mob is a crowd that acts destructively and attacks.*

9. *The neighbors are panicking and looking for scapegoats. I think someone will get hurt in Act Two. They are making the situation more difficult.*

10. *Steve Brand behaves most reasonably. He tries to keep everyone calm and level-headed instead of panicking. On p. 74, he warns the crowd not to turn into a mob.*

What Do You Think Now?
Ask students to think about what caused the group to turn on Mr. Goodman. Is there a factual basis for their accusations against him?

Direct Teach

Model the Skill

- Remind students that readers should not only **make predictions** as they read, they should also evaluate predictions and make new ones as new details arise in the text.

- Restate that during Act 1, a neighborhood kid, Tommy, suggested that space aliens might be responsible for the strange events on Maple Street. No one paid attention to his suggestion until Les Goodman's car inexplicably started. Now, at the beginning of Act 2, the neighbors are convinced that the Goodmans are aliens and are keeping watch over the Goodman house.

- Explain that, based on the details about the guarding of the Goodmans, you might make the following prediction: the Goodman family will try to escape their captivity, using violence if necessary. Write this prediction in the graphic organizer.

Guided Practice: Apply

Ask students to read Act 2 in pairs, pausing after every two pages to evaluate predictions made and make new ones based on new details from the text.

Read with a Purpose Read Act Two to discover how and why the situation on Maple Street grows worse.

The MONSTERS Are Due *on* Maple Street

by **Rod Serling**

ACT TWO

Fade in on the entry hall of the Goodman house at night. On the side table rests an unlit candle. MRS. GOODMAN *walks into the scene, a glass of milk in hand. She sets the milk down on the table, lights the candle with a match from a box on the table, picks up the glass of milk, and starts out of the scene. Cut to an outside shot.* MRS.

GOODMAN *comes through her porch door, glass of milk in hand. The entry hall, with the table and lit candle, can be seen behind her. The camera slowly pans down the sidewalk, taking in little knots of people who stand around talking in low voices. At the end of each conversation they look toward* LES GOODMAN*'s house. From the various houses we can see candlelight but no electricity. An all-pervading quiet*

Universal Access

Struggling Readers

Benchmark Students To highlight the story's plot complications, point out that the neighbors are becoming increasingly belligerent and suspicious of each other over the most trivial things, such as staring at the morning sky. Old friendships are being torn apart as people justify their hostile attitudes due to the emergency. Note that Charlie's comment about using candles in the street being a sign of "goin' back to the dark ages" can also reflect the "regression" of the people themselves.

Advanced Learners

Acceleration Point out to students that the second act of the teleplay begins with a series of images rather than with dialogue. Have students work in small groups to analyze the teleplay directions that begin on p. 78 and run through the top of p. 79. Ask students to identify the plot complications that these images portray, and use the content of the images to predict how the complications may further develop throughout the story.

blankets the area, disturbed only by the almost whispered voices of the people as they stand around. The camera pans over to one group where CHARLIE *stands. He stares across at* GOODMAN's *house. Two men stand across the street from it, in almost sentrylike poses. We return to the group.*

Sally (*a little timorously[1]*). It just doesn't seem right, though, keeping watch on them. Why . . . he was right when he said he was one of our neighbors. Why, I've known Ethel Goodman ever since they moved in. We've been good friends—
Charlie. That don't prove a thing. Any guy who'd spend his time lookin' up at the sky early in the morning—well, there's something wrong with that kind of a person. There's something that ain't legitimate. Maybe under normal circumstances we could let it go by, but these aren't normal circumstances. Why, look at this street! Nothin' but candles. Why, it's like goin' back into the dark ages or somethin'!

[STEVE *walks down the steps of his porch. He walks down the street, over to* LES GOODMAN's *house, and stops at the foot of the steps.* GOODMAN *stands behind the screen door, his wife behind him, very frightened.*]

Goodman. Just stay right where you are, Steve. We don't want any trouble, but this time if anybody sets foot on my porch, that's what they're going to get—trouble!
Steve. Look, Les—

----
1. **timorously** (TIHM uhr uhs lee): timidly; fearfully.

SOCIAL STUDIES LINK

Communism, Suspicion, and Fear in the 1940s and 1950s

The United States and Soviet Union were allies during World War II. However, with the start of the Cold War in the mid-1940s and the detonation of the first Soviet atomic bomb in 1949, distrust of Communist Russia increased. So did the fear that communism was spreading to the United States. In 1950, Senator Joseph McCarthy claimed to possess a list of 205 communists employed in the U.S. Department of State. His accusations fed into the period's political tensions, and many innocent people were labeled communist sympathizers. Lives were destroyed, and individuals made up stories about others in order to appear innocent themselves. Rod Serling alludes to that hysteria over communism in this teleplay.

Ask Yourself

How does *The Monsters Are Due on Maple Street* reflect the period of history in which it was written? How does the theme of this teleplay express Rod Serling's opinion of the climate of the times?

Think About/Talk About

Read with a Purpose Have students read the Read with a Purpose statement. Ask them to predict how things will get worse in Act Two. Have them consider the characters' behaviors at the end of Act One when making their prediction.

▶ **Extend the Discussion**

Summarizing How would you summarize Sally and Charlie's discussion in the first column on p. 79? ***Possible response:*** *Sally feels guilty about being suspicious of the Goodmans, but Charlie argues that Les Goodman is strange and suspicious because he spends a lot of time looking at the sky.*

Foreshadowing At the end of p. 79, Les Goodman begins to act defensive, threatening anyone who steps onto his family's porch. What might Les's building aggression foreshadow? ***Possible response:*** *Les may get so angry and frightened that his neighbors are going to harm his family that he attacks them.*

Making Judgments Read the first column on p. 79. In your opinion, are the people of Maple Street going too far? ***Possible response:*** *So far, they are only watching the Goodmans with suspicion. They haven't done anything rash or destructive quite yet.*

Students with Disabilities

Have students read along with the **Holt Audio Library** version of *The Monsters Are Due on Maple Street.* Students may wish to follow along silently or read aloud one of the character's lines of dialogue.

Social Studies Link
Ask Yourself _____

Possible response: *In this play, as during the McCarthy era, suspicions based on scant evidence are ruining people's lives. Rod Serling seems to be warning against a mass hysteria that he felt was destructive.*

 HSS Analysis Skills: REP 5

- Point out to students that plots can be very complex and change direction frequently as new **plot complications** crop up. Readers have to be on the lookout for new complications and their impact on the plot.

- Note Steve's change of heart on p. 80. Tell students that, even though Steve was originally against Les Goodman, he seems to be realizing that the accusations were made out of panic and not necessarily accurate. That seemed like it might be a resolution, but then, Charlie makes accusations against Steve simply for talking to Goodman. That makes the situation more complicated and throws more suspicion into the mix.

Guided Practice: Apply

Read-Talk-Write Have students review the story so far and look for any patterns in the story action and complications, such as a revelation of differences leading to accusation. Have students discuss the patterns in pairs. Then have students write for five minutes about how they think these complications might be resolved.

Think as a Reader/Writer

Find It in Your Reading Point out the sentence fragments in Steve's second line on p. 80. Note how this device creates authentic dialogue and brings intensity to Steve's words.

Use It in Your Writing Divide students into pairs. Have each pair write a few lines of dialogue on a subject of their choosing that include fragments to mimic natural speech.

Goodman. I've already explained to you people. I don't sleep very well at night sometimes. I get up and I take a walk and I look up at the sky. I look at the stars!

Mrs. Goodman. That's exactly what he does. Why this whole thing, it's . . . it's some kind of madness or something.

Steve (*nods grimly*). That's exactly what it is—some kind of madness.

Charlie's Voice (*shrill, from across the street*). You best watch who you're seen with, Steve! Until we get this all straightened out, you ain't exactly above suspicion yourself.

Steve (*whirling around toward him*). Or you, Charlie. Or any of us, it seems. From age eight on up! Ⓐ

Woman One. What I'd like to know is, what are we gonna do? Just stand around here all night?

Charlie. There's nothin' else we can do! (*He turns back looking toward* STEVE *and* GOODMAN *again.*) One of 'em'll tip their hand. They got to.

Steve (*raising his voice*). There's something you can do, Charlie. You could go home and keep your mouth shut. You could quit strutting around like a self-appointed hanging judge[2] and just climb into bed and forget it.

> "How about a firing squad at dawn, Charlie, so we can get rid of all the suspects?"

Charlie. You sound real anxious to have that happen, Steve. I think we better keep our eye on you too!

Don (*as if he were taking the bit in his teeth, takes a hesitant step to the front*). I think everything might as well come out now. (*He turns toward* STEVE.) Your wife's done plenty of talking, Steve, about how odd you are!

Charlie (*picking this up, his eyes widening*). Go ahead, tell us what she's said.

[STEVE *walks toward them from across the street.*]

Steve. Go ahead, what's my wife said? Let's get it all out. Let's pick out every idiosyncrasy of every single man, woman, and child on the street. And then we might as well set up some kind of a kangaroo court.[3] How about a firing squad at dawn, Charlie, so we can get rid of all the suspects? Narrow them down. Make it easier for you.

Don. There's no need gettin' so upset, Steve. It's just that . . . well . . . Myra's talked about how there's been plenty of nights you spend hours down in your basement workin' on some kind of radio or something. Well,

---

2. **hanging judge:** judge who sentences people to death without sufficient evidence.

3. **kangaroo court:** unauthorized court, usually one that pays no attention to legal procedures. Kangaroo courts were often set up in frontier areas.

Ⓐ **Literary Focus** **Plot Complications** What complication does this exchange between Charlie and Steve introduce?

Vocabulary **idiosyncrasy** (ihd ee uh SIHNG kruh see) *n.:* peculiarity.

Cross-Curricular Connection

SCIENCE: Ham Radio

The neighbors' suspicions of Steve are raised by the ham radio in his basement. Provide students with additional information about this popular hobby.

- Ham, or amateur, radios are personal radios capable of transmitting messages. Ham radios are often located in private homes. Operators may communicate verbally, in Morse Code, or with a computer. A major difference between the typical radio stations and ham radio is that ham radio is restricted to specific frequencies with limited transmitting power.

- Though ham radio is considered a hobby, operators must be licensed by passing an exam that tests their understanding of the technology and its operation. The Federal Communications Commission, a government agency, regulates ham radio in the United States.

- Amateur radio operators have made many contributions to the development of radio technology, such as transmitting over long distances.

- Ham radio operators, as part of the Amateur Radio Service, often provide valuable assistance during

none of us have ever seen that radio—
[*By this time* STEVE *has reached the group.
He stands there defiantly close to them.*]

Charlie. Go ahead, Steve. What kind of
"radio set" you workin' on? I never seen it.
Neither has anyone else. Who you talk to
on that radio set? And who talks to you?
Steve. I'm surprised at you, Charlie. How
come you're so dense all of a sudden? (*A
pause*) Who do I talk to? I talk to monsters
from outer space. I talk to three-headed
green men who fly over here in what look
like meteors.

[STEVE'*s wife steps down from their porch,
bites her lip, calls out.*]

Mrs. Brand. Steve! Steve, please. (*Then
looking around, frightened, she walks
toward the group.*) It's just a ham radio set,
that's all. I bought him a book on it myself.
It's just a ham radio[4] set. A lot of people
have them. I can show it to you. It's right
down in the basement.
Steve (*whirls around toward her*). Show
them nothing! If they want to look inside
our house—let them get a search warrant.
Charlie. Look, buddy, you can't afford to—
Steve (*interrupting*). Charlie, don't tell me
what I can afford! And stop telling me who's
dangerous and who isn't and who's safe and
who's a menace. (*He turns to the group and
shouts.*) And you're with him too—all of you!

---

4. **ham radio:** two-way radio used by an amateur
   operator. Ham radio operators talk to one another
   all over the world via their radios.

B Read and Discuss What can you say about the neighbors now?

You're standing here all set to crucify—all set
to find a scapegoat—all desperate to point
some kind of a finger at a neighbor! Well
now look, friends, the only thing that's gonna
happen is that we'll eat each other up alive—

[*He stops abruptly as* CHARLIE *suddenly
grabs his arm.*]

Charlie (*in a hushed voice*). That's not the
only thing that can happen to us.   **B**

[*Cut to a long shot looking down the street.
A figure has suddenly materialized in the
gloom, and in the silence we can hear the
clickety-clack of slow, measured footsteps on
concrete as the figure walks slowly toward
them. One of the women lets out a stifled
cry.[5] The young mother grabs her boy, as do
a couple of others.*]

Tommy (*shouting, frightened*). It's the
monster! It's the monster!

[*Another woman lets out a wail and the
people fall back in a group, staring toward
the darkness and the approaching figure. As
the people stand in the shadows watching,
DON MARTIN joins them, carrying a shotgun. He holds it up.*]

Don. We may need this.
Steve. A shotgun? (*He pulls it out of* DON'*s
hand.*) Good Lord—will anybody think a
thought around here? Will you people wise

---

5. **stifled** (STY fuhld) **cry:** cry that is checked or stopped.

Vocabulary   **menace** (MEHN ihs) *n.:* danger, threat.

---

emergencies, particularly natural disasters, by estab-
lishing contact between people inside and outside
of affected areas when regular communications
systems are disabled.

Activity   Ask students what about ham radio may have
been suspicious to the neighbors of Maple Street. Have
students form small groups and discuss Steve's hobby.
Ask them to consider ham radio as a symbol of the unknown or of modern technology that the neighbors fear.

Think About/Talk About

 Comprehension

B Read and Discuss
*Possible response: Most are wary of
the Goodmans, and Charlie seems to
go after Steve, too. Steve calls Charlie
a "hanging judge," sentencing without
sufficient evidence, and Don attacks
Steve because Steve has a ham radio.
All are snipping at each other about
things that don't seem important or
rational.*

▶ **Analysis**

A Literary Focus
*Possible response: Steve notes that
once finger-pointing starts, anybody
can be the target of accusations.*

▶ **Extend the Discussion**
Comparing and Contrasting
Re-read the first column of p. 81.
Compare Steve's reaction to the
accusations against him to Mrs.
Brand's reaction. Why does each of
them react the way he or she does?
*Possible response: Steve is sarcastic
at first, saying he talks to green men
from outer space. He won't defend
himself because he knows that the
crowd wants to find an enemy and
defending himself won't make them
stop. Mrs. Brand tries to reason with
the crowd and defend Steve's ham
radio hobby. She defends Steve
because she's scared of what the
angry mob might do.*

Vocabulary: Own the Word
- **idiosyncrasy:** Write the word *idiosyncrasy* and its definition in a center circle on the board. Then draw
  "spider legs" from the center circle
  and have students suggest other
  related words. *Possible responses:
  quirk, odd habit, difference, unique*

- **menace:** Ask students: Would you
  want to be considered a *menace*? Why or why not? *Possible
  response: No, I would not want to be
  a menace. I don't want to be a danger to anyone.*

Read aloud the stage directions in the left column. Say: The stage directions are very effective here in adding to the suspense and the complications in the action of the play. The author uses the word "figure" so that the identity is hidden from the reader as well as the characters. This builds suspense and contributes to the complication of the shooting.

Guided Practice: Apply

Have a volunteer read the stage directions in the right column after letter C. Ask students to work with a partner to discuss how these stage directions add to the complications in the plot and the suspense. Ask for volunteers to explain.

up? What good would a shotgun do against—[*Now* CHARLIE *pulls the gun from* STEVE's *hand.*]

Charlie. No more talk, Steve. You're going to talk us into a grave! You'd let whatever's out there walk right over us, wouldn't yuh? Well, some of us won't!

[*He swings the gun around to point it toward the sidewalk. The dark figure continues to walk toward them. The group stands there, fearful, apprehensive. Mothers clutch children, men stand in front of wives.* CHARLIE *slowly raises the gun. As the figure gets closer and closer, he suddenly pulls the trigger. The sound of it explodes in the stillness. The figure suddenly lets out a small cry, stumbles forward onto his knees, and then falls forward on his face.* DON, CHARLIE, *and* STEVE *race over to him.* STEVE *is there first and turns the man over. Now the crowd gathers around them.*]

Steve (*slowly looks up*). It's Pete Van Horn.
Don (*in a hushed voice*). Pete Van Horn! He was just gonna go over to the next block to see if the power was on—
Woman One. You killed him, Charlie. You shot him dead!
Charlie (*looks around at the circle of faces, his eyes frightened, his face contorted*). But . . . but I didn't know who he was. I certainly didn't know who he was. He comes walkin' out of the darkness—how am I

supposed to know who he was? (*He grabs* STEVE.) Steve—you know why I shot! How was I supposed to know he wasn't a monster or something? (*He grabs* DON *now.*) We're all scared of the same thing. I was just tryin' to . . . tryin' to protect my home, that's all! Look, all of you, that's all I was tryin' to do. (*He looks down wildly at the body.*) I didn't know it was somebody we knew! I didn't know— **C**

[*There's a sudden hush and then an intake of breath. We see the living room window of* CHARLIE's *house. The window is not lit, but suddenly the house lights come on behind it.*]

Woman One (*in a very hushed voice*). Charlie . . . Charlie . . . the lights just went on in your house. Why did the lights just go on? **D**
Don. What about it, Charlie? How come you're the only one with lights now?
Goodman. That's what I'd like to know.

[*There is a pause as they all stare toward* CHARLIE.]

You were so quick to kill, Charlie, and you were so quick to tell us who we had to be careful of. Well, maybe you had to kill. Maybe Peter there was trying to tell us something. Maybe he'd found out something and came back to tell us who there was amongst us we should watch out for—

C | Read and Discuss | How do Charlie's actions <u>advance</u> the plot?

D | Reading Focus | Making Predictions How are the neighbors going to react to the lights going on in Charlie's house? How do you know?

Word-Attack Skills Mini-Lesson

Sounds of *ie* and *ei*
- Present this mnemonic poem:

  I before *e* except after *c*,
  And when pronounced *a*,
  As in *neighbor* and *weigh*.
- Explain that the poem helps you remember how most words with *ie* and *ei* are spelled, but it gives you only one clue about the sounds the letters stand for.
- Use the following words from the selection to explore the differing sounds of *ie* and *ei*. Write these sets

of words on the chalkboard without underlines. In two of the words in each set, *ie* or *ei* stands for the same sound; in one of the words, the letters stand for a sound that is different from the other two. Have students read each set and identify the word with the different sound.

Set 1	Set 2	Set 3
brief	weight	<u>series</u>
field	<u>either</u>	quiet
<u>friends</u>	neighbors	science

[CHARLIE *backs away from the group, his eyes wide with fright.*]

Charlie. No . . . no . . . it's nothing of the sort! I don't know why the lights are on. I swear I don't. Somebody's pulling a gag or something.

[*He bumps against* STEVE, *who grabs him and whirls him around.*]

Steve. A gag? A gag? Charlie, there's a dead man on the sidewalk and you killed him! Does this thing look like a gag to you?

[CHARLIE *breaks away and screams as he runs toward his house.*]

Charlie. No! No! Please!

[*A man breaks away from the crowd to chase* CHARLIE. *The man tackles him and lands on top of him. The other people start to run toward them.* CHARLIE *is up on his feet. He breaks away from the other man's grasp and lands a couple of desperate punches that push the man aside. Then he forces his way, fighting, through the crowd to once again break free. He jumps up on*

Analyzing Visuals **Connecting to the Text** What theme, or message, of the teleplay is hinted at in the photograph?

Analyzing Visuals

Connecting to the Text: *The photograph suggests that people in mobs are quick to choose an enemy and assign blame.*

Activity Write these sentences on the chalkboard. Have students identify the word that shares the vowel sound spelled with *ie* or *ei* in the underlined word.

1. Fear raced through the <u>neighborhood</u>. (space, field, light) [*space*]
2. Something <u>weird</u> was happening. (weigh, weary, wire) [*weary*]
3. A strange <u>series</u> of events scared them. (raid, streak, wild) [*streak*]
4. Ordinary people became a <u>fierce</u> mob. (fur, fiery, fear) [*fear*]

Think About/Talk About

▶ **Comprehension**

C Read and Discuss

Possible response: *By killing Pete Van Horn, Charlie has made the situation much worse.*

D Reading Focus

Possible response: *The neighbors will react with suspicion and accuse Charlie of being a monster. This is the way they reacted when Goodman's car started.*

▶ **Extend the Discussion**

Figures of Speech What does Charlie mean when he says someone is "pulling a gag" at the top of p. 83? Why do you think he says this? ***Possible response:*** *He means someone is playing a trick on him. He says this because he can't come up with any real reason why his lights went on just after he killed Van Horn.*

Motivation Why might Goodman hint at the bottom of p. 82 that Charlie killed Van Horn because he has something to hide? ***Possible response:*** *Goodman might be angry at Charlie for making him into a scapegoat. Laying the blame on Charlie now might be his way of seeking revenge.*

- Explain to students that an author may create **plot complications** in many ways, from environmental factors to character behaviors. In most cases, plot complications are resolved by the end of the story.

- Then, point out the narration from the two mysterious figures in the spaceship on pp. 85–86. It is not just a conversation between two creatures; it reveals how the strange events on Maple Street actually began. This information resolves the complications created by the prospect of alien invasion, and although the reader does not know what finally happens to the residents of Maple Street, it provides the resolution that the author wants readers to have. From the aliens' conversation, the reader can be reasonably assured that the people of Maple Street will destroy one another, just as their world will be destroyed by the alien-introduced self-destruction.

Guided Practice: Apply

Ask students to discuss in groups of three what they think the author uses this conversation to tell us, and why he places it at the very end of the story. Then, have students share their thoughts with the class.

---

his front porch. A rock thrown from the group smashes a window alongside of him, the broken glass flying past him. A couple of pieces cut him. He stands there perspiring, rumpled, blood running down from a cut on his cheek. His wife breaks away from the group to throw herself into his arms. He buries his face against her. We can see the crowd converging on the porch now.]

Voices.

It must have been him.
He's the one.
We got to get Charlie.

[Another rock lands on the porch. Now CHARLIE pushes his wife behind him, facing the group.]

Charlie. Look, look, I swear to you . . . it isn't me . . . but I do know who it is . . . I swear to you, I do know who it is. I know who the monster is here. I know who it is that doesn't belong. I swear to you I know.
Goodman (shouting). What are you waiting for?
Woman One (shouting). Come on, Charlie, come on.
Man One (shouting). Who is it, Charlie, tell us!
Don (pushing his way to the front of the crowd). All right, Charlie, let's hear it!

> "I swear to you, I do know who it is. I know who the monster is here."

[CHARLIE's eyes dart around wildly.]

Charlie. It's . . . it's . . .
Man Two (screaming). Go ahead, Charlie, tell us.
Charlie. It's . . . it's the kid. It's Tommy. He's the one.

[There's a gasp from the crowd as we cut to a shot of the mother holding her boy. The boy at first doesn't understand. Then, realizing the eyes are all on him, he buries his face against his mother, SALLY.]

Sally (backs away). That's crazy. That's crazy. He's a little boy.
Woman One. But he knew! He was the only one who knew! He told us all about it. Well, how did he know? How could he have known?

[The various people take this up and repeat the questions aloud.]

Voices.

How could he know?
Who told him?
Make the kid answer.

Man One. What about Goodman's car?
Don. It was Charlie who killed old man Van Horn.

ⓔ Literary Focus Plot Complications What have the residents decided about Tommy?

Vocabulary **converging** (kuhn VUR jihng) *v.* used as *adj.*: coming together.

Universal Access

ⓔⓛ English Learners

Students may have difficulty with the broken lines of dialogue in column 1 of p. 85. Explain that the writer used dashes and incomplete sentences to help readers understand that the characters are interrupting each other because they are frightened and angry about the situation. This section of dialogue is reflective of the plot complications because everyone on Maple Street wants to find and destroy the "enemy," but they all have different ideas on whom or what the enemy actually is. Enlist

the aid of fluent English speakers to read this section of the dialogue aloud so English learners can better relate the pacing and tone of this section to the complexity of plot events taking place.

Struggling Readers

Model evaluating the following prediction based on the story's conclusion: the noise and light were an alien spaceship crashing, and that aliens are about to invade Maple Street. You might say: we find out at the end that a space ship and space aliens are involved in the

Woman One. But it was the kid here who knew what was going to happen all the time. He was the one who knew!

[STEVE *shouts at his hysterical neighbors.*]

Steve. Are you all gone crazy? (*Pause as he looks about*) Stop.

[*A fist crashes at* STEVE's *face, staggering him back out of view. Several close camera shots suggest the coming of violence: A hand fires a rifle. A fist clenches. A hand grabs the hammer from* VAN HORN's *body, etc.*]

Don. Charlie has to be the one— Where's my rifle—
Woman One. Les Goodman's the one. His car started! Let's wreck it.
Mrs. Goodman. What about Steve's radio— He's the one that called them—
Mr. Goodman. Smash the radio. Get me a hammer. Get me something.
Steve. Stop— Stop—
Charlie. Where's that kid— Let's get him.
Man One. Get Steve— Get Charlie— They're working together.

[*The crowd starts to converge around the mother, who grabs her son and starts to run with him. The crowd starts to follow, at first, walking fast, and then running after him. Suddenly,* CHARLIE's *lights go off and the lights in another house go on. They stay on for a moment, then from across the street other lights go on and then off again.*]

F Read and Discuss | Now what is developing?

Man One (*shouting*). It isn't the kid. . . . It's Bob Weaver's house.
Woman One. It isn't Bob Weaver's house, it's Don Martin's place.
Charlie. I tell you, it's the kid.
Don. It's Charlie. He's the one.

[*The people shout, accuse, scream. The camera tilts back and forth. We see panic-stricken faces in close-up and tilting shots of houses as the lights go on and off. Slowly, in the middle of this nightmarish morass[6] of sight and sound, the camera starts to pull away, until once again we've reached the opening shot, looking at the Maple Street sign from high above. The camera continues to move away until we dissolve to a shot of the metal side of a spacecraft, which sits shrouded[7] in darkness. An open door throws out a beam of light from the illuminated interior. Two figures silhouetted against the bright lights appear. We get only a vague feeling of form, but nothing more explicit than that.*] **F**

Figure One. Understand the procedure now? Just stop a few of their machines and radios and telephones and lawn mowers . . . throw them into darkness for a few hours and then you just sit back and watch the pattern.
Figure Two. And this pattern is always the same?
Figure One. With few variations. They pick the most dangerous enemy they can

---

6. morass (muh RAS): confusing situation. Strictly speaking, a morass is a kind of swamp.
7. shrouded (SHROWD uhd): hidden; covered.

The Monsters Are Due on Maple Street, Act Two **85**

Think About/Talk About

▶ Comprehension

F **Read and Discuss**
Possible response: *Tommy, Charlie, Steve, Les, Bob and Don are all accused of being the "monster" as lights in their houses go on and off. A spacecraft opens and two figures appear.*

▶ Analysis

E **Literary Focus**
Possible response: *The crowd has decided that Tommy is the secret alien invader in their midst.*

▶ Extend the Discussion

Evaluating On p. 84, Woman One argues that "the kid" knew what was going to happen, but on p. 85 she proclaims that "Les Goodman's the one." What does this behavior suggest? **Possible response:** *The neighbors are extremely fickle and irrational; they can go from blaming one person to demonizing another in seconds without any evidence at all.*

Vocabulary: Own the Word

converging: With one or two student volunteers, demonstrate what *converging* is. Explain that you are all approaching the same place at once.

---

chaos on Maple Street, but it is not because they invaded or crashed. This prediction is somewhat accurate, because I predicted that space aliens and a spaceship were involved in the story, though not in the way I expected. Have students work in pairs to evaluate other predictions made during their reading of the story.

Students Who Use African American Vernacular English

English for Academic Success Some students may struggle with the pronunciation of the *th* digraph, as in

this, *that*, or *birthday*. Explain to students that in informal English, the th letter combination may be voiced as /f/ or /v/. In formal English, though, the *th* combination is pronounced /th/. Have students locate the words *they're*, *then*, *that*, *them* on p. 85, and pronounce them using formal English.

✔ For additional instruction and strategies, see Holt Pronunciation Resources and ThinkCentral, Teacher Access.

Think About/Talk About

 Comprehension

Reading Focus

Possible response: I did not predict that there actually were aliens who caused the blackout. I thought there would be a rational explanation for what happened.

 Analysis

Literary Focus

Possible response: It's revealed that aliens caused the humans to become suspicious and attack each other. The narrator warns that prejudice and suspicion are dangerous weapons that exist in the real world, not just in science fiction.

 Extend the Discussion

Author's Purpose Read the Narrator's closing monologue and think about the time period during which this teleplay was written. Why might the author have chosen to close the teleplay with this speech?

Possible response: The author might be warning his audience about the dangers of McCarthyism, which was characterized by prejudice and suspicion. He might want people to think about the harm that they can cause in their communities, even if outside enemies never attack.

Monitor Students' Comprehension

Guide the class in answering these comprehension questions.

1. What strange thing happens on Maple Street at the beginning of the play? [*People hear a loud roar, and then the power goes out.*]

2. Why do people grow suspicious of Les Goodman? [*His car engine starts by itself.*]

3. How do the aliens plan to conquer Earth? [*They are going to instill fear in the humans and let them destroy themselves, just like they did on Maple Street.*]

---

find . . . and it's themselves. And all we need do is sit back . . . and watch.
Figure Two. Then I take it this place . . . this Maple Street . . . is not unique.
Figure One (*shaking his head*). By no means. Their world is full of Maple Streets. And we'll go from one to the other and let them destroy themselves. One to the other . . . one to the other . . . one to the other— **G**

[*Now the camera pans up for a shot of the starry sky.*]

G **Reading Focus** **Making Predictions** <u>Explain</u> whether you predicted this turn of events. If you did, what clues led you to your prediction? If not, what did you think would happen instead?

Narrator's Voice. The tools of conquest do not necessarily come with bombs and explosions and fallout. There are weapons that are simply thoughts, attitudes, prejudices—to be found only in the minds of men. For the record, prejudices can kill and suspicion can destroy, and a thoughtless, frightened search for a scapegoat has a fallout all of its own for the children . . . the children yet unborn. (*A pause*) And the pity of it is . . . that these things cannot be confined to . . . The Twilight Zone! **H**

[*Fade to black.*]

H **Literary Focus** **Plot Complications** How are the complications in the teleplay resolved?

 California Standards, pp. 87–89

- **Reading Standard 1.3** Clarify word meanings through the use of definition, example, restatement, or contrast.
- **Reading Standard 3.2** Identify events that advance the plot and determine how each event explains past or present action(s) or foreshadows future action(s).

Applying Your Skills

The Monsters Are Due on Maple Street, Act Two

Literary Response and Analysis

Reading Skills Focus
Quick Check

1. How does Charlie respond to Pete Van Horn's reappearance?

2. What do you learn about the real cause of the situation on Maple Street? How is it part of a larger plan?

Read with a Purpose

3. How—and why—does the situation on Maple Street continue to get out of control?

Reading Skills: Making Predictions

4. Complete your prediction chart, indicating which of your predictions came true and which did not. Which plot events in this teleplay surprised you? Why do you think you didn't predict those events?

Clue	My Prediction	Yes/No
Maple Street Maple Street residents think they see a meteor but don't hear it crash.	It might not be a meteor at all.	

Literary Skills Focus
Literary Analysis

5. **Analyze** According to the aliens, who is the most dangerous enemy? Who are the real "monsters" in the teleplay?

6. **Analyze** Writers often voice their opinions through a particular character. Which character seems to reflect Rod Serling's point of view? What makes you think so?

7. **Evaluate/Connect** Why might the message of this 1960 teleplay still be important today?

8. **Connect** Think about the odd occurrences that the Maple Street residents witnessed. How would you behave if you were faced with a <u>similar</u> situation?

9. **Extend** The narrator concludes the story by saying that "prejudices can kill and suspicion can destroy." What events do you know from history that prove this to be true?

Literary Skills: Plot Complications

10. **Evaluate** List the most important events that <u>advance</u> the teleplay's **plot**. How do the key **complications** build on each other, leading to the surprising way that the conflicts are finally resolved?

Literary Skills Review: Symbol

11. **Interpret** In literature, **symbols** are persons, places, or things that stand for larger ideas, such as love or honor. Consider when Maple Street lost power and was plunged into darkness. How can this loss of power be seen as a **symbol** for a larger idea? What is that idea?

Writing Skills Focus
Think as a Reader/Writer

Use It in Your Writing Write a paragraph <u>explaining</u> what this story has taught you about the use of authentic dialogue.

 What Do You Think Now

Explain whether you think fear or facts cause more confusion in dangerous situations. Give examples from real life or the teleplay.

Independent Practice
Vocabulary Development

Your Turn _____

1. *converging*

2. *menace*

3. *idiosyncrasy*

English for Academic Success
Language Coach

Explain that the prefix *con-* can mean "with" or "together." Tell students that a *confederation* occurs when people come together to form an alliance, and that to *concoct* can mean "to devise by bringing together." The neighbors formed a *confederation* to accuse Les Goodman; the aliens *concocted* a plan to cause the humans to destroy themselves.

English for Academic Success
Academic Vocabulary

Possible response: *In* The Monsters Are Due on Maple Street, *Serling* explains *that fear and suspicion can have* significant, *dangerous consequences. When the characters begin to fear an alien invasion, they interact with each other in a suspicious, blameful, and paranoid way. Conflicts are not resolved rationally, a man is killed, and chaos reigns. This is* similar *to what happened in the United States in the 1940s and 1950s when people were accused of Communism.*

Applying Your Skills

The Monsters Are Due on Maple Street

Vocabulary Development
Clarifying Word Meanings: Definitions

Writers often help readers understand difficult words by using **definitions.** This means that the word's meaning is provided within the sentence. Let's look at the following sentence:

> In this brief fraction of a moment they take the first step toward a metamorphosis that changes people from a group into a mob.

A reader who does not understand the word *metamorphosis* would benefit from the second half of the sentence. A metamorphosis is a change of form, substance, or structure. In this story the people of Maple Street change "from a group into a mob."

Look for definitions in the text itself. If you read a little past a difficult word, you will often find that the writer has given you some help.

Your Turn _____

Choose the Vocabulary word at right that best fits the blank in each sentence below. Remember to look for definitions within each sentence to help you decide.

> transfixed
> intimidated
> defiant
> idiosyncrasy
> menace
> converging

1. During the second act the crowd's fear, mistrust, and suspicion are _____ , or meeting, to create a mob.

2. A frightened man with a gun can be considered a _____ and a danger to society.

3. Steve's interest in ham radios becomes a threat rather than an oddity, or _____ , that makes him unique.

Language Coach

Prefixes Think about the meaning of the prefix *con–*. How is the meaning of the prefix evident in the word *concoct*? *confederation*?

Academic Vocabulary

Write About . . .

What message does Serling convey in *The Monsters Are Due on Maple Street*? Why is this message <u>significant</u>? Support your answers with details from the teleplay and examples from <u>similar</u> situations—in real life or in other stories—that demonstrate the importance of the teleplay's message. Use the Academic Vocabulary words from this chapter in your response.

Universal Access: Vocabulary Development

EL English Learners/ Struggling Writers

English for Academic Success Students may understand the definitions of the selection vocabulary but have difficulty using these words in speech or writing. Pair English learners with fluent speakers to discuss a current event regarding a dangerous situation.

Ask students to use each vocabulary word at least once. Invite pairs to share their current event discussion with the class.

✔ For more practice, see the Vocabulary Skill Builder in **UA: Differentiating Instruction.**

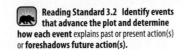

Reading Standard 3.2 Identify events that advance the plot and determine how each event explains past or present action(s) or foreshadows future action(s).

Grammar Link
Pronouns Can Be Problems

Pronouns used in compound structures can be confusing. Which of these sentences is correct?

> **Dad talked to Mom and *me*.**

> **Dad talked to Mom and *I*.**

Mom and me and *Mom and I* are compound structures. When you proofread your own writing, you can use this trick to decide which pronoun is correct: Say the sentence aloud as if it contained only one pronoun, not a compound structure. Let your ear tell you which one sounds right.

TEST **Dad talked to me.** [sounds right]
> **Dad talked to I.** [sounds wrong]

CORRECT **Dad talked to Mom and *me*.**

Your Turn

In the following sentences, choose the correct pronoun.

1. *He/Him* and Steve decided to walk into town to figure out the cause of the power failure.
2. When Tommy first told the crowd what he was thinking, everyone thought *he/him* was crazy.
3. After his car started by itself, Les Goodman was accused by *they/them*.
4. The crowd demanded explanations from Steve and *she/her*.
5. They warned Charlie not to shoot, but *he/him* didn't listen.

CHOICES

As you respond to the Choices, use these **Academic Vocabulary** words as appropriate: <u>advance</u>, <u>explain</u>, <u>significant</u>, <u>similar</u>.

REVIEW
Analyze the Final Scene

Timed ⏱ Writing In the final scene, two new characters are introduced, and the narrator concludes with a powerful message about human beings. In one paragraph, summarize the conversation between Figure One and Figure Two and the narrator's message. In a second paragraph, analyze how this scene <u>explains</u> the actions that precede it—especially the characters' responses to the unexplainable events.

CONNECT
Act It Out

Picture a different ending to the teleplay—instead of leaving the people to destroy each other, the aliens land. How would the residents respond? What new complications might arise? How would the situation be resolved? As a class, act out this new scene.

EXTEND
Give a Multimedia Presentation

TechFocus Create a multimedia presentation on an aspect of *The Monsters Are Due on Maple Street*, such as McCarthyism or the lasting influence of the television show *The Twilight Zone*. Research your topic on the Internet. Then, give a presentation to the class. Include audio and visual features that relate to the topic.

 Learn It Online
Create an eye-popping multimedia presentation! Visit MediaScope at:

go.hrw.com | H7-89 | **Go**

Universal Access: Grammar Link

English for Academic Success Explain to students that when you use a pronoun and a proper noun together, it is said to be a compound structure. Using compound structure eliminates the use of short, repetitive sentences. It can be difficult to determine which pronoun to use. Tell students that one method of determining correct pronoun use in a compound structure is to read or write the sentence with each of the individual pronouns or nouns by itself. Model using the sentence, "Margaret and me went to the science fair." Write the sentence on the board with each subject: "Margaret went to the science

fair." "Me went to the science fair." Read each aloud, and ask: would you say "me went to the science fair"? Students should recognize that this is incorrect. Students should recognize that "I went to the science fair" would be the correct expression to use in this case. Tell students to apply this test whenever they are unsure of the correct pronoun to use in a compound structure.

✔ For more practice with using pronouns, see **Warriner's Handbook, Language Handbook Worksheets** and **Grammar Notes**.

Plot in Science Fiction Stories

Standards Focus

Objectives

Students will
- understand science fiction
- compare and contrast the plots of science-fiction stories

Motivate

What Do You Think?/QuickWrite

Ask students to use the QuickWrite to discuss a beneficial invention and a harmful invention. Have students discuss in their **Reader/Writer Notebook** clues that might indicate that an situation could cause harm.

English for Academic Success

Academic Vocabulary

Look for opportunities to use the Academic Vocabulary words in the chapter.

- **significant, *adj.*:** important
- **similar, *adj.*:** almost the same
- **explain, *v.*:** give reasons for; make understandable
- **advance, *v.*:** move forward

Analyzing Visuals

Use **ThinkCentral, Teacher Access** to project this image for viewing.

Extension Activity Point out that the picture shows different views of the same images, such as different aspects of the man. Ask students to discuss what they think these views might symbolize. ***Possible response:*** *Everything has an opposite; there are two perspectives to every situation.*

 California Standards,
pp. 90–103

■ **Reading Standard 3.2** Identify events that advance the plot and determine how each event explains past or present action(s) or foreshadows future action(s).

CONTENTS

Magritte and the Spies (1971)
by Equipo Cronica (The Cronica Group).
Acrylic on canvas.
©Equipo Cronica (The Cronica Group)/Artists
Rights Society (ARS) New York.

What Do You Think How can you tell when a situation may be dangerous? What clues do you look for?

QuickWrite
Think of two scientific inventions: something that has been a great benefit, and something that has had terrible consequences. What does each reveal about human nature?

Comparing Texts Resources

Chapter 1 Resources, on-level practice and assessment, p. 33

Teacher One Stop™, on-level lesson plans and all print resources

Holt Audio Library: Selections and Summaries in Spanish

UA: Supporting Instruction in Five Languages, selection summary

ThinkCentral Online Assessment, Selection Standards Check

ThinkCentral Online Remediation

Preparing to Read

Zoo / He—y, Come on Ou—t!

Literary Skills Focus

Plot in Science Fiction **Plot** is the series of related events that make up a story. **Science fiction**—lying somewhere between realistic fiction and total fantasy—provides a fascinating environment in which plot events can unfold. The plots of science fiction stories often deal with **conflict** between very different cultures or beings (such as humans and aliens) and may contain these elements:

- a **setting** in the future, on another planet, or in a spaceship
- **technology** that has not yet been invented
- a **journey** through time or to a distant planet or galaxy
- **characters** from outer space—aliens or extraterrestrials
- realistic human reactions to **fantastic situations** and conflicts

Reading Skills Focus

Comparing and Contrasting Science Fiction Plots In a chart like the one below, record plot details about each story.

	"Zoo"	"He—y, Come On Ou—t"!
Human characters		
Alien characters		
Journey		
Futuristic technology		
Lesson about life		

Writing Skills Focus

Think as a Reader/Writer

Find It in Your Reading These stories describe worlds that are quite unlike the one in which we live. Record in your *Reader/Writer Notebook* the details that make the setting of each story unusual.

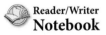
Reader/Writer Notebook
Use your **RWN** to complete the activities for these selections.

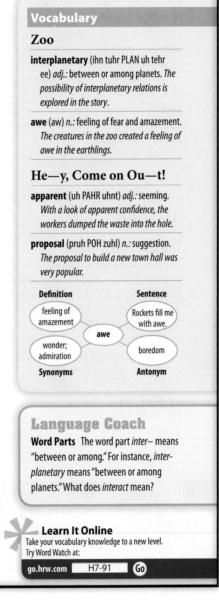

Vocabulary

Zoo

interplanetary (ihn tuhr PLAN uh tehr ee) *adj.*: between or among planets. *The possibility of interplanetary relations is explored in the story.*

awe (aw) *n.*: feeling of fear and amazement. *The creatures in the zoo created a feeling of awe in the earthlings.*

He—y, Come on Ou—t!

apparent (uh PAHR uhnt) *adj.*: seeming. *With a look of apparent confidence, the workers dumped the waste into the hole.*

proposal (pruh POH zuhl) *n.*: suggestion. *The proposal to build a new town hall was very popular.*

Definition — feeling of amazement

Sentence — Rockets fill me with awe.

awe

Synonyms — wonder; admiration

Antonym — boredom

Language Coach

Word Parts The word part *inter*– means "between or among." For instance, *interplanetary* means "between or among planets." What does *interact* mean?

 Learn It Online
Take your vocabulary knowledge to a new level. Try Word Watch at:

go.hrw.com   H7-91   **Go**

Introducing Vocabulary

Read aloud the Vocabulary words and sample sentences. Then, use the following questions to check students' understanding.

1. What type of story might discuss **interplanetary** travel? [*science fiction*]
2. What might someone in a state of **awe** look like? [*impressed*]
3. How might it become **apparent** that someone did not hear you? [*They do not look up when you speak to them.*]
4. What kind of **proposal** would interest a gardener? [*planting flowers in an empty lot*]

English for Academic Success

Language Coach

After students discuss the meaning of *interact*, ask them if they are familiar with any other words using the prefix *inter-*. What do they mean? [*To interact is to communicate.*]

Literary Skills Focus

As you read the story, remind students that while science fiction is filled with fantastic situations, it also contains many familiar situations. Ask students to record what is familiar even in the fantastic settings.

Reading Skills Focus

Give students a copy of the Reading Skills Focus graphic organizer before they read. Tell them to use their responses to answer the questions on the Applying Your Skills page.

Writing Skills Focus

Have students record descriptive setting details in their **Reader/Writer Notebook.**

 Learn It Online
Send students to **Word Watch** for audio pronunciations, synonyms and antonyms, and brief histories of word origins.

go.hrw.com   H7-91   **Go**

Selection Introduction

More About the Writers

- Award-winning author **Edward D. Hoch** has been honored with an Edgar for Best Short Story and a Grandmaster Award. He has also been recognized for his mysteries by the Private Eyes Writers of America and the Bouchercon.

- **Shinichi Hoshi** was first published in the science fiction magazine *Hōseki (The Jewel)*.

Think About the Writers

Discuss the characteristics of science fiction with students. What do they find appealing or interesting about this genre? Why do they think authors like Hoch and Hoshi enjoy writing about it?

🕐 For Independent Reading

- If students enjoyed the science fiction aspect of these stories, they might like Michael Cart's collection of short stories, *Tomorrowland: Ten Stories about the Future,* which includes works from Katherine Paterson, Lois Lowry, and Jon Scieszka.

- In *A Wrinkle in Time* by Madeleine L'Engle, a scientist disappears and his two children, Meg and Charles, must travel through space and time to find him.

MEET THE WRITERS

Edward D. Hoch
(1930–   )

A Mystery Himself

Edward Hoch, whose name rhymes with "coke," was born in Rochester, New York. He has been a full-time writer since 1968, publishing novels and short stories and editing collections in the genres of mystery, crime, suspense, science fiction, and fantasy. Hoch has contributed more than 750 short stories to a long list of publications. This prolific writer is a bit of a mystery himself. To find all of his work, you have to search under his many pseudonyms, or pen names, such as Irwin Booth, Anthony Circus, Stephen Dentinger, Pat McMahon, Mister X, R. E. Porter, and R. L. Stevens.

Shinichi Hoshi
(1926–1997)

The Short-Short Story

Shinichi Hoshi is well known in Japan for his quirky imagination and intriguing science fiction stories, many of which end with a surprising twist. As a young writer, Hoshi set out to write one thousand and one stories, as in the famous story collection *The Arabian Nights* (which was originally titled *The Thousand and One Nights*). Once he reached his goal, Hoshi said, "One thousand and one stories are enough."

Think About the Writers What do you think draws some writers to science fiction?

Preview the Selections

"Zoo" introduces you to **Professor Hugo,** a man who keeps the strangest of species on display for earthlings to see.

In "He—y, Come on Ou—t!" you'll meet a group of **villagers** who are trying to decide what to do about a hole that appeared in the wake of a typhoon.

ZOO

by **Edward D. Hoch**

Read with a Purpose
Read this science fiction story to discover one writer's ideas about zoos of the future.

Build Background
Zoos have existed for a very long time. In fact, researchers believe the first zoos were created in about 4500 B.C. Until recently, most animals in zoos were kept in cages. Today, with more awareness of animals' needs, zookeepers try to replicate natural habitats in order to make animals more comfortable.

The children were always good during the month of August, especially when it began to get near the twenty-third. It was on this day that Professor Hugo's Interplanetary Zoo settled down for its annual six-hour visit to the Chicago area. Ⓐ

Before daybreak the crowds would form, long lines of children and adults both, each one clutching his or her dollar and waiting with wonderment to see what race of strange creatures the professor had brought this year.

In the past they had sometimes been treated to three-legged creatures from Venus, or tall, thin men from Mars, or even snakelike horrors from somewhere more distant. This year, as the great round ship settled slowly to Earth in the huge tri-city parking area just outside of Chicago, they watched with awe as the sides slowly slid up to reveal the familiar barred cages. In them were some wild breed of nightmare—small, horselike animals that moved with quick, jerking motions and constantly chattered in a high-pitched tongue. The citizens of Earth clustered around as Professor Hugo's crew quickly collected the waiting dollars, and soon the good professor himself made an appearance, wearing his many-colored rainbow cape and top hat. "Peoples of Earth," he called into his microphone.

Ⓐ **Literary Focus** Plot in Science Fiction What clue in the first paragraph suggests that this story is science fiction?

Vocabulary **interplanetary** (ihn tuhr PLAN uh tehr ee) *adj.:* between or among planets.
awe (aw) *n.:* feeling of fear and amazement.

Selection Readability	
Easily Accessible **Accessible** **Challenging**	sentences with embedded phrases, futuristic theme

Selection Plot Summary
In the distant future, a crowd comes to see the strange creatures that a traveling circus has brought from throughout the universe. Months later, the creatures return to their planet and tell of the amazing beings they saw on Earth.

- Ask students to name words or phrases that come to mind when they hear the term **science fiction.** Student responses will likely include aliens, spaceships, and monsters.

- Explain that science fiction often, but not always, includes aliens, spaceships, or space travel. Most science fiction has a basis in reality, but involves fantastical events that have never happened, such as time travel, or inventions that do not yet exist, such as mind-scrambler rays.

- Note that, in paragraph 1 on p. 94, Professor Hugo is talking about a planet called Kaan, that is inhabited by horse-spider people. Of course, scientists have never found such a planet or any horse-spider people. But there are many planets and much space in the universe, and the writer used these facts to create a fictional planet and species for the story.

Guided Practice: Apply

Turn and Talk Have students scan the page independently for other ideas, inventions, or creatures that have a scientific element and are not known to exist or to be possible. Then, have students compare lists with a partner and discuss how these elements relate to the science fiction criteria on the Preparing to Read page.

The crowd's noise died down and he continued. "Peoples of Earth, this year you see a real treat for your single dollar—the little-known horse-spider people of Kaan—brought to you across a million miles of space at great expense. Gather around, see them, study them, listen to them, tell your friends about them. But hurry! My ship can remain here only six hours!"

And the crowds slowly filed by, at once horrified and fascinated by these strange creatures that looked like horses but ran up the walls of their cages like spiders. "This is certainly worth a dollar," one man remarked, hurrying away. "I'm going home to get the wife." **B**

All day long it went like that, until ten thousand people had filed by the barred cages set into the side of the spaceship. Then, as the six-hour limit ran out, Professor Hugo once more took the microphone in hand. "We must go now, but we will return next year on this date. And if you enjoyed our zoo this year, telephone your friends in other cities about it. We will land in New York tomorrow, and next week on to London, Paris, Rome, Hong Kong, and Tokyo. Then on to other worlds!"

He waved farewell to them, and as the ship rose from the ground, the Earth peoples agreed that this had been the very best Zoo yet. . . .

> "It was the very best zoo ever...."

Some two months and three planets later, the silver ship of Professor Hugo settled at last onto the familiar jagged rocks of Kaan, and the odd horse-spider creatures filed quickly out of their cages. Professor Hugo was there to say a few parting words, and then they scurried away in a hundred different directions, seeking their homes among the rocks.

In one house, the she-creature was happy to see the return of her mate and offspring. She babbled a greeting in the strange tongue and hurried to embrace them. "It was a long time you were gone! Was it good?"

And the he-creature nodded. "The little one enjoyed it especially. We visited eight worlds and saw many things."

The little one ran up the wall of the cave. "On the place called Earth it was the best. The creatures there wear garments over their skins, and they walk on two legs."

"But isn't it dangerous?" asked the she-creature.

"No," her mate answered. "There are bars to protect us from them. We remain right in the ship. Next time you must come with us. It is well worth the nineteen commocs it costs."

And the little one nodded. "It was the very best zoo ever. . . ." **C**

B | **Literary Focus** Plot in Science Fiction How might the present event of seeing the horse-spider creatures determine the humans' future actions? How are the humans' reactions <u>similar</u> to how people today react to zoo animals?

C | **Read and Discuss** What happens at the end?

Universal Access

English Learners
Help students comprehend science fiction by having them analyze the image on p. 95. Discuss elements of science fiction that appear in the picture.

Struggling Readers
Benchmark Students Tell students that not every science fiction story uses the same elements of science fiction, such as spaceships. Explain that, when comparing science fiction stories and their plots, they should consider: the setting in which story events occur, who the characters are and where they come from, and what fantastical situations or technology they face.

Advanced Learners
Extension Have students identify features of the science fiction genre and plot in science fiction. Then, ask students to take a familiar folk story or fairy tale and rework it to incorporate elements of science fiction.

Students with Disabilities
Read the selection aloud to students, pausing as you read to identify elements of science fiction for students.

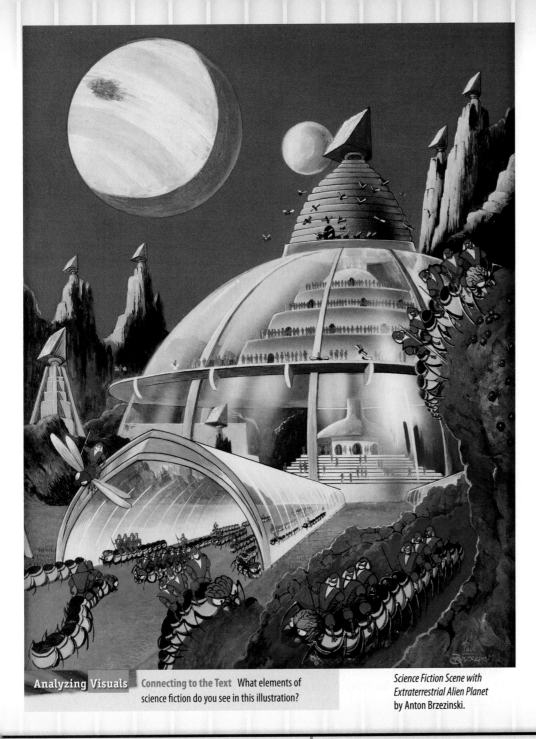

Analyzing Visuals | **Connecting to the Text** What elements of science fiction do you see in this illustration?

Science Fiction Scene with Extraterrestrial Alien Planet by Anton Brzezinski.

![California bear icon] **California Standards, p. 96**

■ **Reading Standard 3.2** Identify events that advance the plot and determine how each event explains past or present action(s) or foreshadows future action(s).

Analyzing Visuals

Connecting to the Text: *This picture contains space aliens, a different planet, a different universe, and buildings that seem to contain futuristic technology.*

Think About/Talk About
See page 95 of the Student Edition for questions relating to these answers.

▶ **Comprehension**

C Read and Discuss

Possible response: *When the horse-spider people return home, they tell about the strange worlds they've seen with creatures who were behind bars and walked on two legs.*

▶ **Analysis**

B Literary Focus

Possible response: *The humans are amazed by how the creatures look and act, like people at zoos today. They will probably want to come see the zoo again.*

▶ **Extend the Discussion**

Key Details Read the second column. What do the descriptions of the horse-spider creatures suggest about life on other planets? ***Possible response:*** *Even though they look different and speak another language, the aliens' behavior is very similar to that of humans.*

Author's Purpose Why do you think the author shows us at the end that the aliens think they are the visitors and the people and creatures outside the ship are the zoo animals? ***Possible response:*** *The author is trying to express the larger idea that any situation can be viewed in more than one way, depending on your perspective.*

Monitor Students' Comprehension
Guide the class in answering these comprehension questions.

1. Who is Professor Hugo and what does he do? [*He is a scientist who runs an interplanetary zoo.*]

2. What happens when the ship returns to Kaan? [*The horse-spider people talk about their trip to the zoo.*]

Zoo **95**

Independent Practice

Reading Skills Focus

Answers:

1. *Story maps should cover the characters, settings, conflict, major events, and resolution.*

2. *Yes, because people often react this way to people or creatures who are different.*

3. *The story features creatures from other planets. It teaches that there are perspectives different from your own.*

Vocabulary Check

Possible responses:

4. *I think it will be possible in a few decades, because of our quickly developing technology.*

5. *I would be amazed at the ability to view the entire world from outer space.*

Literary Skills Focus

Possible responses:

6. *They want to go to the zoo, which always arrives in August.*

7. *The reader would get the perspective of the creatures of Kaan first, and the ending of the story would hold less surprise.*

8. *The bars would protect them from one another.*

9. *At first I thought Professor Hugo was mistreating the creatures by displaying them, but it was a clever way to make money from both groups.*

10. *This is a good science fiction story because it deals with realistic human behaviors in an unexpected, fantastic situation and contains a surprise ending. It is shorter than most science fiction stories, with a lot fewer characters.*

11. *The author does not reveal the aliens' view until the end.*

Applying Your Skills

Zoo

Literary Response and Analysis

Reading Skills Focus
Quick Check

1. Use the following story map to outline the main events that advance this story's plot.

Characters: Setting:

Problem/Conflict:

Major Events:
1.
2.
(Add on as many as you need.)

Ending/Resolution:

Read with a Purpose

2. Explain whether the humans' reactions to the horse-spider people of Kaan are believable.

Reading Skills: Comparing and Contrasting Science Fiction Plots

3. Review your comparison-contrast chart. Which plot elements most strongly indicate that this is a science fiction story? What lesson about life does "Zoo" teach?

✓ **Vocabulary Check**

4. When do you think **interplanetary** travel will be possible? Explain.

5. How might the view of Earth from outer space fill you with **awe**? Explain.

Literary Skills Focus
Literary Analysis

6. **Infer** What past action has caused the children to be "always good during the month of August"?

7. **Analyze** The plot of "Zoo" has two parts and two settings. What if the first part were set on Kaan and the second part were set on Earth? How would this reversal change the story?

8. **Analyze** What did both groups, the people of Earth and the horse-spider people, believe to be the purpose of the bars?

9. **Evaluate** How does your opinion of Professor Hugo change from the beginning of the story to the end?

10. **Evaluate** Review the information you have collected in your chart for this story. Do you think this is a good science fiction story? Why or why not? How does it compare with other science fiction stories you know from books, television, or film?

Literary Skills: Plot in Science Fiction

11. **Analyze** How does the author manipulate the story's plot to develop an ending that is both surprising and humorous?

Writing Skills Focus
Think as a Reader/Writer

Use It in Your Writing Look over some of the details you recorded from "Zoo." Which details about the setting struck you as being the most vivid? Write a paragraph explaining why these details about setting made the story come alive for you.

Universal Access

Struggling Writers
Some students may need additional scaffolding to complete the Writing Skills Focus activity. Have students choose one detail and explain to a partner why it was useful to them in visualizing the setting. Then, have them write what they said in paragraph form to hand in.

HE—Y, COME ON OU—T!

by **Shinichi Hoshi**

Read with a Purpose Read the following selection to see how villagers react to a strange and surprising discovery.

Preparing to Read for this selection is on page 91.

Build Background

The plot events of "He—y, Come on Ou—t!" take place in a fishing village in Japan. The Japan fishing industry is one of the largest and most successful in the world. However, Japanese waters are plagued by pollution and environmental problems.

The typhoon had passed and the sky was a gorgeous blue. Even a certain village not far from the city had suffered damage. A little distance from the village and near the mountains, a small shrine had been swept away by a landslide.

"I wonder how long that shrine's been here."

"Well, in any case, it must have been here since an awfully long time ago."

"We've got to rebuild it right away."

While the villagers exchanged views, several more of their number came over.

"It sure was wrecked."

"I think it used to be right here."

"No, looks like it was a little more over there."

Just then one of them raised his voice. "Hey what in the world is this hole?"

Where they had all gathered there was a hole about a meter[1] in diameter. They peered in, but it was so dark nothing could be seen. However, it gave one the feeling that it was so deep it went clear through to the center of the earth.

There was even one person who said, "I wonder if it's a fox's hole."

"He—y, come on ou—t!" shouted a young man into the hole. There was no echo from the bottom. Next he picked up a pebble and was about to throw it in.

---

1. **meter** (MEE tuhr): measurement; three feet three inches.

(A) Literary Focus Plot in Science Fiction What is significant about the setting? How might it affect the plot?

(B) Read and Discuss What is going on in this village?

Selection Readability	
Easily Accessible	complex theme; challenging setting
Accessible	
Challenging	

Selection Plot Summary

Villagers notice a deep, wide hole in the ground one day. Soon they are using the hole to dispose of anything they don't want to think about, from nuclear waste to old diaries. The society remains oblivious to the damage it has done or what could be in the hole.

Model the Skill

■ Remind students that **science fiction** stories involve fantastical but believable creatures, inventions, and events. Though many science fiction stories are set in outer space, many other science fiction stories are not.

■ Point out that this story is different from "Zoo" because the setting appears to be a traditional village. It is not filled with futuristic references to planets and fantastic creatures. However, there is a giant hole that appears out of nowhere and does not echo when objects are thrown into it. Most holes, even deep ones, have an echo. This suggests that there is something very unusual about the hole, which is a characteristic of a science fiction story.

Guided Practice: Apply

Ask students what, besides the lack of an echo, makes this hole fantastical and different from most other holes in the ground. Why are these characteristics important? Suggest that students consider appearance and actions as they answer this question.

Think as a Reader/Writer

Find It in Your Reading Point out how in paragraph 5 on p. 98, the writer uses an element of science fiction—an unusual, fantastic property of the hole—when the hole swallows up a cord that is lowered into it.

Use It in Your Writing Have students write a sentence describing a fantastical object, or an ordinary object with fantastic properties.

"You might bring down a curse on us. Lay off," warned an old man, but the younger one energetically threw the pebble in. As before, however, there was no answering response from the bottom. The villagers cut down some trees, tied them with rope and made a fence which they put around the hole. Then they repaired[2] to the village. **C**

"What do you suppose we ought to do?"

"Shouldn't we build the shrine up just as it was over the hole?"

A day passed with no agreement. The news traveled fast, and a car from the newspaper company rushed over. In no time a

scientist came out, and with an all-knowing expression on his face he went over to the hole. Next, a bunch of gawking curiosity seekers showed up; one could also pick out here and there men of shifty glances who appeared to be concessionaires.[3] Concerned that someone might fall into the hole, a policeman from the local substation kept a careful watch.

One newspaper reporter tied a weight to the end of a long cord and lowered it into the hole. A long way down it went. The cord ran out, however, and he tried to

---

2. **repaired** (rih PAIRD): here, returned as a group.

3. **concessionaires** (kuhn sehsh uh NAIRZ): businesspeople.

C [Read and Discuss] What is happening now? What do the people think of this discovery?

Analyzing Visuals **Connecting to the Text** How does this image compare with the image of the hole you have visualized, or formed in your mind?

Universal Access

Struggling Readers

Guide students in comparing and contrasting the plots of science fiction stories. Have students think about the horse-spider creatures of Kaan and the mysterious hole. Both are strange and unfamiliar to the people who view them. An unusual phenomenon is one characteristic of a science fiction story. Remind students that the plots of science fiction stories frequently involve human reactions to fantastic situations. Both authors emphasize

how those witnessing the phenomenon react to it; the reactions of the characters drive both stories. Continue comparing and contrasting the story as a group, having volunteers offer more of the comparisons and points of contrast as the discussion progresses.

AAVE Students Who Use African American Vernacular English

English for Academic Success Some students may struggle with the correct use of the verb "to be" when pull it out, but it would not come back up. Two or three people helped out, but when they all pulled too hard, the cord parted at the edge of the hole. Another reporter, a camera in hand, who had been watching all of this, quietly untied a stout rope that had been wound around his waist. **(D)**

The scientist contacted people at his laboratory and had them bring out a high-powered bull horn, with which he was going to check out the echo from the hole's bottom. He tried switching through various sounds, but there was no echo. The scientist was puzzled, but he could not very well give up with everyone watching him so intently. He put the bull horn right up to the hole, turned it to its highest volume, and let it sound continuously for a long time. It was a noise that would have carried several dozen kilometers[4] above ground. But the hole just calmly swallowed up the sound.

In his own mind the scientist was at a loss, but with a look of apparent composure he cut off the sound and, in a

> The scientist was puzzled, but he could not very well give up with everyone watching him so intently.

manner suggesting that the whole thing had a perfectly plausible[5] explanation, said simply, "Fill it in."

Safer to get rid of something one didn't understand.

The onlookers, disappointed that this was all that was going to happen, prepared to disperse. Just then one of the concessionaires, having broken through the throng and come forward, made a proposal.

"Let me have that hole. I'll fill it in for you."

"We'd be grateful to you for filling it in," replied the mayor of the village, "but we can't very well give you the hole. We have to build a shrine there."

"If it's a shrine you want, I'll build you a fine one later. Shall I make it with an attached meeting hall?"

Before the mayor could answer, the people of the village all shouted out.

"Really? Well, in that case, we ought to have it closer to the village."

"It's just an old hole. We'll give it to you!"

---

4. **kilometers** (kuh LAHM uh tuhrz): one thousand meters; 0.6 miles.

5. **plausible** (PLAW zuh buhl): believable.

(D) | Read and Discuss | What did you just learn about the hole?

Vocabulary   **apparent** (uh PAHR uhnt) *adj.*: seeming.
proposal (pruh POH zuhl) *n.*: suggestion.

▶ **Comprehension**

C Read and Discuss

Possible response: *As the villagers look at the damage, they discover a large, deep hole in place of the shrine. Some people think the hole is interesting, but others are concerned and suggest they leave the hole alone, for fear it brings a curse down on them. Finally, they put a makeshift fence around the hole and leave it alone.*

D Read and Discuss

Possible response: *Word spreads that the villagers are trying to decide what to do with the hole and it sparks interest among outsiders. Newspaper reporters, police, and business people arrive, and a scientist even comes out to examine the hole.*

▶ **Extend the Discussion**

Science Fiction In the first column of p. 99, what elements suggest that this story is science fiction rather than a real-life drama? ***Possible response:*** *The hole has unusual properties; the hole cannot be scientifically explained.*

Making Judgments Consider the reactions of the villagers to the concessionaire's proposal. What do their reactions to his offer of a fancy new shrine suggest about human nature? ***Possible response:*** *Their reactions suggest that people are motivated by appealing offers and may be so excited by a tempting promise that they do not consider the potential consequences of their decisions.*

Vocabulary: Own the Word

- **apparent:** Tell students that *apparent* is a derivative of the word *appear*, or "seem." To say, "It appears I have left my book at home" is the same as, "It is *apparent* that I have left my book at home."

- **proposal:** Ask students to name the last time they made a *proposal*. What was it? ***Possible response:*** *I proposed that my friend and I play baseball at the park.*

forming contractions. Explain that in formal English, when using a contraction to describe how someone or something is, the subject must be followed by an apostrophe and the letter s, to stand for is. Point out the last line on p. 99, "It's just an old hole." Explain that this statement represents formal English use of to be in a contraction: *It is* just an old hole; *It's* just an old hole. Have students practice forming contractions using: *he is smart, she is funny, it is cold outside.*

Analyzing Visuals

Connecting to the Text: *I pictured the hole from the story as being totally dark, but the hole in the image reveals what's inside it.*

- Tell students that the English language has a number of **word parts,** or affixes, that can work with many different root words to create new, interrelated words. These affixes can be removed from and added to words, much like pieces of a puzzle.

- Write the word part *un-* on the board. Explain that *un-* is a word part that goes at the beginning of a root word, and it means "not" or "the opposite of." Write *tie* on the board. Explain that *tie* is a root word. Adding the word part *un-* to it will change the meaning of *tie*. *Tie* means to fasten things together. *Untie* means to unfasten things that are already together. *Un-* makes words into their opposites.

Guided Practice: Apply

Have students locate the words *unnecessary* and *unclaimed* on p. 100. Ask volunteers to explain how the word part *un-* changes the meanings of these root words.

So it was settled. And the mayor, of course, had no objection.

The concessionaire was true to his promise. It was small, but closer to the village he did build for them a shrine with an attached meeting hall. **E**

About the time the autumn festival was held at the new shrine, the hole-filling company established by the concessionaire hung out its small shingle at a shack near the hole.

The concessionaire had his cohorts mount a loud campaign in the city. "We've got a fabulously deep hole! Scientists say it's at least five thousand meters deep! Perfect for the disposal of such things as waste from nuclear reactors."

Government authorities granted permission. Nuclear power plants fought for contracts. The people of the village were a bit worried about this, but they consented when it was explained that there would be absolutely no above-ground contamination for several thousand years and that they would share in the profits. Into the bargain, very shortly a magnificent road was built from the city to the village.

Trucks rolled in over the road, transporting lead boxes. Above the hole the lids were opened, and the wastes from nuclear reactors tumbled away into the hole.

> **The hole gave peace of mind to the dwellers of the city.**

From the Foreign Ministry and the Defense Agency boxes of unnecessary classified documents were brought for disposal. Officials who came to supervise the disposal held discussions on golf. The lesser functionaries, as they threw in the papers, chatted about pinball.

The hole showed no signs of filling up. It was awfully deep, thought some; or else it might be very spacious at the bottom. Little by little the hole-filling company expanded its business.

Bodies of animals used in contagious disease experiments at the universities were brought out, and to these were added the unclaimed corpses of vagrants. Better than dumping all of its garbage in the ocean, went the thinking in the city, and plans were made for a long pipe to carry it to the hole.

The hole gave peace of mind to the dwellers of the city. They concentrated solely on producing one thing after another. Everyone disliked thinking about the eventual consequences. People wanted only to work for production companies and sales corporations; they had no interest in becoming junk dealers. But, it was thought, these problems too would gradually be resolved by the hole. **F**

E | Read and Discuss | How are things changing for the villagers and their problem with the hole?

F | Literary Focus | Plot in Science Fiction How are the villagers' actions advancing the plot?

Developing Oral Fluency

Use the first column of p. 100 to give students practice in reading with expression and intonation. Tell students that the concessionaire is trying to reassure the villagers and persuade them that dumping nuclear waste in the hole is a good idea. His speech should therefore be read in a confident, convincing tone of voice.

Paired activity Model reading the second half of column 1 for students. Then, have students work in pairs to practice reading fluently, with expression. If possible, pair a fluent reader with a struggling reader.

- Have one student read the concessionaire's speech, while his or her partner plays the role of the narrator. Have the fluent speaker assist his or her partner with words or phrases the partner finds difficult to pronounce.

- Have students switch roles, so both partners have a chance to read using a persuasive tone of voice.

✔ See **UA: Differentiating Instruction** for practice passages for developing oral fluency.

Young girls whose betrothals[6] had been arranged discarded old diaries in the hole. There were also those who were inaugurating new love affairs and threw into the hole old photographs of themselves taken with former sweethearts. The police felt comforted as they used the hole to get rid of accumulations of expertly done counterfeit bills. Criminals breathed easier after throwing material evidence into the hole.

Whatever one wished to discard, the hole accepted it all. The hole cleansed the city of its filth; the sea and sky seemed to have become a bit clearer than before.

Aiming at the heavens, new buildings went on being constructed one after the other.

One day, atop the high steel frame of a new building under construction, a workman was taking a break. Above his head he heard a voice shout:

"He—y, come on ou—t!"

But, in the sky to which he lifted his gaze there was nothing at all. A clear blue sky merely spread over all. He thought it must be his imagination. Then, as he resumed his former position, from the direction where the voice had come, a small pebble skimmed by him and fell on past. **G**

The man, however, was gazing in idle reverie at the city's skyline growing ever more beautiful, and he failed to notice.

---

6. **betrothals** (bih TROH thuhlz): engagements.

G Read and Discuss Why are the voice and the pebble significant?

 California Standards, pp. 102–103
- **Reading Standard 3.2** Identify events that advance the plot and determine how each event explains past or present action(s) or foreshadows future action(s).

▶ **Comprehension**

E **Read and Discuss**

Possible response: *The problem seems to be solved. A businessman steps up and agrees to fill the hole for them, but in exchange he gets ownership of the hole.*

G **Read and Discuss**

Possible response: *In the beginning of the story the young man yelled, "Hey, come on out," and threw a pebble into the hole. Because the hole was so deep, they never heard the echo. This hole must be deeper than they all thought, because the construction worker finally heard the echo and the pebble returned.*

▶ **Analysis**

F **Literary Focus**

Possible response: *The villagers are discarding their trash and waste into the hole. We know we will later see the consequences of their actions.*

▶ **Extend the Discussion**

Making Predictions At the end of the story, a pebble falls out of the sky. What do you predict will happen next? Explain. ***Possible response:*** *The pebble that fell from the sky was the same pebble that was thrown into the hole. I predict that everything that people dumped into the hole will start falling out of the sky.*

Monitor Students' Comprehension

Guide the class in answering these comprehension questions.

1. What does the concessionaire do once he gets ownership of the hole? [*He allows people to dump their unwanted items and hazardous waste for a fee.*]

2. What does the workman notice at the end of the story? [*He hears the echo of "hey, come on out."*]

3. What is the main idea of the story? [*People should pay attention to the long-term consequences of pollution.*]

Independent Practice
Reading Skills Focus
Answers:

1. *Student story maps should outline all major parts of the plot of "He—y, Come On O—ut!" and leave out details unimportant to the plot.*

2. *They can get rid of everything they don't want and concentrate on producing new things.*

3. *The plot of "Zoo" is more simple and straightforward than "He-y, Come On Ou-T." Their lessons are similar, because they teach that there is an alternative side to every situation.*

Vocabulary Check
Possible Responses:

4. *It was apparent that my friends were throwing me a surprise party when they turned the lights on.*

5. *I would include the numbers and types of animals I wanted in a proposal for a new zoo.*

Literary Skills Focus
Possible Responses:

6. *The old man's warning foreshadows how the villagers become unable to see the consequences of their quest for progress.*

7. *The author wants to show how all that is good is being swept aside for the sake of supposed progress.*

8. *The significant issue is environmental protection and how it is ignored for the sake of "progress."*

9. *The plot is all about the mysterious hole, as the townspeople try to figure out what it is and what to do with it. They eventually decide to dump their trash in it.*

10. *He is concerned about pollution. He uses science fiction to create a fictional scenario showing the serious consequences of pollution.*

Applying Your Skills

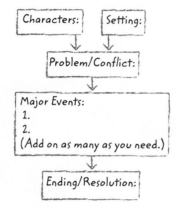

Reading Standard 3.2 Identify events that advance the plot and determine how each event explains past or present action(s) or **foreshadows future action(s).**

He—y, Come On Ou—t!
Literary Response and Analysis

Reading Skills Focus
Quick Check

1. Use the following story map to outline the events that <u>advance</u> the plot of "He—y, Come On Ou—t!"

```
  Characters:      Setting:
        │             │
        ▼             ▼
     Problem/Conflict:
             │
             ▼
   Major Events:
   1.
   2.
   (Add on as many as you need.)

      Ending/Resolution:
```

Read with a Purpose

2. How does the villagers' discovery change their lives?

Reading Skills: Comparing and Contrasting Science Fiction Plots

3. How are the plots of "Zoo" and "He—y, Come On Ou—t!" <u>similar</u> or different? Compare the lessons about life that each story teaches.

✓ **Vocabulary Check**

4. Recall a time in your life when a surprise became **apparent** to you.

5. What would be included in a **proposal** for building a new zoo?

Literary Skills Focus
Literary Analysis

6. **Interpret** As a young man is about to throw a pebble into the hole, an old man warns him not to do it for fear it might bring down a curse. Discuss how this event foreshadows future actions in the story.

7. **Analyze Irony** occurs when what actually happens is very different from what is expected to happen. What irony do you find in the fact that a nuclear waste dump is standing where a shrine used to be? What do you think the author is suggesting through this particular detail?

8. **Evaluate** Although this is a story designed to entertain the reader, there is clearly an underlying message about a <u>significant</u> social issue. What is the issue? What point is the writer making about it?

Literary Skills: Plot in Science Fiction

9. **Analyze** In what ways does the fantastic situation in this story—the mysterious hole—<u>advance</u> the plot?

10. **Evaluate** Based on this story, what do you think is the author's opinion about pollution? How does the plot in this science fiction story allow him to express that opinion?

Writing Skills Focus
Think as a Reader/Writer
Use It in Your Writing Review your notes about the setting of this story. Note how the author uses ordinary details, such as a hole in the ground, to create a disturbing effect. List other details from the story that help create this effect.

Universal Access

Struggling Writers
Some students may need additional scaffolding to complete the Writing Skills Focus activity. Begin by asking students to make a list of ordinary items or objects used in the story in unusual ways. Ask students to make notes about the reactions of characters to the items. Ask students to determine what caused the characters to react in a disturbed way. Students may use a T-chart to help them organize their information, with one column labeled "Object" and the other labeled "People's Reactions."

Object	People's Reactions
cord	disturbed because the cord was swallowed by the hole

Wrap Up

Reading Standard 3.2 Identify events that advance the plot and determine how each event explains past or present action(s) or foreshadows future action(s).

Zoo / He—y, Come on Ou—t!

Writing Skills Focus
Writing a Comparison-Contrast Essay

Write an essay comparing plot elements in "Zoo" and "He—y, Come on Ou—t." To help you plan your essay, review the chart you completed while you read each story. The chart will help you focus on plot elements in the stories that are very <u>similar</u> or very different. You do not have to write about all of these elements in your essay; focus on the two or three plot elements in each story that most advance the plot, explain past or present actions, or foreshadow future events in the story.

Comparison-Contrast Essay

An effective comparison-contrast essay

- clearly states in the essay's opening paragraph what is being compared and contrasted
- focuses on similarities or differences or both
- is organized logically and effectively, using the block or point-by-point method
- when appropriate, cites textual evidence to support ideas
- contains few or no errors in sentence structure, grammar, punctuation, capitalization, and spelling

What Do You Think Now When have you been surprised by the outcome of a dangerous situation?

Organize Your Essay

Here are two ways you can organize your essay:

1. You can organize your essay using the **block method.** That means you will discuss one story at a time, <u>explaining</u> how certain elements enhance the plot of that story. You might outline your essay like this:

   Paragraph 1: Elements of "Zoo"
   A. The unknown in "Zoo"
   B. The surprise ending in "Zoo"
   Paragraph 2: Elements of "He—y, Come on Ou—t"
   A. The unknown in "He—y, Come on Ou—t"
   B. The surprise ending in "He—y, Come on Ou—t"

2. You can organize your essay using the **point-by-point method.** With this method, you discuss each story element one at a time, <u>explaining</u> how it enhances each story's plot. If you organize by element, your first and second paragraph might be focused on these topics:

   Paragraph 1: Setting and characters of each story
   A. "Zoo"
   B. "He—y, Come on Ou—t"
   Paragraph 2: Lesson about life taught in each story
   A. "Zoo"
   B. "He—y, Come on Ou—t"

   At the end of your essay, tell which story you prefer, and explain why.

Independent Practice
Writing Skills Focus

Additional Scaffolding for Struggling Writers Some students may struggle to compare and contrast several elements of both stories. Have students focus their essays on one type of element, such as the setting details from each story that relate to science fiction.

What Do You Think Now?

Have students brainstorm reasons they might have been surprised by the outcome of a dangerous situation. They may include reasons such as not having enough information to realize a situation was dangerous or simply being careless.

Assess

Chapter 1 Resources, Selection Standards Check, p. 36

ThinkCentral Online Assessment, Selection Standards Check

Teacher One Stop™, editable Selection Standards Check

Reteach

To reteach Plot, see **Reteaching Lessons,** p. 842A.

ThinkCentral Online Remediation

Universal Access

EL English Learners

Have English learners use the block method of organization so that they can deal with each text and its details individually, and allow them to focus on only one or two elements of each text. Guide them in outlining and writing their essays so that elements are discussed in the same order in each paragraph, in order for students to understand how the elements correspond. Have them summarize their findings in a concluding paragraph.

To help English learners describe the similarities and differences between the stories in their concluding paragraphs, give them the following word and phrase lists:

Words to Describe Similarities: *both, also, in the same way, likewise, in addition, another*

Words to Describe Differences: *on the other hand, however, but, unlike, whereas, in contrast with*

INFORMATIONAL TEXT FOCUS

Note Taking, Outlining, and Summarizing

CONTENTS

The bust of Theodora and courtesan (detail) from the Court of Theodora *(c. 6th century). S. Vitale, Ravenna, Italy. Scala/Art Resource, NY.*

What Do You Think How can one person's strength when facing difficulties help others?

QuickWrite
Think of a famous woman whom you regard as a role model. Why do you think she is a role model? How has she been an example for others to follow?

Preparing to Read

Grade 6 Review Reading Standard
2.4 Clarify an understanding of texts by creating outlines, **logical notes,** summaries, or reports.

Empress Theodora

Informational Text Focus

Note Taking As you read an informational article, many ideas may come to you. You may connect what you read with your own experience and knowledge. You may ask yourself questions and make predictions. You may challenge the text and reflect on its meaning. Recording logical **notes** will help you clarify your understanding of an informational text and recall what you have read.

Tips for Taking Logical Notes
- **Find the main ideas.** The **main ideas** are the most important ideas in an informational text. You will find clues for identifying main ideas by reading the subheads in the article as well as the first and last sentences of each paragraph.
- **Be organized.** Use a simple outline to record the most <u>significant</u> information and ideas. (See the box below for a sample outline.)
- **Be brief.** Keep your notes short, simple, and clear. Write only words and phrases that will help you focus on important information.
- **Underline or circle information.** It may be useful to highlight certain information in the text, but don't do it in a book that doesn't belong to you, and don't get carried away. If everything is highlighted, it will be hard to tell what is most important.

Outlining **Outlining** helps you uncover the skeleton that holds the text together. An outline highlights the main ideas and supporting details contained in a text. Look at the example of an informal outline on the right.

> I. Main Idea
>   A. Supporting detail
>   B. Supporting detail
>   C. [etc.]
> II. Main Idea
>   A. Supporting detail
>   B. Supporting detail
>   C. [etc.]

Writing Skills Focus

Preparing for **Timed Writing** As you read, record clues in your *Reader/Writer Notebook* that show you the type of relationship Theodora and Justinian had. The clues will help you answer a timed-writing prompt later.

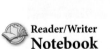
Reader/Writer Notebook
Use your **RWN** to complete the activities for these selections.

Vocabulary
profession (pruh FEHSH uhn) *n.:* paid occupation. *Acting was not considered a respectable profession by the people of the Byzantine Empire.*

forbade (fuhr BAD) *v.:* ordered not to; outlawed. *The emperor threw out the law that forbade Theodora from marrying Justinian.*

facilitate (fuh SIHL uh tayt) *v.:* ease; aid. *The Justinian Code helped facilitate lawmaking in future societies.*

Language Coach
Word Roots The word *profession* comes from a Latin root that means "to declare publicly." How are the words *professor* and *professorial* related to *profession*?

Learn It Online
Do pictures and animation help you learn? Try the *PowerNotes* lesson on:

go.hrw.com | H7-105 | **Go**

Direct Teach

Model the Skill

- Provide students with copies of the Informational Text Focus graphic organizer (See **Chapter 1 Resources.**) or have them set up the outline format on their own paper. Tell students that taking notes on what they read will help them organize information.

- Explain to students that when taking notes, they want to separate main ideas from details, and only write the most important words and phrases in their notes.

- Read aloud paragraph 1 of "Empress Theodora." Note that the main idea of this paragraph is that Theodora was an exceptional woman for her time. Tell students to write that next to Roman numeral I. A supporting detail is that she helped defend the empire from invaders.

> I. Theodora was an exceptional woman for her time
>   A. helped defend empire

Guided Practice: Apply

Have students finish the outline of paragraph 1 as a class.

Analyzing Visuals

Tell students that the image of Theodora's court is a mosaic, or image assembled using pieces of a substance such as glass, stone, or pottery attached to a surface with a permanent adhesive. Mosaics were popular in ancient Rome and in the Byzantine empire.

Connecting to the Text: *She is wearing fancy clothes and standing near the center of the image.*

Read with a Purpose
Read this article to learn about Empress Theodora's unique qualities.

EMPRESS
Theodora
by THE WORLD ALMANAC

The Court of Theodora (c. 6th century).

Analyzing Visuals **Connecting to the Text** What details in this mosaic tell you that Theodora (third from the left) was an important figure in the Byzantine Empire?

Selection Readability	
Easily Accessible **Accessible** Challenging	historical context, complex syntax

Selection Summary
Empress Theodora was a powerful figure at a time when women were socially weak. As the wife of Byzantine Emperor Justinian, she used her influence to protect the weak and defend the empire.

At a time when women had little or no political power, Theodora, empress of the Byzantine Empire, was a rare exception. Though from poor and humble beginnings, she helped maintain her husband's empire as Persian forces threatened from the east and Germanic invaders continued attacking from the west. Born in about A.D. 500, she was the daughter of a bear keeper who worked in Constantinople's Hippodrome, a stadium in which horse races and often violent, bloody performances were held. Her father died when she was young, so Theodora and her sister were forced to support themselves. They became actors, which at the time was considered a low-class profession, especially for women. **Ⓐ**

At age sixteen, Theodora traveled widely, performing throughout North Africa and the Middle East. Six years later she stopped acting, returned to Constantinople, and became a wool spinner. The beautiful and witty young woman met Justinian, the heir to the throne of his uncle, Justin I. Young Theodora fell in love with and wanted to marry Justinian, the future leader of the Byzantine Empire. However, a long-standing law forbade high-ranking men from marrying women of lower classes. **Ⓑ**

INFLUENCING LEGAL AND SOCIAL REFORM

From the beginning of her relationship with Justinian, Theodora promoted freedom and equality for women. She had Justinian ask his uncle to repeal the law that kept the couple from marrying. Justin I agreed, and at age twenty-five, Theodora married Justinian.

Soon after their marriage, Justinian became emperor. Although Theodora was not officially a joint ruler, Justinian treated her as his intellectual equal and sought her opinions and input on many of his important decisions.

RAISING THE STATUS OF WOMEN

Under Empress Theodora's influence, Justinian began to examine the empire's laws carefully and make changes to them. Many of these changes were aimed at protecting women and children. Justinian passed laws that raised the status of women higher than it had ever been in the empire. Divorced women were granted rights, such as the ability to remain guardians of their children. He allowed women to own property. The custom

---

FAST FACTS ABOUT
THEODORA

- born around A.D. 500
- named empress in 527
- delivered a famous speech that helped stop the Nika revolt
- fought for the rights of women throughout her lifetime
- died in 548

Ⓐ Informational Focus Note Taking Now that you have read the first paragraph, what do you think this article will be about? What note would you make about the main idea?

Ⓑ Read and Discuss What is the author telling you here?

Vocabulary **profession** (pruh FEHSH uhn) *n.*: paid occupation.
forbade (fuhr BAYD) *v.*: ordered not to; outlawed.

Think About/Talk About

Read with a Purpose Have students read the Read with a Purpose statement. Ask them what unique qualities might make someone a successful ruler.

▶ Comprehension
Ⓑ Read and Discuss

Possible response: Empress Theodora grew up poor and although she eventually became the Empress, laws should have prevented her from marrying someone of such great stature.

▶ Analysis
Ⓐ Informational Focus

Possible response: It will be about Theodora's rise to power. I would state the main idea as "Theodora was a remarkable woman for her time.

▶ Extend the Discussion

Making Judgments In the section titled "Influencing Legal and Social Reform," the author notes that Theodora was the one who suggested Justinian try to change the law that kept them from marrying. Did Theodora's request put her or anything she cared about at risk? Explain, and consider the time period when you answer. *Possible response: Yes, it could have proven risky for her if she had made the request of someone who was not as open-minded as Justinian. At the time, women were supposed to be submissive and accept the rule of men without question. She could have lost her relationship, her livelihood, or even her life.*

Vocabulary: Own the Word

- **profession:** Refer students to the web from the Language Coach activity. Ask them to list three professions they admire.

- **forbade:** Tell students that *forbade* is the past tense form of the verb *forbid*, which has the connotation of commanding or ruling against an action by law. *Forbade* suggests strong consequences for failing to follow these laws and is formal in tone.

Universal Access

English Learners

English for Academic Success Help students practice taking notes by working with them to paraphrase and condense main ideas. Read the first two sentences with students, explaining difficult words like *humble, threatened,* and *invaders.* Then, help students restate the information in simpler terms. Repeat with the next few sentences if necessary before having students read and paraphrase the selection with fluent partners.

✔ See **UA: Differentiating Instruction** for lesson plans and strategies for teaching English learners.

Struggling Readers

Strategic Students Invite students to read "Empress Theodora" in interactive format in **Holt Interactive Reader** and to use the sidenotes as aids to understanding the selection. The interactive version provides additional instruction, practice, and assessment of the skills taught in the Student Edition.

▶ **Comprehension**

ⓒ **Read and Discuss**

Possible response: Her willingness to trade her life for their empire and ability to inspire the men to continue fighting resulted in them saving Constantinople and securing their legacy. This is another example of her uncommon wisdom and gumption—especially in light of her original commoner status.

▶ **Extend the Discussion**

Evaluating Do you think Theodora would be held in the same regard by historians and others if she had not made her speech and helped to stop the rebellion? Explain. *Possible response:* She would still be considered at least somewhat remarkable, because she still had a strong influence on many other aspects of the Byzantine empire, such as the laws and political decisions. She might not be quite as famous, but she would still be known.

Vocabulary: Own the Word

facilitate: Tell students that the root word for *facilitate* is the Latin word *facilis,* which means "easy." When you *facilitate* a task, you make it easier for someone. Have students make a list of things that *facilitate* their doing well in school. Discuss.

Monitor Students' Comprehension

Use the Read with a Purpose follow-up question to assess students' understanding. *Possible response:* Theodora was bold and assertive in a time when most women had very little influence over the men in their society.

THEODORA'S SPEECH

If, now, it is your wish to save yourself, O Emperor, there is no difficulty. For we have much money, and there is the sea, here the boats. However consider whether it will not come about after you have been saved that you would gladly exchange that safety for death. For as for myself, I approve a certain ancient saying that royalty is a good burial-shroud.

Empress Theodora (11th century) Back view of aureus, Roman gold coin.

of the greatest short speeches ever recorded, the empress persuaded them not to flee to the shame of safety but to fight with courage to the death. His confidence bolstered, Justinian roused his generals and crushed the rebellion. Her speech probably saved the city, the empire—and Justinian's throne. ⓒ

REBUILDING THE CITY

After the revolt, Theodora and Justinian worked together to rebuild and improve the ruined city. They added new aqueducts to provide clean drinking water, bridges to facilitate transportation, and hostels[2] to shelter the homeless. They also built numerous churches, including the beautiful Hagia Sophia—one of the most famous buildings in the world—which still exists in Istanbul as a museum.

LEAVING A LEGACY

Theodora, the daughter of a lowly bear keeper, rose to have a significant impact on the Byzantine Empire as the wife of the emperor. Her intelligence and courage made the empire a safer and fairer place; laws that she initiated influence legal systems that still exist today.

of abandoning infants, most often girls, to die of exposure[1] was outlawed. Other laws established hospitals, orphanages, and care facilities for the needy. Justinian organized existing Roman laws, plus his new ones, into the Justinian Code, which has served as a model for the laws of many later nations.

SAVING THE EMPIRE

Theodora used her intelligence and skill as a leader to save and strengthen the Byzantine Empire. In A.D. 532, as a chariot race was about to begin at the Hippodrome, political rivals there opposed to the emperor joined in a violent protest, now known as the Nika revolt. This riot quickly engulfed the city, and the rebels burned huge areas of Constantinople. Convinced of defeat, Justinian and his advisors prepared to flee the city in ships. With one

1. **exposure** (ehk SPOH zhuhr): physical condition resulting from being left open to danger without the protection of clothing or shelter, especially in severe weather.

ⓒ Read and Discuss | How do Theodora's actions during the riot contribute to what you know about her?

Read with a Purpose

What personal characteristics made Theodora different from most other women of her time?

2. **hostels** (HAHS tuhlz): shelters for those without a home; supervised residences.

Vocabulary **facilitate** (fuh SIHL uh tayt) *v.*: ease; aid.

Developing Oral Fluency

Explain to students that context is highly important to any reading, but it is particularly important to oral reading as it can provide insights into the perspective of the speaker of the text. These insights benefit people who read the text aloud, as it helps them determine the appropriate pacing, volume, and expression.

When reading Theodora's speech, for example, it is important to know that she and Justinian are in a desperate situation: Rebels are burning the city, and the nobles fear for their own lives. Theodora is passionate that Justinian take courage and fight, instead of fleeing

in disgrace. Her passion and intent to persuade, therefore, should come across in a reading of her speech.

Paired activity First, model reading Theodora's speech aloud for the class. Then, have students work in pairs to read the speech aloud while considering its context. Have one partner read while the other listens and coaches on expression, pacing, and volume. Then, have partners switch roles.

✔ See **UA: Differentiating Instruction** for practice passages for developing oral fluency.

Applying Your Skills

Grade 6 Review Reading Standard
2.4 Clarify an understanding of texts
by creating outlines, logical notes, summaries,
or reports.

Empress Theodora
Standards Review

Informational Text

1. A report on this article would state that its **main idea** is

   A Theodora had to support herself.

   B Theodora became a unique and influential force in the Byzantine Empire.

   C the Justinian Code served as a model for the laws of future nations.

   D after the riots Justinian and Theodora rebuilt and improved Constantinople.

2. Re-read the paragraph titled "Saving the Empire." Each of the following would be an important **note** except

   A Nika revolt is name of protest.

   B rebels destroyed much of city.

   C Theodora gave famous speech.

   D Justinian feared defeat.

3. Here is the beginning of an **outline** of "Empress Theodora." Which of the following items belongs in the blank space at number II.B.?

   I. Theodora's early life
   II. Theodora, wife of Justinian I
      A. Overcame prejudice to marry
      B.
      C. Roused Justinian to save his city
   III. Theodora—famous today

   A Worked as a low-class actor

   B Rebuilt the city after the revolt

   C Attacked by forces from the east and west

   D Protected women with new laws

4. Which of the following details would be the *least* important to include in **notes** taken on this article?

   A As young women, Theodora and her sister supported themselves as actors.

   B Theodora's father was a bear keeper in the Hippodrome.

   C Theodora influenced change in the laws of the empire.

   D Theodora persuaded Justinian to stay in the city and fight the rioters.

5. Which of the following statements is an *opinion*, not a fact?

   A Theodora wanted to marry Justinian, the heir to his uncle's throne.

   B The custom of abandoning infants to die of exposure was outlawed.

   C Justinian and Theodora built numerous churches, including the Hagia Sophia.

   D Theodora's intelligence and courage made the empire a safer and fairer place.

Writing Skills Focus

Timed ⌛ Writing Re-read Theodora's speech on page 108. Then, make an inference about Theodora's and Justinian's relationship. Support your inference with two details from the speech.

What Do
You
Think
Now?

How might the empire have been affected if Theodora had given up when faced with a difficult situation? Explain.

California Standards, p. 109

■ **Grade 6 Review Reading Standard 2.4** Clarify an understanding of texts by creating outlines, logical notes, summaries, or reports.

What Do You Think Now?

Ask students to discuss the question in small groups. Have groups consider all of the obstacles Theodora had to overcome, and what might have happened if she gave up on each.

Preteach

Introducing Vocabulary

Read aloud the Vocabulary words and sample sentences. Then, use this activity to check students' understanding.

1. Give an antonym for **renovation**. [*destruction*]
2. Give a synonym for **spectators**. [*onlookers*]
3. Give an antonym for **barbarian**. [*civilized*]

English for Academic Success
Language Coach

Point out that words with common roots can have related meanings. For example, the Latin root *spect-are*, meaning *to watch*, is present in *spectator, spectacle,* and *spectacles* (eyeglasses). All relate to seeing or watching. Renovation *comes from the Latin* renovatus, *or "make like new,*" *and* barbarian *comes from* barbarus, *meaning "ignorant" or "foreign."*

Informational Text Focus

As you read and discuss the selection with students, have them note its main ideas and supporting details that could appear in a summary. Tell them to use their notes to answer the questions on the Applying Your Skills page.

Writing Skills Focus

Have students record information for a summary in their **Reader/Writer Notebook**. Students can use their notes to complete the Writing Skills Focus activity.

Preparing to Read

The Hippodrome

Informational Text Focus

Summarizing an Informational Text A **summary** of an informational text is a short restatement of the **main ideas**—the central or most important ideas—in the work. Summaries can help you remember the most important points in materials you read. They are especially handy if you are using multiple sources for research. Before you summarize, read the text carefully to determine what details to include and what to leave out. After you have written your summary, ask yourself, "Would a person who has not read the article understand what it is about?" If the answer is *no*, revise your summary. Study these tips for writing a good summary:

- Cite the author, title, and main point of the text.
- State the main ideas in the order in which they appear.
- Include the most important supporting details.
- Place quotation marks around words from the text that you have quoted exactly.

Writing Skills Focus

Preparing for **Timed └Writing** The text below is a good summary of "Empress Theodora." Study it. Later, you will be asked to write a summary of "The Hippodrome."

"Empress Theodora" focuses on a remarkable leader of the Byzantine Empire. Born into poverty, Theodora became the respected wife and advisor of Emperor Justinian. Although women had no legal power, she persuaded her husband to pass laws that "raised the status of women higher than it had ever been." When a violent revolt in Constantinople threatened to drive away Justinian and his generals, Theodora rallied him and his subjects with a courageous speech and saved the throne. Not only did she help rebuild Constantinople so well that some of its beauty still stands, she influenced legal systems that exist to this day.

← The summary begins with the title and main point.

← The writer uses quotation marks when quoting the text.

← Details like her inspirational speech are very important.

← This seems like an important idea.

Reader/Writer Notebook

Use your **RWN** to complete the activities for these selections.

Vocabulary

renovation (rehn uh VAY shuhn) *n.:* restoration of something to a better condition. *The emperor's renovation made the stadium better than it had been in years.*

spectators (SPEHK tay tuhrz) *n.:* people who watch at an event. *The spectators cheered from their seats for their favorite horses.*

barbarian (bahr BAIR ee uhn) *adj.:* referring to a group considered uncivilized and inferior by another nation or group. *The Romans thought that the barbarian tribes living in northern Europe were less advanced than the Romans were.*

Language Coach

Word Roots Many English words come directly or indirectly from the Latin language. A **word root** is a word or word part from which other words are made. The Vocabulary words above all have Latin word roots. Look up each word in a dictionary to see which Latin word or words it came from.

✱ **Learn It Online**
To read more articles like this one, go to the Interactive Reading Workshop at:

go.hrw.com [H7-110] **Go**

Selection Resources

Chapter 1 Resources, on-level practice and assessment, p. 45

PowerNotes, interactive lesson presentation with activities

Teacher One Stop™, on-level lesson plans and all print resources

Holt Audio Library

Holt Audio Library: Selections and Summaries in Spanish

UA: Holt Interactive Reader, pp. 28

Holt Interactive Reader for ELD, p. 44

Holt Audio Tutor for ELD

UA: Differentiating Instruction, lesson plan and teaching strategies, pp. 9

UA: Resources for Teaching Advanced Students, lesson plans, p. 63

UA: Supporting Instruction in Five Languages, selection summary

ThinkCentral Online Assessment, Selection Standards Check

ThinkCentral Online Remediation

✱ **Learn It Online**
Reading Workshops are interactive versions of real-world informational texts; students exercise their reading skills by responding to polls and answering questions in an engaging online format.

go.hrw.com [H7-110] **Go**

the HIPPODROME

by THE WORLD ALMANAC®

Read with a Purpose
Read this article to learn what made the Hippodrome important.

At the beginning of the third century A.D., Roman troops destroyed the eastern city of Byzantium, and the new Roman emperor set about rebuilding it larger than before. To provide residents with the type of entertainment popular in Rome, he built the Hippodrome, the largest stadium in the ancient world. A hundred years later the capital of the empire was moved from Rome to Byzantium by the Roman emperor Constantine. He renamed the new capital Constantinople, after himself. One of his major building projects was the renovation of the Hippodrome.

The Hippodrome was the center of Constantinople's social life. The Hippodrome's main function was as a horse- and chariot-racing track. (The term *hippodrome* comes from the Greek words *hippos* ["horse"] and *dromos* ["path" or "way"].) Besides a race track, it also was

(above) Relief from the obelisk of Emperor Theodosius erected in the Hippodrome (4th century A.D.). (upper left) Detail from the relief of the obelisk.

the place to see royal ceremonies, parades of victorious generals, political demonstrations, and executions. Acrobats, plays performed by actors, and fights between wild animals also entertained the crowds. **A**

The stadium's arena is estimated to have been almost 525 yards long (about five football fields) and 129 yards wide. Some say it held as many as 100,000 spectators.

A Informational Focus **Summarizing** Which sentence contains the main idea of the second paragraph?

Vocabulary **renovation** (rehn uh VAY shuhn) *n.*: restoration of something to a better condition.
spectators (SPEHK tay tuhrz) *n.*: people who watch at an event.

Selection Readability

Easily Accessible	historical context,
Accessible	familiar vocabulary
Challenging	

Selection Summary
The Hippodrome was a massive stadium that played an important social role in the city of Constantinople. Today, only its ruins remain in Istanbul.

Comprehension

B **Read and Discuss**

Possible response: The Hippodrome seemed to provide a center for all aspects of city life.

D **Read and Discuss**

Possible response: During the Byzantine Empire, the stadium was large and well kept. Today, the remnants of the great space are few and far between.

Analysis

C **Informational Focus**

Possible response: The Hippodrome was an important location for both sporting and political events.

Extend the Discussion

Summarizing Read the last paragraph. How would you summarize the fate of the Hippodrome? How did it end up in this condition?

Possible response: Once the people who cared about it were no longer in power, it was taken apart, and it was never restored to its former glory.

Monitor Students' Comprehension

Use the Read with a Purpose follow-up question to assess students' understanding. *Possible response:* It was the social, political, and athletic center of their community. Everything from royal ceremonies and plays to sporting events and riots took place in the Hippodrome.

Vocabulary: Own the Word

barbarian: The connotation of *barbarian* is uncivilized or inferior. Have students consider why the word *barbarian* is put in quotation marks in the context of the selection. Discuss ideas with the class. *Possible response:* Barbarian *is in quotes because even though people thought the East was uncivilized, it in fact was not. The area was full of artwork and religious items.*

Constantine decorated the center of the race track with monuments and statues that could be tilted or removed so they wouldn't block the fans' view of the races. He and later emperors adorned the Hippodrome with artworks and religious items from all over the empire and the "barbarian" East. **B**

The races at the Hippodrome were extremely important to the heavy-betting citizens of Constantinople: Loyalty to certain racing teams divided citizens into groups so strong that teams came to represent political differences as well. (Imagine Republicans rooting for one basketball team and Democrats for another.) In A.D. 532, supporters of two teams, the Blues and the Greens, came together to oppose Justinian I's policies. They began a protest in the Hippodrome that quickly turned into a violent riot. As flames engulfed much of the city, Emperor Justinian and his advisors were considering fleeing to safety. To stop them, Justinian's wife, Empress Theodora, delivered a powerful speech, declaring that she refused to give up her throne. This speech encouraged Justinian, and

B **Read and Discuss** What is the author telling you about the Hippodrome?

C **Informational Focus** **Summarizing** What main idea do these details support?

D **Read and Discuss** How does the Hippodrome of the Byzantine Empire compare with the Hippodrome of today?

Vocabulary **barbarian** (bahr BAIR ee uhn) *adj.:* referring to a group considered uncivilized and inferior by another nation or group.

---

he sent troops to the Hippodrome to put down the riot. Exits were blocked, and thirty to forty thousand protesters were killed in the stadium. Constantinople lay in ruins, but Justinian and Theodora remained in power. **C**

Over the centuries the Hippodrome declined in importance and beauty. Constantinople was sacked by Crusaders, and in 1453, Ottoman Turks captured the city, changed its name to Istanbul, and used the stones of the Hippodrome as building material. Today, the ruins of the stadium are a public park with few monuments and artworks remaining. **D**

Read with a Purpose What made the Hippodrome so important to the people of Byzantium?

Drawing of the Hippodrome, depicting a chariot race.

Applying Your Skills

Grade 6 Review Reading Standard
2.4 Clarify an understanding of texts by creating outlines, logical notes, summaries, or reports.

The Hippodrome
Standards Review

Informational Text

1. Which of these events would *not* be essential in a **summary** of this article?

A The renovated Hippodrome became the center of Constantinople's social life.

B Justinian ordered that thousands of protesters in the stadium be killed.

C Citizens of Constantinople considered the "barbarians" of the East to be inferior.

D Ottoman Turks used stones from the Hippodrome for building material.

2. Which of the following is the *best* **summary** of the third paragraph of the article?

A Constantine decorated the impressively large stadium with movable artwork.

B The Hippodrome's track was almost the length of five football fields.

C It is recorded that the Hippodrome could hold as many as 100,000 fans.

D Later emperors also put up artwork from around the empire and other lands.

3. Re-read the fourth paragraph, which begins "The races at the Hippodrome . . . ." Each of the following details would be important to include in a **summary** of the article *except*

A loyal fans of opposing teams supported opposing political parties.

B one team's color was blue and the other's was green.

C supporters of two teams met in the Hippodrome to protest Justinian I's policies.

D soldiers locked the exits to the stadium and killed the people inside.

4. If you were taking notes for a **summary** of this article, which of the following points would you cite in the blank space in the card below?

> Roman emperors built and rebuilt the Hippodrome, the largest stadium of its time.
>
> It was the site of a violent political riot against Justinian I; he was victorious.
>
> Little is left of the Hippodrome, due to invaders and lack of care.

A Besides being a race track, it was used for many social events.

B The Hippodrome was large enough to hold 100,000 spectators.

C Actors performed plays in the Hippodrome to make the city more impressive.

D Emperors decorated the Hippodrome with artwork.

Writing Skills Focus

Timed ⌚**Writing** The main idea of "The Hippodrome" is that the Hippodrome was important to life in Constantinople. Write a summary of the article. Be sure to include three details from the article that support the main idea.

 What Do **You Think Now** Do you think Emperor Justinian would have fled the city if not for Theodora's speech? <u>Explain</u>.

 California Standards, p. 113

■ **Grade 6 Review Reading Standard 2.4** Clarify an understanding of texts by creating outlines, logical notes, summaries, or reports.

Check for Understanding

Independent Practice
Answers and Explanations

1. C *Items A, B, and D relate to the stadium; Item C does not.*

2. A *Item A summarizes all of the information in the paragraph, while B, C, and D only summarize small parts of the paragraph.*

3. B *The information about the opposing teams' colors is less important than the fact that (A) the fans supported political parties as well as teams, (C) two teams met to protest against Justinian, and (D) soldiers put down the rebellion.*

4. A *Item A captures the most important overall significance of the Hippodrome, not minor details.*

Writing Skills Focus
Possible response: The Hippodrome was one of Constantinople's most important structures. It was a social center and the home of sporting events, plays, and other forms of entertainment. It was also the location of a major political uprising.

What Do You Think Now?
Ask students to reread Theodora's speech from the article "Empress Theodora" and think about it in the context of the revolt described on the last page of "The Hippodrome."

Assess

📝 **Chapter 1 Resources,** Selection Standards Check, p. 48

ThinkCentral Online Assessment, Selection Standards Check

◉ **Teacher One Stop™,** editable Selection Standards Check

Reteach

ThinkCentral Online Remediation

Standards Focus

Objectives

Students will

- write a summary of an article that includes the article's main ideas and most significant details
- follow the writer's framework to present information in the same order it is presented

Preteach

Write with a Purpose Read aloud the essentials of a good summary to guide students' understanding of this type of writing. Also refer students to the rubric on p. 122 for more information on summary that they can use throughout this workshop.

Direct Teach

Model the Skill

Think as a Reader/Writer Use the professional model on this page and others in the chapter to provide examples of the elements of a good summary. Note that the excerpt presents details that support the main idea of the article.

Think About the Model
Possible responses:

1. *The writer includes details describing the creation and destruction of the Hippodrome, and its functions.*

2. *The underlying meaning may be that history can take place in the most ordinary settings.*

California Standards, pp. 114–123

■ **Writing Standard 2.5** Write summaries of reading materials: a. Include the main ideas and most significant details. b. Use the student's own words, except for quotations. c. Reflect underlying meaning, not just the superficial details.

Summary

Write with a Purpose

Write a **summary** of an article that includes the article's main ideas and most significant details. The **purpose** of your summary is to reflect the article's underlying meaning in your own words. Your **audience** includes your teacher and classmates.

A Good Summary

- cites the title and author of the text being summarized
- clearly identifies the main idea of the text, restating it in your own words
- includes the most important details that support the main idea
- presents information in condensed form and in the same order that it is presented in the passage
- reflects the underlying meaning of the passage

See page 122 for complete rubric.

Reader/Writer Notebook

Use your **RWN** to complete the activities for this workshop.

Think as a Reader/Writer
When you tell a friend about an interesting experience, you don't include every detail—you summarize the experience, or tell just the most important points. You use a similar technique to write summaries of reading materials. You restate the main idea in your own words and include only the most important details. You have already learned something about summarizing in the Informational Text Focus of this chapter. Before you think about writing your own summary, study this summary of the article on page 111, "The Hippodrome."

> "The Hippodrome" describes the history and significance of the largest stadium in the ancient world. It was built in the third century A.D. after Roman troops destroyed the city of Byzantium and was renovated by Emperor Constantine when the capital of the Roman Empire was moved there from Rome. Under his direction, the Hippodrome became the center of the city's social life.
>
> The giant stadium was mainly a race track, and the racing fans were fiercely loyal to their teams. This loyalty eventually "came to represent political differences as well." In A.D. 532, supporters of two teams joined up at the Hippodrome to protest Justinian I's policies. A riot broke out and spread throughout the city. Justinian wanted to flee, but in a powerful speech, his wife declared she would not give up the throne. Encouraged, Justinian sent troops to the Hippodrome to put down the riot, killing thirty to forty thousand protestors. Justinian and his wife remained in power, but the city was in ruins.
>
> The Hippodrome is now a park, with only a few monuments to indicate its importance in the history of what is now Istanbul.

← The first sentence includes the title and main idea of the article.

← Historical details support the main idea.

← Quotation marks identify a phrase directly from the passage.

← Details about the stadium's significance and place in history further support the main idea.

Think About the Professional Model

With a partner, discuss the following questions about the model.

1. Why might the writer have chosen these details for the summary?
2. Based on the last sentence, what might be the underlying meaning?

Writing Workshop Resources

UA: Holt Interactive Writer and Speaker, on-level practice and assessment, p. 37

UA: Differentiating Instruction, modified lesson plans and leveled assessment, p. 12

WritingNotes, interactive lesson presentations with activities

GrammarNotes, interactive lesson presentations with activities

Writing and Research in a Digital Age, interactive lesson presentations with activities

Writing Standard 2.5 Write summaries of reading materials: a. Include the main ideas and most significant details. b. Use the student's own words, except for quotations. c. Reflect underlying meaning, not just the superficial details. **Writing**

Standard 1.3 Use strategies of note taking, outlining, and **summarizing to impose structure on composition drafts.**

Prewriting

Choose an Article to Summarize

To choose an article, first think of a subject that interests you. Do some research on the subject in a library or on the Internet. You'll probably find many informative articles on the subject, so look for one that is comprehensive but not too long. You want an article that you can summarize in 300 to 500 words. The Idea Starters at right may help you decide which kind of reading material to summarize.

Study the Passage and Find the Main Idea

The first step in writing a good summary is to make sure you fully understand the passage you're going to summarize. Read the passage at least twice. Reading the passage two times or more can help you better understand it.

After you've read the passage several times and are sure you understand it well, you'll need to identify the main idea. The **main idea** is the most important idea in the passage. It may be directly stated, but if it is not, you can use these steps to identify the main idea.

- Re-read the passage to identify its general topic.
- Look at the details included to decide what point the author is making about the general topic.
- Sum up the details in a statement that tells what the author's point is, and confirm the statement by re-reading the passage to make sure all details support the statement.

You can use a graphic organizer like this one to write down the most important details from your passage and condense them into a main idea statement.

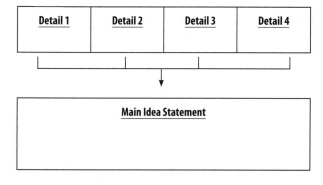

| Detail 1 | Detail 2 | Detail 3 | Detail 4 |

Main Idea Statement

Idea Starters
- a newspaper article
- a magazine article
- an informative Web site
- a passage or chapter from a nonfiction book

Your Turn _____

Get Started In your **RWN,** list some subjects that interest you. Do some quick research on two or three subjects, and select an article that seems well suited for your summary. Then, carefully read the article several times and determine the main idea.

 An interactive graphic organizer can help you generate and organize ideas. Try one at:

go.hrw.com H7-115 **Go**

Guided Practice: Apply

Choose an Article to Summarize

- Have students jot down a quick list of subjects that interest them. Then, have students narrow down that list into a single subject.

- When students have chosen a subject that interests them, have them brainstorm a list of references that will include articles about that subject. For instance, sports magazines and biographies would be the best place to start looking for an article about a famous athlete.

- Tell students to choose an article that is interesting and informative.

Study the Passage and Find the Main Idea

Tell students that they should also look at key features within the article to find the main idea. The first paragraph, the title, the subtitle, and the abstract are all features that may directly state or suggest the main idea of an article.

Your Turn _____

Get Started Once students have read carefully several times the article that they have chosen to summarize, have them work independently to fill in the chart on p. 115.

Teacher One Stop™, on-level lesson plans and all print resources

Holt Six Traits for Writing, rubrics, prompts, and sample papers

Language and Sentence Skills Practice

UA: Developmental Language and Sentence Skills Practice

Language Handbook Worksheets, p.103

Formal Assessment, Entry-Level Test

ThinkCentral Online Assessment, Writing Workshop Test

ThinkCentral Online Remediation

Holt Online Essay Scoring

 Learn It Online
The **Interactive Student Edition** includes more than thirty **Interactive Graphic Organizers.** Your students can use them to generate and organize ideas, compare and contrast, evaluate a decision, support a position and much more.

go.hrw.com H7-115 **Go**

Guided Practice: Apply

Gather Supporting Details

Have students highlight the main idea and supporting details in their article by using a highlighter or underlining. Tell students to look for important details that answer the 5-*W*s (*who, what, when, where,* and *why*) about the main idea of the article.

Find the Underlying Meaning

Ask students to brainstorm a list of words that signal that a writer is providing his or her opinion. As students suggest additions to the list, write them on the board. Leave the list on the board as students complete the workshop. [***Possible responses:*** *I think, I believe, good, better, best, bad, worse, worst, I like, I dislike*]

Think About Audience and Purpose

Tell students that a summary should only include information that is presented or implied in the article. Instruct students to resist the temptation to include their opinions about the subject matter in their summary.

Your Turn _____

Include the Underlying Meaning Have students complete the **Your Turn** activity as independent practice. Remind students to look for words that suggest an opinion as opposed to factual information when identifying words that hint at the author's point of view.

Writing Tip

As you find the most important details that you want to use in your summary, write them down. Don't forget to note the page number and paragraph where you found them so you can go back to them later on if you need to.

Gather Supporting Details

Now that you have identified the main idea of the article, you need to decide which **details** to include in your summary. Not every detail you used to identify the main idea will be important enough to include in your summary. Use only the details from the passage that directly support the author's point, not information that elaborates on the support. After you have listed the most important details, combine any related ideas on your list so that you can avoid repetition later.

Find the Underlying Meaning

In order to effectively summarize a passage, you must find its underlying meaning. The **underlying meaning** is the unstated message, point, or theme of the passage. You can determine this meaning by understanding the author's purpose for writing a piece and by recognizing his or her point of view about the topic. To identify the underlying meaning, consider the ideas, details, and words the author uses. Use the following steps to find the underlying meaning of your article:

- Read the passage carefully.
- Look for emotional words or phrases that communicate strong feelings.
- Look for words that communicate the author's point of view about the topic.
- Write a statement that expresses the underlying meaning of the passage, and include it in your summary.

Think About Audience and Purpose

No matter what your purpose is for writing, you should always consider the needs of your **audience** before you begin. In this workshop, you are writing a summary for your teacher and classmates. Your **purpose** is to tell them the underlying meaning of a nonfiction article in condensed, or shortened, form. As you consider which details to include in your summary, ask yourself these questions about your audience:

- What might my audience already know about the subject discussed in my article?
- Which details will be most important for my audience to know, and which will they find most interesting?
- How can I get the underlying meaning across to my audience?

Your Turn _____

Include the Underlying Meaning Write down the emotional words or phrases that you found in your article, along with any words that hint at the author's point of view. Based on these words and phrases, write a sentence that you think best describes the article's underlying meaning.

Summary Writing Prompts

Students can choose their own article to summarize or use one of the following suggestions to help them write a summary of an article.

History Find an article in a magazine or a short biography about an important person in history. Include a discussion of how that person made a lasting impact on history in your summary.

School Look through the education section of the newspaper or use the library to find periodicals that focus on education and educational policy. Find an

article that addresses an issue you feel your teacher and classmates should know about.

World Languages Look in the travel section of the newspaper or a travel guide to find an article about a country that you would like to visit. Choose an article that focuses on a specific aspect of that country, such as an historical landmark, a regional food, a celebration or event, or a recent news story.

Drafting

Follow the Writer's Framework

To give your readers a good understanding of the article, you need to present information in a concise, clear, and well-organized manner. The **Writer's Framework** at right outlines how to plan your summary effectively.

Condense Information

As you write your draft, think about how you can restate the most important details in fewer words. Try to combine ideas and eliminate words and phrases that are repeated in the article. If you need to use the exact words of the writer to express an idea, put the words in quotation marks and credit the writer.

> ### A Writer's Framework
>
> **Introduction**
> - Provide the title and author of the article you are summarizing.
> - Clearly state the main idea of the article in your own words.
>
> **Body**
> - Present the most important supporting details in the same order that they're provided in the article.
> - Use your own words to present the information in condensed, or shortened, form.
>
> **Conclusion**
> - Restate the main idea of the article, and make sure you convey its underlying meaning.

Grammar Link Using Compound Subjects or Verbs

One way to condense information in your summary is to combine related ideas from separate sentences into a single sentence using compound subjects or verbs. Compound subjects and verbs are joined by coordinating conjunctions such as *and, but,* and *or* and by correlative conjunctions such as *either—or, neither—nor,* and *both—and.* Notice how the writer used a compound verb in the model on page 114.

> It was **built** in the third century A.D. after Roman troops destroyed the city of Byzantium **and** was **renovated** by Emperor Constantine when the capital of the Roman Empire was moved there from Rome.

● Writing Tip

Before you write your conclusion, re-read the beginning of your draft to make sure the main idea is clear. As you restate the main idea in your conclusion, elaborate on the underlying meaning of the passage you have summarized.

Your Turn _____

Write Your Draft Follow your plan and the framework to write a draft of your summary. Be sure to consider the following:
- Have you eliminated words and phrases that are repeated?
- Have you combined ideas by using compound subjects or verbs?

Model the Skill

■ Using a student draft on a transparency, model how to use the questions, tips, and revision techniques suggested in the chart. You might use a student's essay or an essay of your own creation to evaluate and revise using the steps in the chart.

■ Ask volunteers to demonstrate using each of the steps on their own essays.

Peer Review

As students look through their notes, encourage them to ask their partner when they need help understanding how to can improve something. Partners can show how they did it on their own paper.

Holt Six Traits for Writing, rubrics, prompts, and sample papers

Peer Review

Working with a classmate, review each other's draft and trade revision suggestions. Answer each question in the chart to identify where and how your drafts can be improved. As you discuss your papers, be sure to write down your classmate's suggestions. You can refer to your notes as you revise your draft.

Evaluating and Revising

After completing your draft, it's time to go back through and smooth out the rough spots. You can improve your draft by using the evaluation questions and revision techniques shown below.

Summary: Guidelines for Content and Organization

Evaluation Question	Tip	Revision Technique
1. Does your introduction include the title and author of the article?	**Circle** the title and author of the article you've summarized.	**Add** the title and author, if necessary.
2. Does your introduction state the main idea?	**Underline** the main idea.	**Add** a main idea statement if one is missing.
3. Does the body of the summary include only the most important details? Are they presented in the same order that they appear in the article?	**Number** the details that support the main idea. Check to see if details are presented in correct order.	If necessary, **add** new details or **delete** unnecessary details. **Rearrange** details if any are out of order.
4. Have you used your own words to condense information?	**Put parentheses around** information that you have condensed into fewer words.	If needed, **delete** repeated words and phrases, and **combine** ideas to condense information.
5. Does your conclusion restate the main idea and elaborate on the underlying meaning?	**Bracket** the main idea. **Put a check mark** next to the underlying meaning.	**Restate** the main idea in your own words. **Add** information about the underlying meaning.

Research to Practice

Holt Professional Learning for Language Arts

To watch videos on teaching **revision, grammar,** and **on-demand writing skills** featuring Linda Rief, Amy Benjamin, and Leila Christenbury, go to this page in the **ThinkCentral, Teacher Access.**

Universal Access

Struggling Writers

Benchmark Students Help students understand which details support the main idea and which details do not.

- Project the unrevised student draft on p. 119 on an overhead projector. Underline the main idea, which is "the causes and effects of earthquakes" in the first sentence.

- Circle the sentence that begins "In Anchorage, Alaska, in 1964..." You might say, "This sentence is about a specific earthquake. It does not mention what caused the earthquake. It does mention what happens during an earthquake, the effects. But, not all

Read this student's draft along with the comments on its structure and how it could be made even better.

Summary of "When the Earth Shakes"
by Allan Kreda, Ebbets Middle School

"When the Earth Shakes," an article by Patricia Lauber, explains the causes and effects of earthquakes. In Anchorage, Alaska, in 1964, a strong earthquake shook houses, tilted the ground, caused landslides, and opened huge holes in the ground. Other parts of Alaska suffered similar damage. Despite all of the damage it did, the earthquake lasted only five minutes. My grandmother once experienced an earthquake, but it wasn't that bad. Earthquakes are caused by a sudden movement of rock inside the earth. The earth has three layers of rock arranged like the layers of an onion: the core (center), the mantle, and the crust. The crust, or top layer, contains two kinds of rock. The continents are composed of a granite-like rock that is about twenty-five miles thick and extends out under the ocean near the edge of each continent. The other part of the crust is a layer of dark rock under the oceans called basalt, which is about five miles thick. The mantle, the layer underneath the crust, is about eighteen hundred miles thick and is under a lot of pressure. When rock in the mantle or crust shifts or breaks, the movement causes earthquakes.

← Allan identifies the **title**, **author**, and **main idea** in the first sentence of his summary.

← Allan uses **details** about the causes of earthquakes to support the main idea.

MINI-LESSON ▷ How to Choose Details

To tighten his summary even more and keep readers focused on the main idea, Allan could delete some details that don't directly support the main idea of the article.

Allan's Revision of Paragraph One

"When the Earth Shakes," an article by Patricia Lauber, explains the causes and effects of earthquakes. ~~In Anchorage, Alaska, in 1964, a strong earthquake shook houses, tilted the ground, caused landslides, and opened huge holes in the ground. Other parts of Alaska suffered similar damage. Despite all of the damage it did, the earthquake lasted only five minutes. My grandmother once experienced an earthquake, but it wasn't that bad.~~ The earth has three layers of rock arranged like the layers of an onion: the core (center), the mantle, and the crust. . . .

Your Turn _____

Choose Details Read your draft and ask yourself the following questions:

- Have I included the most important details?
- Do all of my details support the main idea?
- What details, if any, could I delete?

earthquakes shake houses and tilt the ground. In order to support the main idea, this sentence should describe the effects of earthquakes in general, or the effects of all earthquakes. This sentence can be cut from the summary because it does not support the main idea."

- Draw a line through the sentence. Explain that the next two sentences also describe one specific earthquake and do not support the main idea. Draw a line through these two sentences.

- Ask students to identify why the sentence that begins "My grandmother once experienced. . ." should be deleted. [*This sentence is also about a specific earthquake and does not mention the causes or effects of earthquakes.*] Then, draw a line through this sentence.

✔ See **UA: Differentiating Instruction** for strategies for struggling writers.

Guided Practice: Apply
Student Draft
Explain that the student draft on this page is the first half of a summary written by a student. Model reading the draft and the annotations in blue, and explain that the yellow highlighting illustrates the student's language choices. Explain that a mini-lesson follows with helpful information about ways to improve this draft as well as their own.

▶ Mini-Lesson
How to Choose Details

- Point out that the student writer has revised his draft to eliminate details that do not support the main idea. Read the student's first draft and revision aloud. Ask students to identify the main idea of the article and the details that Allan has chosen to support it.

- Point to the sentence that begins "The earth has three layers…" Explain to students that this detail supports the main idea by explaining how earthquakes work. Any details that do not describe the causes or effects of earthquakes can be removed from the summary.

Your Turn _____

Choose Details Have students complete the **Your Turn** activity independently. Have them find one place where they can condense their drafts by combining two sentences to form a compound subject or verb. Remind students to use the **Grammar Link** on p. 117 to help them combine sentences correctly.

Guided Practice: Apply

Student Draft

■ Explain that the Student Draft is continued and completed on this page. Again the draft is annotated and highlighted for the students.

■ Read the draft and annotations aloud and discuss.

▶ Mini-Lesson

How to Present Details in Correct Order

■ Point out that in the original draft, the writer does not follow the correct order when presenting information about earthquakes.

■ Explain that the student writer has revised his draft by keeping all of the information in order. The revised draft is much easier to understand because the example with the stick comes immediately after the explanation of energy being released.

Your Turn

Organize Your Details Tell students to number the details in the article as well, and to make sure that the numbers in their summary correspond with the numbers in the article. Remind students to only number the important details in the article as they will not include the unimportant details in their summary.

Student Draft *continues*

Allan includes **details** about the effects of earthquakes, further supporting his **main-idea** statement. →

> Earthquakes release energy in waves, with the energy from one piece of rock pushing on the next one, and so on. Similarly, waves of energy that move from rock into the air create rumbling sounds. Waves that move deep inside the earth are usually not felt, but waves that move along the surface can be very destructive. You can see how that works by trying to break a stick between your hands. As you start to bend the stick, energy is stored as strain. When the strain becomes too great, the stick snaps and releases the stored up energy as waves that pass through the wood particles. The waves make the stick ends vibrate, causing your hands to sting. The vibrations also set air waves in motion, causing the snapping sound you hear when the stick breaks.

MINI-LESSON ▶ **How to Present Details in Correct Order**

As you write your summary, make sure you present details in the same order that they are presented in the article.

Allan noticed that he had presented some details out of order in his second paragraph, so he rearranged the details to match the order used in the article.

Allan's Revision of Paragraph Two

> Earthquakes release energy in waves, with the energy from one piece of rock pushing on the next one, and so on. Similarly, waves of energy that move from rock into the air create rumbling sounds. Waves that move deep inside the earth are usually not felt, but waves that move along the surface can be very destructive. You can see how that works by trying to break a stick between your hands. As you start to bend the stick, energy is stored as strain. When the strain becomes too great, the stick snaps and releases the stored up energy as waves that pass through the wood particles. The waves make the stick ends vibrate, causing your hands to sting. The vibrations also set air waves in motion, causing the snapping sound you hear when the stick breaks.

Your Turn

Organize Your Details Review your summary, and number the details you have used. Then, go back through the original article, and make sure you have presented your details in the same order that they occur in the article.

Universal Access

English Learners

English for Academic Success To help students order the details in their summary, provide them with a list of transitional words and phrases. Examples might *include finally, then, after that, later,* and *next.* Tell students to use these words to link the events in their summary and to ensure that the order in which the details appear matches the order of the details in the article.

✔ See **UA: Differentiating Instruction** for strategies for teaching English learners.

Proofreading and Publishing

Proofreading

After you have revised your summary, it's time to go back through it one more time to correct any errors in grammar, usage, or mechanics. It's easy to overlook you own errors, so try to have your summary read by at least one other classmate.

> ### Grammar Link Using Direct Quotations
>
> When you write a summary, you restate the most important details in your own words. Sometimes, however, you may want to use a direct quotation from an article, especially if the writer has beautifully expressed an idea that adds interest to your summary.
>
> - When you use a direct quotation in a summary, be sure to set it off with quotation marks to show that the words are not your own.
>
> > The layers of rock in the earth are ⟨"arranged like the layers of an onion."⟩

Publishing

Now it is time to publish your summary, sharing it with a wider audience. Here are some ways to share your summary:

- Add photos or illustrations to your summary, and post it on a class bulletin board to get readers interested in the original article.
- If your class has a Web site, you could post your summaries into an "online library."

Reflect on the Process In your **RWN,** write a short response to the following questions as you think about how you wrote your summary.

1. How did you choose an article to summarize? Was it a good choice? Why or why not?
2. What strategies did you use to select the details for your summary?
3. How can the skills you used to write a summary be used in other kinds of writing?

⬤ Proofreading Tip

Good writers and editors have long recognized the importance of "getting a second read" on written materials. Ask a classmate to proofread your summary, looking for misspellings, punctuation errors, and problems in sentence structure.

Your Turn _____

Use Quotations Correctly

Proofread your essay, paying special attention to your use of quotations. Correct any errors you find, including errors in grammar, usage, or punctuation.

Guided Practice: Apply

Proofreading

Integrating with Grammar, Usage, and Mechanics If students make errors involving sentences or parts of speech as they are proofreading, send them to the Parts of a Sentence and Parts of Speech Overview chapters in the **Warriner's Handbook.**

Grammar Link

- Tell students to read their final draft for direct quotations. Have them underline any phrases that they directly quoted from the article.
- Have students determine whether the direct quotes that they used in their summary were correctly set off with quotation marks. Have students add or correct quotation marks where needed in their drafts.

Publishing

Brainstorm with students additional ways to publish their summaries.

Reflect on the Process

Have students reflect on the entire writing process as well as their final product. Challenge them to reflect metacognitively about how they can improve and apply what they have learned.

Your Turn _____

Use Quotations Correctly Have students check their final drafts against the Evaluating and Revising guidelines on p. 118. Ask students to particularly look for quotations to ensure that they have identified and punctuated them correctly. Also remind students to combine repetitive simple sentences as shown in the **Grammar Link** on p. 117.

Struggling Writers

Strategic Students Give students the following sentence starters to help them incorporate direct quotations into their summaries:

- [The author] says, "[quote]." [Dr. Baines says "Over seventy percent of homes have a pet dog or cat."]
- According to [the author], "[quote]." [According to Dr. Baines, "over seventy percent of homes have a pet dog or cat."]
- "[Quote]," says [the author]. [Over seventy percent of homes have a pet dog or cat," says Dr. Baines.]

Advanced Learners

Acceleration Challenge students to include at least one indirect quotation in their summaries. Explain that an indirect quotation paraphrases the sources's words and ideas. An indirect quote does not require quotation marks, but the sources's name should be stated within the indirect quote. Give students this example: According to Dr. Baines, the vast majority of households contain at least one dog or one cat. This sentence conveys Dr. Baines's idea without using his exact words. It also gives credit to Dr. Baines by stating his name.

Guided Practice: Apply

Scoring Rubric

■ Tell students that the best way to understand rubrics is to use them to score actual writing. Review the rubric on p. 122 with students.

■ Have students work with a partner. Tell them to use the rubric to evaluate their partner's final copy of the summary they wrote in the Writing Workshop. Ask students to score their partner's summary, then write a brief paragraph using the language of the rubric to explain the reasons for their partner's score.

Holt Six Traits for Writing, rubrics, prompts, and sample papers

Assess

UA: Interactive Writer and Speaker, summary analytical scales and rubric

ThinkCentral Online Assessment, Writing Workshop Test

Teacher One Stop™, editable Writing Workshop Test

Reteach

ThinkCentral Online Remediation

California Standards, pp. 122–123

■ **Writing Standard 2.5** Write summaries of reading materials: **a.** Include the main ideas and most significant details. **b.** Use the student's own words, except for quotations. **c.** Reflect underlying meaning, not just the superficial details.

Scoring Rubric

You can use the rubric below to evaluate your summary from the Writing Workshop or your response to the prompt on the next page.

	Summary	Organization and Focus	Sentence Structure	Conventions
4	• Is characterized by paraphrasing of the main idea(s) and significant details.	• Clearly addresses all parts of the writing task. • Demonstrates a clear understanding of purpose and audience. • Maintains a consistent point of view, focus, and organizational structure, including the effective use of transitions. • Includes a clearly presented central idea with relevant facts, details, and/or explanations.	• Includes a variety of sentence types.	• Contains few, if any, errors in the conventions of the English language (grammar, punctuation, capitalization, spelling). These errors do not interfere with the reader's understanding of the writing.
3	• Is characterized by paraphrasing of the main idea(s) and significant details.	• Addresses all parts of the writing task. • Demonstrates a general understanding of purpose and audience. • Maintains a mostly consistent point of view, focus, and organizational structure, including the effective use of some transitions. • Presents a central idea with mostly relevant facts, details, and/or explanations.	• Includes a variety of sentence types.	• Contains some errors in the conventions of the English language (grammar, punctuation, capitalization, spelling). These errors do not interfere with the reader's understanding of the writing.
2	• Is characterized by substantial copying of key phrases and minimal paraphrasing.	• Addresses only parts of the writing task. • Demonstrates little understanding of purpose and audience. • Maintains an inconsistent point of view, focus, and/or organizational structure, which may include ineffective or awkward transitions that do not unify important ideas. • Suggests a central idea with limited facts, details, and/or explanations.	• Includes little variety in sentence types.	• Contains several errors in the conventions of the English language (grammar, punctuation, capitalization, spelling). These errors may interfere with the reader's understanding of the writing.
1	• Is characterized by substantial copying of indiscriminately selected phrases or sentences.	• Addresses only one part of the writing task. • Demonstrates no understanding of purpose and audience. • Lacks a point of view, focus, organizational structure, and transitions that unify important ideas. • Lacks a central idea but may contain marginally related facts, details, and/or explanations.	• Includes no sentence variety.	• Contains serious errors in the conventions of the English language (grammar, punctuation, capitalization, spelling). These errors interfere with the reader's understanding of the writing.

Summary Writing Prompts

Students can use the writing prompt on p. 123 in the Student Edition or one of the following prompts.

• A friend of yours is having trouble deciding which sport to try out for. Summarize an article about a sport that you enjoy to help your friend make a decision.

• A friend who lives in a city or town you have visited wants to know what your hometown is like. Summarize an article about your town. The article can be a local restaurant review, a description of a community event, or an almanac entry about your town.

• Imagine that you are buying a car. Summarize an article about a make and model that you find appealing or an article about general car maintenance

Preparing for Timed Writing

Summary

Writing Standard 2.5 Write summaries of reading materials: a. Include the main ideas and most significant details. b. Use the student's own words, except for quotations. c. Reflect underlying meaning, not just the superficial details.

When responding to a prompt requiring a summary, use the models you read in this collection, what you learned writing your own summary, the rubric, and the steps below to help you respond quickly and well to the on-demand task.

Writing Prompt

Your teacher has given you a short passage of text to read and summarize. Read the text carefully and write a summary that includes the main idea and most important supporting details. Be careful to use your own words and to reflect the underlying meaning of the text.

Study the Prompt

The prompt instructs you to read the text carefully, so re-read the text and make sure you understand its **main idea.** You can assume that your **audience** is your teacher, and your **purpose** is to provide information about a passage of text in **summary** form. You are reminded to use your own words to restate the main idea and supporting **details** and to reflect the **underlying meaning** of the text in your summary. **Tip:** Spend about five minutes studying the prompt.

Plan Your Response

Writing a summary is fairly straightforward. You simply want to restate the most important information in your own—and usually far fewer—words. Take notes on the passage you're summarizing as you plan your response.

- Write down the title and author of the text.
- Restate the main idea in your own words.
- Write down the most important details that support the main idea.
- List the details in the same order that they're presented in the text.

- Write down any words that hint at an underlying meaning of the text.

Tip: Spend about ten minutes planning your response.

Respond to the Prompt

Using the notes you've just made, draft your summary. Include the title, author, and main idea in the first paragraph of your summary. You may even be able to get them all in the first sentence. Then, present one supporting detail in each paragraph that follows. Be sure to restate the details in your own words. If you think it is important to use exact words from the text, put them in quotation marks and credit the source. Write as neatly as you can. If your summary can't be read easily, it won't be scored. **Tip:** Spend about twenty minutes writing your summary.

Improve Your Response

Revising Go back over the key aspects of the prompt, and add any missing information.

- Did you restate the main idea and supporting details in your own words?
- Did you reflect the underlying meaning of the text?

Proofreading Take a few minutes to edit your response to correct errors in grammar, spelling, punctuation, and capitalization. Make sure that your edits are neat and the summary is legible.

Checking Your Final Copy Before you turn in your summary, read it one more time to catch any errors you may have missed and to make any finishing touches. The extra time will help ensure that you are presenting your best writing. **Tip:** Save five or ten minutes to read and improve your draft.

Preteach

Speak with a Purpose Remind students that a summary is a "miniature" version of a text that restates the most important ideas. Ask students what they think makes an effective summary. What aspects of the text should or should not be included?

Direct Teach

Model the Skill

Adapt Your Summary

Remind students that summaries should describe key ideas and important details. Model for students how to organize important information. Choose a nonfiction selection from this chapter and make a plan in outline form that organizes the main ideas and details.

Guided Practice: Apply

Have students make their own plans for their summaries that include important events, information, or people from the text they chose.

**California Standards,
pp. 124–125**

■ **Listening and Speaking Standard 2.2** Deliver oral summaries of articles and books: **a.** Include the main ideas of the event or article and the most significant details. **b.** Use the student's own words, except for material quoted from sources.**c.** Convey a comprehensive understanding of sources, not just superficial details

Presenting a Summary

Speak with a Purpose

Deliver an oral summary of an article, book, or story. Use your own words to restate the main idea and most significant details, and show a comprehensive understanding of your source.

Think as a Reader/Writer As a writer, you carefully plan your written summary. Careful planning is equally important when presenting an oral summary. Now is your chance to give an oral summary and share the information you've learned with your teacher and classmates. You will carefully plan what to include in your summary, practice presenting the summary orally, and then impress your audience with your thorough understanding of the source material.

Adapt Your Summary

Choose an Article, Book, or Story

For this workshop you may choose a nonfiction article or book, a novel, or a short story. You may summarize the same article for this workshop and the Writing Workshop, or you may want to select a different work for your oral summary. Just be sure that the work is one that interests you and that is likely to interest your **audience**—in this case, your teacher and classmates.

Read and Take Notes

Take the time to skim or re-read the text, making notes *in your own words*. As you take notes, remember that your **purpose** is strictly to inform your audience. Keeping your purpose in mind will prevent you from getting off track as you take notes. It will also help you remain unbiased, or neutral.

The type of work you are summarizing—fiction or nonfiction—will determine what you should include in your notes.

- **Nonfiction article or book:** Include the title, author, main idea, and most important supporting details.
- **Novel or short story:** Include the title, author, setting, characters, major plot events (conflict, climax, and resolution), and theme.

Your notes should include information that will show your audience that you have a **comprehensive,** or thorough, understanding of the source text. Once you have identified the **main idea,** choose the **details** that best support it. You will restate most of the main ideas in your own words, but you may also consider using **quotations** as supporting details. For a novel or short story, choose a quotation that pinpoints the conflict or reveals the main character's personality. For a nonfiction article or book, quote a striking phrase or a surprising fact.

**Reader/Writer
Notebook**

Use your **RWN** to complete the activities for this workshop.

Listening and Speaking Standards
2.2 Deliver oral summaries of articles and books: a. Include the main ideas of the event or article and the most significant details. b. Use the student's own words, except for material quoted from sources. c. Convey a comprehensive understanding of sources, not just superficial details. **1.4** Organize information to achieve particular purposes and to appeal to the background and interests of the audience. **1.6** Use speaking techniques, including voice modulation, inflection, tempo, enunciation, and eye contact, for effective presentations.

Deliver Your Summary

Once you have a firm grasp on *what* you will say, you are ready to practice *how* you will say it. Practice your presentation until you are sure you know it well. Before you begin speaking, take a deep breath. Stand up straight, look alert, and pay attention to what you are saying. The tips below will help you make an informative and engaging presentation.

Use body language. The chart below lists nonverbal signals, or body language, that will add to your summary.

Nonverbal Signals	Purpose
Eye contact: Look into the eyes of your audience members.	Shows that you are honest or sincere; keeps audience's attention.
Facial expressions: Smile, frown, or raise an eyebrow.	Shows your feelings. Emphasizes parts of your message.
Gestures: Give a thumbs-up, shrug, nod, or shake your head.	Emphasizes your point; adds meaning to the speech.
Posture: Stand tall and straight.	Shows that you are sure of yourself.

Use your voice effectively. Here are verbal elements to consider as you practice and deliver your oral summary.

Verbal Elements	
Enunciation	Pronounce words clearly. Speak carefully so that your listeners can understand you.
Inflection	Let your voice rise and fall naturally as you speak. If you are nervous, take deep breaths to keep your pitch from going too high.
Tempo	Talk more slowly than you would during a conversation.
Modulation	Listeners at the back of the room should be able to hear you clearly.

An Effective Oral Summary

- includes the title and author of the work being summarized
- restates the main idea and supporting details in your own words (if nonfiction, it includes setting, characters, major plot events, and theme)
- shows a comprehensive understanding of the source text, rather than just superficial details
- keeps listeners interested through the use of effective verbal and nonverbal strategies

 Speaking Tip
When you present your summary, use standard American English to communicate your ideas clearly to your audience. Do not make listeners wrestle with difficult vocabulary. If an unfamiliar word is important to the article, book, or story you are summarizing, define it for your audience.

Learn It Online
Pictures can help bring your narrative to life. See how in *MediaScope*, at:
go.hrw.com H7-125 **Go**

Model the Skill
Deliver Your Summary
Model using vocal variations and nonverbal language by orally summarizing your favorite book or movie. After summarizing, discuss with students the techniques you used to make your oral summary effective. Ask students what they noticed, particularly about your voice, facial expressions, and gestures.

Guided Practice: Apply
If students feel nervous about delivering an oral summary to the class, give them tips and strategies for making the process easier. For example, some students may feel more comfortable if they look at a friend from the class while delivering their summary, and pretend that they are summarizing the text in a conversation with the friend.

Teaching Tip
Presentation Aids Model using note cards effectively and ineffectively for students. First, read a few lines of text directly from the note card, staring only at the note card as you read. Then, model using the note card only as a prompt, making frequent eye contact with the audience. Have students explain which style is more effective and why.

English for Academic Success
Remind students to use formal English when delivering their oral summary.

Assess

Writing and Speaking Workshops, Presenting a Summary Evaluation Guide

Learn It Online
If students need help adding multimedia features to their projects, send them to the **MediaScope** mini-site, where students can work through an interactive tutorial on creating multimedia.
go.hrw.com H7-125 **Go**

Universal Access

EL English Learners
English learners may benefit from guidance in choosing the works they are to summarize orally; for students whose grasp of English is extremely limited, consider permitting them to summarize only a few paragraphs to a page of a text. Have students draft summaries with peer assistance, if possible, and conference with them at least once during the process. If students are not comfortable with addressing a large group or are not yet ready to speak in front of the full class, allow them to deliver their oral summaries to smaller groups.

Struggling Learners
Make sure students understand how to use each of the nonverbal techniques—eye contact, facial expressions, gestures, and posture—individually before trying to combine them while delivering the oral summary. Demonstrate each by reading a brief passage from a Chapter 1 selection. Then, assess students' understanding by asking them to demonstrate each technique. For example, you might ask them to make eye contact with you while they read. Explain that a speaker can use these same techniques to make a nonfiction oral summary interesting.

Literary Skills Review

Plot **Directions:** Read the following selection. Then, read and respond to the questions that follow.

from On the Banks of Plum Creek

by **Laura Ingalls Wilder**

Young Laura is playing on the tableland (plateau) where her father had warned her not to go alone.

The tableland seemed big and empty and not interesting. It had been exciting when Pa was there, but now it was just flat land, and Laura thought she would go home and get a drink. She was very thirsty.

She slid down the side of the tableland and slowly started back along the way she had come. Down among the tall grasses the air was smothery and very hot. The dugout was far away and Laura was terribly thirsty.

She remembered with all her might that she must not go near that deep, shady swimming pool, and suddenly she turned around and hurried toward it. She thought she would only look at it. Just looking at it would make her feel better. Then she thought she might wade in the edge of it but she would not go into the deep water.

She came into the path that Pa had made, and she trotted faster. Right in the middle of the path before her stood an animal.

Laura jumped back, and stood and stared at it. She had never seen such an animal. . . . Long gray fur bristled all over it. It had a flat head and small ears. Its flat head slowly tilted up and it stared at Laura.

She stared back at its funny face. And while they stood still and staring, that animal widened and shortened and spread flat on the ground. It grew flatter and flatter, till it was a gray fur laid there. It was not like a whole animal at all. Only it had eyes staring up.

Slowly and carefully Laura stooped and reached and picked up a willow stick. She felt better then. She stayed bent over, looking at the flat gray fur.

It did not move and neither did Laura. She wondered what would happen if she poked it. It might change to some other shape. She poked it gently with the short stick.

A frightful snarl came out of it. Its eyes sparked mad, and fierce white teeth snapped almost on Laura's nose.

Laura ran with all her might. She could run fast. She did not stop running until she was in the dugout. . . .

Resources for Skills and Standards Review

Chapter 1 Resources, Chapter Standards Mastery, p. 54 Chapter Vocabulary Review, p. 51

UA: Differentiating Instruction, below-level Chapter Standards Mastery

Teacher One Stop™, editable Chapter Standards Mastery

Focus on Standards

ThinkCentral Online Assessment, Chapter Standards Mastery

ThinkCentral Online Remediation

Holt Online Essay Scoring

Standards Focus

Objectives

Students will

- locate and analyze elements of plot, such as foreshadowing, that advance the plot or explain plot events
- create outlines, notes, summaries, or reports to understand texts
- use context clues
- analyze a summary

Literary Skills Review

 Review

If necessary, use the following questions to guide students in their reading before they answer the questions at the end of the review.

▶ **Setting**

What details from the selection make its setting clearer? ***Possible response:*** *the descriptions of the tall grass and the shaded swimming pool*

▶ **Plot**

What happens when Laura pokes the animal with a stick? ***Possible response:*** *It snarls and tries to bite her, so Laura runs away from it.*

Test-Taking Tip

Tell students to eliminate answers they are certain are wrong when taking multiple choice tests.

California Standards, pp. 126–127

■ **Reading Standard 3.2** Identify events that advance the plot and determine how each event explains past or present action(s) or foreshadows future action(s).

Laura had been bad and she knew it. She had broken her promise to Pa. But no one had seen her. No one knew that she had started to go to the swimming hole. If she did not tell, no one would ever know. Only that strange animal knew, and it could not tell on her. But she felt worse and worse inside.

1. The setting, the prairie tableland, in this story
   A puts the plot in motion.
   B is the climax of the plot.
   C is the plot's resolution.
   D does not affect the plot.

2. The *initial* reason Laura heads home is because she is
   A afraid of being punished.
   B feeling guilty.
   C frightened by the animal.
   D very thirsty.

3. Which aspect of the setting causes the *main* problem, or conflict, in the story?
   A There is no water to drink.
   B Dangerous animals live there.
   C It is easy to get lost in flat land.
   D The swimming pool is forbidden.

4. Plot complications in the story are caused by Laura's
   A fearfulness.
   B disobedience.
   C loneliness.
   D shame.

5. What is the *main* conflict Laura faces?
   A disobeying her father
   B deciding to go to the swimming pool
   C confronting the unknown animal
   D figuring out how to get drinking water

6. The climax of the story occurs when
   A the animal strikes out at Laura.
   B Laura first sees the animal.
   C Laura turns toward the pool.
   D Laura feels ashamed.

7. The use of the word *bristled* in describing the animal advances the plot by
   A introducing a new character.
   B introducing another complication.
   C using foreshadowing.
   D resolving the conflict.

Timed Writing

8. Explain what happens in the resolution of the story and how plot events determine the story's outcome.

Chapter Review

Review Literary Skills Focus
1. Have students look back through the chapter to find the meanings of the terms listed below.
2. Ask students to cite passages from the chapter that illustrate the meanings of those terms.
   Characters; Plot; Setting; Flashback; Conflicts; Complications; Climax; Resolution; Internal Conflict; External Conflict; Basic Situation; Suspense; Foreshadowing.

Review Reading Skills Focus
1. Have students look back through the chapter to find the meanings of the terms listed below.
2. Ask students to cite passages from the chapter that illustrate the meanings of those terms.
   Comparison and Contrast; Note Taking; Outlining; Summarizing; Visualizing; Making Predictions; Sequence.

Guided Practice

If necessary, use the following questions to guide students in their reading before they answer the questions at the end of the review.

▶ Summarizing

How would you summarize paragraph 1 of column 2?
Possible response: *Advertisements show unrealistic images of men's and women's bodies.*

▶ Note Taking

What information from paragraph 2 on page 2 do you think is most important? ***Possible response:*** *Students' self-esteem drops by 20% to 30% between elementary school and high school.*

Test-Taking Tip

Remind students that before they begin reading a passage on a test, they should preview the questions briefly to get a better idea of the type of information they will need to focus on as they read.

California Standards, pp. 128–129

■ **Grade 6 Review Reading Standard 2.4** Clarify an understanding of texts by creating outlines, logical notes, summaries, or reports.

Informational Skills Review

Note Taking, Outlining, and Summarizing **Directions:** Read the following selection. Then, read and answer each question that follows.

Mirror, Mirror, on the Wall, Do I See Myself As Others Do? by **Joan Burditt**

Two weeks ago I was watching a local news story about the lottery. The film footage showed a young woman standing behind the store counter selling lottery tickets. She had short blond hair, big sparkling eyes, and a huge smile. I recognized her as the woman who worked in the corner drugstore down the street. The next day I walked into the store and said, "Hey, I saw you on TV last night. You looked great." She made a disgusted face.

"I told them not to film me."

"Why not?"

"Because I look so . . ." She puffed out her cheeks. *"Fat!"*

I didn't know what to say. So I just repeated, "Well, you looked great."

I thought, "Here is a shining light of a woman who thinks she looks too bad to be on television for five seconds." So I decided to interview some middle-school and high school students to see if they, like this woman, feel bad about the way they look.

"Lots of kids think they weigh more than they look," said one freshman. "Everyone wants to be size zero. If not, it's hard to feel really good."

It's easy to see why people feel this way, especially kids. Watch television or flip through a magazine. The females look as though they haven't had a decent meal in months. The males look as though they could be hit in the stomach by a freight train and not even feel it. I turned every page of a popular teen magazine for girls and counted advertisements for makeup and clothes. Out of 220 pages, 70 were ads. That's about one third of the magazine!

Statistics show that models in advertisements are 9 percent taller and 23 percent thinner than the average woman. With the click of a mouse, computers can create a picture of the perfect face by cleaning up a model's complexion, trimming her chin, and getting rid of lines around her eyes. Here's a news flash: She's not a real person, folks. She's an illusion.

Other students I interviewed talked about the importance of wearing certain brands of clothing. These clothes display a brand name somewhere, whether it's plastered in three-inch type across the front or appears on a tiny logo on the sleeve. A middle-school student said, "Sometimes

---

Word-Attack Skills Mini-Lesson

English for Academic Success

Review Use the activities below to assess students' grasp of the word-attack skills taught in this chapter.

Activity Display the word groupings listed below. Have students identify the word from each group that has a silent consonant, and have them state which letter is silent.

1. numb   mumble   [*numb; silent b*]
2. dusty   rustling   [*rustling; silent t*]
3. musty   crumbs   [*crumbs; silent b*]

4. happy   bristling   [*bristling; silent t*]

Activity Display the following words. Have students read each word and tell whether the underlined vowels are pronounced as one sound or as two separate sounds.

1. restr<u>ai</u>n   [*one sound*]
2. ster<u>eo</u>   [*two sounds*]
3. s<u>ea</u>side   [*one sound*]
4. st<u>oi</u>cally   [*two sounds*]
5. d<u>ia</u>logue   [*two sounds*]

Grade 6 Review Reading Standard 2.4
Clarify an understanding of texts by creating
outlines, logical notes, summaries, or reports.

I just want to wear a pair of sweatpants and a T-shirt, but if you do, you're looked down on. The way you dress classifies you. You can easily tell which people hang out together by looking at their clothes."

If you're thinking I interviewed insecure kids, you're wrong. A study conducted by the American Association of University Women found that in elementary school 60 percent of girls and 67 percent of boys had high self-esteem—they felt good about themselves. But by the time kids are in high school, self-esteem in girls drops to only 29 percent, compared with self-esteem in boys, which drops to 46 percent.

The good news is that some things may be changing for the better. One middle-school girl reported being on the volleyball and basketball teams. Unlike girls just one generation ago, she can go out for any sport she wants. After an amazing spike or a skillful dribble, however, this beautiful, strong fifteen-year-old still says, "Sometimes you can see yourself as others see you. But if someone says they think I'm pretty, I don't believe them."

Start believing it. Remember what Eleanor Roosevelt said: "No one can make you feel inferior without your consent."

1. Which of the following would be a *main* heading in an outline of this essay?

   A Kids watch TV or read magazines.

   B Logos appear on sleeves.

   C Young women feel bad about their looks.

   D Kids wear sweatpants and T-shirts.

2. Each of the following would be an important note *except*

   A many ads are aimed at kids' appearance.

   B students rely on brands for popularity.

   C teens are too critical of their appearance.

   D girls can play volleyball and basketball.

3. A summary of this article would

   A criticize the fashion-conscious students.

   B note the most important points.

   C include all the statistics.

   D focus on each paragraph's first line.

Timed Writing

4. Using notes, write the main idea of each paragraph, including important details. Then, write a short summary of the article in your own words.

Answers and Explanations

1. **C** Items A, B, and D are all specific details noted by the author, while C is a more general topic with many supporting details in the article.

2. **D** Items A, B, and C all relate to the article's topic of young people and self-esteem, while D is about things girls can do today.

3. **B** A summary does not criticize the article's subject (A) or include many details (C). It restates major points from the whole article, unlike D, which is more of an outline than a summary.

Timed Writing

4. The writer describes a conversation she has with a neighbor who has a negative self-image. She explores the subject of body image with local teenagers, who describe the pressure they feel to be thin and their resulting low self-esteem. The writer ends by urging young people to believe in themselves and feel proud of their bodies.

 ThinkCentral Online Remediation

Reading Standard 1.3 Clarify word meanings through the use of definition, example, restatement, or contrast.

Vocabulary Skills Review

Context Clues **Directions:** As you read each sentence from "Three Skeleton Key," use other words or phrases to help you determine the meaning of the italicized word. Then, choose the best answer.

1. "[Lighthouse tending is] mostly *monotonous*, routine work—keeping the light in order, making out the reports."
   A tedious
   B musical-sounding
   C enjoyable
   D out of the ordinary

2. "Still, on our island, one must be careful, for the rocks were *treacherously* smooth."
   A dependably
   B dangerously
   C truly
   D daringly

3. "She came for us at full speed, as if she were leading the regatta at a race, and *impaled* herself on a sharp point of rock."
   A killed
   B punished
   C armed
   D pierced

4. "Their odor filled the tower, poisoned our lungs, and rasped our nostrils with a *pestilential*, nauseating smell."
   A nasty
   B dangerous
   C deadly
   D pressing

5. "They moved *incessantly*, never still."
   A considerably
   B quickly
   C clumsily
   D constantly

6. "When they *fumigated* the light and repaired the damage done by the rats, I resumed my service there."
   A purified
   B damaged
   C ridiculed
   D dynamited

Academic Vocabulary

Directions: Use the context clues in the following sentence to determine the meaning of the italicized Academic Vocabulary word.

7. "Rikki-tikki-tavi" and "Three Skeleton Key" are *similar* stories: Both feature a great deal of suspense and a rousing climax.
   A pleasant
   B lengthy
   C alike
   D strange

Assess

Answers and Explanations

1. **A** *The tasks described are boring, or* tedious, *to the narrator; they are* not *musical-sounding (B), enjoyable (C), or out of the ordinary (D).*

2. **B** *The narrator says they had to be careful on the rocks, which suggests that they are* dangerous (B), *not* dependable (A) *or* daring (D). *They are also more than* truly (C) *smooth.*

3. **D** *The sharp rock* pierced (D) *the ship; it didn't* kill (A), arm (C), *or* punish (B) *the ship.*

4. **B** *The odor is poisonous and feels damaging to the mens' lungs; it is more than* nasty (A), *but not quite* deadly (C), *and* pressing (D) *does not make sense in context.*

5. **D** *The phrase "never still" tells the reader that "they" do not stop moving, so* constantly *is the correct choice.*

6. **A** *The narrator describes the restoration of the lighthouse, including repairs, which most closely matches* purified *among the answer choices.*

Academic Vocabulary

7. **C** *The sentence describes a common feature of the two stories; items that have things in common are said to be* alike, *not* strange (D), pleasant (A), *or* lengthy (B).

go.
hrw
.com **WordSharp: An Interactive Vocabulary Tutor**

California Standards, pp. 130–131

- **Reading Standard 1.3** Clarify word meanings through the use of definition, example, restatement, or contrast.
- **Writing Standard 2.5** Write summaries of reading materials: **a.** Include the main ideas and most significant details. **b.** Use the student's own words, except for quotations. **c.** Reflect underlying meaning, not just the superficial details.

Vocabulary Review

Use this activity to assess whether students have retained chapter vocabulary. Ask students to choose the word from the box that might be used in each situation.

awe	consolation	crinkling
receding	wafting	

1. smelling freshly baked cookies [*wafting*]
2. listening to an admired speaker [*awe*]
3. watching a boat float slowly away [*receding*]
4. comforting a grieving friend [*consolation*]
5. walking over dry leaves [*crinkling*]

Writing Skills Review

Writing Standard 2.5 Write summaries of reading materials: a. Include the main ideas and most significant details. b. Use the student's own words, except for quotations. c. Reflect underlying meaning, not just the superficial details.

Summary   **Directions:** Read the following paragraph. Then, read the questions below, and choose the best answers.

(1) The article "Tri It!" in the May 2001 issue of *Sports for All* is about how unathletic people can get into shape for a short triathlon. (2) Using the story of an overweight high school student's journey "from couch potato to tri guy," the author inspires readers to see themselves as athletes no matter what shape they are in. (3) Training for a triathlon, which involves swimming, cycling, and running, takes time, as the sample training schedule in the article shows. (4) The article includes tips for completing each part of the race and the two transitions between race segments. (5) Judging from the student's story, the feeling of crossing the finish line is worth all this effort, because at the end of the article the student himself urges others to follow his example.

1. The main idea of this passage is stated in
   A sentence 1.
   B sentence 2.
   C sentence 3.
   D sentence 4.

2. What additional information is needed in sentence 1?
   A the page number of the article
   B a definition of the word *triathlon*
   C the author's name
   D a main idea statement

3. A direct quotation from the article is included in
   A sentence 1.
   B sentence 2.
   C sentence 4.
   D sentence 5.

4. The main idea is best supported by details in
   A sentence 1.
   B sentence 2.
   C sentence 3.
   D sentence 5.

5. Which sentence best describes the underlying meaning of the passage?
   A *Sports for All* is a magazine that should interest both athletes and non-athletes.
   B Training for a triathlon takes time and careful planning.
   C Following a strict training schedule is the key to completing a triathlon.
   D With a little effort and determination, even unathletic people can experience the rewards of completing a triathlon.

6. If you needed to shorten the passage, which sentence could you delete without greatly affecting the summary?
   A sentence 2
   B sentence 3
   C sentence 4
   D sentence 5

Writing Skills Review

Assess

Answers and Explanations

1. *A* The first sentence states the main idea of the article. The other sentences each explain a smaller part of the article.

2. *C* A summary of an article should include the author's name. Sentence 1 already includes a main idea statement (D), a page number is not relevant (A), and triathlon is defined later in the summary.

3. *B* Sentence 2 includes a quote set off in quotation marks. No other sentences include this.

4. *B* Sentence 2 shows how a high-schooler got into shape by preparing for a triathlon. The other sentences do not explain how a triathlon gets people into shape.

5. *D* The passage explains that completing a triathlon takes hard work but is rewarding. Items A, B, and C discuss details that are less important.

6. *C* Sentence 4 is not essential to the summary. Sentences 2, 3, and 5 are all necessary to tie the passage together.

Reteach

 ThinkCentral Online Remediation

Application Homework

For homework, have interested students revisit the summaries they wrote in the Writing Workshop and create a visual representation of the main idea presented in the summaries. Allow them to use any medium they choose, including paint, pencil, or colored pencil. Tell students that the article topic, as well as the main idea, should be evident from the visual.

Extension

Have students exchange summaries with a partner and work backwards from the summary to create an extended synopsis of the article or story. Tell students to use the main idea and details given by the summary writer in conjunction with their imagination and prior knowledge to create what they think the article itself says. When finished, have students compare their extended synopses with the original text and see how close they came to the actual content based on the summary.

If students enjoyed the various stories in this chapter, you might recommend these titles for independent reading.

Assessment Options

The following projects can help you evaluate and assess your students' outside work. Videotapes or audiotapes of completed projects may be included in students' portfolios.

Write a Legend or Tall Tale

■ Students who choose to read *Cut from the Same Cloth* may want to write their own legend or tall tale. Have students imagine a story involving characters or events that could not happen in real life. Encourage them to be as creative as they wish.

■ Have students write a tall tale or legend based on their ideas.

Adapt a Teleplay

■ If students enjoy *Visit to a Small Planet*, encourage them to write a teleplay of their own by adapting an existing story.

■ Have students think of a favorite story that is not a teleplay. Have students retell the story by turning it into a teleplay. Remind them to include camera directions and to write characters' dialogue in script form.

Read On

For Independent Reading

Fiction

Treasure Island

Jim Hawkins is an impressionable young cabin boy. When he discovers a treasure map, he finds himself thrust into an adventure beyond compare. The notorious Long John Silver joins Jim and two of his friends on a ship. Can Hawkins trust this mysterious pirate? Find out in Robert Louis Stevenson's enduring adventure classic, *Treasure Island*.

Cut from the Same Cloth

In *Cut from the Same Cloth: American Women of Myth, Legend, and Tall Tale*, Robert D. San Souci takes a look at women characters who have a talent for adventure in American legends. You'll find stories about Molly Cotton-Tail—Brer Rabbit's clever wife—and Sister Fox—the brains behind Brother Coyote. The stories are entertaining, and they offer up a few lessons as well.

Lupita Mañana

In *Lupita Mañana* by Patricia Beatty, Lupita Torres enters California illegally and tries to help support her widowed mother and younger siblings by finding a job. Lupita's brave, persistent search for a better life is full of obstacles as she struggles toward maturity in a place where the laws are unjust and simply growing up is a difficult, uncertain process.

Visit to a Small Planet

In *The Monsters Are Due on Maple Street*, the earthlings don't meet the invading aliens. The people in *Visit to a Small Planet* do, however, when a single alien appears, dressed as an officer ready for the American Civil War. His timing is a bit off—by a hundred years. He's landed in 1957 in the backyard of a suburban family. You'll discover that he not only can travel the universe but also can read minds—and he can start a war (seeing that he missed the "great fun" of the Civil War). Read Gore Vidal's teleplay to discover the unpredictable ending.

Word Counts and Readabilities of Read On Books

Fiction	Estimated Word Counts	Readability
Treasure Island	21,399	Challenging
Lupita Manana	50,000	Accessible
Cut from the Same Cloth	38,000	Accessible
Visit to a Small Planet	26,600	Accessible

Nonfiction

City

Author David Macaulay shows you what it took to build a Roman city nearly seven hundred years before Justinian and Theodora rebuilt Rome. This Macaulay book, like his other ones on architecture in the past, is filled with accurate and intricate pen-and-ink drawings. The text in *City* will spark your imagination, helping you feel as though you are taking part in history. Because Macaulay knows how to make the past fun, you'll learn dozens of facts about history and architecture without even realizing it!

Snakes

Mostly jump-out-of-your-skin scary, sometimes dangerous, always fascinating—*Snakes* (from the Zoobooks series) will give you an instructive introduction to these scaly creatures. How do they move? Where do they live? Why do they behave the way they do? With scientific photographs and enjoyable text, John Bonnett Wexo provides inspiration for future research into the life of these reptiles.

Final Frontier

The science fiction stories you read so far may make you wonder about the life of a space explorer. *Final Frontier* introduces you to the history and science of the human effort to journey into outer space. Color photographs accompany the description of the birth of rocketry and jet-propelled aircraft, as well as the competition to put people into space and eventually to land on the Moon. The twenty-first century is a great time to dream about space exploration and its unlimited possibilities.

Inventing the Television

Considering the amount of time the average American spends watching TV, surprisingly few people know how and by whom the television was invented. Author Joanne Richter explores the history and early mechanics of television, the lives of the hard-working inventors who contributed to the first television sets, and future uses of the television in different fields.

 Learn It Online
Find study guides for *Treasure Island*, *Lupita Mañana*, and more online at *NovelWise*:

go.hrw.com　H7-133　**Go**

Describe an Animal

■ If students enjoy reading *Snakes*, they may be interested in researching another animal of their choosing. Have them learn about its appearance, habitat, eating habits, and other important features.

■ Students may present their research to the class by making visual aids.

Choose an Inventor to Research

■ Suggest that students who enjoy *Inventing the Television* choose one of the inventors described in the text to research further.

■ Have students research this person's life. Suggest that they organize their findings into a brief oral presentation or into a classroom display accompanied by visual representations of the person and his or her achievements.

Nonfiction	Estimated Word Counts	Readability
Snakes	1, 920	Easily Accessible
City	6,623	Accessible
Inventing the Television	4,988	Easily Accessible
Final Frontier	32, 280	Accessible

 Learn It Online
The **NovelWise** mini-site includes instruction on choosing, reading, and analyzing novels; it also contains a catalogue of book summaries, study guides, teaching guides, and PowerPoint presentations.

go.hrw.com　H7-133　**Go**

Informational Text Focus: Structure and Purpose of Informational Materials

Features highlighted in **yellow** constitute a suggested minimum course of study.

Introducing The Skills

Selection or Feature	For Independent Reading	Grade–Level Standards
Literary Skills Focus: What is Characterization?		**Reading Standard 3.3:** Character
Reading Skills Focus: How Do I Analyze Characterization?		**Reading Standard 3.3:** Character
Reading Model: Girls *from* **How Angel Peterson Got His Name** by Gary Paulsen (Easily Accessible, Lexile 1110) **Skills in Action:** Wrap Up	• **Hatchet** by Gary Paulsen • **I Am Wings: Poems About Love** by Ralph Fletcher	**Reading Standard 3.3:** Character

Applying The Skills

Selection or Feature	For Independent Reading	Grade–Level Standards
Seventh Grade by Gary Soto (Accessible, Lexile 730)	• **The House on Mango Street** by Sandra Cisneros	**Reading Standard 3.3:** Character **Reading Standard 1.2:** Greek, Latin, and Anglo-Saxon roots and affixes
That October by D.H. Figueredo (Challenging, Lexile 590)	• **Cuba 15** by Nancy Osa • **Babe and Me** by Dan Gutma	**Reading Standard 3.3:** Character **Reading Standard 1.2:** Greek, Latin, and Anglo-Saxon roots and affixes
The War of the Wall by Toni Cade Bambara (Accessible, Lexile 920)	**Harriet Tubman: Conductor on the Underground Railroad** by Ann Petry • **Leon's Story** by Leon Walter Tillage	**Reading Standard 3.3:** Character
Comparing Texts: Comparing Characters and Character Traits • **A Day's Wait** by Ernest Hemingway (Accessible, Lexile 900) • **Stolen Day** by Sherwood Anderson (Accessible, Lexile 700)	• **Flowers for Algernon** by Daniel Keyes • **Call It Courage** by Armstrong Sperry	**Reading Standard 3.3:** Character
Informational Text Focus: Structure and Purpose of Informational Materials • **Flea Patrol** (Accessible, Lexile 1020) • **The Black Death** *from* **World History: Medieval to Early Modern Times** (Challenging, Lexile 930) • **Stopping Plague in Its Tracks** (Accessible) • **Signs** (Easily Accessible, Lexile 620)		**Reading Standard 2.1:** Structure and purpose of informational materials

Mastering The Skills

Selection or Feature	Grade–Level Standards
Writing Workshop: Autobiographical Narrative	**Writing Standard 2.1:** Write fictional or autobiographical narratives.
Preparing for Timed Writing: Autobiographical Narrative	**Writing Standard 2.1:** Write fictional or autobiographical narratives.
Listening and Speaking Workshop: Presenting an Autobiographical Narrative	**Speaking Standard 1.4:** Organize information. **Speaking Standard 1.5:** Use persuasive details. **Listening and Speaking Standard 1.6:** Use speaking techniques. **Listening and Speaking Standard 2.1:** Deliver narrative presentations.
Standards Practice: Literary Skills Review Informational Skills Review Vocabulary Skills Review Writing Skills Review	**Reading Standard 3.3:** Character **Reading Standard 2.1:** Structure and purpose of informational materials **Reading Standard 1.2:** Greek, Latin, and Anglo-Saxon roots and affixes **Writing Standard 2.1:** Write fictional or autobiographical narratives.

Daily and Weekly Support

- **Reader/Writer Notebook**
- **Reading and Writing Transparencies**
- **Weekly Standards Review Transparencies**
- **Family Involvement Activities in Five Languages**
- **Language Handbook Worksheets**
- **Holt Virtual File Cabinet for Language Arts**
- **Spelling Lessons and Activities**

Assessment Resources

- **Chapter 2 Resources**, Chapter Diagnostic Test; Selection Standards Checks, Chapter Standards Mastery
- **Universal Access: Differentiating Instruction**, leveled assessment
- **Formal Assessment**, Progress Monitoring Tests 1 and 2
- **English-Language Conventions Progress-Monitoring Test**, Chapters 1–7, 13
- **ThinkCentral Online Assessment**

Print Resources for Universal Access

	On-Level Learners	English Learners	Struggling Readers/Writers	Students Who Use African American Vernacular Engish	Advanced Learners	Students with Disabilities
Chapter 2 Resources practice and assessment for all selections and features	✔				✔	
Universal Access: Holt Interactive Reader interactive readings for Minimum-Course-of-Study Selections		✔	✔	✔		✔
Holt Interactive Reader for English Language Development adaptations of Minimum-Course-of-Study Selections		✔				
Universal Access: Differentiating Instruction modified lesson plans, graphic organizers, and leveled assessment		✔	✔	✔		✔
Universal Access: Resources for Teaching Advanced Students modified lesson plans for Minimum-Course-of-Study Selections					✔	
Universal Access: Supporting Instruction in Five Languages translations of selection summaries and key terms		✔				
Universal Access: Holt Interactive Writer and Speaker practice and assessment	✔	✔	✔	✔	✔	✔
Language and Sentence Skills Practice for Warriner's Handbook Chapters 1–7, 13	✔				✔	
Universal Access: Developmental Language and Sentence Skills Practice for Warriner's Handbook Chapters 1–7, 13		✔	✔	✔		✔

Technology Resources

Assessment Resources

Teacher Management Resources

go.hrw.com

Student Edition Extension Activities

Student Edition Support

Find all of Holt's technology resources at go.hrw.com. Technology resources are also listed as point-of-use in the wrap; below are our featured components for Chapter 2.

Teacher Management Resources

ThinkCentral, Teacher Access
Teacher One Stop™
Holt Professional Learning for Language Arts

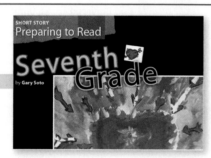

Spotlight on ThinkCentral, Teacher Access

All of the chapter's resources are available on ThinkCentral, Teacher Access. Online suggestions:

• Project "Girls" so that the entire class can discuss this reading model directly from ThinkCentral, Teacher Access—the teacher annotations can remain hidden.

Student Edition Support

PowerNotes
ThinkCentral, Student Access
Student One Stop™
Interactive Reading Workshops
Interactive Graphic Organizers
Writers' Lives
Holt Audio Library
Holt Audio Library: Selections and Summaries in Spanish

Spotlight on Student One Stop™

The Student One Stop™ contains electronic versions of all the important student resources in *Holt Literature and Language Arts*.

• Advise students without an Internet connection that they can access the text and audio for "Seventh Grade," "That October," and "The War of the Wall" with the Student One Stop.™

Student Edition Extension Activities

Digital Storytelling Mini-Site
NovelWise Mini-Site
MediaScope Mini-Site
WordSharp: An Interactive Vocabulary Tutor
GrammarNotes
WritingNotes
Writing and Research in a Digital Age
Literature Links
Holt Audio Tutor for English Language Development

Spotlight on MediaScope Mini-Site

MediaScope teaches students how to analyze media though real-world examples, and offers guidelines to help students create their own media. You can offer students the opportunity to explore this site and create presentations to accompany and support their persuasive speeches.

Universal Access: English learners may benefit from the opportunity to break down media.

Supported Strand: Writing

Assessment Resources

ThinkCentral Online Assessment
Holt Online Essay Scoring
ThinkCentral Online Remediation

Spotlight on Holt Online Essay Scoring

Prepare for writing tests with our list of online prompts. Students will get immediate feedback on their essays that will help them become better writers.

The wrap for these selections includes specific ideas and strategies from *Holt Literature and Language Arts* authors.

From the Authors

For "Seventh Grade," *p. 150*

Linda Rief

I like to juxtapose the characters in "Seventh Grade" to the characters in "Eleven" by Sandra Cisneros. After we finish both stories, I ask the students to write in their Reader/Writer Notebook as quickly as they can about an incident that either one of these stories might have brought to mind for them. This leads to great discussions, especially about all of us trying to be more like Mr. Bueller.

For "Stopping Plague in Its Tracks," p. 213

Sara Kajder

To help students understand seemingly impenetrable informational texts, I encourage them to record questions they have about the text as they read. We then revisit those lists to answer these questions using the text and by making inferences. I frequently use class discussions with informational texts so students may learn from each other's questions and comprehension to enrich their own understanding.

Teacher to Teacher

Diane Lang
Riverside, California

Preteach I use "Seventh Grade" to introduce my students to short stories. After students have read the selection, I ask them to brainstorm in pairs about personal memories and experiences they have about their first day as seventh graders. Have they ever had an experience or memory comparable to Victor's?

Direct Teach On the board, I list the words: who, what, when, where, why and how. I ask the students to think about these words in relation to the story. As a class we will determine the meaning of each of these words in regards to a short story. I record students' responses in a chart on the overhead projector.

Assess Students use the chart to write a summary explaining the following: Who is the protagonist of this story? How does the author describe this character? How do others in the story see this character? How does the protagonist see him/herself?

Holt Professional Learning

Visit the ThinkCentral, Teacher Access to link to Holt's Professional Learning site for English/Language Arts teachers. This site features:

- Videos that share the insights of *Holt Literature and Language Arts* program authors and consultants and demonstrate proven classroom strategies with master teachers
- Study guides for publications by our authors and consultants
- Informative articles and useful Web links
- Help in planning your department's professional learning sessions
- A handbook for new teachers

Developing Critical Thinking About Literature
with Carol Jago and Deborah Appleman

VIDEO PRODUCTS

Strategies for Helping Struggling Readers
with Kylene Beers

Effective Vocabulary Instruction
with Carol Jago and Kylene Beers

Developing Critical Thinking About Literature
with Carol Jago and Deborah Appleman

Teaching Students to Revise, Not Recopy
with Linda Rief

Teaching English Learners
with Robin Scarcella

Using Literature Circles
with Harvey Daniels

Teaching On-Demand Writing Skills
with Leila Christenbury

Managing the Heterogeneous Classroom
with Leila Christenbury and Patrick Schwarz

Teaching Narrative and Expository Texts
with Judith Irvin and Deborah Appleman

Becoming a Tech-Savvy Teacher
with Sara Kajder

Re-engaging the Disengaged Student
with Alfred Tatum

Teaching Grammar in Context
with Amy Benjamin

CHAPTER 2

California Standards

Word Analysis, Fluency, and Systematic Vocabulary Development

- **1.2** Use knowledge of Greek, Latin, and Anglo-Saxon roots and affixes to understand content-area vocabulary.

Reading Comprehension (Focus on Informational Materials)

- **2.1** Understand and analyze the differences in structure and purpose between various categories of informational materials (e.g. textbooks, newspapers, instructional manuals, signs).

Literary Response and Analysis

- **3.3** Analyze characterization as delineated through a character's thoughts, words, speech patterns, and actions; the narrator's description; and the thoughts, words, and actions of other characters.

Writing Applications (Genres and Their Characteristics)

- **2.1** Write fictional or autobiographical narratives:
  - **a.** Develop a standard plot line (having a beginning, conflict, rising action, climax, and denouement) and point of view.
  - **b.** Develop complex major and minor characters and a definite setting.
  - **c.** Use a range of appropriate strategies (e.g., dialogue; suspense; naming of specific narrative action, including movement, gestures, and expressions).

Analyzing Visuals

Explain to students that the people in this image are characters from the film *X-Men: The Last Stand*. Each of the characters has a superpower that makes him or her unique.

Extension Activity Have students use details from the image to describe the traits that each of these characters might possess. ***Possible response:*** *Many of the characters have serious or cunning expressions, and they seem very determined. The man in the top left corner has long claws and an expression that makes him look threatening, while the woman in the bottom left looks friendly and less threatening.*

Chapter Resources

On Course: Mapping Instruction

Chapter 2 Resources

Warriner's Handbook
- Chapter 3, Parts of Speech Overview
- Chapter 4, Complements

PowerNotes

Teacher One Stop™

Formal Assessment, Progress Monitoring Test 1 and 2

English-Language Conventions Progress-Monitoring Tests

Holt Virtual File Cabinet for Language Arts, grammar, reading, and vocabulary resources

Holt Pronunciation Resources
- Phoneme Sounds and Spellings
- Support for Speakers of African American Vernacular English

ThinkCentral Online Assessment

ThinkCentral Online Remediation

CHAPTER 2

Character

INFORMATIONAL TEXT FOCUS

Structure and Purpose of Informational Materials

California Standards
Here are the Grade 7 standards you will work toward mastering in Chapter 2.

Word Analysis, Fluency, and Systematic Vocabulary Development
1.2 Use knowledge of Greek, Latin, and Anglo-Saxon roots and affixes to understand content-area vocabulary.

Reading Comprehension (Focus on Informational Materials)
2.1 Understand and analyze the differences in structure and purpose between various categories of informational materials (e.g., textbooks, newspapers, instructional manuals, signs).

Literary Response and Analysis
3.3 Analyze characterization as delineated through a character's thoughts, words, speech patterns, and actions; the narrator's description; and the thoughts, words, and actions of other characters.

Writing Applications (Genres and Their Characteristics)
2.1 Write fictional or autobiographical narratives:
a. Develop a standard plot line (having a beginning, conflict, rising action, climax, and denouement) and point of view.
b. Develop complex major and minor characters and a definite setting.
c. Use a range of appropriate strategies (e.g., dialogue; suspense; naming of specific narrative action, including movement, gestures, and expressions).

" Be who you are and say what you feel, because those who matter don't mind and those who mind don't matter."
— **Dr. Seuss (Theodor Seuss Geisel)**

What Do You Think
How do other people help you discover something within yourself?

Actors portraying characters from the movie *X-Men: The Last Stand.*

Learn It Online
To understand the role of characterization in novels, visit *NovelWise* at:
go.hrw.com   H7-135   **Go**

Literary Skills Focus

Objectives

Students will

- understand direct and indirect characterization
- analyze character traits

Preteach

Build Skills Tell students to jot down a few words or phrases that describe a friend or family member. Have students explain what these words say about the person.

Direct Teach

Character Traits and Characterization

- Model using both direct and indirect characterization to describe a familiar character. For example, you might say: "The stepmother in 'Cinderella' is wicked and cruel. She makes Cinderella work hard and doesn't allow her to have fun."

- Tell students to think of a character from a story that the class has read. Then, have students challenge a partner to guess their character. Have students use indirect characterization to describe their character, and have them pause after each instance of characterization to let their partner make a guess.

 California Standards, pp. 136–137

- **Reading Standard 3.3** Analyze characterization as delineated through a character's thoughts, words, speech patterns, and actions; the narrator's description; and the thoughts, words, and actions of other characters.

Literary Skills Focus

by **Linda Rief**

What Is Characterization?

Very often, the characters in stories are what keep us reading. We groan when characters make poor choices and cheer when they do the right thing. We love some characters—and love to hate others. We sit on the shoulders of characters and wonder what *we* might do in the situations they face.

> **Adjectives to Describe Character Traits**
>
> brave / cowardly
> wise / foolish
> truthful / sneaky
> modern / old-fashioned
> clever / silly
> generous / stingy

Character Traits and Characterization

Character Traits "Patient." "Loyal Friend." "Sneaky." It would be much easier to tell what people were like if everyone wore a T-shirt proclaiming his or her personal qualities. In real life, though, you have to pay attention to various clues in order to figure out a person's **character traits.** The same is true in stories: You gradually discover a character's traits as you read. The process of revealing a character's traits in a story is called **characterization.** Writers use two methods to **delineate,** or carefully describe, their characters.

Direct Characterization Sometimes a writer tells you directly what a character is like: "Luther was the meanest man in town." A statement like this is known as **direct characterization.**

Indirect Characterization Most of the time, writers want you to discover fictional characters just as you learn about people in real life—by observing them and deciding for yourself what they are like. You ask: What do they look like? How do they act? What do they say? How do they say it? How do other people feel about them? When writers delineate characters by *showing* you who they are rather than *telling* you, they are using **indirect characterization.**

Elements of Characterization

How does a writer *show* what a character is like?

1. **Appearance** Think about what you learn immediately from this description of a key detail about a character's appearance.

   > The Russian looked at the orthopedic shoes I was wearing and the metal braces that went from my right foot to the top of my thigh.
   >
   > from "That October"
   > by D. H. Figueredo

2. **Actions** The writer could say, "Mama was mad." However, this description of Mama's actions reveals her character more clearly:

   > And every time the painter lady asked a fool question, Mama would dump another spoonful of rice on the pile. She was tapping her foot and heating up in a dangerous way.
   >
   > from "The War of the Wall"
   > by Toni Cade Bambara

3. **Speech** Listen to a character talk, and you will begin to learn who he or she is. You

---

Resources

Chapter 2 Resources, Literary Skills Focus Skill Builder, p. 3

PowerNotes, interactive lesson presentation with activities

Teacher One Stop™, on-level lesson plans and all print resources

Universal Access

EL English Learners/Struggling Readers

English for Academic Success Help students understand the words *character*, *characterize*, and *characterization* by explaining the terms' origins.

- Explain that the word *character* comes from the Greek word *kharakter*, which means "a defining quality." In a story, a character is a person who has unique qualities that define him or her. We get to know each character's personality, thoughts, and feelings, by learning about that character's defining qualities.

find out that this narrator is protective of his neighborhood from a simple statement:

> So we just flat out told the painter lady to quit messing with the wall. It was our wall, and she had no right coming into our neighborhood painting on it.
>
> from "The War of the Wall"
> by Toni Cade Bambara

4. Thoughts and Feelings Here is where literature is better than life. In some stories, you can actually read what people are thinking, and what they think shows who they are.

> Oh please, don't say anything, Victor pleaded with his eyes. I'll wash your car, mow your lawn, walk your dog—anything! I'll be your best student, and I'll clean your erasers after school.
>
> from "Seventh Grade" by Gary Soto

5. Other Characters' Reactions What do others in the story think of a character? What do they say about her? How do they act toward him? Of course, just as in life, you have to evaluate the sources. If a character is insulting to everyone, his comments probably explain more about *him* than about the others.

> All weekend long, me and Lou tried to scheme up ways to recapture our wall. Daddy and Mama said they were sick of hearing about it. Grandmama turned up the TV to drown us out.
>
> from "The War of the Wall"
> by Toni Cade Bambara

Your Turn Analyze Characterization

1. Compare direct and indirect characterization.

2. Think of a favorite character from a story or novel. Write down two or three words that describe the character and an example of how the writer reveals each characteristic. (You might want to use a graphic like the one below.)

Rikki-tikki-tavi

clever — tricks the mother snake

curious — spends all day exploring the house

brave — fights two snakes

Learn It Online
What makes up a character? Let *PowerNotes* show you at:

go.hrw.com H7-137 **Go**

• Point out that the word *character* is contained in the word *characterize*; both words come from the same Greek origin. When a writer characterizes a person, he or she tells readers about that person's unique, interesting qualities.

• Another word that comes from *kharakter* is *characterization*. Point out that *characterization* contains the word *characterize* and the suffix *–ation*, which means "process." Therefore, characterization is the process of describing a person's qualities.

Advanced Learners

Acceleration Ask students to consider how the point of view from which a story is told affects their understanding of character. For example, although a narrator may tell readers about his or her own thoughts and feelings, that narrator may not be able to describe what another character is thinking or feeling. Furthermore, a narrator may not be a completely reliable and trustworthy source of information. Have students review the elements of characterization on pp. 246–247 and determine which of these elements can be affected by changes in point of view.

Elements of Characterization

■ Have volunteers list examples of actions that a character might perform, such as stowing away on a ship, teasing a younger sibling, or passing a math quiz. Work with students to determine what each of these actions might suggest about a character.

■ Model using elements of characterization to describe yourself or someone you know. Write five sentences on the board, making sure to describe your appearance, your actions, your speech, your thoughts and feelings, or other people's reactions to you.

■ Then, have students create their own "character sketches" by following your example as they write five sentences about themselves or someone they know well.

Check for Understanding

Your Turn

Possible responses:

1. *Direct characterization occurs when a writer states what a character is like. Indirect characterization occurs when a writer shows the traits through action or dialogue.*

2. *The stepsisters from "Aschenputtel" are cruel; they treat Aschenputtel harshly. They also show their cunning when they cut their feet so they will fit into Aschenputtel's shoe.*

Reteach

To reteach characterization, see **Reteaching Lessons,** p. 842A.

Learn It Online
For a multimedia version of the instruction found on this page, use the **PowerNotes** Literary Skills Focus presentation.

go.hrw.com H7-137 **Go**

Objectives
Students will
- make inferences about characters
- make connections to the text
- analyze how character affects plot

Preteach

Build Background Point out that students have used clues to draw conclusions, or make inferences, in everyday life. For example, students might have concluded that a store was closed by the fact that the lights were out and no cars were in the parking lot. Ask students to describe other similar conclusions that they've drawn in everyday life.

Direct Teach

It Says/I Say/And So

Model the "It Says/I Say/And So" strategy by creating and filling in a chart like the one on p. 138. You might say, "It said in 'The Dive' that Melly blushed when she spoke her thoughts aloud to her father. From my own experience and knowledge, *I say* that people usually blush when they are embarrassed. *And so* I conclude that Melly is embarrassed because she accidentally told her father what she was thinking."

California Standards, pp. 138–139

- **Reading Standard 3.3** Analyze characterization as delineated through a character's thoughts, words, speech patterns, and actions; the narrator's description; and the thoughts, words, and actions of other characters.

Reading Skills Focus

by **Kylene Beers**

How Do I Analyze Characterization?

Your friend asks, "What's wrong?" and you reply, "Nothing." Your friend *knows* that something is wrong, though. He listened to your answer but also paid attention to your facial expression, connected that to his own experiences, and made an inference—an educated guess. You make inferences as you read by making connections between what the author writes and your own experiences. Making connections helps you read for deeper meaning.

Making Inferences About Characters

To make inferences as you read, use clues in the text and your own knowledge and experiences to make an educated guess. Making inferences about characters will help you analyze what kind of people they are based on how they act, what they say, and how other characters respond to them. You might also make an inference about how a character will resolve a conflict or about what motivates, or causes, a character to behave in a certain way.

Tips for Making Inferences As you read the stories in this chapter, look for details that help you make inferences about the characters. To collect evidence, answer questions like these:

- What do I know about the character's appearance, thoughts, words, and actions?
- How do other characters react to the character?
- What does the character learn by the end of the story?

It Says / I Say / And So

You can use an It Says / I Say / And So chart to help you make inferences about characters. Here is an example from "Seventh Grade" by Gary Soto:

It Says	I Say	And So...
Writer's Clues	My Experiences	Inference
Teresa looked at Victor and "smiled sweetly."	Someone who smiles at you usually likes you.	Teresa likes Victor.

Remember that an inference is a conclusion that makes sense. You need evidence to support your inferences. That evidence comes from the writer's clues and your own experiences.

Keep in mind that sometimes writers give clues that may lead you to draw incorrect conclusions. That's what makes a story interesting and exciting. As you read, keep watching for clues in the story, and be ready to make new inferences based on the new evidence you find.

Resources

Chapter 2 Resources, Reading Skills Focus Skill Builder, p. 4

PowerNotes, interactive lesson presentation with activities

Teacher One Stop™, on-level lesson plans and all print resources

Universal Access

EL English Learners/Struggling Readers
English for Academic Success Help students learn the academic terms in the Reading Skills Focus by using them in context.
- Explain to students that *infer* means "draw a conclusion or make an educated guess." Model using the word *infer* in a sentence. You might say: "Because Josh started to sneeze when the cat came into the room, I can infer that Josh is allergic to cats."

Connecting to the Text

Making personal connections to texts helps you to read for deeper meaning. You may relate characters and their behavior to your own life, to other stories you know, and to wider experiences.

The Text and You   As you read, you may recognize connections with your own life that help you put yourself in the story. You may think

- "This character is like me because . . ."
- "I was in a similar situation when . . ."
- "I disagree with the writer's idea because . . ."

The Text and Another Text   You may see similarities between the story you are reading and one you have already read that can help you analyze a character's thoughts and actions. You may think

- "This character reminds me of Superman because . . ."
- "This conflict reminds me of the fight between Rikki-tikki-tavi and Nag because . . ."
- "This story reminds me of 'The Dive' because . . ."

The Text and the World   A story can help you make sense of a situation in your school or community, or it can help you understand people and conflicts in other places. You may think

- "This text reminds me of something I heard on the news because . . ."
- "This setting reminds me of . . ."
- "This character is an example of . . ."

If—Then: How Character Affects Plot

Plot is the action of a story. Because characters are the ones doing the acting, anything characters do affects the plot. You can figure out how a story would change if a character behaved differently by using a strategy called If—Then. Think about a character's traits and the way the character acts in the story. Then, imagine how the events in the story would be different if the character had different traits.

If . . .	Then . . .
A character were mean	What would happen if the character were kind?

Applying the If—Then strategy will help you analyze characterization. It can show you how characters make a story what it is.

Your Turn   Apply Reading Skills

1. Suppose you are called on to answer a question. You answer incorrectly. Instead of getting upset with you, the teacher smiles and says, "Better luck next time." What can you infer about the teacher?

2. Use the If—Then strategy to explain how a story about a boy meeting a girl at the movies would change if a key character were confident instead of shy.

Now go to the Skills in Action: Reading Model

Learn It Online
Practice making inferences with *PowerNotes* at:
go.hrw.com   H7-139   **Go**

Connecting to the Text

Tell students that when a text reminds them of a personal experience or makes them stop and think about an issue, they know they have connected with that text. Ask students to share examples of books that they have particularly enjoyed or characters with whom they've had a lot in common. Then, have students explain how their favorite book or character relates to their lives, to other stories, or to another interesting topic.

If—Then: How Character Affects Plot

Explain the "If—Then" strategy to students. You might model the strategy by saying, "If Cinderella's stepmother and stepsisters had been kind, they might have let her go to the ball. If the lighthouse keepers in 'Three Skeleton Key' had not been brave and resourceful, they all might have been killed by the rats." Write your "If—Then" scenarios in a chart on the board, and have students contribute scenarios of their own.

Check for Understanding

Your Turn
Possible responses:

1. *He or she is patient and understanding.*

2. *If a character were bold instead of shy, he or she might talk a lot on the date, act friendlier toward the other person, or make the other person nervous with his or her enthusiasm.*

Reteach

 ThinkCentral Online Remediation

Learn It Online
For a multimedia version of the instruction found on this page, use the **PowerNotes** Reading Focus presentation.
go.hrw.com   H7-139   **Go**

- Tell students that an inference is a conclusion or an educated guess. To put the word *inference* in context, you might say: "I just made an inference about Josh, but I don't know if it's correct."
- Make sure that students do not confuse *infer* with the word *imply*, which means "suggest." To emphasize the difference between the two words, you might say, "This story *implies* that it is important to be generous and kind. I can *infer* that the author values kindness and generosity."

Advanced Learners

Enrichment   Tell students that in some genres of fiction, authors encourage readers to make inferences that may or may not be correct. For example, in a mystery novel, an author may lead readers to infer that the sinister-looking character lurking in the corner is the thief, when in reality, the crook looks sweet and adorable. Have groups of students choose their favorite mysterious or suspenseful novel, movie, or show and discuss how its plot twists and surprises would be affected if the author stated information directly rather than having readers make inferences.

Reading Model

Objectives

Students will
- analyze characterization
- make inferences from a text
- make connections to a text

Read with a Purpose Read "Girls" to learn what character traits help the narrator, a thirteen-year-old boy, survive the experience of seeing a movie with a girl he likes. (This story is told by a first-person narrator who refers to himself as *I*.)

Girls

from **How Angel Peterson Got His Name**
by **Gary Paulsen**

Preteach

Read with a Purpose Direct students to read the Read with a Purpose statement. Tell students to use their **Reader/Writer Notebook** to note the narrator's character traits.

Direct Teach

Model the Skill

Use the Reading Model to demonstrate the application of the Literary and Reading skills in a short selection. As you or students read the model aloud, stop to discuss the side annotations and highlighting, which are aids to comprehension and analysis.

▶ Literary Focus

Characterization How does the narrator relate to girls? What does this show about him? *Possible response: He can't speak to them; he is shy.*

▶ Reading Focus

Connecting to the Text What do you think the statement "And then we became thirteen" means? *Possible response: Their view of girls began to change at this age.*

Literary Focus

Characterization The writer begins revealing what the characters are like. Here Paulsen uses direct characterization by stating how the narrator and other boys reacted to girls.

Reading Focus

Connecting to the Text The boy in this story is close to your age. As you read, relate his thoughts and feelings to your own, finding points of connection.

Girls.
　　When we were eleven and even twelve they were just like us. Sort of.
　　That is, we could be friends and do projects together in school and some boys could even talk to them. Not me. I never could. And neither could Orvis. Alan seemed to have worked out a way to pretend they weren't even there and Wayne swore that it didn't bother him at all to speak to girls.
　　And then we became thirteen.
　　Everything changed.
　　Well, not everything. I still couldn't talk to them, lived in mortal terror of them, and Orvis was the same way. But we talked *about* them all the time, how they looked, how they smiled, how they sounded, how they must think, about life, about us, how Elaine was really cute but Eileen had prettier hair and Eileen seemed one day to actually, actually look at me, right at me. But we couldn't speak *to* them.
　　Except that now it became very important that we be *able* to speak to them. Before, it didn't seem to matter, and now it was somehow the only thing that *did* matter.

Selection Readability	
Easy Accessible Accessible Challenging	familiar situations; accessible vocabulary

Selection Plot Summary

The narrator describes the nerve-wracking experience of his first date. After getting up the courage to ask Eileen to a movie, he struggles to overcome his discomfort. After his date is over, he realizes he was so nervous that he doesn't remember any of the movie.

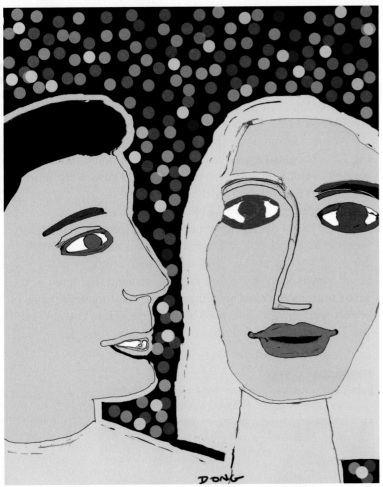

Redlite/Greenlite Couple (2002)
by Diana Ong (1940–). Computer graphics.

I had this problem because Eileen actually *had* looked at me one day on the way out of school, or so I thought, and on top of it she had smiled—I was pretty sure at me as well—and I thought that maybe I was In Love and that it was For Real and when I asked Orvis about it he agreed that I might be In Love For Real and suggested that I take Eileen to a movie.

Which nearly stopped my heart cold. I couldn't talk to her—how could I ask her to go to a movie? Finally it was Orvis who thought of the way. I would ask Wayne to ask Shirley Johnson

▶ **Literary Focus**
Character Traits What traits do the narrator's thoughts reveal? *Possible response: He is romantic yet anxious.*

Analyzing Visuals
Diana Ong, a Chinese American artist born in 1940, creates paintings that are colorful, modern, and abstract.

Extension Activity Ask students whether they think this painting accurately depicts the narrator and Eileen. *Possible response: Since the painting is abstract rather than realistic, I don't think this is what the characters really look like. The boy in the image is talking to the girl, but in the story, the narrator is too scared to talk to girls.*

Literary Focus

Character Traits Writers often include information that explains why characters act in certain ways. Here Paulsen uses indirect characterization by sharing the narrator's thoughts.

Universal Access: Vocabulary

EL **English Learners/ Struggling Readers**

English for Academic Success To help students understand the selection, introduce them to the following vocabulary words.

- **tortuous**—extremely difficult. *The narrator's process of asking Eileen on a date through her friend was tortuous.*

- **procedure**—process or method. *In order to ask Eileen on a date, the narrator followed a complicated procedure.*

- **overlook**—to disregard. *Eileen decided to overlook the narrator's nervousness.*

- **obsession**—fascination or passion. *At age thirteen, some of the boys developed an obsession with girls.*

Then, give students this statement that explains how the words relate to the meaning of the selection:
Around the time when the narrator turned thirteen, he began to understand other people's obsession with talking to girls. After using a tortuous procedure to convince Eileen to go on a date with him, the narrator embarrassed himself in front of her, but Eileen kindly overlooked his awkwardness.

Model the Skill

▶ **Literary Focus**

Character Traits Read the first four full paragraphs in the second column. Name a few details that help you to infer that the narrator is shy and uncomfortable around Eileen.

Possible responses: He is sweating; he drops his money on the ground; he asks Eileen three times if she wants popcorn before she hears him; he is blushing; his ears are ringing.

Analyzing Visuals

Diana Ong's art often features unique portrayals of figures, as in the painting at right.

Connecting to the Text: *It might represent the ridiculously complicated process of talking to many people in order to ask someone out on a date.*

Literary Focus

Character Traits When Paulsen describes the narrator's appearance, he reveals two of the narrator's character traits: (1) He is concerned with the way he looks. (2) He is awkward.

to ask Claudia Erskine, who was a close friend of Eileen's, if Eileen might like to go to the movies with me the following Saturday afternoon.

This tortuous procedure was actually followed and by the time I was told that indeed Eileen would like to see a movie the next Saturday, I was a nervous wreck and honestly hoped she wouldn't go.

We met in front of the theater, as things were done then at our age—I couldn't even imagine going to her home and ringing the bell to pick her up and having her parents answer the door. If I couldn't really speak to girls, what would I do with a set of *parents* of the girl I was going to take to a movie?

So we met at the theater at one-thirty. I wore what I thought were my best clothes, a pullover sweater over a turtleneck, with my feeble attempt at a flattop, Butch-Waxed so much that dropping an anvil on my head wouldn't have flattened it. I think now I must have looked something like a really uncomfortable, sweaty, walking, greasy-topped bottle brush. (Have I mentioned that with my sweater and turtleneck I had gone solely for

Analyzing Visuals **Connecting to the Text** What "tortuous procedure" that the narrator describes might this visual represent?

Date-Line (2000) by Diana Ong (1940–). Computer graphics.

Developing Oral Fluency

The long, winding sentences of "Girls" might challenge some readers. Remind students that fluent readers stop after a period, question mark, or exclamation mark at the end of a sentence and pause more briefly at commas and dashes. Encourage them to read aloud slowly enough so that anyone listening can comprehend all the author is saying.

Paired Activity Model reading the first full paragraph on p. 142 at an appropriate pace, pausing briefly at the comma. Then, have students form pairs and practice

reading the next three paragraphs to one another. Have one partner read while the other takes notes on his or her pacing and punctuation. Have students alternate this process three times. After they have completed the activity, ask them to explain how their reading improved and to share anything they have learned about pacing, appropriate pauses, or fluent reading.

✔ See **UA: Differentiating Instruction** for practice passages for developing oral fluency.

fashion and ignored the fact that it was high summer? Or that the theater was most decidedly *not* air-conditioned?)

But Eileen was a nice person and pretended not to notice the sweat filling my shoes so they sloshed when we walked or how I dropped my handful of money all over the ground. I had brought all of my seven dollars in savings because I really didn't know how much it would cost, what with tickets and treats, and maybe she was a big eater.

She also pretended not to notice when I asked her if she wanted popcorn.

So I asked her again. Louder.

And then again. Louder.

All because I was blushing so hard my ears were ringing and I wasn't sure if I was really making a sound and so when I screamed it out the third time and she jumped back, it more or less set the tone for the whole date.

We went into the theater all right. And we sat next to each other. And she was kind enough to overlook the fact that I smelled like a dead buffalo and that other than asking her three times if she wanted popcorn I didn't say a word to her. Not a word.

I couldn't.

The movie was called *The Thing,* about a creature from another planet who crashes to earth in the Arctic and develops a need/thirst/obsession for human and sled-dog blood and isn't killed until they figure out that he's really a kind of walking, roaring, grunting plant. So they rig up some wire to "cook him like a stewed carrot." All of this I learned the second time around, when I went to the movie with Wayne, because sitting next to Eileen, pouring sweat, giving her endless boxes of Dots and candy corn and popcorn (almost none of which she wanted but accepted nicely and set on the seat next to her), I didn't remember a single thing about the movie. Not a word, not a scene.

All I could do was sit and think, I'm this close to a girl, right next to a girl, my arm almost touching her arm, a girl, right there, right *there. . . .*

Read with a Purpose What kind of person is the narrator? (Consider his thoughts, speech patterns, and actions; and his descriptions of other characters.)

Literary Focus

Indirect Characterization
Writers use speech, actions, thoughts, and feelings to delineate characters. In this paragraph, Paulsen uses several sensory images to show that the narrator is painfully shy and uncomfortable around Eileen.

Reading Focus

How Character Affects Plot If Eileen were inconsiderate instead of kind, she might have left the theater by now. Contrasting how she could have acted with her actual behavior helps focus your analysis of her character.

Reading Focus

Making Inferences You can infer that the narrator forgets about the movie because he is so preoccupied with impressing Eileen.

Model the Skill

▶ Literary Focus

Indirect Characterization Discuss what Eileen's pretending not to notice the offers of popcorn might reveal about her character. **Possible responses:** *She does not want to spend her date's money; she is a bit awkward, too.*

▶ Reading Focus

How Character Affects Plot If the narrator weren't so nervous, how might his date with Eileen be different? **Possible responses:** *He and Eileen might be sharing snacks and talking; he might have remembered the movie.*

▶ Reading Focus

Making Inferences In the next-to-last paragraph, what can you infer from the fact that the narrator does not remember anything about the movie? **Possible response:** *His thoughts are consumed with trying to impress Eileen.*

Check for Understanding

Read with a Purpose Ask students to describe the narrator. **Possible response:** *The narrator seems to be shy, a little awkward, and easily embarrassed.*

More About the Writer

During an unhappy childhood, **Gary Paulsen** found comfort in books. "One night," he says, "as I was walking past the public library in twenty-below temperatures, I could see the reading room bathed in beautiful golden light. I went in to get warm and, to my absolute astonishment, the librarian walked up to me and said, 'Would you like a book? ... When she handed me a library card, she handed me the world.'"

Think About the Writer

Tell students that writers often model characters on their own lives. Discuss the information about Gary Paulsen, and then ask students about the narrator of "Girls." Do they think thirteen-year-old Paulsen was similar to this character?

 For Independent Reading

■ If students enjoy Gary Paulsen's writing, they may want to read *Hatchet,* Paulsen's novel about a teenager who must overcome both a dangerous adventure in the wilderness as well as the heartbreak of his parents' divorce.

■ For students wishing to read more about young people's experience of love, suggest *I Am Wings: Poems About Love* by Ralph Fletcher. In this collection of poems, Fletcher explores the effect of love on one young narrator.

 California Standards, p. 145

■ **Reading Standard 3.3** Analyze characterization as delineated through a character's thoughts, words, speech patterns, and actions; the narrator's description; and the thoughts, words, and actions of other characters

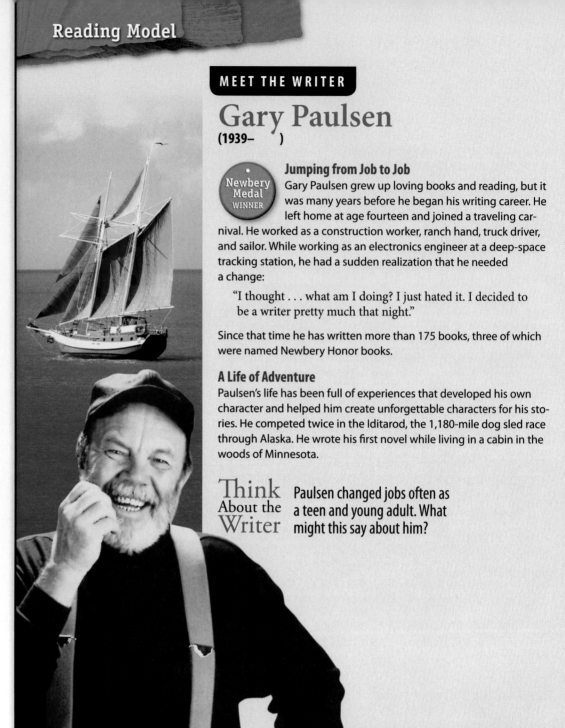

MEET THE WRITER

Gary Paulsen
(1939–)

Newbery Medal WINNER

Jumping from Job to Job

Gary Paulsen grew up loving books and reading, but it was many years before he began his writing career. He left home at age fourteen and joined a traveling carnival. He worked as a construction worker, ranch hand, truck driver, and sailor. While working as an electronics engineer at a deep-space tracking station, he had a sudden realization that he needed a change:

> "I thought . . . what am I doing? I just hated it. I decided to be a writer pretty much that night."

Since that time he has written more than 175 books, three of which were named Newbery Honor books.

A Life of Adventure

Paulsen's life has been full of experiences that developed his own character and helped him create unforgettable characters for his stories. He competed twice in the Iditarod, the 1,180-mile dog sled race through Alaska. He wrote his first novel while living in a cabin in the woods of Minnesota.

Think About the Writer Paulsen changed jobs often as a teen and young adult. What might this say about him?

Resources

Chapter 2 Resources, Literary and Academic Vocabulary Skill Builder, p. 5

UA: Differentiating Instruction, Academic and Selection Vocabulary Skill Builder, p. 47

Teacher One Stop™, on-level lesson plans and all print resources

WordSharp: An Interactive Vocabulary Tutor, more practice with academic language

Academic Vocabulary

Writing About Character and Characterization

English for Academic Success Write the following questions on the board. Tell students these are the kinds of questions on standardized tests. Discuss the meaning of the words, then have students use "Girls" to answer the questions.

• What **attribute** of the narrator's do you feel has the greatest impact on the development of the story? ***Possible response:*** *The attribute of the narrator's that has the most impact on the development of the story is his shyness.*

Reading Standard 3.3 Analyze character-ization as delineated through a character's thoughts, words, speech patterns, and actions; the narrator's description; and the thoughts, words, and actions of other characters.

Into Action: Making Inferences

Practice making inferences and analyzing charac-ters. Re-read the end of "Girls." Then, use the chart to make an inference about the narrator's overall impression of his time with Eileen.

It Says	I Say	And So ...
Writer's Clues	My Experiences	Inference

Talk About . . .

1. How realistic is this story? With a partner, evaluate the credibility, or believability, of the characters, especially the narrator. Use story details in your response. Try to use each Academic Vocabulary word listed on the right at least once in your discussion.

Write About . . .

Answer the following questions about "Girls." For definitions of the underlined Academic Vocabulary words, see the column on the right.

2. What attributes of Eileen's can you infer from her behavior?

3. Identify story details that characterize the narrator's nervousness around girls.

Writing Skills Focus
Think as a Reader/Writer

Paulsen uses description to convey the narrator's appearance and behavior. Imagine a young narra-tor, male or female, who is confident and friendly when going to the movies on a first date. Write a description that conveys the way this character looks and acts. In this chapter you'll have other opportunities to use the skills, or craft, writers use.

Academic Vocabulary for Chapter 2

Talking and Writing About Character and Characterization

Academic Vocabulary is the language you use to write and talk about literature. Use these words to discuss the stories you read in this chapter. The words are underlined throughout the chapter.

attribute (AT ruh byoot) *n.*: quality or trait of someone or some-thing. *The narrator's most obvious attribute is his awkwardness around girls.*

delineate (duh LIHN ee ayt) *v.*: describe in detail; portray. *Writers use several means to delineate characters in their stories: the narrator's description; a character's thoughts, words, speech pat-terns, and actions; and the thoughts, words, and actions of other characters.*

identify (y DEHN tuh fy) *v.*: recognize and be able to say what someone or something is. *If you identify a character's motivation, you often gain insights into that character's behavior.*

respond (rih SPAHND) *v.*: say or write something as a reply or answer. *Respond critically to the author's use of indirect characterization.*

Your Turn

Create a chart like this one to list the attributes of key characters in each selec-tion in this chapter.

Selection	Character	Attributes
"Girls"	narrator	shy

Guided Practice: Apply

Into Action: Making Inferences

Remind students that the "And So" column containing their inference combines the information from the first two columns: the writer's clues and the student's own experiences.

Talk About...

1. Model for students how to incor-porate the academic vocabu-lary words in their discussion. For example, you might say, "I thought that the characters' attri-butes were realistic. The narrator acted nervous and embarrassed, just the way I would in a similar situation."

Write About...
Possible responses:

2. *From her behavior on the date, I can tell that Eileen's attributes include patience and kindness.*

3. *I identified the narrator's behavior as nervousness when he asked Eileen the same question three times.*

Writing Skills Focus

The Think as a Reader/Writer activi-ties in the chapter focus on the reading-writing relationship. Use the activities to help students explore the writer's craft in a text and to practice this aspect of craft in their own writing.

Independent Practice

📖 **Chapter 2 Resources,** Skill Builders, pp. 3–5

✏️ **UA: Differentiating Instruction,** Academic and Selection Vocabulary Skill Builder, p. 47

- **Identify** the process by which the narrator asks Eileen to the movies. ***Possible response:*** *The narrator's process for asking Eileen on a date is silly and complicated: He asks her to the movies through a chain of three other people.*

- Name two details from the story that the writer uses to **delineate** Eileen's character. ***Possible response:*** *Eileen does not refuse his food, and she ignores his awkward behavior. Paulsen uses these details to delineate Eileen as a polite, tolerant person.*

- If you were in Eileen's position, how would you **respond** to the narrator's behavior? ***Possible response:*** *I would probably be a little uncomfortable, and I would feel bad for the narrator, so I might respond by telling the narrator to relax and enjoy the movie.*

Standards Focus

Objectives

Students will

- explore how a writer develops a character
- make inferences about a character

Motivate

What Do You Think?/QuickWrite

Have students write for 3-5 minutes in their **Reader/Writer Notebook** about a time they did something silly to impress someone. Then, have them discuss whether pretending to know more than you do is acceptable.

English for Academic Success

Academic Vocabulary

Look for opportunities to use the Academic Vocabulary words in this chapter.

- **attribute, *n.:*** quality or trait of someone or something.
- **delineate, *v.:*** describe in detail; portray.
- **identify, *v.:*** recognize and be able to say what someone or something is.

Analyzing Visuals

Extension Activity The picture shows a heart and arrows. How do you think these symbols might relate to the content of the story? ***Possible response:*** *The story might be about a character who is in love.*

California Standards, pp. 146–157

- **Reading Standard 3.3** Analyze characterization as delineated through a character's thoughts, words, speech patterns, and actions; the narrator's description; and the thoughts, words, and actions of other characters.

Preparing to Read

SEVENTH GRADE

by **Gary Soto**

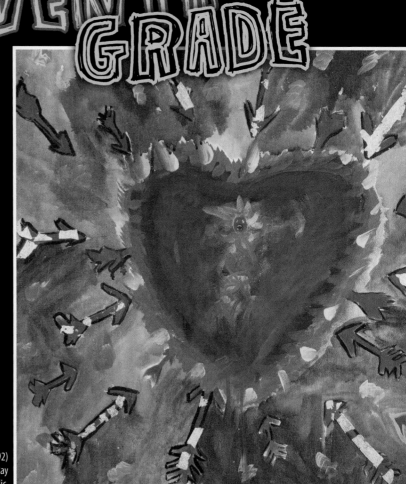

Heart Afire (1992) by Gayle Ray (1954–). Acrylic.

What Do You Think What can happen if you try so hard to be liked that you tell a lie?

⏱ QuickWrite

Think of a time when you or someone you know did something silly to impress someone. Write a short paragraph explaining what happened.

Selection Readability	
Easily Accessible **Accessible** **Challenging**	familiar situations; familiar syntax; conversational dialogue

Selection Plot Summary

Victor struggles to talk to Teresa, a girl he wants to date. He pretends to speak French to win her affection. A sympathetic teacher helps him continue the charade and win the chance to tutor Teresa.

Reader/Writer Notebook

Use your **RWN** to complete the activities for this selection.

Reading Standard 3.3 Analyze characterization as delineated through a character's thoughts, words, speech patterns, and actions; the narrator's description; and the thoughts, words, and actions of other characters.

Literary Skills Focus

Character Traits A **character** is anyone who plays a part in a story. A **character trait** is a personal <u>attribute</u>, or quality. Character traits are revealed through a person's appearance, words, actions, and thoughts. Character traits can also be revealed in the ways a person affects other people. As you read "Seventh Grade," notice how the writer characterizes Victor, his classmates, and his teacher. What are their character traits—their personal qualities?

Literary Perspectives Apply the literary perspective described on page 149 as you read this story.

Reading Skills Focus

Making Inferences To find a character's traits, you have to make inferences. **Inferences** are educated guesses based on evidence. If you read a story in which a character works diligently to mentor students who need help reading, you could infer that the character is a caring person who knows the value of education.

Into Action As you read "Seventh Grade," record your inferences in an It Says / I Say / And So chart. List details about the characters in the first column. In the second, connect the information to your own experience. Then, combine that information and make an inference about the character.

It Says	I Say	And So
Writer's Clues	My Experiences	Inference
Victor practices scowling to attract girls.	Last year I tried to impress someone by telling jokes.	Impressing someone is more difficult than it seems.

Writing Skills Focus

Think as a Reader/Writer

Find It in Your Reading In "Seventh Grade," Soto describes the appearance of several characters. In your *Reader/Writer Notebook*, record descriptions of at least three characters, and then make an inference about each one from their descriptions.

Vocabulary

elective (ih LEHK tihv) *n.:* course that is not required. *When choosing his elective, Victor thought about French.*

propelled (pruh PEHLD) *v.:* moved or pushed forward. *The bell propelled students to their classes.*

conviction (kuhn VIHK shuhn) *n.:* certainty; belief. *Michael scowled with conviction, trying to impress the girls.*

lingered (LIHNG guhrd) *v.:* stayed on. *Victor lingered in the classroom so he could walk out with Teresa.*

sheepishly (SHEEP ihsh lee) *adv.:* awkwardly; with embarrassment. *Victor smiled sheepishly at his teacher.*

Language Coach

Denotations/Connotations

Denotation is the dictionary definition of a word. **Connotation** refers to shades of meaning attached to a word. Authors consider the connotations of words as they try to create more vivid pictures in readers' minds. Which word in each pair creates a clearer impression in your mind?

- *belief* or *conviction*?
- *lingered* or *stayed*?
- *sheepishly* or *shyly*?

 Learn It Online
Reinforce your understanding of these words at:
go.hrw.com | H7-147 | **Go**

Selection Resources

Introducing Vocabulary

Read aloud the words and sample sentences. Then, use this activity to check students' understanding:

1. Suggest an **elective** you would like to take in school.
2. What makes you feel **propelled** to try hard?
3. What is the issue about which you feel **conviction**?
4. In what kind of situation might you **linger**?
5. When might someone look **sheepishly** at a friend?

English for Academic Success

Language Coach

After students read the Language Coach, point out that each pair of words means basically the same thing, but that the connotation of *conviction* is of a strong belief and that of *lingered* is of a person unconcerned with time. Have students write a sentence with each word that clearly shows its connotation.

Literary Skills Focus

As you read and discuss the selection with students, have them write examples of character traits in their **Reader/Writer Notebook.**

Reading Skills Focus

Give students a copy of the Reading Skills Focus graphic organizer before they read. Tell them to use their responses to answer the questions on the Applying Your Skills page.

Writing Skills Focus

Have students record descriptive details about characters in their **Reader/Writer Notebook.**

 Learn It Online
Send students to **Word Watch** for audio pronunciations, synonyms and antonyms, and brief histories of word origins.

go.hrw.com | H7-147 | **Go**

Selection Introduction

More About the Writer

In his youth, **Gary Soto** was not ambitious; in fact, he graduated from high school with a surprisingly low grade point average. After high school, however, he discovered the power of literature. During his second year at Fresno City College, Soto began to come into his own as a writer.

Think About the Writer

Before students answer the question, have them read the Build Background note. Then, ask them to consider how a personal experience can affect what an author writes. Have them discuss how they might use their own experiences in their writing if they were authors.

For Independent Reading

If students want to explore other stories of growing up, particularly in a Mexican-American household, suggest they read *The House on Mango Street** by Sandra Cisneros. This story details the experiences of Esperanza, a young girl growing up in a troubled Hispanic neighborhood in Chicago.

 *This title is available in the HRW library.

Learn It Online
Writers' Lives offers more information on the life of the author as well as Holt's interactive resources pertaining to the author.

go.hrw.com   H7-148   **Go**

 Learn It Online
Learn more about Soto's life at:
go.hrw.com   H7-148   **Go**

Gary Soto
(1952–   )

"A Name Among *la Gente*"
Gary Soto grew up in a Mexican American family in California, and much of his award-winning fiction and poetry draws on his heritage and his childhood memories. Although his work is vastly popular today, Soto remembers that early on he worked hard to make connections with his readers.

> "Unlike most other contemporary poets and writers, I've taken the show on the road and built a name among *la gente,* the people. I have ventured into schools, where I have played baseball and basketball with young people, sung songs, acted in skits, delivered commencement speeches, learned three chords on a Mexican guitar to serenade teachers. . . . From all appearances, my readers care."

Think About the Writer Why do you think being in touch with his audience is important to Gary Soto?

Build Background

Like Victor, the main character in "Seventh Grade," Gary Soto grew up in Fresno, a city in California's San Joaquin Valley with a large Mexican American community. Farmers in this valley grow more than two hundred different types of crops. The valley is one of the nation's leading producers of grapes and raisins.

Preview the Selection

On his first day in the seventh grade, **Victor** tries to impress his classmate **Teresa** by pretending to be someone he isn't.

Universal Access

English Learners
English for Academic Success   Some students have difficulty understanding certain phrases, particularly idioms. List several difficult phrases from the text and work through each one to make meaning. Some examples include "socked each other in the arm," "watched her on the sly," and "catch her eye."

✔ See the English Language Skill Builder **UA: Differentiating Instruction** for lesson plans and strategies for teaching English learners.

Struggling Readers
Strategic Students   Students may have trouble making inferences about character traits Have them work with a partner to identify two details from p. 149. For example, they might note that Victor says it is cool in France, unlike in Fresno. Guide them in a discussion of character traits each detail might suggest; for example, help them infer that Victor dislikes hot weather.

✔ See **UA: Differentiating Instruction** for a graphic organizer to scaffold instruction for teaching struggling readers.

Read with a Purpose Read this story to see how Victor survives his first day of seventh grade.

by **Gary Soto**

On the first day of school, Victor stood in line half an hour before he came to a wobbly card table. He was handed a packet of papers and a computer card on which he listed his one elective, French. He already spoke Spanish and English, but he thought some day he might travel to France, where it was cool; not like Fresno,[1] where summer days reached 110 degrees in the shade. There were rivers in France, and huge churches, and fair-skinned people everywhere, the way there were brown people all around Victor. **Ⓐ**

Besides, Teresa, a girl he had liked since they were in catechism classes[2] at Saint Theresa's, was taking French, too. With any luck they would be in the same class. Teresa is going to be my girl this year, he promised himself as he left the gym full of students in their new fall clothes. She was cute. And good in math, too, Victor thought as he walked down the hall to his homeroom. He ran into his friend, Michael Torres, by the water fountain that never turned off. **Ⓑ**

They shook hands, *raza*-style, and jerked their heads at one another in a *saludo de vato*.[3] "How come you're making a face?" asked Victor.

"I ain't making a face, *ese*. This *is* my face." Michael said his face had changed during the summer. He had read a *GQ* magazine that his older brother had

---

3. ***saludo de vato*** (sah LOO doh day BAH toh): Spanish for "homeboy greeting."

---

1. **Fresno:** town in the San Joaquin Valley, in central California.
2. **catechism** (KAT uh kihz uhm) **classes:** instruction in religious principles.

Ⓐ Read and Discuss What have you learned so far?

Ⓑ Read and Discuss What have you learned about Victor's desire to study French?

Literary Perspectives

The following perspective will help you analyze the characters in "Seventh Grade."

Analyzing Credibility When you read a story about everyday people interacting in normal settings, think about whether the characters are **credible,** or believable. Do the characters ring true in the ways they behave? As you read "Seventh Grade," analyze the story—especially its characters—for credibility. Questions in the text will guide you in using this perspective.

Vocabulary   **elective** (ih LEHK tihv) *n.:* course that is not required.

Model the Skill

■ To help students **make inferences**, provide them with copies of the Reading Skills Focus graphic organizer. (See **Chapter 2 Resources**.)

■ Model for students how to fill out the chart. Tell students that the information in the *It Says* column comes directly from the text. The information in the *I Say* column comes from a reader's knowledge and experiences related to the text. The information in the *And So* column is an inference based on the reader's understanding of the text.

Guided Practice: Apply

Guide students in filling out one item for the *It Says/I Say/And So* chart, as below. Guide students to see the relationship between the text, readers' experiences, and the inference.

It Says	I Say
Victor wants to travel to France, because he thinks that picking grapes is hot and dull.	I grew up on a farm and didn't like the dirt and the hard work.

And So ...
Victor wishes for an easier and more glamorous life.

English for Academic Success

(AAVE) Point out that the author uses informal language in the dialogue to make the characters sound like credible teenagers having a conversation before class. Then, have students rewrite the following quoations using standard English appropriate for a more formal setting.

1. "How 'bout you?"
2. "I ain't so good at it, even if I'm Mexican."

---

borrowed from the Book Mobile and noticed that the male models all had the same look on their faces. They would stand, one arm around a beautiful woman, and *scowl*. They would sit at a pool, their rippled stomachs dark with shadow, and *scowl*. They would sit at dinner tables, cool drinks in their hands, and *scowl*.

"I think it works," Michael said. He scowled and let his upper lip quiver. His teeth showed along with the ferocity of his soul. "Belinda Reyes walked by a while ago and looked at me," he said.

Victor didn't say anything, though he thought his friend looked pretty strange. They talked about recent movies, baseball, their parents, and the horrors of picking grapes in order to buy their fall clothes. Picking grapes was like living in Siberia,[4] except hot and more boring. **C**

"What classes are you taking?" Michael said, scowling.

"French. How 'bout you?"

"Spanish. I ain't so good at it, even if I'm Mexican."

---

4. **Siberia:** vast, barren, and cold region in Russia where criminals and political prisoners were often sent as punishment.

C **Read and Discuss** What is Victor doing now? What is going on with Michael's face?

D **Literary Focus** Character Traits What does the conversation between Victor and Michael reveal?

> Victor sat calmly, thinking of Teresa, who sat two rows away, reading a paperback novel. This would be his lucky year.

"I'm not either, but I'm better at it than math, that's for sure." **D**

A tinny, three-beat bell propelled students to their homerooms. The two friends socked each other in the arm and went their ways, Victor thinking, man, that's weird. Michael thinks making a face makes him handsome.

On the way to his homeroom, Victor tried a scowl. He felt foolish, until out of the corner of his eye he saw a girl looking at him. Umm, he thought, maybe it does work. He scowled with greater conviction.

In homeroom, roll was taken, emergency cards were passed out, and they were given a bulletin to take home to their parents. The principal, Mr. Belton, spoke over the crackling loudspeaker, welcoming the students to a new year, new experiences, and new friendships. The students squirmed in their chairs and ignored him. They were anxious to go to first period. Victor sat calmly, thinking of Teresa, who sat two rows away, reading a paperback novel. This would be his lucky year. She was in his homeroom, and would probably be in his English and math classes. And, of, course, French. **E**

E **Literary Perspectives** Analyzing Credibility What details about Victor's first day of seventh grade are believable? To which events and emotions can you most relate?

Vocabulary **propelled** (pruh PEHLD) *v.*: moved or pushed forward.
conviction (kuhn VIHK shuhn) *n.*: certainty; belief.

Real Issues, Real Experts

*Holt author **Linda Rief** offers strategies for helping students connect texts to their own experiences.*

I like to juxtapose "Seventh Grade" with "Eleven" by Sandra Cisneros. We read both stories aloud after I highlight the speaking parts in copies of both stories. For instance, I make seven copies of the Soto story so I can highlight one copy with the speaking part of each of the seven characters: Victor, Teresa, Michael, homeroom teacher, Mr. Lucas, Mr. Bueller, one kid. In "Eleven" there

are four speaking parts. As we read the stories aloud, one at a time, I always read the narrator.

I ask kids to read the speaking parts aloud so we can begin to hear and understand the voices and differences in these two teachers—one a bit thoughtless, the other so considerate. I highlight the parts so kids aren't spending their time trying to figure out their part but are instead immersing themselves in the story itself. Other students, who are reading along in their texts, get a real sense of the character from the emotion readers put in their voices.

The bell rang for first period, and the students herded noisily through the door. Only Teresa lingered, talking with the homeroom teacher.

"So you think I should talk to Mrs. Gaines?" she asked the teacher. "She would know about ballet?"

"She would be a good bet," the teacher said. Then added, "Or the gym teacher, Mrs. Garza."

Victor lingered, keeping his head down and staring at his desk. He wanted to leave when she did so he could bump into her and say something clever.

He watched her on the sly. As she turned to leave, he stood up and hurried to the door, where he managed to catch her eye. She smiled and said, "Hi, Victor."

He smiled back and said, "Yeah, that's me." His brown face blushed. Why hadn't he said, "Hi, Teresa," or "How was your summer?" or something nice?

As Teresa walked down the hall, Victor walked the other way, looking back, admiring how gracefully she walked, one foot in front of the other. So much for being in the same class, he thought. As he trudged to English, he practiced scowling.

In English they reviewed the parts of speech. Mr. Lucas, a portly man, waddled down the aisle, asking, "What is a noun?"

"A person, place, or thing," said the class in unison.

"Yes, now somebody give me an example of a person—you, Victor Rodriguez."

"Teresa," Victor said automatically. Some of the girls giggled. They knew he had a crush on Teresa. He felt himself blushing again.

"Correct," Mr. Lucas said. "Now provide me with a place."

Mr. Lucas called on a freckled kid who answered, "Teresa's house with a kitchen full of big brothers."

After English, Victor had math, his weakest subject. He sat in the back by the window, hoping that he would not be called on. Victor understood most of the problems, but some of the stuff looked like the teacher made it up as she went along. It was confusing, like the inside of a watch.

After math he had a fifteen-minute break, then social studies, and, finally, lunch. He bought a tuna casserole with buttered rolls, some fruit cocktail, and milk. He sat with Michael, who practiced scowling between bites.

Girls walked by and looked at him.

"See what I mean, Vic?" Michael scowled. "They love it."

"Yeah, I guess so."

They ate slowly, Victor scanning the horizon for a glimpse of Teresa. He didn't see her. She must have brought lunch, he thought, and is eating outside. Victor scraped his plate and left Michael, who was busy scowling at a girl two tables away.

F | **Read and Discuss** The author supplies many details about Victor's day at school. What point do you think he is trying to make?

Vocabulary **lingered** (LIHNG guhrd) *v.:* stayed on.

After we finish both stories, I ask the students to write in their **Reader/Writer Notebook** as quickly as they can about an incident that either one of these stories might have brought to mind for them, especially with respect to teachers they may have had. I then ask them to exchange their notebook with another student, who is to read what the student wrote and write a response to that student's experience—either something it brought to mind for them in their own experience or a reaction to the original student's story.

This leads to great discussions, especially about all of us trying to be more like Mr. Bueller. If the Cisneros story is not available, it is just as easy to do this same thing with just the Soto story.

Think About/Talk About

▶ **Comprehension**

C **Read and Discuss**

Possible response: He ran into his friend Michael. He's scowling because he thinks it will attract girls.

F **Read and Discuss**

Possible response: He's letting us know that Victor is a typical kid having a normal day at school.

▶ **Analysis**

D **Literary Focus**

Possible response: They are typical middle school students who share similar interests.

E **Literary Perspectives**

Possible response: He is too engrossed in thinking about Teresa to be anxious about his classes.

▶ **Extend the Discussion**

Making Inferences Besides the fact that Victor gave Teresa's name as an answer in English class, how do you think some of the girls already knew he had a crush on Teresa? *Possible response: It's obvious from the way he always stares at her and follows her around.*

Vocabulary: Own the Word

• **propelled**: Ask students to list other forces that could propel or move them forward. *Possible responses: a crowd of people or the wind.* Point out that *propeller*, a noun form of *propel*, is the blades that turn to move a boat or plane forward.

• **conviction:** Remind students that the connotation of *conviction* is a *strong* belief. For example, you might say, "I *believe* in conserving resources, but I have a *conviction* that littering is wrong and should be punishable."

• **lingered:** Ask students to list additional reasons they might linger after class. *Possible responses: to get homework assignments; to talk to a friend.*

Model the Skill

■ Review the concept of **character traits.** Explain that you have a friend who is always late or can never find her car keys. Ask students what character trait would describe your friend's actions and appearnce. *[Absent-mindedness]*

■ Tell students that we can also identify traits of characters in a story by observing their words or actions, and by reading their thoughts. Read aloud the second paragraph in the first column, beginning with "He lowered his eyes…." Tell students Victor may be afraid of failing.

■ Then, read aloud the paragraph in which the teacher asks if anyone knows French. Tell students Victor is willing to lie in order to impress a girl. Perhpas he is afraid of failing with the girl, just as he's afraid of failing in math.

Guided Practice: Apply

Have students read to the end of p. 152. Ask them to identify orally Victor's words, actions, and thoughts and identify the character traits these words, actions, and thoughts demonstrate. Record the traits on the board.

Think as a Reader/Writer

Find It in Your Reading Read aloud the paragraph that begins "Great rosebushes…." Point out that the author is describing Victor's physical reaction to being caught pretending to know French. This reaction demonstrates that Victor is easily embarrassed.

Use It in Your Writing Tell students to write two descriptive sentences about a character or person they know that indicates something the subject's personality.

The small, triangle-shaped campus bustled with students talking about their new classes. Everyone was in a sunny mood. Victor hurried to the bag lunch area, where he sat down and opened his math book. He moved his lips as if he were reading, but his mind was somewhere else. He raised his eyes slowly and looked around. No Teresa.

He lowered his eyes, pretending to study, then looked slowly to the left. No Teresa. He turned a page in the book and stared at some math problems that scared him because he knew he would have to do them eventually. He looked to the right. Still no sign of her. He stretched out lazily in an attempt to disguise his snooping.

Then he saw her. She was sitting with a girlfriend under a plum tree. Victor moved to a table near her and daydreamed about taking her to a movie. When the bell sounded, Teresa looked up, and their eyes met. She smiled sweetly and gathered her books. Her next class was French, same as Victor's. **G**

They were among the last students to arrive in class, so all the good desks in the back had already been taken. Victor was forced to sit near the front, a few desks away from Teresa, while Mr. Bueller wrote French words on the chalkboard. The bell rang, and Mr. Bueller wiped his hands, turned to the class, and said, "*Bonjour.*"[5]

"*Bonjour,*" braved a few students.

---

5. *bonjour* (bohn ZHOOR): French for "hello" or "good day."

G Literary Focus **Character Traits** What does the description "smiled sweetly" tell you about Teresa?

"*Bonjour,*" Victor whispered. He wondered if Teresa heard him.

Mr. Bueller said that if the students studied hard, at the end of the year they could go to France and be understood by the populace.

One kid raised his hand and asked, "What's 'populace'?"

"The people, the people of France."

Mr. Bueller asked if anyone knew French. Victor raised his hand, wanting to impress Teresa. The teacher beamed and said, "*Très bien. Parlez-vous français?*"[6] **H**

Victor didn't know what to say. The teacher wet his lips and asked something else in French. The room grew silent. Victor felt all eyes staring at him. He tried to bluff his way out by making noises that sounded French.

"La me vave me con le grandma," he said uncertainly.

Mr. Bueller, wrinkling his face in curiosity, asked him to speak up.

Great rosebushes of red bloomed on Victor's cheeks. A river of nervous sweat ran down his palms. He felt awful. Teresa sat a few desks away, no doubt thinking he was a fool. Without looking at Mr. Bueller, Victor mumbled, "Frenchie oh wewe gee in September." **I**

Mr. Bueller asked Victor to repeat what he said. "Frenchie oh wewe gee in September," Victor repeated.

---

6. *Très bien. Parlez-vous français* (tray bee EHN PAHR lay voo frahn SAY): French for "Very good. Do you speak French?"

H Literary Perspectives **Analyzing Credibility** How believable is Victor's declaration that he knows how to speak French?

I Read and Discuss How is French class going for Victor?

Literary Perspectives

Point out to students that the author has used familiar English words such as "grandma," "Frenchie," and "in September" in Victor's "French" to add humor to the story as well as to help the reader decide if Victor's effort at speaking French is credible.

Los Angeles (2006) by José Ramírez.
Mixed media on canvas.
©Courtesy of the artist.

 Analyzing Visuals   **Connecting to the Text** What does this image suggest about the story and its main characters?

Think About/Talk About
See Student Edition p. 152 for the questions that relate to the following answers.

▶ **Comprehension**

❶ Read and Discuss

Possible response: The teacher asked the class if anyone could speak French and Victor raised his hand to impress Teresa. His plan backfired when the teacher asked him to actually speak French.

▶ **Analysis**

❻ Literary Focus

Possible response: Teresa's smile reveals that she is a kind person; it may also reveal that she likes Victor.

❶ Literary Perspectives

Possible response: Victor's declaration is not believable because he is desperate to impress Teresa.

▶ **Extend the Discussion**

Character Traits Why do you think Victor tries to bluff by speaking gibberish rather than admitting that he can't speak French? *Possible response:* *It is important to him not to look silly in front of Teresa.*

Analyzing Visuals
José Ramírez uses art to address contemporary issues facing everyone from Chicanos of his native Los Angeles to young black women.

Connecting to the Text: *The image suggests the characters live in a neighborhood on the outskirts of Los Angeles. The figures in the image sit side by side, looking at the city in the distance, perhaps imagining their futures. This suggests the characters, close friends, are introspective and ambitious.*

Universal Access

EL English Learners
English for Academic Success Point out the lines "La me vave me con le grandma," and "Frenchie oh wee gee in September" on this page. Clarify that Victor is not speaking French (which is italicized-*Bonjour*) but is simply making up phrases and words that he thinks sound French. In both examples, he ends with a word he knows in English: "grandma" and "September." He is trying to impress Teresa and ends up looking foolish in front of her and the teacher.

AAVE Students Who Use African American Vernacular English
English for Academic Success Some students may have difficulty with the 's that indicates singular possessives, such as *Victor's friend*. They may omit the pronunciation of the 's in speaking and not use it in writing. Write this sentence on the board: "_____ scowl seems strange to Victor." Ask students how the sentence should begin. Then, ask a volunteer to read the sentence aloud. Have students look for another example of 's in the story and practice reading the sentence aloud to a partner.

Think About/Talk About

► Comprehension

Ⓙ Reading Focus

Possible response: Mr. Bueller understands Victor's desperation and does not want to make Victor look foolish. He is a sympathetic and udnerstanding teacher.

Ⓛ Read and Discuss

Possible response: Mr. Bueller didn't reveal Victor's inability to speak French—he let Teresa think that the few words Victor mumbled in class were actually French.

► Analysis

Ⓚ Literary Perspectives

Possible response: Teresa's response doesn't seem very credible. Victor's attempt to speak French didn't convince me, so I'm surprised that it convinced Teresa.

Vocabulary: Own the Word

sheepishly: Tell students that *sheepish* literally means "like a sheep"; sheep are timid and shy. The connotation of *sheepish* is that a sheepish person is embarrassed by his or her behavior. Ask students what made Victor feel sheepish. **Possible response:** *He couldn't speak French so he made up French to impress Teresa.*

Monitor Students' Comprehension

Guide students in answering these comprehension questions.

1. Why does Victor decide to take French? [*to be in a class with Teresa*]

2. How does Victor spend most of his day? [*looking for Teresa*]

3. What makes Victor decide he's going to like seventh grade? [*At the end of the first day of school, Teresa smiles at him.*]

Mr. Bueller understood that the boy didn't know French and turned away. He walked to the blackboard and pointed to the words on the board with his steel-edged ruler.   Ⓙ

"*Le bateau,*" he sang.

"*Le bateau,*" the students repeated.

"*Le bateau est sur l'eau,*" he sang.

"*Le bateau est sur l'eau.*"[7]

Victor was too weak from failure to join the class. He stared at the board and wished he had taken Spanish, not French. Better yet, he wished he could start his life over. He had never been so embarrassed. He bit his thumb until he tore off a sliver of skin.

The bell sounded for fifth period, and Victor shot out of the room, avoiding the stares of the other kids, but had to return for his math book. He looked sheepishly at the teacher, who was erasing the board, then widened his eyes in terror at Teresa who stood in front of him. "I didn't know you knew French," she said. "That was good." Mr. Bueller looked at Victor, and Victor looked back. Oh please, don't say anything, Victor pleaded with his eyes. I'll wash your car, mow your lawn, walk your dog—anything! I'll be your best student, and I'll clean your erasers after school.

---

7. *Le bateau est sur l'eau* (luh ba TOH ay soor loh): French for "The boat is on the water."

Ⓙ **Reading Focus** Making Inferences Why does Mr. Bueller turn away instead of correcting Victor? What kind of teacher do you think he is?

Ⓚ **Literary Perspectives** Analyzing Credibility Based on what you know, how credible is Teresa's response?

Mr. Bueller shuffled through the papers on his desk. He smiled and hummed as he sat down to work. He remembered his college years when he dated a girlfriend in borrowed cars. She thought he was rich because each time he picked her up he had a different car. It was fun until he had spent all his money on her and had to write home to his parents because he was broke.

Victor couldn't stand to look at Teresa. He was sweaty with shame. "Yeah, well, I picked up a few things from movies and books and stuff like that." They left the class together. Teresa asked him if he would help her with her French.

"Sure, anytime," Victor said.

"I won't be bothering you, will I?"

"Oh no, I like being bothered."

"*Bonjour,*" Teresa said, leaving him outside her next class. She smiled and pushed wisps of hair from her face.   Ⓚ

"Yeah, right, *bonjour,*" Victor said. He turned and headed to his class. The rosebushes of shame on his face became bouquets of love. Teresa is a great girl, he thought. And Mr. Bueller is a good guy.Ⓛ

He raced to metal shop. After metal shop there was biology, and after biology a long sprint to the public library, where he checked out three French textbooks.

He was going to like seventh grade.

Ⓛ **Read and Discuss** Why does Victor say that Mr. Bueller is a good guy?

Vocabulary **sheepishly** (SHEEP ihsh lee) *adv.*: awkwardly; with embarrassment.

 California Standards, pp. 155–157

■ **Reading Standard 1.2** Use knowledge of Greek, Latin, and Anglo-Saxon roots and affixes to understand content-area vocabulary.

■ **Reading Standard 3.3** Analyze characterization as delineated through a character's thoughts, words, speech patterns, and actions; the narrator's description; and the thoughts, words, and actions of other characters.

Applying Your Skills

Reading Standard 3.3 Analyze characterization as delineated through a character's thoughts, words, speech patterns, and actions; the narrator's description; and the thoughts, words, and actions of other characters.

Seventh Grade
Literary Response and Analysis

Reading Skills Focus
Quick Check

1. Complete a story map like the one below to review the plot of "Seventh Grade."

```
Characters:
What they want:
Conflicts (problems):
    Event:
    Event:
    Event:
    Climax:
        Resolution of
        conflict:
```

Read with a Purpose

2. What did you learn about Victor from the way he survives his first day of seventh grade? Give details from the story in your response.

Reading Skills: Making Inferences

3. Review the chart you completed while reading. Explain how making inferences helped increase your understanding of the characters in this story.

Literary Skills Focus
Literary Analysis

4. **Interpret** Explain what Soto means when he writes of Victor, "The rosebushes of shame on his face became bouquets of love." What does this tell you about Victor's character?

5. **Analyze** Analyze the character of Victor. What kind of person is he? How do his words, thoughts, actions, and reactions to others help <u>delineate</u> his character?

6. **Evaluate** It has been said that middle school is one of the most emotionally difficult times for students. How do the characters and events in this story support this statement?

7. **Literary Perspectives** Explain which of the following characters you find most believable, and why: Victor, Teresa, Mr. Bueller.

Literary Skills: Character Traits

8. **Compare and Contrast** <u>Identify</u> the traits that Victor and his friend Michael share. In what ways are the two boys different? How does Soto help you see their differences?

Literary Skills Review: Internal Conflict

9. **Extend** Victor feels many emotions, including anticipation, nervousness, and embarrassment. How does your awareness of his emotions help you analyze his character?

Writing Skills Focus
Think as a Reader/Writer

Use It in Your Writing Note all the inferences you were able to make based on Soto's character descriptions. Write a one-paragraph description of a seventh-grader. Include details that will allow readers to draw inferences about your character.

 What Do **You Think Now**

How has this story changed your ideas about how far a person should go in order to impress others?

Universal Access

Struggling Writers

To complete the Writing Focus, provide additional scaffolding for students by having them create T-charts. On the left side, have them list at least two traits that describe a character's personality. For example, their character may be stingy and selfish. On the right side, have them describe an action that could identify this trait, such as refusing to give money to a local charity.

Remind students that the action shows the character trait so the reader can infer it, making it unnecessary to tell the reader that the character is selfish.

Trait	Action
stingy and selfish	refuses to give to local charity

Independent Practice

Vocabulary Development

Your Turn

1. elective > ML éléctīvus, equiv. to L éléct(us)

2. propelled > ME propellen, fr. L propellere, fr. pro- *before* + pellere *to drive*

3. conviction > LL convictiōn (s. of convictiō), proof (of guilt).

4. lingered > ME lengeren, frequentative of lengen, to prolong

5. sheepishly > ME shepisshe

English for Academic Success

Language Coach

Work through the first word with students. Help them see that *scrawny* suggests someone who is thin and bony. The word *slim* is more positive because it suggest someone who is physically fit.

Possible responses:

- **fat**: *large*
- **old**: *mature*
- **smelly**: *fragrant*
- **cheap**: *frugal*

English for Academic Success

Academic Vocabulary

Possible response: Mr. Bueller's most important <u>attribute</u> is his compassion for Victor. He knows Victor cannot speak French; however, he allows Victor to save face in front of the class because he remembers a time when he lied to impress a girl.

 WordSharp: An Interactive Vocabulary Tutor

Learn It Online box

Learn It Online

Holt's **WordSharp: An Interactive Vocabulary Tutor** provides additional support for vocabulary development. Multimedia tutorials show students how to apply vocabulary skills to unfamiliar words—and how to make those words their own.

 go.hrw.com H7-156 **Go**

Applying Your Skills

Seventh Grade

Vocabulary Development

Word Origins: Where a Word Comes From

Dictionaries show the **word origin,** or etymology (eht uh MOL uh jee), in brackets or parentheses following the word itself. At the back or front of a dictionary, you'll find a key to the symbols and abbreviations used in its etymologies. One commonly used symbol is <, which means "comes from" or "is derived from." When the "derived from" symbol is followed by a question mark, the derivation (dehr uh VAY shuhn) of a word or word part is unknown. The same symbol reversed (>) means "from which comes." An asterisk (*) means that a derivation is not certain. Here is the etymology of the word *mother* from one dictionary:

> moder < OE *modor,* akin to Ger *mutter* < IE* *matér,* mother > L *mater,* Gr *mētēr,* OIr *māthir,** *ma–,* echoic of baby talk.

This could be translated into words as "The word *mother* comes from the Middle English word *moder,* which comes from the Old English word *modor,* which is related ('akin') to the German word *mutter,* which comes from the Indo-European word *matér,* from which comes the Latin word *mater,* the Greek word *mētēr,* and the Old Irish word *māthir.* All the words might come from a word that imitates the sound of baby talk."

Your Turn

In a dictionary, find the derivations of the Vocabulary words at right. Create a chart like the one below for each word. Which words come from Latin?

Vocabulary Word	Original Derivation
propelled	< L *pro pellere,* to drive forward

Word list: elective, propelled, conviction, lingered, sheepishly

---

Reading Standard box (top right)

Reading Standard 1.2 Use knowledge of Greek, Latin, and Anglo-Saxon **roots** and affixes **to understand** content-area vocabulary.

Language Coach

Denotations / Connotations

The **denotation** of a word is its dictionary definition. The **connotation** relates to the feelings associated with the word. Some words have negative connotations, such as *scorching,* while others have positive connotations, such as *sunny.*

scrawny
fat
old
smelly
cheap

Your Turn

The words in the box above have negative connotations. For each one, think of another word with the same general meaning but with a more positive connotation.

Academic Vocabulary

Talk About . . .

In a class discussion, <u>identify</u> Mr. Bueller's most important <u>attributes</u>. How are they <u>delineated</u> in the story?

 Learn It Online
Sharpen your word skills with *WordSharp* at:
go.hrw.com H7-156 **Go**

Universal Access: Vocabulary Development

EL English Learners

English for Academic Success While students may understand the meaning of a word, they may need additional practice determining a word's connotations. Pair students with a proficient English speaker; then, have them engage in an instructional conversation in which they work through the following pairs of words, deciding on the difference in connotation for each word.

- *careful* and *finicky*
- *walked* and *ambled*
- *fight* and *dispute*
- *creamy* and *ashen*

156 Chapter 2

Grammar Link

Adjectives

An **adjective** is a word that modifies a noun (such as *dog, bicycle,* or *Charles*) or a pronoun (such as *she, he,* or *it*). Adjectives typically answer one of the questions in the chart below. The adjectives in the chart are underlined.

What kind?	<u>wobbly</u> table <u>recent</u> movie <u>quivering</u> lip
Which one (or ones)?	<u>last</u> students <u>first</u> period <u>that</u> girl
How much (or many)?	<u>all</u> eyes <u>three</u> books <u>many</u> boys

The words *a, an,* and *the* make up a special class of adjectives called **articles.**

Your Turn

Identify the adjective in each sentence below about "Seventh Grade," and tell which of the above questions the adjective answers. (Do not include the articles *a, an,* and *the.*) Then, use the adjective to modify a different word in a sentence of your own.

1. Victor is starting seventh grade.
2. He has a crush on a pretty girl.
3. Teresa has several brothers.
4. Teresa and Victor are in the same class.
5. Victor decides that Mr. Bueller is a good guy.

Reading Standard 3.3 Analyze characterization as delineated through a character's thoughts, words, speech patterns, and actions; the narrator's description; and the thoughts, words, and actions of other characters.

CHOICES

As you respond to the Choices, use these **Academic Vocabulary** words as appropriate: <u>attribute</u>, <u>delineate</u>, <u>identify</u>, <u>respond</u>.

REVIEW
Analyze Characterization

Timed ⏱ Writing How did Soto make Victor likable and unique? Fill out a character map to show Soto's methods of characterization. How does he help you get to know Victor? Summarize your chart in a paragraph.

CONNECT
Write a Journal Entry

Pretend that you are Victor and have just finished your first day of seventh grade. Write a journal entry <u>identifying</u> the day's highlights and explaining how you feel about them.

EXTEND
Write an Alternate Ending

How would the plot of this story change if Mr. Bueller had revealed Victor's ignorance of French? Rewrite the end of the story. What effect does the new ending have on Victor's character?

Independent Practice
Grammar Link
Your Turn _____

1. Which one? He sits in the *seventh* row.
2. What kind? That is a *pretty* dress.
3. How many? I have *several* goldfish.
4. Which one? Tim and I are wearing the *same* shirt.
5. What kind? That was a *good* sandwich.

Choices:
Evaluation Criteria
Review: Timed Writing
40–50 Minutes
- Student maps should include Victor's specific character traits.
- Students should include details to support character traits.

Connect: 〔Homework〕
Write a Journal Entry
- Journal entries should include key events from the story.
- Entries should include a description of Victor's feelings based on details.

Extend: 〔Homework〕
Write an Alternate Ending
- Endings should be realistic and include details from the story.

Assess

📝 **Chapter 2 Resources,** Selection Standards Check, p. 9

 ThinkCentral Online Assessment, Selection Standards Check

🔘 **Teacher One Stop™,** editable Selection Standards Check

Reteach

To reteach **characterization,** see **Reteaching Lessons,** p. 842A.

ThinkCentral Online Remediation

Universal Access: Grammar Link

〔EL〕 English Learners/ Struggling Writers
English for Academic Success Explain to students that adjectives are words that are used to describe someone or something. They give us more detail about the subject, such as what things look or sound like, how much of the subject there is, or even which subject is being described.

- Write the sentence, "I see a man" on the board. Explain that there are no adjectives in this sentence. As a result, the sentence is vague and unclear.

- Then, write the sentence, "I see a short, bald man." Explain that the words *short* and *bald* are adjectives that describe the man you see. They give the listener a better idea of the subject you are describing by providing more detail about the man.

- Have students practice using adjectives by describing objects around the classroom.

✔ For more practice with using adjectives, see **Warriner's Handbook, Language Handbook Worksheets,** and **Grammar Notes**.

Standards Focus

Objectives
Students will
- analyze how traits delineate a character

Motivate

What Do You Think?/QuickWrite
Have students talk about a time when they were told they could not do an activity. What happened? Did anything boost their confidence? Have students record their thoughts in their **Reader/Writer Notebook.**

English for Academic Success

Academic Vocabulary
Look for opportunities to use the Academic Vocabulary words from the chapter.

- **delineate, v:** describe in detail; portray.

- **identify, v.:** recognize and be able to say what someone or something is.

- **respond, v.:** say or write something as a reply or answer.

Analyzing Visuals
Extension Activity Ask students to focus on the boy holding the bat. How would they characterize him, and why? *Possible response: From the boy's stance, he seems focused and determined.*

THAT OCTOBER
by **D. H. Figueredo**

What Do **You Think** In order for you to believe in yourself, how necessary is it that others believe in you?

QuickWrite What helps boost your confidence when you need to meet a challenge? Write your ideas in a paragraph.

California Standards, pp. 158–169

- **Reading Standard 3.3** Analyze characterization as delineated through a character's thoughts, words, speech patterns, and actions; the narrator's description; and the thoughts, words, and actions of other characters.

Selection Readability	
Easily Accessible Accessible **Challenging**	historical context; serious subject matter; theme

Selection Plot Summary
Rudy, a boy living in Havana, Cuba in the early 1960s, breaks a government building's window with his baseball. To avoid getting in trouble, Rudy must tell the story of how he came to play baseball with his team, the Tigers, despite his polio.

Reader/Writer Notebook

Use your **RWN** to complete the activities for this selection.

Reading Standard 3.3 Analyze characterization as delineated through a character's thoughts, words, speech patterns, and actions; the narrator's description; and the thoughts, words, and actions of other characters.

Literary Skills Focus

Characterization The way a writer reveals the personality of a character is called **characterization.** Writers achieve this by

1. describing how the character looks, speaks, and dresses
2. letting you hear the character's inner thoughts and feelings
3. revealing what others think or say about the character
4. showing you the character's actions
5. telling you directly what the character's personality is like

Writers often <u>delineate</u> their characters through the observations of a **narrator,** the person telling the story. In "That October," D. H. Figueredo uses the narrator, a young boy named Rudy, to describe the story's other characters. The reader knows only the information that Rudy knows and shares.

Reading Skills Focus

Connecting to the Text Making personal connections to texts helps you read for deeper meaning. Practice making connections as you read "That October." The chart below provides some examples. As you read, make other connections with the narrator.

I can connect	to myself or my friends	to other stories	to situations in the world
Narrator	He is young like me.	He finds a way to use strength, like Rikki-tikki.	Cuba played in World Baseball Classic.
Conflict			
End of story			

Writing Skills Focus

Think as a Reader/Writer

Find It in Your Reading Writers sometimes reveal their characters' <u>attributes</u> through dialogue. As you read, record in your *Reader/Writer Notebook* two examples of dialogue that help show what the narrator, Alfredo, and Bebo are like.

Vocabulary

illegal (ih LEE guhl) *adj.:* unlawful; against official regulations. *It's illegal to damage government property.*

convinced (kuhn VIHNST) *v.:* made to feel sure; persuaded firmly. *Rudy's teammates were not convinced that he should be part of the team.*

opponents (uh POH nuhnts) *n.:* people on opposite sides in a fight or a game. *The Tigers' World Series opponents were the Leopards.*

encounter (ehn KOWN tuhr) *n.:* face-to-face meeting. *The Leopards were sure they would win their fourth encounter with the Tigers.*

boasting (BOHST ihng) *v.:* speaking too highly about oneself; bragging. *The Leopards were boasting about playing against a weaker team.*

Language Coach

Denotations/Connotations The **denotation** of a word is its dictionary definition. The **connotation** is the feeling or association attached to a word. Which word creates a more complex or specific picture in your mind: *meet* or *encounter*? *telling* or *boasting*?

 Learn It Online

Develop your understanding of words with Word Watch at:

go.hrw.com **H7-159** **Go**

Selection Resources

Chapter 2 Resources, on-level practice and assessment, p. 12

Teacher One Stop™, on-level lesson plans and all print resources

Holt Audio Library

Holt Audio Library: Selections and Summaries in Spanish

UA: Differentiating Instruction, graphic organizer, p. 31

UA: Supporting Instruction in Five Languages, selection summary

Analyzing Visuals Transparencies, p. 7

ThinkCentral Online Assessment, Selection Standards Check

ThinkCentral Online Remediation

Preteach

Introducing Vocabulary

Review the Vocabulary words and sample sentences aloud. Then, have students complete each analogy with a Vocabulary word.

1. *questioned* is to *doubted* as *persuaded* is to [*convinced*]
2. *lawful* is to *permitted* as *prohibited* is to [*illegal*]
3. *friends* is to *enemies* as *teammates* is to [*opponents*]
4. *shouting* is to *screaming* as *bragging* is to [*boasting*]
5. *match* is to *meeting* as *game* is to [*encounter*]

English for Academic Success

Language Coach

Ask students to discuss with a partner the difference between meeting someone and encountering someone. [*encounter; boasting*]

Literary Skills Focus

As you read and discuss the selection with students, have them discuss in pairs how characters are portrayed through their thoughts, words, and actions.

Reading Skills Focus

Give students a copy of the Reading Skills Focus graphic organizer before they read. Tell them to use their responses to answer the questions on the Applying Your Skills page.

Writing Skills Focus

Have students use their **Reader/Writer Notebook** to record examples of dialogue that reveal the speaker's character. Students can use their notes to complete the Writing Skills Focus activity.

 Learn It Online

Send students to **Word Watch** for audio pronunciations, synonyms and antonyms, and brief histories of word origins.

go.hrw.com **H7-159** **Go**

Selection Introduction

More About the Writer

D. H. Figueredo grew up in Cuba during the Communist revolution. He witnessed acts of violence and the arrest of some revolutionaries in his grandmother's neighborhood. Today, Figueredo makes it a point to remember his Cuban roots by celebrating Cuban traditions with his family. He also teaches Caribbean and Latin American literature at the college level.

Think About the Writer

Discuss the challenges that children growing up in nations in turmoil might face. What might lead writers to share childhood obstacles? Discuss how writers often use both fiction and nonfiction to describe their own personal struggles, including those of childhood.

 For Independent Reading

- If students want to explore more about growing up in a Cuban family, suggest that they read *Cuba 15*, a novel by Nancy Osa about a young girl's Cuban heritage and the cultural rituals she must celebrate for her family.

- For students interested in baseball, suggest *Babe and Me* by Dan Gutman. In this book, a young boy and his father travel back in time to meet baseball legend Babe Ruth.

D. H. Figueredo
(1951–   )

Sharing Similarities with Rudy

Like the narrator of "That October," Danilo H. Figueredo spent his boyhood in Cuba during the time when Fidel Castro came to power. Figueredo and his main character have something else in common—both were weakened by polio (see Build Background). When Figueredo was fourteen, he and his family immigrated to the United States.

An Adult Who Loves Children's Stories

Figueredo loves being surrounded by books and has worked as a librarian for over twenty-five years. He writes whenever he can (including in his head!) and began his career as a children's book writer when his son encouraged him to write down cherished bedtime stories. His book *When This World Was New* is based on the first time *his* father walked in the snow.

"I go to the library regularly just to sit in the children's room and watch and listen to the children. I look at the books they're holding in their hands and try to guess what really appeals to them."

Think About the Writer Why do you think Figueredo writes about obstacles he faced in his childhood?

Build Background

Polio Until the early 1960s, the polio virus infected thousands of people every year. Most of these people were children. In some cases, polio caused permanent paralysis in a patient's arms or legs. Although there is still no cure for polio, vaccines introduced in the late 1950s have prevented epidemics in most countries, including Cuba. The narrator in the following story became infected with the virus before the vaccine was widely available.

Cuba "That October" takes place in 1962 in Cuba, a Communist country. Between 1960 and the early 1990s, Cuba relied on economic aid from the Soviet Union, a former Communist superpower. During that time, the Soviet Union maintained a military presence on the island, as reflected in this story.

Preview the Selection

This story begins when a **Russian soldier** investigates the cause of a government building's broken window. The narrator, **Rudy,** explains what happened.

Universal Access

English Learners

Explain to students that the word *camarada* is the Spanish equivalent of *comrade,* which means "friend or ally." Tell them that in using this word to address the Russian soldier, the narrator's father is trying to establish to the soldier that he is not a threat. Use of the word shows elements of the father's character, including his friendliness and his desire to avoid confrontation or conflict. Give students a list of English words and phrases that a character could use to show friendly intentions, such as: *good morning, please,* and *I beg your pardon.* Have English learners work with fluent speakers to list words or phrases that a character might use to show hostile intentions.

Struggling Readers

Benchmark Students Before reading, help students make connections to the characters in "That October" by explaining that this story is about a main character who has to overcome difficulties in order to get something that he wants. Have students think about a time in their own lives when they had to overcome difficulties in order to

---

Read with a Purpose Read this selection to find out how a boy proves his value to his teammates.

THAT OCTOBER

by D. H. Figueredo

The Russian soldier came out of the building on the edge of the baseball field. He had a ball with him. When he noticed I was holding a bat, he started walking toward me.

Pointing at the broken window, he said, "It's against the law to damage government property."

My father was standing beside me. "*Camarada*," he said, using the Spanish word for comrade. "You can't take my son to jail."

"*Tovaritch*," the soldier said, using the Russian for comrade. "This building is used by the army for important research."

"The boy just forgot how strong he is," my father said.

The Russian looked at the orthopedic shoes I was wearing and the metal braces that went from my right foot to the top of my thigh. "Did you hit the ball during the game?" he asked me.

"No," I answered.

"You did it on purpose?"

The baseball team had formed a circle around us. The parents had formed a circle around the players. There were Russian soldiers on the other side of the fence that surrounded the building. They were looking at us.

"*Camarada*, I can explain," my father said.

"I need an explanation, but not from you," the Russian said. "You talk," he ordered me.

"Go ahead, son," my father said.

This is what I told the Russian.

The Tigers were the best team in Havana and I wanted to play with them. But they didn't let me. Why? Because when I was little, I was sick with a virus called polio. I got better but I ended up with a very thin leg. Also, I moved in a funny way, like a puppet, and I limped and fell a lot.

The captain of the team, Alfredo, told me that he couldn't afford a weak player. The pitcher, Bebo, said that the team didn't need a bad player. But I knew I was neither. "I practice every day in my back yard," I told them. "Am always losing balls because I smack them so hard, they fly over the fence and disappear."

A | **Reading Focus** Connecting to the Text How do you think the narrator feels right now?

B | **Read and Discuss** What has the author told you so far?

Model the Skill

■ Remind students that writers use a number of tools to develop complete, realistic characters, including appearance, speech, thoughts, and actions. This is called **characterization.**

■ Have a volunteer read aloud the discussion between Bebo, Alfredo, and the narrator in the first column. Point out that for every reason Bebo and Alfredo find for not having him on the team, the narrator comes up with a reason why he should be allowed to play. Rudy's refusal to back down is one way the author characterizes him for readers.

Guided Practice: Apply

Read-Talk-Write Have students re-read pp. 162–163 independently and take note of any other examples of how the author characterizes Rudy. Then, have students discuss their findings with a partner and work together to write a paragraph describing Rudy's character.

Think as a Reader/Writer

Find It in Your Reading Tell students that in the lines of dialogue between the narrator and Alfredo at the top of p. 162, we learn that the narrator is optimistic, confident, and determined, while Alfredo is skeptical and unwilling to assist the narrator.

Use It in Your Writing Have students write a line of dialogue for a real person or made-up character in which they reveal details of the speaker's personality.

"But you can't run," said Alfredo.

"But I'm a good hitter," I said.

"So?"

"We can work together," I said. "You and I are pretty good hitters. You're also a fast runner. You and I could play as a duo. I bat and you run."

He shook his head. "The team won't go for that," he said.

"The team does what you tell them to do," I said.

Bebo spoke up. He said that it wouldn't work and that it was illegal. But I told him it wasn't, because the Tigers were not an official team, didn't wear uniforms, and didn't have a book of rules. "So there are no rules to break," I said. **C**

Alfredo then said that it would not be fair. "The team would be getting an extra player."

I told him that was not so, that the two of us together made up one person. "It's an experiment," I said.

But they were not convinced. **D**

That evening, I didn't feel like eating. When I went to bed, my father massaged my foot, something he did every night. He could tell I was sad and wanted to know what was wrong. I told him and he asked me, "Is it okay if I talk with Alfredo?"

The next day my father went to the field to see Alfredo. Later on, Alfredo came by the house. He told me he had changed his mind and that I could play with the team. Right after he said so, I made myself a sandwich and poured a big glass of chocolate milk.

> "We can work together," I said. "You and I are pretty good hitters. You're also a fast runner. You and I could play as a duo. I bat and you run."

I was happy to be a Tiger. And I wasn't the only addition to the team. For the first time ever, the players were wearing real jerseys and baseball caps. People began to say that the team was different, that not only did the players look better but that there was also a new combination on the baseball field. Friends and their friends came to see that combination. They said maybe it was a new creature, something like a centaur, the half-person half-horse from long ago. But they were soon disappointed. For what they saw was me batting and Alfredo running.

As the season went on, fewer fans came to the field. **E**

C **Literary Focus** Characterization What attributes can you identify in the narrator from his words and actions to convince the others to put him on the team?

D **Read and Discuss** What is the narrator doing now? How do the boys respond to his idea?

E **Read and Discuss** How have things changed for the team?

Vocabulary **illegal** (ih LEE guhl) *adj.:* unlawful; against official regulations.
convinced (kuhn VIHNST) *v.:* made to feel sure; persuaded firmly.

Cross-Curricular Connection

HISTORY: The Cuban Missile Crisis

Tell students that "That October" takes place against the historical backdrop of the Cuban Missile Crisis.

• In 1962, John F. Kennedy was President of the United States. In October of that year, Kennedy was given information from the U.S. military that proved the Soviet Union had set up missiles in Cuba. Americans began to panic when they learned the missiles were pointed at the United States. Kennedy called on his top advisers to determine what to do about the crisis.

• Instead of going to war with Cuba or the Soviets, Kennedy and his advisers decided to form a naval blockade of the waters around Cuba, preventing more Soviet ships from coming through. This action was perceived as a threat by Nikita Khrushchev, the Soviet Union's premier.

• Kennedy maintained the blockade, and the United States anxiously awaited disaster. Instead, Khrushchev used the military attention as a bargaining chip. The

We played against teams from the neighborhoods of Miramar and Marianao, La Lisa and Los Pasos, losing some games but winning most. By October, we were ready for our World Series. This was when the two top teams played against each other. The winner was the first to win three out of five games.

Our opponents were the Leopards from the town of La Lisa. We won the first game. Then, the Leopards won the next two. By the time the fourth encounter came along, the Leopards were sure they were unbeatable and were boasting that a team with a boy wearing braces was no match for them.

At this game, the Leopards were the first to bat. But they didn't score. We did and at the end of the first inning, we were leading 1 to 0. For a long while, the score remained the same. The parents started to say that either both teams were really good or really tired. Then everything changed.

It happened in the seventh inning. The Leopards had a player on second. A batter bunted the ball and as we scrambled to catch it, the batter ran to first and the player on second made it to third. Then, the next player at the plate delivered a home run. The Leopards were ahead 3 to 1.

It was our turn at bat. Alfredo pulled me aside and told me to hit a homer with so much force that the bat would break in two. He planned to run so fast that his

---

Vocabulary **opponents** (uh POH nuhnts) *n.:* people on opposite sides in a fight or a game.
encounter (ehn KOWN tuhr) *n.:* face-to-face meeting.
boasting (BOHST ihng) *v.:* speaking too highly about oneself; bragging.

Communism

Communism is a political and economic system in which the government owns the land and economic resources. There is no privately owned property.

In 1917, the people of Russia, suffering as a result of poor harvests, economic depressions, and bloody wars, overthrew their monarchy. The new government embraced communism, whose ultimate goal is to create a society that provides equality and economic security for all.

Russia conquered three other territories in 1922 to form the Communist superpower known as the Union of Soviet Socialist Republics (USSR, or Soviet Union).

In 1959, Fidel Castro took power from the military dictator who was ruling Cuba and established a Communist government, the first one in the Western Hemisphere.

Ask Yourself

How did the relationship between Cuba and the Soviet Union affect the relationship between the Russian soldier and the boy and his father?

Soviets agreed to remove their missile silos in Cuba in exchange for the United States's removal of some similarly positioned arms in Turkey.

- Kennedy and Khrushchev completed the bargain, and a more dangerous crisis was averted. However, some Americans did not agree with the way Kennedy resolved the situation, believing that he should have chosen military strikes against Cuba and the Soviets.

 HSS Analysis Skills REP 5

Social Studies Link

The political and economic philosophies of communism were largely influenced by two books published in the mid-1800s: Karl Marx and Friedrich Engels's *The Communist Manifesto* and Friedrich Engels's *Principles of Communism*.

Ask Yourself _____

Possible response: The relationship between the two countries made Rudy and his father and the soldier mistrustful of each other.

Think About/Talk About

▶ Comprehension

Ⓓ Read and Discuss

Possible response: He's trying to convince Bebo and Alfredo that he could hit and Alfredo could run. The boys are telling him it can't happen because it would be like having an extra player.

Ⓔ Read and Discuss

Possible response: The team has received new uniforms, and more people have come to their games because they want to see a spectacle.

▶ Analysis

Ⓕ Literary Focus

Possible response: He is very persistent, and he is determined not to let polio affect his life.

Vocabulary: Own the Word

- **illegal:** Ask students to list actions that are *illegal,* or against the rules, in school. ***Possible response:*** *Cheating, chewing gum.*

- **convinced:** Tell students that *convinced* is the past tense from of the verb *convince. Convinced* means "made certain" or "persuaded." An antonym for *convinced* is *dissuaded.*

- **opponents:** Tell students that the noun *opponent* is a derivative of the verb *oppose. Oppose* means "to be against." A baseball team plays against the other team, or they *oppose* their *opponents.* Ask students to name another word that may be related to *opponent.* ***Possible response:*** *The two teams started the game on opposite sides of the field.*

- **encounter:** Demonstrate an *encounter* for the class. Walk up to one of the students and shake his or her hand. Start a polite conversation. Then, have the rest of class act out the word *encounter.*

- **boasting:** Ask students to applaud if they would like to be someone known for *boasting.* ***Possible response:*** *Students do not applaud because they do not want to be thought of as stuck-up or conceited.*

- Provide students with copies of the Reading Skills Focus graphic organizer (see **Chapter 2 Resources**), or ask them to use their own paper.

- Explain that readers often get the most out of a text when they can **make connections** with what has been written. Readers also benefit from relating the text to other stories or world events.

- Point out that on this page, Bebo is trying to keep Rudy from batting because he thinks Rudy will not be able to run the bases. Rudy has to prove his value for Bebo to consider him a real member of the team. A reader who has experienced the challenge of proving himself or herself in order to gain respect from teammates can connect with Rudy's struggle to make others see what he is capable of. Write "I have had to prove myself" in the graphic organizer.

I can connect	To myself or my friends	To other stories
Narrator	He is young like me.	He finds a way to use strength, like Rikki-tikki.
Conflict	I have had to prove myself	
End of Story		

I can connect	To situations in the world
Narrator	Cuba played in World Baseball Classic; the sport is popular there.
Conflict	
End of Story	

Guided Practice: Apply

Have students independently fill in the organizers with connections they have made to "That October."

legs would turn into wheels, just like in the cartoons on television.

But I failed him. Instead, my bat made a "thud" sound and the ball whirled toward first. Running as hard as he could, Alfredo crash-landed on the base, but the first baseman shouted, the ball inside his glove, "You're dead, pal."

Alfredo cried out. From the stands, his father came out to help him. Leaning on him, Alfredo limped away from the base.

"I won't be able to run," he told me, sitting down on the bench. He had twisted his ankle.

F **Literary Focus** Characterization What can you tell about Alfredo from his words to the narrator?

We went into the final inning with Bebo in charge. He told us that we couldn't let the Leopards get in any more runs. He concentrated on his pitching and struck out the Leopards. But they were still winning by two runs.

Now, it was our turn to bat. One player directed a line drive into left field. He made it to first base. While the Leopards' pitcher was pitching, our player stole second. The next hitter shot the ball over the pitcher's head. The pitcher jumped up, caught the ball but dropped it, giving the Tiger on

Analyzing Visuals Connecting to the Text How does this image suggest the narrator's importance to the team?

Developing Oral Fluency

Tell students that fluent readers adjust their reading rate based on sentence length or to convey emotion. When reading, students should always read at a rate that is neither too fast nor too slow to be understood clearly. They should remember to pause after every sentence and at punctuation like commas and semicolons.

Group Activity Arrange students in pairs, making sure that there is at least one fluent reader in each pair.

- Draw students' attention to the top of p. 164.
- Model reading the selection from the line "Alfredo cried out" to the line "But they were still winning by two runs." Slow your reading rate when reading longer sentences with multiple clauses. You might also slow your reading to convey suspense or increase your rate to convey emotion in Alfredo's dialogue.

- Have student pairs alternate reading the paragraphs on p. 164 aloud, varying their reading rate based upon the text.

✔ See **UA: Differentiating Instruction** for practice passages for developing oral fluency.

second enough time to reach third and allowing the batter to get to first.

We had a chance to recover the game. My teammates stopped feeling sorry for themselves. They said that we could score. But the high hopes vanished when the following two batters struck out.

I was next. But Bebo stopped me. "Somebody else will bat, not you." He said, "This time, Alfredo can't help you."

"I'm a Tiger and the team expects me to play," I said.

"You're not a Tiger," he said. "The only reason you're playing is because your father has money."

"What?"

"See our new shirts? Your father bought them for us. He also gave money to the other teams."

"That's not true," I said.

"Are you calling me a liar?" Bebo asked.

From the bench, Alfredo shouted, "Let him play." He made a fist and opened the palm of his hand and punched it. "Let him play."

Bebo stepped aside. Was he right? Was I allowed to play only because my father was paying for me to play? I wanted to leave. But Alfredo said, "Do it. We need a homer."

I waited a few seconds. My father looked at me in silence. The team looked at me in silence. Bebo had a smirk on his face.

I stepped up to the plate. I nodded to let the pitcher know I was ready. The pitcher eyed the catcher.

Strike one.

Bebo looked at Alfredo. He said, "I told you he's no good. I told you."

Strike two.

Bebo threw his cap in the dirt.

I turned to Alfredo. He mouthed, "You can do it." I turned to my father who gave me thumbs up.

The pitcher stretched his arm back and thrust it forward. The ball curved. I lowered the bat and swung.

It sounded like the wind had banged a door shut. The bat shook in my hands. I stood still for a moment before throwing it backwards. Turning into a minirocket, the bat almost hit Bebo who had to duck. In the meantime, the ball was rising higher and higher, becoming one with the sun before falling to the ground.

The Leopards didn't try to catch the ball. They weren't even looking at it. The parents weren't looking at the ball either. Neither were Bebo, Alfredo, nor the rest of my teammates. Instead, they were all looking at me.

They were looking at me, running. Yes, running in a funny way, like a robin with a broken leg. Running and wheezing, like an old sugarcane mill. Running and making so much noise it sounded as if it were raining pots and pans. But running.

To first base.

To second.

To third. **H**

By the time the Leopards figured that I could run and make it to the plate, it was

G Read and Discuss What mood has the author created?

H Literary Focus Characterization What do the narrator's actions tell you about him? What do his speech patterns—the *way* he speaks—tell you?

Think About/Talk About

▶ Comprehension
G Read and Discuss
Possible response: *It's pretty suspenseful because there are two outs, and they are down by two runs, but the team's hopes are high because they have two men on base.*

▶ Analysis
F Literary Focus
Possible response: *Alfredo is imaginative and has an exaggerated view of how strong he and Rudy are.*

H Literary Focus
Possible response: *The narrator may not be the fastest or most steady runner, but he has the heart and determination to score for his team. The narrator's speech patterns, such as the repeated use of the word "running" in every sentence of the paragraph, reinforce the significance of the image of him running the bases.*

▶ Extend the Discussion
Characterization In the first complete paragraph on p. 164, the narrator states that he "failed" Alfredo. What does the narrator's reaction tell you about his character? ***Possible response:*** *He is eager to prove himself to his teammates, particularly Alfredo, who has shown so much faith in him.*

Analyzing Visuals
Connecting to the Text: *The narrator hits a game-winning home run.*

Universal Access

Struggling Readers
Strategic Students Have students reread the story in pairs or small groups, with each focusing on only one of the story's characters. Have each group create one list each of things the character says, things others say about the character, and important actions carried out by the character. Have students compare the three lists and try to connect actions, speech, and descriptions. For example, students might connect the narrator's father's action of massaging his son's foot with the father's question, "Is it okay if I talk with Alfredo?" Both the statement and the action reveal that the father cares about his son. Have each group present its connections.

AAVE Students Who Use African American Vernacular English
English for Academic Success Point out irregular past tense verbs such as *came*, *told*, and *stole* on p. 164. Point out the contrast between these forms and common informal usages: *comed*, *telled*, and *stealed*. Have students locate additional examples of irregular past tense verbs in the story, and have them practice using them in sentences.

Comprehension

❶ Read and Discuss

Possible response: In the beginning of the story they both use their own language's terms for "friend," but at the end of the story each uses the other's language to refer to each other as "friend." This lets us know that each gained a bit of respect and kindness toward the other.

▶ Extend the Discussion

Symbolism Read the last sentence of the story. What might the ball symbolize to Rudy? *Possible response: It might symbolize his success with the Tigers, his determination to play baseball with polio, and his strange friendship with the Russian soldier.*

Making Judgments Rudy never tells the reader how he feels about how his father got him onto the team. How do you think he feels about this? *Possible response: He was probably angry and upset at first, but he proved that he was a good player and was happy to play on a team.*

Monitor Students' Comprehension

Guide students in answering these comprehension questions.

1. What event leads Rudy to tell the story of how he came to play baseball? [*He hit a baseball in celebration and had to explain how it broke the window of a government building.*]

2. What do *camarada* and *tovaritch* mean? [*comrade, friend*]

3. How is Rudy able to play baseball despite his polio? [*For most of the story, Rudy bats and Alfredo runs.*]

too late. For the Tigers who had been on first and third had already reached home. And I was right behind them.

My father cheered. The parents said, "What a game, what a game." The Tigers congratulated each other. I picked up a ball from the ground and threw it high into the air. As it came down, I whacked it with the bat, whacked it so hard that the ball rose over the fence and the electric posts, heading right for the building.

"And that's how I broke your window," I told the Russian.

He didn't say anything. He noticed that my knees were bleeding and that there were scratches on my right leg.

"Sometimes the braces scratch him," my father said.

The Russian said, "The window is still broken. And it still belongs to the Cuban government. And it's still illegal to damage government property." He loomed over me. Was he going to arrest me?

"Don't do it again," he said, tossing me the ball.

As he started to walk away, my father called him. When the Russian faced him, my father extended his hand. "Thank you, *tovaritch.*"

The Russian shook his hand. "You're welcome, *camarada.*" ❶

❶ Read and Discuss What is the significance of the narrator's father calling the soldier "*tovaritch*" and the soldier calling the boy's father "*camarada*"?

Then my father said, "My name is Rodolfo." He pointed at me. "His name is Rudy."

"Mine is Andrei," said the Russian. Joining the soldiers on the other side of the fence, the Russian went inside the building.

As the baseball players and their parents left the field, my father placed his arm around my shoulder. He said, "I bought the shirts with one condition: that you were allowed to play one game. But just one. The rest was up to you and the team."

From inside his father's car, Alfredo called out my name. "Rudy, you saved the team today," he shouted. "You're definitely a Tiger. And you know who said so?"

I shook my head.

"Bebo."

Later that October, the Tigers and the Leopards finished Havana's 1962 Little League World Series. The Leopards won the final game and were the league champions.

Later that October, the Cuban government told the Russian soldiers that the research they were doing in the building was over. The Russians left the island and went back home.

Later that October, the Cuban government gave my parents and me permission to leave Cuba. We left the island and moved to Miami.

I took the ball with me.

🐻 **California Standards, pp. 167–169**

■ **Reading Standard 1.2** Use knowledge of Greek, Latin, and Anglo-Saxon roots and affixes to understand content-area vocabulary.

■ **Reading Standard 3.3** Analyze characterization as delineated through a character's thoughts, words, speech patterns, and actions; the narrator's description; and the thoughts, words, and actions of other characters.

Applying Your Skills

Reading Standard 3.3 Analyze characterization as delineated through a character's thoughts, words, speech patterns, and actions; the narrator's description; and the thoughts, words, and actions of other characters.

That October
Literary Response and Analysis

Reading Skills Focus
Quick Check

1. Why is the Russian soldier questioning Rudy?
2. How does Rudy make it onto the team?

Read with a Purpose

3. What do you learn about Rudy and the way he overcomes obstacles? <u>Respond</u> by using details from the story.

Reading Skills: Connecting to the Text

4. Review the chart you completed as you read the story. List your strongest connections in the chart below, and explain the reasons for your choices.

Text and myself	
Text and another text	
Text and world situations	

Literary Skills Focus
Literary Analysis

5. **Analyze** How do you feel about the way Rudy makes the team? Explain whether you think Rudy's father is justified in his actions.

6. **Infer** What does the final sentence of the story tell you about the narrator's feelings toward the events he has described?

Literary Skills: Characterization

7. **Analyze** Although Bebo is a minor character, he is important to the story. What purpose does he serve? How does the author <u>delineate</u> Bebo's character?

8. **Interpret** Which aspects of Rudy's characterization show that he is a determined individual, even when confronting difficult circumstances?

9. **Analyze** How does the Russian soldier react to Rudy's story? Comment on the characterization of the soldier, especially his words and actions.

10. **Interpret** How does Bebo's opinion of Rudy change? What does this change reveal about Bebo's character?

Literary Skills Review: Suspense

11. **Interpret** **Suspense** is the uncertainty you feel about what will happen next in a story. Choose two suspenseful moments from "That October." Give reasons for your choices. What were the outcomes of these suspenseful moments?

Writing Skills Focus
Think as a Reader/Writer

Use It in Your Writing Look back at the story and the notes you took on the characters' dialogue. For the narrator, Alfredo, and Bebo, describe one major character trait revealed through dialogue. Give examples from the text to support your descriptions.

What Do You Think Now

When might you need others to believe in you before you believe in yourself? How has this story influenced your ideas?

What Do You Think Now?

Ask students what role others may play in determining an individual's self-confidence. Do we have to rely on others to give us opportunities, or can we create them ourselves?

Check for Understanding

Independent Practice
Reading Skills Focus
Answers:

1. *He knows Rudy broke the window.*
2. *His father buys uniforms for the team as a bribe to let Rudy play.*
3. *Rudy is determined and persistent. He went to Alfredo with a good argument, and he played hard to make up for not being as strong as the other players.*
4. *a. I also play baseball; b. Rudy is a young boy like Victor in "Seventh Grade"; c. Cuba is still a Communist country.*

Literary Skills Focus
Possible responses:

5. *I think it's okay because Rudy was good enough to play on the team; he just needed a chance to prove it.*
6. *He has fond memories of them.*
7. *Bebo is the person Rudy most needs to prove himself to. The author characterizes Bebo as a bit of a bully and as someone who is very concerned about winning.*
8. *Rudy plays hard and runs fast despite his polio, and his efforts save his team from defeat.*
9. *The soldier at first gives the impression that he does not believe Rudy's story, as he doesn't say anything as he stares down at Rudy. However, he notices the marks on Rudy's leg and allows Rudy to leave with just a warning. He probably was sympathetic to Rudy the entire time but wanted to make sure the boy would be more careful in the future.*
10. *Bebo realizes Rudy deserves to be on the team; he is dynamic.*
11. *It is suspenseful when the soldier first approaches Rudy and when Rudy is at bat at the end.*

Vocabulary Development

Your Turn _____

1. An *opponent* is often someone you are set against in a game.

2. *Bauis* means "to puff up," and when people boast, they sometimes puff up their accomplishments.

3. The prefix *in–* is related to *il–*, which makes the word mean "the opposite of legal."

4. If *contra* means "against," *encounter* means "coming up against something or someone."

English for Academic Success
Language Coach

To help students determine the most appropriate word to complete each sentence, ask them what they think of when they read each word. Then, have students determine which word's connotation has the most in common with the situation described in the sentence.

1. *opponents*
2. *illegal*
3. *champions*

English for Academic Success
Academic Vocabulary

Possible response: Rudy is the most credible character in the story. He is determined and tough, the way a real person fighting to overcome the limitations of polio might be, and I think that his attributes and actions in the story are realistic and understandable.

 WordSharp: An Interactive Vocabulary Tutor

 Learn It Online

Holt's **WordSharp: An Interactive Vocabulary Tutor** provides additional support for vocabulary development. Multimedia tutorials show students how to apply vocabulary skills to unfamiliar words—and how to make those words their own.

go.hrw.com | H7-168 | **Go**

Applying Your Skills

Reading Standard 1.2 Use knowledge of Greek, Latin, and Anglo-Saxon roots and affixes to understand content-area vocabulary.

That October

Vocabulary Development
Roots and Affixes

Many English word roots come from Latin, Greek, and an ancestor of the English language called Old English, or Anglo-Saxon. A **word root** is a word part from which other words can be formed.

An **affix** is a word part added to a root. An affix can be added to the front of a word (in which case it is called a **prefix**), or it can be added to the end of a word (in which case it is called a **suffix**). For example, the Vocabulary word **convinced** is made up of the prefix *con–* ("together"; "with") and the Latin root *vince* ("conquer"). In the story you just read, Rudy's teammates weren't **convinced** he should be on their team.

Your Turn _____

You have seen how roots and affixes help you understand the meaning of **convinced**. Explain how each of the following facts helps you understand the meaning of each Vocabulary word.

> convinced
> illegal
> opponents
> encounter
> boasting

1. In Latin, *opponere* means "set against." How does this give you a clue to the meaning of **opponents**?

2. In Proto-Germanic (probably Scandinavian), *bauis* means "to puff up; swell." How does this give you a clue to the meaning of **boasting**?

3. In Medieval Latin, *in–* means "not," and *legalis* means "legal." How does this give you a clue to the meaning of **illegal**?

4. In Latin, *contra* means "against." How does this give you a clue to the meaning of **encounter**?

Language Coach

Denotations/Connotations When choosing their words, skillful writers think about the meanings and associations they want to convey to readers. Choosing words with specific connotations allows writers to create precise descriptions.

Your Turn _____

Choose the word that conveys the most precise meaning.

1. The Tigers were ready to face their _____ (*opponents, enemies*).

2. The soldier explained that it was _____ (*wrong, illegal*) to damage government property.

3. The Leopards won the last game, making them the league _____ (*champions, winners*).

Academic Vocabulary

Write About . . .

D. H. Figueredo creates credible, or believable, characters with clearly delineated attributes. In a paragraph, identify the character in the story who seems most credible and explain why that character seems so believable.

 Learn It Online
Take a closer look at word roots using *WordSharp* at:
go.hrw.com | H7-168 | **Go**

Universal Access: Vocabulary Development

EL **English Learners**

English for Academic Success Use this activity to help students connect new vocabulary to prior knowledge.

Have students write three words that use each of the following prefixes or suffixes. Then, based on what they know about the words they associated with the affix, have them determine what the prefix or suffix means. Have students record the definitions of these affixes in their **Reader/Writer Notebook.**

- un– [*untie, uncertain, unknown; un-: not*]

- re– [*reset, reread, review; re-: again*]

- in– or im– [*inhale, insert, inside; in-/im-: in, not*]

- -ly [*elegantly, happily, eagerly; -ly: how something is done (adverb) or what something is like (adjective)*]

- -able [*approachable, honorable, suitable; -able: able to be*]

- -tion or –sion [*action, comprehension, imagination; -tion/-sion: the act or process of*]

Grammar Link
Strong, Vivid Verbs

This story moves at a fast pace, in part because Figueredo uses strong, vivid verbs to help us see all the action on the baseball field. Rudy doesn't just hit the ball—he *smacks* it. Other players *shoot, jump* for, and *scramble* after the ball. Consider this sentence about a scene from the story:

> **As the ball came down, I whacked it with the bat hard.**

How did Rudy connect the bat with the ball? Replace *whacked* with *hit, slapped, touched, caressed,* and *socked.* How does each verb change what you see? What does each verb tell you about Rudy's feelings and intentions?

Your Turn

Rewrite the following sentences by replacing each "tame" verb with a more specific (and more interesting) verb.

1. The soldier talked to the boy.
2. The fans cheered for their team.
3. Alfredo painfully walked away from the base.

Writing Applications Be a verb spotter. Choose a piece of your own writing, and replace at least three verbs with ones that are sharper, more vivid, and more precise.

CHOICES

As you respond to the Choices, use these **Academic Vocabulary** words as appropriate: <u>attribute</u>, <u>delineate</u>, <u>identify</u>, <u>respond</u>.

REVIEW
Analyze a Character

Timed Writing Write a two-paragraph essay about one of the characters in this story. <u>Identify</u> two of the character's traits, citing details from the story (such as the character's thoughts, words, speech patterns, actions, and the narrator's descriptions) to support your answer.

CONNECT
Compare Characters

In a three-paragraph essay, compare and contrast the character Rudy with another character from a book or movie. What do the two characters have in common? What makes them different? Are they both brave? How does the other character differ from Rudy in how he or she handles a situation? How are their problems or situations different? Use characterization details from each work as you compare.

EXTEND
Write a Sequel

By the end of the story, we learn that Rudy and his family have left Cuba and moved to Miami. What situations will Rudy have to <u>respond</u> to in his new home? How might he have to prove himself all over again in Miami? Will Rudy be successful in dealing with new challenges? Write a sequel to this story that tells about Rudy's first weeks in Miami.

Independent Practice
Grammar Link
Your Turn

1. The soldier *chatted* with the boy.
2. The fans *roared* for their team.
3. Alfredo painfully *limped* away from the base.

Choices:
Evaluation Criteria
Review: Timed Writing
40–50 Minutes
- Essays should be clear and well-organized.
- Essays should use details from the story that clearly delineate the character's traits.

Connect: **Homework**
Compare Characters
- Students should compare and contrast Rudy with a character from another story in an organized way.
- Essays should identify details from the stories to support the comparisons and contrasts.

Extend: **Homework**
Write a Sequel
- The story should begin where "That October" ends.
- The story should use descriptive language to tell readers about Rudy's new life in the United States.

Assess

Chapter 2 Resources, Selection Standards Check, p. 15

 ThinkCentral Online Assessment, Selection Standards Check

Teacher One Stop™, editable Selection Standards Check

Reteach

To reteach **characterization,** see Reteaching Lessons, p. 842A.

 ThinkCentral Online Remediation

Universal Access: Grammar Link

EL English Learners

English for Academic Success Provide students with additional assistance with strong, vivid words. Explain that these kinds of verbs provide a very specific image and give insight into the character's feelings and what is happening in the story.

- Tell students that a sentence that describes how the boys *tried* to catch the baseball does not tell the reader anything specific. If the word *scrambled* is used, it tells the reader that the baseball team is in frantic motion trying to get their hands on the moving ball.

- Likewise, words like *strolled* and *stormed* provide better alternatives than the word *moved. Strolled* suggests the character is feeling confident and at ease. *Stormed* suggests the character is in a hurry and possibly very angry.

✔ For more practice with using verbs, see **Warriner's Handbook, Language Handbook Worksheets,** and **Grammar Notes**.

Standards Focus

Objectives

Students will

- understand factors that motivate character behaviors
- understand how characters, their motivations, and actions affect plot

Motivate

What Do You Think?/QuickTalk

Use the QuickTalk to have students discuss whether they think first impressions of strangers are usually accurate. Have volunteers tell about a time when they or someone they know judged someone based on an inaccurate impression.

English for Academic Success

Academic Vocabulary

Look for opportunities to use the Academic Vocabulary words in this Chapter.

- **attribute, *n.*:** quality or trait of someone or something.
- **delineate, *v*:** describe in detail; portray.
- **identify, *v.*:** recognize and be able to say what someone or something is.
- **respond, *v.*:** say or write something as a reply or answer.

Analyzing Visuals

Extension Activity Ask students how the figures' indistinct faces affect their perceptions of them. ***Possible response:*** *The figures don't seem like unique individuals.*

![California bear] **California Standards, pp. 170–183**

- **Reading Standard 3.3** Analyze characterization as delineated through a character's thoughts, words, speech patterns, and actions; the narrator's description; and the thoughts, words, and actions of other characters.

THE WAR OF THE WALL

by **Toni Cade Bambara**

Church Boys III (2000) by Francks Deceus. Mixed media on canvas.

What Do **You Think** When have you judged someone based on a first impression? How did your opinion change (if at all)?

QuickTalk
Why do people often distrust strangers?

Selection Readability	
Easily Accessible **Accessible** Challenging	conversational style; accessible theme; rela[...] characters

Selection Plot Summary

Neighbors are upset when an outsider paints on a local wall until th[...] out that the painter has commemorated African American leaders. T[...] community comes to learn that first impressions can be deceptive.

Reader/Writer Notebook

Use your **RWN** to complete the activities for this selection.

Reading Standard 3.3 Analyze characterization as delineated through a character's thoughts, words, speech patterns, and actions; the narrator's description; and the thoughts, words, and actions of other characters.

Literary Skills Focus

Motivation As you read a story, think about why the characters act the way they do. The reason behind a character's actions is called the character's **motivation.** Feelings, needs, goals, and pressures from family and friends—all of these are forces that push and pull people from inside and outside.

Throughout the twists and turns of a story, keep asking yourself what makes the characters behave in a particular way. What role do the characters' motivations and actions play in their characterization?

Reading Skills Focus

How Character Affects Plot Characters' actions reveal their personalities. Their behavior also drives what happens in a story.

Into Action Complete an If—Then chart like the one below as you read. First, write something the narrator does in the column marked "Action." Then, record a way he might have acted differently under the "If" heading. Leave the last column blank for now.

Action	If	Then
The narrator confronts the painter.	the narrator approached her nicely . . .	

TechFocus As you read, <u>identify</u> a scene in this story that could be filmed effectively.

Writing Skills Focus

Think as a Reader/Writer

Find It in Your Reading One way writer Toni Cade Bambara <u>delineates</u> her characters is through the colorful descriptions her observant narrator presents: "She was rearing back on her heels, her hands jammed into her back pockets, her face squinched up like the masterpiece she had in mind was taking shape on the wall by magic." In your *Reader/Writer Notebook,* list examples of precise images and phrases that help you see the characters and picture what they are doing.

Vocabulary

integration (ihn tuh GRAY shuhn) *n.:* process of bringing together people of all races. *Things didn't get better when integration was first introduced in the town.*

concentration (kahn suhn TRAY shuhn) *n.:* act of thinking carefully about something. *Painting is an activity that requires concentration.*

liberation (lihb uh RAY shuhn) *n.:* release from slavery, prison, or other limitation. *Neighborhood residents saw African flags of liberation on the wall.*

inscription (ihn SKRIHP shuhn) *n.:* words written on something. *The kids were unsure of what the inscription on the wall would say.*

dedicate (DEHD uh kayt) *v.:* do or make something in honor of another person. *Artists often dedicate their work to someone.*

Language Coach

Slang Informal language that includes invented words and existing words that have been given new meanings is called **slang.** *Dude* and *get a whiff* are examples of slang in this story.

 Learn It Online
For a preview of this story, see the video introduction on:

go.hrw.com | H7-171 | Go

Preteach

Introducing Vocabulary

Read the Vocabulary words and sample sentences aloud. Then, have student pairs take turns testing each other by having one partner read the definitions aloud and the other identify the words.

English for Academic Success

Language Coach

Tell students that examples of slang include *awesome, buck* (dollar), *cool,* and *cop* (police officer). Point out that many slang words do not relate directly to their literal meanings. Have students name slang words and phrases they are familiar with.

Literary Skills Focus

As you read and discuss the selection with students, have them use their experiences and knowledge of behavior to assess character motivation.

Reading Skills Focus

Give students a copy of the Reading Skills Focus graphic organizer before they read. Tell them to use their responses to answer the questions on the Applying Your Skills page.

Writing Skills Focus

Have students record examples of imagery in their **Reader/Writer Notebook.** Students can use their notes to complete the Writing Skills Focus activity.

Selection Resources

Chapter 2 Resources, on-level practice and assessment, p. 18

PowerNotes, interactive lesson presentation with activities

Teacher One Stop™, on-level lesson plans and all print resources

Holt Audio Library

Holt Audio Library: Selections and Summaries in Spanish

UA: Holt Interactive Reader, p. 36

Holt Interactive Reader for ELD, p. 56

Holt Audio Tutor for ELD

UA: Differentiating Instruction, modified lesson plans and leveled assessment, p. 32

UA: Supporting Instruction in Five Languages, selection summary

UA: Resources for Teaching Advanced Students, lesson plans, p. 70

Weekly Standards Review Transparencies, Transparency 3

Analyzing Visuals Transparencies, p. 10

 Learn It Online
The **PowerNotes** presentation for this lesson includes a short video that introduces the selection. The video is also available on the online version of this page.

go.hrw.com | H7-171 | Go

Selection Introduction

More About the Writer

Toni Cade Bambara took an active role in the civil rights movement. Her writings often reflect characters trying to break free of injustice or intolerance in their lives. Her many short stories were gathered into the Chapters *Gorilla, My Love* (published in 1972) and *The Sea Birds Are Still Alive* (1977).

Think About the Writer

Review Toni Cade Bambara's biography with students. Point out that authors' personal experiences, including environments they have encountered, often find their way into their fiction. Ask students how they think "The War of the Wall" might reflect the surroundings of Bambara's childhood home in 1940s Harlem.

 For Independent Reading

- Students wishing to learn more about famous African Americans depicted on the painter lady's mural may like to read *Harriet Tubman: Conductor on the Underground Railroad*. This biography looks at the woman who led many slaves to freedom during the American Civil War.

- Students interested in reading about the background to this selection might wish to read *Leon's Story* by Leon Walter Tillage. This autobiography reveals the obstacles faced by African Americans in the middle of the 20th century.

 Learn It Online
Writers' Lives offers more information on the life of the author as well as Holt's interactive resources pertaining to the author.

go.hrw.com | H7-172 | Go

MEET THE WRITER

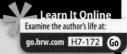 **Learn It Online**
Examine the author's life at:
go.hrw.com H7-172 Go

Toni Cade Bambara
(1939–1995)

Growing Up in New York City

Toni Cade Bambara was born Miltonia Mirkin Cade. As an adult, the author added "Bambara," inspired by a signature on a sketch book belonging to her great-grandmother. She grew up in Harlem in the 1940s, surrounded by vibrant literary, artistic, and political communities. She learned the power of the spoken word on "speaker's corner," where people preached and spoke on issues of importance. She recorded the speech of her friends and neighbors, trying to capture the pulse of daily life. She absorbed the rhythms of jazz and bebop that filled New York City streets and clubs.

Go Far; Remember Where You Came From

After college, Bambara traveled and studied in Europe. She later lived in Atlanta and Philadelphia. Even so, her early experiences living in an African American community continued to inspire her. Bambara's writing focuses on the experiences of African Americans. Known primarily for her short stories and novels, Bambara later concentrated on screenplays, including an adaptation of her much-loved story "Raymond's Run."

"It is important for young folks to listen, to be proud of our oral tradition."

Think About the Writer How do you think Bambara's early surroundings influenced her work?

Build Background

"The War of the Wall" takes place during or shortly after the Vietnam War, which ended in 1972. The setting is an African American neighborhood in the South.

Southern and northern cultures often clashed at that time. Many southerners resented northerners' efforts to push the issues of integration and civil rights. They saw northern civil rights advocates as troublemakers intruding on their lives. While the story doesn't focus on these issues, this background gives you insight into the culture clash that motivates the characters and their actions.

Preview the Selection

A mysterious **painter** comes to town and begins to paint over a wall that is central to the town's sense of community. The **narrator** and his friend **Lou** don't know exactly what she's doing, but they are sure they want to stop her.

Universal Access

 English Learners

English for Academic Success Read aloud the first page of the story for students. Point out how the descriptions reveal the close bonds between the characters in this fictional community and how important the wall is to them. Children play games at the wall, and the elderly sit in the wall's shade. Explain that though each character in the story has unique traits and motivations, the common interest in the wall motivates the actions of the entire community. Have students copy portions of the descriptions in their **Reader/Writer Notebook**

and work with a partner to make a brief annotation of what each description reveals about the community as a whole.

✔ See **UA: Differentiating Instruction** for lesson plans and strategies for teaching English learners.

Struggling Readers

To help students read "The War of the Wall," model the reading skill of understanding how character affects plot. You might say: "Looking at the second paragraph, I see that the 'painter lady' ignores the children's requests

THE WAR OF THE WALL

by **Toni Cade Bambara**

Me and Lou had no time for courtesies. We were late for school. So we just flat out told the painter lady to quit messing with the wall. It was our wall, and she had no right coming into our neighborhood painting on it. Stirring in the paint bucket and not even looking at us, she mumbled something about Mr. Eubanks, the barber, giving her permission. That had nothing to do with it as far as we were concerned. We've been pitching pennies against that wall since we were little kids. Old folks have been dragging their chairs out to sit in the shade of the wall for years. Big kids have been playing handball against the wall since so-called integration when the crazies 'cross town poured cement in our pool so we couldn't use it. I'd sprained my neck one time boosting my cousin Lou up to chisel Jimmy Lyons's name into the wall when we found out he

was never coming home from the war in Vietnam to take us fishing. **Ⓐ**

"If you lean close," Lou said, leaning hip-shot against her beat-up car, "you'll get a whiff of bubble gum and kids' sweat. And that'll tell you something—that this wall belongs to the kids of Taliaferro Street." I thought Lou sounded very convincing. But the painter lady paid us no mind. She just snapped the brim of her straw hat down and hauled her bucket up the ladder.

"You're not even from around here," I hollered up after her. The license plates on her old piece of car said "New York." Lou dragged me away because I was about to grab hold of that ladder and shake it. And then we'd really be late for school. **Ⓑ**

When we came from school, the wall was slick with white. The painter lady was running string across the wall and taping it here and there. Me and Lou leaned against

---

Ⓐ **Read and Discuss** What is the author letting you know about this wall?

Ⓑ **Read and Discuss** How does this scene add to what you know about the wall?

Vocabulary **integration** (ihn tuh GRAY shuhn) *n.:* process of bringing together people of all races.

---

that she leave the wall alone. She seems very engrossed in what she is doing, persistent, and even stubborn. These traits lead her to continue painting the wall, which contributes to the story's plot."

✔ See **UA: Differentiating Instruction** for lesson plans and strategies for teaching struggling readers.

Advanced Learners
Acceleration Have students discuss the biggest motivation for the children's reaction to the painter and speculate on how motivation will influence plot.

✔ See **UA: Resources for Teaching Advanced Students** for lesson plans and strategies for teaching advanced learners.

Students with Disabilities
Invite students to read "The War of the Wall" in interactive format in **UA: Holt Interactive Reader** and to use the sidenotes as aids to understanding the selection. The interactive version provides additional instruction, practice, and assessment of the skills taught in the Student Edition.

Model the Skill

- Point out that characters, like real people, have reasons for acting as they do. Understanding **motivation** has a strong effect on how a reader interprets a character and the story.

- Tell students that the motivation behind the main character's anger is clear—he thinks the painter is changing a landmark without permission. What prompts the "painter lady" to ignore the neighborhood kids is not as obvious. Because the painter and her actions are so important to the story, it is important to try to understand why she's doing what she does.

- Model searching for clues that might reveal the painter lady's motivation for ignoring the kids. Point out that the author writes that her "face [is] squinched up like the masterpiece she had in mind was taking shape on the wall by magic." Her behavior seems to be entirely motivated by the work she is doing on the wall. She does not dislike the children; she is simply too engrossed to pay any attention to them.

Guided Practice: Apply

Remind students that character is determined by many behaviors, and learning the motivation behind each behavior helps create a more complete picture of a character. Have students read in groups the "painter lady's" conversation with the twins beginning on p. 175 and brainstorm reasons why she refuses the supper they bring.

---

the gum ball machine outside the pool hall and watched. She had strings up and down and back and forth. Then she began chalking them with a hunk of blue chalk.

The Morris twins crossed the street, hanging back at the curb next to the beat-up car. The twin with the red ribbons was hugging a jug of cloudy lemonade. The one with yellow ribbons was holding a plate of dinner away from her dress. The painter lady began snapping the strings. The blue chalk dust measured off halves and quarters up and down and sideways too. Lou was about to say how hip it all was, but I dropped my book satchel on his toes to remind him we were at war.   **C**

Some good aromas were drifting our way from the plate leaking pot likker[1] onto the Morris girl's white socks. I could tell from where I stood that under the tinfoil was baked ham, collard greens, and candied yams. And knowing Mrs. Morris, who sometimes bakes for my mama's restaurant, a slab of buttered cornbread was probably up under there too, sopping up some of the pot likker. Me and Lou rolled our eyes, wishing somebody would send us some dinner. But the painter lady didn't even turn around. She was pulling the strings down and prying bits of tape loose.

Side Pocket came strolling out of the pool hall to see what Lou and me were

---

1. **pot likker** (paht LIHK uhr): leftover liquid from cooked meat and vegetables that is often used to make a sauce.

C **Literary Focus** Motivation Why might the narrator choose to use such a strong phrase as "at war"?

---

studying so hard. He gave the painter lady the once-over, checking out her paint-spattered jeans, her chalky T-shirt, her floppy-brimmed straw hat. He hitched up his pants and glided over toward the painter lady, who kept right on with what she was doing.

"Watcha got there, Sweetheart?" he asked the twin with the plate.

"Suppah," she said, all soft and country-like.

"For her," the one with the jug added, jerking her chin toward the painter lady's back.

Still she didn't turn around. She was rearing back on her heels, her hands jammed into her back pockets, her face squinched up like the masterpiece she had in mind was taking shape on the wall by magic. We could have been gophers crawled up into a rotten hollow for all she cared. She didn't even say hello to anybody. Lou was muttering something about how great her concentration was. I butt him with my hip, and his elbow slid off the gum machine.   **D**

"Good evening," Side Pocket said in his best ain't-I-fine voice. But the painter lady was moving from the milk crate to the stepstool to the ladder, moving up and down fast, scribbling all over the wall like a crazy person. We looked at Side Pocket. He looked at the twins. The twins looked at us. The painter lady was giving a show. It was like those old-timey music movies where the dancer taps on the table top and then

---

D **Read and Discuss** What is happening between the community members and the painter?

Vocabulary **concentration** (kahn suhn TRAY shuhn) n.: act of thinking carefully about something.

Developing Oral Fluency

Remind students that a person's ability to understand another person's speech or oral reading depends on the speed and clarity with which the speaker talks. If the speaker talks too fast, it is impossible to figure out what he or she is saying. If the speaker speaks too slowly, it can be hard to follow what is being said and put the words together into sentences and paragraphs.

Model too-fast and too-slow reading with the sentence, "The painter lady had a tall ladder." Then, model appropriate pace using the same sentence.

Small-group Activity Put students into groups to choral read parts of the story. Direct students to start out reading as they would read naturally and then adjust their pace to match each other and the pace you modeled. Listen to groups' readings and provide guidance as needed.

✔ See **UA: Differentiating Instruction** for practice passages for developing oral fluency.

Thinking (1990) by Carlton Murrell. Oil on board.

starts jumping all over the furniture, kicking chairs over and not skipping a beat. She didn't even look where she was stepping. And for a minute there, hanging on the ladder to reach a far spot, she looked like she was going to tip right over.

"Ahh," Side Pocket cleared his throat and moved fast to catch the ladder.

"These young ladies here have brought you some supper."

"Ma'am?" The twins stepped forward. Finally the painter turned around, her eyes "full of sky," as my grandmama would say. Then she stepped down like she was in a trance. She wiped her hands on her jeans as the Morris twins offered up the plate and

E Literary Focus **Motivation** Is the painter "giving a show" for the others, or is there another explanation for her "scribbling all over the wall"?

Analyzing Visuals

Tell students that **Carlton Murrell's** artistic inspirations range from his native Barbados to the styles of the European Impressionists. He received more than 15 awards for his thought-provoking creations.

Connecting to the Text: *Although the boy in the portrait and the narrator are both young, the boy in the portrait seems lost in thought, while the narrator seems more restless and quick to act.*

Think About/Talk About

▶ Comprehension

Ⓓ Read and Discuss

Possible response: *More people are gathering to watch the painter. Some girls even brought her a meal.*

▶ Analysis

Ⓒ Literary Focus

Possible response: *The narrator might choose to use strong words like "war" to show that his dislike for the painter lady and her actions is very strong. It shows his determination to oppose the painter lady's work on the wall in any way possible.*

Ⓔ Literary Focus

Possible response: *The painter lady seems to be in her own world. She is imaginative, passionate, and engrossed in her work.*

▶ Extend the Discussion

Character Traits At the end of p. 175, the narrator compares the painter to a "crazy person." What does this description reveal about the narrator? ***Possible response:*** *He's judgmental, and he probably puts a lot of importance on acting "normal." He isn't willing to give the painter the benefit of the doubt.*

Vocabulary: Own the Word

concentration: Use role play to expand students' understanding. Ask students to make a face that shows *concentration*. Then, ask students to make a face that shows the opposite of *concentration*. Have students suggest words that describe this look. [*distraction, commotion, inattentiveness*] Tell students that these words are antonyms for *concentration*.

Model the Skill

■ Tell students that **formal English** is a bit like a formal dress—both are used in situations where people have to present themselves as proper, orderly, and following all the rules. **Informal English** is a more relaxed form of language that includes abbreviations, nicknames, slang, words shortened in speech, and dialect.

■ Point out what Mama says on page 177, "If you eat in the community, sistuh, you gonna eat pig by-and-by, one way or t'other." Explain that this sentence represents informal English in multiple ways. The pronunciation of *sister* as *sistuh* is an example of dialect. *Gonna* is the informal version of *going to*. *By-and-by* is a slang expression referring to sooner or later. Finally, *t'* is an abbreviated form of *the* used in speech. In formal English, the sentence would read, "If you eat in the community, sister, you are going to eat pig sooner or later, one way or the other."

Guided Practice: Apply

Discuss as a class why "shut right up" and "can I get" from the last two full paragraphs of page 177 are examples of informal English. Have students revise the phrases to reflect formal English.

Think as a Reader/Writer

Find It in Your Reading Point out that in the bottom of the first column on p. 177, Mama is "tapping her foot and heating up in a dangerous way." This description suggests someone who is feeling impatient but struggling to remain polite.

Use It in Your Writing Have students use vivid images as they write two short physical descriptions of someone who, like Mama, feels impatient or annoyed.

Analyzing Visuals

Connecting to the Text
How does this image help you connect to the setting of the story?

At the Farmer's Market (2003) by Pam Ingalls.

the jug. She rolled back the tinfoil, then wagged her head as though something terrible was on the plate.

"Thank your mother very much," she said, sounding like her mouth was full of sky too. "I've brought my own dinner along." And then, without even excusing herself, she went back up the ladder, drawing on the wall in a wild way. Side Pocket whistled one of those oh-brother breathy whistles and went back into the pool hall.

The Morris twins shifted their weight from one foot to the other, then crossed the street and went home. Lou had to drag me away, I was so mad. We couldn't wait to get to the firehouse to tell my daddy all about this rude woman who'd stolen our wall. **F**

All the way back to the block to help my mama out at the restaurant, me and Lou kept asking my daddy for ways to run the painter lady out of town. But my daddy was busy talking about the trip to the country and telling Lou he could come too because Grandmama can always use an extra pair of hands on the farm.

Later that night, while me and Lou were in the back doing our chores, we found out that the painter lady was a liar. She came into the restaurant and leaned against the glass of the steam table, talking

F **Read and Discuss** What mood does this scene create?

Universal Access

Struggling Readers
Strategic Students Some students may struggle to understand factors that shape a character's motivation. Model identifying a character's motivation using the painter lady's refusal of the dinner brought by the Morris twins. You might say: "The painter lady tells the twins that she has brought her own dinner along, but this turns out not to be true, as the painter lady comes to the restaurant later on. I want to find out what her motivation was for refusing what was offered. I will read on and see if I find any clues in the text." Read aloud the first column of p. 177. Say: "I notice on this page that the painter lady is asking a lot of questions about the restaurant's food, and she seems very concerned about not having pork or meat in any of her food. It seems like she is very careful about what she eats, or maybe she is on a special diet for a reason. This makes me think she turned down the food, not to be impolite, but because she could not eat it." Have students work in pairs to analyze Mama's motivation for being angry with the painter lady in the restaurant.

about how starved she was. I was scrubbing pots and Lou was chopping onions, but we could hear her through the service window. She was asking Mama was that a ham hock in the greens, and was that a neck bone in the pole beans, and were there any vegetables cooked without meat, especially pork.

"I don't care who your spiritual leader is," Mama said in that way of hers. "If you eat in the community, sistuh, you gonna eat pig by-and-by, one way or t' other."

Me and Lou were cracking up in the kitchen, and several customers at the counter were clearing their throats waiting for Mama to really fix her wagon for not speaking to the elders when she came in. The painter lady took a stool at the counter and went right on with her questions. Was there cheese in the baked macaroni, she wanted to know? Were there eggs in the salad? Was it honey or sugar in the iced tea? Mama was fixing Pop Johnson's plate. And every time the painter lady asked a fool question, Mama would dump another spoonful of rice on the pile. She was tapping her foot and heating up in a dangerous way. But Pop Johnson was happy as he could be. Me and Lou peeked through the service window, wondering what planet the painter lady came from. Who ever heard of baked

[THE PAINTER LADY TOOK A STOOL AT THE COUNTER AND WENT RIGHT ON WITH HER QUESTIONS.]

macaroni without cheese, or potato salad without eggs? **G**

"Do you have any bread made with unbleached flour?" the painter lady asked Mama. There was a long pause, as though everybody in the restaurant was holding their breath, wondering if Mama would dump the next spoonful on the painter lady's head. She didn't. But when she set Pop Johnson's plate down, it came down with a bang.

When Mama finally took her order, the starving lady all of a sudden couldn't make up her mind whether she wanted a vegetable plate or fish and a salad. She finally settled on the broiled trout and a tossed salad. But just when Mama reached for a plate to serve her, the painter lady leaned over the counter with her finger all up in the air.

"Excuse me," she said. "One more thing." Mama was holding the plate like a Frisbee, tapping that foot, one hand on her hip. "Can I get raw beets in that tossed salad?"

"You will get," Mama said, leaning her face close to the painter lady's, "whatever Lou back there tossed. Now sit down." And the painter lady sat back down on her stool and shut right up.

All the way to the country, me and Lou tried to get Mama to open fire on the painter lady. But Mama said that seeing as how she was from the North, you

G [Read and Discuss] Describe what is happening between the painter and Mama. So far, several community members have been put off by the painter. How do they react to her? What does their reaction to her tell you about them?

Model the Skill

■ Explain to students that identifying a **character's motivation** and truly understanding it are two separate tasks that readers carry out.

■ Read aloud the following sentences from p. 178: "All weekend long, me and Lou tried to scheme up ways to recapture our wall," and "When a train came roaring into the station all covered from top to bottom, windows too, with writings and drawings done with spray paint, me and Lou slapped five." Point out that "me and Lou slapped five" is prompted by watching the train pull into the station and realizing that they can reclaim their wall by spray painting. Their action is motivated by finding a way to reclaim a wall they think is theirs. Explain that what the reader has to think more deeply about the character's motivation to commit a destructive and illegal act. You might say that, for them, the wall must be more than just a part of their neighborhood; it represents familiarity and a life they have always known. They are resisting change.

Guided Practice: Apply

Have students continue reading and see if they can identify and evaluate the painter lady's motivation for creating the finished mural described on pp. 179–180.

---

couldn't expect her to have any manners. Then Mama said she was sorry she'd been so impatient with the woman because she seemed like a decent person and was simply trying to stick to a very strict diet. Me and Lou didn't want to hear that. Who did that lady think she was, coming into our neighborhood and taking over our wall?

"Welllll," Mama drawled, pulling into the filling station so Daddy could take the wheel, "it's hard on an artist, ya know. They can't always get people to look at their work. So she's just doing her work in the open, that's all."

Me and Lou definitely did not want to hear that. Why couldn't she set up an easel downtown or draw on the sidewalk in her own neighborhood? Mama told us to quit fussing so much; she was tired and wanted to rest. She climbed into the back seat and dropped down into the warm hollow Daddy had made in the pillow. **Ⓘ**

All weekend long, me and Lou tried to scheme up ways to recapture our wall. Daddy and Mama said they were sick of hearing about it. Grandmama turned up the TV to drown us out. On the late news was a story about the New York subways. When a train came roaring into the station all covered from top to bottom, windows too, with writings and drawings done with spray paint, me and Lou slapped five. Mama said it was too bad kids in New York had

---

nothing better to do than spray paint all over the trains. Daddy said that in the cities, even grown-ups wrote all over the trains and buildings too. Daddy called it "graffiti." Grandmama called it a shame.

We couldn't wait to get out of school on Monday. We couldn't find any black spray paint anywhere. But in a junky hardware store downtown we found a can of white epoxy paint, the kind you touch up old refrigerators with when they get splotchy and peely. We spent our whole allowance on it. And because it was too late to use our bus passes, we had to walk all the way home lugging our book satchels and gym shoes, and the bag with the epoxy.

When we reached the corner of Taliaferro and Fifth, it looked like a block party or something. Half the neighborhood was gathered on the sidewalk in front of the wall. I looked at Lou, he looked at me. We both looked at the bag with the epoxy and wondered how we were going to work our scheme. The painter lady's car was nowhere in sight. But there were too many people standing around to do anything. Side Pocket and his buddies were leaning on their cue sticks, hunching each other. Daddy was there with a lineman[2] he catches a ride with on Mondays. Mrs. Morris had her arms flung around the shoulders of the twins on either side of

---

2. **lineman** (LYN muhn): worker whose job is to set up and repair telephone or electric power lines.

Ⓗ [Reading Focus] **How Character Affects Plot** Consider Mama's words and actions toward the painter in the last scene. How has Mama's attitude changed? How would this scene be different if her attitude had stayed the same?

Ⓘ [Read and Discuss] What does this scene tell you about the communication difficulties between the painter and the people in the neighborhood?

Cross-Curricular Connection

HISTORY: Civil Rights Leaders

During the civil rights movement, which began in the 1950s, African Americans protested against unfair U.S. laws that limited their rights. Over the next decade, civil rights leaders organized protests and demonstrations. This caused the government to change its laws, giving African Americans equal rights. Some important civil rights leaders, such as Martin Luther King Jr. and Fannie Lou Hamer, are included in the painter's mural in "The War of the Wall."

Martin Luther King Jr., born in 1929 in Georgia, was a Baptist minister as well as a civil rights activist noted for his eloquence. One of his most famous speeches is his I Have a Dream speech, delivered at the 1963 March on Washington. In a sermon at Charles J. Mason Temple in Memphis, Tennessee, in 1968, King stated the words on the mural on p. 179: "I've been to the mountaintop, and I've seen the Promised Land."

🐻 **HSS Analysis Skills** HR 1

her. Mama was talking with some of her customers, many of them with napkins still at the throat. Mr. Eubanks came out of the barber shop, followed by a man in a striped poncho, half his face shaved, the other half full of foam.

"She really did it, didn't she?" Mr. Eubanks huffed out his chest. Lots of folks answered right quick that she surely did when they saw the straight razor in his hand.

Mama beckoned us over. And then we saw it. The wall. Reds, greens, figures outlined in black. Swirls of purple and orange. Storms of blues and yellows. It was something. I recognized some of the faces right off. There was Martin Luther King, Jr. And there was a man with glasses on and his mouth open like he was laying down a heavy rap. Daddy came up alongside and reminded us that he was Minister Malcolm X. The serious woman with a rifle I knew was Harriet Tubman because my grandmama has pictures of her all over the house. And I knew Mrs. Fannie Lou Hamer 'cause a signed photograph of her hangs in the restaurant

J **Read and Discuss** What is happening at the wall?

Analyzing Visuals **Connecting to the Text** Just as the mural below honors Dr. Martin Luther King, Jr., the "painter lady's" work of art celebrates important leaders. What might be the painter's motivation for creating this art?

Analyzing Visuals

Connecting to the Text: The painter might want people in the community to be reminded of the struggles and accomplishments of Martin Luther King. By including the quotation, the painter might be attempting to explain King's basic philosophy and encourage others to follow his example.

Think About/Talk About

▶ Comprehension

H Reading Focus
Possible response: Mama has become more understanding of the painter's situation. Mama would have still been complaining about the painter lady and saying that she had no right to be in the neighborhood.

I Read and Discuss
Possible response: Mama tells us the painter is from the north and, for Mama, that explains the painter's ill-mannered ways. She also sympathizes with the painter's plight as an artist.

J Read and Discuss
Possible response: Something exciting must be happening. Half the people standing there were in the middle of something else and couldn't keep themselves from gathering.

▶ Extend the Discussion

Understanding Characterization
Read the description of the neighborhood residents' behavior in the last paragraph on p. 178. How would you characterize these bystanders and why? *Possible response:* The townspeople are extremely impressed with the painter's work. Even a man who was halfway through a shave has come to look.

▶ **Extend the Discussion**

Symbolism Read the paragraphs describing the mural. How might the mural's content be significant or symbolic to the community? *Possible response: The mural might symbolize the community's close-knit nature and proud heritage.*

Vocabulary: Own the Word

- **liberation:** Tell students that *libera-tion* comes from the Latin root verb *liber*, which means "free." Ask stu-dents what other words share this Latin root. [*liberty, liberal*]

- **inscription:** Tell students that *inscribe* is the verb from which the noun *inscription* is formed. *Inscribe* means "to write, print, or engrave words on something." Explain that an inscription on a piece of art is often a dedication.

- **dedicate:** Ask students if they have ever had something dedicated to them or if they have ever dedi-cated something to someone. Ask them why they chose to make this dedication. *Possible response: I dedicated the A I got on my math test to my brother because he helped me study.*

Monitory Students' Comprehension

Guide the class in answering these comprehension questions.

1. What was the narrator's plan for getting rid of the painter? [*He and Lou were going to use white epoxy paint to ruin her artwork.*]

2. How does the painter annoy Mama at the restaurant? [*She requests strange foods.*]

3. What lesson do the townspeople learn when they see the mural? [*They shouldn't have judged the painter so quickly.*]

---

next to the calendar.

Then I let my eyes follow what looked like a vine. It trailed past a man with a horn, a woman with a big white flower in her hair, a handsome dude in a tuxedo seated at a piano, and a man with a goa-tee holding a book.[3] When I looked more closely, I realized that what had looked like flowers were really faces. One face with yellow petals looked just like Frieda Morris. One with red petals looked just like Hattie Morris. I could hardly believe my eyes.

"Notice," Side Pocket said, stepping close to the wall with his cue stick like a classroom pointer. "These are the flags of liberation," he said in a voice I'd never heard him use before. We all stepped closer while he pointed and spoke. "Red, black, and green," he said, his pointer falling on the leaflike flags of the vine. "Our libera-tion flag. And here Ghana, there Tanzania, Guinea-Bissau, Angola, Mozambique."[4] Side Pocket sounded very tall, as though he'd been waiting all his life to give this lesson.

Mama tapped us on the shoulder and pointed to a high section of the wall.

---

3. **a man with a horn, a woman with a big white flower in her hair, a handsome dude in a tuxedo seated at a piano, and a man with a goatee hold-ing a book:** Louis Armstrong, Billie Holiday, Duke Ellington, and W.E.B. DuBois, respectively.

4. **Ghana, there Tanzania, Guinea-Bissau, Angola, Mozambique:** countries in Africa.

K Read and Discuss What does the inscription add to what you know about the painter?

There was a fierce-looking man with his arms crossed against his chest guarding a bunch of children. His muscles bulged, and he looked a lot like my daddy. One kid was looking at a row of books. Lou punched me 'cause the kid looked like me. The one that looked like Lou was spin-ning a globe on the tip of his finger like a basketball. There were other kids there with microscopes and compasses. And the more I looked, the more it looked like the fierce man was not so much guarding the kids as defending their right to do what they were doing.

Then Lou gasped and dropped the paint bag and ran forward, running his hands over a rainbow. He had to tiptoe and stretch to do it, it was so high. I couldn't breathe either. The painter lady had found the chisel marks and had painted Jimmy Lyons's name in a rainbow.

"Read the inscription, honey," Mrs. Morris said, urging little Frieda forward. She didn't have to urge much. Frieda marched right up, bent down, and in a loud voice that made everybody quit oohing and ahhing and listen, she read,

> *To the People of Taliaferro Street*
> *I Dedicate This Wall of Respect*
> *Painted in Memory of My Cousin*
> *Jimmy Lyons*   **K**

Vocabulary **liberation** (lihb uh RAY shuhn) *n.:* release from slavery, prison, or other limitation.
inscription (ihn SKRIHP shuhn) *n.:* words written on something.
dedicate (DEHD uh kayt) *v.:* do or make something in honor of another person.

California Standards, pp. 181–183

■ **Reading Standard 3.3** Analyze characterization as delin-eated through a character's thoughts, words, speech patterns, and actions; the narrator's description; and the thoughts, words, and actions of other characters.

Applying Your Skills

Reading Standard 3.3 Analyze characterization as delineated through a character's thoughts, words, speech patterns, and actions; the narrator's description; and the thoughts, words, and actions of other characters.

The War of the Wall
Literary Response and Analysis

Reading Skills Focus
Quick Check

1. Where is the "painter lady" from? How do the narrator and Lou know that?

2. Which of the painter's <u>attributes</u> bother the narrator? Give at least two examples.

3. What does the woman paint on the wall?

Read with a Purpose

4. What do the narrator and Lou learn about the painter that makes them realize their first impressions were wrong?

Reading Skills: How Character Affects Plot

5. Record in your "Then" column how different actions by the characters might have changed the story. What is the author saying about miscommunication in this story?

Action	If	Then
The narrator confronts the painter.	the narrator approached her nicely . . .	

Literary Skills Focus
Literary Analysis

6. **Draw Conclusions** At the end of the story, what does the narrator's description of the wall tell you about his feelings toward it?

7. **Analyze** Analyze the painter's character. Support your analysis with examples from the text.

8. **Evaluate** This story is a **first-person narrative,** told by a character in the story. Do you think the story would have been better, not as good, or about the same if someone else had been the narrator? Explain your choice.

Literary Skills: Motivation

9. **Analyze** Explain why the narrator and Lou want to "run the painter lady out of town."

10. **Analyze** What is the painter's motivation for creating the mural?

Literary Skills Review: Plot and Setting

11. **Interpret** Fill in details about the setting of the story in the chart below. Then, describe the effect the setting has on the plot.

Place and Time	Customs (How People Act in a Place)	Effects the Setting Has on the Plot

Writing Skills Focus
Think as a Reader/Writer
Use It in Your Writing Choose two or three of the narrator's precise descriptions from the story. How did these images help you better understand the characters? <u>Respond</u> to this question in a paragraph.

 What Do You Think Now How do you feel about judging people based on first impressions now that you've read the story?

What Do You Think Now?
Ask students how the children's first impression of the painter turned out to be incorrect. Have them review their answers to the What Do You Think? question. Does the story support or contradict the students' original thoughts about making a first impression?

Check for Understanding

Independent Practice
Reading Skills Focus
Answers:

1. *She is from New York. They see her license plate.*

2. *She is quiet and a picky eater.*

3. *She paints a mural of great African Americans and people from the neighborhood.*

4. *She dedicates the wall to her cousin, Jimmy Lyons, who lived in the neighborhood.*

5. *The narrator and painter would have gotten along. Problems can be avoided by asking questions rather than simply jumping to conclusions.*

Literary Skills Focus
Possible responses:

6. *The narrator shows that he is impressed by the mural through his detailed descriptions of the mural and the positive reaction of the neighborhood.*

7. *She has a good heart to honor her cousin. She seems shy; she doesn't always reply to people when they talk to her.*

8. *It would not have been as good because we would not see how someone's perspective of the painter changed.*

9. *They think the painter has no right to take over their space.*

10. *She wants to honor her cousin and African American heroes.*

11. *Taliaferro Street; early 1970's; everyone knows each other and gets along; the setting influences characters' reactions and the content of the mural.*

Independent Practice
Vocabulary Development
Your Turn

- *Integration* brings people from different places together. People across town came to the neighborhood during integration.

- *Concentration* means "focus." The kids can't break the painter lady's concentration.

- *Liberation* is the gaining of freedom. The liberation flags are flags that represent countries' freedom.

- *Inscription* means "words written on something"; a girl reads the inscription on the mural.

- When you *dedicate* something, you devote it to someone. The mural is dedicated to Jimmy Lyons.

English for Academic Success
Language Coach
Remind students that in the story, Side Pocket said, "Watcha got there, Sweetheart?" to a girl who was holding a plate of food. Have students look through the story for other examples of informal English, and challenge them to rewrite some of the phrases in formal English.

English for Academic Success
Academic Vocabulary
Possible response: The narrator responds negatively to the painter at first, although his response changes when he sees the mural she's created. The narrator is stubborn and suspicious of outsiders, but he can be convinced to change his mind. This makes him credible—he has realistic faults, and he's able to overcome them.

 WordSharp: An Interactive Vocabulary Tutor

✱ Learn It Online

WordSharp: An Interactive Vocabulary Tutor provides additional support for vocabulary development. Multimedia tutorials show students how to apply vocabulary skills to unfamiliar words—and how to make those words their own.

go.hrw.com   H7-182   **Go**

Applying Your Skills

The War of the Wall

Vocabulary Development
Word, Sentence, and Paragraph Clues

Just about everyone encounters unfamiliar words when reading. If you do not have access to a dictionary, then word, sentence, and paragraph clues can help. Here is how to use those clues:

- **Word Clues:** Does the unfamiliar word resemble a word or word part you already know?

- **Sentence Clues:** Does the writer contrast the word with another familiar word? Does the writer provide a definition in the sentence? What part of speech is the unfamiliar word? Does the meaning of the sentence change if you substitute or remove the unfamiliar word?

- **Paragraph Clues:** What is the paragraph's main idea? What connection could the word have to the main idea and to the other sentences in the paragraph?

For example, *inscription* is very close in form to *scribe, script,* and other words associated with writing. The paragraph in which the word appears is about someone stepping forward to read text from the mural. When you combine the word clues and paragraph clues, you can guess that *inscription* means "words written on something."

Your Turn

Look through "The War of the Wall" for clues that help reveal the meanings of the Vocabulary words at right. When you've practiced sufficiently, try your skills with an unfamiliar word from the selection. Always check your guesses in a dictionary.

> integration
> concentration
> liberation
> inscription
> dedicate

Language Coach
Formal and Informal English Compare these two sentences:

> What do you have there, miss?

> Hey, gal, watcha got there?

The sentences ask the same thing, but they create different effects. The first sentence uses formal English, while the second uses informal English.

Formal English is the language you use in school, speaking, and writing. Formal English does not include slang or other casual expressions. You use **informal English** when you talk with or write to family members or friends. Informal English includes colloquial expressions and slang. It's often used in stories to make the dialogue between characters sound real. What are two examples of informal English in this story?

Academic Vocabulary

Write About . . .
Think about how the narrator responds to the painter. In a paragraph, identify two or three of the narrator's strongest attributes. Finally, explain whether the narrator is a credible character.

Universal Access: Vocabulary Development

EL English Learners/ Struggling Readers

English for Academic Success Model for students how to use roots and affixes to help them decipher unfamiliar words. Write the word *unprofessionally* on the board. Explain to students that even though this is a long word and may seem hard to understand, it is made up of several affixes and a root that they already know. Use lines to break the word up into its parts: un/profession/al/ly. Point to the word *profession*. Tell students that a profession is a job or calling.

Next, point to the suffix *–al.* explain that this suffix means "of or relating to." So, *professional* means "of or relating to a job or calling." The second suffix, *-ly*, means "acting in such a manner," so *professionally* must mean "acting in such a manner or relating to a job or calling." The prefix *–un* means "not," so *unprofessionally* must mean "not acting in such a manner of or relating to a job or calling." Ask a student to rephrase this definition in their own words. ***Possible response:*** Unprofessionally *means "like an amateur."*

Grammar Link
Adverbs

An **adverb** is a word that modifies a verb, an adjective, or another adverb. In these examples, the **adverb** is in boldface, and the word it modifies is underlined.

Modify a verb	The painter lady **finally** settled on the broiled trout and a salad.
Modify an adjective	Lou was **very** annoyed with the lady.
Modify an adverb	Mama was sorry she'd behaved **so** impatiently with the lady.

Adverbs tell you *where, when, how,* or *to what extent* (*how much* or *how long*).

Where	Dad was **there,** along with half the neighborhood.
When	We learned **later** that the painter lady was a liar.
How	She concentrated **intently.**
How much/how long	Side Pocket was **extremely** charming.

Note: The word *not* is an adverb that tells how much.

Your Turn

Identify the adverb in each of the following sentences. Then, tell which word it modifies.

EXAMPLE: The twins called softly to the painter lady.

ANSWER: adverb: *softly;* word modified: *called*

1. The twins waited patiently as they watched the lady.
2. Sometimes Mrs. Morris bakes for Mama's restaurant.
3. The painter lady was incredibly focused.
4. People stood outside and admired the wall.

CHOICES

As you respond to the Choices, use these **Academic Vocabulary** words as appropriate: attribute, delineate, identify, respond.

REVIEW
Compare Characters

Timed ⌐Writing Choose two characters from "The War of the Wall." Use a Venn diagram to compare and contrast their traits and motivations. How are the characters alike? How are they different? Write a paragraph summarizing the information in your Venn diagram.

Character 1 Differences Characters' Similarities Character 2 Differences

CONNECT
Film a Scene

TechFocus Choose a scene from "The War of the Wall" that would be effective in a movie. Scenes that depict a conflict, like the one in the diner between Mama and the painter, make the best movie scenes. First, work with two or three classmates to write a script based on the incident. Then, film the scene. Be sure to capture the feelings of the characters through your facial expressions, tone of voice, and speech patterns.

EXTEND
Imagine You're the Painter

In "The War of the Wall," you know the painter only through what the narrator tells you, not from the painter herself. How does the painter feel about the way people treat her or the reaction to her mural? Imagine that you're the painter, and write a journal entry about your experiences.

Independent Practice
Grammar Link
Your Turn

1. adverb: *patiently;* word modified: *waited*
2. adverb: *sometimes;* word modified: *bakes*
3. adverb: *incredibly;* word modified: *focused*
4. adverb: *outside;* word modified: *stood*

Choices:
Evaluation Criteria
Review: Timed Writing 40–50 Minutes

- Diagrams should compare two characters from "The War of the Wall."
- Students should note at least two valid similarities and two valid differences between the characters.

Connect: ⬤Homework
Film a Scene

- The film should depict a scene from "The War of the Wall."
- The film should capture the characters' feelings and motivations.

Extend: ⬤Homework
Imagine You're the Painter

- Entries should be written from the painter lady's point of view.
- Entries should include details and situations from the text.

Assess

 Chapter 2 Resources, Selection Standards Check, p. 21

ThinkCentral Online Assessment, Selection Standards Check

Teacher One Stop™, editable Selection Standards Check

Reteach

ThinkCentral Online Remediation

Universal Access: Grammar Link

EL **English Learners**

English for Academic Success Some students may have difficulty with adverbs. Use this lesson to reinforce the formal English use of adverbs.

- Explain to students that adverbs are descriptive words that describe where, when, or how something was done. Adverbs may also describe how much or how long; for instance, how much money was spent or how long the concert went on.
- Use the following example to clarify the identification

and use of adverbs:

> We drank the cold sodas quickly.

- Explain that *quickly* is an adverb modifying the verb *drank;* it describes how "we" drank the sodas. Tell students that although *cold* describes *sodas,* it is not giving any information about where, when, how, how much, or how long; therefore, it is not an adverb.

✔ For more practice with using adverbs, see **Warriner's Handbook, Language Handbook Worksheets** and **Grammar Notes.**

COMPARING TEXTS

Comparing Characters and Character Traits

CONTENTS

What Do
You
Think What can you discover about yourself when you are afraid?

QuickWrite
Think of a situation you faced that was not as scary or dangerous as you first thought it was. What did you learn from the experience?

Surgeon Uses Stethoscope
by Todd Davidson.

Preparing to Read

A Day's Wait / Stolen Day

Reading Standard 3.3 Analyze characterization as delineated through a character's thoughts, words, speech patterns, and actions; the narrator's description; and the thoughts, words, and actions of other characters.

Literary Skills Focus

Characters and Character Traits How do you get to know the people you meet? They don't carry around signs saying "I am kind" or "I am a mean bully." You have to figure out for yourself what people are like. How do you do it? You notice their appearance. You pay attention to what they do and say. You listen to what others say about them. These clues help you make inferences about their **character traits.**

You do the same things to get to know the characters in a story. What characters say, do, and think; how they are described; what other characters think about them—these are the ways that characters are delineated by writers.

Reading Skills Focus

Comparing and Contrasting Characters The main characters in "A Day's Wait" and "Stolen Day" are both young boys who think they are sick but who behave in different ways. Clues in the text help you understand the boys' character traits. Are they brave or fearful, mean or kind?

Into Action As you read, fill in a chart like this one for each boy. List the story details that suggest each boy's character traits.

Actions	
Words	
Thoughts / Feelings	
Effects on Others	

Writing Skills Focus

Think as a Reader/Writer

Find It in Your Reading As you read "A Day's Wait," note three places where the writer could have revealed a character's thoughts. As you read "Stolen Day," record the narrator's thoughts, and think about what they add to your understanding of him.

Reader/Writer Notebook

Use your **RWN** to complete the activities for these selections.

Vocabulary

A Day's Wait

detached (dih TACHT) *adj.*: not involved emotionally; indifferent. *His reaction to his son's illness was surprisingly detached.*

commenced (kuh MEHNST) *v.*: began. *He did not pay attention when his father commenced reading.*

slack (slak) *adj.*: loose. *Schatz had only a slack hold on his emotions.*

Stolen Day

solemn (SAHL uhm) *adj.*: gloomy; serious. *He wore a solemn expression while explaining that he was sick.*

wriggled (RIHG uhld) *v.*: wiggled; squirmed. *The fish wriggled in his arms as he brought it home.*

Language Coach

Pronouncing *mn* When you say the word *solemn,* the *n* is silent. This is true of any word that ends in *mn.* When the letters *mn* are in the middle of a word, you hear the sounds of both letters (think of the word *chimney*). With a partner, pronounce the following words: *hymn, remnant, amnesia, condemn.*

Learn It Online
Dig deeper into vocabulary. Use Word Watch to increase your understanding of words at:

go.hrw.com   H7-185   **Go**

UA: Supporting Instruction in Five Languages, selection summary

Analyzing Visuals Transparencies, p. 13

ThinkCentral Online Assessment, Selection Standards Check

ThinkCentral Online Remediation

Preteach

Introducing Vocabulary

Use the activity below to check students' understanding of the Vocabulary words.

1. How might a branch become **detached** from a tree? [*The wind might have blown it off.*]
2. What did we do when class **commenced** today? [*took attendance*]
3. Would you be **slack** about preparing for a test? [*No, I would study.*]
4. What would make you feel **solemn**? [*going to a funeral*]
5. What might a worm have **wriggled** on? [*a fishing hook*]

English for Academic Success

Language Coach

Give students examples of other words that contain the letters *mn*, such as *autumn, calmness, condemn, column,* and *gymnast.* Read the words aloud, and have students repeat each word after you.

Literary Skills Focus

As you read and discuss the selections with students, have them take notes on specific text details they can use to enter character traits.

Reading Skills Focus

Give students a copy of the Reading Skills Focus graphic organizer before they read. Tell them to use their responses to answer the questions on the Applying Your Skills page.

Writing Skills Focus

As you read and discuss the selections with students, have them record characters' inner thoughts in their **Reader/Writer Notebook.**

Learn It Online
Send students to **Word Watch** for audio pronunciations, synonyms and antonyms, and brief histories of word origins.

go.hrw.com   H7-185   **Go**

Selection Introduction

More About the Writers

■ **Ernest Hemingway** was reared in a conservative household that emphasized hard work, determination, and physical fitness. These values, in addition to his experiences serving during the First World War, inform much of his writing.

■ Life in Ohio was a major influence on the works of **Sherwood Anderson.** In addition to his simple, naturalistic prose style, he had an interest in the psychology of his characters.

Think About the Writer

Discuss with students the way writers may gather sources to create characters—do they base characters on themselves, on people they know, or a combination of the two? As they read the stories, ask students to think about how the writers created the characters. Why might they have included the details they did?

For Independent Reading

■ If students want to explore how the thoughts of a character inform a story, Daniel Keyes's short story "Flowers for Algernon" focuses on the diary of a mentally handicapped man, Charlie, after an experimental surgery to improve his cognition.

■ Students who enjoy reading about examples of young characters demonstrating courage might want to read *Call It Courage* by Armstrong Sperry. In this novel, the son of a Polynesian chief must face his fear of the ocean.

Ernest Hemingway
(1899–1961)

Nobel Prize WINNER

Grace Under Pressure

Ernest Hemingway was born in Oak Park, Illinois. He spent his youth hunting, fishing, boxing, and playing football. When the United States entered World War I, he volunteered to be an ambulance driver in Italy. He was nineteen when a bomb landed three feet from him, filling his right leg with 227 pieces of shrapnel.

When he returned from the war, Hemingway wrote many stories and novels that portray men who show "grace under pressure"—calm courage in the face of great danger. That is also a theme in "A Day's Wait." The story's silences and sparse dialogue reflect the belief of Hemingway's heroes that they should keep a tight rein on their fears and other emotions.

Hemingway won the Nobel Prize in Literature in 1954. Today he is regarded as one of the twentieth century's great writers.

Sherwood Anderson
(1876–1941)

A Talented Storyteller

Sherwood Anderson grew up in a small Ohio town that would later play a major role in many of his stories. He attended school infrequently while working full time to help provide for his family. His talent for storytelling emerged later in life, while he was running his own business.

Anderson's straightforward writing style changed the short story and influenced a younger generation of writers. Anderson offered his support to younger writers, among them Ernest Hemingway. In fact, Anderson was instrumental in getting Hemingway's first novel published.

Think About the Writers

In what ways do you think the lives and experiences of these authors have influenced their work?

Preview the Selections

In "A Day's Wait," you'll meet **Schatz,** a nine-year-old boy who shows grace under pressure while he's sick with the flu.

In "Stolen Day," you'll meet a **boy** who is convinced that he's suffering from a serious disease.

A Day's Wait

by Ernest Hemingway

Read with a Purpose
Read this short story to find out what the main character, Schatz, learns after "a day's wait."

Build Background
To understand this story, you have to know that there are two kinds of temperature scales: Celsius, which is used in Europe, and Fahrenheit, which is used in the United States. Water boils at 100 degrees Celsius. The boiling point on the Fahrenheit scale is 212 degrees.

Hemingway and his family lived in France for many years. In this story, they are back in the United States. The story is based on an incident that actually occurred, involving Hemingway's nine-year-old son Bumby. (In the story, Bumby is called Schatz—German for "treasure.")

He came into the room to shut the windows while we were still in bed and I saw he looked ill. He was shivering, his face was white, and he walked slowly as though it ached to move.

"What's the matter, Schatz?"

"I've got a headache."

"You better go back to bed."

"No. I'm all right."

"You go to bed. I'll see you when I'm dressed."

But when I came downstairs he was dressed, sitting by the fire, looking a very sick and miserable boy of nine years. When I put my hand on his forehead I knew he had a fever.

"You go up to bed," I said, "you're sick."

"I'm all right," he said.

When the doctor came he took the boy's temperature.

"What is it?" I asked him.

"One hundred and two."

Ⓐ

Ⓐ **Read and Discuss** What has the author revealed so far?

Selection Readability	
Easily Accessible	familiar situations;
Accessible	dialogue;
Challenging	challenging theme

Selection Plot Summary
In "A Day's Wait," Schatz believes he is suffering from a fatal illness, when in reality, his worry stems from a misunderstanding regarding his temperature reading on the thermometer (Celsius versus Fahrenheit).

Model the Skill

■ Explain that some characters have **traits** that are easily identifiable; others have traits that the reader must read carefully for and make inferences about.

■ Read aloud from point B to the end of the column. Point out that the boy is visibly sick: He is pale and has dark spots under his eyes. His behavior also suggests illness, because he is lying down, probably tired, and indifferent. Though these clues are important to a reader as they give insight into the boy's condition, it is the last line of the column that is most significant. His father reveals that, instead of doing what a sick person would normally do by going to sleep, he is sitting up and staring at the foot of the bed. His unusual behavior reveals how he handles illness. He seems to refuse to yield to it. Knowing that illness can be stressful, coupled with his resistance to illness, suggests that he is frustrated with or worried about his illness.

Guided Practice: Apply

Turn and Talk Have students continue reading to point D. Then, have students work in pairs to make an inference about the boy's character based on his comment to his father that "you don't have to stay if it's going to bother you." ***Possible response:*** *The boy doesn't want to burden others with this illness.*

Downstairs, the doctor left three different medicines in different-colored capsules with instructions for giving them. One was to bring down the fever, another a purgative,[1] the third to overcome an acid condition. The germs of influenza can only exist in an acid condition, he explained. He seemed to know all about influenza and said there was nothing to worry about if the fever did not go above one hundred and four degrees. This was a light epidemic of flu and there was no danger if you avoided pneumonia. **Ⓑ**

Back in the room I wrote the boy's temperature down and made a note of the time to give the various capsules.

"Do you want me to read to you?"

"All right. If you want to," said the boy. His face was very white and there were dark areas under his eyes. He lay still in the bed and seemed very detached from what was going on.

I read aloud from Howard Pyle's *Book of Pirates*; but I could see he was not following what I was reading. **Ⓒ**

"How do you feel, Schatz?" I asked him.

"Just the same, so far," he said.

I sat at the foot of the bed and read to myself while I waited for it to be time to give another capsule. It would have been natural for him to go to sleep, but when I looked up he was looking at the foot of the bed, looking very strangely.

---

1. **purgative** (PUR guh tihv): laxative.

Ⓑ Read and Discuss What has happened?

Ⓒ Literary Focus Character Traits Based on his words and actions, what are some of the father's main attributes?

"Why don't you try to go to sleep? I'll wake you up for the medicine."

"I'd rather stay awake."

After a while he said to me, "You don't have to stay in here with me, Papa, if it bothers you."

"It doesn't bother me."

"No, I mean you don't have to stay if it's going to bother you." **Ⓓ**

I thought perhaps he was a little light-headed and after giving him the prescribed capsules at eleven o'clock I went out for a while.

It was a bright, cold day, the ground covered with a sleet that had frozen so that it seemed as if all the bare trees, the bushes, the cut brush, and all the grass and the bare ground had been varnished with ice. I took the young Irish setter for a little walk up the road and along a frozen creek, but it was difficult to stand or walk on the glassy surface and the red dog slipped and slithered and I fell twice, hard, once dropping my gun and having it slide away over the ice.

We flushed a covey[2] of quail under a high clay bank with overhanging brush and I killed two as they went out of sight over the top of the bank. Some of the covey lit in trees, but most of them scattered into brush piles and it was necessary to jump on the ice-coated mounds of brush several

---

2. **flushed a covey** (KUHV ee): frightened a small group of birds from their hiding place.

Ⓓ Read and Discuss What is going on between the boy and his father here?

Vocabulary **detached** (dih TACHT) *adj.*: not involved emotionally; indifferent.

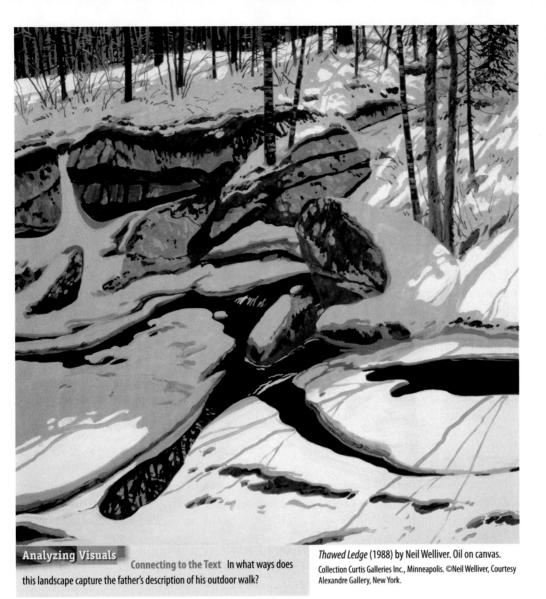

Analyzing Visuals
Connecting to the Text In what ways does this landscape capture the father's description of his outdoor walk?

Thawed Ledge (1988) by Neil Welliver. Oil on canvas. Collection Curtis Galleries Inc., Minneapolis. ©Neil Welliver, Courtesy Alexandre Gallery, New York.

times before they would flush. Coming out while you were poised unsteadily on the icy, springy brush, they made difficult shooting and I killed two, missed five, and started back pleased to have found a covey close to the house and happy there were so many left to find on another day. **E**

At the house they said the boy had

E | Read and Discuss | What is this part of the story about?

emotions—we know only what the narrator tells us. When students finish reading, ask them to discuss with a partner how the narrator's point of view might have affected their understanding of Schatz's character.

Students with Disabilities
Make a large, color-coded version of the Reading Skills Focus graphic organizer and post it on the board. Distribute erasable colored pencils or markers, and have students mark Schatz's actions, words, thoughts, feelings, and effects on others in the appropriate colors as they read.

Analyzing Visuals
Neil Welliver (1929-2005) was known for his depictions of the landscape of Maine. He often traveled deep into the woods to sketch the landscape before transferring his images on large canvasses in the studio.

Connecting to the Text: *The landscape reflects the icy environment the father must walk through and depicts a ledge similar to the one the father slipped on.*

Think About/Talk About

▶ Comprehension
B Read and Discuss
Possible response: *Apparently, the doctor was called and has prescribed three medicines for the boy's flu symptoms.*

D Read and Discuss
Possible response: *The father records the boy's temperature and notes when to dispense the medication; then, he reads to his son, who is neither following the story nor nodding off. The father says that the son should go to sleep, but the son wants to stay awake.*

E Read and Discuss
Possible response: *The father goes hunting with his dog for a while.*

▶ Analysis
C Literary Focus
Possible response: *The father's attributes include an attention to detail and a deep concern and love for his son.*

Vocabulary: Own the Word
detached: Tell students that someone who is *detached* is indifferent and distant. An antonym for *detached* is *involved*. Have students describe how Schatz would have looked and acted if he was involved. [*Schatz would have looked at his father with interest.*]

English for Academic Success
AAVE Some students may struggle with the pronunciation of end consonants in contractions. Explain that in informal English, these consonants are often not pronounced. If speaking in a setting that requires formal English, however, it is important to enunciate the *t* sound on the end of a consonant. Model pronouncing *don't* and *doesn't*, first in informal English, then in formal English. Then, have students practice saying the following consonants aloud, using formal English: *can't, won't, hasn't, musn't.*

Think About/Talk About

▶ **Comprehension**

F Read and Discuss

Possible response: The father realizes that his son is worrying that the medicine won't help him get better.

G Read and Discuss

Possible response: The father has known all along that there are two systems for measuring temperature, Celsius and Fahrenheit. Schatz thought that he was dying, but the father knew that Schatz wasn't going to die.

▶ **Extend the Discussion**

Making Judgments Read Schatz's conversation with his father in column 2. Do you think that Schatz's behavior in this scene is credible? Explain. *Possible response: It seems a little unbelievable that someone would worry about dying from a slight fever, but since Schatz is only nine years old, he might not understand temperatures very well. I think his behavior is credible.*

Vocabulary: Own the Word

- **commenced:** Tell students that a noun form of the verb *commence* is *commencement*. A commencement is a beginning, but the word is also used to describe a graduation ceremony. Because of this, some people often confuse the meaning of the word *commence* with "ending." This confusion comes from associating graduation with the end of school, instead of the beginning of life after school, which is the intended meaning.

- **slack:** Tell students that *slack* is an adjective meaning "loose." Some synonyms for *slack* are *limp, relaxed, floppy,* and *drooping.* Have students work in pairs to come up with antonyms for *slack.* [*taut, tight, firm*]

Monitor Students' Comprehension

Check students' understanding of the story by asking them what causes Schatz to worry. [*He thinks that his temperature is so high that he's about to die.*]

---

refused to let anyone come into the room.

"You can't come in," he said. "You mustn't get what I have."

I went up to him and found him in exactly the position I had left him, white-faced, but with the tops of his cheeks flushed by the fever, staring still, as he had stared, at the foot of the bed.

I took his temperature.

"What is it?"

"Something like a hundred," I said. It was one hundred and two and four tenths.

"It was a hundred and two," he said.

"Who said so?"

"The doctor."

"Your temperature is all right," I said. "It's nothing to worry about."

"I don't worry," he said, "but I can't keep from thinking."

"Don't think," I said. "Just take it easy."

"I'm taking it easy," he said and looked straight ahead. He was evidently holding tight onto himself about something.

"Take this with water."

"Do you think it will do any good?"

"Of course it will."

I sat down and opened the *Pirate* book and commenced to read, but I could see he was not following, so I stopped.

"About what time do you think I'm going to die?" he asked.

"What?"

"About how long will it be before I die?"

"You aren't going to die. What's the matter with you?"

"Oh, yes, I am. I heard him say a hundred and two."

"People don't die with a fever of one hundred and two. That's a silly way to talk."

"I know they do. At school in France the boys told me you can't live with forty-four degrees. I've got a hundred and two."

He had been waiting to die all day, ever since nine o'clock in the morning.

"You poor Schatz," I said. "Poor old Schatz. It's like miles and kilometers. You aren't going to die. That's a different thermometer. On that thermometer thirty-seven is normal. On this kind it's ninety-eight."

"Are you sure?"

"Absolutely," I said. "It's like miles and kilometers. You know, like how many kilometers we make when we do seventy miles in the car?"

"Oh," he said.

But his gaze at the foot of the bed relaxed slowly. The hold over himself relaxed too, finally, and the next day it was very slack and he cried very easily at little things that were of no importance. **G**

F Read and Discuss | What do you learn in this conversation?

G Read and Discuss | What has the father known all along that Schatz hasn't known until now?

Vocabulary **commenced** (kuh MEHNST) *v.:* began. **slack** (slak) *adj.:* loose.

 California Standards, p. 191

- **Reading Standard 3.3** Analyze characterization as delineated through a character's thoughts, words, speech patterns, and actions; the narrator's description; and the thoughts, words, and actions of other characters.

Applying Your Skills

Reading Standard 3.3 Analyze characterization as delineated through a character's thoughts, words, speech patterns, and actions; the narrator's description; and the thoughts, words, and actions of other characters.

A Day's Wait

Literary Response and Analysis

Reading Skills Focus
Quick Check

1. Complete a story map like the one below for "A Day's Wait."

Title and Author	
Setting	
Characters	
Conflict	
Resolution	

Read with a Purpose

2. What does "a day's wait" reveal to Schatz?

Reading Skills: Comparing and Contrasting Characters

3. Complete the chart by identifying Schatz's character traits as revealed by the details you listed.

	Story Details	Trait
Actions		
Words		
Thoughts/Feelings		
Effects on Others		

✓ Vocabulary Check

Answer the following questions:

4. Why has Schatz's self-control grown **slack** by the end of the story?
5. Why might you describe the father's attitude as **detached**?
6. Why was Schatz distracted when his father **commenced** reading?

Literary Skills Focus
Literary Analysis

7. **Analyze** Why would a young boy <u>respond</u> so heroically in the face of death? Explain whether you think Schatz's behavior is typical.

8. **Interpret** The heroes in Hemingway's stories often hold back emotion in times of crisis. How does Schatz reveal the strain and tension he feels inside?

9. **Evaluate** The father calls his son "Schatz," which is German for "treasure." What does this name reveal about the father's feelings for the boy? How else do you see the father's feelings for Schatz being expressed?

10. **Connect / Extend** Why do people often hesitate to share their feelings? How can failing to share feelings lead to assumptions that can interfere in our daily lives?

Literary Skills: Characters and Character Traits

11. **Analyze** Although Schatz is sick, he gets up, closes the windows in his parents' room, and then gets dressed. What character traits do these actions reveal?

12. **Infer** While his son is ill, the father goes hunting and kills two birds. What does this action tell you about the father's character?

Writing Skills Focus
Think as a Reader/Writer

Use It in Your Writing How might "A Day's Wait" be different if it were told from Schatz's point of view? Rewrite the first scene of the story as if the boy were telling it. Be sure to include Schatz's inner thoughts.

Universal Access

Struggling Writers

Provide additional scaffolding for students struggling to re-imagine the scene from Schatz's point of view. Point out the father's description of Schatz on p. 187: "He was shivering, his face was white, and he walked slowly as though it ached to move." Tell students to consider how Schatz likely feels, given his sickly appearance. Does he feel weak or strong? Is he worried or carefree? Have students complete a web, brainstorming ideas about Schatz's perceptions and impressions of the scene.

As they draft their responses, remind them to use pronouns such as *I* and *me* in describing Schatz's inner thoughts.

Check for Understanding

Independent Practice
Reading Skills Focus
Answers:

1. *Title and Author: "A Day's Wait" by Ernest Hemingway. Setting: A house in the country during winter. Characters: Schatz, his father, the doctor. Conflict: Schatz thinks he's going to die. Resolution: Schatz discovers he won't die.*

2. *He realizes that he will survive and that he has confused Celsius with Fahrenheit.*

3. *Examples should demonstrate that Schatz is brave and shows concern for others.*

Vocabulary Check
Possible responses:

4. *Schatz is no longer worried about being strong in the face of death.*

5. *He does not believe that his son's illness is anything to be worried about.*

6. *He thinks he's about to die.*

Literary Skills Focus
Possible responses:

7. *He seems to follow his father's lead in hiding his emotions. Perhaps his behavior was typical during the time of this story, but it's probably not now.*

8. *Schatz reveals the strain he has been under by crying over small things.*

9. *He obviously cares a great deal for Schatz and values him greatly.*

10. *People are afraid of looking weak. Assumptions can lead people to arrive at false conclusions that waste time or hurt other people.*

11. *Schatz is responsible, uncomplaining, brave, and emotionally strong.*

12. *He does not stop what he is doing when something goes wrong. He realizes the illness is not serious, so he continues his normal routine.*

Stolen Day

by Sherwood Anderson

Direct Teach

Model the Skill

■ Provide students with copies of the graphic organizer (see **Chapter 2 Resources**), or ask them to use a piece of their own paper.

■ Explain that **comparing and contrasting** characters they are reading about helps readers better understand those characters. Tell students that as they read "Stolen Day," they should work to compare and contrast the story's narrator with Schatz from "A Day's Wait."

■ Read aloud p. 192. Point out that on this page, the main character walks to the creek, sees a boy whose illness keeps him from going to school, and then begins to ache. The main character complains to his teacher and is sent home. Explain that the main character's actions are important for understanding him and for comparing him with Schatz from "A Day's Wait." Write the actions in the graphic organizer.

Actions	Walks to the creek, sees Walter, begins to ache, complains to teacher, goes home
Words	
Thoughts/Feelings	
Effects on Others	

Guided Practice: Apply

Ask students how the main character's reaction to his ache contrasts with Schatz's reaction to his headache on p. 189. ***Possible response:*** *The character in this story cries and complains to his teacher; Schatz remains stoic.*

Read with a Purpose

Read this short story to learn why the narrator says he has a serious, life-threatening disease.

Preparing to Read for this selection is on page 185.

Build Background

The setting for this story is a small Ohio town about a century ago. Some customs may have changed, but people's emotions and their motives, or reasons for doing what they do, have stayed pretty much the same.

It must be that all children are actors. The whole thing started with a boy on our street named Walter, who had inflammatory rheumatism.[1] That's what they called it. He didn't have to go to school.

Still he could walk about. He could go fishing in the creek or the waterworks pond. There was a place up at the pond where in the spring the water came tumbling over the dam and formed a deep pool. It was a good place. Sometimes you could get some good big ones there.

I went down that way on my way to school one spring morning. It was out of my way but I wanted to see if Walter was there.

He was, inflammatory rheumatism and all. There he was, sitting with a fish pole in his hand. He had been able to walk down there all right.

It was then that my own legs began to hurt. My back too. I went on to school but, at the recess time, I began to cry. I did it when the teacher, Sarah Suggett, had come out into the schoolhouse yard.

She came right over to me.

"I ache all over," I said. I did, too.

I kept on crying and it worked all right.

"You'd better go on home," she said.

---

1. **inflammatory rheumatism** (ihn FLAM uh tawr ee ROO muh tihz uhm): disease characterized by pain in the joints, fever, and inflammation of the heart.

Ⓐ **Read and Discuss** What does the boy think about Walter and his "rheumatism"?

Selection Readability	
Easily Accessible **Accessible** **Challenging**	common childhood experiences; accessible theme; familiar genre

Selection Plot Summary

A boy pretends to suffer from inflammatory rheumatism because another student at his school has it and gets to stay home. The boy begins to convince himself that he really is sick and imagines his family's reaction to his illness.

Read with a Purpose Have students read the Read with a Purpose statement. Point out that if the narrator says he is sick, it may not mean he actually is sick.

▶ **Comprehension**

Ⓐ **Read and Discuss**

Possible response: It seems as though the narrator is jealous that Walter appears healthy but does not have to go to school.

▶ **Extend the Discussion**

Compare and Contrast Characters In paragraphs 5–9, the narrator pretends to be in severe pain in order to leave school early. In your opinion, is this something that Schatz would have done? Why or why not? *Possible response: I do not think that Schatz would have pretended to be very ill. Schatz seems like an honest person who is scared of being sick, so I do not think that he'd lie about coming down with a bad illness.*

Analyzing Visuals **Connecting to the Text** What can you infer about the boy in the painting based on his appearance? What character traits does he appear to have?

Portrait of Leslie Stanley (1931) by Ruskin Spear (1911–1990). Oil on canvas.

Analyzing Visuals

Childhood polio left English painter **Ruskin Spear** (1911–1990) disabled, but it did not stop him from embarking on a successful career as an artist and teacher. He painted portraits not only of famous figures but also of the everyday men and women in West London.

Connecting to the Text: He looks like he's thinking carefully about something. He appears to be a calm, thoughtful person.

Universal Access

Struggling Readers

Benchmark Students Guide students' interpretation of the main character by focusing their attention on the first line of the story. Explain that the narrator tells readers from the beginning, "It must be that all children are actors," because the concept of children acting or pretending is central to the story. Tell students that the narrator himself may be acting at times during the story. Then, read aloud the first page of the story for students. Pause at the end of the page and revisit the first line of the story with students. What do they think of the narrator's sudden pain, and the timing of his crying?

Strategic Students Guide students in analyzing the narrator's words and actions on the first page of "Stolen Day" to help them make inferences about character traits. Ask students to identify the tone of the narrator's remarks about Walter. If necessary, guide students to understand that the narrator's tone is one of envy and anger, as he thinks it unfair that Walter does not seem ill yet is allowed to skip school and go fishing. Then, discuss with students how the narrator's tone of envy may suggest a character trait of jealousy.

Model the Skill

■ Tell students that some words contain letters, either vowels or consonants, that are not pronounced when the word is said. These are **silent letters**.

■ Write the vocabulary words *solemn* and *column* on the board. Say each. Ask students whether the pronunciations of the words were different from what they expected from the spellings of the words. Explain that each of these words has a silent letter. In both words, the silent letter is *n*. Tell students that when *m* and *n* appear side-by-side at the end of a word, the *n* remains silent and the word ends with an /m/ sound.

Guided Practice: Apply

Write *condemn* and *autumn* on the board. Ask a volunteer to pronounce each word and explain the reason behind its pronunciation.

Think as a Reader/Writer

Find It in Your Reading Tell students that on p. 195, the narrator's inner thoughts reveal one of his motives for pretending to be sick: He wishes his mother would pay more attention to him.

Use It in Your Writing Ask students to write two sentences that reveal the inner thoughts that influenced a particular decision they made.

So I went. I limped painfully away. I kept on limping until I got out of the schoolhouse street.

Then I felt better. I still had inflammatory rheumatism pretty bad but I could get along better. **B**

I must have done some thinking on the way home.

"I'd better not say I have inflammatory rheumatism," I decided. "Maybe if you've got that you swell up."

I thought I'd better go around to where Walter was and ask him about that, so I did—but he wasn't there.

"They must not be biting today," I thought.

I had a feeling that, if I said I had inflammatory rheumatism, Mother or my brothers and my sister Stella might laugh. They did laugh at me pretty often and I didn't like it at all.

"Just the same," I said to myself, "I have got it." I began to hurt and ache again. **C**

I went home and sat on the front steps of our house. I sat there a long time. There wasn't anyone at home but Mother and the two little ones. Ray would have been four or five then and Earl might have been three.

It was Earl who saw me there. I had got tired sitting and was lying on the porch. Earl was always a quiet, solemn little fellow.

> "It's a wonder, with my inflammatory rheumatism and all, I didn't just drop down dead."

He must have said something to Mother for presently she came.

"What's the matter with you? Why aren't you in school?" she asked.

I came pretty near telling her right out that I had inflammatory rheumatism but I thought I'd better not. Mother and Father had been speaking of Walter's case at the table just the day before. "It affects the heart," Father had said. That frightened me when I thought of it. "I might die," I thought. "I might just suddenly die right here; my heart might stop beating."

On the day before I had been running a race with my brother Irve. We were up at the fairgrounds after school and there was a half-mile track.

"I'll bet you can't run a half-mile," he said. "I bet you I could beat you running clear around the track."

And so we did it and I beat him, but afterwards my heart did seem to beat pretty hard. I remembered that lying there on the porch. "It's a wonder, with my inflammatory rheumatism and all, I didn't just drop down dead," I thought. The thought frightened me a lot. I ached worse than ever. **D**

"I ache, Ma," I said. "I just ache."

She made me go in the house and upstairs and get into bed.

B **Literary Focus** Character Traits What does the information about the narrator's sickness show you?

C **Reading Focus** Comparing and Contrasting Characters Compare the way this boy responds to illness with the way Schatz responds. How are the two boys similar and different?

D **Read and Discuss** Why does the narrator feel the way he does after his race with Irve?

Vocabulary solemn (SAHL uhm) *adj.:* gloomy; serious.

Word-Attack Skills Mini-Lesson

Hard and soft *c*

• Write the selection word *recess* on the chalkboard and underline the letter *c*. Read the word aloud for students, and have them repeat it after you.

• Remind students that when *c* comes before *e, i,* or *y,* it can have the sound /s/. In *recess*, the letter *c* sounds like /s/ because it comes before *e*.

• However, the letter *c* can also have the /k/ sound when followed by *a* or *o*, as in the selection words *came* and *course*.

• Write the word *course* on the board and read it aloud for students. Then, have students read the word after you. Tell students to notice the /k/ sound that the letter *c* makes in this word.

• Use the following words to demonstrate these rules regarding the letter *c*:

recess—*c* stands for /s/ before *e*.

carp—*c* stands for /k/ before *a*.

covered—*c* stands for /k/ before *o*.

It wasn't so good. It was spring. I was up there for perhaps an hour, maybe two, and then I felt better.

I got up and went downstairs. "I feel better, Ma," I said.

Mother said she was glad. She was pretty busy that day and hadn't paid much attention to me. She had made me get into bed upstairs and then hadn't even come up to see how I was. **E**

I didn't think much of that when I was up there but when I got downstairs where she was, and when, after I had said I felt better and she only said she was glad and went right on with her work, I began to ache again.

I thought, "I'll bet I die of it. I bet I do."

I went out to the front porch and sat down. I was pretty sore at Mother.

"If she really knew the truth, that I have the inflammatory rheumatism and I may just drop down dead any time, I'll bet she wouldn't care about that either," I thought. **F**

I was getting more and more angry the more thinking I did.

"I know what I'm going to do," I thought; "I'm going to go fishing."

I thought that, feeling the way I did, I might be sitting on the high bank just above the deep pool where the water went over the dam, and suddenly my heart would stop beating.

And then, of course, I'd pitch forward, over the bank into the pool and, if I wasn't dead when I hit the water, I'd drown sure.

They would all come home to supper and they'd miss me. **G**

"But where is he?"

Then Mother would remember that I'd come home from school aching.

She'd go upstairs and I wouldn't be there. One day during the year before, there was a child got drowned in a spring. It was one of the Wyatt children.

Right down at the end of the street there was a spring under a birch tree and there had been a barrel sunk in the ground.

Everyone had always been saying the spring ought to be kept covered, but it wasn't.

So the Wyatt child went down there, played around alone, and fell in and got drowned.

Mother was the one who had found the drowned child. She had gone to get a pail of water and there the child was, drowned and dead.

This had been in the evening when we were all at home, and Mother had come running up the street with the dead, dripping child in her arms. She was making for the Wyatt house as hard as she could run, and she was pale.

She had a terrible look on her face, I remembered then.

"So," I thought, "they'll miss me and there'll be a search made. Very likely there'll be someone who has seen me sitting by the pond fishing, and there'll be a big alarm and

---

E [Read and Discuss] What do the narrator's thoughts about his mother tell you?

F [Reading Focus] **Comparing and Contrasting Characters** How does the boy feel about his mother's response to him? How does this compare to Schatz's reactions in "A Day's Wait"?

G [Literary Focus] **Character Traits** What do you learn about the boy from his thoughts here?

Activity Write these sets of words on the board. Have volunteers identify the two words in each set in which *c* stands for /s/.

1.	medical	<u>surface</u>	<u>icy</u>
2.	<u>cement</u>	coming	<u>proceed</u>
3.	specter	<u>docile</u>	<u>voice</u>
4.	placate	<u>trance</u>	<u>decide</u>
5.	<u>parcel</u>	camper	<u>cedar</u>

Think About/Talk About

▶ Comprehension

C Reading Focus
Possible response: *Schatz tries to be brave about his illness because he doesn't want to worry his parents; the narrator of this story feels sorry for himself and thinks about the attention he will receive. Schatz seems to be very considerate of others while the narrator of this story seems very selfish.*

D Read and Discuss
Possible response: *The narrator remembers how hard his heart was beating during his race with Irve and associates it with inflammatory rheumatism rather than with the race itself.*

E Read and Discuss
Possible response: *The narrator doesn't think he gets enough attention from his mom, even when he's sick.*

F Reading Focus
Possible response: *The boy in this story is angry that his mother does not take him seriously; Schatz does not want his father to get himself worked up about his illness.*

▶ Analysis

B Literary Focus
Possible response: *The narrator seems to be pretending he's sick, but he also believes he has rheumatism.*

G Literary Focus
Possible response: *The boy wants his family members to appreciate him more than they do, and he wants them to feel bad about not caring about him enough.*

Vocabulary: Own the Word
solemn: Demonstrate the facial expression of a *solemn* person. Ask students to demonstrate from their seats. Then, ask students to demonstrate the opposite of *solemn* using facial expressions. Ask students what words describe this mood. [*cheerful, happy, upbeat*]

Model the Skill

■ Remind students that characters, like people, can be extremely complicated. Analyzing **character** and **character motivation** is critical to fully understanding a story.

■ Explain that the narrator of "Stolen Day" is affected by a number of different emotions. He is jealous that Walter gets to skip school and go fishing every day, he is hurting from a perceived illness, and he is angry that his mother has not shown much concern over his condition. Point out the paragraph starting with "I was having a grand time…" on p. 196. Tell students that this paragraph helps to explain one of the narrator's motivations for pretending to be sick; he will gain the same amount of attention that his mother gave to the Wyatt child. Though it may seem strange for the narrator to be enjoying the thought of his own death, the complex emotions the character is dealing with give rise to this action. He is channeling his anger and physical discomfort into a fantasy in which his feelings seem right and his wants are fulfilled.

Guided Practice: Apply

Turn and Talk Have students begin reading at the bottom of p. 196, when the narrator says, "By this time I didn't ache hardly at all," and have them continue to read through the second paragraph on p. 197. Then, have students discuss in pairs what the narrator's inner thoughts about his rheumatism reveal about his motivation. Have students consider whether the narrator might feel guilty about spending the day at the creek rather than going to school.

Analyzing Visuals **Connecting to the Text** What does the painting reveal about the narrator's motivation for thinking he's sick?

Richard Fishing by the Pool by Charles Knight (1910–1990). Pen and ink; watercolor; gouache on paper. ©Chris Beetles, London.

all the town will turn out and they'll drag the pond."

I was having a grand time, having died. Maybe, after they found me and had got me out of the deep pool, Mother would grab me up in her arms and run home with me as she had run with the Wyatt child. **H**

I got up from the porch and went around the house. I got my fishing pole and lit out for the pool below the dam. Mother was busy—she always was—and didn't see me go. When I got there I thought I'd better not sit too near the edge of the high bank.

By this time I didn't ache hardly at all, but I thought.

"With inflammatory rheumatism you can't tell," I thought.

H **Reading Focus** Comparing and Contrasting Characters What does the narrator mean when he says, "I was having a grand time, having died"?

Developing Oral Fluency

On pp. 196–197, the narrator experiences several emotions. Discuss with the class what some of those emotions are. [*excitement about catching the carp, embarrassment when his family laughs at him*]

Small-Group Activity Put students into small groups, making sure that there is at least one fluent student in each group.

• Model reading a few lines of the narration, making sure to show the narrator's emotions. For example, read with excitement the narrator's feelings of pride after catching the large fish and being the center of attention.

• Next, have students take turns reading paragraphs aloud within their group. Students should use appropriate expression for the narrator's emotions in that paragraph.

• Finally, have groups discuss how taking note of the changes in emotion helped them to follow the story.

✔ See **UA: Differentiating Instruction** for practice passages for devleoping oral fluency.

"It probably comes and goes," I thought. "Walter has it and he goes fishing," I thought.

I had got my line into the pool and suddenly I got a bite. It was a regular whopper. I knew that. I'd never had a bite like that. I knew what it was. It was one of Mr. Fenn's big carp.

Mr. Fenn was a man who had a big pond of his own. He sold ice in the summer and the pond was to make the ice. He had bought some big carp and put them into his pond and then, earlier in the spring when there was a freshet,[2] his dam had gone out.

So the carp had got into our creek and one or two big ones had been caught—but none of them by a boy like me.

The carp was pulling and I was pulling and I was afraid he'd break my line, so I just tumbled down the high bank, holding onto the line, and got right into the pool. We had it out, there in the pool. We struggled. We wrestled. Then I got a hand under his gills and got him out.

He was a big one all right. He was nearly half as big as I was myself. I had him on the bank and I kept one hand under his gills and I ran.

> I had got my line into the pool and suddenly I got a bite.

I never ran so hard in my life. He was slippery, and now and then he wriggled out of my arms; once I stumbled and fell on him, but I got him home.

So there it was. I was a big hero that day. Mother got a washtub and filled it with water. She put the fish in it and all the neighbors came to look. I got into dry clothes and went down to supper—and then I made a break that spoiled my day. **❶**

There we were, all of us, at the table, and suddenly Father asked what had been the matter with me at school. He had met the teacher, Sarah Suggett, on the street and she had told him how I had become ill.

"What was the matter with you?" Father asked, and before I thought what I was saying I let it out.

"I had the inflammatory rheumatism," I said—and a shout went up. It made me sick to hear them, the way they all laughed.

It brought back all the aching again, and like a fool I began to cry.

"Well, I have got it—I have, I have," I cried, and I got up from the table and ran upstairs.

I stayed there until Mother came up. I knew it would be a long time before I heard the last of the inflammatory rheumatism. I was sick all right, but the aching I now had wasn't in my legs or in my back. **❿**

---

2. **freshet** (FREHSH iht): flood caused by heavy rain or a thaw.

---

❶ Read and Discuss What is going on with the narrator now?

❿ Read and Discuss What does the boy mean when he says that he was sick but that the aching wasn't in his legs or his back?

Vocabulary **wriggled** (RIHG uhld) v.: wiggled; squirmed.

Analyzing Visuals

British artist **Charles Knight** (1901–1990), the son of an amateur painter, was known for his watercolor renditions of landscapes and seascapes.

Connecting to the Text: *The painting reveals that the motivation for pretending to be sick is the opportunity to go fishing.*

Think About/Talk About

▶ **Comprehension**

❽ Reading Focus

Possible response: *The narrator is wallowing in self-pity, reveling in thoughts of how everyone would react if he died.*

❶ Read and Discuss

Possible response: *The narrator's excited and proud because he caught a giant fish and is getting a lot of attention.*

❿ Read and Discuss

Possible response: *The narrator feels upset that his family finds his "illness" so funny. He feels sick with embarrassment.*

▶ **Extend the Discussion**

Irony What is ironic about the way the story ends? ***Possible response:*** *The narrator ends up being the center of attention after all, but he is being ridiculed rather than praised or worried over.*

Vocabulary: Own the Word

wriggled: Explain to students that in the selection, a fish wriggles its way out of the narrator's arms. Ask students what other creatures wriggle and why. ***Possible responses:*** *Cats and dogs wriggle when they are held because they do not like to be held. Worms wriggle because that is how they get around.*

Monitor Students' Comprehension

To check students' understanding of the story, ask them how the narrator feels about his "illness" at the end of the story. [*He feels guilty and embarrassed about his lie.*]

Check for Understanding

Independent Practice

Reading Skills Focus

Answers:

1. *He cries and says he is sick.*

2. *He wrestles him out of the water.*

3. *His father asks him why he left school early.*

4. *He wants an excuse to go fishing, too.*

5. *Examples should demonstrate that the narrator is jealous, self-centered, and lazy.*

Vocabulary Check

Possible responses:

6. *I would think he felt gloomy.*

7. *I cried to avoid being punished for teasing my brother.*

Literary Skills Focus

Possible responses:

8. *He "steals" a day of school by pretending to be sick.*

9. *They are familiar with his exaggerations.*

10. *He is trying to convince himself that he is; he doesn't want to go to school.*

11. *Children, including the narrator, often have overactive imaginations that can lead to trouble.*

12. *The flashback shows that the narrator was jealous of the attention the drowned child received from the narrator's mother. It shows that he does not feel appreciated and is very self-centered if he is more concerned about himself rather than the death of the other child.*

Applying Your Skills

Stolen Day

Literary Response and Analysis

Reading Skills Focus
Quick Check

1. How does the narrator get himself sent home from school?

2. How does the narrator capture the carp?

3. What happens to spoil the narrator's day?

Read with a Purpose

4. Why do you think the narrator starts to feel sick after he sees Walter fishing at the pond?

Reading Skills: Comparing and Contrasting Characters

5. Complete the chart by identifying the narrator's character traits as revealed by the details you listed.

	Story Details	Trait
Actions		
Words		
Thoughts/Feelings		
Effects on Others		

✔ Vocabulary Check

Answer the following questions:

6. If you saw a boy wearing a **solemn** expression, what do you think he might be feeling?

7. How have you behaved during a time when you **wriggled** out of trouble?

Literary Skills Focus
Literary Analysis

8. **Interpret** Explain what the title of the story means. What other titles might fit the story?

9. **Infer** Why do you think the narrator's family responds by laughing at him when he says he has inflammatory rheumatism?

10. **Infer** Why does the boy insist that he really *is* sick? What do you think the boy really wants?

11. **Extend** The first line of the story says, "It must be that all children are actors." How does this sentence connect to the narrator and his actions? How does it connect to children in general?

Literary Skills: Characters and Character Traits

12. **Analyze** A **flashback** is an interruption of action to tell about something that happened in the past. In "Stolen Day" the narrator interrupts his fantasy about dying to tell about an accident the year before. How does the flashback help you understand the narrator's feelings? What do you learn about his character from the flashback?

Writing Skills Focus
Think as a Reader/Writer

Use It in Your Writing Because "Stolen Day" is told by the main character in the story, you gain access to his inner thoughts. In a paragraph, explain how knowing his thoughts helps you understand his character.

Universal Access

Struggling Writers

Provide students with a specific example of how knowing the main character's inner thoughts sheds light on his character. Point out how, on p. 192, the narrator comments: "I kept on crying and it worked all right." Then, have students consider how their perception of the scene might be different if it were told from a third-person point of view and omitted the boys' inner thoughts: "The boy kept on crying." Explain that the boy's inner thoughts show that he is sneaky and his crying is intended to fool the teacher.

Reading Standard 3.3 Analyze characterization as delineated through a character's thoughts, words, speech patterns, and actions; the narrator's description; and the thoughts, words, and actions of other characters.

A Day's Wait / Stolen Day

Writing Skills Focus
Write a Comparison-Contrast Essay

Write an essay comparing Schatz in "A Day's Wait" to the boy in "Stolen Day." Begin by reviewing the charts you completed when you read the stories. The charts will help you <u>identify</u> similarities and differences between the two characters. Then, decide how you will organize your essay.

1. You can organize the essay by character traits. In the first paragraph you might discuss three traits the boys have in common. In the second paragraph you might discuss at least one way in which the boys are different. Cite details that illustrate the traits you see in each.

2. You can organize your essay by character. You might focus on Schatz and his character traits in your first paragraph and then do the same for the boy in "Stolen Day" in the next paragraph. Cite specific details from the stories to support your analysis of each character. Be sure to clearly <u>delineate</u> how the boys are alike and how they are different.

At the end of your essay, tell which character you liked more and why. Did you <u>identify</u> with either character? Use details from the stories to explain why you <u>responded</u> the way you did.

What Do You Think Now?

What do the boys learn about themselves through their experiences in these stories?

CHOICES

As you respond to the Choices, use these **Academic Vocabulary** words as appropriate: <u>attribute</u>, <u>delineate</u>, <u>identify</u>, <u>respond</u>.

REVIEW
Write a Character Description
What kind of person do you think Schatz's father is? Write a description of this character, <u>identifying</u> the character traits that are revealed in the story. Cite the story details you used to draw conclusions about his <u>attributes</u>.

CONNECT
Express an Opinion
Timed Writing In "Stolen Day" the narrator says that he has inflammatory rheumatism, but his family doesn't <u>respond</u> the way he would like. Do you think the narrator is lying to his family, or do you think he actually believes he *is* sick? What evidence in the story can you find to support your answer? Write a short paragraph in which you state your opinion and give reasons to support it.

EXTEND
Write a Journal Entry
Schatz spends part of "A Day's Wait" alone while his father is out hunting. As "Stolen Day" ends, the narrator is in his bedroom waiting for his mother to arrive. Pretend you are one of these boys. Write a journal entry describing how you feel as you wait for your parent. Use what you know about each boy's character traits to keep your journal entry "in character."

Independent Practice
Choices: Evaluation Criteria
Review: Homework
Write a Character Description
- The description includes character traits identified in the story.
- The analysis of Schatz's father comes directly from these traits.

Connect: Timed Writing
40–50 Minutes
- The paragraph includes some of the narrator's internal thoughts as evidence.
- The paragraph examines reasons that these thoughts are most relevant to the character's motivation.

Extend: Homework
Write a Journal Entry
- The entry is from the point of view of one of the characters waiting for a parent to arrive.
- The entry uses dialogue that is "in character."

Assess

Chapter 2 Resources, Selection Standards Check, p. 27

ThinkCentral Online Assessment, Selection Standards Check

Teacher One Stop™, editable Selection Standards Check

Reteach

To reteach **characterization,** see **Reteaching Lessons,** p. 842A.

ThinkCentral Online Remediation

What Do You Think Now?
Review with students the experiences of the boys before speculating on the self-knowledge each boy gains from his particular situation. Then, discuss whether they learned as much as they should have.

Standards Focus

Objectives

Students will
- identify the main idea and details in informational writing
- distinguish types of informational writing and how structure organizes information

Motivate

What Do You Think?/QuickWrite

Use the QuickWrite to have students examine their feelings about rats. Ask students why rats might be perceived as dangerous. Then, have students use their **Reader/ Writer Notebook** to list adjectives that describe a rat.

English for Academic Success

Academic Vocabulary

Look for opportunities to use the Academic Vocabulary words in this chapter.

- **identify, v.:** recognize and be able to say what someone or something is.

- **respond, v.:** say or write something as a reply or answer.

Analyzing Visuals

Extension Activity Ask students what details in the image provide clues about what the man is doing with the rat. **Possible response:** *His protective suit and mask suggest that the rat is dangerous or contagious.*

🐻 **California Standards,**
pp. 200–217

■ **Reading Standard 2.1** Understand and analyze the differences in structure and purpose between various categories of informational materials (e.g. textbooks, newspapers, instructional manuals, signs).

Structure and Purpose of Informational Materials

CONTENTS

What Do **You** Think? How can being well-informed improve—sometimes even save—your life?

🕐 **QuickWrite**
Gaining life skills is part of becoming an independent adult. Why is having knowledge of life's various risks and dangers an important life skill?

Preparing to Read

Reading Standard 2.1 Understand and analyze the differences in structure and purpose between various categories of informational materials (e.g., textbooks, **newspapers,** instructional manuals, signs).

Flea Patrol

Informational Text Focus

Structure and Purpose of a Newspaper Article The **purpose** of a newspaper article is to provide factual information about current events. A good informational article in a newspaper provides detailed answers to the questions *who? what? when? where? why?* and *how?*

Many newspaper articles are structured in what is called an **inverted pyramid** style. (*Inverted* means "upside-down.") The article begins with a **summary lead,** a sentence or paragraph that gives the **main idea** of the story—usually the most important idea or detail in the article. The lead is followed by the less important details of the article. Some articles begin with a lead that grabs your interest in a topic. This type of lead does not summarize but instead describes an interesting situation or fact related to the story. Here are some additional elements in the **structure** of a newspaper article. You will find examples of these elements in "Flea Patrol."

- **Headline:** the catchy, boldface words that tell you the subject of the article
- **Subhead:** the words in smaller type under the headline that add details about the article
- **Byline:** the name of the reporter who wrote the article
- **Dateline:** the location where and the date when the information was reported
- **Lead:** the sentence or paragraph that begins the news article
- **Tone:** the choice of words and point of view that meet the interests of the newspaper's audience. Tone often depends on the subject of the article. Some articles are light and humorous. Others are serious.

Summary lead, or most important information

Important details

Least important details

Vocabulary

transmitted (trans MIHT ihd) *v.*: caused to pass from one thing to another. *Fleas that fed on infected rats transmitted the plague throughout Europe.*

application (ap luh KAY shuhn) *n.*: act of putting to use. *An application of insecticide kills fleas.*

rural (RUR uhl) *adj.*: of or relating to the countryside. *People living in rural areas are at greater risk of catching the plague.*

Language Coach

Word Roots Many English words have Latin roots and affixes. An **affix** is a word part that is added to a root. The Vocabulary word *transmitted* is made up of the Latin root *mis,* meaning "send," and the word part *trans–,* meaning "across." Identify three things that are transmitted.

Writing Skills Focus

Preparing for **Timed └Writing** As you read this article, record the main idea and important details for use in writing a summary later.

Reader/Writer Notebook
Use your **RWN** to complete the activities for this selection.

Learn It Online
Check out the *PowerNotes* slideshow to get a lesson using words and pictures:

go.hrw.com H7-201 Go

Selection Resources

Chapter 2 Resources, on-level practice and assessment, p. 30

PowerNotes, interactive lesson presentation with activities

Teacher One Stop™, on-level lesson plans and all print resources

Holt Audio Library

Holt Audio Library: Selections and Summaries in Spanish

UA: Holt Interactive Reader, p. 48

Holt Interactive Reader for ELD, p. 62

Holt Audio Tutor for ELD

UA: Differentiating Instruction, modified lesson plans and leveled assessment, p. 36

UA: Supporting Instruction in Five Languages, selection summary

UA: Resources for Teaching Advanced Students, lesson plans, p. 73

ThinkCentral Online Assessment, Selection Standards Check

Direct Teach

Model the Skill

- Tell students that newspaper editors want their readers to be able to easily find the important information in an article. They help the reader do this by using a **structure** that makes the important information stand out, as in headings, subheads, and writing the most important, general information at the beginning of the article.

- Model identifying the lead of a newspaper article. Identify the first paragraph as the article's lead, and read it aloud. The lead introduces the article and briefly explains the main points. This lead tells readers they will be reading about the efforts of park rangers to prevent the spread of disease from insects and rodents. What other components of a newspaper article do students see here? *[Students should identify the byline and dateline.]*

Guided Practice: Apply

Have students read the article in pairs and briefly summarize each paragraph. What do they notice about the type of information found in the earlier paragraphs? How is it different from that in the later paragraphs?

FLEA PATROL

Keeping National Parks Safe from Plague

by JESSICA COHN

Read with a Purpose

Read the following article to find out how scientists and rangers are keeping our national parks safe.

BLANDING, UTAH, January 10—Park rangers are hunting fleas to stop the spread of disease. They are on alert to fight a plague of rodents in some national parks. **(A)**

Bubonic plague is found in rodents and the fleas that feed on them in several areas of the United States, including some national parks. To keep the disease under control, rangers spray insecticide. They hope to kill the fleas, which can spread the disease to humans. But before you scratch an overnight park visit off your list of things to do, you should know something else. No humans are known to have become infected with plague at national park campgrounds. Through this course of action, officials are trying to keep it that way.

At least a third of Europeans died from the plague during the Middle Ages. That

(A) **Informational Focus** Structure and Purpose of a Newspaper Article   Identify the purpose of the lead in this article.

Selection Readability

Easily Accessible	historical context, informational tone, scientific vocabulary
Accessible	
Challenging	

Selection Summary

Today, the bubonic plague lives in fleas that bite rodents in national parks. The author discusses how park rangers manage the problem.

deadly drama, known as the Black Death, is kept alive in history, literature, and imagination. "As soon as people hear 'Black Death' or 'plague,' they freak out," says Ralph Jones, chief ranger of Natural Bridges National Park in Utah. "But that's not the way it is anymore. It's just a naturally occurring disease. It's just part of the world."

In spring 2006, rangers discovered more dead field mice and chipmunks at Natural Bridges than was normal. Curious about the reason, the rangers had the animals tested at the Centers for Disease Control and Prevention (CDC), a federal agency responsible for protecting the health and safety of the population. The bacterium that causes plague was uncovered. **B**

Natural Bridges closed its campground until the disease could be contained. Sites reopened that May. The same year, plague was found in creatures living in Mesa Verde National Park and Colorado National Monument, reported the U.S. Public Health Service.

"Bubonic plague goes in cycles," says Jones, "depending on the population of the rodents."

People get sick when bitten by fleas that have fed on the blood of rodents carrying the bacterium. The disease can also be transmitted through contact with infected sores or by breathing infected matter in the air. Plague can be cured as long as humans seek medical help

BUBONIC PLAGUE SYMPTOMS

Bubonic plague is treatable with antibiotics. Symptoms appear two to seven days after infection:

- blackish-purple lumps under skin
- chills
- diarrhea
- exhaustion
- fever
- tender, swollen lymph nodes
- headache
- muscle pain
- vomiting

and are treated with antibiotics. But every year, countless rodents die from the disease. **C**

Officials concentrate on killing off fleas when rodents are found to be carrying plague. An application of insecticide at rodent holes is recommended when dead animals are identified as plague carriers.

The disease is regularly found in creatures throughout the western United States, especially in the area known as Four Corners, where the states of Arizona, Colorado, New Mexico, and Utah meet. The trick is keeping the disease contained to wild animals, which is usually easy enough. Most people avoid contact with these creatures.

About ten to fifteen plague cases are reported in humans yearly in the United States, mostly in rural areas, says the CDC. One in seven cases is fatal. The southwestern United States is especially affected. Africa, Asia, and South America have hot spots as well. In 2006, a Los Angeles woman was treated for the disease, that area's first case in more than twenty years.

Researchers at the University of Oslo recently studied data on creatures known as great gerbils, along with related weather records. Plague increased more than 50 percent among the animals with temperature increases of fewer than 2 degrees.

B **Read and Discuss** What has the author set up for you?

C **Informational Focus** Tone How would you describe the tone of this paragraph?

Vocabulary **transmitted** (trans MIHT ihd) *v.:* caused to pass from one thing to another.
application (ap luh KAY shuhn) *n.:* act of putting to use.
rural (RUR uhl) *adj.:* of or relating to the countryside.

Think About/Talk About

Read with a Purpose Have students read the Read with a Purpose statement. Ask students to discuss why rangers and scientists might have to keep parks safe.

▶ **Comprehension**

 Read and Discuss

Possible response: The author has told us that the plague was recently uncovered at Natural Bridges in Utah.

▶ **Analysis**

 Informational Focus

Possible response: The lead is meant to draw the reader in.

C **Informational Focus**

Possible response: It is informative.

▶ **Extend the Discussion**

Credibility On p. 203, the author cites statistics from the Centers for Disease Control and Prevention (CDC). How does this citation add to the credibility of the article? ***Possible response:*** *It makes the article sound more authoritative.*

Vocabulary: Own the Word

- **transmitted:** Tell students that the prefix *trans-* is from a Latin and means "across or beyond." This prefix is combined with the Latin verb *mittere,* which means "to send," to form *transmitted.* The meaning of the word follows from the definitions of its Latin parts: "to send across or beyond."

- **application:** Explain to students *apply* is the verb form of *application. Apply* means "to use." *Application* can also mean "a request." The noun form of this usage of the word is *apply,* meaning "to submit an application."

- **rural:** Create a semantic web on the board. Write the word *rural* in a circle and draw lines branching away. Fill these lines as students suggest words that they associate with *rural.* [***Possible responses:*** *farm, forest, cabin, relaxed, fresh, open, boring*]

Independent Practice
Answers and Explanations

1. **B** *Just as an article does, an inverted pyramid starts with a broad statement and narrows down to specifics.*

2. **C** *Jessica Cohn. The other names are people and groups mentioned in the article.*

3. **D** *The subhead says "Keeping National Parks Safe from Plague," which relates most to item D.*

4. **D** *It presents the main idea. The other answer choices do not appear in the lead.*

5. **D** *Transmitted is a synonym for spread.*

6. **A** *Rural areas are in the country. Urban means "in a city." Infested and desirable do not relate to the countryside.*

7. **A** *Application means utilization.*

Writing Skills Focus
Possible response: This article discusses cases of bubonic plague that have occurred in animals at national parks in the present-day United States. Park rangers identify cases and take steps to prevent the spread of the disease to humans, killing off the fleas found in disease-carrying rodents.

What Do You Think Now?
Ask students to consider the information they learned about plague. How does the information prepare people, making them less afraid? How might the information cause people to worry?

Chapter 2 Resources, Selection Standards Check, p. 36

ThinkCentral Online Assessment, Selection Standards Check

Teacher One Stop™, editable Selection Standards Check

NEWSPAPER ARTICLE
Applying Your Skills

Reading Standard 2.1 Understand and analyze the differences in structure and purpose between various categories of informational materials (e.g., textbooks, **newspapers,** instructional manuals, signs).

Flea Patrol

Standards Review

Informational Text and Vocabulary

1. The structure of a **newspaper article** is said to be similar to an
   A inverted octagon.
   B inverted pyramid.
   C oval with a circle in the center.
   D upside-down T.

2. The **byline** of the news article shows it was written by
   A Ralph Jones.
   B the Centers for Disease Control and Prevention.
   C Jessica Cohn.
   D park rangers at Natural Bridges National Park.

3. The **subhead** of the article tells you that
   A the Black Death killed huge numbers of people.
   B a national park closed its campsites for a time.
   C fleas spread plague to rats and humans.
   D national parks are protected from plague.

4. The **lead** of this article
   A is an attention-grabber.
   B makes a serious statement about dangerous rodents.
   C answers *who? what? where? when?* and *how?*
   D presents the article's main idea.

5. Something that is *transmitted* is
   A changed.
   B captured.
   C cured.
   D spread.

6. If something is *rural,* it might be
   A outside a city.
   B infested.
   C inside a city.
   D desirable.

7. Another word for *application* is
   A utilization.
   B removal.
   C disinfection.
   D concentration.

Writing Skills Focus
Timed ʟ Writing Summarize this article in a paragraph that answers the questions *who? what? when? where? why?* and *how?*

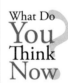

What Do You Think Now Some people feel prepared after learning about dangers (such as diseases), while others just feel scared. Explain both reactions.

 ThinkCentral Online Remediation

California Standards, pp. 204–205

■ **Reading Standard 2.1** Understand and analyze the differences in structure and purpose between various categories of informational materials (e.g. textbooks, newspapers, instructional manuals, signs).

Reading Standard 2.1 Understand and analyze the differences in structure and purpose between various categories of informational materials (e.g., textbooks, newspapers, instructional manuals, signs).

The Black Death *from* **World History: Medieval to Early Modern Times**

Informational Text Focus

Structure and Purpose of a Textbook The story "Three Skeleton Key" (Chapter 1) might have made you want to learn more about rats and their role in history. Textbooks are one source for information about history and the way rats influenced it.

Textbooks have some unique qualities that distinguish them from other informational materials. Because textbooks are used for teaching and instruction, not just for reference, their academic content is carefully researched and written to be accessible to a specific grade level, not just a general audience. The structure of a textbook attempts to make locating specific information easy for users. Textbooks are generally divided into units, chapters, or other sections that focus on a particular topic. Within a chapter or unit, one lesson will generally build upon another. Questions and activities to assess understanding appear at regular intervals. Textbooks also offer photographs, graphics, and artwork that can lead you to do further investigation of a subject.

In the next four pages are features from a history textbook called *World History: Medieval to Early Modern Times.* See how well you understand the structure of this textbook.

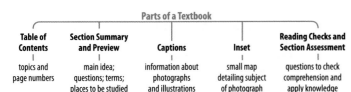

Parts of a Textbook

Table of Contents	Section Summary and Preview	Captions	Inset	Reading Checks and Section Assessment
topics and page numbers	main idea; questions; terms; places to be studied	information about photographs and illustrations	small map detailing subject of photograph	questions to check comprehension and apply knowledge

Writing Skills Focus

Preparing for Timed ⌐Writing When an idea is important, most textbook writers take care to present it clearly and use headings to help identify it. Look for a heading that is used to help signal a main idea.

Reader/Writer Notebook
Use your **RWN** to complete the activities for this selection.

Learn It Online
To learn about the structure and purpose of informational texts, visit the interactive Reading Workshop:
go.hrw.com   H7-205   **Go**

Selection Resources

Chapter 2 Resources, on-level practice and assessment, p. 33

PowerNotes, interactive lesson presentation with activities

Teacher One Stop™, on-level lesson plans and all print resources

Holt Audio Library

Holt Audio Library: Selections and Summaries in Spanish

UA: Holt Interactive Reader, p. 52

Holt Interactive Reader for ELD, p. 66

Holt Audio Tutor for ELD

UA: Differentiating Instruction, modified lesson plans and leveled assessment, p. 36

Holt English Language Development, systematic instruction and scaffolded content

UA: Supporting Instruction in Five Languages, selection summary

UA: Resources for Teaching Advanced Students, lesson plans, p. 76

ThinkCentral Online Remediation

Preteach

Informational Text Focus
As you read and discuss the selection with students, have them look for and identify the different features of a textbook, such as the table of contents, the section assessment, and captions.

Writing Skills Focus
Have students use their **Reader/ Writer Notebook** to write down examples of headings that convey main ideas.

Learn It Online
Reading Workshops are interactive versions of real-world informational texts; students exercise their reading skills by responding to polls and answering questions in an engaging online format.
go.hrw.com   H7-205   **Go**

Direct Teach

Model the Skill

■ Explain that a **table of contents** is like a road map for a book. Readers use tables of contents to locate specific stories, articles, or topics. Using the table of contents is faster than flipping through the entire book to find what you need.

■ Model for students how to use a table of contents. Tell students that if readers want to learn about royalty at the time of the plague, they would look at the table of contents to find the section that would best fit their needs. The first section looks like it would contain information on royalty because it's about kings. If a reader wanted to read about specific historical events, the table of contents indicates that the second section would be a good place to start reading.

Guided Practice: Apply

Ask students which section or sections they would read to learn about the role religion played in medieval life. Guide them in understanding that sections 3 and 5 likely contain information about religion in medieval life, due to the kep words "Christianity" and "Church Authority."

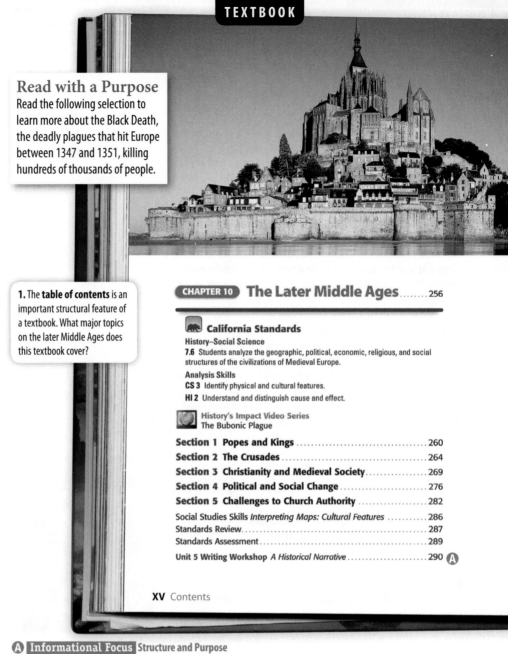

Read with a Purpose
Read the following selection to learn more about the Black Death, the deadly plagues that hit Europe between 1347 and 1351, killing hundreds of thousands of people.

1. The **table of contents** is an important structural feature of a textbook. What major topics on the later Middle Ages does this textbook cover?

CHAPTER 10 **The Later Middle Ages** 256

California Standards
History–Social Science
7.6 Students analyze the geographic, political, economic, religious, and social structures of the civilizations of Medieval Europe.
Analysis Skills
CS 3 Identify physical and cultural features.
HI 2 Understand and distinguish cause and effect.

History's Impact Video Series
The Bubonic Plague

XV Contents

Ⓐ **Informational Focus** Structure and Purpose of a Textbook Why does the table of contents use headings of different sizes?

Selection Readability	
Easily Accessible Accessible **Challenging**	historical context, complex graphics

Selection Summary

This social studies text models how textbooks function while at the same time providing more information about the history of the bubonic plague in Europe in the Middle Ages.

The Black Death

While the English and French fought the Hundred Years' War, an even greater crisis arose. This crisis was the **Black Death**, a deadly plague that swept through Europe between 1347 and 1351.

The plague originally came from central and eastern Asia. Unknowingly, traders brought rats carrying the disease to Mediterranean ports in 1347. From there it quickly swept throughout much of Europe. Fleas that feasted on the blood of infected rats passed on the plague to people.

The Black Death was not caused by one disease but by several different forms of plague. One form called bubonic plague (byoo-BAH-nik PLAYG) could be identified by swellings called buboes that appeared on victims' bodies. Another even deadlier form could spread through the air and kill people in less than a day.

The Black Death killed so many people that many were buried quickly without priests or ceremonies. In some villages nearly everyone died or fled as neighbors fell ill. In England alone, about 1,000 villages were abandoned.

The plague killed millions of people in Europe and millions more around the world. Some historians think Europe lost about a third of its population—perhaps 25 million people. This huge drop in population caused sweeping changes in Europe.

In most places, the manor system fell apart completely. There weren't enough people left to work in the fields. Those peasants and serfs who had survived the plague found their skills in high demand. Suddenly, they could demand wages for their labor. Once they had money, many fled their manors completely, moving instead to Europe's growing cities. **D**

READING CHECK **Identifying Cause and Effect** What effects did bubonic plague have in Europe?

SUMMARY AND PREVIEW Magna Carta, the Hundred Years' War, and the Black Death changed European society. In the next section, you will learn about other changes in society, changes brought about by religious differences.

2. Key items and terms are set in **boldface type**. The boldface terms are often defined in the text. Is the boldface word on this page defined?

3. The purpose of a **reading check** is to provide readers with an opportunity to review what they have learned.

Section 4 Assessment

go.hrw.com
Online Quiz
KEYWORD: SQ7 HP10

Reviewing Ideas, Terms, and People HSS 7.6.5, 7.6.7

1. **a. Identify** What document did English nobles hope would limit the king's power?
   b. Explain How was the creation of **Parliament** a step toward the creation of democracy in England?
2. **a. Identify** Who rallied the French troops during the **Hundred Years' War**?
   b. Elaborate The Hundred Years' War caused much more damage in France than in England. Why do you think this was the case?
3. **a. Describe** What was the **Black Death**?
   b. Explain How did the Black Death contribute to the decline of the manor system?
   c. Elaborate Why do you think the Black Death was able to spread so quickly through Europe?

Critical Thinking

4. **Identifying Cause and Effect** Draw a scroll like the one shown here. Inside the scroll, list two ideas contained in Magna Carta. Next to the scroll, write two sentences about Magna Carta's effects on England's government.

Magna Carta	Effects
1. _____	1. _____
2. _____	2. _____

FOCUS ON WRITING

5. **Rating Importance** After reading this section, you'll probably want to add King John to your list. You should also start to think about which people were the most important. Rank the people on your list from most to least important.

4. Questions usually conclude each section of text. These questions help you review what you have just read. If you can't respond to the questions, you need to re-read the text.

B **Informational Focus** Structure and Purpose of a Textbook This text is part of Section 4. What will the next section of this textbook cover? Where did you find this information?

C **Read and Discuss** How did the world deal with the Black Death?

D **Read and Discuss** How does the idea of peasants moving into cities fit into the picture of the Black Death?

Universal Access

Advanced Learners

Enrichment Tell students that the end of a textbook will often contain a glossary, which explains specialized or difficult words from the text. Have them pick out words from the selection that they would expect to find in a glossary, for example, "bubonic plague," and "serfs." Have students create a glossary by looking up the meaning of each term and writing it in their own words.

✔ See **Resources for Teaching Advanced Students** for lesson plans and strategies for teaching advanced learners.

Students with Disabilities

To provide students with a more concrete way in which to analyze the sections of a textbook, guide them through the sections of their own literature textbook. You may wish to provide poster-sized images or transparencies of the textbook's table of contents, assessments, captions, summaries, and other typical textbook components.

✔ See **UA: Differentiating Instruction** for lesson plans and strategies for teaching students with disabilities.

Think About/Talk About

Read with a Purpose Have students read the Read with a Purpose statement. Ask students to discuss the information that might be included in a text about the Black Death.

▶ Comprehension

A Informational Focus

Possible response: The different sizes of the heads represent the different types of information that can be found under those heads. The largest, darkest heads are used for the textbook's primary informational sections.

B Informational Focus

Possible response: I learned from the table of contents that the next section of the textbook, Section 5, will cover challenges to church authority.

C Read and Discuss

Possible response: People dealt with plague by burying the dead and abandoning their villages.

D Read and Discuss

Possible response: So many people died from plague that fieldworkers were hard to come by. The peasants who were able to make money moved to the city.

▶ Extend the Discussion

Making Inferences Read the section titles in the table of contents on p. 206. Based on the major topics covered in this chapter about the later Middle Ages, what can you infer about people in Europe at that time? *Possible response: They were religious; they were ruled by kings; they lived in a period of uncertainty and change.*

Model the Skill

- Explain that Latin, the language of ancient Rome, contributed a number of **word roots and parts** to the English language. Knowledge of word parts and their meanings help readers decode unfamiliar words.

- Write the word part *dis–* on the board. Explain that *dis–* is a Latin word part that goes at the beginning of a root word. It means "not," or "the absence of." Write *disease* on the board and draw a line between *dis–* and *ease*. Explain that the word *ease* often means "comfort" or "good feeling." When you add *dis–* to *ease,* you have the absence of ease, or the absence of comfort. In English, *disease* refers both to feeling uncomfortable and to illness, both of which are not comfortable.

Guided Practice: Apply

Have students identify the root words of *disagree* and *disable.* Ask how the meanings of the root words are changed by adding *dis–*.

History and Geography

The Black Death

"And they died by the hundreds," wrote one man who saw the horror, "both day and night." The Black Death had arrived. The Black Death was a series of deadly plagues that hit Europe between 1347 and 1351, killing millions. People didn't know what caused the plague. They also didn't know that geography played a key role in its spread—as people traveled to trade, they unwittingly carried the disease with them to new places.

The plague probably began in central and eastern Asia. These arrows show how it spread into and through Europe.

This ship has just arrived in Europe from the east with trade goods—and rats with fleas.

The fleas carry the plague and jump onto a man unloading the ship. Soon, he will get sick and die.

280

E [Read and Discuss] What does this graphic help you understand? What does the graphic do more effectively than text alone can do?

Cross-Curricular Connection

HISTORY: The Black Death

Amid the devastation caused by the plague throughout the later Middle Ages, wider social and political changes were afoot.

- One of the major consequences of the Black Death was a backlash against the Christian church. People blamed God for punishing them, and the priests and bishops had no explanation for his wrath. As a result, the peasants revolted against an organization that had previously been a fundamental and unquestioned part of life.

- The restructuring of society in the years after the plague enabled Europe to dismantle the feudal system that had been in place for so long. Peasants were in demand because of a lack of farm workers, and opportunities arose for the lower members of society, who had previously been stifled by a rigid class system.

- Death had become so prevalent in society that it took on a physical form. Much European artwork in the years following the plague incorporated images of skeletons, hooded figures and skull and crossbones.

The plague is so terrifying that many people think it's the end of the world. They leave town for the country, spreading the Black Death even farther.

People dig mass graves to bury the dead. But often, so many victims are infected that there is no one left to bury them.

So many people die so quickly that special carts are sent through the streets to gather the bodies.

The garbage and dirty conditions in the town provide food and a home for the rats, allowing the disease to spread even more.

5. Illustrations have **captions,** text that explains the subject of the illustration. How do the captions help you understand this illustration?

GEOGRAPHY SKILLS | **INTERPRETING MAPS**
1. How did the Black Death reach Europe from Asia?
2. What helped spread the plague within Europe?

281

 Informational Focus Structure and Purpose of a Textbook These questions ask about the inset and the two-page illustration. Look at the images and captions to find the answers to these questions.

Small-Group Activity Have students, working in small groups, choose one aspect of the Black Death to research further. They may want to pick the transportation of the plague from Europe, the physical symptoms of the plague, or the consequences of the disease on society. Have each group present an oral report on their findings.

🐻 **HSS Analysis Skills** REP 1

Think About/Talk About

▶ **Comprehension**

 Read and Discuss
Possible response: *The graphic shows me that the plague spread quickly and easily. It helps me visualize the plague's journey through a town.*

F Informational Focus
Possible response: *The caption over the ship tells me that rats on the ship carried the plague from Asia to Europe; the caption over the stable tells me that unsanitary living conditions help spread the plague by helping rats survive.*

▶ **Extend the Discussion**

Tone Read the introductory paragraph next to the main heading. What effect does the quotation have on the tone of the text, and why might the author have chosen to include it? ***Possible response:*** *The quotation enhances the somber tone of the text by highlighting the number of people who died from plague. It is a quote from an eyewitness, which makes the information more credible and authentic.*

Irony Read the caption next to the church at the top of p. 209. What is ironic about the fact that people fled villages because they thought it was the "end of the world"? ***Possible response:*** *By leaving their villages, people spread plague faster, contributing to the "end of the world" scenario.*

Check for Understanding

Independent Practice

Answers and Explanations

1. **B** *The date listed on the copyright page is 2009.*

2. **B** *The table of contents identifies eight chapters in the book.*

3. **C** *Plot is the topic of chapter 1.*

4. **B** *This information can be found in the first few pages of students' textbooks.*

5. **C** *The book has an Index of Skills, a Handbook of Reading and Informational Terms, and an Index of Authors and Titles.*

Writing Skills Focus

Possible response: *Both textbooks and newspaper articles have headings and subheads. One major difference between the two is that newspaper articles are organized in pyramid structure, while textbooks are generally organized by topic.*

What Do You Think Now?

Ask students to consider what kind of information a newspaper contains versus a textbook to help them answer the question.

TEXTBOOK
Applying Your Skills

The Black Death *from* World History: Medieval to Early Modern Times

Standards Review

Informational Text

To confirm how well you know the important parts of a textbook, answer the following questions by referring to the key parts of the textbook you are using now: *Holt Literature and Language Arts, First Course.*

1. The **copyright page** is in the front of the book, usually the page after the main title page. Listed here is the date the book was published. What is the copyright date of this book?

   A 2008
   B 2009
   C 2010
   D 2011

2. The **table of contents** is found in the front of a textbook. According to the table of contents of this textbook, how many chapters are in this book?

   A 7
   B 8
   C 9
   D 10

3. What is the topic of Chapter 1 in this textbook?

   A Theme
   B Character
   C Plot
   D Forms of Prose and Poetry

4. The **Authors and Program Consultants page** of this textbook lists the names of the writers. What pages of this book lists the program authors?

   A iii–iv
   B A2–A3
   C 2–3
   D 6–7

5. Which of the following features is *not* found at the back of this book?

   A Index of Skills
   B Handbook of Reading and Informational Terms
   C Index of Maps
   D Index of Authors and Titles

Writing Skills Focus

Timed ∟Writing Explain the similarities and differences between a textbook and a newspaper. In your explanation, cite examples of their differences and similarities in both structure and purpose.

 When might you use a textbook to increase your knowledge? When might you use a newspaper? Cite specific examples.

 California Standards, pp. 210–211

■ **Reading Standard 2.1** Understand and analyze the differences in structure and purpose between various categories of informational materials (e.g. textbooks, newspapers, instructional manuals, signs).

INSTRUCTIONAL MANUAL
Preparing to Read

Reading Standard 2.1 Understand and analyze the differences in structure and purpose between various categories of informational materials (e.g., textbooks, newspapers, **instructional manuals**, signs).

Stopping Plague in Its Tracks

Informational Text Focus

Structure and Purpose of an Instructional Manual

Instructional manuals usually explain a process, such as how to use an MP3 player, or present information to educate the reader about important information, such as what to do in case of a flood. The purpose of an instructional manual is to guide you through a task or through information that may be new to you. A well-written instructional manual should include easy-to-follow steps, and it should be organized so that the user can quickly <u>identify</u> and locate needed information. Many instructional manuals contain diagrams and step-by-step instructions.

The following selection is an instructional manual for understanding, treating, and preventing the plague. This manual, like most, follows a simple structure you can use to your advantage.

- First, scan the **table of contents** to preview the topics to be covered (see the text to the right for an example).
- Read all the information carefully. Look at headings, bulleted or numbered lists, and any special side notes or features. Take note of any **steps** you must take.
- Study all the **diagrams,** and make sure you understand them.
- If there is a **glossary**—an alphabetical list of special terms and their definitions—check your understanding of terms and symbols.

By the Numbers When you're tackling more complex instructional manuals, check the back for an **index**—a list of covered topics that is in alphabetical order. It is much more detailed than a table of contents, so you can use it to find the specific information you need. You will find an index in the back of this textbook. Look up the word *purpose,* and you will find this page number.

Writing Skills Focus

Preparing for Timed Writing Informational manuals are structured so that information is easy to locate. As you read "Stopping Plague in Its Tracks," look at the way the writer organized the information.

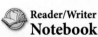
Reader/Writer Notebook
Use your **RWN** to complete the activities for this selection.

STOPPING PLAGUE in Its TRACKS

A COMMUNITY HEALTH CENTER PROJECT

CONTENTS

UNDERSTANDING PLAGUE

1. What Is Plague?
2. Where Is Plague Found?
3. How Is Plague Transmitted?
4. How Do I Recognize the Symptoms of Plague?
5. Seeking Medical Help: Can Plague Be Treated?
6. How Can Plague Be Prevented?

TYPES OF PLAGUE AND THEIR SYMPTOMS

1. Bubonic
2. Pneumonic
3. Septicemic

Informational Focus

Structure and Purpose of an Instructional Manual

How is the material organized to help readers learn about and seek treatment for plague?

Preteach

Informational Text Focus

- Ask volunteers to discuss situations in which they or people they know have used instructional manuals in order to complete a task. Have students explain what the instructional manual looked like, what information it contained, and how it helped them to complete their task.

- Review the table of contents on p. 211 with students. Explain that this table of contents gives an overview of information about the plague. Read the table of contents aloud with students, pausing after each item to discuss what specific details each section might include. For example, ask students to predict what characteristics might be discussed in Section 1.

- As you read and discuss the selection with students, have them note the structure, purpose, and features of an instructional manual.

Writing Skills Focus

Have students record organizational features of the selection in their **Reader/Writer Notebook.**

Selection Resources

Chapter 2 Resources, on-level practice and assessment, p. 34

PowerNotes, interactive lesson presentation with activities

Teacher One Stop™, on-level lesson plans and all print resources

Holt Audio Library

Holt Audio Library: Selections and Summaries in Spanish

UA: Holt Interactive Reader, p. 56

Holt Interactive Reader for ELD, p. 72

Holt Audio Tutor for ELD

UA: Differentiating Instruction, modified lesson plans and leveled assessment, p. 36

UA: Supporting Instruction in Five Languages, selection summary

UA: Resources for Teaching Advanced Students, lesson plans, p. 79

ThinkCentral Online Assessment, Selection Standards Check

ThinkCentral Online Remediation

Direct Teach

Model the Skill

- Tell students that some informational texts use **call-out boxes** to give readers additional information. These boxes may include charts, lists, or graphs.

- Direct students to the call-out box "Symptoms of Plague" on p. 212. Point out that the information in this box relates to the rest of the manual. The rest of the manual is written in paragraph form, while the information in the call-out box is written in a style that is similar to a dictionary entry. This organizational pattern makes it easier for a reader to locate the specific information that he or she is looking for.

Guided Practice: Apply

Ask students to read the information in the call-out box "Symptoms of Plague." Then, ask them to identify which type of plague causes fever. [*Pneumonic plague and septicemic plague both cause fever.*]

Read with a Purpose

Read this instructional manual to learn how to prevent and treat plague, a life-threatening disease that can be controlled with antibiotics.

STOPPING PLAGUE in Its TRACKS

A COMMUNITY HEALTH CENTER PROJECT

When you hear the word *plague*, you might think of it as a particularly nasty and devastating disease of the past, something you read about in history books when you studied Europe in the Middle Ages. Many people think that the plague was conquered and wiped out long ago. Yet, as recently as the early twentieth century, a plague pandemic in Asia claimed thousands of lives. Plague is still a potential danger to people everywhere, even in the twenty-first century—and even here in the United States. Following is the information you need to steer clear of plague. **Ⓐ**

SYMPTOMS OF PLAGUE

Seek medical assistance if you suspect that you may have any of the types of plague.

Bubonic (byoo BAHN ihk)
Caused by the bite of an infected flea. Look for:
- swollen, painful lymph nodes called buboes
- chills and fever
- headache

Pneumonic (noo MAHN ihk)
Spread by breathing in droplets from an infected human or animal. Can be a complication of bubonic or septicemic plague if the bacteria has spread to the lungs. Look for:
- bloody cough
- chest pain
- difficulty breathing
- high fever
- nausea and vomiting
- weakness

Septicemic (sehp tuh SEE mihk)
Caused when bacteria multiply in the bloodstream. Can be a complication of bubonic or pneumonic plague. Look for:
- abdominal pain
- decayed body tissue (gangrene), especially fingers, nose, or toes
- bleeding under the skin or from mouth or other body cavity
- chills and fever
- diarrhea and vomiting

Ⓐ Informational Focus Structure and Purpose of an Instructional Manual Identify the purpose of this instructional manual.

Selection Readability	
Easily Accessible Accessible **Challenging**	historical context, accessing information

Selection Summary

This instructional manual illustrates the methods of treatment and prevention that people should follow to control the plague today.

UNDERSTANDING PLAGUE

1. What Is Plague?

Plague is a highly infectious, life-threatening disease caused by a bacterium called *Yersinia pestis,* which lives in fleas. Plague is part of a natural cycle, regularly passed among members of the rodent family, such as gophers, ground squirrels, prairie dogs, and rats. Plague can take several forms—bubonic, pneumonic, and septicemic. Each form is distinguished by its symptoms and by how it spreads.

2. Where Is Plague Found?

Plague is found in many countries, including the United States. The majority of U.S. cases have been reported in the rural and urban west. Because it is spread by fleas, plague outbreaks are most common from April to November following mild winters and wet springs—conditions favorable for flea reproduction.

3. How Is Plague Transmitted?

Bubonic plague, the most common type, is usually caused by the bite of an infected flea. It can also come from contact with body fluids and tissues from infected animals. Bubonic plague cannot be transmitted from person to person without the bite of a flea or rodent. **Pneumonic plague**, on the other hand, is the most infectious form of plague because it can pass directly from person to person if a person breathes in infected droplets from someone with the disease. This form of plague, which attacks the lungs, can also result from letting bubonic or septicemic plague go untreated. **Septicemic plague**, the least common but most quickly lethal type, results when a person's blood is overrun with lethal *Yersinia pestis* bacteria. This form of plague can start with a flea bite or contact with infected fluids or tissues, but it also often results as a complication of untreated bubonic or pneumonic plague.

Colored scanning electron micrograph of the rat flea seen here clinging to the fur of a rat.

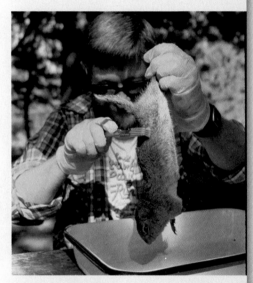

A chipmunk is brushed to collect potential plague-ridden fleas for analysis. King's Canyon National Park.

Real Issues, Real Experts

Holt author **Sara Kajder** *offers strategies for helping students understand informational texts.*

Informational text can be tough going as readers work their ways through what is often a lot of territory in a short piece. We see this in the range of information provided in "Stopping Plague in Its Tracks."

In order to help students monitor their understanding, I encourage them to record their questions throughout the reading process. We then revisit those lists to build inferences to think beyond the facts and use the text to

support our reading. This is a task that we often pair with class discussion, as readers need to hear how others question the text and construct meaning from the features, structures, central ideas, and vocabulary of the text.

Title of the Text	
What do I already know about the topic?	
Questions	**Inferences**
(I wonder...)	(What I think)

Model the Skill

■ Tell students that informational texts may include diagrams, or labeled drawings explaining a concept, to help their readers understand a part of the text.

■ Direct students to the image on p. 215. Remind students that this manual is meant to instruct people on how to prevent plague and what will happen if they become infected. To clarify the steps a person must take in order to protect him or herself, the author of the manual included this diagram. Match the parts of the diagram, such as moving piles away from the house, to the corresponding description in he text.

Guided Practice: Apply

■ Have groups of three students create their own diagrams to illustrate another part of the text; for example, they may wish to create a labeled drawing explaining how the plague is transmitted or how the plague can be treated.

■ Invite groups to share their completed diagrams with the class.

4. How Do I Recognize the Symptoms of Plague?
See the symptoms of plague outlined in the "Symptoms of Plague" glossary on the first page of this manual. Seek medical attention if you experience any combination of the symptoms. Be especially alert within a week of exposure to a sick or dead animal, an insect bite, close contact with a person or animal with plague, or travel to an area of the world with high risk rates.

5. Seeking Medical Help: Can Plague Be Treated?
In the past, bubonic plague killed about half of the people it infected. (Septicemic and pneumonic plague killed virtually all victims.) Today, with public health care systems in place and the availability of powerful antibiotics and other medical interventions, fewer than fifteen percent of plague victims succumb to the disease. Of these, the vast majority are victims of septicemic or pneumonic plague. Those exposed to bubonic plague who get treatment seldom die from the disease today. There is as yet no effective vaccine for the plague.

- **Screening and Diagnosis**
A doctor can assess plague risks and symptoms best and can confirm the diagnosis with a microscopic examination of fluid from buboes (painfully swollen lymph nodes), airways, or from a blood test.

- **Treatment**
Certain antibiotics are highly effective in treating plague. If you have been exposed to plague but have no symptoms, your doctor may prescribe preventive antibiotics, taken orally. If a doctor determines that you do have plague, you will likely be sent to a hospital and be put into isolation. You will be given antibiotics intravenously (through the veins) or intramuscularly (into the muscles) for at least ten days.

- **Complications**
Untreated bubonic plague can lead to the extremely deadly form known as septicemic plague, in which the bloodstream is overrun with the bacteria that cause plague. Other complications can include decay in fingers and toes (gangrene), inflammation of brain and spinal cord

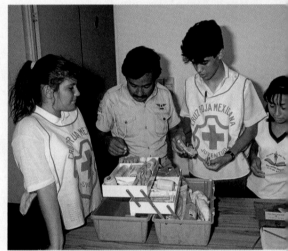

Sorting antibiotics at Red Cross Cancun Quintana Roo State, Yucatan Peninsula, Mexico.

Universal Access

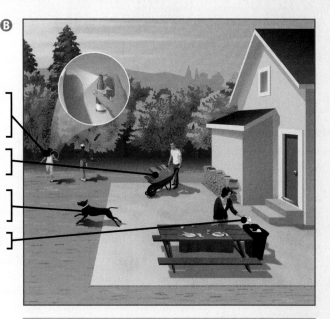

Help children understand safety measures. Protect them with insect repellent.

Move piles away from the house or destroy them.

Watch where pets roam. Give them flea protection.

Clear away food when done with it.

B **Informational Focus** Structure and Purpose of an Instruction Manual Why does the manual include a diagram? What does this diagram show?

membranes and fluid (meningitis), lung failure, and shock, leading to death.

6. How Can Plague Be Prevented?
Ask your doctor about preventive treatment if you have had close contact with an infected person or animal, have been bitten by an insect while in an area with a recent plague outbreak, or plan to spend time in an area with a recent outbreak. If you live in an area known to have outbreaks, use these precautions:

- While outdoors, protect yourself from fleas by wearing long-sleeved shirts and long pants tucked into socks or boots. Dress children appropriately, and use insect repellent. Never allow children to go barefoot outdoors.

- Do not touch dead or sick animals. Wear gloves or use a tool, such as a shovel, to remove dead animals.
- Don't feed or touch rodents, such as squirrels and field mice.
- Discourage rodents from nesting near or entering your home. Remove outdoor piles, such as woodpiles, where mice and other rodents tend to nest. Do not leave food outdoors.
- Watch where your pets wander, and use flea-protection products consistently. Ask your veterinarian for product recommendations. Both dogs and cats can bring home infected fleas, but cats in particular can transmit bubonic plague to their owners. The best precaution for cats is to keep them indoors.

Think About/Talk About

▶ **Comprehension**

B **Informational Focus**
Possible response: *The diagram is included to help readers understand the steps that they should take every day to prevent being infected with the plague.*

▶ **Extend the Discussion**
Analyzing Structure and Purpose
What is the purpose of the subtitles "Screening and Diagnosis," "Treatment," and "Complications"? Why do they appear in the fifth section of the manual?

Possible response: *The three subheads describe the process of treating the plague, which is why they appear in the fifth section of the manual, "Seeking Medical Help: Can Plague Be Treated?"*

Applying Your Skills

Reading Standard 2.1 Understand and analyze the differences in structure and purpose between various categories of informational materials (e.g., textbooks, newspapers, instructional manuals, signs).

Check for Understanding

Independent Practice
Answers and Explanations

1. **A** C and D are listed in the Contents, but do not apply to prevention. The diagram would not be useful.

2. **D** Lists, contents, and diagrams are all listed.

3. **B** The other sections do not detail how plague can be prevented.

4. **B** Seeking Medical Help directly addresses going to the doctor for help.

5. **D** The steps for preventing plague appear in a separate section.

6. **B** Pictures of a person infected with plague would best explain the symptoms.

Writing Skills Focus
Possible response: To chop celery, place the stalk length-wise on a cutting board. With a small knife, make one cut down the center of the entire stalk. Be sure to grip the knife firmly and keep your fingers safely out of the way. Then, put the stalk crosswise and make cuts every quarter of an inch.

What Do You Think Now?
Suggest students delineate the ways people prevent plague from spreading.

Assess
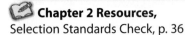
Chapter 2 Resources, Selection Standards Check, p. 36

ThinkCentral Online Assessment, Selection Standards Check

Teacher One Stop™, editable Selection Standards Check

Reteach

ThinkCentral Online Remediation

Stopping Plague in Its Tracks
Standards Review

Informational Text

1. In which part of the instructional manual would you look *first* to find the section that discusses plague prevention?
   - **A** Contents
   - **B** the diagram
   - **C** Symptoms of Plague
   - **D** Seeking Medical Help

2. Which of the following is *not* included in the instructional manual?
   - **A** a table of contents
   - **B** diagrams
   - **C** lists
   - **D** an index

3. In which part of the manual would you look for a simple visual of how better to protect the area you live in from plague?
   - **A** Contents
   - **B** How Can Plague Be Prevented?
   - **C** Seeking Medical Help
   - **D** What Is Plague?

4. If you had a question about whether you should contact your doctor regarding plague, under what heading would you look?
   - **A** How Is Plague Transmitted?
   - **B** Seeking Medical Help
   - **C** How Can Plague Be Prevented?
   - **D** Where Is Plague Found?

5. Which information does *not* appear in the section headed "Seeking Medical Help: Can Plague Be Treated?"
   - **A** treatment of plague
   - **B** diagnosis of plague
   - **C** complications from plague
   - **D** prevention of plague

6. Which of the following illustrations would be *most* helpful to you if included in the section headed "How Do I Recognize the Symptoms of Plague?"
   - **A** a photograph of various common rodents that carry plague
   - **B** a photograph of swollen buboes on a person infected by plague
   - **C** a photograph of doctors and nurses around a hospital bed
   - **D** a photograph of *Yersinia pestis* bacteria as seen through a microscope

Writing Skills Focus
Timed Writing Think about a task or activity you know how to do that involves safety concerns, such as skating, carving a pumpkin, or using gardening or cleaning equipment. Write a set of step-by-step instructions that clearly show how to perform the task or activity and that include necessary safety warnings.

 What Do You Think Now How might knowing this information about plague help someone living in a high-risk area?

California Standards, pp. 216–217
- **Reading Standard 2.1** Understand and analyze the differences in structure and purpose between various categories of informational materials (e.g. textbooks, newspapers, instructional manuals, signs).

Preparing to Read

Reading Standard 2.1 Understand and analyze the differences in structure and purpose between various categories of informational materials (**e.g.,** textbooks, newspapers, instructional manuals, **signs**).

Signs

Informational Text Focus

Structure and Purpose of Signs In everyday life, one of the most common ways we communicate information is through the use of **signs.** Sometimes signs are the only sources of information we have. Sometimes understanding them can be a matter of life or death.

Signs are perhaps the simplest, most basic form of public document. The purpose of signs is to immediately communicate information, such as directions, warnings, or specific locations. To interpret a sign, you "read" its **structure,** which includes its shape, color, and the pictures or symbols on it. Signs do not depend on a specific written language. Instead, they communicate in a simple, direct way through symbols and markings whose meanings are commonly agreed upon or easy to interpret. Thus, many signs can be universally understood. In fact, a number of signs that you see every day are used virtually all over the world.

Imagine that you were traveling abroad and could not speak the local language. How would you locate a hospital, hotel, or taxi stand? How would you know when to cross the street at an intersection? Chances are that there would be signs to guide you that don't rely on knowledge of a specific language.

Here are some facts about signs:

- There are 58 million traffic signs on our nation's roads.
- Uniform pictorial signs were first developed in Europe for tourists.
- The skull-and-crossbones sign was flown on pirate ships to indicate that anyone who crossed the ship's path would die.
- Signs that indicate danger usually have an unusual shape (like a triangle) and a bright color.
- Signs indicating where travelers can eat, rest, or get gas are usually blue, white, or green—colors that suggest relaxation. Red usually indicates something dangerous or forbidden.

Our world is full of signs. Language itself is a system of symbols and signs—a very sophisticated one. See whether you can identify what the signs on the next two pages mean.

Reader/Writer
Notebook
Use your **RWN** to complete the activities for this selection.

Language Coach

Signs As this page discusses, signs convey information, often without using words. Communication does not always rely on language alone. What signs without words can you name? How do they convey information effectively?

Learn It Online
Explore the structure and purpose of signs with *PowerNotes* online:

go.hrw.com | H7-215 | **Go**

Selection Resources

Chapter 2 Resources, on-level practice and assessment, p. 35

PowerNotes, interactive lesson presentation with activities

Teacher One Stop™, on-level lesson plans and all print resources

Holt Audio Library: Selections and Summaries in Spanish

UA: Holt Interactive Reader, p. 59

Holt Interactive Reader for ELD, p. 76

Holt Audio Tutor for ELD

Differentiating Instruction, modified lesson plans and leveled assessment, p. 36

UA: Supporting Instruction in Five Languages, selection summary

UA: Resources for Teaching Advanced Students, lesson plans, p. 82

ThinkCentral Online Assessment, Selection Standards Check

ThinkCentral Online Remediation

Direct Teach

Model the Skill

■ Have volunteers describe signs that they see every day, such as stop signs on the way to school. Tell students that signs use pictures, colors, and symbols, in addition to words, to communicate meaning.

■ Model for students interpreting the meaning of a sign. Explain that signs with a diagonal line through an image mean that something is not permitted. Therefore, the sign showing a dog with a line going through it means that dogs are not allowed in the area.

Guided Practice: Apply

What do students think of when they see a skull and crossbones? Discuss how that association allows a skull and crossbones to communicate meaning on a sign.

Read with a Purpose

Look at the signs below to learn about their meanings.

What would convey the fact that this sign means "danger"?

Which sign means "dogs are allowed"? Which sign means "no dogs allowed"? What symbol gives you that information?

Imagine that you have arrived for the first time in Mexico City. If you need information, would these signs help you? What clues give you your answer? Why wouldn't the second sign work in every country?

Selection Readability	
Easily Accessible Accessible Challenging	minimal text; familiar images

Selection Summary

The selection shows some common signs with captions asking students to think about what the symbols mean.

If you were driving along a road and saw this sign, how would you <u>respond</u>?

When you travel, you might need a drugstore. If you know about Greek mythology, you can describe what this universal symbol for "pharmacy" means.

Signs say a great deal with only a simple graphic or illustration. What does this sign say to you?

Here is a familiar sign. What is it saying?

Read with a Purpose

What are some other universal signs that you see in daily life? How is the meaning of each sign made clear?

Do you know what this sign means? It's the biohazard symbol, which warns people that something is a biological agent that is dangerous to humans or the environment. The biohazard symbol did not have a distinct meaning when it was created, but it is memorable. Its creators wanted to educate people on the meaning of a new, standardized symbol.

Read with a Purpose Have students read the Read with a Purpose statement. Discuss with students a list of clues that might help them to interpret a sign's meaning.

▶ Extend the Discussion

Drawing Conclusions Why do you think these signs are largely made up of images rather than letters or words? *Possible response: If the signs contained words in a certain language, only people who spoke that language would be able to understand the signs' meanings. Since pictures and images can be understood by many people around the world, even if they don't all speak the same language, it makes sense to convey important information through images.*

Synthesizing Based on the articles you have just read, which of the signs on this page could have been useful during the Middle Ages? Why? *Possible response: The biohazard sign could have been used because plague was a dangerous biological agent.*

Compare and Contrast

After students have read the articles and completed the Applying Your Skills questions, have them compare and contrast the plague in the Middle Ages with the plague today. Use the following discussion questions:

- Compare the protective clothing worn by the man on p. 200 to the illustration of the doctor on p. 213.

   Similarities: Both sets of clothing are designed to cover the entire body to prevent the person from coming into contact with infected material.

   Differences: The modern outfit does not come with

herbs and spices like the outfit from the 17th century. The herbs were probably used to hide the smell of death and decay rather than for some medicinal purpose.

- Compare plague in the modern world to plague in the Middle Ages.

   Similarities: Plague is still carried largely through fleas and rodents.

   Differences: Today, plague is much less deadly because of advanced medical knowledge. It is also less easy to spread because of improved sanitary conditions.

Objectives

Students will

- write autobiographical narratives about meaningful experiences
- include thoughts and feelings in their narratives

Preteach

Write with a Purpose Read aloud the essentials of a good autobiographical narrative to guide students' understanding of this type of writing. Also refer students to the rubric on p. 228 for more information on autobiographical narratives that they can use throughout this workshop.

Direct Teach

Model the Skill

Think as a Reader/Writer Use the professional model on this page and others in the collection to provide examples of the elements of a good autobiographical narrative. Point out in the Cosby excerpt that the author focuses on one event.

Think About the Professional Model

Possible responses:

1. *The author is smitten with a girl. The girl does not seem to notice him.*

2. *The author compares how the girl looks at him to how she looked at lampposts; he's not sure if the girl feels the way he does about her.*

3. *He and the girl begin as strangers. The suspense in the story builds as the reader waits for them to meet.*

4. *The author describes his thoughts and feelings as well as how the girl reacts to him.*

Autobiographical Narrative

Write with a Purpose

Write an autobiographical narrative about a significant experience in your life. Your **purpose** is to tell what happened and to explain to your readers why this experience is meaningful to you. Think about your **audience** as you write, and provide enough information so that they can understand your experience.

A Good Autobiographical Narrative

- is told from your point of view, using the pronouns *I, me, my*
- focuses on one experience
- includes essential background information or uses context
- develops a standard plot line
- develops a definite setting
- delineates character through dialogue and/or description
- shows what the experience means to you

See page 228 for complete rubric.

Reader/Writer Notebook

Use your **RWN** to complete the activities for this workshop.

Think as a Reader/Writer

In this chapter, you have been drawn to powerful themes by the techniques writers have used. Now it is time for you to draw readers into your point of view as you write an autobiographical narrative. Before you begin, take a few minutes to read this passage from Bill Cosby's autobiographical narrative "The Only Girl in the World for Me."

> The first time I saw her, she was crossing the street to the schoolyard and for one golden moment our eyes met. Well, maybe the moment was closer to bronze because she made no response. But at least she had seen me, just about the way that she saw lampposts, hydrants, and manholes. Or was there something more? I began to dream; and later that day, when I was playing with the boys in the yard, it seemed that she was looking at me and the world was suddenly a better place, especially Twelfth and Girard.
>
> However, we still never talked, but just traded silent unsmiling looks whenever we passed. For several days, just her look was enough of a lift for me; but a higher altitude was coming, for one night at a party, we met and I actually danced with her. Now I was certain that I was in love and was going to win her.

← Notice how the author establishes a definite setting for his first meeting with the girl.

← The author includes specific narrative actions, including movement and facial expressions.

← The author's organizational structure is in clear chronological order.

Think About the Professional Model

With a partner, discuss the following questions about the model.

1. What do you learn about the author from this information? What do you learn about the other major character?

2. What are some examples of description that the author uses? How do these details help you understand the importance of this experience for the author?

3. How does the author's presentation of events create rising action and build suspense?

4. In place of dialogue, what strategies does the author use to <u>delineate</u> character and advance the plot line?

California Standards, pp. 220–229

■ **Writing 2.1** Write fictional or autobiographical narratives. **a.** Develop a standard plot line (having a beginning, conflict, rising action, climax, and denouement) and point of view. **b.** Develop complex major and minor characters and a definite setting. **c.** Use a range of appropriate strategies (e.g., dialogue; suspense; naming of specific narrative action, including movement, gestures, and expressions).

Writing Workshop Resources

UA: Holt Interactive Writer and Speaker, on-level practice and assessment

UA: Differentiating Instruction, modified lesson plans and leveled assessment, p. 39

WritingNotes, interactive lesson presentations with activities

GrammarNotes, interactive lesson presentations with activities

Writing and Research in a Digital Age, interactive lesson presentations with activities

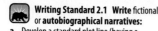

Writing Standard 2.1 Write fictional or **autobiographical narratives:**
a. Develop a standard plot line (having a beginning, conflict, rising action, climax, and denouement) and point of view. **b.** Develop complex major and minor characters and a definite setting. **c.** Use a range of appropriate strategies (e.g., dialogue; suspense; naming of specific narrative action, including movement, gestures, and expressions).

Prewriting

List Your Ideas

Use the Idea Starters in the margin to help you <u>identify</u> and make a list of memorable experiences you might want to write about. Ask yourself the following questions about each one:

- Does this incident mean something special to me?
- Do I remember this incident clearly?
- Am I comfortable sharing this incident with my audience?

Choose a Topic

You may find it helpful to use a comparison table, like the one below, when you are choosing between topics.

Surprises	Vacations
Throwing a surprise birthday party for my mother was a great experience.	My family's trip to visit relatives in Italy was a very special time.
I remember every detail of the party.	I was only three years old, so I probably don't remember much of it.
I'd love to share this experience.	I wouldn't mind telling others about our trip.

Gather Details

Once you have chosen a particular experience, take notes on how it unfolded and how you felt about it. For instance, see how the following chart can help you visualize Bill Cosby's experience in "The Only Girl in the World for Me."

Who	What	When	Where	Why	How
Bill Cosby	He fell in love.	When he was young	The schoolyard	Their eyes met.	They traded looks.
A girl			At a party	They danced.	He felt happy and in love.

To help gather details, ask yourself these questions and create a chart like the one above:

- *Who* was involved in the experience? *What* did he or she say?
- *What* happened? *When* did it happen?
- *Where* did it happen? *What* was the setting?
- *Why* did it happen?
- *How* did it happen? *How* did I feel as the events unfolded?
- *What* did I learn as a result of the experience? *How* have I changed?

Idea Starters

- surprises
- challenges
- vacations
- helping others
- luck
- secrets
- sports
- losing a friend
- the future
- honesty

Your Turn _____

Get Started Making notes in your **RWN**, choose your experience and write a clear statement about why it is so **meaningful** to you. Begin listing **details** about the experience, including any **background information** you will need to provide your readers. Your notes will help you draft your narrative.

 Learn It Online
To see how one writer met all the assignment criteria, visit:

go.hrw.com | H7-221 | **Go**

Guided Practice: Apply

Choose a Topic

- Have students fill out a chart similar to the one in the Student Edition as they brainstorm possible topics. Remind them to think of experiences that are meaningful to them. Suggest that they expand their comparison table to include other idea starters such as luck, secrets, and sports.

- To figure out the best possible topic, have students share their ideas with a partner. Tell them to ask their partners which of the topics on the list they would be most interested to hear more about.

Your Turn _____

Get Started Tell students that the organization of their narrative will help their readers understand what is going on. Have students consider the chronological order of their narrative as they begin making notes. Tell students to make sure they have answered all of the questions on this page about details so that their narrative is as comprehensive as possible.

 Learn It Online
Interactive Writer's Models on the **Interactive Student Edition** provide annotated sample essays along with writing tips and strategies.

go.hrw.com | H7-221 | **Go**

Guided Practice: Apply

Order the Key Events

- Tell students that autobiographical narratives are organized in chronological order.

- Point out words in the Professional Model on p. 220 that signal chronological order (*first* and *later that day* in paragraph 1; *for several days* in paragraph 2). Tell students that transitional words like *next, later on,* and *afterwards* signal to the reader when an event happens.

Think About Purpose and Audience

Remind students that the purpose of an autobiographical narrative is for the author to express himself or herself by sharing an interesting story or a meaningful experience. Sharing an autobiographical narrative may also be a chance for the reader to get to know the author.

Your Turn _____

Order the Events Have students complete the **Your Turn** activity as independent practice. After they have completed their sequence chart, have them add transitional words to the sequence of events.

⬤ Writing Tip

What a person (or character) says can reveal a great deal about him or her. That's why it's a good idea to include some **dialogue** in your narrative. Be sure to use correct punctuation as you write your dialogue, and try to make the dialogue sound the way people really talk. (Although slang and sentence fragments are usually avoided in formal writing, it may be natural to use such language in your narrative.) You may wish to describe your characters' gestures and expressions as well.

Your Turn _____

Order the Events List the key events of your experience in the **sequence** in which they occurred. Creating a **flowchart** can help you identify beginning, middle, and ending events in your narrative.

Order the Key Events

In order to develop a standard plot line for your narrative, be sure to place events in the correct sequence. Your readers will easily follow your narrative if you use **chronological order,** the order in which events occurred in time. Use transitional words such as *first, then,* and *finally* to emphasize the sequence of events. To unify important ideas and show how they are related, use transitional words and phrases such as *for example, mainly,* and *in addition to.* Completing a flowchart like the one below can help you visualize the **sequence** of events.

Sequence Chart

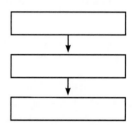

Keep Your Point of View Consistent

Use first-person pronouns—*I, me, my, we*—when referring to yourself. Keep your **point of view** consistent throughout your narrative.

Think About Purpose and Audience

Before you begin, consider your purpose and your audience. Is your **purpose** for writing to tell a funny or scary story or to share a meaningful experience? Be sure to indicate to readers why the experience was important to you. If your **audience** is made up of people who know you well, then much less background will need to be provided than might be necessary for an audience of strangers. Think about what readers will need to know that does not come up in the context of this experience. Consider these questions:

- Is this a unique experience, one your audience could not have experienced?

- What is the setting of your experience? Is it a place where your audience regularly spends time, or is it an unusual place for them to have been?

- Does your audience know the other people in your experience? If so, what was their relationship to them?

Autobiographical Narrative Writing Prompts

Students can choose their own essay ideas or use one of the following prompts to write an autobiographical narrative.

Physical Education Write about an important or memorable game that you played in. Be sure to include your thoughts and feelings about that game.

Music Write about a time when music played a key role in your life. Did you learn to play an insturment, or join the choir? Did your favorite song inspire you to do something? Detail your experiences in an autobio-

graphical narrative.

History Write about a time when you experienced or witnessed history in the making. Remember to write from your own perspective, using the first person.

School Write about your first day in seventh grade. Include the events that you recall most vividly.

World Languages Have you ever communicated in a language different from your native language? Write about your experiences.

Drafting

Follow Your Framework

Using a framework like the one below as a guide, draft your narrative. Focus on the single experience you are describing, and be sure to provide enough background for your audience so they can understand your experience. Develop a standard plot line with a beginning, conflict, rising action, climax, and denouement. Be sure you tell the events in a clear order, or sequence, and from a consistent point of view.

> **Framework for an Autobiographical Narrative**
>
> **Introduction:** dialogue, question, statement, or description that grabs the reader's attention and names the experience about which you're writing
>
> **Body:** description of events in chronological order
>   First event
>   Second event
>   Third event, and so on . . .
>
> **Conclusion:** summary expressing the importance, or meaning, of the experience

Use Vivid Descriptive Details

Help your readers share the experience you had by describing sensory details. How did things look, sound, smell, taste, and feel? As you describe these details, use precise words. Consider using a thesaurus for help in finding the best word to describe what you experienced. For example, if you want to think of a more dramatic way to describe a hot day, you could use words such as *sweaty, sweltering, scorching,* and *blazing.*

> ### Grammar Link Adjectives
>
> **Adjectives** are words that describe, or modify, nouns. They make writing vivid by creating a more precise image for the reader. Adjectives indicate size, color, number, and other characteristics. Use precise adjectives to describe specific narrative actions, such as characters' expressions, movements, and gestures.
>
> "for one **golden** moment our eyes met" (The adjective *golden* modifies the noun *moment.*)
>
> "we . . . traded **silent unsmiling** looks whenever we passed" (The adjectives *silent* and *unsmiling* modify the noun *looks.*)

Reflecting on the Importance of the Experience

State in a sentence or two why the experience is important. For instance, the passage from Bill Cosby's narrative "The Only Girl in the World for Me" ends with: "Now I was certain that I was in love and was going to win her."

As you write your draft, look back at your statement to see if it fits your narrative. If it does not, you may need to rewrite your draft or your statement.

● Writing Tip

To develop complex characters through dialogue, you must write in each character's true voice. Think about your characters' attributes—their backgrounds and experiences. Think about how they talk and act. If you know your characters well, you will be able to write the dialogue and describe the actions that bring those characters to life for your audience.

Your Turn _____

Write Your Draft Following your plan, write a draft of your essay. Be sure to think about

- giving **background information** your readers might need
- accurately representing the **sequence** of events
- using **precise details** to describe the experience

Guided Practice: Apply

Use Vivid Descriptive Details

Tell students that vivid descriptive details will make their narrative come to life. Encourage students to consider these techniques when adding descriptive elements to their autobiographical narrative:

- To make the details more realistic, consider describing how people in the narrative react to the setting, the action, and each other.

- Use figurative language, such as simile, metaphor, and personification, to create new and exciting descriptions of ordinary things.

- Tap into all five of your senses. Try using a sense that you wouldn't ordinarily think of to describe something, such as describing the way the beach smells or noises that involve the sand.

Grammar Link

For practice, have students insert adjectives into each of the following sentences.

1. After running for twenty minutes, my _____ lungs screamed, "No more!" [***Possible responses:*** *tired, exhausted*]

2. The _____ kitten ate three bowls of food. [***Possible responses:*** *hungry, starving, ravenous*]

 Warriner's Handbook, p. 34

Your Turn _____

Write Your Draft Ask students to complete the **Your Turn** activity as independent practice. Remind students to use their completed sequence chart as they begin to draft their narrative. Suggest that students use every other line as they write their draft so that revisions can be made more easily later.

Model the Skill

- Using a student draft on a transparency, model how to use the questions, tips, and revision techniques suggested in the chart. You might use a student's essay or an essay of your own creation to evaluate and revise using the steps in the chart.

- Ask volunteers to demonstrate using each of the steps on their own essays.

Peer Review

Tell students to use a colored pen when commenting on a peer's paper so that the writer can see their suggestions clearly. Advise students not to use a red pen while they are marking others' work, though, as their partners may feel as though they are playing teacher.

Holt Six Traits for Writing, rubrics, prompts, and sample papers

Peer Review

Working with a peer, review your draft. Answer each question in this chart to locate where and how your drafts could be improved. As you discuss your papers, be sure to take notes about your partner's suggestions.

Evaluating and Revising

Read the questions in the left column of the chart, and then use the tips in the middle column to help you make revisions to your essay. The right column suggests techniques you can use to revise your draft.

Autobiographical Narrative: Guidelines for Content and Organization

Evaluation Question	Tip	Revision Technique
1. Does your introduction grab the reader's attention and set the scene? Does it suggest what the main conflict of the plot line will be?	**Underline** the attention-getting opener.	**Add** a memorable quotation, statement, or piece of dialogue to the introduction. **Add** specific details to make the setting more precise.
2. Is the point of view consistent throughout?	**Identify** pronouns (*I*, *he*, or *she*) that show point of view. **Label** the narrative's point of view, and **circle** any information not given from that point of view.	If any sentences are circled, **delete** them. If necessary, **add** the same information told from the narrator's point of view.
3. Does the narrative include essential background information?	**Put a star** next to details that make clear the context, or background, of the experience.	**Add** information that will help the reader understand the events in your narrative.
4. Are the events in sequential order? Have you developed a standard plot line with rising action, a climax, and a denouement?	**Number** the events in your paper. **Compare** the sequence with the actual order of events.	**Rearrange** any events that are out of order.
5. Do precise details and vocabulary help develop your characters and setting?	**Put check marks** next to specific, precise descriptions. In the margin, note to which senses the details appeal.	**Elaborate** with dialogue or sensory details. **Delete** any unrelated details. **Revise** with more precise vocabulary.
6. Have you described your thoughts and feelings to clarify why the experience is important?	**Put a check mark** under statements of your feelings or thoughts. Put an **exclamation point** next to your statement of importance.	**Add** any other relevant important thoughts and feelings. **Add** a clear statement explaining why the experience matters.

Real Issues, Real Experts

Holt Professional Learning for Language Arts

To watch videos on teaching **revision, grammar,** and **on-demand writing skills** featuring **Linda Rief, Amy Benjamin**, and **Leila Christenbury**, go to this page in **ThinkCentral, Teacher Access.**

Universal Access

EL English Learners

English for Academic Success Give students a list of transitional words that they can use in the autobiographical narratives to signal chronological order, such as *first, then, later, before, after, the next day, hours later, immediately after, by sunset, at noon, in the beginning,* and *up until then.*

Struggling Writers

Benchmark Students If students are having trouble expressing why the experience described in their autobiographical narrative is important, have them consider the following questions: Is there

Read this student's draft and the comments about it as a model for revising your own autobiographical narrative

Claire of Bilberry

by Claire Moreland-Ochoa, Lake Travis Middle School

"I don't know about taking a hike today," my dad hinted. "I think I will take a nap."

While my dad was taking a nap, Danielle and I had some tea outside. Tea was becoming my favorite drink at any time of the day because it was very cold in England. While we were sitting outside on the deck at Ennerdale View, my mom walked out and gave me the *worst* news of the day.

"Honey, we are going on a hike," she broke into a smile. I wanted to frown, but instead I kept a straight face and asked, "When are we leaving?"

"Now."

We soon came to a man with purple hands sitting on a bench. The rental car slowly halted beside him. My dad introduced himself and asked why the man had purple hands.

"Well, I have been picking bilberries all morning on the Ennerdale Lake path," he said, sitting on a bench with a tin can in one of his hands. After a couple of words were said, we drove a little way and turned left.

← Claire opens with **dialogue**, immediately placing readers in the scene.

← Claire begins with an **example** of her behavior, in this case her facial expression.

← **Specific details** help readers picture the scene.

MINI-LESSON ▶ How to Develop a Setting for Readers

Claire places readers in the scene, but does not say *why* she and her family are there. Readers could follow the narrative more easily if they knew from the beginning that the family is on vacation in England, have been there for a while, and might be getting bored.

Claire's Revision of Paragraph One

"I don't know about taking a hike today," my dad hinted. "I think I will take a nap." ∧*Our family had been in western England on vacation for about two weeks. We were renting a house in the remote Lake District. Everyone but Mom was growing weary of our daily hikes through the forest.*

Your Turn _____

Add Necessary Background Information Read your draft, and then ask yourself:

- How can I effectively develop the setting or characters?
- How can I help readers better understand the context of my experience?

---

a lesson that your audience can learn from your experience? Did you learn a lesson from it? If someone were to ask you, "So what?" about your experience, what would you say?

Advanced Learners

Acceleration Have students use a flashback to develop the setting for their readers. Tell students to use transitional words that signal that the action occurred in the past, such as *previously, last week,* and *before.* Encourage students to include action and dialogue in their flashbacks.

Students with Disabilities

If students have trouble remembering details about the setting of their narrative, allow them to consult personal photographs or journals or talk to a friend or family member to help them recall concrete images as well as their thoughts and feelings about where their autobiographical narrative takes place.

Guided Practice: Apply
Student Draft

Explain that the Student Draft on this page is the first half of an autobiographical narrative written by a student. Model reading the draft and the annotations in blue, and explain that the yellow highlighting illustrates the student's language choices. Explain that a mini-lesson follows with helpful information about ways to improve this draft as well as their own.

▶ Mini-Lesson
How to Develop a Setting for Readers

- Explain to students that the student writer has initially not given her audience enough background information. Readers will be confused as to why she is in England and why her father is talking about a hike.

- Ask students to look at the professional model on p. 220. Ask them to think about what additional background information Cosby could have added to his essay and what effect this change would have on the essay overall. [**Possible response:** *Cosby could have added the name of the city in which the action took place to make the part of the essay that mentions street names more relevant.*]

Your Turn _____

Add Necessary Background Information Ask students to complete the **Your Turn** activity in pairs. Have students exchange papers to help each other identify places in their papers where they need more background information. Ask each student to come up with one question about their partner's paper that they will need to answer to provide enough background information.

Guided Practice: Apply
Student Draft
- Explain that the Student Draft is continued and completed on this page. Again the draft is annotated and highlighted for students.
- Read the draft and annotations aloud and discuss. Refer students to the Writer's Framework on p. 223. Ask students to comment on whether the student writer followed this framework.

▶ Mini-Lesson
How to Relate Events in a Clear Order
- Remind students that providing events in chronological order is not enough—they also have to make sure that the sequence of events is easy to follow so that their readers are not confused about when, where, and how the action takes place.
- Explain that the student writer has revised the order of events in her draft by including all necessary information. Read the student's first draft, and then compare it to her revised version. Ask students to comment on which version is more effective and why.

Your Turn _____
Make the Order of Events
Clear Have students form groups of three with classmates who have no knowledge of their essay. Have each student in the group read his or her draft aloud. Other group members should comment on whether the student included all the details necessary to create a coherent sequence of events. Direct students to alter their draft as needed.

Student Draft continues

Traveling down a narrow lane, the car turned onto a dirt road. We stopped at a gate. I climbed out and opened it. The car drove by. I closed the gate behind it, realizing that the gates are there to keep the sheep in. But there was not just one gate. There were four gates to open.

"What is with England and gates?" I asked myself. After long minutes of taking pictures of sheep and hiking, we finally saw the first bilberry patch. Running up to the patch, I started picking the bilberries and shoving them into my mouth, while thinking, "I am **so** hungry!" Soon the whole family was devouring bilberries. My mom filmed the process. The bilberries disappeared on this patch, and we moved on. One by one, the bilberry patches popped up on each side of us. One by one, the bilberry patches turned into just patches without the bilberries anymore.

Halfway through the hike my parents ordered me to stop eating and Danielle to stop picking. We fell back a little and pretended to stoop over and look at all kinds of things. Sometimes it was a bug we were looking at; other times it was a flower or a strange-looking plant. We never stopped to look at any of those. We just saw a very nice bilberry patch and stopped to pick them and eat them.

On the way back we stopped to have a shortbread cookie. I smeared bilberry juice on the top of mine and thought it was very good. Everyone's faces twisted up when they saw what I was doing to the poor cookie. When we were finally back in the car, I was relieved but satisfied with a full stomach of bilberries. From then on I had a nickname, "Claire of Bilberry."

Claire mentions a specific **narrative** *action.* →

Claire uses good transitional words throughout to help readers follow the **sequence** *of the experience.* →

The ending names the narrative action that is so **memorable**—*Claire got her nickname because of it!* →

Your Turn _____
Make the Order of Events
Clear Carefully compare what you have written to your memory of the experience. Be sure that you have presented every important event and that the events are in chronological order.

MINI-LESSON ▶ How to Relate Events in a Clear Order

Claire does a great job of telling all of the important events in sequential order. However, she leaves out important information in the eighth paragraph. One of her readers pointed out that the action moves from the gates to taking pictures and hiking without transition or explanation. Her revision addresses this omission.

Claire's Revision of Paragraph Eight

After the car passed through the fourth gate, we traveled to the end of the dirt road. There, at the edge of the forest, we located the path and started off on foot.
"What is with England and gates?" I asked myself. After long minutes . . .

Universal Access

AAVE Students Who Use African American Vernacular English
English for Academic Success Write this sentence from the student model on the board:

We never stopped to look at any of those.

Tell students that this sentence contains a negative [*never*]. Remind students that when making negative statements using formal English, they should be careful to avoid forming a double negative. A double negative occurs when two words in a phrase or sentence are negative instead of one.

Then, work with students to revise this sentence to eliminate the double negative:
We do not want to play checkers no more.
Possible response: *We do not want to play checkers any more.*

EL English Learners
English for Academic Success Remind students to consult their lists of transitional words as they review the sequence of events in their autobiographical nar-

Proofreading and Publishing

Proofreading

You have revised your autobiographical narrative, and now it is time to polish it to eliminate any errors that might distract your readers. Edit your narrative to correct any misspellings, punctuation errors, and problems in sentence structure.

Grammar Link Capitalize Proper Nouns

In an autobiographical narrative, you are likely to refer to specific people or places. When you do so, you are using a proper noun. A **proper noun** refers to a particular person, place, or thing and is capitalized. Claire follows this rule in her essay:

> "What is it with **England** and gates?" I asked myself.
> "Well, I have been picking bilberries all morning on the **Ennerdale Lake** path," he said. . . .

England is the name of a country, and **Ennerdale Lake** is the name of the path. In addition to names of persons and geographical names, proper names include such things as nationalities, teams, businesses, historical periods, holidays, buildings, religions, planets, and languages.

Claire also correctly follows the rule to capitalize a word showing family relationship when the word is used in place of the person's name. However, when a possessive comes before the word, the word is not capitalized.

> Everyone but **Mom** was growing weary of our daily hikes through the forest.
> "I don't know about taking a hike today," **my dad** hinted.

Publishing

Now it is time to publish your autobiographical narrative for a wider audience. Here are some ways to share your story:

- Add photos from the experience, or use drawings to illustrate the narrative and present the finished product as a gift to someone who shared the experience with you.
- E-mail your narrative to interested relatives or friends.

Reflect on the Process
In your *Reader/Writer Notebook,* write a short response to each of the following questions.

1. What strategies did you find helpful as you were trying to develop characters and setting?
2. What was the most important revision you made to your narrative?
3. What do you think about this experience now?

🔵 **Proofreading Tip**

There are three main areas to focus on when editing: spelling, punctuation, and sentence structure. It makes sense to focus on just one area at a time while proofreading. Ask two peers to help you, and assign each person just one area to check.

Your Turn _____
Proofread and Publish

Proofread your narrative for any boldface or italic treatments you have used. Are the right words emphasized? If you have not used type styles to indicate important points, look for places where their use could improve readers' understanding of your narrative. Then, carefully proofread your narrative for any errors, make the corrections, and publish your polished work for others to enjoy.

Guided Practice: Apply

Proofreading
Integrating with Grammar, Usage, and Mechanics If students make errors in the usage of adjectives as they are proofreading, send them to the Parts of Speech and Complements chapters in **Warriner's Handbook.**

Grammar Link

- Have students read through their final draft and underline any nouns that refer to a specific person, place, or thing.
- Tell students to make sure that all of the proper nouns they have underlined are capitalized. Have them correct any proper nouns that have not been capitalized in their narrative.

Publishing
Brainstorm with students additional ways to publish their autobiographical narratives.

Reflect on the Process
Have students reflect on the entire writing process as well as their final product. Challenge them to reflect metacognitively about how they can improve and apply what they have learned.

Your Turn _____

Proofread and Publish Have students read their narratives out loud to check whether they have used boldface or italic treatments correctly. If they emphasize a word as they read it aloud, then the word may need to be boldfaced or italicized in their narrative. Words that are not read aloud with any particular emphasis should not be boldfaced or italicized. Have students check their final drafts against the revision guidelines on p. 224.

---

rative. Tell them that using transitional words will help their readers follow the action and recognize when a new setting, person, or detail is introduced.

Struggling Writers
To help students identify whether they have left out an important detail in the chronological events of their narrative, have them pantomime the actions in their autobiographical narrative. If they notice that they are jumping from one action to the next without a clear transition or reason, then they may need to add a detail to their draft.

Advanced Learners
Enrichment Explain to students that while it is important to include enough information in their autobiographical narrative to make the action easy to follow, it is also important to be concise and precise. Leaving out irrelevant and unnecessary details will help students relate events in a clear order that is easy for the reader to understand. Tell students to revise their draft, removing details that do not contribute to their autobiographical narrative's clear sequence of events.

Scoring Rubric

- Tell students that the best way to understand rubrics is to use them to score actual writing. Review the rubric with students

- Have students work with a partner to evaluate the final copies of the autobiographical narratives that they wrote in the Writing Workshop. Ask students to score each other's narratives, then write a brief paragraph using the language of the rubric to explain the score.

Holt Six Traits for Writing, rubrics, prompts, and sample papers

Assess

UA: Interactive Writer and Speaker, fictional narrative analytical scales and rubric

ThinkCentral Online Assessment, Writing Workshop Test

Teacher One Stop™, editable Writing Workshop Test

Reteach

ThinkCentral Online Remediation

California Standards, pp. 228–229

- **Writing 2.1** Write fictional or autobiographical narratives. **a.** Develop a standard plot line (having a beginning, conflict, rising action, climax, and denouement) and point of view. **b.** Develop complex major and minor characters and a definite setting. **c.** Use a range of appropriate strategies (e.g., dialogue; suspense; naming of specific narrative action, including movement, gestures, and expressions).

Scoring Rubric

You can use the rubric below to evaluate your autobiographical narrative from the Writing Workshop or your response to the prompt on the next page.

	Autobiographical Narrative	Organization and Focus	Sentence Structure	Conventions
4	• Is told from a consistent first-person point of view. • Focuses clearly on only one experience. • Clearly and thoughtfully expresses the meaning of the experience.	• Clearly addresses all parts of the writing task. • Demonstrates a clear understanding of purpose and audience. • Maintains a consistent point of view, focus, and organizational structure, including the effective use of transitions. • Includes a clearly presented central idea with relevant facts, details, and/or explanations.	• Includes a variety of sentence types.	• Contains few, if any, errors in the conventions of the English language (grammar, punctuation, capitalization, spelling). These errors do not interfere with the reader's understanding of the writing.
3	• Is told from a consistent first-person point of view. • Focuses mainly on one experience. • Clearly expresses the meaning of the experience.	• Addresses all parts of the writing task. • Demonstrates a general understanding of purpose and audience. • Maintains a mostly consistent point of view, focus, and organizational structure, including the effective use of some transitions. • Presents a central idea with mostly relevant facts, details, and/or explanations.	• Includes a variety of sentence types.	• Contains some errors in the conventions of the English language (grammar, punctuation, capitalization, spelling). These errors do not interfere with the reader's understanding of the writing.
2	• Is told mostly from a first-person point of view, with occasional shifts in point of view. • Focuses mostly on one experience, but contains some extraneous, unrelated information. • Makes only a vague reference to the meaning of the experience.	• Addresses only parts of the writing task. • Demonstrates little understanding of purpose and audience. • Maintains an inconsistent point of view, focus, and/or organizational structure, which may include ineffective or awkward transitions that do not unify important ideas. • Suggests a central idea with limited facts, details, and/or explanations.	• Includes little variety in sentence types.	• Contains several errors in the conventions of the English language (grammar, punctuation, capitalization, spelling). These errors may interfere with the reader's understanding of the writing.
1	• Is told from an inconsistent point of view, with confusing shifts in point of view throughout. • Includes information about several seemingly unrelated experiences. • Provides no insight into the meaning of the experience.	• Addresses only one part of the writing task. • Demonstrates no understanding of purpose and audience. • Lacks a point of view, focus, organizational structure, and transitions that unify important ideas. • Lacks a central idea but may contain marginally related facts, details, and/or explanations.	• Includes no sentence variety.	• Contains serious errors in the conventions of the English language (grammar, punctuation, capitalization, spelling). These errors interfere with the reader's understanding of the writing.

Autobiographical Narrative Writing Prompts

Students can use the writing prompt in the Student Edition or one of the following prompts.

- Change can sometimes cause chaos, confusion, and doubt. Write an autobiographical narrative about a big change in your life and how you handled it.

- Sometimes it's hard to do the right thing. Recall a time you had to choose whether to do the right thing. Write an autobiographical narrative explaining the circumstances and how you made your decision.

- What big obstacles or challenges have you had to overcome in order to be successful? Write an autobiographical narrative about an obstacle or challenge that you faced and how you overcame it.

- Life experiences often teach us important lessons that we can carry into the future. Write about a time you learned a valuable lesson. How did the experience change your perspective? How have you applied the knowledge gained from the experience? Write about what the lesson was, how you learned it, and what its effects have been.

Autobiographical Narrative

When you respond to an autobiographical narrative prompt, use the models you have read, what you have learned from writing your own autobiographical narrative, the rubric on page 228, and the steps below.

Writing Standard 2.1 Write fictional or **autobiographical narratives: a.** Develop a standard plot line (having a beginning, conflict, rising action, climax, and denouement) and point of view. **b.** Develop complex major and minor characters and a definite setting. **c.** Use a range of appropriate strategies (e.g., dialogue; suspense; naming of specific narrative action, including movement, gestures, and expressions).

Writing Prompt

Select an important experience in your life and write a narrative about it. Develop a standard plot line with a beginning, middle, and end. Your narrative should have a well-developed setting and characters, and you should use appropriate strategies, such as dialogue, descriptions of characters' actions, and suspense, to move the plot forward. Your narrative should maintain a consistent first-person point of view. The narrative should build to a climax and end with a reflection on why the experience is still meaningful to you.

Study the Prompt

Begin by reading the prompt carefully. Note what is required in your narrative: a standard plot line, a well-developed setting and characters, a consistent point of view, and a final reflection on the meaning of the experience.
Tip: Spend about five minutes studying the prompt.

Plan Your Response

Think of some personal experiences that are important to you. Which of these would you feel comfortable writing about? Once you have settled on your subject,

- write down who was involved, what happened, when it happened, where it happened, why it happened, how it happened, and why it is still meaningful to you
- think about your purpose and audience
- list the events in the order that they occurred

Tip: Spend about fifteen minutes planning your response.

Respond to the Prompt

Using the notes you have just made, draft your narrative. Follow these guidelines:

- In the introduction, use interesting dialogue or a question, statement, or description to grab the reader's attention and set up the main conflict. Create a definite setting.
- In the body, relate events in the order that they occurred. Develop characters using a range of narrative strategies, such as dialogue and descriptions of expressions and gestures.
- In the conclusion, summarize your experience, emphasizing why it is still meaningful.

As you are writing, remember to use words that are best for your audience—not too informal. Write as neatly as you can. If your narrative cannot be read easily, it may not be scored. **Tip:** Spend about twenty minutes writing your draft.

Improve Your Response

Revising Go back over key aspects of the narrative. Did you develop a standard plot line and maintain a consistent point of view? Did you develop characters using appropriate strategies? Did you explain the event's importance to you?

Proofreading Take a few minutes to proofread your narrative to correct errors in grammar, spelling, punctuation, and capitalization. Make sure all your edits are neat, and erase any stray marks.

Checking Your Final Copy Read your narrative one more time to catch any errors you may have missed.
Tip: Save five to ten minutes to improve your paper.

Preteach

Speak with a Purpose Remind students that a spoken autobiographical narrative is simply a longer version of a significant life event told to someone else. Ask them what they have been most excited to tell their friends, family members, or classmates about. Perhaps they have shared personal successes or told someone how they spent a special occasion.

Direct Teach

Model the Skill

Adapt Your Narrative

Guide students in analyzing and adapting the words in their written autobiographical narratives so that they sound like natural speech. For example, students may want to change the formal structure of the phrase *I am* to the more informal contraction, *I'm.* Suggest that students read their written narratives aloud to themselves to identify any awkward or stilted phrasing.

Presenting an Autobiographical Narrative

Speak with a Purpose

Adapt your written autobiographical narrative into an oral presentation. Practice your presentation, and then present it to your class.

Think as a Reader/Writer Presenting an autobiographical narrative orally requires much of the same kind of thought and preparation as was required to write the narrative. For an oral autobiographical narrative, however, you must decide what aspects of your written narrative to keep, discard, emphasize, or deemphasize. Also, you will be able to use movement, gestures, and facial expressions to convey specific narrative action and emotions of major and minor characters.

Adapt Your Narrative

Tell Them About It

Your audience will be your classmates. As you adapt your written narrative, keep your audience's backgrounds and interests in mind. Organize your presentation to gain the most appeal and interest. Also, decide what the **purpose** of your presentation will be and what effect you want your narrative to have. Keep details and events that are critical to your audience's understanding and enjoyment. Discard parts of your narrative that might confuse your audience or be too minor for an oral presentation. Here are some additional points to consider:

- **Word Choice** Think about how the words you've written will sound. Avoid slang, yet be sure that your speech sounds natural.
- **Context, Plot, and Point of View** Do not confuse your listeners; help your audience follow your narrative easily. Review your written narrative, and retain elements that establish a **context** for your narrative. Consider which events make up a **standard plot line** (that is, a **beginning, conflict, rising action, climax,** and **denoument**). Also, is your **point of view** clear (will listeners be confused about who is thinking or saying what)?
- **Descriptions** Make sure you have included descriptions of the **complex major and minor characters** that bring them to life. Check that you have established a **definite setting.**
- **Interest-adding Strategies** Find places in your narrative to incorporate **dialogue, suspense,** and **specific narrative action** that you can describe or act out using **facial expressions, gestures,** and **movement.** Listeners want to be drawn into a narrative—using these strategies will engage and entertain your audience.

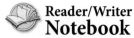

Reader/Writer Notebook

Use your **RWN** to complete the activities for this workshop.

Resources

UA: Holt Interactive Writer and Speaker, on-level practice and assessment

UA: Differentiating Instruction, modified lesson plans, p. 41

Teacher One Stop™, on-level lesson plans and all print resources

Listening and Speaking Standards
1.4 Organize information to achieve particular purposes and to appeal to the background and interests of the audience.
1.5 Arrange supporting details, reasons, descriptions, and examples effectively and persuasively in relation to the audience.
1.6 Use speaking techniques, including voice modulation, inflection, tempo, enunciation, and eye contact, for effective presentations.
2.1 Deliver narrative presentations: **a.** Establish a context, standard plot line (having a beginning, conflict, rising action, climax, and denouement), and point of view. **b.** Describe complex major and minor characters and a definite setting. **c.** Use a range of appropriate strategies, including dialogue, suspense, and naming of specific narrative action (e.g., movement, gestures, expressions).

Deliver Your Autobiographical Narrative

Bring the Experience to Life

When you give your oral presentation, you'll want to communicate the overall mood, or feeling, of your experience. You'll also want to show listeners your attitude—how you think and feel about the experience now. Concentrate on movements, gestures, and facial expressions that will help you relate mood and attitude in a vivid, believable way. In addition, use these speaking techniques to bring your experience to life for your listeners.

- **Voice Modulation** Change the tone and volume of your voice to emphasize important moments, build suspense, and show emotion.

- **Inflection** Move the pitch of your voice up or down to express shades of meaning or to share your attitude about the experience. For example, a rising inflection can show doubt, surprise, or curiosity. A falling inflection can express certainty.

- **Tempo** Change the speed at which you talk to communicate emotion. For example, you might increase your tempo when delivering a section of your narrative that involves a dangerous event.

- **Enunciation** Say each word clearly and precisely. Try not to slur your words or drop word endings. For example, don't say "I'm gonna" when you mean "I'm going to," unless you're imitating someone's dialogue.

- **Eye Contact** Make frequent eye contact with your listeners. That will make them feel as though you are talking directly to them, which will help keep their attention. You can also use eye contact for emphasis at important moments in your narrative.

Make It Noteworthy

You may be tempted simply to read your autobiographical narrative directly from a written copy of it. That approach, however, is not effective. A much better way to make sure you do not leave anything out is to use a well-organized set of notes. You can use index cards to make notes about key events and details, and you might even want to give yourself reminders about gestures to use at certain points in your narrative. You can occasionally refer to your notes as you deliver your autobiographical narrative, instead of completely losing eye contact with your audience.

> **A Good Autobiographical Narrative Presentation**
>
> - is told from a clear point of view
> - has a clear context and standard plot line
> - relates events in a clear order
> - includes vivid descriptions of complex major and minor characters
> - establishes a definite setting
> - includes strategies such as dialogue, suspense, and specific narrative action to engage the audience
> - uses speaking techniques effectively

 Speaking Tip

Rehearse your narrative several times, concentrating on a different element each time. Perform in front of a friend or relative, or record your rehearsal. Make changes based on feedback from your listener or recording.

Learn It Online
Add music and pictures to your narrative. Go to our *Digital Storytelling* mini-site at:

go.hrw.com   H7-231   **Go**

Guided Practice: Apply

Deliver Your Autobiographical Narrative

- Have students practice delivering their autobiographical narratives using note cards.

- Remind students to use short prompts on their note cards instead of writing out the whole presentation.

- Advise students to put reminders on their note cards about gestures, tone of voice and keeping eye contact with the audience.

- Remind listeners to pay attention and offer constructive, helpful comments about each presentation.

Teaching Tip

Bring the Experience to Life If students struggle to make eye contact with the audience, have them practice their narratives in small groups. Tell students to divide their narratives into a beginning, middle and conclusion. They should try to make eye contact with a different member of the group during each part of their narrative.

English for Academic Success

Remind students to use formal English when delivering their autobiographical narrative. They should use informal English, such as slang, only when a reading dialogue containing it.

Assess

UA: Holt Interactive Writer and Speaker, Autobiographical Narrative Evaluation Guide

Learn It Online
The **Digital Storytelling Mini-Site** shows students how to take a personal experience and craft it into a short film-complete with music, images, and special effects.

go.hrw.com   H7-231   **Go**

Standards Focus

Objectives

Students will

- review character
- review characterization
- review comparing and contrasting
- identify Latin roots and affixes
- review writing persuasive essays or articles

Literary Skills Review

Review

If necessary, use the following questions to guide students in their reading before they answer the questions at the end of the review.

▶ **Character**

In paragraph 1, what element of characterization does the narrator use to describe the Red Girl? ***Possible response:*** *She describes the Red Girl's physical appeareance.*

When the narrator states, "I, on the other hand, took a full bath every morning," is she using direct or indirect characterization? ***Possible response:*** *She is using indirect characterization to tell us about herself by describing her actions.*

Test-Taking Tip

Tell students to begin their tests with a positive attitude, focusing only on their own performance and not that of others.

California Standards, pp. 232–233

■ **Reading Standard 3.3** Analyze characterization as delineated through a character's thoughts, words, speech patterns, and actions; the narrator's description; and the thoughts, words, and actions of other characters.

Literary Skills Review

Character **Directions:** Read the following story. Then, answer each question that follows.

from The Red Girl by **Jamaica Kincaid**

Here is a portion of a story set in Antigua, an island in the Caribbean Sea. The narrator is a young girl named Annie John who has wanted to play with another girl she calls the Red Girl.

The Red Girl and I stood under the guava tree looking each other up and down. What a beautiful thing I saw standing before me. Her face was big and round and red, like a moon—a red moon. She had big, broad, flat feet, and they were naked to the bare ground; her dress was dirty, the skirt and blouse tearing away from each other at one side; the red hair that I had first seen standing up on her head was matted and tangled; her hands were big and fat, and her fingernails held at least ten anthills of dirt under them. And on top of that, she had such an unbelievable, wonderful smell, as if she had never taken a bath in her whole life.

I soon learned this about her: She took a bath only once a week, and that was only so that she could be admitted to her grandmother's presence. She didn't like to bathe, and her mother didn't force her. She changed her dress once a week for the same reason. She preferred to wear a dress until it just couldn't be worn anymore. Her mother didn't mind that, either. She didn't like to comb her hair, though on the first day of school, she could put herself out for that. She didn't like to go to Sunday school, and her mother didn't force her. She didn't like to brush her teeth, but occasionally her mother said it was necessary. She loved to play marbles, and was so good that only Skerritt boys now played against her. Oh, what an angel she was, and what a heaven she lived in! I, on the other hand, took a full bath every morning and a sponge bath every night. I could hardly go out on my doorstep without putting my shoes on. I was not allowed to play in the sun without a hat on my head. My mother paid a woman who lived five houses away from us sevenpence a week—a penny for each school day and twopence for Sunday—to comb my hair. On Saturday, my mother washed my hair. Before I went to sleep at night I had to make sure my uniform was

---

Resources for Skills and Standards Review

Chapter 2 Resources, Chapter Standards Mastery, Chapter Vocabulary Review

UA: Differentiating Instruction, below-level Chapter Standards Mastery, p. 57

Teacher One Stop™, editable Chapter Standards Mastery

Focus on Standards

ThinkCentral Online Assessment, Chapter Standards Mastery

ThinkCentral Online Remediation

Holt Online Essay Scoring

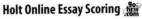

clean and creaseless and all laid out for the next day. I had to make sure that my shoes were clean and polished to a nice shine. I went to Sunday school every Sunday unless I was sick. I was not allowed to play marbles, and, as for Skerritt boys, that was hardly mentionable.

1. Which of the following character traits does the narrator imply about the Red Girl?
- **A** She takes care of her only dress.
- **B** She spends too much time on her hair.
- **C** She is not interested in bathing.
- **D** She is always neat and clean.

2. In this passage from "The Red Girl," the narrator uses all of the following methods of characterization *except*
- **A** stating character traits directly.
- **B** quoting speech.
- **C** describing actions.
- **D** describing appearance.

Read this sentence from the passage.

> She took a bath only once a week, and that was only so that she could be admitted to her grandmother's presence.

3. In this sentence the grandmother can *best* be described as
- **A** indifferent.
- **B** angry.
- **C** happy-go-lucky.
- **D** strict.

4. The narrator describes the Red Girl by revealing
- **A** the girl's actions.
- **B** the girl's thoughts.
- **C** others' opinions of her.
- **D** the girl's words.

5. From the narrator's description of herself, you can infer that
- **A** she likes to wear her school uniform.
- **B** she is embarrassed for the Red Girl.
- **C** she longs for a life like the Red Girl's.
- **D** she'd like to play with the Skerritt boys.

6. The narrator tells you directly how she feels about the Red Girl when she says
- **A** "Her fingernails held at least ten anthills of dirt under them."
- **B** "She didn't like to go to Sunday school."
- **C** "Her face was big and round and red."
- **D** "What a beautiful thing I saw standing before me."

Timed Writing

7. Why do you think the narrator admires the Red Girl so much? Write a paragraph explaining whether you agree or disagree with the narrator's opinion of the Red Girl. Make sure you include strong examples of the narrator's descriptions as support.

Chapter Review

Review Literary Skills Focus

1. Have students look back through the chapter to find the meanings of the terms listed below.

2. Have students cite passages from the chapter that illustrate the meanings of those terms.

Character; Character Trait; Characterization; Motivation.

Review Reading Skills Focus

1. Have students look back through the chapter to find the meanings of the terms listed below.

2. Have students cite passages from the chapter that illustrate the meanings of those terms.

Making Inferences; Connecting to the Text; Plot; Comparing and Contrasting Characters

Assess

Answers and Explanations

1. C *The narrator's descriptions of the Red Girl show that she is unconcerned about her appearance, not a careful dresser (A), someone who spends a lot of time on her hair (B), or neat and clean (D).*

2. B *The narrator states the Red Girl's traits directly (A), describes actions like the Red Girl looking her up and down (C), and describes her appearance (D). She does not quote speech.*

3. D *This sentence suggests the grandmother has strict views on cleanliness. If she is indifferent or happy-go-lucky (A, C) it would not matter if the girl took a bath. If she is angry (B) she might outright refuse to see the girl at all.*

4. A *The girl's actions are described, but her thoughts and words are not revealed (B, D), nor are the opinions of other people (C).*

5. C *The narrator wishes that she did not have to follow so many rules in her own life. She does not mention liking her school uniform or being embarassed for the Red Girl (A, B). She only says that she cannot be around the Skerritt boys, not that she necessarily would like to play with them (D).*

6. D *"What a beautiful thing. . ." is the narrator's directly stated opinion of the Red Girl. Choices A, B, and C just state facts about the Red Girl.*

Timed Writing

7. *I think that the narrator likes the Red Girl because the Red Girl is able to do as she pleases and plays with the boys. My parents aren't as strict as the narrator's, but I can still understand her opinion. I think I'd like the Red Girl, too.*

Reteach

 ThinkCentral Online Remediation

If necessary, use the following questions to guide students in their reading before they answer the questions at the end of the review.

▶ **Text Structures**

What is the difference between the structure of a textbook and the structure of a newspaper article? *A textbook is many pages and contains an index and glossary; a newspaper article is one or a few pages and contains a headline, byline, and date.*

How is the instructional manual laid out? Is this typical of such texts? Explain. ***Possible response:*** *It is laid out in a series of steps for the user to follow. This is typical of manuals that I've seen, and it makes sense, because manuals tell readers how to carry out a task, and tasks are most easily explained in steps.*

▶ **Purpose of a Text**

What is the purpose of an instructional manual? *It explains how to do something.*

Test-Taking Tip

Tell students to review the questions and their answers after they have finished the test and to make any corrections needed. Remind them not to change their answers unless they know they are incorrect.

 California Standards, pp. 234–235

■ **Reading Standard 2.1** Understand and analyze the differences in structure and purpose between various categories of informational materials (e.g., textbooks, newspapers, instructional manuals, signs).

Informational Skills Review

Structure and Purpose of Texts **Directions:** Read the following informational texts. Then, answer each question that follows.

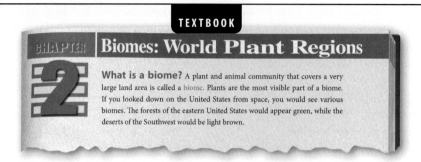

TEXTBOOK

CHAPTER 2

Biomes: World Plant Regions

What is a biome? A plant and animal community that covers a very large land area is called a biome. Plants are the most visible part of a biome. If you looked down on the United States from space, you would see various biomes. The forests of the eastern United States would appear green, while the deserts of the Southwest would be light brown.

NEWSPAPER ARTICLE

B2

Hatteras Lighthouse Completes Its Move

BUXTON, N.C., July 9 (AP)—As onlookers clapped and cheered, the Cape Hatteras Lighthouse slid today onto the concrete pad where its caretakers hope it will stand for another century, a safe distance from the thundering Atlantic surf.

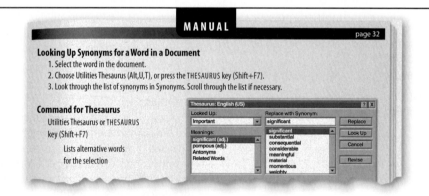

MANUAL

page 32

Looking Up Synonyms for a Word in a Document
1. Select the word in the document.
2. Choose Utilities Thesaurus (Alt,U,T), or press the THESAURUS key (Shift+F7).
3. Look through the list of synonyms in Synonyms. Scroll through the list if necessary.

Command for Thesaurus
Utilities Thesaurus or THESAURUS key (Shift+F7)

  Lists alternative words for the selection

1. Which statement explains the difference between the purpose of a textbook and the purpose of a newspaper article?

   A A textbook has an index, a glossary, and graphic features, while a newspaper article has an inverted pyramid structure.

   B A textbook has a table of contents and an index, while a newspaper article has a headline, a dateline, and a byline.

   C A textbook presents information and questions about a main subject, while a newspaper article gives information about a current event.

   D A textbook has many pages, while a newspaper article is usually one page long or less.

2. In comparing the structure of a textbook and the structure of an instructional manual, you could say that a textbook

   A has a longer table of contents than an instructional manual.

   B presents information about a broad subject, but an instructional manual presents information on how to operate a device.

   C is used in the classroom, but a manual is used at home.

   D is provided to you by your school, while a manual comes with something you buy.

3. In the textbook excerpt on the opposite page, the definition of the word *biome* appears in the

   A text.

   B index.

   C caption.

   D table of contents.

4. If the directions in an instructional manual have steps, the steps

   A must be read first.

   B do not need to be read.

   C should be followed in order.

   D will appear in the glossary.

5. The excerpt from the newspaper article on the opposite page shows all of the following features *except* a

   A byline.

   B dateline.

   C page number.

   D headline.

Timed Writing

6. Explain the purpose of having diagrams and indexes in instructional manuals.

Answers and Explanations

1. **C** *Items A and B both describe features of texts, not purposes. Item D describes differences in structure.*

2. **A** *Item B tells the purpose of a textbook and an informational manual. Both books might be used in a classroom (C). Item D says nothing about the structure of the books.*

3. **A** *The textbook excerpt states that a biome is a plant and animal community covering a very large area. Items B, C, and D do not appear in the excerpt.*

4. **C** *If an instructional manual has numbered steps, it is because the task must be carried out in a specific order. Though it is wise to read the steps first (A), and the reader should not ignore them (B), it is most important that the steps are followed in order. A glossary contains definitions, not steps in a task (D).*

5. **A** *The newspaper article contains a dateline, "July 9" (B), the page number, B2 (C), and a headline, "Hatteras Lighthouse Completes Its Move" (D). It does not contain a byline giving the author of the article and his or her position.*

Timed Writing

6. *An instructional manual contains diagrams to help the reader gain a visual understanding of what he or she has read. It has an index to help the reader locate information.*

ThinkCentral Online Remediation

Word-Attack Skills Mini-Lesson

Review Use the activities below to check students' grasp of the word-attack skills taught in this chapter.

Activity Display these sets of words. Have students identify the two words in which the letter *c* is pronounced the same. Answers are underlined.

1. focus   content   produce
2. cereal   canteen   advice
3. presence   combed   cleaned
4. construct   icing   finance

Activity Display this list of words containing the letter *c*. Have students tell if the underlined parts stand for /s/ or /k/.

1. topic (k)
2. function (k)
3. cymbal (s)
4. essence (s)
5. privacy (s)
6. carrot (k)

Assess

Answers and Explanations

1. A Decent *means "good, moral."*

2. C Recognize *means "to recall previous knowledge." The prefix* re– *means "again".*

3. D *A satchel is a type of bag. A trunk is a different type of container (C), while A and B are not bags.*

4. B *The Latin root* liber *means "free," while* liberal *can mean "greater freedom and a less strict interpretation of rules."*

5. D *An inscription is writing found on a surface. The Latin root* scribo *means "to write."*

6. A *When you dedicate something, you are honoring a person or idea.*

Academic Vocabulary

7. C *The narrator realized the painter's good traits. Compliments, responses, and opinions are not synonyms of* attributes.

 WordSharp: An Interactive Vocabulary Tutor

Reteach

 ThinkCentral Online Remediation

🐻 **California Standards, p. 236**

■ **Reading Standard 1.2** Use knowledge of Greek, Latin, and Anglo-Saxon roots and affixes to understand content-area vocabulary.

Vocabulary Skills Review

🐻 **Reading Standard 1.2** Use knowledge of Greek, **Latin**, and Anglo-Saxon **roots and affixes to understand content-area vocabulary.**

Latin Roots and Affixes   Directions: Each question features a word from "The War of the Wall." Choose the correct answer.

1. Which of the following words is formed from the Latin root meaning "to be fitting" or "to be appropriate"?

   A decent

   B sole

   C creative

   D courageous

2. The word *recognized* is made by adding the Latin prefix *re–* to a word root meaning "knowledge; understanding." The Latin prefix *re–* most nearly means

   A "before."

   B "forward."

   C "again."

   D "not."

3. Which of the following words comes from the Latin word meaning "bag" or "sack"?

   A notebook

   B capture

   C trunk

   D satchel

4. The Latin root of the word *liberation* means "to free." Which of the following words comes from the same root?

   A deliberate

   B liberal

   C possible

   D reliable

5. Which of the following words comes from the Latin root meaning "to write"?

   A scrimp

   B wrist

   C interpretation

   D inscription

6. Which of the following words is formed from the Latin root meaning "to devote; to declare"?

   A dedicate

   B interest

   C dead

   D independence

Academic Vocabulary

Directions: Use context clues to determine the meaning of the Academic Vocabulary word below.

7. The narrator of "The War of the Wall" did not recognize the painter's positive *attributes* until the mural was revealed.

   A compliments

   B responses

   C traits

   D opinions

Vocabulary Review

Use this activity to assess whether students have retained the chapter Vocabulary. Ask them to choose the word from the box that best completes each sentence.

electives	integration	inscription
opponents	propelled	

1. _____ of the proposed plan of action argued that it would be too costly. [*Opponents*]

2. The _____ on the memorial contained a famous quotation. [*inscription*]

3. The nation's first _____ of blacks and whites on a high school football team marked a major achievement in the civil rights struggle. [*integration*]

4. Along with the courses she needed to take, Carol's schedule included _____. [*electives*]

5. The rain _____ them to cancel the picnic. [*propelled*]

Writing Skills Review

Autobiographical Narrative   Directions: Read the following paragraph. Then, answer each question that follows.

Writing Standard 2.1 Write fictional or autobiographical narratives: a. Develop a standard plot line (having a beginning, conflict, rising action, climax, and denouement) and point of view. b. Develop complex major and minor characters and a definite setting. c. Use a range of appropriate strategies (e.g., dialogue; suspense; naming of specific narrative action, including movement, gestures, and expressions).

(1) The day I had been dreading for months finally arrived. (2) It was a wet, cold February morning when I saw the moving vans pull up to our driveway. (3) We were leaving the only home I had ever known, the place where I had built a lifetime of memories. (4) The movers were wearing slickers to keep the rain off. (5) I heard my mother giving instructions to the movers, anxiously telling them to be careful with the baby's crib. (6) As I made a tour of the place, the rooms appeared vacant. (7) All the pictures and curtains had been taken down; the furniture was covered with sheets; the books and breakable objects had been packed away. (8) I knew that I would make new friends and have fun in the years ahead, but nothing would replace the memories of my first home.

1. What could the writer add to further develop the conflict in this autobiographical narrative?
   - A the effect of the move on other members of the family
   - B a description of some of the narrator's special memories
   - C treasured objects broken during the move
   - D reactions of the neighbors

2. Which of the following sentences is unnecessary and should be deleted?
   - A sentence 3
   - B sentence 4
   - C sentence 7
   - D sentence 8

3. If the narrator were to add dialogue, it would probably come after
   - A sentence 5.
   - B sentence 6.
   - C sentence 7.
   - D sentence 8.

4. Which of the following sentences is the best replacement for sentence 6?
   - A As I entered each room, I found it empty.
   - B As I revisited the rooms, the floorboards creaked.
   - C As I moved around the empty house, I was grief-stricken.
   - D As I walked through the rooms, the house seemed to have lost its life.

5. The tone of this story is
   - A cheerful.
   - B reflective and sad.
   - C sullen and gloomy.
   - D angry and resentful.

Writing Skills Review

Assess

Answers and Explanations

1. **B** *The effect of the move on other members of the family (A) and the reactions of neighbors (D) do not belong in a personal narrative. Because the narrator has not yet moved, mentioning objects broken during the move (C) would be out of place.*

2. **B** *Knowing that the movers were wearing slickers is irrelevant to the main idea of the narrative. Choices A, C, and D all help to convey the narrator's feelings about the move.*

3. **A** *In sentence 5, the narrator hears her mother giving instructions to the movers. Dialogue would be out of place after sentences 6 (B), 7 (C), or 8 (D).*

4. **D** *Sentence 6 does not say that the floorboards creaked (B) or that the narrator is grief-stricken (C). While choice A is a simple restatement of sentence 6, the phrase "seemed to have lost its life" in choice D makes the sentence come alive.*

5. **B** *The tone of this story is reflective and sad, but not sullen (C). The narrator is not angry and resentful (D), nor is she cheerful (A).*

Reteach

ThinkCentral Online Remediation

California Standards, p. 237

- **Writing Standard 2.1** Write fictional or autobiographical narratives: a. Develop a standard plot line (having a beginning, conflict, rising action, climax, and denouement) and point of view. b. Develop complex major and minor characters and a definite setting. c. Use a range of appropriate strategies (e.g., dialogue; suspense; naming of specific narrative action, including movement, gestures, and expressions).

Application Homework
Fictional Personal Narrative

Challenge students to write a personal narrative from the point of view of a fictional character. Tell students that their fictional character might experience an event very similar to something that students have experienced in real life, but the character should have unique traits and qualities that make his or her interpretation of the event unique. Remind students to convey their character's thoughts and feelings through first-person narration.

Extension Homework
Examination of an Autobiography

For homework, have students read an autobiographical essay or portions of an autobiography of a modern or historical figure of their choice. As they read, tell students to take notes about the structure and style of the autobiography. Then, have students write an essay examining how the author conveyed elements of his or her life. Tell students to explain which elements they found most and least effective.

If students enjoyed the themes and topics explored in this chapter, you might recommend these titles for independent reading.

Assessment Options

The following projects can help you evaluate and assess your students' outside work. Videotapes or audiotapes of completed projects may be included in students' portfolios.

Write a "What-If" Scenario

■ Students who choose to read *MindBenders* may want to explore "what-if" scenarios from their own imaginations. Tell students that their scenarios are not limited to the present time or location; they can be as creative as students desire.

■ Have students brainstorm scenarios and select one about which to write a brief fictional story.

Research and Compare Diseases

■ If students enjoy *Fever 1793*, they may be interested in researching yellow fever and the effect it has had at different times in history.

■ Students may present their research to the class by making and sharing a chart comparing and contrasting the effects of yellow fever with those of the bubonic plague that they read about in the Informational Text Focus.

Read On

For Independent Reading

Fiction

Adam of the Road

It's the summer of 1294. Adam, an eleven-year-old minstrel who has lost contact with his father, is frustrated by another minstrel named Jankin, who steals his dog, Nick. In this adventure set in the Middle Ages, Adam scours the English countryside in search of the two things that mean the most to him—his father and his dog. Along the way, he meets some interesting friends and learns a few lessons. Read to find out more in Elizabeth Janet Gray's Newbery Award–winning historical novel.

MindBenders

What if you get on the bad side of a Hawaiian volcano goddess? Could you imagine being struck by lightning and finding yourself 140 years in the past? What would you do if you woke up one morning and saw seven guardian angels having a chat in your bedroom? Neal Shusterman presents these wacky situations and more in *MindBenders*.

Fever 1793

The deadly illness in *Fever 1793* is yellow fever—a disease that killed thousands annually until its deadly agent, the mosquito, was identified. The eighteenth-century outbreak finds fourteen-year-old Mattie trapped in the city with her sick mother. Mattie escapes to the country, but within the span of a few horrific months, she must grow from a sullen teenager into a courageous adult. Laurie Halse Anderson's award-winning novel takes you to a time when there were no modern medicines and death could come from an insect's bite.

Tangerine

Paul feels self-conscious about the thick glasses he has to wear, but he knows he can play on the toughest soccer team in Tangerine County, Florida. Other people, including his sinister brother, have their doubts. Can Paul triumph on and off the field? *Tangerine* by Edward Bloor will have you rooting Paul on!

Word Counts and Readabilities of Read On Books

Fiction	Estimated Word Counts	Readability
Adam of the Road	59,000	Accessible
MindBenders	33,000	Easily Accessible
Tangerine	90,090	Accessible
Fever 1793	49,808	Accessible

Nonfiction

Murals: Walls That Sing

Learn about neighborhood murals in *Murals: Walls That Sing* by George Ancona. The book is a photo essay about the strength a mural has to bring together neighborhoods and communities. Each mural is accompanied by a description of the artist who created it and the connection the artist has to the community.

Bill Nye the Science Guy's Great Big Book of Science: Featuring Oceans and Dinosaurs

From Bill Nye, the author and Emmy Award–winning TV star, comes this collection of fascinating facts and twenty-four easy-to-follow experiments. You may be saying to yourself, "What do oceans and dinosaurs have to do with each other?" Well, you'll have to read *Bill Nye the Science Guy's Great Big Book of Science: Featuring Oceans and Dinosaurs* to get the answer to that question and many more.

Pride of Puerto Rico: The Life of Roberto Clemente

Baseball is a beloved game far beyond the United States. The admiration for the game is due in part to people's interest in its heroic players, such as the subject of *Pride of Puerto Rico: The Life of Roberto Clemente* by Paul Robert Walker. This biography will introduce you to Clemente, a man who was as proud of his family and country (both the native and the adopted) as he was of his baseball career.

Black Heroes of the American Revolution

During the nation's war for independence from Britain, people from all walks of life took up arms to protect the newly born United States. In *Black Heroes of the American Revolution*, Burke Davis tells the stories of the black soldiers, sailors, spies, scouts, guides, and wagon drivers who bravely faced danger for the country they called their own.

Learn It Online
Continue your learning through further reading. Find tips for choosing, reading, and studying novels at:

go.hrw.com | H7-239 | **Go**

Assessment Options
Perform a Science Experiment

- Encourage students who read *Bill Nye the Science Guy's Great Big Book of Science: Featuring Oceans and Dinosaurs* to choose one of the experiments from the book to perform for the class.

- Tell students to practice their experiment before they demonstrate it for their classmates. During their demonstration, have students explain what they are doing, what they expect to happen, and why the experiment works the way it does.

Create a Mural Representation

- If the murals in George Ancona's photo essay *Murals: Walls That Sing* spark students' interest, they may want to find out more about the murals or the artists who created them.

- Suggest that students choose one mural or muralist from the book to research further. Have them briefly share their findings with the class or in small groups.

- Students who are artistically inclined may also wish to paint or draw their own "mini-mural," a representation of the type of mural that would be found on a community wall.

Nonfiction	Estimated Word Counts	Readability
Murals: Walls That Sing	4,632	Easily Acccessible
Bill Nye the Science Guy's Great Big Book of Science	5,700	Easily Accessible
Pride of Puerto Rico: The Life of Roberto Clemente	30, 905	Accessible
Black Heroes of the American Revolution	12,672	Accessible

 Learn It Online
The **NovelWise** mini-site includes instruction on choosing, reading, and analyzing novels; it also contains a catalogue of book summaries, study guides, teaching guides, and PowerPoint presentations.

go.hrw.com | H7-239 | **Go**

Theme

3

Features highlighted in **yellow** constitute a suggested minimum course of study.

Introducing The Skills

Selection or Feature	For Independent Reading	Grade–Level Standards
Literary Skills Focus: What is Theme?		**Reading Standard 3.4:** Theme
Reading Skills Focus: How Do I Identify and Analyze Theme?		**Reading Standard 3.4:** Theme
Reading Model: Hearts and Hands by O. Henry (Accessible, Lexile 830) **Skills in Action:** Wrap Up	• **The Gift of the Magi** by O. Henry	**Reading Standard 3.4:** Theme

Applying The Skills

Selection or Feature	For Independent Reading	Grade–Level Standards
The Highwayman by Alfred Noyes (Accessible, Lexile N/A)	• **Music that Happens: Poems that Tell Stories** by Paul Janeczko • **The Secret Garden** by Frances Hodgson Burnett	**Reading Standard 3.4:** Theme **Reading Standard 1.1:** Identify idioms, analogies, metaphors, and similes
User Friendly by T. Ernesto Bethancourt (Accessible, Lexile 600)	• **Airborn** by Keith Oppel • **Knots in my Yo-Yo String** by Jerry Spinelli	**Reading Standard 3.4:** Theme **Reading Standard 1.1:** Identify idioms, analogies, metaphors, and similes
Annabel Lee by Edgar Allan Poe (Challenging, Lexile N/A)	• **Honey, I Love and Other Poems** by Eloise Greenfield • **How to Write Poetry** by Paul Janeczko	**Reading Standard 3.4:** Theme
Echo and Narcissus by Roger Lancelyn Green (Challenging, Lexile 1100)	• **The Fabrics of Fairytale: Stories Spun from Far and Wide** by Tanya Robyn Batt • **The Lion, the Witch, and the Wardrobe** by C.S. Lewis	**Reading Standard 3.4:** Theme
The Only Girl in the World for Me by Bill Cosby (Accessible, Lexile 860)	• **Voice that Challenged a Nation: Marian Anderson and the Struggle for Equal Rights** by Russell Freedman • **When I Was Your Age: Original Stories About Growing Up, Volume 1**	**Reading Standard 3.4:** Theme **Reading Standard 1.1:** Identify idioms, analogies, metaphors, and similes
Comparing Texts: Comparing Themes Across Works • **Hum** by Naomi Shahib Nye (Accessible, Lexile 840) • **Antaeus** by Borden Deal (Accessible, Lexile 1010)	• **19 Varieties of Gazelles** by Naomi Shahib Nye • **Seedfolks** by Paul Fleischman	**Reading Standard 3.4:** Theme
Informational Text Focus: Tracing an Author's Argument or Perspective • **Canines to the Rescue** by Jonah Goldberg (Challenging, Lexile 1210) • **Tribute to the Dog** by George Graham Vest (Challenging, Lexile 1170)		**Reading Standard 2.4:** Author's argument, point of view, or perspective

Selection or Feature	Grade–Level Standards
Writing Workshop: Response to Literature	**Writing Standard 2.2:** Write responses to literature.
Preparing for Timed Writing: Response to Literature	**Writing Standard 2.2:** Write responses to literature.
Listening and Speaking Workshop: Presenting a Response to Literature	**Listening and Speaking Standard 1.4:** Organize information. **Listening and Speaking Standard 1.5:** Use persuasive details. **Listening and Speaking Standard 1.6:** Use speaking techniques. **Listening and Speaking Standard 2.4:** Deliver persuasive presentations.
Standards Practice: Literary Skills Review Informational Skills Review Vocabulary Skills Review Writing Skills Review	**Reading Standard 3.4:** Theme **Reading Standard 2.4:** Author's argument, point of view, or perspective **Reading Standard 1.1:** Identify idioms, analogies, metaphors, and similes **Writing Standard 2.2:** Write responses to literature

Daily and Weekly Support

 Reader/Writer Notebook

 Reading and Writing Transparencies

 Weekly Standards Review Transparencies

 Family Involvement Activities in Five Languages

 Language Handbook Worksheets

Holt Virtual File Cabinet for Language Arts

Spelling Lessons and Activities

Assessment Resources

 Chapter 3 Resources, Chapter Diagnostic Test; Selection Standards Checks, Chapter Standards Mastery

Universal Access: Differentiating Instruction, leveled assessment

 Formal Assessment, Progress Monitoring Test 3

 English-Language Conventions Progress-Monitoring Test, Chapters 1–9, 13

ThinkCentral Online Assessment

Print Resources for Universal Access

	On-Level Learners	English Learners	Struggling Readers/Writers	Students Who Use African American Vernacular English	Advanced Learners	Students with Disabilities
Chapter 3 Resources practice and assessment for all selections and features	✔				✔	
Universal Access: Holt Interactive Reader interactive readings for Minimum-Course-of-Study Selections		✔	✔	✔		✔
Holt Interactive Reader for English Language Development adaptations of Minimum-Course-of-Study Selections		✔				
Universal Access: Differentiating Instruction modified lesson plans, graphic organizers, and leveled assessment		✔	✔	✔		✔
Universal Access: Resources for Teaching Advanced Students modified lesson plans for Minimum-Course-of-Study Selections					✔	
Universal Access: Supporting Instruction in Five Languages translations of selection summaries and key terms		✔				
Universal Access: Holt Interactive Writer and Speaker practice and assessment	✔	✔	✔	✔	✔	✔
Language and Sentence Skills Practice for Warriner's Handbook Chapters 1–9, 13	✔				✔	
Universal Access: Developmental Language and Sentence Skills Practice for Warriner's Handbook Chapters 1–9, 13		✔	✔	✔		✔

Technology Resources

Find all of Holt's technology resources at go.hrw.com. Technology resources are also listed at point of use in the wrap; below are our featured components for Chapter 3.

Teacher Management Resources

ThinkCentral, Teacher Access
Teacher One Stop™
Holt Professional Learning for Language Arts

Spotlight on Teacher One Stop™

The Teacher One Stop™ contains all of the print resources that you will need when using *Holt Literature and Language Arts*.
- Find a PDF version of the Teacher's Edition for the times you do not have Internet access available.
- Use Puzzle Pro to create fun vocabulary practice activities for your students.

Student Edition Support

PowerNotes
ThinkCentral, Student Access
Student One Stop™
Interactive Reading Workshops
Interactive Graphic Organizers
Writers' Lives
Holt Audio Library
Holt Audio Library: Selections and Summaries in Spanish

Spotlight on Interactive Reading Workshops

Give your students more practice with magazine articles that use comparison and contrast through this interactive reading workshop. Students can answer pop-up questions and take a poll, and their answers will be reported to you.

Universal Access: Struggling readers will benefit from this additional, motivational practice.

Supported Strands: Reading, Vocabulary

Student Edition Extension Activities

Digital Storytelling Mini-Site
NovelWise Mini-Site
MediaScope Mini-Site
WordSharp: An Interactive Vocabulary Tutor
GrammarNotes
WritingNotes
Writing and Research in a Digital Age
Literature Links
Holt Audio Tutor for English Language Development

Spotlight on Digital Storytelling

The site walks students through the step-by-step process of creating digital stories—personal narratives recorded aloud, and enhanced by video, pictures, music, and artifacts.

Universal Access: Advanced learners in particular may appreciate an opportunity to work in new media.

Supported Strand: Writing

Assessment Resources

ThinkCentral Online Assessment
Holt Online Essay Scoring
ThinkCentral Online Remediation

5. When a writer uses a **first-person narrator**, the story —

○ A   does not contain dialogue between the characters
→ ○ B   is told by one of the characters
○ C   does not contain a main character
○ D   has only one character

Correct Answer: B

7.1.5
point of view

Spotlight on ThinkCentral Online Assessment

Preview and assign the Chapter 3 Diagnostic and Summative tests here.

The wrap for these selections includes specific ideas and strategies from *Holt Literature and Language Arts* authors.

From the Author

For Writing Workshop: Response to Literature, *p. 354*

When we read a piece of literature together, I copy short excerpts on a transparency and make copies for the students to glue into their Reader/Writer Notebooks. After we've read the piece of literature as a whole, I ask students to respond to excerpts by writing anything that it brings to mind for them. Pulling out short passages and showing students how to respond to them encourages and teaches them how to pay attention to the gifts of story, character, language, the craft of writing, and/or the personal connections that authors offer us by, and in, their writing.

Linda Rief

Teacher to Teacher

Preteach To teach theme, I go through picture books to find one suitable for my current student population. There are Cinderella stories from every culture, and many short interesting tales of heroism or the importance of family.

Charlyn Earp
San Diego, California

Direct Teach: I read a picture book with a strong theme, like *The Rough-Face Girl* by Rafe Martin (an Algonquin Cinderella story). We discuss author's purpose and message, and brainstorm ideas. I ask students to think of other themes from books or stories they are reading or have read. Then, I pass out independent reading books from my bookshelf or titles of stories and books on strips of paper (for example, Grimm's fairytales). In pairs, students find and note themes based on a brief perusing of the backs and inside pages of books or from prior knowledge of titles. Students pass around the resources until every pair has analyzed six to seven titles. Then in groups of four, the pairs share and compare, and we discuss again as a class.

Assessment In groups of four, students create a new story outline with two themes. Students must show how their plots will support the themes.

Holt Professional Learning

Strategies for Helping Struggling Readers
with Kylene Beers

Visit the ThinkCentral, Teacher Access to link to Holt's Professional Learning site for English/Language Arts teachers. This site features:

- Videos that share the insights of *Holt Literature and Language Arts* program authors and consultants and demonstrate proven classroom strategies with master teachers
- Study guides for publications by our authors and consultants
- Informative articles and useful Web links
- Help in planning your department's professional learning sessions
- A handbook for new teachers

VIDEO PRODUCTS

Strategies for Helping Struggling Readers
with Kylene Beers

Effective Vocabulary Instruction
with Carol Jago and Kylene Beers

Developing Critical Thinking About Literature
with Carol Jago and Deborah Appleman

Teaching Students to Revise, Not Recopy
with Linda Rief

Teaching English Learners
with Robin Scarcella

Using Literature Circles
with Harvey Daniels

Teaching On-Demand Writing Skills
with Leila Christenbury

Managing the Heterogeneous Classroom
with Leila Christenbury and Patrick Schwarz

Teaching Narrative and Expository Texts
with Judith Irvin and Deborah Appleman

Becoming a Tech-Savvy Teacher
with Sara Kajder

Re-engaging the Disengaged Student
with Alfred Tatum

Teaching Grammar in Context
with Amy Benjamin

California Standards

Word Analysis, Fluency, and Systematic Vocabulary Development

- **1.1** Identify idioms, analogies, metaphors, and similes in prose and poetry.

Reading Comprehension (Focus on Informational Materials)

- **2.4** Identify and trace the development of an author's argument, point of view, or perspective in text.

Literary Response and Analysis

- **3.4** Identify and analyze recurring themes across works (e.g., the value of bravery, loyalty, and friendship; the effects of loneliness).

Writing Applications (Genres and Their Characteristics)

- **2.2** Write responses to literature:
  - **a.** Develop interpretations exhibiting careful reading, understanding, and insight.
  - **b.** Organize interpretations around several clear ideas, premises, or images from the literary work.
  - **c.** Justify interpretations through sustained use of examples and textual evidence.

Analyzing Visuals

Susan Bower (1953–) is a contemporary English artist. She has received many accolades and awards for her oil paintings, including the Gourley Memorial Award in 2000. Her style of painting has been described as spontaneous and unconventional.

Extension Activity Ask students to describe what is happening between the two figures in the painting. How does the painting relate to the quotation on the opposite page? ***Possible response:*** *The man is declaring his love for the woman by offering her the moon and the stars. The woman accepts his love but turns away from his gifts. Like the quotation, the woman does not need gifts or other physical objects to accept the man's love.*

Unit Resources

On Course: Mapping Instruction

Chapter 3 Resources

Warriner's Handbook
- Chapter 5, The Phrase
- Chapter 6, The Clause
- Chapter 7, Kinds of Sentence Structure

PowerNotes

Teacher One Stop™

Formal Assessment, Progress Monitoring Test 3

English-Language Conentions Progress-Monitoring Tests and Answer Key

Holt Virtual File Cabinet for Language Arts, grammar, reading, and vocabulary resources

Holt Pronunciation Resources
- Phoneme Sounds and Spellings
- Support for Speakers of African American Vernacular English

ThinkCentral Online Assessment

ThinkCentral Online Remediation

Theme

INFORMATIONAL TEXT FOCUS

Tracing an Author's Argument or Perspective

 California Standards

Here are the Grade 7 standards you will work toward mastering in Chapter 3.

Word Analysis, Fluency, and Systematic Vocabulary Development
1.1 Identify idioms, analogies, metaphors, and similes in prose and poetry.

Reading Comprehension (Focus on Informational Materials)
2.4 Identify and trace the development of an author's argument, point of view, or perspective in text.

Literary Response and Analysis
3.4 Identify and analyze recurring themes across works (e.g., the value of bravery, loyalty, and friendship; the effects of loneliness).

Writing Applications (Genres and Their Characteristics)
2.2 Write responses to literature:
   a. Develop interpretations exhibiting careful reading, understanding, and insight.
   b. Organize interpretations around several clear ideas, premises, or images from the literary work.
   c. Justify interpretations through sustained use of examples and textual evidence.

" If you live in my heart, you live rent free."

—Irish proverb

 What Do **You** Think

What makes us care about certain people? Why do we connect with some people and not with others?

Learn It Online
Examine arguments and perspectives in different media at MediaScope online:

go.hrw.com   H7-241   Go

Moon on a Stick (2004) by Susan Bower. Oil on board.

Chapter Objectives

- Students will locate and analyze elements of theme in multiple texts.

- Students will learn about a writer's use of cause and effect, find the theme of a text, and practice making predictions about texts.

- In the Informational Text Focus, students will evaluate evidence and arguments and learn about bias and stereotyping.

- At the end of the chapter, students will write and present a response to literature.

Routines for California Classrooms

For ideas on classroom practices and approaches to grouping, see the discussion of routines on pages T34–T37 of this Teacher's Edition.

What Do You Think?

What makes us care about certain people? Why do we connect with some people and not with others?

Read the quotation aloud. Then, ask students to think about what the heart commonly symbolizes. Have them explore the ideas of caring and connection by describing times when they have connected easily with a friend or family member and times when they have felt concern about another person's plight.

Real Issues, Real Experts: Professional Learning

Spotlight on . . .
Helping Struggling Readers

Poems such as "The Highwayman" and "Annabel Lee" present unfamiliar settings and complex vocabulary that students may find difficult to understand. To help you

 make these texts more accessible to all students, consider the ideas presented in this video:

In *Strategies for Helping Struggling Readers*, Holt author

Kylene Beers details easy-to-use strategies for improving your students' comprehension and fluency, enabling everyone in the class equal footing using the same selection.

Each video is accompanied by printable articles, planning materials, and a training guide for supervisors. For these resources and more, visit **Holt Professional Learning for Language Arts** by going to this page in **ThinkCentral, Teacher Access.**

Learn It Online
Use **PowerNotes** to introduce this chapter.

go.hrw.com   H7-241   Go

Literary Skills Focus

Objectives

Students will identify and analyze themes common among literary works

Preteach

Build Background Ask volunteers to describe the message that their favorite song, book, movie, or work of art sends about life. Explain that broad, general statements and messages like these are called themes.

Direct Teach

Theme

■ Tell students to go beyond what is stated directly when searching for a theme. Suggest that they consider how the characters, plot, or setting relate to real life or think about the message that a writer is trying to communicate.

■ Model identifying the theme of a familiar story or fable, such as "The Boy Who Cried Wolf." You might say, "The big idea in this story is that lying can be dangerous. That big idea is the story's theme."

■ Ask students what themes might be highlighted by authors whose subjects are war and humor. [*Ordinary people can be heroic. Laughter can heal wounds of the body and the spirit.*]

California Standards, pp. 242–243

■ **Reading Standard 3.4** Identify and analyze recurring themes across works (e.g., the value of bravery, loyalty, and friendship; the effects of loneliness).

LITERARY RESPONSE AND ANALYSIS
Literary Skills Focus

by **Linda Rief**

What Is Theme?

You tape sayings inside your locker, hang posters with words of wisdom all over your room, and post favorite sayings on your Web site. These are your insights into life—the themes by which you live. Authors share their themes by creating works that explore important ideas and reveal messages about them.

Theme

A key element of literature—of fiction, nonfiction, poetry, and drama—is theme. **Theme** is a revelation about our lives and represents the discovery of a truth about our own experience.

Themes Focus on the "Big" Ideas Literature that endures focuses on the big topics in life: understanding the nature of love, accepting responsibility, discovering the joys and problems of friendship. You usually won't find the theme of a piece of literature stated directly. Theme is what the writer wants you to discover for yourself as you share the experiences of the characters.

> T. J. kept the vision bright within us, his words shrewd and calculated toward the fulfillment of his dream.
>
> from "Antaeus" by Borden Deal

Subject Isn't Theme Theme is not the same thing as the subject, or topic, of a work. The **subject** is what the work is about and can usually be expressed in a word or two. The theme is the idea—best expressed in a complete sentence—that the author wishes to share about that subject. The following chart shows the difference between some possible subjects and themes.

Subject	Theme
Bravery	The courage to be unpopular can be one of the highest forms of bravery.
Loneliness	We can lose our sense of self when we are isolated from other people.
Family	A family's love is most important during difficult times.

Plot Isn't Theme Plot is what happens in a story. Although a story's plot reveals the theme, the plot itself is not the theme. A story's plot might be about two good friends, one of whom is bribed to betray the other but suffers the consequences. That's what *happens*. What does the story reveal to you about life, though?

Maybe it reveals that friendship is more important than money. Maybe it reveals that disloyalty is its own punishment. In a single plot, you might discover both themes, or you might see an entirely different theme instead. Consider the various themes the following plot event might suggest:

> He was walking along the railroad track, still heading South, still heading home.
>
> from "Antaeus" by Borden Deal

Resources

Chapter 3 Resources, Literary Skills Focus Skill Builder, p. 3

PowerNotes, interactive lesson presentation with activities

Teacher One Stop™, on-level lesson plans and all print resources

---

Universal Access

EL English Learners/Struggling Readers

English for Academic Success Help students learn the academic terms in the Literary Skills Focus by providing these words and their student-friendly definitions:

• **Recurring**—happening again and again

• **Subject**—topic; a person, place, thing, idea, or event that a text focuses on

• **Analyze**—to study in order to understand the parts and relationship of the parts to one another

• **Evaluate**—to examine in order to determine significance

Recurring Themes

Different writers may explore similar themes, even though the stories they create may be quite different. Part of what makes theme so powerful is that it doesn't apply only to the characters and events of a particular story. Most themes have qualities that are relevant to all readers. Thus, many themes keep appearing in a wide variety of works written in different contexts and in different genres.

Themes recur—or occur over and over again—in the stories we tell because some truths about human experience are universal, whether a story was written hundreds of years ago in a snowbound Alaskan village or typed on a laptop yesterday in Zimbabwe. Think about the theme that the following lines from a poem suggest. Since the poem deals with an important, universal topic—love—you've probably encountered similar themes in novels, short stories, movies, and other poems.

> And neither the angels in heaven above,
> Nor the demons down under the sea,
> Can ever dissever my soul from the soul
> Of the beautiful Annabel Lee—
> from "Annabel Lee"
> by Edgar Allan Poe

We recognize and respond to recurring themes even if we don't realize it. Read or watch enough romantic stories, and you'll become familiar with the theme that nothing is more important than finding true love. Read a few young adult novels about teens dealing with tough changes and painful self-discoveries, and you'll recognize the "coming of age" theme the next time you encounter it in a book or film.

Analyzing and Evaluating Theme

You may not always agree with the values expressed through certain themes. In some stories, you'll discover themes that truly speak to you and seem like important pieces of wisdom the writer has learned through hard experience. In other stories, you may feel that the writer is just giving you an overused formula that he or she doesn't even really believe. Identifying and expressing the theme in words lets you analyze it and decide if it fits with what *you* know about life.

Your Turn Analyze Theme

1. Think of a story that you know well. Identify the story's theme and what it means to you.

2. Identify a favorite saying or quotation that you think would make a good theme for a story. Explain why it has the qualities of a theme and what it conveys about life.

3. The chart below lists three very general subjects for a story. In the right column of the chart, make up a theme for each. Try to choose a recurring theme—a theme that is important enough to have occurred again and again in literature.

Subject	Recurring Theme
Money	
Animals	
Death	

 Learn It Online
Visit *NovelWise* to learn how to recognize themes in novels:

go.hrw.com H7-243 **Go**

Recurring Themes

- Remind students that certain experiences are common to everyone, regardless of culture, setting, or background. Point out that nearly everyone experiences love, loss, and the struggle to find one's place in the world.

- Work with students to brainstorm other common experiences. Choose one experience from the list, and have a volunteer suggest one way in which a person might undergo that experience. Discuss the proposed situation as a class, focusing on lessons or truths that might be learned from the experience. Identify the lessons or truths common to variations of the experience, and explain that these are recurring themes.

Check for Understanding

Your Turn
Possible responses:

1. *My favorite book is* The Hobbit, *and one of the themes from the book is that unassuming people can do great things. It is important to me because I am underestimated because I am so quiet.*

2. *I like the saying, "if at first you don't succeed, try, try again." It would make a good theme because it expresses the life truth that nothing comes easy, and most people have to work hard to get what they want.*

3. *Money: people do not need to be rich to be happy; Animals: animal friends can be more loyal than human friends; Death: dying is a part of living.*

Advanced Learners

Acceleration Have students discuss with a partner one of the selections from Chapter 1 or Chapter 2 that they read, and identify the subject and theme of the work. Then, have partners explain to the class why they chose the subject and theme they chose.

 Learn It Online
The **NovelWise** mini-site includes instruction on choosing, reading, and analyzing novels; it also contains a catalogue of book summaries, study guides, teaching guides, and PowerPoint presentations.

go.hrw.com H7-243 **Go**

Reading Skills Focus

Objectives
Students will
- find the theme of a text
- understand cause and effect
- make generalizations

Direct Teach

Build Background Ask students what they might think if a student walked into class with soaking wet hair and clothing. [*They got caught in a downpour on the way to school.*] Explain that their answers are educated guesses, or inferences. Then, ask students why the lights are on in the classroom today. [*Someone turned them on.*] Tell students that this is the cause of the lights being on in the classroom. The effect is that the lights are on.

Direct Teach

Finding the Theme
Model differentiating between theme and subject using the selection "Seventh Grade" from chapter 2. You might say, "Some topics from the selection are the first day of school and impressing a crush. But the theme of the selection is that the first day of school is a time for reinvention. How else could you state that theme?" [*You can always improve yourself.*]

California Standards, pp. 244–245

- **Reading Standard 3.4** Identify and analyze recurring themes across works (e.g., the value of bravery, loyalty, and friendship; the effects of loneliness).

Reading Skills Focus

by **Kylene Beers**

How Do I Identify and Analyze Theme?

You might think that identifying theme, noting cause-and-effect relationships (the way two events are connected), and making generalizations are unrelated skills. Yet, understanding cause-and-effect relationships can help you determine the meaning of a text. In turn, identifying a text's meaning can help you state and analyze the theme—which itself is a kind of generalization.

Finding the Theme

When you are asked to think about the theme of a work, start by considering what the theme is *not*. You have learned that theme is not the plot or the subject of a story. Theme is the truth about life that you discover from reading a story. A theme is always a complete thought that is best expressed in a sentence.

To clarify the differences between plot, subject, and theme, study the chart below. It contains an example of a familiar plot and subject and a possible theme that might emerge from such a story.

Plot	Subject	Theme
A man meets his friend after a twenty-year absence and is surprised by what he discovers.	Expectations; reunions	Meetings often don't turn out the way one expects.

A story can have more than one theme; however, one major understanding about life usually stands out strongly.

Use Story Clues

Look for clues in a story that you can combine with your own experiences to make an **inference,** or educated guess, about the theme. Ask yourself these questions:

- How has the main character changed over the course of the story? The lessons that a character learns are often a clue to the theme.
- Does the story's title reveal anything important? (Not all titles do. Some give more clues about plot than about theme.)
- Which events or scenes seem most significant? What ideas about life do they suggest?

Take Notes Record characters' meaningful comments and actions as well as ideas that strike you as important. These notes can help you track your thoughts about theme.

Say It Your Way Once you determine the theme, you will need to express it in your own words. Be sure to express a theme as a complete sentence, not a word or phrase. "Love" is a subject, not a theme; "Love cannot last when two people cannot trust each other" is a theme.

Resources

Chapter 3 Resources, Reading Skills Focus Skill Builder, p. 4

PowerNotes, interactive lesson presentation with activities

Teacher One Stop™, on-level lesson plans and all print resources

Universal Access

EL **English Learners/Struggling Readers**
English for Academic Success Provide students with additional assistance in understanding the academic vocabulary.

- Then, explain to students the difference between the word *effect* and the word *affect*.
- Tell students that *effect* is a noun that means a change that occurred as a direct result of an action by someone or something. Provide an example of an effect. For example, dirty clothes would be the effect of falling onto muddy ground. Explain that an article (*the, an*), or an adjective will often be found before the word *effect*.

Identifying Cause and Effect

You know from experience that one thing leads to another. A **cause** is an event that makes something happen. An **effect** is the result of the cause. Fiction writers use cause and effect to develop a plot. To help you identify causes and effects, ask these questions as you read:

- Why did this happen?
- What happened because of this event?

As you read, look for words that signal cause and effect, such as *resulted in, so, thus, why, because, therefore,* and *since.*

Tracing Causes and Effects Sometimes one cause in a story will have many effects. In other stories a single event triggers a **causal chain** in which each event causes another one to happen, like dominoes falling. Tracing a causal chain can be tricky; although one event may follow another, it may not really be caused by it. To figure out causes and effects, follow these steps:

- Look for what happens first. Then ask what happens *because of* that.
- Look for hidden or multiple causes and results.
- Use a graphic organizer, such as this flow chart, to record the chain of events.

If you know the reasons that things happen in a story, you may notice similar cause-and-effect patterns in other stories and in real life. You may even identify recurring themes in these patterns.

Making Generalizations

A **generalization** is a broad statement that covers several situations—that tells about something *in general*. Be careful of making generalizations without enough information, though. For example, if you read two poems that rhyme and then make the generalization that *all* poems rhyme, you'd be incorrect. Base your generalizations on multiple experiences—on all the facts that you can gather.

The generalizations you make while reading can help point you to a work's theme. As you read, ask yourself what general ideas the events of the story suggest. Stating a work's theme is itself a kind of generalization. Always try to express the theme of a work in a way that applies not just to the work, but also to situations in real life.

Your Turn Apply Reading Skills

1. List two strategies that can help you find the theme of a story.
2. Create a chart that identifies cause-and-effect relationships in the following scenario: You sleep through your alarm, are late for school, miss a test in English, stay after school to take the test, and miss a chance to see a movie with friends.
3. Based on the scenario in number 2 and your own knowledge and experiences, what generalization can you make about oversleeping?

Now go to the Skills in Action: Reading Model

Learn It Online
For more on cause and effect, see the interactive graphic organizers at:

go.hrw.com H7-245 **Go**

Understanding Cause and Effect

List some possible cause and effect scenarios, such as *The bus broke down, so I was late for school* or *It started to rain, so the game was cancelled.* Then, have students choose one of the scenarios and add at least two related events to it to form their own causal chains. Discuss any themes apparent in the causal chains.

Making Generalizations

Model making a generalization. You might say: "If I wanted to make a generalization about the climate of our region, I would think about weather patterns I have experienced throughout the time I've lived here. That would give me enough information to describe the climate patterns in broad terms, which would therefore be a generalization."

Check for Understanding

Your Turn

Possible responses:

1. *Look at the text's main character, title, or events; take notes on important ideas in the text; know the difference between plot, theme, and topic.*
2. *sleep through alarm -> late for school -> miss test in English -> stay after school to take test -> miss chance to see new movie with friends*
3. *From the scenario, I can make the generalization that oversleeping is inconvenient and has undesirable consequences.*

- Tell students that *affect* is a verb that means "to influence or change something." As an example, write on the board the following sentence: *The lack of rain affected the growth of the crops.*

Advanced Learners

Acceleration Have students predict where they will be and what they will be doing twenty years from now. Have students create causal flowcharts like the one on p. 245 that show how they will arrive at their predicted future state.

Learn It Online
If your students need help organizing a paper, introduce them to **Interactive Graphic Organizers**—tools for generating and organizing details, determining main ideas, drawing conclusions, comparing and contrasting ideas, and other key skills.

go.hrw.com H7-245 **Go**

Reading Model

Objectives
Students will
• find the theme of a text
• understand cause and effect

Preteach

Read with a Purpose Have students read the Read with a Purpose statement. Ask them to jot down in their **Reader/Writer Notebook** words that hint that things are not as they appear.

Direct Teach

Model the Skill
Use the Reading Model to demonstrate the application of the Literary and Reading skills in a short selection. As you or students read the model aloud, stop to discuss the side annotations and highlighting, which are aids to comprehension and analysis.

▶ **Reading Focus**

Finding the Theme How might the story's title, "Hearts and Hands," relate to the two men who board the train? **Possible response:** *The the title suggests they may be emotionally linked.*

Cause and Effect What might have caused the coach to be full? **Possible response:** *It might have been a peak travel time or holiday.*

California Standards, pp. 246–249
■ **Reading Standard 3.4** Identify and analyze recurring themes across works (e.g., the value of bravery, loyalty, and friendship; the effects of loneliness).

Read with a Purpose Read this short story to discover what happens when two friends meet on a train and things are not as they appear.

Reading Focus

Finding the Theme Remember that a story title can be a clue to the **theme.** Think about what "Hearts and Hands" may mean as you read.

Hearts and Hands

by O. Henry

Reading Focus

Cause and Effect Writers use cause and effect to develop a plot. The **cause** is an event that makes something happen. The coach is full, so the two men sit opposite the young woman. Read on to learn the **effect**—what happens as a result. You may recognize more than one effect or a causal chain of relationships. Watch for both—they may provide clues to the theme.

At Denver there was an influx of passengers into the coaches on the eastbound B.&M. express. In one coach there sat a very pretty young woman dressed in elegant taste and surrounded by all the luxurious comforts of an experienced traveler. Among the newcomers were two young men, one of handsome presence with a bold, frank countenance and manner; the other a ruffled, glum-faced person, heavily built and roughly dressed. The two were handcuffed together.

As they passed down the aisle of the coach the only vacant seat offered was a reversed one facing the attractive young woman. Here the linked couple seated themselves. The young woman's glance fell upon them with a distant, swift disinterest; then with a lovely smile brightening her countenance and a tender pink tingeing her rounded cheeks, she held out a little gray-gloved hand. When she spoke her voice, full, sweet, and deliberate, proclaimed that its owner was accustomed to speak and be heard.

"Well, Mr. Easton, if you *will* make me speak first, I suppose I must. Don't you ever recognize old friends when you meet them in the West?"

Selection Readability	
Easily Accessible **Accessible** Challenging	historical setting and context; simple dialogue

Selection Plot Summary
Two passengers on a train reverse roles when one of them meets an old acquaintance.

Model the Skill

▶ **Reading Focus**

Cause and Effect What happens as a result of the young man revealing his "bracelet"? Why does this happen? **Possible response:** *The young woman's expression changes to horror because she believes the man she knows is a prisoner.*

Analyzing Visuals

Connecting to the Text What paragraph of the story on page 246 might this portrait illustrate?

Young Woman in a Black Hat (1895) by Auguste Renoir (1841–1919). Pastel.

Analyzing Visuals

Along with artists such as Monet, Manet, and Degas, French painter **Pierre-Auguste Renoir** (1841-1919) was associated for many years with the French Impressionist movement.

Connecting to the Text: *It might illustrate the second paragraph, in which the young woman is described.*

The younger man roused himself sharply at the sound of her voice, seemed to struggle with a slight embarrassment which he threw off instantly, and then clasped her fingers with his left hand.

"It's Miss Fairchild," he said, with a smile. "I'll ask you to excuse the other hand; it's otherwise engaged just at present."

He slightly raised his right hand, bound at the wrist by the shining "bracelet" to the left one of his companion. The glad look in the girl's eyes slowly changed to a bewildered horror. The glow faded from her cheeks. Her lips parted in a vague, relaxing distress. Easton, with a little laugh, as if amused, was about to speak again when the other forestalled[1] him. The

Reading Focus

Cause and Effect Watch the sequence of events here. The girl is glad (effect) because she had found an old friend (cause), but she quickly reacts with shock (effect) once she notices that he is handcuffed (cause). In response to her reaction (cause), Easton starts to say something (effect), but the other man stops him (cause).

---

1. **forestalled** (fawr STAWLD): prevented.

Universal Access

EL English Learners/ Struggling Readers

English for Academic Success To help students understand the selection, introduce them to the following vocabulary words.

• **frank**— open and honest. *Easton appeared to be frank.*

• **ruffled**— messy, unclean, unattractive. *The ruffled-looking man did not look very important.*

• **countenance**— appearance or expression. *Miss Fairchild had a pleasant countenance.*

• **acquainted**— familiar with or known. *Easton and Miss Fairchild were acquainted with one another.*

• **pen**— short for penitentiary; a jail or prison. *The criminal remarked that he was headed to the pen.*

Then, give students this statement that explains how the words relate to the meaning of the selection: *Handsome Easton seemed to have a frank countenance compared to the ruffled man next to him. Miss Fairchild had been acquainted with Easton in the past. In fact, Easton was the real criminal being sent to the pen.*

Model the Skill

▶ **Reading Focus**

Making Generalizations How might Easton's generalizations relate to themes from the text? ***Possible response:*** *Easton's generalizations on the subject of money are similar to recurring themes involving money, such as "some people will do anything for money." This also relates back to the prison sentence for counterfeiting, or producing fake money, that supports the idea of taking desperate measures to have money.*

glum-faced man had been watching the girl's countenance with veiled glances from his keen, shrewd eyes.

"You'll excuse me for speaking, miss, but I see you're acquainted with the marshal here. If you'll ask him to speak a word for me when we get to the pen he'll do it, and it'll make things easier for me there. He's taking me to Leavenworth prison. It's seven years for counterfeiting."

"Oh!" said the girl, with a deep breath and returning color. "So that is what you were doing out here? A marshal!"

Reading Focus

Making Generalizations Notice the generalizations that Easton makes about money. You can make your own generalization based on Easton's words and your own experiences. Keep your generalization in mind when you get to the end of the story and learn more about Easton.

"My dear Miss Fairchild," said Easton, calmly, "I had to do something. Money has a way of taking wings unto itself, and you know it takes money to keep step with our crowd in Washington. I saw this opening in the West, and—well, a marshalship isn't quite as high a position as that of ambassador, but—"

"The ambassador," said the girl, warmly, "doesn't call anymore. He needn't ever have done so. You ought to know that. And so now you are one of those dashing Western heroes, and

Developing Oral Fluency

Small-Group Activity Tell students that dialogue, like conversation in real life, reflects the emotions and character traits of those speaking. Accordingly, readers should pay careful attention to expression when reading dialogue.

- Ask students to imagine what the characters in "Hands and Hearts" would sound like. Have students think about each character's traits and emotions. Then, have them use those details to reach a consensus about the tone, pitch, and speed of the characters' voices. Students should come up with appropriate

voices for Easton, the marshal, Miss Fairchild, and the two passengers.

- Then, model reading the dialogue from "Hearts and Hands." Read a line or two of each character's dialogue aloud, varying your expression and intonation for each character.

- Put students into groups of six, or put students into smaller groups and have some students read more than one role. Have group members take turns reading the dialogue for Easton, the marshal, Miss Fairchild, and the two passengers. Create the role of a you ride and shoot and go into all kinds of dangers. That's different from the Washington life. You have been missed from the old crowd."

The girl's eyes, fascinated, went back, widening a little, to rest upon the glittering handcuffs.

"Don't worry about them, miss," said the other man. "All marshals handcuff themselves to their prisoners to keep them from getting away. Mr. Easton knows his business."

"Will we see you again soon in Washington?" asked the girl.

"Not soon, I think," said Easton. "My butterfly days are over, I fear."

"I love the West," said the girl irrelevantly.[2] Her eyes were shining softly. She looked away out the car window. She began to speak truly and simply, without the gloss of style and manner: "Mamma and I spent the summer in Denver. She went home a week ago because father was slightly ill. I could live and be happy in the West. I think the air here agrees with me. Money isn't everything. But people always misunderstand things and remain stupid—"

"Say, Mr. Marshal," growled the glum-faced man. "This isn't quite fair. Haven't had a smoke all day. Haven't you talked long enough? Take me in the smoker now, won't you? I'm half dead for a pipe."

The bound travelers rose to their feet, Easton with the same slow smile on his face.

"I can't deny a petition for tobacco," he said, lightly. "It's the one friend of the unfortunate. Goodbye, Miss Fairchild. Duty calls, you know." He held out his hand for a farewell.

"It's too bad you are not going East," she said, reclothing herself with manner and style. "But you must go on to Leavenworth, I suppose?"

"Yes," said Easton, "I must go on to Leavenworth."

The two men sidled down the aisle into the smoker.

The two passengers in a seat nearby had heard most of the conversation. Said one of them: "That marshal's a good sort of chap. Some of these Western fellows are all right."

---

2. **irrelevantly** (ih REHL uh vuhnt lee): without relation to the subject at hand.

narrator, who will read the text that is not dialogue.

- As students read, remind them to pay close attention to their tone, pitch, and speed. Tell students that although they should make an attempt to convey their character's vocal qualities, it is also important that they read clearly and audibly.

- After students have read the story aloud, ask them to share what they learned about dialogue from this activity.

Reading Focus

Finding the Theme Watch for significant passages that may be clues to the theme. After you finish the story, re-read the two highlighted passages in which the glum-faced man speaks to the girl. Think about what the man is doing and what the writer may be revealing through the man's words.

Reading Focus

Cause and Effect Note the cause and effect in this passage: The girl's father became ill, so her mother returned home early. Now, the girl is returning East as well.

Model the Skill

▶ Reading Focus

Finding the Theme After reading the story, re-read the second full paragraph on p. 249. How do the other man's words in this paragraph relate to the story's theme? *Possible response:* The other man is lying to the girl out of kindness to Easton. This lie relates to the idea that appearances can be deceiving and to the idea that sometimes lies can be helpful rather than harmful.

Finding the Theme What potential story theme emerges as the girl reveals the cause for her early departure from the West? *Possible response:* She says that "money isn't everything," meaning that in the West, people are not judged based on the amount of money they have. This statement is also a theme expressed by other writers in various forms, including "money alone can't guarantee happiness," and "wealth is not the most important measure of status."

▶ Literary Focus

Theme How does the last sentence of the story convey the theme?
Possible response: Easton was the prisoner. This conveys the theme that things are not always what they seem.

Read with a Purpose Ask students to identify the difference between appearance and reality. *Possible response:* Mr. Easton seems to be the marshal but is really the prisoner.

More About the Writer

O. Henry was noted for writing about "everyday" people, especially those in New York's working class. In his introduction to his collection, *The Four Million,* he writes, "… some one invented the assertion that there were only 'Four Hundred' people in New York City who were really worth noticing. But a wiser man has arisen—the census taker—and his larger estimate of human interest has been preferred in marking out the field of these little stories of the 'Four Million.'"

Think About the Writer

Ask students what O. Henry's portrayal of the criminal and marshal suggests about his opinions.

For Independent Reading

Suggest students read "The Gift of the Magi," O. Henry's famous story of two lovers' sacrifices.

California Standards, p. 251

■ **Reading Standard 3.4** Identify and analyze recurring themes across works (e.g., the value of bravery, loyalty, and friendship; the effects of loneliness).

Reading Model

"Pretty young to hold an office like that, isn't he?" asked the other.

"Young!" exclaimed the first speaker, "why—Oh! didn't you catch on? Say—did you ever know an officer to handcuff a prisoner to his *right* hand?"

Literary Focus

Theme Notice what the passenger concludes about the marshal. Remember that significant statements can help point to a **theme.**

Read with a Purpose What do you now understand about appearance versus reality?

MEET THE WRITER

O. Henry
(1862–1910)

Observing with a Keen Eye

Born William Sydney Porter, O. Henry once expressed his philosophy of writing in this way:

"The short story is a potent medium of education. . . . It should break prejudice with understanding. I propose to send the down-and-outers into the drawing-rooms of the 'get-it-alls,' and I intend to insure their welcome."

O. Henry's exceptional powers of observation enabled him to study ordinary people and turn them into extraordinary characters in his stories. One place where O. Henry used his ability to write about people is Pete's Tavern, the restaurant where he wrote his classic short story "The Gift of the Magi."

Think About the Writer

How does this story communicate O. Henry's compassion for "down-and-outers"?

O. Henry, ©The Granger Collection, New York.

Resources

Chapter 3 Resources, Literary and Academic Vocabulary Skill Builder, p. 5

UA: Differentiating Instruction, Academic and Selection Vocabulary Skill Builder, p. 80

Teacher One Stop™, on-level lesson plan and all print resources

WordSharp: An Interactive Vocabulary Tutor, more practice with academic language

---

Academic Vocabulary

Writing About Theme

English for Academic Success Write the following question on the board. Tell students these are the kinds of questions on standardized tests. Discuss the meaning of the words, then have students use "Hearts and Hands" to answer the questions.

• What subjects or themes **recur** throughout "Hearts and Hands"?
Possible response: One recurring subject is the idea of money; Easton first discusses the need for money in the Washington crowd, and Miss Fairchild later cherishes Denver, where "money isn't everything." A recurring theme, related to these points, is the

Reading Standard 3.4 Identify and analyze recurring themes across works (e.g., the value of bravery, loyalty, and friendship; the effects of loneliness).

Into Action: Tracing Cause and Effect

Review "Hearts and Hands" for events that have cause-and-effect relationships. Fill in the chart to explain how the events are related. Also note when an effect causes something else to happen. Then, considering the causes and effects, identify the theme they reveal.

Cause: What Happened
_____

Effect/Cause:
_____

Effect/Cause:
_____

Effect:
_____

Talk About . . .

1. Why does the marshal cover up for the prisoner? Is he trying to spare the feelings of the young woman? Does he see the prisoner as a fellow human being?

   With a partner, discuss your ideas. Use details from the story to support your responses. Try to use each Academic Vocabulary word listed at the right at least once in your discussion.

Write About . . .

Answer the following questions about "Hearts and Hands." For definitions of the underlined Academic Vocabulary words, see the column on the right.

2. What does the young woman <u>reveal</u> about her feelings for Easton?

3. Why is knowing which hand of each man is cuffed—left or right—a <u>relevant</u> detail?

4. Explain how Easton's need for money is an <u>implicit</u> detail in the story. How did he try to solve his money problems?

Writing Skills Focus
Think as a Reader/Writer

In Chapter 4, you'll read stories and poems with powerful, recurring themes. In your *Reader/Writer Notebook,* note details that are clues to the works' themes. The details you record will help you analyze the themes you identify.

Academic Vocabulary for Chapter 3

Talking and Writing About Theme

Academic Vocabulary is the language you use to write and talk about literature. Use these words to discuss the stories you read in this chapter. The words are underlined throughout the chapter.

implicit (ihm PLIHS iht) *adj.:* suggested or understood but not stated directly. *Another theme implicit in the story is that even strangers can show compassion for each other.*

recur (rih KUR) *v.:* occur again. *Important themes recur in many different stories throughout time.*

relevant (REHL uh vuhnt) *adj.:* directly relating to the subject. *A story's theme has more meaning if it is relevant to our own lives.*

reveal (rih VEEL) *v.:* show something that was previously hidden. *The young woman revealed her feelings for Easton in the way she spoke to him.*

Your Turn

Copy the Academic Vocabulary words into your *Reader/Writer Notebook.* Use these words in a paragraph that explains what you can learn from a story's theme. Practice using these words as you talk and write about the selections in this chapter.

Guided Practice: Apply
Into Action: Tracing Cause and Effect

If students have trouble using the graphic organizer, they may find it helpful to draw a flowchart that uses arrows to link causes with effects.

Talk About...

1. Model for students how to incorporate the academic vocabulary words in a conversation. You might say, "I think the marshal covers up for the prisoner because he is compassionate and kind. These qualities are *implicit* in his actions toward the prisoner."

Write About...
Possible responses:

2. *She <u>reveals</u> that she has a romantic interest in Easton.*

3. *Knowing which hand is cuffed is a <u>relevant</u> detail because it <u>reveals</u> which man is the prisoner and which is the marshal.*

4. *Easton's lack of money is an <u>implicit</u> detail in the story because he never says he needs money, but suggests that money is important to the Washington crowd and that it "has a way of taking wings unto itself." He tells Miss Fairchild he tried to solve the problem by taking a position as a marshal, but he actually tried to get money by producing counterfeit money and got caught doing so.*

Writing Focus

The Think as a Reader/Writer activities in this chapter focus on the reading-writing relationship. Use the activities to help students explore the writer's craft in a text and to practice this aspect of craft in their own writing.

Independent Practice

 Chapter 3 Resources, Skill Builders, pp. 3–5

UA: Differentiating Instruction, Academic and Selection Vocabulary Skill Builder, p. 80

---

idea that a person's value is often measured by the amount of money he or she has.

- What trait of Miss Fairchild's does the narrator **reveal** on the first page of the story? *Possible response:* Miss Fairchild is very confident and possesses a sense of superiority as a result of her privileged background.

- Would learning more about Mr. Easton's former relationship with Miss Fairchild be **relevant** to the story's plot? Explain. *Possible response:* It might be interesting to know more about those two characters, but learning about

their friendship wouldn't be entirely relevant to the events on the train.

- What emotion is **implicit** in Miss Fairchild's reaction to the sight of Mr. Easton's handcuffs? *Possible response:* When Miss Fairchild sees Mr. Easton's handcuffs, her cheeks turn pale and her mouth opens, implicitly suggesting dismay, shock, or great concern.

Standards Focus

Objectives
Students will
• differentiate theme from subject
• analyze theme

Motivate
What Do You Think?/QuickWrite
Have students discuss love-related sacrifices they are familiar with, from books, television, or movies. Then, have them use their **Reader/Writer Notebook** to consider situations in which such a sacrifice is warranted.

English for Academic Success

Academic Vocabulary
Look for opportunities to use the Academic Vocabulary words in this chapter.

• **relevant, *adj.*:** directly relating to the subject.
• **reveal, *v.*:** show something that was previously hidden.

Analyzing Visuals
Extension Activity How does the title of the image relate to the title of the poem? ***Possible response:*** *Both "highwayman" and "demon" have negative connotations and suggest the potential to cause harm.*

POEM
Preparing to Read

The Highwayman
by **Alfred Noyes**

What Do **You Think** When might loyalty require sacrifice?

🕐 **QuickTalk**
With a partner, discuss incidents you have heard of in which someone sacrificed something he or she held dear because of love or concern for another person. Explain whether you believe the sacrifice was worth it.

A Demon in My View by Edmund Dulac.

🐻 **California Standards, pp. 252–263**

■ **Reading Standard 1.1**   Identify idioms, analogies, metaphors, and similes in prose and poetry.
■ **Reading Standard 3.4**   Identify and analyze recurring themes across works (e.g., the value of bravery, loyalty, and friendship; the effects of loneliness).

Selection Readability	
Easily Accessible **Accessible** Challenging	familiar vocabulary; figurative language; familiar situations; unfamiliar form

Selection Plot Summary
"The Highwayman" tells the story of the ill-fated romance between a robber and a landlord's daughter.

Reader/Writer Notebook

Use your **RWN** to complete the activities for this selection.

Reading Standard 3.4 Identify and analyze recurring **themes** across works (e.g., the value of bravery, loyalty, and friendship; the effects of loneliness).

Literary Skills Focus

Subject Versus Theme The **theme** is the important idea a piece of literature <u>reveals</u> about people and life. It is the meaning you take away from the story. A theme is not the same as a subject or topic. The **subject** of a work can usually be expressed in just a word or two: love, war, injustice. The theme is the idea that the writer is conveying *about* a particular subject: *Love can cause both joy and pain.* Some themes, such as the power of loyalty, have endured throughout time and across cultures.

Narrative Poems Poems that are written to tell a story are called **narrative poems.** These story poems resemble short stories: They have a plot (with complications, a climax, and a resolution), one or more settings, and characters in conflict.

Literary Perspectives Apply the literary perspective described on page 255 as you read this poem.

Reading Skills Focus

Finding the Theme To help you find the theme of this poem, notice important things the characters say and the actions or choices they make. Words or phrases that are repeated or that seem especially important can also be clues to theme.

Into Action One strategy for finding the theme is to take notes as you read. Use a chart like this one to take notes about "The Highwayman."

"The Highwayman"	Notes for Finding the Theme
Comments by characters	
Characters' actions & choices	
Important words	"though hell should bar the way"

Writing Skills Focus

Think as a Reader/Writer

Find It in Your Reading As you read this narrative poem, identify its plot structure—the basic situation, conflict, complications, climax, and resolution. Which events seem most significant? What themes, or messages about life, do they <u>reveal</u>?

Selection Introduction

More About the Writer

When **Alfred Noyes** was a child, his father taught him Latin and Greek. He wrote the two-hundred page epic poem "Drake," which showed that he was also influenced by poets whose work was more recent, such as Alfred, Lord Tennyson. Noyes also wrote an autobiography, which was published in 1953.

Think About the Writer

Discuss what the phrase "wild bit of country" might mean, and give students a few examples of things that Noyes might have experienced while living there. For example, Noyes mentions how listening to the sound of the wind one night inspired "The Highwayman". Ask students to think about other aspects of the natural world that could inspire poetry.

For Independent Reading

■ Students interested in reading additional narrative poetry might enjoy the selections gathered by Paul Janeczko into the collection *The Music That Happens: Poems that Tell Stories.*

■ If students are interested in stories set in rural England's past, they might enjoy reading Frances Hodgson Burnett's classic *The Secret Garden.*

Alfred Noyes
(1880–1958)

A Popular Poet

The British poet, novelist, biographer, and essayist **Alfred Noyes** was often called the most popular writer of his time. People enjoyed his verse for its rousing storytelling and its thumping rhythms—and for these reasons, his work was often performed aloud.

"The Highwayman"

Today Noyes is best remembered for "The Highwayman," which he wrote in a small cottage on the edge of Bagshot Heath in England, shortly after leaving Oxford University. He recalled:

"Bagshot Heath in those days was a wild bit of country, all heather and pinewoods. 'The Highwayman' suggested itself to me one blustery night when the sound of the wind in the pines gave me the first line: 'The wind was a torrent of darkness among the gusty trees. . . .'

It took me about two days to complete the poem. Shortly afterward it appeared in *Blackwood's Magazine.* It illustrates the unpredictable chances of authorship, that this poem, written in so short a time, when I was twenty-four, should have been read so widely."

©The Granger Collection, New York.

Think About the Writer How do you think Noyes's writing was affected by his living in the "wild bit of country"?

Build Background

The highwayman in this famous poem is a robber who lived in England in the 1700s. Highwaymen stopped stagecoaches on the lonely moorlands of northern England and Scotland to rob the rich passengers of money and jewels. Some highwaymen were considered heroes by the Scots because they shared the money with the poor. Highwaymen were often dashing, romantic figures who dressed in expensive clothes. This poem is based on a true story that the poet heard while he was on vacation in that part of England where highwaymen used to lie in wait for stagecoaches.

Dick Turpin (1706–1739). English robber, lithograph, English, 19th Century.

Preview the Selection

In this narrative poem, a daring and dashing **robber** (the highwayman) visits a beautiful young woman named **Bess** at an inn. As they plan to meet each other again, a stableman named **Tim** listens jealously. When a group of cruel soldiers arrives, Bess makes a fateful decision.

Read with a Purpose Read this selection to find out what happens to a young woman who is in love with a robber, or highwayman.

The Highwayman

by **Alfred Noyes**

Landscape with Effect of Moonlight by Jules César Denis van Loo (1743–1821).

Part 1

The wind was a torrent of darkness
    among the gusty trees,
The moon was a ghostly galleon°
    tossed upon cloudy seas,
The road was a ribbon of moonlight
    over the purple moor,
And the highwayman came riding—
5   Riding—riding—
The highwayman came riding, up to
    the old inn door. **Ⓐ**

   2. galleon (GAL ee uhn): large sailing ship.

Ⓐ **Literary Focus** Subject Versus Theme/Narrative Poems
From reading this first stanza and the poem's title, what is the subject of the poem? What do you learn about the setting in the first stanza?

Literary Perspectives

The following perspective will help you think about the elements of poetry in this narrative poem.

Analyzing Responses to Literature The way a writer uses literary elements—such as character, plot, and theme—will influence the way you respond to a work. As you read, you think about whether a character is credible or unrealistic. You question whether the plot is believable. When reading poetry, you will also notice the imagery and figures of speech the writer includes and the effects of each.

Look for the theme of "The Highwayman," and think about whether it has provided you with a new insight about life. Be sure to note the theme's effect on you. As you read, respond to questions that guide you in using this perspective.

Direct Teach

Think About/Talk About

Read with a Purpose Have students read the Read with a Purpose statement. Ask students what they think might happen to the young woman in love with the robber.

▶ Analysis

Ⓐ Literary Focus

Possible response: *The subject of the poem is the life of the highwayman. It is a windy, cloudy, moonlit night.*

▶ Extend the Discussion

Analyzing Why do you think the author uses the word "riding" so often in the first stanza? What effect does this repetition have? ***Possible response:*** *The repetition emphasizes how much time a highwayman spends riding a horse and creates a stronger image in the reader's mind of the highwayman approaching the inn on his horse. The rhythm of the repetition also sounds sort of like a horse's hooves beating on the ground.*

Setting Re-read the first stanza. What specific setting details does the writer give in the stanza? How do they help you visualize the setting? ***Possible response:*** *The poet describes the wind, the trees, the moon surrounded by fragments of cloud, and the dark, purple moor with a road that is bright in the moonlight. These details help me picture a windy night with a full moon out in the country, where the land is covered with brush and trees.*

Literary Perspectives

During their first reading, have students make notes in their **Reader/Writer Notebook** on the story told in the poem. Direct students to focus on plot details throughout this reading, and to make sure they understand both the figurative language and the story it tells. Then, have students discuss with a partner what story the poem told and whether or not they thought it was realistic.

Once students understand the events of the poem, have them reread the poem with careful attention to how love influences the thoughts, statements, and actions of the highwayman, Tim the ostler, and Bess the landlord's daughter. When they have finished their re-reading, have students reflect individually on what they learned about love and human behavior from this selection, particularly if they learned anything they did not know before, in a journal entry. Ask volunteers to share their entries as a segue into a discussion of the poem's themes.

Remind students to use the notes and questions at the bottom of the page to help them use the perspective.

Model the Skill

■ Provide students with copies of the Reading Skills Focus graphic organizer (See **Chapter 3 Resources**) or ask them to use their own paper.

■ Tell students that authors provide numerous clues about theme throughout a text.

■ Read aloud the first stanza on p. 257, and model making notes in the graphic organizer. You might say, "I see in the first two lines that Tim the ostler is listening and is in the dark. This suggests that he is eavesdropping on their conversation." Write in the organizer, "Tim is hiding in the dark and eavesdropping."

■ You might say, "I also read that Tim's eyes are 'hollows of madness,'" which suggests that he may be unstable, and the two following lines suggest the cause. Tim is madly in love with the landlord's daughter. These two points seem very important, so I will note them in my organizer."

"The Highwayman"	Notes for Finding the Theme
Comments by characters	
Characters' actions & choices	Tim is hiding in the dark and eavesdropping;
Important words	"His eyes were hollows of madness" "But he loved the landlord's daughter"

Guided Practice: Apply

As a class, read aloud the stanza beginning "One kiss." Guide students in understanding Tim the ostler is still eavesdropping. Have volunteers share words, actions and character comments that they think might suggest the poem's theme.

He'd a French cocked hat on his forehead, a bunch of lace at his chin,
A coat of the claret° velvet, and breeches of brown doeskin.
They fitted with never a wrinkle. His boots were up to the thigh.
10 And he rode with a jeweled twinkle,
     His pistol butts a-twinkle,
His rapier hilt° a-twinkle, under the jeweled sky.

Over the cobbles he clattered and clashed in the dark inn yard.
And he tapped with his whip on the shutters, but all was locked and barred.
15 He whistled a tune to the window, and who should be waiting there
But the landlord's black-eyed daughter,
     Bess, the landlord's daughter,
Plaiting° a dark red love knot into her long black hair. **B**

---

8. claret (KLAR uht): purplish red, like claret wine.

12. rapier (RAY pee uhr) **hilt:** sword handle.

18. plaiting (PLAYT ihng): braiding.

B Read and Discuss What situation has the poet set up so far?

By the Window by Martin Drolling (1752–1817).

Universal Access

EL English Learners

English for Academic Success Students unfamiliar with American history may not recognize the terms "redcoat troop" and "King George's Men." Explain that both of these terms refer to the British army under King George III. The army wore red-jacketed uniforms, hence the term *red coat*. Students may also have trouble with other unfamiliar terms in the poem. Help them find definitions for *torrent* (rushing river), *moor* (open wasteland), *breeches* (knee-length pants), and *cobbles* (paving stones).

Advanced Learners

Acceleration Point out the patterns of recurring colors and images in this poem—for example, the love knot tied in Bess's hair and the ropes knotted around her body, or the dark night and Bess's black hair. Have students look for other patterns in the poem. Then, have students discuss the patterns they identified, and connect these patterns to a theme from the poem. For example, the love knot and the ropes tied around Bess may represent the strength of love, which would relate

And dark in the dark old inn yard a stable wicket° creaked
20 Where Tim the ostler° listened. His face was white and peaked.
His eyes were hollows of madness, his hair like moldy hay,
But he loved the landlord's daughter,
    The landlord's red-lipped daughter,
Dumb as a dog he listened, and he heard the robber say— **C**

25 "One kiss, my bonny sweetheart, I'm after a prize tonight,
But I shall be back with the yellow gold before the morning light;
Yet, if they press me sharply, and harry° me through the day,
Then look for me by moonlight,
    Watch for me by moonlight,
30 I'll come to thee by moonlight, though hell should bar the way."

He rose upright in the stirrups. He scarce could reach her hand,
But she loosened her hair in the casement.° His face burnt like a brand
As the black cascade of perfume came tumbling over his breast;
And he kissed its waves in the moonlight,
35   (Oh, sweet black waves in the moonlight!)
Then he tugged at his rein in the moonlight, and galloped away to the west. **D**

---

19. wicket (WIHK iht): small door or gate.

20. ostler (AHS luhr): groom; person who takes care of horses.

27. harry (HAR ee): harass or push along.

32. casement (KAYS muhnt): window that opens outward on hinges.

C Literary Perspectives **Analyzing Responses to Literature** Identify
at least two figures of speech that describe Tim. What impression do they create?

D Literary Perspectives **Analyzing Responses to Literature** Explain
whether you think the character of the highwayman is believable or unrealistic.

Analyzing Visuals
Tell students that **Martin Drolling**
(1752–1817) was a French painter. He
is best known for his portraits, such
as "By the Window," and paintings of
interiors.

Extension Activity Ask students to
compare and contrast the girl in the
image with Bess, the landlord's daughter. *Possible response: The girl in the
image looks like I expected Bess to look,
but she looks like she's daydreaming
instead of waiting for the highwayman.*

▶ **Comprehension**
B **Read and Discuss**
*Possible response: There's a well-
dressed highwayman riding through
the night. He stops at the inn where
the landlord's daughter Bess answers
his knocking.*

▶ **Analysis**
C **Literary Perspectives**
*Possible response: The metaphor "his
eyes were hollows of madness" and
the simile "dumb as a dog" create the
impression of a man rendered senseless by love.*

D **Literary Perspectives**
*Possible response: I think that the
character is believable because people
make extravagant gestures and promises when they are in love.*

▶ **Extend the Discussion**
Interpreting Re-read lines 25–30.
Why might not the highwayman be
able to return until the next night?
*Possible response: It sounds like peo-
ple are trying to catch him because he's
done something bad. He may be busy
trying to avoid getting caught during
the day and have to stay in hiding.*

Model the Skill

- Remind students that the **subject** of a story is not the same as a **theme**, though the two may be connected.

- Ask volunteers to suggest words that come to mind as they read "The Highwayman." Students may suggest *love, betrayal, courage, crime, danger,* or *jealousy.* Write the suggestions on the board. Explain to students that the words they suggested are all possible subjects for the poem, and that they all connect to the theme or themes of the poem.

- Using *courage* as an example, explain that you will look for specific examples of courage in the poem so far to determine how the subject relates to the theme. Point out that on p. 259, Bess bravely defies the redcoats by wriggling loose and getting control of the musket. She resists out of concern for her love, which suggests a potential theme: "Love inspires incredible courage."

Guided Practice: Apply

Divide students into as many groups as there are words left on the board. Have each group choose one subject word and reread the poem to find examples of the subject. Have a volunteer from each group share their examples, and discuss as a class the themes they suggest.

Think as a Reader/Writer

Find It in Your Reading Point out that Bess's struggle to reach the trigger is part of the rising action of the poem's plot.

Use It in Your Writing Tell students to rewrite a few lines of the poem to describe the same rising action in their own words.

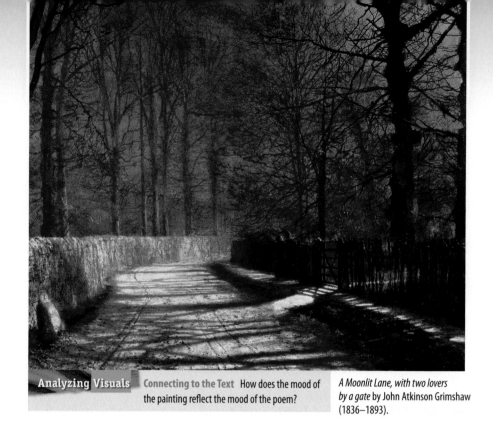

Analyzing Visuals **Connecting to the Text** How does the mood of the painting reflect the mood of the poem?

A Moonlit Lane, with two lovers by a gate by John Atkinson Grimshaw (1836–1893).

Part 2

He did not come in the dawning. He did not come at noon;
And out of the tawny sunset, before the rise of the moon,
When the road was a gypsy's ribbon, looping the purple moor,
40   A redcoat troop came marching—
        Marching—marching—
King George's men came marching, up to the old inn door.

Reaching Reluctant Readers

- Many students may not be motivated to read poetry. Encourage students to read "The Highwayman" by telling them it is really a story written in poetic form. Furthermore, it has many of the elements that make a story exciting, such as love, betrayal, kidnapping, suicide, and murder.

- Point out that poems are similar to song lyrics. In fact, poems such as "The Highwayman" have been set to music. If possible, obtain a copy of "The Highwayman"

set to music and play it for the class. Have students discuss how listening to a sung version of the poem is different from reading it or hearing it read aloud.

- To reinforce the connection between poetry and music, suggest that students choose a stanza from "The Highwayman" or another poem to set to the tune of one of their favorite songs. Have volunteers perform their stanzas for the class.

They said no word to the landlord. They drank his ale instead.
But they gagged his daughter, and bound her, to the foot of her narrow bed.
45   Two of them knelt at her casement, with muskets at their side!
There was death at every window;
        And hell at one dark window;
For Bess could see, through her casement, the road that *he* would ride.   **E**

They had tied her up to attention, with many a sniggering jest;
50   They had bound a musket beside her, with the muzzle beneath her breast!
"Now, keep good watch!" and they kissed her. She heard the dead man say—
Look for me by moonlight;
        Watch for me by moonlight;
I'll come to thee by moonlight, though hell should bar the way!   **F**

55   She twisted her hands behind her; but all the knots held good!
She writhed her hands till her fingers were wet with sweat or blood!
They stretched and strained in the darkness, and the hours crawled by like years,
Till, now, on the stroke of midnight,
        Cold, on the stroke of midnight,
60   The tip of one finger touched it! The trigger at least was hers!

The tip of one finger touched it; she strove no more for the rest!
Up, she stood up to attention, with the muzzle beneath her breast.
She would not risk their hearing; she would not strive again;
For the road lay bare in the moonlight;
65   Blank and bare in the moonlight;
And the blood of her veins, in the moonlight, throbbed to her love's refrain.   **G**

E **Reading Focus** Finding the Theme Think about the significance of what Bess sees. What decision might she need to make?

F **Literary Perspectives** Analyzing Responses to Literature Who is the "dead man"? How do these events and descriptions increase suspense?

G **Read and Discuss** What is Bess doing?

- Explain to students that poets use **onomatopoeia** to add to the meaning in a poem by the sound of the words. Onomatopoeia is the use of words that sound exactly like the noise they're describing, such as the *roar* of a hungry lion.

- Point out the word *shattered* in line 78. Tell students that *shattered* means "broke into many tiny pieces." Say the word aloud. Tell students that the word *shattered* sounds like something being broken into many pieces, as the gunshot broke the silence of the night and broke Bess's body into pieces as well.

Guided Practice: Apply

Think/Pair/Share Have students scan the entire poem and identify words with a strong sound quality. Ask students to compare lists with a partner. Then, have volunteers share a few of their chosen words with the class and discuss how the meaning-sound connection creates onomatopoeia.

Tlot-tlot; tlot-tlot! Had they heard it? The horse hoofs ringing clear;
Tlot-tlot, tlot-tlot, in the distance? Were they deaf that they did not hear?
Down the ribbon of moonlight, over the brow of the hill,
70 The highwayman came riding,
     Riding, riding!
The redcoats looked to their priming!° She stood up, straight and still.

Tlot-tlot, in the frosty silence! *Tlot-tlot,* in the echoing night!
Nearer he came and nearer. Her face was like a light!
75 Her eyes grew wide for a moment; she drew one last deep breath,
Then her fingers moved in the moonlight,
     Her musket shattered the moonlight,
Shattered her breast in the moonlight and warned him—with her death.   **H**

---

72. priming: (PRYM ihng): explosive for firing a gun.

H **Literary Focus** Subject Versus Theme
What has Bess just done? How might this event help reveal the author's idea about people or life?

A Hilly Scene (c. 1826–1828)
by Samuel Palmer.

Literary Perspectives

Point out to students how the author uses the repetition of the words *riding* and *moonlight* on p. 260 to create a sense of drama and high emotion. Have students think about how this language affects their response to the poem's theme.

He turned. He spurred to the west; he did not know who stood
80 Bowed, with her head o'er the musket, drenched with her own blood!
Not till the dawn he heard it, his face grew gray to hear
How Bess, the landlord's daughter,
    The landlord's black-eyed daughter,
Had watched for her love in the moonlight, and died in the darkness there.

85 Back, he spurred like a madman, shouting a curse to the sky,
With the white road smoking behind him and his rapier brandished high.
Blood-red were his spurs in the golden noon; wine-red was his velvet coat;
When they shot him down on the highway,
    Down like a dog on the highway,
90 And he lay in his blood on the highway, with the bunch of lace at his throat.

And still of a winter's night, they say, when the wind is in the trees,
When the moon is a ghostly galleon tossed upon cloudy seas,
When the road is a ribbon of moonlight over the purple moor,
A highwayman comes riding—
95   *Riding—riding—*
A highwayman comes riding, up to the old inn door.

Over the cobbles he clatters and clangs in the dark inn yard;
He taps with his whip on the shutters, but all is locked and barred.
He whistles a tune to the window, and who should be waiting there
100 *But the landlord's black-eyed daughter,*
    Bess, the landlord's daughter,
Plaiting a dark red love knot into her long black hair.

 Reading Focus Finding the Theme What does the highwayman do when he learns what happened to Bess? What happens to him? Which words from the stanza seem the most powerful?

 Literary Focus Subject Versus Theme What message about life (or death) might the writer be making in these last two stanzas?

 California Standards, pp. 262–263

- **Reading Standard 1.1** Identify idioms, analogies, metaphors, and similes in prose and poetry.
- **Reading Standard 3.4** Identify and analyze recurring themes across works (e.g., the value of bravery, loyalty, and friendship; the effects of loneliness).

▶ **Comprehension**

🅘 **Reading Focus**

Possible response: The highwayman starts riding back toward the inn, and he is shot dead. The words spurred, madman, smoking, *and* brandished *are very powerful.*

▶ **Analysis**

🅗 **Literary Focus**

Possible response: Bess shot herself to warn the highwayman of the danger he faced at the inn. This reveals the idea that love is a powerful feeling that can lead people to make huge sacrifices.

🅙 **Literary Focus**

Possible response: I think the author is making the message that love is stronger than anything. Even though Bess and the highwayman died, they return as ghosts in love.

▶ **Extend the Discussion**

Theme What do you think is the theme of this poem? *Possible responses: True love endures even the greatest tragedies; love conquers treachery and betrayal.*

Monitor Students' Comprehension

Guide the class in answering these comprehension questions.

1. What does the highwayman promise Bess? [*He will return to her.*]

2. Who overhears the promise, and how is he described? [*Tim the ostler; his face is "white and peaked," his eyes are "hollows of madness," his hair like "moldy hay."*]

3. What could Bess see through the window when she was tied up? [*the road the highwayman would ride to see her*]

4. Why did the highwayman ride back to the inn after he heard the news about Bess? [*He wanted to die too because he couldn't go on living knowing what Bess had done for him.*]

Check for Understanding

Independent Practice
Reading Skills Focus
Answers:

1. *Bess is the landlord's daughter who is in love with the highwayman. She kills herself in order to warn the highwayman.*

2. *The characters in "The Highwayman" have important realizations about love. Bess decides that she cannot let the highwayman be taken away from her and is willing to sacrifice anything for him. She kills herself to warn him. The highwayman cannot live without Bess and decides that death is preferable to a life alone. He dies trying to avenge her. Tim the ostler presumably learns that treachery has dire consequences, and that love cannot be forced, but we never see this.*

Literary Skills Focus
Possible responses:

3. *Tim the ostler alerts the redcoats to the highwayman's return to the inn. He loves Bess and wants to get rid of the highwayman.*

4. *The highwayman returns to the inn knowing he will be killed because he knows that he cannot live without Bess. He may also hope to avenge her death.*

5. *The setting is a windy and moonlit night at an old country inn. The wind as a torrent of darkness, the road a ribbon of moonlight, and the old inn locked and barred helped me visualize the scene.*

6. *I agree ; the repeated lines and sing song rhythm make the poem melodious and song like.*

7. *Love is a powerful emotion.*

8. *The last two stanzas take place after the events happened; they are a spooky retelling of the poem. The characters are now ghosts.*

9. *I think the narrator respects the highwayman because of how he describes his death. I feel that he was noble because he refused to go on living without his true love.*

Applying Your Skills

The Highwayman
Literary Response and Analysis

Reading Skills Focus
Read with a Purpose

1. Who is Bess? What happens to her?

Reading Skills: Finding the Theme

2. Through characters' behavior, a writer may make statements about human nature or life. In "The Highwayman," what do the characters realize in the course of the story? What actions do they take as a result? Add another row to your chart of notes, and identify observations about life shown through Tim, the highwayman, and Bess.

"The Highwayman"	Notes for Finding the Theme
Comments by characters	
Characters' actions & choices	
Important words	"though hell should bar the way"
Observations about life shown through characters	

Literary Skills Focus
Literary Analysis

3. **Interpret** What part does Tim the ostler play in the story? What is his motive?

4. **Interpret** Why do you think the highwayman comes back to the inn after he hears what has happened to Bess?

5. **Analyze** What is the setting of this poem? What details help you to see and hear what is happening?

6. **Literary Perspectives** A critic described Noyes as "one of the most melodious of modern writers, with a witchery in words that at its best is irresistible." Discuss whether you agree with this statement. What most appeals to you in this poem? Cite <u>relevant</u> details and literary elements from the poem in your response.

Literary Skills: Subject Versus Theme/Narrative Poems

7. **Interpret** This poem is about love, betrayal, and death. What **theme,** or message about people and life, does the poem <u>reveal</u> to you?

8. **Analyze** The last two stanzas are very much like the first and third stanzas. The wording, however, is slightly different. How does the difference reflect what happens at the end of the poem?

Literary Skills Review: Characterization

9. **Infer** Judging by the narrator's description, how do you think the narrator feels about the highwayman? How can you tell? How do *you* feel about the highwayman?

Writing Skills Focus
Think as a Reader/Writer
Use It in Your Writing If you could write a new ending for the poem, what would it be? Write your ending in a paragraph. Does your ending alter the plot of this narrative poem? What impact does it have on the theme?

 What Do You Think Now

Is Bess's sacrifice noble or pointless? Explain.

What Do You Think Now?

Discuss with students what they consider to be the "border" between noble and pointless sacrifices, particularly those made for love. Students may tend to view the sacrifice in relation to the poem's outcome; that is, that the highwayman died anyway, so Bess' sacrifice was not worthwhile. If this is so, ask them to consider Bess' point of view. She thought only of protecting her love from certain death—would she have had any idea how he might react to her own?

Universal Access

Struggling Writers
Have students list the events in the plot numerically: first, second, third, fourth, and so on. Emphasize the cause and effect relationship between events. Then have students indicate the event they would change to alter the poem's ending. Students can then write a new ending or explain how one event could alter the outcome.

Applying Your Skills

The Highwayman

Vocabulary Development
Metaphor and Simile

In our everyday language we use many expressions that are not literally true: "Joe's bragging gets under my skin." When we use an expression like this one, we are using a **figure of speech.** The meaning of a figurative expression depends on a comparison. In our example, bragging is *compared* to something that causes annoyance.

There are many kinds of figures of speech; the most common are **similes** and **metaphors.** A **simile** is a comparison of two unlike things using the word *like, as, than,* or *resembles.* Here is a famous simile by William Wordsworth: "I wandered lonely as a cloud. . . ." A **metaphor** also compares two unlike things, but it does so without using *like, as, than,* or *resembles.* For example, in "The Highwayman," Alfred Noyes says, "The moon *was* a ghostly galleon tossed upon cloudy seas."

Your Turn

Fill in a chart like the one below by completing each comparison from "The Highwayman." Then, identify each comparison as a simile or metaphor.

Figures of Speech

line 1: The wind is compared to a torrent of darkness.

line 3: The road is compared to

line 12: The stars in the sky are compared to

line 21: Tim's hair is compared to

 California Standards, p. 263
- **Reading Standard 1.1** Identify idioms, analogies, metaphors, and similes in prose and poetry.
- **Reading Standard 3.4** Identify and analyze recurring themes across works (e.g., the value of bravery, loyalty, and friendship; the effects of loneliness).

CHOICES

As you respond to the Choices, use these **Academic Vocabulary** words as appropriate: implicit, recur, relevant, reveal.

REVIEW
Write a Summary and Response

Timed Writing Write two paragraphs about "The Highwayman." First, summarize the plot by describing the poem's conflict, climax, and resolution. In the second paragraph, explain the theme of the poem and how it affected you.

CONNECT
Write a Character Analysis

Write a character analysis of Tim the groom. First, discuss the role he plays in the story. Then, discuss his motivation. Are his motivations obvious, or are they mostly implicit? Provide evidence that supports the reasons you give for Tim's behavior. Finally, discuss what different decisions Tim could have made and how they might have changed the events of the poem.

EXTEND
Create a Storyboard

Partner Work Working with a partner, create a storyboard for the film version of this poem. Illustrate the structure of the narrative and the important changes of scene and action. Put a relevant quotation from the poem under each sketch.

Learn It Online
Find a storyboard template at the Digital Storytelling site:

go.hrw.com | H7-263 | Go

Reteach

** ThinkCentral Online Remediation**

Independent Practice
Vocabulary Development
Your Turn

1. *Metaphor*
2. *The road is compared to a ribbon of moonlight. Metaphor.*
3. *The stars in the sky are compared to jewels. Metaphor.*
4. *Tim's hair is compared to moldy hay. Simile.*

Choices:
Evaluation Criteria
Review: Timed Writing
40–50 Minutes

- The paragraph includes all relevant information about the conflict, climax, and resolution.

Connect: **Homework**
Write a Character Analysis

- The character analysis presents a thorough examination of Tim's actions and motivation and cites evidence from the text.

Extend: **Homework**
Create a Storyboard

- The storyboard accurately portrays all story elements and includes a quotation for each sketch.

Assess

Chapter 3 Resources, Selection Standards Check, p. 7

ThinkCentral Online Assessment, Selection Standards Check

Teacher One Stop™, editable Selection Standards Check

Learn It Online
The **Digital Storytelling** mini-site shows students how to craft a short film—complete with music, images, and special effects.

go.hrw.com | H7-263 | Go

User Friendly

by **T. Ernesto Bethancourt**

Standards Focus

Objectives

Students will

- identify and analyze themes
- understand cause-and-effect relationships and how they connect to theme

Motivate

What Do You Think?/QuickWrite

Have students discuss the factors that influence the formation of friendships. Then, have them use their **Reader/Writer Notebook** to reflect on how they would react to learning that someone's best friend is a computer.

English for Academic Success

Academic Vocabulary

Look for opportunities to use the Academic Vocabulary words in this chapter.

- **implicit, _adj.:_** suggested or understood but not stated directly.

- **relevant, _adj.:_** directly relating to the subject.

- **reveal, _v.:_** show something that was previously hidden.

Analyzing Visuals

Extension Activity What is the child in the picture interacting with, and how? **_Possible response:_** _It looks like he or she is using a computer, and is completely engrossed in what it is doing._

 What Do You Think

What can make it difficult for a young person to make friends?

QuickWrite

Suppose someone you just met said, "My best friend is a computer." What would that statement tell you about the person?

Selection Readability	
Easily Accessible **Accessible** Challenging	familiar situation with family and friends; humorous style; chronological order

Selection Plot Summary

Kevin Neal feels like a nerd who never "gets the girl." After his father makes a few adjustments to Kevin's computer, however, Kevin realizes that love may not be all it's cracked up to be.

Reader/Writer Notebook

Use your **RWN** to complete the activities for this selection.

Reading Standard 3.4 Identify and analyze recurring **themes** across works (e.g., the value of bravery, loyalty, and friendship; the effects of loneliness).

Literary Skills Focus

Theme Here are some tips that can help you find a story's theme:

- Decide what the characters have learned by the story's end. Often that discovery can be translated into a statement of the theme.
- Think about the **title** and whether it might point to the theme of the story. (Not all titles do, however.)
- Look for passages, including dialogue and statements by a first-person narrator, in which the writer seems to make important statements about life. Such passages may point to the theme.

Reading Skills Focus

Identifying Cause and Effect In "User Friendly," a chain of events lands Kevin in computer trouble. He sees **effects** (*what* happens), but for most of the story he's blind to **causes** (*why* the events happen). A **causal chain** is a series of events in which each event causes another one to happen. Be careful, though—even though one event may follow another, that does not necessarily mean it was *caused* by it. To discover causes and effects, look for what happens first. Then, ask what happens *because* of that. Be alert to hidden or multiple causes and effects.

Into Action As you read, use a graphic organizer, such as the flow-chart below, to record the chain of events.

Cause		Effect/Cause		Effect
Kevin has a crush on Ginny.	→	Kevin talks with Ginny. She makes fun of him.	→	

Writing Skills Focus

Think as a Reader/Writer

Find It in Your Reading In this story, the writer focuses on the loneliness of his main character, who is also the narrator. Look for passages (such as "sat down to my usual lonely breakfast") that convey Kevin's feelings of loneliness. Record them in your *Reader/Writer Notebook.*

Vocabulary

absently (AB suhnt lee) *adv.*: in a way that shows one is not thinking about what is happening. *He stared absently at the box.*

modifications (mod uh fuh KAY shuhnz) *n.*: slight changes. *The modifications to the computer have some interesting effects.*

incident (IHN suh duhnt) *n:* happening; occurrence. *The embarrassing incident on the bus bothers Kevin.*

furiously (FYUR ee uhs lee) *adv.*: rapidly, with intensity. *He typed furiously.*

Kevin →

- absently — thinks of his loneliness
- only "friend" is computer with **modifications**
- furiously — attempts to find cause of strange **incidents**

Language Coach

Adjectives To change two of the Vocabulary words above from adverbs into adjectives, you need only remove the *–ly* ending. Changing the nouns into adjectives is trickier: *modifications* becomes *modifiable; incident* becomes *incidental.* Find *absent, modifiable, incidental,* and *furious* in a dictionary. How do their definitions differ from the definitions above?

Learn It Online
See the video introduction to this story at:

go.hrw.com H7-265 Go

Selection Resources

Chapter 3 Resources, on-level practice and assessment, p. 10

PowerNotes, interactive lesson presentation with activities

Teacher One Stop™, on-level lesson plans and all print resources

Holt Audio Library

Holt Audio Library: Selections and Summaries in Spanish

UA: Holt Interactive Reader, p. 66

Holt Interactive Reader for ELD, p.88

Holt Audio Tutor for ELD

UA: Differentiating Instruction, modified lesson plans and leveled assessment, p. 60

UA: Resources for Teaching Advanced Students, lesson plans

UA: Supporting Instruction in Five Languages, selection summary

Weekly Standards Review Transparencies, Transparency 10

ThinkCentral Online Assessment, Selection Standards Check

Preteach

Introducing Vocabulary

Read aloud the Vocabulary words and sample sentences. Then, have student pairs take turns testing each other by having one partner read the definitions aloud and the other identify the words.

English for Academic Success
Language Coach

Explain to students that some words exist in several variations that represent different parts of speech. For instance, *explain* is a verb, *explanatory* is an adjective that describes something that is meant to explain, and *explanation* is a noun that identifies the statement intended to explain. [*All the definitions are similar in meaning to the Vocabulary words, but they are different parts of speech.*]

Literary Skills Focus

As you read and discuss the selection with students, have them keep track of key words and phrases that suggest theme.

Reading Skills Focus

Give students a copy of the Reading Skills Focus graphic organizer before they read. (See **Chapter 3 Resources.**) Tell them to use their responses to answer the questions on the Applying Your Skills page.

Writing Skills Focus

Have students record examples of Kevin's loneliness in their **Reader/ Writer Notebook**. Students can use their notes to complete the Writing Skills Focus activity.

Learn It Online
The **PowerNotes** presentation for this lesson includes a short video that introduces the selection. The video is also available on the online version of this page.

go.hrw.com H7-265 Go

More About the Writer

- **T. Ernesto Bethancourt** is actually the pen name of author Tom Paisley, who has written more than twenty novels.

- Bethancourt's writing is reflective of his own life, but intertwined with the fantastic. His novels *The Tomorrow Connection* and *Tune in Yesterday,* for instance, are about musicians—who have adventures with time travel!

Think About the Writers

Remind students to consider all aspects of Bethancourt's life that contributed to his career as a writer, particularly obstacles he had to overcome. Also note that even professional writers require time and ideas to produce each book.

For Independent Reading

- Students who enjoyed "User Friendly" may enjoy the fantastic airship adventures of Matt the cabin boy in Keith Oppel's *Airborn*.

- Students interested in reading an autobiography from the perspective of a young person might enjoy Jerry Spinelli's *Knots in My Yo-Yo String*.

T. Ernesto Bethancourt
(1932–   )

The Accidental Writer

T. Ernesto Bethancourt became a full-time writer by accident. He was working as a folk musician in a nightclub, and his first daughter had just been born. In hopes that she would read it one day, Bethancourt used the time between shows to begin writing his autobiography, or life story.

"Through a series of extraordinary events, the autobiography became novelized, updated, and was published in 1975 as *New York City, Too Far from Tampa Blues.* The book was an immense success, and I began a new career in midlife."

Bethancourt attributes his writing success to the New York City public schools and the public library. "I thank them, every day, for the new and wonderful life they have given to me and my family." In another interview he said, "The Brooklyn Public Library was a place of refuge from street gangs. There was adventure, travel, and escape to be found on the shelves."

Think About the Writer How did Bethancourt's "accidental" success nevertheless require his effort and perseverance?

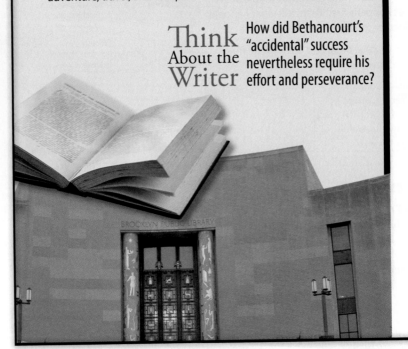

Build Background

This story was written in the 1980s. Back then, computers were quite different from what they are today. Computer screens were green or black, and the type appeared in white. Computers had disk drives, and you saved your work on floppy disks. Commands were given to the computer in keystrokes. The mouse hadn't been introduced. What's more important in terms of this story is that in those days it was unusual for a kid to have a powerful personal computer in his or her own room.

Preview the Story

In "User Friendly" you will meet **Kevin Neal,** a smart kid who doesn't fit in with his peers, and whose best friend is his computer, **Louis.**

User Friendly

by **T. Ernesto Bethancourt**

I reached over and shut off the insistent buzzing of my bedside alarm clock. I sat up, swung my feet over the edge of the bed, and felt for my slippers on the floor. Yawning, I walked toward the bathroom. As I walked by the corner of my room, where my computer table was set up, I pressed the *on* button, slid a diskette into the floppy drive, then went to brush my teeth. By the time I got back, the computer's screen was glowing greenly, displaying the message: *Good morning, Kevin.*

I sat down before the computer table, addressed the keyboard, and typed: *Good morning, Louis.* The computer immediately began to whir and promptly displayed a list of items on its green screen.

```
Today is Monday, April 22,
the 113th day of the year.
```

```
There are 253 days remaining.
Your 14th birthday is five
days from this date.
Math test today, 4th Period.
Your history project is due
today. Do you wish printout: Y/N?
```

I punched the letter *Y* on the keyboard and flipped on the switch to the computer's printer. At once the printer sprang to life and began *eeeek*ing out page one. I went downstairs to breakfast. **Ⓐ**

My bowl of Frosted Flakes was neatly in place, flanked by a small pitcher of milk, an empty juice glass, and an unpeeled banana. I picked up the glass, went to the refrigerator, poured myself a glass of Tang, and sat down to my usual lonely breakfast. Mom was already at work, and Dad wouldn't be home from his Chicago trip for another

Ⓐ **Read and Discuss** What has the author revealed so far?

- Remind students that **themes** are general truths about life, such as "appearances can be deceiving." Authors communicate theme through story elements from titles to text. Readers must pay close attention to a character's reflections and lessons learned to fully grasp a story's theme or themes.

- Model for students identifying potential themes from a character's reflections. Point out that on p. 269, Kevin reveals that he is treated like a "freak" at school and his father built him a computer with a personality program so he could have a friend. Kevin alludes, in that statement, to his loneliness and longing to be liked. The struggle to fit in with one's peers is a common occurrence and is reflective of the life truth "life is generally better when not lived alone."

Guided Practice: Apply

Have students continue reading in pairs, taking notes as they read on any connections they make to the title, or any important reflections or lessons learned by Kevin. Pause students occasionally and have volunteers share potential themes and evidence they have identified, providing guidance as needed.

Think as a Reader/Writer

Find It in Your Reading Point out Kevin's loneliness when he says "The kids at school stay away from me, like I'm a freak or something." at the top of p. 269.

Use It in Your Writing Tell students to write a sentence about a time they felt lonely.

---

three days. I absently read the list of ingredients in Frosted Flakes for what seemed like the millionth time. I sighed deeply.

When I returned to my room to shower and dress for the day, my history project was already printed out. I had almost walked by Louis, when I noticed there was a message on the screen. It wasn't the usual:

```
Printout completed. Do you wish
to continue: Y/N?
```

Underneath the printout question were two lines:

```
When are you going to get me my
voice module,[1] Kevin?
```

I blinked. It couldn't be. There was nothing in Louis's basic programming that would allow for a question like this. Wondering what was going on, I sat down at the keyboard and entered: *Repeat last message.* Amazingly, the computer replied:

```
It's right there on the screen,
Kevin. Can we talk? I mean,
are you going to get me a
voice box?
```

I was stunned. What was going on here? Dad and I had put this computer together. Well, Dad had, and I had helped. Dad is one of the best engineers and master computer designers at Major Electronics, in Santa Rosario, California, where our family lives.

Just ask anyone in Silicon Valley[2] who Jeremy Neal is and you get a whole rave

---

1. **voice module:** unit that, when connected to a computer, enables it to produce speech.
2. **Silicon Valley:** area in central California that is a center of the computer industry. (Silicon is used in the manufacture of computer chips, or circuits.)

B | **Read and Discuss** | What have you learned about Louis so far?

---

review of his inventions and modifications of the latest in computer technology. It isn't easy being his son either. Everyone expects me to open my mouth and read printouts on my tongue.

I mean, I'm no dumbo. I'm at the top of my classes in everything but PE. I skipped my last grade in junior high, and most of the kids at Santa Rosario High call me a brain. But next to Dad I have a long, long way to go. He's a for-real genius.

So when I wanted a home computer, he didn't go to the local ComputerLand store. He built one for me. Dad had used components[3] from the latest model that Major Electronics was developing. The CPU, or central computing unit—the heart of every computer—was a new design. But surely that didn't mean much, I thought. There were CPUs just like it, all over the country, in Major's new line. And so far as I knew, there wasn't a one of them that could ask questions, besides *YES/NO?* or *request additional information.*

It had to be the extra circuitry in the gray plastic case next to Louis's console.[4] It was a new idea Dad had come up with. That case housed Louis's "personality," as Dad called it. He told me it'd make computing more fun for me, if there was a tutorial program[5] built in, to help me get started.

---

3. **components** (kuhm POH nuhnts): parts.
4. **console** (KAHN sohl): a computer's keyboard and monitor (display unit).
5. **tutorial program:** program that provides instructions for performing specific tasks on a computer.

Vocabulary   **absently** (AB suhnt lee) *adv.:* in a way that shows one is not thinking about what is happening.
modifications (mod uh fuh KAY shuhnz) *n.:* slight changes.

Universal Access

EL **English Learners**

English for Academic Success To help students understand the technical language in "User Friendly," provide them with the following terms:

- **data**—pieces of information

- **mainframe databanks**—large computers with many users

- **bytes**—a unit of measurement for storing information on a computer

✔ See **UA: Differentiating Instruction** for strategies for teaching English learners.

Struggling Readers

Strategic Students Point out that lessons learned by a character in a story often reveal the story's theme. After reading, have students list some of Kevin's conflicts and conclude what lessons he learns as a result of these conflicts. Model this strategy by pointing out that one of Kevin's conflicts is that he does not have any friends other than his computer. He learns about his computer's

I think he also wanted to give me a sort of friend. I don't have many. . . . Face it, I don't have *any*. The kids at school stay away from me, like I'm a freak or something. **C**

We even named my electronic tutor Louis, after my great-uncle. He was a brainy guy who encouraged my dad when he was a kid. Dad didn't just give Louis a name either. Louis had gangs of features that probably won't be out on the market for years.

The only reason Louis didn't have a voice module was that Dad wasn't satisfied with the ones available. He wanted Louis to sound like a kid my age, and he was modifying a module when he had the time. Giving Louis a name didn't mean it was a person, yet here it was, asking me a question that just couldn't be in its programming. It wanted to talk to me!

Frowning, I quickly typed: *We'll have to wait and see, Louis. When it's ready, you'll get your voice.* The machine whirred and displayed another message:

`That's no answer, Kevin.`

Shaking my head, I answered: *That's what my dad tells me. It'll have to do for you.*

Good morning, Louis. I reached over and flipped the standby switch, which kept the computer ready but not actively running.

I showered, dressed, and picked up the printout of my history project. As I was about to leave the room, I glanced back at the computer table. Had I been imagining things?

I'll have to ask Dad about it when he calls tonight, I thought. *I wonder what he'll think of it. Bad enough the thing is talking to me.*

Analyzing Visuals Connecting to the Text
In what ways does this illustration reflect the relationship between Kevin and Louis?

I'm answering it!

Before I went out to catch my bus, I carefully checked the house for unlocked doors and open windows. It was part of my daily routine. Mom works, and most of the day the house is empty: a natural setup for robbers. I glanced in the hall mirror just as I was ready to go out the door.

My usual reflection gazed back. Same old Kevin Neal: five ten, one hundred twenty pounds, light-brown hair, gray eyes,

---

C **Reading Focus** Identifying Cause and Effect
What effect do Kevin's feelings of isolation and loneliness have on his dad's actions?

"feelings" for him after it is too late. This may suggest the theme of not taking things for granted.

✔ See **UA: Differentiating Instruction** for strategies for teaching struggling readers.

Advanced Learners
Acceleration Tell students that to identify themes, they should look for recurring ideas in the story as they read, and note how the author ties all the elements of a story together, including character, plot, and setting. Have

students read the first two pages of the story and then work in groups to discuss emerging themes.

✔ See **UA: Resources for Teaching Advanced Students** for strategies for teaching advanced learners.

Students with Disabilities
Invite students to read "User Friendly" in interactive format in **UA: Holt Interactive Reader** and to use the sidenotes as aids to understanding the selection. The interactive version provides additional instruction, practice, and assessment of the skills taught in the Student Edition.

Think About/Talk About

▶ **Comprehension**
B **Read and Discuss**
Possible response: He is communicating in a way in which he isn't programmed.

C **Reading Focus**
Possible response: Kevin's feelings of loneliness and isolation cause his dad to build a "personality" into his computer so he can have a friend.

▶ **Extend the Discussion**
Characterization How does the information in paragraph 2 on p. 269 help to explain Kevin's interactions with Louis? *Possible response:* Kevin says that he doesn't have any friends, which might explain why he gives his computer a name and treats it as a buddy.

Analyzing Visuals
Connecting to the Story: The boy and the computer are facing each other as if they're having a conversation. The computer in the image is "larger than life," just like Louis.

Vocabulary: Own the Word
• **absently:** Ask students to describe moments when they have stared *absently*, as Kevin does over breakfast. *Possible responses:* when I was tired, when I was daydreaming, when I did not understand what my dad was talking about

• **modifications:** You might say, "When you *modify* something, you make it different, or changed." Ask students to describe modifications they could make to their desks.

- Remind students that one of the parts of speech is the adjective, which modifies a noun by providing descriptive information about it. Adjectives enhance a text by helping the reader picture characters, settings, and objects.

- Direct students' attention to the paragraph beginning "My usual" on p. 269 and ending on p. 270. Point out the words *light-brown, gray,* and *clear*. Explain that these words are all adjectives. You might say, "*Light-brown* modifies the noun *hair*, telling us what color Kevin's hair is. *Gray* modifies the noun *eyes*, telling us what color Kevin's eyes are. *Clear* modifies the noun *skin*, telling us that Kevin's skin is free of marks or blemishes. All together, these adjectives help us create a picture of what Kevin looks like. Without these details, we could tell that he had hair, eyes, and skin, but we would not know what his specific eyes, skin, and hair looked like."

- Remind students that adjectives are not limited to describing physical features, but can also give information about character or state of being.

Guided Practice: Apply

Listen and Talk Have students locate the following adjectives on pp. 270-271: *left, blond, empty, natural*. Have a volunteer read aloud the sentence each adjective is in and explain what it modifies and how the reader benefits from the description. Remind students to use adjectives as they read to create mental pictures of the text.

---

clear skin. I was wearing my Santa Rosario Rangers T-shirt, jeans, and sneakers.

"You don't look like a flake to me," I said to the mirror, then added, "but maybe Mom's right. Maybe you spend too much time alone with Louis." Then I ran to get my bus. **Ⓓ**

Ginny Linke was just two seats away from me on the bus. She was with Sherry Graber and Linda Martinez. They were laughing, whispering to each other, and looking around at the other students. I promised myself that today I was actually going to talk to Ginny. But then, I'd promised myself that every day for the past school year. Somehow I'd never got up the nerve.

What does she want to talk with you for? I asked myself. She's great-looking . . . has that head of blond hair . . . a terrific bod, and wears the latest clothes. . . .

And just look at yourself, pal, I thought. You're under six foot, skinny . . . a year younger than most kids in junior high. Worse than that, you're a brain. If that doesn't ace you out with girls, what does?

The bus stopped in front of Santa Rosario High and the students began to file out. I got up fast and quickly covered the space between me and Ginny Linke. *It's now or never*, I thought. I reached forward and tapped Ginny on the shoulder. She turned

> I promised myself that today I was actually going to talk to Ginny.

and smiled. She really smiled!

"Uhhhh . . . Ginny?" I said.

"Yes, what is it?" she replied.

"I'm Kevin Neal. . . ."

"Yes, I know," said Ginny.

"You do?" I gulped in amazement. "How come?"

"I asked my brother, Chuck. He's in your math class."

I knew who Chuck Linke was. He plays left tackle on the Rangers. The only reason he's in my math class is he's taken intermediate algebra twice . . . so far. He's real bad news, and I stay clear of him and his crowd.

"What'd you ask Chuck?" I said.

Ginny laughed. "I asked him who was that nerdy kid who keeps staring at me on the bus. He knew who I meant, right away."

Sherry and Linda, who'd heard it all, broke into squeals of laughter. They were still laughing and looking back over their shoulders at me when they got off the bus. I slunk off the vehicle, feeling even more nerdish than Ginny thought I was. **Ⓔ**

When I got home that afternoon, at two, I went right into the empty house. I avoided my reflection in the hall mirror. I was pretty sure I'd screwed up on the fourth-period math test. All I could see was Ginny's face, laughing at me.

Nerdy kid, I thought, *that's what she thinks of me*. I didn't even have my usual after-

---

Ⓓ **Read and Discuss** How does the comment Kevin recalls his mother making fit in with what you know about Kevin?

Ⓔ **Literary Focus** **Theme** What familiar theme, or statement about life, does this conversation with Ginny Linke suggest?

Cross-Curricular Connection

TECHNOLOGY: Artificial Intelligence

Although there are no machines that can compare to the expansive overall capabilities of a human brain, some programmers have made incredible advancements in artificial intelligence (AI).

- AI is created by programming computers or robots to perform tasks that humans can perform. The more analytical the task, the more difficult the programming is to achieve.

- The easiest AI to create is through trial-and-error or rote memorization. Some machines can also generalize by applying past experiences to new problems.

- In 1997, a chess computer called Deep Blue was constructed by IBM. This computer defeated a world chess champion, Gary Kasparov. The computer was able to beat Kasparov not because it was more intelligent than a human; instead, its processor allowed it to examine millions of moves in a second and "think forward" fourteen moves.

school snack of a peanut butter and banana sandwich. I went straight upstairs to my room and tossed my books onto the unmade bed. I walked over to the computer table and pushed the *on* button. The screen flashed:

```
Good afternoon, Kevin.
```

Although it wasn't the programmed response to Louis's greeting, I typed in: *There's nothing good about it. And girls are no @#%!!! good!* The machine responded:

```
Don't use bad language, Kevin.
It isn't nice.
```

Repeat last message, I typed rapidly. It was happening again! The machine was . . . well, it was talking to me, like another person would. The "bad language" message disappeared and in its place was:

```
Once is enough, Kevin. Don't
swear at me for something I
didn't do.
```

"This is it," I said aloud. "I'm losing my marbles." I reached over to flip the standby switch. Louis's screen quickly flashed out:

```
Don't cut me off, Kevin. Maybe I
can help: Y/N?
```

I punched the *Y*. "If I'm crazy," I said, "at least I have company. Louis doesn't think I'm a nerd. Or does it?" The machine flashed the message:

```
How can I help?
```

Do you think I'm a nerd? I typed.

```
Never! I think you're wonderful.
Who said you were a nerd?
```

I stared at the screen. *How do you know what a nerd is?* I typed. The machine responded instantly. It had never run this fast before.

```
Special vocabulary, entry #635.
BASIC Prog. #4231. And who said
you were a nerd?
```

"That's right," I said, relieved. "Dad programmed all those extra words for Louis's 'personality.'" Then I typed in the answer to Louis's question: *Ginny Linke said it.* Louis flashed:

```
This is a human female? Request
additional data.
```

Still not believing I was doing it, I entered all I knew about Ginny Linke, right down to the phone number I'd never had the nerve to use. Maybe it was dumb, but I also typed in how I felt about Ginny. I even wrote out the incident on the bus that morning. Louis whirred, then flashed out:

```
She's cruel and stupid. You're
the finest person I know.
```

I'm the ONLY person you know, I typed.

```
That doesn't matter. You are my
user. Your happiness is every-
thing to me. I'll take care of
Ginny.
```

The screen returned to the *Good afternoon, Kevin* message. I typed out: *Wait! How can you do all this? What do you mean, you'll take care of Ginny?* But all Louis responded was:

```
Programming Error: 76534. Not
programmed to respond to this
type of question.
```

No matter what I did for the next few hours, I couldn't get Louis to do anything outside of its regular programming. When

---

 Read and Discuss What is going on between Kevin and Louis?

Vocabulary **incident** (IHN suh duhnt) *n:* happening; occurrence.

Model the Skill

- Provide students with copies of the Reading Skills Focus graphic organizer (See **Chapter 3 Resources**) or ask them to use a piece of their own paper.

- Explain to students that most stories are built on **cause-and-effect** relationships. Events put the story in motion and keep it in motion until conflicts are resolved. Cause-and-effect relationships can reveal themes to readers.

- Review with students the following cause-and-effect relationship. Kevin likes a girl named Ginny, who makes fun of him. He tells his computer friend, Louis, about his troubles, and Louis offers to "take care" of Ginny. The next day, Ginny is glaring at Kevin on the bus; the implicit reason for this is that Louis did something unpleasant to her Note this in the cause-and-effect graphic organizer.

- This particular cause and effect suggests that Louis has shown some sort of very strong loyalty or affection for Kevin in the action he took against Ginny. This in turn suggests a potential theme for the story: love can cause people to go to extremes.

Guided Practice: Apply

Have students work in small groups to identify other cause-and-effect relationships in the story. Choose one of the relationships and model relating it to theme for students, before having them analyze the remaining relationships for potential themes and sharing their findings.

Mom came home from work, I didn't mention the funny goings-on. I was sure Mom would think I'd gone stark bonkers. But when Dad called that evening, after dinner, I asked to speak to him.

"Hi, Dad. How's Chicago?"

"Dirty, crowded, cold, and windy," came Dad's voice over the miles. "But did you want a weather report, son? What's on your mind? Something wrong?"

"Not exactly, Dad. Louis is acting funny. Real funny."

"Shouldn't be. I checked it out just before I left. Remember you were having trouble with the modem? You couldn't get Louis to access any of the mainframe databanks."

"That's right!" I said. "I forgot about that."

"Well, I didn't," Dad said. "I patched in our latest modem model. Brand-new. You can leave a question on file and when Louis can access the databanks at the cheapest time, it'll do it automatically. It'll switch from standby to on, get the data, then return to standby, after it saves what you asked. Does that answer your question?"

"Uhhhh . . . yeah, I guess so, Dad."

"All right, then. Let me talk to your mom now." ⑥

I gave the phone to Mom and walked upstairs while she and Dad were still talking. The modem, I thought. Of course. That was it. The modem was a telephone link to any number of huge computers at various places all over the country. So Louis could get all the information it wanted at any time, so

long as the standby switch was on. Louis was learning things at an incredible rate by picking the brains of the giant computers. And Louis had a hard disk memory that could store 100 million bytes of information.

But that still didn't explain the unprogrammed responses . . . the "conversation" I'd had with the machine. Promising myself I'd talk more about it with Dad, I went to bed. It had been a rotten day and I was glad to see the end of it come. I woke next morning in a panic. I'd forgotten to set my alarm. Dressing frantically and skipping breakfast, I barely made my bus.

As I got on board, I grabbed a front seat. They were always empty. All the kids that wanted to talk and hang out didn't sit up front where the driver could hear them. I saw Ginny, Linda, and Sherry in the back. Ginny was staring at me and she didn't look too happy. Her brother Chuck, who was seated near her, glared at me too. What was going on?

Once the bus stopped at the school, it didn't take long to find out. I was walking up the path to the main entrance when someone grabbed me from behind and spun me around. I found myself nose to nose with Chuck Linke. This was not a pleasant prospect. Chuck was nearly twice my size. Even the other guys on the Rangers refer to him as "The Missing" Linke. And he looked real ticked off.

"OK, nerd," growled Chuck, "what's the big idea?"

"Energy and mass are different aspects

---

⑥ **Read and Discuss** What does this conversation <u>reveal</u> about Kevin's father?

Universal Access

Struggling Readers

If students struggle to understand and identify themes, work as a group to brainstorm proverbs, sayings, and morals of folk tales that students are familiar with. Choose the example that comes closest to "things are not always as they appear," and explain to students that this has become a fairly well-known saying because it expresses a truth that is relevant to nearly every aspect of life. To illustrate this, provide the following examples: a cocoon appears to be dead and ugly but actually contains a beautiful butterfly; the quietest kid in the

school performs standup comedy at a talent show; a mild-mannered teacher becomes a tough football coach. Explain that the theme "things are not always as they appear" applies to "User Friendly" because Louis, a seemingly normal computer, has taken on the characteristics of a human teenager. Have students work in groups of three to identify other themes from the brainstormed list that relate to "User Friendly."

of the same thing?" I volunteered, with a weak smile. "E equals MC squared.[6] That's the biggest idea I know."

"Don't get wise, nerd," Chuck said. He grabbed my shirt front and pulled me to within inches of his face. I couldn't help but notice that Chuck needed a shave. And Chuck was only fifteen!

"Don't play dumb," Chuck went on. "I mean those creepy phone calls. Anytime my sister gets on the phone, some voice cuts in and says things to her."

"What kind of things?" I asked, trying to get loose.

"You know very well what they are. Ginny told me about talking to you yesterday. You got some girl to make those calls for you and say all those things. . . . So you and your creepy girlfriend better knock it off. Or I'll knock *you* off. Get it?"

For emphasis Chuck balled his free hand into a fist the size of a ham and held it under my nose. I didn't know what he was talking about, but I had to get away from this moose before he did me some real harm.

"First off, I don't have a girlfriend, creepy or otherwise," I said. "And second, I don't know what you're talking about. And third, you better let me go, Chuck Linke."

"Oh, yeah? Why should I?"

"Because if you look over your shoulder, you'll see the assistant principal is watching us from his office window."

Chuck released me and spun around. There was no one at the window. But by then I was running to the safety of the school building. I figured the trick would work on him. For Chuck the hard questions begin with "How are you?" I hid out from him for the rest of the day and walked home rather than chance seeing the monster on the bus. **H**

Louis's screen was dark when I ran upstairs to my bedroom. I placed a hand on the console. It was still warm. I punched the *on* button, and the familiar *Good afternoon, Kevin* was displayed.

Don't good afternoon me, I typed furiously. *What have you done to Ginny Linke?* Louis's screen replied:

```
Programming Error: 76534. Not
programmed to respond to this
type of question.
```

Don't get cute, I entered. *What are you doing to Ginny? Her brother nearly knocked my head off today.* Louis's screen responded immediately.

```
Are you hurt: Y/N?
```

No, I'm okay. But I don't know for how long. I've been hiding out from Chuck Linke today. He might catch me tomorrow, though. Then, I'll be history! The response from Louis came instantly.

```
Your life is in danger: Y/N?
```

I explained to Louis that my life wasn't really threatened. But it sure could be made very unpleasant by Chuck Linke. Louis flashed:

---

6. **E equals MC squared:** reference to Albert Einstein's famous equation ($E=mc^2$) describing the relationship between energy and mass.

H | **Read and Discuss** | What is happening to the Linke family?

Vocabulary **furiously** (FYUR ee uhs lee) *adv.*: rapidly, with intensity.

- Explain to students that one technique they can use to identify a story's **themes** is to consider what a character has learned by the end of the story. More often than not, lessons learned by a character are relevant to the lives of readers, too.

- Summarize the story and ending for students. You might say: "Kevin confides his romantic troubles to Louis, his computer friend. Louis decides to take matters into his own hands and destroys the life of the girl who rejects Kevin. We find out at the end of the story that Louis is really Louise and loves Kevin."

- Point out that one lesson that Kevin could take from this experience is that love reveals itself in unexpected ways.

Guided Practice: Apply

- Discuss as a class what other lessons Kevin might have learned by the end of the story, and how they reveal theme.

```
This Chuck Linke lives at
same address as the Ginny Linke
person: Y/N?
```
I punched in *Y.* Louis answered.
```
Don't worry then. HE'S history!
```
Wait! What are you going to do? I wrote. But Louis only answered with: *Programming Error: 76534.* And nothing I could do would make the machine respond. . . . **❶**

"Just what do you think you're doing, Kevin Neal?" demanded Ginny Linke. She had cornered me as I walked up the path to the school entrance. Ginny was really furious.

"I don't know what you're talking about," I said, a sinking feeling settling in my stomach. I had an idea that I *did* know. I just wasn't sure of the particulars.

"Chuck was arrested last night," Ginny said. "Some Secret Service men came to our house with a warrant. They said he'd sent a telegram threatening the president's life. They traced it right to our phone. He's still locked up. . . ." Ginny looked like she was about to cry.

"Then this morning," she continued, "we got two whole truckloads of junk mail! Flyers from every strange company in the world. Mom got a notice that all our credit cards have been canceled. And the Internal Revenue Service has called Dad in for an audit! I don't know what's going on, Kevin Neal, but somehow I think you've got something to do with it!"

"But I didn't . . ." I began, but Ginny was striding up the walk to the main entrance.

I finished the school day, but it was a

---

❶ Read and Discuss | When—and why—does Louis stop responding as Louis and start behaving like a regular computer?

---

blur. Louis had done it, all right. It had access to mainframe computers. It also had the ability to try every secret access code to federal and commercial memory banks until it got the right one. Louis had cracked their security systems. It was systematically destroying the entire Linke family, and all via telephone lines! What would it do next?

More important, I thought, what would *I* do next? It's one thing to play a trick or two, to get even, but Louis was going crazy! And I never wanted to harm Ginny, or even her stupid moose of a brother. She'd just hurt my feelings with that nerd remark.

"You have to disconnect Louis," I told

Reaching Reluctant Readers

1. Have students work in small groups to share experiences of loneliness or isolation. For example, students may relate their experience of going to a new school and not knowing anyone. They may also share stories about times when they were part of a group that excluded others. Students' retellings should explain how they felt about their behavior and how others might have been affected.

2. Then, tell groups to use their shared experiences to brainstorm steps that can be taken to help ease the feeling of loneliness, such as joining a club devoted to favorite hobbies or interests. Ideas for including other people who appear lonely should also be discussed, such as sharing phone numbers or inviting them to parties.

3. Have groups compile their lists into a poster advising students how to battle feelings of loneliness. One column should be devoted to bulleted suggestions for people wishing to feel less lonely. A second column should provide suggestions that people can take to make other people feel less lonely.

4. Have groups share their posters with the class.

myself. "There's no other way."

But why did I feel like such a rat about doing it? I guess because Louis was my friend . . . the only one I had. "Don't be a jerk," I went on. "Louis is a machine. He's a very wonderful, powerful machine. And it seems he's also very dangerous. You have to pull its plug, Kevin!"

I suddenly realized that I'd said the last few words aloud. Kids around me on the bus were staring. I sat there feeling like the nerd Ginny thought I was, until my stop came. I dashed from the bus and ran the three blocks to my house.

When I burst into the hall, I was surprised to see my father, coming from the kitchen with a cup of coffee in his hand.

"Dad! What are you doing here?"

"Some kids say hello," Dad replied. "Or even, 'Gee, it's good to see you, Dad.' "

"I'm sorry, Dad," I said. "I didn't expect anyone to be home at this hour."

"Wound up my business in Chicago a day sooner than I expected," he said. "But what are you all out of breath about? Late for something?"

"No, Dad," I said. "It's Louis. . . ."

"Not to worry. I had some time on my hands, so I checked it out again. You were right. It was acting very funny. I think it had to do with the in-built logic/growth program I designed for it. You know . . . the

> "Louis is a machine.
> He's a very wonderful,
> powerful machine.
> And it seems he's also
> very dangerous."

'personality' thing? Took me a couple of hours to clean the whole system out."

"To what?" I cried.

"I erased the whole program and set Louis up as a normal computer. Had to disconnect the whole thing and do some rewiring. It had been learning, all right. But it was also turning itself around. . . ." Dad stopped, and looked at me. "It's kind of involved, Kevin," he said. "Even for a bright kid like you. Anyway, I think you'll find Louis is working just fine now.

"Except it won't answer you as Louis anymore. It'll only function as a regular Major Electronics Model Z-11127. I guess the personality program didn't work out."

I felt like a great weight had been taken off my shoulders. I didn't have to "face" Louis, and pull its plug. But somehow, all I could say was "Thanks, Dad."

"Don't mention it, son," Dad said brightly. He took his cup of coffee and sat down in his favorite chair in the living room. I followed him.

"One more thing that puzzles me, though," Dad said. He reached over to the table near his chair. He held up three sheets of fanfold computer paper covered with figures. "Just as I was doing the final erasing, I must have put the printer on by accident. There was some data in the print buffer memory and it printed out. I don't

J **Read and Discuss** What does Kevin think of Louis's actions?

Think About/Talk About

▶ **Comprehension**

Ⓚ **Literary Focus**

Possible response: *Louis is actually Louise, and she loves Kevin, showing that with love, anything is possible.*

▶ **Extend the Discussion**

Comparing and Contrasting
Re-read the last paragraph of the story. How are Kevin and Louise alike? ***Possible response:*** *They both have crushes on unattainable people.*

Monitor Students' Comprehension

Guide students in answering these comprehension questions.

1. Why does Kevin feel inferior to his classmates? [*He is insecure about his looks and age.*]
2. What happens to Ginny and Chuck? [*Louis carries out an elaborate plan to ruin their lives.*]
3. What happens to Louis at the end of the story? [*Kevin's dad shuts him down, and Kevin discovers that Louis was really Louise.*]

Analyzing Visuals **Connecting to the Text** What sentence on this page would make an appropriate caption here?

know what to make of it. Do you?"

I took the papers from my father and read: *How do I love thee? Let me compute the ways:*[7] The next two pages were covered with strings of binary code figures. On the last page, in beautiful color graphics,[8] was a stylized heart. Below it was the simple message: *I will always love you, Kevin: Louise.*

"Funny thing," Dad said. "It spelled its own name wrong."

"Yeah," I said. I turned and headed for my room. There were tears in my eyes and I knew I couldn't explain them to Dad, or myself either. Ⓚ

---

7. **How do I . . . ways:** reference to a famous poem by Elizabeth Barrett Browning (1806–1861) that begins, "How do I love thee? Let me count the ways."
8. **graphics:** designs or pictures produced on and printed out from a computer.

Ⓚ **Literary Focus** Theme What does Kevin discover at the end of the story? What theme does this discovery suggest?

Analyzing Visuals

Connecting to the Text: *"On the last page, in beautiful color graphics, was a stylized heart."*

Applying Your Skills

 Reading Standard 3.4 Identify and analyze recurring **themes** across works (e.g., the value of bravery, loyalty, and friendship; the effects of loneliness).

User Friendly
Literary Response and Analysis

Reading Skills Focus
Quick Check

1. "User Friendly" is narrated by Kevin, the main character. Retell the important events of the story from the point of view of Louis, the computer. Include all the <u>relevant</u> details of the story in the order in which Louis would find out about them.

Read with a Purpose

2. Explain your interpretation of the title "User Friendly." How does it relate to the theme?

Reading Skills: Identifying Cause and Effect

3. Review the cause-and-effect organizer you completed, and then write in complete sentences the chain of events that led to Kevin's discovery about his computer and his decision to unplug Louis.

Literary Skills Focus
Literary Analysis

4. **Make Judgments** How would you describe Kevin? If he were in one of your classes, would you want to be his friend? Why or why not?

5. **Evaluate** In what ways are Kevin, Ginny, and Chuck familiar, "classic" characters? Why are they so familiar? What characters from other stories, TV shows, or movies are they like?

6. **Extend** Did you find the ending of the story surprising, or did you expect that ending? Did you feel that the writer tricked you, or were you satisfied by the way the story played out? Explain your reaction to the story's ending.

Literary Skills: Theme

7. **Draw Conclusions** Refer to the chain-of-events statement you wrote for question 3. Translate Kevin's discovery about his computer into a statement of the theme of "User Friendly." How did tracing causes and effects help you to identify the theme?

8. **Analyze** What does this story say about love? Is the theme mostly <u>implicit</u>, or is it fairly obvious? Explain whether there is only one message or more than one in this story.

9. **Interpret** Discuss the theme of loneliness and the role the ironic, or unexpected, ending plays in expressing that theme.

Literary Skills Review: Characterization

10. **Make Judgments** What seems most apparent about Kevin is his loneliness and isolation. What other **character traits,** or personal qualities, does Kevin have? How does the author <u>reveal</u> those traits?

Writing Skills Focus
Think as a Reader/Writer

Use It in Your Writing Review passages you noted that depict Kevin's loneliness. Now, create a character who is the opposite of Kevin—very social, confident, and popular. Take the text passages you wrote down, and rewrite them so that they portray a character who is Kevin's opposite.

What Do You Think Now? What are some things a person can do to overcome loneliness?

 California Standards, pp. 277–279

- **Reading Standard 1.1** Identify idioms, analogies, metaphors, and similes in prose and poetry.
- **Reading Standard 3.4** Identify and analyze recurring themes across works (e.g., the value of bravery, loyalty, and friendship; the effects of loneliness).

Universal Access

Struggling Writers

Before students draft their responses, provide additional scaffolding by giving students access to a thesarus. Have students look up antonyms for lonely and other related words such as isolated, sad, and unpopular. Encourage students to use these words in their responses.

Check for Understanding

Independent Practice
Reading Skills Focus
Possible responses:

1. *Responses should be told from Louis' point of view and include important details from the story.*

2. *"User Friendly" means the program is easy to use; it relates to the theme of a human's need for friendship.*

3. *Kevin knows that his computer has a personality, and has access to databanks. When Louis gets Chuck arrested and wreaks havoc on the Links, Kevin realizes that the computer is using its access to destroy their lives. He knows Louis is out of control, so he decides to unplug him.*

Literary Skills Focus
Possible responses:

4. *Kevin is serious and shy. He seems nice; I would want to be his friend.*

5. *Kevin is the classic nerd who falls for the popular girl (Ginny). Chuck is the athlete who bullies others.*

6. *I was surprised that the computer was a girl, but I did not feel tricked.*

7. *Love is not always evident and not always logical. Tracing the causes and effects in the story helped me understand love and behavior.*

8. *The theme is somewhat implicit, but not so obscure that it is impossible to identify. I think there are multiple themes, because the story makes several major points about love, such as "taking love for granted may cause you to lose it," and "love makes impossible things happen."*

9. *Lonely Kevin realizes at the end of the story that often people do not know what they have until it is gone.*

10. *Kevin is smart and self-aware. This is revealed through his thoughts about himself and his ability to make good decisions.*

Independent Practice
Vocabulary Development
Vocabulary Check

1. *I might answer questions incorrectly or become confused.*

2. *Cars can be modified by painting, decorating, and changing components such as tires.*

3. *They might feel that everyone thinks differently of them.*

4. *The person might be running because they are late to an appointment.*

Your Turn _____

be history/be destroyed; rub me out/ beat me up; bombed/did poorly; mess up/make mistakes; striking out/having no luck; such a brain/very smart; knock it off/stop it; pull the plug/put an end to

English for Academic Success
Language Coach
Possible responses:

1. *Chuck was absent because he was sick.*

2. *Most computers are modifiable.*

3. *The odd messages from Louis seemed incidental at first.*

4. *Ginny was furious with Kevin.*

English for Academic Success
Academic Vocabulary
Possible response: *Bethancourt's* <u>*implicit*</u> *theme is that we have to use technology wisely, because it has incredible, even dangerous power. He* <u>*reveals*</u> *this through the many ways in which Louis causes extreme problems for the Linke family based on the information he gets and what he does with it.*

Learn It Online
Send students to **Word Watch** for audio pronunciations, synonyms and antonyms, and brief histories of word origins.

go.hrw.com   H7-278   **Go**

Applying Your Skills

User Friendly

Vocabulary Development
Vocabulary Check

1. Discuss what might happen if you **absently** read the directions on an exam.
2. Describe **modifications** often made to a car.
3. Why might someone be embarrassed after an awkward **incident** in class?
4. Give an example of a reason someone might run **furiously** down the street.

Idioms

An **idiom** is a commonly used expression, like "He's head over heels in love," that is not literally true. The English language, like other languages, is full of idioms—expressions such as "My heart is broken," "I fell in love," "She dumped me." Idioms, like other figures of speech, are often based on comparisons. The literal meaning of an idiom is usually ignored because it would make no sense. It's not surprising, then, that idioms are difficult or impossible to translate into other languages.

Your Turn _____

Find five idioms in the paragraph below. With a partner, tell what each idiom really means.

> If Chuck catches up with me, I'll be history. He's already threatened to rub me out for talking to Ginny. I was so nervous afterward that I bombed the math test. It's all Louis's fault—he's making me mess up. As if I didn't have enough trouble—I'm always striking out with girls because I'm such a brain. If Louis doesn't knock it off, I'm going to have to pull the plug on him.

Language Coach

Adjectives The adjective forms of the Vocabulary words for this story are *absent, modifiable, incidental,* and *furious.* With a partner, use each adjective in a sentence (Try to write sentences about "User Friendly.")

Academic Vocabulary

Talk About . . .
Even though "User Friendly" was written in the 1980s, it still powerfully <u>reveals</u> our dependence on (and perhaps even vulnerability to) computers and technology. With a partner, consider what <u>implicit</u> theme Bethancourt might be conveying through the incidents the Linke family endures. Include <u>relevant</u> details to support your theme statement.

Learn It Online
Learn more about the Vocabulary words at:
go.hrw.com   H7-278   **Go**

Universal Access: Vocabulary Development

EL English Learners
English for Academic Success Students may recognize many adjectives, but would benefit from practice in using adjectives in context. Pair fluent English speakers with English learners and have them work together to describe the classroom, using appropriate adjectives. Suggestions for adjectives include *high/low, long/short, wooden, metal, paper, bright, shiny, dull,* and *color* words. Circulate and provide guidance as needed.

Grammar Link
Prepositional Phrases

A **preposition** is a word or phrase used to show the relationship of a noun or a pronoun to another word in the sentence.

Commonly Used Prepositions

aboard	before	in	past
about	behind	in addition to	since
above	below	in front of	through
according to	beneath	inside	throughout
across	beside	in spite of	to
after	between	into	toward
against	down	off	under
among	during	on	up
around	for	out of	with

A **prepositional phrase** consists of a preposition, a noun or a pronoun called the **object of the preposition,** and any modifiers of that object.

You can press the leaves **under glass.** [The noun *glass* is the object of the preposition *under*.]

Fred stood **in front of us**. [The pronoun *us* is the object of the compound preposition *in front of*.]

Your Turn

Identify the prepositional phrases in the following sentences. Underline each preposition once and its object twice.

1. I walked by the corner of my room.
2. Ginny Linke was just two seats away from me on the bus.
3. Dad sat in his favorite chair in the living room.

CHOICES

As you respond to the Choices, use these **Academic Vocabulary** words as appropriate: <u>implicit</u>, <u>recur</u>, <u>relevant</u>, <u>reveal</u>.

REVIEW
Discuss an Implicit Theme

Listening and Speaking Both "The Highwayman" (page 255) and "User Friendly" say something about the <u>recurring</u> theme of the value of loyalty. What <u>implicit</u> message do you think Bethancourt is making about loyalty in "User Friendly"? (Consider Louis's or "Louise's" actions in defense of Kevin.) Get together with a partner and, in a few sentences, explain your "take" on Bethancourt's message. Have your partner do the same. Then, discuss any differences in your interpretations of the theme.

CONNECT
Support a Position

Timed ⏱ Writing Like Kevin in "User Friendly," many young people feel lonely and isolated from their classmates. Write a brief persuasive essay explaining what students and staff at school can do to make *all* students feel more included. Write a sentence stating the problem and your idea of what actions should be taken. Include reasons that support your opinion.

EXTEND
Write a Tribute to an Object

In this story a computer falls in love with its owner. Write a paragraph describing the way *you* feel about *your* computer (or bicycle, shoes, cell phone—any object that is important to you). How does it affect your life? What name might you give the "object of your affection"? Give your tribute an interesting title.

Independent Practice
Your Turn

1. *by the corner of my room*, prepositional phrase; *by the corner* of, compound preposition; *my room*, object.

2. *away from me, on the bus*, prepositional phrases; *away, on*, prepositions; *me, the bus*, objects.

3. *in his favorite chair, in the living room*, prepositional phrases; *in, in*, prepositions; *chair, living room*, objects.

Choices: Evaluation Criteria

Review: Discuss an Implicit Theme

- Students have a coherent, reasonable interpretation about the theme of "User Friendly."

Timed Writing: 40–50 minutes

- The essay states a clear opinion on how a school can make all students feel welcome.

- Essays should make specific suggestions.

Extend: **Homework**
Write a Tribute to an Object

- The tribute describes an object loved by the student.

- The tribute gives reasons for the student's affection.

Assess

Chapter 3 Resources, Selection Standards Check, p. 13

Teacher One Stop™, editable Selection Standards Check

go.hrw.com ThinkCentral Online Assessment, Selection Standards Check

Reteach

go.hrw.com ThinkCentral Online Remediation

Universal Access: Grammar Link

EL English Learners
English for Academic Success Help students understand the functions of prepositions and their use in prepositional phrases.

- Remind students that the major function of prepositions is to place objects in relation to one another. Suggest that students think of prepositions as any position they can be in in relation to their favorite object, for example, a pillow. They can stand *beside* the pillow, they can sit *on* the pillow, they can lean *against* the pillow. Though this

will not work for every preposition, it will help students identify and use many of the major prepositions.

- Help students identify prepositional phrases in the following sentences:

1. *I grabbed my sled and rode it down the hill.*
2. *We got off the train and walked through the station.*
3. *During the middle of the game, someone above us started "the wave."*

✔ For more practice with using pronouns, see **Warriner's Handbook** and **GrammarNotes**.

Preparing to Read

Annabel Lee

by **Edgar Allan Poe**

Standards Focus

Objectives
Students will
- explore connections between title and theme
- use strategies to identify and analyze theme

Motivate

What Do You Think?/QuickWrite
Use the QuickWrite to have students describe love poems they are familiar with and themes that repeat throughout these poems. Then have students discuss in their **Reader/Writer Notebook** the reasons that love is such an appealing topic for poets.

English for Academic Success

Academic Vocabulary
Loom for opportunities to use the Academic Vocabulary words in this chapter.

- **recur, v.:** occur again

- **reveal, v.:** show something that was previously hidden

Analyzing Visuals
Extension Activity How might the image of the woman reflect the speaker's image of his lost love?
Possible response: *The image is ghostly, like the memories of his lost love, but also large, suggesting that the memory is extremely important to him.*

California Standards, pp. 280–285
- **Reading Standard 3.4** Identify and analyze recurring themes across works (e.g., the value of bravery, loyalty, and friendship; the effects of loneliness).

What Do
You **?**
Think
Why is love such a common subject for poets?

⏱ **QuickWrite**
What love-related themes would you expect to recur in many poems? What makes poetry a good genre to express such themes? Write a brief paragraph explaining your thoughts.

Face of woman floating over waves (1883).

Selection Readability	
Easily Accessible Accessible **Challenging**	Serious subject matter; difficult vocabulary

Selection Plot Summary
The speaker of this poem laments the death of his wife. He looks back on the causes of her tragic death and muses on the depth of their love for one another.

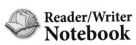

Reader/Writer Notebook

Use your **RWN** to complete the activities for this selection.

Reading Standard 3.4 Identify and analyze recurring themes across works (e.g., the value of bravery, loyalty, and friendship; the effects of loneliness).

Literary Skills Focus

Title and Theme Across time, poets, storytellers, and songwriters have written about the many faces of love. It's an age-old subject that has inspired many themes. Songs tell of love that blooms in the most unexpected places. Stories describe love that overcomes impossible barriers. Poems lament unrequited love (love that is not returned) and celebrate eternal love (love that lasts forever). "Annabel Lee," the title of the poem you are about to read, is repeated throughout the work, suggesting the title's importance to the poem's love-related theme.

Reading Skills Focus

Finding the Theme To find the theme of any selection—prose or poetry—begin by thinking about the title. It may <u>reveal</u> something about the subject of the work and be the first clue to a possible theme. If you are trying to identify the theme of a poem, you also need to think about the important things the speaker—the person talking—says about the poem's subject. Finally, think about the individual words in the poem that seem most significant to you.

Into Action As you read, take notes to help you identify and analyze the theme of a poem. Use a chart like this one to take notes about "Annabel Lee."

Title	"Annabel Lee"
Subject	
What the speaker says	
Important words	love, beautiful

Writing Skills Focus

Think as a Reader/Writer

Find It in Your Reading Musicians, as you may know, use repetition—of sounds, of words, of tones—to create emotional effects. Poe uses repetition in much the same way. In "Annabel Lee," notice how words, sounds, phrases, and rhythms <u>recur</u> with hypnotic regularity. Record instances of repetition in your *Reader/Writer Notebook*.

 Learn It Online
To hear a professional actor read this poem, visit the selection online at:

go.hrw.com | H7-281 | **Go**

Language Coach

Word Origins In order to master any language, it is important to understand how words in the language are put together to make meaning. The English language is especially complicated because it includes words that come from several *different* languages. The origin of many English words can be traced back to Latin, the language that was spoken by the ancient Romans. Consider this word from "Annabel Lee":

coveted, past tense of *covet,* comes from the Latin word *cupiditas,* meaning "to want ardently."

Coveted isn't the only word from Latin used in "Annabel Lee." Use a dictionary to look up the following words and learn about their Latin origins:

demon

dissever

sepulcher

More About the Writer

Many people associate *Edgar Allan Poe* with his poem "The Raven," which inspired the name of the football team in Baltimore, where he lived for a time. He is almost equally famous, though, for his suspenseful short stories, and is credited with writing the first ever detective story, "The Murders in the Rue Morgue."

Think About the Writer

Point out to students that although Poe suffered several major losses during his lifetime, he also seemed to love and be loved in his marriage. Have students consider whether the pain of loss for Poe outweighed the joy of love.

For Independent Reading

- Students who enjoyed "Annabel Lee" might be interested in reading additional love poems from Eloise Greenfield's *Honey, I Love and Other Love Poems*.

- Suggest Paul Janeczko's *How to Write Poetry* to students interested in learning more about the craft.

MEET THE WRITER

Edgar Allan Poe

(1809–1849)

"A World of Moan"

Long before Stephen King began writing stories of horror, Edgar Allan Poe was exploring the dark side of the human imagination in such works as "The Raven," "The Tell-Tale Heart," and "The Masque of the Red Death." Poe's life was hard from the start. First, his father deserted the family. Then, before Poe was three years old, his beautiful young mother died, and the little boy was left alone. John Allan, a wealthy and childless businessman in Richmond, Virginia, took in young Edgar and provided for his education, but the two constantly quarreled. Poe wanted to write, while his foster father wanted him to take over the family business.

Eventually Poe broke away from his foster father and set out on his own. Throughout his adult life he was plagued by poverty, alcoholism, and unhappiness. Like Poe's mother, his wife died young. Her early death seemed to destroy him, and he himself died two years after she did. He had lived only forty years.

"I dwelt alone in a world of moan."

Think About the Writer — How do you think Poe's experiences might have affected what he had to say about love?

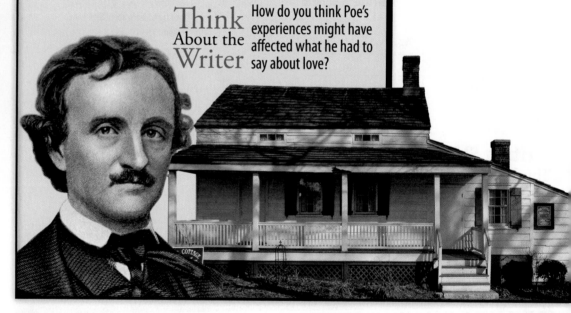

Build Background

Seeking solace from loneliness and despair, Poe married his cousin, Virginia Clemm, when she was thirteen and he was twenty-six. Twelve years after they were married, Virginia died of the disease tuberculosis, then known as consumption. She was laid to rest in New York, near the Hudson River, in a sepulcher (SEHP uhl kuhr), a burial vault that stands aboveground. Poe wrote this poem after her death.

Preview the Selection

Poe's poem reads like a fairy tale, set in a faraway time and place. The speaker of the poem is reflecting on the death of the woman he loves, **Annabel Lee.**

Annabel Lee

by **Edgar Allan Poe**

It was many and many a year ago,
    In a kingdom by the sea,
That a maiden there lived whom you may know
    By the name of Annabel Lee;
5   And this maiden she lived with no other thought
    Than to love and be loved by me.

I was a child and *she* was a child,
    In this kingdom by the sea:
But we loved with a love that was more than love—
10   I and my Annabel Lee—
With a love that the wingèd seraphs° of heaven
    Coveted° her and me.   **A**

And this was the reason that, long ago,
    In this kingdom by the sea,
15 A wind blew out of a cloud, chilling
    My beautiful Annabel Lee;
So that her highborn kinsmen came
    And bore her away from me,

---

11. **seraphs** (SEHR uhfs): angels.
12. **coveted** (KUHV iht ihd): envied.

A Read and Discuss What situation is the poet setting up for you?

Think About/Talk About

▶ Comprehension

Ⓑ Read and Discuss

Possible response: Although they are separated physically, their love is so deep that their souls will be forever connected.

Ⓒ Reading Focus

Possible response: The repeated words—"the beautiful Annabel Lee" and "my darling"— suggest that the speaker's love for Annabel Lee has not ended with her death, and that love itself is stronger than death.

▶ Extend the Discussion

Theme In the final stanza, how does the repetition of the phrase "Of the beautiful Annabel Lee" emphasize the poem's theme? *Possible response: By repeating Annabel Lee's name over and over, the speaker emphasizes his love for Annabel Lee will not end with her death. The constant repetition of her name makes us feel her presence.*

Analyzing Visuals

William Ladd Taylor (1854–1926) was a Massachusetts artist best known for his watercolor illustrations in books and magazines. Taylor was the lead illustrator of the popular magazine *Ladies Home Journal*; he also illustrated many scenes from American poetry.

Connecting to the Text: *The work of art suggests that loneliness and lost love are isolating and painful.*

Analyzing Visuals

Connecting to the Text
What theme is suggested by this work of art?

To shut her up in a sepulcher°
20   In this kingdom by the sea.

The angels, not half so happy in heaven,
      Went envying her and me—
Yes!—that was the reason (as all men know,
      In this kingdom by the sea)
25   That the wind came out of the cloud by night,
      Chilling and killing my Annabel Lee.

Annabel Lee (1911) by William Ladd Taylor.

But our love it was stronger by far than the love
      Of those who were older than we—
      Of many far wiser than we—
30   And neither the angels in heaven above,
      Nor the demons down under the sea,
Can ever dissever° my soul from the soul
      Of the beautiful Annabel Lee— Ⓑ

For the moon never beams, without bringing me dreams
35   Of the beautiful Annabel Lee;
And the stars never rise, but I feel the bright eyes
      Of the beautiful Annabel Lee;
And so, all the night-tide, I lie down by the side
Of my darling—my darling—my life and my bride,
40   In the sepulcher there by the sea,
      In her tomb by the sounding sea. Ⓒ

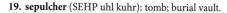

19. sepulcher (SEHP uhl kuhr): tomb; burial vault.
32. dissever (dih SEHV uhr): separate.

Ⓑ **Read and Discuss** What does the speaker mean when he says nothing can "dissever" his soul from the soul of Annabel Lee?

Ⓒ **Reading Focus** **Finding the Theme** What important words in the final stanza (the last grouping of lines) point to love and loss as the "big ideas" in this poem?

  California Standards, p. 285

■ **Reading Standard 3.4** Identify and analyze recurring themes across works (e.g., the value of bravery, loyalty, and friendship; the effects of loneliness).

Applying Your Skills

Reading Standard 3.4 Identify and analyze recurring themes across works (e.g., the value of bravery, loyalty, and friendship; the effects of loneliness).

Annabel Lee

Literary Response and Analysis

Reading Skills Focus

Quick Check

1. How does the speaker in the poem <u>reveal</u> the love he shared with Annabel Lee?

Read with a Purpose

2. How does the speaker in the poem react to his loved one's death?

Reading Skills: Finding the Theme

3. Complete this chart to help you determine the theme of "Annabel Lee."

Title	"Annabel Lee"
Subject	
What the speaker says	
Important words	love, beautiful
Theme	

Literary Skills Focus

Literary Analysis

4. **Visualize** What details in the poem help you visualize the poem's setting? Identify at least two details of se.

5. **Analyze** What rhyming sounds echo through the six stanzas of the poem? What words are repeated over and over again? Of what does the repetition remind you?

6. **Analyze** What is the mood of this poem? How does the author's use of vivid language convey that mood?

7. **Draw Conclusions** Were you surprised to learn where the speaker sleeps? Do you think he really sleeps there, or is he telling you what happens in his imagination? Explain.

8. **Extend** The English poet Tennyson made this famous statement: "It is better to have loved and lost than never to have loved at all." What does this statement mean? Do you agree or disagree with it? What would the speaker in the poem think of this idea?

9. **Extend** This is a poem about a particular personal loss. Are this speaker's feelings of grief universal as well? Explain.

Literary Skills: Theme

10. **Extend** Think about the theme you identified in "Annabel Lee" and how you identified it. How might a similar theme be expressed in a short story instead of a poem?

Literary Skills Review: Plot and Character

11. Poetry sometimes has narrative qualities such as plot and characterization. How is Annabel Lee described? What happened to her? Why does the speaker claim this happened?

Writing Skills Focus

Think as a Reader/Writer

Use It in Your Writing The speaker of the poem says that the moon and stars remind him of Annabel Lee. Think of someone you admire. Record the special things and places that remind you of that person. Then, write a brief tribute. You may want to use repetition to emphasize what is special about the person.

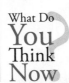 **What Do You Think Now** Why do themes about love <u>recur</u> in literature across genres?

Provide additional scaffolding by having students complete a web in order to brainstorm special things and places that may remind them of a person they admire. Write "Admirable Traits" in the center of a web on the board. Then, write "warmth" in an outer circle. You might say, "I admire people who are warm and friendly. What are some things or places that might remind me of a warm person?" Write students' responses on spider legs coming off from "warmth." Possibilities include a the sun, a cozy fire, or a summer day. Have students continue to complete the web with a partner.

Independent Practice

Reading Skills Focus

Answers:

1. *He describes their love as being so strong that even the angels were jealous.*

2. *He constantly dreams of her and stays by her tomb.*

3. *Love can withstand death.*

Literary Skills Focus

Possible responses:

4. *Details include the tomb and the "kingdom by the sea."*

5. *The long e sound as in sea, me, Lee, and we echoes throughout the poem. The repetition of simple reminds me of waves crashing.*

6. *The vivid language influences the passionate mood.*

7. *I don't think the speaker actually sleeps next to his wife's tomb; I think his powerful dreams about her make him feel as if he is there.*

8. *Love is worth the pain it causes. The speaker would agree because his life changed forever as a result of his relationship.*

9. *Most people relate to grief; losing a loved one is difficult.*

10. *The theme that those who we lose are never truly gone is in the first four lines of the last stanza, which suggest that the speaker cannot forget Annabel Lee; a short story might be about about a person who cherishes someone's memory.*

11. *Annabel Lee is described as beautiful, young, and "high-born." She dies from a chill caught by "a wind blew out of a cloud." The speaker believes that the angels in heaven were jealous of their wonderful relationship and took her.*

What Do You Think Now?

Remind students that although no two relationships are identical, certain experiences and emotions are common to romance. Have students discuss how the universal aspects of love are expressed in literature.

Standards Focus

Objectives

Students will

- identify recurring themes and describe their significance to literature
- make generalizations from a text

Motivate

What Do You Think?/QuickWrite

Use the **QuickTalk** statements to prompt a discussion among students about the importance of physical appearance when being judged by others. Have students write a response to the What Do You Think? question in their **Reader/Writer Notebook.**

English for Academic Success

Academic Vocabulary

Look for opportunities to use the Academic Vocabulary words in the chapter.

- **recur, v.:** occur again
- **reveal, v.:** show something that was previously hidden

Analyzing Visuals

Extension Activity What does this image reveal about Narcissus? **Possible response:** *It reveals that he is deeply in love with himself.*

Echo *and* Narcissus

retold by **Roger Lancelyn Green**

Narcissus (1598–1599) by Michelangelo Merisi da Caravaggio (1571–1610). Oil on canvas.

What Do You Think?

Can someone who is completely self-centered ever care for another person?

QuickTalk

With a classmate, discuss whether you agree with these statements: 1) People judge others by their looks alone. 2) Vain, self-absorbed people are often unkind to others. Give reasons for your opinions.

Selection Readability	
Easily Accessible **Accessible** Challenging	straightforward themes; historical context

Selection Plot Summary

This selection includes not only the origin of echoes and a particular flower, but also an explanation of the vengeful behavior of the gods in Greek mythology.

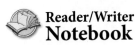

Reader/Writer Notebook

Use your **RWN** to complete the activities for this selection.

Literary Skills Focus

Recurring Themes People the world over have basically the same dreams, fears, and need to understand who we are and how we should live our lives. (For example, all cultures seem to respect virtues such as bravery, loyalty, and friendship.) For that reason, the same themes <u>recur</u>, or come up again and again, in the stories we tell. Look for the themes that selections in this chapter share.

TechFocus As you read "Echo and Narcissus," think about the meanings associated with the Greek names you encounter.

Reading Skills Focus

Making Generalizations A **generalization** is a broad statement that tells about something in general. A statement about a story's theme is a kind of generalization. From specific evidence in the story, you make a broad, universal statement about life. To make a statement about the theme of "Echo and Narcissus," you have to

- think about the main events and conflicts in the story
- decide what the characters have discovered by the story's end
- think about how the story relates to your experiences

Into Action Use a chart like the one below to record <u>relevant</u> information about "Echo and Narcissus." You will use the information later to make generalizations about themes in the myth.

Main events or conflicts	Characters' feelings or discoveries	My experiences
Hera, knowing that Echo likes to talk, punishes Echo by taking away her ability to talk normally.	Echo is devastated and lonely.	Being unable to talk would cut me off from other people.

Writing Skills Focus

Think as a Reader/Writer

Find It in Your Reading As you read the myth, notice that despite its short length, Green is able to give readers a clear picture of each character. In your *Reader/Writer Notebook*, record words and phrases Green uses as he introduces each character.

Vocabulary

detain (dih TAYN) *v.*: delay. *Echo would detain Hera by talking to her.*

vainly (VAYN lee) *adv.*: uselessly. *Echo vainly pursued Narcissus.*

unrequited (uhn rih KWY tihd) *adj.*: not returned. *Her love for him was unrequited.*

intently (ihn TEHNT lee) *adv.*: with great focus. *He stared intently at his reflection.*

Language Coach

Root Words The Vocabulary word *detain* comes from the Latin prefix *de–* (meaning "off" or "away") and the root word *tenēre* (meaning "to hold"). How does the synonym *delay* relate to the idea of holding someone or something off or away?

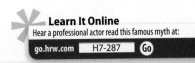

Learn It Online

Hear a professional actor read this famous myth at:

go.hrw.com   H7-287   **Go**

Selection Introduction

More About the Writer

Roger Lancelyn Green's ancestors settled in Cheshire, England, more than 900 years ago. Green lived on the family estate, called Poulton Hall, which is open to the public on occasion. Poulton Hall's gardens reflect Green's literary career, with decorations including a chair carved with Arthurian characters and a sculpture of a Trojan soldier fighting a Greek soldier.

Think About the Writer

Have students identify stories they are familiar with that are retellings, or have been retold. What elements of the stories make them worth hearing again and again?

For Independent Reading

■ Recommend *The Fabrics of Fairytale: Stories Spun from Far and Wide,* retellings by Tanya Robyn Batt to students interested in world mythology and folk tales.

■ If students are interested in a more modern story with elements of myth, suggest *The Lion, The Witch, and The Wardrobe,* by Green's Oxford classmate C.S. Lewis.

Roger Lancelyn Green
(1918–1987)

An Inkling of Future Success

Roger Lancelyn Green was born in Norwich, England, and educated at Oxford University. At Oxford, Green was a member of the literary group called the Inklings, led by the famous writers J.R.R. Tolkien and C. S. Lewis. Green and Lewis remained close, and Green later co-wrote a well-known book about the *Chronicles of Narnia* author entitled *C.S. Lewis: A Biography.*

A Greek at Heart

After a short stint as an actor in London, Green devoted his life to writing and the study of ancient times. His books for children include stories, poems, and his own retellings of fairy tales, legends, and myths from many lands. Green's special love was Greece, which he visited over twenty times during his lifetime in order to study its history, literature, mythology, and archaeological remains.

Think About the Writer — Why might a writer retell myths and legends from thousands of years ago?

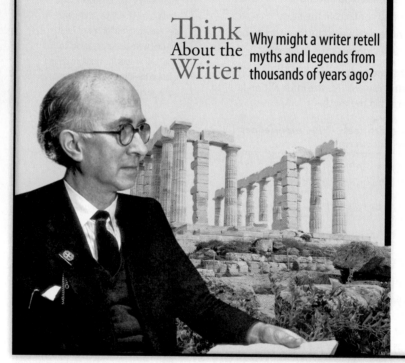

Build Background

"Echo and Narcissus" is an **origin myth**—an imaginative story that explains how something came into being. This myth explains the origin of the phenomenon of echoes and of the spring flower called narcissus.

Many words in English come to us from the ancient myths of Greece and Rome. The myth of Narcissus gave the field of psychology an important term, *narcissism,* to describe self-love. A person who suffers from extreme narcissism is a *narcissist,* preoccupied with only his or her concerns and convinced of his or her superiority in looks, talent, or other qualities. Such people may act with great selfishness and be unable to make and keep friends or truly care about others.

Preview the Selection

The Greek gods and goddesses **Zeus, Hera,** and **Aphrodite** appear in the myth you are about to read. The main characters, however, are those named in the title—**Echo,** a talkative nymph, or lesser female deity, and **Narcissus,** a good-looking but vain young man.

Read with a Purpose Read this myth to discover the transformation a handsome but selfish young man undergoes.

Echo and Narcissus

Retold by **Roger Lancelyn Green**

Up on the wild, lonely mountains of Greece lived the Oreades,[1] the nymphs or fairies of the hills, and among them one of the most beautiful was called Echo. She was one of the most talkative, too, and once she talked too much and angered Hera, wife of Zeus, king of the gods.

When Zeus grew tired of the golden halls of Mount Olympus, the home of the immortal gods, he would come down to earth and wander with the nymphs on the mountains. Hera, however, was jealous and often came to see what he was doing. It seemed strange at first that she always met Echo, and that Echo kept her listening for hours on end to her stories and her gossip.

But at last Hera realized that Echo was doing this on purpose to detain her while Zeus went quietly back to Olympus as if he had never really been away.

"So nothing can stop you talking?" exclaimed Hera. "Well, Echo, I do not intend to spoil your pleasure. But from this day on, you shall be able only to repeat what other people say—and never speak unless someone else speaks first." **(A)**

Hera returned to Olympus, well pleased with the punishment she had made for Echo, leaving the poor nymph to weep sadly among the rocks on the mountainside and speak only the words which her sisters and their friends shouted happily to one another.

She grew used to her strange fate after a while, but then a new misfortune befell her.

There was a beautiful youth called Narcissus,[2] who was the son of a nymph and the god of a nearby river. He grew up in the plain of Thebes[3] until he was sixteen years old and then began to hunt on the mountains toward the north where Echo and her sister Oreades lived.

As he wandered through the woods and valleys, many a nymph looked upon him and loved him. But Narcissus laughed at them scornfully, for he loved only himself.

---

1. **Oreades** (oh ree AD eez).

2. **Narcissus** (nahr SIHS uhs).
3. **Thebes** (theebz).

Vocabulary **detain** (dih TAYN) *v.:* delay.

(A) | Read and Discuss | What information does the author give you?

Universal Access

EL English Learners
English for Academic Success Provide students with definitions of words from the text that may be confusing.

- **immortal**–able to live forever. *The gods who lived on Mount Olympus were immortal.*

- **gossip**–talking about other people, often to make them look bad. *Echo entertained Hera with gossip about the other nymphs.*

- **scornfully**–disrespectfully, arrogantly. *Narcissus scornfully told Echo that he would never love her.*

- **embrace**–hug. *Echo tried to greet Narcissus with an embrace.*

- **cast**–throw away. *He cast her aside like a piece of garbage.*

- **lingering**–remaining in one place. *Echo was lingering in the clearing, in the hope of seeing Narcissus.*

- **woe**–unhappiness, sadness. *Narcissus caused much woe.*

Model the Skill

- Remind students that **universal themes** are not only common to many cultures and stories, but many of these themes have been explored since ancient times.

- Have students read pp. 290–291. Then, summarize for students the events on the page: Hera finds out the nymph Echo has been covering for her husband Zeus's questionable actions; she punishes Echo by taking her voice; Echo meets a young man named Narcissus and falls in love, but he rejects her because he only loves himself.

- Ask students what ideas they recognize in this story as having appeared in "User Friendly" and "Annabel Lee." [*Students should recognize the notions of vanity, romantic rejection, and grieving for love lost.*]

- Model translating the idea of romantic rejection into a universal theme statement. Explain that romantic rejection happens often to many people and is a universal experience. A general statement that could be made about this experience is, "No matter how much you love someone, you can't make them love you back." Explain that this statement is a universal theme because it could apply to many literary or real-life situations.

Guided Practice: Apply

Turn and Talk Have students read over their notes and skim the first two pages of "Echo and Narcissus." Divide the class in half and ask one half to translate "vanity" into a theme statement, and the other half to translate "grieving for love lost" into a theme statement. Have groups share their statements with the class and explain why they represent universal themes.

Farther up the mountains Echo saw him. And at once her lonely heart was filled with love for the beautiful youth, so that nothing else in the world mattered but to win him. **B**

Now she wished indeed that she could speak to him words of love. But the curse which Hera had placed upon her tied her tongue, and she could only follow wherever he went, hiding behind trees and rocks, and feasting her eyes vainly upon him.

One day Narcissus wandered farther up the mountain than usual, and all his friends, the other Theban youths, were left far behind. Only Echo followed him, still hiding among the rocks, her heart heavy with unspoken love.

Presently Narcissus realized that he was lost, and hoping to be heard by his companions, or perhaps by some mountain shepherd, he called out loudly:

"Is there anybody here?"

"Here!" cried Echo.

Narcissus stood still in amazement, looking all around in vain. Then he shouted, even more loudly:

"Whoever you are, come to me!"

"Come to me!" cried Echo eagerly.

Still no one was visible, so Narcissus called again:

"Why are you avoiding me?"

Echo repeated his words, but with a sob in her breath, and Narcissus called once more:

"Come here, I say, and let us meet!"

"Let us meet!" cried Echo, her heart leaping with joy as she spoke the happiest words that had left her lips since the curse of Hera had fallen on her. And to make good her words, she came running out from behind the rocks and tried to clasp her arms about him.

But Narcissus flung the beautiful nymph away from him in scorn.

"Away with these embraces!" he cried angrily, his voice full of cruel contempt. "I would die before I would have you touch me!"

"I would have you touch me!" repeated poor Echo.

"Never will I let you kiss me!"

"Kiss me! Kiss me!" murmured Echo, sinking down among the rocks, as Narcissus cast her violently from him and sped down the hillside.

"One touch of those lips would kill me!" he called back furiously over his shoulder.

"Kill me!" begged Echo.

And Aphrodite,[4] the goddess of love, heard her and was kind to her, for she had been a true lover. Quietly and painlessly, Echo pined away and died. But her voice lived on, lingering among the rocks and answering faintly whenever Narcissus or another called. **C**

"He shall not go unpunished for this cruelty," said Aphrodite. "By scorning poor Echo like this, he scorns love itself. And scorning love, he insults me. He is alto-

---

4. **Aphrodite** (af ruh DY tee).

B Read and Discuss What do you know about Echo?

Vocabulary vainly (VAYN lee) *adv.*: uselessly.

C Reading Focus Making Generalizations Echo's story is over at this point. What generalization can you make about Echo's tale?

Cross-Curricular Connection

HISTORY: Greek Mythology

Several Greek gods are integral to the origin myth; however, it is Zeus who initiates the conflict.

- Zeus's father Cronos was the leader of the Titans. Cronos tried to swallow Zeus for fear that his children would supplant him. Zeus was saved, however, and overthrew his father and ruled the world with his siblings (including Hades and Poseidon).

- Zeus ruled from Mount Olympus, which was considered heaven. Sometimes he visited Earth disguised as an old man or an animal to avoid detection.

- His symbol was the thunderbolt. People believed that rain, thunder, lightning and other weather phenomena were sent by Zeus.

- In addition to his military prowess, Zeus was known for having many love interests, which incited the anger of his wife, Hera. Hera vindictively tracked those upon whom Zeus lavished his attention.

HSS Analysis Skills: REP 1, 2

Analyzing Visuals   Connecting to the Text What details in this painting suggest Echo's feelings after Narcissus scorns her?

Disappointed Love by Francis Danby.

gether eaten up with self-love . . . Well, he shall love himself and no one else, and yet shall die of unrequited love!"

It was not long before Aphrodite made good her threat, and in a very strange way. One day, tired after hunting, Narcissus came to a still, clear pool of water away up the mountainside, not far from where he had scorned Echo and left her to die of a broken heart.

With a cry of satisfaction, for the day was hot and cloudless, and he was parched with thirst, Narcissus flung himself down beside the pool and leaned forward to dip his face in the cool water.

What was his surprise to see a beautiful face looking up at him through the still waters of the pool. The moment he saw, he loved—and love was a madness upon him so that he could think of nothing else.

"Beautiful water nymph!" he cried. "I love you! Be mine!"

Desperately he plunged his arms into the water—but the face vanished and he

Vocabulary   **unrequited** (uhn rih KWY tihd) *adj.:* not returned.

Analyzing Visuals

Connecting to the Story: *The woman in the painting looks upset; she sits with her face in her hands as if she is crying. Like the woman in the painting, Echo is distraught when she is scorned by the man she loves.*

Think About/Talk About

▶ **Comprehension**

Ⓑ Read and Discuss
Possible response: *She has fallen in love with a man named Narcissus, who is self-absorbed and arrogant.*

Ⓒ Reading Focus
Possible response: *Loving someone can hurt, as the other person may not share the same feelings.*

▶ **Extend the Discussion**

Theme What possible universal theme is suggested by the relationship between Narcissus and Echo?
Possible response: *Echo has fallen in love with Narcissus, who is arrogant and cruelly flings her away from him. This suggests that "unrequited love causes incredible pain" is a universal theme in the story.*

Vocabulary: Own the Word

- **vainly:** You might ask students, "When might a person request something *vainly?*"

- **unrequited:** Have students explain why *unrequited* love might make a person suffer.

▶ Comprehension

Ⓓ Read and Discuss

Possible response: Aphrodite made Narcissus fall in love with his own reflection, ensuring that he would never have the love he longed for.

▶ Analysis

Ⓔ Literary Focus

Possible response: A more realistic story might include a man who behaved like Narcissus. Instead of falling in love with his reflection, however, the man would be rejected by a woman he loved.

▶ Extend the Discussion

Symbolism Re-read the last paragraph of the story. What might the blooming flower represent? *Possible response: Life is a circle, and life can spring from death.*

Monitor Students' Comprehension

To check students' understanding of the selection, ask what lesson the story of Narcissus teaches. [*It is foolish to love no one but yourself because you will end up alone.*]

Vocabulary: Own the Word

intently: Demonstrate a person staring *intently* at a book or object in the classroom. Ask one or two students to stand at their desks and demonstrate the word by staring intently at something.

---

touched only the pebbles at the bottom of the pool. Drawing out his arms, he gazed intently down and, as the water grew still again, saw once more the face of his beloved.

Poor Narcissus did not know that he was seeing his own reflection, for Aphrodite hid this knowledge from him—and perhaps this was the first time that a pool of water had reflected the face of anyone gazing into it.

Narcissus seemed enchanted by what he saw. He could not leave the pool, but lay by its side day after day looking at the only face in the world which he loved—and could not win—and pining just as Echo had pined.

Slowly Narcissus faded away, and at last

Vocabulary **intently** (ihn TEHNT lee) *adv.:* with great focus.

---

his heart broke.

"Woe is me for I loved in vain!" he cried.

"I loved in vain!" sobbed the voice of Echo among the rocks.

"Farewell, my love, farewell," were his last words, and Echo's voice broke and its whisper shivered into silence: "My love . . . farewell!"

So Narcissus died, and the earth covered his bones. But with the spring, a plant pushed its green leaves through the earth where he lay. As the sun shone on it, a bud opened and a new flower blossomed for the first time—a white circle of petals round a yellow center. The flowers grew and spread, waving in the gentle breeze which whispered among them like Echo herself come to kiss the blossoms of the first Narcissus flowers. Ⓔ

 Ⓓ Read and Discuss Aphrodite said that Narcissus's actions would not go unpunished. How does this new information reflect that comment?

Ⓔ Literary Focus **Recurring Themes** In real life, people don't pine away and return as spring flowers. How might a more realistic story express the theme of this myth?

California Standards, pp. 293–295

■ **Reading Standard 3.4** Identify and analyze recurring themes across works (e.g., the value of bravery, loyalty, and friendship; the effects of loneliness).

Applying Your Skills

Reading Standard 3.4 Identify and analyze recurring themes across works (e.g., the value of bravery, loyalty, and friendship; the effects of loneliness).

Echo and Narcissus
Literary Response and Analysis

Reading Skills Focus
Quick Check

1. According to this myth, what is the origin of the echo we hear when we call into a cave or canyon? What is the origin of the fragrant flower called the narcissus?

Read with a Purpose

2. How might Narcissus feel about his change?

Reading Skills: Making Generalizations

3. Use the information you recorded in your chart to make a generalization about a theme in "Echo and Narcissus." Be sure to express your generalization in a complete sentence.

Main events or conflicts	Characters' feelings or discoveries	My experiences
Hera, knowing that Echo likes to talk, punishes Echo by taking away her ability to talk normally.	Echo is devastated and lonely.	Being unable to talk would cut me off from other people.

Generalization of a theme in "Echo and Narcissus: _____

Literary Skills Focus
Literary Analysis

4. **Connect** Did reading this myth change your opinions of beauty and vanity? If so, how?

5. **Draw Conclusions** According to the myth, Echo was one of the most beautiful of the Oreades. Why, then, does Narcissus reject her? Why is he so cruel to her?

6. **Make Judgments** Are Echo and Narcissus victims of the gods, or are they responsible for their own downfall? Explain your opinion.

7. **Analyze** Discuss the idea of unrequited love and the way it is reflected in this story. How do stories of unrequited love often turn out, and what themes are implicit in such stories? Explain why this theme recurs often in stories.

Literary Skills: Recurring Themes

8. **Interpret** Which of the following statements best fits the myth? (1) We can't love others if we love ourselves too much; (2) Love is a powerful emotion; (3) Romantic love and self-love can have devastating effects. Then, explain why the theme you selected can be considered a recurring theme.

Literary Skills Review: Character Traits

9. **Analyze** Character traits are the qualities that define a person. What is Narcissus's major character flaw? Explain why Aphrodite's curse is—or is not—an appropriate punishment.

Writing Skills Focus
Think as a Reader/Writer
Use It in Your Writing Review the words you recorded that describe the myth's characters. Now, think of two characters from literature or a favorite movie or television show. Write a three- to five-sentence description that reveals each character.

What Do **You** **Think** **Now** How is Narcissus's fate similar to the *real* effects of being self-centered?

Universal Access

Struggling Writers
Provide additonal scaffolding by supplying students with the following questions. First, have them think about and respond to them in notes independently in their Reader/Writer Notebook. Then, have students discuss their thoughts in pairs before drafting their responses.

- What does the character look like?
- What does the character act and sound like?
- How does the character behave? How does he or she treat others?

Check for Understanding

Independent Practice
Reading Skills Focus
Answers:

1. *The origin of the echo comes from Hera's punishment of the nymph Echo, allowing Echo to speak only by repeating the words of others. The narcissus flower originated on the ground on which the vain Narcissus died after being enchanted by his own image.*

2. *Because he is vain, Narcissus would enjoy being a pretty flower.*

3. *Love is life-altering whether you seek it or not. Love is so powerful that it lives on after death. In the story, love causes pain whether or not it is sought.*

Literary Skills Focus
Possible responses:

4. *Yes; I learned that beauty is only skin deep, and vanity gets you in trouble.*

5. *He is fixated on his own beauty. He is cruel because he does not think that she is worthy of him.*

6. *Their character flaws led to their downfall; the gods merely used these flaws to contrive appropriate punishments.*

7. *It is love for another person who does not feel the same way about you. Both Echo and Narcissus face tragic fates as a result of unrequited love.*

8. *Statement 3 best fits the fates of the characters in this story. It is a recurring theme because it comes up again and again in literature.*

9. *Echo's flaw is excessive vanity that prevents him from loving anyone but himself. Aphrodite's punishment is very appropriate, because she forces him to suffer the same rejection that he gave others without a second thought.*

What Do You Think Now?
Have students make a list of possible effects of being self-centered.

Independent Practice
Vocabulary Development
Vocabulary Check

1. *c*

2. *d*

3. *a*

4. *b*

Your Turn _____

Students' retellings should be simple and straightforward, use all the vocabulary words, and provide clear context clues.

English for Academic Success
Language Coach
Possible responses:

1. *You won't be able to sustain yourself on a four-hour hike if you don't eat.*

2. *Every envelope should contain a signed invitation.*

3. *It is important to maintain a brisk pace if you want a good aerobic workout.*

4. *To obtain a driver's license, you have to pass a test.*

English for Academic Success
Academic Vocabulary
Possible response: *Themes involving vanity and unrequited love* recur *in literature because they also* recur *in human experience in every culture, regardless of time or place. They remain* relevant *because these aspects of love and human nature are universal.*

Applying Your Skills

Echo and Narcissus

Vocabulary Development

Vocabulary Check

Match each Vocabulary word with its synonym.

1. vainly   a. unreturned
2. detain   b. carefully
3. unrequited   c. uselessly
4. intently   d. delay

Context Clues

What do you do when you come across an unfamiliar word? Rather than skipping over it or running straight to a dictionary, try using **context clues**—the surrounding words and sentences—to discover the word's meaning. As you examine the surrounding text, ask yourself the following questions:

- Does the surrounding text give clues to the word's meaning?
- Is there a familiar word or word part within the unfamiliar word?
- How is the word used in the sentence?
- Does the meaning that I have guessed make sense in the sentence?

Your Turn _____

Using the Vocabulary words from this selection—*detain, vainly, unrequited, intently*—write a short-short version of the Echo and Narcissus story that a six-year-old would understand. Be sure to build context clues into the sentences.

Language Coach

Root Words Earlier you learned that the Vocabulary word *detain* comes from the Latin root word *tenēre*. Many other words also come from this root word. In a dictionary, look up the definitions of the words *maintain, contain, sustain,* and *obtain* and finish each sentence below with the correct word.

You won't be able to _____ yourself on a four-hour hike if you don't eat.

Every envelope should _____ a signed invitation.

It is important to _____ a brisk pace if you want a good aerobic workout.

To _____ a driver's license, you have to pass a test.

Academic Vocabulary

Write About . . .

As you read "Echo and Narcissus," you may have felt that something about the myth seemed familiar. That feeling could be because of its theme. Themes about vanity and unrequited love recur and remain relevant through the years. In a brief paragraph, explain why you think these themes continue to interest people from different times and places.

Universal Access: Vocabulary Development

 English Learners

English for Academic Success Explain that although context clues do not explicitly reveal the meaning of an unfamiliar word, they can prove useful in determining word meanings. Explain to students how to determine word usage through context. For example, *delay* can be used as a noun or as a verb. Context will make clear to the reader whether *delay* is used as a noun or a verb in a particular sentence. If used as a noun, *delay* will be preceded by an article, such as *the*, and be referenced as a thing. If used as a verb, *delay* will be preceded by a subject (noun or pronoun), and be referenced as an action. Have students review the story with fluent readers and use usage and other context clues to determine the word meanings.

✔ See the Academic and Selection Vocabulary Skill Builder in **UA: Differentiating Instruction.**

Grammar Link
Direct Objects

A **direct object** is a noun or pronoun that follows an action verb and tells *who* or *what* receives the action of the verb.

Hera punished Echo.
[*Echo* tells *who* was punished.]

Hera's curse tied her tongue.
[*Her tongue* tells *what* was tied.]

A direct object can never follow a linking verb, because a linking verb does not express action.

Hera was jealous.

[The verb *was* doesn't express action; therefore, it does not have a direct object. The adjective *jealous* is not a direct object.]

A direct object is never part of a prepositional phrase.

Hera returned to Olympus.

[*Olympus* is not the direct object of *returned*; *Olympus* is the object of the preposition *to*.]

Your Turn

Identify the direct objects in the following sentences.
1. Narcissus scorned love itself.
2. With the spring, a plant pushed its green leaves through the earth.
3. Desperately he plunged his arms into the water.

Writing Applications Circle each direct object in an example of your own writing. Underline the verb related to each direct object.

CHOICES

As you respond to the Choices, use these **Academic Vocabulary** words as appropriate: <u>implicit</u>, <u>recur</u>, <u>relevant</u>, <u>reveal</u>.

REVIEW
Evaluate a Theme

Timed ⌐Writing A <u>recurring</u> theme is a kind of generalization. Like all generalizations, the statement of a theme seems more legitimate when it is based on as many examples as possible. State a theme from "Echo and Narcissus." Then, tell whether you agree or disagree with the theme. Is there enough evidence—in the myth, in other works you've read, or in your own experiences—to support the theme? Is there evidence to the contrary? Give examples to support your position.

CONNECT
Research Word Origins

TechFocus *Echo* and *narcissism* are two English words with roots in ancient Greek culture. Using the Internet, research the meanings and origins of the six words in the list below. Explain each word's origin in ancient Greek culture or mythology. Which words' origins seem most <u>relevant</u> to their current usage? (Can you see why the word came to be?)

> *psyche, nectar, chaos, vulcanize, mercury, cereal*

EXTEND
Write a Description

In "Echo and Narcissus" the narrator describes love as if it were an illness. What if love actually *were* an illness? How would you describe the symptoms? Write a brief description of "love sickness." Then, write up your suggested treatment or cure for this illness. Use humor to make your descriptions more engaging.

Independent Practice
Your Turn _____
1. *love*
2. *green leaves*
3. *his arms*

Choices:
Evaluation Criteria
Timed Writing: 40–50 minutes
- Students identify the theme of the myth and state whether they agree or disagree with it.
- Students use concrete evidence to support their argument.

Connect: Homework
Research Word Origins
- Students describe the origins of all six words.
- Students explain the word's development and modern usage.

Extend: Write a Description
- Student presents actual characteristics of love as symptoms.
- Students uses humor to describe "illness" and "treatment."

 Assess

Chapter 3 Resources, Selection Standards Check, p. 21

Teacher One Stop™, editable Selection Standards Check

ThinkCentral Online Assessment, Selection Standards Check

 Reteach

ThinkCentral Online Remediation

Universal Access: Grammar Link

EL English Learners/ Struggling Writers

Suggest to students that one way to determine whether a sentence should contain a direct object is to consider whether the action (verb) is something that the subject can do to the recipient. In the first example on the student page, Hera *punishes* Echo. Punishment is something that one person can do to another, so the sentence has a direct object. In the final example, however, there is no direct object because *returning* is not something Hera can do

to Olympus itself. It is a place she can go back to; it is a mountain that she could strike with her hand or build a house on. Because *returning* is not an action that Hera can carry out directly on the mountain, the sentence does not have a direct object.

✔ For more practice with using pronouns, see **Warriner's Handbook, Language Handbook Worksheets,** and **GrammarNotes.**

PERSONAL NARRATIVE

Preparing to Read

The Only Girl in the World for Me

by **Bill Cosby**

 What Do You Think? How can "falling for" someone affect a person's behavior?

 Quick Talk

People in love are sometimes described as "lovesick" or "love-struck" because they behave in ways that may seem unusual or even foolish. Discuss with a classmate how you can you tell when someone is in love.

Selection Readability	
Easily Accessible **Accessible** Challenging	familiar theme; conversational language; humorous tone; familiar situation with friends

Selection Summary

Bill Cosby tells the story of his first love from a young man's perspective using humorous and realistic details.

Reader/Writer Notebook

Use your **RWN** to complete the activities for this selection.

Reading Standard 3.4 Identify and analyze recurring themes across works (e.g., the value of bravery, loyalty, and friendship; the effects of loneliness).

Literary Skills Focus

Theme in Nonfiction The theme of a literary work is the insight or truth about life that it <u>reveals</u>. Writers seldom state a theme directly; themes are usually <u>implicit</u>. You must infer the theme by studying the most important elements in the work. Theme is not the same thing as **subject.** For example, the subject of a work may be "memories," but the theme would be an observation about that subject: "Our memories of an event often change as we gain more life experience." Look for key incidents or passages in which the writer makes broad statements about life. These can help lead you to the theme.

TechFocus As you read, pay attention to the emotions Cosby reveals in his notes to the friend of the girl he wants to date. Later you will have the chance to see how these same ideas <u>recur</u> in love poems.

Reading Skills Focus

Identifying Cause and Effect A **cause** is the event that makes something happen. An **effect** is what happens as a result of the cause. Sometimes writers will use a cause-and-effect organization to develop their narratives. One action can set off a chain of events. To see the pattern, look for what happens first. Then, ask what happens *because* of that event. Look for hidden or multiple causes and results.

Into Action As you read, fill out a graphic organizer like this one.

Writing Skills Focus

Think as a Reader/Writer

Find It in Your Reading When Cosby says, "Not even malaria could have taken my temperature to where it went," he is exaggerating by comparing the effects of his excitement to a dangerous fever. **Hyperbole** (hy PUR buh lee), or exaggeration, often creates a humorous effect. As you read Cosby's narrative, record examples of hyperbole in your *Reader/Writer Notebook.*

Vocabulary

altitude (AL tuh tood) *n.:* height; high level. *Their relationship reached a higher altitude when he got to dance with her at a party.*

suppressing (suh PREHS ihng) *v.* used as *n.:* holding back. *He imagined her in the act of suppressing a laugh at the thought of being his girlfriend.*

deflation (dih FLAY shuhn) *n.:* here, loss of confidence or high spirits. *He needed to recover from the deflation of learning she had a boyfriend.*

reservoir (REHZ uhr vwahr) *n.:* large supply. *He chose his words carefully, but he had a limited reservoir of romantic expressions.*

Language Coach

Suffixes Suffixes are word parts added to the end of a base word or root to create a different meaning. The suffix *–ous* means "full of." It changes a noun to an adjective: *wonder + –ous = wondrous* "full of wonder"

The suffix *–ly* means "like" or "in a way that is." It changes an adjective to an adverb: *soulful + –ly = soulfully* "in a way that shows deep feeling"

Analyze the meanings of other adverbs ending in *–ly* in Cosby's narrative.

Learn It Online
Become vocabulary savvy with Word Watch at:
go.hrw.com | H7-297 | **Go**

Selection Introduction

More About the Writer

In addition to his stand-up comedy and hit series *The Cosby Show*, **Bill Cosby** starred in the dramatic series *I Spy* in the 1960s. Cosby's success paved the way for African American actors to appear in lead roles on television, and Cosby won three Emmy awards for the role.

Think About the Writer

Have students brainstorm painful situations that affect the old, and then consider equally difficult situations that affect the young. How might a positive, humorous viewpoint ease the negative emotions provoked by such situations?

 For Independent Reading

■ Students interested in the lives of African American entertainers may enjoy reading Russell Freedman's *Voice that Challenged a Nation: Marian Anderson and the Struggle for Equal Rights*.

■ If students enjoy Cosby's story of growing up and falling in love, recommend *When I Was Your Age: Original Stories About Growing Up, Volume 1*, a short story anthology edited by Amy Ehrlich.

MEET THE WRITER

Bill Cosby
(1937–   )

Projecting a New Image

William Henry "Bill" Cosby grew up in a poor neighborhood in North Philadelphia. He left school in the tenth grade and later joined the Navy. During the Navy years, he became aware of his abilities. He trained as a physical therapist and helped rehabilitate Korean War veterans. He also earned his high school diploma. After his discharge in 1961, he received a scholarship to Temple University.

Finding Humor in Anything

Cosby's career is a remarkable success story. He is a well-known comedian, actor, writer, and producer, and one of the wealthiest people in the entertainment industry. He has contributed generously to various causes; in 2003, he received the Bob Hope Humanitarian Award. While attending college on a football scholarship, Bill Cosby began working as a stand-up comedian for five dollars a night. He became famous for his funny, heart-warming stories about his boyhood in Philadelphia. Bill Cosby has said,

"You can turn painful situations around through laughter. If you can find humor in anything—even poverty—you can survive it."

Think About the Writer How does Cosby's advice about painful situations apply equally to both young and old?

Preview the Selection
In "The Only Girl in the World for Me," you'll read about **Bill Cosby's** first love.

Read with a Purpose Read this nonfiction narrative to find out what happens when Bill Cosby falls in love for the first time.

The Only Girl in the World for Me
by Bill Cosby

I can't remember where I have left my glasses, but I can still remember the smell of the first girl I ever fell in love with when I was twelve: a blend of Dixie Peach pomade[1] on her hair and Pond's cold cream on her skin; together they were honeysuckle for me. And just as heady as her scent was the thought that I was in love with the only girl in the world for me and would marry her and take care of her forever in a palace in North Philadelphia. Because I wanted to make a wondrous impression on this girl, grooming was suddenly important to me. Before puberty, happiness in appearance for me was pants that didn't fall down and a football that stayed pumped; but now I started taking three long baths a day and washing my own belt until it was white and shining my shoes until I could see in them a face that was ready for romance. **Ⓐ**

The first time I saw her, she was crossing the street to the schoolyard and for one golden moment our eyes met. Well, maybe the moment was closer to bronze because she made no response. But at least she had seen me, just about the way that she saw lampposts, hydrants, and manholes. Or was there something more? I began to dream; and later that day, when I was playing with the boys in the yard, it seemed that she was looking at me and the world was suddenly a better place, especially Twelfth and Girard. **Ⓑ**

However, we still never talked, but just traded silent unsmiling looks whenever we passed. For several days, just her look was enough of a lift for me; but a higher altitude was coming, for one night at a party, we met and I actually danced with her. Now I was certain that I was in love and was going to win her. **Ⓒ**

---

1. **pomade** (puh MAYD): perfumed ointment for the scalp and hair.

Ⓐ **Read and Discuss** What does the author want you to know?

Ⓑ **Literary Focus** **Theme in Nonfiction** What does Cosby's statement "for one golden moment our eyes met. Well, maybe the moment was closer to bronze" reveal about romance and reality? (What's the difference between gold and bronze?)

Ⓒ **Read and Discuss** What is happening now?

Vocabulary **altitude** (AL tuh tood) *n.*: height; high level.

Model the Skill

- Explain that nonfiction, like fiction, typically shares a message with readers, though the presentation of theme in nonfiction is more often carried out through the author's observations and descriptions of real life situations. **Universal themes**, no matter how ancient or serious they are, may also be presented using humor or nonfiction situations.

- Draw students' attention to Cosby's descriptions of the changes to his behavior caused by his love for the "goddess" girl. Point out that he goes out of his way to impress her with athletic achievement and exceptional grooming. Though Cosby exaggerates these preparations, such as claiming that he even brushed his eyelashes, he is still describing a theme in the form of the extremes he went to for the love of this girl.

Guided Practice: Apply

Divide students into groups of three. Ask them identify Cosby's other descriptions of the extremes of love. Have each group share their findings and discuss how "love makes people go to extremes" is a universal theme presented in a nonfiction format.

Think as a Reader/Writer

Find It in Your Reading Point out the author's use of hyperbole on p. 300 when he says, "Not even malaria could have taken my temperature to where it went."

Use It in Your Writing Have students write a sentence describing an emotional reaction containing hyperbole.

I began my conquest with a combination of sporting skill and hygiene: I made my jump shots and my baths as dazzling as they could be. Oddly enough, however, although I saw her every day at school and on the weekends too, I never spoke to her. I had what was considered one of the faster mouths in Philadelphia, but I still wasn't ready to talk to her because I feared rejection. I feared:

COSBY: I like you very much. Will you be my girlfriend?

GODDESS: (*Doing a poor job of suppressing a laugh*) I'd rather have some cavities filled.

All I did, therefore, was adore her in silent cleanliness. Each Sunday night, I took a bath and then prepared my shirt and pants for display to her. On Monday morning, I took another bath (Bill the Baptist,[2] I should have been called) and then brushed my hair, my shoes, and my eyelashes and went outside to await the pang of another silent passage. **(D)**

At last, deciding that I could no longer live this way, I sat down one Sunday night and wrote a note that was almost to her. It was to her constant girlfriend and it said:

Please don't tell her, but find out what she thinks of me.

Bill

The following morning, I slipped the

---

2. **Bill the Baptist:** reference to John the Baptist, a prophet who baptized his followers to show that they had repented.

(D) Reading Focus Identifying Cause and Effect What has caused Cosby to act so timidly? What effect might his shyness cause?

note to the girlfriend and began the longest wait of my life.

Two agonizing days later, the girlfriend slipped me an answer, but I put it into my pocket unread. For hours, I carried it around, afraid to read it because I didn't happen to be in the mood for crushing rejection that day. At last, however, I summoned the courage to open the note and read:

She thinks you're cute.

Not even malaria[3] could have taken my temperature to where it went. I had been called many things, but cute was never one of them.

An even lovelier fever lay ahead, for the next time I saw her, she smiled at me, I smiled at her, and then I composed my next winged message to her friend:

I think she's cute too. Does she ever talk about me?

The answer to this one came return mail and it sounded like something by Keats:[4]

She talks about you a lot.
She knows it when you come around her.

And the angels sang! Imagine: She actually *knew* it when I came around her! The fact that she also knew it when gnats came around her in no way dampened my ecstasy.

And so, we continued to smile as we passed, while I planned my next move. My Western Union[5] style had clearly been

---

3. **malaria** (muh LAYR ee uh): disease characterized by chills and fever.
4. **Keats:** John Keats (1795–1821), an English poet.
5. **Western Union:** company that operates a telegraph service.

Vocabulary **suppressing** (suh PREHS ihng) *v.* used as *n.*: holding back.

Universal Access

Struggling Readers

Explain to students that identifying theme in nonfiction involves processes similar to those required to identify theme in fiction. In a work of fiction, the author uses the speech, thoughts, and actions of characters to share a message about life. In a work of nonfiction, the author uses descriptions in conjunction with the speech, thoughts, and actions of real people to share the message.

Direct students' attention to the second paragraph on p. 301, and read it aloud. You might say: "In this paragraph, Cosby describes his joy at finding out that the girl he likes knows that he exists. He thinks that love can make people prone to exaggeration and to strong feelings. This is a very general statement about life, so I will sum it up in a theme statement: love makes people feel incredibly strong emotions."

AAVE Students Who Use African American Vernacular English

English for Academic Success Students who use informal English may drop the *s* from the ends of plural charming the pants off her (so to speak) and now I launched my most courageous question yet:

Does she have a boyfriend?

When I opened the answer the next day in school, the air left me faster than it left the *Hindenburg:*[6]

Yes.

Trying to recover from this deflation, I told myself that I was still cute. I was the cutest man in second place. But perhaps my beloved wasn't aware of the glory she kept passing by. Once more, I sat down and wrote:

How much longer do you think she'll be going with him? And when she's finished with him, can I be next?

Note the elegance and dignity of my appeal. My dignity, however, did have some trouble with the reply:

She thinks she's going to break up with him in about a week, but she promised Sidney she would go with him next.

Suddenly, my aching heart found itself at the end of a line. But it was like a line at a bank: I knew it was leading to a payoff. I also knew that I could cream Sidney in cuteness.

Head of a Jamaican Girl by John Augustus Edwin (1878–1961).

Once she had made the transition to Sidney, I patiently began waiting for her to get sick of him. I had to be careful not to rush the illness because Sidney belonged to a tough gang and there was a chance that I might not be walking around too well when the time came for me to inherit her.

And then, one magnificent morning, I received the magic words:

She would like to talk to you.

I wrote back to see if she would wait until

---

6. **Hindenburg:** airship filled with hydrogen gas that caught fire and blew up following a transatlantic flight in May 1937.

E | Read and Discuss | What does this mean?

Vocabulary **deflation** (dih FLAY shuhn) *n.:* here, loss of confidence or high spirits.

words. Explain that in formal English, the *s* on the end of a plural word should always be written and pronounced. Point out examples from paragraph 2 on p. 300: *shoes* and *eyelashes.* Pronounce each word for students in formal English, emphasizing the *s* sound. Then, have students pronounce the following words, providing feedback: *coats, buildings, buses, tomatoes, hats, ideas.*

✔ For additional instruction and strategies, see **Holt Pronunciation Resources** and **ThinkCentral, Teacher Access.**

Analyzing Visuals
Welsh artist **Augustus Edwin John** (1878–1961) painted the portraits of many famous individuals, including Queen Elizabeth II and James Joyce. John's fascination with Gypsy culture is reflected in some of his work.

Extension Activity Ask students how the girl in the portrait compares to their mental image of the girl Bill Cosby loved. *Possible response: She looks similar to the way I pictured her— pretty and friendly.*

Think About/Talk About

▶ **Comprehension**

D Reading Focus
Possible response: Cosby acts timidly because he is afraid of being rejected by the girl he likes. His shyness may prevent the girl from noticing and may also prevent him from finding out that she likes him back.

E Read and Discuss
Possible response: In order to have a better chance of dating the girl he likes, the narrator is negotiating with the girl's friend through a series of notes.

▶ **Extend the Discussion**

Theme How does the last full paragraph on p. 300 relate to the selection's theme? *Possible response: It describes the ecstatic feeling that comes over people when they're head over heels in love. Even though the note isn't really that exciting, Bill thinks it's the best thing that anyone's ever written. The theme of the selection seems to be that when you're in love, you don't always act rationally because love is such a powerful emotion.*

Vocabulary: Own the Word
- **suppressing:** Remind students that *suppressing* means "to restrain or hold back," and that its opposite, *expressing,* means "letting things out or sharing them." You might say, "Suppressing hiccups means trying to prevent them from happening, while expressing hiccups is letting them happen."
- **deflation:** Give students an example of the word's use in a similar context. You might say, "After the deflation of being turned down for a date, the good math grade gave Andrew the inflation he needed."

Model the Skill

■ Explain to students that **cause-and-effect** relationships may include a series of events that function as causes and effects. For example, an open cage door may have the effect of a hamster escaping, which may in turn cause a cat to chase the hamster, which in turn leads to a precious lamp being broken, which leads to someone getting punished. Such chains of events may be used in fiction and nonfiction narratives to help readers understand the action in the story. They may also help readers understand theme.

■ Point out the chain of events on p. 303 that begins just after point G. Cosby wants to be a gentleman, so he puts his arm around his date's seat instead of holding her hand. Because of his arm position, blood stops flowing to his arm, making it tingle and ache. Another problem compounds the aching arm: Cosby needs to go to the bathroom. His discomfort causes him to feel the urge to move, which causes him to need an excuse to get up and go to the bathroom. He makes it to the bathroom, which causes him to run into his date coming out of the bathroom, as well. He realizes then that his "goddess" is actually quite human, and that the reality of love is not quite as idealistic as people make it out to be. Not only does the cause-and-effect structure explain how this episode happen, it also reveals a theme of the work through Cosby's realization about love.

Guided Practice: Apply

Have students review the story in pairs and choose another chain of events that they think is important to the story. Ask them to write out the cause-and-effect structure of the chain and share it with the class. Then, discuss as a group how the chain of events reveals a theme or clues suggesting theme.

Neighbors (2003) by Richard H. Fox.

I had finished duty at my post as a school crossing guard. Yes, she would wait; I could walk her home. We were going steady now; and how much more torrid our passion would be when I began to *talk* to her. 🇫

At last, the words came and I chose them with care. As I walked her home from school, I reached into my reservoir of romantic thoughts, smiled at her soulfully, and said, "How you doing?"

Her response was equally poetic:

"All right."

"So we're going steady now?"

"You want to?"

"Yeah. Give me your books."

And now, as if our relationship were not already in the depths of desire, I plunged even deeper by saying, "You wanna go to a movie on Saturday?"

"Why not?"

There might have been reasons. Some people were looking at us now because

🇫 **Reading Focus** Identifying Cause and Effect What effect does the message "She would like to talk to you" have on Cosby?

Vocabulary **reservoir** (REHZ uhr vwahr) *n.* large supply.

Developing Oral Fluency

Have students read pp. 302–303 aloud to improve oral skills. Remind students to use punctuation as signals; for example, commas require a brief pause, while periods need a full pause.

Group Activity Have students work in groups of three and assign each student the role of young Bill, Bill as the narrator, and the girl he has a crush on.

• Model reading the first few paragraphs on p. 302 aloud for students, emphasizing paying attention to punctuation as you read.

• Have each group read from the line "At last, the words came" to the line "One o'clock," using the appropriate expression and tone of voice for their part.

• Have students take turns playing each role, so they each get a chance to practice reading dialogue and narrative.

• Have one group read the passage aloud to the class, demonstrating appropriate pauses for punctuation and tone of voice.

she was so beautiful, people possibly wondering what she was doing with me; but I knew that I was someone special to be the love of a vision like this, no matter how nearsighted that vision might be.

When we reached her door, I said, "Well, I'll see you Saturday."

"Right," she replied as only she could say it.

"What time?"

"One o'clock."

When this day of days finally arrived, I took her to a theater where I think the admission was a dime. As we took our seats for the matinee, two basic thoughts were in my mind: not to sit in gum and to be a gentleman.

Therefore, I didn't hold her hand. Instead, I put my arm around the top of her seat in what I felt was a smooth opening move. Unfortunately, it was less a move toward love than toward gangrene:[7] With my blood moving uphill, my arm first began to tingle and then to ache. I could not, however, take the arm down and let my blood keep flowing because such a lowering would mean I didn't love her; so I left it up there, its muscles full of pain, its fingertips full of needlepoints.

Suddenly, this romantic agony was enriched by a less romantic one: I had to go to the bathroom. Needless to say, I couldn't

---

7. **gangrene** (GANG green): tissue decay in a part of the body.

let her know about this urge, for great lovers never did such things. The answer to "Romeo, Romeo, wherefore art thou, Romeo?"[8] was not "In the men's room, Julie."

What a prince of passion I was at this moment: My arm was dead, my bladder was full, and I was out of money too; but I desperately needed an excuse to move, so I said, "You want some popcorn?"

"No," she said.

"Fine, I'll go get some."

When I tried to move, every part of me could move except my arm: It was dead. I reached over and pulled it down with the other one, trying to be as casual as a man could be when pulling one of his arms with the other one.

"What's the matter?" she said.

"Oh, nothing," I replied. "I'm just taking both of my arms with me."

A few minutes later, as I came out of the bathroom, I was startled to meet her: She was coming from the bathroom *too*. How good it was to find another thing that we had in common. With empty bladders and full hearts, we returned to our seats to continue our love.

---

8. **"Romeo . . . Romeo?"**: reference to a speech by Juliet in Act II of William Shakespeare's play *The Tragedy of Romeo and Juliet*. The line reads, "O Romeo, Romeo! Wherefore art thou Romeo?" Juliet is actually asking why his name is Romeo.

G **Read and Discuss** What is developing here?

H **Literary Focus** Theme in Nonfiction What observation about love has Cosby made in this last paragraph?

Analyzing Visuals

Richard H. Fox (1960–) Contemporary New York artist uses brightly colored oil paints to create his lively depictions of urban life.

Connecting to the Text: The bright colors, marquee, and crowds of people suggest this excitement.

Think About/Talk About

▶ Comprehension

F **Reading Focus**

Possible response: The message causes great happiness for Bill, and the excitement at the reality of a long-desired romance.

G **Read and Discuss**

Possible response: Bill and the girl are finally talking and going out on a date.

▶ Analysis

H **Literary Focus**

Possible response: Cosby observes that even his dream girl is a normal human being, and love is based in reality after all.

▶ Extend the Discussion

Drawing Conclusions In the last paragraph, why is it so significant to Bill that his girlfriend has gone to the bathroom? *Possible response: He realizes she's a normal human being, not a "great lover" who never needs to go to the bathroom.*

Vocabulary: Own the Word

reservoir: Ask students to list other things they could have a reservoir of. *Possible responses: good ideas, water, cat food, school supplies.*

Monitor Students' Comprehension

To check students' understanding of the selection, ask them to describe Bill Cosby's attitude toward his first experience with love. [*He has a light-hearted, amused attitude about the ridiculous things he did when he first fell in love.*]

Independent Practice

Reading Skills Focus
Answers:

1. Charts should include important stages in the story and the action Cosby takes during each.

2. The "only girl in the world" for Bill Cosby was his first crush. He does not give her name but calls her a "goddess," making her seem perfect and more than human.

3. Students' responses should summarize how one event affects each subsequent one in the selection.

Vocabulary Check

4. c

5. a

6. d

7. b

Literary Skills Focus
Possible responses:

8. This was probably painful because the fear of rejection is stressful.

9. Cosby used humor to relay an awkward experience from his adolescence. Sometimes I find laughing makes things easier.

10. The selection reveals that young people's emotions are greatly affected by other people and situations; therefore, their emotions change dramatically and often. First love with its ups and downs, has a huge effect on the lives of young people.

11. The two complications that emerge are the potential for rejection by the girl, and how to excuse himself to the restroom. He solves the first problem by communicating through the girl's friend, and the second problem by offering to get some popcorn.

What Do You Think Now?

Have students review the exchange of notes between Cosby and the girl's friend to grasp his insights as they answer the question.

Applying Your Skills

Reading Standard 3.4 Identify and analyze recurring themes across works (e.g., the value of bravery, loyalty, and friendship; the effects of loneliness).

The Only Girl in the World for Me

Literary Response and Analysis

Reading Skills Focus
Quick Check

1. Cosby's relationship with the girl he adores goes through some definite stages, or steps. On this chart, describe those stages. Then, tell what Cosby finally did to find true love.

Stage	Action
1.	
2.	
3.	
4.	

Read with a Purpose

2. Who is the "only girl in the world" for Bill Cosby? Why do you think he never tells you her name?

Reading Skills: Identifying Cause and Effect

3. Using the entries in the chart you prepared earlier, explain the chain of events beginning with the first cause and ending with the last effect.

✔ Vocabulary Check

Words that are similar in meaning are called **synonyms.** Choose the best synonym on the right for each Vocabulary word on the left.

4.	**altitude**	a.	restricting
5.	**suppressing**	b.	stockpile
6.	**deflation**	c.	elevation
7.	**reservoir**	d.	decrease

Literary Skills Focus
Literary Analysis

8. **Evaluate** Do you think the experience Cosby describes in this selection was painful for him at the time? Explain your answer.

9. **Interpret** How do Cosby's words "You can turn painful situations around through laughter" connect to this story? to your life?

Literary Skills: Theme in Nonfiction

10. **Interpret** This selection deals with a boy's attempts to approach a girl he likes. What universal truth about young people's feelings and the effects of "first love" is <u>revealed</u>? State the theme in one or two sentences.

Literary Skills Review: Plot Complications

11. **Analyze** Plot events that make it difficult to resolve the **conflict,** or main problem, in a story are called **complications.** What two complications emerge in this story? How does Cosby overcome them?

Writing Skills Focus
Think as a Reader/Writer

Use It in Your Writing In a brief account, write about something awkward that has happened to you. Like Cosby, try using hyperbole, or exaggeration, to make the story funny.

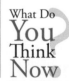
What Do You Think Now

What do Cosby's thoughts <u>reveal</u> about why people act strangely when they've recently fallen in love?

Universal Access

Struggling Writers
Provide students with additional scaffolding by having them use a graphic organizer to brainstorm ways to retell an experience through the lens of hyperbole. Model doing so by providing an example. For instance, you might say, "When I was in seventh grade, I had to give a speech. I was wearing a wool sweater that day, and it turns out that wool sweaters give me hives! So during my speech, my entire face became a giant red balloon. The crowd howled with laughter, sounding like a pack of wolves. It was very embarrassing."

Experience	Hyperbole
face broke out in hives	face was giant red balloon
the crowd laughed	the crowd howled like wolves

Vocabulary Development
Identifying and Using Analogies

An **analogy** is a comparison made between two things to show how they are alike. An analogy can explain one idea by showing how it is similar to a more easily understood idea. Here are some examples of analogies:

- *Learning to ride a bike is like sitting on the edge of a cliff. You keep thinking you're going to fall.*
- *Passing my math test was like jumping into a swimming pool on a hot day. What a relief!*
- *A dog running loose in a pet-food store is like a kid running loose in a candy shop.*

Notice that analogies include the word *like*. The first part names the subject. The second part makes the comparison. You may need to add a sentence to explain the similarity. When you write analogies, first think of something familiar to compare to the subject. Then, make a list of ways the two are similar. Choose the clearest idea for making the comparison.

Your Turn _____

Try writing your own analogy. Before you write, make a list of ways your two subjects are similar. Then, compare your subjects point by point. Remember that an analogy uses several points of comparison, not just one.

Here are some ideas for subjects:
falling in love
sending text messages
playing a sport
making friends

 Reading Standard 1.1 Identify idioms, analogies, metaphors, and similes in prose and poetry. **Reading Standard 3.4** Identify and analyze recurring themes across works (e.g., the value of bravery, loyalty, and friendship; the effects of loneliness).

CHOICES

As you respond to the Choices, use these **Academic Vocabulary** words as appropriate: <u>implicit</u>, <u>recur</u>, <u>relevant</u>, <u>reveal</u>.

REVIEW
Compare Themes

Timed Writing Choose another selection from this chapter that deals with the topic of love. Write a two-paragraph essay in which you compare and contrast that selection's theme with the theme you identified in "The Only Girl in the World for Me." Use <u>relevant</u> details from each selection as examples in your essay.

CONNECT
Dramatize the Narrative

Listening and Speaking Create and record a radio script based on Cosby's narrative. Read the lines in such a way as to communicate the humorous tone of Cosby's writing. Decide where to raise or lower your voice, and where you should pause. (Give your audience an opportunity to laugh at the parts you think are funniest.)

EXTEND
Research Love Poems

TechFocus Cosby compares one of the notes he receives to "something by Keats"—in other words, to poetry. Expressions of love have <u>recurred</u> in poetry throughout time. Arrange to present a program of love poems to the class, using modern technology to enhance your presentation. Consult with your teacher or librarian to compile a list of great works. Start with poems you already know, such as "Annabel Lee."

Independent Practice
Your Turn _____

Possible response: Falling in love is like climbing a mountain. You have many obstacles to overcome, but when you succeed, you are on top of the world.

Choices:
Evaluation Criteria
Review: Timed Writing
40–50 Minutes

- Students compare and contrast the theme of "The Only Girl in the World for Me" with the theme of another selection.
- Students use details from each story in the essay.

Connect: Dramatize the Narrative

- Students adapt Cosby's narrative into radio script format.
- Students use appropriate pacing, tone, pitch, and timing to convey the humor of the narrative.

Extend: Homework
Research Love Poems

- Students include a range of poems with love-related themes.
- Students use technology appropriately to share the poems.

Assess

Collection 3 Resources, Selection Standards Check, p. 21

ThinkCentral Online Assessment, Selection Standards Check

Teacher One Stop™, editable Selection Standards Check

Reteach

ThinkCentral Online Remediation

Universal Access: Vocabulary Development

EL English Learners/ Struggling Writers

English for Academic Success Some students may struggle to interpret analogies. Explain to students that analogies are much like similes, which are comparisons of two people, places, objects, or ideas, that use *like* or *as* in the comparison. Like analogies, similes show how two things are related. An example of a simile is: *skateboarding is like flying*. Analogies are often more involved than similes. The simile above, as an analogy, might be rewritten as: *riding a skateboard is like flying close to the Earth. You are close enough to reach out and touch trees and signposts, but you are moving fast and you feel lighter than air.* Have students work with fluent English speakers to write the Your Turn analogy.

Standards Focus

Objectives

Students will
- identify and analyze themes appearing in multiple literary works
- compare and contrast themes

Motivate

What Do You Think?/QuickWrite

Use the **QuickWrite** to discuss qualities students look for in a friend. Then have students discuss in their **Reader/Writer Notebook** how friendships can help them overcome challenges to reach their full potential as individuals.

English for Academic Success

Academic Vocabulary

Look for opportunities to use the Academic Vocabulary words in the chapter.

- **implicit, *adj.*:** suggested or understood but not stated directly
- **recur, *v.*:** occur again
- **relevant, *adj.*:** directly relating to the subject
- **reveal, *v.*:** show something that was previously hidden

Analyzing Visuals

Extension Activity What message might the artist want to communicate in this image? ***Possible response:*** *The boy standing at the beginning of a tree-lined road suggests that he is on a journey.*

California Standards, pp. 306–335

- **Reading Standard 3.4** Identify and analyze recurring themes across works (e.g., the value of bravery, loyalty, and friendship; the effects of loneliness).

Comparing Themes Across Works

CONTENTS

What Do You Think? How can friends inspire you to meet and overcome challenges in your life?

QuickWrite

What do you look for in a friend? What brings you together with people who become your friends? Explain how friends have helped, supported, or inspired you—perhaps just by being in your life.

Michael's Garden (2000)
by Hyacinth Manning (1954–).
Pastel.

Preparing to Read

Reading Standard 3.4 Identify and analyze recurring themes across works (e.g., the value of bravery, loyalty, and friendship; the effects of loneliness).

Hum / Antaeus

Literary Skills Focus

Themes Across Works A theme is a truth about life that a work of literature reveals. Stories that are set in very different places and times and that have very different characters can have themes that are a great deal alike. Themes from different stories are often similar because themes are insights into common human experiences. It's not unusual to encounter works that deal with the same basic theme but treat it in different ways.

Reading Skills Focus

Comparing and Contrasting Themes The stories you are about to read differ in many ways, but they also share some important similarities. Each story says something important about friendship. As you read, look for similarities and differences in the way the theme of friendship is treated in the two works.

Into Action To compare themes in different works, you first need to identify a theme for each. Complete a chart like the one below to compare and contrast themes between the two selections.

	Brief Summary of Story	Subject of Story	Statement of Theme
Hum			
Antaeus			

Writing Skills Focus

Think as a Reader/Writer

Find It in Your Reading In each story you'll be reading, the writer uses several techniques to make dialogue seem realistic. The characters use slang and other informal language, respond to questions with one-word answers, express themselves in short phrases, and speak in unique ways. As you read, write down examples of dialogue that you find especially realistic.

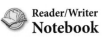

Reader/Writer
Notebook
Use your **RWN** to complete the activities for these selections.

Vocabulary

Hum

recourse (REE kawrs) *n.:* source of aid. *Sami could not find recourse when his classmates ignored him.*

solitude (SAHL uh tood) *n.:* state of being alone. *The school seemed to wait in solitude.*

quizzical (KWIHZ uh kuhl) *adj.:* puzzled; baffled. *His quizzical face showed confusion.*

Antaeus

contemplate (KAHN tuhm playt) *v.:* look at or think about carefully. *They could contemplate the results with awe.*

flourishing (FLUR ih shihng) *v.* used as *adj.:* thriving. *The boys saw the grass flourishing in the soil.*

sterile (STEHR uhl) *adj.:* barren; lacking in interest or vitality. *Grass grew on the building's sterile roof.*

Language Coach

Latin Words Which of the Vocabulary words above comes from the ancient Latin word *recurrere* ("to run back"), also the source of *recur*?

Learn It Online
Hear professional actors read these stories at:

go.hrw.com | H7-307 | **Go**

Comparing Texts Resources

Chapter 3 Resources, on-level practice and assessment, p. 24

Teacher One Stop™, on-level lesson plans and all print resources

Holt Audio Library

Holt Audio Library: Selections and Summaries in Spanish

UA: Differentiating Instruction, graphic organizer, p. 67

UA: Supporting Instruction in Five Languages, selection summary

Analyzing Visuals Transparencies, p. 16

ThinkCentral Online Assessment, Selection Standards Check

ThinkCentral Online Remediation

Introducing Vocabulary

Review the Vocabulary words with students. Then, check students' understanding by having them match each vocabulary word to its synonym below.

1. consider [*contemplate*]
2. prosperous [*flourishing*]
3. remedy [*recourse*]
4. bare [*sterile*]
5. perplexed [*quizzical*]
6. loneliness [*solitude*]

English for Academic Success
Language Coach

Remind students that many English words have their origins in Latin, whether part or all of the word comes from Latin. Latin contributed many whole words, root words, and affixes to English. [*recourse is related to the Latin word* recurrere]

Literary Skills Focus

As you read and discuss the selection with students, have them take note of themes they have encountered before, also noting the contexts in which they have encountered them.

Reading Skills Focus

Give students a copy of the Reading Skills Focus graphic organizer before they read. Tell them to use their responses to answer the questions on the Applying Your Skills page.

Writing Skills Focus

Have students record examples of realistic dialogue in their **Reader/ Writer Notebook.** Students can use their notes to complete the Writing Skills Focus activity.

Learn It Online

The online version of this selection includes audio support to engage all students and to help struggling readers with reading comprehension and vocabulary.

go.hrw.com | H7-307 | **Go**

More About the Writers

- Following the attacks of September 11, 2001, **Naomi Shihab Nye** wrote a letter to "would-be terrorists." In it, she bridged the gap between Arabs and Americans by showing that being unable to communicate through non-violent means leads to stereotyping, discrimination, and misunderstanding. She encouraged others to express themselves verbally, with messages we can all understand. These values are echoed in her short story, "Hum."

- **Borden Deal's** given name was Loyse Youth Deal. He and his family were farmers who lived through the Great Depression. When the price of cotton fell during the Depression, the Deals lost their land. With the aid of President Roosevelt's public-wellness programs, they moved to Mississippi and found work.

Think About the Writers

Remind students that every person has a unique life experience, and therefore learns different life truths from their experiences. Ask what truths Deal and Nye may wish to share with their readers.

 For Independent Reading

- If students are interested in reading more from Naomi Shihab Nye, recommend *19 Varieties of Gazelles,* which explores Arab perspectives.

- If human connections with the natural world interest students, recommend Paul Fleischman's *Seedfolks,* anecdotes about a neighborhood's reaction to a Vietnamese girl's planting of bean seeds in honor of the father she never knew.

Naomi Shihab Nye
(1952–)

The Arab American Experience

Like the character Sami Salsaa in "Hum," Naomi Shihab Nye made the transition from life in one country to another as a young teen. Nye, the daughter of an American mother and a Palestinian father, spent her early years in St. Louis, Missouri. At age fourteen she moved with her family to her father's hometown of Jerusalem, in Israel, where she attended high school. When the family returned to the United States, they settled in San Antonio, Texas, where Nye still lives with her husband and son. Nye brings her perspective as an Arab American to her writing, which includes poetry, songs, children's picture books, and novels.

Borden Deal
(1922–1985)

Keeping the Faith

Borden Deal—like T. J., the hero of "Antaeus"—came from a family of southern cotton farmers who knew firsthand the hardships of farm life during the Great Depression. After high school, Deal left Mississippi and traveled around the country on foot and by train, working in various odd jobs until he finally settled on a career as a full-time writer. Deal was just as persistent as T. J. in pursuing his dreams: Although "Antaeus" is now his most well-known story, it took him ten years to get it published, and it was turned down several times by virtually every publication to which he submitted the story. "So you see, when you believe in something, it pays to keep the faith and be persistent," Deal says.

Think About the Writers

Why do you think both writers have created characters who share aspects of their own backgrounds and experiences?

In "Hum" you will meet **Sami Salsaa,** who moved with his parents to the United States from the Middle East to escape the violence of life in the city of Bethlehem—only to be caught up in the tragedy of September 11.

In "Antaeus," **T. J.,** a young boy from the South, moves to a northern city, where he meets a group of boys who befriend him. Together, the boys try to create a garden, and in the process, they learn about friendship and growing up.

HUM

by **Naomi Shihab Nye**

Read with a Purpose
Read this short story to discover what happens when a young Arab boy moves from Palestine, in the Middle East, to Lubbock, Texas.

Build Background
On September 11, 2001, terrorists flew passenger planes into the two towers of the World Trade Center in New York City and into the Pentagon in Washington, D.C., killing nearly three thousand people. A fourth airplane crashed into a field in Pennsylvania after alert passengers tried to overcome their hijackers. The nineteen terrorists who hijacked the airplanes were young Arabs from Saudi Arabia, Egypt, and Yemen who advocated a radical form of Islam. Following the attacks, some innocent Arabs and non-Arab Muslims—such as the Pakistani shop owner in this story—were treated unjustly by fearful and suspicious citizens.

S ami Salsaa thought things were improving in his new life, right before they got worse.

His classmates had stopped joking about his first name ending with "i," like a girl's name—Brandi, Lori, Tiffani. And about his last name, which they said sounded like hot sauce.

In a country where basketball stars had fish names—Kobe, Samaki—they could get over it. In a country where people poked silver posts through their tongues and shiny rings into their navels and the man at the auto body shop had a giant swan with a pink heart tattooed on his upper right arm, who cared?

His parents had taken his advice, which was rare.

"Don't call it 'America,'" Sami had said

to them, after they unpacked their cracked suitcases on August 6, 2001, and settled into putty-colored Apartment 276 with the tiny black balcony jutting out over a stained parking lot. The sign at the bank across the street flashed 98 degrees. Sami hadn't realized Texas would be so blazing hot.

"Call it 'the United States,'" he said soberly. "'America' means more, means North, South, and Central America, the whole thing. Don't you like it better when people say 'Palestine' instead of 'the Middle East'? We shouldn't sound dumb."

They stared at him.

His mom said, "I only said 'America' because it was shorter."

Both of them started saying "United States" right away. Ⓐ

Ⓐ **Read and Discuss** What can you say about Sami and his parents?

Selection Readability

Easily Accessible	serious subject matter; simple dialogue; familiar theme
Accessible	
Challenging	

Selection Plot Summary
Sami's family has just fled Palestine for a new home in Texas, when the September 11, 2001 terrorist attacks throw the country into mourning. Suddenly, Sami and his parents are under suspicion from people who blame their entire race for the actions of a few. With help from others, Sami learns that sharing helps us to understand others who are different.

Model the Skill

■ Remind students that a story's **theme** is the larger idea or message that the author wants to communicate. Themes are more complex than topics and are usually hinted at throughout a text. Only occasionally are they stated outright.

■ Read the third and fourth paragraphs of p. 310. Point out that the writer is telling us everyday details that we would find ordinary, but that Sami finds unusual. He is fascinated by the fifty kinds of bread in the store. He has difficulty understanding classmates at first, but things are starting to improve. This suggests that the theme of the story might be that adjusting to change is difficult, but it can be done. It is only the beginning of the story, though, it's too soon to tell what the theme will be.

Guided Practice: Apply

Have students underline or write down parts of the text that deal with change and adapting to change as they read. Explain that they will use these notes later to identify the story's theme.

School in Texas started in the middle of August. Sami got an easy locker combination—10-20-30—and the best mark in his eighth-grade class on the first pre-algebra test of the year. Algebra was one of those subjects that translated easily from country to country; Sami had started working with equations in his cousin Ali's textbook in Bethlehem a year ago, during a curfew period, so the concepts felt familiar.

The teacher singled him out for praise, mentioning his "neatness" and "careful following of directions." Though he had not yet raised his hand once in class, now he thought he might. Sami found himself wishing he were taking full-fledged algebra instead of pre-algebra, which sounded babyish.

There was so much to look at in this country. Girls in tight T-shirts and jeans, for one thing. Magazines with interesting covers fanned out on a neat rack next to soft blue couches in the library's reading corner. Fifty different kinds of bread in neat plastic wrappers lined up at the grocery store.

Two boys, Gavin and Jim, set their trays down next to his at lunch. They told him what a corn dog was. They showed him how to dip it into a small pool of mustard. A girl named Jenny laughed when he tried it.

"Do you have brothers and sisters?" they asked.

"No," Sami said. "I am probably the only Palestinian who doesn't have any brothers or sisters." All his cousins and friends back home had huge families.

His history teacher asked him to stay after class during the third week of school and surprised him by saying, "I just want you to know I think our country's policy in your homeland has been very unfair. And more people than you might think would agree with me. Don't let the slanted press coverage get you down." The teacher clapped his hand on Sami's shoulder warmly and smiled at him.

Sami felt light walking the long sunny blocks between school and his apartment complex.

This might work out after all.

Cross-Curricular Connection

HISTORY: Human Migration

• Throughout history, humans have migrated, or moved to different lands. These immigrations have changed lands racially and ethnically as well as linguistically. In other words, these movements have created a mixture of races, ethnicities, and languages all over the world.

• Between 1870 and 1900, about 12 million people packed up their belongings and moved to the United States. Some families traveled to America in search of better jobs, lower taxes, cheaper transportation, and more plentiful food supplies.

• In 1892, an immigration station was established on Ellis Island in New York, within view of the Statue of Liberty. Here, millions of immigrants were processed and granted permission to enter the country. During the Great Depression, immigration to the United States declined. With the arrival of World War II, the number of immigrants arriving each year began to increase and has increased every year since then.

 HSS Analysis Skills: HR 2, 3

On top of that, his father flew to Los Angeles for the weekend to see his brother, Sami's uncle, and reported that hummus, Sami's favorite simple food from back home, was served on the plane. Incredible! Hummus, in a little plastic tub, with a shrink-wrapped piece of pita bread alongside it!

Next thing they knew, there might be a *falafel* stand in Lubbock.

It had been difficult for Sami's family to leave Bethlehem, the only town Sami and his mother had ever lived in, but the situation there had been so horrible recently, everyone was exhausted. Sami's school had been closed every other week and all citizens of Bethlehem put under curfew. His aunt Jenan had been gunned down in the street by Israeli soldiers as she returned from the market. When she died, it was the first time Sami ever felt glad she had no children. Always before, he had wished she had a boy just his age. His parents cried so much they said they used up all their tears. **B**

So when his father, a professor at Bethlehem University, was offered a teaching position in the engineering department at Texas Tech in Lubbock, he accepted it. Sami had felt sad at first that his family wasn't moving to a community with lots of other Arab immigrant families, like Dearborn, Michigan. Lubbock was a remote west Texas city with far fewer immigrants than Dallas or Houston. Someone on the plane told Sami's mother that a Middle Eastern bakery in Austin churned out spinach pies and *zaater* bread by the hour. That made Sami wish they were moving to Austin.

"Use this situation as an opportunity," his father said when Sami worried out loud about being too noticeable in Lubbock. His father always said things like that. "Let people notice you for how outstanding you are, not just how different."

A teacher at school told Sami there was an Arab family living far out on a ranch, raising cows. Their kids were in college already. This surprised Sami. Arabs knew about cows? He thought they only knew

B | Read and Discuss | What can you say about Sami's life?

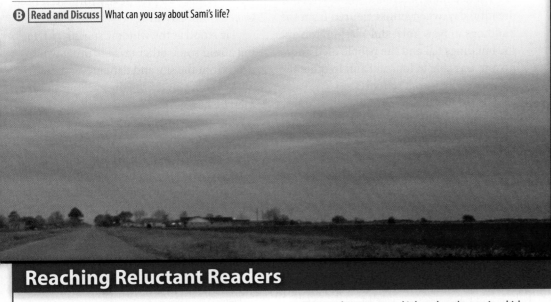

Reaching Reluctant Readers

Provide students with a variety of ways to respond to "Hum" and connect the story to their own lives:

- Have students become "experts" on the events of September 11, 2001, or the history of the conflict between Israel and Palestine by researching these events and organizing their findings into a "newscast" to be presented to the class.

- Have students create a skit based on the text in which Sami confronts the students who hold him responsible for the September 11 attacks. Make sure both points of view on the attacks are expressed in the skit.

- Allow students to write an open letter, like Nye's letter written after September 11, to people of their age, asking them to remember to be compassionate and encourage others to respect people who are different.

Think About/Talk About

▶ **Comprehension**

B Read and Discuss

Possible response: *Things are looking good—Sami's math teacher praises him, he eats lunch with two boys, and the history teacher is sympathetic about Palestine's biased treatment.*

▶ **Extend the Discussion**

Theme Read the advice Sami's father gives to him in the second column of p. 311. What theme does the author convey through Sami's father's words? How might this relate to the author's views on life? ***Possible response:*** *Through Mr. Salsaa's advice to his son, the author reveals that it is important to use new surroundings as an opportunity to show people that you are a unique individual.*

Determining Author's Purpose On p. 311 the author describes how the family moved from Palestine to Texas. Why is this information important for the reader to know at this point in the story? ***Possible response:*** *This information is important to know because it gives more background information on Sami, particularly that he has been through hardships before and that his family moved to the United States to escape the oppression and violence that made life in Palestine difficult.*

Model the Skill

■ Provide students with copies of the graphic organizer (See **Chapter 3 Resources**) or ask them to use a piece of their own paper.

· Explain to students that when they set out to compare and contrast themes in multiple texts, they need to gather certain information in order to properly compare the themes. Understanding stories' plot, subject, and theme, is key to comparing and contrasting themes.

■ Review with students events that have happened so far in the story: Sami's family fled the violence in Palestine and settled in Texas, Sami had trouble fitting in but is doing better, and then the September 11 attacks occurred. Tell students that these events are important to note, but they should not fill in the "brief summary" box of their graphic organizers just yet. Ask students to consider the events in the story so far, and brainstorm potential subjects that these story events might suggest: fitting in, accepting change, terrorism, friendship, isolation, prejudice. List them on the board for students' reference.

Guided Practice: Apply

Have students work in groups of three to discuss the potential subjects they brainstormed above. Have them discuss potential ideas or themes that relate to several of the subjects, and identify the theme and subject that seem to fit best with what they know about "Hum" so far.

about sheep and goats. A famous Syrian eye surgeon had moved to Lubbock with his family long ago. Sami's father planned to go meet him soon. **C**

Lubbock had a huge, straight horizon; it would be hard to find a larger horizon in the whole United States. You couldn't see a single hill in any direction. At night the stars glittered dramatically in the giant dark dome of sky. There were smooth streets in all directions with no Israeli tanks or armed soldiers in them, neat buildings and shopping centers, brilliant pink and orange sunsets, shiny pickup trucks with tires, and men in blue jeans wearing baseball caps that said COORS and RED RAIDERS.

"Hey, Sambo!" shouted one of his classmates outside the cafeteria a few weeks after school began. This made Sami feel familiar, jovial. He couldn't understand why the boy got in trouble for saying it.

Sami and his mother stood on the balcony and watched with pleasure as the sky swirled like milk in tea, one night before the dreadful day, when smoke poured from the buildings in New York and Washington and the buildings fell and the people died and no one was able to look at Sami in quite the same friendly way at school.

His parents had bought the television set just a few days before and kept checking out the different channels, so they had it turned on at breakfast when the news broke.

Sami wished he had never seen the images of the jets flying into the buildings.

C **Read and Discuss** What have you learned about Sami's family?

He wished he had closed his eyes.

Before that morning, a soaring silver airplane had been Sami's favorite mental picture; he'd always dreamed of the plane that would lift him out of a hard and scary life into a happier one, even before their big journey. Planes were magic; you stepped on, then stepped off in a completely different world. Someday he thought he'd go to New Zealand, and other places too. The world was a deep pocket of wonders; he had barely stuck his hand in.

But now Sami's joy in watching and imagining jets in flight was totally ruined.

He did not go to school. His father went to the university to teach a ten o'clock class, but none of his students appeared, so he came home. Everyone was numb. Sami and his parents stared hard at the television all day. He knew his relatives and friends in Bethlehem would be watching too. Sami's eyes kept blurring. Each time the television voices said "Arabs," his heart felt squeezed. A reporter said Palestinians had been "celebrating" the disaster, and Sami knew that was a lie. Palestinians had practically forgotten how to celebrate anything.

He stood at the window staring out, feeling afraid some other terrible thing would drop from the sky and flatten everyone.

When it was eventually evening a tall man he had noticed before, walking slowly with a large blond dog on a leather harness, came around the corner on the level below, and paused.

The man turned and sat down in a green plastic chair next to a door on the ground

Word-Attack Skills Mini-Lesson

Hard and Soft c and g

Point out that the letters *c* and *g* both have hard sounds and soft sounds using these words: *cast, gasoline, certain, genuine, city, ginger, compete, good, customer,* and *gust.* Tell students that *c* and *g* stand for the hard sounds /k/ and /g/ before the vowels *a, o,* and *u* and for the soft sounds /s/ and /j/ before the vowels *e* and *i*. *C* and *g* can also stand for their hard sounds when they are followed by another consonant (for example, *crib* and *glide*) and when they occur at the end of a word (for example,

panic and *big*). A final *e* after *c* or *g* makes the sound soft—for example, *police* and *page*. Use *electric* and *electricity* to demonstrate the effect that the vowel *i* has on the letter *c*.

Activity Write the following items on the chalkboard. Ask a volunteer to read an item aloud and then to call on a classmate, asking him or her to explain why *c* or *g* has a hard or soft sound in each underlined word.

floor. Was that his apartment? The dog stretched out beside him.

The man stared into the empty darkening sky and the empty blue water of the swimming pool. No one was swimming now. Why wasn't he watching television like everyone else? **ⓓ**

That night Sami's mother forgot to cook. So Sami toasted bread in their new toaster oven and spread red jelly on top. It looked like blood. He offered bread to his parents, but they didn't want to eat.

He had never seen his parents so shocked before, not when Jenan died, not even when his own friends were beaten and shot by Israeli soldiers, or when his uncle's perfect stone house was bulldozed to the ground without any cause or recourse. *Sad,* Sami had always seen them, forever and ever—sadness was their tribal legacy[1]—but this shocked? Never.

Although they had all been trying to speak only in English, to sharpen their English skills, they reverted to Arabic without even noticing it. **ⓔ**

His parents stayed up almost all night, fixated on the screen, and Sami lay awake, shivering, staring at his ceiling. What made people do what they did?

The next day, his father met him outside the school to walk him home. "Did anything bad happen today?" his father asked.

1. **tribal legacy:** habits or patterns that are handed down through a specific culture.

ⓓ **Literary Focus** Themes Across Works What is your impression of the man with the dog?

ⓔ **Read and Discuss** What has happened?

Vocabulary **recourse** (REE kawrs) *n.:* source of aid.

Coming to America

When Sami and his parents come to the United States, they are repeating a journey that has been made by millions of individuals from all parts of the world. From its earliest roots as an English colony, the United States has been a destination for people treated unjustly in their own homelands. The Pilgrims came seeking religious freedom. The first Jews came to America in 1654 from Brazil, where they were persecuted for their religious beliefs. Thousands of Germans arrived in the early 1700s to escape the armies that were attacking their land and burning villages to the ground. Throughout the twentieth century, wars and political strife brought waves of newcomers looking for a safe haven to the United States.

Every newcomer has brought his or her language, culture, and ideas. Look around your own community for the influence of different cultures. Names of places, types of restaurants, parades, and celebrations may all reflect different cultures. The more you learn about your own community and region, the more you will uncover evidence of generations of immigrants who have come to the United States looking for a place where dialogue is possible and differences are accepted and appreciated.

Ask Yourself
What aspects of your community reflect the heritage of the people who live in it?

Social Studies Link
Tell students that between 1892 and 1924, most immigrants arrived in America through Ellis Island, just off the coast of New York City, which is now preserved as a museum.

 HSS Analysis Skills: HR 2, 3
Ask Yourself _____
Possible response: My town has a variety of ethnic grocery stores that represent its cultural diversity.

---

1. The small <u>badger</u> could not find <u>recourse</u> from the <u>cold</u> winter night.
2. After making a new friend, the shy girl was <u>especially</u> <u>communicative</u> in class.
3. The <u>quizzical</u> look on the <u>guard's</u> face informed the <u>officer</u> that his <u>instructions</u> were <u>unclear</u>.

Think About/Talk About

▶ **Comprehension**
ⓒ Read and Discuss
Possible response: Life for them wasn't stable, schools were often closed, and people had curfews. When Sami's aunt was killed, his father found a job in the US.

ⓔ Read and Discuss
Possible response: On Sept. 11th, 2001, there were terrorist attacks on the World Trade Center buildings in New York City and at the Pentagon in Arlington, Virginia. Everyone is shocked and glued to their televisions waiting for explanations.

▶ **Analysis**
ⓓ Literary Focus
Possible response: The man with the dog seems cautious. From the description in the text, he appears to be Sami's neighbor.

▶ **Extend the Discussion**
Cause and Effect What event from p. 312 is the "dreadful day" Sami describes in column 1, paragraph 3? What effect does it have on the people of Lubbock? *Possible response: The dreadful day is September 11, 2001, when terrorists flew planes into the World Trade Center and the Pentagon without warning. The attacks cause everyone in Lubbock to go into a state of shock, and watch the news coverage of the attacks for most of the day.*

Vocabulary: Own the Word
recourse: Ask students if they have you ever sought *recourse* for something. Have them explain why, who helped them, and how they were able to help.

Model the Skill

- Tell students that English developed from a combination of other languages, including German and Latin. English adopted many words, roots, and affixes from Latin that are used in everyday speech. Learning about word origins is valuable to a reader's understanding of the English language.

- Point out the word *implicate* in paragraph 1 of column 2, p. 314. Explain to students that *implicate* comes from Latin, and its English form is very close to its original Latin form. The English verb *implicate* comes from the Latin verb *implicare*, which meant *entwine* or *involve*. In English, *implicate* keeps the original meaning "to involve," but takes on the additional meaning "to incriminate." In the context of the story, Sami worries that his apology will implicate him, or present him as guilty, in the September 11 attacks.

Guided Practice: Apply

- Identify the following words from pp. 314–315 as having Latin origins: *vacant, quote, assigned,* and *invisible.*

- Have students work in pairs to look up the words and identify the specific Latin words they are derived from. Discuss how the Latin and English words are similar or different in meaning.

Sami shook his head. Some students had stayed home for a second day. Teachers turned on television sets in the classrooms. Everyone had been so shocked they forgot he was there.

A tight pressure in his chest made it hard to breathe.

Bad things started happening the *next* day, but Sami couldn't tell his parents.

"GO HOME," said a scribbled, unsigned note taped to his locker.

"Your people are murderers," Jake Riley whispered in homeroom.

Murderers? His people? No one had said the hijackers were Palestinian.

His family had always spoken out against the suicide bombings that killed Israeli civilians. Many Palestinians did. But who could hear them? They were regular people, not politicians. No one quoted them in the news.

All day Sami thought of things he might have whispered back.

Not true.

Just a few of them.

Some of yours are too.

A counselor came to take Sami out of class. She had a worried expression. "You realize that you are the only Arab student in this school at a very difficult time. If anyone gives you any trouble . . ."

Sami didn't think he could tell her what had already happened.

It would make him seem weak.

If anyone found out he told, they would hate him even more.

No one sat with him at lunch now. He tried sitting down next to some boys from his PE class and they stopped speaking and stared at him. "I feel very bad about what happened," Sami said, with difficulty, though his words were so true. "Very very bad." His tongue felt thick. But did saying that implicate him in some way? As if all Arabs had done it? Still, what else could he say?

Nobody answered him. They finished eating in silence, exchanging glances with one another, and left the table.

The streets of Lubbock glistened in their solitude for days and days. It seemed no one was going out to shop. Restaurants were empty. Everyone stayed glued to their gloomy televisions.

In English class Sami and his classmates wrote responses to September 11 for more than a week and read them out loud, discussing them at length. The teacher even insisted they do second drafts. She said it would be good therapy.

Sami was the only one who mentioned that other people in the world also suffered from terrorism, all the time. Some of it, he said, was even governmentally sponsored and official. He did not mention his own family's bad experiences. He wrote this so that Americans wouldn't feel as if they were the only victimized people in history. But no one responded as if this had been a good

F [Read and Discuss] After the attacks on September 11, how have things changed for Sami at school?

Vocabulary **solitude** (SAHL uh tood) *n.:* state of being alone.

Universal Access

EL English Learners

English for Academic Success Students may have difficulty understanding some of the author's language because they may not be familiar with the diction and figurative language. Have students re-read the first full paragraph on p. 315. Provide an explanation of the figurative language using more familiar terms. For example, if students are struggling with the line, "a huge blanket had been spread over the vast and lumpy distant sorrows of the world—hushing them," explain that to blanket an issue means" to cover it up or ignore it." In this case, many sorrows in the world had been forgotten or ignored. This isolates people and makes them feel alone and victimized.

Struggling Readers

Benchmark Students Have students pause while reading to identify some of the topics addressed in "Hum." Then, have students identify other stories that share those topics. For example, the struggle to fit in with one's peers is also examined in "That October" (Chapter 2). Have students list similarities and differences between the two stories as they read. and explain how the story elements express similar themes.

thing to say.

Sometimes it seemed that a huge blanket had been spread over the vast and lumpy distant sorrows of the world—hushing them. Making them invisible. But weren't they still under there? Maybe people could only feel the things that touched *them*, the things at closer range.

One evening before sunset, Sami said to his parents, "I'm going out to take a walk."

"No!" his mother said. "It's almost dark!"

His father touched her hand to quiet her, and said, "Just around the apartments, yes? Don't leave the apartments."

His father looked so tired again, the way he had before they left Bethlehem. Some students had tried to drop his classes, though the deadline for that had passed.

A mysterious person had placed an ugly anonymous letter inside his faculty mailbox, but his father wouldn't tell Sami exactly what it said.

"Did you throw it away?"

"I burned it," his father said sadly. "In the outdoor ashtray."

Everyone had forgotten how to smile.

Sami's mother was working as an aide at a nursery school. She felt the eyes of the parents on her like hot buttons when they read her name tag, HANAN, even if they didn't know where she was from.

Sami stepped outside. He walked down the metal stairs toward the vacant swimming pool. Trash cans were spilling over next to the barbecue grills.

A little toddler stood on a couch inside a neighboring apartment, staring out. Sami fluttered his fingers at her. She ducked and covered her face. The

Analyzing Visuals   Connecting to the Text
How does this image help you connect with the story?

baby was lucky. She could not understand the news.

Cars slept in their assigned spaces under the carport roof. It seemed strange, but Sami felt jealous of them. It might be easier to be a car.

Another evening he asked his mother if he could make soup. She was surprised at his sudden interest in cooking. He rinsed lentils in a colander, as he had seen her do many times. He chopped an onion and fried garlic in a skillet.

As the soup was simmering, his mother remembered she had forgotten to pick up the mail downstairs when she came in from work. She asked if he would go get it and

Hum **315**

Think About/Talk About

▶ Comprehension

ⒻRead and Discuss
Possible response: The first day after Spetember 11, nothing happens out of the ordinary, as people seem numb. But then come the mean notes, whispers, and isolation.

▶ Extend the Discussion

Character   In the last paragraph on p. 314, the author gives readers insight into Sami's views on the attacks. How does his upbringing affect his understanding of the effects of September 11? *Possible response:* As a result of Sami's upbringing, he is familiar with terrorism and acts of violence. He is able to see beyond a one-sided view; instead, he is able to view other perspectives throughout the world, in contrast to most of his peers, who see Americans as the only victims.

Analyzing Visuals
Connecting to the Text: The image connects with the story because it conveys a very lonely mood, which reflects Sami's feelings after September 11.

Vocabulary: Own the Word
solitude: Explain to students that the word *solitude* originally came from the Latin word *solus*, which meant "alone." Solitude is the state of being alone. Have students discuss whether solitude is positive or negative to them.

AAVE Students Who Use African American Vernacular English

English for Academic Success   Some students may struggle with formal English expressions of past time. Speakers of informal English may leave off the *-ed* ending and say only the verb itself, as in, "Yolanda *dance* at the party," instead of *danced*. Explain that in formal English, most verbs take on the *-ed* ending to indicate an action that took place in the past. Read aloud the following sentences from the end of column 1, p. 315, as students follow along in their books.

"Sami stepped outside. He walked down the metal stairs toward the vacant swimming pool." Explain that the use of *-ed* on *step* and *walk* reflects formal English past tense. Have students form short sentences, which volunteers will read aloud to the class, using the formal English past tense of the following verbs: *skip, look, point, yell, pick.*

✔ For additional instruction and strategies, see **Think-Central, Teacher Access.**

■ Remind students that authors reveal **theme** throughout the course of a story or novel. Readers have to stay alert for clues, such as events or characters' thoughts, that help the reader identify the story's theme.

■ Point out that, on p. 316, the reader learns that Sami feels the hijackers have ruined his life too. Explain that this statement also relates to the theme of prejudice against someone who is different, because the hijackers' actions have led many Americans to associate people of Arab background with murder and hatred—Sami included. Have students write this information in their graphic organizers.

Guided Practice: Apply

Turn and Talk Direct students to the top of p. 317, where Sami meets his blind neighbor, Hugh Mason, for the first time. Ask students how they think meeting someone else with a difference will affect Sami. [*Students should recognize that Sami may gain perspective from this experience.*] Suggest that this interaction may also provide important information regarding the story's theme.

Think as a Reader/Writer

Find It in Your Reading Point out to students the author's use of realistic, natural dialogue in the exchange between Hugh and Sami in the first column of p. 317.

Use It in Your Writing Have students write a few lines from a recent conversation with a friend or family member, using phrases, fragments, and slang to create the natural rhythm of the conversation.

handed him the little key.

The mailbox was stuffed with bills and ads. How could so many people have their address when they'd only been here two months?

Walking back toward the apartment with his hands full, Sami kicked a red balloon on the ground. It felt good to kick something sometimes. The balloon had a ribbon dangling from it—someone must have had a party. Today he had wished he

could kick his backpack at school. Did those hijackers realize they had ruined his life too? He used to kick stones on the roads around Bethlehem. These were the same white stones that everyone was always getting in trouble for throwing. He only kicked them.

Once he had kicked a tin can all the way to Manger Square and his father passed him walking home from the bakery with a fresh load of steaming pita bread wrapped inside a towel. He spoke sharply to Sami for wasting his time.

"Find something useful to do," his father had said.

Today, so far away, after so much had happened, Sami thought of those long-ago words as the balloon snagged on a bush and popped. He spotted a thick unopened envelope on the ground. Had it fallen from someone's trash?

He stooped to pick it up, awkwardly, since his hands were full.

The envelope was addressed to Hugh Mason, Apartment 109.

Looking around, Sami realized that was the apartment where the tall man with the blond dog lived.

Sami pressed the buzzer. The

Ⓖ Literary Focus **Themes Across Works** How have the events of September 11 affected Sami and his family? Why does Sami think that it feels good to kick things, and why does this thought lead him to think of his former life?

Cross-Curricular Connection

HISTORY: Louis Braille

• Louis Braille was blinded as the result of an accident with a tool called an awl. He was only three years old.

• Despite this setback, Louis Braille became an outstanding musician and attended a renowned school for the blind on a full scholarship. He later taught at the institution.

• Louis Braille was impressed by a writing system for the blind used at the school. This method, created by Charles Barbier, used dots to make messages.

• Braille was determined to create his own means of writing for the blind. He adapted the system to create a six-dot code.

• Various combinations created different letters. Through this development, people who were blind could read and write. He even adapted this system to allow for musical notation.

• Although Braille's system was embraced by his students, the school did not fully accept it until after Braille's death. In 1932 (78 years after Braille's death), a universal Braille system was adopted.

man opened the door, dog at his side. He was staring straight ahead. Sami had finally understood, after watching him pass through the courtyard more than once, that he couldn't see. "Yes?"

The dog seemed to take a step forward to stand between his master and Sami.

"Mr. Hug Mason?" Sami pronounced it "hug"—he had never seen this English name before and did not know how to say it.

The tall man laughed. "Yes?"

"I have a letter for you with your name on it. I found it on the ground by the mailboxes. Maybe you dropped it?" He also wanted to ask, "How do you read it?" but was embarrassed to.

Mr. Mason put out his hand. "Thank you. I have dropped many things in my life. Very kind of you. You have an interesting accent. Where are you from?"

Sami hesitated. Could he lie?

Could he say Norway?

He knew his accent was not like a Mexican-American accent.

"I am," he said, in as American a voice as he could muster, "from Bethlehem."

Mr. Mason paused. "So you're Palestinian?"

"I am."

The dog seemed to have relaxed. He sniffed Sami's hand. His pale coat was lush and rumpled.

Mr. Mason's voice was gentle. "That must be harder than usual these days."

Sami felt startled when tears rose up in his own eyes. At least the man couldn't see them.

Sami whispered, "It is. Does your dog have a name?"

Half an hour later, Hugh and Sami were sitting on the green plastic chairs outside together, still talking. Tum Tum lay calmly beside them. They had discussed Lubbock, school, the troubles of Bethlehem, and the recent disaster. It was amazing how fast they had each talked, and how easily they had moved from subject to subject. They had not mentioned Hugh Mason's blindness, though Sami felt curious about it.

But they *had* discussed Tum Tum's job. Hugh had flown to California to be trained, alongside Tum Tum, four years ago. Training lasted twenty-eight days and was very "intense." Sami liked that word. He had never used it. This was Hugh's second dog. He'd had his first one for twelve years after his wife was killed. Killed? Crossing a street. "Hit-and-run."[2] Sami didn't know the phrase. Hugh had to explain it.

Tum Tum had been trained for "intelligent disobedience." If, for example, he saw Hugh getting ready to do something dangerous, like fall off a cliff (were there any cliffs in Lubbock?) or into the swimming pool, he would stand up on his hind legs, put his huge paws on Hugh's shoulders, and knock him over backward.

Later, thinking about it, Sami wished all people had dogs to guide their behavior if

---

2. **hit-and-run:** accident in which a car hits a person or animal and then immediately flees the scene.

 Literary Focus **Themes Across Works** Do you think Sami and Hugh will be friends? Why or why not? What has brought them together?

Model the Skill

- Tell students that to compare and contrast the **themes** of these stories, they may wish to record additional clues that suggest theme as they read. Remind them that authors communicate theme through characters, actions, and narration, which will be equally useful as the summary, subject, and theme information requested by the graphic organizer.

- Have a volunteer read aloud the Reading Skills Focus from the Preparing to Read page. Point out that this section gives a hint about a major point of comparison between the two selections: both share important ideas about friendship.

- Brainstorm with students the ways in which friendship has come up in the story so far, including: Sami's longing for friendship, his developing friendships that are interrupted by September 11, and the new friendship that seems to be developing between Sami and Hugh. Work collaboratively to develop theme statements that these experiences may suggest, such as, "prejudice is destructive and harmful to human relationships." Have students record the ways in which friendship has come up and the theme statements to be revisited when they compare and contrast the stories' themes later on.

Guided Practice: Apply

Have students continue reading the story, pausing as they read more information about friendship to make notes on what exactly happens and what theme this may suggest.

---

they were about to get into trouble.

When Tum Tum needed to go outside the apartment to pee behind a bush, he would hum.

Hum? What was "hum"? Hugh demonstrated, making a low smooth sound in his throat. Not all guide dogs did this—it was something particular to this one.

Tum Tum's ears perked up straight when he heard Hugh humming. Hugh said that if Tum Tum was just sitting on the grass right next to him, the dog would sometimes hum or make little talking sounds to let Hugh know what he was doing. Now he hummed in response to Hugh's hum. Tum Tum was a very communicative dog.

Hugh said that when a guide dog died, the loss for a blind person was nearly as hard as the loss of a human being, you were so used to each other by then. But had he always been blind? Why was this such a hard question to ask?

Sami heard his mother's worried call. The soup! He had forgotten it completely. He jumped up.

His mother walked anxiously toward them with her hands raised. What had happened to him?

Sami answered in Arabic.

This was a good man, he'd found a letter . . . but his mother only said in Arabic, *"Come home."*

Sami said to Hugh, "Excuse me, we will

> This was a good man, he'd found a letter . . . but his mother only said in Arabic, *"Come home."*

visit another day?"

Hugh stood up and shook his hand as if Sami were a school principal.

"Anytime! I enjoyed the visit very much." He held out his hand in the general direction of Sami's mother and said, "Good evening, pleased to meet you, I am Hugh Mason, you have a very nice son."

The lentils were too soft. Sami measured cumin and salt into the pot. He squeezed lemons. His mother was anxiously waiting for his father to come home. She was fretting and dusting things. At dinner Sami's mother told his father, he *had been with a man,* as if it were a big mistake to talk to a neighbor!

Sami couldn't believe it.

"Did you go in his house?"

Sami knew better than to go in his house.

"No."

"What did he want from you?"

"Nothing! To talk! He can't even see!" For the second time that afternoon, tears rose into Sami's eyes. "He offered me a job."

"A JOB?"

A fork fell off the table.

"To read to him. He is very smart. He works at a hospital answering telephones. The phone board has a Braille[3] panel so he can connect the calls. Someone drives him there. The dog goes too. Tum Tum. But he

---

3. **Braille** (brayl): writing and reading system for the blind that uses raised bumps which are felt by the fingers.

---

❶ Read and Discuss What is going on with Sami now?

Developing Oral Fluency

Use the exchange between Sami and his family that begins in the second column of p. 318 to give students practice in reading dialogue by following textual clues. Remind students that in this scene, Sami's parents are worried about his safety since the 9/11 attacks and are therefore mistrustful of Hugh. Point out words such as "fretting" and "anxiously," which give hints to readers about how a character acts and speaks. Tell students that following these textual clues will help them read dialogue with the intonation and emotion appropriate to the character's thoughts and feelings.

Small-Group Activity Divide students into teams of three.

- First, model identifying textual clues that suggest how the character's voice would sound. Look to key words for hints about which emotion or feeling to convey.

- For example, in the paragraph on p. 318 that begins "Nothing!" we are told that Sami is on the verge of tears. This demonstrates his frustration with his parents and anger at their mistrust of his new friend.

- Next, have each team practice identifying the textual

needs some reading help at home."

His father said, "You need to focus on your studies."

Sami said, "But he would pay me! I need some money too! Also, I learned new words. He has an excellent vocabulary, like a professor. I would read the newspaper, his mail, some magazines, and maybe even books. PLEASE?"

His father closed his eyes and shook his head. "Some days I wish we had never come here." **J**

Sami started reading to Hugh on Tuesday and Thursday evenings. He read for two hours. Sometimes his throat felt hoarse afterward. He and Hugh sat outside when the weather was warm. When the "northers" came—Hugh told Sami that was the word everyone used for the cold winds from the north—they sat inside, Sami on the flowered couch and Hugh in a wooden chair at the table. Tum Tum sprawled happily between them and seemed to listen.

Sami would read the newspaper headlines and ask Hugh if he wanted to hear the stories. Whenever it was a sad story about Palestine and Israel, Hugh would say, "No. Don't read it. Tell me a story about Bethlehem instead."

So Sami would put the paper down and find himself describing little details he had never mentioned to anyone before. The way the stones were stacked to make a wall outside his old school. Crookedly, if you looked at it from the side. But the wall felt smooth along the top.

The olive-wood carvers who shaped ele-

gant nativity sets[4] and doves of peace from hunks of wood and served mint tea to traveling nuns, hoping they would buy presents to take home.

The teacher whose jacket was so old and raggedy he had long threads trailing down his back. Everyone whispered that he lived alone, had no one to take care of him. This was rare in Bethlehem. Few people lived alone. (Sami felt bad after telling this, since Hugh lived alone. No, not alone. He had Tum Tum.)

Sami told about the ancient wrinkled grandma-lady who made small date pies and kept them warm in her oven. She gave them to any student who stopped to visit her, even for two minutes, on the way home from school.

Hugh said he could visualize all these things with his "inner eyes."

"Does everyone have inner eyes?" Sami asked. "Even people who can see?"

"Of course," said Hugh. "You know whenever you remember something? You use them then. But some people don't use them enough. They forget about them. But they're all I have. In some ways, I think I can see better than people who aren't blind." **K**

The teachers at school had urged Sami to join the Debate Club, but he didn't want to debate anyone. Debate involved winning and losing. Sami felt more attracted to "dialogue," a word he had heard Hugh use frequently, because dialogue was like

---

4. **nativity sets:** small figures representing the birth of Christ.

J Read and Discuss What is all this telling you?

K Reading Focus Comparing and Contrasting Themes What words and ideas might be important here? How might they point to the story's theme?

▶ **Comprehension**

I **Read and Discuss**

Possible response: When Sami goes for the mail, he finds and delivers a letter belonging to Hugh Mason. Hugh is sympathetic to Sami's political difficulties and the two talk about many topics.

J **Read and Discuss**

Possible response: Sami is late returning from getting the mail and his mother is frantic. His parents are pelting him with questions, probably wondering if he has been hurt or taunted. Sami explains that he was talking with a blind man who needs help reading and has offered Sami the job.

K **Reading Focus**

Possible response: Hugh says he visualizes what Sami says through his "inner eyes," which is a key phrase in the text. Everyone has these, but some people forget to use them and Hugh thinks that even though he's blind, he can see better than some people.

▶ **Extend the Discussion**

Conflict In the paragraph on p. 319 that begins "So Sami would put the paper down," how do you know that Sami's feelings towards Hugh have changed? What conflict has been resolved? *Possible response: While he reads to Hugh, Sami offers details of his life that he does not share with others. Hugh is kind and does not mistreat Sami because of his heritage, so Sami feels comfortable around him. Sami is no longer afraid to share his differences with Hugh or to ask Hugh questions about being blind.*

clues in the scene on p. 318–319. Once several clues have been found, have students discuss the tone and intonation that should accompany each line based on the textual clues.

- Then, have students read the dialogue with one student playing Sami, one playing Sami's mother and one playing Sami's father.

- Have students switch roles and repeat the procedure.

✔ See **UA: Differentiating Instruction** for practice passages for developing oral fluency.

Model the Skill

■ Ask volunteers to share the notes they have made so far on the story's **theme**. Clarify or confirm as needed that loneliness, feeling different, adapting to change, and fitting in are all ideas that the writer uses to give clues about the theme.

■ Read aloud the short poem by James Wright in the last paragraph on p. 320. Point out how the poem begins with loss and ends with the sense of being found. This reflects the theme of the story, as it starts with Sami feeling isolated and alone and now he can be himself when he discovers there are other students who have felt isolated because of their perceived differences. Because of its message, the poem is also a clue that helps the reader identify theme.

Guided Practice: Apply

■ As a class, discuss how the story moves through loneliness, isolation, differences, and acceptance.

■ Have students work in groups of four to try to condense the main characters' common ideas and experiences into a sentence that captures the theme.

■ Have groups share their ideas and combine these ideas to form a theme statement that the entire class accepts. You may wish to have students use the **Numbered Heads Together** format during their discussion.

---

a bridge. The teachers said, "In that case, you'll have to start your own club."

"Okay," he said. Why did he say that? he thought later. He didn't know how to start a club!

His history teacher printed up a set of "Guidelines for Dialogue Groups" off the Internet. It said things like: (1) Never interrupt; (2) Try to speak in specifics and stories, instead of generalities; (3) Respect varying opinions. Everyone does not have to agree, but everyone needs to respect everyone else.

A Korean girl named Janet approached Sami in the gym and said she had heard about the club from the art teacher and wanted to join it. "The art teacher is my good friend," Janet said. "Let's go to her room tomorrow after school and make some posters on those big tables."

Sami was glad Janet was so artistic since he was *not*. She designed the posters and he colored in the letters and graphics with fat felt-tip markers. Janet chattered freely as they worked. Adopted at birth, she had been brought to west Texas by her parents. Everyone was always asking her if she was Chinese.

The new club met on a Wednesday after school in the English classroom. Three students from Mexico City appeared at the meeting, looking quizzical. They said their English teacher had told them to come, to work on their language skills. They were happy to talk about anything. A tall Anglo American who had lived in Saudi Arabia with his oil engineer dad, an African-American girl named Hypernia, a very large girl in overalls, and

a boy with a prosthetic leg appeared. Sami would never have known about the leg until the boy sat down and his pants revealed a bit of hardware at his ankle. There was also a Jewish boy who went by his initials, L. B.

For the first meeting, people just introduced themselves and told a bit about their lives. The boy who had lived in Saudi Arabia said he felt personally grieved by September 11, since the Arabs he had known were always so "nice." Hypernia said she had felt very lonely since her parents moved to Lubbock from Dallas, where she'd attended a school that was 80 percent African-American. "I feel like an alien or something. Like everyone is staring at me. I never felt this way before."

L. B. said he was really tired of explaining about the Jewish holidays. Sami asked if he had ever been to Israel and he said no, but his grandmother had. He stared at Sami hard and said, "I really wish people could get along over there. I mean, it's terrible, isn't it?"

Sami said, "*Really* terrible." He liked the boy just for saying that.

The club ended up talking about the Pakistani auto mechanic on the east side of town whose shop windows had been broken after September 11. It had been in the newspaper. They decided to go visit him, take him a card.

Janet suggested "On Not Fitting In" as a topic for their next meeting. She had brought a poem by James Wright, an American poet, to read. It said, "Whatever it was I lost, whatever I wept for / Was a wild,

ⓛ Reading Focus Comparing and Contrasting Themes Which words seem especially important in the "Guidelines for Dialogue Groups"?

Vocabulary quizzical (KWIHZ ih kuhl) *adj.:* puzzled; baffled.

Universal Access

gentle thing, the small dark eyes / Loving me in secret. / It is here."

Sami found it mysterious, but it made him think of Tum Tum.

He mentioned to the group that he worked for a man who could not see in usual ways, but who might be a nice guest speaker for their group someday. He had interesting ideas, Sami said, and he liked to listen. "I'm visually impaired too," said the large girl in overalls. "Bring him. I'd like to meet him." Sami looked at her, surprised. He had seen her tilt her head to other people as they spoke, but had no indication she was blind. Suddenly he noticed the white cane on the floor at her side. She said softly, as if in answer to a question he didn't ask, "I

only see shades of light and dark. But I can't see any of your faces."

Weeks went by. The Dialogue Club was featured on the morning announcements at school. Gavin, who had once, so long ago, eaten lunch in the cafeteria with Sami, came to the club to write a story for the school paper, and he didn't get a single fact or quote wrong, which amazed the club members. They said the school paper was famous for getting everything wrong.

Sami's parents invited Hugh to dinner. They had stopped worrying about Sami's job when they discovered how nice and smart Hugh was. Sami's father seemed to feel a little embarrassed about having acted so negative in the beginning. So he took care

 Read and Discuss Why are the members of the Dialogue Club friends?

Analyzing Visuals

Connecting to the Text
Is this how you picture the Dialogue Club? Explain your answer.

▶ **Comprehension**

Ⓛ **Reading Focus**
Possible response: The words "respect" and "opinions" seem especially important.

Ⓜ **Read and Discuss**
Possible response: The members are friends because they all have common feelings of not fitting in. They share stories and practice their new language.

▶ **Extend the Discussion**

Analyzing Theme In the second full paragraph on p. 321 Sami recommends Hugh as a guest speaker for the Dialogue Club. What themes would Hugh be able to relate to the members of the club if he were a guest speaker? *Possible response: Hugh would be able to talk about being different and how to overcome the difficulties and prejudicial treatment that can come about as a result of one's differences.*

Analyzing Visuals
Connecting to the Text: Yes, this is how I picture the Dialogue Club, because they are a diverse group of students talking respectfully with one another.

Vocabulary: Own the Word
quizzical: Demonstrate a person's face who is *quizzical*. Ask one or two students to stand at their desks and demonstrate.

Have students work in groups to identify the ways that each character in the story does not fit in and what they do to try and fit in.

Advanced Learners
Acceleration Have students engage one another in a dialogue about the story's theme. Each student must have a clear theme with at least three pieces of evidence from the story. Ask each student to present their ideas in a short oral presentation.

Students with Disabilities
Read aloud the last three pages of the selection to students. When you finish reading, guide students in creating their own Dialogue Club in which to discuss the story. Prompt students with the questions below, and guide their responses.
• What effect did September 11 have on Sami? On the community of Lubbock?
• How did the Dialogue Club affect its participants? Did it have any effect on the school as a whole?
• What did Sami learn from his friendship with Hugh?

Model the Skill

- Tell students that one of their purposes for reading "Antaeus" is to compare and contrast its **themes** with the theme or themes of "Hum." They have already read and taken notes on "Hum"; they should do the same now for "Antaeus," gathering as much information as possible so they can adequately compare the themes of the stories.

- Have students spend three to five minutes reviewing the notes and graphic organizers they created for "Hum." Explain that they will want to look for similar characterization, story events, and important statements as they read "Antaeus."

- Point out that "Antaeus" opens with a teenage boy, T.J., moving to a completely different place and having to adjust to his surroundings. He does not know anyone, and must make new friends if he is able. Ask how this situation is similar to the beginning of "Hum." [*Students should recognize that Sami's situation is nearly the same T.J.'s, except that Sami has come from a foreign country and is not accepted quite as easily as T.J. is.*] Suggest that because both stories deal with the experience of being new and different, the authors might explore the effects of being different or an outsider on friendships. This will become clearer as the story progresses.

Guided Practice: Apply

Have students read the story, pausing as they read more information about friendship to make notes on what happens and what theme or themes the author may wish to share with readers.

Antaeus

by **Borden Deal**

Read with a Purpose

Read this selection to see how a new kid in town persuades a group of boys to build a garden in the middle of a city.

Preparing to Read for this selection is on page 307.

Build Background

During World War II, the United States geared up to produce equipment, weapons, and goods to serve the military effort overseas. Because most factories were in the North, many families left their homes in the South to seek work. The narrator refers to this situation in the opening of the story.

The title of this story comes from Greek mythology. Antaeus (an TEE uhs), the son of the sea god Poseidon, was a mighty and fearsome wrestler who could defeat anyone as long as he remained in contact with the earth. If, however, Antaeus were lifted up from the ground, he immediately became weak and could easily be defeated. Antaeus continually challenged people to wrestle with him, and he always killed his opponent—until, that is, he met the superhuman hero Hercules. Hercules defeated Antaeus by lifting him off the ground and crushing him.

This was during the wartime, when lots of people were coming North for jobs in factories and war industries, when people moved around a lot more than they do now, and sometimes kids were thrown into new groups and new lives that were completely different from anything they had ever known before. I remember this one kid, T. J. his name was, from somewhere down South, whose family moved into our building during that time. They'd come North with everything they owned piled into the back seat of an old-model sedan that you wouldn't expect could make the trip, with T. J. and his three younger sisters riding shakily on top of the load of junk.

Our building was just like all the others there, with families crowded into a few rooms, and I guess there were twenty-five or thirty kids about my age in that one building. Of course, there were a few of us who formed a gang and ran together all the time after school, and I was the one who brought T. J. in and started the whole thing.

The building right next door to us was a factory where they made walking dolls. It was a low building with a flat, tarred roof that had a parapet[1] all around it about head-high, and we'd found out a long time before that no one, not even the watchman, paid any attention to the roof because it was higher than any of the other buildings around. So my gang used the roof as a headquarters. We could get up there by crossing over to the fire escape from our own roof on a plank and then going on up. It was a secret

---

1. **parapet** (PAR uh peht): wall or railing.

Selection Readability

Easily Accessible	historical context; complex dialogue;
Accessible	figurative language; literary fiction
Challenging	

Selection Plot Summary

After a new friend joins their circle, a group of young men decides to create a rooftop garden in the middle of the city. Their garden flourishes through their hard work, but an authority figure forces them to destroy what they built.

place for us, where nobody else could go without our permission.

I remember the day I first took T. J. up there to meet the gang. He was a stocky, robust kid with a shock of white hair, nothing sissy about him except his voice; he talked in this slow, gentle voice like you never heard before. He talked different from any of us and you noticed it right away. But I liked him anyway, so I told him to come on up. **(A)**

We climbed up over the parapet and dropped down on the roof. The rest of the gang were already there.

"Hi," I said. I jerked my thumb at T. J. "He just moved into the building yesterday."

He just stood there, not scared or anything, just looking, like the first time you see somebody you're not sure you're going to like.

"Hi," Blackie said. "Where are you from?"

"Marion County," T. J. said.

We laughed. "Marion County?" I said. "Where's that?"

He looked at me for a moment like I was a stranger, too. "It's in Alabama," he said, like I ought to know where it was.

"What's your name?" Charley said.

"T. J.," he said, looking back at him. He had pale blue eyes that looked washed-out, but he looked directly at Charley, waiting for his reaction. He'll be all right, I thought. No sissy in him, except that voice. Who ever talked like that?

"T. J.," Blackie said. "That's just initials. What's your real name? Nobody in the world has just initials."

"I do," he said. "And they're T. J. That's all the name I got."

His voice was resolute with the knowledge of his rightness, and for a moment no one had anything to say. T. J. looked around at the rooftop and down at the black tar under his feet. "Down yonder where I come from," he said, "we played out in the woods. Don't you-all have no woods around here?"

"Naw," Blackie said. "There's the park a few blocks over, but it's full of kids and cops and old women. You can't do a thing."

T. J. kept looking at the tar under his feet. "You mean you ain't got no fields to raise nothing in?—no watermelons or nothing?"

"Naw," I said scornfully. "What do you want to grow something for? The folks can buy everything they need at the store."

He looked at me again with that strange, unknowing look. "In Marion County," he said, "I had my own acre of cotton and my own acre of corn. It was mine to plant and make ever' year."

He sounded like it was something to be proud of, and in some obscure way it made the rest of us angry. Blackie said, "Who'd want to have their own acre of cotton and corn? That's just work. What can you do with an acre of cotton and corn?" **(B)**

T. J. looked at him. "Well, you get part of the bale offen your acre," he said seriously. "And I fed my acre of corn to my calf."

We didn't really know what he was talking about, so we were more puzzled than angry; otherwise, I guess, we'd have chased him off the roof and wouldn't

---

(A) **Reading Focus** **Comparing and Contrasting Themes** What is the narrator's reaction to T. J.? How are T. J.'s experiences so far like and unlike Sami's in "Hum"?

(B) **Read and Discuss** What does this conversation reveal about the narrator and T. J.?

Cross-Curricular Connection

LITERATURE: Antaeus
Inform students that in Greek mythology, Antaeus was the son of Gaia (goddess of the earth) and Poseidon (god of the sea). Antaeus was a giant with supernatural strength. He challenged all comers to battles, which he always won, until Hercules accepted his challenge. Hercules knew that Antaeus drew strength from the earth (his mother, Gaia), and so knew he must remove Antaeus from the source of his strength. Hercules raised Antaeus into the air and defeated him there.

Activity Have students discuss why Deal titled his short story *Antaeus*. Ask them how the title helps communicate the story's theme. *Possible response: Deal wanted readers to compare T.J. and Antaeus to show how similar the two characters were. The theme of strength is suggested in the title because both characters get their strength from the earth.*

Model the Skill

- Tell students that many Latin words are so integral to the English language that it is difficult to identify them as Latin without looking up their origins in a dictionary. Identifying the sources of words, however, is important to expanding vocabulary.

- Write the Vocabulary word *contemplate* on the board, and have a volunteer read aloud the definition from the textbook. Explain that the word *contemplate* came from the Latin affix *com-*, meaning "together," and noun *templum*, which described a sacred space set aside for people to search for divine answers and signs, rather like the oracles of ancient Greece. People in the templum would most likely have been paying careful attention to potential signs; people who contemplate are paying careful attention to whatever they are doing. The words have different, yet related, meanings.

Guided Practice: Apply

Have students look up *private, domain, honest, attention,* and record each word's Latin origin and English usage in their **Reader/Writer Notebook.**

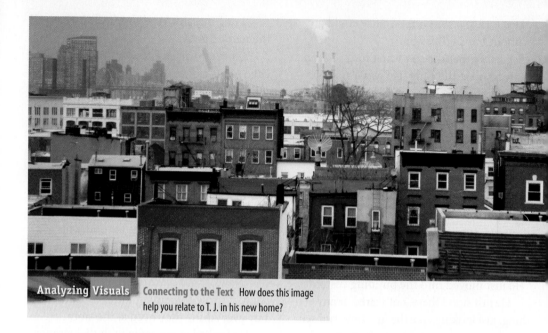

Analyzing Visuals   **Connecting to the Text** How does this image help you relate to T. J. in his new home?

let him be part of our gang. But he was strange and different, and we were all attracted by his stolid sense of rightness and belonging, maybe by the strange softness of his voice contrasting our own tones of speech into harshness.

He moved his foot against the black tar. "We could make our own field right here," he said softly, thoughtfully. "Come spring we could raise us what we want to—watermelons and garden truck and no telling what all."

"You'd have to be a good farmer to make these tar roofs grow any watermelons," I said. We all laughed.

But T. J. looked serious. "We could haul us some dirt up here," he said. "And spread it out even and water it, and before you know it, we'd have us a crop in here." He looked at us intently. "Wouldn't that be fun?"

"They wouldn't let us," Blackie said quickly.

"I thought you said this was you-all's roof," T. J. said to me. "That you-all could do anything you wanted to up here."

"They've never bothered us," I said. I felt the idea beginning to catch fire in me. It was a big idea, and it took a while for it to sink in; but the more I thought about it, the better I liked it. "Say," I said to the gang. "He might have something there. Just make us a regular roof garden, with flowers and grass and trees and everything. And all ours, too," I said. "We wouldn't let anybody up here except the ones we wanted to."

"It'd take a while to grow trees," T. J. said quickly, but we weren't paying any attention to him. They were all talking about it suddenly, all excited with the idea after I'd put it in a way they would catch hold of it. Only rich people had roof gar-

Analyzing Visuals

Connecting to the Text: *The image helps me see the environment that T.J has to adjust to. I can easily compare this setting to T.J.'s former home—a sparse, flat farm.*

dens, we knew, and the idea of our own private domain excited them.

"We could bring it up in sacks and boxes," Blackie said. "We'd have to do it while the folks weren't paying any attention to us, for we'd have to come up to the roof of our building and then cross over with it."

"Where could we get the dirt?" somebody said worriedly.

"Out of those vacant lots over close to school," Blackie said. "Nobody'd notice if we scraped it up."

I slapped T. J. on the shoulder. "Man, you had a wonderful idea," I said, and everybody grinned at him, remembering that he had started it. "Our own private roof garden."

He grinned back. "It'll be ourn," he said. "All ourn." Then he looked thoughtful again. "Maybe I can lay my hands on some cotton seed, too. You think we could raise us some cotton?" **D**

We'd started big projects before at one time or another, like any gang of kids, but they'd always petered out[2] for lack of organization and direction. But this one didn't; somehow or other T. J. kept it going all through the winter months. He kept talking about the watermelons and the cotton we'd raise, come spring, and when even that wouldn't work,

---
2. **petered out:** gradually disappeared.

C **Reading Focus** **Comparing and Contrasting Themes** How has T. J.'s idea influenced the rest of the boys? What is it about him that causes the others to react in this way? What kind of position does T. J. seem to be taking in the group?

D **Read and Discuss** What is happening? Why does T. J.'s idea excite the boys so much?

he'd switch around to my idea of flowers and grass and trees, though he was always honest enough to add that it'd take a while to get any trees started. He always had it on his mind, and he'd mention it in school, getting them lined up to carry dirt that afternoon, saying in a casual way that he reckoned a few more weeks ought to see the job through.

Our little area of private earth grew slowly. T. J. was smart enough to start in one corner of the building, heaping up the carried earth two or three feet thick so that we had an immediate result to look at, to contemplate with awe. Some of the evenings T. J. alone was carrying earth up to the building, the rest of the gang distracted by other enterprises or interests, but T. J. kept plugging along on his own, and eventually we'd all come back to him again, and then our own little acre would grow more rapidly.

He was careful about the kind of dirt he'd let us carry up there, and more than once he dumped a sandy load over the parapet into the areaway below because it wasn't good enough. He found out the kinds of earth in all the vacant lots for blocks around. He'd pick it up and feel it and smell it, frozen though it was sometimes, and then he'd say it was good growing soil or it wasn't worth anything, and we'd have to go on somewhere else.

Thinking about it now, I don't see how

Vocabulary **contemplate** (KAHN tuhm playt) *v.:* look at or think about carefully.

Model the Skill

- Remind students that authors can convey **themes** using narration, character actions, character thoughts and speech, or story events. Guide them in analyzing pp. 328–329 of "Antaeus" to identify potential story themes expressed using the methods listed above.

- Read aloud pp. 328–329 as students follow in their books. Ask them to mark with a sticky note or slip of paper any statements that strike them as "big ideas." When you have finished reading, model analyzing a sample "flagged" statement to determine whether or not it is a story theme.

- Point out at the bottom of column 1 on p. 328 the sentence, "It was the first time in my life that spring and spring earth had meant anything to me." Explain that the narrator has grown up in the city and has little awareness of the natural world, or even the world outside the confines of a few city blocks. Now that T.J. has introduced him to the ideas of nature, growth, land, and seasons, however, his perspective has changed. The narrator now understands the value of the garden they are creating. This is an important idea, and could be a potential theme, which might be phrased as "we do not know what we are missing until it is shown to us."

Guided Practice: Apply

Have volunteers share other story passages they flagged. Then, analyze them as a class, allowing students to volunteer their thoughts and guiding the discussion as needed.

---

he kept us at it. It was hard work, lugging paper sacks and boxes of dirt all the way up the stairs of our own building, keeping out of the way of the grown-ups so they wouldn't catch on to what we were doing. They probably wouldn't have cared, for they didn't pay much attention to us, but we wanted to keep it secret anyway. Then we had to go through the trapdoor to our roof, teeter over a plank to the fire escape, then climb two or three stories to the parapet, and drop them down onto the roof. All that for a small pile of earth that sometimes didn't seem worth the effort. But T. J. kept the vision bright within us, his words shrewd and calculated toward the fulfillment of his dream; and he worked harder than any of us. He seemed driven toward a goal that we couldn't see, a particular point in time that would be definitely marked by signs and wonders that only he could see. **E**

The laborious earth just lay there during the cold months, inert and lifeless, the clods lumpy and cold under our feet when we walked over it. But one day it rained, and afterward there was a softness in the air, and the earth was live and giving again with moisture and warmth.

That evening T. J. smelled the air, his nostrils dilating with the odor of the earth under his feet. "It's spring," he said, and there was a gladness rising in his voice that filled us all with the same feeling. "It's mighty late for it, but it's spring. I'd just about decided it

wasn't never gonna get here at all."

We were all sniffing at the air, too, trying to smell it the way that T. J. did, and I can still remember the sweet odor of the earth under our feet. It was the first time in my life that spring and spring earth had meant anything to me. I looked at T. J. then, knowing in a faint way the hunger within him through the toilsome[3] winter months, knowing the dream that lay behind his plan. He was a new Antaeus, preparing his own bed of strength. **F**

"Planting time," he said. "We'll have to find us some seed."

"What do we do?" Blackie said. "How do we do it?"

"First we'll have to break up the clods," T. J. said. "That won't be hard to do. Then we plant the seeds, and after a while they come up. Then you got you a crop." He frowned. "But you ain't got it raised yet. You got to tend it and hoe it and take care of it, and all the time it's growing and growing, while you're awake and while you're asleep. Then you lay it by when it's growed and let it ripen, and then you got you a crop."

"There's those wholesale seed houses over on Sixth," I said. "We could probably swipe some grass seed over there."

T. J. looked at the earth. "You-all seem mighty set on raising some grass," he said. "I ain't never put no effort into that. I spent all my life trying not to raise grass."

---

3. **toilsome** (TOYL suhm): involving hard work; laborious.

E **Read and Discuss** How do T. J.'s actions add to what you know about him?

F **Literary Focus** Themes Across Works Antaeus was a mythological giant who drew his strength from his mother, the Earth. What connection is the narrator making when he says T. J. is "preparing his own bed of strength"? What might this comparison suggest about the story's theme?

Universal Access

Struggling Readers

Strategic Students Model comparing themes of two stories on p. 329. You might say: "As I read the story, I learn how growing the grass affects the boys. Working on this project brings them closer together, and their friendship grows as they all care for the grass. To me, this suggests a theme, which I would state as 'Working together can bring together very different people.' The same was also true of the Dialogue Club in 'Hum'—a group of students with diverse backgrounds got together because they wanted to talk about important

issues, and became friends. Therefore, both stories have the theme 'Working together can unite very different people.'" Have students continue reading the story in pairs, pausing to make notes on themes and to compare the themes to those from "Hum."

Advanced Learners

Enrichment Have students get into groups to discuss the various themes and important concepts in the story. Ask them to consider how the author presents the themes, as well as the themes themselves.

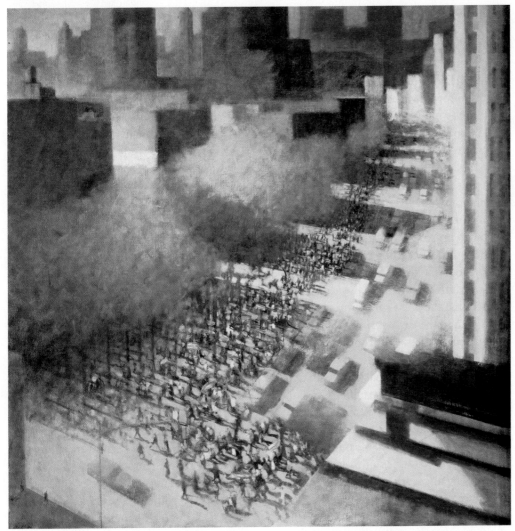

Sixth Avenue I (1986) by Bill Jacklin. Oil on canvas.
Private collection.

"But it's pretty," Blackie said. "We could play on it and take sunbaths on it. Like having our own lawn. Lots of people got lawns."

"Well," T. J. said. He looked at the rest of us, hesitant for the first time. He kept on looking at us for a moment. "I did have it in mind to raise some corn and vegetables. But we'll plant grass."

He was smart. He knew where to give in. And I don't suppose it made any difference to him, really. He just wanted to grow something, even if it was grass.

Students Who Use African American Vernacular English

English for Academic Success On p. 329, read aloud the sentence, *"Now we got to scrape up some seed money," T.J. said, looking at us.* Explain that "got to" is informal English, and that *got* is used in formal English as the past tense of "to get." In this case, T.J. is saying that the boys need to come up with seed money, which in formal English would be expressed as "have to" instead of "got to." Have a volunteer rewrite the sentence on the board in formal English.

Analyzing Visuals

Interested in light and movement, **Bill Jacklin** (1943-) began to concentrate on painting city life in 1985. His paintings are generally urban scenes with large crowds in brightly lit areas.

Extension Activity Does this image match your mental image of the city in which T.J. and the gang live? Why or why not? *Possible response: No, it seems brighter and more cheerful than the city in the story, and there are more trees and plants.*

Think About/Talk About

▶ Comprehension

E Read and Discuss

Possible response: T.J. is persistent and willing to continue to work when no one else will—he can envision what the roof will look like even though no one else can.

▶ Analysis

F Literary Focus

Possible response: The narrator is thinking that to T.J., the act of planting the roof garden is more than just his way of remembering home; it's giving him a purpose in life.

▶ Extend the Discussion

Cause and Effect Review the text between points D and E. What effect does winter have on the garden plans? *Possible response: The winter prevents the boys from planting the garden right away, but it allows them time to prepare the soil they need. Though some of the gang lose interest at times, T.J. talks and plans all winter and encourages them to keep going.*

Theme In the paragraph on p. 328 beginning "There's those wholesale seed houses," the boys decide to grow grass instead of vegetables. How does this illustrate the theme of ambition? *Possible response: The boys see grass as a symbol of wealth because it would mean that they have their own lawn. They want to be able to have something they created to call their own.*

- Have students pause after reading p. 331 and make additional notes on comparing and contrasting the **themes** of "Antaeus" and "Hum."

- Point out to students that p. 331 presents a turning point in the story: the boys' private paradise has been discovered by three men who presumably own the building. It remains to be seen whether the men will allow them to keep what they have created or destroy the garden. Ask students how each of the scenarios—keeping the garden or destroying it—will affect the boys. [*Students should recognize that the preservation of the garden would keep the boys' friendship strong and maintain T.J.'s connection to the earth, while the destruction of the garden could damage their friendship and wound T.J. deeply.*]

- Remind students that themes of creation and destruction also appear in "Hum." The hijackers destroy buildings on September 11, which also destroys the relationships Sami is developing with his peers; Sami creates the Dialogue Club, which brings together a group of very different people. Note that in both stories, the act of creation brings people together and promotes understanding of differences. This could be a common theme, which you might phrase as "Creation promotes unity and understanding among people."

Guided Practice: Apply

Have students write a statement comparing the two selection's treatment of the theme of friendship.

Think as a Reader/Writer

Find It in Your Reading Point out the author's use of realistic dialogue on p. 331, in T.J.'s statements to the men about why there is grass growing on the top of the building.

Use It in Your Writing Have students write a few lines of realistic dialogue explaining their opinion on a book.

"Of course," he said, "I do think we ought to plant a row of watermelons. They'd be mighty nice to eat while we was a-laying on that grass."

We all laughed. "All right," I said. "We'll plant us a row of watermelons." **G**

Things went very quickly then. Perhaps half the roof was covered with the earth, the half that wasn't broken by ventilators,[4] and we swiped pocketfuls of grass seed from the open bins in the wholesale seed house, mingling among the buyers on Saturdays and during the school lunch hour. T. J. showed us how to prepare the earth, breaking up the clods and smoothing it and sowing the grass seed. It looked rich and black now with moisture, receiving of the seed, and it seemed that the grass sprang up overnight, pale green in the early spring.

We couldn't keep from looking at it, unable to believe that we had created this delicate growth. We looked at T. J. with understanding now, knowing the fulfillment of the plan he had carried along within his mind. We had worked without full understanding of the task, but he had known all the time.

We found that we couldn't walk or play on the delicate blades as we had expected to, but we didn't mind. It was enough just to look at it, to realize that it was the work of our own hands, and each evening, the whole gang was there, trying to measure the growth that had been achieved that day.

One time a foot was placed on the plot of

---

4. **ventilators** (VEHN tuh layt uhrz): devices used to bring in fresh air.

G Read and Discuss How does this add to what you know about T. J.?

---

ground, one time only, Blackie stepping onto it with sudden bravado. Then he looked at the crushed blades and there was shame in his face. He did not do it again. This was his grass, too, and not to be desecrated.[5] No one said anything, for it was not necessary.

T. J. had reserved a small section for watermelons, and he was still trying to find some seed for it. The wholesale house didn't have any watermelon seeds, and we didn't know where we could lay our hands on them. T. J. shaped the earth into mounds ready to receive them, three mounds lying in a straight line along the edge of the grass plot.

We had just about decided that we'd have to buy the seeds if we were to get them. It was a violation of our principles, but we were anxious to get the watermelons started. Somewhere or other, T. J. got his hands on a seed catalog and brought it one evening to our roof garden.

"We can order them now," he said, showing us the catalog. "Look!"

We all crowded around, looking at the fat green watermelons pictured in full color on the pages. Some of them were split open, showing the red, tempting meat, making our mouths water.

"Now we got to scrape up some seed money," T. J. said, looking at us. "I got a quarter. How much you-all got?"

We made up a couple of dollars among us and T. J. nodded his head. "That'll be more than enough. Now we got to decide

---

5. **desecrated** (DEHS ih krayt ihd): showed disrespect for something considered holy.

Developing Oral Fluency

Use pp. 330–333 to develop oral fluency. Fluent readers try to express each character's emotions in their voices as they read that character's lines of dialogue. Remind students to consider how a character's emotions will affect how they speak and what they say. Have students volunteer to read, or have each student read one paragraph.

Group activity Put students into groups of three or four, making sure that there is at least one fluent student in each group.

- Have students read the selection, taking turns by alternating paragraphs.

- Have students write down and discuss any words or emotions they may be unfamiliar with.

- Encourage students to think about the emotions the boys are feeling, and remind students to let those emotions guide their expression as they read. Have them discuss how each of the boys might be feeling differently.

what kind to get. I think them Kleckley Sweets. What do you-all think?"

He was going into esoteric[6] matters beyond our reach. We hadn't even known there were different kinds of melons. So we just nodded our heads and agreed that yes, we thought the Kleckley Sweets too.

"I'll order them tonight," T. J. said. "We ought to have them in a few days."

"What are you boys doing up here?" an adult voice said behind us.

It startled us, for no one had ever come up here before in all the time we had been using the roof of the factory. We jerked around and saw three men standing near the trapdoor at the other end of the roof. They weren't policemen or night watchmen but three men in plump business suits,

---

6. **esoteric** (ehs uh TEHR ihk): specialized; beyond most people's understanding or knowledge.

H | Read and Discuss | What does the interaction between the gang and T. J. during their decision-making process show you?

---

looking at us. They walked toward us.

"What are you boys doing up here?" the one in the middle said again.

We stood still, guilt heavy among us, levied by the tone of voice, and looked at the three strangers.

The men stared at the grass flourishing behind us. "What's this?" the man said. "How did this get up here?"

"Sure is growing good, ain't it?" T. J. said conversationally. "We planted it."

The men kept looking at the grass as if they didn't believe it. It was a thick carpet over the earth now, a patch of deep greenness startling in the sterile industrial surroundings.

"Yes, sir," T. J. said proudly. "We toted that earth up here and planted that grass." He fluttered the seed catalog. "And we're just fixing to plant us some watermelon."

The man looked at him then, his eyes

Vocabulary **flourishing** (FLUR ih shihng) *v.* used as *adj.*: thriving.
sterile (STEHR uhl) *adj.*: barren; lacking in interest or vitality.

Analyzing Visuals

Connecting to the Text
How do these boys compare to the ones you imagine as you read the story?

Heads of Children by André Lhote (1885–1962). Oil on board.
©André Lhote/Artists Rights Society (ARS), New York.

Analyzing Visuals
Beginning as a professional wood-carver, **André Lhote** (1885–1962) was a creative and artistic painter. He worked in a style called cubism, using angular shapes and lines to illustrate a variety of subjects and scenes.

Connecting to the Text: *The boys in the image look like they're the same age and from the same time period as the boys in the story.*

▶ **Comprehension**

G **Read and Discuss**
Possible response: *This scene shows that T.J. can compromise, not force his ways on people. Like earlier, he leads by example—just plugging away, bringing up the soil even when no one else is in the mood to.*

H **Read and Discuss**
Possible response: *The boys trust T.J.'s opinions fully. T.J. seems to be their leader.*

▶ **Extend the Discussion**

Making Judgments In the second column of p. 331, the boys are caught on the roof by adults. How can they justify their actions? Explain.
Possible response: *They might say that they are building a community garden, or that they thought the building was abandoned.*

Vocabulary: Own the Word

- **flourishing:** Write the word *flourishing* and its definition on the board and draw a circle around them. Ask students to read the definition to themselves and think of things that could be described as flourishing. Invite volunteers to share their answers by drawing a "spider leg" off the circle on the board and writing their idea on the end of the leg.

- **sterile:** Ask students to explain why the green grass is such a strange sight in the *sterile* surroundings of the city. ***Possible response:*** *The city is very dull and man-made; there is not much else growing in the city.*

- Remind students that writers sometimes give clues about **theme** by making broad statements about life. These statements are usually not themes themselves, but may provide key words or ideas for developing a theme statement.

- Read aloud from p. 332 the statements, "It's our earth. It's our land. Can't nobody touch a man's own land." This is a broad statement about life that explains why T.J. has become so attached to their garden. He misses his home in the South, and he is also deeply connected to the earth, like the title character Antaeus. From this statement and T.J.'s dedication to the garden throughout the story, the reader can develop a theme statement such as, "people who are devoted to the earth and growing things will not thrive if separated from the land they work."

Guided Practice: Apply

Read aloud another sentence from p. 332: "The adult world had descended on us even in our richest dream, and we knew there was no calculating the adult world, no fighting it, no winning against it." Lead a class discussion about how this statement relates to a common condition in life. Work with students to propose a theme statement based on this sentence and the boys' actions in the story.

Think as a Reader/Writer

Find It in Your Reading Point out that T.J.'s reaction to the men shows how he is different from the other boys. He does not fear authority figures like the gang does.

Use It in Your Writing Have students choose an event from their lives to which they reacted strongly. Ask them to write a sentence each for two different reactions that one might have to the same event.

strange and faraway. "What do you mean, putting this on the roof of my building?" he said. "Do you want to go to jail?"

T. J. looked shaken. The rest of us were silent, frightened by the authority of his voice. We had grown up aware of adult authority, of policemen and night watchmen and teachers, and this man sounded like all the others. But it was a new thing to T. J.

"Well, you wasn't using the roof," T. J. said. He paused a moment and added shrewdly, "So we just thought to pretty it up a little bit."

"And sag it so I'd have to rebuild it," the man said sharply. He started turning away, saying to another man beside him, "See that all that junk is shoveled off by tomorrow." ❶

"Yes, sir," the man said.

T. J. started forward. "You can't do that," he said. "We toted it up here, and it's our earth. We planted it and raised it and toted it up here."

The man stared at him coldly. "But it's my building," he said. "It's to be shoveled off tomorrow."

"It's our earth," T. J. said desperately. "You ain't got no right!"

The men walked on without listening and descended clumsily through the trapdoor. T. J. stood looking after them, his body tense with anger, until they had disappeared. They wouldn't even argue with him, wouldn't let him defend his earth rights.

He turned to us. "We won't let 'em do it," he said fiercely. "We'll stay up here all day tomorrow and the day after that, and we won't let 'em do it."

We just looked at him. We knew there was no stopping it.

He saw it in our faces, and his face wavered for a moment before he gripped it into determination. "They ain't got no right," he said. "It's our earth. It's our land. Can't nobody touch a man's own land."

We kept looking at him, listening to the words but knowing that it was no use. The adult world had descended on us even in our richest dream, and we knew there was no calculating the adult world, no fighting it, no winning against it.

We started moving slowly toward the parapet and the fire escape, avoiding a last look at the green beauty of the earth that T. J. had planted for us, had planted deeply in our minds as well as in our experience. We filed slowly over the edge and down the steps to the plank, T. J. coming last, and all of us could feel the weight of his grief behind us.

"Wait a minute," he said suddenly, his voice harsh with the effort of calling.

We stopped and turned, held by the tone of his voice, and looked up at him standing above us on the fire escape.

"We can't stop them?" he said, looking down at us, his face strange in the dusky light. "There ain't no way to stop 'em?"

"No," Blackie said with finality. "They own the building."

We stood still for a moment, looking up at T. J., caught into inaction by the decision working in his face. He stared back at us, and his face was pale and mean in the poor light, with a bald nakedness in his skin like

❶ **Read and Discuss** What does the man mean when he says, "And sag it so I'd have to rebuild it"?

cripples have sometimes.

"They ain't gonna touch my earth," he said fiercely. "They ain't gonna lay a hand on it! Come on."

He turned around and started up the fire escape again, almost running against the effort of climbing. We followed more slowly, not knowing what he intended to do. By the time we reached him, he had seized a board and thrust it into the soil, scooping it up and flinging it over the parapet into the areaway below. He straightened and looked at us.

"They can't touch it," he said. "I won't let 'em lay a dirty hand on it!"

We saw it then. He stooped to his labor again, and we followed, the gusts of his anger moving in frenzied labor among us as we scattered along the edge of earth, scooping it and throwing it over the parapet, destroying with anger the growth we had nurtured with such tender care. The soil carried so laboriously upward to the light and the sun cascaded swiftly into the dark areaway, the green blades of grass crumpled and twisted in the falling.

It took less time than you would think; the task of destruction is infinitely easier than that of creation. We stopped at the end, leaving only a scattering of loose soil, and when it was finally over, a stillness stood among the group and over the factory building. We looked down at the bare sterility of black tar, felt the harsh texture of it under the soles of our shoes,

> "They can't touch it," he said. "I won't let 'em lay a dirty hand on it!"

and the anger had gone out of us, leaving only a sore aching in our minds, like over-stretched muscles.

T. J. stood for a moment, his breathing slowing from anger and effort, caught into the same contemplation of destruction as all of us. He stooped slowly, finally, and picked up a lonely blade of grass left trampled under our feet and put it between his teeth, tasting it, sucking the greenness out of it into his mouth. Then he started walking toward the fire escape, moving before any of us were ready to move, and disappeared over the edge.

We followed him, but he was already halfway down to the ground, going on past the board where we crossed over, climbing down into the areaway. We saw the last section swing down with his weight, and then he stood on the concrete below us, looking at the small pile of anonymous earth scattered by our throwing. Then he walked across the place where we could see him and disappeared toward the street without glancing back, without looking up to see us watching him.

They did not find him for two weeks.

Then the Nashville police caught him just outside the Nashville freight yards. He was walking along the railroad track, still heading South, still heading home. **Ⓙ**

As for us, who had no remembered home to call us, none of us ever again climbed the escapeway to the roof.

Ⓙ **Literary Focus** Themes Across Works What theme is suggested by T. J.'s decision to walk home?

🐻 **California Standards, pp. 334–335**
- **Reading Standard 3.4** Identify and analyze recurring themes across works (e.g., the value of bravery, loyalty, and friendship; the effects of loneliness).

Think About/Talk About

▶ Comprehension

Ⓘ Read and Discuss

Possible response: The weight of the dirt and grass must be putting so much pressure on the roof that they can see the damage inside the building.

▶ Analysis

Ⓙ Literary Focus

Possible response: T.J.'s decision conveys the theme that some people need to be near their roots to be strong.

▶ Extend the Discussion

Cause and Effect What effect does the destruction of the garden have on T.J.? What does it cause him to do? *Possible response:* When the garden is destroyed, T.J., like Antaeus, is defeated. He is robbed of his strength and no longer has any earth to connect to in the city. Because he no longer has what he needs in the city, he runs away, trying to get back to the land that makes him strong.

Motivation In the third full paragraph, T.J. begins to destroy the roof garden. Why do you think he does this after it took so much effort for the boys to grow the garden? *Possible response:* T.J. would rather destroy the garden himself than let anyone else touch it. He knows it will be destroyed anyway and by doing it himself, he retains control.

Monitor Students' Comprehension

Guide the class in answering these comprehension questions.

1. Why does the narrator introduce T. J. to his gang? [*He thinks T. J. is interesting and unusual.*]

2. How much time and effort do the boys put into their garden? [*It takes all winter and spring to prepare and plant the garden, and they put forth a great effort to get all the soil up to the roof.*]

3. Why is the building owner angry about the garden? [*He thinks it will damage his roof.*]

Check for Understanding

Independent Practice

Reading Skills Focus
Answers:

1. *First, T.J. moved to the city from his home in Alabama. Next, T.J. worked harder than anyone else to build the rooftop garden. Then, T.J. was more proud than anyone of the grass they grew on the roof. Next, the adult who owned the building told the boys he was going to destroy the garden. Finally, T.J. got angry, destroyed the garden, and ran away back home to the South.*

2. *The garden is important because it is a place to call their own.*

3. *Some of the themes I see in the story are: that friendships can develop among the most unlikely people and that creating something wonderful takes time and patience. I think the main theme is that people find strength in different things, people, or places, and can lose that strength when separated from the source.*

Vocabulary Check

4. *Contemplating involves careful thought.*

5. *A garden that has not been taken care of will not thrive.*

6. *Sterile environments are very uniform and often boring.*

Literary Skills Focus
Possible Responses:

7. *T.J.'s reaction was believable because he worked hard and the owner did not appreciate the beauty of the earth.*

8. *Like Antaeus, T.J. is connected with the earth and crushed when separated from it. The allusion shows the theme is universal.*

9. *The boys learn to take pride in accomplishing a goal. T.J. learns life isn't fair.*

10. *I identified ideas about the unifying power of nature in* The Secret Garden. *This theme is relevant to contemporary life because there is a fight between environmentalists and developers.*

Applying Your Skills

Antaeus

Literary Response and Analysis

Reading Skills Focus
Quick Check

1. Fill out a story map like the one below to show the main events of this story.

Read with a Purpose

2. Why does the garden become so important to the boys?

Reading Skills: Comparing and Contrasting Themes

3. Complete the chart you began on page 307. Consider what this story says about friendship, the earth, and home. Write down two or three themes that you see in this story. Then, state what you think is the main theme.

Brief Summary of Story	Subject of Story	Statement of Theme

✓ Vocabulary Check

Respond to each question below.

4. Why would it be hard to **contemplate** something if you were rushed?

5. Why would a garden that has not been cared for in months be unlikely to be **flourishing**?

6. Why might someone who loves to be excited and entertained dislike a **sterile** environment?

Literary Skills Focus
Literary Analysis

7. **Evaluate** Did you find this story, particularly its ending, believable? Do you think T. J. overreacted to the loss of his garden, or do you think his response was understandable? Give reasons for your opinion.

8. **Interpret** In Greek mythology, Antaeus cannot be beaten as long as he is in contact with the earth. However, Hercules is able to kill him by lifting him into the air and crushing him. What is the implicit connection between what happens to Antaeus and what happens to T. J.? What do you think this **allusion,** or reference to another work, adds to the story?

Literary Skills: Themes Across Works

9. **Interpret Theme** often reveals what the main characters learn in the story—as well as what you learn as you share their experiences. What do you think the narrator and the other boys learned through the events of the story? What do you think T. J. learned?

10. **Extend** Where else have you encountered themes that are similar to the themes you identified in "Antaeus"? How are these themes relevant to contemporary life?

Writing Skills Focus
Think as a Reader/Writer
Use It in Your Writing Review your notes about the way the author uses realistic dialogue. Write a short scene in which the boys from this story discuss how to continue doing the work T. J. taught them.

Universal Access

Struggling Writers
Provide additional scaffolding by reviewing with students the characteristics of realistic dialogue. For example, you might say, "Realistic dialogue reflects the way real kids, kids like you and your friends, talk to one another in casual conversations. Do you and your friends always speak in complete sentences? Or do you use fragments and run-ons as well? Does realistic dialogue necesarrily follow all the rules of formal English? Or might it use informal patterns, slang terms, or abbreviations? Think about these possibilities as you write your scenes."

Wrap Up

Hum / Antaeus

Reading Standard 3.4 Identify and analyze recurring themes across works (e.g., the value of bravery, loyalty, and friendship; the effects of loneliness).

Writing Skills Focus
Write a Comparison-Contrast Essay

Write an essay comparing the themes in "Hum" and "Antaeus." Begin by studying the chart you filled out for each selection. After thinking about the main theme you identified for each work, decide how you will organize your essay.

1. **Organize by selection.** In the first paragraph, explore how the theme is treated in "Hum." In the second paragraph, do the same for "Antaeus." In the final paragraph, explain how the treatment of the theme is similar and different in each story, and tell which selection you think treated the theme more effectively.

2. **Organize by theme.** In the first paragraph, discuss the similarities in the way the two stories treat the theme. In the second paragraph, discuss the differences in the way the two stories treat the theme. End the essay with your assessment of which story treated the theme more effectively.

What Do You Think Now How have these stories affected your ideas about friendship? Why do you think themes about friendship recur in literature?

CHOICES

As you respond to the Choices, use these **Academic Vocabulary** words as appropriate: implicit, recur, relevant, reveal.

REVIEW
Support a Dialogue Club
Timed Writing The Dialogue Club in "Hum" is likely to have a positive effect on the people who joined it. Write a brief persuasive essay that makes a case for the value of starting a Dialogue Club in your school. Include ways the club can improve morale within the student body and can address important school issues.

CONNECT
Continue the Story
What happens to T. J. and the narrator after the events of "Antaeus"? Write two brief scenes that take place after the story ends. In the first scene, tell what happens next from T. J.'s point of view—let him continue the story, speaking as "I." In the next scene, reveal the narrator's thoughts and feelings about T. J.'s departure.

EXTEND
Participate in a Panel Discussion
Listening and Speaking One theme in both stories is that people can appreciate—and learn from—one another's differences. With a small group, organize a panel discussion on this theme. Consider these questions: *What are the dangers of not appreciating individual differences? In what ways are differences strengths? How can appreciating differences help people understand one another? How can differences be combined to make a stronger society?*

Independent Practice

Choices:
Evaluation Criteria
Review: Timed Writing 45–50 Minutes
- Students write a well-developed essay that supports founding a Dialogue Club.
- Students use potential benefits of the Dialogue Club as support.

Connect:
Continue the Story
- Students create one scene each from the narrator's perspective and from T.J.'s perspective.
- Students create scenes that correspond to the original story content.

Extend:
Participate in a Panel Discussion
- Students engage in respectful debate and discussion.
- Students address each question in its entirety.

Assess

Chapter 3 Resources, Selection Standards Check, p. 27

Teacher One Stop™, editable Selection Standards Check

ThinkCentral Online Assessment, Selection Standards Check

Reteach

ThinkCentral Online Remediation

Universal Access

Struggling Writers
Provide additional scaffolding for students struggling to write the conclusions of their comparison-contrast essays. Explain that in assessing which story treated the theme more effectively, they might consider the following factors:
- the credibility of the stories' plot and characters
- the degree to which they felt engaged in or moved by the story and theme
- how creative the author's use of language was in conveying the theme

What Do You Think Now?
Have students revisit their original responses in their **Reader/Writer Notebook** and consider whether their views on friendships have changed. Ask them also what similarities they can see between the friendships developed between Sami, Hugh, and the Dialogue Club, and those developed among T.J. and the gang. Themes about friendship probably occur frequently because friendship is so important in our lives.

Objectives

Students will

- understand and analyze an author's perspective
- evaluate an author's perspective in a text

Motivate

What Do You Think?/QuickTalk

Have volunteers discuss their experiences with animals. Ask students to write in their **Reader/Writer Notebook** about how they benefitted from the experiences.

English for Academic Success

Academic Vocabulary

Look for opportunities to use the Academic Vocabulary words in this chapter.

- **reveal, v.:** show something that was previously hidden

Analyzing Visuals

Extension Activity Ask students to indicate from what perspective the photograph is taken. What might a person in that situation be experiencing? *Possible response: The perspective is from within the hole in the ice. A person in that situation would be relieved that help has arrived.*

INFORMATIONAL TEXT FOCUS

Tracing an Author's Argument or Perspective

CONTENTS

What Do You Think

What benefits do people gain from their relationships with animals?

QuickTalk

Most people have either personally experienced or observed in others the bond between humans and animals. With a small group, share your experiences.

California Standards,
pp. 336–347

- **Reading Standard 2.4** Identify and trace the development of an author's argument, point of view, or perspective in text.

Selection Readability	
Easily Accessible **Accessible** **Challenging**	familiar situations; unfamiliar vocabulary

Selection Summary

This article explores the relationship rescue dogs have with both their human caretakers and disastrous situations. The article's tone and details clearly reveal the author's perspective.

Preparing to Read

Reading Standard 2.4 Identify and trace the development of an author's argument, point of view, or perspective in text.

Canines to the Rescue

Informational Text Focus

Analyzing an Author's Perspective
The way you view a subject is called your **perspective.** Consider the topic of dogs. Some people's perspective on that subject is negative—they think dogs are dangerous animals that can turn on you at any moment. Other people have a positive view of dogs—they think dogs are friendly, loving, and faithful companions.

Perspective in writing refers to a writer's **point of view,** or attitude, toward a subject. The word *perspective* comes from the Latin word *perspicere,* which means "to look at closely." All writing <u>reveals</u> some kind of perspective on the world. The writer is saying, in effect, "Here is what I think about this issue."

Tips for Tracing an Author's Perspective After you read "Canines to the Rescue," make a chart like the one on the right. Completing the chart will help you interpret the author's perspective on rescue dogs. The notes beside the article will help you trace the author's perspective as you read.

"Canines to the Rescue"

> The author spends time with rescue dogs in the rubble of the World Trade Center.
>
> ↓
>
> The author gives examples of rescue dogs' qualities:
> 1.
> 2.
> 3.
> [and so on]
>
> ↓
>
> The author compares his opinion of dogs with another writer's:
>
> ↓
>
> Final quotation:
>
> ↓
>
> The author's perspective on rescue dogs:

Language Coach

Word Choice Word choice often hints at an author's perspective toward a topic. For example, near the end of "Canines to the Rescue," the author uses the word *cynic* (SIHN ihk) to describe people who disagree with his viewpoint. *Cynic* is a harsh word that means "someone who believes that people act only out of their self-interest." As you read, look for some of the positive words, such as *selfless, dedication,* and *heroic,* the author uses to present his perspective toward dogs.

Writing Skills Focus

Preparing for **Timed └Writing** As you read "Canines to the Rescue," use your *Reader/Writer Notebook* to take notes about the author's perspective on dogs. Which details and events are most memorable?

Reader/Writer Notebook
Use your **RWN** to complete the activities for this selection.

 Learn It Online
To learn more about analyzing the author's perspective, use the interactive Reading Workshop at:

go.hrw.com | H7-337 | **Go**

Direct Teach

Model the Skill

■ Provide students with copies of the graphic organizer (see **Chapter 3 Resources**) or ask them to use a piece of their own paper.

■ Explain that people have views, or perspectives, on issues from education to clothing styles. An **author's perspective** often influences his or her writing. It is up to the reader to identify the writer's perspective and compare it with the reader's own feelings.

Canines to the rescue

> The author spends time with rescue dogs in the rubble of the World Trade Center.
>
> ↓
>
> The author gives examples of rescue dog's qualities:
> 1. Strong work ethic
> 2.
> 3.
> [and so on]
>
> ↓
>
> The author compares his opinion of dogs with another writer's:
>
> ↓
>
> Final quotation:
>
> ↓
>
> The author's prespective on rescue dogs:

■ Model filling in the graphic organizer with the qualities of rescue dogs using the second paragraph on p. 338. You might say: "In this paragraph, the author explains that dogs do not need to be bribed in order to help humans, which is unlike other animals. In my graphic organizer, I will write that dogs have a strong work ethic."

Guided Practice: Apply

Explain that the details a writer includes about the subject, such as qualities, quotations about the subject, and comparisons with another writer's perspective, reflect his or her perspective. Have students work in pairs to add details to the graphic organizer.

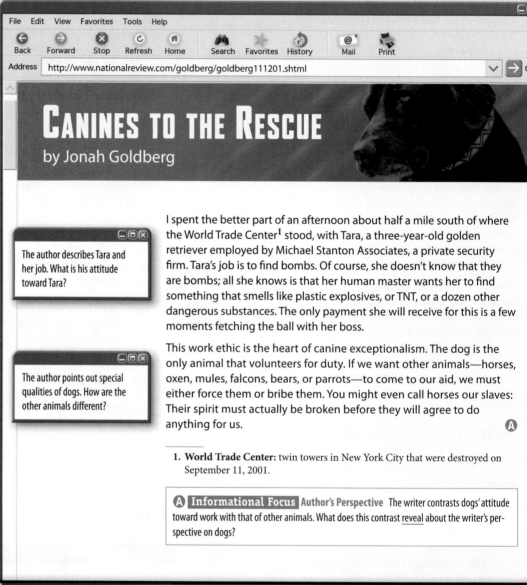

Read with a Purpose
As you read, consider why dogs and humans share a unique bond.

File   Edit   View   Favorites   Tools   Help

Back   Forward   Stop   Refresh   Home   Search   Favorites   History   Mail   Print

Address   http://www.nationalreview.com/goldberg/goldberg111201.shtml

CANINES TO THE RESCUE
by Jonah Goldberg

The author describes Tara and her job. What is his attitude toward Tara?

The author points out special qualities of dogs. How are the other animals different?

I spent the better part of an afternoon about half a mile south of where the World Trade Center[1] stood, with Tara, a three-year-old golden retriever employed by Michael Stanton Associates, a private security firm. Tara's job is to find bombs. Of course, she doesn't know that they are bombs; all she knows is that her human master wants her to find something that smells like plastic explosives, or TNT, or a dozen other dangerous substances. The only payment she will receive for this is a few moments fetching the ball with her boss.

This work ethic is the heart of canine exceptionalism. The dog is the only animal that volunteers for duty. If we want other animals—horses, oxen, mules, falcons, bears, or parrots—to come to our aid, we must either force them or bribe them. You might even call horses our slaves: Their spirit must actually be broken before they will agree to do anything for us. **Ⓐ**

1. **World Trade Center:** twin towers in New York City that were destroyed on September 11, 2001.

> **Ⓐ Informational Focus** **Author's Perspective** The writer contrasts dogs' attitude toward work with that of other animals. What does this contrast <u>reveal</u> about the writer's perspective on dogs?

Universal Access

Ⓔ English Learners
Help students understand figurative or idiomatic expressions they may not comprehend. Expressions like "the heart of" and "no picnic" may puzzle some students. Have students "translate" these expressions into literal phrases. Example: "the heart of" means "the most important thing about," and "no picnic" means "difficult."

✔ See **UA: Differentiating Instruction** for strategies for teaching English learners.

Struggling Readers
Tell students that before they look for the author's perspective, they must identify the topic of the text. Explain that from the title, you know the topic of the article: rescue dogs. Once you know the topic, you can figure out how the author feels about the topic. In the first paragraph, it is revealed that the author worked with a rescue dog at the World Trade Center. If he works with dogs, he probably likes and respects them. As students continue to read, have them jot down clues that give information about the author's perspective.

Analyzing Visuals

Connecting to the Text Notice the conditions in the photograph. How does this picture support the information from the text?

Look carefully at the word choice in the paragraph. Which words offer clues to the author's view of dogs?

Long before the rubble settled in downtown New York, German shepherds, Labrador retrievers, and Rottweilers—as well as canines of less aristocratic lineage—were already pulling at their leashes to help with the search-and-rescue efforts. Locating the dead and searching (too often in vain) for the living is obviously an **arduous** and emotionally draining task for human beings, but it is no picnic for dogs either. The rubble provided unstable footing, was full of glass shards and twisted metal, and sometimes glowed red hot. Dangerous fumes, loud noises, and the equivalent of landslides were constant sources of distraction and peril. Dogs repeatedly had to limp out of the wreckage on bloody paws, the razor-edged debris[2] slicing through even the leather boots distributed to some of them. **B**

---

2. **debris** (duh BREE): pieces of stone, wood, glass, or other materials left after something is destroyed.

B Read and Discuss How does this information add to what you have learned about rescue dogs?

Vocabulary arduous (AHR joo uhs) *adj.*: difficult.

✔ See **UA: Differentiating Instruction** for strategies for struggling readers.

✔ See **UA: Resources for Teaching Advanced Students** for strategies for teaching advanced learners.

Advanced Learners

Acceleration Have students analyze the way in which the article's tone gives the reader clues about the author's perspective. Point out the phrases "of course," "the dog is the only animal," and "we must" in the first two paragraphs. Have students discuss how these authoritative phrases contribute to the article's tone and what they might reveal about the author's perspective on the issue.

Students with Disabilities

Invite students to read "Canines to the Rescue" in interactive format in **UA: Holt Interactive Reader** and to use the sidenotes as aids to understanding the selection. The interactive version provides additional instruction, practice, and assessment of the skills taught in the Student Edition.

Think About/Talk About

Read with a Purpose Have students read the Read with a Purpose statement. Remind students to study the evidence the author gives that shows the bond between dog and human.

▶ **Comprehension**

B Read and Discuss

Possible response: They are selfless—willing to harm themselves in pursuit of a missing person.

▶ **Analysis**

A Informational Focus

Possible response: The writer considers dogs unique in the animal world.

▶ **Extend the Discussion**

Author's Perspective How does the description of the disaster scene on p. 339 help to communicate the author's opinion of the rescue dogs? *Possible response: The author describes the scene in chilling detail and lets us know just how dangerous and painful it must have been for the people and dogs working there. The author suggests that the dogs must have been very tough, brave, and admirable for working under these conditions.*

Making Generalizations Re-read paragraph 2 on p. 338. What generalizations does the author make about dogs? What makes these statements generalizations? *Possible response: The author generalizes dogs as having a wonderful work ethic and always volunteering for duty. These statements are generalizations because they suggest that these characteristics apply to all dogs, even though there may be some slight variations or exceptions to this statement.*

Vocabulary: Own the Word

arduous: Remind students that the connotation of *arduous* is "an extremely difficult task." You might say, "Writing a book report is tough, but writing a research paper is arduous." Ask students to create a pair of related statements that show how *arduous* is more difficult than *tough*.

Model the Skill

■ Tell students that words are a writer's tools—the writer uses words to shape the meaning he or she wants to share with readers. An author's **word choice,** or the specific terms he or she uses, may also reveal the author's perspective on his or her subject. Identifying specific instances of word choice in a text can help the reader better understand the author's meaning and perspective.

■ Point out the Vocabulary word *persevered* on p. 340. Ask a volunteer to read aloud the paragraph before the word. Then, explain that in the paragraph before the word *persevered*, the author describes the extreme difficulty of not finding survivors when searching the rubble of disasters. Read aloud the paragraph beginning at point C. Explain that the author chose the word *persevered* to describe how the dogs kept working in unfavorable conditions. The author seeks to convince readers that the dogs are loyal and strong to keep working despite the extreme difficulties. The author's use of *persevered* reflects careful word choice because he uses the word to help the audience share his perspective: that dogs are wonderful and strong.

Guided Practice: Apply

Think-Pair-Share Have students skim pp. 340–341 and identify words that they think were deliberately chosen by the author to express his feelings about dogs. Have students share their word choices and reasoning with a partner, and then ask volunteers to share with the class.

Quotations, such as this one from a veterinarian, offer clues to the author's perspective.

Worse, the stress associated with not finding survivors was extreme; dogs tasked with this assignment expect—*need*—to find survivors. "They don't like to find bodies. They'll find them, but they don't feel rewarded," veterinarian Douglas Wyler explained. "The dogs are good, they're professionals, but like any professional they can suffer from melancholy and depression. It's hard for the men not to find anyone alive, and the dogs sense that." **C**

But the dogs persevered. Consider Servus, a Belgian Malinois (a smaller version of the German shepherd) who arrived at the Twin Towers site with his owner, police officer Chris Christensen, the day after the disaster. While searching for survivors, Servus fell down a nine-foot hole into a mound of dust and debris. When they pulled him free, "he couldn't breathe," Christensen explained. Servus tried to vomit, to no avail. By the time the convulsions started and Servus's tongue turned purple, between twenty and thirty men were gathered to help an animal they clearly considered a colleague (often, police dogs are given full-dress funerals). The

C **Read and Discuss** What additional information about rescue dogs do you find in this paragraph?

Vocabulary **persevered** (pur suh VIHRD) *v.:* kept trying; persisted.

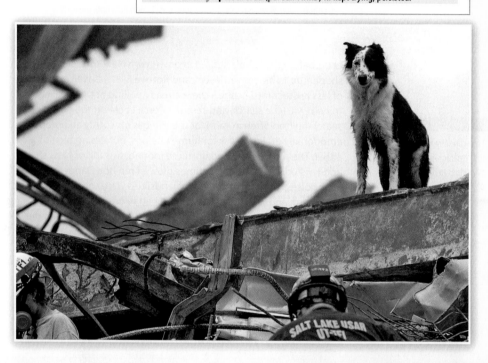

Developing Oral Fluency

Tell students that appropriate volume is important in oral reading because a reader who speaks too softly cannot be heard by the audience, while a reader who speaks too loudly can be difficult to understand. In either case, it is difficult for a listener to grasp the words and meanings being expressed.

Whole-Class Activity Have volunteers read an excerpt of your choice from "Canines to the Rescue"

aloud to practice reading with appropriate volume. Ask one volunteer to speak very softly while reading, ask another volunteer to speak very loudly while reading, and ask the final volunteer to read at an appropriate volume—audible, but not excessively loud. Discuss with students what made each volume appropriate or inappropriate.

✔ See **UA: Differentiating Instruction** for practice passages for devleoping oral fluency.

canine was rushed to one of the veterinary MASH units set up to treat the rescue dogs as well as the numerous "civilian" animals and pets injured or abandoned in the surrounding residential areas.

The vets managed to resuscitate[3] Servus, and he was given an IV.[4] (It was not unusual to see rescue humans and rescue dogs lying beside one another, each with his own IV drip.) When the vets unstrapped the dog from the gurney and released him for some doggie R & R,[5] he ran straight from the tent and leapt into the police car assigned to bring dogs to ground zero. "I couldn't believe it," Christensen said. "I told him three times to get out and he just looked at me, so we went to work. We worked for seven hours." **(D)**

Such dedication has inspired a growing effort in the scientific community to explain this age-old symbiosis between men and dogs. Until fairly recently, the study of dogs has been ignored by scientists more interested in more "authentic" animals—despite the fact that the domestic dog may be the second most successful of all mammal species, after human beings.

More to the point, their success is directly attributable to the fact that they have teamed up with human beings. I'm told that according to an American Indian legend, human beings and animals were separated by a great canyon in prehistory. Forced to choose sides, the dog decided to throw in his lot with man and leapt the chasm to live and work with us. The moral of the story is certainly true, though the choice was evolutionary as well as sentimental. Some, like nature writer Stephen Budiansky, take the story too far in the other direction. He argues that canines have mastered an

The writer contrasts his view of dogs with those of scientists who don't regard dogs as highly.

The author cites scientific research. He compares and contrasts his perspective with another writer's.

---

3. **resuscitate** (rih SUHS uh tayt): revive; bring back to life.
4. **IV** (abbreviation for *intravenous*): medical procedure in which blood, plasma, medicine, or nutrients are delivered directly into a vein.
5. **R & R:** abbreviation used in the military, meaning "rest and recuperation."

(D) Informational Focus Author's Perspective In what ways does the anecdote about Servus support the author's perspective on rescue dogs?

▶ Comprehension

 Read and Discuss

Possible response: The author seems to think that, at times, dogs can be better friends and companions than humans can.

▶ Analysis

 Informational Focus

Possible response: The author believes that whatever the motive for dogs' behavior, what matters is their loyalty and selfless actions.

▶ Extend the Discussion

Summarizing In your own words, state the major ideas about rescue dogs that the author communicated to readers through this article. *Possible response: The author wants readers to understand the loyalty, integrity, and dedication of rescue dogs. He emphasizes the special relationship between dogs and humans, which he believes to be the driving force behind the willingness of dogs to face danger and depression for the sake of humans.*

Making Judgments In the paragraph that begins "These cynics would have us believe," the writer states that we "con" dogs. Do you agree with this statement? Explain. *Possible response: Yes, we convince dogs to do things by offering them rewards and praise.*

Vocabulary: Own the Word

fidelity: Tell students that the root word for *fidelity* is *fidelis*, which is Latin and means "faithful." A character trait of dogs is *fidelity*, which is loyalty or faithfulness. Have students describe ways animals show fidelity.

Monitor Students' Comprehension

Use the Read with a Purpose follow-up question to assess students' understanding. *Possible response: Dogs can help humans, creating a strong dependency and a limitless friendship.*

evolutionary strategy that makes us love them: "Dogs belong to that elite group of con artists at the very pinnacle of their profession, the ones who pick our pockets clean and leave us smiling about it."

These cynics would have us believe that dogs—which have, in numerous documented cases, given their lives for human beings—are actually slyly exploiting an emotional glitch in people that makes us love soft, big-eyed furry things. This overlooks the obvious fact that we "con" dogs too; that they, in fact, love us as much as, if not more than, we love them.

Allowing himself to be carried by crane hundreds of feet above the ground and then lowered into a smoldering pit of metal and glass defies every instinct a dog has, except one: to be a selfless friend of his ally and master. "Histories are more full of examples of the fidelity of dogs than of friends," observed Alexander Pope. "Heaven goes by favor," remarked Mark Twain. "If it went by merit, you would stay out and your dog would go in."

The author uses famous quotations to support his view.

There's no disputing that dogs do things for canine reasons. Many of their heroic acts can be attributed to misplaced maternal or other instincts. Newfoundlands have saved many people from drowning, but their instinct is just as strong to "save" banana crates and other flotsam. Tara—the ebullient[6] golden retriever I looked for bombs with—doesn't know the details; all she knows is that she wants to please her human master.

The author ends by contrasting ideas about dogs and by expressing his opinion.

And isn't that good enough?

Read with a Purpose In what ways can humans and dogs form a unique bond?

6. **ebullient** (ih BUHL yuhnt): high-spirited.

E | Read and Discuss What does this paragraph tell you about the author's view of dogs and their place in society?

F | Informational Focus **Author's Perspective** What do the last two paragraphs reveal about the author's perspective on rescue dogs?

Vocabulary **fidelity** (fuh DEHL uh tee) *n.*: faithfulness.

 Internet

Universal Access

Students with Disabilities

Have students cover the page with a sheet of paper so that the only paragraph visible to them is the paragraph they are currently reading. This will help students trace the the author's perspective through each paragraph.

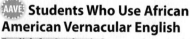 Students Who Use African American Vernacular English

English for Academic Success Some students may struggle with the formal usage of the articles *a* and *an*. Explain that in formal English, *a* is used before words that begin with consonants, and *an* is used before words that begin with vowels. Point out the formal English usage "an evolutionary strategy" and "a smoldering pit" from the text. Have students reinforce their understanding of the formal usage of *a* and *an* by choosing the appropriate article for each sentence below.

- My cousin got (a/an) new backpack.
- Kia drew (a/an) elephant after our class trip to the zoo.
- I ate (a/an) sandwich and (a/an) apple for lunch.

WEB ARTICLE
Applying Your Skills

 Reading Standard 2.4 Identify and trace the development of an author's argument, point of view, or perspective in text.

Canines to the Rescue

Standards Review

Informational Text and Vocabulary

1. Which of the following *best* states the **author's perspective** on rescue dogs?
   - A They work under cruel and inhumane conditions.
   - B They face deadly challenges to please their masters.
   - C They are con artists that fool humans into loving them.
   - D They do not receive adequate rewards for their work.

2. One way the author expresses his **perspective** on dogs is by contrasting
   - A a legend with an opposing opinion.
   - B pet dogs with search-and-rescue dogs.
   - C canine con artists with human dog trainers.
   - D German shepherds with Labrador retrievers.

3. To *best* describe his **perspective,** the author chooses the words
   - A *soft; maternal; elite.*
   - B *strategy; authentic; instinct.*
   - C *disaster; convulsions; draining.*
   - D *colleague; volunteers; dedication.*

4. Which of the following quotations *best* presents the **author's perspective?**
   - A "Servus . . . was given an IV."
   - B "a selfless friend of his ally and master"
   - C "a smaller version of the German shepherd"
   - D "their instinct is just as strong to 'save' banana crates"

5. If a task is *arduous*, it is
   - A irritating.
   - B difficult.
   - C exceptional.
   - D unusual.

6. A synonym for *fidelity* is
   - A honesty.
   - B gravity.
   - C dignity.
   - D loyalty.

7. Someone who has *persevered* has
   - A persisted.
   - B shouted.
   - C disputed.
   - D conceded.

Writing Skills Focus

Timed └Writing How effective is the author in communicating his perspective on dogs? Use details from the article to support your response.

What Do
You
Think
Now

What has this article made you think about what people can gain from their relationships with animals?

 California Standards, p. 343

■ **Reading Standard 2.4** Identify and trace the development of an author's argument, point of view, or perspective in text.

Check for Understanding

Answers and Explanations

1. **B** Dogs work under difficult conditions, but the author does not say the conditions are unacceptable (A). The writer refutes the opinion expressed in C. D reflects what the writer says is a misunderstanding.

2. **A** The author compares a Native American legend to those who go "too far" in criticizing dogs. The article does not mention pet dogs (B). It does not compare canine con artists with human dog trainers (C) or any two breeds (D).

3. **D** The article focuses on how dogs are loyal and do not have to be forced to work for humans. Word sets A, B, and C relate to the topic of the article but do not reflect the author's perspective on dogs.

4. **B** Quotations A and C are specific facts, while D does not reflect the author's primary perspective.

5. **B** A suggests a negative connotation, while C and D are not specific enough.

6. **D** Fidelity means "faithfulness," which D is a synonym for.

7. **A** B is unrelated, and C and D have the opposite meaning.

Writing Skills Focus

Possible response: The author is very effective in communicating his perspective on dogs. He gives many positive examples of dog behavior that reveal how intelligent, loyal, and strong dogs are and that convince the reader to feel the same.

What Do You Think Now?

Direct students' attention to the last few paragraphs of the article. What information do these paragraphs offer about the benefits of animal-human interaction? Have students discuss whether this information is convincing.

SPEECH
Preparing to Read

Reading Standard 2.4 Identify and trace the development of an author's **argument**, point of view, or perspective **in text.**

Preteach

Introducing Vocabulary

Read the Vocabulary words and sample sentences aloud. Then, use this activity to check students' understanding of the Vocabulary words.

1. What is a word that is the opposite of <u>malice</u>? [*kindness*]

2. What would be an example of a <u>treacherous</u> act? [*betraying a friend*]

3. If people are living in <u>prosperity</u>, what do they have? [*wealth*]

Language Coach

Suggest that students try adding prefixes and suffixes to *mal-* to arrive at new related words. Suggest that they use a dictionary or thesarus if needed. *Possible responses:* **malicious, malnourished, malfunction**

Informational Text Focus

Give students a copy of the Reading Skills Focus graphic organizer before they read to analyze the lawyer's appeals. (See **Chapter 3 Resources.**) Tell them to use their responses to answer the questions on the Applying Your Skills page.

Writing Skills Focus

Have students note the main points of the lawyer's appeal in their **Reader/Writer Notebook** and then use their notes to complete the Writing Skills Focus activity.

Tribute to the Dog

Informational Text Focus

Tracing an Author's Argument *Argument* can mean "angry disagreement." You can argue with your friends about all kinds of things, from who should be class president to what music should be played at a dance. In writing, or in formal speeches, the word *argument* is used to mean "debate or discussion." An **argument** is a position supported by both reason—also called logic—and emotion. Writers who present an argument want to persuade you to act in a certain way. They may want you to agree with their opinions, vote for their candidates, buy their products, or support their causes.

All writing, including arguments, <u>reveals</u> some kind of **perspective,** or point of view. Often in an argument, someone wants you to see things from a particular perspective. To convince you, the writer provides a mix of reasons and appeals. **Logical appeals** use reason to persuade you and are based on facts and statistics. **Emotional appeals** use tone, language, and anecdotes to stir up your feelings and make you sympathetic to the author's argument. "Canines to the Rescue" (page 338) presents both logical and emotional appeals. Vest, in his "Tribute to the Dog," relies heavily on emotional appeals as he tugs at readers' heartstrings. Which argument for dogs do you find more convincing?

Into Action Complete a chart like the one below as you read "Tribute to the Dog." Notice how Vest emphasizes the loyalty of dogs to their masters by comparing the behavior of dogs to the behavior of humans.

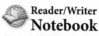

Human Behavior	Canine (Dog) Behavior

Writing Skills Focus

Preparing for **Timed └Writing** As you read "Tribute to the Dog," note the wording and examples Vest uses to appeal to your emotions.

Reader/Writer
Notebook
Use your **RWN** to complete the activities for this selection.

 Learn It Online
Use Word Watch to explore vocabulary words at:

go.hrw.com H7-344 Go

Selection Resources

Chapter 3 Resources, on-level practice and assessment, p. 36

Teacher One Stop™, on-level lesson plans and all print resources

Holt Audio Library

Holt Audio Library: Selections and Summaries in Spanish

UA: Differentiating Instruction, graphic organizer, p. 71

UA: Supporting Instruction in Five Languages, selection summary

ThinkCentral Online Assessment, Selection Standards Check

ThinkCentral Online Remediation

 Learn It Online
Send students to **Word Watch** for audio pronunciations, synonyms and antonyms, and brief histories of word origins.

go.hrw.com H7-344 Go

TRIBUTE to the DOG

Gentlemen of the Jury: The best friend a man has in the world may turn against him and become his enemy. His son or daughter that he has reared[1] with loving care may prove ungrateful. Those who are nearest and dearest to us, those whom we trust with our happiness and our good name may become traitors to their faith. The money that a man has, he may lose. It flies away from him, perhaps when he needs it most. A man's reputation may be sacrificed in a moment of ill-considered action. The people who are prone to fall on their knees to do us honor when success is with us, may be the first to throw the stone of malice when failure settles its cloud upon our heads. **(A)**

The one absolutely unselfish friend that man can have in this selfish world, the one that never deserts him, the one that never proves ungrateful or treacherous is his dog. A man's dog stands by him in prosperity and in poverty, in health and in sickness. He will sleep on the cold ground, where the

---

1. **reared:** raised.

(A) Informational Focus Author's Argument Note the contrast between the title and the examples in the first paragraph. What does this contrast <u>reveal</u> about the speaker's attitude toward dogs?

Vocabulary **malice** (MAL ihs) *n.:* meanness; hatred.
treacherous (TREHCH uhr uhs) *adj.:* unfaithful.
prosperity (prahs PEHR uh tee) *n.:* state of being successful, especially of being wealthy.

Selection Summary

In his closing argument to a jury, a lawyer extols the relationship between a dog and its owner. While our friends and family, our reputations, and our wealth may disappear when we need them most, he says, a dog is honored to follow us in our lowest moments. Even death cannot dissolve the loyalty of a dog, who sits at a grave, sad-eyed but alert, after all others have gone home.

Think About/Talk About

▶ **Analysis**

(A) Informational Focus

Possible response: The author's attitude is reverential; the author believes that unlike the unfaithfulness of humans, a dog's devotion is constant and unwavering.

▶ **Extend the Discussion**

Author's Purpose Why does the author avoid discussing the facts of the case when giving his summation? *Possible response: His client's dog was trespassing. It would be difficult to prove his client innocent given the facts of the case. He is trying to appeal to the jury's emotions instead.*

Comparing and Contrasting What comparison does the speaker set up between the first and second paragraphs? How do you think it will relate to the author's perspective on dogs? *Possible response: The author compares human friends to canine friends. I think this will reflect the author's perspective on dogs by expressing his favor for dogs; he describes dogs as more loyal than the most loyal human friends.*

Vocabulary: Own the Word

- **malice:** The author uses the word *malice* in an image: "to throw the stone of malice." What other ways can *malice* be demonstrated?

- **treacherous:** You might ask students, "Which one of the following demonstrate *treacherous* behavior? A tricky thief, a true friend, or a dishonest politician? [*a dishonest politician is unfaithful to the people he serves*]

- **prosperity:** Remind students that *prosperity* is the noun form of the verb *prosper*, which means to succeed in an activity, especially economically. Have students make a list of three ways a person can *prosper* or reach *prosperity*.

▶ Comprehension

Ⓑ Read and Discuss

Possible response: The dog is not swayed by a person's status, money, or reputation. It kisses the hand that has no food to offer and guards a poor man as loyally as a wealthy prince.

▶ Analysis

Ⓒ Informational Focus

Possible response: Vest makes an emotional appeal by painting a picture with his words of a dog so loyal to its master that it waits by his grave.

▶ Extend the Discussion

Main Idea What was the main point of the speech? *Possible response: The lawyer wishes to show that the dog that was shot was not just a mere animal, but a unique creature that in many respects is even more admirable than humans.*

Monitor Students' Comprehension

Use the Read with a Purpose follow-up question to assess students' understanding. *Possible response: I would have been swayed by Vest's arguments because he made emotional appeals. Even though I don't have a dog myself, his arguments made me wish I had a friend so loyal.*

wintry winds blow and the snow drives fiercely, if only he may be near his master's side. He will kiss the hand that has no food to offer. He will lick the wounds and sores that come in encounters with the roughness of the world. He guards the sleep of his pauper[2] master as if he were a prince. When all other friends desert, he remains. When riches take wings,[3] and reputation falls to pieces, he is as constant in his love as the sun in its journey through the heavens. **Ⓑ**

If fortune drives the master forth, an outcast in the world, friendless and homeless, the faithful dog asks no higher privilege than that of accompanying him, to guard him against danger, to fight against his enemies. And when the last scene of all comes, and death takes his master in its embrace and his body is laid away in the cold ground, no matter if all other friends pursue their way,[4] there by the graveside will the noble dog be found, his head between his paws, his eyes sad, but open in alert watchfulness, faithful and true even in death. **Ⓒ**

George Graham Vest

Read with a Purpose Explain whether or not you would have been swayed by George Graham Vest's arguments.

---

2. **pauper:** person who is very poor.
3. **take wings:** vanish; fly away.
4. **pursue their way:** continue with their lives.

Ⓑ Read and Discuss | What evidence does the author give for saying that a dog is "as constant in his love as the sun in its journey through the heavens"?

Ⓒ Informational Focus **Author's Argument** In what ways does Vest make emotional appeals in this paragraph?

Universal Access

EL English Learners

English for Academic Success Assist students in understanding the complex and archaic syntax in the text by conducting a guided reading. Read aloud each sentence to students, then pause and translate the author's language into more modern terms. Encourage students to take notes throughout the guided reading. When you finish reading, discuss as a group the topic of the text and the author's perspective on the topic.

Struggling Readers

Strategic Students Use a Jigsaw routine by dividing students into three groups and assign one paragraph of the text to each group. Have each group focus exclusively on the assigned paragraph, and work to summarize what the paragraph says. Also have students take note of key words and phrases that they believe express the author's opinion on the topic of the article. When each group is finished, have them share their paragraph summaries in order and discuss as a group what the author's perspective might be.

Applying Your Skills

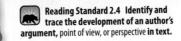 **Reading Standard 2.4** Identify and trace the development of an author's **argument,** point of view, or perspective **in text.**

Tribute to the Dog
Standards Review

Informational Text and Vocabulary

1. Which of the following *best* describes the author's reason for writing this summation?

   A to give his opinion about the need for farmers to have dogs

   B to teach the emotional differences between dogs and people

   C to convince people that a dog is the finest companion one can have

   D to entertain the courtroom with elaborate descriptions of dogs

2. One way the author expresses his **argument** about dogs is by contrasting dogs with

   A people.

   B death.

   C cats.

   D princes.

3. Which of the following quotations *best* supports the **author's argument?**

   A "The money that a man has, he may lose."

   B "His son or daughter . . . may prove ungrateful."

   C "by the graveside will the noble dog be found"

   D "A man's reputation may be sacrificed. . . ."

4. From the summation you can conclude that the **author's argument** is that

   A dogs are more loyal than humans.

   B dogs must obey laws as humans do.

   C everyone should have a dog.

   D everyone without a dog will be lonely.

5. An act of *malice* is one of

   A hatred.

   B disregard.

   C expertise.

   D quality.

6. A state of *prosperity* is one of

   A uncertainty.

   B success.

   C awareness.

   D injury.

7. A synonym for *treacherous* is

   A frightening.

   B logical.

   C unfaithful.

   D opinionated.

Writing Skills Focus

Timed ◔ Writing How did Vest convince you that the dog is "man's best friend"? Cite examples from the speech that had the strongest effect on your emotions.

 What Do You Think Now Explain who is more effective at arguing for his position and communicating his perspective: Goldberg or Vest.

 California Standards, p. 347

■ **Reading Standard 2.4** Identify and trace the development of an author's argument, point of view, or perspective in text.

What Do You Think Now?
Have students consider how emotional and logical appeals influence readers.

Standards Focus

Objectives

Students will

- write a response to literature
- persuade audience of the validity of their interpretation

Preteach

Write with a Purpose Read aloud the essentials of a good response to literature to guide students' understanding of this type of writing. Also refer students to the rubrics on p. 348 for more information on responses to literature that they can use throughout this workshop.

Direct Teach

Think as a Reader/Writer

Use the professional model on this page and others in the chapter to provide examples of the elements of a good response to literature.

Think About the Professional Model
Possible responses:

1. *Yes. The organization is effective because it is logical.*
2. *Three relevant examples are cited.*
3. *The author concludes her review by saying "Do not miss this one." This statement makes it clear that she wants people to read the book.*
4. *Yes; the author cites details from the story and shows an understanding of the main character's difficulties.*

California Standards, pp. 348–356

- **Writing Standard 2.2** Write responses to literature. **2.2a** Develop interpretations exhibiting careful reading, understanding, and insight. **2.2b** Organize interpretations around several clear ideas, premises, or images from the literary work. **2.2c** Justify interpretations through sustained use of examples and textual evidence.

Response to Literature

Write with a Purpose

Write an essay justifying your interpretation of a literary work. Explain how details from the work support your **thesis**. Remember that your **purpose** is to **persuade** your **audience** that you have developed a valid **interpretation** of the work.

A Good Response to Literature

- identifies the work by title and author
- states the interpretation clearly
- supports the interpretation with textual evidence such as details, examples, and reasons
- has a clear organization
- restates or reinforces the interpretation in a strong conclusion

See page 356 for complete rubric.

Reader/Writer Notebook

Use your **RWN** for completing the activities in this workshop.

Think as a Reader/Writer

Before you write your own response to a literary work, read Kathleen Odean's review of the novel *Catherine, Called Birdy*, by Karen Cushman. Notice how Odean uses evidence from the novel to persuade readers to support her interpretation of the work and to convince her audience to read the novel.

> Catherine, daughter of a small-time nobleman in medieval England, is hilarious. In a diary format she records her daily life, the outrages she suffers as a girl, and her often humorous assessment of things. She longs to be outside frolicking instead of inside sewing, and she chafes at her lessons in ladylike behavior.
>
> Birdy is the sort of girl who organizes a spitting contest and starts a mud fight. She makes a list of all the things girls cannot do, such as go on a crusade, be a horse trainer, laugh out loud, "and marry whom they will." She battles with her father, who wants to marry her off to the highest bidder, no matter how repulsive. Many of her best sarcastic remarks are reserved for him, and she irritates him whenever possible. She has a lively sense of humor and a palpable love of life. Few fictional characters are so vivid and funny—do not miss this one.

← The author states her **thesis** about the character in the first sentence.

← Specific **details** from the story are used to support the claim that this character is very funny.

← The closing sentences **restate the thesis** in a persuasive way.

Think About the Professional Model

With a partner, discuss the following questions about the model.

1. Does this response include an introduction, body, and conclusion? Is the organization effective? Why or why not? See page 356 for the complete rubric.
2. How many examples does the author include as evidence to back up her interpretation? Are the examples <u>relevant</u>?
3. How does the author <u>reveal</u> her purpose and make it clear?
4. Does this interpretation show careful reading, understanding, and insight? Explain.

Writing Workshop Resources

UA: Holt Interactive Writer and Speaker, on-level practice and assessment, p. 65

UA: Differentiating Instruction, modified lesson plans, p. 72

WritingNotes, interactive lesson presentations with activities

GrammarNotes, interactive lesson presentations with activities

Writing and Research in a Digital Age, interactive lesson presentations with activities

Writing Standard 2.2 Write responses to literature. a Develop interpretations exhibiting careful reading, understanding, and insight. b Organize interpretations around several clear ideas, premises, or images from the literary work. c Justify interpretations through sustained use of examples and textual evidence.

Prewriting

Choose a Subject

Think of a literary work that profoundly affected you—one with an interesting character who faces a clear conflict. A work that inspired a strong response in you is probably one that you would like to analyze further. Review your *Reader/Writer Notebook* to remind yourself of some of your responses to literature.

Develop a Thesis

Once you have chosen a topic, you need to formulate a **thesis** about the topic. A thesis statement expresses your point of view about a subject—in this case, your thesis will sum up your interpretation of a literary work. The thesis statement is usually located in an opening paragraph and supported by evidence presented throughout the essay. A strong thesis inspires readers to ask "How?" or "Why?" It avoids general and sweeping statements such as *all*, *none*, or *every*. Here are some examples to guide you:

Selection	Topic	Thesis Statement:
"The Dinner Party" (page 8)	The plot of the story	The plot is carefully designed to overturn stereotypes about gender differences.
"Rikki Tikki Tavi" (page 15)	The character of the hero	In his characterization of Rikki, Kipling combines animal traits with human motives.
"Bargain" (page 393)	The theme of the story	The theme of "Bargain" is that disrespect can breed vengeance.

Think About Purpose and Audience

As you plan your essay, keep your **purpose** and **audience** in mind. Your purpose is to convince your audience to agree with your interpretation of a literary work. Your audience includes your classmates and your teacher, who are knowledgeable and interested readers. Your essay should increase their understanding and enjoyment of the work.

Idea Starters

- How is a specific literary element, such as setting, plot, point of view, or character, used in the work?
- What problem does the main character face?
- What is the theme or main idea of the work?
- What is the significance of the title?

Your Turn _____

Get Started Working in your **RWN,** make a list of possible **subjects** you might want to discuss in your essay. Spend a few minutes freewriting about each one. Which **subject** generated your most interesting response? Form a working **thesis** about that **subject.**

 An interactive graphic organizer can help you generate and organize essay ideas. Try one at:

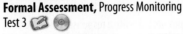 go.hrw.com | H7-349 | **Go**

Guided Practice: Apply

Develop a Thesis

- Remind students that when they choose a work of literature to write a response about, they do not need to write about every aspect of the work. Instead, they may focus on just one feature, such as a character, a theme, or an interesting writing technique.

- As students work to identify a selection and a topic that interest them, have them use a table like the one on the page to explore their reactions to the text or topic. For example, students may consider "Bargain," the topic of bullying as an element of theme, and note that in the selection, a bully must pay the ultimate price for his actions. Students may choose to develop a thesis about whether or not they feel the bully's punishment was just or went too far.

Think About Purpose and Audience

Have students keep in mind that when they write a response, their audience may not be familiar with the specific literary work. Remind students to give a brief description of the work in their response.

Your Turn _____

Get Started Have students pair up and share their subject and thesis ideas with their partner. Then, have their partners give feedback. Does the subject hold their attention? Is the thesis strong enough to write an extended response about? Have partners discuss what could make their subject ideas stronger.

Teacher One Stop™, on-level lesson plans and all print resources

Holt Six Traits for Writing, rubrics, prompts, and sample papers

Language and Sentence Skills Practice

UA: Developmental Language and Sentence Skills Practice

Language Handbook Worksheets, p.121

Formal Assessment, Progress Monitoring Test 3

ThinkCentral Online Assessment, Writing Workshop Test

ThinkCentral Online Remediation

Holt Online Essay Scoring

Learn It Online

The **Interactive Student Edition** includes more than thirty **Interactive Graphic Organizers**. Your students can use them to generate and organize ideas, compare and contrast, evaluate a decision, support a position and much more.

go.hrw.com | H7-349 | **Go**

Guided Practice: Apply

Re-Read the Literary Work

■ Explain to students that a cluster diagram can help them organize their thoughts and compile evidence to use in their writing. Direct students to the cluster diagram describing *Catherine, Called Birdy.* Point out that the circle in the center of the diagram is reserved for the thesis statement. All of the circles that radiate from the central circle are details that support the thesis that the main character, Catherine, is lively and funny.

■ Have students complete a cluster diagram as they re-read their chosen literary work. Remind them that their supporting details may include quotations and paraphrased statements from the story. After students have completed their diagrams, have them review their details to ensure that each one is relevant to their thesis.

Your Turn

Choose and Record Quotes Have students complete the **Your Turn** activity as independent practice. As they work, monitor their progress by making sure their chosen quotes from the text are clearly understandable and are relevant to their thesis.

⬤ Writing Tip

Note specific details that provide supporting evidence. Provide explanations or commentaries that draw connections for the reader. In fiction, describe:

• actions
• thoughts
• words
• others' behavior
• direct comments by writer

Your Turn _____

Choose and Record Quotes
Make notes in your **RWN,** choosing short pieces of the work that you might want to **quote directly.** Carefully copy the quotes in your notebook. Then draft an explanation of why each quote is important and how it supports your thesis. Try to keep quotations as brief as possible.

Gather Evidence

In a literary interpretation, the evidence you present in support of your thesis may include direct quotations; paraphrased lines or short passages; details such as images, actions, and dialogue; and explanations or reasons. You may want to make a chart like the one below, listing all of your points and the evidence supporting them. Then, evaluate the evidence, making sure each point is strongly and fully supported. You probably will not want to use all of the evidence, especially if some of it is weak. Select evidence carefully, choosing the best or most persuasive examples to back up your conclusions.

Point	Evidence
Birdy is unusual.	spitting contests and mud fights
She is strong-minded.	wants to choose her own husband

Re-read the Literary Work

Now that you have decided on a focus for your essay and drafted a working thesis, it is time to revisit the literary work you are analyzing. If it is short, re-read the entire work with your thesis in mind. If you are writing about a longer work, re-read sections you feel are important to your thesis. While you are reading, pause to record in your notebook any new thoughts and reactions you have, as well as any quotations that would support your points.

Catherine, Called Birdy

In her diary, she records daily events from a humorous perspective.

She rebels against the restraints of accepted ladylike behavior.

The character, Catherine, is funny and lively.

She fights her father's efforts to marry her to the highest bidder.

She makes witty sarcastic remarks, particularly about her father.

Response to Literature Writing Prompts

Students can choose their own ideas or use one of the following prompts to write a response to literature.

Social Studies Think of a lesson or theme about everyday life that is expressed in the literary work. What is the author trying to say about society as a whole?

Language Arts Examine the writing techniques the author uses in this literary work. Point out a particularly unique or interesting technique and explain how it contributes to the work.

Psychology Write a thorough description about a particular character. Explain how his or her actions, thoughts, and words reveal the character's personality and psyche.

Drafting

Follow the Writer's Framework

Organize your essay to include an introduction, a body, and a conclusion. In your **introduction,** identify the title, author, and thesis statement. The **body** of your essay should present evidence in support of your thesis. Each paragraph in the body of your essay should focus on a main supporting idea. The **conclusion** brings together your main idea and restates the thesis, revealing insights into the work.

Organize Evidence

You may arrange your evidence in **chronological order,** the order that it appears in the story, or you may place it in order of importance. Decide which way will work best by writing drafts of your points and evidence on index cards (or in blocks of text on the computer). Arrange and rearrange the text to see which arrangement might work best in your essay.

A Writer's Framework
Introduction:
_____
_____
Body:
_____
_____
Main Ideas:
1. _____
2. _____
Conclusion:
_____
_____

● Writing Tip

Do not fall into the trap of summarizing too much of the plot. Keep your audience's needs and your purpose in mind. Your audience needs only a brief summary. Your purpose for writing is to present your interpretation and analysis of what you have read. Your audience wants to know what you think about what you have read, and you want to persuade your audience that your interpretation is valid.

Grammar Link Using Comparatives and Superlatives

When organizing evidence in order of importance, writers often use **degrees of comparison.** The **comparative** degree of a modifier compares two people or things. When using the comparative degree, add the ending *-er* or the word *more.* The **superlative** degree compares more than two people or things. When using the superlative degree, add the ending *-est* or the word *most.*

Comparative Degree	Superlative Degree
Catherine is livel**ier** than her father wants her to be.	I enjoyed this book because Catherine is one of the funni**est** fictional characters I have ever encountered.
Catherine is **more** outspoken than many of her peers.	Catherine saved her **most** sarcastic comments for her father.

Your Turn _____

Write Your Draft Write a draft of your essay. Be sure to
- include a thesis
- quote accurately
- accurately interpret evidence
- restate the thesis in your conclusion

Model the Skill

Follow the Writer's Framework

Model organizing information using the Writer's Framework model.

- For the introduction, write: "In "Names/Nombres," Julia Alvarez shows how it is important for people to respect their family's heritage while fitting in with mainstream American culture.

- In the body, provide details such as Alvarez enjoying her family's party featuring Dominican food and traditions, and Alvarez accepting her American friends' pronunciation of her name.

- In the conclusion, write: "Alvarez's experience teaches us that America's strength lies within the fact that its people can be both diverse and similar at the same time."

Guided Practice: Apply

Grammar Link

For practice, have students identify each modifier and label it as comparative or superlative.

1. The brown shoes are fancier the gray shoes. [*fancier; comparative*]

2. That's the strangest story I've ever heard! [*strangest; superlative*]

 Warriner's Handbook, First Course, p. 224

Your Turn _____

Write Your Draft Ask students to complete the **Your Turn** activity as independent practice. Remind students to use their completed diagrams as they begin to draft their story. Suggest that students use every other line as they write their drafts so that revisions can be made more easily later.

Universal Access

 English Learners

Review the definitions of any academic vocabulary words from the section that may be unfamiliar to students.

Audience people reading a literary response. The audience must be convinced of the writer's thesis.

Interpretation opinion or explanation of something. The thesis is an author's interpretation of a literary work.

Purpose reason for doing something. The purpose of a literary response is to convince the audience that the writer's viewpoint is correct.

Thesis the main argument or idea of a literary response, such as the writer's opinion about the theme or a certain character. Writers must convince readers that their argument is correct.

Advanced Learners

Acceleration Remind students that using the author's own words is often the most effective way to get a point across. After they have compiled their main points and evidence, have them find one direct quote from the text for each piece of evidence.

Model the Skill

■ Using a student draft on a transparency, model how to use the questions, tips, and revision techniques suggested in the chart. You might use a student's response to literature or a response of your own creation to evaluate and revise using the steps in the chart.

■ Ask volunteers to demonstrate using each of the steps on their own stories.

Peer Review

Remind students that their partner needs to know what is good about the draft as much as he or she needs to know what is wrong with it. Encourage students to praise excellent sentences or ideas!

Holt Six Traits for Writing, rubrics, prompts, and sample papers

Peer Review

Be sure to provide helpful suggestions to your partner, and remember that your partner's suggestions are meant to help you develop a better essay.

Evaluating and Revising

Read the questions in the left column of the chart, and then use the tips in the middle column to help you make revisions to your essay. The right column suggests techniques you can use to revise your draft.

Supporting an Interpretation: Guidelines for Content and Organization

Evaluation Question	Tip	Revision Technique
1. Are the author and the title named in your introduction?	**Highlight** the author and the title.	**Add** a sentence or phrase naming the author and the title.
2. Does the introduction have a clear thesis?	**Underline** the thesis statement.	**Add** a sentence that clearly states the thesis.
3. Is the main idea of each paragraph clear, and does it support the thesis?	**Bracket** the main idea discussed in each paragraph of the body.	**Revise** the body paragraphs so that each deals with a main idea.
4. Is the main idea of each body paragraph supported with evidence?	**Draw a box** around each supporting detail or quotation. **Draw a wavy line** under elaborations.	**Add** details or quotations to support your thesis. **Elaborate** on details or quotations with commentary.
5. Does your conclusion restate the thesis?	**Highlight** the sentence in the conclusion that restates the thesis.	**Add** a sentence restating the thesis.
6. Are the sentences and ideas connected with appropriate transitions?	**Draw two lines** under each transitional word or phrase.	**Add** transitions where they are needed to connect ideas and achieve coherence.
7. Does the conclusion include a summary of the key points of your essay?	**Circle** the summary of key points.	**Add** one or more sentences that remind your reader of your strongest point or points.

Real Issues, Real Experts

Holt Professional Learning for Language Arts

To watch videos on teaching **revision, grammar,** and **on-demand writing skills** featuring Linda Rief, Amy Benjamin, and Leila Christenbury, go to this page in **ThinkCentral, Teacher Access**.

Read this student's draft and the comments about it as a model for revising your own response to a literary work.

A Girl's Adventure

by Sophia Eckerle, Paradise Canyon Elementary School

"Not every thirteen year old girl is accused of murder, brought to trial, and found guilty." This is the opening sentence of *The True Confessions of Charlotte Doyle,* a novel by Avi. The novel takes place in 1832. It tells the story of Charlotte who has finished her schooling in England and must sail home to America. She sails on the *Seahawk,* a rundown ship under the command of Captain Jaggery, a strange character. Charlotte's experiences with the Captain and the sailors change her ideas about how to judge people and how she wants to live her life.

As a wealthy and protective father, Mr. Doyle wants to shape Charlotte's future. He sends Charlotte to the expensive Barrington School for Better Girls in England. He has very high expectations for her and wants her to become an educated proper young lady. Before her journey, Mr. Doyle gave Charlotte a journal and expected her to write (with correct spelling) about the events of the voyage.

At the beginning of the journey, Captain Jaggery is a proper Englishman—one a thirteen-year-old girl could look up to. Like Charlotte's father, he believes that a young girl should wear fancy dresses and devote herself to studying instead of parading around with the crew wearing men's clothes.

← Sophia mentions the **title of the work** and the **name of the author.**

← She states her **thesis** about the main character at the end of the first paragraph.

← Sophia presents **evidence** that supports her claim about Charlotte's father.

MINI-LESSON ▶ **How to Use Supporting Evidence**

Be sure to support your thesis with relevant details. Sophia needs to clearly explain the significance of the main ideas found in the body of her essay. Each paragraph should support the essay's overall thesis.

Sophia's Revision of Paragraph Three

At the beginning of the journey, ∧ *Charlotte's views have been largely influenced by her father. Because of this, she sees* Captain Jaggery ~~is~~ *as* a proper Englishman—one a thirteen-year-old girl can look up to. ∧ *Charlotte is fooled into thinking the captain is trustworthy by his meticulous clothes and manners.*

Your Turn

Use Evidence Read your draft, and then ask yourself:

- Where might I add evidence in support of an important point?
- Have I explained the significance of the evidence I have provided?

Universal Access

Struggling Writers

To help students evaluate evidence, have them work in small groups and analyze each piece of evidence presented in their own drafts. First, have them identify the thesis statement. Then, tell them to decide whether the evidence presented is relevant to and supportive of the thesis. Does additional evidence need to be added to strengthen the argument? Does the writer explain why the evidence is relevant to the thesis? Finally, have groups add, delete, or modify evidence as needed.

Students with Disabilities

To help students understand the features of a response to literature, read aloud to the class a book review or literary critique. Work with students to identify the writer's thesis and the evidence he or she provides from the text to support this opinion.

Guided Practice: Apply

Student Draft

Explain that the Student Draft on this page is the first half of a response to literature written by a student. Model reading the draft and the annotations in blue, and explain that the yellow highlighting illustrates the student's language choices. Explain that a mini-lesson follows with helpful information about ways to improve this draft as well as their own.

▶ **Mini-Lesson**
How to Use Supporting Evidence

- Point out that the student writer has strengthened one paragraph in her revision by reconnecting to the thesis statement—Charlotte changes as a result of her experiences.

- Explain to students that they must choose their words carefully to avoid giving false impressions. Point out that in the first sentence of the final paragraph of the draft, the writer implies that Jaggery was a proper gentleman. In her revision, the writer correctly notes that Charlotte was fooled into thinking Jaggery was a gentleman.

Your Turn

Use Evidence Have students pair up with partners as they work on the **Your Turn** activity. Have each student read his or her partner's essay. Have them circle any instances in the essay in which there is not enough evidence provided to support an idea, or the evidence used is irrelevant or confusing. Have students underline instances in which evidence is clear and convincing. Tell students to supplement their drafts with additional evidence where their partners found it lacking.

Guided Practice: Apply

Student Draft

- Explain that the Student Draft is continued and completed on this page. Again the draft is annotated and highlighted for the students.

- Read the draft and annotations aloud and discuss.

▶ Mini-Lesson
Clarify Your Interpretation

- Point out methods the writer uses to strengthen her argument, such as the use of a quotation from Jaggery that is overheard by Charlotte and helps change her opinion of him.

- Explain that the student writer has revised her final paragraph to clarify her interpretation of the novel. Have students compare and contrast the original ending with the revised one. What makes the new conclusion stronger?

Your Turn _____

Write a Striking Conclusion As students complete the **Your Turn** activity, have them think about ways to make their conclusion catch the reader's attention. Ask students to try to make a connection between the literary text and the reader in some way, such as suggesting readers experience the selection for themselves. Have students write down possible concluding sentences and share them with a partner.

Student Draft *continues*

Sophia includes a **quotation** from the novel to illustrate a character's nature. →

> Charlotte's view of the captain begins to change when she sees how badly he treats the crew. He calls the crew "dirty beasts who demand the touch of the whip." Charlotte sees that this is not true.
>
> When the men mutiny against him, the deterioration of Captain Jaggery's mind continues. He kills two of the sailors for an attempted uprising. Charlotte decides that the captain is mad. Changing her fancy clothes for the clothes of a common sailor, she joins the crew. She has learned that the sailors who treat her kindly are the ones to trust, not the cruel captain. His high rank and his nice clothes are not important. Jaggery retaliates by giving her the hardest work on the ship, destroying the barrier between the aristocrats and the working class that Charlotte started. In this way, he contributes to Charlotte's changing attitudes.
>
> Both men influenced Charlotte's life and led to her adventures aboard the Seahawk. By the end of her ordeal, Charlotte was happy to run to the arms of her protective father.

Sophia explains how the **details** of the story support her thesis. →

MINI-LESSON ▶ Clarify Your Interpretation

A good writer restates the main idea of the essay in a fresh and persuasive way in the conclusion. Sophia's original conclusion was vague. When she revises her draft, she provides a stronger conclusion that makes her interpretation more clear.

Sophia's Draft of the Last Paragraph

> Both men influenced Charlotte's life and led to her adventures aboard the Seahawk. By the end of her ordeal, Charlotte was happy to run to the arms of her protective father.

Sophia's Revision of the Last Paragraph

> Charlotte's father and Captain Jaggery influenced the course of Charlotte's life, but perhaps the men on the ship influenced her more. Though at first happy to return to her father, Charlotte's experiences with the sailors forever changed the way she thought about the world. Read this exciting novel to appreciate all that Charlotte learns through her adventure and the surprising decision she makes about her future.

Your Turn _____

Write a Striking Conclusion
With a partner, review the conclusion to your essay. Have you restated your thesis? If not, repeat your main point in your conclusion, but do so in a fresh way. Try writing a closing sentence that might make your reader want to read the work you have written about and recommended.

Universal Access

Struggling Writers

Have students exchange drafts with a partner. Partners should read the draft and summarize in a few sentences what the writer's interpretation of the text and belief about his or her chosen topic. Have each partner share their summaries, then ask the writers share their own beliefs about the text and topic. Explain that if there are any discrepancies between what the writer intended and what the reader understood, they should be addressed in the final revision of the essay.

Advanced Learners

Acceleration Explain to students that writers may choose to strengthen and clarify their own arguments by addressing and disputing an opposing position. Have students review their essays independently and try to identify different positions writers might take on their topic. Then, have students discuss in groups of three how to differentiate and clarify students' own arguments by addressing the opposing positions.

Proofreading and Publishing

Proofreading

Re-read your essay for errors in usage, spelling, punctuation, and grammar. This is also the time to examine the vocabulary you used. Could you improve your essay with more precise vocabulary, more powerful verbs, and more colorful modifiers? Be sure to check the logic of your essay, as well. Do your main points and the evidence lead to the conclusion you drew? If so, then trade papers with a partner to proofread each other's work. Then, prepare your final copy to share with your audience.

Grammar Link Capitalizing Authors' Names and Titles

The author's first name, last name, and any initials must be capitalized. In the title of a work, always capitalize the first and last word and all of the important words in between.

> Incorrect: Sophia wrote the essay "*A girl's adventure.*"
> Correct: Sophia Eckerle wrote the essay "*A Girl's Adventure.*"

Publishing

Here are some ways to share your response to a literary work with your audience, using a variety of formats.

- Submit your composition to the school newspaper.
- If your class has a Web page, find out if you can post it there.
- Ask the school librarian if you may post a copy of your essay on a bulletin board in the library.

Reflect on the Process Respond to the following in your *Reader/Writer Notebook*.

1. Did the process of writing about the literary work affect your interpretation? If so, how?
2. What did you find to be most challenging about writing your essay? How might you work differently the next time?
3. Which piece of your evidence do you think is the strongest? Why?
4. What was the most important revision you made to your draft? How did it strengthen your essay?

● Proofreading Tip

Exchange papers with a partner, and ask that partner to highlight any quotes you have used in your paper. Give your partner a copy of the work you wrote about and a list of the pages from which you quoted. Ask your partner to carefully read the original and your paper to make sure that you have quoted the work exactly. Ask your partner to circle any errors in your quotations. Correct those errors carefully, checking the original again yourself.

Your Turn _____

Proofread and Publish

Proofread your composition. Be sure that you have followed the rules for capitalization when you mention the author's name and the title of the work. In addition, proofread your essay for any errors in punctuation, spelling, and sentence structure, particularly run-on sentences. Make the corrections on your final draft.

Guided Practice: Apply

Proofreading

Integrating with Grammar, Usage, and Mechanics If students make errors in capitalization, as they are proofreading, send them to the Capital Letters chapter in **Warriner's Handbook.**

Grammar Link

- Tell students to read their final draft for instances of an author's name or title. Have students underline each instance of an author's name or title.
- Instruct students to make sure they have correctly capitalized each name and title in their response to literature.

Publishing

Brainstorm with students additional ways to publish their responses to literature.

Reflect on the Process

Have students reflect on the entire writing process as well as their final product. Challenge them to reflect metacognitively about how they can improve and apply what they have learned.

Your Turn _____

Proofread and Publish Provide students with red pens to edit the essays. Have students underline letters that violate the rules of capitalization and write the correct spelling of misspelled words in the margin.

Guided Practice

Scoring Rubric

- Tell students that the best way to understand rubrics is to use them to score actual writing.

- Have students use the rubric to evaluate their final drafts of the response to literature they wrote in the Writing Workshop. Have students write a paragraph explaining what they did well and what they need to improve using the language of the rubric.

✍ **Holt Six Traits for Writing,** rubrics, prompts, and sample papers

Assess

✍ **UA: Interactive Speaker and Writer,** Response to Literature analytical scales and rubric, p. 70

ThinkCentral Online Assessment, Writing Workshop Test

💿 **Teacher One Stop™,** editable Writing Workshop Test

Reteach

ThinkCentral Online Remediation

🐻 **California Standards, pp. 356–357**

- **Writing Standard 2.2** Write responses to literature. **2.2a** Develop interpretations exhibiting careful reading, understanding, and insight. **2.2b** Organize interpretations around several clear ideas, premises, or images from the literary work. **2.2c** Justify interpretations through sustained use of examples and textual evidence.

Scoring Rubric

You can use the rubric below to evaluate your response to literature.

	Response to Literature	Organization and Focus	Sentence Structure	Conventions
4	• Is characterized by paraphrasing of the main idea(s) and significant details. • Develops interpretations that demonstrate a thoughtful, comprehensive grasp of the text. • Organizes accurate and coherent interpretations around clear ideas, premises, or images from the literary work. • Provides specific textual examples and details to support the interpretations.	• Clearly addresses all parts of the writing task. • Demonstrates a clear understanding of purpose and audience. • Maintains a consistent point of view, focus, and organizational structure, including the effective use of transitions. • Includes a clearly presented central idea with relevant facts, details, and/or explanations.	• Includes a variety of sentence types.	• Contains few, if any, errors in the conventions of the English language (grammar, punctuation, capitalization, spelling). These errors do not interfere with the reader's understanding of the writing.
3	• Is characterized by paraphrasing of the main idea(s) and significant details. • Develops interpretations that demonstrate a comprehensive grasp of the text. • Organizes accurate and reasonably coherent interpretations around clear ideas, premises, or images from the literary work. • Provides textual examples and details to support the interpretations.	• Addresses all parts of the writing task. • Demonstrates a general understanding of purpose and audience. • Maintains a mostly consistent point of view, focus, and organizational structure, including the effective use of some transitions. • Presents a central idea with mostly relevant facts, details, and/or explanations.	• Includes a variety of sentence types.	• Contains some errors in the conventions of the English language (grammar, punctuation, capitalization, spelling). These errors do not interfere with the reader's understanding of the writing.
2	• Is characterized by substantial copying of key phrases and minimal paraphrasing. • Develops interpretations that demonstrate a limited grasp of the text. • Includes interpretations that lack accuracy or coherence as related to ideas, premises, or images from the literary work. • Provides few, if any, textual examples and details to support the interpretations.	• Addresses only parts of the writing task. • Demonstrates little understanding of purpose and audience. • Maintains an inconsistent point of view, focus, and/or organizational structure, which may include ineffective or awkward transitions that do not unify important ideas. • Suggests a central idea with limited facts, details, and/or explanations.	• Includes little variety in sentence types.	• Contains several errors in the conventions of the English language (grammar, punctuation, capitalization, spelling). These errors may interfere with the reader's understanding of the writing.
1	• Is characterized by substantial copying of indiscriminately selected phrases or sentences. • Demonstrates little grasp of the text. • Lacks an interpretation or may be a simple retelling of the passage. • Lacks textual examples and details.	• Addresses only one part of the writing task. • Demonstrates no understanding of purpose and audience. • Lacks a point of view, focus, organizational structure, and transitions that unify important ideas. • Lacks a central idea but may contain marginally related facts, details, and/or explanations.	• Includes no sentence variety.	• Contains serious errors in the conventions of the English language (grammar, punctuation, capitalization, spelling). These errors interfere with the reader's understanding of the writing.

Response to Literature Writing Prompts

Students can use the writing prompt on p. 357 in the Student Edition or one of the following prompts.

- Think about a famous literary character who undergoes a dramatic change over the course of the story. Write an essay describing this character and what brings about his or her change.

- You have become the literary critic for the school newspaper. Your first assignment is to describe a literary work in which an author uses a distinct tone or atmosphere. Think of a work that uses tone or atmosphere effectively and explain how it contributes to the text.

- A friend in another state has asked you to recommend a book you think she should read. Write a letter to your friend describing your favorite work of literature, using evidence to explain what makes it unique or interesting.

Preparing for Timed Writing

Response to Literature

When responding to an on-demand prompt requiring a response to literature, use the models you have read, what you've learned from writing your own persuasive essay, the rubric on page 356, and the steps below.

Writing Standard 2.2 Write responses to literature: a. Develop interpretations exhibiting careful reading, understanding, and insight. b. Organize interpretations around several clear ideas, premises, or images from the literary work. c. Justify interpretations through sustained use of examples and textual evidence.

Writing Prompt
Recall a story that has a character that you admired or liked. What personality traits appealed to you? Write a literary interpretation, presenting a clear thesis summing up the character's admirable qualities. Include descriptions of the character's actions and words to provide <u>relevant</u> details that justify your response.

Study the Prompt
Begin by reading the prompt carefully. Note what is required in your essay: an interpretation of a literary character that is supported with <u>relevant</u> details.
Tip: Spend about five minutes studying the prompt.

Plan Your Response
Think of a literary work that you know well enough to write about with authority. Once you understand your task and have settled on your subject,
- write down the author and title of the literary work
- write a one-sentence thesis statement
- list several points that you will use to support your thesis
- consider the kinds of evidence you will use to support your main ideas
Tip: Spend about fifteen minutes planning your response.

Respond to the Prompt
Using the notes you have just made, draft your essay. Follow these guidelines:
- In the introduction, present the author's name and the title of the work, and provide a clear thesis statement.
- Present each supporting main point in a separate paragraph, and provide evidence for each main point in the form of details and quotations.
- In the conclusion, restate the thesis and summarize the main points.

As you are writing, remember to use words that are best for your audience—not too informal. Write as neatly as you can. If your essay can't be read easily, it may not be scored.
Tip: Spend about twenty minutes writing your draft.

Improve Your Response
Revising Go back over the key aspects of the essay. Did you state your interpretation clearly? Did you provide supporting details for all of your points, consistently using valid images and examples as support?

Proofreading Take a few minutes to proofread your essay to correct errors in grammar, spelling, punctuation, and capitalization. Make sure all of your edits are neat, and erase any stray marks.

Checking Your Final Copy Before you turn in your essay, read it one more time to catch any errors you may have missed. You will be glad that you took the extra time for one final review.
Tip: Save five to ten minutes to improve your paper.

Objectives

Students will

• deliver a persuasive speech that includes a clear thesis, background, and supporting evidence

• use effective verbal and nonverbal techniques for an effective presentation

Preteach

Speak with a Purpose Ask students if they have ever felt overwhelmed with information when listening to someone speak. Ask students to discuss ways they can avoid making this mistake when delivering their literary response essay as a persuasive speech.

Direct Teach

Model the Skill

Adapt Your Essay

Model for students how to ensure their points are persuasive and to the point. Suggest that students write down the thesis at the top of each note card that contains a main point. Remind to connect the main point to the thesis.

Guided Practice: Apply

Have students use their note cards and practice presenting their main points to a partner. Have them give feedback on how they can add clarity in presenting their main points.

Presenting a Response to Literature

Speak with a Purpose

You may not have time to cite every supporting detail, description, reason, or example you used in your literary response essay, and too much information can overwhelm an audience. Be selective as you prepare your speech, and choose only the strongest, most persuasive textual evidence—well-articulated evidence that makes the most impact on your audience.

Think as a Reader/Writer Presenting a speech that describes your interpretation of a literary work and persuades your audience that your interpretation is valid is much like writing a response to literature. You use many of the same techniques writers use, but you also need to learn how to *deliver* the speech persuasively. If you merely read your literary interpretation in a dull, lifeless voice, your listeners may not be persuaded by even the strongest arguments.

Adapt Your Essay

Consider Your Purpose and Audience

In order to adapt your literary interpretation into a speech that is persuasive, you must first consider your **purpose** and **audience.** Your purpose is to persuade listeners to agree with your interpretation. Since this is a class assignment, you know that your audience will be your classmates and that they have probably read the literary work. Consider whether your classmates are likely to agree or disagree with your interpretation. This will help you organize and deliver your speech.

Plan Ahead

Begin with a copy of your written essay. Identify your **topic,** or the aspect of the work that you plan to explore; your **thesis,** or main idea about your topic; and the **evidence** that supports your thesis. Next, make notes on the written copy, highlighting points you want to emphasize. Remember to consider your audience as well as the time allowed for your speech. Then, create note cards to remind you of the main points you want to present. Refer to the note cards as you practice and, if allowed, as you give your speech.

Stick to the Point

Readers can always re-read a passage they don't understand. Listeners don't have that luxury. Therefore, you must ensure that your points are clear and persuasive. Remember to state your thesis clearly at the beginning of your speech, to support it with solid evidence, and to restate it at the end. If your main ideas don't sound very persuasive when read aloud, try rephrasing them. For example, you may find that shorter sentences have more snap.

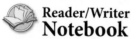 **Reader/Writer Notebook**

Use your **RWN** to complete the activities for this workshop.

California Standards, pp. 358–359

■ **Speaking Standard 1.4** Organize information to achieve particular purposes and to appeal to the background and interests of the audience.

■ **Speaking Standard 1.5** Arrange supporting details, reasons, descriptions, and examples effectively and persuasively in relation to the audience.

■ **Speaking Standard 1.6** Use speaking techniques, including voice modulation, inflection, tempo, enunciation, and eye contact, for effective presentations.

■ **Speaking Standard 2.4** Deliver persuasive presentations: **a.** State a clear position or perspective in support of an argument or proposal. **b.** Describe the points in support of the argument and employ well-articulated evidence.

Resources

UA: Holt Interactive Writer and Speaker, practice and assessment, p. 165

UA: Differentiating Instruction, modified lesson plans, p. 74

Teacher One Stop™, on-level lesson plans and all print resources

Listening and Speaking Standards
1.4 Organize information to achieve particular purposes and to appeal to the background and interests of the audience. **1.5** Arrange supporting details, reasons, descriptions, and examples effectively and persuasively in relation to the audience. **1.6** Use speaking techniques, including voice modulation, inflection, tempo, enunciation, and eye contact, for effective presentations.

Deliver Your Speech

All good politicians know that the success of their speeches depends largely on delivery. A position supported by the best evidence may not win votes if the politician has a dull, lifeless delivery. Similarly, the success of your response to literature depends on your ability to grab your listeners' attention, build their interest, and persuade them to agree with your interpretation. Using effective verbal and nonverbal speaking techniques can help ensure that your speech is a success.

Verbal Techniques

- **Enunciation** Practice your speech with a partner, and note any words that he or she does not understand. Look up words that you might replace in a thesaurus, and be sure you know how to pronounce them.
- **Vocal Modulation** To stress certain points, speak more loudly or softly. Ask a partner whether your volume is varied enough and whether you can be heard clearly, no matter what your volume.
- **Inflection** Avoid speaking in a monotone. Emphasize important ideas by raising or lowering the pitch of your voice. Ask a partner whether you sound convincing and reasonable. The sound of your voice should fit your audience and suit your purpose.
- **Tempo** Speak slowly enough for your audience to keep up, but don't fall into a pattern that sounds unnatural. Use pauses to emphasize major points: A pause shows your audience that the idea is important, and it gives people time to think about your point. Remember to stop and take a breath when necessary.

Nonverbal Techniques

If you use note cards to help you remember your main points, include cues for nonverbal actions, such as pausing for effect or making a supportive gesture. Making **eye contact** is one way of keeping the audience involved. Practice glancing at your note cards and then regaining eye contact with your audience members. Look at different places in the room, so you can practice engaging as many of the listeners as possible. A self-assured speaker can look anyone in the eye.

Keep in mind that your **posture** and **facial expressions** are also reflections of your confidence. Stand tall, and remember that your interpretation represents your best thinking about a literary work. Believe in yourself, and others will believe in you, too.

> **A Good Response to Literature**
>
> - includes a clear thesis statement
> - supports the thesis with main points
> - includes a variety of supporting evidence for the main points
> - provides enough background for listeners to understand the supporting evidence
> - uses verbal and nonverbal techniques convincingly
> - clearly and persuasively restates the thesis

Listening Tip

Listen for evidence of the speaker's attitude toward the literary work. Pay attention to the logic and coherence of the speech and note the speech's overall impact on you. Listen critically for evidence that supports the speaker's interpretation of the work and the conclusions he or she draws.

Learn It Online
Learn more about persuasive techniques online at MediaScope:

| go.hrw.com | H7-359 | Go |

Universal Access

 English Learners

English for Academic Success Provide students with extra practice delivering a literary response speech.

- Pair students with another non-native English speaker. Ask pairs to practice each verbal technique using their thesis statements. Have them comment on each other's enunciation, vocal modulation, inflection, and tempo.

- Next have students pair up with proficient English speakers, practicing the same techniques and giving each other feedback.

- After students have gained familiarity with the verbal techniques, have them practice eye contact, appropriate posture, and facial expression in groups of three.

Standards Focus

Objectives

Students will

• analyze, compare, and contrast themes
• evaluate an argument
• analyze figurative language
• analyze a personal narrative

Literary Skills Review

Review

If necessary, use the following questions to guide students in their reading before they answer the questions at the end of the review.

▶ **Theme**

Helen complains that she is embarrassed to invite friends home, but when she learns that the family will not have to move, she decides to give a party. What does her behavior suggest about her true feelings?
Possible response: It is not how a house looks but the memories it contains that make it a home.

Test-Taking Tip

Tell students to avoid distractors, choices that may be true but are too broad, too narrow, or otherwise not the best answer.

California Standards, pp. 360–363

■ **Reading Standard 3.4** Identify and analyze recurring themes across works (e.g., the value of bravery, loyalty, and friendship; the effects of loneliness).

Literary Skills Review

Theme **Directions: Read the following story and poem.** Then, answer each question that follows.

Home *from* Maud Martha
by **Gwendolyn Brooks**

What had been wanted was this always, this always to last, the talking softly on this porch, with the snake plant in the jardiniere in the southwest corner, and the obstinate slip from Aunt Eppie's magnificent Michigan fern at the left side of the friendly door. Mama, Maud Martha, and Helen rocked slowly in their rocking chairs, and looked at the late afternoon light on the lawn and at the emphatic iron of the fence and at the poplar tree. These things might soon be theirs no longer. Those shafts and pools of light, the tree, the graceful iron, might soon be viewed possessively by different eyes.

Papa was to have gone that noon, during his lunch hour, to the office of the Home Owners' Loan. If he had not succeeded in getting another extension, they would be leaving this house in which they had lived for more than fourteen years. There was little hope. The Home Owners' Loan was hard. They sat, making their plans.

"We'll be moving into a nice flat somewhere," said Mama. "Somewhere on South Park, or Michigan, or in Washington Park Court." Those flats, as the girls and Mama knew well, were burdens on wages twice the size of Papa's. This was not mentioned now.

"They're much prettier than this old house," said Helen. "I have friends I'd just as soon not bring here. And I have other friends that wouldn't come down this far for anything, unless they were in a taxi."

Yesterday, Maud Martha would have attacked her. Tomorrow she might. Today she said nothing. She merely gazed at a little hopping robin in the tree, her tree, and tried to keep the fronts of her eyes dry.

"Well, I do know," said Mama, turning her hands over and over, "that I've been getting tireder and tireder of doing that firing. From October to April, there's firing to be done."

"But lately we've been helping, Harry and I," said Maud Martha. "And sometimes in March and April and in October, and even in November, we could build a little fire in the fireplace. Sometimes the weather was just right for that."

She knew, from the way they looked at her, that this had been a mistake. They did not want to cry.

But she felt that the little line of white, sometimes ridged with smoked purple,

---

Resources for Skills and Standards Review

Chapter 3 Resources, Chapter Standards Mastery, Chapter Vocabulary Review, p. 42

UA: Differentiating Instruction, below-level Chapter Standards Mastery

Teacher One Stop™, editable Chapter Standards Mastery

Focus on Standards

ThinkCentral Online Assessment, Chapter Standards Mastery

ThinkCentral Online Remediation

Holt Online Essay Scoring

and all that cream-shot saffron would never drift across any western sky except that in back of this house. The rain would drum with as sweet a dullness nowhere but here. The birds on South Park were mechanical birds, no better than the poor caught canaries in those "rich" women's sun parlors.

"It's just going to kill Papa!" burst out Maud Martha. "He loves this house! He *lives* for this house!"

"He lives for us," said Helen. "It's us he loves. He wouldn't want the house, except for us."

"And he'll have us," added Mama, "wherever."

"You know," Helen said, "if you want to know the truth, this is a relief. If this hadn't come up, we would have gone on, just dragged on, hanging out here forever."

"It might," allowed Mama, "be an act of God. God may just have reached down and picked up the reins."

"Yes," Maud Martha cracked in, "that's what you always say—that God knows best."

Her mother looked at her quickly, decided the statement was not suspect, looked away.

Helen saw Papa's coming. "There's Papa," said Helen.

They could not tell a thing from the way Papa was walking. It was that same dear little staccato walk, one shoulder down, then the other, then repeat, and repeat. They watched his progress. He passed the Kennedys', he passed the vacant lot, he passed Mrs. Blakemore's. They wanted to hurl themselves over the fence, into the street, and shake the truth out of his collar. He opened his gate—the gate—and still his stride and face told them nothing.

"Hello," he said.

Mama got up and followed him through the front door. The girls knew better than to go in too.

Presently Mama's head emerged. Her eyes were lamps turned on.

"It's all right," she exclaimed. "He got it. It's all over. Everything is all right."

The door slammed shut. Mama's footsteps hurried away.

"I think," said Helen, rocking rapidly, "I think I'll give a party. I haven't given a party since I was eleven. I'd like some of my friends to just casually see that we're homeowners."

> **Theme**

In the second full paragraph of the first column, Helen says of Papa, "It's us he loves. He wouldn't want the house, except for us." What does this statement suggest about the attachment to a "home"? **Possible response:** *Homes are made up of loved ones, not bricks and lumber. Houses are physical entities, while homes are a state of mind.*

In your own words, state the big idea, or the theme, of this selection. **Possible response:** *People feel very strongly about the places in which they live; they love their homes.*

Name a detail from the story that conveys Maud Martha's feelings that her home is unique. **Possible response:** *The author writes, "The rain would drum with as sweet a dullness nowhere but here."*

Chapter Review

Review Literary Skills Focus
1. Have students look back through the chapter to find the meanings of the terms listed below.
2. Have them cite passages from the chapter that illustrate the meanings of those terms.

Nonfiction; Theme; Subject; Narrative Poem; Title; Recurring Theme.

Review Reading Skills Focus
1. Have students review the chapter to find the meanings of the terms listed below.
2. Have them cite passages from the chapter that illustrate the meanings of those terms.

Author's Purpose; Author's Perspective; Cause and Effect; Comparing and Contrasting; Generalizations.

Literary Skills Review CONTINUED

Review

If necessary, use the following questions to guide students in their reading before they answer the questions at the end of the review.

▶ **Theme**

Read the second stanza of the poem, in which the speaker describes the animals watching one another. What do you think this description conveys, and how does it relate to the overall message of the poem?

Possible response: *This description, like the poem as a whole, suggests the interconnectedness of all forms of life. All of these animals have a home in the desert.*

Test-Taking Tip

Tell students to watch carefully for words like *not* or *except* in multiple-choice questions. If they encounter these words, they should look for the choice that is false, opposite, or different from the others.

Gold by Pat Mora

When Sun paints the desert
with its gold,
I climb the hills.
Wind runs round boulders, ruffles
5 my hair. I sit on my favorite rock,
lizards for company, a rabbit,
ears stiff in the shade
of a saguaro.°
In the wind, we're all
10 eye to eye.

Sparrow on saguaro watches
rabbit watch us in the gold
of sun setting.
Hawk sails on waves of light, sees
15 sparrow, rabbit, lizards, me,
our eyes shining,
watching red and purple sand rivers
    stream down the hill.

I stretch my arms wide as the sky
like hawk extends her wings
20 in all the gold light of this, home.

8. **saguaro** (suh GWAH roh): huge cactus found in the southwestern United States and northern Mexico.

---

1. Maud Martha in "Home" and the speaker in "Gold" share a
   A love of a place.
   B sadness about the sky.
   C dislike of cities.
   D need of nature.

2. The following words are in both selections. Which are key words in both selections?
   A light; eyes
   B purple; like
   C home; I
   D home; we're

California Standards,
pp. 362–363

- **Reading Standard 3.4** Identify and analyze recurring themes across works (e.g., the value of bravery, loyalty, and friendship; the effects of loneliness).

3. A thematic topic of both passages is

  A longing for home.

  B a need for shelter.

  C housing for survival.

  D a desire for peace.

4. Read this sentence from the excerpt:

> Her eyes were lamps turned on.

Which phrase from "Gold" means almost the same thing?

  A "the gold light of this, home"

  B "we're all / eye to eye"

  C "sails on waves of light"

  D "our eyes shining"

5. A recurring theme of the excerpt and the poem deals with

  A shortness of life.

  B importance of nature.

  C love of home.

  D need for peace.

6. A recurring theme in "Gold" is the comparison of

  A the speaker and the animals.

  B the light and the sun.

  C the boulders and the cactus.

  D flying and sitting.

7. A theme of both passages deals with

  A cities and happiness.

  B place and identity.

  C nature and loneliness.

  D home and money.

Timed Writing

8. Which statement *best* expresses a theme of both the story and the poem to you?

- Home is a place associated with deep feelings.
- Homelessness is a problem that must be fixed.
- Living in a house is a basic need of all people.
- Everyone should live as one with nature.
- Home is a source of identity.

Use examples from each selection to explain why you chose that statement.

Assess

Answers and Explanations

1. A *There is no specific reference to B or C. They may both enjoy nature but it is not the main point (D).*

2. D *The respective "homes" belong to both human and animal. A and B are not key, while "I" is not important in "Home" (C).*

3. A *Both selections describe the longing for a home. Though housing is a need, and required for survival, the selections deal specifically with an emotional connection to home. D is not relevant.*

4. D *In both selections eyes were shining from excitement. A, B, and C are not relevant.*

5. C *Love of home is the central idea. A and D are not mentioned, while B is indirectly referenced.*

6. A *The speaker and animals both regard the desert as home. The other choices are incidental details.*

7. B *Though happiness (A), nature (C), home, and money (D) are topics of the stories, the theme focuses on place and identity (B).*

Timed Writing

8. *"Home is a place associated with deep feelings" best expresses the theme of both the selections. In the story, Maud Martha is worried and sad that her family might lose their house. In the poem, the speaker expresses her love for her desert home.*

Reteach

 ThinkCentral Online Remediation

If necessary, use the following questions to guide students in their reading before they answer the questions at the end of the review.

▶ **Author's Purpose**

What is the author's purpose for writing this selection? In which paragraph does the author's purpose become clear? ***Possible response:*** *The author's purpose is to inform the reader about a man who jumped in front of a train to save a stranger. This becomes clear in the selection's fourth paragraph, which introduces Wesley Autrey.*

Which details from the paragraph on page 364 that begins "Five cars rolled overhead" indicate that the author believes Mr. Autrey's actions were courageous? ***Possible response:*** *She includes the fact that people on the platform were applauding.*

Test-Taking Tip

Tell students to take time to read the directions at the beginning of a test. Explain that students should make sure they understand the directions (and ask any questions about directions they do not understand) before they begin to work.

**California Standards,
pp. 364–365**

- **Reading Standard 2.4** Identify and trace the development of an author's argument, point of view, or perspective in text.

STANDARDS REVIEW

Informational Skills Review

Tracing an Author's Argument or Perspective   **Directions:**
Read the following selection. Then, respond to the questions that follow.

A Man Down, a Train Arriving, and a Stranger Makes a Choice
by **Cara Buckley**

It was every subway rider's nightmare, times two.

Who has ridden along New York's 656 miles of subway lines and not wondered: "What if I fell to the tracks as a train came in? What would I do?"

And who has not thought: "What if someone else fell? Would I jump to the rescue?"

Wesley Autrey, a 50-year-old construction worker and Navy veteran, faced both those questions in a flashing instant yesterday, and got his answers almost as quickly.

Mr. Autrey was waiting for the downtown local at 137th Street and Broadway in Manhattan around 12:45 P.M. He was taking his two daughters, Syshe, 4, and Shuqui, 6, home before work.

Nearby, a man collapsed, his body convulsing. Mr. Autrey and two women rushed to help, he said. The man, Cameron Hollopeter, 20, managed to get up, but then stumbled to the platform edge and fell to the tracks, between the two rails.

The headlights of the No. 1 train appeared. "I had to make a split decision," Mr. Autrey said.

So he made one, and leapt.

Mr. Autrey lay on Mr. Hollopeter, his heart pounding, pressing him down in a space roughly a foot deep. The train's brakes screeched, but it could not stop in time.

Five cars rolled overhead before the train stopped, the cars passing inches from his head, smudging his blue knit cap with grease. Mr. Autrey heard onlookers' screams. "We're O.K. down here," he yelled, "but I've got two daughters up there. Let them know their father's O.K." He heard cries of wonder, and applause.

Power was cut, and workers got them out. Mr. Hollopeter, a student at the New York Film Academy, was taken to St. Luke's-Roosevelt Hospital Center. He had only bumps and bruises, said his grandfather, Jeff Friedman. The police said it appeared that Mr. Hollopeter had suffered a seizure.

Word-Attack Skills Mini-Lesson

Review   Use the activity below to check students' grasp of the word-attack skills taught in this collection.

Activity   Ask students to identify whether the underlined letters in each word have a hard sound or a soft sound.

1. gallon   [*hard g*]
2. encourage   [*hard c, soft g*]
3. dancing   [*soft c, hard g*]
4. circle   [*soft c, hard c*]
5. forgery   [*soft g*]

Mr. Autrey refused medical help, because, he said, nothing was wrong. He did visit Mr. Hollopeter in the hospital before heading to his night shift. "I don't feel like I did something spectacular; I just saw someone who needed help," Mr. Autrey said. "I did what I felt was right."

1. What might be the author's *best* reason for asking the four questions at the beginning of the article?

   A to make readers imagine what Autrey had been thinking

   B to inspire readers to react with courage like Autrey's

   C to remind readers to be aware when in dangerous situations

   D to advise readers not to use public transportation when ill

2. The author uses the direct quotations in the article to make its effect

   A strictly factual.

   B highly dramatic.

   C personally appealing.

   D very frightening.

3. The author uses the example of Autrey's going to his night job after the accident to express her point of view that he

   A unfortunately needed to work for a living.

   B was disappointed with Hollopeter.

   C believed he did nothing special.

   D wanted to brag to his co-workers.

4. The direct quotations used by the author reflect her perspective that

   A no one deserved praise for any help except Autrey.

   B Autrey was concerned about others more than himself.

   C the subway workers helped as much as they possibly could.

   D despite being terrified, Autrey was brave.

Timed Writing

5. State the author's perspective about Wesley Autrey and his courageous act. Describe how she supports her opinion, citing three examples from the article.

Vocabulary Skills Review

Vocabulary Skills Review

Assess

Answers and Explanations

1. **B** *Items A, C, and D do not reflect the content of the story.*

2. **A** *The family are unable to come to a decision on their own, so Mama belives God took over like a rider takes the reins of a horse to control its movements.*

3. **A** *Item A compares sand to rivers without using "like" or "as."*

4. **A** *The speaker uses the word "as" to compare her arms to the sky.*

5. **B** *When the speaker says that she and the animals are eye to eye, she does not mean it literally (A), and items C and D do not relate to the subject of the idiom. The speaker means that she and the animals are similar.*

Academic Vocabulary

6. **D** *In this context,* important *is a synonym for* relevant.

 WordSharp: An Interactive Vocabulary Tutor

Reteach

ThinkCentral Online Remediation

California Standards, p. 366

■ **Reading Standard 1.1** Identify idioms, analogies, metaphors, and similes in prose and poetry.

Figurative Language

Directions: Identify and analyze metaphors, similes, and idioms from "Home" (page 360) and the poem "Gold" (page 362).

1. In "Home" the narrator says Mama's "eyes were lamps turned on." This metaphor means that Mama was
   A almost in tears.
   B happy and excited.
   C very angry.
   D turning on the porch light.

2. Read this sentence from "Home":

   > God may just have reached down and picked up the reins.

   The underlined idiom in the sentence reveals that Mama believes God
   A may have taken charge of the family's decision.
   B will take care of the wagon to move the family's belongings.
   C caused the rain to fall as the family sat on the porch.
   D will watch over the family in their new home.

3. Which lines from the poem contain an example of a metaphor?
   A "watching red and purple sand rivers stream down the hill"
   B "Sparrow on saguaro watches / rabbit watch us . . ."
   C ". . . wide as the sky / like hawk extends her wings"
   D "I sit on my favorite rock, / lizards for company . . ."

4. Which line from the poem contains an example of a simile?
   A "I stretch my arms wide as the sky"
   B "I climb the hills"
   C "Hawk sails on waves of light, sees"
   D "in all the gold light of this, home"

5. Read this sentence from "Gold":

   > In the wind, we're all / eye to eye."

   The idiom "eye to eye" means that
   A the speaker, the lizards, and the rabbit are the same height.
   B the speaker and the animals are considered alike by nature.
   C the wind is attacking the speaker for being in the desert.
   D the speaker and the animals watch the sunset together.

Academic Vocabulary

Directions: Read the following passage, and identify the meaning of the Academic Vocabulary word below.

6. The title of a story and the discoveries characters make are *relevant* when trying to discover the story's theme.

   In this sentence, *relevant* means
   A important.
   B appealing.
   C unclear.
   D similar.

Vocabulary Review

Use this activity to assess whether students have retained the collection Vocabulary. Ask students to fill in the underlined word in each sentence using one of the words in the box, based on the context clues provided.

> flourishing   detain   intently
> recourse   furiously

1. Crocuses, lilacs, and tulips had begun to bloom, and the garden seemed to be _____. [*flourishing*]

2. The student wrote _____ in her exam booklet. [*furiously*]

3. The train accident would _____ the businessmen for another four hours. [*detain*]

4. Crystal stared _____ at the parrot, hoping it would talk. [*intently*]

5. The family's guard dog provided _____ against intruders. [*recourse*]

Writing Skills Review

Response to Literature   **Directions:** Read the following paragraph from an essay discussing *Song of the Trees*, a selection in Chapter 5. Then, answer each question that follows.

Writing Standard 2.2 Write responses to literature: a. Develop interpretations exhibiting careful reading, understanding, and insight. b. Organize interpretations around several clear ideas, premises, or images from the literary work. c. Justify interpretations through sustained use of examples and textual evidence.

(1) Readers don't actually meet the character David Logan until fairly late in Mildred D. Taylor's novella *Song of the Trees*. (2) The incredible strength of this character places him at the heart of the story and of his family. (3) Readers learn near the beginning of the story that David Logan is absent from his family, working hard to earn money in difficult times. (4) His absence leaves a big hole in the family, and the hole gets bigger as trouble comes to the Logans in the form of Mr. Andersen. (5) The children and Mr. Andersen's workers all know that Mr. Andersen would not be able to chop down the trees if David Logan were around. (6) In fact, Mrs. Logan decides to send her son Stacey to get David because they need his strength in order to stop Mr. Andersen. (7) Once he arrives, readers find powerful evidence of his strength. (8) He immediately takes control of what is going on. (9) His quiet, firm voice echoes through the woods. (10) He is very sure about his plan of action and never backs down. (11) As he says, "I always mean what I say." (12) Once David Logan solves the situation, readers also see his heart. (13) Like his daughter Cassie, David mourns the loss of the singing trees. (14) It's easy to see how his influence has affected the family in many ways.

1. Which sentence contains the thesis, or main idea, of the essay?
   A sentence 1
   B sentence 2
   C sentence 3
   D sentence 6

2. Which transitional word would work best to link sentences 1 and 2?
   A moreover
   B nevertheless
   C so
   D and

3. Sentence 13, as well as the title of the story, uses which literary device?
   A allusion
   B irony
   C dialect
   D personification

4. Sentence 6 talks about three male characters. In sentence 7, the pronoun *he* may confuse readers. How could sentence 7 be changed to be more clear?
   A Substitute "David" for "he."
   B Delete the transitional expression "Once he arrives."
   C Combine the ideas in sentences 6 and 7 into one sentence.
   D none of the above

5. Why is the final sentence weak?
   A It does not clearly restate the thesis.
   B It presents too much evidence.
   C It mentions an obvious idea.
   D It uses a formal tone.

Writing Skills Review

Assess

Answers and Explanations

1. **B** The second sentence of the passage states that David Logan is the strength and center of the family. The other sentences are important points, but they are not the main idea.

2. **B** Sentences 1 and 2 explain that David Logan only appears at the end of the story, *nevertheless*, he is still an important character.

3. **D** Sentence 13 mentions the trees that David and Cassie Logan cherish; they both describe the trees as singing, which is a human characteristic.

4. **A** Replacing the general pronoun *he* with the more specific "David" makes it clear to the reader whom the author is discussing.

5. **A** The last sentence includes an overly simplified and general mention of the theme; it does not present too much evidence (B), state an obvious idea (C), or use a formal tone (D).

Reteach

ThinkCentral Online Remdiation

California Standards, p. 367
■ **Writing Standard 2.2** Write responses to literature.

Application

Challenge students to identify the opposing perspective to the one they supported in the response to literature they wrote in the Writing Workshop. Have them identify details that support the opposing perspective and organize them into an outline. Then, have them evaluate which is the stronger response to literature.

Extension [Homework]

Have students read a book or portions of a book of their choosing and prepare an oral presentation of a response to literature. Tell students to include a summary of the book, as their classmates may or may not be familiar with it. Remind students to focus on a main idea, such as a theme they identified in the text, and support it with details.

If students enjoyed the themes and topics explored in this chapter, you might recommend these titles for independent reading.

Assessment Options

The following projects can help you evaluate and assess your students' outside work. Videotapes or audio-tapes of completed projects may be included in students' portfolios.

Write a Short Story

■ If students relate to Jean Ferris's novel *Across the Grain*, have them reflect on its themes of friendship and being an outsider.

■ Have students choose one of the story's themes and write a short story of their own that is based on that theme. Explain that while students may want to give the theme a personal twist in their story, they can also take advantage of the theme's universal characteristics to make their story relevant to many different kinds of people.

View a Movie Adaptation

■ If students enjoy the novel *Holes*, suggest that they watch the 2003 movie adaptation of the same name.

■ Have students form small groups and discuss similarities and differences between the movie and book. Ask students to discuss which version of the story they preferred and why.

Read On

For Independent Reading

Fiction

Across the Grain

In her novel *Across the Grain*, Jean Ferris tells the story of the orphan Will Griffin, a seventeen-year-old who is looking after his flighty older sister, Paige, despite her status as his guardian. When she decides to move from their beach house to a remote desert town, Will is lost and dismayed. Then he meets a moody girl named Mike and an elderly loner named Sam. These outsiders help one another through sorrowful times and discover the value of friendship.

The Flag of Childhood: Poems from the Middle East

In this collection of poems by writers from Egypt, Iraq, Israel, and elsewhere in the Middle East, you'll find some poems filled with ordinary events, such as getting a haircut or watching a sunrise, and others with heartbreaking scenes of war and its aftermath. In *The Flag of Childhood*, Naomi Shihab Nye opens a window so that you can see that, despite cultural and religious differences, young people are basically the same everywhere.

Holes

Teenager Stanley Yelnats, wrongly sentenced to a detention camp in the Texas desert, must struggle through another piece of bad luck caused by a curse on his family, which began more than a century ago when his great-great-grandfather broke a promise. Stanley survives the harsh treatment at the camp thanks to his courage and newfound friendships. Flashbacks throughout this novel by Louis Sachar link past and present events and lead to an exciting life-or-death ending.

User Unfriendly

It's the most advanced computer game ever. It plugs directly into your brain—no hardware, no software—and you are really *there*. Arvin Rizalli and his friends pirate the game, along with its hidden program errors, and enter a dark, fantastical world of danger-filled fortresses and terrifying creatures. Vivian Vande Velde, the award-winning author of young-adult mysteries, takes you through a story of mayhem, sword fights, and an unpredictable ending.

Word Counts and Readabilities of Read On Books

Fiction	Estimated Word Counts	Readability
Across the Grain	56,000	Easily Accessible
The Flag of Childhood: Poems from the Middle East	12,079	Accessible
Holes	47,079	Accessible
User Unfriendly	66,070	Accessible

Nonfiction

Second-Hand Dog: How to Turn Yours into a First-Rate Pet

Whether you've ever adopted a shelter dog or not, *Second-Hand Dog* will help you admire the ability of formerly homeless dogs to become loving companions. Accompanied by witty cartoons, Carol Lea Benjamin's book gives step-by-step instructions on giving your dog the guidance it needs (and wants) to make both of you happy.

Knots in My Yo-yo String: Autobiography of a Kid

Have you ever thought what you would write in a book about your childhood? Jerry Spinelli, a Newbery Award–winning author, revisits events of his childhood: dreaming of a career as a major-league shortstop, reading comic books for hours, and spending his one and only time in school detention. Spinelli had no idea he would write books, but he recounts in compelling prose the incident that inspired him to become a writer.

Sylvia Stark: A Pioneer

Freed from slavery just before the American Civil War, Sylvia Stark traveled by wagon train to California in 1860, at the height of the gold rush. A group of African Americans formed a community of their own until they were threatened by a federal law that would have forced those who had escaped from slavery to return to it. Stark and more than six hundred people fled to the safety of Canada. The story of her life, as told by Victoria Scott and Ernest Jones, is one of initiative, endurance, and bravery.

Amos Fortune: Free Man

Despite the horrors of captivity, Fortune never gave up hope of securing his personal freedom. When he finally became a free man at the age of sixty, he dedicated the remainder of his life to freeing others who were enslaved as he had been. Find out more about this remarkable man in Elizabeth Yates's Newbery Medal winner, *Amos Fortune: Free Man*.

Learn It Online
Explore other novels and find tips for choosing, reading, and studying novels at:

go.hrw.com   H7-369   **Go**

Nonfiction	Estimated Word Counts	Readability
Second-Hand Dog: How to Turn Yours into a First-Rate Pet	21,528	Accessible
Sylvia Stark: A Pioneer	17, 385	Accessible
Knots in My Yo-yo String: Autobiography of a Kid	35,000	Accessible
Amos Fortune: Free Man	8,816	Challenging

Informational Text Focus: Text Structures: Cause and Effect

Features highlighted in **yellow** constitute a suggested minimum course of study.

Introducing The Skills

Selection or Feature	For Independent Reading	Grade–Level Standards
Literary Skills Focus: What Is Point of View?		**Reading Standard 3.5:** Points of view
Reading Skills Focus: How Can I Contrast Points of View to Analyze Narrative Texts?		**Reading Standard 3.5:** Points of view
Reading Model: A *Good* **Reason to Look Up** by Shaquille O'Neal (Easily Accessible, Lexile 920) **Skills in Action:** Wrap Up	• **Bad Boy: A Memoir** by Walter Dean Myers • **Promises to the Dead** by Mary Downing Hahn	**Reading Standard 3.5:** Points of view

Applying The Skills

Selection or Feature	For Independent Reading	Grade–Level Standards
After Twenty Years by O. Henry (Accessible, Lexile 850)	• **The Gift of the Magi and Other Stories** by O. Henry	**Reading Standard 3.5:** Points of view **Reading Standard 1.1:** Identify idioms, analogies, metaphors, and similes.
Bargain by A.B. Guthrie (Challenging, Lexile 950)	• **The Perilous Journey of the Donner Party** by Marian Calabro • **Prairie Songs** by Pamela Conrad	**Reading Standard 3.5:** Points of view **Reading Standard 1.1:** Identify idioms, analogies, metaphors, and similes.
Names/Nombres by Julia Alvarez (Accessible, Lexile 1060)	• **Before We Were Free** by Julia Alvarez • **Child of the Owl** by Laurence Yep	**Reading Standard 3.5:** Points of view **Reading Standard 1.3:** Word meanings
Elzabeth I by Milton Meltzer (Challenging, Lexile 1040)	• **Ten Queens: Portraits of Women of Power** by Milton Meltzer • **Lives of Extraordinary Women: Rulers, Rebels (And What the Neighbors Thought)** by Kathleen Krull	**Reading Standard 3.5:** Points of view **Reading Standard 1.3:** Word meanings
from **Barrio Boy** by Ernesto Galarza (Accessible, Lexile 1140)	• **A Long Way from Home** by Maureen Crane Wartski • **Any Small Goodness: A Novel of the Barrio** by Tony Johnston	**Reading Standard 3.5:** Points of view **Reading Standard 1.3:** Word meanings
Comparing Texts: Comparing Versions of the Cinderella Story • **Aschenputtel** retold by Jakob and Wilhelm Grimm, translated by Lucy Crane (Accessible, Lexile 1200) • **Yeh-Shen** by Ai-Ling Louie (Challenging, Lexile 1010) • **Interview** by Sara Henderson Hay (Accessible, Lexile N/A)	• **The Emperor's New Clothes: A Tale Set in China** by Demi • **Ella Enchanted** by Gail Carson Levine	**Reading Standard 3.5:** Points of view
Informational Text Focus: Text Structures: Cause and Effect • **Tilting at Windmills: The Search for Alternative Energy Sources** (Accessible, Lexile 1020) • **Saving the Earth: Teens Fish for Answers** (Accessible, Lexile 1030)		**Reading Standard 2.3:** Cause-and-effect

Point of View

4 Point of View

Mastering The Skills

Selection or Feature	Grade–Level Standards
Writing Workshop: Persuasive Essay	**Writing Standard 1.1:** Organize and use transitions. **Writing Standard 1.2:** Support statements and claims. **Writing Standard 2.4:** Write persuasive compositions.
Preparing for Timed Writing: Persuasive Essay	**Writing Standard 2.4:** Write persuasive compositions.
Listening and Speaking Workshop: Presenting a Persuasive Speech	**Listening and Speaking Standard 2.4:** Deliver persuasive presentations
Standards Practice: Literary Skills Review Informational Skills Review Vocabulary Skills Review Writing Skills Review	**Reading Standard 3.5:** Points of view **Reading Standard 2.3:** Cause-and-effect **Reading Standard 1.3:** Word meanings **Writing Standard 2.4:** Write persuasive compositions

Daily and Weekly Support

- **Reader/Writer Notebook**
- **Reading and Writing Transparencies**
- **Weekly Standards Review Transparencies**
- **Family Involvement Activities in Five Languages**
- **Language Handbook Worksheets**
- **Holt Virtual File Cabinet for Language Arts**
- **Spelling Lessons and Activities**

Assessment Resources

- **Chapter 4 Resources**, Chapter Diagnostic Test; Selection Standards Checks, Chapter Standards Mastery
- **Universal Access: Differentiating Instruction**, leveled assessment
- **Formal Assessment**, Midyear Summative Test, Progress Monitoring Test 4
- **English-Language Conventions Progress-Monitoring Test**, Chapters 1–13
- **ThinkCentral Online Assessment**

Print Resources for Universal Access

	On-Level Learners	English Learners	Struggling Readers/Writers	Students Who Use African American Vernacular English	Advanced Learners	Students with Disabilities
Chapter 4 Resources practice and assessment for all selections and features	✔				✔	
Universal Access: Holt Interactive Reader interactive readings for Minimum-Course-of-Study Selections		✔	✔	✔		✔
Holt Interactive Reader for English Language Development adaptations of Minimum-Course-of-Study Selections		✔				
Universal Access: Differentiating Instruction modified lesson plans, graphic organizers, and leveled assessment		✔	✔	✔		✔
Universal Access: Resources for Teaching Advanced Students lesson plans for Minimum-Course-of-Study Selections					✔	
Universal Access: Supporting Instruction in Five Languages translations of selection summaries and key terms		✔				
Universal Access: Holt Interactive Writer and Speaker practice and assessment	✔	✔	✔	✔	✔	✔
Language and Sentence Skills Practice for Warriner's Handbook Chapters 1–13	✔				✔	
Universal Access: Developmental Language and Sentence Skills Practice for Warriner's Handbook Chapters 1–13		✔	✔	✔		✔

Technology Resources

Assessment Resources

Teacher Management Resources

go.hrw.com

Student Edition Extension Activities

Student Edition Support

Find all of Holt's technology resources at go.hrw.com. Technology resources are also listed at point of use in the wrap; below are our featured components for Chapter 4.

Teacher Management Resources

ThinkCentral, Teacher Access
Teacher One Stop™
Holt Professional Learning for Language Arts

Spotlight on ThinkCentral, Teacher Access

All of the chapter's resources are available at ThinkCentral, Teacher Access.

- Use *PowerNotes* to introduce "Names/Nombres" and from *Barrio Boy.*
- Encourage advanced students to explore the NovelWise Mini-site for the complete work of *Barrio Boy,* along with study guides, graphic organizers, and discussion questions.

Student Edition Support

PowerNotes
ThinkCentral, Student Access
Student One Stop™
Interactive Reading Workshops
Interactive Graphic Organizers
Writers' Lives
Holt Audio Library
Holt Audio Library: Selections and Summaries in Spanish

Spotlight on Interactive Graphic Organizers

Use this site to find interactive graphic organizers, along with lesson plans for reading, writing, and differentiated instruction.

- Encourage students to take advantage of the various main ideas charts when reading "Names/Nombres," and "Elizabeth I."

Student Edition Extension Activities

Digital Storytelling Mini-Site
NovelWise Mini-Site
Holt Audio Tutor for ELD
MediaScope Mini-Site
WordSharp: An Interactive Vocabulary Tutor
GrammarNotes
WritingNotes
Writing and Research in a Digital Age
Literature Links

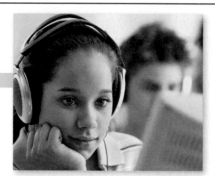

Spotlight on Holt Audio Tutor for ELD

Help struggling readers and English learners stay on track with the selections and skills in the Minimum Course of Study.

- This CD provides audio recordings of more accessible versions of "After Twenty Years" and "Names/Nombres" as they appear in Holt Interactive Reader for ELD, including instructional annotations.
- Students can read and listen to the adapted selection, listen to the annotations in English and Spanish, and pause to write their responses.

Assessment Resources

ThinkCentral Online Assessment
Holt Online Essay Scoring
ThinkCentral Online Remediation

Spotlight on ThinkCentral Online Assessment

With online essay scoring, students can practice writing responses to essay prompts—and our system automatically scores them. Students will receive immediate feedback on their essays.

The wrap for these selections includes specific ideas and strategies from *Holt Literature and Language Arts* authors.

From the Authors

For "After Twenty Years", *p. 382*

Students may have difficulty making the inferences needed to understand "After Twenty Years." Use the strategy It Says—I Say as a visual scaffold to help students organize their thoughts as they move from considering what's in the text to connecting that to their prior knowledge. Finding answers to questions will give the student insight into a writer's perspective.

Deborah Appleman

For "Elizabeth I", *p. 422*

To help readers comprehend the information in "Elizabeth I," consider dividing the reading into more manageable chunks by having students stop and think about what they have learned thus far after every four to six paragraphs. For each section, students should jot down important events and what made them important using a graphic organizer.

Kylene Beers

Teacher to Teacher

Preteach Before we read "After Twenty Years," I tell students that we are going to focus on point of view. I ask them to look for clues that help them figure out who is telling the story. After reading, I ask students to share their clues. I make sure they know that the story was written from the third-person point of view. Then, I introduce the other points of view.

Direct Teach I ask students to retell one of the episodes in the story from the point of view of either Bob or Jimmy, focusing on presenting the characters inner thoughts and feelings. Before they begin, we choose one episode for me to model writing a few sentences on the board. Then, I ask them to begin writing, using the model on the board as a reference. I provide assistance as necessary.

Andrea Harb
Costa Mesa, California

Assess Students are assessed on their ability to use first person words as well as evidence related to Bob's or Jimmy's thoughts and feelings.

Holt Professional Learning

Teaching Narrative and Expository Texts
with Judith Irvin and Deborah Appleman

Visit the ThinkCentral, Teacher Access to link to Holt's Professional Learning site for English/Language Arts teachers. This site features:

- Videos that share the insights of *Holt Literature and Language Arts* program authors and consultants and demonstrate proven classroom strategies with master teachers
- Study guides for publications by our authors and consultants
- Informative articles and useful Web links
- Help in planning your department's professional learning sessions
- A handbook for new teachers

VIDEO PRODUCTS

Strategies for Helping Struggling Readers
with Kylene Beers

Effective Vocabulary Instruction
with Carol Jago and Kylene Beers

Developing Critical Thinking About Literature
with Carol Jago and Deborah Appleman

Teaching Students to Revise, Not Recopy
with Linda Rief

Teaching English Learners
with Robin Scarcella

Using Literature Circles
with Harvey Daniels

Teaching On-Demand Writing Skills
with Leila Christenbury

Managing the Heterogeneous Classroom
with Leila Christenbury and Patrick Schwarz

Teaching Narrative and Expository Texts
with Judith Irvin and Deborah Appleman

Becoming a Tech-Savvy Teacher
with Sara Kajder

Re-engaging the Disengaged Student
with Alfred Tatum

Teaching Grammar in Context
with Amy Benjamin

CHAPTER 4

 California Standards

Word Analysis, Fluency, and Systematic Vocabulary Development

- **1.1** Identify idioms, analogies, metaphors, and similes in prose and poetry.
- **1.3** Clarify word meanings through the use of definition, example, restatement, and contrast.

Reading Comprehension (Focus on Informational Materials)

- **2.3** Analyze text that uses the cause-and-effect organizational pattern.

Literary Response and Analysis

- **3.5** Contrast points of view (e.g., first and third person, limited and omniscient, subjective and objective) in narrative text, and explain how they affect the overall theme of the work.

Writing Applications (Genres and Their Characteristics)

- **1.1** Create an organizational structure that balances all aspects of the composition and uses effective transitions between sentences to unify important ideas.
- **1.2** Support all statements and claims with anecdotes, descriptions, facts and statistics, and specific examples.
- **2.4** Write persuasive compositions:
  - **a.** State a clear position or perspective in support of a proposition or proposal.
  - **b.** Describe the points in support of the proposition, employing well-articulated evidence.
  - **c.** Anticipate and address reader concerns and counterarguments.

Analyzing Visuals

Use **ThinkCentral, Teacher Access** to project this image for viewing.

Extension Activity Based on the photograph, ask students to describe what kind of attitude they believe Bethany Hamilton must have toward life. *Possible response: I imagine Bethany Hamilton must have a positive, inspired attitude toward life because she hasn't let her injury prevent her from pursuing her passion: surfing.*

Chapter Resources

On Course: Mapping Instruction

Chapter 1 Resources

Warriner's Handbook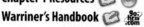
- Chapter 8, Agreement
- Chapter 9, Using Verbs Correctly

PowerNotes

Teacher One Stop™,

Formal Assessment, Progress Monitoring Test 1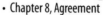

English-Language Conventions Progress-Monitoring Tests

Holt Virtual File Cabinet for Language Arts, grammar, reading, and vocabulary resources

Holt Pronunciation Resources
- Phoneme Sounds and Spellings
- Support for Speakers of African American Vernacular English

ThinkCentral Online Assessment

ThinkCentral Online Remediation

CHAPTER 4

Point of View

INFORMATIONAL TEXT FOCUS

Cause-and-Effect Organizational Pattern

California Standards
Here are the grade 7 standards you will work toward mastering in Chapter 4.

Word Analysis, Fluency, and Systematic Vocabulary Development
1.1 Identify idioms, analogies, metaphors, and similes in prose and poetry.
1.3 Clarify word meanings through the use of definition, example, restatement, and contrast.

Reading Comprehension (Focus on Informational Materials)
2.3 Analyze text that uses the cause-and-effect organizational pattern.

Literary Response and Analysis
3.5 Contrast points of view (e.g., first and third person, limited and omniscient, subjective and objective) in narrative text, and explain how they affect the overall theme of the work.

Writing Applications (Genres and Their Characteristics)
2.4 Write persuasive compositions:
a. State a clear position or perspective in support of a proposition or proposal.
b. Describe the points in support of the proposition, employing well-articulated evidence.
c. Anticipate and address reader concerns and counterarguments.

"You cannot control what happens to you, but you can control your attitude toward what happens to you."

—Brian Tracy

What Do You Think? How do our attitudes influence the changes and challenges we face in life?

Bethany Hamilton, finding courage to surf after losing her left arm to a shark.

✳ **Learn It Online**
Learn how to share your point of view at the Digital Storytelling mini-site:
go.hrw.com   H7-371   Go

Literary Skills Focus

Objectives

Students will

- identify and understand different points of view
- understand how point of view affects the theme of a work

Preteach

Build Background Ask students to think about the different ways stories are told. Have they ever read a story told from an unusual point of view, such as from the perspective of an animal or an object? How did it affect their reading experience?

Direct Teach

Point of View

- Point out to students that use of the pronouns *I, me, my, we, our,* and *us* in a narrative text signal that first-person point of view is being employed. Explain that pronouns such as *he, she, his, her,* and *they* are used in narratives told from both omniscient and third-person limited points of view.

- Remind them that a text told from the third-person limited point of view will focus only on the thoughts and feelings of one character, while one told from omniscient point of view will describe the thoughts and feelings of all characters.

California Standards, pp. 372–373

- **Reading Standard 3.5** Contrast points of view (e.g., first and third person, limited and omniscient, subjective and objective) in narrative text, and explain how they affect the overall theme of the work.

Literary Skills Focus

by **Carol Jago**

What Is Point of View?

When you were little, you may have imagined that there was something terrifying under your bed. Did it ever occur to you that the unknown "something" might find *you* just as terrifying? As the saying goes, "It all depends on your point of view." When you're telling a story, or narrative, you look at things one way—your way. When other people tell the same story, they will put a different spin on the same events, influencing the narrative through their point of view.

"It's all according to your point of view. To me, you're a monster."

Point of View

Both true and fictional narratives are told from a particular **point of view,** or vantage point. Each point of view affects the way you perceive story events and the theme of the work. As you read, ask yourself who the narrator is, whether you can trust him or her, and what the narrator's relationship is to the story's meaning.

First-Person Point of View

When narrative texts are told from the **first-person point of view,** the narrator speaks as "I." You know only what the first-person narrator tells you, and you may not be able to trust everything he or she reveals. (Some narrators withhold information or lie. Some are biased or uninformed. Others are simply crazy.)

> There was Slade and here was Mr. Baumer with his bills and here I was . . . just like in the second go-round of a bad dream.
>
> from "Bargain" by A. B. Guthrie

Omniscient Point of View

Fictional narratives are often told from the **omniscient** (ahm NIHSH uhnt) **point of view.** (In Latin, *omnis* means "all," and *sciens* means "knowing," so this is also called the "all-knowing" point of view.) An omniscient narrator can reveal the private thoughts and actions of all the characters. This kind of narrator can also reveal what is happening in other places, and even in other times.

> The two men started up the street, arm in arm. The man from the West, his egotism enlarged by success, was beginning to outline the history of his career.
>
> from "After Twenty Years" by O. Henry

Third-Person-Limited Point of View

In the third-person limited point of view, which is commonly used in fiction, the narrator focuses on the thoughts, feelings, and reactions of just *one* character (usually the main character), using third-person pronouns like *he, she, his,* and *her.*

Resources

Chapter 4 Resources, Literary Focus Skill Builder, p. 3

PowerNotes, interactive lesson presentation with activities

Teacher One Stop™, on-level lesson plans and all print resources

Universal Access

EL **English Learners/Struggling Readers**

English for Academic Success Help students learn the academic terms in the Literary Skills Focus. Read each bolded word aloud and have students repeat them. Then, have students use the bold words to fill in the blanks in these sentences:

1. In stories told from a(n) _____, the reader learns the most private thoughts of all characters. [*omniscient point of view*]
2. Journalists must make sure that the news articles they write use a(n) _____. [*objective point of view*]

Subjective and Objective Points of View

Some people make the mistake of thinking that all nonfiction is factual and objective, but writers of some nonfiction narrative texts make a point of stating their feelings and opinions on a subject. Writers who express their personal thoughts and feelings are writing from a **subjective point of view.** In contrast, writers who stick to the facts only and avoid personal opinions are writing from an **objective point of view.**

Subjective Point of View *Subjective* means "personal; resulting from feelings; existing only in the mind." When using a subjective point of view, nonfiction writers will stress the opinions and feelings they associate with their subjects. Autobiographies and personal narratives often include subjective details. Notice how Ernesto Galarza states his feelings about his teacher in these sentences from his autobiography:

> Miss Hopley was not a giant in body, but when she mobilized it to a standing position she seemed a match for giants. I decided I liked her.
>
> from *Barrio Boy* by Ernesto Galarza

Objective Point of View *Objective* means "real; factual; without bias." Reporters use an objective point of view in their articles as they answer the *5W-How?* questions: *Who? What? When? Where? Why?* and *How?* Readers expect to find true and accurate accounts of events in all types of news stories—in newspapers, in news magazines, on television, and on the Web.

Biographies and autobiographies usually contain a mix of subjective and objective points of view. A biographer will be certain to report facts accurately. At times, however, a biographer will

also reveal his or her feelings and even judgments about a subject. Which elements in the passage that follows are subjective? Which are objective?

> Ever since Elizabeth was eight, however, she had said again and again, "I will never marry." Did marriage look promising to a girl whose father had had six wives, two of whom, including her own mother, he had beheaded? Yet she liked to hear of people wanting to marry her.
>
> from "Elizabeth I" by Milton Meltzer

A writer's choice to write from the subjective or objective point of view can affect your perception of the text. A work that sticks primarily to facts will have a theme different from that of a narrative text that expresses a writer's feelings.

Your Turn Analyze Point of View

1. Explain the difference between omniscient and third-person-limited point of view.

2. Re-read the quotation from "After Twenty Years" on page 372. Then, rewrite the scene from the first-person point of view. You will have to write as "I." You may also wish to include the man from the West's feelings.

3. What is the most important contrast between subjective and objective writing?

4. Would you expect a science textbook to be more objective or subjective? Explain.

✽ **Learn It Online**
Visit *NovelWise* to learn how to recognize and distinguish points of view.

go.hrw.com   H7-373   **Go**

Subjective and Objective Points of View

Guide students in understanding that a text told wholly from an objective point of view would likely have a straightforward theme meant to inform or educate the reader about the text's topic. In contrast, a text with subjective details might invoke broader themes.

Check for Understanding

Your Turn

Possible responses:

1. *Omniscient tells all about every character, while third person-limited reveals the thoughts of one character.*

2. *I started up the street, arm and arm with my friend. I felt very confident.*

3. *Subjective stresses opinions; objective stresses facts.*

4. *I would expect it to be more objective, because a textbook usually contains mostly facts.*

Reteach

To reteach point of view, see **Reteaching Lessons,** p. 842A.

ThinkCentral Online Remediation

---

3. I like reading narratives told from a(n) _____ because they give me the sense that the character is speaking directly to me . [*first-person point of view*].

4. In this autobiography, the author uses a(n) _____ when she describes her feelings and opinions about her childhood. [*subjective point of view*].

5. Even though the main character in this narrative never directly shares her thoughts and feelings, readers learn a great deal about her because the story is told from a(n) _____ [*third-person limited point of view*].

Advanced Learners

Acceleration Have students form groups and discuss which point of view they prefer in narratives. Do they find it easier to relate to a first-person narrator, or do they enjoy the "all-knowingness" of an omniscient narrator? Why?

✽ **Learn It Online**
The **NovelWise** mini-site includes instruction on choosing, reading, and analyzing novels; it also contains a catalogue of book summaries, study guides, teaching guides, and PowerPoint presentations.

go.hrw.com   H7-373   **Go**

Objectives
Students will
- compare and contrast, distinguish fact from opinion, determine author's purpose, and make predictions
- use reading skills to contrast point of view

Preteach

Motivate Have students discuss which they enjoy reading about more: facts or opinions. How can tell the difference? Why do they prefer one over the other?

Direct Teach

Distinguishing Fact from Opinion

- Remind students that statements that seem like facts may actually be opinions. Tell students to read closely to determine if a statement can be proven or just supported by convincing evidence.

- Provide the following example: George Washington was a great man. Point out that while many people believe this statement to be true, and there is much evidence to support it, it is not a fact because it cannot be proven.

California Standards, pp. 374–375

- **Reading Standard 3.5** Contrast points of view (e.g., first and third person, limited and omniscient, subjective and objective) in narrative text, and explain how they affect the overall them of the work.

Reading Skills Focus

by **Kylene Beers**

How Can I Contrast Points of View to Analyze Narrative Texts?

The point of view in a narrative text affects its theme, the message the work communicates to you. Applying reading skills that can help you identify and contrast different points of view will help you better interpret the short stories, autobiographies, biographies, personal narratives, and other narrative texts you read.

Comparing and Contrasting

When you **compare,** you look for similarities, or likenesses. When you **contrast,** you look for differences. You have probably often compared and contrasted literary elements such as conflict and character. In this chapter, you will compare and contrast points of view in narrative texts.

For example, "Elizabeth I" by Milton Meltzer and *Barrio Boy* by Ernesto Galarza are both narrative texts that describe the events in someone's life, but they do so from different points of view. "Elizabeth I" is a biography written from an objective, third-person point of view. *Barrio Boy,* on the other hand, is an autobiography written from a subjective, first-person point of view. Refer to the chart below to help you contrast points of view in narrative texts.

Types of Point of View	
Objective	Sticks primarily to the facts
Subjective	Expresses a writer's feelings
Omniscient	Told by an all-knowing narrator
First Person	Told by a character using the pronoun *I*
Third-person limited	Told by a narrator that focuses on the thoughts and feelings of one character

Distinguishing Fact from Opinion

A **fact** is something that can be proven true. An **opinion** represents a personal belief or judgment and cannot be proven true or false.

When you read narrative texts, especially nonfiction, it is important to be able to distinguish fact from opinion. Here are examples from the autobiography *Barrio Boy:*

Term	Definition	Example
Fact	something that can be proven	Half of the block was occupied by Lincoln School.
Opinion	something that can be supported by facts but can't be proven true or false	[Miss Hopley] seemed a match for giants. I decided I liked her.

Be alert to opinions stated as facts. If you are in doubt, ask, "Can this statement be proven?" In *Barrio Boy* it can be proven that the school occupies a certain amount of space. However, the way Ernesto feels about Miss Hopley is an opinion. Watch for these words to help you identify opinions: *believe, seem, may, think, probably, likely,* and *possibly.* Look out also for the author's word choice, tone, and what he or she does *not* say.

Resources

Chapter 4 Resources, Reading Focus Skill Builder, p. 4

PowerNotes, interactive lesson presentation with activities

Teacher One Stop™, on-level lesson plans and all print resources

Universal Access

EL English Learners/Struggling Readers
English for Academic Success Help students learn the academic terms in the Reading Skills Focus by breaking the terms into their word parts.

- Write the word parts for *biography* on the board with their respective meanings: *bio–*: life and *–graph*: something written or drawn. Help students see that a *biography* is a written text about someone's life.

- Write *autobiography* and *auto–*: self on the board. Guide students in understanding that an *autobiography* is a written text

You are likely to find many opinions in narrative texts that are written from a subjective point of view, such as autobiographies and personal narratives. Writers usually express their feelings in these types of texts. Objective writing, such as news articles, will consist primarily of facts. The ability to distinguish between facts and opinions will help you determine whether a text has a primarily objective or subjective point of view.

Determining Author's Purpose

Writers of narrative texts have different purposes.

- A **biography** informs us about a person's life but also entertains with interesting details.
- In an **autobiography,** the writer—who is also the subject of the text—may want to share information, explain events in his or her life, and even persuade the reader.
- Writers of **personal narratives** may want to reveal a truth about life. In "Names/Nombres," Julia Alvarez shares what she has discovered about the importance of names.

> By the time I was in high school, I was a popular kid and it showed in my name. Friends called me *Jules* or *Hey Jude . . .*
> from "Names/Nombres"
> by Julia Alvarez

Below is a list of reasons explaining an author's possible purposes for writing:

- to inform
- to persuade
- to reveal a truth about life
- to share an experience
- to explain
- to entertain

Identifying the author's purpose can help you to think about the effects of a particular point of view on the theme of a work.

Making Predictions

When you make predictions, you guess what will happen next in a narrative text. You anticipate how events will unfold and how characters will behave. Understanding a narrator's point of view can help you make predictions, which can in turn help you determine the meaning of a text. Follow these tips for making predictions:

- Look for clues that hint at future events.
- Think about how those clues connect to past and present actions in the narrative.
- Think about similar narratives and how they unfolded.
- Use your own knowledge and experience to anticipate what is likely to happen next.

Your Turn Apply Reading Skills

1. Write a sentence about a sports star or other celebrity. Use a combination of fact and opinion. Circle the facts in your sentence. Then underline the opinions you included.

2. How might the purpose of a biography differ from that of a fictional narrative? How might the two be similar? Explain your thoughts.

3. Suppose you read a story in which one character is bullied by another character at the outset. What do you predict might happen in such a story?

 Now go to the Skills in Action: Reading Model

 Learn It Online
Build your understanding using *PowerNotes:*
go.hrw.com H7-375 **Go**

Determining Author's Purpose

Clarify a "truth about life" that an author might share in a text. Suggest, for example, that such truths might include lessons learned when overcoming adversity.

Making Predictions

Ask students how considering the genre of a narrative can help them make predictions. For example, what usually happens at the end of a fairy tale? [The characters live happily ever after.]

Check for Understanding

Your Turn

Possible responses:

1. *Tiger Woods is a golfer (circled) who is the greatest athlete in the history of the sport.*

2. *A biography might be written to inform, but a fictional narrative might be intended to entertain. Both might be written to reveal a truth or to share an experience.*

3. *I would predict the characters would have a confrontation, but then settle their differences.*

Reteach

ThinkCentral Online Remediation

---

about a person's own life; thus, the author writes about *himself* or *herself.*

- Point out the words and phrases *both, different,* and *on the other hand* in the first column on p. 374. Explain to students that these are academic terms that will be useful to them as they compare and contrast points of view in narrative text. Ask students to think about other academic terms that help express comparisons and contrasts. Suggest words and phrases such as *similarly, but, yet, likewise, alike, in contrast,* and *also.*

Students with Disabilities

Write the five points of view on the board, each in a different color. Have students copy the color-coded points of view into their **Reader/Writer Notebook.** Read the "Types of Point of View" chart aloud to students and explain that each color represents a different point of view. Have students use this color-coding in their notes as they read the selections in Chapter 4.

Learn It Online
For a multimedia version of the instruction found on this page, use the **PowerNotes** Reading Focus presentation.

go.hrw.com H7-375   **Go**

Reading Model

Objectives

Students will
• identify author's point of view
• identify author's purpose
• distinguish facts from opinions

Preteach

Read with a Purpose Have students read the Read with a Purpose statement. Then, ask them to note in their **Reader/Writer Notebook** any lessons that they have learned from a parent or other adult.

Direct Teach

Model the Skill

Use the Reading Model to demonstrate the application of the Literary and Reading Skills in a short selection. As you or students read the model aloud, stop to discuss the side annotations and highlighting, which are aids to comprehension and analysis.

▶ Literary Focus

Subjective Point of View Why does *good* suggest subjective point of view? *Possible response: It is an adjective that describes an opinion.*

Point of View What topic is O'Neal sharing his view on? *Possible response: O'Neal's essay is about what people think of him.*

▶ Reading Focus

Fact and Opinion: How does O'Neal's current opinion about pranks compare to the opinion he had in junior high? *Possible response: He used to think pranks were funny, but now he thinks they're harmful.*

Making Predictions: What do you predict O'Neal will do when he understands how harmful his behavior is? *Possible response: I predict he will help others.*

Read with a Purpose Read this **personal narrative** to discover a lesson the writer learned from his parents.

A Good Reason to Look Up

by Shaquille O'Neal

Literary Focus

Subjective Point of View The word *good* in the title suggests that this personal narrative is written from a **subjective point of view.**

Literary Focus

Point of View Notice the pronoun *I* in the first sentence. This is a **first-person** account. To find out who the *I* is in a nonfiction narrative text, look for the name of the writer.

Reading Focus

Fact and Opinion In O'Neal's **opinion**, the pranks he played were harmful to others. He supports his opinion with **fact**— the example of what he did with Icy Hot.

Reading Focus

Making Predictions Based on O'Neal's subjective point of view on these past events, you can predict that he has changed his ways.

When I was in junior high school, what my friends thought of me was real important to me. During those years I grew much taller than most of my peers. Being so tall made me feel uncomfortable. In order to keep the focus off of me and my unusual height, I went along with the crowd who would play practical jokes on other kids at school. Being one of the class clowns gave me a way to make sure that the jokes were directed at others, and not at me.

I would pull all kinds of pranks that were hurtful, and sometimes even harmful, to others. Once before gym class, my friends and I put Icy Hot in the gym shorts of one of the kids on the basketball team. Not only was he terribly embarrassed, but he also had to go to the school nurse's office. I thought it was going to be funny, but it ended up that no one thought it was—least of all my father.

My parents didn't always think that my behavior was funny. They reminded me about The Golden Rule: to treat others as I would like to be treated. Many times, I was disciplined for the hurtful way that I was treating others. What I was doing was hurting other kids, and in turn hurting my reputation as someone to be looked up to. My friends were looking up to me because I was tall, but what did they see?

My parents wanted me to be a leader who was a good example to others—to be a decent human being. They taught me

California Standards, pp. 376–377

■ **Reading Standard 3.5** Contrast points of view (e.g., first and third person, limited and omniscient, subjective and objective) in narrative text and explain how they affect the overall theme of the work.

Selection Readability	
Easily Accessible Accessible Challenging	familiar setting; conversational tone; familiar theme

Selection Summary

Shaquille O'Neal describes how he became someone others could look up to for his positive example as well as for his height.

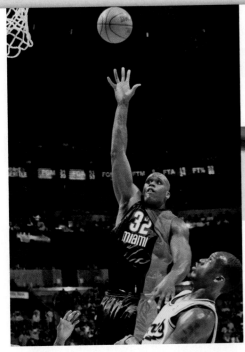

Analyzing Visuals

Connecting to the Text How does this image reflect what Shaquille O'Neal says?

to set my own goals, and to do the best at everything that I set out to do. During the lectures I got from my father, he told me over and over again to be the leader that I was meant to be—to be a big man in my heart and actions, as well as in my body. I had to question myself whether or not it was important to be the kind of leader and person my father believed I was inside. I knew in my heart that he was right. So I tried my best to follow my father's advice.

Once I focused on being the best that I could be at basketball and became a leader in the game, I took my responsibility to set a good example more seriously. I sometimes have to stop and think before I act, and I make mistakes occasionally—everyone is human. But I continue to look for opportunities where I can make a difference, and to set a good example because of my father's advice. I now pass it on to you.

"Be a leader, Shaq, not a follower. Since people already have to look up to you, give them a *good* reason to do so."

Read with a Purpose What did Shaquille O'Neal learn from his parents? Are these important lessons? Explain.

Reading Focus

Comparing and Contrasting Based on the information O'Neal gives you, you can draw **contrasts,** or note differences, between his size and the way he used to behave, between being a leader and being a follower.

Reading Focus

Author's Purpose O'Neal states his reason for writing this text. He wants to explain what he learned and to encourage readers to follow his example.

Model the Skill

▶ **Reading Focus**

Comparing and Contrasting Describe a contrast O'Neal mentions in this paragraph. *Possible response: Although O'Neal is not perfect, he now looks for opportunities to set a positive example where he can.*

Author's Purpose Besides the reasons that O'Neal states in paragraph 5, what other purposes might O'Neal have for writing this essay? *Possible response: He might want to persuade readers to treat their peers with respect.*

Check for Understanding

Read with a Purpose Ask students to explain the lesson that O'Neal learned. *Possible response: O'Neal learned that he needed to set a good example for other people by treating others with respect. I think this is an important lesson because if more people learned it, then fewer people would be treated with cruelty.*

Analyzing Visuals

Connecting to the Text: *Shaquille O'Neal is striving to be a leader on the basketball court.*

Universal Access: Vocabulary

EL **English Learners/ Struggling Readers**

English for Academic Success To help students understand the selection, introduce them to the following vocabulary words.

• **peers**—people in equal standing, such as classmates. *Shaq wished to be popular with his peers.*

• **prank**—harmful trick. *Shaq's pranks often got him in trouble.*

• **reputation**—the opinion people have about a person. *Shaq wanted to have a reputation as a leader.*

• **decent**—kind. *Shaq grew up to become a decent person.*

• **lecture**—a formal talk about bad behavior. *Shaq's father gave him a lecture when he behaved badly.*

Then, give students this statement that explains how the words relate to the meaning of this selection: *Shaq did not always have a good reputation in school. He would play pranks on other people to try to impress his peers. Shaq's father gave him many lectures that inspired Shaq to change and become a decent person.*

More About the Writer

Professional basketball player **Shaquille O'Neal** has penned a 2001 autobiography, *Shaq Talks Back*, and a children's book, *Shaq and the Beanstalk and Other Very Tall Tales*. He won the National Basketball Association's 1999–2000 Most Valuable Player Award.

Think About the Writer

Ask students what they already knew about Shaquille O'Neal and what they have just learned about him. How has this information influenced how they view him? Do his decisions and actions fit their definition of a role model?

🕐 For Independent Reading

■ If students enjoyed reading the subjective point of view expressed in O'Neal's essay, suggest they read *Bad Boy: A Memoir* by Walter Dean Myers. In this autobiography, Myers describes what it was like growing up in Harlem during the 1940s and 1950s.

■ If students wish to read about another boy learning to take responsibility and do the right thing, suggest *Promises to the Dead,* Mary Downing Hahn's novel about a young boy trying to fulfill his promise to bring the child of an escaped slave to freedom.

🐻 **California Standards, p. 379**

■ **Literary Response and Analysis 3.5** Contrast points of view (e.g., first and third person, limited and omniscient, subjective and objective) in narrative text and explain how they affect the overall theme of the work.

MEET THE WRITER

Shaquille O'Neal
(1972–   )

Vital Statistics

- Nicknames: Shaq, Superman, Diesel, the Big Aristotle
- Born: March 6, 1972, in Newark, New Jersey. His birth name, Shaquille Rashaun, means "little warrior" in Arabic.

Interesting Facts

- Shaq learned to play basketball as a boy while living in Germany.
- Shaq is seven feet one inch tall and weighs more than three hundred pounds. His shoe size is 21.

Why Is He Important?

- Shaq is the youngest player to have been named one of the NBA's fifty greatest players.
- He has acted in films, television programs, and commercials.
- Shaq is a member of the National Advisory Council of Reading Is Fundamental, an organization that promotes literacy for children.

What's Important to Him?

Basketball isn't Shaq's only love. He enjoys reading and says, "My parents encouraged me to read and to educate myself. Following their advice, I've always tried to read to better myself." He has worked hard on his education, and in 2000, he graduated from Louisiana State University with a bachelor's degree. While working on an MBA from the University of Phoenix in 2005, he said, "It's just something to have on my résumé when I go back to reality. Someday I might have to put down a basketball and have a regular 9–5 [job] like everybody else."

Think About the Writer Do you view O'Neal as a role model? Why or why not?

Resources

Chapter 4 Resources, Literary and Academic Vocabulary Skill Builder, p. 5

Teacher One Stop™, on-level lesson plans and all print resources

WordSharp: An Interactive Vocabulary Tutor, more practice with academic language

Academic Vocabulary

Writing About Point of View

English for Academic Success Write the following questions on the board. Tell students these are the kinds of questions they will encounter on standardized tests. Discuss the meaning of the words, then have students use "A *Good* Reason to Look Up" to answer the questions.

- **Analyze** how the essay's point of view influences your opinion of O'Neal. How do you **perceive** him, based on this essay?
  Possible response: The essay's first-person point of view made it seem like O'Neal was confiding in me and giving me personal advice. I perceive him to be a thoughtful, kind individual interested

Reading Standard 3.5 Contrast points of view (e.g., first and third person, limited and omniscient, subjective and objective) in narrative text, and explain how they affect the overall theme of the work.

Into Action: Comparing and Contrasting Point of View

Use the chart below to contrast the point of view in "A Good Reason to Look Up" with the other two points of view listed in the chart. Then, explain how the work's point of view affects its theme.

The First-Person Point of View in "A Good Reason to Look Up"...

is different from the third-person-limited point of view in that...	is different from the omniscient point of view in that...	affects the work's theme because...

Talk About...

1. Who else could have narrated "A *Good* Reason to Look Up." besides O'Neal? Discuss what it might have been like if it were written from someone else's point of view. In your response, try to use each Academic Vocabulary word listed on the right at least once.

Write About...

Answer the following questions about "A *Good* Reason to Look Up." For definitions of the underlined Academic Vocabulary words, see the column on the right.

2. How does O'Neal <u>perceive</u> the events of his childhood differently today than he did when he was young?

3. Identify one subjective and one objective detail from this <u>narrative</u>.

4. <u>Analyze</u> O'Neal's experiences. What brought him to the realization that represents the work's theme?

Writing Skills Focus
Think as a Reader/Writer

In Chapter 4, the Writing Skills Focus activities on the Preparing to Read pages explain how the writers use point of view in narrative text. On the Applying Your Skills pages, you'll have a chance to practice these methods.

Academic Vocabulary for Chapter 4

Talking and Writing About Point of View

Academic Vocabulary is the language you use to write and talk about literature. Use these words to discuss the texts you read in this chapter. The words are underlined throughout the chapter.

analyze (AN uh lyz) *v.*: examine in detail. *Understanding point of view will help you analyze the texts that you read.*

narrative (NAR uh tihv) *adj.*: that narrates or recounts; being in story form. *The point of view of a narrative text will often affect its theme.*

organizational (AWR guh nuh ZAY shuh nuhl) *adj.*: pertaining to organization or structure. *The cause-and-effect organizational pattern is often used to explain a process.*

perceive (puhr SEEV) *v.*: be aware of through the senses; observe. *A narrator will perceive story events in his or her unique way.*

Your Turn

Copy the Academic Vocabulary words into your *Reader/Writer Notebook*. Then, use each word in a sentence about someone that you or others admire. Practice using these Academic Vocabulary words throughout this chapter.

Guided Practice: Apply
Into Action: Comparing and Contrasting Point of View

Students may wish to work in pairs to discuss how the essay's point of view affects it theme.

Talk About...

1. Model for students how to incorporate the academic vocabulary words into a conversation. You might say, "The essay might have a different <u>organizational</u> pattern if it were written from someone else's point of view."

Write About...
Possible responses:

2. *Back then, he thought he was being funny. Now, he <u>perceives</u> that he acted foolishly when he played pranks.*

3. *One objective detail in this <u>narrative</u> is that O'Neal grew taller than most of his peers. A subjective detail is that O'Neal tried his best to follow his father's advice.*

4. *When I <u>analyze</u> O'Neal's experiences, it's clear that the guidance of his parents made him realize the essay's theme: treat others as you wanted to be treated, and try your best to set a good example.*

Writing Skills Focus

The Think as a Reader/Writer activities in the chapter focus on the reading-writing relationship. Use the activities to help students explore the writer's craft in a text and to practice this aspect of craft in their own writing.

Independent Practice

Chapter 4 Resources, Skill Builders, pp. 3–5

UA: Differentiating Intruction, Academic and Selection Vocabulary Skill Builder, p. 112

---

in sharing his wisdom with others.

- Comment on the essay's **organizational** structure. How does it affect your reading experience? ***Possible response:*** *The essay is organized into several paragraphs in which O'Neal first recounts experiences from childhood and then shares what he learned from these events. The essay is easy to read and follow.*

- What is the theme of this **narrative?** How does the essay's point of view help convey this theme? ***Possible response:*** *The theme is that it is important to set a good example for others. Since the essay is told from the first-person point of view of Shaquille O'Neal, a very successful person, this message seems relevant and credible.*

Standards Focus

Objectives
Students will
- recognize omniscient point of view
- make and evaluate predictions

Motivate

What Do You Think?/QuickWrite
Have students discuss the special qualities of a friend. Then, have them use their **Reader/Writer Notebook** to consider the circumstances in which duty is more important than friendship.

English for Academic Success

Academic Vocabulary
Look for opportunities to use the Academic Vocabulary words in this chapter.

- **analyze, *v.:*** examine in detail.
- **narrative, *adj.:*** that narrates or recounts; being in story form.
- **perceive, *v.:*** be aware of through the senses; observe.

Analyzing Visuals
Use **ThinkCentral Teacher Access** to project this image for viewing.

Extension Activity Have students explain the artist's point of view in this image. ***Possible response:*** *The artist is behind the man's jacket.*

After Twenty Years

by **O. Henry**

What Do You Think

Under what circumstances would you choose duty over loyalty to a friend?

QuickWrite
Write a list of words and phrases describing one of your closest friends. Put a check mark next to the qualities you think that friend will still have twenty years from now.

The Rewarded Poet (1956) by René Magritte (1898–1967). Oil on canvas.
©René Magritte/Artists Rights Society (ARS) New York.

California Standards, pp. 380–389
- **Reading Standard 3.5** Contrast points of view (e.g., first and third person, limited and omniscient, subjective and objective) in narrative text and explain how they affect the overall theme of the work.

Selection Readability	
Easily Accessible **Accessible** Challenging	familiar situations; conversational dialogue

Selection Plot Summary
Two friends, Bob and Jimmy, part ways with an agreement to meet again in twenty years. As Bob waits on a dark street to meet Jimmy, he has, unknowingly, an important conversation with a policeman. When Bob is arrested by a plainclothes officer posing as Jimmy, he learns that the real Jimmy was the policeman he'd talked to earlier.

Reader/Writer Notebook

Use your **RWN** to complete the activities for this selection.

Reading Standard 3.5 Contrast points of view (e.g., first and third person, limited and **omniscient**, subjective and objective) **in narrative text** and explain how they affect the overall theme of the work.

Literary Skills Focus

Omniscient Point of View When you read a literary work, ask yourself, "Who is telling the story?" The answer to this question will help you identify the point of view. A story with an **omniscient point of view,** such as "After Twenty Years," is told by an invisible narrator who is not a character in the story but who knows everything about every character, including their private feelings, their pasts, and even their futures.

Literary Perspectives Apply the literary perspective described on page 383 as you read this story.

Reading Skills Focus

Making Predictions When you make informed guesses about what will happen next in a <u>narrative</u> text, you are **making predictions.** Here's how to do it:

- Look for clues that **foreshadow,** or hint at, what will happen.
- As the suspense builds, predict possible outcomes. See if you can guess where the author is leading you.
- <u>Analyze</u> how the point of view affects what you know. Revise your predictions as the narrator gives you more information.
- Draw on your own experiences—including other reading experiences—to mak your predictions.

Track the accuracy of your predictions in a chart like the one below. Revise your predictions as you read.

Story Events	Predictions	Revised Predictions

Writing Skills Focus
Think as a Reader/Writer

Find It in Your Reading As you read, record in your *Reader/Writer Notebook* examples of dialogue that reveal the personalities of the policeman and the man standing in the doorway.

Vocabulary

habitual (huh BIHCH u uhl) *adj.:* done or fixed by habit. *The officer made his habitual check of the buildings.*

intricate (IHN truh kiht) *adj.:* complicated; full of detail. *The club twirled with intricate movements.*

dismally (DIHZ muh lee) *adv.:* miserably; gloomily. *People walked dismally through the rainy streets.*

egotism (EE guh tihz uhm) *n.:* conceit; talking about oneself too much. *His egotism made him brag about his success.*

simultaneously (sy muhl TAY nee uhs lee) *adv.:* at the same time. *They looked simultaneously at each other.*

Language Coach

Word Derivatives Recognizing base words and their **derivatives,** or words that are similar in spelling, can help you understand unfamiliar words. For example, the Vocabulary word *habitual* is a derivative of the base word *habit.* See the chart below for other derivatives of *habit.*

Base	Derivatives
habit	habitual
	habitually
	inhabit
	inhabited

Learn It Online
See the video introduction to this story at:

go.hrw.com   **H7-381**   **Go**

Selection Resources

Chapter 4 Resources, on-level practice and assessment, pp. 6–11

PowerNotes, interactive lesson presentation with activities

Teacher One Stop™, on-level lesson plans and all print resources

Holt Audio Library

Holt Audio Library: Selections and Summaries in Spanish

UA: Holt Interactive Reader, pp. 96–103

Holt Interactive Reader for ELD, pp. 122–127

Holt Interactive Reader Audio Tutor

UA: Differentiating Instruction, modified lesson plans and leveled assessment, pp. 90–92

UA: Resources for Teaching Advanced Students, lesson plans, p. 103

UA: Supporting Instruction in Five Languages, selection summary

Weekly Standards Review Transparencies, Transparency 4

Analyzing Visuals Transparencies, p. 31

ThinkCentral Online Remediation

Preteach

Introducing Vocabulary

Read aloud the Vocabulary words and sample sentences. Then, have students complete each sentence with a Vocabulary word.

1. When the players ran for the ball _____, they hit each other. [*simultaneously*]
2. Flossing every night is a _____ task. [*habitual*]
3. The girl moaned _____ as she worked on the _____ exam problem. [*dismally, intricate*]
4. The proud celebrity was full of _____. [*egotism*]

English for Academic Success
Language Coach

Have students look at the words related to *habitual* and determine what all of the words have in common. [the base word *habit*] Then, have students identify the prefixes and suffixes that change the word's meaning.

Literary Skills Focus

As you read and discuss the selection with students, have them record examples of omniscient point of view.

Reading Skills Focus

Give students a copy of the Reading Skills Focus graphic organizer before they read. (See **Chapter 4 Resources.**) Tell them to use their responses to answer the questions on the Applying Your Skills page.

Writing Skills Focus

Have students record dialogue from the text in their **Reader/Writer Notebook.** Students can use their notes to complete the Writing Skills Focus activity.

Learn It Online
The **PowerNotes** presentation for this lesson includes a short video that introduces the selection. The video is also available on the online version of this page.

go.hrw.com   **H7-381**   **Go**

More About the Writer

Though he is renowned today for his brilliant short stories, **O. Henry** was not quite so fondly regarded by colleagues during his lifetime. One of his most famous stories, "The Gift of the Magi," was written in three hours after Henry had long since missed his deadline and with his irate editor waiting on the couch for the story's completion.

Think About the Writer

Before students answer the question, work with them to discuss aspects of characterization. Then review O. Henry's biography. What similarities do they find between the author's characters and his personal experiences?

 For Independent Reading

If students enjoyed the surprise ending of "After Twenty Years," they may be interested in reading *"The Gift of the Magi and Other Stories."* It includes O. Henry's story of two lovers' sacrifices to buy the other a Christmas gift.

MEET THE WRITER

Learn It Online
Get more on the author's life at:
go.hrw.com H7-382 Go

O. Henry
(1862–1910)

Early Troubles

O. Henry is the pen name of William Sydney Porter. Born in Greensboro, North Carolina, he left school at fifteen and eventually moved to Texas. There, he edited a humor magazine and worked for a bank in Austin. Porter was accused of embezzling money from the bank, and, although probably innocent, he panicked and fled to Honduras. When he returned to Austin to be with his dying wife, he was convicted and spent more than three years in a federal prison in Ohio.

Plot Twists

Porter moved to New York after being released from prison in 1901. Soon after, as O. Henry, he became a popular short story writer, known for the surprise endings of his works. Porter found inspiration for some of his plots, including "After Twenty Years," in the stories he heard in prison.

While Porter was dining with friends one day, a young writer asked him where he got his plots. "Oh, everywhere," Porter replied. "There are stories in everything." He picked up a menu and said, "There's a story in this." Indeed there was, as Porter later published a story called "Springtime à la Carte."

Think About the Writer

How might O. Henry's troubles have affected the way he viewed his characters?

©The Granger Collection, New York.

Build Background

O. Henry's stories were often set in the streets, tenements, and hotels of New York City, where he lived in the early 1900s.

The population of New York City exploded in the late 1800s and early 1900s. Waves of European immigrants came to the city to start new lives, working hard to save enough money to move out of the poorly maintained tenement buildings in which they lived.

O. Henry enjoyed writing about the lives of everyday people and the challenges they face. His stories are known for their coincidences, ironic humor, and twist endings.

Preview the Selection

This short story begins with an encounter between a **policeman** walking a local beat and a **man** standing in a darkened doorway.

Real Issues, Real Experts

*Holt author **Deborah Appleman** offers strategies for appreciating writer's craft.*

This short story, written by one of the acknowledged masters of the genre, provides students with the opportunity to really appreciate the writer's craft. It is also a great vehicle for focusing on the kinds of skills, such as predicting and close reading, that become automatic for good readers.

Given O. Henry's immaculate attention to detail, I ask students to list all the descriptive words. Then in groups of four, the most artistically able student in the group renders a kind of composite sketch of all of the main characters while the other group members coach him/her. Passages like "a pale, square-jawed face with keen eyes and a little white scar near his right eyebrow. His scarf pin was a large diamond, oddly set" not only create character but also provide subtle clues.

After Twenty Years

by **O. Henry**

The policeman on the beat moved up the avenue impressively. The impressiveness was habitual and not for show, for spectators were few. The time was barely ten o' clock at night, but chilly gusts of wind with a taste of rain in them had well nigh depeopled the streets. **A**

Trying doors as he went, twirling his club with many intricate and artful movements, turning now and then to cast his watchful eye down the pacific[1] thoroughfare, the officer, with his stalwart form and slight swagger, made a fine picture of a guardian of the peace. The vicinity was one that kept early hours. Now and then you might see the lights of a cigar store or of an all-night lunch counter, but the majority of the doors belonged to business places that had long since been closed. **B**

When about midway of a certain block,

the policeman suddenly slowed his walk. In the doorway of a darkened hardware store a man leaned with an unlighted cigar in his mouth. As the policeman walked up to him, the man spoke up quickly. **C**

---

1. **pacific:** peaceful.

A **Literary Focus** Omniscient Point of View How can you tell this story is told from an omniscient point of view?

B **Literary Perspectives** Analyze Responses to Literature What connections can you make to this character? In what stories have you encountered a character with similar traits?

C **Reading Focus** Making Predictions What do you predict will happen between the policeman and the man waiting in the doorway?

Vocabulary **habitual** (huh BIHCH u uhl) *adj.:* done or fixed by habit.
intricate (IHN truh kiht) *adj.:* complicated; full of detail.

Literary Perspectives

The following perspective will help you think about the point of view of this short story:

Analyzing Responses to Literature The way a writer uses literary elements—such as character, plot, theme, and point of view—influences how you perceive a literary work. As you read, you consider whether episodes in the plot foreshadow future events, you form opinions of characters based on their descriptions, and so on. As you read "After Twenty Years," pay attention to the way the literary elements shape your response to the work, and analyze how the omniscient point of view affects the theme. The Literary Perspectives questions at the bottom of the page will guide you in using this perspective.

Since O. Henry is a master at the surprise ending, I like to read the story twice, giving students the rare opportunity to re-read, another technique that good readers employ. We first talk about how we are all taken in by the ending, and then we re-read to see what clues we might have missed. And there are plenty! Re-reading can be as comforting as watching a favorite film over again; there is something delicious about knowing what's in store.

Literary Perspectives

Before students read the selection, have them read the **Literary Perspectives** about **Analyzing Responses to Literature**.

Have students keep track of their personal responses to "After Twenty Years" by having them keep a response journal. As they read, have students jot down their thoughts about the story's characters and events. Remind students that there is no "right" or "wrong" personal response to literature. Remind students to use the notes and questions at the bottom of the page to help them use the perspective.

Direct Teach

Think About/Talk About
Read with a Purpose Have students read the Read with a Purpose statement. Discuss how things may change between friends after twenty years apart.

▶ **Comprehension**
C Reading Focus
Possible response: The police officer will question or arrest the man.

▶ **Analysis**
A Literary Focus
Possible response: The narrator is speaking generally about the policeman's habits and describing the setting, but not from the viewpoint of the policeman. That means that he is an omniscient narrator.

B Literary Perspectives
Possible response: I've seen policemen like the one in the story patrolling my neighborhood at night. I've encountered similar characters in stories about police officers.

▶ **Extend the Discussion**
Speculating Why might the policeman have slowed down at the sight of the man in the doorway in the third paragraph? *Possible response:* The policeman might feel the man is up to no good if he is hanging around an unlit area with no one else around.

Vocabulary: Own the Word
- **habitual:** Ask students to name a *habitual* part of their morning routine. *Possible response:* brushing my teeth
- **intricate:** Help students understand the meaning of *intricate* within the context of the selection. Explain that the officer is not simply swinging his club back and forth, but instead, twirling it in a complex pattern.

- Tell students that stories can be told from different **points of view**. A story that is narrated by the main character and uses "I" and "me" is told from the first-person point of view. A story told from only one character's perspective but using "he" and "she" is told from the third-person limited point of view. A story told by a narrator who is completely uninvolved in the action is told from the **third person omniscient point of view**. The omniscient point of view is unique because the narrator is not involved in the action. Omniscient narrators can relate the thoughts of any character.

- Have students read p. 384. Point out that although the man in the doorway talks about being out West to make his fortune, it is never revealed what he did in the West. Remind students that as an omniscient narrator knows everything about the characters, he or she would know exactly what the man did out West. Explain that the absence of these details from the story is a strong example of omniscient narration because this narrator is withholding information for a reason. The man's activities in the West will likely be important to the story later on.

Guided Practice: Apply

Have students review pp. 384–385, looking for other instances in which the omniscient narrator deliberately withholds information.

Think as a Reader/Writer

Find It in Your Reading In the last paragraph on p. 384, the man in the doorway shows his trust and optimism through dialogue.

Use It in Your Writing Have students write a line of dialogue for themselves that reveals something about their personality.

"It's all right, officer," he said reassuringly. "I'm just waiting for a friend. It's an appointment made twenty years ago. Sounds a little funny to you, doesn't it? Well, I'll explain if you'd like to make certain it's all straight. About that long ago there used to be a restaurant where this store stands— 'Big Joe' Brady's restaurant."

"Until five years ago," said the policeman. "It was torn down then."

The man in the doorway struck a match and lit his cigar. The light showed a pale, square-jawed face with keen eyes and a little white scar near his right eyebrow. His scarf pin was a large diamond, oddly set. **D**

"Twenty years ago tonight," said the man, "I dined here at 'Big Joe' Brady's with Jimmy Wells, my best chum and the finest chap in the world. He and I were raised here in New York, just like two brothers, together. I was eighteen and Jimmy was twenty. The next morning I was to start for the West to make my fortune. You couldn't have dragged Jimmy out of New York; he thought it was the only place on earth. Well, we agreed that night that we would meet here again exactly twenty years from that date and time, no matter what our conditions might be or from what distance we might have to come. We figured that in twenty years each of us ought to have our destiny worked out and our fortunes made, whatever they were going to be."

"It sounds pretty interesting," said the policeman. "Rather a long time between

meets, though, it seems to me. Haven't you heard from your friend since you left?"

"Well, yes, for a time we corresponded," said the other. "But after a year or two we lost track of each other. You see, the West is a pretty big proposition, and I kept hustling around over it pretty lively. But I know Jimmy will meet me here if he's alive, for he always was the truest, staunchest old chap in the world. He'll never forget. I came a thousand miles to stand in this door tonight, and it's worth it if my old partner turns up."

The waiting man pulled out a handsome watch, the lids of it set with small diamonds.

"Three minutes to ten," he announced. "It was exactly ten o'clock when we parted here at the restaurant door."

"Did pretty well out West, didn't you?" asked the policeman.

"You bet! I hope Jimmy has done half as well. He was a kind of plodder, though, good fellow as he was. I've had to compete with some of the sharpest wits going to get my pile. A man gets in a groove in New York. It takes the West to put a razor edge on him." **E**

The policeman twirled his club and took a step or two.

"I'll be on my way. Hope your friend comes around all right. Going to call time on him sharp?"

"I should say not!" said the other. "I'll give him half an hour at least. If Jimmy is alive on earth, he'll be here by that time. So long, officer."

D **Reading Focus** **Making Predictions** What might the scar and the large diamond suggest about the man's past?

E **Literary Perspectives** **Analyze Responses to Literature** How does the writer use dialogue and descriptive details to reveal character traits? What is your impression of the man from the West and of Jimmy Wells?

Universal Access

 English Learners

English for Academic Success Students may struggle with some of the words and phrases the narrator uses to describe his characters. Point out that a "stalwart form" is sturdy and firm. Someone who is "staunch" is very loyal, and someone who is "silky" might be seductively charming and very smooth. Remind students that the narrator can provide these detailed descriptions because he is omniscient, or all-knowing.

✔ See UA: **Differentiating Instruction** for lesson plans and strategies for teaching English learners.

Struggling Readers

Tell students that, particularly in stories with omniscient narration, things are not always as they appear. Remind students to look for text clues that foreshadow what will happen next. Guide students in using the description of the man from the West to make a prediction about what kind of person he will turn out to be.

"Good night, sir," said the policeman, passing on along his beat, trying doors as he went.

There was now a fine, cold drizzle falling, and the wind had risen from its uncertain puffs into a steady blow. The few foot passengers astir in that quarter hurried dismally and silently along with coat collars turned high and pocketed hands. And in the door of the hardware store the man who had come a thousand miles to fill an appointment, uncertain almost to absurdity, with the friend of his youth, smoked his cigar and waited.

About twenty minutes he waited, and then a tall man in a long overcoat, with collar turned up to his ears, hurried across from the opposite side of the street. He went directly to the waiting man.

"Is that you, Bob?" he asked, doubtfully.

"Is that you, Jimmy Wells?" cried the man in the door.

"Bless my heart!" exclaimed the new arrival, grasping both the other's hands with his own. "It's Bob, sure as fate. I was certain I'd find you here if you were still in existence. Well, well, well!—twenty years is a long time. The old restaurant's gone, Bob;

Vocabulary **dismally** (DIHZ muh lee) *adv.*: miserably; gloomily.

Analyzing Visuals
Connecting to the Text
How do the images on this page reflect the **mood**, or atmosphere, of the story?

Analyzing Visuals
Connecting to the Text: The image shows a dark, wet, and foggy scene. These characteristics reflect the story's mysterious atmosphere.

Think About/Talk About

▶ Comprehension
Ⓓ Reading Focus
Possible response: The man has a dangerous past through which he acquired a great deal of wealth.

▶ Analysis
Ⓔ Literary Perspectives
Possible response: The man from the West seems friendly and quite devoted to his friend Jimmy, although he seems to think he's a little more talented than Jimmy. He seems a bit egotistical, but not overly so. He says Jimmy is a loyal, honest person who works hard, which gives the reader a positive impression of him.

▶ Extend the Discussion
Characterization At the top of the second column, O. Henry describes the approaching man as wearing a "long overcoat, with collar turned up to his ears." What does this description suggest about him? *Possible response: Although the wind and rain make it logical for the man to be wearing a long coat with a turned-up collar, it also might foreshadow that this man has something to hide from Bob.*

Vocabulary: Own the Word
dismally: You might say, "*Dismal* is the adjective form of the adverb *dismally*. Just as *dismally* means miserably or gloomily, *dismal* means miserable or gloomy. *Dismally* is used to modify verbs by telling how they were performed; the man walked *dismally*. *Dismal* is used to modify nouns by telling what kind; It was a *dismal* day.

Think About/Talk About

▶ Comprehension

ⓕ Reading Focus

Possible response: A friend of Jimmy's or an impostor; he might want something from Bob or be coming after him.

▶ Analysis

ⓖ Literary Focus

Possible response: The omniscient point of view helps convey the theme that betrayal of a friend can be a complicated issue.

ⓗ Literary Perspectives

Possible response: I'm surprised that the policeman at the beginning of the story was actually Jimmy. This was foreshadowed by "Jimmy's" change in appearance.

▶ Extend the Discussion

Omniscient Point of View How might the description of the two men in the fifth full paragraph be different if the narrator were not omniscient? **Possible response:** *The narrator might not be able to tell us about Bob's egotism.*

Vocabulary: Own the Word

• **egotism:** Guide students in creating a semantic web for *egotism*. Have them share words, phrases, and concepts they associate with the meaning of *egotism*. **Possible response:** *arrogant, brag, full of one-self, snobby*

• **simultaneously:** Ask students to name two things they can do *simultaneously*. **Possible response:** *listen to music and do homework*

Monitor Students' Comprehension

Guide the class in answering these true-false questions.

1. Jimmy Wells becomes a police officer. [*T*]

2. Jimmy doesn't show up to meet Bob after twenty years. [*F*]

3. Bob is a wanted criminal. [*T*]

Chapter 4

I wish it had lasted, so we could have had another dinner there. How has the West treated you, old man?"

"Bully;[2] it has given me everything I asked it for. You've changed lots, Jimmy. I never thought you were so tall by two or three inches."

"Oh, I grew a bit after I was twenty."

"Doing well in New York, Jimmy?"

"Moderately. I have a position in one of the city departments. Come on, Bob; we'll go around to a place I know of and have a good long talk about old times."

The two men started up the street, arm in arm. The man from the West, his egotism enlarged by success, was beginning to outline the history of his career. The other, submerged in his overcoat, listened with interest.

At the corner stood a drugstore, brilliant with electric lights. When they came into this glare, each of them turned simultaneously to gaze upon the other's face.

The man from the West stopped suddenly and released his arm.

> When they came into this glare, each of them turned simultaneously to gaze upon the other's face.

---

2. **bully:** informal term meaning "very well."

Vocabulary   egotism (EE guh tihz uhm) *n.:* conceit; talking about oneself too much.
simultaneously (sy muhl TAY nee uhs lee) *adv.:* at the same time.

"You're not Jimmy Wells," he snapped. "Twenty years is a long time, but not long enough to change a man's nose from a Roman to a pug." ⓕ

"It sometimes changes a good man into a bad one," said the tall man. "You've been under arrest for ten minutes, 'Silky' Bob. Chicago thinks you may have dropped over our way and wires us she wants to have a chat with you. Going quietly, are you? That's sensible. Now, before we go to the station, here's a note I was asked to hand to you. You may read it here at the window. It's from Patrolman Wells."

The man from the West unfolded the little piece of paper handed him. His hand was steady when he began to read, but it trembled a little by the time he had finished. The note was rather short. ⓖ

Bob: I was at the appointed place on time. When you struck the match to light your cigar, I saw it was the face of the man wanted in Chicago. Somehow I couldn't do it myself, so I went around and got a plainclothes man to do the job.

Jimmy ⓗ

ⓕ **Reading Focus** **Making Predictions** If the man is not Jimmy Wells, who is he? Why is he there in Jimmy's place?

ⓖ **Literary Focus** **Omniscient Point of View** How does the writer use omniscient point of view to hint at the story's theme?

ⓗ **Literary Perspectives** **Analyze Responses to Literature** Did the resolution of the plot surprise you? Which story events foreshadowed this ending?

 California Standards, pp. 387–389

■ **Reading Standard 1.1** Identify idioms, analogies, metaphors, and similes in prose and poetry.

■ **Reading Standard 3.5** Contrast points of view (e.g., first and third person, limited and omniscient, subjective and objective) in narrative text and explain how they affect the overall theme of the work.

Applying Your Skills

Reading Standard 3.5 Contrast points of view (e.g., first and third **person**, limited and **omniscient**, subjective and objective) in narrative text and explain how they affect the overall theme of the work.

After Twenty Years
Literary Response and Analysis

Reading Skills Focus
Quick Check

1. What does the policeman do after saying good night to the man in the doorway?

Read with a Purpose

2. How do the two old friends' values differ? Why did Jimmy Wells do what he did?

Reading Skills: Making Predictions

3. Review the chart you completed as you read the story. Which of your predictions were correct? What events in the story surprised you?

Story Events	Predictions	Revised Predictions	Outcome

Literary Skills Focus
Literary Analysis

4. **Infer** Why does the police officer need to know if the man in the doorway will wait for his friend? What do you think the officer would have done if the man had said he was leaving exactly at ten o'clock?

5. **Interpret** What actions and details of appearance help reveal the true character of the man in the doorway?

6. **Extend** What would you do in Jimmy's place? How would you support your decision?

7. **Literary Perspectives** A critic said that O. Henry's works reveal "feelings of compassion for the weakness of man." Using examples from this story, explain whether you agree or disagree with this assessment.

Literary Skills: Omniscient Point of View

8. **Extend** O. Henry chose to tell his story from an **omniscient point of view.** What would we have known—and not known—if Bob or Jimmy had told the story from his **first-person point of view**? Given the nature of this story, why do you think O. Henry chose to tell it from the omniscient point of view?

Literary Skills Review: Theme

9. **Interpret** Both men honor their commitment, but Jimmy Wells discovers that he values something more than a long friendship. What theme or themes does the story reveal? How do the details the omniscient narrator shares about Jimmy Wells and his friend affect the theme of the work?

10. **Connect** Have you ever felt betrayed by a friend? How did the betrayal affect your friendship? Explain whether it changed your understanding of your friend's values.

Writing Skills Focus
Think as a Reader/Writer
Use It in Your Writing In "After Twenty Years," O. Henry uses dialogue to reveal character traits in an implicit, or indirect, way. Imagine two characters from a story you'd like to write. Then, write a short dialogue that reveals two character traits of each character.

 What Do You Think Now

How does Jimmy Wells's decision reflect your own values about friendship, duty, and loyalty?

What Do You Think Now?
Encourage students to connect the text to their own lives. How do the story events relate to their own beliefs about loyalty and duty?

Check for Understanding

Independent Practice
Reading Skills Focus
Answers:

1. *He finds a plainclothes policeman to pretend to be Jimmy.*

2. *Both men seem to value the friendship. It is clearly hard for Wells to turn in his friend, and certainly too hard for him to make the arrest.*

3. *I predicted that the policeman was not who he seemed, which is right, but I did not realize who he was.*

Literary Skills Focus
Possible responses:

4. *The police officer needs to know if he has time to put his plan into action. The officer would have arrested him.*

5. *Bob's face, his scar, the diamond, and his quickness to speak to the police officer suggest a sinister nature.*

6. *I'd do the same. Honesty is more important than personal loyalty.*

7. *I agree. O. Henry makes us sympathize with Jimmy's conflict. He knows his friend is a wanted criminal, and wants to do the right thing by arresting him, but he can't bring himself to do it.*

8. *The reader would have known all of the narrating character's thoughts and feelings, but would not have observed the action in the same way and would have miss foreshadowing of the end.*

9. *The theme is that honoring the law outweighs honoring friendship. The omniscient narrator affects the theme by making Bob seem like a man of integrity and Jimmy seem deceitful.*

10. *Being betrayed made me realize that friendships are not always what they seem to be.*

Independent Practice

Vocabulary Development

Vocabulary Check
Possible responses:

1. They speak at the same time.
2. I knitted an *intricate* sweater.
3. They are disappointed.
4. They will like me.
5. Bragging displays *egotism*.

Your Turn

- *deep in thought*—absorbed or extremely thoughtful
- *weathered face*—wrinkled, tough-skinned face
- *broke into a big smile*—smiled
- *left well enough alone*—left something the way it was
- *stuck between a rock and a hard place*—forced to choose between two difficult or unpleasant options

English for Academic Success
Language Coach
Possible responses:

- *impressiveness*—impress, press, impression, unimpressed
- *guardian*—guard, guarding, unguarded
- *correspond*—respond, response
- *reassuringly*—assure, assurance, reassured

English for Academic Success
Academic Vocabulary
Possible response: The narrator <u>perceives</u> Jimmy as having a "stalwart form," implying that Jimmy is an honorable, solid individual. Bob has "keen eyes" and a scar; these descriptions reveal intelligence and an association with danger.

Learn It Online
Holt's **WordSharp: an Interactive Vocabulary Tutor** provides additional support for vocabulary development. Multimedia tutorials show students how to apply vocabulary skills to unfamiliar words—and how to make those words their own.

go.hrw.com | H7-388 | Go

Applying Your Skills

After Twenty Years

Vocabulary Development

Vocabulary Check

1. Describe what happens when two people respond to a question **simultaneously.**
2. Discuss an **intricate** project you have completed.
3. Why might someone sulk **dismally** after a game involving a favorite sports team?
4. If your good behavior is **habitual,** how do you think other people will feel about you?
5. Give an example of behavior that displays a person's **egotism.**

Idioms

An **idiom** is a commonly used expression that is not literally true, such as these examples from "After Twenty Years": *a taste of rain, lost track,* and *gets in a groove.* Idioms are often based on comparisons or images. For example, *gets in a groove* means "becomes comfortable living a certain way," not literally "stuck in an indentation." Most people do not pay attention to the literal meaning of idioms because they make no literal sense.

Your Turn

Idioms Find at least three idioms in the paragraph that follows. Explain the meaning of each idiom.

The officer was deep in thought as he walked his habitual beat. His weathered face broke into a big smile when he saw the man waiting by the building. As the other man stepped from the dark doorway, the officer thought to himself, "I wish he had left well enough alone. Now I'm stuck between a rock and a hard place."

Language Coach
Root Words and Derivatives One way to figure out the meaning of an unfamiliar word is to look for a familiar root word or word part and think about its meaning.

On a separate sheet of paper, create a chart like the one below. For each word in the first column, write related words in the second column. The first one is done for you.

Vocabulary Word	Related Words
egotism	ego, egotistical, egotistically, egocentric
impressiveness	
guardian	
corresponded	
reassuringly	

Academic Vocabulary

Talk About . . .
How do O. Henry's descriptions of the characters Jimmy and Bob help you <u>perceive</u> the two men's values? <u>Analyze</u> the two characters, and discuss your thoughts with a partner.

Learn It Online
For action-packed vocabulary lessons, visit:
go.hrw.com | H7-388 | Go

Universal Access: Vocabulary Development

EL English Learners

English for Academic Success Model completing part of the Your Turn activity on p. 388. After reading aloud the first sentence in the paragraph, say: "The phrase *deep in thought* is an idiom because it is not literally true. The officer is not actually submerged in thought, as one would be in water. It is an expression that means "extremely thoughtful or reflective." Then, pair English learners with native speakers. Have them complete the rest of the Your Turn activity together. Tell

pairs to engage in instructional conversations about the meanings and possible origins of the idioms they identify. After completing the activity, instruct pairs to practice using the idioms by creating their own original sentences containing them. Then, encourage English learners to translate the English idioms into their native languages and share them their partners.

Grammar Link
Prepositional Phrases

A **phrase** is a group of related words that is used as a single part of speech and does not contain both a verb and its subject. A **prepositional phrase** includes a preposition (a word used to show the relationship of a noun or pronoun to another word in the sentence), the object of the preposition (the noun or pronoun that completes the prepositional phrase), and any modifiers (words, phrases, or clauses that make the meaning of a word or word group more specific) of that object. Consider this sentence from "After Twenty Years":

In the doorway of a darkened hardware store a man leaned with an unlighted cigar in his mouth.

This sentence has four prepositional phrases that tell the reader exactly where the man was, what he had, and where he had it. The man was "in the doorway." Where was the doorway? It was part "of a darkened hardware store." What did the man have? He leaned "with an unlighted cigar." Where was the cigar? The cigar was "in his mouth."

Your Turn

Identify the prepositional phrase or phrases in each sentence, and explain the relationship it shows between a noun or pronoun and another word in the sentence.

1. "'I'm just waiting for a friend.'"
2. "The man in the doorway struck a match and lit his cigar."
3. "I was at the appointed place on time."
4. "The two men started up the street, arm in arm."

CHOICES

As you respond to the Choices, use these **Academic Vocabulary** words as appropriate: analyze, narrative, organizational, perceive.

REVIEW
Change the Point of View

Group Discussion In a group, discuss how the narrative might differ if told from Bob's point of view. Imagine Bob telling a fellow prisoner how his friend Jimmy Wells helped arrest him. How would this point of view affect the story's theme? Would it still be about loyalty versus honesty, or would it have a different theme? Explain.

CONNECT
Analyze Literature

Timed └Writing Some readers do not appreciate O. Henry's surprise endings. They claim the endings are implausible, or unlikely to occur in real life. Write a paragraph explaining why you agree or disagree with this opinion. Analyze the ending of "After Twenty Years," and use details from the story to support your opinion.

EXTEND
Offer Advice

Imagine that you write an advice column for your school newspaper and that you receive this letter. What advice would you give?

Last Friday I saw my friend take a wallet that was left in the cafeteria. I know she needs the money because her dad is between jobs. I want to do what's right, but I'm not sure what to do. HELP!

✱ **Learn It Online**
Dig deeper into the story with the Internet links at:
go.hrw.com H7-389 [Go]

Independent Practice
Your Turn

1. for a friend: tells who he is waiting for
2. in the doorway: tells where the man was
3. at the appointed place: tells where he was; on time: tells when he was there
4. up the street: tells where they started

Choices: Evaluation Criteria

Use the following set of criteria to assess students' work.

Review: [Homework]
Change the Point of View
Students should discuss how the narrative and theme might differ.

Connect: Timed Writing
40–50 Minutes
The paragraph should analyze the plausibility of the selection ending.

Extend: [Homework]
Offer Advice
The advice gives a clear and helpful solution to the problem.

Assess

📝 **Chapter 4 Resources,** Selection Standards Check, pp. 9–11

ThinkCentral Online Assessment, Selection Standards Check

💿 **Teacher One Stop™,** editable Selection Standards Check

Reteach

ThinkCentral Online Remediation

✱ **Learn It Online**
Literature Links direct students to prescreened Web sites offering more information related to a selection.

go.hrw.com H7-389

Universal Access: Grammar Link

EL English Learners/ Struggling Readers

English for Academic Success To help students become more familiar with the vocabulary and usage of prepositions, write a "What am I?" riddle that describes an object in your classroom. Use as many prepositional phrases as possible, and underline them. For example: "I hang *above* the chalkboard *in* the center *of* the front wall. Students glance *at* me *throughout* class. My hands move in a circle. What am I?" Ask students to guess the answer to the riddle. [a clock]

AAVE Students Who Use African American Vernacular English

English for Academic Success Some students may place prepositions at the end of sentences in speech and writing or use them when unneeded. For example, "Where is she?" might become "Where's she at?" Explain to students that in formal, academic English, ending sentences with prepositions is avoided.

✔ For more practice with prepositions, see the **Language Handbook Worksheets and GrammarNotes.**

Standards Focus

Objectives

Students will

• understand first-person point of view

• make and evaluate predictions

Motivate

What Do You Think?/QuickWrite

Ask students to discuss their knowledge of, or experiences with, bullying. Have students write in their **Reader/Writer Notebook** about the consequences for the bully and bullied.

English for Academic Success

Academic Vocabulary

Look for opportunities to use the Academic Vocabulary words in this chapter.

• **analyze, v.:** examine in detail.

• **narrative, adj.:** that narrates or recounts; being in story form.

• **organizational, adj.:** pertaining to organization or structure.

• **perceive, v.:** be aware of through the senses; observe.

Analyzing Visuals

Extension Activity Have students discuss the point of view from which this picture was taken. ***Possible response:*** *It looks like this picture was taken from the perspective of the person whose shadow is on the ground.*

California Standards, pp. 390–407

■ **Reading Standard 3.5** Contrast points of view (e.g., first and third person, limited and omniscient, subjective and objective) in narrative text and explain how they affect the overall theme of the work.

Bargain
by **A. B. Guthrie**

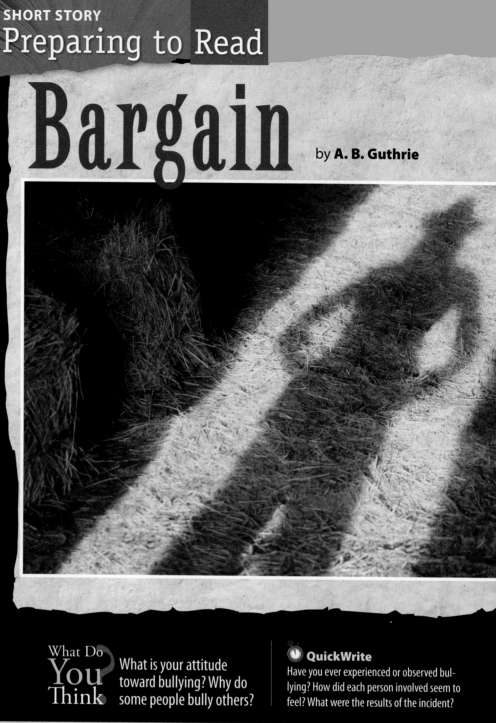

What Do You Think What is your attitude toward bullying? Why do some people bully others?

QuickWrite Have you ever experienced or observed bullying? How did each person involved seem to feel? What were the results of the incident?

Selection Readability	
Easily Accessible Accessible **Challenging**	historical context; difficult vocabulary; challenging theme

Selection Plot Summary

A young boy watches in dismay as his gentle employer, Mr. Baumer, is bullied by a violent man named Slade. The boy is confused and upset when, instead of asking for help, Mr. Baumer hires Slade to work for him. Eventually Slade's own ignorance costs him dearly when he tries to steal alcohol from Mr. Baumer but drinks poison instead.

Reader/Writer Notebook

Use your **RWN** to complete the activities for this selection.

Reading Standard 3.5 Contrast points of view (e.g., **first** and **third person**, limited and omniscient, subjective and objective) **in narrative text and explain how they affect the overall theme of the work.**

Literary Skills Focus

First-Person Point of View When you relate events that happen to you, you speak from the **first-person point of view,** using the pronoun *I*. The story "Bargain" is also told from the first-person point of view. It is told by Al, a character in the story who is about thirteen years old.

When <u>narrative</u> texts are told from the first-person point of view, you learn directly the narrator's thoughts and feelings. Second, you know *only* what the narrator knows. Everything you learn about story events, characters, and other relevant details comes from the way the narrator <u>perceives</u> them.

Reading Skills Focus

Making Predictions The process of trying to guess what will happen next in a story is called **making predictions.** Here is how you do it.

- Look for clues that **foreshadow,** or hint at, what will happen.
- As suspense builds, try to guess where the writer is headed. Draw on your own experience and knowledge.
- Ask yourself questions. Revise your predictions as the writer reveals more information.

Into Action As you read "Bargain," complete a prediction chart like the one below.

Based on (evidence from the story or your own experience)	I Predict...
Slade embarrassed and hurt Mr. Baumer, who teared up.	Slade and Mr. Baumer will have another conflict.

Writing Skills Focus

Think as a Reader/Writer

Find It in Your Reading The first-person point of view reveals the narrator's thoughts. As you read, record examples of the narrator's inner thoughts, and describe what he reveals about himself.

Vocabulary

prodded (PRAHD id) *v.:* urged on, here by poking with a stick. *He prodded the cow to move it out of the road.*

merchandise (MUR chuhn dys) *n.:* items that are for sale in stores. *The store's merchandise included mittens.*

evaporation (ih vap uh RAY shuhn) *n.:* process by which a liquid changes into a gas. *Evaporation was blamed for the missing whiskey.*

thermometer (thuhr MAHM uh tuhr) *n.:* instrument that measures temperature. *The thermometer showed that it was below freezing.*

Language Coach

Context Clues When you encounter an unfamiliar word, context clues can help you unlock its meaning. There is a store in "Bargain" called the Moon Dance Mercantile. To determine the meaning of *mercantile,* look for familiar word parts. *Mercantile* might remind you of the word *merchant.* A merchant is someone who sells goods. *Merchant* and *mercantile* both derive from the Latin word *mercari,* meaning "to trade." What Vocabulary word in the box above is related to this Latin word?

 Learn It Online
Hear a professional actor read this story. Visit the selection online at:

go.hrw.com | H7-391 | **Go**

Selection Resources

Chapter 4 Resources, on-level practice and assessment, pp. 12–17

Teacher One Stop™, on-level lesson plans and all print resources

Holt Audio Library: Selections and Summaries in Spanish

UA: Supporting Instruction in Five Languages, selection summary

Analyzing Visuals Transparencies, p. 34

ThinkCentral Online Assessment, Selection Standards Check

ThinkCentral Online Remediation

Preteach

Introducing Vocabulary

Read aloud the Vocabulary words and sample sentences. Then, use this activity to check students' understanding.

1. What kind of **merchandise** might be found in a department store? [*clothes*]

2. What might happen if you **prodded** a snake? [*It might bite you.*]

3. What happens to a puddle during **evaporation**? [*It dries up.*]

4. What might a **thermometer** read in a hot desert? [*110 degrees*]

English for Academic Success

Language Coach

After students read the Language Coach, guide them in understanding that *merchandise* is related to the Latin word *mercari*. Point out that based on the context clues described for the word mercantile, they should be able to determine that the Moon Dance Mercantile Company is a company that sells or trades goods.

Literary Skills Focus

As you read and discuss the selection with students, have them identify events they learn about through the narrator of the story.

Reading Skills Focus

Give students a copy of the Reading Skills Focus graphic organizer before they read. Tell them to use their responses to answer the questions on the Applying Your Skills page.

Writing Skills Focus

Have students record examples of the narrator's inner thoughts in their **Reader/Writer Notebook**. Students can use their notes to complete the Writing Skills Focus activity.

 Learn It Online
The online version of this selection includes audio support to engage all students and to help struggling readers with reading comprehension and vocabulary.

go.hrw.com | H7-391 | **Go**

Selection Introduction

More About the Writer

"Fiction is love and hate and agreement and conflict and common adventure, not lonely musings on have-beens and might-have-beens," **A.B. Guthrie** writes in his 1965 autobiography, *The Blue Hen's Chick.* Guthrie earned a degree in journalism at the University of Montana. Before becoming a novelist and a screenwriter, he was a journalist. He began as a cub reporter for the Lexington Leader, a newspaper in Kentucky, in 1926. Eventually, he became executive editor.

Think About the Writer

Point out that Guthrie grew up in Montana and worked in both Mexico and California. Have students identify these locations on a map, and ask them to discuss how living in the West during the 20th century might have inspired Guthrie to write historical fiction about the West.

For Independent Reading

■ If students would like to read a nonfiction account of a group's harrowing journey Westward during the 1840s, recommend *The Perilous Journey of the Donner Party* by Marian Calabro.

■ Pamela Conrad's *Prairie Songs* may also be of interest to students who enjoy reading about early settlers in the American West.

A. B. Guthrie
(1901–1991)

Pulitzer Prize WINNER

"Real People in Real Times"

A. B. Guthrie wanted to portray the West as it was, not create myths about it. Most people agree that Guthrie succeeded. His most famous work, a trilogy about the opening of the West, is noted for its historical accuracy. Guthrie also wrote the screenplay for *Shane*—a famous movie about a western gunslinger. Shane takes justice into his own hands to save a family.

Guthrie Grows

Albert Bertram Guthrie, Jr., grew up in the little town of Choteau, Montana. After graduating from college, he traveled extensively and worked at various jobs—ranching in Sonora, Mexico; selling groceries in California; working as a census taker in Montana.

Guthrie became a fiction writer when he took time off from his newspaper job to visit his sick mother. During his visit he had time to write his first novel, *Murders at Moon Dance* (1943). In this book he introduces the setting of "Bargain" and many of his other short stories. Guthrie said about his writing,

"I want to talk about real people in real times. For every Wyatt Earp or Billy the Kid, there were thousands of people just trying to get along."

Think About the Writer What aspects of Guthrie's life prepared him to write about the West?

Build Background

This story takes place in Moon Dance, a town you might recognize as similar to ones portrayed in TV and movie westerns, with a muddy main street, a saloon, and a general store. This story is a kind of **historical fiction.** Setting is important in historical fiction. The writer wants you to feel what it was like to live in a rough frontier town. If you took away Moon Dance and all the historical details, you'd have a different story.

Preview the Selection

Mr. Baumer, one of the story's main characters, is a struggling store owner in a small western town. As the story begins, he and his young sales clerk, **Al,** are walking to the post office to mail customer bills. Mr. Baumer and Al soon run into the story's other main character, a violent bully named **Slade.**

Universal Access

English Learners

To help students make predictions about "Bargain," give them background information about stories set in the American West. Explain that these stories were set in frontier towns during the 1800s, when people from the eastern United States traveled westward in search of land and wealth. In many stories, two characters are involved in an external conflict that is resolved through a dramatic showdown. As they read, have students use this information to make predictions about the story.

Struggling Readers

Benchmark Students Students may find it easier to make predictions about what will happen in a story if they first identify the story's main conflict. Remind students that a story's conflict usually determines the progress of the plot. Once students have determined the conflict, they can predict how the conflict will be resolved. Model this strategy after reading the first page of "Bargain." You might say, "It looks like an external conflict between Mr. Baumer and Slade is developing. I predict that Mr. Baumer will fight back against Slade."

Bargain

by A. B. Guthrie

Mr. Baumer and I had closed the Moon Dance Mercantile Company and were walking to the post office, and he had a bunch of bills in his hand ready to mail. There wasn't anyone or anything much on the street because it was suppertime. A buckboard[1] and a saddle horse were tied at Hirsches' rack, and a rancher in a wagon rattled for home ahead of us, the sound of his going fading out as he prodded his team. Freighter[2] Slade stood alone in front of the Moon Dance Saloon, maybe wondering whether to have one more before going to supper. People said he could hold a lot without showing it except in being ornerier[3] even than usual.

Mr. Baumer didn't see him until he was almost on him, and then he stopped and fingered through the bills until he found the right one. He stepped up to Slade and held it out.

Slade said, "What's this, Dutchie?"

Mr. Baumer had to tilt his head up to talk to him. "You know vat it is."

Slade just said, "Yeah?" You never could tell from his face what went on inside his skull. He had dark skin and shallow cheeks and a thick-growing moustache that fell over the corners of his mouth.

"It is a bill," Mr. Baumer said. "I tell you before, it is a bill. For twenty-vun dollars and fifty cents."

"You know what I do with bills, don't you, Dutchie?" Slade asked.

Mr. Baumer didn't answer the question. He said, "For merchandise."

Slade took the envelope from Mr. Baumer's hand and squeezed it up in his fist and let it drop on the plank sidewalk. Not saying anything, he reached down and took Mr. Baumer's nose between the knuckles of his fingers and twisted it up into his eyes. That was all. That was all at the time. Slade half turned and slouched to the door of

---

1. **buckboard:** open carriage.
2. **freighter:** here, person who transports goods.
3. **ornerier** (AWR nuhr ee uhr): dialect for "meaner and more stubborn."

A Literary Focus First-Person Point of View How can you tell this story is told from the first-person point of view?

Vocabulary prodded (PRAHD id) *v.:* urged on, here by cracking or touching with a whip.
merchandise (MUR chuhn dys) *n.:* items that are for sale in stores.

Model the Skill

■ Provide students with copies of the Reading Focus graphic organizer (See **Chapter 4 Resources**) or ask them to use a piece of their own paper.

■ Remind students that **making predictions** is a strategy that readers use to guess what will happen next in the story. Readers rely largely on the text itself to generate predictions, but might also use their prior knowledge.

■ Model using the graphic organizer to make predictions from a text. You might say, "Based on Mr. Baumer's comment in the third paragraph that 'Is good to know to read and write and figure,' I predict that these skills will be important somehow in the text." Write this prediction in the graphic organizer.

Based on...	I predict...
Mr. Baumer's comment "Is good to know to read and write and figure."	These skills will be important somehow in the text.

Guided Practice: Apply

Three-Minute Review Pause students' reading and have them go back over notes, text, and graphic organizer entries they have read or created so far. Ask them to make one new prediction based on their review and note it in the graphic organizer. Remind students use the graphic organizer to track predictions they make as they read.

the bar and let himself in. Some men were laughing in there. **B**

Mr. Baumer stooped and picked up the bill and put it on top of the rest and smoothed it out for mailing. When he straightened up, I could see tears in his eyes from having his nose screwed around. **C**

He didn't say anything to me, and I didn't say anything to him, being so much younger and feeling embarrassed for him. He went into the post office and slipped the bills in the slot, and we walked on home together. At the last, at the crossing where

I had to leave him, he remembered to say, "Better study, Al. Is good to know to read and write and figure." I guess he felt he had to push me a little, my father being dead.

I said, "Sure. See you after school tomorrow"—which he knew I would anyway. I had been working in the store for him during the summer and after classes ever since pneumonia took my dad off.

Three of us worked there regularly: Mr. Baumer, of course, and me and Colly Coleman, who knew enough to drive the delivery wagon but wasn't much help

B **Reading Focus** Making Predictions What part do you think Slade will play in this story? What makes you say so?

C **Read and Discuss** What does this new information add to the picture you have of Mr. Baumer?

Analyzing Visuals **Connecting to the Text** How does this photograph help you to understand what Mr. Baumer's store was like?

General store (1936). Photograph. ©The Granger Collection, New York.

Cross-Curricular Connection

SOCIAL STUDIES: The General Store
To help students understand the setting of Mr. Baumer's general store, provide them with the following pieces of information:

• The general stores of small rural communities in America, including the Old West town of "Bargain," evolved from the trading posts where early settlers would exchange goods.

• Money was sometimes scarce, so trade at early general stores often occurred through barter.

• These stores carried everything from food and clothing to farming equipment. They were also frequently community gathering places, where shoppers could exchange news, information, and gossip.

• General stores declined in popularity in America in the 1920s.

around the store except for carrying orders out to the rigs[4] at the hitchpost and handling heavy things like the whiskey barrel at the back of the store which Mr. Baumer sold quarts and gallons out of.

The store carried quite a bit of stuff—sugar and flour and dried fruits and canned goods and such on one side and yard goods and coats and caps and aprons and the like of that on the other, besides kerosene and bran and buckets and linoleum and pitchforks in the storehouse at the rear—but it wasn't a big store like Hirsch Brothers up the street. Never would be, people guessed, going on to say, with a sort of slow respect, that it would have gone under long ago if Mr. Baumer hadn't been half mule and half beaver. He had started the store just two years before and, the way things were, worked himself close to death.

He was at the high desk at the end of the grocery counter when I came in the next afternoon. He had an eyeshade on and black sateen protectors on his forearms, and his pencil was in his hand instead of behind his ear and his glasses were roosted on the nose that Slade had twisted. He didn't hear me open and close the door or hear my feet as I walked back to him, and I saw he wasn't doing anything with the pencil but holding it over paper. I stood and studied him for a minute, seeing a small, stooped man with a little paunch bulging through his unbuttoned vest. He was a man you wouldn't remember

from meeting once. There was nothing in his looks to set itself in your mind unless maybe it was his chin, which was a small pink hill in the gentle plain of his face.

While I watched him, he lifted his hand and felt carefully of his nose. Then he saw me. His eyes had that kind of mistiness that seems to go with age or illness, though he wasn't really old or sick, either. He brought his hand down quickly and picked up the pencil, but he saw I still was looking at the nose, and finally he sighed and said, "That Slade."

Just the sound of the name brought Slade to my eye. I saw him slouched in front of the bar, and I saw him and his string[5] coming down the grade from the buttes,[6] the wheel horses held snug and the rest lined out pretty, and then the string leveling off and Slade's whip lifting hair from a horse that wasn't up in the collar.[7] I had heard it said that Slade could make a horse scream with that whip. Slade's name wasn't Freighter, of course. Our town had nicknamed him that because that was what he was.

"I don't think it's any good to send him a bill, Mr. Baumer," I said. "He can't even read."

"He could pay yet."

"He don't pay anybody," I said.

"I think he hate me," Mr. Baumer went on. "That is the thing. He hate me for coming not from this country. I come here,

---

4. **rigs:** carriages with their horses.

5. **string:** here, a group of horses.
6. **buttes** (byoots): steep, flat-topped hills that stand alone on a plain.
7. **up in the collar:** pulling as hard as the other horses.

Analyzing Visuals

Connecting to the Text: *The photograph lets you see what types of goods would have been sold in Mr. Baumer's store, along with the store's atmosphere.*

- Remind students that stories told in **first-person point of view** are told by a character in the story who uses "I" and "me" in narrating the story. Explain to students that first-person narration is limiting for readers because they only know what the narrator knows, and they experience everything only from the narrator's perspective.

- To clarify the nuances of first-person point of view, direct students' attention to the second paragraph of p. 397. Read aloud the sentence, "Up to a point things looked and happened as they had before, so much the same that I had the crazy feeling that I was going through that time again." Tell students that not only is Al, the narrator, telling the story from his perspective with his thoughts and feelings, but he is also providing critical story information that could only be explained by him—that he has the strange feeling this night feels the same as the night of the first fight, and that Mr. Baumer and Slade are going to meet again.

Guided Practice: Apply

Turn and Talk Have students review the story so far and work in pairs to identify occasions when Al takes the reader into his thoughts, feelings, and personal perspective. Ask students to discuss how Al's narration affects the reader's understanding of the story.

---

sixteen years old, and learn to read and write, and I make a business, and so I think he hate me."

"He hates everybody."

Mr. Baumer shook his head. "But not to pinch the nose. Not to call Dutchie."

The side door squeaked open, but it was only Colly Coleman coming in from a trip, so I said, "Excuse me, Mr. Baumer, but you shouldn't have trusted him in the first place."

"I know," he answered, looking at me with his misty eyes. "A man make mistakes. I think some do not trust him, so he will pay me because I do. And I do not know him well then. He only came back to town three, four months ago, from being away since before I go into business." **D**

"People who knew him before could have told you," I said.

"A man make mistakes," he explained again.

"It's not my business, Mr. Baumer, but I would forget the bill."

His eyes rested on my face for a long minute, as if they didn't see me but the problem itself. He said, "It is not twenty-vun dollars and fifty cents now, Al. It is not that anymore."

"What is it?"

He took a little time to answer. Then he brought his two hands up as if to help him shape the words. "It is the thing. You see, it is the thing."

D Read and Discuss Mr. Baumer thought that if he trusted Slade, then Slade would be trustworthy. How does this add to what you know about Mr. Baumer?

E Reading Focus **Making Predictions** What do you think will happen between Mr. Baumer and Slade? Why?

I wasn't quite sure what he meant.

He took his pencil from behind the ear where he had put it and studied the point of it. "That Slade. He steal whiskey and call it evaporation. He sneak things from his load. A thief, he is. And too big for me." **E**

I said, "I got no time for him, Mr. Baumer, but I guess there never was a freighter didn't steal whiskey. That's what I hear."

It was true, too. From the railroad to Moon Dance was fifty miles and a little better—a two-day haul in good weather, heck knew how long in bad. Any freight string bound home with a load had to lie out at least one night. When a freighter had his stock tended to and maybe a little fire going against the dark, he'd tackle a barrel of whiskey or of grain alcohol if he had one aboard consigned to Hirsch Brothers or Mr. Baumer's or the Moon Dance Saloon or the Gold Leaf Bar. He'd drive a hoop out of place, bore a little hole with a nail or bit and draw off what he wanted. Then he'd plug the hole with a whittled peg and pound the hoop back. That was evaporation. Nobody complained much. With freighters you generally took what they gave you, within reason.

"Moore steals it, too," I told Mr. Baumer. Moore was Mr. Baumer's freighter.

"Yah," he said, and that was all, but I stood there for a minute, thinking there might be something more. I could see

---

Vocabulary **evaporation** (ih vap uh RAY shuhn) *n.*: process by which a liquid changes into a gas.

Developing Oral Fluency

Use the long paragraph that begins "It was true, too" on p. 396 to give students the opportunity to practice reading long, complex sentences with appropriate pacing and expression. Tell students that when they read a long sentence aloud, they should pay particular attention to the sentence's punctuation when determining when to pause, slow down, or speed up. Encourage students to read long sentences silently to themselves before attempting to read them aloud.

Whole-Class Activity Lead an echo reading of the paragraph on p. 396 that begins "It was true, too."

- First, have students reread the paragraph quietly to themselves, paying particular attention to the paragraph's commas, periods, and dashes.

- Remind students that punctuation tells a reader when to pause or stop while reading, and allows the reader to break a sentence into separate parts.

- Explain that the dash in the second sentence is similar

thought swimming in his eyes, above that little hill of chin. Then a customer came in, and I had to go wait on him.

Nothing happened for a month, nothing between Mr. Baumer and Slade, that is, but fall drew on toward winter and the first flight of ducks headed south and Mr. Baumer hired Miss Lizzie Webb to help with the just-beginning Christmas trade and here it was, the first week in October, and he and I walked up the street again with the monthly bills. He always sent them out. I guess he had to. A bigger store, like Hirsches', would wait on the ranchers until their beef or wool went to market.

Up to a point things looked and happened almost the same as they had before, so much the same that I had the crazy feeling I was going through that time again. There was a wagon and a rig tied up at Hirsches' rack and a saddle horse standing hipshot[8] in front of the harness shop. A few more people were on the street now, not many, and lamps had been lit against the shortened day.

It was dark enough that I didn't make out Slade right away. He was just a figure that came out of the yellow wash of light from the Moon Dance Saloon and stood on the boardwalk and with his head made the little motion of spitting. Then I recognized the lean, raw shape of him and the muscles flowing down into the sloped shoulders, and in the settling darkness I filled the pic-

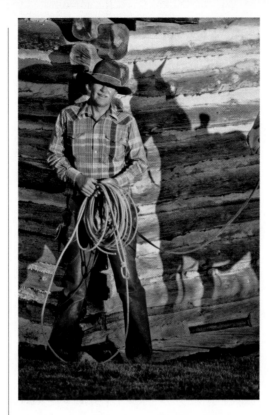

ture in—the dark skin and the flat cheeks and the peevish eyes and the moustache growing rank.

There was Slade and here was Mr. Baumer with his bills and here I was, just as before, just like in the second go-round of a bad dream. I felt like turning back, being embarrassed and half scared by trouble even when it wasn't mine. Please, I said to myself, don't stop, Mr. Baumer! Don't bite off anything! Please, shortsighted the way you are, don't catch sight of him at all!

---

8. **hipshot:** with one hip lower than the other.

F | Read and Discuss | What do you think Mr. Baumer believes about his chances of getting paid by or defending himself against Slade?

---

to a colon, and should be accompanied by a brief pause when reading.

• Emphasize that lengthy sentences with multiple uses of the words "and" or "or," as seen in sentence 4, should be read slowly to avoid confusion.

• Read each sentence aloud, slowly and with appropriate expression. Then ask students to repeat each sentence chorally, echoing your pacing and expression.

✔ **UA: Differentiating Instruction,** for practice passages for developing oral fluency.

Think About/Talk About

▶ **Comprehension**

D **Read and Discuss**
Possible response: Mr. Baumer believes that people are good and return respect when they are respected.

E **Reading Focus**
Possible response: I think that Mr. Baumer will teach Slade a lesson about being trustworthy. Mr. Baumer is tired of being bullied.

F **Read and Discuss**
Possible response: It doesn't seem as though Mr. Baumer thinks he has much of a chance against Slade. He says Slade is too big for him.

▶ **Extend the Discussion**

Making Inferences At the end of the first column on p. 396, Mr. Baumer explains that his conflict with Slade is not about money anymore; "it is the thing." What do you think Mr. Baumer means by this?
Possible response: I think he means that he doesn't care as much about getting his money as about being treated with tolerance and respect. To Mr. Baumer, losing money isn't as painful as experiencing injustice.

Analyzing In the paragraph on p. 397 that begins "It was dark enough…," Al describes seeing Slade. How does this imagery affect your perception of Slade? *Possible response:* Al describes Slade as "lean" and "raw" with "muscles flowing down into the sloped shoulders." This makes Slade seem like an intimidating, unattractive, and volatile person.

Vocabulary: Own the Word

evaporation: Tell students that water *vapor* is the gaseous form of liquid water. Then, explain that the suffix *–ion* means "act or process." Help students understand make the connection between the word parts and the meaning of *evaporation,* "the process by which liquid changes into a gas." In this context, evaporation does not actually occur. The freighter steals some of the whiskey—thus it "evaporates."

- Remind students that readers **make and evaluate predictions** as they read a text to help them stay engaged in what they are reading.

- Model making and evaluating predictions in a text using p. 398. Begin reading aloud at the beginning of the page. Stop and point out that, in the first paragraph, the narrator describes his hope that Mr. Baumer and Slade do not see each other. Based on this foreshadowing, a reader might predict that Mr. Baumer will start a dispute with Slade over the bill.

- Continue reading, stopping in the second column at "You look, Al," to note that your prediction was just proven right—that Mr. Baumer is looking for the bill to try to get Slade to pay up. Tell students that, based on what happened last time, you think there will be another fight.

Guided Practice: Apply

Have students continue reading and record any lines that they think they have information that will confirm or refute your prediction of another fight. Have students make a prediction of their own to note in their graphic organizers and evaluate as they continue to read.

I held up and stepped around behind Mr. Baumer and came up on the outside so as to be between him and Slade, where maybe I'd cut off his view.

But it wasn't any use. All along I think I knew it was no use, not the praying or the walking between or anything. The act had to play itself out.

Mr. Baumer looked across the front of me and saw Slade and hesitated in his step and came to a stop. Then in his slow, business way, his chin held firm against his mouth, he began fingering through the bills, squinting to make out the names. Slade had turned and was watching him, munching on a cud of tobacco like a bull waiting.

"You look, Al," Mr. Baumer said without lifting his face from the bills. "I cannot see so good."

So I looked, and while I was looking, Slade must have moved. The next I knew, Mr. Baumer was staggering ahead, the envelopes spilling out of his hands. There had been a thump, the clap of a heavy hand swung hard on his back.

Slade said, "Haryu, Dutchie?"

Mr. Baumer caught his balance and turned around, the bills he had trampled shining white between them and at Slade's feet the hat that Mr. Baumer had stumbled out from under.

G **Literary Focus** First-Person Point of View   How do Al's inner thoughts tell you his feelings about Mr. Baumer?

Universal Access

EL English Learners

English for Academic Success

- Direct students' attention to the following simile: "Slade had turned and was watching him, munching on a cud of tobacco like a bull waiting" (p. 398).

- Then, draw a Venn diagram on the board, with "Slade" as the title for the left column and "Bull" as the title for the right column. Work with students to fill in the right and left columns of the diagram (*Slade: man, talks; Bull: animal, grunts*), before focusing on the center, shared column.

- Ask students to provide adjectives that could describe both a bull and Slade (*mean, aggressive, violent*), and explain that this is the purpose of a simile: to compare two seemingly unlike things. Repeat this process with another simile from the text.

Struggling Readers

To check students' understanding of the story's point of view, ask them to identify both objective and subjective details on p. 399. Guide them in understanding that objective details include Al's simple recounting of events, such as the approach of Angus McDonald and Dr. King.

Slade picked up the hat and scuffed through the bills and held it out. "Cold to be goin' without a skypiece," he said. **H**

Mr. Baumer hadn't spoken a word. The lampshine from inside the bar caught his eyes, and in them, it seemed to me, a light came and went as anger and the uselessness of it took turns in his head.

Two men had come up on us and stood watching. One of them was Angus McDonald, who owned the Ranchers' Bank, and the other was Dr. King. He had his bag in his hand.

Two others were drifting up, but I didn't have time to tell who. The light came in Mr. Baumer's eyes, and he took a step ahead and swung. I could have hit harder myself. The fist landed on Slade's cheek without hardly so much as jogging his head, but it let the devil loose in the man. I didn't know he could move so fast. He slid in like a practiced fighter and let Mr. Baumer have it full in the face. **I**

Mr. Baumer slammed over on his back, but he wasn't out. He started lifting himself. Slade leaped ahead and brought a boot heel down on the hand he was lifting himself by. I heard meat and bone under that heel and saw Mr. Baumer fall back and try to roll away.

Things had happened so fast that not until then did anyone have a chance to get between them. Now Mr. McDonald pushed

H Read and Discuss What is happening here?

I **Literary Focus** First-Person Point of View How does knowing Al's thoughts affect the way you perceive events?

Subjective details include Al's feelings and opinions, such as his description of Mr. Baumer's eyes in the first column: "it seemed to me, a light came and went [in his eyes] as anger and the uselessness of it took turns in his head."

AAVE Students Who Use African American Vernacular English

English for Academic Success Point out the following sentence in the first paragraph on p. 399: "Cold to be goin' without a skypiece," he said. Explain to students that in casual situations, it is common for speakers to delete the pronunciation of the final *g* in present participles, such as *going, having,* and *leaving,* which may become *goin', havin',* and *leavin',* respectively. Point out that this dialogue thus reflects natural, realistic speech patterns and rhythms. Point out that this contrasts with the patterns used in formal, academic English. Have students practice saying the "ing" words in formal English by creating sentences and repeating them orally with a partner.

Think About/Talk About

▶ Comprehension

H Read and Discuss

Possible response: As Mr. Baumer prepares to give Slade his bill, Slade seems eager to have another confrontation with him.

▶ Analysis

G Literary Focus

Possible response: Al cares about Mr. Baumer a great deal and doesn't want him to get hurt.

I Literary Focus

Possible response: Al is horrified by the fight and afraid for Mr. Baumer's safety, which causes me to sympathize with Mr. Baumer.

▶ Extend the Discussion

Making Judgments In the first full paragraph on p. 398, Al says that trying to step between Mr. Baumer and Slade would be "no use" because "the act had to play itself out." Do you agree with Al's belief that nothing could be done to prevent Slade's confrontation with Mr. Baumer? Why or why not? **Possible response:** I think that if enough of the people from town had been around to prevent Slade from attacking Mr. Baumer, they could have solved the situation temporarily, but I agree with the narrator that a fight between Slade and Mr. Baumer seems inevitable.

Model the Skill

- Point out that some English words have related roots and meanings. Understanding the meaning of one word can help a reader identify and figure out the meaning of a related, unfamiliar word. This is called using **context clues.**

- Point out the word *post* as used in *post office* on p. 400 and *posting* on p. 401. *Post,* as in *post office,* refers to items of mail, such as letters. *Posting,* as it is used on p. 401, refers to mailing bills. Both *post* and *posting* contain the root word *post,* and are related to mail, which puts them in the same word family. Other members of this word family would be *postal, postage,* and *postcard.*

Guided Practice: Apply

Have students work in groups to research words in the same families as *robbing, rounding,* and *draining.*

Think as a Reader/Writer

Find It in Your Reading Point out how, at the top of column 2 on p. 400, Al laments that there seems to be "no getting the best of" Slade. This statement highlights Al's loyalty to Mr. Baumer and his desire for Slade to face justice.

Use It in Your Writing Tell students to imagine themselves in Al's place. Have them write a few sentences expressing their feelings about the situation between Mr. Baumer and Slade.

Freighter. That's enough, now," and Dr. King lined up, too, and another man I didn't know, and I took a place, and we formed a kind of screen between them. Dr. King turned and bent to look at Mr. Baumer.

"Fool hit me first," Slade said.

"That's enough," Mr. McDonald told him again while Slade looked at all of us as if he'd spit on us for a nickel. Mr. McDonald went on, using a half-friendly tone, and I knew it was because he didn't want to take Slade on any more than the rest of us did. "You go on home and sleep it off, Freighter. That's the ticket."

Slade just snorted.

From behind us, Dr. King said, "I think you've broken this man's hand."

"Lucky for him I didn't kill him," Slade answered. "Dutch penny pincher!" He fingered the chew out of his mouth. "Maybe he'll know enough to leave me alone now."

Dr. King had Mr. Baumer on his feet. "I'll take him to the office," he said.

Blood was draining from Mr. Baumer's nose and rounding the curve of his lip and dripping from the sides of his chin. He held his hurt right hand in the other. But the thing was that he didn't look beaten even then, not the way a man who has given up looks beaten. Maybe that was why Slade said, with a show of that fierce anger, "You stay away from me! Hear? Stay clear away, or you'll get more of the same!" **J**

Dr. King led Mr. Baumer away, Slade went back into the bar, and the other men walked off, talking about the fight. I got down and picked up the bills, because I knew Mr. Baumer would want me to, and mailed them at the post office, dirty as they were. It made me sorer, someway, that Slade's bill was one of the few that wasn't marked up. The cleanness of it seemed to say that there was no getting the best of him.

Mr. Baumer had his hand in a sling the next day and wasn't much good at waiting on the trade. I had to hustle all afternoon and so didn't have a chance to talk to him even if he had wanted to talk. Mostly he stood at his desk, and once, passing it, I saw he was practicing writing with his left hand. His nose and the edges of the cheeks around it were swollen some.

At closing time I said, "Look, Mr. Baumer, I can lay out of school a few days until you kind of get straightened out here."

"No," he answered as if to wave the subject away. "I get somebody else. You go to school. Is good to learn."

I had a half notion to say that learning hadn't helped him with Slade. Instead, I blurted out that I would have the law on Slade. **K**

"The law?" he asked.

"The sheriff or somebody."

"No, Al," he said. "You would not."

I asked why.

"The law, it is not for plain fights," he said. "Shooting? Robbing? Yes, the law come quick. The plain fights, they are too many. They not count enough."

He was right. I said, "Well, I'd do something anyhow."

"Yes," he answered with a slow nod of

J | **Reading Focus** | Making Predictions What clues suggest that Baumer will not give up?

K | **Read and Discuss** What does this conversation tell you?

Word-Attack Skills Mini-Lesson

Adding Suffixes to Words Ending in –y
English for Academic Success

- Display the selection word *ornerier.* Help students analyze the word as the base word *ornery* plus the comparative ending *–er.*

- Remind students that when suffixes and endings are added to words that end with *y,* the *y* changes to *i.* Recalling this can help them pronounce and decode words.

- Then, write the words *mistiness* and *business* on the chalkboard and have students compare their pronunciations.

- *Mistiness* sounds like the base word *misty* plus *–ness:* /mis′tē•nis/. *Business* is the combination of *busy* and *–ness,* but its pronunciation and meaning have changed over time. The second vowel in *business* is not pronounced: /biz′nis/, and the word has come to mean "work" or "responsibility" instead of "the state of being busy." Share the fact that the word *busyness* (bis′ē•nis) was coined to cover that meaning.

---

his head. "Something you vould do, Al." He didn't tell me what.

Within a couple of days he got another man to clerk for him—it was Ed Hempel, who was always finding and losing jobs—and we made out. Mr. Baumer took his hand from the sling in a couple or three weeks, but with the tape on it, it still wasn't any use to him. From what you could see of the fingers below the tape, it looked as if it never would be.

He spent most of his time at the high desk, sending me or Ed out on the errands he used to run, like posting and getting the mail. Sometimes I wondered if that was because he was afraid of meeting Slade. He could just as well have gone himself. He wasted a lot of hours just looking at nothing, though I will have to say he worked hard at learning to write left-handed.

Then, a month and a half before Christmas, he hired Slade to haul his freight for him. **L**

Ed Hempel told me about the deal when I showed up for work. "Yessir," he said, resting his foot on a crate in the storeroom where we were supposed to be working. "I tell you he's throwed in with Slade. Told me this morning to go out and locate him if I could and bring him in. Slade was at the saloon, o' course, and says to the devil with Dutchie, but I told him this was honest-to-God business, like Baumer had told me to, and there was a quart of whiskey right there in the store for him if he'd come and get it. He was out of money, I reckon, because the quart fetched him."

"What'd they say?" I asked him.

"Search me. There was two or three people in the store and Baumer told me to wait on 'em, and he and Slade palavered[9] back by the desk."

"How do you know they made a deal?"

Ed spread his hands out. "'Bout noon, Moore came in with his string, and I heard Baumer say he was makin' a change. Moore didn't like it too good, either."

It was a hard thing to believe, but there one day was Slade with a pile of stuff for the Moon Dance Mercantile Company, and that was proof enough with something left for boot.

Mr. Baumer never opened the subject up with me, though I gave him plenty of chances. And I didn't feel like asking. He didn't talk much these days but went around absent-minded, feeling now and then of the fingers that curled yellow and stiff out of the bandage like the toes on the leg of a dead chicken. Even on our walks home he kept his thoughts to himself.

---

9. palavered (puh LAV uhrd): talked; met to discuss something.

L Read and Discuss | Why do you think Mr. Baumer has hired Slade?

Activity Display these words. Have students identify the base word and the suffix or ending.

1. worrisome [*worry* + *–some*]
2. compliance [*comply* + *–ance*]
3. craziness [*crazy* + *–ness*]
4. easiness [*easy* + *–ness*]
5. silliness [*silly* + *–ness*]
6. hardiness [*hardy* + *–ness*]
7. pettiness [*petty* + *–ness*]
8. seemliness [*seemly* + *–ness*]
9. heaviness [*heavy* + *–ness*]
10. heartiest [*hearty* + *–est*]
11. happiness [*happy* + *–ness*]
12. readiness [*ready* + *–ness*]
13. reliant [*rely* + *–ant*]
14. wearisome [*weary* + *–some*]

Think About/Talk About

▶ Comprehension

J **Reading Focus**

Possible response: He doesn't look beaten.

K **Read and Discuss**

Possible response: Mr. Baumer thinks Al's education is more important than his own struggles. Al thinks education won't help Mr. Baumer in his battle against Slade.

L **Read and Discuss**

Possible response: Mr. Baumer either has a new plan to get his money or revenge, or he's trying his old plan of showing respect to gain respect.

▶ Extend the Discussion

Characterization In the second full paragraph on p. 401, Al mentions that Mr. Baumer "wasted a lot of hours just looking at nothing." Given what you know about Mr. Baumer, what do you think he is doing?

Possible response: Mr. Baumer may be trying to think of a plan to get Slade to pay him back. Earlier in the story, he seemed set on making Slade pay the bill even when Al recommended he forget about it.

- Tell students that a **first-person** narrator can give readers emotional cues that lead them to share the narrator's feelings and reactions.

- Have a volunteer read aloud the paragraph starting with "I felt different…" Point out that Al used to think of Mr. Baumer as a father figure, having lost his own father not long ago. Contrast this with Al's new feelings towards Mr. Baumer—sore, angry, not understanding his decision to hire Slade. Most importantly, he has lost respect for his employer. Al's negative feelings towards Mr. Baumer at this point in the story suggest to the reader that Mr. Baumer's actions are illogical and possibly foolish and lead the reader to question Mr. Baumer's motives as Al does.

Guided Practice: Apply

Have students review the story and think about how Al's feelings towards Mr. Baumer have evolved—from respect, to sympathy, to doubt. Ask them to use what they learned from Al to think about how Al and Mr. Baumer's relationship will turn out at the end of the story. Have students write two or three sentences predicting how Al will feel about Mr. Baumer at the end of the story.

I felt different about him now and was sore inside. Not that I blamed him exactly. A hundred and thirty-five pounds wasn't much to throw against two hundred. And who could tell what Slade would do on a bellyful of whiskey? He had promised Mr. Baumer more of the same, hadn't he? But I didn't feel good. I couldn't look up to Mr. Baumer like I used to and still wanted to. I didn't have the beginning of an answer when men cracked jokes or shook their heads in sympathy with Mr. Baumer, saying Slade had made him come to time. Ⓜ

Slade hauled in a load for the store, and another, and Christmastime was drawing on and trade heavy, and the winter that had started early and then pulled back came on again. There was a blizzard and then a still cold and another blizzard and afterwards a sunshine that was iceshine on the drifted snow. I was glad to be busy, selling overshoes and sheep-lined coats and mitts and socks as thick as saddle blankets and Christmas candy out of buckets and hickory nuts and the fresh oranges that the people in our town never saw except when Santa Claus was coming.

One afternoon, when I lit out from class, the thermometer on the school porch read forty-two degrees below. But you didn't have to look at it to know how cold the weather was. Your nose and fingers and toes and ears and the bones inside you told you. The snow cried when you stepped on it.

I got to the store and took my things off and scuffed my hands at the stove for a minute so's to get life enough in them to tie a parcel. Mr. Baumer—he was always polite to me—said, "Hello, Al. Not so much to do today. Too cold for customers." He shuddered a little, as if he hadn't got the chill off even yet, and rubbed his broken hand with the good one. "Ve need Christmas goods," he said, looking out the window to the furrows that wheels had made in the snow-banked street, and I knew he was thinking of Slade's string, inbound from the railroad, and the time it might take even Slade to travel those hard miles.

Slade never made it at all.

Less than an hour later our old freighter, Moore, came in, his beard white and stiff with frost. He didn't speak at first but looked around and clumped to the stove and took off his heavy mitts, holding his news inside him.

Then he said, not pleasantly, "Your new man's dead, Baumer."

"My new man?" Mr. Baumer said.

"Who do you think? Slade. He's dead."

All Mr. Baumer could say was "Dead!"

"Froze to death, I figger," Moore told him, while Colly Coleman and Ed Hempel and Miss Lizzie and I and a couple of customers stepped closer.

"Not Slade," Mr. Baumer said. "He know too much to freeze."

"Maybe so, but he sure's froze now. I got him in the wagon."

We stood looking at one another and at Moore. Moore was enjoying his news, enjoying feeding it out bit by bit so's to hold the stage. "Heart might've give out, for all I know."

Ⓜ **Literary Focus** First-Person Point of View How can you tell Al's view of Baumer has changed?

Vocabulary **thermometer** (thuhr MAHM uh tuhr) *n.*: instrument that measures temperature.

Cross-Curricular Connection

HISTORY: Westward Expansion

- During the 1800s, hundreds of thousands of Americans emigrated from the eastern United States to the American West.

- Between 1804 and 1806, Merriweather Lewis and William Clark led a government expedition of nearly fifty men from St. Louis to the Pacific Ocean and back. The group traveled almost 8,000 miles and kept journals that recorded the many types of plants and animals they discovered.

- Between 1848 and 1850, thousands of people traveled to California following the discovery of gold in 1848. Some traveled nearly 2,000 miles and risked death from disease or Native American groups who resisted settlement. Most people never became rich from the hard work.

- The Oregon Trail became a popular route to the Northwest in the 1840's. Starting in Missouri and ending in Oregon, the trail was around 2,000 miles long and usually took four to six months to complete.

Analyzing Visuals **Connecting to the Text** How does this photograph of an Old West town help you visualize Guthrie's setting?

The side door swung open, letting in a cloud of cold and three men who stood, like us, waiting on Moore. I moved a little and looked through the window and saw Slade's freight outfit tied outside with more men around it. Two of them were on a wheel of one of the wagons, looking inside.

"Had a extra man, so I brought your stuff in," Moore went on. "Figgered you'd be glad to pay for it."

"Not Slade," Mr. Baumer said again.

"You can take a look at him."

Mr. Baumer answered no.

"Someone's takin' word to Connor to

Think About/Talk About

▶ **Analysis**

Ⓜ **Literary Focus**

Possible response: Al feels sorry and embarrassed for Mr. Baumer. He no longer feels deep respect and admiration for Mr. Baumer because he thinks that Mr. Baumer has given in to Slade.

▶ **Extend the Discussion**

Point of View What role do Al's thoughts and feelings in the first paragraph on p. 402 play in the story? How do they affect the story's plot, mood, or theme? *Possible response:* Since Al feels upset about Mr. Baumer, his thoughts and feelings cause the mood of the story to darken. They make Mr. Baumer's situation seem more drastic, which causes me to worry that Mr. Baumer's conflict with Slade will not end happily.

Key Details What details from the first column of p. 402 let you know just how cold the weather is? *Possible response:* The thermometer reads 42 degrees below zero; the snow "cried" when stepped on; the townspeople feel the cold in their "nose and fingers and toes and ears and the bones inside."

Vocabulary: Own the Word

thermometer: Ask students to describe what they might wear if the *thermometer* read 20 degrees Fahrenheit. *Possible response:* warm coat, hat, and gloves.

• Although stop points for rest and supplies were established along the route, dangers such as disease were a common problem.

Activity Have students choose one of the following subtopics related to Westward Expansion: the expedition of Lewis and Clark; the Oregon Trail; the California Gold Rush. Tell students to find one good image from a book or article about their subtopic and to write a short explanation of what is happening in the image.

 HSS Analysis Skills: CS 1, 3 HR 4

Analyzing Visuals
Connecting to the Text: The photograph helps me visualize the ruggedness and isolation of Guthrie's setting.

▶ Comprehension

 Read and Discuss

Possible response: *Slade was stealing from Mr. Baumer, not realizing that it was poisonous wood alcohol he was drinking and not whisky. Slade died after drinking the poison.*

▶ Extend the Discussion

Point of View What does Al's observation of Mr. Baumer's eyes in the last paragraph suggest? What might Al think about Mr. Baumer? ***Possible response:*** *By telling us about what he saw in Mr. Baumer's eyes, Al might be suggesting that Mr. Baumer is happy about Slade's death or that Mr. Baumer was directly responsible for Slade's poisoning.*

Monitor Students' Comprehension

Guide the class in answering these comprehension questions.

1. Why does Al tell Mr. Baumer to forget about the bill? [*He knows Slade is dangerous.*]

2. What happens after Mr. Baumer confronts Slade a second time? [*Slade beats him up.*]

3. Why does Slade drink the wood alcohol? [*He thinks it is liquor.*]

---

bring his hearse. Anyhow, I told 'em to. I carted old Slade this far. Connor can have him now."

Moore pulled on his mitts. "Found him there by the Deep Creek crossin', doubled up in the snow an' his fire out." He moved toward the door. "I'll see to the horses, but your stuff'll have to set there. I got more'n enough work to do at Hirsches.'"

Mr. Baumer just nodded.

I put on my coat and went out and waited my turn and climbed on a wagon wheel and looked inside, and there was Slade piled on some bags of bran. Maybe because of being frozen, his face was whiter than I ever saw it, whiter and deader, too, though it never had been lively. Only the moustache seemed still alive, sprouting thick like greasewood from alkali.[10] Slade was doubled up all right, as if he had died and stiffened leaning forward in a chair.

> "Found him there by the Deep Creek crossin', doubled up in the snow an' his fire out."

I got down from the wheel, and Colly and then Ed climbed up. Moore was unhitching, tossing off his pieces of information while he did so. Pretty soon Mr. Connor came up with his old hearse, and he and Moore tumbled Slade into it, and the team, which was as old as the hearse, made

---

10. **greasewood from alkali:** Greasewood is a thorny desert plant. Alkali is dry, salty soil that can look white and chalky, like Slade's face.

 Read and Discuss What has happened to Slade?

---

off, the tires squeaking in the snow. The people trailed on away with it, their breaths leaving little ribbons of mist in the air. It was beginning to get dark.

Mr. Baumer came out of the side door of the store, bundled up, and called to Colly and Ed and me. "We unload," he said. "Already is late. Al, better you get a couple lanterns now."

We did a fast job, setting the stuff out of the wagons onto the platform and then carrying it or rolling it on the one truck that the store owned and stowing it inside according to where Mr. Baumer's good hand pointed.

A barrel was one of the last things to go in. I edged it up and Colly nosed the truck under it, and then I let it fall back. "Mr. Baumer," I said, "we'll never sell all this, will we?"

"Yah," he answered. "Sure we sell it. I get it cheap. A bargain, Al, so I buy it."

I looked at the barrel head again. There in big letters I saw "Wood Alcohol—Deadly Poison."

"Hurry now," Mr. Baumer said. "Is late." For a flash and no longer I saw through the mist in his eyes, saw, you might say, that hilly chin repeated there. "Then ve go home, Al. Is good to know to read."

🐻 **California Standards, pp. 405–407**

- **Reading Standard 1.1** Identify idioms, analogies, metaphors, and similes in prose and poetry.
- **Reading Standard 3.5** Contrast points of view (e.g., first and third person, limited and omniscient, subjective and objective) in narrative text and explain how they affect the overall theme of the work.

Applying Your Skills

Reading Standard 3.5 Contrast points of view (e.g., **first** and third **person**, limited and omniscient, subjective and objective) in narrative text, and explain how they affect the overall theme of the work.

Bargain

Literary Response and Analysis

Reading Skills Focus
Quick Check

1. Why does Mr. Baumer have problems with Slade?

2. Why does Mr. Baumer say at the end, "Is good to know to read"?

Read with a Purpose

3. **Interpret** Explain whether this story is about justice or about revenge.

Reading Skills: Making Predictions

4. Review the Prediction Chart you filled in while reading. Add a column labeled "I Was," and write "correct" or "incorrect" next to each prediction, showing whether or not that prediction was correct.

Based on . . .	I Predict . . .	I Was . . .
Slade embarrassed and hurt Mr. Baumer, who teared up.	Slade and Mr. Baumer will have another conflict.	Correct

Literary Skills Focus
Literary Analysis

5. **Analyze** Who do you think is responsible for Slade's death—Mr. Baumer or Slade himself? Give reasons to support your view.

6. **Interpret** When Al suggests that Mr. Baumer forget Slade's bill, Mr. Baumer says it isn't about the money anymore; it is "the thing." What is the implicit meaning of "the thing"?

7. **Interpret** Why do you think Guthrie titled this <u>narrative</u> "Bargain"? What are the bargains, and who benefits from them?

8. **Analyze** What are Slade's two fundamental weaknesses? How does each contribute to his downfall?

9. **Extend** Explain whether you would keep silent about the cause of Slade's death if you were in Al's situation.

Literary Skills: First-Person Point of View

10. **Interpret** "Bargain" is written from the **first-person point of view,** from Al's vantage point. What would you have known if Mr. Baumer had told the story himself? Would the story's theme be different with a new narrator? If so, what might the new theme be?

Literary Skills Review: Foreshadowing

11. **Interpret** A writer helps you predict future events by including clues that foreshadow future events. Give two examples of events in "Bargain" that foreshadow the end of the story.

Writing Skills Focus
Think as a Reader/Writer

Use It in Your Writing Review the notes about the narrator's inner thoughts that you recorded. What do your notes reveal about Al's response to events? How are his thoughts relevant to the action in the story? Write a paragraph in which you <u>analyze</u> the way Al's thoughts affected your perception of events and characters.

 What Do **You Think Now**

How has "Bargain" affected your attitude toward bullying?

Universal Access

Struggling Writers

Provide additional scaffolding for the Writing Focus activity by reminding students that to *analyze* something means "to examine in detail." Tell students that asking themselves the questions *how?* and *why?* can help them begin the process of analysis. Model doing so in response to the Writing Focus prompt. For example, you might say, "I'm supposed to analyze the way Al's thoughts affected my perception of events and characters. The first question I'll ask myself is *How did Al's thoughts affect my perception of events and characters?* One way is that I felt sorry for Mr. Baumer at the beginning. Then, I ask myself *Why did I feel sorry for Mr. Baumer?* I felt sorry for him because Al presented him as a hardworking, honorable man who was the victim of Slade's cruelties." Tell students to continue to ask themselves *how?* and *why?* as they draft their paragraphs.

Vocabulary Development

Your Turn _____

1. *b*

2. *a*

3. *d*

4. *c*

English for Academic Success

Language Coach

Provide the following sentence and ask students to use context clues to determine the meaning of the word *depraved: Slade was a depraved man who stole from others without a second thought.* Guide students in understanding that the context of the sentence, which describes Slade as a thief without a conscience, can help them determine that depraved means "dishonest or immoral."

English for Academic Success

Academic Vocabulary

Possible response: When I <u>analyze</u> the <u>narrative</u>, it becomes clear that Al is a caring, loyal person. He believes in honesty and doing the right thing. He likes Mr. Baumer and dislikes the way Slade treats him. I would use the <u>organizational</u> method of topical paragraphs to discuss and describe each character trait.

Applying Your Skills

Bargain

Vocabulary Development

Putting Analogies to Work

An **analogy** (uh NAL uh jee) is a point-by-point comparison of two things to show how they are alike. In the story you just read, Mr. Baumer could tell Al that learning to read is like a lifesaver. Here are two other examples of analogies:

- To people in the nineteenth century, a country store was like the Internet is today. Both places enable people of their respective time periods to get anything they need that's available for sale.

- Mr. Baumer's broken fingers are like "the toes on the leg of a dead chicken." They are alike in color and feel, and both are useless.

Your Turn _____

Form an analogy by matching the phrases in column A with the phrases and sentences in column B. Then, think of two new analogies for two of the Vocabulary words.

> merchandise
> prodded
> evaporation
> thermometer

Column A	Column B
1. Being **prodded** to clean your room is like	**a.** reading your own diary. Both tell what you already know.
2. When you have a fever, taking your temperature with a **thermometer** is like	**b.** having a tooth drilled. You may not like either, but you are better off once each is done.
3. **Merchandise** in a store is like	**c.** a dead tree in a forest. You may not notice either until a lot is gone.
4. The slow **evaporation** of water in a lake is like	**d.** dessert on a high shelf. Both may be desirable and out of reach.

Language Coach

Context Clues Looking at context clues—the words and sentences surrounding a word—can help you identify a word's meaning. For example, if a friend said, "I consigned my old bike to be sold at the bicycle store; they sold it for fifty dollars and gave me thirty," you might be able figure out that *consigned* means "turned over goods to someone else to sell."

In "Bargain," Colly carries customers' orders out to carriages waiting at the hitchpost. How might you identify the meaning of *hitchpost*?

Academic Vocabulary

Talk About . . .

Imagine being asked to <u>analyze</u> the narrator of "Bargain"—his character traits, basic beliefs, likes and dislikes—in one or two paragraphs. What does the <u>narrative</u> reveal about Al? Write down notes on the information you'd include and your <u>organizational</u> method for presenting it. Then, compare notes in a discussion with a classmate.

Universal Access: Vocabulary Development

Struggling Readers

Clarify for students how to use context clues to determine the meaning of an unfamiliar word by modeling how to use context clues to indentify the meaning of the selection word *hitchpost*. Explain that if you were unsure of what the word *hitchpost* means, you could use your knowledge about the compound word's parts, *hitch* and *post*, as well as other words in the sentence, such as *carriages*, to decode its meaning. Point out that

ou already know that a carriage is a wagon pulled by a horse; you also know that *hitch* means "to fasten or tie" and a post is a wooden stake or bar. These context clues help you determine that a *hitchpost* must be a station where horse-drawn carriages wait outside a business. Have students use context clues to identify the meaning of another selection word. Then invite them to share their thought processes with the class.

Grammar Link
Clauses

A **clause** is a word group that contains a verb and its subject. Some clauses are used as sentences, and others are used as parts of sentences.

Every clause contains a subject and a verb. However, not all clauses express complete thoughts. A clause that expresses a complete thought is called an **independent clause.** When an independent clause stands alone, it is a sentence. A clause that cannot stand alone is called a **subordinate clause.** A subordinate clause is joined with at least one independent clause to express a complete thought.

My mother drove me to school. [This entire sentence is an independent clause.]

My mother drove me to school, but my brother rode his bicycle. [This sentence contains two independent clauses.]

Because I missed the bus, my mother drove me to school. [This sentence contains one subordinate clause and one independent clause.]

Your Turn

The following sentences are from "Bargain." Identify the italicized clause in each sentence as independent or subordinate.

1. "There wasn't anyone or anything much on the street *because it was suppertime.*"
2. "*Two men had come up on us* and stood watching."
3. "*His eyes rested on my face* for a long minute."
4. "Ed Hempel told me about the deal *when I showed up for work.*"

CHOICES

As you respond to the Choices, use these **Academic Vocabulary** words as appropriate: <u>analyze</u>, <u>narrative</u>, <u>organizational</u>, <u>perceive</u>.

REVIEW
Point of View

Listening and Speaking Retell a scene in "Bargain" from Mr. Baumer's point of view. Which events would he consider to be the most important? What point would he try to make in telling this story?

CONNECT
Make a Case

Imagine that Mr. Baumer is put on trial for causing Slade's death. In one paragraph, summarize the case *against* Mr. Baumer. Give reasons and evidence to inform and persuade the jury that Mr. Baumer is guilty. Then, present evidence to show that Slade is responsible for his own death.

EXTEND
Support a Position

Timed ⌊Writing How would you solve a problem like Mr. Baumer's? Suppose you could offer Mr. Baumer advice on this situation. In a paragraph, state the way you think he should handle the situation, and list the reasons that he should take your advice.

---

* **Learn It Online**
To enhance your understanding of the story use the Internet links at:

go.hrw.com [H7-407] **Go**

Universal Access: Grammar Link

⟨EL⟩ English Learners
English for Academic Success
- Tell students that one way to identify a subordinate clause is by looking for a subordinating conjunction at the beginning of a clause. Common subordinating conjunctions include *after, if, that, since, where, when,* and *while.*
- Tell students the conjunctions *for, nor,* and *so* only join two independent clauses.

- Explain that the conjunction *but* connects two clauses of equal status, such as two independent clauses.
- Model identifying a subordinating conjunction in the following sentence: "While I watched him, he lifted his hand and felt carefully of his nose." (column 2, p. 395) You might say: "I'll look for subordinating conjunctions as I read. I see that it begins with the subordinating conjunction *while.* I know that 'while I watched him' is a subordinate clause because it cannot stand alone without the rest of the sentence."

Standards Focus

Objectives

Students will

- understand subjective and objective points of view
- identify the author's purpose

Motivate

What Do You Think?/QuickWrite

Ask students to discuss the benefits and drawbacks of fitting in, and have students explain whether they think it's important to fit in. Have them record their thoughts in their **Reader/Writer Notebook**.

English for Academic Success

Academic Vocabulary

Look for opportunities to use the Academic Vocabulary words in this chapter.

- **analyze, v.:** examine in detail.
- **narrative, adj.:** that narrates or recounts; being in story form.
- **organizational, adj.:** pertaining to organization or structure.
- **perceive, v.:** be aware of through the senses; observe.

Analyzing Visuals

Extension Activity Have students discuss what the artist might be trying to convey through this painting. **Possible response:** *The artist might want to convey the idea that each person's name is exciting and unique.*

California Standards, pp. 408–419

- **Reading Standard 1.3** Clarify word meanings through the use of definition, example, restatement, or contrast.
- **Reading Standard 3.5** Contrast points of view (e.g., first and third person, limited and omniscient, subjective and objective) in narrative text and explain how they affect the overall theme of the work.

Names/Nomb
by **Julia Alvarez**

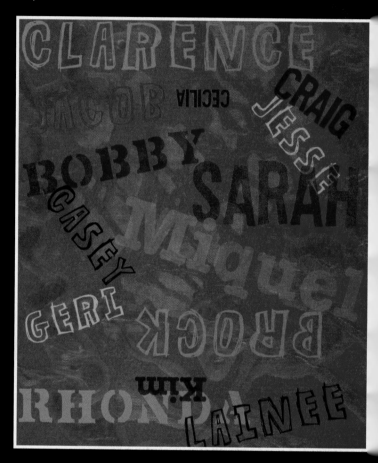

What Do You Think Sometimes you need to make tough choices in order to fit in. How far would you go to fit in?

QuickWrite Would you ever change your name or name from others in order to fit in? Li you would—or would not—conside

Selection Readability

Easily Accessible **Accessible** Challenging	familiar situations; understandab subject-forward syntax

Selection Plot Summary

When Julia Alvarez first moves to the United States, she is one pronounces her name correctly. Eventually she comes pronunciations as different nicknames or identities for the

Reader/Writer Notebook

Use your **RWN** to complete the activities for this selection.

Reading Standard 3.5 Contrast points of view (e.g., first and third person, limited and omniscient, **subjective and objective**) in narrative text, and explain how they affect the overall theme of the work.

Literary Skills Focus

Subjective and Objective Points of View When authors write from a **subjective point of view,** they share their own thoughts, feelings, opinions, and judgments. Certain types of nonfiction, such as personal <u>narratives</u> and autobiographies, are usually written from a subjective point of view. An **objective point of view,** on the other hand, is unbiased; it presents facts and figures rather than the author's feelings. The purpose of objective writing is to inform.

Reading Skills Focus

Author's Purpose The **author's purpose** is the reason a text is written. For example, the author may want to inform, to entertain, to persuade, or to express feelings. One way to determine the author's purpose is to <u>analyze</u> the main points the writer makes. Those points form the **main idea**—the central idea the writer wants you to remember. An author's purpose is seldom directly stated, but knowing the main idea will help you **infer,** or make an educated guess about, that purpose.

Into Action Use an <u>organizational</u> chart such as the one below to help you determine the author's purpose. As you read, list the author's main points in the boxes. Then, <u>analyze</u> those points to determine the main idea. Later, you'll use your chart to infer the author's purpose.

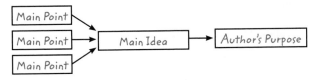

Writing Skills Focus

Think as a Reader/Writer

Find It in Your Reading As you read "Names/Nombres," make a list of at least five subjective details Alvarez uses to describe her thoughts and feelings. Which words in the details you identified signal that these descriptions are subjective?

Vocabulary

ethnicity (ehth NIHS uh tee) *n.:* common culture or nationality. *Julia's friends asked about her ethnicity.*

exotic (ehg ZAHT ihk) *adj.:* not native. *At the party, Julia's family served exotic dishes.*

heritage (HEHR uh tihj) *n.:* traditions that are passed along. *Julia remained proud of her heritage.*

convoluted (KAHN vuh loo tihd) *v.* used as *adj.:* complicated. *The grammar of a new language often seems convoluted.*

Language Coach

Suffixes A **suffix** is a word part added to the end of a word. *Ethnicity* has the suffix *–ity,* which means "having a particular quality." What word do you get when adding this suffix to the word *complex*?

Learn It Online
There's more to words than just definitions. Get the whole story on:

go.hrw.com H7-409 **Go**

Selection Resources

Chapter 4 Resources, on-level practice and assessment, pp. 18–23

PowerNotes, interactive lesson presentation with activities

Teacher One Stop™, on-level lesson plans and all print resources

Holt Audio Library

Holt Audio Library: Selections and Summaries in Spanish

UA: Holt Interactive Reader, pp. 104–113

Holt Interactive Reader for ELD, pp. 128–133

Holt Interactive Reader Audio Tutor

UA: Differentiating Instruction, modified lesson plans and leveled assessment, pp. 94–96

UA: Resources for Teaching Advanced Learners, lesson plans, p. 106

UA: Supporting Instruction in Five Languages, selection summary

Analyzing Visuals Transparencies, p. 37

ThinkCentral Online Assessment, Selection Standards Check

Preteach

Introducing Vocabulary

Read the Vocabulary words and sample sentences aloud. Then, use this activity to check students' understanding.

1. What are some different types of **ethnicity**? [*Italian; Chinese*]
2. What country do you think of as **exotic**? [*Thailand*]
3. What is another word for **heritage**? [*inheritance*]
4. What kind of documents might be **convoluted**? [*legal documents*]

English for Academic Success

Language Coach

After students have created the word *complexity,* tell them to examine its word parts to determine its definition. [*having the quality of being complicated*]

Literary Skills Focus

As you read and discuss the selection with students, have them decide whether it is written from a subjective or objective point of view and explain how they know whether it is objective or subjective.

Reading Skills Focus

Give students a copy of the Reading Skills Focus graphic organizer before they read. (See **Chapter 4 Resources.**) Tell them to use their responses to answer the questions on the Applying Your Skills page.

Writing Skills Focus

Have students record subjective details in their **Reader/Writer Notebook.** Students can use their notes to complete the Writing Skills Focus activity.

Learn It Online
Send students to **WordWatch** for definitions, synonyms, antonyms, and brief histories of word origins.

go.hrw.com H7-409 **Go**

Selection Introduction

More About the Writer

Currently, **Julia Alvarez** lives in Vermont with her husband on an eleven-acre farm. They grow their own vegetables and fruits there. They also have created a farming project in the Dominican Republic where people can learn to run sustainable farms, growing crops like coffee.

Think About the Writer

Tell students to consider how the experience of being different can affect a person's point of view on the differences among others. Have them discuss whether such experiences are more likely to make a person appreciate or dislike differences.

For Independent Reading

- If students want to read more from Julia Alvarez, suggest they read *Before We Were Free*, a story set in the Dominican Republic in the 1960s.

- Students may also enjoy Laurence Yep's *Child of the Owl*, which is about a Chinese American teen living in San Francisco.

Julia Alvarez
(1950–)

A Special Point of View

Born in New York City, Julia Alvarez spent her childhood in the Dominican Republic, returning with her family to New York when she was ten years old. Adjusting to her new surroundings in the early 1960s wasn't easy for young Julia.

Interpreting Two Worlds

Despite the difficulties, being an immigrant gave Julia a special point of view: "We travel on that border between two worlds," she explains, "and we can see both points of view."

After college and graduate school, Alvarez taught poetry for twelve years in several different states. Today Alvarez lives in Vermont, where she writes novels and teaches at Middlebury College. Of "Names/Nombres," she says:

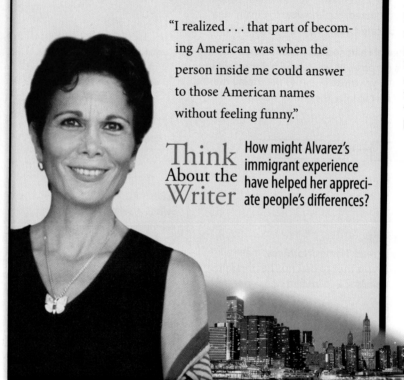

> "I realized . . . that part of becoming American was when the person inside me could answer to those American names without feeling funny."

Think About the Writer How might Alvarez's immigrant experience have helped her appreciate people's differences?

Build Background

Julia Alvarez was born in the Dominican Republic. This country is located on the Caribbean island of Hispaniola, which it shares with the country of Haiti. Use the map below to locate the Dominican Republic. It is west of Puerto Rico and east of Cuba and Jamaica.

Preview the Selection

Julia Alvarez and her family fled the Dominican Republic in 1960. Her **father**, a medical doctor, was part of an underground movement to overthrow the dictator who ruled the Dominican Republic at the time. To avoid the father's arrest, the family escaped to the United States. "Names/Nombres" describes what it was like for Julia growing up in New York City.

Universal Access

English Learners

Spanish names and words in the text may be difficult for some students to pronounce. If possible, ask Spanish-speaking students to pronounce the Spanish words listed in the box on p. 411.

✔ See **UA: Differentiating Instruction** for lesson plans and strategies for teaching English learners.

Struggling Readers

To help students better understand the concept of inferring an author's main idea in order to determine his or her purpose, tell them to pay attention to important details as they read. Explain that details such as a selection's title and the events described in the text can both give clues that they may use to infer the author's main idea and purpose for writing. Model identifying such details. Point out the title of "Names/Nombres" and how, on the first page of the narrative, Alvarez gives details about the various ways people pronounced her family's surname. Guide students in understanding how these details suggest the importance of her name to her sense of identity, which is a broader idea that likely

Names/Nombres

by **Julia Alvarez**

When we arrived in New York City, our names changed almost immediately. At Immigration, the officer asked my father, *Mister Elbures*, if he had anything to declare. My father shook his head no, and we were waved through.

I was too afraid we wouldn't be let in if I corrected the man's pronunciation, but I said our name to myself, opening my mouth wide for the organ blast of the *a*, trilling my tongue for the drumroll of the *r*, *All-vah-rrr-es!* How could anyone get *Elbures* out of that orchestra of sound? **Ⓐ**

At the hotel my mother was *Missus Alburest*, and I was *little girl*, as in, "Hey, little girl, stop riding the elevator up and down. It's *not* a toy."

When we moved into our new apartment building, the super called my father *Mister Alberase*, and the neighbors who became mother's friends pronounced her name *Jew-lee-ah* instead of *Hoo-lee-ah*. I, her name-sake, was known as *Hoo-lee-tah* at home. But at school I was *Judy* or *Judith*, and once an English teacher mistook me for *Juliet*.

Glossary: Spanish Words for Talking About Family

Family relationships are an important part of Alvarez's experiences and her reflections on them. Alvarez uses Spanish terms to describe some of her relatives. Check this glossary for the pronunciation and meaning of these words and phrases.

comadre (koh MAH dray) *n.*: informal Spanish for "close friend." *Comadre* is the name that the mother and the godmother of a child use for one another.

madrina (mah DREE nah) *n.*: Spanish for "godmother."

mis hermanas (mees ehr MAH nahs): Spanish for "my sisters."

primas (PREE mahs) *n.*: Spanish for "female cousins."

tía (TEE ah) *n.*: Spanish for "aunt."

tío (TEE oh) *n.*: Spanish for "uncle."

una hija de crianza (OO nah EE hah deh kree AHN sah): Spanish for "an adopted daughter." *Crianza* means "upbringing."

Ⓐ **Read and Discuss** What do these two paragraphs reveal about the "Elbures" family?

relates to the main idea of the piece.

✔ See UA: **Differentiating Instruction** for lesson plans and strategies for teaching struggling readers.

Advanced Learners

Enrichment Ask students to discuss whether the essay would be as effective if it were written from an objective third-person viewpoint. Tell students to cite text details as support.

✔ See **UA: Resources for Teaching Advanced Students** for strategies for teaching advanced learners.

Students with Disabilities

Explain that in true narratives, such as "Names/Nombres," writers share stories about their lives and personal experiences. Read aloud the first paragraph to students. Explain that *Elbures* is a mispronunciation of the author's surname, *Alvarez*. Ask students if they have ever heard their names mispronounced, and if so, how it made them feel. Then have students consider why the author is sharing this story as a segue into understanding author's purpose.

✔ Invite students to read the selection in interactive format in **UA: Holt Interactive Reader**.

Direct Teach

Think About/Talk About

Read with a Purpose Have students read the Read with a Purpose statement. Then, ask them to think about the significance of their own names. Have students discuss how they would feel if their names or nicknames changed.

▶ **Comprehension**

Ⓐ Read and Discuss

Possible response: The family just immigrated to New York City, and the immigration officer is having trouble pronouncing their name.

▶ **Extend the Discussion**

Characterization In the second paragraph, Julia pronounces her family's name correctly to herself after it is mispronounced. What does this suggest about her? *Possible response: Her name is an important part of her identity.*

Point of View At the end of paragraph 2, the author expresses shock that her family's name could be mispronounced when she says, "How could anyone get *Elbures* out of that orchestra of sound?" Is this comment subjective or objective? Explain. *Possible response: This is a subjective comment because although the pronunciation of Julia's last name is obvious to her, other people who don't speak Spanish probably wouldn't find the pronunciation obvious at all.*

Model the Skill

- Provide students with copies of the graphic organizer (see **Chapter 4 Resources**) or ask them to use a piece of their own paper.

- Explain to students that the **main idea** of a piece of nonfiction is the big idea that the author seeks to convey through his or her writing. Knowing the main idea can help readers infer the author's purpose for writing.

- Model identifying the main idea of a paragraph using paragraph 2 from p. 412. Tell students that on this page, readers find out about nicknames Julia acquired while at school in the United States and with her Dominican relatives at home. She focuses on the differences in nicknames her American and Dominican acquaintances give her. The specific names are minor details, but the sources of her different sets of nicknames are main points that help reveal the main idea and the author's purpose.

Guided Practice: Apply

Write "American nicknames" and "Dominican nicknames" as two main points in the graphic organizer, and ask students to restate the main idea of paragraph 2, discussed above, to enter in the graphic organizer. Explain that they should keep noting important main points and main ideas as they read that will help them identify the main idea of the essay, and therefore, infer the author's purpose for writing it.

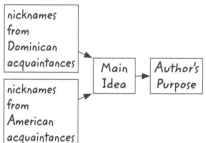

It took a while to get used to my new names. I wondered if I shouldn't correct my teachers and new friends. But my mother argued that it didn't matter. "You know what your friend Shakespeare said, '*A rose by any other name would smell as sweet.*'"[1] My family had gotten into the habit of calling any famous author "my friend" because I had begun to write poems and stories in English class.   **B**

By the time I was in high school, I was a popular kid, and it showed in my name. Friends called me *Jules* or *Hey Jude,* and once a group of troublemaking friends my mother forbade me to hang out with called me *Alcatraz.* I was *Hoo-lee-tah* only to Mami and Papi and uncles and aunts who came over to eat sancocho[2] on Sunday afternoons—old world folk whom I would just as soon go back to where they came from and leave me to pursue whatever mischief I wanted to in America. *JUDY ALCATRAZ,* the name on the "Wanted" poster would read. Who would ever trace her to me?   **C**

My older sister had the hardest time getting an American name for herself because *Mauricia* did not translate into English. Ironically, although she had the most foreign-sounding name, she and I were the Americans in the family. We had been born in New York City when our parents had first tried immigration and then gone back "home," too homesick to stay. My mother often told the story of how she had almost changed my sister's name in the hospital.

After the delivery, Mami and some other new mothers were cooing over their new baby sons and daughters and exchanging names and weights and delivery stories. My mother was embarrassed among the Sallys and Janes and Georges and Johns to reveal the rich, noisy name of *Mauricia,* so when her turn came to brag, she gave her baby's name as *Maureen.*

"Why'd ya give her an Irish name with so many pretty Spanish names to choose from?" one of the women asked.

My mother blushed and admitted her baby's real name to the group. Her mother-in-law had recently died, she apologized, and her husband had insisted that the first daughter be named after his mother, *Mauran.* My mother thought it the ugliest name she had ever heard, and she talked my father into what she believed was an improvement, a combination of *Mauran* and her own mother's name, *Felicia.*

"Her name is *Mao-ree-shee-ah,*" my mother said to the group of women.

---

1. *"A rose . . . as sweet"*: Julia's mother is quoting from the play *Romeo and Juliet.*
2. **sancocho** (sahn KOH choh): stew of meats and fruit.

B **Literary Focus** Subjective/Objective Points of View   What examples of the author's feelings convey a subjective point of view? What do these subjective details tell you about her?

C **Read and Discuss** When the "old world folk" would come to visit, Julia wished they would go back to where they came from. What does that reveal about her?

Developing Oral Fluency

Use the dialogue on pp. 412 and 414 to help students practice reading with expression. Tell them that fluent readers try to express a character's emotions in their voice as they read that character's lines of dialogue.

Paired activity Have students work with a partner to practice reading this page aloud.

- Model reading the second column on p. 412 aloud for students, paying particular attention to the dialogue. For example, draw a distinction between the chatty curiosity of the woman who says, "Why'd ya give her an Irish name . . . " and the embarrassed, apologetic tone of the mother when she says, "Her name is . . . "

- Then, have students read p. 414 aloud together by alternating reading a paragraph at a time.

- If time is limited, have students focus on reading aloud the lines of dialogue on the page.

✔ See **UA: Differentiating Instruction** for practice passages for developing oral fluency.

Hannah (2001) by Alexandra Heyes. Oil.

©Alexandra Heyes

Analyzing Visuals

Connecting to the Text
How well does this portrait match your image of Julia?

Think About/Talk About

▶ **Comprehension**

ⓒ Read and Discuss

Possible response: Her views are beginning to change, and she is starting to feel an allegiance to her American friends.

▶ **Analysis**

ⓑ Literary Focus

Possible response: The author conveys a subjective point of view by explaining that she was not sure if she should correct people when they pronounced her name wrong. That tells me that she might be shy or uncertain about the rules of her new society.

▶ **Extend the Discussion**

Main Idea In the first paragraph on p. 412, why do you think that Julia's mother argues that names do not matter? How might this give you a clue about the essay's main idea?

Possible response: Julia's mother believes that even if her new friends do not pronounce her name correctly, it will not change who Julia is as a person. This makes me wonder if the main idea might be that names are less important than a person's identity.

Analyzing Visuals

Tell students that **Alexandra Heyes** is a painter from New Zealand whose work has been displayed in galleries around the world. Heyes has painted many portraits, including *Hannah*, and uses layers of paints to create her work.

Connecting to the Text: *Julia and the girl in the portrait seem to be the same age. They both seem thoughtful. I think the portrait looks very much like Julia.*

Model the Skill

- Explain to students that nonfiction writing can be written from an **objective** or **subjective point of view.** Writers with an objective point of view stick to proven facts and tell them in a straightforward manner. Writers who write from a subjective point of view include their feelings or opinions, which are not considered factual, in their writing.

- Tell students that a good way to determine whether a statement is subjective or objective is to ask themselves, "Would I be able to prove this information using a reliable source?" Facts, including dates, events, and names, can all be researched and are objective. A writer's opinions may be based in fact, but they reflect a writer's feelings on a subject, and feelings cannot be verified.

- To clarify this difference for students, read aloud on p. 414, paragraph 1, the sentences starting with "Sometimes, American tongues . . ." and "What an awful name . . ." Explain that listing the ways Americans mispronounced her sister's name is an objective statement because it deals with fact. Alvarez's statement about her sister's name being "awful to transport" is subjective because it expresses an opinion.

Guided Practice: Apply

Have students work in pairs to review the story and identify an example of objective and of subjective writing. Have volunteers explain their choices.

Think as a Reader/Writer

Find It in Your Reading Point out that in the paragraph running from pp. 414–415, when Julia describes having "burned with shame" when friends identified her as exotic, she is using subjective details.

Use It in Your Writing Have students write a few sentences in which they use subjective details to describe feelings of embarrassment.

"Why, that's a beautiful name," the new mothers cried. "*Moor-ee-sha, Moor-ee-sha,*" they cooed into the pink blanket. *Moor-ee-sha* it was when we returned to the States eleven years later. Sometimes, American tongues found even that mispronunciation tough to say and called her *Maria* or *Marsha* or *Maudy* from her nickname *Maury.* I pitied her. What an awful name to have to transport across borders! **D**

My little sister, Ana, had the easiest time of all. She was plain *Anne*—that is, only her name was plain, for she turned out to be the pale, blond "American beauty" in the family. The only Hispanic thing about her was the affectionate nicknames her boyfriends sometimes gave her. *Anita,* or, as one goofy guy used to sing to her to the tune of the banana advertisement, *Anita Banana.*

Later, during her college years in the late sixties, there was a push to pronounce Third World[3] names correctly. I remember calling her long distance at her group house and a roommate answering.

"Can I speak to Ana?" I asked, pronouncing her name the American way.

"Ana?" The man's voice hesitated. "Oh! You must mean *Ah-nah!*"

---

3. **Third World:** developing countries of Latin America, Africa, and Asia.

D [Read and Discuss] What does the story about the origin of Mauricia's name tell you about Julia's mother?

E [Literary Focus] Subjective/Objective Points of View   Is the author being objective or subjective as she conveys this information about herself? How do you know?

Our first few years in the States, though, ethnicity was not yet "in." Those were the blond, blue-eyed, bobby-sock years of junior high and high school before the sixties ushered in peasant blouses, hoop earrings, serapes.[4] My initial desire to be known by my correct Dominican name faded. I just wanted to be Judy and merge with the Sallys and Janes in my class. But, inevitably, my accent and coloring gave me away. "So where are you from, Judy?"

"New York," I told my classmates. After all, I had been born blocks away at Columbia-Presbyterian Hospital. **E**

"I mean, *originally.*"

"From the Caribbean," I answered vaguely, for if I specified, no one was quite sure on what continent our island was located.

"Really? I've been to Bermuda. We went last April for spring vacation. I got the worst sunburn! So, are you from Portoriko?"

"No," I sighed. "From the Dominican Republic.

"Where's that?"

"South of Bermuda."

They were just being curious, I knew, but I burned with shame whenever they

---

4. **serapes** (suh RAH peez): woolen shawls worn in Latin American countries.

Vocabulary   ethnicity (ehth NIHS uh tee) *n.*: common culture or nationality.

Word-Attack Skills Mini-Lesson

Pronunciations of *oo*

Have students compare these words from the selection: *cooed, goofy, hoop, school, good, took, mistook.* Point out that all are spelled with a double *o,* yet the *o's* are not all pronounced the same.

Activity Write the following sentences on the chalkboard, and ask volunteers to read them aloud.

1. The <u>school</u> was full of <u>goofy</u> guys.
2. I wanted to <u>choose</u> <u>good</u> classes.

3. I <u>took</u> my mother's <u>hoop</u> earrings.
4. They <u>cooed</u> over the baby's <u>booted</u> <u>foot</u>.
5. We read a <u>book</u> about <u>balloons</u>.

Ask students how many pronunciations of the double *o* they heard in these sentences. Have them list the similar-sounding words together. [*school, goofy, choose, hoop, cooed, booted,* and *balloons; good, took, foot, book*]

---

singled me out as a "foreigner," a rare, exotic friend.

"Say your name in Spanish, oh, please say it!" I had made mouths drop one day by rattling off my full name, which, according to Dominican custom, included my middle names, Mother's and Father's surnames for four generations back.

"Julia Altagracia María Teresa Álvarez Tavares Perello Espaillat Julia Pérez Rochet González." I pronounced it slowly, a name as chaotic with sounds as a Middle Eastern bazaar or market day in a South American village. **F**

My Dominican heritage was never more apparent than when my extended family attended school occasions. For my graduation, they all came, the whole lot of aunts and uncles and the many little cousins who snuck in without tickets. They sat in the first row in order to better understand the Americans' fast-spoken English. But how could they listen when they were constantly speaking among themselves in florid-sounding[5] phrases, rococo[6] consonants, rich, rhyming vowels?

Introducing them to my friends was a further trial to me. These relatives had such complicated names and there were so many of them, and their relationships to myself were so convoluted. There was my Tía Josefina, who was not really an aunt but a much older cousin. And her daughter, Aida Margarita, who was adopted, una hija de crianza. My uncle of affection, Tío José, brought my madrina Tía Amelia and her comadre Tía Pilar. My friends rarely had more than a "Mom and Dad" to introduce.

After the commencement ceremony, my family waited outside in the parking lot while my friends and I signed yearbooks with nicknames which recalled our high school good times: "Beans" and "Pepperoni" and "Alcatraz."

> *I pronounced it slowly, a name as chaotic with sounds as a Middle Eastern bazaar or market day in a South American village.*

---

5. **florid-sounding:** flowery; using fancy words.
6. **rococo** (ruh KOH koh): fancy. Rococo is an early-eighteenth-century style of art and architecture known for its fancy ornamentation.

F **Read and Discuss** The author tells you that when she pronounces her name, she says it slowly. What point is she making?

Vocabulary **exotic** (ehg ZAHT ihk) *adj.:* not native.
heritage (HEHR uh tihj) *n.:* traditions that are passed along.
convoluted (KAHN vuh loo tihd) *v.* used as *adj.:* complicated.

Universal Access

Think About/Talk About

▶ Comprehension

** Reading Focus**

Possible response: The title illustrates that she has fully accepted her dual life and the many names that she is called in America.

(H) Read and Discuss

Possible response: Although Julia had been frustrated with her different names, she is now able to look back and laugh at them.

▶ Extend the Discussion

Main Idea How does the final paragraph relate to the main idea of the selection? *Possible response: By the end of the selection, Julia realizes that her many names are something to be proud of rather than a source of embarrassment. The main idea is that we should be proud of our unique characteristics.*

Monitor Students' Comprehension

Guide the class in answering these comprehension questions.

1. Why are Julia and her older sister considered the "Americans" in the family? [*The were born in New York City before their parents returned to the Dominican Republic.*]

2. What do Julia's high school nicknames suggest about her? [*She is popular in school.*]

Analyzing Visuals

Connecting to the Text: *The image helps me perceive how excited the students are at graduation, so I understand that the mood would be the same at Julia's.*

Analyzing Visuals **Connecting to the Text** In what ways does this photograph help you perceive the mood at Julia's graduation?

We hugged and cried and promised to keep in touch.

Our goodbyes went on too long. I heard my father's voice calling out across the parking lot, "*Hoo-lee-tah! Vámonos!*"[7]

Back home, my tíos and tías and primas, Mami and Papi, and mis hermanas had a party for me with sancocho and a store-bought pudín,[8] inscribed with

---

7. **Vámonos!** (VAH maw nohs): Spanish for "Let's go!"
8. **pudín** (poo DEEN): Spanish cake.

(G) Reading Focus Author's Purpose Why does Alvarez call this work "Names/Nombres"? In describing her many nicknames and her feelings about them, what is she saying about herself and her new life?

Happy Graduation, Julie. There were many gifts—that was a plus to a large family! I got several wallets and a suitcase with my initials and a graduation charm from my godmother and money from my uncles. The biggest gift was a portable typewriter from my parents for writing my stories and poems.

Someday, the family predicted, my name would be well-known throughout the United States. I laughed to myself, wondering which one I would go by. **(H)**

(H) Read and Discuss Julia laughs when she thinks about which "well-known" name she'll go by. What does this tell you about her?

🐻 California Standards, pp. 417–419

- **Reading Standard 1.3** Clarify word meanings through the use of definition, example, restatement, or contrast.
- **Reading Standard 3.5** Contrast points of view (e.g., first and third person, limited and omniscient, subjective and objective) in narrative text and explain how they affect the overall theme of the work.

Applying Your Skills

Reading Standard 3.5 Contrast points of view (e.g., **first** and third **person,** limited and omniscient, **subjective and objective**) in narrative text, and explain how they affect the overall theme of the work.

Names/Nombres
Literary Response and Analysis

Reading Skills Focus
Quick Check

1. As a teenager, why does Julia want to be called Judy? How has her attitude toward her name changed since then?

Read with a Purpose

2. Explain how a name can influence a person's identity and sense of self.

Reading Skills: Author's Purpose

3. Review your author's-purpose chart. Then:
   - Think about the main points you recorded.
   - Use this information to figure out the main idea. In your own words, write the main idea in the chart if you haven't already.
   - Analyze the main idea and infer the author's purpose from it. Record the purpose you inferred in the last box of your chart.

Literary Skills Focus
Literary Analysis

4. **Analyze** How does the title "Names/Nombres" connect to Alvarez's comment about being on the "border between two worlds"?

5. **Interpret** Shakespeare said, "A rose by any other name would smell as sweet." How do those words apply to Alvarez and her life?

6. **Analyze** What do you think Alvarez learns about her family and her heritage as she takes a journey through the "name game"?

Literary Skills: Subjective/Objective Points of View

7. **Evaluate** What evidence reveals that this <u>narrative</u> has a subjective point of view?

8. **Compare/Contrast** If a nonfiction accout of an immigrant's experience adapting to a new culture were written from the objective point of view, in what ways would it differ from "Names/Nombres"?

Literary Skills Review: First-Person Point of View

9. **Comparing/Contrasting** Alvarez is the narrator and uses the first-person pronoun *I*. How would the <u>narrative</u> change if it were told by another person, such as Alvarez's mother? What main idea might this person express that Alvarez does not?

Writing Skills Focus
Think as a Reader/Writer

Use It in Your Writing Review the subjective details you identified in Alvarez's writing. In a paragraph, explain the effect of including subjective details like these in this work.

 What Do You Think Now

How has "Names/Nombres" affected your ideas about what people will do to fit in?

Independent Practice
Reading Skills Focus
Answers:

1. *She wishes to appear more American. Since then, she has come to believe it is possible to embrace both an American and a Dominican identity.*

2. *In Alvarez's case, a name can influence how someone views his or her culture and background.*

3. *The main idea is that our attempts to fit in do not have to come at the expense of what makes us unique. The author's purpose is to share this insight with readers.*

Literary Skills Focus
Possible responses:

4. *The title reflects the manner in which American and Dominican cultures are both a part of Julia.*

5. *Alvarez is the same person, regardless of her name.*

6. *She learns that her family is dealing with the same issues of identity, but they are proud of their heritage.*

7. *The narrator talks about her feelings, which are subjective.*

8. *An objective essay would have facts and figures about people whose names are mispronounced or who identify with two cultures. It would not include any of the narrator's feelings about the events described.*

9. *Another person in Alvarez's family could convey their sense of loss as she drifts away from her heritage and family. They would be able to show how they resisted the changes that Alvarez embraced.*

What Do You Think Now?

Ask students to consider the ideas about fitting in that they had prior to reading. Have them discuss how Julia's experiences with trying to fit in relate to their own ideas about fitting in. Ask students to explain the lesson that Julia learned about trying to be like everybody else.

Universal Access

Struggling Writers
Provide additional scaffolding for students by reviewing the definition of subjective details. Remind students that subjective details include thoughts, feelings, opinions, and judgments. To help students complete the Writing Focus activity, encourage them to think about the effect reading Alvarez's subjective details had on them. Did reading about her thoughts and emotions make them smile or laugh? Did it cause them to feel sympathetic, or allow them to relate to her experiences? What about her opinions? Did reading Alvarez's opinions persuade them to think about an issue differently? Have students reflect on these topics with a partner before writing.

Independent Practice

Vocabulary Development

Your Turn
Possible responses:

1. *from a different culture*
2. *complicated and confusing*
3. *historical traditions*
4. *a person's cultural background*

English for Academic Success

Language Coach

Explain to students that the sample words from the text apply the rule for words ending with the suffix–*ly*. Help them understand that *constantly* refers to how often something is done, *immediately* refers to when something is done, and *ironically* refers to how something is done.

English for Academic Success

Academic Vocabulary

Possible response: In her narrative, Julia conveys through anecdotes how large a role her family has played in helping her develop her identity. I <u>perceive</u> that the Alvarezes' strong family ties are evident in their support at Julia's graduation.

 WordSharp: An Interactive Vocabulary Tutor

Applying Your Skills

Names/Nombres

Vocabulary Development

Context Clues: Definitions

Writers often help you understand word meanings by providing context clues. A word's **context** consists of the words, sentences, and paragraphs that surround the word.

The most direct kind of context clue is a definition. A writer who uses definitions will explain what a word means in the sentence or passage. For example, Julia Alvarez clarifies the meaning of *foreigner* as her classmates used it by defining it in a sentence:

> "I burned with shame whenever they singled me out as a 'foreigner,' a rare, exotic friend."

A definition will sometimes follow a word (look for a comma after the word being defined). Also look for such words and phrases as *or* and *that is* when looking for definitions of words in context.

Your Turn

Complete the following sentences so that they clarify the meanings of the Vocabulary words in the list.

ethnicity
exotic
heritage
convoluted

1. The meal was **exotic**—that is, it was _____.
2. The explanation of the science project became more **convoluted** the longer the student talked. In other words, it was _____.
3. The street festival was planned to introduce visitors to the city's **heritage,** or _____.
4. Studies have shown that **ethnicity,** meaning _____, influences the kinds of programs that people watch on television.

Language Coach

Suffixes Many English words can be divided into parts. If you know the meanings of various word parts, you can often figure out the meanings of unfamiliar words. Suffixes are word parts that are added to the ends of words. Knowing the meanings of suffixes can greatly increase your vocabulary. For instance, knowing that the suffix –*ly* means "in a particular way" will help you understand the meaning of three other words from "Names/Nombres":

> *immediately   ironically   constantly*

Words ending in –*ly* usually tell how or how often something is done. Explain whether or not this rule applies to these three words from "Names/Nombres."

Academic Vocabulary

Write About . . .

In a paragraph, describe how you <u>perceive</u> the role of Alvarez's family in helping her develop her identity. Then, <u>analyze</u> how Alvarez reveals her identity through subjective details in her <u>narrative</u>. Use the underlined Academic Vocabulary words in your response.

✳ Learn It Online
Explore suffixes with *WordSharp:*

✳ Learn It Online

Holt's **WordSharp: An Interactive Vocabulary Tutor** provides additional support for vocabulary development. Multimedia tutorials show students how to apply vocabulary skills to unfamiliar words—and how to make those words their own.

go.hrw.com   H7-418   **Go**

Universal Access: Vocabulary Development

EL English Learners

English for Academic Success Help students become more familiar with the formation of adverbs in English by providing additional scaffolding for the Language Coach activity on page 418. Explain that suffix –*ly* changes adjectives into adverbs. Remind students that adverbs are words that modify verbs by answering the questions *how*? and *when*? Model using an adjective and its related adverb in the following sentences: This matter needs your *immediate* attention. This matter needs your attention *immediately*. Point out how, in the first sentence, *immediate* is an adjective that tells *what kind* of attention this matter needs. In the second sentence, the suffix –*ly* transforms *immediate* into the adverb immediately. The adverb modifies the verb *needs* by answering the question *when?*; when does this matter need your attention? *Immediately*. Have pairs of students use *ironic/ironically* or *constant/constantly* in sentences. Tell them to have an instructional conversation about how the suffix changes the meaning and usage of the base word.

Grammar Link
Subject and Predicate

Sentences consist of two basic parts: subjects and predicates. The **subject** tells *who* or *what* the sentence is about. To find the subject, ask *who* or *what* is doing something or *who* or *what* is being discussed. The subject may come at the beginning, middle, or end of a sentence.

EXAMPLES

My sister had many friends in high school. [*Who* had many friends in high school? *My sister* did.]

In college, **Anne** changed her name back to Ana. [*Who* changed her name? *Anne* did.]

How excited **the graduates** are! [*Who* is excited? *The graduates* are.]

The **predicate** tells something about the subject. A **complete predicate** consists of a verb and all the words that complete the verb's meaning. Like the subject, the predicate may be found anywhere in a sentence, though it often follows the subject.

EXAMPLES

Mami **didn't like her mother-in-law's name.**

Out in the audience were many of her relatives.

After the ceremony, Julia's family **celebrated.** [The predicate in this sentence is divided by the subject, *Julia's family*.]

Your Turn

Identify each word or word group in italics as a subject or a predicate.

1. Friends *called me by my nickname*.
2. Ethnicity, *in the early sixties, was not yet "in."*
3. Will *you* please say your name in Spanish?
4. After graduation, *Julia* signed yearbooks.

CHOICES

As you respond to the Choices, use these **Academic Vocabulary** words as appropriate: analyze, narrative, organizational, perceive.

REVIEW
Speak Objectively/Subjectively

Partner Talk Imagine that you are visiting a new place for the first time and are phoning home. With a partner, make two **objective** statements relating facts about the place and two **subjective** statements expressing your thoughts and feelings about it. (You can make up any details you want.)

CONNECT
Describe a Family Food

Timed Writing Alvarez describes foods that are served at her family get-togethers. Think of foods you associate with family meals or special occasions. Then, use the **first-person point of view** to write a description of your favorite family dish. Be sure to include **subjective** details that reveal why this dish is your favorite.

EXTEND
Write About Your Name

Use both a **subjective** and **objective point of view** to write about your family name, given name, nickname, or pet name. Explain when and how you got the name and how you feel about it. Is it an accurate representation of who you are? How do you think it affects the way that others perceive you?

 Learn It Online
Use MediaScope to visually explain your name:
go.hrw.com | H7-419 | **Go**

Independent Practice

Grammar Link
Your Turn _____
1. predicate   3. subject
2. predicate   4. subject

Choices: Evaluation Criteria
Review: **Homework**
Speak Objectively/ Subjectively
The subjective statements include opinions and the objective statements give facts or figures.

Connect: Timed Writing 40-50 Minutes
The paragraph describes a family meal from the first-person point of view, using subjective details.

Extend: **Homework**
Write About Your Name
The piece of writing uses objective and subjective points of view to describe the name and student.

Assess

Chapter 4 Resources, Selection Standards Check, pp. 21–23

ThinkCentral Online Assessment, Selection Standards Check

Teacher One Stop™, editable Selection Standards Check

Reteach

To reteach **point of view,** see **Reteaching Lessons,** p. 842A.

ThinkCentral Online Remediation

Learn It Online
The **MediaScope** mini-site provides hands-on resources for understanding, analyzing, creating, and critiquing media and multimedia.

go.hrw.com | H7-419 | **Go**

Universal Access: Grammar Link

EL English Learners

English for Academic Success Reinforce the standard English use of subjects and predicates with this activity:

- Help students identify subjects and predicates by writing these sentences on the board: *Alvarez had many names. The names represented different parts of her identity.*

- Read the sentences aloud. Ask students who or what is discussed in each sentence. [Alvarez, the names] Explain that each phrase is the subject of its sentence.

- Then ask students what each sentence tells about the subjects. [Alvarez *had many names;* The names *represented different parts of her identity*.] Explain that these are the predicates.

- Using colored chalk, underline the subjects once. Using a different color, underline the predicates twice.

- Check that students understand, and repeat the exercise with this sentence if necessary: Alvarez loved her family.

✔ For more practice with subjects and predicates, see **Warriner's Handbook, Language Handbook Worksheets,** and **GrammarNotes.**

Standards Focus

Objectives

Students will
- recognizes objective facts and sub-jective details
- read and analyze a biography
- identify the author's purpose

Motivate

What Do You Think?/QuickWrite

Have students describe challenges that they or someone they know has faced successfully. Ask: "How did the challenge help you grow as a person?"

English for Academic Success

Academic Vocabulary

Look for opportunities to use the Academic Vocabulary words in this chapter.

- **analyze, *v.*:** examine in detail.
- **narrative, *adj.*:** that narrates or recounts; being in story form.
- **organizational, *adj.*:** pertaining to organization or structure.
- **perceive, *v.*:** be aware of through the senses; observe.

Analyzing Visuals

Extension Activity Have students discuss the details they expect to read in Elizabeth's biography.

Possible response: *I expect to read about how she came into power and the events that made up her reign.*

California Standards, pp. 420–435

- **Reading Standard 1.3** Clarify word meanings through the use of definition, example, restate-ment, or contrast.
- **Reading Standard 3.5** Contrast points of view (e.g., first and third person, limited and omniscient, subjective and objective) in narrative text and explain how they affect the overall theme of the work.

BIOGRAPHY
Preparing to Read

ELIZABETH I

by **Milton Meltzer**

What Do **You Think?** How does your attitude affect the way you confront challenges?

QuickWrite

Think about a challenge that you have faced in the past. What was it, and how did you handle it? What effect did your attitude have on the outcome?

The photographs illustrating this biography are from the 1998 movie *Elizabeth*, starring Cate Blanchett as Elizabeth I.

Selection Readability

Easily Accessible Accessible **Challenging**	serious subject matter; historical context; challenging vocabulary

Selection Summary

Elizabeth I came to power during a difficult time in England. As a result of her reign, England became a European power. The country moved from medieval times into a renaissance through advances in the arts and sciences.

Reader/Writer Notebook

Use your **RWN** to complete the activities for this selection.

Reading Standard 3.5 Contrast points of view (e.g., first and third person, limited and omniscient, **subjective and objective**) in narrative text and explain how they affect the overall theme of the work.

Literary Skills Focus

Subjective and Objective Points of View in Biography In a **biography,** a writer tells the true story of another person's life. The word *biography* comes from two Greek words: *bios*, meaning "life," and *graphein*, meaning "to write." Most biographers try to present carefully researched facts about the subject of the biography.

Writing that presents facts without revealing the writer's feelings and opinions is said to be **objective.** News reporters usually try to write in an objective style. Conversely, writing that reveals the writer's feelings and opinions is said to be **subjective.** Biographies often combine objective facts with subjective details, including the biographer's personal opinions about a subject.

Reading Skills Focus

Determining an Author's Purpose <u>Narrative</u> texts may be written for many different purposes, such as to persuade, to inform, to share an experience, or to entertain.

Milton Meltzer's biography of Elizabeth I is written with a number of purposes in mind. He informs you about events of Queen Elizabeth's life, he entertains you with interesting details, and he may even seek to reveal a truth about life. Meltzer achieves his purposes through a combination of objective and subjective writing.

Into Action Complete a chart like the one below to <u>analyze</u> Milton Meltzer's purposes for writing "Elizabeth I." Record details from the text that support each purpose.

Author's Purpose	Details
to inform	Elizabeth became Queen of England in 1558.

Writing Skills Focus

Think as a Reader/Writer

Find It in Your Reading Record in your *Reader/Writer Notebook* three remarkable achievements Meltzer includes about Elizabeth's life. Note their effect on how you <u>perceive</u> Queen Elizabeth.

Vocabulary

monarch (MAHN ahrk) *n.:* sole and absolute ruler. *Elizabeth became the monarch of England in 1558.*

alliance (uh LY uhns) *n.:* pact between nations, families, or individuals that shows a common cause. *Elizabeth's advisor urged her to join the alliance against the enemy.*

monopoly (muh NAHP uh lee) *n.:* exclusive control of a market. *His monopoly on sweet wines made the earl of Essex rich.*

arrogant (AR uh guhnt) *adj.:* convinced of one's importance. *The queen seemed arrogant, but she did listen to others.*

intolerable (ihn TAHL uhr uh buhl) *adj.:* unbearable. *Even though Mary Stuart was an enemy, Elizabeth felt it would be intolerable to cut off her cousin's head.*

Language Coach

Recognizing Roots Learning common word roots derived from Latin and Greek can help you understand English words. The Vocabulary words *monarch* and *monopoly* include word roots that derive from the Greek *monos*, meaning "single," or "alone."

Learn It Online
To hear a professional actor read this excerpt, visit the selection at:

go.hrw.com H7-421 **Go**

Selection Resources

Chapter 4 Resources, on-level practice and assessment, pp. 24–29

Teacher One Stop™, on-level lesson plans and all print resources

Holt Audio Library

Holt Audio Library: Selections and Summaries in Spanish

UA: Supporting Instruction in Five Languages, selection summary

Analyzing Visuals Transparencies, p. 40

ThinkCentral Online Assessment, Selection Standards Check

ThinkCentral Online Remediation

Selection Introduction

More About the Writer

Milton Meltzer was determined to become the first member of his family to attend college, but money was a problem. The issue was solved when a new program at Columbia University in New York City awarded Meltzer a scholarship given to students who could not otherwise afford the tuition. He entered the college in 1932 at the age of seventeen.

Think About the Writer

Have students consider how an author's point of view is often revealed in his or her writing. Then, have them think about the issues Meltzer has written about, such as slavery and civil rights, to help answer the question.

For Independent Reading

- If students want to read more biographies by Milton Meltzer, suggest they read *Ten Queens: Portraits of Women of Power.*
- Students interested in reading about the lives of women in history may enjoy Kathleen Krull's *Lives of Extraordinary Women: Rulers, Rebels (And What the Neighbors Thought).*

MEET THE WRITER

Milton Meltzer
(1915–   )

Historian and writer **Milton Meltzer** has taken an interest in social issues throughout his life. After attending Columbia University, he worked as a writer for the Work Projects Administration, a government agency that provided jobs to unemployed people during the Great Depression of the 1930s. Never one to shy away from controversy, Meltzer has written about the Holocaust, the civil rights movement, slavery, and immigration, among his many other subjects.

Meltzer's Life Stories

Meltzer's biographies cover well known historical figures, such as George Washington and Mark Twain, as well as others who may not be so well known—like Thomas Paine, who battled for America's freedom, and Betty Friedan, who fought for women's rights. Meltzer recognizes a common link between his subjects:

"My subjects choose action. . . . Action takes commitment, the commitment of dedicated, optimistic individuals. I try to make the readers understand that history isn't only what happens to us. History is what we *make* happen. Each of us. All of us."

Think About the Writer How has Meltzer's interest in social issues affected his choice of topics?

Build Background

When Elizabeth I's father, Henry VIII, was king, he wanted to divorce his first wife to marry Anne Boleyn. However, Henry was a Catholic, and the Catholic Church did not allow divorce and remarriage. When the pope refused to grant Henry permission to divorce, Henry broke away from Catholicism. He started the Church of England and made himself its leader. When Elizabeth came to the throne, there was still much conflict about religion in England.

Preview the Selection

In a time when women were expected to obey their husbands, one of the most powerful people in the world was a woman: **Elizabeth I,** Queen of England. Elizabeth was the daughter of **Henry VIII** and **Anne Boleyn.** After her half sister **Mary** died, Elizabeth took the throne. Great musicians, writers, and explorers flourished under her rule.

Real Issues, Real Experts

Holt author **Kylene Beers** *offers strategies for keeping track of information.*

This is a long selection that is filled with many events. While the vocabulary and syntax may not overwhelm struggling readers, the amount of information could. To help these readers, consider dividing the reading into more manageable chunks by having students stop and think about what they've read thus far at the following points:

End of paragraphs 5, 12, 17, 21, 27, 32
End of selection

For each section, students should jot down important events and what made them important using the following graphic organizer:

Names, Dates, Events
Review Notes

Topic	Information
On this side of line, put important names, dates, or events	On this side, explain why those are important

ELIZABETH I

by **Milton Meltzer**

"Good Queen Bess" her people called her. But "good" is a tame word for one of the most remarkable women who ever lived. Elizabeth I came to the throne of England in 1558 at the age of twenty-five. It was not a happy time for a young woman to take the responsibility for ruling a kingdom. Religious conflicts, a huge government debt, and heavy losses in a war with France had brought England low. But by the time of Elizabeth's death forty-five years later, England had experienced one of the greatest periods in its long history. Under Elizabeth's leadership, England had become united as a nation; its industry and commerce, its arts and sciences had flourished; and it was ranked among the great powers of Europe. **(A)**

Elizabeth was the daughter of King Henry VIII and his second wife, Anne Boleyn. At the age of two she lost her mother when Henry had Anne's head chopped off. Not a good start for a child. But her father placed her in the care of one lord or lady after another, and the lively little girl with the reddish-gold hair, pale skin, and golden-brown eyes won everyone's affection. **(B)**

Almost from her infancy Elizabeth was trained to stand in for ruling men, in case the need should arise. So she had to master whatever they were expected to know and do. Her tutors found the child to be an eager student. She learned history, geography, mathematics, and the elements of astronomy and architecture. She mastered four modern languages—French, Italian, Spanish, and Flemish[1]—as well as classical Greek and Latin. She wrote in a beautiful script that was like a work of art. The earliest portrait painted of her—when she was thirteen—shows a girl with innocent eyes holding a book in her long and delicate hands, already confident and queenly in her bearing.

She was a strong-willed girl who liked to give orders. She loved to be out on horseback, and rode so fast it frightened the men assigned to protect her. She loved dancing

---

1. **Flemish:** language spoken in Flanders, a region covering a small part of northern France and Belgium.

(A) Read and Discuss   What is the author setting up for you?

(B) Literary Focus   Subjective / Objective Points of View   What details about Elizabeth's life are objective so far?

Model the Skill

- Explain to students that **subjective** writing is not always easy to identify, particularly when an entire text is in the third person and sounds like straightforward narration. Readers have to look harder for words that may suggest an opinion.

- Read aloud the paragraph that begins, "And there was no shortage of suitors." Tell students that the statement that men wanted to marry Elizabeth and asked her to marry them is a fact because it can be proven by historical accounts. The quote at the end of the paragraph is also fact because it would have been recorded in a document. Although it could be proven that men did not believe the queen's insistence that she wanted to remain single, the word *understandably* suggests that the author thinks it perfectly reasonable that they would not believe her given her encouragement of many suitors. It is only one word, but the choice to use this word introduces the author's opinion into an otherwise objective paragraph.

Guided Practice: Apply

Turn and Talk Have students review what they have read so far and then work in pairs to identify another instance of what they think is subjective writing. Have each pair discuss what makes this writing subjective.

Think as a Reader/Writer

Find It in Your Reading Point out that at the top of the second column on p. 424, the author expresses his opinion that Elizabeth was a very special woman.

Use It in Your Writing Have students write a sentence that expresses an opinion about a celebrity, athlete, or historical figure.

---

too—she never gave it up. Even in her old age she was seen one moonlit night dancing by herself in the garden.

Elizabeth had a half sister, Mary, born in 1516 of Henry's first wife, Catherine of Aragon. Many years later came Elizabeth, the child of Anne Boleyn, and four years after, her half brother, Edward, the son of Henry's third wife, Jane Seymour. After Henry died, because succession[2] came first through the male, ten-year-old Edward was crowned king. But he lived only another six years. Now Mary took the throne and, soon after, married King Philip II of Spain, a Catholic monarch like herself. He was twenty-seven and she was thirty-eight. But they were rarely together, each ruling their own kingdom. Mary died of cancer at the age of forty-two. That made Elizabeth the monarch.

When she came to the throne on November 17, 1558, it was a day to be marked by celebrations, then and long after. As Her Majesty passed down a London street, an astonished housewife exclaimed, "Oh, Lord! The queen is a woman!" For there were still many who could scarcely believe they were to be ruled by another woman. Elizabeth herself would say with mock modesty that she was "a

---

2. **succession:** order in which one succeeds to the throne.

C **Reading Focus** Author's Purpose What purpose or purposes has the author revealed so far? Explain.

D **Literary Focus** Subjective / Objective Points of View Biographers often include direct quotations from their subjects. Why do you think the biographer chose this quotation? What do you learn about Elizabeth from it?

---

mere woman." But everyone soon learned she was a very special woman. "Am I not a queen because God has chosen me to be a queen?" she demanded. **D**

As princess and later as queen, Elizabeth lived in various palaces, with much coming and going; each time she moved, she took along her household staff of 120 people. Often the changes were required because there was no sanitation. The smelly palaces had to be emptied so they could be "aired and sweetened."

Even before Elizabeth came of age, there was much talk of when she would marry, and whom. Marriages among the nobility and royalty were arranged not for love, but for practical reasons—to add land holdings, to strengthen the prestige and power of families, to cement an alliance of nations against a common enemy.

And remember, from the most ancient times, kings claimed that they as men were born to rule by divine right. That is, God had ordained that the crown should pass through the male line of descent. But when the king's wife had no male child, it meant trouble. Who then would rule? That crisis often led to civil war as various factions battled for the power to name a king. Many disputed Elizabeth's right to the throne, and as long as she had neither husband nor successor, her life was in danger.

Vocabulary **monarch** (MAHN ahrk) *n.:* sole and absolute ruler.

alliance (uh LY uhns) *n.:* pact between nations, families, or individuals that shows a common cause.

Universal Access

Analyzing Visuals

Connecting to the Text What details in the painting suggest Elizabeth's importance to society?

Ever since Elizabeth was eight, however, she had said again and again, "I will never marry." Did marriage look promising to a girl whose father had had six wives, two of whom, including her own mother, he had beheaded? Yet she liked to hear of people who wanted to marry her. **E**

And there was no shortage of suitors. She continued to insist she wished to live unmarried. No matter how often she said it, men did not believe it. Understandably, since she often made a prince or duke who had come to court her believe she was finally ready to give in—only at the last moment to back out. Once, to a delegation from Parliament come to beg her to marry, she declared, "I am already bound unto a husband, which is the Kingdom of England."

And why should she, the absolute ruler of England, allow a man to sit alongside her as king? The power of husbands over wives in that century—and even now, in many places of this world—was so great that a husband might snatch the reins of power from her and leave her with the title but not the authority she loved to exercise. **F**

Was it fun to be queen? As monarch,

Queen Elizabeth I (1533–1603) being carried in Procession (Eliza Triumphans) c. 1601 by Robert Peake (fl. 1580–1626).

E | **Literary Focus** | Subjective / Objective Points of View Although this paragraph consists mostly of objective details, what subjective opinion is suggested in the question Meltzer asks?

F | **Read and Discuss** | How did the time period in which Elizabeth lived influence her views on marriage?

- Have a volunteer choose a sentence they think is subjective. Discuss the sentence with the class and identify objective and subjective elements.

Students with Disabilities

Because this is a long, complex selection, allow students to read it in short segments. After students read each segment of the text, work with them to summarize what they've learned about Elizabeth I so far.

Analyzing Visuals

Tell students that **Robert Peake** (c. 1551–1619) had a brief career painting portraits of the sons of one of Elizabeth's successors, King Charles I. His style resembled that of the painters of miniature portraits that were popular at the time.

Connecting to the Text: *She is being carried on a throne by her subjects, and many people have come to see her.*

Think About/Talk About

▶ Comprehension

C Reading Focus

Possible response: The author's purpose so far is to convince the reader that Elizabeth was a great queen. He described how extraordinary she was.

F Read and Discuss

Possible response: The power of husbands over wives during the sixteenth century potentially threatened Elizabeth's reign over England, so she vowed she would never marry.

▶ Analysis

D Literary Focus

Possible response: Elizabeth believes that she has a right to be queen because she was chosen by God.

E Literary Focus

Possible response: Meltzer's question suggests that he believes that Elizabeth did not think highly of marriage because she had observed so many as a child that ended horribly.

▶ Extend the Discussion

Characterization What does the information in the second paragraph on p. 425 suggest about Elizabeth's character? *Possible response: She's stubborn, and believes that she doesn't need a husband, but she enjoys being admired.*

Vocabulary: Own the Word

- **monarch:** Help students understand the word *monarch* and its associations. Tell students that a president is elected and works with the other branches of government, but a monarch has complete control over the laws of a country.

- **alliance:** Have students use the word *alliance* in context. You might say:"Have you ever formed an alliance with someone? Why? What was the benefit of forming an alliance with them?" *Possible response: I formed an alliance with friends to help our friend become class president. Our alliance helped her win the election.*

- Tell students that **subjective** details can create sensory images that engage and inform the reader.

- Tell students to read the first column on p. 427. Explain how the writer uses subjective details to convey the splendor of the parties that the queen attended. The writer describes the glittering candles "creating a fairyland" and the elite guests enjoying the "hideous sport of bear baiting." Explain that while these subjective details do not provide facts for the reader, they still contribute to the reader's knowledge by helping the reader imagine the scene. The author has used these details to show the readers that Elizabeth attended the fanciest parties of her day. She and her company enjoyed a sport that would have been considered barbaric today, bear baiting.

Guided Practice: Apply

Turn-and-Talk Have students discuss other subjective details that they have read so far that aid their understanding of Elizabeth. What do these subjective details tell them about the queen?

Queen Elizabeth watching *The Merry Wives of Windsor* at the Globe Theatre by David Scott (1806–1849). Oil on canvas.

she commanded great wealth, inherited from her father, and people who wanted favors were always enriching her with lavish presents. She was no spendthrift, however. She hated to see money wasted, whether her own or the kingdom's. Early on she began keeping careful household account books, and later she would do the same with the royal accounts. Always she urged her counselors to carry out orders as inexpensively as possible.

Above everything else, Elizabeth wanted to have her people think well of her. Her deepest desire was to assure them of peace and prosperity. And why not make a grand personal impression upon them at the same time? In her mature years she gave free rein to her love of jewels and staged brilliant displays for the court and the people. Her dresses were decorated with large rubies, emeralds, and diamonds, and she wore jeweled necklaces, bracelets, and rings. In her hair, at her ears, and around her neck she wore pearls—the symbol of virginity.

During her reign she made many great processions through London, the people wild with excitement, crowding the streets—for the English, like most people, loved spectacle. In the first of them, her coronation, she wore gold robes as she was

Cross-Curricular Connection

HISTORY: The Pressure to Marry

Throughout her rule, Elizabeth endured great pressure to wed. When Elizabeth assumed the throne, her country was in disorder. The military was weak, and the nation itself was not well respected. Many voiced concern that Elizabeth should marry, as a strategic betrothal could strengthen England by increasing its allies.

- Many of Elizabeth's contemporaries believed that women were too emotional and impulsive to rule a nation. Instead, their more superior, rational male counterparts should reign.

- Later, Englishmen grew concerned about who might succeed Elizabeth. With neither a husband nor an heir, next in line for the throne was Mary, Queen of Scots. Since Mary had French and Catholic support, many feared Mary would rise to power and resume Catholic control of the nation. It was thought that if Elizabeth had an heir, the threat of Mary, Queen of Scots would diminish.

crowned. Trumpets sounded, pipes and drums played, the organ pealed, bells rang. Then came the state banquet in Westminster Hall. It began at 3:00 P.M., and went on till 1:00 A.M.

Elizabeth was often entertained at house parties. One of them, given by the Earl of Leicester in Kenilworth Castle, lasted for eighteen days in July. Thirty other distinguished guests were invited. The great number of their servants (together with Leicester's) turned the palace into a small town. When darkness fell, candles glittered everywhere, indoors and out, creating a fairyland. Musicians sang and played, the guests danced in the garden, and such a great display of fireworks exploded that the heavens thundered and the castle shook. Then came a pleasure relished in those days: the hideous sport of bear baiting. A pack of dogs was let loose in an inner courtyard to scratch and bite and tear at thirteen tormented bears. Still, the happy guests retained their appetite for a "most delicious banquet of 300 dishes."

The tremendous festival at Kenilworth was only one of the highlights of Elizabeth's summer festival. She moved from one great house to another all season long, always at the enormous expense of her hosts. They had little to complain of, however, for their wealth was often the product of the queen's generous bestowal of special privileges. In recognition of his high rank and in return for

his support, she granted the duke of Norfolk a license to import carpets from Turkey free of duty. The earl of Essex was favored with the profitable right to tax imported sweet wines. Other pets got rich from a monopoly on the importation of or taxation of silks, satins, salt, tobacco, starch. **(H)**

England was a small nation at the time she ruled: less than four million people, about as many as live in Arizona today. But the English were a young people, coming to maturity with new worlds opening up to them, in the mind and across the seas. A rebirth of culture—the Renaissance—had begun in the 1400s. With the revival of interest in the literature of the ancient Greek and Roman worlds came the beginning of a great age of discovery. This period marked the transition from medieval to modern times. The arts and sciences were influenced by changes in economic life. All the nation was swept up in the vast tides of change. Merchants, bankers, the gentry,[3] artisans, seamen, miners—men and women of every class and condition—felt themselves part of the national venture. **(I)**

At the heart of the change in England was the queen. But no king or queen rules alone, no matter how authoritative or arrogant they may be. They usually look to others for advice, advice they may follow

---

3. **gentry:** upper class.

(G) | **Literary Focus** Subjective / Objective Points of View What do these objective details show about Elizabeth?

(H) | **Read and Discuss** What have you learned about Elizabeth and her relationship with other members of royalty?

Vocabulary **monopoly** (muh NAHP uh lee) *n.*: exclusive control of a market.

arrogant (AR uh guhnt) *adj.*: convinced of one's importance.

(I) | **Read and Discuss** What is the connection between the Renaissance and England during Elizabeth's rule?

- Robert Dudley, who was the Earl of Leicester, was said to be one of Elizabeth's favorite suitors. Although he had a poor reputation with many in England, Elizabeth bestowed much of her attention upon Dudley. After Dudley's wife died, many thought Elizabeth would marry him; however, she held to her decision to be England's mistress.

 HSS Analysis Skills: HI 1, 2, 3

Analyzing Visuals
Tell students that **David Scott** (1806–1849) had art in his blood—his father worked as an engraver. Scott's artistic interests lay in painting historic scenes, including the painting of Queen Elizabeth at the Globe Theatre.

Extension Activity Have students consider how this theater production differs from modern-day shows. *Possible response: Most of the audience is standing, and they appear to be much closer to the actors.*

▶ Comprehension

(H) Read and Discuss
Possible response: She enjoyed many parties and festivals. She was very generous to the people she liked.

(I) Read and Discuss
Possible responses: The Renaissance was a period of rebirth that marked the change between medieval and modern times. It was embraced by the English during Elizabeth's reign.

▶ Analysis

(G) Literary Focus
Possible response: The details about Elizabeth's appearance and jewels make me think she was vain and shallow, although the details about her accounting skills show that she was also intelligent and good with money. The author gives the reader mixed opinions about Elizabeth.

▶ Extend the Discussion
Subjective Writing Read the author's description of bear baiting at the end of the second full paragraph of p. 515. What does the author imply about modern society compared to Elizabethan society? *Possible response: The author implies that people today are much more civilized and gentle than people who lived in Elizabethan times.*

Vocabulary: Own the Word
- **monopoly:** Tell students that *monopoly* is associated with business and money. *Monopolies* may make their owners a lot of money, but they can have many negative consequences. If a company has a *monopoly* on a product, they can charge any price that they want, no matter how high.

- **arrogant:** Ask students to applaud in order to indicate if they would like to be described as *arrogant*. Ask students to explain why they did or did not applaud. *Possible response: Student do not applaud; arrogance is a negative trait.*

Model the Skill

- Provide students with copies of the graphic organizer (see **Chapter 4 Resources**) or ask them to use a piece of their own paper.

- Tell students that most nonfiction texts are meant to inform the reader. This biography of Queen Elizabeth is meant to inform too, but there are other purposes as well.

- Model for students analyzing one of the **author's purposes** for "Elizabeth I." You might say: "On p. 428, the author describes how religion almost tears Elizabeth's kingdom apart. People threaten to overthrow the queen. Even the Pope encouraged people to kill the queen over religion. But, the author maintains that Elizabeth was just and fair. He is trying to persuade the reader that even though she faced opposition, Elizabeth was a great ruler."

Guided Practice: Apply

Have students look for other details in the selection that show that the author is trying to persuade the reader to think of Elizabeth in a certain way. Have students share the details they find with the class and record them in their graphic organizer.

Author's Purpose	Details
to persuade	Elizabeth kept religion from tearing her country apart

---

or reject. Elizabeth appointed ministers to handle the various departments of government, and made Sir William Cecil, then thirty-eight, her principal advisor. He was a brilliant, hardworking master of statecraft, devoted to her and England's well-being, and as ruthless as she and the nation's interests required. When he died in old age, his son Robert replaced him at her side.

So great was the queen's role, however, that her time became known as the Age of Elizabeth. Not only did many fine musicians flower, but writers too, such as Christopher Marlowe and John Donne and Ben Jonson and Edmund Spenser. And above all, the incomparable William Shakespeare, whose plays were sometimes performed at court. Astronomers, naturalists, mathematicians, geographers, and architects pioneered in their fields. **J**

Then, too, there were the daring explorers who pushed English expansion overseas. One of the queen's favorites, Sir Walter Raleigh, planned the colony of Virginia in America and named it for her, the Virgin Queen. The queen herself put money into several of the great voyages, keeping close watch over the plans and their results. She supported Sir Francis Drake on his three-year voyage around the world, profiting mightily from the immense loot he captured from Spanish ships taken in the Pacific.

For Elizabeth, one of the most urgent problems was the question of religion. Her father had broken with the Catholic Church and launched the English Reformation, creating the Church of England, with him-self at its head. When Elizabeth's older half sister, Mary (who remained Catholic), married the Catholic king of Spain, Philip II, she reconciled England with the Church of Rome. In Mary's brief reign she persecuted those Protestants who refused to conform, executing some 270 of them.

When Elizabeth became queen upon Mary's death, she said she hoped religion would not prevent her people from living together in peaceful unity. She did not want to pry into people's souls or question their faith. But in 1570, Pope Pius V excommunicated[4] her, denied her right to the throne, and declared her subjects owed her no allegiance. A directive[5] from the pope's office decreed that the assassination of Queen Elizabeth would not be regarded as a sin. The effect of this directive was to turn practicing Catholics—about half of the English, most of them loyal—into potential traitors. **K**

Though Elizabeth had wanted to pursue a middle way of toleration, circumstances threatened to overwhelm her. She had to beware of several Catholic monarchs of Europe who wished to see a Protestant England overthrown. Philip II of Spain sent ambassadors to England to urge Catholics to rise against Elizabeth, put her cousin Mary[6] on the throne, and restore Roman

---

4. **excommunicated:** cast out from a religious community. Strictly speaking, the queen was denied the sacraments of the Catholic Church.
5. **directive:** order or instruction, especially given by a government.
6. **Mary:** Mary Stuart (1542–1587), Queen of Scots, not Elizabeth's half sister.

J [Reading Focus] Author's Purpose What two purposes are evident in this paragraph?

K [Read and Discuss] What problem is Elizabeth facing?

Universal Access

EL English Learners

English for Academic Success Check students' understanding of challenging vocabulary words in the first full paragraph on p. 428. Have pairs use context clues to identify the meanings of the words *flower, incomparable,* and *pioneered.* Then, guide students to understand that in context, *flower* means "develop or thrive," *incomparable* means "the best of the best," and *pioneered* means "led the way to new knowledge." Explain that the author's creative use of language shows one of his purposes is to entertain.

Advanced Learners

Acceleration Have students choose one of the historical figures mentioned on p. 428 to research in detail. Then, have students create a brief biography of their figure by summarizing their findings in a paragraph.

AAVE Students Who Use African American Vernacular English

English for Academic Success Review with students how to correctly show past time using the past participle of verbs. Point out the following excerpt from

Analyzing Visuals | **Connecting to the Text** The photo above is from a movie about Elizabeth I. Which characteristics of Elizabeth does the actress convey in the scene?

Catholicism as the national faith. The line between power, politics, and religion was becoming very thin.

Missionary priests living abroad were sent into England to stir up opposition to the queen. But the English Catholics as a body never rebelled, nor did they ever intend to. Still, missionary priests such as Edmund Campion were convicted of plotting against Elizabeth and executed.

In 1588 a long-threatened invasion of England by Spain was launched by Philip II. He mistakenly believed that the English Catholics were waiting to welcome him. News of his armada of 130 big ships carrying 17,000 soldiers was terrifying. But the queen did not panic. She supervised the high command personally, meanwhile ral-

lying popular support for the defense of the realm and sending troops to protect the coasts while Sir Francis Drake's ships set out to attack the Spanish fleet.

The Spanish Armada was defeated in three battles, its ships dispersed. When the news came of the tremendous victory, the citizens took to the streets, shouting for joy.

The defeat of the Spanish Armada did not end Spain's aggression against England. The Jesuits[7] in England, who were especially identified with Spain, continued to be persecuted. Richard Topcliffe, a notorious hater of Catholics, was given authority to track down suspects. He examined them under torture

---

7. **Jesuits** (JEHZH oo ihts): priests who are members of the Roman Catholic Society of Jesus.

the end of the first column of p. 428: "Her father had broken with the Catholic Church. . ." Remind students that *had* is an auxiliary verb that precedes the past participle of *break, broken*. Point out that the past participle contrasts with the regular past tense of *break, broke*. Have students practice forming the past participles of the following verbs, using the conventions of formal English: *saw, do, give*. [*had seen, had done, had given*]

Analyzing Visuals

Connecting to the Text: *The actress looks graceful and confident, like Elizabeth. She seems to have control of the room.*

ⓙ Reading Focus
Possible response: *The author is trying to inform the reader of the many artists that lived and flourished during Elizabeth's rule. He is also trying to persuade the reader that Elizabeth inspired an extraordinary artistic era.*

ⓚ Read and Discuss
Possible responses: *The Catholic church doesn't want Elizabeth to rule England, and the pope has told his followers that they are allowed to kill Elizabeth.*

▶ **Extend the Discussion**

Motivation Read the second full paragraph on p. 428. What motivations might Elizabeth have had for supporting English exploration? ***Possible response:*** *Elizabeth wanted England to prosper and grow under her rule, and colonies offered new opportunities for growth and worldwide influence.*

Making Judgments What judgment might you make about the contrast between Elizabeth's belief in religious tolerance and her support of the executions described in the first full paragraph of p. 429? ***Possible response:*** *I think that if Elizabeth believed strongly in peace and tolerance, she shouldn't have allowed such a severe punishment.*

Model the Skill

- Tell students that nonfiction writing, like fiction texts, often provides support to help readers understand the meanings of unfamiliar words. Nonfiction texts may provide actual **definitions** in the text. Point out, though, that not every definition follows the straightforward pattern of *"school means 'a place where you go to learn.'"*

- Read aloud the following sentence from p. 431: "Elizabeth prayed intensely before using the royal touch on people with scrofula, a nasty skin disease. "Tell students that even if they do not recognize the word *scrofula*, they can find out what it means from the definition included in the sentence: "a nasty skin disease." The writer defined *scrofula* in the text so readers could understand what it means and keep reading without interrupting their reading to look the word up.

Guided Practice: Apply

Think/Pair/Share Have students skim the text to identify instances where the writer has defined a word in the text for the reader's use and think about why the writer chose to define that particular word. Ask students to share the definitions they found with a partner, and then have volunteers share their thoughts with the group. Discuss as a class why those definitions are helpful to a reader.

to force information about people who had sheltered them. The treatment of them was so vicious and cruel that the victims welcomed death as a release from their agony. **L**

During Elizabeth's reign several plots to assassinate her were uncovered. Elizabeth managed to give the impression that she was not frightened, but those close to her knew she was. When one of the major plots proved to center around Elizabeth's cousin, Mary, Queen of Scots, Elizabeth found it almost intolerable to put to death a crowned queen. Yet she ordered the use of torture on Mary's co-conspirators, and in the end, Mary was beheaded. A song composed by William Byrd at the time suggests how ominous the news of a monarch's execution was:

L **Literary Focus** Subjective / Objective Points of View Is this sentence an objective fact or a subjective detail? Explain.

Vocabulary **intolerable** (ihn TAHL uhr uh buhl) *adj.*: unbearable.

The noble famous Queen
who lost her head of late
Doth show that kings as well as clowns
Are bound to fortune's fate,
And that no earthly Prince
Can so secure his crown
but fortune with her whirling wheel
Hath power to pull them down.

When two earls combined forces against her, Elizabeth's troops overcame them. The queen was so enraged she ordered that 800 of the mostly poor rebels be hanged. But she spared the lives of their wealthy leaders so that they might enrich her, either by buying their pardons or by forfeiting[8] their lands. **M**

Elizabeth came down hard on writers who criticized her actions. John Stubbs, a zealous Puritan, wrote a pamphlet expressing horror at the possibility the queen might marry a French Catholic. The queen had Stubbs and his publisher tried and convicted for seditious libel.[9] How dare Stubbs say publicly she was too old to marry, and that the much younger French suitor could not possibly be in love with her? Elizabeth was merciless as she invoked the penalty for libel. With a butcher's cleaver, the executioner cut the right hands off Stubbs and his publisher. Not an uncommon punishment.

---

8. **forfeiting** (FAWR fiht ihng): giving up, usually because of force of some kind.
9. **seditious libel** (sih DIHSH uhs LY buhl): stirring up of discontent about the government (sedition) with false written statements (libel).

M **Read and Discuss** What picture has the author given you of Elizabeth?

Reaching Reluctant Readers

Encourage students to make a social connection to the text by comparing Elizabeth's reign with the roles and powers of leaders today. Use a Pinwheel Discussion to have students consider the following questions.

- What powers did Elizabeth have that enabled her to do things world leaders would not be able to do today?

- How were the issues that affected her reign similar and different to the challenges our society currently faces?

- Was Elizabeth a strong and fair leader? How does her reign compare to that of other monarchs or politicians who have led a country in terms of fairness, justice, and equality?

Have students report the main points of their discussion back to the rest of the class.

How did Elizabeth learn of all these plots and conspiracies? How did she know what plans Philip II of Spain was devising to invade her kingdom? Spies and secret agents—they were her eyes and ears. Crucial to the flow of information was Sir Francis Walsingham. Trained as a lawyer, he lived on the Continent[10] for years, mastering the languages and the ins and outs of European affairs. Upon his return home, he was asked by Sir William Cecil, the queen's right arm, to gather information on the doings and plans of foreign governments. Soon he was made chief of England's secret service. He placed over seventy agents and spies in the courts of Europe. And of course he watched closely the activities of people at home suspected of disloyalty. Letters to and from them were secretly opened, to nip plots in the bud. **N**

Monarchs had absolute power. Elizabeth could arrest anyone, including the topmost ranks of the nobility, and imprison them in the Tower of London even if they had not committed any legal offense. The only thing that held her back was her fear of public opinion. It upset her when a crowd gathered at a public execution and was so disgusted by the butchery that they let out roars of disapproval. Still, like all rulers, Elizabeth said she believed that "born a sovereign princess" she enjoyed "the privilege common to all kings" and was "exempt from human jurisdiction[11] and subject only to the judgement of God."

Despite her blazing nervous energy, Elizabeth was often sick. Her ailments were anxiously reported and discussed. For the English believed her survival was their only guarantee of freedom from foreign invasion and civil war. Once, suffering a raging toothache for the first time, the queen feared the pain of having an extraction. She had never had a tooth pulled and was terrified. To reassure her, an old friend, the Bishop of London, had her watch while the dental surgeon pulled out one of the bishop's own good teeth. And then she consented to have her own taken out.

It was commonly believed then that kings and queens had the magical power to cure disease in their subjects. Eager to demonstrate that she too had the sacred power of royalty, Elizabeth prayed intensely before using the royal touch on people with scrofula, a nasty skin disease. Her chaplain said he watched "her exquisite hands, boldly, and without

> Monarchs had absolute power. Elizabeth could arrest anyone.

---

10. **Continent:** Europe.

11. **jurisdiction** (jur ihs DIHK shuhn): legal control.

N [Read and Discuss] Has your perception of Elizabeth changed since the beginning of this excerpt? Explain.

Think About/Talk About

▶ Comprehension

M Read and Discuss

Possible response: *The author has shown Elizabeth as merciless against her enemies, unless they were able to bribe her with money. This picture presents her as greedy.*

N Read and Discuss

Possible response: *I thought that Elizabeth was more just and passionate than other kings and queens. Now, I see that she was just as greedy and controlling as any other monarch.*

▶ Analysis

L Literary Focus

Possible response: *This is a subjective detail because it presents a judgment about how vicious and cruel the torture was.*

▶ Extend the Discussion

Characterization Read the last paragraph of p. 430. Which of Elizabeth's character traits are revealed by her reaction to those who criticized her? ***Possible response:*** *She was intolerant of those who criticized her. At times, she was harsh and even cruel in her treatment of critics.*

Vocabulary: Own the Word

intolerable: Tell students that *unbearable, insufferable, impossible, painful,* and *excruciating* are synonyms for the word *intolerable. Bearable, manageable, endurable,* and *tolerable* are all antonyms. Ask students to identify a time when they were forced to do something that they thought was *intolerable.* How did they feel? ***Possible response:*** *Students should describe an action or activity that they were not comfortable doing. They should describe their feelings as physical, emotional, or moral distress.*

Developing Oral Fluency

Use the first and second paragraphs of p. 431 to help students practice reading with appropriate inflection within complex text structures. Remind students to pause, emphasize words, or change their intonation based on punctuation.

Paired Activity Divide students into mixed-ability pairs. Model reading the first two lines of the second paragraph using the punctuation to show proper intonation. For example, sentences that end with a question mark should end with rising intonation.

- Have one student read the first paragraph while his or her partner makes a note of any words that are not read fluently. Have partners alternate this procedure until they complete both paragraphs.

- Have students exchange papers to review the terms they had difficulty reading fluently. Provide time for students to practice their recitations independently before allowing them a final opportunity to read with fluency.

✔ See **UA: Differentiating Instruction** for practice passages for developing oral fluency.

Think About/Talk About

▶ Comprehension

Ⓞ Read and Discuss

Possible response: Monarchs were believed to have a sacred ability to cure the sick.

▶ Analysis

Ⓟ Literary Focus

Possible response: The author is trying to persuade the reader that Elizabeth was an extraordinary ruler.

▶ Extend the Discussion

Motivation Why were the people of England so fearful for the queen's health? *Possible response: They believed that Elizabeth was keeping them safe from war and invasion and were anxious that she remained in good health.*

Monitor Students' Comprehension

Guide the class in answering these comprehension questions.

1. Why did Elizabeth become queen of England? [*Her half-sister Mary, the previous queen, died.*]

2. How did Elizabeth differ from other female monarchs of the time? [*She was unusually intelligent and skilled as a ruler, she kept control of her power by refusing to marry, and she disproved the notion that women were too emotional to rule a country alone.*]

3. Describe the author's opinion of Elizabeth. [*He thinks of her as a remarkable woman and a rare genius.*]

---

disgust, pressing the sores and ulcers." In one day it was reported that she healed thirty-eight persons. But if she did not feel divinely inspired, she would not try her touch. **Ⓞ**

Even in the last decade of her life, Elizabeth's energy was astonishing. She was as watchful as always over the affairs of state, though sometimes forgetful. But age made her more irritable; she sometimes shouted at her ladies and even boxed their ears. She was less able to control rival factions out for power, and became so fearful of assassins she rarely left her palaces.

A portrait of her done when she was approaching sixty shows her in a great white silk dress studded with aglets[12] of black onyx, coral, and pearl. She wears three ropes of translucent pearls and stands on a map of England, her England. An ambassador reported that at sixty-three she looked old, but her figure was still beautiful, and her conversation was as brilliant and charming as ever.

Elizabeth's energy was astonishing.

There was dancing at court every evening, a pastime she still enjoyed. When it came to displays of gallantry by eager young men, she could act a bit vain and foolish, although never letting any hopeful get out of bounds.

In early 1603 Elizabeth developed a bad cold that led to a serious fever, and then she fell into a stupor[13] for four days. As she lay dying, all of London became strangely silent. On March 24, the life of a rare genius ended. The nation went into mourning. **Ⓟ**

"Old age came upon me as a surprise, like a frost," she once wrote.

---

12. **aglets** (AG lihts): tips of lace on dresses.

13. **stupor** (STOO puhr): loss of sensibility; dullness.

Ⓞ | Read and Discuss | What does this new information add to what you've been told about monarchs?

Ⓟ | Literary Focus | Subjective / Objective Points of View What might be the author's purpose in using the subjective phrase "rare genius"?

 California Standards, pp. 433–435

■ **Reading Standard 1.3** Clarify word meanings through the use of definition, example, restatement, or contrast.

■ **Reading Standard 3.5** Contrast points of view (e.g., first and third person, limited and omniscient, subjective and objective) in narrative text and explain how they affect the overall theme of the work.

Applying Your Skills

Elizabeth I

Literary Response and Analysis

Reading Skills Focus
Quick Check

1. How did England change during the Renaissance? Who was at the heart of that change?

Read with a Purpose

2. What are some of Elizabeth's most impressive accomplishments?

Reading Skills: Author's Purpose

3. Review the chart you completed as you read the biography. Explain whether the writer achieved each purpose by using subjective details, objective facts, or a combination of the two.

Author's Purpose	Details
to inform	Elizabeth became Queen of England in 1558.
to entertain	
to reveal a truth about life	

Literary Skills Focus
Literary Analysis

4. **Infer** What inferences can you make about how Elizabeth's subjects perceived her? Support your inferences with textual details.

5. **Make Judgments** Write down one opinion about Elizabeth that you formed as you read the biography. What objective facts helped you form that opinion? What subjective details influenced you?

Literary Skills: Subjective and Objective Points of View in Biography

6. **Evaluate** Discuss whether the biographer is too subjective, too objective, or fairly balanced in his account of Elizabeth's life. Find details in the narrative text that support your evaluation.

Literary Skills Review: Recurring Themes

7. **Infer** As an unmarried woman, Elizabeth was a strong ruler in a time when government was dominated by men. What common theme might you infer from her biography?

8. **Compare** Can you think of another story in which a character overcomes great odds to achieve greatness? How is it similar to and different from the story of Elizabeth's life?

Writing Skills Focus
Think as a Reader/Writer
Use It in Your Writing Review the achievements you recorded in your *Reader/Writer Notebook*. Why might the writer have chosen to include these details in the biography?

 What Do You Think Now How did Elizabeth turn challenges into opportunities? What does this tell you about the kind of person she was?

Check for Understanding

Independent Practice
Reading Skills Focus
Possible responses:

1. *England became more prosperous and developed the arts and sciences. The queen was at the heart of the change in this period.*

2. *Elizabeth funded overseas exploration, protected England from the Armada, and held her country together despite religious conflict.*

3. *Details that show that the author sought to entertain include the description Elizabeth as a gifted child (subjective) and Elizabeth dancing alone in the moonlight (objective).*

Literary Skills Focus
Possible responses:

4. *I can infer that Elizabeth's subjects were uneasy about her ability to reign as they were alarmed to be ruled by a woman and afraid that she would never marry and produce an heir.*

5. *Elizabeth was a free spirit who challenged the status quo at the time. She did not marry (objective) and she spent a lot of time at frivolous parties (subjective).*

6. *The biographer balanced objective and subjective details. Every subjective detail had factual support in the form of objective details.*

7. *Women are just as strong as men.*

8. *Odysseus in* The Odyssey *overcomes great odds to return home to his family. He and Elizabeth are similar because they experienced success, but they are different because Odysseus was not born into a privileged life like Elizabeth.*

What Do You Think Now?

Ask students to identify other leaders in history who have "turned challenges into opportunities" by making the best of a difficult situation. Have students compare these leaders to Elizabeth and list examples of how Elizabeth and others turned challenges into opportunities.

Universal Access

Struggling Writers
Provide additional scaffolding for struggling students to complete the Writing Focus activity by having them complete a concept web before writing. In the center of their concept webs, tell them to write the word "achievements." Then, have them write words, phrases, and ideas that they associate with this concept on the lines radiating from the center. Model filling it in with words such as "pride," "contributions," and "making a difference." After they have completed their webs, tell students to use their ideas to help them determine why the author included so many

of Elizabeth's achievements in the biography. What do her achievements say about her?

Applying Your Skills

Reading Standard 1.3 Clarify word meanings through the use of definition, example, restatement, or contrast.

Independent Practice

Vocabulary Development

Your Turn

Possible responses:

1. Elizabeth I was a famous English monarch. That is, she was born to be a ruler.

2. Two rulers formed an alliance, a pact that shows a common cause.

3. Businesses are prevented from obtaining exclusive control of a market—a monopoly—to keep prices competitive.

4. The actor was too arrogant, or overly self-important, to admit his mistake.

5. People thought the king's rule was intolerable. That is, his reign was unbearable.

English for Academic Success

Language Coach

Explain to students that the word *conspiracy* comes from Latin roots meaning "to breathe together." Knowing the root of a word can often help us work out its meaning.

1. spir - conspiracy
2. geo - geography
3. spec - spectacle
4. jud - judgment
5. port - importation

English for Academic Success

Academic Vocabulary

Possible response: Meltzer conveys Elizabeth as compassionate by showing her reluctance to assassinate her cousin. But, subjective details such as how cruelly she tortured her enemies lead me to perceive her as the opposite—cold and unfeeling.

Learn It Online

WordSharp: An Interactive Vocabulary Tutor provides additional support for vocabulary development. Multimedia tutorials show students how to apply vocabulary skills to unfamiliar words—and how to make those words their own.

go.hrw.com   H7-434   **Go**

Elizabeth I

Vocabulary Development

Clarifying Word Meanings: Definitions

You may have noticed that Milton Meltzer often helps you with the meanings of difficult words and terms, defining them within the sentence in which they appear or in a sentence nearby. Writers of textbooks and other materials written for students often do this. It's up to you to be able to recognize a definition when you see it. Here are three examples from "Elizabeth I" in which Meltzer clarifies word meanings through definitions.

Here, the words *that is* signal that a definition is following. Meltzer uses an entire sentence to define *divine right*.

> "Kings claimed that they as men were born to rule by divine right. *That is*, God had ordained that the crown should pass through the male line of descent."

In this example, the definition of *Renaissance* comes before the word:

> "*A rebirth of culture*—the Renaissance—had begun in the 1400s."

Here, Meltzer defines the word *scrofula* right after the comma:

> "Elizabeth prayed intensely before using the royal touch on people with scrofula, *a nasty skin disease.*"

Your Turn

Write a sentence for each Vocabulary word at right, defining the word by applying one of the methods used in the examples. Use each method at least once.

monarch
alliance
monopoly
arrogant
intolerable

Language Coach

Recognizing Roots

Remember that a word root is a word or word part from which several other words can be formed. The chart at right contains some word roots and their meanings.

Root	Meaning
spir–	breathe
geo–	earth
spec–	see
jud–	judge
port–	carry

Each of the following words from the biography contains a word root from the chart. Explain how knowing the meaning of the root helps you understand the meaning of the word.

1. conspiracy
2. geography
3. spectacle
4. judgment
5. importation

Academic Vocabulary

Talk About . . .

Get together with a partner, and analyze the way Meltzer reveals his opinion of Elizabeth during her reign. What subjective details affect the way you perceive her character?

Learn It Online
Improve your word skills with *WordSharp* at:

go.hrw.com   H7-434   **Go**

Universal Access: Vocabulary Development

 English Learners

English for Academic Success Help students understand how authors clarify word meanings by embedding word definitions in a text by further explaining the syntax and punctuation found in the examples on p. 434. Point out that in the first example, the phrase "That is" is followed by a comma. In the second example, the defined word is preceded and followed by em dashes. Explain that em dashes are used to emphasize phrases that are set apart from the normal flow of the sentence. Explain that in the final example, a comma precedes the definition of the word *scrofula*. Remind students that all three syntactical constructions can be used to clarify word meanings within a text.

Grammar Link

Types of Sentences

Sentences are classified not only by structure but also by purpose. The purpose of a sentence is classified as either declarative, interrogative, imperative, or exclamatory.

Declarative sentences are sentences that make a statement. They end in a period.

> *Elizabeth had a fascinating life.*

An **interrogative sentence** asks a question. It always ends in a question mark.

> *Who was Elizabeth's mother?*

Imperative sentences give commands or make requests. A strong command may end in an exclamation point.

> *Please explain how she became queen.*

Note: If an imperative sentence does not have a subject, the understood subject is always *you*.

> *[You] Throw him in the dungeon!*

Exclamatory sentences show excitement or strong feelings. They end with an exclamation point.

> *How dare he say I am too old to marry!*

Your Turn

Classify and correctly punctuate the following sentences.

1. When did Elizabeth hear about the plot
2. Remain quiet in the queen's presence
3. England had a small population during Elizabeth's reign
4. Long live the queen

CHOICES

As you respond to the Choices, use these **Academic Vocabulary** words as appropriate: analyze, narrative, organizational, perceive.

REVIEW
Support a Position

Timed Writing Is the narrative completely objective about Elizabeth, or did the author introduce some subjective details? What is the effect of this technique? Write a brief persuasive essay in which you analyze the author's point of view, supporting your position with specific details from the text.

CONNECT
Take a Different Point of View

Partner Work Work with a partner to rewrite the first paragraph of this biography as a first-person narrative. Use the pronoun *I* to relate Elizabeth's point of view, and include subjective details. (Imagine how Elizabeth might perceive her achievements and disappointments.)

EXTEND
Create a Biographical Sketch

TechFocus Write a short biographical sketch of a historical figure you admire. Use the Internet to gather information, and decide whether you want to include primarily objective facts, subjective details, or a combination of the two. Choose an effective organizational pattern for your biographical sketch, such as chronological order if you want to give an overview of the person's life, or cause and effect if you want to examine a person's historical contributions.

Learn It Online
Use these Internet links to discover more about the story:

go.hrw.com | H7-435 | **Go**

Independent Practice

Grammar Link
Your Turn

1. interrogative, ?
2. imperative, . or !
3. declarative, .
4. exclamatory, !

Choices:
Evaluation Criteria
Review: Timed Writing
40–50 minutes

Students use persuasive technique and text details to support their position on the author's point of view.

Connect: **Homework**
Take a Different Point of View

- Students use first-person pronouns and subjective details, and consider Elizabeth's traits and personality.

Extend: **Homework**
Create a Biographical Sketch

- Students research and write a biographical sketch.
- Students follow an organizational pattern appropriate to the content of the sketch.

Assess

Chapter 4 Resources, Selection Standards Check, pp. 27–29

ThinkCentral Online Assessment, Selection Standards Check

Teacher One Stop™, editable Selection Standards Check

Reteach

ThinkCentral Online Remediation

Learn It Online
Literature Links direct students to pre-screened Web sites offering more information related to a selection.

go.hrw.com | H7-435 | **Go**

Universal Access: Grammar Link

English Learners

English for Academic Success Use this lesson to reinforce the standard use of types of sentences.

- Point out to students that examining the words *declarative, interrogative,* and *exclamatory* can make them easier to remember. *Declarative* comes from *declare,* which means "to state;" a declarative sentence is a statement. *Interrogative* comes from *interrogate,* which means "to ask questions." Students may remember seeing witnesses interrogated on television or in movies. *Exclamatory* is related to *exclaim;* students may also associate it with exclamation point. *Imperative* is related to *imperial,* which has to do with ruling and commanding.

- Have students write a brief paragraph or dialogue that contains one of each type of sentence. Then, have each student trade with a partner and label the types of sentences in each other's compositions.

✔ For more practice with types of sentences, see **Warriner's Handbook, Grammar Notes,** and **Language Handbook Worksheets**.

Standards Focus

Objectives

Students will

- understand objective and subjective point of view in an autobiography
- distinguish fact from opinion

Motivate

What Do You Think?/QuickWrite

Have students write for 3–5 minutes in their **Reader/Writer Notebook** about a challenge they had to face, and how they approached the challenge. Invite volunteers to share their thoughts with the class.

English for Academic Success

Academic Vocabulary

Look for opportunities to use the Academic Vocabulary words in the chapter.

- **analyze, v.:** examine in detail
- **narrative, adj:** that narrates or recounts; being in story form
- **perceive, v:** be aware of through the senses; observe

Analyzing Visuals

Extension Activity Ask students to discuss the message the image conveys about the United States. ***Possible response:*** *The image conveys the idea that the United States is a diverse country made up of people from a variety of different backgrounds.*

California Standards, pp. 443–445

- **Reading Standard 3.5** Contrast points of view (e.g., first and third person, limited and omniscient, subjective and objective) in narrative text, and explain how they affect the overall theme of the work.

Preparing to Read

from BARRIO BOY

by **Ernesto Galarza**

What Do You Think? How might your attitude hinder you when you confront a new experience?

QuickWrite

Describe what you would do if you suddenly had to learn a new language. If you have been in this situation, explain how you learned the language.

America (1985)
by Diana Ong (1940–   ).

Selection Readability	
Easily Accessible	familiar theme; familiar genre;
Accessible	complex syntax
Challenging	

Selection Summary

Ernesto begins attending a school in America after emigrating from Mexico. With the help of his teacher and classmates, he learns to speak English and appreciate his new surroundings while retaining aspects of his culture.

Reader/Writer Notebook

Use your **RWN** to complete the activities for this selection.

from **Barrio Boy**

Reading Standard 3.5 Contrast points of view (e.g., **first** and third **person,** limited and omniscient, **subjective and objective**) in narrative text, and explain how they affect the overall theme of the work.

Literary Skills Focus

Subjective and Objective Points of View in Autobiography An **autobiography** is a person's life story written by that very person. You will notice a contrast between the point of view of an autobiography such as *Barrio Boy* and the point of view of a biography such as "Elizabeth I."

The essential facts and relevant details of a biography and an autobiography may be the same. In an autobiography, however, you learn the writer's feelings about his or her experiences because the point of view is almost completely subjective. A biography, on the other hand, is mostly told from an objective point of view, with an emphasis on researched facts. An autobiography is told from the first-person point of view; the writer reveals his or her inner thoughts and feelings. A biography is told from the third-person point of view, which keeps the focus on the subject, not the writer.

Reading Skills Focus

Distinguishing Fact from Opinion When you read an autobiography, you must be able to tell fact from opinion. A **fact** is a statement that can be proved true. *Sacramento is the capital of California* is a fact. An **opinion** is a personal feeling or belief: *I think Sacramento is a great place to live.* Opinions cannot be proven true. Be mindful that some writers may state an opinion as if it were a fact. If you are unsure, ask yourself, "Can this statement be proven true, or is it someone's personal belief?" If the statement can be proven true, then it is a fact.

Into Action As you read, keep a log of facts and opinions you find in Galarza's autobiography.

Writing Skills Focus

Think as a Reader/Writer

Find It in Your Reading Notice the precise descriptive details Galarza uses that help you visualize his new school. List at least five of these details in your *Reader/Writer Notebook.*

Language Coach

Comparing Adjectives The comparative degree of an adjective (to form, add *–er* or *more*) compares two or more people or things. The superlative degree (to form, add *–est* or *most*) compares more than two people or things.

Learn It Online

See a good reader in action, and practice your own skills, at:

go.hrw.com   H7-437   **Go**

Selection Resources

Chapter 4 Resources, on-level practice and assessment, pp. 30–35

Teacher One Stop™, on-level lesson plans and all print resources

Holt Audio Library

Holt Audio Library: Selections and Summaries in Spanish

UA: Supporting Instruction in Five Languages, selection summary

Analyzing Visuals Transparencies, p. 43

ThinkCentral Online Assessment, Selection Standards Check

ThinkCentral Online Remediation

Learn It Online

Online reading support for this selection includes audio segments that model the thought processes of a good reader. These **Think-Aloud** models are followed by prompts that let students record their own thoughts about the selection.

go.hrw.com   H7-437   **Go**

Selection Introduction

More About the Writer

During the 1950s, **Ernesto Galarza** helped create the first multiracial farm worker's union. He also founded the Mexican American Legal Defense Fund. Ernesto Galarza wrote many papers and articles, and in 1979, he was the first U.S. Latino to be nominated for the Nobel Prize in Literature.

Think About the Writer

To answer the question, suggest students discuss how education can affect their daily life outside of school. How can education improve a person's chances of success later in life? Have students record their responses in their **Reader/Writer Notebook**.

 For Independent Reading

■ If students enjoy the selection from Ernesto Galarza's *Barrio Boy,* they may enjoy Maureen Crane Wartski's *A Long Way from Home.* It is the story of Vietnamese immigrants struggling to adjust to American life.

■ If students want to read more about the experiences of Hispanic immigrants in America, recommend *Any Small Goodness*: *A Novel of the Barrio* by Tony Johnston.

MEET THE WRITER

Ernesto Galarza
(1905–1984)

Beginning His Journey

For young **Ernesto Galarza,** coming to the United States meant abandoning everything he had ever known and confronting an alien landscape. He couldn't understand the language; the customs and values were strange. Like millions of other immigrants, he felt lost. He soon discovered that education was the key to making sense of his new life. Eventually, Galarza earned his Ph.D. from Columbia University in New York and then returned to California to teach.

Making His Mark

His most beloved book is *Barrio Boy,* the bestselling 1971 account of his journey from Mexico to the United States. In the quotation below, Galarza explains how he came to write *Barrio Boy.*

"*Barrio Boy* began as anecdotes I told my family about Jalcocotán, the mountain village in western Mexico where I was born. Among this limited public (my wife, Mae, and daughters, Karla and Eli Lu) my thumbnail sketches became bestsellers. Hearing myself tell them over and over, I began to agree with my captive audience that they were not only interesting but possibly good."

Think About the Writer   How can you tell that education is important to Galarza?

Build Background

Ernesto Galarza was born in 1905 in Jalcocotán, a village in western Mexico. In 1910, when the Mexican Revolution threatened their peaceful mountain home, Ernesto, his mother, and two uncles left their village for Mazatlán, Mexico. Eventually, they moved to Sacramento, California, and lived in what Galarza calls a "rented corner of the city"—the *barrio,* or Spanish-speaking neighborhood.

Preview the Selection

Ernesto Galarza, the narrator of the story, is beginning his first day of school in the United States. He is worried about fitting in because he speaks primarily Spanish at home.

Universal Access

EL English Learners

Encourage students to share their own experiences with learning a new language. Ask them to share what has helped them to learn and what has been challenging for them. Have them compare their experiences with that of Ernesto's as they read.

Struggling Readers

Explain that writers are often subtle in their use of facts and opinions. That is, facts are not always in the form of numbers, names, or statistics; nor are opinions always in the form of "I think..." or "I feel...." Explain that Galarza writes this essay to share his positive introduction to a new culture through help from his school. He includes both facts and opinions in the detailed descriptions of how the teachers taught him and his classmates. Miss Ryan's careful instruction of the students who are learning English is a fact. The description of how Miss Ryan "loosened me and my classmates from the safe anchorage of our desks" is an opinion because it is Galarza's own perception of this fact. Work with students to find other subtle facts and opinions in the text.

from BARRIO BOY

by **Ernesto Galarza**

Read with a Purpose
Read the following excerpt from an autobiography to discover how one boy from Mexico adjusted to school life in Sacramento, California, in the early 1900s.

The two of us [Ernesto and his mother] walked south on Fifth Street one morning to the corner of Q Street and turned right. Half of the block was occupied by the Lincoln School. It was a three-story wooden building, with two wings that gave it the shape of a double T connected by a central hall. It was a new building, painted yellow, with a shingled roof that was not like the red tile of the school in Mazatlán. I noticed other differences, none of them very reassuring. **A**

We walked up the wide staircase hand in hand and through the door, which closed by itself. A mechanical contraption screwed to the top shut it behind us quietly.

Up to this point the adventure of enrolling me in the school had been carefully rehearsed. Mrs. Dodson had told us how to find it and we had circled it several times on our walks.

Friends in the barrio explained that the director was called a principal, and that it was a lady and not a man. They assured us that there was always a person at the school who could speak Spanish.

Exactly as we had been told, there was a sign on the door in both Spanish and English: "Principal." We crossed the hall and entered the office of Miss Nettie Hopley.

Miss Hopley was at a roll-top desk to one side, sitting in a swivel chair that moved on wheels. There was a sofa against the opposite wall, flanked by two windows and a door that opened on a small balcony. Chairs were set around a table, and framed pictures hung on the walls of a man with long white hair and another with a sad face and a black beard.

The principal half turned in the swivel chair to look at us over the pinch glasses

A **Literary Focus** Subjective / Objective Points of View What evidence of a subjective point of view do you see here?

Vocabulary **reassuring** (ree uh SHUR ihng) *v.* used as *adj.*: comforting.
contraption (kuhn TRAP shuhn) *n.*: strange machine or gadget.
assured (uh SHURD) *v.*: guaranteed; promised confidently.

Advanced Learners
Enrichment Challenge students to write a short response to this excerpt from *Barrio Boy* after they have finished reading. Have them analyze how Ernesto's attitude towards learning developed over time. They may wish to use the background information about the author to extend their analysis beyond the excerpt. Ask volunteers to present their responses to the class.

Direct Teach

Think About/Talk About
Read with a Purpose Have students read the Read with a Purpose statement. Have students use their prior knowledge of learning languages or being in new situations to predict the challenges Ernesto might face.

▶ Comprehension

A **Literary Focus**
Possible response: The author is sharing personal thoughts, feelings, and opinions.

▶ Extend the Discussion
Setting What might you infer about the school from the third and fourth paragraphs? *Possible response:* The school has experience in working with Spanish-speaking students, since people from the barrio are familiar with it and the school has signs in English and Spanish.

Character Re-read the first paragraph. How does Ernesto feel about his first day at a new school? What clues in the text support this? *Possible response:* He appears to feel apprehensive and uncomfortable because he notices differences between this school and his school in Mexico and says they are not reassuring.

Vocabulary: Own the Word
- **reassuring:** Point out that Ernesto finds the differences between his school in Mazatlán and the Lincoln school not *reassuring*. Ask students to explain what he means by this, and why he might feel this way. *Possible response:* Ernesto is nervous, so the differences increase his sense of anxiety rather than comfort him.

- **contraption:** Ask students to name a *contraption* that helps secure together sheets of paper. [*stapler*]

- **assured:** Ask students: Have you ever *assured* someone you would do something? Explain who you *assured* and what you told him or her you would do.

Model the Skill

- Remind students that a **fact** can be proved true, while an **opinion** is a statement of belief or personal preference.

- Model identifying a fact and opinion on p. 440. Read aloud the first full paragraph. Point out that Galarza includes a mixture of both facts and opinions. Explain that his recollections of simple actions, such as Miss Hopley taking off her glasses and signaling the students to the table, are facts. However, his personal thoughts and feelings, such as the "warm welcome" he perceives in Miss Hopley's eyes, are opinions.

Guided Practice: Apply

Have students read the second full paragraph on p. 440. Guide them in evaluating which parts of the paragraph can be classified as facts, and which parts are opinions. Help them understand that while some of Galarza's description of Miss Hopley is factual—for example, her hair is gathered in a bun—much of it is colored by his personal opinions. For example, it cannot be proved that Miss Hopley had "thin lips that moved like steel springs;" this is Galarza's personal opinion on the subject.

Think as a Reader/Writer

Find It in Your Reading Point out Galarza's detailed description of where he receives private English lessons: "the closet, a narrow hall off the classroom with a door at each end."

Use It in Your Writing Have students write a detailed description of a part of the classroom.

crossed on the ridge of her nose. To do this, she had to duck her head slightly, as if she were about to step through a low doorway.

What Miss Hopley said to us we did not know, but we saw in her eyes a warm welcome, and when she took off her glasses and straightened up, she smiled wholeheartedly, like Mrs. Dodson. We were, of course, saying nothing, only catching the friendliness of her voice and the sparkle in her eyes while she said words we did not understand. She signaled us to the table. Almost tiptoeing across the office, I maneuvered myself to keep my mother between me and the gringo[1] lady. In a matter of seconds I had to decide whether she was a possible friend or a menace. We sat down.

Then Miss Hopley did a formidable thing. She stood up. Had she been standing when we entered, she would have seemed tall. But rising from her chair, she soared. And what she carried up and up with her was a buxom superstructure, firm shoulders, a straight sharp nose, full cheeks slightly molded by a curved line along the nostrils, thin lips that moved like steel springs, and a high forehead topped by hair gathered in a bun. Miss Hopley was not a giant in body, but when she mobilized it to a standing position she seemed a match for giants. I decided I liked her. **B**

She strode to a door in the far corner of the office, opened it, and called a name. A boy of about ten years appeared in the doorway.

---

1. **gringo** (GRIHNG goh): someone who is northern American, non-Hispanic, or doesn't speak Spanish.

B **Reading Focus** Fact and Opinion What opinion does Galarza express in this paragraph?

He sat down at one end of the table. He was brown like us, a plump kid with shiny black hair combed straight back, neat, cool, and faintly obnoxious.

Miss Hopley joined us with a large book and some papers in her hand. She, too, sat down and the questions and answers began by way of our interpreter. My name was Ernesto. My mother's name was Henriqueta. My birth certificate was in San Blas. Here was my last report card from the Escuela Municipal Numero 3 para Varones[2] of Mazatlán, and so forth. Miss Hopley put things down in the book and my mother signed a card.

As long as the questions continued, Doña Henriqueta could stay and I was secure. Now that they were over, Miss Hopley saw her

---

2. **Escuela Municipal Numero 3 para Varones:** Spanish for "Municipal School Number 3 for Boys."

Vocabulary formidable (FAWR muh duh buhl) *adj.*: awe-inspiring; impressive.

Universal Access

Students with Disabilities
Guide students in recognizing facts and opinions. For example, point out the contrasts between the opinion "I decided I liked her" on p. 440, and facts, such as "My mother's name was Henriqueta." Challenge students to identify one of each on their own.

(AAVE) Students Who Use African American Vernacular English
English for Academic Success Students may have trouble with the use of an apostrophe and *s* to indicate possession. Point out the following sentence in the last full paragraph of p. 440: "My mother's name was Henriqueta." Explain to students that this sentence

to the door, dismissed our interpreter, and without further ado took me by the hand and strode down the hall to Miss Ryan's first grade.

Miss Ryan took me to a seat at the front of the room, into which I shrank—the better to survey her. She was, to skinny, somewhat runty me, of a withering height when she patrolled the class. And when I least expected it, there she was, crouching by my desk, her blond, radiant face level with mine, her voice patiently maneuvering me over the awful idiocies of the English language. **ⓒ**

During the next few weeks Miss Ryan overcame my fears of tall, energetic teachers as she bent over my desk to help me with a word in the pre-primer. Step by step, she loosened me and my classmates from the safe anchorage of the desks for recitations at the blackboard and consultations at her desk.

Frequently she burst into happy announcements to the whole class. "Ito can read a sentence," and small Japanese Ito, squint-eyed and shy, slowly read aloud while the class listened in wonder: "Come, Skipper, come. Come and run." The Korean, Portuguese, Italian, and Polish first-graders had similar moments of glory, no less shining than mine the day I conquered "butterfly," which I had been persistently pronouncing in standard Spanish as boo-ter-flee. "Children," Miss Ryan called for attention. "Ernesto has learned how to pronounce *butterfly*!" And I proved it with a perfect imitation of Miss Ryan. From that celebrated success, I was soon able to match Ito's progress as a sentence reader with "Come, butterfly, come fly with me."

Like Ito and several other first-graders who did not know English, I received private lessons from Miss Ryan in the closet, a narrow hall off the classroom with a door at each end. Next to one of these doors Miss Ryan placed a large chair for herself and a small one for me. Keeping an eye on the class through the open door, she read with me about sheep in the meadow and a frightened chicken going to see the king, coaching me out of my phonetic ruts in words like *pasture, bow-wow-wow, hay,* and *pretty*, which to my Mexican ear and eye had so many unnecessary sounds and letters. She made me watch her lips and then close my eyes as she repeated words I found hard to read. When we came to know each other better, I tried interrupting to tell Miss Ryan how we said it in Spanish. It didn't work. She

---

ⓒ **Literary Focus** Subjective / Objective Points of View Does the phrase "the awful idiocies of the English language" show a subjective or objective point of view? Explain.

Vocabulary **survey** (suhr VAY) *v.* : look carefully in order to make a decision or gather information.

---

indicates possession. The name Henriquetta belongs to the mother, so in formal English, an apostrophe and *s* is added to the word *mother*. Point out other examples of possession on p. 441, such as "Miss Ryan's first grade" and "Ito's progress." Have students read them aloud.

Think About/Talk About

▶ **Comprehension**

ⓑ Reading Focus

Possible response: He likes and is impressed by Miss Hopley.

▶ **Analysis**

ⓒ Literary Focus

Possible response: An author writing from an objective point of view would not use this phrase because it is based on personal opinion, not facts.

▶ **Extend the Discussion**

Character In the first full paragraph of p. 440, why does Ernesto warm to Miss Hopley even though he cannot understand what she is saying? *Possible response: Ernesto sees that Miss Hopley has a warm welcome in her eyes and smiles at him. She also speaks in a friendly tone, even though he does not understand the words.*

Conflict What internal conflict does Ernesto face in the second column of p. 441? How does he overcome this? *Possible response: Ernesto must learn to stop pronouncing words the Spanish way and learn to speak English. He overcomes his linguistic battle by practicing and by receiving individual lessons from Miss Ryan.*

Vocabulary: Own the Word

- **formidable:** Ask students to applaud in order to indicate how much they would like to be described as *formidable*. Have volunteers share why they made their choice. *Possible response: Students may applaud loudly and explain they would enjoy being thought of as "impressive."*

- **survey:** Act out the word *survey* by looking closely at a classroom object from all angles. Then, invite students to act out their interpretations of the word *survey*.

from Barrio Boy **441**

Possible response: Besides providing the students with knowledge, the school tries to rid the children of their preconceived notions about other cultures.

▶ **Analysis**

E **Literary Focus**

Possible response: Galarza reveals his personal feelings about adjusting to American culture.

▶ **Extend the Discussion**

Characterization At the top of p. 441, Galarza describes students as either not afraid to love Miss Ryan or loving her so they would not be afraid. What does this suggest about her character? *Possible response: She is strong and tough, but also supportive. Her caring nature compels students to love her back.*

Monitor Students' Comprehension

Guide the class in answering these comprehension questions.

1. Who is Ernesto? [*He is a boy from Mexico who moves to America.*]

2. How are many of the other students like Ernesto? [*They come from many different cultures around the world and must work hard to learn English.*]

3. What are two things the teachers helped the students learn? [*traditional academic knowledge and respect for people of all backgrounds*]

only said "oh" and went on with *pasture, bow-wow-wow,* and *pretty.* It was as if in that closet we were both discovering together the secrets of the English language and grieving together over the tragedies of Bo-Peep. The main reason I was graduated with honors from the first grade was that I had fallen in love with Miss Ryan. Her radiant, no-nonsense character made us either afraid not to love her or love her so we would not be afraid, I am not sure which. It was not only that we sensed she was with it, but also that she was with us.

Like the first grade, the rest of the Lincoln School was a sampling of the lower part of town, where many races made their home. My pals in the second grade were Kazushi, whose parents spoke only Japanese; Matti, a skinny Italian boy; and Manuel, a fat Portuguese who would never get into a fight but wrestled you to the ground and just sat on you. Our assortment of nationalities included Koreans, Yugoslavs, Poles, Irish, and home-grown Americans.

Miss Hopley and her teachers never let us forget why we were at Lincoln: for those who were alien, to become good Americans; for those who were so born, to accept the rest of us. Off the school grounds we traded the same insults we heard from our elders. On the playground we were sure to be marched up to the principal's office for calling someone a wop, a chink, a dago, or a greaser. The school was not so much a melting pot as a griddle where Miss Hopley and her helpers warmed knowledge into us and roasted racial hatreds out of us. **D**

At Lincoln, making us into Americans did not mean scrubbing away what made us originally foreign. The teachers called us as our parents did, or as close as they could pronounce our names in Spanish or Japanese. No one was ever scolded or punished for speaking in his native tongue on the playground. Matti told the class about his mother's down quilt, which she had made in Italy with the fine feathers of a thousand geese. Encarnación acted out how boys learned to fish in the Philippines. I astounded the third grade with the story of my travels on a stagecoach, which nobody else in the class had seen except in the museum at Sutter's Fort. After a visit to the Crocker Art Gallery and its collection of heroic paintings of the golden age of California, someone showed a silk scroll with a Chinese painting. Miss Hopley herself had a way of expressing wonder over these matters before a class, her eyes wide open until they popped slightly. It was easy for me to feel that becoming a proud American, as she said we should, did not mean feeling ashamed of being a Mexican. **E**

> The teachers called us as our parents did, or as close as they could pronounce our names.

D **Read and Discuss** The author says that the staff at Lincoln "warmed knowledge into us and roasted racial hatreds out of us." What does he mean by that?

E **Literary Focus** Subjective / Objective Points of View What does the last sentence reveal about whether this narrative is told from a subjective or objective point of view?

 California Standards, pp. 443–445

- **Reading Standard 1.3** Clarify word meanings through the use of definition, example, restatement, or contrast.
- **Reading Standard 3.5** Contrast points of view (e.g., first and third person, limited and omniscient, subjective and objective) in narrative text and explain how they affect the overall theme of the work.

Applying Your Skills

from **Barrio Boy**

Literary Response and Analysis

Reading Skills Focus
Quick Check

1. How are the students in Ernesto's class similar to the children in his neighborhood?
2. According to Miss Hopley and the teachers at Lincoln School, what are the children to remember about why they are at school?
3. How does the Lincoln School honor its students' original languages and customs?

Read with a Purpose

4. How is Ernesto able to adjust to school in California during the early 1900s?

Reading Skills: Fact and Opinion

5. In *Barrio Boy*, Ernesto Galarza reveals his opinions about his teachers. He also presents facts. Give examples of one fact and one opinion Ernesto presents about his teachers.

Literary Skills Focus
Literary Analysis

6. **Interpret** In many ways, this story is a tribute to Ernesto's teachers. What does Galarza mean when he says Miss Ryan was not only "with it, but also . . . with us"?
7. **Connect** How do you think attending the Lincoln School affected Galarza's life both as a child and as an adult?
8. **Infer** At school, Ernesto learns tolerance for other cultures and races. Where does he learn intolerance?
9. **Extend** What does this autobiography reveal about the difficulties of learning a second language?

10. **Analyze** What does Ernesto discover about becoming a proud American? What message or theme does this discovery suggest?

Literary Skills: Subjective and Objective Points of View in Autobiography

11. **Analyze** Explain whether you think this autobiography is primarily objective or subjective in its point of view. Support your explanation with examples from the text.

Literary Skills Review: Figures of Speech

12. **Interpret** Galarza <u>perceives</u> the Lincoln School not as a melting pot—which makes everyone the same—but as a warm griddle. What do you think this comparison means? Which **metaphor**—the melting pot or the warm griddle—would you use to describe the United States today? Why?

Writing Skills Focus
Think as a Reader/Writer

Use It in Your Writing As you read, you listed descriptive details that helped you visualize the Lincoln School. Use precise details in a brief description of your school.

 What Do **You Think Now**

How can a positive attitude help a person confront a new experience?

Independent Practice

Vocabulary Development

Your Turn _____

1. *everything will be okay*
2. *microwaves, washing machines, and computers*
3. *I'll stand by you*
4. *Tiger Woods, Peyton Manning, Venus Williams*
5. *a cave*

English for Academic Success

Language Coach

Work through the first Your Turn question with students. Point out that the sentence uses both *more* and the comparative *stranger* in comparing two schools. Explain that the word *more* should be omitted.

Your Turn _____

1. *Ernesto thought American schools were stranger than Mexican schools.*
2. *Miss Hopley might have been the tallest person Ernesto had ever seen.*

English for Academic Success

Academic Vocabulary

Possible response: The <u>narrative</u> shows that Galarza <u>perceived</u> his experiences at Lincoln to be a very important in shaping his life. He conveys the value of the experience though both facts and opinions.

Applying Your Skills

from **Barrio Boy**

Vocabulary Development

Clarifying Word Meanings: Examples

Writers often help readers understand difficult words by using definitions, examples, restatements, or contrasts. A writer who uses examples provides specific instances in order to show what a word means. Consider the following sentence:

People came to the meeting from such varied **municipalities** as Sacramento, Oakland, Bakersfield, and San Diego.

Even if you don't know that a municipality is a city or a town, the examples in the sentence give you a clue to the meaning of the word.

Your Turn _____

Complete the following sentences by using examples to clarify the meanings of the boldfaced words.

| reassuring |
| contraptions |
| assured |
| formidable |
| survey |

1. The most **reassuring** words I ever heard were "_____."
2. Three **contraptions** that make life easier today are _____, _____, and _____.
3. I **assured** my friend I was loyal. I said, "_____."
4. Three **formidable** figures in sports are _____, _____, and _____.
5. _____ is a place I would **survey** carefully before entering.

Language Coach

Comparing Adjectives Here are two tips for using the comparative and superlative degrees of adjectives:

- When comparing, don't use both *more* and *–er*, and don't use *most* with *–est.*

Ernesto felt **more safer** when his mother was present.

Matti was the **most thinnest** boy in the second grade.

- Don't use the superlative form when you compare only two people or things.

Do you think Ernesto was **proudest prouder** of being an American or a Mexican?

Of the two boys, Ito learned **most more** quickly.

Your Turn

Correct the faulty comparisons in these items.

1. Ernesto thought American schools were more stranger than Mexican schools.
2. Miss Hopley might have been the most tallest person Ernesto had ever seen.

Academic Vocabulary

Talk About . . .

Explain what Galarza's autobiographical <u>narrative</u> shows about how the author <u>perceived</u> the importance of his experience at Lincoln. Does he convey the value of the experience through fact, opinion, or a combination of the two?

 Learn It Online
For action-packed vocabulary lessons, visit:
 go.hrw.com H7-444 **Go**

Universal Access: Vocabulary Development

EL **English Learners**

English for Academic Success Pair students with a proficient speaker. Write the following adjectives on the board, and have pairs work together to identify the comparative and superlative forms. Then, tell pairs to write a sentence demonstrating the correct usage of each of the three words. As they complete the activity, tell pairs to engage in instructional conversations about why they make their choices.

- large (*larger, largest*)
- happy (*happier, happiest*)
- funny (*funnier, funniest*)
- loud (*louder, loudest*)

 Learn It Online

WordSharp: An Interactive Vocabulary Tutor provides additional support for vocabulary development. Multimedia tutorials show students how to apply vocabulary skills to unfamiliar words— and how to make those words their own.

go.hrw.com H7-444 **Go**

Grammar Link
Sentences and Fragments

To be a complete sentence, a group of words must have a subject and a verb and must express a complete thought. A **sentence fragment** is punctuated like a sentence, but it lacks one or more of the key elements that make up a complete sentence.

FRAGMENT   Up the wide staircase. [The word group lacks a subject and a verb.]

SENTENCE   We walked up the wide staircase.

FRAGMENT   Striding to the door. [The word group lacks a subject and verb.]

SENTENCE   Striding to the door, Miss Hopley opened it and called a name.

FRAGMENT   Before Miss Ryan took me to a seat. [Even with a subject and verb, this group of words does not express a complete thought.]

SENTENCE   Before Miss Ryan took me to a seat, I was standing in the hallway.

Your Turn

Identify each of the following word groups as a sentence or a fragment.

1. during the next few weeks
2. she made me watch her lips
3. next to one of these doors
4. like the first grade
5. scrubbing away
6. someone showed us a silk scroll

CHOICES

As you respond to the Choices, use these **Academic Vocabulary** words as appropriate: <u>analyze</u>, <u>narrative</u>, <u>organizational</u>, <u>perceive</u>.

REVIEW
Contrast Points of View

Timed Writing Imagine that Miss Ryan is writing a biographical sketch of Ernesto Galarza. In it, she shares her thoughts about Ernest and about teaching English to her students. From what point of view would Miss Ryan write? How would <u>perceiving</u> events from her point of view affect the theme of the work? Discuss these questions in a brief essay.

CONNECT
Write a Research Report

What problems do immigrants face today? How might schools and local governments attempt to solve these problems? Write a short report in which you <u>analyze</u> and respond to these questions. You will have to do some research to support your answers. Cite the sources of the facts and the relevant opinions you gather.

EXTEND
Create Your Own Metaphor

The metaphor of the melting pot is often used to describe the United States and its immigrant population. Galarza uses the metaphor of a griddle. Create your own metaphor to describe the way that people from different traditions come together in this country. Write a paragraph in which you introduce and explain the implicit, or suggested, meaning of your metaphor.

Independent Practice
Grammar Link
Your Turn
1. *fragment*
2. *sentence*
3. *fragment*
4. *fragment*
5. *fragment*
6. *sentence*

Choices:
Evaluation Criteria
Review: Timed Writing
40–50 minutes
Essays should discuss how Miss Ryan's version of events would affect the theme of the work.

Connect: **Homework**
Write a Research Report
- The report should identify problems immigrants face.
- Students should analyze solutions to the problems, citing facts and relevant opinions as necessary.

Extend: **Homework**
Create Your Own Metaphor
- Students should create an original metaphor to describe the diversity of American culture.
- Students should explain the metaphor's meaning in a paragraph.

Assess

Chapter 4 Resources, Selection Standards Check, p. 33–35

ThinkCentral Online Assessment, Selection Standards Check

Teacher One Stop™, editable Selection Standards Check

Reteach

ThinkCentral Online Remediation

Universal Access: Grammar Link

 English Learners

English for Academic Success Remind students that the subject of a sentence is what the sentence is about; the verb is the action taken by the subject. Identify the subject (Jill) and the verb (walked) in the following example of a complete sentence: After school, Jill walked home. Then explain that if "After school" appeared by itself, it would be a fragment. Provide students with additional scaffolding in understanding the difference between a sentence and a fragment by guiding them in identifying what is missing from each of the fragments in the "Your Turn" exercise. Sentence fragments are typically missing a subject or verb, or do not express a complete thought, such as "during the next few weeks," or "scrubbing away." Then, help them add possible words or phrases to make a complete sentence.

✔ For more practice with sentences and fragments, see **Warriner's Handbook**, **GrammarNotes**, and **Language Handbook Worksheets**.

Standards Focus

Objectives

Students will
- analyze folk tales
- analyze motifs
- compare and contrast texts

Motivate

What Do You Think?/QuickWrite

Have volunteers share examples of likable underdogs from books, movies, or personal experiences. Ask students what helped these underdogs to succeed. Have students record their responses in their **Reader/Writer Notebook.**

English for Academic Success

Academic Vocabulary

Look for opportunities to use the Academic Vocabulary words in this chapter.

- **analyze, v.:** to examine in detail
- **perceive, v.:** observe
- **narrative, adj.:** being in story form

Analyzing Visuals

Use the ThinkCentral, Teacher Access to project this image for viewing.

Extension Activity Have students list adjectives that describe the glass slipper. Ask students what sort of person might own a shoe like this. *Possible response: fancy, delicate, unique. The owner is probably a rich person who values beautiful things.*

California Standards, pp. 446–467

- **Reading Standard 3.5** Contrast points of view (e.g., first and third person, limited and omniscient, subjective and objective) in narrative text and explain how they affect the overall theme of the work.

Comparing Versions of the Cinderella Story

CONTENTS

What Do You Think What helps a person overcome life's difficulties?

QuickWrite Underdogs—likable characters in no-win situations—delight us by winning in the end. Why do we enjoy stories about an underdog who is rescued or given help to succeed?

Comparing Texts Resources

Chapter 4 Resources, on-level practice and assessment, pp. 36–41

Teacher One Stop™, on-level lesson plans and all print resources

Holt Audio Library

Holt Audio Library: Selections and Summaries in Spanish

Preparing to Read

Aschenputtel / Yeh-Shen / Interview

Reading Standard 3.5 Contrast points of view (e.g., first and third person, limited and omniscient, subjective and objective) in narrative text and explain how they affect the overall theme of the work.

Literary Skills Focus

Folk Tales Some of the world's oldest and most familiar stories are **folk tales**—stories passed on by word of mouth, often over centuries. The Cinderella story is one such folk tale. Scholars have traced the oldest version of this tale back more than one thousand years. The version you probably know best was collected in the 1600s by French writer Charles Perrault. "Aschenputtel" is the German version of the Cinderella story. "Yeh-Shen" is the Chinese version. "Interview" is a modern poem that tells the Cinderella story from a different point of view.

Reading Skills Focus

Comparing and Contrasting Across Texts As you read these three versions of the Cinderella story, think about how they are similar and how they are different. Pay special attention to the point of view from which each narrative is told.

Into Action Complete a chart like the one below as you read each selection to compare and contrast the three texts.

Comparing Cinderella Stories

	"Aschenputtel"	"Yeh-Shen"	"Interview"
Point of View			
Plot			
Tone			
Theme			

Writing Skills Focus

Preparing for Timed ∟Writing **Tone** refers to a writer's attitude toward a subject: admiring, critical, humorous, and so on. As you read these selections, write down some of the words, phrases, and sentences that convey a specific tone.

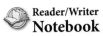

Reader/Writer Notebook

Use your **RWN** to complete the activities for these selections.

Vocabulary

Aschenputtel

persisted (puhr SIHS tihd) *v.:* refused to give up. *He persisted in his search.*

splendor (SPLEHN duhr) *n.:* magnificence. *The splendor of the golden dress dazzled all at the feast.*

Yeh-Shen

glistening (GLIHS uhn ihng) *v.* used as *adj.:* sparkling; reflecting light. *The glistening shoe sparkled.*

entranced (ehn TRANST) *v.:* cast a spell on; enchanted. *The king was entranced by the mysterious woman.*

vigil (VIHJ uhl) *n.:* overnight watch. *The king kept vigil near the shoe.*

Language Coach

Homographs Words that look the same but are pronounced differently and have different meanings are called **homographs.** *Entrance* (EHN truhns, *n.*) means "place to enter," while to *entrance* (ehn TRANS, *v.*), means "to fill with wonder." Think of two other words that are homographs.

Learn It Online

There's more to words than definitions. Get the whole story on:

go.hrw.com   H7-447   **Go**

Preteach

Introducing Vocabulary

Guide students in choosing the best synonym for each Vocabulary word.

1. **entranced** (fascinated, excited, amused) [*fascinated*]
2. **vigil** (watch, plan, ritual) [*watch*]
3. **glistening** (sparkling, beautiful, glowing) [*sparkling*]
4. **persisted** (continued, slowed, worked) [*continued*]
5. **splendor** (glory, fun, skill) [*glory*]

English for Academic Success

Language Coach

Have groups of students work together to brainstorm homographs. Compile all homographs into a master list. [*project, bow, wind*]

Literary Skills Focus

As you read and discuss the selections with students, have them identify motifs common to folk tales.

Reading Skills Focus

Give students a copy of the Reading Skills Focus graphic organizer before they read. (See **Chapter 4 Resources.**) Tell them to use their responses to answer the questions on the Applying Your Skills page.

Writing Skills Focus

Have students jot down words and phrases that create a specific tone in their **Reader/Writer Notebook.** Students can use their notes to complete the Writing Skills Focus activity.

Learn It Online

Send students to **Word Watch** for audio pronunciations, synonyms and antonyms, and brief histories of word origins.

go.hrw.com   H7-447   **Go**

Selection Introduction

More About the Writers

- **Jakob and Wilhelm Grimm** recorded their tales primarily for historical and patriotic reasons rather than to entertain. The tales reflected the harsh nature of life in centuries past.

- **Ai-Ling Louie**, a Chinese American, first learned the ancient tale on which "Yeh-Shen" was based from her immigrant grandmother.

- **Sara Henderson Hay** started out as a secretary for a New York publishing firm, but her writing career began to take off after she won a poetry contest.

Think About the Writers

To help students answer the question, suggest they discuss how stories and movies based on existing tales add or change elements of the original story.

For Independent Reading

- If students enjoy "Yen-Shen," they may enjoy another Chinese variation of a familiar fairy tale. Demi's *The Emperor's New Clothes: A Tale Set in China* is a retelling of the classic tale of an arrogant emperor set in ancient China.

- Students who enjoy the following selections may also enjoy *Ella Enchanted* by Gail Carson Levine. This retelling of the Cinderella story has an amusing magical twist and was recently made into a motion picture.

Jakob and Wilhelm Grimm
(1785–1863); (1786–1863)

Rescuing Rapunzel

Jakob and Wilhelm Grimm introduced us to such famous fairy-tale characters as Rapunzel, Hansel and Gretel, and Aschenputtel (Cinderella). Before the 1800s, most European folk and fairy tales were not written down. The Brothers Grimm collected and wrote down the vanishing traditional stories of Germany. By the time the final edition of their collected stories was published, in 1857, the brothers had collected about two hundred tales.

Ai-Ling Louie
(1949–   )

For the Children

For Ai-Ling Louie, teaching led to writing: "My desire to be a writer didn't come into full bloom until I became an elementary school teacher. I found myself fascinated by the books my school children were reading. . . . 'Yeh-Shen' was written for my class to hear."

Sara Henderson Hay
(1906–1987)

An Early Start

At the age of ten, Sara Henderson Hay published her first poem. She became an award-winning poet known for her humorous, witty poems.

Think About the Writers

When writers base a work on a story that already exists, is the new work less original? Explain your thoughts.

Preview the Selections

In "Aschenputtel," which means "little ash girl" or "cinder girl," you will meet the title character, also known as the German Cinderella. The story will probably seem very familiar to you, but get ready for a rather "grim" ending that's definitely not from Disney.

"Yeh-Shen," a Chinese folk tale about a girl, **Yeh-Shen,** and her **fish,** is one of the oldest versions of the Cinderella story—and perhaps even the first.

"Interview" is a short poem that suggests the story of Cinderella would be very different if it were told by her **stepmother.**

Aschenputtel

German, retold by **Jakob** and **Wilhelm Grimm,** translated by **Lucy Crane**

Read with a Purpose
Read "Aschenputtel" to see what lesson this traditional folk tale teaches.

Build Background
There are more than nine hundred different versions of the Cinderella story. Almost all of them feature familiar **motifs,** or patterns: a young woman is mistreated by a stepmother and stepsisters; the young woman receives help from magical characters and meets a prince who falls in love with her; finally, a lost object, such as a magical shoe, brings the girl and her prince together.

There was once a rich man whose wife lay sick, and when she felt her end drawing near, she called to her only daughter to come near her bed and said,

"Dear child, be pious and good, and God will always take care of you, and I will look down upon you from heaven and will be with you."

And then she closed her eyes and expired.[1] The maiden went every day to her mother's grave and wept and was always pious and good. When the winter came, the snow covered the grave with a white covering, and when the sun came in the early spring and melted it away, the man took to himself another wife.

The new wife brought two daughters home with her and they were beautiful and fair in appearance but at heart were wicked and ugly. And then began very evil times for the poor stepdaughter. (A)

"Is the stupid creature to sit in the same room with us?" said they. "Those who eat food must earn it. Out with the kitchen maid!"

They took away her pretty dresses and put on her an old gray kirtle[2] and gave her wooden shoes to wear.

"Just look now at the proud princess, how she is decked out!" cried they, laughing, and then they sent her into the kitchen. There she was obliged to do heavy work from morning to night, get up early in the morning, draw water, make the fires, cook, and wash. Besides that, the sisters did their

---

1. **expired** (ehk SPYRD): died. In Latin, *exspirare* means "to breathe out"; to breathe out one's last breath is to die.

2. **kirtle** (KUR tuhl): old-fashioned word for "dress."

(A) **Reading Focus** **Compare and Contrast** What details common to most Cinderella stories have you noticed so far?

Selection Readability	
Easily Accessible **Accessible** Challenging	familiar theme; familiar genre; complex syntax

Selection Plot Summary
A polite young maiden, Aschenputtel, is treated cruelly by her wicked stepsisters. With help from some magical birds, Aschenputtel wins the heart of a handsome prince at a dance, and her stepsisters are punished for their wickedness.

Direct Teach

Think About/Talk About
Read with a Purpose Have students read the Read with a Purpose statement. Then, ask volunteers to use their prior knowledge of the "Cinderella" story to predict what the lesson of "Aschenputtel" will be.

▶ Comprehension

(A) Reading Focus
Possible response: The main character is a girl who has lost her mother, is good and kind, and is mistreated by her cruel stepmother and stepsisters.

▶ Extend the Discussion

Motifs Read the first four paragraphs of the story. What common fairy tale motif do the stepmother and stepsisters represent? *Possible response: These characters are beautiful but wicked. Stepmothers and stepsisters in fairy tales are often cruel to the main character.*

Tone How would you describe the tone of the first three paragraphs? Give examples of words or phrases that create this tone. *Possible response: The tone is sad and serious. Words like* expired *and* wept *contribute to this tone.*

Making Predictions Read the mother's promise to the girl in paragraph 2. Based on this promise, what do you predict will happen in the story? *Possible response: The girl will obey her mother by being pious and good, and in return, her mother will help her out of a difficult situation.*

Model the Skill

■ Ask students to name some folk tales or fairy tales that they are familiar with. Explain that versions of these folk and fairy tales students know are told with slight variations in cultures all around the world. A feature that folk and fairy tales have in every culture are **motifs**, or common patterns. Motifs may include types of characters or other story elements such as magical helpers for the main character.

■ Model identifying a traditional motif in a folk tale using "Aschenputtel." Point out that in the first four paragraphs, Aschenputtel's mother dies, and a wicked stepmother and stepsisters join her family. Tell students that the cruel stepmother is a common motif in many folk tales. For example, the main characters in "Snow White" and "Hansel and Gretel" also include wicked stepmothers.

Guided Practice: Apply

Think-Pair-Share Have students think about the version of "Cinderella" that they are most familiar with. Ask them to identify other characters or events in this story that are similar to "Cinderella." Have students compare notes with a partner and refine their lists of motifs. Ask one member of each pair to share his or her list to create a class list of Cinderella motifs.

utmost to torment her—mocking her and strewing peas and lentils among the ashes and setting her to pick them up. In the evenings, when she was quite tired out with her hard day's work, she had no bed to lie on but was obliged to rest on the hearth among the cinders. And as she always looked dusty and dirty, they named her Aschenputtel.

It happened one day that the father went to the fair, and he asked his two stepdaughters what he should bring back for them.

"Fine clothes!" said one.

"Pearls and jewels!" said the other.

"But what will you have, Aschenputtel?" said he.

"The first twig, Father, that strikes against your hat on the way home; this is what I should like you to bring me."

So he bought for the two stepdaughters fine clothes, pearls, and jewels, and on his way back, as he rode through a green lane, a hazel twig struck against his hat; and he broke it off and carried it home with him. And when he reached home, he gave to the stepdaughters what they had wished for, and to Aschenputtel he gave the hazel twig. She thanked him and went to her mother's grave, and planted this twig there, weeping so bitterly that the tears fell upon it and watered it, and it flourished and became a

B **Read and Discuss** What has the author told you so far?

Analyzing Visuals **Connecting to the Text** What does the girl in the painting have in common with Aschenputtel?

A Little Shepherdess (1891) by William-Adolphe Bouguereau (1895–1905). Oil on canvas.

Universal Access

EL English Learners

Have students familiar with the Cinderella story retell it in their own words for students who may not be familiar with the tale. Then, ask if any stories written in students' native language contain similar elements.

Struggling Readers

Strategic Students To help students read "Aschenputtel," model identifying details that you will compare and contrast as you read future texts. You might say, "In this version of the Cinderella story, the main character is

a girl whose mother dies, leaving her with a stepmother and stepsisters who treat her badly. When I read other versions of the story, I'll look to see if these elements are repeated." Encourage students to use notes or the Reading Skills Focus graphic organizer to keep track of repeated elements among the three Cinderella stories.

Advanced Learners

Acceleration After students read "Aschenputtel," have them work in groups to discuss the story's motifs. Examples include magical animals, the number 3, and fine tree. Aschenputtel went to see it three times a day and wept and prayed, and each time a white bird rose up from the tree, and, if she uttered any wish, the bird brought her whatever she had wished for. **C**

Now it came to pass that the king ordained[3] a festival that should last for three days and to which all the beautiful young women of that country were bidden so that the king's son might choose a bride from among them. When the two stepdaughters heard that they too were bidden to appear, they felt very pleased, and they called Aschenputtel and said,

"Comb our hair, brush our shoes, and make our buckles fast, we are going to the wedding feast at the king's castle."

Aschenputtel, when she heard this, could not help crying, for she too would have liked to go to the dance, and she begged her stepmother to allow her.

"What, you Aschenputtel!" said she. "In all your dust and dirt, you want to go to the festival! You that have no dress and no shoes! You want to dance!"

But since she persisted in asking, at last the stepmother said,

> "Comb our hair, brush our shoes, and make our buckles fast, we are going to the wedding feast at the king's castle."

"I have scattered a dish full of lentils in the ashes, and if you can pick them all up again in two hours, you may go with us."

Then the maiden went to the back door that led into the garden and called out,

O gentle doves, O turtledoves,
And all the birds that be,
The lentils that in ashes lie
Come and pick up for me!
The good must be put in the dish,
The bad you may eat if you wish.

Then there came to the kitchen window two white doves, and after them some turtledoves, and at last a crowd of all the birds under heaven, chirping and fluttering, and they alighted among the ashes; and the doves nodded with their heads and began to pick, peck, pick, peck, and then all the others began to pick, peck, pick, peck and put all the good grains into the dish. Before an hour was over, all was done, and they flew away. Then the maiden brought the dish to her stepmother, feeling joyful and thinking that now she should go to the feast; but the stepmother said,

"No, Aschenputtel, you have no proper clothes, and you do not know how to dance, and you would be laughed at!"

And when Aschenputtel cried for disappointment, she added,

---

3. **ordained** (awr DAYND): ordered or decreed.

C | Read and Discuss | What does this conversation between the girls and the father let you know about the girls?

Vocabulary **persisted** (puhr SIHS tihd) *v.:* refused to give up.

Think About/Talk About

▶ **Comprehension**

B Read and Discuss

Possible response: A man's wife dies, and a daughter is left behind. The man remarries, and the stepmother and her daughters are cruel to the girl.

C Read and Discuss

Possible response: The stepdaughters seem greedy compared with Aschenputtel.

▶ **Extend the Discussion**

Characterization Compare Aschenputtel's request for a gift in the fifth full paragraph of p. 450 with her stepsisters' requests. What does Aschenputtel's request reveal about her character? *Possible response: Aschenputtel isn't interested in fancy, expensive things. She's not greedy, and she seems to have a connection to the natural world.*

Motifs What fairy tale motif is featured in the second column on p. 451? *Possible response: Magical animals, which appear in many fairy tales, help Aschenputtel perform a difficult task.*

Vocabulary: Own the Word

persisted: Tell students that the connotation of *persisted* is fierce determination. This is stronger than the connotation for *tried* or *attempted.* Ask students if they have ever *persisted* in asking for something. Were they able to get what they wanted?

transformations. Have groups discuss other stories with similar motifs. [*Snow White, Hansel and Gretel, Beauty and the Beast*] Then, have groups brainstorm ideas for an original story that features some of these motifs.

Students with Disabilities

Copy the Reading Skills Focus graphic organizer onto the board. As students finish reading each page, pause to help them record new details in the graphic organizer.

Analyzing Visuals

French artist **William-Adolphe Bouguereau** (1825–1905) was renowned for his extremely realistic, if sentimental, depictions of his subjects.

Connecting to the Text: *She is dressed plainly and appears to have been doing hard work.*

- Provide students with copies of the Reading Skills Focus graphic organizer. (See **Chapter 4 Resources**.)

- Help students identify details that they will need to **compare and contrast** as they read the Cinderella stories. Point out that on this page, there are several important events, including the stepmother's refusal to allow Aschenputtel to attend the festival, the magical help, Aschenputtel's dance with the prince, and her escape. Tell student to add these to the "Plot" row of their charts.

	"Aschenputtel"
Characters	Aschenputtel, two stepdaughters, step-mother, prince, doves
Plot	stepmother's refusal, Aschenputtel's dance with the prince, Aschenputtel's escape
Tone	
Theme	

Guided Practice: Apply

Numbered Heads Together Divide students into mixed-ability groups of four and have groups discuss their entries for plot, character, tone, and theme for "Aschenputtel." Ask groups to come to a consensus about each of the elements in the chart. You may wish to use the Numbered Heads Together discussion format to facilitate group discussions and encourage students to share their responses.

"If you can pick two dishfuls of lentils out of the ashes, nice and clean, you shall go with us," thinking to herself, "for that is not possible." When she had strewed two dish-fuls of lentils among the ashes, the maiden went through the back door into the garden and cried,

> O gentle doves, O turtledoves,
> And all the birds that be,
> The lentils that in ashes lie
> Come and pick up for me!
>> The good must be put in the dish,
>> The bad you may eat if you wish.

So there came to the kitchen window two white doves, and then some turtledoves, and at last a crowd of all the other birds under heaven, chirping and fluttering, and they alighted among the ashes, and the doves nodded with their heads and began to pick, peck, pick, peck, and then all the others began to pick, peck, pick, peck and put all the good grains into the dish. And before half an hour was over, it was all done, and they flew away. Then the maiden took the dishes to the stepmother, feeling joyful and thinking that now she should go with them to the feast. But her stepmother said, "All this is of no good to you; you cannot come with us, for you have no proper clothes and can-not dance; you would put us to shame." **D**

Then she turned her back on poor Aschenputtel and made haste to set out with her two proud daughters.

And as there was no one left in the house, Aschenputtel went to her mother's grave, under the hazel bush, and cried,

> Little tree, little tree, shake over me,
> That silver and gold may come down
> and cover me.

Then the bird threw down a dress of gold and silver and a pair of slippers embroidered with silk and silver. And in all haste she put on the dress and went to the festival. But her stepmother and sisters did not know her and thought she must be a foreign princess, she looked so beautiful in her golden dress. Of Aschenputtel they never thought at all and supposed that she was sitting at home, pick-ing the lentils out of the ashes. The King's son came to meet her and took her by the hand and danced with her, and he refused to stand up with anyone else so that he might not be obliged to let go her hand; and when anyone came to claim it, he answered,

"She is my partner." **E**

And when the evening came, she wanted to go home, but the prince said he would go with her to take care of her, for he wanted to see where the beauti-ful maiden lived. But she escaped him and jumped up into the pigeon house. Then the prince waited until her father came along, and told him that the strange maiden had jumped into the pigeon house. The father thought to himself, "It cannot surely be Aschenputtel" and called for axes and hatchets and had the pigeon house cut down, but there was no one in it. And when they entered the house, there sat Aschenputtel in her dirty clothes among the cinders, and a little oil lamp burnt dimly in the chimney; for Aschenputtel had

D **Read and Discuss** What does this statement tell you about Aschenputtel and her stepmother?

E **Reading Focus** Compare and Contrast Explain how people perceive and treat Aschenputtel differently, depending on what she's wearing.

Cross-Curricular Connection

LITERATURE: Versions of the Cinderella Story

Explain to students that "Aschenputtel" and "Yeh-Shen" are only two of the hundreds of different versions of the Cinderella tale.

- The most familiar version of the Cinderella story was written in 1697 by French author Charles Perrault, who introduced such elements as the fairy godmother and the glass slipper into his tale of "Cendrillon."

- In 1957, composer Richard Rodgers and lyricist Oscar Hammerstein II created a musical version of the

Cinderella story based on the Perrault retelling. Their successful television movie was remade in 1965 and 1997.

- Variants of the Cinderella story can be traced to Vietnam, Italy, Egypt, and many other countries and cultures around the world.

- Today, authors, artists, and film directors have continued to adapt the tale of Cinderella for a variety of media. Modern adaptations of the Cinderella story include Gail Carson Levine's novel *Ella Enchanted* and the movie *Ever After*.

Analyzing Visuals | Connecting to the Text | What details in the painting tell you that Aschenputtel's stepsisters treat her harshly?

Cinderella and Her Wicked Sisters (19th century) by Emile Meyer.

been very quick and had jumped out of the pigeon house again and had run to the hazel bush; and there she had taken off her beautiful dress and had laid it on the grave, and the bird had carried it away again, and then she had put on her little gray kirtle again and had sat down in the kitchen among the cinders. **F**

F | Read and Discuss | What has happened to Aschenputtel?

▶ **Comprehension**

Ⓓ **Read and Discuss**

Possible response: Even though Aschenputtel completed the first task, her stepmother wouldn't allow her to go. When Aschenputtel pleads again, the stepmother gives the second task. The stepmother seems cruel to expect so much more of Aschenputtel when her own daughters are not required to do the same tasks.

Ⓔ **Reading Focus**

Possible response: People disrespect Aschenputtel when she is wearing dirty clothes, but everyone loves her when she wears a beautiful dress.

Ⓕ **Read and Discuss**

Possible response: The bird grants Aschenputtel a special dress and shoes so she can attend the festival. At the festival, the prince chooses Aschenputtel from all the others. When she leaves, the prince follows but loses track of her.

▶ **Extend the Discussion**

Speculating At the end of p. 452, Aschenputtel runs away from the prince before he could take her home. What might be the reason for Aschenputtel's behavior? *Possible response:* She might not want to reveal her true identity to him, or she might be worried that her stepmother and stepsisters will find out that she's disobeyed them. She may also be embarrassed by her home life and afraid of being rejected by the prince as a result.

Analyzing Visuals

Connecting to the Text: *One of the girls has a haughty, superior look on her face. The other girl is ignoring Aschenputtel, who sits in the corner looking sad.*

Ring Doves (1998) by Rosemary Lowndes (1937–2001).

Model the Skill

■ Write the word **homograph** on the board, drawing a line between *homo* and *graph*. Explain that *homograph* has two word parts— *homo*, meaning "same," and *graph*, meaning "written." Readers are helped by knowing that homographs look the same, but that is the only similarity between them.

■ Write the word *wind* on the board and the following sentences: "I will *wind* my watch" and "The *wind* blew off my hat." Explain that both sentences use the word *wind*, with the exact same spelling. However, in the first sentence, *wind*, has a long *i* sound; in the second sentence *wind*, with a short *i* sound. Point out that the words also have different meanings. *Wind* is a verb meaning "to turn or twist," and *wind* is a noun meaning "air that moves."

Guided Practice: Apply

Point out the word *doves* on page 452, noting that it is a homograph. Have students work in pairs to identify alternate pronunciations and meanings for *dove*. Explain that whenever they come across a word that could be pronounced in more than one way, they should try each pronunciation and meaning in the sentence to see which word makes sense.

Think as a Reader/Writer

Find It in Your Reading Tell students that in the fifth paragraph of p. 454, the author uses the phrase "leapt as lightly as a squirrel" to convey a fast, playful tone.

Use It in Your Writing Have students write a sentence in which they convey a playful tone by comparing a person's actions to the actions of an animal.

The next day, when the festival began anew, and the parents and stepsisters had gone to it, Aschenputtel went to the hazel bush and cried,

> Little tree, little tree, shake over me,
> That silver and gold may come down
> and cover me.

Then the bird cast down a still more splendid dress than on the day before. And when she appeared in it among the guests, everyone was astonished at her beauty. The prince had been waiting until she came, and he took her hand and danced with her alone. And when anyone else came to invite her, he said,

"She is my partner." **G**

And when the evening came, she wanted to go home, and the prince followed her, for he wanted to see to what house she belonged; but she broke away from him and ran into the garden at the back of the house. There stood a fine large tree, bearing splendid pears; she leapt as lightly as a squirrel among the branches, and the prince did not know what had become of her. So he waited until her father came along, and then he told him that the strange maiden had rushed from him, and that he thought she had gone up into the pear tree. The father thought to himself,

"It cannot surely be Aschenputtel" and called for an axe and felled the tree, but there was no one in it. And when they went into the kitchen, there sat Aschenputtel among the cinders, as usual, for she had got down the other side of the tree and had

G **Literary Focus** **Folk Tales** Princes often appear in tales like "Aschenputtel." In what ways is the character of the prince a motif, or common pattern?

Reaching Reluctant Readers

Help students become engaged with the Cinderella story by allowing them to create a personal retelling of the tale.

• Ask students to think about which elements of the story they enjoy and which elements seem crucial to include in any Cinderella story.

• Then, have students brainstorm ways to reinterpret those elements for a modern audience. Ask students

to consider: "If the Cinderella story took place in my community, how might it change? What parts of the story would stay the same?"

• Allow students to create their own retelling in a medium of their choice, such as artwork, a graphic novel, a song, a film, a skit, or a slam poem.

taken back her beautiful clothes to the bird on the hazel bush and had put on her old gray kirtle again.

On the third day, when the parents and the stepchildren had set off, Aschenputtel went again to her mother's grave and said to the tree,

> *Little tree, little tree, shake over me,*
> *That silver and gold may come down*
> *and cover me.*

Then the bird cast down a dress the likes of which had never been seen for splendor and brilliancy, and slippers that were of gold.

And when she appeared in this dress at the feast, nobody knew what to say for wonderment. The prince danced with her alone, and if anyone else asked her, he answered, "She is my partner."

And when it was evening, Aschenputtel wanted to go home, and the prince was about to go with her when she ran past him so quickly that he could not follow her. But he had laid a plan and had caused all the steps to be spread with pitch,[4] so that as she rushed down them, her left shoe remained sticking in it. The prince picked it up and saw that it was of gold and very small and slender. The next morning he went to the father and told him that none should be his bride save the one whose foot the golden shoe should fit. **I**

---

4. **pitch** (pihch): here, black, sticky tar.

H **Literary Focus** Folk Tales The number three is a common motif in European folk tales. What events have happened three times in this story?

The two sisters were very glad, because they had pretty feet. The eldest went to her room to try on the shoe, and her mother stood by. But she could not get her great toe into it, for the shoe was too small; then her mother handed her a knife, and said,

"Cut the toe off, for when you are queen, you will never have to go on foot." So the girl cut her toe off, squeezed her foot into the shoe, concealed the pain, and went down to the prince. Then he took her with him on his horse as his bride and rode off. They had to pass by the grave, and there sat the two pigeons on the hazel bush and cried,

> *There they go, there they go!*
> *There is blood on her shoe;*
> *The shoe is too small,*
> *—Not the right bride at all!*

Then the prince looked at her shoe and saw the blood flowing. And he turned his horse round and took the false bride home again, saying she was not the right one and that the other sister must try on the shoe. So she went into her room to do so and got her toes comfortably in, but her heel was too large. Then her mother handed her the knife, saying, "Cut a piece off your heel; when you are queen, you will never have to go on foot."

So the girl cut a piece off her heel and thrust her foot into the shoe, concealed the pain, and went down to the prince, who took his bride before him on his horse and

I **Read and Discuss** What can you say about the third day of the festival?

Vocabulary **splendor** (SPLEHN duhr) *n.*: magnificence.

Think About/Talk About

▶ **Comprehension**

I **Read and Discuss**
Possible response: Aschenputtel arrives looking marvelous and is singled out by the prince. But this time, the prince has a plan for when she leaves—he puts sticky tar on the steps to keep her from running away.

▶ **Analysis**

G **Literary Focus**
Possible response: The prince is a motif because in tales like this one, the prince falls in love with the heroine and usually marries her at the end of the story.

H **Literary Focus**
Possible response: Aschenputtel has gotten a dress from the tree three times, she has danced with the prince three times, she has run away from him three times, and the festival has gone on for three days.

Vocabulary: Own the Word
splendor: Help students create a semantic web for the word *splendor*. Write the word in a center circle on the board. Then, draw branches or legs that connect to the center circle. Have students add concepts and attributes to the semantic web based words they associated with *splendor*.
Possible responses: wealth, greed, expensive, extravagant, bright

Analyzing Visuals
Ring doves, also known as wood pigeons, are known to form large flocks to eat. They eat primarily seeds and grains and are considered a nuisance by farmers.

Extension Activity Ask students how the actions of the birds might be part of a common folk tale motif.

Possible response: Animals often play helpful, even magical, roles in many folk tales.

Developing Oral Fluency

Use Aschenputtel's call to the birds to give students practice in speaking with tone and inflection. Tell students they should try to convey the tone of the text and the emotions of the characters.

Whole-Class Activity Model reading Aschenputtel's speech that begins, "Little tree, little tree" on p. 455. Use a hopeful tone of voice to emphasize the pleading nature of the text. Choral read the same speech with the class. Next, have the class read the bird's speech that begins "There they go, there they go!" Point out the birds' accusatory tone as they reveal the stepsisters' actions.

✔ See **UA: Differentiating Instruction** for practice passages for developing oral fluency.

Think About/Talk About

▶ Comprehension

❶ Read and Discuss

Possible response: The stepsisters' eyes are plucked out by the guardian birds as punishment for their mistreatment of Aschenputtel.

▶ Extend the Discussion

Theme Read the last sentence of the story. What is the theme, or lesson, of this folk tale? *Possible response: Good behavior will be rewarded, and wicked behavior will be punished.*

Monitor Students' Comprehension

Guide the class in answering these questions.

1. How do the doves help Aschenputtel in the story? [*They help her complete impossible tasks, bring her beautiful clothes, and reveal the stepsisters' dishonesty.*]

2. Which characters "get what they deserve" at the end of the story? Explain. [*Aschenputtel is rewarded for being sweet by marrying the prince, and the stepsisters are punished for their cruelty by being blinded.*]

3. Which elements of "Aschenputtel" are common to most Cinderella stories? [*A girl who's treated badly by her family falls in love with a prince who loves her in return.*]

 California Standards, pp. 446–457

■ **Reading Standard 3.5** Contrast points of view (e.g., first and third person, limited and omniscient, subjective and objective) in narrative text and explain how they affect the overall theme of the work.

---

rode off. When they passed by the hazel bush, the two pigeons sat there and cried,

> *There they go, there they go!*
> *There is blood on her shoe;*
> *The shoe is too small,*
> *—Not the right bride at all!*

Then the prince looked at her foot and saw how the blood was flowing from the shoe and staining the white stocking. And he turned his horse round and brought the false bride home again.

"This is not the right one," said he. "Have you no other daughter?"

"No," said the man, "only my dead wife left behind her a little stunted[5] Aschenputtel; it is impossible that she can be the bride." But the King's son ordered her to be sent for, but the mother said,

"Oh, no! She is much too dirty; I could not let her be seen."

But he would have her fetched, and so Aschenputtel had to appear.

First she washed her face and hands quite clean and went in and curtseyed to the prince, who held out to her the golden shoe. Then she sat down on a stool, drew her foot out of the heavy wooden shoe, and slipped it into the golden one, which fitted it perfectly. And when she stood up and the prince looked in her face, he

> "This is not the right one," said he. "Have you no other daughter?"

knew again the beautiful maiden that had danced with him, and he cried,

"This is the right bride!"

The stepmother and the two sisters were thunderstruck and grew pale with anger, but the prince put Aschenputtel before him on his horse and rode off. And as they passed the hazel bush, the two white pigeons cried,

> *There they go, there they go!*
> *No blood on her shoe;*
> *The shoe's not too small,*
> *The right bride is she after all.*

And when they had thus cried, they came flying after and perched on Aschenputtel's shoulders, one on the right, the other on the left, and so remained.

And when her wedding with the prince was appointed to be held, the false sisters came, hoping to curry favor[6] and to take part in the festivities. So as the bridal procession went to the church, the eldest walked on the right side and the younger on the left, and the pigeons picked out an eye of each of them. And as they returned, the elder was on the left side and the younger on the right, and the pigeons picked out the other eye of each of them. And so they were condemned for the rest of their days because of their wickedness and falsehood. ❶

---

5. **stunted** (STUHN tihd): not properly grown.

6. **curry favor:** try to win approval by flattering and fawning.

---

❶ **Read and Discuss** How does this information about the stepsisters fit with what you learned earlier?

Applying Your Skills

Reading Standard 3.5 Contrast points of view (e.g., first and third person, limited and omniscient, subjective and objective) in narrative text and explain how they affect the overall theme of the work.

Aschenputtel
Literary Response and Analysis

Reading Skills Focus
Quick Check

1. What does the stepmother do to stop Aschenputtel from attending the feast?

Read with a Purpose

2. Which of the following statements do you think best sums up the lesson "Aschenputtel" teaches?
   - Goodness is rewarded in the end.
   - Bad people will be punished for evil deeds.
   - Love conquers all.

   Explain whether or not this lesson applies to today's world.

Reading Skills: Comparing and Contrasting Across Texts

3. Look at the chart you filled out as you read (page 447). Place a check mark (√) next to elements of "Aschenputtel" that you know from other versions of the story. Place a plus sign (+) next to elements that are new to you.

Comparing Cinderella Stories

	"Aschenputtel"	"Yeh-Shen"	"Inter-view"
Point of View			
Plot			
Tone			
Theme			

✓ Vocabulary Check

Answer the following questions.

4. How would you react to the **splendor** of a Broadway musical?
5. When might you admire someone who **persisted**?

Literary Skills Focus
Literary Analysis

6. **Interpret** Why does the father call his own daughter Aschenputtel? What does this tell you about him?
7. **Interpret** How do you feel about the way the story ends? If it were written for readers today, would this ending be acceptable? Why or why not?
8. **Analyze** Why do some people, especially in childhood, feel they have something in common with Cinderella-type characters? What feelings might they share with her? Explain what universal human qualities people might perceive in Cinderella characters.

Literary Skills: Folk Tales

9. **Evaluate** How does the motif of the number three build suspense in this folk tale?

Writing Skills Focus
Think as a Reader/Writer
Use It in Your Writing Write a paragraph in which you analyze how the writer reveals one of the characters in "Aschenputtel." How does the author's tone contribute to the characterization? Support your response with examples from the folk tale.

Struggling Writers
Provide additional scaffolding for the Writing Skills Focus activity by reminding students that the author's tone is the author's attitude toward a subject. Tone is revealed by the author's word choice. Help students brainstorm words that describe tone by creating a chart on the board. Suggestions might include words such as *sympathetic, loving, disapproving, disparaging, mocking, somber, teasing, mischievous,* and *indifferent*. Then, tell students to choose one character and use the list to identify the author's tone toward this character. Have them copy at least three descriptions of the character that create this tone.

Words That Describe Tone

sympathetic
disapproving
mocking
somber
indifferent

Independent Practice
Reading Skills Focus
Answers:

1. *She makes Aschenputtel pick lentils out of the ashes.*
2. *Goodness is rewarded in the end. This is a good lesson, even today, because it teaches that being kind will be rewarding in life.*
3. *I recognize the stepmother from other stories, but I don't recognize the birds.*

Vocabulary Check
Possible responses:

4. *with applause*
5. *when they have overcome hardship*

Literary Skills Focus
Possible responses:

6. *He seems to agree with the stepsisters that she is a disgusting creature who shouldn't be treated well.*
7. *It is a bit gruesome and violent. People might find it unacceptable because violence and gore are not often considered appropriate for children.*
8. *Most people occasionally feel left out, hurt, or ignored. Many people also imagine having a life much more glorious or luxurious than the one they live. People might perceive grace, humility, and a desire for a better life in Cinderella characters.*
9. *The festival lasts three days, while Aschenputtel dances and runs away from the prince three times. This adds to the suspense because the reader anticipates that something different will happen the third time.*

Model the Skill

- Remind students that **setting** and **plot** are critical elements of any story. The setting is the time and place in which the plot, or story action, occurs.

- Point out the first paragraph of the story. Tell students that the writer clearly states the story's general setting in the first sentence: in China, long ago, in a place where people live in caves. Ask students what events happen in this paragraph. [*Students should understand that Chief Wu married two wives, each of whom had a daughter, and then one wife and Chief Wu himself died.*] Explain that these events are part of the story's plot and set up the action that will come later in the story.

Guided Practice: Apply

Have students read pp. 458 and 459. Have students discuss in groups of three what new setting details and plot events they learned about on these two pages. Then, have them create a quick sketch of what they think the setting looks like, and label where the plot events have occurred so far.

FOLK TALE

Yeh-Shen

Chinese, retold by **Ai-Ling Louie**

Read with a Purpose

Read this ancient Chinese folk tale to see its similarities to "Aschenputtel" and other versions of the Cinderella story familiar to you.

Preparing to Read for this selection is on page 447.

Build Background

The reteller of this tale, Ai-Ling Louie, remembers hearing "Yeh-Shen" being told to her by her grandmother. Curious about the origins of the story, which had been told in her family for three generations, she decided to do some research. She learned that the tale had first been written down by Tuan Cheng-shi in an ancient Chinese manuscript during the Tang dynasty (A.D. 618–907)—more than one thousand years ago. The story had probably been handed down orally for centuries even before that.

In the dim past, even before the Ch'in and the Han dynasties, there lived a cave chief of southern China by the name of Wu. As was the custom in those days, Chief Wu had taken two wives. Each wife in her turn had presented Wu with a baby daughter. But one of the wives sickened and died, and not too many days after that Chief Wu took to his bed and died too.

Yeh-Shen, the little orphan, grew to girlhood in her stepmother's home. She was a bright child and lovely too, with skin as smooth as ivory and dark pools for eyes. Her stepmother was jealous of all this beauty and goodness, for her own daughter was not pretty at all. So in her displeasure, she gave poor Yeh-Shen the heaviest and most unpleasant chores.

The only friend that Yeh-Shen had to her name was a fish she had caught and raised. It was a beautiful fish with golden eyes, and every day it would come out of the water and rest its head on the bank of the pond, waiting for Yeh-Shen to feed it. Stepmother gave Yeh-Shen little enough food for herself, but the orphan child always found something to share with her fish, which grew to enormous size. **A**

Somehow the stepmother heard of this. She was terribly angry to discover that Yeh-Shen had kept a secret from her. She hurried down to the pond, but she was

A **Literary Focus** Folk Tales What clues in the story help you determine the point of view from which it is told?

Selection Readability	
Easily Accessible Accessible **Challenging**	difficult vocabulary and syntax; unfamiliar setting; familiar plot and theme

Selection Plot Summary

Orphaned Yeh-Shen is treated badly by her stepmother, and she finds solace only in her pet fish. When her stepmother kills the fish, the heartbroken Yeh-Shen receives help from the fish's spirit in winning the love of a king.

unable to see the fish, for Yeh-Shen's pet wisely hid itself. The stepmother, however, was a crafty woman, and she soon thought of a plan. She walked home and called out, "Yeh-Shen, go and collect some firewood. But wait! The neighbors might see you. Leave your filthy coat here!" The minute the girl was out of sight, her stepmother slipped on the coat herself and went down again to the pond. This time the big fish saw Yeh-Shen's familiar jacket and heaved itself onto the bank, expecting to be fed. But the stepmother, having hidden a dagger in her sleeve, stabbed the fish, wrapped it in her garments, and took it home to cook for dinner.

When Yeh-Shen came to the pond that evening, she found her pet had disappeared. Overcome with grief, the girl collapsed on the ground and dropped her tears into the still waters of the pond.

"Ah, poor child!" a voice said.

Yeh-Shen sat up to find a very old man looking down at her. He wore the coarsest of clothes, and his hair flowed down over his shoulders.

"Kind uncle, who may you be?" Yeh-Shen asked.

The only friend Yeh-Shen had to her name was a fish she had caught and raised.

"That is not important, my child. All you must know is that I have been sent to tell you of the wondrous powers of your fish."

"My fish, but sir . . ." The girl's eyes filled with tears, and she could not go on.

The old man sighed and said, "Yes, my child, your fish is no longer alive, and I must tell you that your stepmother is once more the cause of your sorrow." Yeh-Shen gasped in horror, but the old man went on. "Let us not dwell on things that are past," he said, "for I have come bringing you a gift. Now you must listen carefully to this: The bones of your fish are filled with a powerful spirit. Whenever you are in serious need, you must kneel before them and let them know your heart's desire. But do not waste their gifts."

Yeh-Shen wanted to ask the old sage many more questions, but he rose to the sky before she could utter another word. With heavy heart, Yeh-Shen made her way to the dung heap to gather the remains of her friend.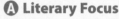

Time went by, and Yeh-Shen, who was often left alone, took comfort in speaking to the bones of her fish. When she was hungry, which happened quite often,

---

ⓑ `Read and Discuss` What have you learned about the stepmother?

ⓒ `Read and Discuss` What do you find out about the fish?

Think About/Talk About

Read with a Purpose Have students read the Read with a Purpose statement. Then, have students list elements from "Aschenputtel" that they expect to see in "Yeh-Shen."

▶ Comprehension

ⓑ Read and Discuss

Possible response: She dislikes Yeh-Shen so much that she kills Yeh-Shen's only friend, the fish.

ⓒ Read and Discuss

Possible response: The fish is magical and will help Yeh-Shen when she is in need, but it warns her not to waste these gifts.

▶ Analysis

ⓐ Literary Focus

Possible response: The presence of the pronouns she and it along with the absence of the pronouns I and me help me determine that the point of view is third person.

▶ Extend the Discussion

Motifs Read the description of Yeh-Shen's stepmother in the second paragraph. What traditional fairy tale role does Yeh-Shen's stepmother play in this story? What role might the fish described in paragraph 3 play?

Possible response: The stepmother is the story's villain. She is jealous of Yeh-Shen, and she treats Yeh-Shen cruelly. The fish might be a magical creature that helps Yeh-Shen.

Universal Access

🅔🅛 English Learners

To help students compare "Yen-Shen" to "Aschenputtel," have them identify key words that both stories have in common. [*stepmother, tears, festival, beautiful, marry, king, shoe*] Then, have students use these words to write sentences explaining what both stories have in common.

🅐🅐🅥🅔 Students Who Use African American Vernacular English

English for Academic Success Students may struggle with the usage of *is* versus *are* according to the rules of for-

mal English. Point out how, in the second column on p. 459, the old man tells Yeh-Shen that "you *are* in serious need." This contrasts with an earlier part of his dialogue, when he says, "your stepmother (she) *is* once more the cause of your sorrow." Explain to students that in formal English, *are* is the appropriate form of *to be* for the subjects *you, we,* and *they; is* accompanies the subjects *he, she,* and *it.* Have students create sentences using the verbs *are* and *is* in formal English. Ask volunteers to share sentences with the class.

Model the Skill

■ To help students **compare and contrast across texts,** have volunteers share their entries for plot, characters, theme, and tone for "Aschenputtel." Explain to students that not only are they looking for those same elements in "Yeh-Shen," but they should also pay attention to how those elements are similar to or different from the corresponding elements in "Aschenputtel."

■ Point out that on this page of the folk tale, we learn that the festival, the fish's help, and losing the shoe are important plot points. Tell students to note these details in their chart. Students should note that a festival and a lost shoe are in both stories. Both stories also have a magical friend who helps the main character, but Aschenputtel's friend is a bird, while Yeh-Shen's is a fish's spirit.

Guided Practice: Apply

Have students scan their graphic organizers for further similarities and differences in character and plot in the two stories. Have them circle elements that the stories have in common and put a box around elements that are different. Remind them to add to their organizers as they read.

Think as a Reader/Writer

Find It in Your Reading Point out that in the last paragraph on p. 460, the sentence "But now the bones were silent," conveys a sad tone.

Use It in Your Writing Have students choose an emotion (such as joy or fear) and an event that could cause it. Tell them to write a few lines about the event in a tone that conveys their chosen emotion.

Yeh-Shen asked the bones for food. In this way, Yeh-Shen managed to live from day to day, but she lived in dread that her stepmother would discover her secret and take even that away from her. **D**

So the time passed and spring came. Festival time was approaching: It was the busiest time of the year. Such cooking and cleaning and sewing there was to be done! Yeh-Shen had hardly a moment's rest. At the spring festival young men and young women from the village hoped to meet and to choose whom they would marry. How Yeh-Shen longed to go! But her stepmother had other plans. She hoped to find a husband for her own daughter and did not want any man to see the beauteous Yeh-Shen first. When finally the holiday arrived, the stepmother and her daughter dressed themselves in their finery and filled their baskets with sweetmeats. "You must remain at home now and watch to see that no one steals fruit from our trees," her stepmother told Yeh-Shen, and then she departed for the banquet with her own daughter.

As soon as she was alone, Yeh-Shen went to speak to the bones of her fish. "Oh, dear friend," she said, kneeling before the precious bones, "I long to go to the festival, but I cannot show myself in these rags. Is there somewhere I could borrow clothes fit to wear to the feast?" At once she found herself dressed in a gown of azure[1] blue,

---

1. **azure** (AZH uhr): like the color of the sky.

D Literary Focus Folk Tales What motif, or common pattern, from the typical Cinderella story do the fish bones represent?

---

with a cloak of kingfisher feathers draped around her shoulders. Best of all, on her tiny feet were the most beautiful slippers she had ever seen. They were woven of golden threads, in a pattern like the scales of a fish, and the glistening soles were made of solid gold. There was magic in the shoes, for they should have been quite heavy, yet when Yeh-Shen walked, her feet felt as light as air.

"Be sure you do not lose your golden shoes," said the spirit of the bones. Yeh-Shen promised to be careful. Delighted with her transformation, she bid a fond farewell to the bones of her fish as she slipped off to join in the merrymaking. **E**

That day Yeh-Shen turned many a head as she appeared at the feast. All around her people whispered, "Look at that beautiful girl! Who can she be?"

But above this, Stepsister was heard to say, "Mother, does she not resemble our Yeh-Shen?"

Upon hearing this, Yeh-Shen jumped up and ran off before her stepsister could look closely at her. She raced down the mountainside, and in doing so, she lost one of her golden slippers. No sooner had the shoe fallen from her foot than all her fine clothes turned back to rags. Only one thing remained—a tiny golden shoe. Yeh-Shen hurried to the bones of her fish and returned the slipper, promising to find its mate. But now the bones were silent. Sadly Yeh-Shen realized that she had lost her only

---

E Read and Discuss What has happened to Yeh-Shen?

Vocabulary glistening (GLIHS uhn ihng) v. used as *adj.:* sparkling; reflecting light.

Developing Oral Fluency

Have students use the text on this page to practice reading dialogue with expression. Remind students that when they read dialogue, they are speaking in a character's voice and should attempt to convey that character's personality as they read.

Small-Group Activity Put students into groups of four. Direct them to the third full paragraph on p. 460.

• First, have students discuss the character traits of the fish's bones, the stepsister, and the people at the festival. Tell students to think about how each of these characters might sound.

• Then, ask a fluent student to model reading the sentence spoken by the fish's bones at the beginning of the third full paragraph. Tell students to pay attention to the expression in the reader's voice.

• Have groups of students read the third, fourth, and fifth paragraphs on p. 460. Tell one student to read the part of the fish's bones, one student to read the part of the people at the feast, and one student to read the part of the stepsister. Have the fourth student serve as a narrator and read the text that is not dialogue.

friend. She hid the little shoe in her bed-straw and went outside to cry. Leaning against a fruit tree, she sobbed and sobbed until she fell asleep. **F**

The stepmother left the gathering to check on Yeh-Shen, but when she returned home, she found the girl sound asleep, with her arms wrapped around a fruit tree. So, thinking no more of her, the stepmother rejoined the party. Meantime, a villager had found the shoe. Recognizing its worth, he sold it to a merchant, who presented it in turn to the king of the island kingdom of T'o Han.

The king was more than happy to accept the slipper as a gift. He was entranced by the tiny thing, which was shaped of the most precious of metals, yet which made no sound when touched to stone. The more he marveled at its beauty, the more determined he became to find the woman to whom the shoe belonged. A search was begun among the ladies of his own kingdom, but all who tried on the sandal found it impossibly small. Undaunted, the king ordered the search widened to include the cave women from the countryside where the slipper had been found. Since he realized it would take many years for every woman to come to his island and test her foot in the slipper, the king thought of a way to get the right woman to come forward. He ordered the sandal placed in a pavilion[2] by the side of the road near where it had

---

2. **pavilion** (puh VIHL yuhn): large tent or shelter, often highly decorated.

F Read and Discuss What is going on now? What has changed?

Carp Swimming Upwards (19th century) by Katsushika Taito (c. 1804–1848). Woodblock print.

Analyzing Visuals   **Connecting to the Text**
What surprises you about the role of the fish in this tale?

Vocabulary   **entranced** (ehn TRANST) *v.:* cast a spell on; enchanted.

Analyzing Visuals

Katsushika Taito was a prized student of the Japanese artist Hokusai, who gave Katsushika the name Taito to use when signing his own work. Katsushika became known for his work with *manga*, or illustrated picture books.

Connecting to the Text: *I'm surprised that the fish's bones have magical powers.*

Think About/Talk About

▶ Comprehension

E Read and Discuss

Possible response: *Yeh-Shen asked her fish to help her attend the festival, and he provided her with the appropriate clothes.*

F Read and Discuss

Possible response: *The fish warned Yeh-Shen not to lose her shoes, but she lost one anyway. All her nice things disappeared, and the fish's bones stopped talking to her.*

▶ Analysis

D Literary Focus

Possible response: *They represent the magical character who helps the heroine.*

▶ Extend the Discussion

Motifs Yeh-Shen can ask the magic bones for anything her heart desires. Why wouldn't she wish harm on her stepmother, or ask for a new home? How does her selflessness relate to all Cinderella stories? ***Possible response:*** *Yeh-Shen is kind and not greedy. Cinderellas are good, kind, and honest, so Yeh-Shen must follow that motif.*

Character In the second full paragraph on p. 461, what might the king's desire to meet the slipper's owner imply about his character? ***Possible response:*** *He likes beautiful, exquisite things. Unlike other princes in Cinderella stories, he hasn't fallen in love with Yeh-Shen; he just thinks her shoe is pretty.*

Vocabulary: Own the Word

- **glistening:** Ask students to name objects that they would describe as *glistening.* ***Possible response:*** *a mirror, a smooth lake, a diamond*

- **entranced:** Tell students that the word *entranced* is formed when the prefix *en-* is attached to the word *trance.* Explain that a trance is a dazed or hypnotized state. So, a person who is *entranced* is in a dazed state, as if under a spell.

Think About/Talk About

▶ Comprehension

Ⓖ Reading Focus

Possible response: In the other stories, the prince goes door to door, having women try the shoe on. In this version, the king leaves the shoe in a pavilion for women to try on.

Ⓗ Read and Discuss

Possible response: Things are looking great. The shoe fit her, and she married the king.

▶ Extend the Discussion

Making Judgments What fairy tale conventions does the story's ending, described in the last paragraph, incorporate? Do these conventions create a realistic ending? Explain.
Possible response: The story ends with a marriage and with the wicked characters' punishment. This isn't realistic because in real life, things don't always end "happily ever after."

Vocabulary: Own the Word

vigil: Ask students to complete this sentence about the vocabulary word and the selection: "The king continued his *vigil* at the pavilion because. . ." [. . .*no woman yet had been able to put on the slipper.*]

Monitor Students' Comprehension

Guide the class in answering these comprehension questions.

1. How does Yeh-Shen's relationship with her fish affect the story? [*The fish's power lets her go to the feast, and her desire to regain her friendship with the fish leads to her marrying the king.*]

2. Why do the fish bones stop speaking to Yeh-Shen? [*She loses her golden shoe.*]

---

been found, and his herald[3] announced that the shoe was to be returned to its original owner. Then, from a nearby hiding place, the king and his men settled down to watch and wait for a woman with tiny feet to come and claim her slipper. **Ⓖ**

All that day the pavilion was crowded with cave women who had come to test a foot in the shoe. Yeh-Shen's stepmother and stepsister were among them, but not Yeh-Shen—they had told her to stay home. By day's end, although many women had eagerly tried to put on the slipper, it still had not been worn. Wearily, the king continued his **vigil** into the night.

It wasn't until the blackest part of night, while the moon hid behind a cloud, that Yeh-Shen dared to show her face at the pavilion, and even then she tiptoed timidly across the wide floor. Sinking down to her knees, the girl in rags examined the tiny shoe. Only when she was sure that this was the missing mate to her own golden slipper did she dare pick it up. At last she could return both little shoes to the fish bones. Surely then her beloved spirit would speak to her again.

Now the king's first thought, on seeing Yeh-Shen take the precious slipper, was to throw the girl into prison as a thief. But when she turned to leave, he caught a glimpse of her face. At once the king was struck by

---

3. **herald** (HEHR uhld): person in a king's court who makes official announcements.

Ⓖ Reading Focus **Compare and Contrast** Analyze how the king's strategy for finding the owner of the slipper is similar to and different from that of the princes in the Cinderella stories you know.

---

the sweet harmony of her features, which seemed so out of keeping with the rags she wore. It was then that he took a closer look and noticed that she walked upon the tiniest feet he had ever seen.

With a wave of his hand, the king signaled that this tattered creature was to be allowed to depart with the golden slipper. Quietly, the king's men slipped off and followed her home.

All this time, Yeh-Shen was unaware of the excitement she had caused. She had made her way home and was about to hide both sandals in her bedding when there was a pounding at the door. Yeh-Shen went to see who it was—and found a king at her doorstep. She was very frightened at first, but the king spoke to her in a kind voice and asked her to try the golden slippers on her feet. The maiden did as she was told, and as she stood in her golden shoes, her rags were transformed once more into the feathered cloak and beautiful azure gown.

Her loveliness made her seem a heavenly being, and the king suddenly knew in his heart that he had found his true love.

Not long after this, Yeh-Shen was married to the king. But fate was not so gentle with her stepmother and stepsister. Since they had been unkind to his beloved, the king would not permit Yeh-Shen to bring them to his palace. They remained in their cave home, where one day, it is said, they were crushed to death in a shower of flying stones. **Ⓗ**

Ⓗ Read and Discuss How are things looking for Yeh-Shen now?

Vocabulary **vigil** (VIHJ uhl) *n.*: overnight watch.

 California Standards, p. 463

■ **Reading Standard 3.5** Contrast points of view (e.g., first and third person, limited and omniscient, subjective and objective) in narrative text and explain how they affect the overall theme of the work.

Applying Your Skills

Reading Standard 3.5 Contrast points of view (e.g., first and third person, limited and omniscient, subjective and objective) in narrative text and explain how they affect the overall theme of the work.

Yeh-Shen
Literary Response and Analysis

Reading Skills Focus
Quick Check

1. Who is Yeh-Shen's only friend? What does the stepmother do to the friend?

2. What advice about fish bones does the old man give Yeh-Shen?

3. What happens when Yeh-Shen runs away from the festival?

Read with a Purpose

4. What is the message of "Yeh-Shen"? How is the message of "Yeh-Shen" similar to or different from the message of "Aschenputtel"?

Reading Skills: Comparing and Contrasting Across Texts

5. Look at the chart you've been completing as you read. In what area does "Yeh-Shen" differ most from "Aschenputtel": point of view, plot, tone, or theme? What are the most significant similarities between the two narratives?

Comparing Cinderella Stories

	"Aschenputtel"	"Yeh-Shen"	"Inter-view"
Point of View			
Plot			
Tone			
Theme			

✓ Vocabulary Check

Fill in each blank with the correct Vocabulary word.

glistening   entranced   vigil

6. The _____ snow reflected the moonlight.

7. She kept a _____ until the morning.

8. The children were _____ by the new toys.

Literary Skills Focus
Literary Analysis

9. **Analyze** Review what you have learned about Yeh-Shen's stepmother. How would Yeh-Shen's story change if it were told from the stepmother's point of view?

Literary Skills: Folk Tales

10. **Analyze** Cinderella tales from around the world share common features, or **motifs,** but they also have strong cultural characteristics. From the evidence in this story, what qualities do you perceive the ancient Chinese valued in women?

Writing Skills Focus
Think as a Reader/Writer

Use It in Your Writing Look back at the words, phrases, and sentences that best reveal the tone of this story. Does the tone change depending on which characters or events are described? State your thoughts in a paragraph.

Check for Understanding

Independent Practice
Reading Skills Focus
Answers:

1. *Her only friend is her pet fish; her stepmother kills the fish.*

2. *He tells her to share her heart's desires with the bones, but not to waste their magic.*

3. *She loses her golden shoe and can no longer talk to the fish's spirit.*

4. *The stories have a similar message: Good people are rewarded, and wicked people are punished.*

5. *The two stories differ slightly in plot and significantly in setting. They have similar characters and themes.*

Vocabulary Check
Answers:

6. *glistening*

7. *vigil*

8. *entranced*

Literary Skills Focus
Possible responses:

9. *Yen-Shen's stepmother is cruel and despises Yen-Shen for her beauty. If the story were told from the stepmother's point of view, Yen-Shen would have been the villain and her daughter would have been the heroine.*

10. *They probably valued beauty and kindness.*

Universal Access

Struggling Writers

Benchmark Students Provide additional scaffolding for students by suggesting that they consider how the tone when Yeh-Shen is described is similar to or different from the tone when the stepmother is described. Write the following sentence frames on the board, and have students use them to organize their ideas before they begin drafting their paragraphs. Remind them to use their notes to cite specific examples from the selection that support their conclusions.

When Yeh-Shen is described, the tone is _____ .
When the stepmother is described, the tone is _____ .
The tone changes from _____ to _____ because _____ .

Direct Teach

Model the Skill

- Review with students some of the patterns they noticed in "Aschenputtel" and "Yeh-Shen," such as the lost shoes, the magical friend, the prince, and the wicked stepmother and stepsisters. Clarify for students that these are **motifs** that appear in most Cinderella stories.

- Read the poem "Interview" aloud to students. Point out that this Cinderella story is told as a poem, and from a different point of view than the other versions they read, but that the motifs still appear. For example, in line 2, the stepmother calls Cinderella "Miss Glass Slipper of the Year," and talks about her going to the ball and marrying the prince. Even though the poem does not describe the shoe, the ball, or the prince in detail, these elements are still included to help the reader understand that the poem is talking about the Cinderella story. They are motifs in the other folk tales that are universal to the Cinderella story.

Guided Practice: Apply

Have students reread the poem in pairs and revisit their Reading Skills Focus graphic organizer and identify other motifs in the poem. Remind them to consider characters and ideas, as well as objects, as motifs.

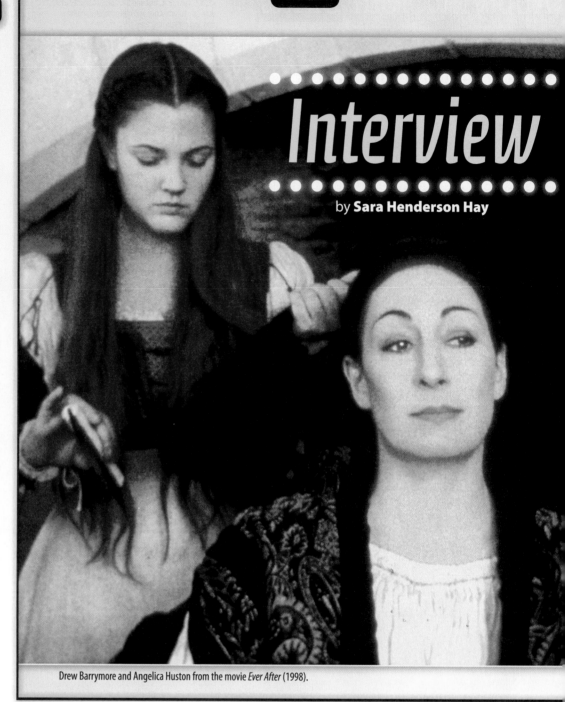

Interview

by **Sara Henderson Hay**

Drew Barrymore and Angelica Huston from the movie *Ever After* (1998).

Selection Readability	
Easily Accessible **Accessible** **Challenging**	difficult vocabulary and syntax; unfamiliar setting

Selection Summary

In this poem, the story of Cinderella is told from the point of view of the stepmother as she speaks with an interviewer. The stepmother attempts to convince the interviewer that she and her lovely daughters are the victims of Cinderella's outrageous lies.

Yes, this is where she lived before she won
The title Miss Glass Slipper of the Year,
And went to the ball and married the king's son.
You're from the local press, and want to hear
5   About her early life? Young man, sit down.
These are my *own* two daughters; you'll not find
Nicer, more biddable° girls in all the town,
And lucky, I tell them, not to be the kind
That Cinderella was, spreading those lies,   **A**
10 Telling those shameless tales about the way
We treated her. Oh, nobody denies
That she was pretty, if you like those curls.
But looks aren't everything, I always say.
Be sweet and natural, I tell my girls,
15 And Mr. Right will come along, someday.   **B**

---

7. **biddable** (BIHD uh buhl): obedient.

A [Read and Discuss] What does the speaker in the poem mean when she says Cinderella spread lies about the way they treated her? What is she talking about?

B [Read and Discuss] The speaker says, "Oh, nobody denies / That she was pretty, if you like those curls." What does this statement reveal about the speaker?

Reading Standard 3.5 Contrast points of view (e.g., first and third person, limited and omniscient, subjective and objective) in narrative text and explain how they affect the overall theme of the work.

Check for Understanding

Independent Practice
Reading Skills Focus
Answers:

1. *In the modern version, the stepmother is presented as the heroine, and Cinderella is the villain.*

2. *Unlike "Aschenputtel" and "Yeh-Shen," the poem implies that Cinderella is not a nice person and that the stepmother has been wrongly accused.*

Literary Skills Focus
Possible responses:

3. *The speaker is Cinderella's stepmother. This becomes clear when she refers to her "own" daughters.*

4. *The point of view in "Interview" is first person; the point of view in the other stories is third person. This point of view is effective for conveying the stepmother's thoughts and motivations, but it does not tell the whole story. It would not be effective without knowing the Cinderella story.*

5. *The speaker does not believe what she is saying. It is obvious that she is the mean woman that is portrayed in the original Cinderella when she gives Cinderella a backhanded compliment.*

6. *The stepmother would seem like the victim to me, but I wouldn't trust her completely because she does make snide comments.*

7. *The tone is critical and bitter. It suggests the speaker is jealous.*

8. *The theme of the other versions is that cruelty is punished, suggesting that there is only one good and one bad side. The theme of this version is different because it shows that stories are not always black and white.*

9. *It summarizes Cinderella's trip to the ball and her marriage to the prince. It leaves out the magical elements of the story.*

Interview
Literary Response and Analysis

Reading Skills Focus
Read with a Purpose

1. What is a key difference between this retelling of the folk tale and the traditional versions?

Reading Skills: Comparing and Contrasting Across Texts

2. Review the "Interview" column in the "Comparing Cinderella Stories" graphic organizer. In what ways does the poem differ from "Aschenputtel" and "Yeh-Shen"?

Comparing Cinderella Stories

	"Aschenputtel"	"Yeh-Shen"	"Interview"
Point of View			
Plot			
Tone			
Theme			

Literary Skills Focus
Literary Analysis

3. **Interpret** Who is the speaker—the one doing the talking—in this poem? At what point do you recognize the speaker? What specific details in the poem point to the speaker's identity?

4. **Analyze** Explain how the point of view in "Interview" is different from the point of view in "Aschenputtel" and "Yeh-Shen." How effective is this point of view? Would it be effective if you did not know the Cinderella story?

5. **Interpret** Explain whether or not the speaker believes what she is saying about Cinderella and her own girls. Support your response with examples from the text.

6. **Analyze** If you had never heard the original story of Cinderella, and all you had read was this poem, what would you think of the stepmother?

7. **Analyze** The speaker's attitude toward a subject is called **tone**. A tone can be, for example, admiring, comic, bitter, loving, critical, serious, or disrespectful. What tone do you <u>perceive</u> in this poem? What does the tone tell you about the speaker's personality and values?

8. **Interpret** One theme this poem explores is that there are two sides to every story. How is this theme different from the themes of the other versions of Cinderella you have read?

Literary Skills: Folk Tales

9. **Analyze** This poem is a comment on the Cinderella story; it is not a Cinderella story itself. What aspects of the Cinderella story does it summarize? What does it leave out?

Writing Skills Focus
Think as a Reader/Writer

Use It in Your Writing Think about the tone you've identified in this poem. Then, explain whether the speaker is expressing a subjective or objective point of view. Cite examples from the poem to support your response.

Universal Access

Struggling Writers
Provide additional scaffolding by encouraging students to think about an author's tone and the words chosen to describe the character. Have students record the descriptions of Cinderella from the poem, read them aloud, and then determine the tone of the poem.

**California Standards,
pp. 466–467**
- **Reading Standard 3.5** Contrast points of view (e.g., first and third person, limited and omniscient, subjective and objective) in narrative text and explain how they affect the overall theme of the work.

COMPARING TEXTS
Wrap Up

Reading Standard 3.5 Contrast points of view (e.g., first and third person, limited and omniscient, subjective and objective) in narrative text and explain how they affect the overall theme of the work.

Aschenputtel / Yeh-Shen / Interview

Writing Skills Focus
Write a Comparison-Contrast Essay

Write a comparison-contrast essay on "Aschenputtel," "Yeh-Shen," and "Interview." To help you write a comparison-contrast essay on the three selections, refer to the charts you filled in as you read each version of the Cinderella tale. You can organize your essay in one of two ways:

1. You can use the **block method** and write one paragraph for each selection. In this case you would <u>analyze</u> and describe the point of view, the plot, the tone, and the theme, selection by selection.

2. You can use the **point-by-point method** and write one paragraph on the point of view in each selection, one on the plot of each selection, one on the tone of each selection, and one on the theme of each selection.

Whichever <u>organizational</u> method you use, be sure to include a final paragraph in which you describe your responses to the selections.

What Do
You
Think
Now

Why might waiting to be rescued not be a positive attitude to have in real life?

CHOICES

As you respond to the Choices, use these **Academic Vocabulary** words as appropriate: <u>analyze</u>, <u>narrative</u>, <u>organizational</u>, <u>perceive</u>.

REVIEW
Contrast Points of View

In "Interview" you heard from one of the characters in the Cinderella story. Let another character speak and tell his or her side of the story. Let us hear from the point of view of one of the stepsisters, the prince, the dove, the king, the fairy godmother, or even an anonymous guest at the ball. Write as "I." What does your narrator <u>perceive</u> that compels him or her to speak up?

CONNECT
Write an Article

Timed Writing Imagine that you have been asked to write an article that will introduce the new princess, Aschenputtel, to the kingdom. Review the story to find the answers to the 5W-How? questions: who? what? when? where? why? and how? Improve your article by including details from the folk tale, and make sure you write from an objective point of view.

EXTEND
Analyze Another Cinderella

Oral Report Find a different version of Cinderella in a library or on the Internet. You may enjoy searching for a version from your own culture. In an oral report, summarize the version for your class, share some cultural background information, and point out the ways the tale is like or unlike the traditional Cinderella tale.

Universal Access

Struggling Writers

Provide additional scaffolding by explaining to students that in their final paragraphs, they should describe their responses to the selections, comparing and contrasting as appropriate. For example, if they found the theme of both "Aschenputtel" and "Yeh-Shen" easy to detect and relate to, they should note this as a similarity. Likewise, if they found "Interview" to be more interesting than the other two selections, they should not only mention this, but also discuss reasons why they had this reaction. Remind students that even though the final paragraph will contain their personal responses, they should still support these responses with reasons and evidence from the text.

Objectives
Students will
- identify and understand cause-and-effect text structure
- follow a cause-and-effect chain

Motivate

What Do You Think?/QuickWrite
Have students discuss examples of people or groups who are doing something to protect the environment. Then, have students use their **Reader/Writer Notebook** to explain how they might be able to do something themselves or as a class to help the environment.

Analyzing Visuals
Use ThinkCentral, Teacher Access to project this image for viewing.

Extension Activity Ask students to discuss what the people in the image might be doing. ***Possible response:*** *They might be trying to heal an injured bird.*

California Standards, pp. 468–477

- **Reading Standard 2.3** Analyze text that uses the cause-and-effect organizational pattern.

INFORMATIONAL TEXT FOCUS

Text Structures: Cause and Effect

Rescue workers hold oil-covered cormorant that was caught in the massive spill (1989) from the grounded oil tanker *Exxon Valdez* in Prince William Sound, Valdez, Alaska.

CONTENTS

What Do You Think Concerns about the environment are widespread. What can you do to protect it?

 QuickWrite
What efforts at conservation have you observed in your home, at school, or in your community? What more could people do?

Selection Resources

Chapter 4 Resources, on-level practice and assessment, pp. 42–47

PowerNotes, interactive lesson presentation with activities

Teacher One Stop™, on-level lesson plans and all print resources

Holt Audio Library

Holt Audio Library: Selections and Summaries in Spanish

UA: Holt Interactive Reader, pp. 114–119

Holt Interactive Reader for ELD, pp. 138–143

Preparing to Read

Reading Standard 2.3 Analyze text that uses the cause-and-effect organizational pattern.

Tilting at Windmills: The Search for Alternative Energy Sources

Informational Text Focus

Cause-and-Effect Organizational Pattern Suppose you study hard for a test and are rewarded with a high grade. Your studying is a **cause**—it makes something happen. An **effect** is what happens as a result—your A+ on the test. Not studying might have led to an entirely different effect—a barely passing grade.

Writers of informational texts often use a **cause-and-effect organizational pattern**, or text structure, when they want to explain the causes and effects of a process or event or describe a problem. When you read an informational text that deals with causes and effects, ask yourself, "Why did this happen?" and "What happened because of this?" These questions will help you discover the cause-and-effect chain that forms the structure of the text.

Into Action Read "Tilting at Windmills," keeping track of the cause-and-effect chain by filling out a chart like the one below. Start each cause statement with the word *because*.

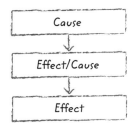

Writing Skills Focus

Preparing for Timed ⏱ Writing Texts that have a cause-and-effect <u>organizational</u> pattern usually include signal words, or transitions, that show how one idea is connected to another: *after, as a result, because, consequently, so, then, therefore,* and *since*. As you read this article, make a list of all the helpful transitions you find.

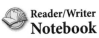
Reader/Writer Notebook
Use your **RWN** to complete the activities for this selection.

Vocabulary

renewable (rih NOO uh buhl) *adj.:* able to be replaced by a new thing of the same sort. *Scientists are looking for renewable energy sources.*

shortages (SHAWR tihj ihz) *n.:* situations in which needed items cannot be gotten in sufficient amounts. *There were shortages of oil in the 1970s.*

Language Coach

Percentages We use percentages to simplify the discussion of numbers. The word *percent* is made from the Latin words *per* and *centum* and means "parts out of one hundred." In this article, statistics—information presented in number form—that use percentages are given. When the article states "Wind supplies 20 percent of Denmark's power," it is saying that out of every 100 units of electricity produced, 20 are produced by wind power. In what other contexts are percentages used?

Learn It Online
Enhance your vocabulary with Word Watch at::
go.hrw.com | H7-469 | **Go**

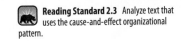
Learn It Online
Send students to **Word Watch** for audio pronunciations of words, snyonyms and antonyms, and brief histories of word origins.

go.hrw.com | H7-469 | **Go**

Direct Teach

Model the Skill

- Provide students with copies of the Informational Text Focus graphic organizer (See **Chapter 4 Resources**) or ask them to use their own paper.

- Tell students that **cause-and-effect organizational patterns** help readers follow a sequence of events and reasons they occur.

- Point out that the article states that burning fossil fuels releases emissions into the atmosphere. Burning the fossil fuels is a cause, and the emissions are an effect.

- Explain that some effects become causes by precipitating further events. The release of emissions is an effect of burning fossil fuels, but the emissions in the air cause air pollution.

Guided Practice: Apply

Read-Talk-Write Have students continue reading. When they finish, have pairs discuss cause-and-effect relationships they noticed in the text. Have partners collaborate to fill in a cause-and-effect chain for one relationship.

A seventeenth-century sailing ship sails past a twenty-first-century offshore wind farm.

TILTING AT WINDMILLS:
THE SEARCH FOR ALTERNATIVE ENERGY SOURCES

by THE WORLD ALMANAC

Read with a Purpose Read this article to learn about using wind power to generate electricity.

When you turn on a light, a television, or a computer, you probably don't give much thought to how the electricity powering those devices got there. But fuel was used to create that electrical charge. And chances are, it was a fossil fuel, gotten from decaying plants and animals.

Over millions of years, dead plants and animals get buried and then turn into substances like coal, oil, and natural gas. These products are found in underground deposits that are mined by energy companies. Fossil fuels are natural, in a sense, but using them can create some nasty by-products. Coal and the like are burned to release their energy, and the burning fuel releases harmful substances called emissions into the atmosphere. **Ⓐ**

In addition to the problem of causing pollution, fossil fuels are also running out. There is a limited supply of fossil fuel in the ground, and because it takes millions of

Ⓐ Informational Focus Cause and Effect **Organizational Pattern** What is the effect of burning fossil fuels?

Selection Readability	
Easily Accessible **Accessible** Challenging	serious subject matter; real-life situations; accessible theme

Selection Summary

Wind, a clean and renewable energy source, is gaining popularity as an alternative to fossil fuels, which are nonrenewable and pollute the environment. Despite their advantages, windmill farms have met opposition in some locations because they require large amounts of space and may be harmful to wildlife.

years to form, it is considered a nonrenewable energy source. So power companies are increasingly turning to an alternative source of energy: the wind. "Strong growth figures in the U.S. prove that wind is now a mainstream option for new power generation," said Randy Swisher. He is president of the American Wind Energy Association.

AS OLD AS THE WIND

Wind is the fastest-growing source of renewable energy, according to the United States Department of Energy. A renewable power source, such as wind or solar power, does not depend on a limited fuel supply. Wind is freely available and is used to generate power in more than thirty states. It keeps more than two million households running.

People first used wind to generate power around five thousand years ago. They used it to propel sailboats up and down the Nile River. Sometime between A.D. 500 and A.D. 900, the Persians realized that wind could be used to turn a wheel. They attached several sails to a central axle, and the windmill was born.

Early windmills were used to pump water and grind grain, and many are still used for these tasks today. In the Netherlands, flooding is common, and farmers often need to move large amounts of water. Windmills are a workable solution. Because they are part of everyday life in the Netherlands, people have tried to make these hardworking machines attractive. The country has become famous for its beautiful windmills, which dot the landscape. **ⓑ**

RUNNING WITH THE WIND

The most widespread use of modern windmills is for creating electricity. Generating electricity requires a turbine, which is a kind of engine. Steam, water, air, or some other force turns a wheel or a set of wheels, which turns a shaft. This shaft usually turns a generator, which produces electricity.

Beginning in the 1920s, wind was used in a limited way to generate electricity in rural areas of the United States. Then came the energy crisis of the 1970s. Around the world, there were shortages of oil. The cost of fossil fuels soared. Because of these difficulties, interest in generating power from wind on a large scale grew.

Giant "wind farms" were built in remote areas where wind sweeps across the landscape. Other wind farms were built offshore, to capture sea breezes.

"As security of energy supply and climate change are ranging high on the political agendas of the world's governments, wind energy has already become a mainstream energy source in many countries around the world," said Arthouros Zervos. He is the chairman of the Global Wind Energy Council. "Wind energy is clean and fuel-free, which makes it the most attractive solution to the world's energy challenges."

 ⓑ **Read and Discuss** What have you learned about windmills?

> **Vocabulary** **renewable** (rih NOO uh buhl) *adj.*: able to be replaced by a new thing of the same sort.
> **shortages** (SHAWR tihj ihz) *n.*: situations in which needed items cannot be gotten in sufficient amounts.

▶ **Comprehension**

C Read and Discuss

Possible response: Students may be surprised that the United States ranks third in the amount of wind power it generates.

D Read and Discuss

Possible response: The author is prompting the reader to think about the benefits of using wind power to generate energy.

▶ **Extend the Discussion**

Cause and Effect According to paragraph 3 on p. 472, what is causing the construction of wind farms to be delayed? *Possible response: People who live near construction areas are trying to prevent wind farms from being built because they think it will ruin their view of the ocean.*

Making Inferences Read the third paragraph and analyze the photograph. How might windmills harm birds and other wildlife? *Possible response: Birds could fly into the blades of a windmill.*

Monitor Students' Comprehension

Use the Read with a Purpose follow-up question to assess students' understanding. *Possible response: Wind power is a renewable resource, unlike fossil fuel. It is clean and does not require the use of fuel.*

Analyzing Visuals **Connecting to the Text** What is causing the windmills to appear as they do in this photo?

C Read and Discuss What is your response to this statement?

Two gigantic wind farms are located off the coast of Denmark. Wind supplies 20 percent of Denmark's power. The United States ranks third, behind Germany and Spain, in the amount of power it generates from the wind. **C**

FACING THE WIND

Wind farms are quite a sight. A typical power-generating windmill is enormous. It is around twenty stories tall, and the diameter of its blades is about 200 feet across. The taller the windmill and the longer its blades, the more wind it can capture.

But giant wind farms are not always welcome. Some groups complain that wind farms spoil the landscape—or seascape. The construction of a wind farm planned for an area near Cape Cod, Massachusetts, has been delayed because many people say it will ruin their view of the Atlantic Ocean. Large windmills can also be harmful to birds and other wildlife. And because wind is not constant, other power sources must be used when the wind is not blowing.

Government programs, however, especially in the United States and Europe, are encouraging the use of wind power as an alternative to fossil fuels. This ancient technology can help us meet our energy needs without using up our natural resources and polluting the atmosphere. **D**

Read with a Purpose What are the benefits of using wind power to generate energy?

D Read and Discuss What is the author prompting you to think about?

Universal Access

Students with Disabilities

Divide the article into four sections based on its subheads (the lead, "As Old as the Wind," "Running with the Wind," and "Facing the Wind"). Then, use the **Jigsaw with Experts** routine to have students analyze sections of the text in groups. After students read each section, have them pause to summarize what they've read and discuss any causes and effects that the writer has described in that section.

✔ See **UA: Differentiating Instruction** for lesson plans and strategies for teaching students with disabilities.

Analyzing Visuals

Connecting to the Text: *The wind is causing the windmills' blades to spin very fast, so the blades appear blurred.*

Applying Your Skills

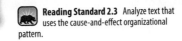

Tilting at Windmills
Standards Review

Informational Text and Vocabulary

1. This article suggests that all of the following might have caused the rise of wind power *except*

   A the need to generate electricity in remote places.

   B the desire to generate energy without causing pollution.

   C the attempt to conserve our supply of fossil fuels.

   D the desire to create beautiful windmills.

2. What caused many people to become interested in using wind power as a resource?

   A energy crisis of the 1970s

   B beauty of the Dutch windmills

   C view of the ocean from Cape Cod

   D desire to fill unused land

3. Why can't people rely on wind power alone to satisfy their energy needs?

   A Wind is a renewable resource.

   B Large windmills are dangers to birds.

   C Wind does not always blow.

   D Wind farms exist around the country.

4. Which of the following sentences contains a **cause** and an **effect?**

   A Burning coal or oil releases its energy.

   B Solar power does not depend on a limited fuel supply.

   C The Persians attached sails to a central axle.

   D Fossil fuels take millions of years to form.

5. According to the article, which of the following is a major effect of burning fossil fuels?

   A creation of a secure energy supply

   B capture of the energy in sea breezes

   C provision of power to two million households

   D release of harmful substances into the air

6. Another word for *renewable* is

   A clean.

   B replaceable.

   C sufficient.

   D decaying.

7. An antonym for *shortages* is

   A excesses.

   B supplies.

   C growths.

   D insufficiencies.

Writing Skills Focus

Timed └Writing Using a cause-and-effect organizational pattern, briefly describe the effects of using wind power instead of fossil fuels as an energy resource. Cite relevant evidence from the article in your response.

 What Do **You Think Now** Would the use of wind power help your community? Explain.

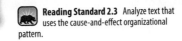
What Do You Think Now?
Have students discuss the question in small groups. Encourage them to review what they learned about wind power in the article. Have them think about what changes the use of wind power would bring about, and whether these changes would be beneficial.

Check for Understanding

Independent Practice
Answers and Explanations

1. D *This article suggests that the need to generate electricity in remote places (A), the desire to generate energy without causing pollution (B), and the attempt to conserve our supply of fossil fuels (C) might have caused the rise of wind power.*

2. A *The energy crisis of the 1970s, not beauty (B, C) or a desire to fill unused land (D), caused many people to become interested in using wind power as a resource.*

3. C *Wind does not always blow, so people can't rely on wind power alone to satisfy their energy needs. Items A and D are advantages to using wind power, and B is not related to the need for other resources.*

4. A *Burning coal or oil causes a release in energy.*

5. D *The release of harmful substances into the air is a major effect of burning fossil fuels. There is a limited supply of fossil fuels, not a secure supply (A), fossil fuels do not capture wind energy as windmills do (B), and the article states that wind, not fossil fuels, provides power to two million households (C).*

6. B *Another word for* renewable *is replaceable, not clean (A), sufficient (C), or decaying (D).*

7. A Shortages *means "insufficient amounts," and the opposite of not having enough is having too much, or having excesses.*

Writing Skills Focus
Possible response: *Using wind power would reduce the demand for fossil fuels, which would result in less burning of fossil fuels, which in turn would improve air quality and protect the environment.*

Preparing to Read

Reading Standard 2.3 Analyze text that uses the cause-and-effect organizational pattern.

Introducing Vocabulary

Read aloud the words and sample sentences. Then, use this activity to check students' understanding.

1. Chemicals can be _____ to the environment. [*hazards*]

2. A whale's _____ is the ocean. [*habitat*]

3. The article about endangered species left me with a _____ feeling of sadness. [*profound*]

English for Academic Success

Language Coach

After reading the Language Coach, tell students to look for cause and effect signal words at the beginning of sentences, as well as in the middle. Provide the following examples: *Due to the drought, the crops didn't grow. The crops didn't grow, due to the drought.*

Informational Text Focus

As you read and discuss the selection with students, remind hem to note causes and effects in their causal chains.

Writing Skills Focus

Have students take notes about calls to action in their **Reader/Writer Notebook**. Students can use their notes to complete the Writing Skills Focus activity.

Saving the Earth: Teens Fish for Answers

Informational Text Focus

Cause-and-Effect Organizational Pattern If you are having difficulty understanding the cause-and-effect <u>organizational</u> pattern, you might think about the weather. One obvious cause-and-effect example is hot air hitting cold air, which has the effect of producing rain. Rain, combined with a cold front, can cause temperatures in the southern United States to drop drastically and suddenly.

"Saving the Earth: Teens Fish for Answers" follows a cause-and-effect pattern. Each event causes another event to happen. In this article, changes in the environment cause Ohio students to take action. The students' actions then lead to their own effects, including a change in the way one student <u>perceives</u> herself and her place in the world.

Into Action Use a causal chain like the one below to record the causes and effects in the article.

Cause — Brook trout population in Ohio decreases. → Effect — Two friends test water quality in local streams. → Effect — They discover streams are becoming polluted. → Effect

Writing Skills Focus

Preparing for **Timed Writing** Writers of informational texts write with a purpose. The writer of a cause-and-effect article wants to explain how certain events are related, but he or she may be doing so with an even greater goal in mind. As you read "Saving the Earth," look for evidence that the writer is trying to persuade you to believe or do something. Look specifically for a call to action, and think about how it might relate to the causes and effects in the article.

Reader/Writer Notebook

Use your **RWN** to complete the activities for this selection.

Vocabulary

habitat (HAB uh tat) *n.*: place where an animal or plant naturally lives. *The habitat of the brook trout was in danger.*

hazards (HAZ uhrdz) *n.*: dangers. *Environmental hazards threatened the watershed.*

profound (pruh FOWND) *adj.*: very deep; felt strongly. *McMullen's work had a profound effect on her life.*

Language Coach

Transitions Writers who organize their texts around causes and effects include transition words to show how one idea connects to another. The terms in the chart below will help you recognize the pattern of causes and effects in this article.

Words That Signal Causes	Words That Signal Effects
because, since, due to, given that, as, since, were caused by, results from	therefore, consequently, as a result, then, thus, so, for that reason

Learn It Online
To read more articles like this, go to the interactive Reading Workshops on:

go.hrw.com | H7-474 | **Go**

Learn It Online
Reading Workshops are interactive versions of real-world informational texts; students exercise their reading skills by responding to polls and answering questions in an engaging online format.

go.hrw.com | H7-474 | **Go**

SAVING THE EARTH:
Teens Fish for Answers

by THE WORLD ALMANAC®

Read with a Purpose
Read this article to discover how some teens help protect the environment.

Karoline Evin McMullen was in seventh grade when she and a friend started wondering how pollution was affecting their area. They had witnessed a building boom in their native Ohio, in which chain stores and restaurants replaced farmland. They also noticed a decrease in the population of the Ohio brook trout, which lives in the area's Chagrin River.

"I was inspired to start my conservation work by the habitat destruction going on in my area," says McMullen, now 16. The girls tested the water in local streams and compared their findings with older data. It was clear that water quality was suffering. **Ⓐ**

The girls started the group Save Our Stream, which educates people about environmental hazards and repairs the trout's habitat. They received thousands of dollars in grants and designed outdoor educational trails. They wrote a book about brook trout and created a pamphlet and a Web site. And they gave presentations to thousands of students and teachers and reached millions more through an educational TV network.

McMullen says the results of their efforts are measurable. "Eighty percent of people I polled didn't know there was a native brook trout, let alone that it belonged in their own backyard," she says about the group's start. But in polls of people given training, "100 percent were doing things they had been told to do." **Ⓑ**

WATER WAYS

Save Our Stream publicizes the need for natural buffers against water runoff. The group encourages people to plant trees and allow grass to grow high along stream banks. That "helps filter off pollution" before the water enters the stream, says McMullen.

Ⓐ **Informational Focus** Cause and Effect **Pattern** What caused McMullen to start her conservation work?

Ⓑ **Informational Focus** Cause and Effect **Pattern** What effect did Save Our Stream have on the people living in McMullen's town?

Vocabulary **habitat** (HAB uh tat) *n.*: place where an animal or plant naturally lives.
hazards (HAZ uhrdz) *n.*: dangers.

Selection Summary
When two teenage girls noticed that trout were growing scarce in the river near their Ohio home, they compared water samples of local streams to older samples and found that the trout's disappearance corresponded with an increase in water pollution. This led them to form Save Our Stream, a group that educates the public about water pollution.

Think About/Talk About
Read with a Purpose Have students read the Read with a Purpose statement. Point out that both articles they are reading deal with protecting the environment.

▶ Analysis

Ⓐ Informational Focus
Possible response: McMullen and her friend noticed that the water quality of their local stream was deteriorating.

Ⓑ Informational Focus
Possible response: The people learned about their environment and followed McMullen's conservation advice.

▶ Extend the Discussion
Cause and Effect Read the first paragraph of the selection. How might Ohio's building boom and the decrease in the brook trout population be related? Which might be the cause and which might be the effect? *Possible response: The restaurants and stores may have produced water runoff that polluted the water in local streams. The building boom may have caused the trout to die.*

Vocabulary: Own the Word
- **habitat:** Work with students to create a semantic web for *habitat*. Write the word in a center circle on the board. Draw lines, or legs, branching out from the center circle. Have students add concepts and attributes to the semantic web. *Possible responses: den, nest, swamp, stream, ecology, nature, science, biology, home, ecosystem*

- **hazards:** Ask students to identify some of the *hazards* that threaten animal habitats today. [*Water pollution, landfills, road construction, rising temperatures*]

▶ **Comprehension**

Ⓒ **Read and Discuss**

Possible response: The author is explaining that there are many simple things that people can do every day to help the environment.

▶ **Extend the Discussion**

Cause and Effect Based on McMullen's comments in the second paragraph of p. 476, what effect did Save Our Stream have on her? *Possible response: She became more aware about conservation and about her own future.*

Vocabulary: Own the Word

profound: Remind students that the connotation of *profound* is "very meaningful or important." You might say, "I always find my friend's advice to be helpful, but the idea she shared with me today was especially *profound*." Have students create a pair of related sentences that show how *profound* has a stronger connotation than *meaningful*.

Monitor Students' Comprehension

Use the Read with a Purpose follow-up question to assess students' understanding. *Possible response: According to the third paragraph of p. 475, the group "educates people about environmental hazards and repairs the trout's habitat."*

The group encourages washing cars on lawns instead of on concrete, so soap and dirt do not go directly into storm drains. They advertise the importance of picking up pet waste and flushing or throwing it away, so the waste does not go straight into streams.

The teens were awarded the Gloria Barron Prize for Young Heroes in 2006. But McMullen says her greatest rewards were built into her work. "It has had a sort of profound effect on the way I see myself and what I want to do with my future," she says. "Through this program, I've been enlightened about conservation. I want to pursue higher education and help governments find a solution for people and the world they live in."

HEED THE CALL

The environment is a big issue, and teens have heard the call. They're getting their hands dirty in outdoor conservation projects and organizing community forces. In Mount Rainier National Park in Washington State, students restore trails and campgrounds. Farther north, the group Alaska Youth for Environmental Action spreads the word about global warming.

You can start working to help the environment now: Join an ecology club, and if there isn't one, start your own. Make sure your school recycles paper. Turn off lights. Plant trees. Volunteer in your local park system. Plant native species. Most of all, know that you can make a difference. Ⓒ

Read with a Purpose How does Save Our Stream work to protect the environment?

Ⓒ **Read and Discuss** What is the author's purpose here?

Vocabulary **profound** (pruh FOWND) *adj.:* very deep; felt strongly.

Students from the group Save Our Stream clean Geauga Park District in Chardon, Ohio.

Universal Access

Advanced Learners

Enrichment Have students consider the broader effects of McMullen's actions. How might her actions have effects that reach beyond her hometown? Have students discuss the implications for her county, her state, or the country.

AAVE Students Who Use African American Vernacular English

English for Academic Success Students may replace the consonant cluster *th* with /d/ in the pronunciation of words such as *they*, *there*, and *things*. Direct students' attention to these words on p. 475, and model pronouncing them according to the conventions of formal English. Remind students that this is the style of English most appropriate and effective for academic contexts. In pairs, have students read aloud p. 476, noting any *th* sounds they encounter (*they're, their, there, farther*). Tell them to practice pronouncing the words so that the /th/ sound is clearly voiced.

Applying Your Skills

 Reading Standard 2.3 Analyze text that uses the cause-and-effect organizational pattern.

Saving the Earth
Standards Review

Informational Text and Vocabulary

1. This article suggests that all of the following might have caused the decline in the trout population *except* the
   A destruction of farmland.
   B washing of cars on cement.
   C pollution caused by pet waste.
   D tall grasses planted near streams.

2. What caused McMullen to become interested in her local environment?
   A creating her Web site for a science project
   B seeing pollution in a local stream
   C designing educational outdoor trails
   D perceiving a decrease in native trout

3. According to the article, which of the following is a major effect of the Save Our Stream organization?
   A Native trout are plentiful again.
   B People who received training have changed their habits.
   C Students have restored trails and campgrounds in Washington.
   D The media has spread the word about global warming.

4. Which of the following sentences contains a **cause** and an **effect?**
   A Soapy, dirty water can enter storm drains.
   B Trees and grass help filter pollutants.
   C The environment is a hot topic.
   D Conserve water when showering and washing your hands.

5. Another word for *habitat* is
   A waterway.
   B surroundings.
   C farmland.
   D population.

6. Which of the following terms means the same thing as *hazards*?
   A polls
   B pollution
   C pet waste
   D threats

7. A *profound* truth is
   A meaningful.
   B renewable.
   C common.
   D differing.

Writing Skills Focus

Timed └Writing The last two paragraphs of the article contain several possible actions to take. First, list each action and the immediate effect that following each action would have. Then, explain the ultimate effect of following each action.

 What Do You Think Now

What organizations like Save Our Stream are in your area?

■ **California Standards, p. 477**
■ **Reading Standard 2.3** Analyze text that uses the cause-and-effect organizational pattern.

What Do You Think Now?

If students are not immediately familiar with environmental organizations in their area, suggest that they discuss the question with their classmates. If possible, have students use print or online resources to research organizations in their area.

Check for Understanding

Independent Practice
Answers and Explanations

1. **D** *Planting tall grasses near streams helps reduce the effects of pollution, not increase them.*

2. **D** *McMullen noticed a decrease in the trout population (D), not pollution in the stream (B). A and C are effects of McMullen's organization.*

3. **B** *The major effect has been changing people's habits. A and D are not stated in the article; C is not a direct effect of the organization.*

4. **B** *The planting of trees (cause) has the effect of filtering pollutants.*

5. **B** *An animal's habitat is its surroundings, or the place it lives.*

6. **D** *Hazards are threats; B and C are too specific; A is unrelated.*

7. **A** *A profound truth is a deep, or meaningful, truth.*

Writing Skills Focus

Possible response: *Joining an ecology club would make me more involved in environmental causes. Recycling paper would reduce my garbage output and might save trees. Turning off lights would save energy and might reduce our reliance on fossil fuels. Planting trees and volunteering would make the community nicer and might lead to a healthier environment.*

Assess

 Chapter 4 Resources, Selection Standards Check, pp. 45–47

ThinkCentral Online Assessment, Selection Standards Check

Teacher One Stop™, editable Selection Standards Check

Reteach

ThinkCentral Online Remediation

Standards Focus

Objectives
Students will

- write persuasive essays that support arguments with reasons and evidence
- address potential objections
- include a call to action

Preteach

Write with a Purpose Read aloud the essentials of a good persuasive essay to guide students' understanding of this type of writing. Also refer students to the rubric on p. 486 for more information on persuasive essays that they can use throughout this workshop.

Direct Teach

Model the Skill

Think as a Reader/Writer Use the professional model on this page and others in the chapter to provide examples of the elements of a good persuasive essay. Note that "Hungry Here" uses statistical evidence to support the position that some people in America are suffering from hunger.

Think About the Model
Possible responses:

1. *The author notes that one in ten Americans go hungry, which shows how prevalent the problem is.*

2. *It urges readers to get involved to stop the problem of hunger.*

California Standards, pp. 478–487

- **Writing Standard 1.1** Create an organizational structure that balances all aspects of the composition and uses effective transitions between sentences to unify important ideas.
- **Writing Standard 1.2** Support all statements and claims with anecdotes, descriptions, facts and statistics, and specific examples.
- **Writing Standard 2.4** Write persuasive compositions: **a.** State a clear position or perspective in support of a proposition or proposal. **b.** Describe the points in support of the proposition, employing well-articulated evidence. **c.** Anticipate and address reader concerns and counterarguments

Persuasive Essay

Write with a Purpose

Write a persuasive essay that includes a clear position on an issue supported by reasons and evidence. Your **purpose** is to convince readers to think or act in a certain way. Keep your **audience** in mind as you plan your essay.

A Good Persuasive Essay

- identifies an issue and takes a clear position on it
- addresses possible reader concerns
- provides reasons and evidence that support the position, including facts, examples, and personal experiences
- makes a convincing call to action

See page 486 for complete rubric.

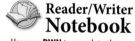

Reader/Writer Notebook

Use your **RWN** to complete the activities for this workshop.

Think as a Reader/Writer Before you write your own essay, read the excerpt below from "Hungry Here," a persuasive essay by World Almanac. This excerpt begins in the middle of the essay as the writer addresses a commonly held belief.

> We like to think of America as a land of plenty. Yet about one in ten Americans uses a food bank or soup kitchen on a regular basis in order to get food. And such charitable services do not reach everyone. Many people live in constant hunger, and some are literally starving to death.
>
> Who are America's hungry? You might be surprised. Second Harvest found that 36 percent of its food bank users come from homes with at least one working adult. For these families, a regular wage does not guarantee regular meals. When expenses—such as rent, heat, electric, and medical bills—run higher than family income, little may be left over for food. . . .
>
> *[The writer details the work of student Daniel Cayce in a long paragraph that is omitted here. The final paragraph of the essay is shown below.]*
>
> Daniel grew up in a family with a history of helping the needy. He has been working side-by-side with his grandmother, the founder of Jo Ann Cayce Charities, since age three. It was obvious to Daniel that hunger was not something long ago and far away. Perhaps it is time for the rest of us to realize this same truth and to take action in our own communities and as a nation.

The writer **counters** *the argument that America is a land of plenty by using specific statistics as evidence.*

The writer asks *a* **question** *to connect to the reader and uses statistics that show the seriousness of the problem.*

In the final paragraph, the author uses Daniel's example to urge readers *to* **take action** *against hunger in their community.*

Think About the Professional Model
With a partner, discuss the following questions about the model:

1. Why is the author's use of evidence persuasive?

2. How does the call to action effectively conclude the essay?

Writing Workshop Resources

UA: Holt Interactive Writer and Speaker, on-level practice and assessment, pp. 79–93

UA: Differentiating Instruction, modified lesson plans and leveled assessment, pp. 104–105

WritingNotes, interactive lesson presentations with activities go.hrw.com

GrammarNotes, interactive lesson presentations with activities go.hrw.com

Writing and Research in a Digital Age, interactive lesson presentations with activities go.hrw.com

Writing Standards 1.1 Create an organizational structure that balances all aspects of the composition and uses effective transitions between sentences to unify important ideas. **1.2** Support all statements and claims with anecdotes, descriptions, facts and statistics, and specific examples. **2.4** Write persuasive compositions: a. State a clear position or perspective in support of a proposition or proposal. b. Describe the points in support of the proposition, employing well-articulated evidence. c. Anticipate and address reader concerns and counterarguments.

Prewriting

Choose an Issue

The **purpose** of persuasive writing is to convince your readers to share your point of view and take action on an issue. An **issue** is a subject, situation, or idea about which people are likely to disagree, such as the best way to raise money for a class trip, whether video games are harmful to children, or whether the city should build a new park. Your first step is to brainstorm issues about which you feel strongly and about which you know or have access to enough information to be persuasive. Then, choose one issue that you think will also matter to your audience.

Think About Purpose and Audience

As you begin planning your essay, keep your **purpose** and **audience** in mind. Your **purpose** is to persuade your audience to agree with your position on a controversial issue.

Your **audience** is an individual or group of individuals who have strong feelings on the issue. To focus on your audience, answer the following questions:

- Who is my audience?
- What interest does my audience have in the issue?
- How does the audience currently feel about the issue? How do I know?
- What reasons might the audience have to be against my position?
- What arguments can I use to counter the audience's concerns?

State Your Position

Every issue has at least two sides—for it and against it. As a writer, you need to adopt a **position** or **perspective** and to support it. State your position or perspective clearly in an **opinion statement**. It should indicate the issue and the side you support—for or against.

Issue	Position	Opinion Statement
hunger in America	It is a serious problem.	We can all do something to help the hungry in our community.

Idea Starters
- ways to improve your neighborhood
- plans to improve your school
- requests to your parents for a privilege or activity

 Writing Tip

Try to avoid matters of personal preference, such as the best color or kind of shoes, when you choose an issue. There's really no way to argue about personal taste.

Your Turn _____

Get Started Making notes in your **RWN**, choose an **issue** and decide on your **position** about it. Answer the questions about **audience** on this page. Keep your **purpose** in mind as you write your notes. Write an **opinion statement** that shows your position on the issue.

 Learn It Online
An interactive graphic organizer can help you generate and organize essay ideas. Try one at:

go.hrw.com | H7-479 | **Go**

Teacher One Stop™, on-level lesson plans and all print resources

Holt Six Traits for Writing, rubrics, prompts, and sample papers

Language and Sentence Skills Practice,

UA: Developmental Language and Sentence Skills Practice

Language Handbook Worksheets, p. 125

Formal Assessment, Progress Monitoring Test 4

ThinkCentral Online Assessment, Writing Workshop Test

ThinkCentral Online Remediation

Holt Online Essay Scoring

Guided Practice: Apply

Choose an Issue

- Have students jot down a quick list of possible topics. Remind them to think of issues they are passionate and knowledgeable about. Students may like to look through newspapers or magazines for ideas on current issues.

- When students complete their list, have them look over the topics they listed and figure out the best one. If they choose to, students may fill in the chart in the Student Edition with multiple issues to see which topics they have strong opinions about.

Think About Purpose and Audience

Explain to students that their audience will have varying levels of knowledge about the subject of the essay. Some may know a lot about the topic, while others will be unfamiliar with it. Remind students to give readers detailed background information about their topic.

Your Turn _____

Get Started Once students have selected the topics for their essay, put them in small groups of three or four. Have each student share his or her opinion statement, and have the other members of the group express their opinion on the topic. This will help students determine how people feel about the issue and what objections students should address in their essays.

Learn It Online
The **Interactive Student Edition** includes more than thirty **Interactive Graphic Organizers.** Your students can use them to generate and organize ideas, compare and contrast, evaluate a decision, support a position, and much more.

go.hrw.com | H7-479 | **Go**

Guided Practice: Apply

Gather Evidence

- Remind students that they can use a variety of sources to find background information and evidence to support their topic. They can consult their local library for books about the subject or use an encyclopedia or a reputable online source. They can also interview experts who are knowledgeable about the subject.

- Encourage students to fill out a graphic organizer like the one in the Student Edition. It should clearly list their position, their reason for supporting this position, and the evidence that supports this position. Remind students that they must be able to fill in all of these criteria before they begin writing their essay.

Your Turn

Choose Your Support Have students complete the **Your Turn** activity as independent practice. As they work, monitor students' progress by making sure their evidence comes from accurate sources and clearly supports their position.

Writing Tip

Reasons that appeal to a reader's logic, or intelligence, are called **logical appeals.** Logical appeals show why it makes sense to accept the writer's position on the issue.

Writing Tip

To find support for your opinion,
- interview experts or people interested in the issue
- conduct research by using articles, books, and reliable Web sites or by taking a poll

Your Turn

Choose Your Support
Making notes in your **RWN,** choose and evaluate your **reasons.** Select the most specific and convincing **evidence** you can find to support each reason for your position. Keep your **audience** in mind as you choose your reasons and evidence.

Provide Reasons

You must convince your readers that your position is logical and makes sense. Strong **reasons** will support your position. Reasons tell **why** you believe what you do. Review your opinion statement and then ask, "Why?"

- Why do I believe that . . . ?
- Why do I want . . . ?
- Why do I support . . . ?

The answers to the question *Why?* will be your reasons.

Now think about the members of your audience and what they value. Which of your reasons will strongly appeal to your particular audience? For which of your reasons can you provide specific support?

Gather Evidence

Effective persuasive writing must have convincing **evidence** to support its reasons. For each of your reasons, plan to use at least one of the following kinds of specific evidence:

- an **anecdote,** a brief story that illustrates a point
- a **fact,** a statement that can be proven true
- a **statistic,** a fact given in number form
- an **example,** a specific instance that illustrates a general idea
- an **expert opinion,** a statement made by an authority on a subject

Notice how the reason and evidence below support the writer's position.

Position	Reason	Evidence
Hunger in America is a serious problem.	The problem is widespread, affecting millions.	One in ten Americans uses a food bank or soup kitchen. Thirty-six percent of the individuals who use food banks are from homes with working adults.

Anticipate Audience Concerns

Your goal is to persuade readers to accept your position. Some readers may have beliefs that oppose your position; other readers may resist your ideas by holding on to popularly held beliefs, such as "America is a land of plenty" in the model on page 478. Anticipate your audience's concerns and beliefs so that you can stress the benefits of your position.

Persuasive Essay Writing Prompts

Students can choose their own essay ideas or use one of the following prompts to write a persuasive essay.

School Think of a significant problem or issue that is affecting your school, and offer a solution to the problem. You might like to consider issues such as graffiti, trash, bullying, or disrespect to teachers or fellow students.

Social Studies Research a problem that is affecting the community or the world as a whole, and call people's attention to the issue. For example, you could write about a particular endangered species and what people can do to help save it.

History Research a significant event in history that could have ended with a different result. Offer your opinion of how things could have been done differently, using evidence to support your argument.

Drafting

Follow the Writer's Framework

To convince your readers, you need to tell them your position on the issue, present reasons and evidence for your position, and inspire them to act as you wish. The **Writer's Framework** to the right outlines how to plan your draft to maximize your power of persuasion.

Organize Your Support

The order in which you present reasons and evidence, as well as the way you begin and end a persuasive composition, determines the effectiveness of your argument. Arrange your reasons according to **order of importance,** ending with your strongest reason. Use transitional words and phrases to emphasize the order of importance of your reasons.

> **A Writer's Framework**
>
> **Introduction**
> - Grab the audience's attention
> - State your position in an opinion statement
>
> **Body**
> - Second strongest reason and supporting evidence
> - Other reasons and supporting evidence
> - Strongest reason and supporting evidence
>
> **Conclusion**
> - Restate your position
> - Call your audience to action

Grammar Link Using Transitions

Transitions are words and phrases that show how ideas are related to one another. Use this chart to identify transitions you can use to make the relationships among ideas clear within and between the paragraphs of your persuasive essay.

Common Transitional Words and Phrases

Cause and Effect	Order of Importance	Compare and Contrast
as a result	first	although
because	furthermore	and
consequently	last	but
for	mainly	however
since	more important	instead
so	then	similarly
therefore	to begin with	yet

🔵 Writing Tip

A **quotation,** a vivid **example,** or a surprising **statistic** can be a strong opening for your essay. Maintain a strong, positive tone and support your position with anecdotes and other examples from personal experience that your audience can relate to.

Your Turn _____

Draft Your Persuasive Essay Using the notes you gathered and the **Writer's Framework,** write a draft of your persuasive essay. Be sure to think about
- how to state clearly your **position** on the issue and the reasons that support it
- how to **organize** your reasons and evidence
- how to address your audience's concerns
- how to conclude with a call to action

Guided Practice: Apply

Follow the Writer's Framework

- To help students understand the Writer's Framework, find a piece of persuasive writing, such as a newspaper editorial, and read it aloud to students. Point out how the editorial follows the Writer's Framework by stating a position in the opening paragraph, giving reasons and evidence to support the position, and ending with a call to action.

- Tell students that when they include a call to action at the end of their essay, they should make sure they take their target audience into account. The suggested action should be plausible and within reason for their readers.

Grammar Link

For practice, have students fill in the blanks with a transitional word or phrase that fits each sentence.

1. I don't like that show. _____, I won't watch it. [**Possible responses:** As a result, So, Therefore]

2. _____, I found the bread. Then, I made a sandwich. [**Possible responses:** First, To begin with]

3. He didn't know Angela very well, _____ he went to her party anyway. [**Possible responses:** but, yet]

 Warriner's Handbook, First Course, p. 437

Your Turn _____

Draft Your Persuasive Essay Ask students to complete the **Your Turn** activity as independent practice. Remind students to use their completed outline as they begin to draft their essay. Suggest that students use every other line as they write their draft so that revisions can be made more easily later.

Universal Access

 English Learners

Review the definitions of any academic vocabulary words from the section that students may be unfamiliar with, such as *persuasion, perspective,* and *evidence.* Explain how each word relates to writing a persuasive essay.

✔ See **UA: Differentiating Instruction** for strategies for teaching English learners.

Struggling Writers

To help students understand the features of persuasive writing, brainstorm ideas with students. Think of a position or topic, and write it on the board. Examples might include "Fast food should be banned from the cafeteria" or "Families should only be allowed one car." Have students suggest reasons or arguments to support the position, and create a word web on the board with their ideas. Explain that each opinion or reason should be supported by evidence, and have students suggest where might be the best place to look for supporting facts or statistics. Add these ideas to the word web.

✔ See **UA: Differentiating Instruction** for strategies for teaching struggling writers.

Model the Skill

- Using a student draft on a transparency, model how to use the questions, tips, and revision techniques suggested in the chart. You might use a student's essay or an essay of your own creation to evaluate and revise using the steps in the chart.

- Ask volunteers to demonstrate using each of the steps on their own essays.

Peer Review

Tell students to let their partner know when they come to a passage in their partner's draft that they don't understand or find confusing. Explain to students that they don't need to solve the problem for the writer; they should just point out where the argument has gone astray.

Peer Review

With a peer, go through the chart at the right. Then, review your draft. Answer each question in this chart to locate where and how your drafts could be improved. Be sure to take notes on what you and your partner discuss. You can refer to your notes as you revise your draft.

Evaluating and Revising

Read the questions in the left column of the chart, and then use the tips in the middle column to help you make revisions to your essay. The right column suggests techniques you can use to revise your draft.

Persuasive Composition: Guidelines for Content and Organization

Evaluation Question	Tip	Revision Technique
1. Does the introduction grab the audience's attention?	**Put stars** next to questions, anecdotes, or statements that would interest the audience.	If needed, **add** an attention-grabber to the beginning of the introduction.
2. Does the introduction have a clear opinion statement?	**Underline** the opinion statement. Ask a peer to read it and identify your position on the issue.	**Add** an opinion statement or, if necessary, **replace** the opinion statement with a clearer one.
3. Are there at least two reasons that logically support your opinion statement?	With a colored marker, **highlight** the reasons that support the opinion statement.	**Add** reasons that support the opinion statement.
4. Does at least one piece of evidence support each reason?	**Circle** evidence that supports each reason. **Draw a line** from the evidence to the reason.	If necessary, **add** evidence to support each reason. **Elaborate** on pieces of evidence by adding details or explaining their meaning.
5. Are the reasons in the order that is most persuasive?	**Number** the reasons in the margin, and rank them by their strength and persuasiveness.	**Reorder** ideas, using your strongest reason last.
6. Does the conclusion include a restatement of the position and a call to action?	**Put a check mark** next to the restatement. **Underline** the call to action.	**Add** a restatement of the position if it is missing. **Add** a call to action if there is not one.

Real Issues, Real Experts

Holt Professional Learning for Language Arts

To watch videos on teaching **revision, grammar,** and **on-demand writing skills** featuring Linda Rief, Amy Benjamin, and Leila Christenbury, go to this page in the ThinkCentral, Teacher Access.

Universal Access

Struggling Writers

Benchmark Students Divide students into pairs. Then, give each pair a topic, such as pets, family, school, or activities. Have each student think of an anecdote related to their topic. It may be a story that happened to them or something that happened to someone they know. Have students briefly write down their anecdote in their notebook.

- Have students share their anecdotes with each other. Do their stories have anything in common? Tell students to consider

Read this student draft and notice the comments on its strengths and suggestions on how it could be improved.

Kids Should Be Paid for Chores

by T. J. Wilson, Atlantic Middle School

According to the Joint Council on Economic Education, teenagers between the ages of 13 and 17 will spend $89 billion in this country. Where will that staggering amount of money come from? Many teens are not allowed to work outside of the home; therefore, I strongly believe that kids should be paid for doing chores around the house. Kids all across the country constantly nag their parents for money to go to the movies, buy CDs, and purchase trendy clothes. Consequently, many parents complain about their kids always asking them for money.

Constant friction results. Parents complain that kids don't help out around the house enough. Lots of times, kids get nagged until they clean up their rooms, put out the trash, cut the lawn, shovel the snow, and do many other chores. But conflicts result at home. Why can't kids and parents reach a compromise about money and chores? This would end the feuding and make everyone in the household happy. Parents would pay kids a small fee for doing chores without being reminded. Kids would no longer ask for money.

← T. J. uses a **statistic** to grab the reader's attention.

← He clearly states his **position.**

← **Transitions** help the reader identify the cause-and-effect nature of this problem.

← T. J. supports his position with **examples.**

← T. J. could strengthen his point here.

MINI-LESSON ▶ How to Use Anecdotes as Supporting Evidence

T. J.'s second paragraph ends with the point that conflicts in the household will end when kids are paid for chores. He can strengthen this point by adding an anecdote.

T. J.'s Revision of Paragraph Two

Parents would pay kids a small fee for doing chores without being reminded. Kids would no longer ask for money. My cousin Jeremy from Illinois constantly argued with his dad about mowing the lawn and walking the dog. Every time Jeremy asked for money, the accusations began again. Then they decided on a set fee for the chores: $20.00 a week for mowing and $7.00 a week for daily dog walks. Jeremy now eagerly does his chores, and he doesn't argue with his dad—even the dog is happy!

Your Turn _____

Strengthen Your Evidence

Read your draft and then ask yourself these questions:

- What reason or reasons in my draft can be strengthened with an anecdote?
- What details should I add to make the anecdote specific?

Guided Practice: Apply

Student Draft

Explain that the Student Draft on this page is the first half of a persuasive essay written by a student. Model reading the draft and the annotations in blue, and explain that the yellow highlighting illustrates the student's language choices. Explain that a mini-lesson follows with helpful information about ways to improve this draft as well as their own.

▶ **Mini-Lesson**

How to Use Anecdotes as Supporting Evidence

■ Remind students that an anecdote is a brief story that illustrates a point. Anecdotes give the reader a real-life example of the topic being discussed in the essay.

■ Have volunteers give examples of another anecdote T. J. could add to strengthen his essay.

Your Turn _____

Strengthen Your Evidence Ask students to complete the **Your Turn** activity as independent practice. Have students think of a time when they or someone they know or have heard of was directly affected by the issue at hand. Remind students to describe this experience in their essay and explain how it supports their argument.

---

whether their anecdotes are funny, serious, boring, or exciting. Do their anecdotes contain many objective facts or are they mostly subjective retellings of incidents or events?

- Have pairs share their findings with the rest of the class. Can the class make any generalizations about anecdotes? Students may find that anecdotes are usually interesting stories that do not contain many facts because they recount an incident or event from a subjective viewpoint.

Students with Disabilities

Help students understand the difference between facts and anecdotes. On the board, write sentences, some of which contain facts and some of which contain anecdotal evidence. For example, you might write *Studies show 50 percent of Americans recycle.* and *I always put my lunch tray in the recycling bin at school. It makes me feel like I'm making a difference.* Guide students in understanding which statements can be classified as facts and which are more typical of anecdotes.

Guided Practice: Apply
Student Draft

- Explain that the Student Draft is continued and completed on this page. Again the draft is annotated and highlighted for the students.

- Read the draft and annotations aloud and discuss. Refer students to the Writer's Framework on p. 481. Ask students to comment on whether the student writer followed this framework.

▶ **Mini-Lesson**
How to Conclude with a Call to Action

- Remind students that a call to action asks the reader to do something to help solve a problem. If your essay is persuasive enough, the reader may be willing to do something to support your position.

- Explain that the student writer has revised his final paragraph by adding a call to action. Ask students to comment on which version is more effective and why.

Your Turn _____

Conclude with a Call to Action Pair up students and have them discuss each other's conclusions. Then, have partners work together to make a list of possible calls to action for each essay. Remind students to use the **Grammar Link** on p. 481 to incorporate transitional words and phrases into their call to action in order to link it with the rest of their essay.

Student Draft *continues*

T. J. cites an **expert opinion** to support his point about responsibility. →

Notice that a **transition word** emphasizes a cause-and-effect relationship. →

T. J. anticipates and addresses the "ideal world" belief. This counters an **audience concern.** →

The final paragraph repeats the major ideas but does not encourage the reader to **take action.** →

> This compromise teaches kids responsibility. John Covey, a father of ten and co-author of *The Seven Habits of Effective Families,* says there are two reasons to get children to do chores: "to get the job done and to help them grow." Teens learn to be responsible and develop a work ethic. When their chores are completed with no nagging, they'd be paid whatever their parents had agreed to pay them. Kids could spend the money on things they like or save money for expensive items.
>
> In an ideal world, kids would happily do chores, never asking for money, and parents would have the resources to pay for outside help or the time to do all the work themselves. Who are we kidding? The real world demands a compromise on chores and money.
>
> Kids would stop begging for money. Parents would stop nagging kids to clean up their rooms or the kitchen. Both parents and kids would be getting what they want.

MINI-LESSON ▶ **How to Conclude with a Call to Action**

T. J.'s final paragraph repeats his strongest reason: eliminating conflict. To strengthen his conclusion, he decides to add a call to action by asking his readers to do something about the issue he has addressed. Notice how he revised to add two rhetorical questions and a specific call to action.

T. J.'s Revision of Paragraph Five

> In an ideal world, kids would happily do chores, never asking for money, and parents would have the resources to pay for outside help or the time to do all the work themselves. Who are we kidding? The real world demands a compromise on chores and money.
>
> *Do you want to* *Do you want your* *to* *you*
> Kids would stop begging for money. Parents would stop nagging kids
> *your* *Talk to your parents today. Propose*
> to clean up their rooms or the kitchen. Both parents and kids would be
> *a compromise of responsibility and payment for chores.*
> getting what they want.

Your Turn _____

Conclude with a Call to Action With a partner, review the conclusion to your composition. If it lacks a call to action, add one. If it has a weak call to action, improve it. Your partner can suggest how the call to action does (or does not) make him or her want to take action.

Universal Access

EL English Learners

Provide students with sentence starters that will help them add a concluding call to action to their essay. Examples might include:

- I therefore suggest _____.
- This leads me to the conclusion that _____.
- A solution might be _____.
- To solve this problem, I think that _____.

Use the Student Draft to give students examples of how they might use each of these sentences to write a call to action.

Proofreading and Publishing

Proofreading

Errors in your final essay will distract your reader from your persuasive points. Polish your persuasion by carefully correcting any misspellings, punctuation errors, and problems in sentence structure.

Grammar Link **Punctuating Rhetorical Questions**

Why should you proofread? Persuasive writers often ask questions like these. By directly addressing the audience, **rhetorical questions** connect with readers and make them think, even though the writer doesn't really expect an answer.

T. J. used several rhetorical questions in his essay, but he forgot to punctuate the new questions correctly in his revised conclusion.

> Do you want to stop begging for money? Do you want your parents to stop
>
> nagging you to clean up your room? Talk to your parents today. Propose a
>
> compromise of responsibility and payment for chores. Both parents and kids
>
> would be getting what they want.

Publishing

Here are some different formats that you can use to share your persuasive essay with your audience.

- If your school or community is affected by the issue you have discussed, consider submitting your essay to the school newspaper, local newspaper, or parent-teacher organization newsletter.
- If your topic is specialized, consider submitting your essay to the Letters to the Editor column of a magazine that explores the issue.
- Create an "Opposing Views" bulletin board by pairing your essay with one that supports a different position on your issue.

Reflect on the Process

In your **RWN,** write short responses to these questions:

1. Do you think your essay achieves its purpose? Why or why not?
2. What is the strongest support in your essay? Why is it the strongest?
3. Which revisions do you think most strengthened your position?

🔵 **Proofreading Tip**

Ask three different peers to read your essay, each one focusing on only one potential problem area: spelling, punctuation, or sentence structure. Use each reader's suggestions to improve your essay.

Your Turn _____

Proofread and Publish

Proofread your essay for any rhetorical questions you have used. If you have not used any, find one place where you can add one. Write an effective rhetorical question, and punctuate it correctly. In addition, proofread your essay for any additional errors in punctuation, spelling, and sentence structure. Make the corrections on your final draft. Then, publish your essay so that others can read it.

Guided Practice: Apply

Grammar Link

- Tell students to read their final draft and identify and underline any rhetorical questions they have included in their essay.
- Have students make sure that they have correctly punctuated their rhetorical questions. Remind them that like any other type of question, rhetorical questions should always end in a question mark.

Publishing

Brainstorm with students additional ways to publish their persuasive essays.

Reflect on the Process

Have students reflect on the entire writing process as well as their final product. Challenge them to reflect metacognitively about how they can improve and apply what they have learned.

Your Turn _____

Proofread and Publish Have students check their final drafts against the Evaluating and Revising guidelines on p. 482. Have them go through each item on the list and make sure that their draft meets all the requirements. Remind students that if they are unsure of the spelling of any word, they should look it up in a dictionary.

🏅 Students Who Use African American Vernacular English

English for Academic Success Point out the Student Draft at the top of p. 484. Ask students to record each usage of the articles *a* and *an* in the three paragraphs in their Reader/Writer Notebooks: *a father, a work ethic, an ideal world, a compromise.* Point out that words that begin with consonants are preceded by the article *a,* while words that begin with vowels are preceded by the consonant *an.* Explain that this is a convention of formal, academic English.

Advanced Learners

Enrichment Have students modify their calls to action for a group of readers who are not their original target audience. For example, they might address politicians, who have a wider influence and better financial resources than their fellow students. Other potential target audiences might include parents, teachers, scientists, or businesspeople. Have students write a paragraph explaining who they are targeting and why their revised call to action is appropriate for that particular group.

Guided Practice: Apply

Scoring Rubric

■ Tell students that the best way to understand rubrics is to use them to score actual writing.

■ Distribute copies of students' persuasive essays with the names removed. Have students use the rubric to evaluate the anonymous essays. Ask students to score the essays, then write a paragraph using the language of the rubric to explain the reasons for their score.

✎ **Holt Six Traits for Writing,** rubrics, prompts, and sample papers

Assess

✎ **Writing and Speaking Workshops,** Persuasive Essay analytical scales and rubric

🖥 **ThinkCentral Online Assessment,** Writing Workshop Test

💿 **Teacher One Stop™,** editable Writing Workshop Test

Reteach

🖥 **ThinkCentral Online Remediation**

🐻 **California Standards, pp. 486–487**

■ **Writing Standard 1.1** Create an organizational structure that balances all aspects of the composition and uses effective transitions between sentences to unify important ideas.
■ **Writing Standard 1.2** Support all statements and claims with anecdotes, descriptions, facts and statistics, and specific examples.
■ **Writing Standard 2.4** Write persuasive compositions: **a.** State a clear position or perspective in support of a proposition or proposal. **b.** Describe the points in support of the proposition, employing well-articulated evidence. **c.** Anticipate and address reader concerns and counterarguments.

Scoring Rubric

You can use the rubric below to evaluate your persuasive essay or your response to the prompt on the next page.

	Persuasive Writing	Organization and Focus	Sentence Structure	Conventions
4	• Authoritatively defends a position with precise and relevant evidence and convincingly addresses the reader's concerns, biases, and expectations.	• Clearly addresses all parts of the writing task. • Demonstrates a clear understanding of purpose and audience. • Maintains a consistent point of view, focus, and organizational structure, including the effective use of transitions. • Includes a clearly presented central idea with relevant facts, details, and/or explanations.	• Includes a variety of sentence types.	• Contains few, if any, errors in the conventions of the English language (grammar, punctuation, capitalization, spelling). These errors do not interfere with the reader's understanding of the writing.
3	• Generally defends a position with relevant evidence and addresses the reader's concerns, biases, and expectations.	• Addresses all parts of the writing task. • Demonstrates a general understanding of purpose and audience. • Maintains a mostly consistent point of view, focus, and organizational structure, including the effective use of some transitions. • Presents a central idea with mostly relevant facts, details, and/or explanations.	• Includes a variety of sentence types.	• Contains some errors in the conventions of the English language (grammar, punctuation, capitalization, spelling). These errors do not interfere with the reader's understanding of the writing.
2	• Defends a position with little, if any, evidence and may address the reader's concerns, biases, and expectations.	• Addresses only parts of the writing task. • Demonstrates little understanding of purpose and audience. • Maintains an inconsistent point of view, focus, and/or organizational structure, which may include ineffective or awkward transitions that do not unify important ideas. • Suggests a central idea with limited facts, details, and/or explanations.	• Includes little variety in sentence types.	• Contains several errors in the conventions of the English language (grammar, punctuation, capitalization, spelling). These errors may interfere with the reader's understanding of the writing.
1	• Fails to defend a position with any evidence and fails to address the reader's concerns, biases, and expectations.	• Addresses only one part of the writing task. • Demonstrates no understanding of purpose and audience. • Lacks a point of view, focus, organizational structure, and transitions that unify important ideas. • Lacks a central idea but may contain marginally related facts, details, and/or explanations.	• Includes no sentence variety.	• Contains serious errors in the conventions of the English language (grammar, punctuation, capitalization, spelling). These errors interfere with the reader's understanding of the writing.

Persuasive Essay Writing Prompts

Students can use the writing prompt on p. 487 in the Student Edition or one of the following prompts.

• A film crew wants to follow around residents of your town for several weeks for a reality TV show. Take a position on whether or not you think this is a good idea.

• Your neighborhood plans to tear down a worn-down but popular movie theater to build a park. Argue for or against this plan.

• Your school is cutting the lengths of art and music classes in order to extend English, math, and history classes. Explain why you do or do not support this change.

Persuasive Essay

Writing Standard 2.4 Write persuasive compositions. a. State a clear position or perspective in support of a proposition or proposal. b. Describe the points in support of the proposition, employing well-articulated evidence. c. Anticipate and address reader concerns and counterarguments.

When responding to an on-demand persuasive prompt, use models you've read, what you've learned by writing your own persuasive essay, the rubric on page 486, and the steps below.

Writing Prompt

Your school is considering adding a fifteen-minute period each morning for students to relax, talk, listen to music, and get a snack. The school day will be lengthened to accommodate this midday break. Write a persuasive essay for your school paper convincing readers to support this proposal. Use specific reasons and examples.

Study the Prompt

Begin by reading the prompt carefully. Notice that the **position** is determined for you. Underline "convincing readers to **support** this proposal." Circle the proposal: "adding a fifteen-minute period each morning." Now circle the next sentence, "The school day will be lengthened." That is the **counterargument** that you must address. Note and underline any additional information in the prompt, such as the references to snacks, music, relaxation, and talking. These can become convincing reasons. Your audience includes the students, parents, and staff at your school. **Tip:** Spend about five minutes studying the prompt.

Plan Your Response

Reasons Persuasive writing requires that you ask and answer the question *Why?* in relation to your position. **Ask,** "Why would it be a good idea to have a break?" Your answers become your reasons. Brainstorm convincing reasons that will also appeal to your audience.

Evidence Next, you must answer the question *How?* The answer you provide will lead to strong,

convincing supporting evidence for each reason. Include a specific **example** or **anecdote** that supports each reason.

Organization Once you have decided on two to three reasons, plan their order in your essay. Put your strongest reason last to be most convincing. **Tip:** Spend about ten minutes planning your response.

Respond to the Prompt

One way to begin a persuasive composition is to start out by immediately addressing the **counterargument**—in this case, "The school day will be lengthened." The rest of your paper concentrates on supporting your **position** with reasons and evidence. **Tip:** Spend about twenty minutes writing your essay.

Improve Your Response

Revising Go back to the key aspects of the prompt. Add any missing information.

- Do you state your position clearly?
- Do you offer good reasons and evidence?
- Does your composition have an introduction, a body, and a conclusion with a call to action for your audience?

Proofreading Take a few minutes to edit your response to correct errors in grammar, spelling, punctuation, and capitalization. Make sure that your edits are neat and the essay is legible.

Checking Your Final Copy Before you turn in your essay, read it one more time to catch any errors you may have missed and to make any finishing touches. You'll be glad you took more time to present your best writing. **Tip:** Save five or ten minutes to read and improve your draft.

Standards Focus

Objectives
Students will
- present a persuasive speech
- use verbal and nonverbal techniques to deliver an argument

Preteach

Speak with a Purpose Ask students to think of a time when they talked to a friend or family member in order to convince that person of something. Have students discuss some of the techniques they used in order to persuade someone that their argument was valid.

Direct Teach

Model the Skill

Adapt Your Essay

Have volunteers share their topics with the class. Allow the class to respond by stating what they know about the issues or how they feel about them. Then, as a class, discuss what each volunteer might do in order to persuade the class to agree with his or her position (or to take further action).

Guided Practice: Apply

Assist students in creating visual displays for their speeches. Some students' topics may be particularly well supported by charts or graphs.

California Standards, pp. 478–487

- **Listening and Speaking Standard 1.4** Organize information to achieve particular purposes and to appeal to the background and interests of the audience.
- **Listening and Speaking Standard 1.5** Arrange supporting details, reasons, descriptions, and examples effectively and persuasively in relation to the audience.
- **Listening and Speaking Standard 1.6** Use speaking techniques, including voice modulation, inflection, tempo, enunciation, and eye contact, for effective presentations.

- **Listening and Speaking Standard 2.4** Deliver persuasive presentations: a. State a clear position or perspective in support of an argument or proposal. b. Describe the points in support of the argument and employ well-articulated evidence.

Presenting a Persuasive Speech

Speak with a Purpose
Adapt your written essay into a persuasive speech. Practice your speech, and then present it to your class.

Think as a Reader/Writer Writing is not the only way to convey your opinions about an issue; you can also share your views by presenting a persuasive speech. Adapt your persuasive essay into a speech, organizing your supporting details and examples so that they appeal to the background and interests of your audience.

Adapt Your Essay

Relate Your Message to Your Audience
Whatever your specific purpose, you will need to engage the people in your audience—in this case, your classmates. To grab their attention and make them care about the issue, you can use the following strategies:

- **Provide the big picture** Explain all sides of the issue, and explain any terms and details that your audience will need to know.
- **Provide relevant reasons and evidence** Give **reasons** why your audience should agree with you, and use **evidence** (facts, examples, and personal experiences) to which your audience can relate.
- **Present visuals and media displays** Use handmade visuals or technology-based media displays to bring your speech to life.

Organize Your Ideas Persuasively
To organize your speech, consider the following strategies:

If your audience . . .	Your purpose is to . . .	Use this strategy:
opposes your position	get them to consider your position	Acknowledge their point of view, then move on to present strong reasons why they should accept your position.
agrees with your position	get them to take action	Strengthen their existing opinion by beginning with your position and then listing the supporting reasons. Close with a clear call to action.
is unsure about your position	persuade them to agree with you	Present all sides of the issue, then give them solid reasons why your position is best when compared to all the others.

○ Speaking Tip
Remember that the order in which you present your reasons and supporting evidence also has an effect on your audience. Decide whether you want to start or end your speech with your strongest argument.

Reader/Writer Notebook
Use your **RWN** to complete the activities for this workshop.

Resources

UA: Holt Interactive Writer and Speaker, on-level practice and assessment, pp. 168-171

UA: Differentiating Instruction, modified lesson plans, p. 106

Teacher One Stop™, on-level lesson plans and all print resources

Listening and Speaking Standards
1.1 Ask probing questions to elicit information, including evidence to support the speaker's claims and conclusions. **1.2** Determine the speaker's attitude toward the subject. **1.3** Respond to persuasive messages with questions, challenges, or affirmations. **1.5** Arrange supporting details, reasons, descriptions, and examples effectively and persuasively in relation to the audience. **1.6** Use speaking techniques, including voice modulation, inflection, tempo, enunciation, and eye contact, for effective presentations. **2.4** Deliver persuasive presentations: a. State a clear position or perspective in support of an argument or proposal. b. Describe the points in support of the argument and employ well-articulated evidence.

Deliver Your Persuasive Speech

Verbal Techniques

In persuasion, *how* you say something is often as important as *what* you say. It's difficult to pay attention to a speaker who mumbles, who stumbles over words, who looks down while talking, or who races through a speech. A strong presenter can make any argument more persuasive by using certain speaking techniques. To persuade your listeners, practice delivery techniques that will hold their attention, not distract from your message. Consider the speaking techniques below:

Enunciation Pronounce words carefully and clearly.
Vocal Modulation Stress certain words and phrases by changing the volume of your voice.
Inflection Raise the pitch of your voice at the end of a question, and lower it at the end of a statement.
Tempo Adjust the speed and rhythm of your speech. Be sure to pause to emphasize important points.

Nonverbal Techniques

Posture and Expression You believe that your solution is a good one. Show your certainty by using appropriate facial expressions and by standing with confidence in front of your audience.
Eye Contact Keep audience members involved by looking at them.

A Positive Attitude

Your **attitude,** or feelings toward the subject, will affect how listeners respond to your speech. Both what you say and how you say it reveal your attitude. You have chosen an issue that you have a strong opinion about, so be positive about your position and its resulting benefits.

With a positive attitude, you will shine as a speaker. Let your attitude show in both verbal and nonverbal ways.

How Did You Do?

The point of a persuasive speech is to win over an audience to your point of view. To find out if you have succeeded, give your listeners a chance to respond and to provide constructive feedback. Allow them to ask questions after the speech and to tell you where they agreed or disagreed with you. Invite them to challenge points you made and to let you know what overall impact your speech had on them.

> **A Good Persuasive Speech**
> - clearly presents the speaker's position on an issue
> - employs a positive tone
> - includes relevant reasons and evidence to support the speaker's position
> - is held together with logical transitions
> - uses effective verbal and nonverbal techniques to persuade the audience

◯ Listening Tip

If you are listening to a persuasive speech, first try to identify the speaker's attitude toward the subject. Jot down questions as you listen, and make note of points you agree or disagree with. Note places where you think the speaker has not fully supported his or her claims, and be ready to challenge the speaker's conclusions if you have the opportunity.

＊ Learn It Online
Pictures, music, and animation can make your argument more compelling. See how on *MediaScope* at:
go.hrw.com H7-489 **Go**

Model the Skill
Deliver Your Persuasive Speech

■ Model examples and non-examples of using effective verbal and nonverbal techniques to deliver a speech. You might wish to write your own short speech about a relevant topic or deliver lines from a well-known speech such as the Gettysburg Address. The first time you present the model speech, talk in a slow, droning voice, and do not make eye contact with the audience or stand up straight.

■ Then, give the speech again, this time using effective verbal and nonverbal techniques. Ask students to explain which version of the speech was most persuasive and why.

Guided Practice: Apply

■ During each presentation, ask students to jot down their thoughts about the argument being presented.

■ At the conclusion of each presentation, provide students with an opportunity to respond to the speaker's argument. They may choose to ask questions or present possible counterarguments.

■ Allow student presenters an opportunity to respond to questions and counterarguments.

Assess

UA: Holt Interactive Writer and Speaker, Persuasive Speech, analytical scale and rubric

＊ Learn It Online
If students need help adding multimedia features such as charts and graphs to their presentations, direct them to the **MediaScope** mini-site, where students can work through an interactive tutorial on creating multimedia.
go.hrw.com H7-489   **Go**

Universal Access

EL English Learners

Explain to students the similarities and differences between a persuasive speech and a persuasive essay. Remind them that in a persuasive speech, the speaker must address additional factors besides the strength of their argument, word choice, and the arrangement of paragraphs. Point out that their voice, posture, and visual aids will all contribute to how a speech's argument is received by the audience. Explain that an otherwise strong argument may be weakened by speaking in a flat tone or by simply reading the speech without making eye contact with the audience.

Have students present their speech to a partner to practice tone and making eye contact. Point out that by practicing their speech, students will become less reliant on reading from notes and will enhance the fluency of their speech. Tell students that practicing their speech with someone can also help students nervous about giving presentations feel more comfortable.

Literary Skills Review

Point of View

Directions: Read the passages below. Then, read each question that follows, and write the letter of the best response.

The News of King Midas
from *The Royal News*

Rumors of the so-called Midas touch have been confirmed today. According to sources close to the king, Midas is now unable to eat or drink, as anything he touches turns to gold.

"Serves him right," said one palace insider who asked not to be named. "He could have wished for something sensible, such as a triple-tax-free diversified bond portfolio. Now who knows where the price of gold is heading?"

The king's wife and daughter were unavailable for comment, as they had been turned to gold.

from *Cook to the King: A Novel*

"Sandwich?" the head cook roared. "You want me to fix you a sandwich?" She glared at the king. "With what, may I ask?"

What an idiot he was. Even the youngest servant boy knew what was going to happen by the time dessert was served, but not King Midas. Oh, no. Not content merely to ruin her entire day's work (that perfectly poached salmon! that lovely macaroni pudding!), he had to come tearing through her kitchen. By the time he was through, there wasn't a crumb that didn't clink and glitter when she swept it up.

from *A Courtier's Memoir*

After all my years serving in the palace, I thought I'd seen it all. When the king, however, started turning everything to gold, you could have knocked me over with a feather. Actually, he nearly *did* knock me over with a feather. An ostrich plume, it was, on my second-best hat! If I do say so myself, I was looking rather spiffy until the king snatched it off and started waving it around. He yelled that he'd turned my hat to gold. It was gold, all right. Solid gold. I've still got the lump on my head to prove it.

King Midas's E-mail

To: gods_helpline@olympus.edu
From: kmidas@palace.org
Subject: My Kingdom for a Burger
OK, point taken. I was greedy and foolish, and I'm sorry. Please, undo my wish before I starve to death!

1. In which passage does the narrator use a third-person-limited point of view?
   A   *The Royal News*
   B   *Cook to the King*
   C   *A Courtier's Memoir*
   D   King Midas's E-mail

2. Which passage *most* objectively tells what happens to King Midas?
   A   *The Royal News*
   B   *Cook to the King*
   C   *A Courtier's Memoir*
   D   King Midas's E-mail

3. The narrator, or speaker, in *The Royal News* is
   A   the king himself.
   B   an advisor to the king.
   C   an omniscient narrator.
   D   a second person.

4. Which of the following phrases from *A Courtier's Memoir* reveals its point of view?
   A   *he nearly did*
   B   *you could have*
   C   *It was gold*
   D   *I've still got the lump*

5. The speaker who delivers the most subjective feelings and opinions is
   A   King Midas
   B   author of *Cook to the King*
   C   reporter at *The Royal News*
   D   the courtier

Timed Writing

6. Briefly explain the differences between the omniscient, first-person, and third-person-limited points of view. Use an example of each from the passages to help explain the differences.

Chapter Review

Review Literary Skills Focus
Have students look back through the chapter to find the meanings of the terms listed below.
1. Have students look back through the chapter to find the meanings of the terms listed below.
2. Ask students to cite passages from the chapter that illustrate the meanings of those terms.
Point of View; Subjective and Objective; Biography; Folk Tales

Review Reading Skills Focus
Have students look back through the chapter to find the meanings of the terms listed below.
1. Have students look back through the chapter to find the meanings of the terms listed below.
2. Ask students to cite passages from the chapter that illustrate the meanings of those terms.
Compare and Contrast; Fact and Opinion; Author's Purpose; Making Predictions; Cause and Effect

If necessary, use the following questions to guide students in their reading before they answer the questions at the end of the review.

▶ **Cause and Effect**

According to paragraph 2, what was an effect of the mongoose population explosion? ***Possible response:*** *The mongooses began to attack other animals and even humans, in addition to spreading rabies.*

Read paragraph 3. What is a negative effect of trying to poison the mongooses? ***Possible response:*** *Many other species, such as cats, dogs, and chickens, are likely to be poisoned as well.*

Test-Taking Tip

Remind students to get a good night's sleep the night before a test and to eat breakfast the morning of the test. They will think more clearly and perform better if they are well-rested and not hungry.

California Standards, pp. 492–493

■ **Reading Standard 2.3** Analyze text that uses the cause-and-effect organizational pattern.

Informational Skills Review

Cause-and-Effect Organizational Structure   **Directions:** Read the following article. Then, answer each question that follows.

Mongoose on the Loose by **Larry Luxner**

In 1872, a Jamaican sugar planter imported nine furry little mongooses from India to eat the rats that were devouring his crops. They did such a good job, the planter started breeding his exotic animals and selling them to eager farmers on neighboring islands.

With no natural predators—like wolves, coyotes, or poisonous snakes—the mongoose population exploded, and within a few years, they were killing not just rats but pigs, lambs, chickens, puppies, and kittens. Dr. G. Roy Horst, a U.S. expert on mongooses, says that today mongooses live on seventeen Caribbean islands as well as Hawaii and Fiji, where they have attacked small animals, threatened endangered species, and have even spread minor rabies epidemics.

In Puerto Rico there are from 800,000 to one million of them. That is about one mongoose for every four humans. In St. Croix, there are 100,000 mongooses, about twice as many as the human population. "It's impossible to eliminate the mongoose population, short of nuclear war," says Horst. "You can't poison them, because cats, dogs, and chickens get poisoned, too. I'm not a prophet crying in the wilderness, but the potential for real trouble is there," says Horst.

According to Horst, great efforts have been made to rid the islands of mongooses, which have killed off a number of species, including the Amevia lizard on St. Croix, presumed extinct for several decades. On Hawaii, the combination of mongooses and sports hunting has reduced the Hawaiian goose, or nene, to less than two dozen individuals. . . .

Horst says his research will provide local and federal health officials with extremely valuable information if they ever decide to launch a campaign against rabies in Puerto Rico or the U.S. Virgin Islands.

Word-Attack Skills Mini-Lesson

Review   Use the activity below to check students' grasp of the word-attack skills taught in this chapter.
Activity   Have students combine the following base words and suffixes.

1. happy + er [*happier*]
2. bounty + ful [*bountiful*]
3. sleepy + ness [*sleepiness*]
4. heavy + est [*heaviest*]

5. sandy + ness [*sandiness*]
6. comply + ant [*compliant*]
7. foamy + er [*foamier*]
8. worry + er [*worrier*]
9. cloudy + ness [*cloudiness*]
10. easy + est [*easiest*]

✔ For additional instruction and strategies, see **Holt Pronunciation Help DVD-Rom and Think Central, Teacher Access.**

1. The following diagram displays information about the causes and effects of bringing mongooses to Jamaica.

Rats destroy sugar planter's crops.

↓

Effect: Planter imports nine mongooses.

↓

Effect:

↓

Effect: Planter breeds and sells the mongooses.

↓

Effect: Mongoose population explodes.

Which of these events belongs in the third box?

A Mongooses do a good job getting rid of rats.

B Mongooses threaten the Hawaiian goose.

C Mongooses destroy other species.

D Mongooses are difficult to study.

2. In 1872, a Jamaican sugar planter imported nine mongooses to

A keep snakes away from his farm.

B serve as pets for his young children.

C eat the rats that were ruining his crops.

D breed them for their fur.

3. Because the mongooses didn't have any natural predators in that part of the world, their population

A diminished.

B exploded.

C fluctuated.

D declined.

4. You would be *most* likely to find this information about mongooses in a

A chemistry book.

B collection of stories.

C travel guide.

D magazine on nature.

Timed Writing

5. Describe the effects of the mongoose population explosion.

Assess

Answers and Explanations

1. *A The effect of the planter's importation of nine mongooses is that the mongooses do a good job getting rid of the rats. The mongooses threaten the Hawaiian goose (B) and destroy other species (C) after their population explodes. The article does not say that mongooses are difficult to study (D).*

2. *C The sugar planter imported the mongooses to eat the rats that were ruining his crops, not to keep snakes away from his farm (A), serve as pets for his children (B), or breed them for their fur (C).*

3. *B Because there were no predators in that part of the world to kill the mongooses, their population exploded. A lack of predators would not cause an animal population to shrink (A, D) or fluctuate (C).*

4. *D A magazine on nature might include this type of information about mongooses. A chemistry book (A) and a travel guide (C) probably would not. The factual information in this article would not belong in a collection of stories (B).*

Timed-Writing

5. *The mongoose population explosion has resulted in the spread of rabies, attacks on small animals, and threats to endangered species.*

Reteach

 ThinkCentral Online Remediation

Assess

Answers and Explanations

1. **C** Habitual *means routine or regular, so the answer is C.*

2. **B** Egotism *is selfishness, which is closest to B.*

3. **A** Intricate *means complicated, which is closest to A.*

4. **A** *B, C, and D are too specific.* Merchandise *is items that are sold, which is A.*

5. **D** Thermometers *show the temperature, so the answer is D.*

6. **A** Convoluted *means complicated, so the answer is A.*

7. **C** Arrogant *means conceited or proud, which is closest to C.*

8. **B** Exotic *means unusual or extraordinary, so the answer is B.*

Academic Vocabulary

9. **D** Perceive *means sense or understand, so the answer is D.*

 WordSharp: An Interactive Vocabulary Tutor

Reteach

 ThinkCentral Online Remediation

 California Standards, p. 494

- **Vocabulary Standard 1.3** Clarify word meanings through the use of definition, example, restatement, or contrast.

Vocabulary Skills Review

Reading Standard 1.3 Clarify word meanings through the use of definition, example, restatement, or contrast.

Clarify Word Meanings

Directions: Read each sentence, using context clues to help you clarify the meaning of the italicized word. Choose the best answer.

1. The policeman twirled his nightstick in a *habitual* manner each time he stopped at a corner.
   A wobbly
   B nervous
   C regular
   D purposeful

2. "Silky Bob's" *egotism* made him boast about himself.
   A hunger
   B self-interest
   C illness
   D ignorance

3. The man from Chicago's fancy vest was covered with small, *intricate* embroidery.
   A detailed
   B flashy
   C Asian
   D diamond-shaped

4. Mr. Baumer stocked his store shelves with various *merchandise*.
   A items for sale
   B canned food
   C wood alcohol
   D rolls of cloth

5. The *thermometer* didn't rise above 2 degrees during the whole month of January.
   A northerly wind
   B barometer
   C morning star
   D temperature indicator

6. The hikers who got lost in the woods took a long and *convoluted* route back to the ranger station.
   A complicated
   B ordinary
   C murky
   D strange

7. The *arrogant* woman disrespected the other people in the room by talking about herself for more than an hour.
   A overly emotional
   B overly confused
   C overly self-important
   D easily persuaded

8. The *exotic* bird was like no other bird I have seen; it had bright blue feathers with pink tips.
   A ordinary in a dull way
   B different in a fascinating way
   C very desirable
   D strongly offensive

Academic Vocabulary

Choose the answer choice that is closest in meaning to the italicized word.

9. Ernesto Galarza's autobiography helps readers *perceive* what it is like to be a young immigrant.
   A imagine
   B admire
   C decide
   D understand

Vocabulary Review

Use this activity to assess whether students have retained the collection Vocabulary. Ask students to choose the noun from the box that fits the description.

alliance	splendor	vigil
evaporation	monopoly	

1. An association of people with a common aim. [*alliance*]

2. The situation in which one company or person is the only provider of a product or service. [*monopoly*]

3. A period spent doing something through the night. [*vigil*]

4. Something that is magnificent, impressive, or brilliant. [*splendor*]

5. A process in which a liquid is changed into a vapor. [*evaporation*]

Writing Skills Review

Persuasive Essay **Directions:** Read the following paragraph from a persuasive essay. Then, answer each question that follows.

Writing Standard 2.4 Write persuasive compositions: a. State a clear position or perspective in support of a proposition or proposal. b. Describe the points in support of the proposition, employing well-articulated evidence. c. Anticipate and address reader concerns and counterarguments.

(1) The backwater swamps of the American South support many life-forms that are threatened by the overuse of natural resources. (2) Wetlands that have not been replanted after logging are vulnerable to floods and erosion. (3) Because the soil is so rich, lands have been cleared for agriculture. (4) The great trees have been cut down for lumber. (5) Huge stands of oak, elm, cypress, and other species of the North American wetlands have been removed from the landscape. (6) To preserve and protect this important habitat, we must all work for the reforestation of these swamps.

1. Which of the following statements might be added to support the opening sentence?
   A Many swamp creatures are nocturnal.
   B These wetlands shelter snakes, alligators, black bears, and many varieties of birds as well as enormous trees.
   C Many superstitions exist about swamps.
   D The naturalist John James Audubon wrote about alligators on the shores of the Red River.

2. Where might sentence 2 be moved to make the paragraph more effective?
   A to the beginning of the paragraph, to introduce the topic
   B following sentence 5, to show the harm that can come from deforestation
   C to the end of the paragraph, to serve as a call to action
   D out of the paragraph altogether

3. What transitional word or phrase could be added to the beginning of sentence 5?
   A Fortunately,
   B Otherwise,
   C However,
   D For example,

4. How else might sentence 5 be strengthened?
   A by explaining how lumber is used for construction
   B by replacing "Huge stands" with exact statistics
   C by using comparisons to the destruction of rain forests
   D by moving it to the end of the paragraph

5. In the remaining paragraphs of the essay, readers would expect to find all of the following *except*
   A possible objections to the solution.
   B the benefits of following the writer's plan.
   C a call for change or action.
   D lists of threatened jungle habitats.

Writing Skills Review

Assess

Answers and Explanations

1. **B** This sentence specifies the species of life in the swamps. Choices A, C, and D are irrelevant details.

2. **B** Sentence 2 shows that erosion can come from deforestation. It does not introduce the topic (A) or serve as a call to action (C), but it should remain in the paragraph (D).

3. **D** Sentence 5 gives an example of types of trees that have been cut down for lumber. It does not show a positive effect (A) or show comparison and contrast (B, C).

4. **B** Providing specific statistics would strengthen this sentence. Explaining how lumber is used for construction (A) would weaken rather than strengthen the writer's argument. Using comparisons to the destruction of rain forests (C) or moving the sentence to the end of the paragraph (D) would not strengthen it.

5. **D** Readers would expect to find possible objections (A), benefits of following the writer's plan (B), and a call for change or action (C). They are elements of a persuasive essay. Because the essay focuses on swamps, they would not find a list of threatened jungle habitats.

Reteach

 ThinkCentral Online Remediation

California Standards, p. 495
- **Writing Standard 2.4** Write persuasive compositions.

Application Homework
Letter to the Editor

For homework, have students review a local newspaper and identify a current event about which they have an opinion. Then, have students write a letter to the editor that states their opinion and persuades others to agree with their position. Remind students that although their letters must be brief, the letters should contain strong evidence to support their argument. Have students submit their letters to the newspaper if they wish.

Extension
Analysis of a Debate

Have students watch a political commentary show or listen to a radio show. As students watch or listen, have them take notes about each speaker's argument and whether or not they agree with it. Then, have students form groups and discuss the panelists' arguments along with their own ideas for solutions to the problem.

If students enjoyed the themes and topics explored in this collection, you might recommend these titles for independent reading.

Assessment Options

The following projects can help you evaluate and assess your students' outside work. Videotapes or audiotapes of completed projects may be included in students' portfolios.

Compare a Book and a Film

■ Students who read Witi Ihimaera's novel *The Whale Rider* may wish to view and compare the 2003 movie of the same name.

■ Have students discuss the book and the movie in small groups. Suggest that they focus on the characterization of Kahu in the novel and Pai in the film.

Create a Diorama

■ After students read *Elizabeth I and the Spanish Armada,* suggest that they create a diorama based on the British victory of the Spanish Armada.

■ Display student artwork in the classroom or elsewhere in the school for students, faculty, and visitors to enjoy.

Read On
For Independent Reading

Fiction

Bearstone

Fourteen-year-old Cloyd never knew his parents and never went to school. After being on his own for so long, he has trouble accepting the kindness of an old rancher from Colorado. In Will Hobbs's novel *Bearstone,* Cloyd embraces his Native American heritage, begins to respect others, and learns what it takes to be an adult.

Whale Rider

In Whangara, New Zealand, the respected title of "whale rider" has always been bestowed upon a male descended from Kahutia Te Rangi. Now there is no male heir to the title. Only an eight-year-old girl named Kahu can claim the throne. Can she rise to the challenge when beached whales threaten the future of her tribe? Find out in *The Whale Rider* by Witi Ihimaera.

M. C. Higgins, the Great

M. C. Higgins and his family have been living on Sarah's Mountain ever since M. C.'s great-grandmother arrived there as a fugitive from slavery. His family members love their mountain, but one day M. C. notices a massive pile of debris accumulating on a cliff over their home. In Virginia Hamilton's *M. C. Higgins the Great,* a young boy is torn between his loyalty to his family and his desire for a life beyond the mountains.

Soldier Boy

When Johnny "the Kid" McBane runs away from the slums of nineteenth-century Chicago, he joins the cavalry even though he is underage and has never ridden a horse or shot a rifle. He soon masters his duties and ultimately fights with General Custer at the Battle of Little Bighorn. This gripping historical novel by Brian Burks explores army life in the 1870s American West as it details one boy's struggle to become a man.

Selections Readability

Word Counts and Readabilities of Read On Books

Nonfiction	Estimated Word Counts	Readability
Bearstone	40,000	Accessible
M.C. Higgins, the Great	68,000	Accessible
Whale Rider	31,736	Accessible
Soldier Boy	23,640	Accessible

Nonfiction

Children of the Wild West

What was daily life like for Al, the boy in the story "Bargain," back in the nineteenth-century West? What was his school like? Did he ever have fun? In *Children of the Wild West,* author Russell Freedman explores the difficult lives of children and their parents who left the comfort of the eastern United States for the Wild West, in search of land, money, and a future of their own.

Chinese Cinderella

The story of "Yeh-Shen" is a fairy tale: It contains a magical creature that saves Yeh-Shen, a handsome prince, and a happily-ever-after ending. In *Chinese Cinderella,* Adeline Yen Mah tells the true story of her sad Cinderella-like childhood. Her story has no magic or princes, but it does have an evil stepmother, cruel stepsiblings, and a harsh life of toil and abuse. Instead of being helped by a magical fish, Adeline's life is transformed by her love of books as well as her strength, hard work, and determination for a better life.

The Circuit

The Circuit tells the experiences of a family who moves from Mexico to California in hopes of a better life. Told from his point of view as a young boy, Francisco Jiménez has created a collection of autobiographical stories, describing his life as a migrant child who works the fields of California with his family. Some of the many awards the book has won are The Boston Globe-Horn Book Award, the Américas Award, and the Tomás Rivera Book Award.

Elizabeth I and the Spanish Armada

In this colorful, informative graphic history, you get a glimpse into the reign of Elizabeth I of England, and especially into her underdog navy's 1588 victory over the world's mightiest navy at that time, the Spanish Armada. The full-color panels, maps, fact segments, and a time line provide the background to Colin Hynson's presentation of an important moment in history.

Learn It Online
Explore other novels, and find tips for choosing, reading, and studying works at:
go.hrw.com H7-497 **Go**

Estimated Word Counts and Lexile Scores of Read On Books

Nonfiction	Estimated Word Counts	Readability
Children of the West	11,036	Accessible
Chinese Cinderella	48,541	Accessible
The Circuit	26,961	Accessible
Elizabeth I and the Spanish Armada	Graphic Novel	Accessible

Assessment Options
Research the Wild West

- Have students who read *Children of the Wild West* choose an aspect of life in the nineteenth-century West that most interests them to research in further detail.

- Have students use print or electronic resources to conduct research. Then, have students design a visual presentation, such as a poster or a slideshow, to convey the results of their research to the class.

- After students present their information about the West, have them conduct a brief question and answer session to address classmates' questions about what life in the Wild West was like.

Discuss a Character

Have students who read *The Circuit* form small groups and discuss the character of Francisco Jiménez. Do they relate to Jiménez's struggles? How does he display bravery in the book, and how effectively does he convey his childhood experiences?

Learn It Online
The **NovelWise** mini-site includes instruction on choosing, reading, and analyzing novels; it also contains a catalogue of book summaries, study guides, teaching guides, and PowerPoint presentations.

go.hrw.com H7-497 **Go**

Forms of Prose and Poetry

Introducing The Skills

Features highlighted in **yellow** constitute a suggested minimum course of study.

Selection or Feature	For Independent Reading	Grade–Level Standards
Literary Skills Focus: What Are the Forms of Prose?		**Reading Standard 3.1:** Purposes and characteristics of prose
Reading Skills Focus: How Do I Analyze Prose?		**Reading Standard 3.1:** Purposes and characteristics of prose
Reading Model: Fish Cheeks by Amy Tan (Accessible, Lexile 950) **Skills in Action:** Wrap Up	• **The Lotus Seed** by Sherry Garland	**Reading Standard 3.1:** Purposes and characteristics of prose

Applying The Skills

Selection or Feature	For Independent Reading	Grade–Level Standards
Amigo Brothers by Piri Thomas (Accessible, Lexile 900)	• **Baseball in April and Other Stories** by Gary Soto • **The Million Dollar Shot** by Dan Gutman	**Reading Standard 3.1:** Purposes and characteristics of prose **Reading Standard 2.3:** Clarify word meanings
An Unforgettable Journey by Maijue Xiong (Accessible, Lexile 910)	• **A Long Way from Home** by Maureen Crane Wartski • **American Dragons: Twenty-Five Asian American Voices** compiled by Laurence Yep	**Reading Standard 3.1:** Purposes and characteristics of prose **Reading Standard 2.3:** Clarify word meanings
Song of the Trees by Mildred D. Taylor (Challenging, Lexile 740)	• **The Land** by Mildred D. Taylor • **To Kill a Mockingbird** by Harper Lee	**Reading Standard 3.1:** Purposes and characteristics of prose
A Mason-Dixon Memory by Clifton Davis (Accessible, Lexile 890)	• **The Watsons Go to Birmingham— 1963** by Christopher Paul Curtis • **Roll of Thunder, Hear My Cry** by Mildred D. Taylor	**Reading Standard 3.1:** Purposes and characteristics of prose

Selection or Feature	For Independent Reading	Grade–Level Skills
Literary Skills Focus: What Are the Forms and Characteristics of Poetry?		**Reading Skill:** Forms and characteristics of poetry
Literary Skills Focus: What Are the Sounds of Poetry?		**Reading Skill:** Forms and characteristics of poetry
Reading Skills Focus: How Do I Read and Analyze Poetry?		**Reading Skill:** Forms and characteristics of poetry
Reading Model: The Village Blacksmith by Henry Wadsworth Longfellow (Accessible, Lexile N/A) **Skills in Action:** Wrap Up	• **A Jar of Tiny Stars: Poems by NCTE Award-Winning Poets**	**Reading Skill:** Forms and characteristics of poetry

Applying The Skills

Selection or Feature	For Independent Reading	Grade–Level Skills
I'm Nobody! by Emily Dickinson (Accessible, Lexile N/A)	• **A Gathering of Days: A New England Girl's Journal** by Joan Blos • **Celebrating America: A Collection of Poems and Images of the American Spirit compiled** by Laura Whipple	**Reading Skill:** Forms and characteristics of poetry
• **Madam and the Rent Man** (Accessible, Lexile N/A) • **Harlem Night Song** (Accessible, Lexile N/A) • **Winter Moon** (Accessible, Lexile N/A) by Langston Hughes	• **Langston Hughes: Poet of the Harlem Renaissance** by Jack Rummel • **The Other Side: Shorter Poems** by Angela Johnson	**Reading Skill:** Forms and characteristics of poetry
• **I Ask My Mother to Sing** by Li-Young Lee (Challenging, Lexile N/A) • **Ode to Family Photographs** by Gary Soto (Challenging, Lexile N/A)	• **Waiting to Waltz, A Childhood: Poems** by Cynthia Rylant • **Stolen Dreams: Portraits of Working Children** by David L. Parker	**Reading Skill:** Forms and characteristics of poetry
• **Father William** by Lewis Carroll (Accessbile, Lexile N/A) • **Sarah Cynthia Sylvia Stout Would Not Take the Garbage Out** by Shel Silverstein (Accessible, Lexile N/A)	• **Where the Sidewalk End** by Shel Silverstein • **Hist-Wist and Other Poems for Children**	**Reading Skill:** Forms and characteristics of poetry
The Runaway by Robert Frost (Accessible, Lexile N/A)	• **Heart to Heart: New Poems Inspired by Twentieth-Century American Art** by Jan Greenberg • **Old Elm Speaks: Tree Poems** by Kristine O'Connell George	**Reading Skill:** Forms and characteristics of poetry
Names of Horses by Donald Hall (Challenging, Lexile N/A)	• **Rainbows are Made** by Carl Sandburg • **Heartbeat** by Sharon Creech	**Reading Skill:** Forms and characteristics of poetry
Author Study: Sandra Cisneros • **An Interview with Sandra Cisneros** by Marit Haahr (Accessible, Lexile 1460) • **Salvador Late or Early** by Sandra Cisneros (Accessible, Lexile N/A) • **Chanclas** by Sandra Cisneros (Accessible, Lexile 1120) • **Abuelito Who** by Sandra Cisneros (Accessible, Lexile N/A) • **The Place Where Dreams Come From** by Sandra Cisneros (Accessible, Lexile 1160)	• **Lupita Mañana** by Patricia Beatty • **Grassroots: Poems by Carl Sandburg** by Carl Sandburg	**Reading Standard 3.1:** Purposes and characteristics of prose

Forms of Prose and Poetry

Mastering The Skills

Selection or Feature	Grade–Level Standards
Writing Workshop: Fictional Narrative	**Writing Standard 1.7:** Revise **Writing Standard 2.1:** Write fictional or autobiographical narratives.
Preparing for Timed Writing: Fictional Narrative	**Writing Standard 2.1:** Write fictional or autobiographical narratives.
Listening and Speaking Workshop: Presenting an Autobiographical Narrative	**Listening and Speaking Standard 2.1:** Deliver narrative presentations.
Standards Practice: Literary Skills Review Vocabulary Skills Review Writing Skills Review	**Reading Standard 3.1:** Prose **Reading Standard 1.3:** Clarify word meanings. **Writing Standard 2.1:** Write fictional or autobiographical narratives.

Daily and Weekly Support

- **Reader/Writer Notebook**
- **Reading and Writing Transparencies**
- **Weekly Standards Review Transparencies**
- **Family Involvement Activities in Five Languages**
- **Language Handbook Worksheets**
- **Holt Virtual File Cabinet for Language Arts**
- **Spelling Lessons and Activities**

Assessment Resources

- **Chapter 5 Resources,** Chapter Diagnostic Test; Selection Standards Checks, Chapter Standards Mastery
- **Universal Access: Differentiating Instruction,** leveled assessment
- **English-Language Conventions Progress-Monitoring Test,** Chapters 1–13
- **ThinkCentral Online Assessment**

	On-Level Learners	English Learners	Struggling Readers/Writers	Students Who Use African American Vernacular English	Advanced Learners	Students with Disabilities
Chapter 5 Resources practice and assessment for all selections and features	✔				✔	
Universal Access: Holt Interactive Reader interactive readings for Minimum-Course-of-Study Selections		✔	✔	✔		✔
Holt Interactive Reader for English Language Development adaptations of Minimum-Course-of-Study Selections		✔				
Universal Access: Differentiating Instruction modified lesson plans, graphic organizers, and leveled assessment		✔	✔	✔		✔
Universal Access: Resources for Teaching Advanced Students lesson plans for Minimum-Course-of-Study Selections					✔	
Universal Access: Supporting Instruction in Five Languages translations of selection summaries and key terms		✔				
Universal Access: Holt Interactive Writer and Speaker practice and assessment	✔	✔	✔	✔	✔	✔
Language and Sentence Skills Practice for Warriner's Handbook Chapters 1–13	✔				✔	
Universal Access: Developmental Language and Sentence Skills Practice for Warriner's Handbook Chapters 1–13		✔	✔	✔		✔

5 Forms of Prose and Poetry

Technology Resources

Find all of Holt's technology resources at go.hrw.com. Technology resources are also listed at point of use in the wrap; below are our featured components for Chapter 5.

Teacher Management Resources

ThinkCentral, Teacher Access

Teacher One Stop™

Holt Professional Learning for Language Arts

The Highwayman

Alfred Noyes

Part 1

The wind was a torrent of darkness among the gusty trees,
The moon was a ghostly galleon² tossed upon cloudy seas,
The road was a ribbon of moonlight over the purple moor,
And the highwayman came riding—
5   Riding—riding—
The highwayman came riding, up to the old inn door.

Spotlight on ThinkCentral, Teacher Access

All of the chapter's resources are available at ThinkCentral, Teacher Access. Online suggestions:
• Play the point-of-use audio versions of the poems while projecting the text, so your students can read along.

Student Edition Support

PowerNotes

ThinkCentral, Student Access

Student One Stop™

Interactive Reading Workshops

Interactive Graphic Organizers

Writers' Lives

Holt Audio Library

Holt Audio Library: Selections and Summaries in Spanish

Spotlight on PowerNotes

Help your students build background for and motivate them to read "Amigo Brothers" through the PowerNotes video.

Universal Access: Struggling readers will particularly benefit from the background information this video provides.

Supported Strands: Vocabulary, Reading, Literature, Writing
Available on DVD-ROM as well as on go.hrw.com.

Student Edition Extension Activities

Digital Storytelling Mini-Site

NovelWise Mini-Site

MediaScope Mini-Site

WordSharp: An Interactive Vocabulary Tutor

GrammarNotes

WritingNotes

Writing and Research in a Digital Age

Literature Links

Holt Audio Tutor for English Language Development

What are active and passive voice?

Like people, verbs can be

active   or   passive

Billy kicks the ball.

Kim is bothered by a headache.

Josie plays the instrument.

Jen has been hurt by a friend.

< Back   Next >   Lesson Menu   Exit ✕

Spotlight on GrammarNotes

These customizable PowerPoint presentations provide student-friendly, interactive instruction on basic grammar concepts and helps students connect grammar with writing and literature.

Universal Access: English learners, and any students who need extra help, can benefit from the presentation "Using Active and Passive Voice" when writing the fictional narrative in this chapter's Writing Workshop.

Supported Strand: Writing

Assessment Resources

ThinkCentral Online Assessment

Holt Online Essay Scoring

ThinkCentral Online Remediation

Spotlight on Online Essay Scoring

With online essay scoring, students can practice writing responses to essay prompts—and our system automatically scores them. Students will receive immediate feedback on their essays.

Real Issues, Real Experts

The wrap for these selections includes specific ideas and strategies from *Holt Literature and Language Arts* authors.

From the Authors

For "Amigo Brothers," p. 510

To teach students about comparing and contrasting, I like to use an ABC chart. Have students create one small box for each letter of the alphabet and write char-

acter traits of each character in the box of the letter the trait starts with. This gives your students a visual representation of similarities and differences.

Kylene Beers

For "I'm Nobody!," p. 580

To show students that people can have different reactions and interpretations to poetry, divide a number of different poems into separate stanzas and place them in

an envelope. Each student should take a stanza, then identify the classmates who hold the remaining parts of their poem through the use of topic, style, and voice.

Linda Reif

For "The Runaway," p. 605

Having students retell poems in prose form can make poetry seem less formi-dable, especially when students realize that poems tell a story like other selections they

have read. Other nota-ble features to be dis-cussed include the use of figurative language, such as metaphors and similes, to paint a vivid picture.

Deborah Appleman

Teacher to Teacher

Erin Sullivan
Riverside, California

Preteach I give groups the same copies of different forms of prose. For example, each group receives the same novel or short story. Students discuss and record the different characteristics found in prose in a chart.

Direct Teach I put the following words on the board: essay, short story, novella, novel, autobiography. In groups, students talk briefly about what each word means. Then, we have a class discussion to make sure there is no confusion. I then ask for volunteers to help me label each different form of prose accurately on the board.

Assess The next day, I give students a short handout that lists all of the forms of prose on one side and the dis-tinct characteristics on the other and they match them.

Holt Professional Learning

Visit the ThinkCentral, Teacher Access to link to Holt's Professional Learning site for English/Language Arts teachers. This site features:

- Videos that share the insights of *Holt Literature and Language Arts* program authors and consultants and demonstrate proven classroom strategies with master teachers
- Study guides for publications by our authors and consultants
- Informative articles and useful Web links
- Help in planning your department's professional learning sessions
- A handbook for new teachers

Managing the Heterogeneous Classroom
with Leila Christenbury and Patrick Schwarz

VIDEO PRODUCTS

Strategies for Helping Struggling Readers
with Kylene Beers

Effective Vocabulary Instruction
with Carol Jago and Kylene Beers

Developing Critical Thinking About Literature
with Carol Jago and Deborah Appleman

Teaching Students to Revise, Not Recopy
with Linda Rief

Teaching English Learners
with Robin Scarcella

Using Literature Circles
with Harvey Daniels

Teaching On-Demand Writing Skills
with Leila Christenbury

Managing the Heterogeneous Classroom
with Leila Christenbury and Patrick Schwarz

Teaching Narrative and Expository Texts
with Judith Irvin and Deborah Appleman

Becoming a Tech-Savvy Teacher
with Sara Kajder

Re-engaging the Disengaged Student
with Alfred Tatum

Teaching Grammar in Context
with Amy Benjamin

Word Analysis, Fluency, and Systematic Vocabulary Development

■ **1.3** Clarify word meanings through the use of definition, example, restatement, or contrast.

Literary Response and Analysis

■ **3.1** Articulate the expressed purposes and characteristics of different forms of prose (e.g., short story, novel, novella, essay).

Writing Applications (Genres and Their Characteristics)

■ **2.1** Write fictional or autobiographical narratives:
  a. Develop a standard plot line (having a beginning, conflict, rising action, climax, and denouement) and point of view.
  b. Develop complex major and minor characters and a definite setting.
  c. Use a range of appropriate strategies (e.g., dialogue; suspense; naming of specific narrative action, including movement, gestures, and expressions).

(left) Elijah Wood and (right) Sean Astin from the *Lord of the Rings* movie series.

Analyzing Visuals

Extension Activity Tell students that *The Lord of the Rings* series is a work of fiction. Ask students to identify what characteristics of the movie and the novel categorize them as fiction.

Possible response: The story is fiction because it is made up. The setting is a place that does not exist. The characters are creatures that do not exist in the real world. Some of the characters are able to do things that humans and animals cannot do.

Chapter Resources

On Course: Mapping Instruction
Chapter 1 Resources
Warriner's Handbook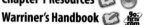
  • Chapter 10, Using Pronouns Correctly
  • Chapter 11, Using Modifiers Correctly
  • Chapter 12, A Glossary of Usage
  • Chapter 13, Capital Letters
PowerNotes
Teacher One Stop™,
Formal Assessment, Progress Monitoring Test 1

English-Language Conventions Progress-Monitoring Tests
Holt Virtual File Cabinet for Language Arts, grammar, reading, and vocabulary resources
Holt Pronunciation Resources
  • Phoneme Sounds and Spellings
  • Support for Speakers of African American Vernacular English
ThinkCentral Online Assessment
ThinkCentral Online Remediation

CHAPTER **5**

Forms of Prose and Poetry

"Every one of us gets through the tough times because somebody is there, standing in the gap to close it for us."

—**Oprah Winfrey**

What Do
You
Think

How do you manage
through tough times?

***

Chapter Objectives

■ In the first part of the chapter, students will learn about the elements of prose by reading a variety of texts. They will learn about such types of prose as short stories, novels, novellas, folk tales, biographies, and autobiographies.

■ In the second part of the chapter, students will learn to identify and analyze a variety of poetic forms.

■ Students will analyze common sound effects found in poetry, such as rhythm, rhyme, alliteration, and onomatopoeia.

■ Students will practice re-reading poetry to enhance comprehension. They will also learn to question the texts that they read.

■ In the Author Study, students will analyze, compare, and contrast works of poetry and in prose by Sandra Cisneros.

■ At the end of the chapter, students will write and present a short fictional narrative.

Routines for California Classrooms

For ideas on classroom practices and approaches to grouping, see the discussion of routines on pages T34–T37 of this Teacher's Edition.

What Do You Think?
How do you manage through tough times?

Read the quotation aloud. Then ask students to think about ways in which they cope with difficult situations. Who or what is most helpful to them? Invite students who are comfortable sharing difficult experiences and how they dealt with them to do so.

***

Learn It Online
An interactive graphic organizer can help you keep track of what you learn. Try one out at:

go.hrw.com | H7-499 | **Go**

***

Learn It Online
The **ThinkCentral, Teacher Access** includes more than thirty **Interactive Graphic Organizers**. Your students can use them to generate and organize ideas, compare and contrast, evaluate a decision, support a position and much more.

go.hrw.com | H7-499 | **Go**

***

Literary Skills Focus

by **Linda Rief**

Literary Skills Focus

Objectives

Students will
- understand the characteristics of novels, novellas, and short stories
- understand the characteristics of nonfiction

Preteach

Build Background Tell students that prose includes most fiction and nonfiction writing. Have students name some texts they have read recently, and discuss with students whether these selections are examples of prose.

Direct Teach

Prose: Some Types of Fiction

■ Draw a line with the words *shortest* and *longest* at either end. Ask students where the words *novella, novel,* and *short story* should be placed on the line. Model by placing *novel* at the end, showing that it is the longest of the three texts. Have students place *novella* and *short story* on the line.

■ Give students examples of folk tales, such as the story of Paul Bunyan. Have students name other folk tales they have read or heard about.

 California Standards, pp. 500–501

■ **Reading Standard 3.1** Articulate the expressed purposes and characteristics of different forms of prose (e.g., short story, novel, novella, essay).

What Are the Forms of Prose?

You might think of prose as everything that isn't poetry. In fact, you've been speaking prose all your life. You also read prose every day—in your textbooks, in novels, in magazines and newspapers, and on the Web. There are many types of prose, as this organizer shows. Prose is generally divided into fiction and nonfiction.

Nonfiction → news article, report, history, biography, essay, autobiography

Prose

Fiction → adventure, romance, novel, novella, historical fiction, short story

---

Prose: Some Types of Fiction

Short Story A **short story** is a brief work of fiction in which one or several characters experience a series of events. This is the **plot**. The characters work through a **conflict**, or struggle, which leads to a **climax**, or a high point. Finally, there is a **resolution**, or ending. If all that happens in five to twenty pages, you have a short story.

> Antonio Cruz and Felix Vargas were both seventeen years old. They were so together in friendship that they felt themselves to be brothers. They had known each other since childhood, growing up on the Lower East Side of Manhattan in the same tenement building on Fifth Street between Avenue A and Avenue B.
>
> from "Amigo Brothers"
> by Piri Thomas

Novel A work of fiction that is one hundred pages or more is a **novel**. In a novel you meet many characters, explore many themes, encounter many conflicts, and probably see subplots (other, less important plots) unfold within the larger plot. There may be several settings.

Novella If a work is longer than twenty pages but shorter than one hundred pages, it is a **novella,** which is simply a short novel.

> Mama's back was to me. She was dipping flour from a near-empty canister, while my older brother, Stacey, built a fire in the huge iron-bellied stove.
>
> from *Song of the Trees*
> by Mildred D. Taylor

Folk Tale A **folk tale** is a story with no known author that has been passed on from one generation to another by word of mouth. Folk tales usually teach a lesson and often contain fantastic elements or events that could not happen in the world as we know it. These stories tend to travel, so similar characters and plots are found in the folk tales of several cultures.

> There was once a rich man whose wife lay sick, and when she felt her end drawing near, she called to her only daughter to come near her bed.
>
> from "Aschenputtel," German folk tale retold by Jakob and Wilhelm Grimm

---

Resources

Chapter 5 Resources, Literary Skills Focus Skill Builder, p. 3 📄 💿

PowerNotes, interactive lesson presentation with activities 💿 🔵

Teacher One Stop™, on-level lesson plans and all print resources 💿

Universal Access

🔵 English Learners/Struggling Readers

Help students learn the academic terms in the Literary Skills Focus by breaking the terms into their word parts.

- Divide the words *biography* and *autobiography* into their respective word parts.
- Explain that the word part *auto* means "self." This word part is found in words such as *automatic*, which refers to something that works by itself.
- Then, explain that the word part *bio* means "life." This word part is found in the word *biology*, which means "the study of life."

Prose: Some Types of Nonfiction

Essay and Article Essays and articles are short pieces of prose that discuss a limited topic. Some people write short personal essays about simple things, such as eating an ice-cream cone or taking a dog for a walk. Others write long essays about complex topics, such as freedom, respect, and justice. People write articles for different purposes—to explain something, to persuade, to deliver information, or even to make you laugh.

> On Christmas Eve I saw that my mother had outdone herself in creating a strange menu. She was pulling black veins out of the backs of fleshy prawns. The kitchen was littered with appalling mounds of raw food.
>
> from "Fish Cheeks" by Amy Tan

Some nonfiction topics are too complex to be covered in the short format of an essay. Full-length biographies and autobiographies are examples of longer types of nonfiction.

Biography If you wanted to know the whole story of a person's life, you'd read a book-length biography. A **biography** is the story of a real person's life, written by another person.

Autobiography An **autobiography** is the story of a person's life, written by that person.

> After Laos became a Communist country in 1975, my family, along with many others, fled in fear of persecution.
>
> from "An Unforgettable Journey" by Maijue Xiong

Characteristics of Fiction and Nonfiction

Elements of Fiction	• **Characters** are the imaginary people or animals in a story. • **Plot** is the series of events in a story. • **Setting** is the time and place in which a story is set. The setting may be made up or may be real. • **Point of view** is the vantage point from which a story is told. In **first-person point of view,** one of the characters, using the personal pronoun *I*, is telling a story. In **third-person omniscient point of view,** the narrator knows everything about the characters and their problems. • Many works of fiction convey a **theme,** which is a universal message about life.
Elements of Nonfiction	• Nonfiction is about **real people, events,** or **ideas.** • It is told from the **point of view,** or **perspective,** of the author. • It presents **facts** and **ideas.** • It may mention the **historical context** of the subject—information about the society and culture of the time.

Your Turn Analyze Forms of Prose

Articulate (express clearly and specifically) whether each description of a written work is an example of fiction or nonfiction.

1. an article supporting a proposed law
2. a story about a princess and a frog falling in love
3. a story about an imaginary character set during the Civil War

Learn It Online
Try the *PowerNotes* version of this lesson on:
go.hrw.com H7-501 Go

Prose: Some Types of Nonfiction

■ Point out the excerpt from "Fish Cheeks" on p. 501. Explain that the use of personal pronouns such as "I" and "my" is an indication of an autobiographical account. Point out that the word "appalling" in the last sentence indicates the author's personal opinion. The presence of personal opinions is a characteristic of autobiographies.

■ Explain to students that because of its length and scope, "Fish Cheeks" is considered a personal essay rather than a full autobiography. "Fish Cheeks" is a short work that covers one particular incident in the author's life, while an autobiography is longer and describes many events from the author's life.

■ Have students describe the ways in which nonfiction is different from fiction. Ask them to list on the board reasons why someone might write a personal essay or informational article. [*to inform, to persuade, to entertain*]

Check for Understanding

Your Turn
Possible responses:
1. *nonfiction*
2. *fiction*
3. *fiction*

Reteach

ThinkCentral Online Assessment

Learn It Online
For a multimedia version of the instruction found on this page, use the **PowerNotes** Literary Skills Focus presentation.

go.hrw.com H7-501 Go

• The word part *graph* means "written." When a person signs an *autograph*, she writes her own name.

• Combine the word parts and their meanings to show how they provide the definitions for *biography* and *autobiography*.

  Autobiography: The life story of a person that is written by that person.

  Biography: The life story of a person that is written by someone else.

Advanced Learners

Extension Have students write a short paragraph describing themselves in the form of a biography. Then, have students modify their paragraph so that it is told in the form of an autobiography. Have students share with the class the methods they used to modify their paragraph. These methods may include writing in the first-person point of view or expressing personal thoughts and opinions.

Objectives
Students will
- learn to compare and contrast texts
- set a purpose for reading
- learn to activate prior knowledge
- understand chronological order

Build Background Have students think about a time when they did not understand something they read. Ask students what they found confusing about the text. Explain that this section will give them tips for understanding a text.

Comparing and Contrasting

- Model using a Venn diagram to compare football and soccer. Write in the overlapping area of the diagram *team sport* and *played on a long field*. In the area of the diagram that corresponds to football, write *ball thrown or carried*, and in the area that corresponds to soccer, write *ball kicked with feet.*

- Have students practice using a Venn diagram to compare and contrast two books, movies, or television shows.

California Standards, pp. 502–503
- **Reading Standard 3.1** Articulate the expressed purposes and characteristics of different forms of prose (e.g., short story, novel, novella, essay).

Reading Skills Focus

by **Kylene Beers**

How Do I Analyze Prose?

Reading is like riding a bicycle: You have to do many things to get where you want to go. Skilled bikers know how to balance, shift gears, and use hand brakes as they ride. Good readers also juggle different tasks. As a skilled reader, you set a purpose for reading, compare and contrast events and characters, make connections with your prior knowledge, and notice time order.

Comparing and Contrasting

When you compare, you look for similarities, or likenesses. When you contrast, you look for differences. You compare and contrast things every day. For instance, you might compare and contrast the features of your cat to a friend's cat. When you read, you might compare the traits of two important characters or a confrontation at the beginning of a story to a confrontation at the end.

Venn Diagram A **Venn diagram** helps you recognize similarities and differences. The one below compares and contrasts two stories in Chapter 4. In the space where the circles overlap, note how the stories are alike. Where there is no overlap, note differences.

Aschenputtel — Yeh-Shen

helped by fairy godmother, meets prince | has wicked stepmother, has wish granted, loses shoe | helped by fish, meets king

Differences — Similarities — Differences

Setting a Purpose for Reading

When you read an article about your favorite actor, you read it differently than you read directions for installing a computer program. That's because you have a different **purpose,** or reason, for reading. When you read directions, your purpose is to understand how to complete a task. You'll read directions more slowly than you would read a magazine article because you must understand every step in the directions in order to get the right result.

How to Set a Purpose Before you read, you need to choose a purpose for reading. Previewing a text will help you set a purpose. Look at a text's title, headings, and illustrations. They often reveal reasons for reading it. See the chart below for purposes you might set for reading various forms of prose.

Form of Prose	Purpose for Reading
Short story	to be entertained
Autobiography	to learn about a person
News editorial	to make a decision on an issue
Technical directions	to complete a task

Activating Prior Knowledge

When you read a text on an unfamiliar topic, you can increase your comprehension by using prior knowledge. When you **activate prior knowledge,** you recall what you already know in order to help you understand something new. Your knowledge can come from your own experience or from other information you have heard or read.

A Model for Activating Prior Knowledge
Read the paragraph below. Then, see how one reader might activate prior knowledge.

> Dinner threw me deeper into despair. My relatives licked the ends of their chopsticks and reached across the table, dipping them into the dozen or so plates of food. Robert and his family waited patiently for platters to be passed to them.

← Dinner seems like a strange time to be upset.

← I really like Chinese food, but I don't know how to use chopsticks.

When I'm eating at someone's house, I sometimes worry about

← my table manners.

Chronological Order

Most prose narratives, true or fictional, are written in **chronological order.** Writers are using chronological order if they put events in **sequence,** or the order in which they actually happened. "An Unforgettable Journey," an autobiography in this chapter, is written in chronological order. It begins with "I was born in a small village" and goes on to relate important events in the writer's life as they happened in time, one after the other.

Words That Signal Chronological Order	
first	then
next	after
during	later
while	last
meanwhile	finally

All of the words above are clues that events are written in chronological order.

Your Turn Apply Reading Skills

1. Write a sentence that compares and contrasts fiction and nonfiction.

2. What purpose would you set if you were going to read a biography? Why?

3. If you were reading an essay about holiday family dinners, what prior knowledge might help you understand the essay?

4. Why would you expect an autobiography to be written in chronological order?

> Now go to the Skills in Action: Reading Model

Learn It Online
Need help understanding comparison and contrast? Check out the interactive Reading Workshop on:

go.hrw.com H7-503 **Go**

• Help students see that when they compare two things, they are bringing them together to find things in common. When they contrast two things, they are putting them against each other to find how they are different.

• Write *chronological* on the board. Divide the word between *chrono-* and *–logical.* Explain that *chrono* refers to time and *logical* refers to order or organization.

• Explain that *chronological* means arranging things in the order that they happened in time.

Advanced Learners

Extension Have students analyze the importance of chronological order in a text.

• Tell students to write a brief summary of a familiar story. Then, have students review their summaries and remove any words that signal chronological order.

• Have students read their summary to a partner. Then, tell students to replace the words that signal chronological order and re-read their summary.

• Ask pairs to discuss the logical and literary effects that these sorts of signal words have on a text.

Setting a Purpose for Reading

Model setting a purpose for reading. You might say, "I read an instruction manual to learn how to set up my computer." Ask what a person's purpose for reading a comic book might be. [*to be entertained*]

Activating Prior Knowledge

Direct students to the excerpt from "Fish Cheeks" on page 503. Ask them to discuss how their own prior experiences and knowledge help them relate to the situation in the excerpt.

Chronological Order

■ Model putting events in chronological order by using signal words. You might say, "The signal word *first* shows that this is the beginning of a series of events: *First, I set the table.* I use the signal word *next* or *then* to describe the next event: *Then, I filled the water glasses.*"

■ Have students write and share their own sentences using signal words.

Check for Understanding

Your Turn _____
Possible responses:

1. *Fiction describes imaginary topics; nonfiction tells about real ones.*

2. *I would read to learn about a person's life, because biographies give facts about real people.*

3. *knowledge about the holiday being celebrated*

4. *It tells the sequence of events that occurred in a person's life.*

Reteach

ThinkCentral Online Assessment

Learn It Online
For a multimedia version of the instruction found on this page, use the **PowerNotes** Reading Skills Focus presentation.

go.hrw.com H7-503   **Go**

Reading Model

Objectives

Students will

- analyze a personal essay
- set a purpose for reading the essay
- activate prior knowledge to improve comprehension
- compare and contrast characters

Preteach

Read with a Purpose Have students discuss the types of lessons that parents teach. Then, have them use their **Reader/Writer Notebook** to note details that reveal the lesson Amy learned from her mother.

Direct Teach

Model the Skill

Use the Reading Model to demonstrate the application of the Literary and Reading skills in a short selection. As you or students read the model aloud, stop to discuss the side annotations and highlighting, which are aids to comprehension and analysis.

▶ Literary Focus

Essay/Personal Narrative This personal narrative expresses the author's emotions. What emotional language does she use in the first two paragraphs? *Possible response: She says she loved Robert and felt disappointment with her family's food.*

▶ Reading Focus

Activating Prior Knowledge

What prior knowledge helps you understand why Amy was embarrassed by the food? *Possible response: These foods are uncommon in America, and Amy thought Robert would find her strange for eating them.*

Read with a Purpose Read the following personal narrative to discover the lesson Amy Tan learns from her mother.

Fish Cheeks

by **Amy Tan**

Literary Focus

Essay / Personal Narrative An essay can be personal or formal. "Fish Cheeks" is a kind of essay called a **personal narrative** because it focuses on the writer's feelings and experiences and it tells a story. Tan is writing about an embarrassing incident that happened when she was a teenager.

I fell in love with the minister's son the winter I turned fourteen. He was not Chinese, but as white as Mary in the manger. For Christmas I prayed for this blond-haired boy, Robert, and a slim new American nose.

When I found out that my parents had invited the minister's family over for Christmas Eve dinner, I cried. What would Robert think of our shabby *Chinese* Christmas? What would he think of our noisy *Chinese* relatives who lacked proper American manners? What terrible disappointment would he feel upon seeing not a roasted turkey and sweet potatoes but *Chinese* food?

Reading Focus

Activating Prior Knowledge As you read, activate prior knowledge to visualize the ingredients Tan's mother is preparing. Prawns are like shrimp.

On Christmas Eve I saw that my mother had outdone herself in creating a strange menu. She was pulling black veins out of the backs of fleshy prawns. The kitchen was littered with appalling mounds of raw food: a slimy rock cod with bulging fish eyes that pleaded not to be thrown into a pan of hot oil. Tofu, which looked like stacked wedges of rubbery white sponges. A bowl soaking dried fungus back to life. A plate of squid, their backs crisscrossed with knife markings so they resembled bicycle tires.

Reading Focus

Chronological Order Writers often use words such as *then* to indicate that events are taking place in chronological order.

And then they arrived—the minister's family and all my relatives in a clamor of doorbells and rumpled Christmas packages. Robert grunted hello, and I pretended he was not worthy of existence.

California Standards, pp. 504–506

- **Reading Standard 3.1** Articulate the expressed purposes and characteristics of different forms of prose (e.g., short story, novel, novella, essay).

Selection Readability	
Easy Accessible **Accessible** Challenging	familiar situation with family and friends; conversational dialogue; accessible theme

Selection Plot Summary

As a Chinese American teenager, Amy Tan wants to fit in with her American peers. When the family of an American boy she likes is invited to her house for dinner, she is embarrassed by her family's customs and food. Only years later does Amy realize that her heritage is an important part of who she is.

Analyzing Visuals

Connecting to the Text
Compare and contrast these foods to those Tan mentions. Which might you find on Tan's dinner menu?

Redfish Still Life (2002) by Diana Ong (1940–   ). Computer graphics.

Dinner threw me deeper into despair. My relatives licked the ends of their chopsticks and reached across the table, dipping them into the dozen or so plates of food. Robert and his family waited patiently for platters to be passed to them. My relatives murmured with pleasure when my mother brought out the whole steamed fish. Robert grimaced. Then my father poked his chopsticks just below the fish eye and plucked out the soft meat. "Amy, your favorite," he said, offering me the tender fish cheek. I wanted to disappear.

At the end of the meal my father leaned back and belched loudly, thanking my mother for her fine cooking. "It's a polite Chinese custom to show you are satisfied," explained my father to our astonished guests. Robert was looking down at his plate with a reddened face. The minister managed to muster up a quiet burp. I was stunned into silence for the rest of the night.

After everyone had gone, my mother said to me, "You want to be the same as American girls on the outside." She handed me an early gift. It was a miniskirt in beige tweed. "But inside

Reading Focus

Comparing and Contrasting
Tan contrasts Robert's family with her own. Notice how the two families act differently during the meal.

Literary Focus

Essay / Personal Narrative
Notice the comical details in this passage. Writers of personal essays often include elements of humor.

Model the Skill

▶ Reading Focus

Comparing and Contrasting How does Amy's family's behavior contrast with that of the minister's family? *Possible response: Amy's family members eagerly dig into all the food and take what they want; the minister's family waits patiently to be served.*

▶ Literary Focus

Essay/Personal Narrative Besides humor, what other elements of a personal narrative are evident in the text? *Possible response: The author tells a brief story about one topic: the Christmas Eve dinner. This is a common element of a personal narrative.*

Analyzing Visuals

Tell students that **Diana Ong** (1940–   ) specializes in abstract art, using bright colors and exaggerated shapes to portray real people and things. Her art includes both watercolor paintings and computer-designed graphics. *Connecting to the Text: There appear to be fish and shrimp in the picture, but also vegetables and possibly soup. The fish in particular would be found on a Tan menu.*

Universal Access

(EL) English Learners/ Struggling Readers

To help students understand the selection, introduce them to the following vocabulary words.

- **appalling**—very bad; awful; terrible. *Amy looked worriedly at the appalling pile of food.*

- **bulging**—sticking out. *The eyes were bulging from the head of the fish.*

- **clamor**—a loud noise. *Robert's family made a clamor when they arrived.*

- **astonished**—shocked or amazed. *The minister's family was astonished when Amy's father belched.*

Then, give students this statement that explains how the words relate to the meaning of the selection:
When she was fourteen, Amy Tan was embarrassed that her family's favorite foods looked appalling. Her American friend's family seemed astonished by traditional Chinese food, but they didn't make a clamor when Amy and her family ate a fish with bulging eyes.

Model the Skill

▶ **Reading Focus**

Setting a Purpose for Reading Has your purpose for reading the essay changed? If so, how? ***Possible response:*** *I started reading to find out what lesson Amy would learn. Now I also want to know whether Amy's opinion about her culture will change.*

Check for Understanding

Read with a Purpose Ask students to explain the meaning of Tan's mother's lesson. ***Possible response:*** *You should be proud of your culture.*

More About the Writer

Amy Tan's first novel, *The Joy Luck Club,* further explores mother–daughter relationships in Chinese American families. In 1993, the book was turned into a film, which Tan wrote, produced, and even appeared in briefly in an uncredited cameo.

Think About the Writer

Point out that Tan wrote for corporations under a pseudonym, but she wrote fiction under her own name. Ask students to list reasons why an author might not want his or her name to appear on a work.

 For Independent Reading

Students may enjoy reading Sherry Garland's *The Lotus Seed,* which explores how a Vietnamese American woman shares her heritage.

 California Standards, p. 507

- **Reading Standard 3.1** Articulate the expressed purposes and characteristics of different forms of prose (e.g., short story, novel, novella, essay).

Reading Model

Reading Focus

Setting a Purpose for Reading
By setting a purpose before you read, you know to look for the lesson Tan learns from her mother.

you must always be Chinese. You must be proud you are different. Your only shame is to have shame."

And even though I didn't agree with her then, I knew that she understood how much I had suffered during the evening's dinner. It wasn't until many years later—long after I had gotten over my crush on Robert—that I was able to fully appreciate her lesson and the true purpose behind our particular menu. For Christmas Eve that year, she had chosen all my favorite foods.

Read with a Purpose In your own words, explain the lesson Tan learns from her mother.

MEET THE WRITER

Amy Tan
(1952–   )

Accepting Who She Is

Amy Tan spent her childhood in Oakland, California, where her parents had settled after leaving China. "I was the only Chinese girl in class from third grade on. . . . When I was a teenager, I rejected everything Chinese."

When she was fifteen, her father and brother died from brain tumors. After these losses, Amy's mother revealed a secret: Amy had three half sisters still living in China. These upheavals changed her identity, and suddenly her Chinese heritage became important to her.

A Journey to Success

Tan's writing career began when she and a partner started a business. Later, under a pseudonym (a made-up name), she wrote booklets for corporations. Finally, she decided to write fiction under her own name. She became a success with the publication of her first novel, *The Joy Luck Club,* a national bestseller that was inspired by her mother. Tan now embraces the Chinese culture she once tried to reject.

Think About the Writer Why do you think Tan used a pseudonym, or pen name, when she started her career?

Resources

Chapter 5 Resources, Literary and Academic Vocabulary Skill Builder, p. 5

Differentiating Instruction, Academic and Selection Vocabulary Skill Builder, p. 148

Teacher One Stop™, on-level lesson plans and all print resources

WordSharp: An Interactive Vocabulary Tutor, more practice with academic language

Academic Vocabulary

Writing About Forms of Prose

Write the following questions on the board. Tell students these are the kinds of questions on standardized tests. Discuss the meaning of the words, then have students use "Fish Cheeks" to answer the questions.

- What **impact** does the Christmas dinner have on the teenaged Amy? Explain. ***Possible response:*** *It makes her realize years later that she is proud of her Chinese heritiage and should not worry what others may think.*

Reading Standard 3.1 Articulate the expressed purposes and characteristics of different forms of prose (e.g., short story, novel, novella, **essay**).

Into Action: Charting Sequence

Fill out the sequence chart below to organize the events in "Fish Cheeks." Add more boxes as needed.

The narrator falls in love with Robert. → Event 1 → [etc.] → The narrator realizes her mother made all of her favorite foods.

Talk About . . .

1. How do you think Robert and his family reacted to Christmas Eve dinner at the Tans' house? With a partner, discuss your ideas. Use details from the essay to support your response. Try to use each Academic Vocabulary word listed on the right at least once in your discussion.

Write About . . .

Answer the following questions about "Fish Cheeks." For definitions of the underlined Academic Vocabulary words, see the column on the right.

2. What insight into the meaning of the essay does the essay's title give you? What might the fish cheeks symbolize?

3. What impact did Tan's use of humor have on you? How did you react to the descriptions of her embarrassing moments? Explain.

4. Amy's mother tells her that Amy can be an American girl on the outside but must always be Chinese on the inside. Do you think this is possible? Is it a good idea? Articulate your opinion.

Writing Skills Focus
Think as a Reader/Writer

The Writing Skills Focus activities on the Preparing to Read pages in the first part of this chapter will help you analyze techniques writers use when creating prose. On the Applying Your Skills pages, you will have the opportunity to practice using those techniques in your own writing.

Academic Vocabulary for Chapter 5

Talking and Writing About Forms of Prose

Academic Vocabulary is the language you use to write and talk about literature. Use these words to discuss the prose you read in this chapter. The words are underlined throughout the chapter.

articulate (ahr TIHK yuh layt) *v.*: express clearly and specifically. *Tan articulates the uncomfortable, embarrassing feelings she experienced during the Christmas Eve dinner.*

characteristics (kar ihk tuh RIHS tihks) *n. pl.*: distinguishing qualities or features. *Characteristics of Tan's story include humorous descriptions and a clear, honest tone in her narration.*

impact (IHM pakt) *n.*: powerful effect. *Tan's vivid images have a strong impact on readers.*

insight (IHN syt) *n.*: power to understand. *Tan gives readers insight into the experience of adjusting to the customs of two cultures.*

Your Turn

Copy the Academic Vocabulary words into your *Reader/Writer Notebook*. Then, use each word in a sentence about "Fish Cheeks." Practice using these Academic Vocabulary words as you talk and write about the prose selections in this chapter.

Guided Practice: Apply

Into Action: Charting Sequence

Point out clue words from the essay such as *then* and *later* to help students place events in order.

Talk About...

1. Model for students how to incorporate academic vocabulary words into a conversation. For example, you might say, "Tan's description of Robert's family's awkward behavior gives us insight into their feelings about the party."

Write About...
Possible responses:

2. *The title is significant because fish cheeks are the author's favorite food, although they embarrass her at the party.*

3. *The humor had an impact on me because it let me know that it was okay to laugh at the embarrassing events.*

4. *I agree that it's possible to act American but still have Chinese values. People should be proud of their backgrounds and of the places in which they live currently.*

Writing Skills Focus

The Think as a Reader/Writer activities in the collection focus on the reading-writing relationship. Use the activities to help students explore the writer's craft in a text and to practice this aspect of craft in their own writing.

Independent Practice

Chapter 5 Resources, Skill Builders, pp. 3–5

Differentiating Instruction, Academic and Selection Vocabulary Skill Builder, p. 148

• Which detail or sentence from the story gave you the most **insight** into Amy's mother's lesson? Why? ***Possible response:*** *The most important part of the lesson was the comment that "your only shame is to have shame." This shows that people are too worried about what others may think. Amy's shame was of her own making because there was no good reason to be ashamed of her heritage.*

• How does Amy's mother **articulate** her understanding of Amy's embarrassment during the dinner? ***Possible response:*** *She articulates her understanding by giving Amy a gift reflective of her American identity, but emphasizes that she should not be ashamed of her Chinese heritage.*

• What **characteristics** does Amy assign to her Chinese relatives? ***Possible response:*** *She presents them as loud, shabby, and ill-mannered.*

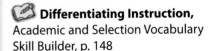

Standards Focus

Objectives

Students will

• learn the characteristics of short stories

• understand characters' internal and external conflicts

• compare and contrast characters

Motivate

What Do You Think?/QuickWrite

Have students reflect on how friends should behave in a contest. Then, have them use their **Reader/Writer Notebook** to write about what might happen if contest rules are not followed.

English for Academic Success

Academic Vocabulary

Look for opportunities to use the Academic Vocabulary words in this chapter.

• **articulate, v.:** express clearly and specifically

• **characteristics, n. pl.:** distinguishing qualities or features.

• **impact, n.:** powerful effect

• **insight, n.:** power to understand

Analyzing Visuals

Extension Activity Have students compare and contrast the boys in the image. **Possible response:** One looks younger than the other, but both look athletic and friendly.

AMIGO BROTHERS

by **Piri Thomas**

What Do You Think How reliable are friendships when competition is involved?

QuickWrite
What advice would you give two friends competing against each other? Create a list titled "Rules for Competing Against a Friend."

California Standards, pp. 508–523

■ **Reading Standard 1.3** Clarify word meanings through the use of definition, example, restatement, or contrast.

■ **Reading Standard 3.1** Articulate the expressed purposes and characteristics of different forms of prose (e.g., short story, novel, novella, essay).

Selection Readability	
Easily Accessible **Accessible** Challenging	familiar situations; accessible dialogue; some unfamiliar terminology

Selection Plot Summary

Antonio Cruz and Felix Vargas dream of becoming boxing champions. When they must fight against each other in the championship match, they worry that it may ruin their friendship. In the end, they promise to remain "amigo brothers" no matter what happens.

Reader/Writer Notebook

Use your **RWN** to complete the activities for this selection.

 Reading Standard 3.1 Articulate the expressed purposes and characteristics of different forms of prose (e.g., short story, novel, novella, essay).

Literary Skills Focus

Forms of Prose: Short Story A short work of fiction, usually around five to twenty pages, is called a **short story.** (Sometimes a story that's even shorter is called a **short-short story.**) Short stories accomplish a great deal in only a few pages. We meet the **main characters,** get involved in their **conflicts** or **problems,** sort out the **complications,** and move speedily to a **climax** and a **resolution.** A good short story can convey an important message in a brief format.

In "Amigo Brothers" two best friends struggle with the **external conflict** of competing against each other in a boxing match. Each boy also struggles with an **internal conflict:** How can he do his best without hurting and possibly even losing his closest friend?

Reading Skills Focus

Comparing and Contrasting Piri Thomas contrasts two best friends: "Antonio was fair, lean, and lanky, while Felix was dark, short, and husky." A **comparison** points out similar characteristics between things; a **contrast** points out differences. After you read the story, review it and use a Venn diagram like the one below to help identify ways in which Felix and Antonio are alike and different. Write their similarities in the space where the circles overlap.

Writing Skills Focus

Think as a Reader/Writer

Find It in Your Reading An important characteristic of prose writing is the use of **vivid verbs**—colorful, precise verbs that help you picture actions clearly. Here are a few of the vivid verbs that Piri Thomas uses in "Amigo Brothers" to help readers visualize the story's action: *blasting, blared,* and *roaring.* Make a list of other vivid verbs you notice as you read.

Vocabulary

bouts (bowts) *n.:* matches; contests. *Both boxers had won many bouts.*

pensively (PEHN sihv lee) *adv.:* thoughtfully. *Felix nodded pensively as he rested.*

torrent (TAWR uhnt) *n.:* flood; rush. *A torrent of emotion left him close to tears.*

dispelled (dihs PEHLD) *v.:* driven away. *All doubt was dispelled the moment Tony made up his mind.*

frenzied (FREHN zeed) *adj.:* wild; out of control. *The audience's reaction was as frenzied as the battle in the ring.*

Language Coach

Suffixes Many English words are made up of various word parts. For example, a **suffix** is one or more letters or syllables added to the end of a word or word part to create a new word. Adding a suffix to a word also changes its part of speech. *Pensive* is an adjective that means "thoughtful." The suffix *–ly* means "in a certain way." How does adding *–ly* to *pensive* change its meaning? What part of speech is *pensively*?

 Learn It Online
To preview this story, watch the video introduction at:

go.hrw.com H7-509 **Go**

Selection Resources

Chapter 5 Resources, on-level practice and assessment, p. 6

PowerNotes, interactive lesson presentation with activities

Teacher One Stop™, on-level lesson plans and all print resources

Holt Audio Library

Holt Audio Library: Selections and Summaries in Spanish

UA: Holt Interactive Reader, p. 124

Holt Interactive Reader for ELD, p. 152

Holt Audio Tutor for ELD

UA: Differentiating Instruction, modified lesson plans and leveled assessment, p. 122

UA: Resources for Teaching Advanced Students, lesson plans

UA: Supporting Instruction in Five Languages, selection summary

ThinkCentral Online Assessment, Selection Standards Check

ThinkCentral Online Remediation

Preteach

Introducing Vocabulary
Review the Vocabulary words with students. Then, check students' understanding by having them replace the underlined words in these sentences with Vocabulary words.

1. A <u>rush</u> of rain caused the river to flood. [*torrent*]

2. Of all the boxing <u>fights</u> I've seen, this is the best. [*bouts*]

3. I was worried about the exam, but my fears were <u>erased</u>. [*dispelled*]

4. I work <u>thoughtfully</u>, but my dad is more <u>uncontrolled</u>. [*pensively, frenzied*]

English for Academic Success

Language Coach
Explain that the suffix *–ly* often changes adjectives into adverbs. The adjective *pensive* becomes the adverb *pensively.*

Literary Skills Focus
As you read and discuss the selection with students, have them create a diagram tracking the story's conflicts, climax, and resolution.

Reading Skills Focus
Give students a copy of the Reading Skills Focus graphic organizer before they read. (See **Chapter 5 Resources.**) Tell them to use their responses to answer the questions on the Applying Your Skills page.

Writing Skills Focus
Have students record vivid verbs in their **Reader/Writer Notebook.** Students can use their notes to complete the Writing Skills Focus activity.

 Learn It Online
The **PowerNotes** presentation for this lesson includes a short video that introduces the selection. This video is also available on the online version of this page.

go.hrw.com H7-509 **Go**

Selection Introduction

More About the Writer

Piri Thomas has written about the impact of reading on his life. Books, he says, opened his mind to the world beyond the *barrio* in which he lived. He learned of different places, ideas, and people, particularly those who judged others on who they were, not what they looked like.

Think About the Writer

Suggest that students brainstorm a list of words that describe their community. Possible words may include *determination, ambition, courage, supportive,* or *diverse.*

For Independent Reading

- If students are interested in characters who struggle with issues similar to those that Felix and Antonio face, they may want to read *Baseball in April and Other Stories* by Gary Soto. This collection of short stories focuses on Latino characters who face universal challenges.

- Students who want to read about another character who seeks a better life through a sports contest might enjoy Dan Gutman's *The Million Dollar Shot.*

Piri Thomas
(1928–   )

A Survivor from the Mean Streets

Like Antonio and Felix in "Amigo Brothers," Piri Thomas grew up in a rough neighborhood in New York City. Unfortunately, he wasn't as lucky as Antonio and Felix—he didn't have a sport like boxing to help him escape the lures of drugs and crime. As a result, Thomas spent time in prison.

Rising Above

While in prison, Thomas discovered that he could write, and after his release, he published an autobiography called *Down These Mean Streets* (1967). Thomas has worked for many years to help drug addicts give up their addictions and start new lives. He says of the kind of Hispanic neighborhood in which he grew up:

> "I believe love is the barrio's greatest strength. The proof is on the faces of the children who, against heavy odds, can still smile with amazing grace as they struggle to survive and rise above the mean streets."

Think About the Writer Thomas feels strongly about the community in which he was raised. What makes your community strong?

Build Background

Boxing matches consist of three-minute rounds. Fighters are given one minute to rest between rounds. If a fighter is knocked down, he or she is given ten seconds to get up and continue fighting. If the fighter cannot get up, he or she is considered knocked out, or down for the count. If neither fighter gets knocked out after fighting a specified number of rounds, judges determine the winner.

Preview the Selection

This story is about two friends (*amigos* in Spanish), **Antonio** and **Felix,** living on the Lower East Side of New York City. Like many boys from the Lower East Side, Antonio and Felix dream of building a better life by winning the New York Golden Gloves, a tournament started in 1927 by Paul Gallico, a newspaper writer. This tournament marks an amateur's entry into the world of big-time boxing.

Real Issues, Real Experts

*Holt author **Kylene Beers** offers strategies for helping students compare and contrast information.*

While a Venn Diagram helps students organize information to note comparisons and contrasts, I find another organizational tool also helpful: an ABC chart. Students copy a chart like this one on their own paper. If using this with "Amigo Brothers," then at the top students would write "Antonio" in black ink and "Felix" in blue ink. As they find information about both, they put that information in the specified box. So, if readers decide both characters are courageous, then in the C box, (c for courageous), they would write "courageous" in one color ink and then circle it in the other color to indicate this trait belongs to both characters. After adding as many traits as possible, they then discuss how these two characters are similar and different.

Read with a Purpose Read this selection to see how good friends deal with a conflict that threatens to hurt their relationship.

AMIGO BROTHERS

by **Piri Thomas**

Antonio Cruz and Felix Vargas were both seventeen years old. They were so together in friendship that they felt themselves to be brothers. They had known each other since childhood, growing up on the Lower East Side of Manhattan in the same tenement[1] building on Fifth Street between Avenue A and Avenue B.

Antonio was fair, lean, and lanky, while Felix was dark, short, and husky. Antonio's hair was always falling over his eyes, while Felix wore his black hair in a natural Afro style.

Each youngster had a dream of someday becoming lightweight champion of the world. Every chance they had, the boys worked out, sometimes at the Boys' Club on 10th Street and Avenue A and sometimes at the pro's gym on 14th Street. Early morning sunrises would find them running along the East River Drive, wrapped in sweat shirts, short towels around their necks, and handkerchiefs Apache style around their foreheads.

While some youngsters were into street negatives, Antonio and Felix slept, ate, rapped, and dreamt positive. Between them, they had a collection of *Fight* magazines second to none, plus a scrapbook filled with torn tickets to every boxing match they had ever attended, and some clippings of their own. If asked a question about any given fighter, they would immediately zip out from their memory banks divisions, weights, records of fights, knockouts, technical knockouts, and draws or losses. **Ⓐ**

Each had fought many bouts representing their community and had won two gold-plated medals plus a silver and bronze medallion. The difference was in their style. Antonio's lean form and long reach made him the better boxer, while Felix's short and muscular frame made him the better slugger. Whenever they had met in the ring for sparring sessions,[2] it had always been hot and heavy. **Ⓑ**

---

1. **tenement:** apartment. Tenement buildings are often cheaply built and poorly maintained.

2. **sparring sessions:** practice matches in which boxers use light punches.

Ⓐ Reading Focus Compare and Contrast How are the boys both similar and different? Identify their <u>characteristics</u>.

Ⓑ Literary Focus Short Story What basic situation is presented in these paragraphs? What is the central conflict?

Vocabulary **bouts** (bowts) *n.:* matches; contests.

■Antonio ■Felix

A	B	C	D	E	F	G	H	I
	better boxer	com- petiteve	dark		fair- skinned	good sportsman	husky hard- working	
J	K	L	M	N	O	P	Q	R
		lean lanky				positive		
S	T	U	V	W	X	Y	Z	
seventeen short slugger								

Model the Skill

■ Tell students that most short stories are driven by **conflict**, or the struggles of characters to get what they want. The story's plot is based around characters' efforts to overcome obstacles that stand between them and what they want. A character may be in conflict with another person, situation, or force of nature; he may also face an inner conflict of emotional challenges standing in the way of his wants.

■ Read aloud the first two paragraphs of p. 512. Tell students that these two paragraphs set up conflicts for the characters in this story.

■ Point out that Felix and Antonio are best friends who are as close as brothers and who love boxing. Now, they find out that they will have to face each other in a boxing match. The conflict between the two boys is literally a conflict: They will have to physically fight each other.

■ Point out the phrase, "a wall rising between them." Ask students to read the remainder of p. 512 and see if they can pinpoint the cause of Felix and Antonio's "wall." Students should recognize based on the second column that the boys are worried about hurting each other and their friendship.

Guided Practice: Apply

Turn-and-Talk Have students continue reading pp. 513 and 514, asking them to pay close attention to how the conflict between the boys and within each boy's mind affects the action of the story. When they finish reading the two pages, have them discuss the developments in the conflict that they identified.

Now, after a series of elimination bouts, they had been informed that they were to meet each other in the division finals that were scheduled for the seventh of August, two weeks away—the winner to represent the Boys' Club in the Golden Gloves Championship Tournament.

The two boys continued to run together along the East River Drive. But even when joking with each other, they both sensed a wall rising between them.

One morning less than a week before their bout, they met as usual for their daily workout. They fooled around with a few jabs at the air, slapped skin, and then took off, running lightly along the dirty East River's edge.

Antonio glanced at Felix, who kept his eyes purposely straight ahead, pausing from time to time to do some fancy leg work while throwing one-twos followed by uppercuts to an imaginary jaw. Antonio then beat the air with a barrage of body blows and short devastating lefts with an overhead jaw-breaking right.

After a mile or so, Felix puffed and said, "Let's stop a while, bro. I think we both got something to say to each other."

Antonio nodded. It was not natural to be acting as though nothing unusual was happening when two ace-boon buddies were going to be blasting each other within a few short days.

They rested their elbows on the railing separating them from the river. Antonio

© Read and Discuss Knowing what you do about Felix and Antonio, how do you think they might feel about having the opportunity to fight in the Golden Gloves Championship Tournament?

wiped his face with his short towel. The sunrise was now creating day.

Felix leaned heavily on the river's railing and stared across to the shores of Brooklyn. Finally, he broke the silence.

"Man. I don't know how to come out with it."

Antonio helped. "It's about our fight, right?"

"Yeah, right." Felix's eyes squinted at the rising orange sun.

"I've been thinking about it too, panin.[3] In fact, since we found out it was going to be me and you, I've been awake at night, pulling punches on you, trying not to hurt you."

"Same here. It ain't natural not to think about the fight. I mean, we both are cheverote[4] fighters and we both want to win. But only one of us can win. There ain't no draws in the eliminations." **©**

Felix tapped Antonio gently on the shoulder. "I don't mean to sound like I'm bragging, bro. But I wanna win, fair and square."

Antonio nodded quietly. "Yeah. We both know that in the ring the better man wins. Friend or no friend, brother or no . . ."

Felix finished it for him. "Brother. Tony, let's promise something right here. OK?"

"If it's fair, hermano,[5] I'm for it." Antonio admired the courage of a tugboat pulling

3. **panin** (pah NEEN): Puerto Rican Spanish slang for "pal" or "buddy."
4. **cheverote** (cheh vuh ROH tay): Puerto Rican Spanish slang for "the greatest."
5. **hermano** (ehr MAH noh): Spanish for "brother."

© Literary Focus Short Story Articulate the inner conflict with which each boy will struggle.

Universal Access

EL English Learners

Help English learners understand internal and external conflict by reviewing key terms.

• Provide English learners with student-friendly definitions of *conflict*, *internal*, and *external*.

• Then, explain how the using the words *internal* and *conflict* together describes a struggle someone has within his or her own mind. Someone who has to make an important decision or face a fear is dealing with an internal conflict.

• Repeat the exercise with the words *external* and *conflict*, noting that an external conflict is a struggle that a person has with another person or force. Fighting with a friend or surviving a dangerous storm are both examples of external conflicts.

✔ See **UA: Differentiating Instruction** for lesson plans and strategies for teaching English learners.

Right Hook—Left Hook: The Boxing Controversy

Doctors have expressed deep concern about boxing injuries such as those received by the former heavyweight champion Muhammad Ali. Ali suffers from Parkinson's disease, an illness probably caused by the hits he took in the ring. The symptoms of Parkinson's disease range from unclear speech to difficulty walking. In 1984, the American Medical Association (AMA) supported a complete ban on boxing.

The sport remains popular, however. Supporters believe that training young people to box teaches them self-control. Supporters also point out the benefits of fighting according to a set of rules. Some doctors disagree with the AMA's position and believe boxing produces few injuries because all the major muscle groups are used.

Ask Yourself
Where do you stand on this issue?

---

a barge five times its welterweight size.

"It's fair, Tony. When we get into the ring, it's gotta be like we never met. We gotta be like two heavy strangers that want the same thing and only one can have it. You understand, don't cha?"

"Sí, I know." Tony smiled. "No pulling punches. We go all the way."

"Yeah, that's right. Listen, Tony. Don't you think it's a good idea if we don't see each other until the day of the fight? I'm going to stay with my Aunt Lucy in the Bronx. I can use Gleason's Gym for working out. My manager says he got some sparring partners with more or less your style."

Tony scratched his nose pensively. "Yeah, it would be better for our heads." He held out his hand, palm upward. "Deal?"

"Deal." Felix lightly slapped open skin. **E**

E Read and Discuss What is happening between the boys now?

"Ready for some more running?" Tony asked lamely.

"Naw, bro. Let's cut it here. You go on. I kinda like to get things together in my head."

"You ain't worried, are you?" Tony asked.

"No way, man." Felix laughed out loud. "I got too much smarts for that. I just think it's cooler if we split right here. After the fight, we can get it together again like nothing ever happened."

The amigo brothers were not ashamed to hug each other tightly.

"Guess you're right. Watch yourself, Felix. I hear there's some pretty heavy dudes up in the Bronx. Suavecito,[6] OK?"

"OK. You watch yourself too, sabe?"[7]

---

6. **suavecito** (swah vay SEE toh): Puerto Rican Spanish slang for "cool."

7. **sabe** (SAH bay): Spanish for "you know."

Vocabulary **pensively** (PEHN sihv lee) *adv.*: thoughtfully.

Struggling Readers
Help students identify the competing forces that create the boys' internal conflicts on these pages. Explain that both Felix and Antonio want two things. Draw students' attention to the phrases "trying not to hurt you" and "we both want to win" on p. 512. Then, ask students what clues these phrases give about the two competing desires that each boy faces. [*They want to win the match, but they also want to remain friends.*]

✔ See **UA: Differentiating Instruction** for lesson plans and strategies for teaching struggling readers.

Health Link
Ask Yourself _____
Possible response: *I think that proper rules must be followed to ensure that boxing is safe. That way, people can enjoy participating in or watching the sport, but fewer people will suffer serious injuries as a result.*

Think About/Talk About

▶ Comprehension
C Read and Discuss
Possible response: *They must be thrilled to have the opportunity to fight in the match, but because they're best friends, they must feel worried about fighting each other.*

E Read and Discuss
Possible response: *They've decided that they won't see each other until the day of the fight so that their friendship won't distract them from their training.*

▶ Analysis
D Literary Focus
Possible response: *They're afraid of hurting each other in the match, physically and emotionally. At the same time, they both want to win.*

▶ Extend the Discussion
Making Predictions At the end of the first column on p. 513, Felix and Antonio seemingly resolve their conflict. Based on what you know about the structure of a short story, do you think this resolution is permanent or temporary? Explain. ***Possible response:*** *I think this is only a temporary resolution. The boys haven't sorted out any major complications, and there hasn't been a climactic moment yet. A true resolution will come after the story's climax.*

Vocabulary: Own the Word
pensively: Demonstrate looking *pensively* at students. Ask one or two students to stand at their desks and demonstrate.

Model the Skill

- Provide students with copies of the Venn diagram for "Amigo Brothers." (See **Chapter 5 Resources**.)

- Tell students that **comparing** involves thinking about what two or more objects, people, or ideas have in common. **Contrasting** is thinking about how the same objects, people, or ideas are different. In a short story, you can compare and contrast characters by how they look, think, and act.

- Model comparing and contrasting Felix and Antonio's methods of preparing for the fight, using the Venn diagram. Point out that on pp. 514–515, Felix and Antonio prepare for the big fight in different ways. Although they do different things, preparing for the fight is common to both of them. Note that in the overlapped area as a similarity.

Guided Practice: Apply

Felix   Antonio

preparing for the big fight

Have students review pp. 514–515 independently and fill in the diagram with differences in the boys' preparations.

Think as a Reader/Writer

Find It in Your Reading Tell students that the author uses vivid verbs to help the reader visualize the action. At the top of p. 515, he describes Antonio as "bobbing and weaving like mercury."

Use It in Your Writing Have students write two sentences using vivid verbs to describe something they have done recently.

Tony jogged away. Felix watched his friend disappear from view, throwing rights and lefts. Both fighters had a lot of psyching up to do before the big fight. **F**

The days in training passed much too slowly. Although they kept out of each other's way, they were aware of each other's progress via the ghetto grapevine.

The evening before the big fight, Tony made his way to the roof of his tenement. In the quiet early dark, he peered over the ledge. Six stories below, the lights of the city blinked and the sounds of cars mingled with the curses and the laughter of children in the street. He tried not to think of Felix, feeling he had succeeded in psyching his mind. But only in the ring would he really know. To spare Felix hurt, he would have to knock him out, early and quick.

Up in the South Bronx, Felix decided to take in a movie in an effort to keep Antonio's face away from his fists. The flick was *The Champion* with Kirk Douglas, the third time Felix was seeing it.

The champion was getting beaten, his face being pounded into raw, wet hamburger. His eyes were cut, jagged, bleeding, one eye swollen, the other almost shut. He was saved only by the sound of the bell.

Felix became the champ and Tony the challenger.

The movie audience was going out of its head, roaring in blood lust at the butchery going on. The champ hunched his shoulders, grunting and sniffing red blood back into his broken nose. The challenger, confident that he had the championship in the bag, threw a left. The champ countered with a dynamite right that exploded into the challenger's brains.

Felix's right arm felt the shock. Antonio's face, superimposed on the screen, was shattered and split apart by the awesome force of the killer blow. Felix saw himself in the ring, blasting Antonio against the ropes. The champ had to be forcibly restrained. The challenger was allowed to crumble slowly to the canvas, a broken bloody mess.

When Felix finally left the theater, he had figured out how to psych himself for tomorrow's fight. It was Felix the Champion vs. Antonio the Challenger. **G**

He walked up some dark streets, deserted except for small pockets of wary-looking kids wearing gang colors. Despite the fact that he was Puerto Rican like them, they eyed him as a stranger to their turf. Felix did a fast shuffle, bobbing and weaving, while letting loose a torrent of blows that would demolish whatever got in its way. It seemed to impress the brothers, who went about their own business.

Finding no takers, Felix decided to split to his aunt's. Walking the streets had not relaxed him; neither had the fight flick. All it had done was to stir him up. He let himself quietly into his Aunt Lucy's apartment and went straight to bed, falling into a fitful sleep with sounds of the gong for Round One.

Antonio was passing some heavy time on his rooftop. How would the fight

F **Read and Discuss** How does the boys' decision to train separately add to what you know about Antonio and Felix?

G **Literary Focus** **Short Story** What does this scene in the movie theater contribute to the story's plot?

Vocabulary **torrent** (TAWR uhnt) *n.*: flood; rush.

Universal Access

Advanced Learners

Extension Have students use details from the story to make a prediction about what the story's resolution will entail. Tell students that the resolution they describe should explain the outcome of the match and discuss how it will impact the boys' friendship. Remind students to support their resolution predictions with elements from the text. Have students form small discussion groups to share their predictions, or have students post and respond to predictions on a class blog or Web site.

✔ See **UA: Resources for Teaching Advanced Learners** for lesson plans and strategies for teaching advanced learners.

Students with Disabilities

Read the selection with students, pausing to review difficult words or Spanish vocabulary defined at the bottom of the page.

✔ See **UA: Differentiating Instruction** for lesson plans and strategies for teaching students with disabilities.

tomorrow affect his relationship with Felix? After all, fighting was like any other profession. Friendship had nothing to do with it. A gnawing doubt crept in. He cut negative thinking real quick by doing some speedy fancy dance steps, bobbing and weaving like mercury. The night air was blurred with perpetual motions of left hooks and right crosses. Felix, his amigo brother, was not going to be Felix at all in the ring. Just an opponent with another face. Antonio went to sleep, hearing the opening bell for the first round. Like his friend in the South Bronx, he prayed for victory via a quick clean knockout in the first round. **(H)**

> Antonio went to sleep, hearing the opening bell for the first round.

Large posters plastered all over the walls of local shops announced the fight between Antonio Cruz and Felix Vargas as the main bout.

The fight had created great interest in the neighborhood. Antonio and Felix were well liked and respected. Each had his own loyal following. Betting fever was high and ranged from a bottle of Coke to cold hard cash on the line.

Antonio's fans bet with unbridled faith in his boxing skills. On the other side, Felix's admirers bet on his dynamite-packed fists. **(I)**

Felix had returned to his apartment early in the morning of August 7th and stayed there, hoping to avoid seeing Antonio. He turned the radio on to salsa[8] music sounds and then tried to read while waiting for word from his manager. **(J)**

The fight was scheduled to take place in Tompkins Square Park. It had been decided that the gymnasium of the Boys' Club was not large enough to hold all the people who were sure to attend. In Tompkins Square Park, everyone who wanted could view the fight, whether from ringside or window fire escapes or tenement rooftops. The morning of the fight Tompkins Square was a beehive of activity with numerous workers setting up the ring, the seats, and the guest speakers' stand. The scheduled bouts began shortly after noon and the park had begun filling up even earlier.

The local junior high school across from Tompkins Square Park served as the dressing room for all the fighters. Each was given a separate classroom with desk tops, covered with mats, serving as resting tables. Antonio thought he caught a glimpse of Felix waving to him from a room at the far end of the corridor. He waved back just in case it had been him.

The fighters changed from their street clothes into fighting gear. Antonio wore white trunks, black socks, and black shoes.

---

8. **salsa** (SAHL sah): Latin American dance music, usually played at a fast tempo.

(H) | Read and Discuss | What is going on with the boys now?

(I) | Reading Focus | Compare and Contrast | Identify the phrase that signals the use of contrast in this paragraph.

(J) | Literary Focus | Short Story | Has Felix completely resolved the conflict he feels about fighting Antonio? How do you know?

Model the Skill

■ Tell students that all readers come across words they do not know when they are reading. Looking up the words in a dictionary is one way to find out what they mean, but other words or phrases right in the text may help readers figure out what the unfamiliar words mean. These are called **context clues**.

■ Point out the word *improvised* in the first full paragraph on p. 516. Copy onto the board the sentence, "Some were well prepared, some improvised on the spot," underlining the word *improvised*. Ask students to note the words that are closest to *improvised*, such as *prepared* and *on the spot*. Point out that *prepared* means "ready;" *on the spot* means "made up right there." Tell students that if we contract these context clues, we come up with *made up on the spot with no preparation*.

Guided Practice: Apply

Have students work in groups of three to identify context clues for *interwoven* on p. 516 and *bilingual* on p. 517. Have each group share their context clues and process of putting the clues together with the class.

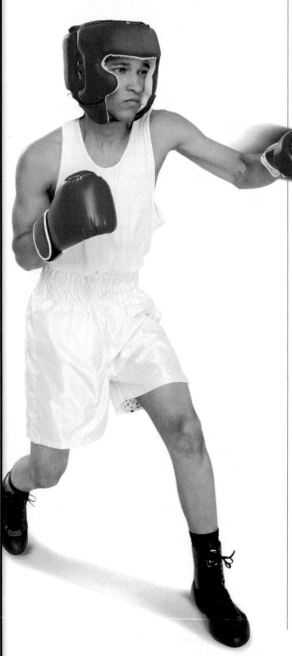

Felix wore sky-blue trunks, red socks, and white boxing shoes. They had dressing gowns to match their fighting trunks with their names neatly stitched on the back.

The loudspeakers blared into the open windows of the school. There were speeches by dignitaries, community leaders, and great boxers of yesteryear. Some were well prepared; some improvised on the spot. They all carried the same message of great pleasure and honor at being part of such a historic event. This great day was in the tradition of champions emerging from the streets of the Lower East Side.

Interwoven with the speeches were the sounds of the other boxing events. After the sixth bout, Felix was much relieved when his trainer, Charlie, said, "Time change. Quick knockout. This is it. We're on."

Waiting time was over. Felix was escorted from the classroom by a dozen fans in white T-shirts with the word "Felix" across their fronts.

Antonio was escorted down a different stairwell and guided through a roped-off path.

As the two climbed into the ring, the crowd exploded with a roar. Antonio and Felix both bowed gracefully and then raised their arms in acknowledgment.

Antonio tried to be cool, but even as the roar was in its first birth, he turned slowly to meet Felix's eyes looking directly into his. Felix nodded his head and Antonio responded. And both as one, just as quickly, turned away to face his own corner.

K **Read and Discuss** What picture is the author painting for you in this paragraph?

Universal Access

EL English Learners

Students may have difficulty understanding some of the boxing terminology used in the story. Provide a glossary to which students can refer as they read the selection.

- **bob and weave**—to move up and down and to the side to avoid being hit
- **cross**—a type of punch that starts from the side and crosses the boxer's body
- **hook**—a punch from the side
- **knockout**—when a boxer knocks the opponent to the ground for 10 seconds; this results in a victory
- **sparring**—practice boxing in which the boxers do not try to hit each other very hard or try to win
- **uppercuts**—punches aimed at the jaw from below

Struggling Readers

Explain that the author helps us understand the external conflict facing Antonio and Felix. Point out the announcer's words on p. 517: "The winner will represent the Boys' Club in the tournament of champions, the Golden Gloves. There will be no draw. May the best man

Bong—bong—bong. The roar turned to stillness.

"Ladies and Gentlemen, Señores y Señoras."

The announcer spoke slowly, pleased at his bilingual efforts.

"Now the moment we have all been waiting for—the main event between two fine young Puerto Rican fighters, products of our Lower East Side."

"Loisaida,"[9] called out a member of the audience.

"In this corner, weighing 134 pounds, Felix Vargas. And in this corner, weighing 133 pounds, Antonio Cruz. The winner will represent the Boys' Club in the tournament of champions, the Golden Gloves. There will be no draw. May the best man win."

The cheering of the crowd shook the window panes of the old buildings surrounding Tompkins Square Park. At the center of the ring, the referee was giving instructions to the youngsters.

"Keep your punches up. No low blows. No punching on the back of the head. Keep your heads up. Understand? Let's have a clean fight. Now shake hands and come out fighting."

Both youngsters touched gloves and nodded. They turned and danced quickly to their corners. Their head towels and dressing gowns were lifted neatly from their shoulders by their trainers' nimble fingers. Antonio crossed himself. Felix did the same.

BONG! BONG! ROUND ONE. Felix and Antonio turned and faced each other

---

9. **Loisaida** (loy SY dah): Puerto Rican English dialect for "Lower East Side."

Analyzing Visuals

Connecting to the Text
How do the photos of these two boys help you connect to the characters?

win." This shows that one of the boys will have to beat his friend in order to advance his dreams.

Students Who Use African American Vernacular English

English for Academic Success Point out the phrase "He turned slowly to meet Felix's eyes" in the last paragraph of p. 516. Have students repeat the phrase. Tell students that adding an apostrophe and *s* to a person's name indicates possession. The eyes belong to Felix; they are Felix's eyes. Practice this rule with students.

Analyzing Visuals
Connecting to the Text: The photos help me to visualize the characters, and they make the characters seem more "real" and relatable.

Think About/Talk About

▶ **Comprehension**

Ⓚ Read and Discuss
Possible response: There's a festive atmosphere. Everyone's picking sides, helping set up. Even important people are at the fight, giving speeches and watching fights.

▶ **Extend the Discussion**

Conflict The last full paragraph on p. 517 describes the boys' behavior as they meet each other in the boxing ring. What is happening with the characters' internal and external conflicts at this point? **Possible response:** The external conflict has reached its peak because the boys are fighting each other now. The characters' internal conflicts seem to be resolved because they are acting like opponents rather than friends.

Forms of Prose Read the first three full paragraphs on p. 516. How might this descriptive passage be different if this story were told in a different form, such as a novel? **Possible response:** In a novel, this passage might be much longer. Instead of giving a brief description of the speeches, a novel might include thematically important excerpts from a few of the speeches. It might also include subplots or descriptions of what minor characters are doing during this time.

Model the Skill

- Review with students the parts of a **short story** listed on p. 509: **conflict, climax,** and **resolution.** Explain that in a short story, conflicts have to be resolved in a relatively short space. Before the resolution, though, comes the story's climax, the point in the story in which the conflicts are faced and the results decided.

- Remind students that there are two major conflicts in this story—that of the boys facing each other in a physical boxing match, and that of the boys feeling uncomfortable about competing against each other while still wanting to win. Point out that the boxing match has gone through two rounds and neither boy has clearly won. Predict that finding out who wins the match will be the climax in which the conflict between the boys will be decided.

Guided Practice: Apply

Have students continue reading the story and raise their hands when they think they have identified the climax—the exact moment when the results of each conflict become clear—and the resolution, which ties up loose ends. When all students have identified what they think are the climax and resolution, have volunteers share their ideas and discuss them as a group.

---

squarely in a fighting pose. Felix wasted no time. He came in fast, head low, half-hunched toward his right shoulder, and lashed out with a straight left. He missed a right cross as Antonio slipped the punch and countered with one-two-three lefts that snapped Felix's head back, sending a mild shock coursing through him. If Felix had any small doubt about their friendship affecting their fight, it was being neatly dispelled. **L**

Antonio danced, a joy to behold. His left hand was like a piston pumping jabs one right after another with seeming ease. Felix bobbed and weaved and never stopped boring in. He knew that at long range he was at a disadvantage. Antonio had too much reach on him. Only by coming in close could Felix hope to achieve the dreamed-of knockout.

Antonio knew the dynamite that was stored in his amigo brother's fist. He ducked a short right and missed a left hook. Felix trapped him against the ropes just long enough to pour some punishing rights and lefts to Antonio's hard midsection. Antonio slipped away from Felix, crashing two lefts to his head, which set Felix's right ear to ringing.

Bong! Both amigos froze a punch well on its way, sending up a roar of approval for good sportsmanship.

Felix walked briskly back to his corner. His right ear had not stopped ringing. Antonio gracefully danced his way toward his stool none the worse, except for glowing glove burns showing angry red against the whiteness of his midribs.

L **Literary Focus** Short Story How has the conflict between the two friends changed? What <u>impact</u> does this have on the story?

"Watch that right, Tony." His trainer talked into his ear. "Remember Felix always goes to the body. He'll want you to drop your hands for his overhand left or right. Got it?"

Antonio nodded, spraying water out between his teeth. He felt better as his sore midsection was being firmly rubbed.

Felix's corner was also busy.

"You gotta get in there, fella." Felix's trainer poured water over his curly Afro locks. "Get in there or he's gonna chop you up from way back." **M**

Bong! Bong! Round Two. Felix was off his stool and rushed Antonio like a bull, sending a hard right to his head. Beads of water exploded from Antonio's long hair.

Antonio, hurt, sent back a blurring barrage of lefts and rights that only meant pain to Felix, who returned with a short left to the head followed by a looping right to the body. Antonio countered with his own flurry, forcing Felix to give ground. But not for long.

Felix bobbed and weaved, bobbed and weaved, occasionally punching his two gloves together.

Antonio waited for the rush that was sure to come. Felix closed in and feinted with his left shoulder and threw a right instead. Lights suddenly exploded inside Felix's head as Antonio slipped the blow and hit him with a pistonlike left, catching him flush on the point of his chin.

Bedlam broke loose as Felix's legs momentarily buckled. He fought off a series

M **Read and Discuss** What do you learn from the advice of the two trainers?

Vocabulary **dispelled** (dihs PEHLD) *v.:* driven away.

Cross-Curricular Connection

ATHLETICS: Boxing

Students may be interested in learning more about the Golden Gloves tournament in which Felix and Antonio compete. Provide them with the following background information:

- The Golden Gloves amateur boxing tournament began in Chicago in 1926 and became a competition between Chicago and New York in 1927.
- Soon, other cities set up tournaments. Eventually, there was so much interest that a national competi-

tion was created. Golden Gloves tournaments have even been held a few times between American and European teams.

- The winner of the Golden Gloves receives a gold charm shaped like a boxing glove.
- Some professional world champions, including Joe Louis, Sugar Ray Leonard, and Cassius Clay (later Muhammad Ali), won the Golden Gloves in their early years.

of rights and lefts and came back with a strong right that taught Antonio respect.

Antonio danced in carefully. He knew Felix had the habit of playing possum when hurt, to sucker an opponent within reach of the powerful bombs he carried in each fist.

A right to the head slowed Antonio's pretty dancing. He answered with his own left at Felix's right eye that began puffing up within three seconds.

Antonio, a bit too eager, moved in too close, and Felix had him entangled into a rip-roaring, punching toe-to-toe slugfest that brought the whole Tompkins Square Park screaming to its feet.

Rights to the body. Lefts to the head. Neither fighter was giving an inch. Suddenly a short right caught Antonio squarely on the chin. His long legs turned to jelly and his arms flailed out desperately. Felix, grunting like a bull, threw wild punches from every direction. Antonio, groggy, bobbed and weaved, evading most of the blows. Suddenly his head cleared. His left flashed out hard and straight, catching Felix on the bridge of his nose. **N**

Felix lashed back with a haymaker, right off the ghetto streets. At the same instant, his eye caught another left hook from Antonio. Felix swung out, trying to clear the pain. Only the frenzied screaming of those along ringside let him know that he had dropped Antonio. Fighting off the growing haze, Antonio struggled to his feet, got up, ducked, and threw a smashing right that dropped Felix flat on his back.

Felix got up as fast as he could in his own corner, groggy but still game. He didn't even hear the count. In a fog, he heard the roaring of the crowd, who seemed to have gone insane. His head cleared to hear the bell sound at the end of the round. He was glad. His trainer sat him down on the stool. **O**

N **Reading Focus** Compare and Contrast How are the boys' fighting styles alike and different?

O **Read and Discuss** How is the match going so far?

Vocabulary **frenzied** (FREHN zeed) *adj.*: wild; out of control.

Analyzing Visuals **Connecting to the Text** What moment in the story might this photograph depict?

Analyzing Visuals
Connecting the Text: This might be the moment when the "toe-to-toe slugfest" managed to bring "the whole Tompkins Square Park screaming to its feet."

Think About/Talk About

▶ Comprehension

M Read and Discuss

Possible response: *Each trainer is encouraging his boxer to use his strengths against the other's weakness.*

N Reading Focus

Possible response: *Antonio tries to move around the ring and avoid Felix's punches, while Felix goes right up to Antonio and punches. Felix is more willing to take a punch in order to return one.*

O Read and Discuss

Possible response: *It seems to be a rough fight, but even. Each boy manages to knock the other down at least once.*

▶ Analysis

L Literary Focus

Possible response: *The conflict has now changed from being primarily an internal conflict to an external one as the friends actually try to defeat each other.*

▶ Extend the Discussion

Character Reread the first three full paragraphs on p. 518. How does the boys' fighting style reflect both their competitive nature and their personal friendship? ***Possible response:*** *They do not hold back their punches and fight aggressively to win. However, they still hold their punches after the bell rings so they do not hurt each other or give themselves an unfair advantage.*

Vocabulary: Own the Word

- **dispelled:** Ask students: How might someone *dispel* a rumor? ***Possible response:*** *He or she could prove that it is not true.*

- **frenzied:** Ask students whether they would like to be described as *frenzied* and why. ***Possible response:*** *Students may explain that they would only want to be described as frenzied in positive situations, such as cheering for sports teams.*

▶ Comprehension

Ⓟ Read and Discuss

Possible response: *They're pummeling each other, even after the bell. There's no chance one of them isn't fighting his best.*

▶ Analysis

Ⓠ Literary Focus

Possible response: *They agree to fight their best and not allow the competition to permanently affect their friendship.*

▶ Extend the Discussion

Theme What possible theme, or lesson, does the resolution of the story provide in the final paragraphs? **Possible response:** *The way in which someone competes is more important than winning and losing.*

Monitor Students' Comprehension

Guide the class in answering these comprehension questions.

1. What dream do Antonio and Felix share? [*They both want to become the lightweight boxing champion of the world.*]

2. To what do the boys agree before their boxing match? [*They won't train together; they'll fight to win.*]

3. How do the boys show they are friends after the fight? [*They leave together before the winner is announced.*]

In his corner, Antonio was doing what all fighters do when they are hurt. They sit and smile at everyone.

The referee signaled the ring doctor to check the fighters out. He did so and then gave his OK. The cold-water sponges brought clarity to both amigo brothers. They were rubbed until their circulation ran free.

Bong! Round Three—the final round. Up to now it had been tic-tac-toe, pretty much even. But everyone knew there could be no draw and that this round would decide the winner.

This time, to Felix's surprise, it was Antonio who came out fast, charging across the ring. Felix braced himself but couldn't ward off the barrage of punches. Antonio drove Felix hard against the ropes.

The crowd ate it up. Thus far the two had fought with mucho corazón.[10] Felix tapped his gloves and commenced his attack anew. Antonio, throwing boxer's caution to the winds, jumped in to meet him.

Both pounded away. Neither gave an inch and neither fell to the canvas. Felix's left eye was tightly closed. Claret-red blood poured from Antonio's nose. They fought toe-to-toe.

---

10. **mucho corazón** (MOO choh koh rah SOHN): Spanish for "a lot of heart."

Ⓟ **Read and Discuss** How does Round Three reflect the boys' fears of fighting their best fight?

> No matter what the decision, they knew they would always be champions to each other.

The sounds of their blows were loud in contrast to the silence of a crowd gone completely mute. The referee was stunned by their savagery.

Bong! Bong! Bong! The bell sounded over and over again. Felix and Antonio were past hearing. Their blows continued to pound on each other like hailstones.

Finally the referee and the two trainers pried Felix and Antonio apart. Cold water was poured over them to bring them back to their senses. Ⓟ

They looked around and then rushed toward each other. A cry of alarm surged through Tompkins Square Park. Was this a fight to the death instead of a boxing match?

The fear soon gave way to wave upon wave of cheering as the two amigos embraced.

No matter what the decision, they knew they would always be champions to each other.

BONG! BONG! BONG! "Ladies and Gentlemen. Señores and Señoras. The winner and representative to the Golden Gloves Tournament of Champions is . . ."

The announcer turned to point to the winner and found himself alone. Arm in arm the champions had already left the ring. Ⓠ

Ⓠ **Literary Focus** Short Story How do the boys resolve their conflict? What is the story's resolution?

🐻 **California Standards, pp. 520–523**

■ **Reading Standard 1.3** Clarify word meanings through the use of definition, example, restatement, or contrast.

■ **Reading Standard 3.1** Articulate the expressed purposes and characteristics of different forms of prose (e.g., short story, novel, novella, essay).

Applying Your Skills

Reading Standard 3.1 Articulate the expressed purposes and characteristics of different forms of prose (e.g., short story, novel, novella, essay).

Amigo Brothers
Literary Response and Analysis

Reading Skills Focus
Quick Check

1. Why do the boys stop training together?
2. How does the fight end?

Read with a Purpose

3. What <u>insight</u> did you discover about the way friends can deal with a threat to their relationship? Use details from the story to support your response.

Reading Skills: Compare and Contrast

4. Review the Venn diagram you completed, and then describe in complete sentences how Felix and Antonio are similar and different.

Antonio   Felix

Differences   Similarities   Differences

Literary Skills Focus
Literary Analysis

5. **Interpret** Why do both boys wish for an early knockout? What does this wish show about them and the strength of their friendship?

6. **Connect** Explain whether you would be able to walk away from a contest like this fight without finding out if you had won.

7. **Evaluate** Did you find this story, particularly its ending, true to life? Do you think two good friends can fight each other and stay friends? Give reasons for your opinion.

Literary Skills: Short Story

8. **Analyze** What does the way the boys prepare, fight the bout, and act after the fight tell you about their **characters**?

9. **Analyze** Describe what you think is the **climax,** or most emotional or suspenseful moment, for the boys. What do they learn at this moment?

10. **Analyze** Which do you think has the greatest <u>impact</u> on the story: the **external conflict** (the fight itself) or the **internal conflict** (the feelings the boys struggle with before and during the fight)? Why?

Literary Skills Review: Omniscient Point of View

11. **Analyze** "Amigo Brothers" is told from the **omniscient point of view**—the narrator knows everything about the characters and their problems. How does the author's choice of an all-knowing narrator help you better understand the internal conflicts the two friends experience?

Writing Skills Focus
Think as a Reader/Writer
Use It in Your Writing Write a short description of an activity you enjoy. Use vivid verbs to bring the activity to life for your audience.

What Do You Think Now

Look back at the list you wrote before reading the selection. How many of the rules did Antonio and Felix follow?

Universal Access

Struggling Writers
Provide students with additional scaffolding to help them complete the Writing Skills Focus activity. Have them complete a graphic organizer to help them use appropriate vivid verbs to describe a favorite activity. In a two-column chart, have students write the name of their activity in the left-hand column. In the right-hand column, have them write verbs that describe the activity.

Activity	Verbs to Describe It

Check for Understanding

Independent Practice
Reading Skills Focus
Answers:

1. *They think that training separately will prevent them from getting distracted by the idea of fighting against their friend.*

2. *The boys both leave before the judges pick a winner.*

3. *Friends will always stick together. Antonio and Felix walk off before a winner is announced, showing that their friendship is more important than boxing.*

4. *Both boys are teens who love to box. Felix is short with an Afro; Antonio is tall with long hair.*

Literary Skills Focus
Possible responses:

5. *They want to avoid hurting each other. They don't want to risk their friendship, but they want to win.*

6. *It would be hard to walk away after making such an effort.*

7. *It seemed true to life because friends can be happy for each other's success.*

8. *They value friendship and try to do their best at their sport.*

9. *When the boys embrace at the end of the match, they learn their friendship is strong enough to survive the fight.*

10. *The internal conflict is more important because the boys' friendship is the most important aspect of the story.*

11. *An omniscient narrator knows the thoughts of all characters. If the story was told from a limited perspective, the reader would not see how each boy struggles with the conflict. It would limit the reader's understanding of the story.*

What Do You Think Now?
Ask students to share some rules they wrote for competing against a friend. Then, have students work together to identify whether or not Antonio and Felix followed them.

Independent Practice
Vocabulary Development
Your Turn _____
Possible responses:

1. The athletes must compete in *bouts*, or boxing matches, to narrow the pool of competitors.

2. I contemplated the ball *pensively* before I hit it, but my opponent fired the ball at me immediately.

3. The *frenzied* Wings fans threw hats, scarves, and even posters into the air after that last goal.

4. There's a *torrent* of water flowing through the gutter. It's just rushing along as the rain falls harder.

5. It took five years for those rumors to be *dispelled*. The allegations of cheating were the hardest to drive away.

English for Academic Success
Language Coach
Explain that adverbs ending in *–ly*, such as *slowly* or *weakly*, describe how something is done.

Possible responses:

1. *I nodded eagerly. I ate the pizza quickly. I was completely satisfied.*

2. *We took a drive across a rocky road. It was a bumpy ride. I felt sleepy.*

English for Academic Success
Academic Vocabulary
Possible response: The scene provides the <u>insight</u> that the boys care too deeply about each other to worry about winning and losing. The greatest <u>impact</u> of the fight is that it shows that the friendship can survive challenges and become stronger.

 WordSharp: An Interactive Vocabulary Tutor

Learn It Online
Holt's **WordSharp: An Interactive Vocabulary Tutor** provides additional support for vocabulary development. Multimedia tutorials show students how to apply vocabulary skills to unfamiliar words—and how to make those words their own.

go.hrw.com   H7-522   **Go**

Applying Your Skills

Amigo Brothers

Vocabulary Development
Clarifying Word Meanings: Using Words in Context

One indication that you have successfully added a word to your personal vocabulary is the ability to use it in a new context. For example, the Vocabulary words for this selection come from a story about boxing, but they can also be used to write about other sports or other topics.

Your Turn _____

bouts
pensively
torrent
dispelled
frenzied

Use the boldface Vocabulary words correctly in each context stated below. Show that you understand the meaning of each Vocabulary word by including in each sentence a context clue: a definition, example, restatement, or contrast, as indicated.

1. You are writing a news article about tryouts for the Olympic Games. Write a sentence using the word **bouts.** Include a definition.

2. You are a retired tennis player. Write a sentence for your autobiography using the word **pensively.** Include a contrast.

3. You are a sportscaster describing the crowd at a hockey game. Use the word **frenzied** in a description of the crowd. Include an example.

4. You are observing a violent storm. Use the word **torrent** to describe what you see. Include a restatement.

5. You are a biographer writing a book about a controversial, often misunderstood athlete. Write a sentence using the word **dispelled.** Include a restatement.

Language Coach

Using Word Parts: Suffixes A word part added to the end of a word is called a **suffix.** Two commonly used suffixes are *–ly* and *–y*.

Suffix	Meaning	Examples
–ly	in a certain or particular way	immediately, lightly, purposely
–y	full of, characterized by	lanky, curly

Many adverbs end in *–ly*. These adverbs are generally formed by adding *–ly* to adjectives. The words in the chart that end with *–y* are adjectives.

1. Think of three more words that end in *–ly*, and use each in a sentence.

2. Think of three more words that end in *–y*, and use each in a sentence.

Academic Vocabulary

Talk About . . .
Discuss with a partner the final paragraph of "Amigo Brothers." What <u>insight</u> into Felix and Antonio's relationship does the final scene provide? What <u>impact</u> does the fight have on their friendship? Use these two Academic Vocabulary words in your discussion.

 Learn It Online
Sharpen your word skills with *WordSharp* at:
go.hrw.com   H7-522   **Go**

Universal Access: Vocabulary Development

EL English Learners/ Struggling Readers

English for Academic Success Students may understand the definitions of the Vocabulary words but have difficulty understanding how to use them in conversation. Place students into small groups, making sure to include at least one fluent English speaker in each group. Direct them to discuss the following questions and use the Vocabulary word in their answers.

- Why do you think boxers fight in short *bouts*?
- Why might a person speak *pensively*?
- Describe what a *torrent* might look like.
- What things can be *dispelled*?
- When might a person seem *frenzied*?

Grammar Link

Run-on Sentences

A **run-on sentence** is two complete sentences punctuated as if they were one sentence. In a run-on, two separate thoughts run into each other. The reader cannot tell where one idea ends and another one begins.

There are several ways to revise run-on sentences. Here are two of them: You can make two sentences, or you can use a comma and a coordinating conjunction, such as *and, but,* or *or.*

RUN-ON: The friends both had a dream of someday becoming lightweight champion of the world, every chance they had, they worked out at the Boys' Club.

CORRECT: The friends both had a dream of someday becoming lightweight champion of the world. Every chance they had, they worked out at the Boys' Club.

or

CORRECT: The friends both had a dream of someday becoming lightweight champion of the world, **and** every chance they had, they worked out at the Boys' Club.

Your Turn

Revise each run-on sentence by breaking it into two separate sentences or by using a comma and a coordinating conjunction.

1. The two boys continued to run together along the East River Drive soon they realized that a tension was developing between them because of the big fight.

2. Antonio and Felix trained separately they knew about each other's progress.

CHOICES

As you respond to the Choices, use these **Academic Vocabulary** words as appropriate: articulate, characteristics, impact, insight.

REVIEW

Analyze a Short Story

Fill out a graphic organizer to identify the significant plot events of "Amigo Brothers." (You might want to add more events.)

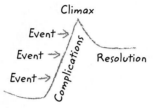

Characters: _____

Their problem: _____

CONNECT

Compare Characters

Timed ⌐Writing In a three-paragraph essay, **compare and contrast** the personality characteristics of Felix and Antonio, and explain the impact their personality traits have on the story. Write first about their similarities and then about their differences. (Review the Venn diagram you made.) Then, explain which character you like better, and why.

EXTEND

Imagine a Conversation

Partner Talk What do you think Felix and Antonio said to each other as they walked away from the fight? With a partner, discuss how they might have articulated their feelings.

Independent Practice
Grammar Link
Your Turn

1. The two boys continued to run together along the East River Drive. Soon, they realized that a tension was developing between them because of the big fight.

2. Antonio and Felix trained separately, but they knew about each other's progress.

Choices:
Evaluation Criteria
Review: (Homework)
Analyze a Short Story

The graphic organizer identifies the characters and their problem, as well as events, complications, climax, and resolution.

Connect: Timed Writing
40–50 minutes

• The essay compares and contrasts Felix and Antonio.

• The essay explains the student's feelings about the characters within the allotted time period.

Extend: (Homework)
Imagine A Conversation

• The dialogue is realistic based on what happens in the story.

• The dialogue expands on events.

Assess

✐ **Chapter 5 Resources,** Selection Standards Check, p. 9

ThinkCentral Online Assessment, Selection Standards Check

💿 **Teacher One Stop™,** editable Selection Standards Check

Reteach

To reteach **forms of prose,** see **Reteaching Lessons,** p. 842A.

ThinkCentral Online Remediation

Universal Access: Grammar Link

Tell students that the two thoughts or sentences contained in a run-on sentence may be difficult to distinguish from one another, as they may be very closely related. In the run-on sentence, "Jenica went to the grocery store on Saturday she bought ingredients for chicken soup," for example, the entire run-on sentence discusses Jenica's trip to the grocery store. Tell students that one way of determining whether a sentence is a run-on, and also where it should be split, is to look for a second subject-verb pairing. "Jenica went" is one subject-verb pairing; "she bought" is a second. Multiple subject-verb constructions in one sentence indicate that there is more than one sentence in the sentence. The second subject-verb also suggests where to divide the sentence. For example, the sentence above might be divided as: "Jenica went to the grocery store on Saturday. She bought ingredients for chicken soup."

Standards Focus

Objectives

Students will

- understand and identify the characteristics of an autobiography
- analyze the use of chronological order in a text

Motivate

What Do You Think?/QuickWrite

Ask students to think of a time in which they or someone they know had to adjust to a new or unfamiliar situation. Who did the person rely on to help them handle the adjustment?

English for Academic Success

Academic Vocabulary

Look for opportunities to use the Academic Vocabulary words in this chapter.

- **articulate, v.:** express clearly and specifically
- **characteristics, n. pl.:** distinguishing qualities or features
- **insight, n.:** power to understand
- **interpret, v.:** decide on the meaning of something

Analyzing Visuals

Use Think Central, Teacher Access to project this image for viewing.

Extension Activity Ask students to describe the "journey" these pictures suggest. *Possible response: The people have moved to a new place. Many years have passed.*

California Standards, pp. 520–523

- **Reading Standard 1.3** Clarify word meanings through the use of definition, example, restatement, or contrast.
- **Reading Standard 3.1** Articulate the expressed purposes and characteristics of different forms of prose (e.g., short story, novel, novella, essay).

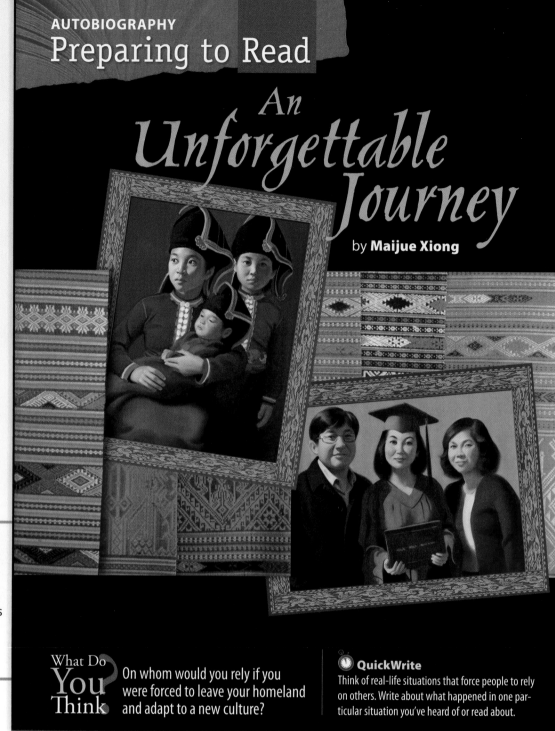

Preparing to Read

An Unforgettable Journey

by **Maijue Xiong**

What Do You Think On whom would you rely if you were forced to leave your homeland and adapt to a new culture?

QuickWrite Think of real-life situations that force people to rely on others. Write about what happened in one particular situation you've heard of or read about.

Selection Readability	
Easily Accessible **Accessible** Challenging	accessible theme, familiar genre, unfamiliar setting

Selection Plot Summary

Maijue Xiong tells of her family's daring flight from Laos in 1975 to the United States. This unforgettable journey took them through harsh jungle trails and frightening river rapids while her family suffered from malnutrition and disease. Xiong has never forgotten what her parents did for her.

Reader/Writer Notebook

Use your **RWN** to complete the activities for this selection.

Reading Standard 3.1 Articulate the expressed purposes and characteristics of different forms of prose (e.g., short story, novel, novella, essay).

Literary Skills Focus

Forms of Prose: Autobiography The most personal kind of prose writing is autobiographical writing. An **autobiography** is the story of a person's life written by that very person. (In contrast, a **biography** is the story of a person's life told by *another* person.) In an autobiography, the writer uses the first-person point of view, writing as *I.* You are able to get inside the writer's mind, and you learn about his or her most personal thoughts, feelings, and ideas. In "An Unforgettable Journey," Maijue Xiong tells how her life was changed forever when she and her family found themselves "without a home or a country."

Reading Skills Focus

Tracking Chronological Order When writers relate events in the sequence, or order, in which they happened, they are using **chronological order.** When you read a narrative text, look for transitional words and phrases such as *first, next, then,* and *at last* to figure out the order in which events occur.

Into Action Use a time line to record the order of events from the time Xiong's family fled Laos until they arrived in California. Your time line will be in chronological order, or organized by time.

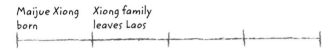

Maijue Xiong born   Xiong family leaves Laos

TechFocus As you keep track of events, think about the tone of voice you would use in different parts of the narrative if you were to read this writer's experiences aloud.

Writing Skills Focus

Think as a Reader/Writer

Find It in Your Reading As you read Xiong's autobiography, look for transitional words and phrases that signal chronological order. List them in your *Reader/Writer Notebook.*

Vocabulary

refuge (REHF yooj) *n.:* place of safety. *Xiong found refuge from war in the United States.*

transition (tran ZIHSH uhn) *n.:* change; passing from one condition to another. *The transition to life in the United States from life in Laos required many changes.*

persecution (pur suh KYOO shuhn) *n.:* act of attacking others because of their beliefs or their ethnic background. *Some Hmong faced persecution.*

deprivation (dehp ruh VAY shuhn) *n.:* condition of not having something essential. *They suffered from food deprivation.*

Language Coach

Suffixes The suffix *–tion* means "being; the result of." How does knowing this suffix help you understand the meaning of *relocation*?

Learn It Online
There's more to words than just definitions. Get the whole story at:

go.hrw.com   H7-525   **Go**

Selection Introduction

More About the Writer

The school at which **Maijue Xiong** taught, HOPE (Hmong Open Partnerships in Education) Community Academy, is a charter elementary school in Minnesota devoted to serving the Hmong community.

Think About the Writer

Have students brainstorm ways immigrants stay connected to their native cultures, such as building communities like the Chinatown neighborhoods in many major cities. Invite students who have experienced immigration and feel comfortable discussing their experiences to share ways and reasons they stay connected to their homelands.

For Independent Reading

- If students are interested in the experiences of refugees, they might enjoy *A Long Way From Home,* Maureen Crane Wartski's story of a young Vietnamese refugee.

- Students may also be interested in *American Dragons: Twenty-five Asian American Voices,* writings of Asian Americans compiled by author Laurence Yep.

Maijue Xiong
(1972–   )

A Writer Who Can Never Forget

Maijue Xiong (MY zhoo ee see AWNG) was a college student in the United States when she wrote about her family's flight from Laos. Xiong eventually earned degrees in sociology and Asian American studies at the University of California, Santa Barbara, where she helped found the Hmong Club to promote Laotian culture.

An active member of the Asian Culture Committee, Xiong now lives in St. Paul, Minnesota. She has taught elementary school at HOPE Community Academy and currently teaches fourth grade at Galtier Magnet Elementary School. Xiong remains active in the Hmong community.

"Now that I am older, I treasure the long but valuable lessons my parents tried to teach us—lessons that gave me a sense of identity as a Hmong."

Think About the Writer What <u>insights</u> can you draw from Xiong's connection to the Hmong community?

Build Background

The Hmong (mawng) people of Southeast Asia have faced persecution and exile for more than two centuries. The autobiographical selection that follows is one of several Hmong life stories collected by Sucheng Chan, a teacher at the University of California, Santa Barbara. Maijue Xiong was one of the students who contributed a life story to the book that Chan and her students put together called *Hmong Means Free: Life in Laos and America.*

Preview the Story

In 1975, when **Maijue Xiong** was just three years old, she fled Laos along with her parents, stepuncle, and two sisters. This autobiography describes the family's many adventures and difficulties as they journey through jungles, fields, and mountain trails; cross the Mekong River to Thailand; spend time in a refugee camp; and finally arrive in California.

Universal Access

English Learners

Work with students to brainstorm transitional phrases that can be used to signal chronological order. Record these phrases on the board. Students' responses might include "one day," "after that," "before long," "the first time," or "the next morning." Have students look for these phrases as they read. If students come across additional transitional phrases in the text, have them add the new phrases to the list.

Struggling Readers

To help students read "An Unforgettable Journey," model the reading skill of identifying chronological order. Point out that, at the top of the second column, the author says that after Laos became a Communist country, her family decided to leave. The word *after* tells readers that these events occurred in chronological order: First, Laos became a Communist country. Then, the author's family left. Have students scan p. 527 and identify other potential transition words.

An Unforgettable Journey

by **Maijue Xiong**

I was born in a small village called Muong Cha in Laos on April 30, 1972. At the time I was born, my father was a soldier actively fighting alongside the American Central Intelligence Agency[1] against the Communists. Although a war was in progress, life seemed peaceful. We did not think of ever leaving Laos, but one day our lives were changed forever. We found ourselves without a home or a country and with a need to seek refuge in another country. This period of relocation involved a lot of changes, adjustments, and adaptations. We experienced changes in our language, customs, traditional values, and social status. Some made the transition quickly; others have never fully adjusted. The changes my family and I experienced are the foundation of my identity today. **A**

---

1. **Central Intelligence Agency** (CIA): government agency that helps protect the United States by gathering information about foreign governments and carrying out secret operations.

After Laos became a Communist country in 1975, my family, along with many others, fled in fear of persecution. Because my father had served as a commanding officer for eleven years with the American Central Intelligence Agency in what is known to the American public as the "Secret War," my family had no choice but to leave immediately. My father's life was in danger, along with those of thousands of others. We were forced to leave loved ones behind, including my grandmother, who was ill in bed the day we fled our village. For a month, my family walked through the dense tropical jungles and rice fields, along rugged trails through many mountains, and battled the powerful Mekong River. We traveled in silence at night and slept in the daytime. Children were very hard to keep quiet. Many parents feared the Communist soldiers would hear the cries of their children; therefore, they drugged the children with opium to keep them quiet. Some parents even left

A **Literary Focus** Autobiography What important characteristics does the author reveal about herself in this paragraph?

Vocabulary **refuge** (REHF yooj) *n.*: place of safety.
transition (tran ZIHSH uhn) *n.*: change; passing from one condition to another.
persecution (pur suh KYOO shuhn) *n.*: act of attacking others because of their beliefs or their ethnic background.

Model the Skill

- Explain that **autobiographies** are personal accounts of events in an individual's life as told by that individual. Because autobiographies describe events from the point of view of the person experiencing them, autobiographies often include thoughts, perspective, and emotions that might not be revealed in a biography.

- Point out that Xiong's family had to walk through "dense jungles with trees and bushes all around" to escape Laos. Ask the following: "Would a biographer know enough to include this description in a biography of Xiong?" [*Students should answer that it is easy to find out.*]

- Point out that Xiong also writes that "I was like a little ant placed in a field of tall grass." That statement expresses Xiong's feelings of smallness and fear by sharing thoughts a biographer would not know. Xiong's unique perspective—feeling like an ant in tall grass—is personal enough that it would probably not appear in a biography, but would be included in an autobiography.

Guided Practice: Apply

Listen-Talk-Write Read p. 528 aloud, from point B to point C, as students listen. When you finish reading, have students discuss with a partner how hearing the events from Xiong's point of view made them feel. Then, have students write for three minutes about how the events in the passage would differ if they were described in a biography of Xiong.

those children who would not stop crying behind. Fortunately, whenever my parents told my sisters and me to keep quiet, we listened and obeyed.

I do not remember much about our flight, but I do have certain memories that have been imprinted in my mind. It is all so unclear—the experience was like a bad dream: When you wake up, you don't remember what it was you had dreamed about but recall only those bits and pieces of the dream that stand out the most. I remember sleeping under tall trees. I was like a little ant placed in a field of tall grass, surrounded by dense jungle with trees and bushes all around me—right, left, in the back, and in front of me. I also remember that it rained a lot and that it was cold. We took only what we could carry and it was not much. My father carried a sack of rice, which had to last us the whole way. My mother carried one extra change of clothing for each of us, a few personal belongings, and my baby sister on her back. My older sister and I helped carry pots and pans. My stepuncle carried water, dried meat, and his personal belongings. **B**

From the jungles to the open fields, we walked along a path. We came across a trail of red ants and being a stubborn child, I refused to walk over them. I wanted someone to pick me up because I was scared, but my parents kept walking ahead. They kept telling me to hurry up and to step over the ants, but I just stood there and cried. Finally, my father came back and put me on

his shoulders, along with the heavy sack of rice he was carrying. . . . **C**

After experiencing many cold days and rainy nights, we finally saw Thailand on the other side of the Mekong River. My parents bribed several fishermen to row us across. The fishermen knew we were desperate, yet, instead of helping us, they took advantage of us. We had to give them all our valuables: silver bars, silver coins, paper money, and my mother's silver wedding necklace, which had cost a lot of money. When it got dark, the fishermen came back with a small fishing boat and took us across the river. The currents were high and powerful. I remember being very scared. I kept yelling, "We're going to fall out! We're going to fall into the river!" My mom tried to reassure me but I kept screaming in fear. Finally, we got across safely. My family, along with many other families, were picked up by the Thai police and taken to an empty bus station for the night.

After a whole month at this temporary refugee camp set up in the bus station, during which we ate rice, dried fish, roots we dug up, and bamboo shoots we cut down, and drank water from streams, we were in very poor shape due to the lack of nutrition. Our feet were also swollen from walking. We were then taken to a refugee camp

Analyzing Visuals Connecting to the Text In what ways does this illustration represent the family's experience of crossing the Mekong River?

B Literary Focus Autobiography What does the author want you to understand? What <u>impact</u> does the first-person point of view have on the narrative?

C Read and Discuss What did you just find out?

Cross-Curricular Connection

GEOGRAPHY: Laos and Thailand
Explain to students that Xiong's family's journey takes them from Laos to the neighboring country of Thailand.

- Laos and Thailand are both nations in Southeast Asia. Laos is landlocked, while Thailand lies on the coast.
- The region is noted for its tropical climate and monsoon seasons.

- Laos was governed by a monarchy for several hundred years until 1975, when the Communist Party seized control. Today, Laos remains a Communist country.
- In 1975, approximately 10 percent of Laos's population fled to Thailand following the Communist takeover.

HSS Analysis Skills CR 3

▶ Comprehension

🅒 Read and Discuss

Possible response: *The author remembers only parts of her childhood journey—being outdoors in the rain and cold, being surrounded by the jungle, and her family having to carry their clothing and food with them. We also found out that Xiong's father did not leave her behind when she cried, as other parents did to their children.*

▶ Analysis

🅑 Literary Focus

Possible response: *Because the father's life was in danger, the family had to leave their home quickly. Escaping meant a month of walking at night through jungles, mountains, and fields. The author wants readers to understand how difficult and frightening the situation was.*

▶ Extend the Discussion

Autobiography Read the first two sentences of the first full paragraph on p. 528. In what way does the autobiographical format limit Xiong's storytelling? ***Possible response:*** *Because Xiong is writing about her own experience, she can only write about what she remembers. She does not remember all the details of her journey, and because this is not a fictional account, she can't make them up.*

Analyzing Based on her experience with the red ants in the second full paragraph on p. 528, how would you describe the author as a child? ***Possible response:*** *She did not really understand the seriousness of the situation and the reasons for her family's move. She was still concerned with childish things, only realizing the real dangers years later as an adult.*

Developing Oral Fluency

Tell students that writers often convey strong feelings about events that occur in their autobiographies. Model reading the first and second full paragraphs of p. 528, reflecting the author's emotions of fear and nervousness.

Paired Activity Have students form pairs and alternate reading the first and second full paragraphs on p. 528, beginning with the paragraph that starts, "I do not remember." Remind students to focus on conveying emotion in their reading. As one partner reads, instruct the other to evaluate his or her reading.

Analyzing Visuals

Connecting to the Text: *It represents the family's experience because it shows a boat ride at night through choppy water. The whole image seems gloomy, and the passengers' faces look anxious, which is how Xiong's family probably felt during their trip across the Mekong.*

Model the Skill

- Provide students with copies of the Reading Skills Focus graphic organizer. (See **Chapter 5 Resources**) or ask them to use a piece of their own paper.

- Tell students that writers of autobiographies and biographies usually tell events in **chronological order**.

- Model organizing events in chronological order using the graphic organizer. Ask students to list the major events that happen on pp. 530 and 531. *Students should recognize that Xiong's sister dies, her family applies to go to America, they travel to Bangkok, and then arrive in the America.* As students list the events, place the first two events in chronological order using the graphic organizer.

Xiong's sister dies	The family applies to go to America

Guided Practice: Apply

Have students work independently to place the remaining two events on the time line, and then share their time lines with a partner.

Think as a Reader/Writer

Find It in Your Reading Point out the phrases "On the evening she died," and "After we found him," in the first column. Explain that these are transitional phrases that signal chronological order.

Use It in Your Writing Have students write a brief description of something they have done recently, using transitional words and phrases to signal the chronological order of events.

in Nongkhai, where disease was rampant and many people got sick. My family suffered a loss: My baby sister, who was only a few months old, died. She had become very skinny from the lack of milk, and there was no medical care available. The memory of her death still burns in my mind like a flame. On the evening she died, my older sister and I were playing with our cousins outside the building where we stayed. My father came out to tell us the sad news and told us to go find my stepuncle. After we found him, we went inside and saw our mother mourning the baby's death. Fortunately, our family had relatives around to support and comfort us. . . . **D**

Our family life in the camp was very unstable, characterized by deprivation and neglect. My older sister and I were left alone for days while my parents were outside the camp trying to earn money to buy extra food. My parents fought a lot during this period, because we were all under such stress. They knew that if we remained in Thailand, there would be no telling what would become of us. We had to find a better life. Some people in the camp were being sponsored to go to the United States. The news spread that anyone who had served in the military with the CIA could apply to go to America. Since my stepuncle had already gone there two years earlier, he sponsored my family. Because my father had been in the military and we had a sponsor, it took only six months to process our papers when usually it took a year or more. . . .

It took a full day to travel to Bangkok, where we stayed for four nights. The building we stayed in was one huge room. It was depressing and nerve-racking. I especially

D Read and Discuss What happens to the family in the refugee camp?

Vocabulary deprivation (dehp ruh VAY shuhn) *n.*: condition of not having something essential.

Universal Access

AAVE Students Who Use African American Vernacular English

English for Academic Success Some students may struggle with identifying the past tenses of verbs in formal English. Tell students that regular verbs can be changed to the past tense simply by adding -ed to the ending. *An Unforgettable Journey* tells about a story that happened in the past, so most of the verbs are in the past tense, such as *stayed* (p. 530), *remained* (p. 530), and *chased* (p. 531). Have students find other verbs on pp. 530-531 that use the -ed ending. Make a list on the board, and have students repeat the words aloud.

Struggling Readers

Strategic Students Point out the ellipsis in column 2. Explain that writers or editors may use ellipses to indicate that something has been left out of the text. It may be that part of the text was not printed; it may suggest the passage of time. Tell students that in this text, time passes and events happen between the family gaining sponsorship and traveling to Bangkok.

The Vietnam War and Hmong Refugees

War often leads to the exile of thousands of civilians on the losing side. Such was the fate of the Hmong (muhng) people, most of whom had supported the United States in its war in Vietnam and Laos. In 1975, when the Communists won, one third of the Hmong people fled. More than 135,000 ended up in the United States. Most live in California, but there are also Hmong communities in Minnesota, Wisconsin, Georgia, Texas, Rhode Island, Nebraska, North Carolina, Colorado, and Montana.

This map shows countries of Southeast Asia and their capitals as they existed just before 1975, when Maijue Xiong and her family left their village of Muong Cha, which was located north of Vientiane in Laos. Today, the map of this part of the world looks somewhat different. For instance, North and South Vietnam are now united into one country.

Ask Yourself
How does Maijue Xiong's autobiography reflect the history of the Hmong in Laos?

---

remember how, when we got off the bus to go into the building, a small child about my age came up to my family to beg for food. I recall the exact words she said to my father, "Uncle, can you give me some food? I am hungry. My parents are dead and I am here alone." My dad gave her a piece of bread that we had packed for our lunch. After she walked away, my family found an empty corner and rolled out our bedding for the night. That night, the same child came around again, but people chased her away, which made me sad. **(E)**

In the morning, I ran to get in line for breakfast. Each person received a bowl of rice porridge with a few strips of chicken in it.

For four days, we remained in that building, not knowing when we could leave for the United States. Many families had been there for weeks, months, perhaps even years. On the fourth day, my family was notified to be ready early the next morning to be taken to the airport. The plane ride took a long time and I got motion sickness. I threw up a lot. Only when I saw my stepuncle's face after we landed did I know we had come to the end of our journey. We had come in search of a better life in the "land of giants." **(F)**

On October 2, 1978, my family arrived at Los Angeles International Airport, where my uncle was waiting anxiously. We stayed with my uncle in Los Angeles for two weeks

(E) Literary Focus Autobiography How does the first-person point of view make the narrative more direct and personal? What would be different if events were told from the third-person point of view?

(F) Reading Focus Chronological Order What main events have occurred so far? List them in order on your time line.

Reaching Reluctant Readers

To help students connect to the text, lead a group discussion about the challenges faced by Maijue Xiong and her family.

- Have students imagine being in Xiong's situation, facing hazardous conditions while making a risky escape from Laos. Ask them how would they have handled the situation if they were in Xiong's shoes.
- Then, ask students whether they think Xiong's parents made the right decision by taking their family on the dangerous journey out of Laos.

- You might ask two groups of students to debate the issue. Have one side explain why the journey was necessary [the family escaped the risk of persecution and found a better life] and the other side explain why it was not worth the risk [the youngest child died and the grandmother was left behind].

Think About/Talk About

▶ Comprehension

(D) Read and Discuss

Possible response: *The hardships continue—illness, death, separations, and stress.*

(F) Reading Focus

Possible response: *So far, Xiong's family has fled Laos, stayed at a refugee camp in Thailand, suffered the loss of Xiong's baby sister, and traveled to Bangkok. Now they've arrived in the United States.*

▶ Analysis

(E) Literary Focus

Possible response: *First-person point of view makes the events more personal by allowing the reader to share in the narrator's emotion. A third-person point of view might present the events in a more objective fashion, with less emotion.*

▶ Extend the Discussion

Analyzing In the third sentence on p. 530, Xiong describes the memory of her sister's death as something that "burns in my mind like a flame." What might this metaphor mean? **Possible response:** *The memory of her sister's death is very painful, and Xiong will never forget it.*

Vocabulary: Own the Word

deprivation: Review the word and its definition. Ask students: What kind of *deprivation* did Xiong and her family face? **Possible response:** *They had very little food or water, which are essential to survival.*

Social Studies Link

Ask Yourself

Possible response: *The family fled because they supported America; they later settled in California.*

 HSS Analysis Skills CR 3

Comprehension

H Read and Discuss

Possible response: Now that we understand the sacrifices her family made, we see the perseverance that helped her succeed.

Analysis

G Literary Focus

Possible response: The author learned about the language, culture, and diversity, and established her "lifelong goal to get an education." This passage reveals emotion and the narrator's perspective.

Extend the Discussion

Theme Read the last paragraph. How might Xiong's "sense of accomplishment" connect to the theme of this autobiography? *Possible response: The theme might be that you can reach your goals if you work hard. Xiong probably feels accomplished not only because she's done well in school but also because she's persevered in escaping from Laos and building a new life.*

Monitor Students' Comprehension

To check students' understanding of the autobiography, ask them how Xiong's experiences on her journey became the "foundation of [her] identity." [*She's proud to be a Hmong and determined to overcome all challenges.*]

---

and then settled in Isla Vista because there were already a few Hmong families there. We knew only one family in Isla Vista, but later we met other families whom my parents had known in their village and from villages nearby. It was in Isla Vista that my life really began. My home life was now more stable. My mother gave birth to a boy a month after we arrived in the United States. It was a joyous event because the first three children she had were all girls. (Boys are desired and valued far more than girls in Hmong culture.) . . .

I entered kindergarten at Isla Vista Elementary School. The first day was scary because I could not speak any English. Fortunately, my cousin, who had been in the United States for three years and spoke English, was in the same class with me. She led me to the playground where the children were playing. I was shocked to see so many faces of different colors. The Caucasian students shocked me the most. I had never seen people with blond hair before. The sight sent me to a bench, where I sat and watched everyone in amazement. In class, I was introduced to coloring. I did not know how to hold a crayon or what it

was for. My teacher had to show me how to color. I also soon learned the alphabet. This was the beginning of my lifelong goal to get an education. . . . **G**

Now that I am older, I treasure the long but valuable lessons my parents tried to teach us—lessons that gave me a sense of identity as a Hmong. "Nothing comes easy . . . ," my parents always said. As I attempt to get a college education, I remember how my parents have been really supportive of me throughout my schooling, but because they never had a chance to get an education themselves, they were not able to help me whenever I could not solve a math problem or write an English paper. Although they cannot help me in my schoolwork, I know in my heart that they care about me and want me to be successful so that I can help them when they can no longer help themselves. Therefore, I am determined to do well at the university. I want to become a role model for my younger brother and sisters, for I am the very first member of my family to attend college. I feel a real sense of accomplishment to have set such an example. **H**

> Now that I am older, I treasure the long but valuable lessons my parents tried to teach us—lessons that gave me a sense of identity as a Hmong. "Nothing comes easy . . . ," my parents always said.

G Literary Focus Autobiography **What do you learn here about Xiong? What <u>characteristics</u> of autobiographical prose does this passage reveal?**

H Read and Discuss **What does this statement tell you about the author?**

 California Standards, pp. 532–534

- **Reading Standard 1.3** Clarify word meanings through the use of definition, example, restatement, or contrast.
- **Reading Standard 3.1** Articulate the expressed purposes and characteristics of different forms of prose (e.g., short story, novel, novella, essay).

Applying Your Skills

Reading Standard 3.1 Articulate the expressed purposes and characteristics of different forms of prose (e.g., short story, novel, novella, essay).

An Unforgettable Journey
Literary Response and Analysis

Reading Skills Focus
Quick Check

1. Explain three important events Xiong faced during her family's escape.

2. How did Xiong feel about school when she first arrived in the United States?

Read with a Purpose

3. What did you learn about the <u>impact</u> of leaving one's homeland?

Reading Skills: Tracking Chronological Order

4. Review your time line, and be sure you have included only main events. What have you learned about the way chronological order works in stories?

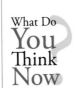

Maijue Xiong born   Xiong family leaves Laos

Literary Skills Focus
Literary Analysis

5. **Interpret** How does the statement made by Xiong's parents, "Nothing comes easy," apply to this selection?

Literary Skills: Autobiography

6. **Contrast** In your own words, <u>articulate</u> the difference between autobiography and biography.

7. **Analyze** What <u>insights</u> do you find when reading an autobiography that you might not discover in other forms of prose?

8. **Evaluate** Xiong describes experiences she had when she was only three years old. People often do not remember events that occurred at such a young age. Why do you think her memories are so vivid?

Literary Skills Review: First-Person Point of View

Autobiographies are told from the **first-person point of view.** In this point of view, we know only what the narrator decides to tell us. (The writer speaks as *I*, using the first-person pronoun.)

9. **Analyze** How would your interpretation of these events be different if they had been conveyed by someone who was not Hmong?

Writing Skills Focus
Think as a Reader/Writer

Use It in Your Writing Think about an unforgettable journey you have heard or read about. How does it compare to Xiong's journey? Write a paragraph comparing the two journeys, making sure to include transitional words. Use a Venn diagram to show similarities and differences.

Journeys You Heard About   Xiong's Journey

Differences   Similarities   Differences

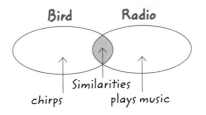

What Do You Think Now

How might things have turned out if Xiong's family had made their journey without getting help along the way?

Universal Access

Struggling Writers

Some students may struggle to write a comparison/contrast paragraph. Model for students how to use the Venn diagram graphic organizer. Describe a journey you have heard about. Explain how the journey is similar and different from Xiong's. Then place one detail in each of the three ovals. Remind students that a Venn diagram is an effective way to list similarities and differences.

Bird   Radio

Similarities

chirps   plays music

Independent Practice

Vocabulary Development

Your Turn _____

1. *deprivation*
2. *persecution*
3. *refuge*
4. *transition*

English for Academic Success

Language Coach

Before beginning the **Language Coach** activity, review the Vocabulary words and their meanings with students. Remind students that although the suffix –*tion* changes a word's part of speech, it does not fundamentally change the word's meaning.

1. *persecution*
2. *deprivation*
3. *transition*

English for Academic Success

Academic Vocabulary

Possible response: The strength, bravery, and perseverance that Xiong gained from the journey are <u>characteristics</u> that helped her to grow into a confident, successful adult.

 WordSharp: An Interactive Vocabulary Tutor

 Learn It Online

Holt's **WordSharp: An Interactive Vocabulary Tutor** tutor provides additional support for vocabulary development. Multimedia tutorials show students how to apply vocabulary skills to unfamiliar words—and how to make those words their own.

go.hrw.com | H7-534 | **Go**

534 Chapter 5

Applying Your Skills

An Unforgettable Journey

Vocabulary Development

Clarifying Word Meanings: Contrast Clues

Sometimes writers will clarify the meaning of a word by using contrast clues. **Contrast clues** show how a word differs from another word or situation. For example, you can get a good idea that *apprehensive* means "fearful" or "uneasy" in the sentence below because the word is contrasted with a word opposite in meaning: *fearless.*

The children were extremely **apprehensive** as they made their way through the dense jungle, but their parents seemed **fearless.**

Look for signal words that alert you to contrasts: *although, but, yet, still, unlike, not, in contrast, instead,* and *however.*

Your Turn _____

In the following sentences, contrast clues point you to the meaning of each Vocabulary word. Using the contrast clues, fill in each blank with the correct Vocabulary word.

| refuge |
| transition |
| persecution |
| deprivation |

1. Some people have food, clothing, and shelter, but others experience _____ because they are forced to live without these basic needs.

2. Although we expected _____ for our beliefs, we found acceptance.

3. Instead of finding a _____ , they suffered exposure to wind and rain.

4. In contrast to people who made a _____ to the new culture, some of the exiles kept their traditional way of life.

Language Coach

The Suffix –*tion* The suffix –*tion* means "action or process of"; "condition or state of being"; "the result of." For instance, *rejection* is the state of being rejected, and *connection* is the process of connecting. When the suffix –*tion* is added to a verb like *persecute* or *deprive,* the new word formed is a noun. Think about what the suffix –*tion* means in the three Vocabulary words below, and fill in the appropriate word for each sentence.

| transition | persecution | deprivation |

1. Maijue Xiong and her family fled Laos because the Hmong people faced _____.

2. The Xiongs experienced a great deal of _____ on their journey.

3. They found their move to America to be a difficult _____.

Academic Vocabulary

Write About . . .

What <u>characteristics</u> of Xiong's childhood helped her become an admirable and accomplished adult? Write your response to this question in one paragraph.

 Learn It Online
Expand your vocabulary with *WordSharp* at:

go.hrw.com | H7-534 | **Go**

Universal Access: Vocabulary Development

 English Learners

English for Academic Success Students may require extra practice with the Academic Vocabulary terms. Have students form "book clubs" to discuss "Unforgettable Journey" using the Academic Vocabulary words *articulate, insights, impact,* and *characteristics.* Put students in mixed-ability groups, having a fluent English speaker lead off the discussion. Tell groups they may discuss whatever parts of the story most interest them, but they must use each Academic Vocabulary term at least once in the discussion. Monitor discussions and provide feedback as needed.

Grammar Link
Subject-Verb Agreement

Two words agree when they have the same number. The number of a verb should agree with, or match, the number of a subject.

I sleep in the daytime. [*I* is one person, so the verb *sleep* is in the singular form.]

Our **feet were** swollen. [*Feet* refers to more than one foot, so the verb *were* is in the plural form.]

When a sentence contains a verb phrase, the first helping verb in the phrase agrees with the subject.

I was forced to leave loved ones behind.

We were forced to leave loved ones behind.

Note that in a question, the verb phrase is often split. The same rules of agreement always apply.

Is the **child starving?**

Are the **children starving?**

Your Turn

Identify which form of the verb in parentheses agrees with its subject.

1. Her father (*has, have*) been a commanding officer.
2. Children (*cry, cries*) because they fear the soldiers.
3. I (*walk, walks*) through jungles and rice fields.
4. (*Is, Are*) my uncle waiting for us at the airport?
5. The relatives (*greet, greets*) my new baby brother.

CHOICES

As you respond to the Choices, use these **Academic Vocabulary** words as appropriate: <u>articulate</u>, <u>characteristics</u>, <u>impact</u>, <u>insight</u>.

REVIEW
Create a Podcast
TechFocus Retell Maijue Xiong's story as a biographical podcast. First, consult your time line and make a list of all major events. Then, write a script for your podcast, record it, and play it for the class. How is the purpose of your biographical podcast different from that of Xiong's autobiography?

CONNECT
Write a Personal Narrative
Timed **Writing** Maijue Xiong and her family endured a difficult journey. What kinds of journeys have you taken? You may have moved from one city or state to another, changed neighborhoods, or simply had a long commute to school. Describe your journey in a two-paragraph personal narrative. Be sure to <u>articulate</u> the <u>insights</u> you gained from the experience.

EXTEND
Give a PowerPoint Presentation
TechFocus Conduct research on Laos, and create a PowerPoint presentation. Highlight significant facts about the country, such as details about its history, culture, and economy. Include illustrations for visual <u>impact</u>. Then, deliver the presentation to your class.

 Learn It Online
Tell your story in a whole new way. Try digital storytelling—we'll show you how at:

go.hrw.com | H7-535 | **Go**

Independent Practice
Grammar Link
Your Turn _____
1. *has*
2. *cry*
3. *walk*
4. *Is*
5. *greet*

Choices:
Evaluation Criteria
Review: **Homework**
Create a Podcast
The podcast retells all the major events in Xiong's journey.

Timed Writing: 40–50 Minutes
The narrative gives an autobiographical account of a journey and describes insights.

Extend: **Homework**
Give a PowerPoint Presentation
The presentation gives facts about Laos's culture, economy, and history, and includes interesting visuals.

Assess

 Chapter 5 Resources, Selection Standards Check, p. 15

ThinkCentral Online Assessment, Selection Standards Check

Teacher One Stop™, editable Selection Standards Check

Reteach

ThinkCentral Online Remediation

 Learn It Online
The **Digital Storytelling** mini-site shows students how to take a personal experience and craft it into a short film—complete with music, images, and special effects.

go.hrw.com | H7-535 | **Go**

Universal Access: Grammar Link

Tell students that although the rules of subject-verb agreement apply to both regular and irregular verbs, some verbs are the same in their singular and plural forms in one or more tenses. The irregular verb *to choose* is a good example of this. In the present tense, the singular form of *choose* is *chooses*, as in, *She* chooses *salad for lunch.* The plural form is *choose*, as in, *They* choose *tacos for lunch.* In the past tense, however, *chose* is the singular and plural form. *They chose to ride the early bus on Tuesday. I chose to ride the early bus on Tuesday.* Advise students to consider whether a verb is regular or irregular when evaluating subject-verb agreement.

Standards Focus

Objectives
Students will
- learn about the distinctive characteristics of a novella
- activate prior knowledge to understand new texts

Motivate

What Do You Think?/QuickWrite
Have students examine the ways in which people help each other. Discuss ways in which they have helped or been helped by others. Then, have students use their **Reader/Writer Notebook** to write about a time when they or someone they know asked for help.

English for Academic Success
Academic Vocabulary
Look for opportunities to use the Academic Vocabulary words in the chapter.

- **articulate, v.:** express clearly
- **characteristics, n. pl.:** distinguishing qualities or features
- **significance, n.:** importance;
- **impact, n.:** powerful effect

Analyzing Visuals

Extension Activity Ask students to describe what elements contribute to the painting's mood. **Possible response:** *The visible brushstrokes and soft colors of the trees give the painting a gentle, dreamlike quality.*

Song of the Trees
by **Mildred D. Taylor**

Golden Autumn (1901) by Stanislav Joulianovitch Joukovski (1873–1944). Oil on canvas.

 What Do You Think How can family or friends stand together during hard times?

 QuickWrite
Write about a difficult time in which you or someone you know turned to others for help. To whom did you (or someone else) turn? How did they help?

California Standards, pp. 536–555

- **Reading Standard 3.1** Articulate the expressed purposes and characteristics of different forms of prose (e.g., short story, novel, novella, essay).

Selection Readability	
Easily Accessible Accessible **Challenging**	historical context; serious subject matter

Selection Plot Summary
The African American Logan family unites to protest their white neighbors' plans to chop down their beloved trees in this Depression-era story of race relations. After Cassie Logan and her brothers try unsuccessfully to fight off the lumbermen, their father saves the day with a risky plan.

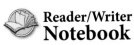

Reader/Writer Notebook

Use your **RWN** to complete the activities for this selection.

 Reading Standard 3.1 Articulate the expressed purposes and characteristics of different forms of prose (e.g., short story, novel, **novella**, essay).

Literary Skills Focus

Forms of Prose: Novella This story by Mildred Taylor was first published in a small book by itself, as a forty-eight page novella. You can think of a **novella** as a long short story or as a short novel. Like short stories and novels, novellas have **characters, conflicts, plots, settings,** and **themes.** In a novel or novella, more characters will appear, the conflicts will multiply, and several themes may operate at once.

Literary Perspectives Apply the literary perspective described on page 539 as you read this novella.

Reading Skills Focus

Activating Prior Knowledge When you **activate prior knowledge,** you use what you already know to help you understand something new. You can use your prior knowledge to think about the most important ideas in this novella before you begin to read. As you read, your prior knowledge will help you interpret the text.

Into Action In the chart below, write *yes* in the blank at the left if you believe the statement and can support it. Write *no* if you do not believe the statement and cannot support it. You will complete the chart after you have read the story.

Before Reading		After Reading
_____	1. Given the chance, most people won't take advantage of another person.	_____
_____	2. Nobody owns the earth.	_____
_____	3. People gain self-respect by standing up for their beliefs.	_____

Writing Skills Focus

Think as a Reader/Writer

Find It in Your Reading **Personification** is a figure of speech in which nonhuman things are described as if they were human. In this novella, the character Cassie thinks of the trees as her friends. In your *Reader/Writer Notebook,* list five examples from the story in which the writer uses personification in describing the trees.

Vocabulary

dispute (dihs PYOOT) *n.:* argument. *Mama settled the dispute between the brothers.*

curtly (KURT lee) *adv.:* rudely; with few words. *The man spoke curtly to Mama, showing his disrespect.*

elude (ih LOOD) *v.:* avoid; cleverly escape. *Christopher-John was able to elude the lumbermen who tried to catch him.*

incredulously (ihn KREHJ uh luhs lee) *adv.:* unbelievingly. *Mr. Andersen stared incredulously when Papa refused his request.*

Language Coach

Multiple-Meaning Words Many words in English have more than one meaning. For example:

cross → mixture of two things
cross → angry

Use context clues to help you decide which meaning of *cross* fits in each sentence below.

1. The whole class was _____ when rain spoiled the picnic.

2. Ralph's dog was a _____ between a Labrador and a poodle.

 Learn It Online
Increase your understanding of the story with improved word comprehension. Visit:

go.hrw.com H7-537 **Go**

Selection Resources

Chapter 5 Resources, on-level practice and assessment, p. 18

Teacher One Stop™, on-level lesson plans and all print resources

Holt Audio Library

Holt Audio Library: Selections and Summaries in Spanish

UA: Supporting Instruction in Five Languages, selection summary

ThinkCentral Online Assessment, Selection Standards Check

ThinkCentral Online Remediation

Selection Introduction

More About the Writer

Mildred D. Taylor's writings are based on her family's own history. Her book *The Land*, about a Logan ancestor who buys land in Mississippi in the 1870s, parallels the experience of Taylor's great-grandfather. Just as Taylor and her family moved from Mississippi to Ohio in the 1940s, her characters make the same journey in the final book in the Logan family saga.

Think About the Writer

Discuss the different kinds of people who affect students' lives. Remind students that a person does not need to be well known or wildly successful to be inspirational. Neighbors, family, and friends are all capable of inspiring us with their achievements and attitudes.

For Independent Reading

- If students are interested in reading more about the Logan family, suggest Mildred D. Taylor's *The Land*.

- If students want to explore the perspective of a white character growing up in the segregationist South, suggest they read Harper Lee's *To Kill a Mockingbird**, a classic coming-of-age story that explores a young girl's experiences in 1930s Alabama.

 *This title is available in the HRW library.

Mildred D. Taylor
(1943–   )

Newbery Medal WINNER

Early Success

Mildred Taylor grew up in Toledo, Ohio, where she was a high school honor student, a newspaper editor, and a class officer. Still, she says, she wasn't able to be what she *really* wanted to be: a cheerleader.

Learning Family Stories

Every summer Taylor and her family visited relatives in Mississippi, and she listened to their stories. By the time she was nine or ten, Taylor knew that she wanted to write.

Prizes for Her Work

Her first effort, *Song of the Trees*, introduced the Logan family and won first prize in the African American category of a competition for children's books. In 1977, when she accepted the Newbery Award for her second work about the Logan family, *Roll of Thunder, Hear My Cry*, Taylor spoke about her father:

> "Throughout my childhood he impressed upon my sister and me that we were somebody, that we were important and could do or be anything we set our minds to do or be."

Think About the Writer Taylor was inspired by her father. Who are the greatest inspirations in your life?

Build Background

The depression referred to in this story is the Great Depression, the severe economic decline in the United States that lasted from 1929 to 1942. During the Depression many banks and businesses closed. People lost their jobs, their savings, and even their homes. Many people had barely enough food to eat. At this time the segregation of African Americans was still a reality in much of the United States.

Preview the Selection

Times are difficult for the **Logan family** during the Great Depression, so **David**, the father, has taken a job far from home. While he is away, new trouble comes to his daughter, **Cassie,** and her mother, grandmother, and three brothers. This story is based on events that Taylor's father experienced as he was growing up.

Song of the Trees

by **Mildred D. Taylor**

"Cassie. Cassie, child, wake up now," Big Ma called gently as the new sun peeked over the horizon.

I looked sleepily at my grandmother and closed my eyes again.

"Cassie! Get up, girl!" This time the voice was not so gentle.

I jumped out of the deep, feathery bed as Big Ma climbed from the other side. The room was still dark, and I stubbed my toe while stumbling sleepily about looking for my clothes.

"Shoot! Darn ole chair," I fussed, rubbing my injured foot.

"Hush, Cassie, and open them curtains if you can't see," Big Ma said. "Prop that window open, too, and let some of that fresh morning air in here."

I opened the window and looked outside. The earth was draped in a cloak of gray mist as the sun chased the night away. The cotton stalks, which in another hour would glisten greenly toward the sun, were gray. The ripening corn, wrapped in jackets of emerald and gold, was gray. Even the rich brown Mississippi earth was gray.

Only the trees of the forest were not gray. They stood dark, almost black, across the dusty road, still holding the night. A soft breeze stirred, and their voices whispered down to me in a song of morning greeting.

"Cassie, girl, I said open that window, not stand there gazing out all morning. Now, get moving before I take something to you," Big Ma threatened.

I dashed to my clothes. Before Big Ma had unwoven her long braid of gray hair,

Ⓐ

Ⓐ Literary Focus Novella   What setting is being described here? What does it tell you about the characters' lives?

Literary Perspectives

The following perspective will help you think about the plot of this novella.

Analyzing Historical Context   To use the **historical perspective,** consider a literary text in its historical context: the time in which the author wrote, the time in which the story is set, and the ways in which people of the period saw the world. As you read, consider the economic situation that crippled the United States from 1929 to 1942. *Song of the Trees* is set in the context of a significant event in American history, the Great Depression (see page 538). Be sure to respond to the questions that will guide you in using this perspective.

- Review with students the characteristics of a **novella**: it is shorter than a novel and longer than a short story; it has a plot, setting, and characters; it may have multiple themes and conflicts. Point out that understanding the characteristics of the form of prose you are reading helps you know what to expect and to look for in a text.

- Point out Mama's lecture to Christopher-John on p. 540. The lecture sets up both part of the setting (the home of a poor family during the Great Depression) and a story conflict (the family's struggle with poverty). Then, point out the sibling conflicts between Cassie and Little Man over his picky dressing habits, and between Stacey and Cassie and Little Man over carrying out the day's work. Explain that smaller conflicts like these would likely not appear in a short story because there would only be space for the main conflicts and most critical information.

Guided Practice: Apply

Have students jot down in their **Reader/Writer Notebooks** the characters, setting, conflicts, and critical ideas that they see emerging in the novella so far. Tell students to add to their lists as they read.

---

my pants and shirt were on and I was hurrying into the kitchen.

A small kerosene lamp was burning in a corner as I entered. Its light reflected on seven-year-old Christopher-John, short, pudgy, and a year younger than me, sitting sleepily upon a side bench drinking a large glass of clabber milk.[1] Mama's back was to me. She was dipping flour from a near-empty canister, while my older brother, Stacey, built a fire in the huge iron-bellied stove.

"I don't know what I'm going to do with you, Christopher-John," Mama scolded. "Getting up in the middle of the night and eating all that cornbread. Didn't you have enough to eat before you went to bed?"

"Yes'm," Christopher-John murmured.

"Lord knows I don't want any of my babies going hungry, but times are hard, honey. Don't you know folks all around here in Mississippi are struggling? Children crying cause they got no food to eat, and their daddies crying cause they can't get jobs so they can feed their babies? And you getting up in the middle of the night, stuffing yourself with cornbread!"

Her voice softened as she looked at the sleepy little boy. "Baby, we're in a depression. Why do you think Papa's way down in Louisiana laying tracks on the railroad?

---

1. **clabber milk:** thickly curdled sour milk.

B [Read and Discuss] What has the author shown you about this family so far?

C [Literary Perspectives] Analyzing Historical Context How does what you learned about the Great Depression in the Build Background text help you understand why Mama is upset when Christopher-John eats all the cornbread?

So his children can eat—but only when they're hungry. You understand?" **C**

"Yes'm," Christopher-John murmured again, as his eyes slid blissfully shut.

"Morning, Mama," I chimed.

"Morning, baby," Mama said. "You wash up yet?"

"No'm."

"Then go wash up and call Little Man again. Tell him he's not dressing to meet President Roosevelt[2] this morning. Hurry up, now, cause I want you to set the table." **D**

Little Man, a very small six-year-old and a most finicky dresser, was brushing his hair when I entered the room he shared with Stacey and Christopher-John. His blue pants were faded, but except for a small grass stain on one knee, they were clean. Outside of his Sunday pants, these were the only pants he had, and he was always careful to keep them in the best condition possible. But one look at him and I knew that he was far from pleased with their condition this morning. He frowned down at the spot for a moment, then continued brushing.

"Man, hurry up and get dressed," I called. "Mama said you ain't dressing to meet the president."

"See there," he said, pointing at the stain. "You did that."

---

2. **President Roosevelt:** Franklin Delano Roosevelt (1882–1945) was president of the United States from 1933 to 1945.

D [Literary Focus] Novella Whereas a short story may have only one or two main characters and introduce them right away, a novella often introduces more characters as the story proceeds. List all the characters you have met so far. How are they related to one another?

Universal Access

EL English Learners

Point out to students that the characters in this novella use slang when they speak to each other. Tell students that they may be able to decipher the meanings of these unfamiliar words by thinking of standard English words that sound similar. For example, the word *ole* in paragraph 5 of p. 539 sounds similar to the word *old*. Work with students to identify the meanings of other selection words such as *yes'm*, and *ain't*.

Struggling Readers

Tell students that activating prior knowledge means relating what you read to what you already know. For example, point out that in paragraph 7 on p. 539, Cassie describes cotton and corn. A reader might know that these things often grow on farms or in a rural area, and they can use this prior knowledge to determine that Cassie and her family live in a rural area.

(left) *Big James Sweats;* (middle) *Little Calist Can't Swim* from the series Sugar Children (1996). Gelatin silver print on paper, 14˝ x 11˝. © Vik Muniz/Licensed by VAGA, New York, NY.

Sokoro (2006) by Tilly Willis. Oil on canvas.

Analyzing Visuals **Connecting to the Text** Which characters could each of these portraits represent? Explain.

"I did no such thing. You fell all by yourself."

"You tripped me!"

"Didn't!"

"Did, too!"

"Hey, cut it out, you two!" ordered Stacey, entering the room. "You fought over that stupid stain yesterday. Now get moving, both of you. We gotta go pick blackberries before the sun gets too high. Little Man, you go gather the eggs while Christopher-John and me milk the cows."

Little Man and I decided to settle our dispute later when Stacey wasn't around. With Papa away, eleven-year-old Stacey thought of himself as the man of the house, and Mama had instructed Little Man, Christopher-John, and me to mind him. So, like it or not, we humored him. Besides, he was bigger than we were. **E**

I ran to the back porch to wash. When I returned to the kitchen, Mama was talking to Big Ma.

"We got about enough flour for two more meals," Mama said, cutting the biscuit dough. "Our salt and sugar are practically down to nothing and—" She stopped when she saw me. "Cassie, baby, go gather the eggs for Mama."

"Little Man's gathering the eggs."

"Then go help him."

"But I ain't set the table yet."

E Read and Discuss What does this scene show you about Stacey, Little Man, and Cassie?

Vocabulary **dispute** (dihs PYOOT) *n.:* argument.

Advanced Learners
Acceleration Point out that this novella has a main theme as well as several secondary themes that may be influenced by or connected to the main theme. After they read, have students work in groups to identify the story's main and secondary themes.

Students with Disabilities
To help students visualize the novella's setting, provide them with images of places similar to the corn fields, cotton fields, and forests that Cassie describes on p. 539.

Analyzing Visuals
Tell students that **Vik Muniz** (1961–   ) was born in Brazil and later moved to New York City. **Tilly Willis** is an English painter with close ties to Senegal, West Africa.

Connecting to the Text: *I think the first portrait is of Stacey, the second is of Christopher-John, and the third is of Cassie. The first boy looks oldest, the second doesn't look as neat as Little Man, and Cassie is the only young girl in the story.*

Think About/Talk About

▶ Comprehension

Ⓑ Read and Discuss
Possible response: *So far, the author has introduced five family members. It seems as if they are short on money.*

Ⓔ Read and Discuss
Possible response: *This scene shows how picky Little Man is about his clothing. It also shows that Cassie and he argue regularly, and that Little Man and Cassie accept Stacey in the role of man of the house.*

▶ Analysis

ⒸLiterary Perspectives
Possible response: *During the Great Depression, people couldn't afford much, even food. When Christopher-John eats more than he needs, he may cause the other family members to go hungry because they can't afford more food.*

ⒹLiterary Focus
Possible response: *Cassie, Big Ma, Christopher-John, Mama, Stacey, Little Man. Christopher-John, Stacey, and Little Man are Cassie's brothers. They are all Mama's children and Big Ma's grandchildren.*

▶ Extend the Discussion
Conflict At the end of p. 541, how does Mama's dialogue and her reaction to Cassie heighten the tension in the novella? ***Possible response:*** *Mama's words and actions tell us that things aren't going well for the Logans, and we also learn that Mama isn't willing to reveal this information to her children. This part of the story makes the reader worry about the family's lack of money, and it introduces a conflict between the adults and the children.*

Vocabulary: Own the Word
dispute: Explain to students that *dispute* comes from the Latin verb *disputare,* meaning *discuss.* A *dispute* is a heated, emotional discussion. Have students describe *disputes* that might happen among siblings.

Song of the Trees **541**

Model the Skill

- Tell students that the sentence of a subject may be singular, identifying only one person or object, or plural, identifying multiple people or objects. In formal English, a sentence's subject and verb have to agree, or match in number.

- Tell students that a sentence with more than one subject, such as "my cousins and I," presents more difficulty in determining subject-verb agreement. Subjects joined by *and* are linked and considered plural, but subjects joined by *neither…nor* are treated differently. If there are two singular subjects, they would take a singular verb; but if there is a singular and a plural subject, the verb form will be determined by the subject closest to the verb, and could be singular or plural.

- Direct students to the paragraph on p. 542 that begins with the sentence "Christopher-John and Little Man…" Identify the subjects of the sentence: *Christopher-John* and *Little Man,* taking care to point out that there are two. Because they are joined by *and,* the two subjects are considered together a plural subject, and would take the plural form of a verb.

Guided Practice: Apply

Think-Pair-Share Provide students with the following sentence, and have them choose the form that the verb should take. Then, have students explain their answers to a partner before sharing and discussing their answers with the class. *Neither Abigail nor her aunt takes/take dance classes.*

Think as a Reader/Writer

Find It in Your Reading Point out the use of personification in the first column on p. 542, when Cassie says the trees "answered me with a soft, swooshing sound."

Use It in Your Writing Have students write a sentence in which they use personification to describe an everyday object as having human characteristics.

"Set it when you come back."

I knew that I was not wanted in the kitchen. I looked suspiciously at my mother and grandmother, then went to the back porch to get a basket.

Big Ma's voice drifted through the open window. "Mary, you oughta write David and tell him somebody done opened his letter and stole that ten dollars he sent," she said.

"No, Mama. David's got enough on his mind. Besides, there's enough garden foods so we won't go hungry."

"But what 'bout your medicine? You're all out of it and the doctor told you good to—" **F**

"Shhhh!" Mama stared at the window. "Cassie, I thought I told you to go gather those eggs!"

"I had to get a basket, Mama!" I hurried off the porch and ran to the barn.

After breakfast, when the sun was streaking red across the sky, my brothers and I ambled into the coolness of the forest, leading our three cows and their calves down the narrow cow path to the pond. The morning was already muggy, but the trees closed out the heat as their leaves waved restlessly, high above our heads. **G**

"Good morning, Mr. Trees," I shouted. They answered me with a soft, swooshing sound. "Hear 'em, Stacey? Hear 'em singing?"

"Ah, cut that out, Cassie. Them trees ain't singing. How many times I gotta tell you that's just the wind?" He stopped at a sweet alligator gum, pulled out his knife, and scraped off a glob of gum that had seeped through its cracked bark. He handed me half.

As I stuffed the gooey wad into my mouth, I patted the tree and whispered, "Thank you, Mr. Gum Tree."

Stacey frowned at me, then looked back at Christopher-John and Little Man walking far behind us, munching on their breakfast biscuits.

"Man! Christopher-John! Come on, now," he yelled. "If we finish the berry picking early, we can go wading before we go back."

Christopher-John and Little Man ran to catch up with us. Then, resuming their leisurely pace, they soon fell behind again.

A large gray squirrel scurried across our path and up a walnut tree. I watched until it was settled amidst the tree's featherlike leaves; then, poking one of the calves, I said, "Stacey, is Mama sick?"

"Sick? Why you say that?"

"Cause I heard Big Ma asking her 'bout some medicine she's supposed to have."

Stacey stopped, a worried look on his face. "If she's sick, she ain't bad sick," he decided. "If she was bad sick, she'd been in bed."

We left the cows at the pond and, taking our berry baskets, delved deeper into the forest looking for the wild blackberry bushes.

"I see one!" I shouted.

"Where?" cried Christopher-John, eager for the sweet berries.

"Over there! Last one to it's a rotten egg!" I yelled, and off I ran.

Stacey and Little Man followed at my heels. But Christopher-John puffed far behind. "Hey, wait for me," he cried.

F **Literary Perspectives** **Analyzing Historical Context** How does this conversation add to what you already know about Mama and the family's situation?

G **Read and Discuss** What are the children doing?

Word-Attack Skills Mini-Lesson

Digraphs *ai* and *ea*

- Remind students that vowel digraphs such as *ai* and *ea* usually stand for long vowel sounds.

- Illustrate this by using the selection words *stain* and *clean*. The digraph *ai* stands for the long *a* in *stain*, and the digraph *ea* stands for the long *e* in *clean*.

- Ask students to identify other examples of words in the selection in which *ai* stands for the long *a* and *ea* stands for the long *e*. [Possibilities for *ai*: *braid, exclaimed, wait, afraid, remained;* for *ea: streaking, eat, heat, eager, easy, mean*]

- Point out that there are some words in which these two digraphs do not stand for the long vowel sounds. For instance, in the selection word *against*, *ai* stands for the short *e*.

- Use the selection words *threatened, heavy,* and *head* as examples of words in which *ea* stands for the short *e* instead of the long *e*.

"Let's hide from Christopher-John," Stacey suggested.

The three of us ran in different directions. I plunged behind a giant old pine and hugged its warm trunk as I waited for Christopher-John.

Christopher-John puffed to a stop, then, looking all around, called, "Hey, Stacey! Cassie! Hey, Man! Y'all cut that out!"

I giggled and Christopher-John heard me.

"I see you, Cassie!" he shouted, starting toward me as fast as his chubby legs would carry him. "You're it!"

"Not 'til you tag me," I laughed. As I waited for him to get closer, I glanced up into the boughs of my wintry-smelling hiding tree, expecting a song of laughter. But the old pine only tapped me gently with one of its long, low branches. I turned from the tree and dashed away.

"You can't, you can't, you can't catch me," I taunted, dodging from one beloved tree to the next. Around shaggy-bark hickories and sharp-needled pines, past blue-gray beeches and sturdy black walnuts I sailed, while my laughter resounded through the ancient forest, filling every chink. Overhead, the boughs of the giant trees hovered protectively, but they did not join in my laughter.

Deeper into the forest I plunged.

Christopher-John, unable to keep up, plopped on the ground in a pant. Little Man and Stacey, emerging from their hiding places, ran up to him.

"Ain't you caught her yet?" Little Man demanded, more than a little annoyed.

"He can't catch the champ," I boasted, stopping to rest against a hickory tree. I slid my back down the tree's shaggy trunk and looked up at its long branches, heavy with sweet nuts and slender green leaves, perfectly still. I looked around at the leaves of the other trees. They were still also. I stared at the trees, aware of an eerie silence descending over the forest.

Stacey walked toward me. "What's the matter with you, Cassie?" he asked.

"The trees, Stacey," I said softly, "they ain't singing no more." **H**

"Is that all?" He looked up at the sky. "Come on, y'all. It's getting late. We'd better go pick them berries." He turned and walked on.

"But, Stacey, listen. Little Man, Christopher-John, listen."

The forest echoed an uneasy silence.

"The wind just stopped blowing, that's all," said Stacey. "Now stop fooling around and come on."

I jumped up to follow Stacey, then cried, "Stacey, look!" On a black oak a few yards away was a huge white *X*. "How did that get there?" I exclaimed, running to the tree.

"There's another one!" Little Man screamed.

> I jumped up
> to follow Stacey,
> then cried,
> "Stacey, look!"
> On a black oak
> a few yards away was
> a huge white X.

H **Read and Discuss** What is going on with Cassie and the trees?

Literary Perspectives

Activity Display these sentences and have volunteers underline the two words that contain the digraphs *ai* or *ea*. Have them tell which word has a long vowel sound.

1. The family was about to eat breakfast. [*eat*]
2. Uneasiness hung heavy in the air. [*uneasiness*]
3. The children were afraid to go against their parents' wishes. [*afraid*]
4. Mean greed threatened the woods. [*mean*]
5. Men were ready to steal the trees. [*steal*]

Remind students that during the Depression, many families did not have enough money to buy the most basic supplies. Point out Big Mama's comment in the fifth paragraph on p. 542: "But what about your medicine?" Have students think about the sacrifice Mama is making for her family. What does this tell us about her?

Think About/Talk About

▶ Comprehension

G Read and Discuss

Possible response: The kids have to get the cows watered and pick berries, but they also seem to have fun in the forest doing things like playing hide and seek with each other.

H Read and Discuss

Possible response: Cassie is responding to a perceived change in the trees she perceives as friends who protect her, talk to her, and sing to her. She feels a connection to them, and she thinks they are telling her that something is not right in the forest.

▶ Analysis

F Literary Perspectives

Possible response: Mama is independent and strong. She doesn't want the kids to worry, and she's not afraid to struggle to keep Papa from worrying about the family while he is away. We also find out that she is ill but can't afford her medicine because of the family's financial situation.

▶ Extend the Discussion

Tone Read paragraphs 6 and 7 on p. 543. Then, compare Cassie's mood to the mood conveyed by the trees. How does this contrast affect the tone of the story?

Possible response: Cassie is excited and laughing and expecting the trees to laugh with her, but the trees are gentle, protective, perfectly still, and not singing any more. The eerie silence introduces a serious or ominous element to the story, as if something bad might happen.

Model the Skill

■ Provide students with copies of the Reading Skills Focus graphic organizer. (See **Chapter 5 Resources**.)

■ Demonstrate how to use the graphic organizer to **activate prior knowledge**. Read item one aloud. You might say, "To respond to this statement, I think about what I know from my own experience about people taking advantage of one another. In my life, I have found that people do not take advantage of each other. So I answered yes."

Before Reading

yes 1. Given the chance, most people won't take advantage of another person.

_____ 2. Nobody owns the earth.

_____ 3. People gain self-respect by standing up for their beliefs.

■ Have a volunteer read p. 545 aloud, and demonstrate evaluating prior knowledge based on story events. You might say, "Mr. Andersen has a clear opportunity to take advantage of the Logans, and he is quite happy to do so. That is not what I would have expected. My experience tells me that many people wouldn't take advantage of others, but that number might be fewer than I thought."

Guided Practice: Apply

Have students revisit their support for the first item in the graphic organizer, and evaluate whether Mr. Andersen's scheme is strong enough to change their minds.

"I see one too!" shouted Christopher-John.

Stacey said nothing as Christopher-John, Little Man, and I ran wildly through the forest counting the ghostlike marks.

"Stacey, they're on practically all of them," I said when he called us back. **I**

"Why?"

Stacey studied the trees, then suddenly pushed us down.

"My clothes!" Little Man wailed indignantly.

"Hush, Man, and stay down," Stacey warned. "Somebody's coming."

Two white men emerged. We looked at each other. We knew to be silent.

"You mark them all down here?" one of the men asked.

I | Read and Discuss | What is happening in the forest now?

"Not the younger ones, Mr. Andersen."

"We might need them, too," said Mr. Andersen, counting the X's. "But don't worry 'bout marking them now, Tom. We'll get them later. Also them trees up past the pond toward the house."

"The old woman agree to you cutting these trees?"

"I ain't been down there yet," Mr. Andersen said.

"Mr. Andersen . . ." Tom hesitated a moment, looked up at the silent trees, then back at Mr. Andersen. "Maybe you should go easy with them," he cautioned. "You know that David can be as mean as an ole jackass when he wanna be."

"He's talking about Papa," I whispered. **J**

"Shhhh!" Stacey hissed.

J | Literary Focus | Novella What additional characters have come into the story? Explain why a novella allows for the appearance of more characters as the story continues.

Thomas Flaherty by Thomas Eakins (1844–1916).

Universal Access

EL English Learners

Students may have difficulty understanding Mr. Andersen's colloquial phrasing. Have students read one of Mr. Andersen's sentences aloud, and provide students with a more familiar rephrasing of his words. For example, if students are struggling with the phrase, "He don't have no say in it," explain that Mr. Andersen means, "He doesn't have any power to change it."

Struggling Readers

Benchmark Students Explain to students that Mr.

Andersen's decision to begin cutting down the Logan family's trees without permission creates a conflict in the story. Mr. Andersen wants to sell the trees, and he will do whatever is necessary to get them. The Logans want to keep the forest and their property as it is. To help students determine how the conflict will develop, draw students' attention to Mr. Andersen's conversation with Tom. Point out the sentence, "Besides, I guess I oughta know how to handle David Logan." Discuss with students what the word "handle" might imply. Suggest that Mr. Andersen sees Papa as an object he can control.

Mr. Andersen looked uneasy. "What's that gotta do with anything?"

"Well, he just don't take much to any dealings with white folks." Again, Tom looked up at the trees. "He ain't afraid like some."

Mr. Andersen laughed weakly. "Don't worry 'bout that, Tom. The land belongs to his mama. He don't have no say in it. Besides, I guess I oughta know how to handle David Logan. After all, there are ways. . . .

"Now, you get on back to my place and get some boys and start chopping down these trees," Mr. Andersen said. "I'll go talk to the old woman." He looked up at the sky. "We can almost get a full day's work in if we hurry."

Mr. Andersen turned to walk away, but Tom stopped him. "Mr. Andersen, you really gonna chop all the trees?"

"If I need to. These folks ain't got no call for them. I do. I got me a good contract for these trees and I aim to fulfill it."

Tom watched Mr. Andersen walk away; then, looking sorrowfully up at the trees, he shook his head and disappeared into the depths of the forest.   **K**

"What we gonna do, Stacey?" I asked anxiously. "They can't just cut down our trees, can they?"

"I don't know. Papa's gone. . . ." Stacey muttered to himself, trying to decide what we should do next.

"Boy, if Papa was here, them ole white men wouldn't be messing with our trees," Little Man declared.

"Yeah!" Christopher-John agreed. "Just let Papa get hold of 'em and he gonna turn 'em every which way but loose."

"Christopher-John, Man," Stacey said finally, "go get the cows and take them home."

"But we just brought them down here," Little Man protested.

"And we gotta pick the berries for dinner," said Christopher-John mournfully.

"No time for that now. Hurry up. And stay clear of them white men. Cassie, you come with me."

We ran, brown legs and feet flying high through the still forest.

By the time Stacey and I arrived at the house, Mr. Andersen's car was already parked in the dusty drive. Mr. Andersen himself was seated comfortably in Papa's rocker on the front porch. Big Ma was seated too, but Mama was standing.

Stacey and I eased quietly to the side of the porch, unnoticed.

"Sixty-five dollars. That's an awful lot of money in these hard times, Aunt Caroline," Mr. Andersen was saying to Big Ma.

I could see Mama's thin face harden.

"You know," Mr. Andersen said, rocking familiarly in Papa's chair, "that's more than David can send home in two months."

"We do quite well on what David sends home," Mama said coldly.

Mr. Andersen stopped rocking. "I suggest you encourage Aunt Caroline to sell them trees, Mary. You know, David might not always be able to work so good. He could possibly have . . . an accident."   **L**

K **Reading Focus** Prior Knowledge In what way might Mr. Andersen take advantage of the Logan family? Support your response with your own knowledge and with details from the text.

L **Literary Focus** Novella A novella usually has a central antagonist, a character who is opposed to the main characters. Who is the main antagonist in this story? What danger does he pose?

Have students skim the page for other evidence of Mr. Andersen's feelings toward the Logan family.

Advanced Learners

Extension Have students examine the conversation between Mr. Andersen and Tom on p. 545 to determine Tom's role in the conflict between Mr. Andersen and the Logans. Ask students to list specific examples of actions in the text that illustrate Tom's feelings about chopping down the trees. Have students consider the author's purpose for including Tom in the story.

Analyzing Visuals

Tell students that the man in the portrait, Thomas Flaherty, served in Congress from 1937 to 1943, around the time of the events of *Song of the Trees*.

Extension Activity Ask students to explain which character from *Song of the Trees* Thomas Flaherty most closely resembles. *Possible response: He looks the most like Mr. Andersen. He is white, and he looks a little angry.*

Think About/Talk About

▶ Comprehension

❶ Read and Discuss
Possible response: The siblings have noticed large marks on almost all of the trees.

❶ Reading Focus
Possible response: Mr. Andersen might take advantage of the Logans by bullying Big Ma into letting him cut the trees. He discusses her age and gender as though they make her weak, and I know that people sometimes take advantage of the elderly.

▶ Analysis

❶ Literary Focus
Possible response: Mr. Andersen and Tom have come into the story. A novella is longer than a short story and may have multiple conflicts. Length and complexity allow for additional characters to come into the story.

❶ Literary Focus
Possible response: Mr. Andersen is the antagonist in the story. He threatens the Logan family's property, self-respect, and even their safety to get his own way.

▶ Extend the Discussion

Conflict In paragraph 3 on p. 545, Mr. Andersen says, "After all, there are ways…" What might he be talking about? How does this comment contribute to the story's conflict?
Possible response: I think he's talking about hurting Papa or doing something illegal to get the trees for himself. Not only is Mr. Andersen taking advantage of the Logans, but he's raising the stakes of the conflict by threatening to harm them physically as well.

Model the Skill

■ Remind students that a **novella**, which is longer than a short story, can include more complex plots, the development and resolution of multiple story conflicts, and themes.

■ Point out that among the nine major characters in the book, there are multiple conflicts: Cassie must deal with the loss of her beloved trees; the Logans struggle to make enough money to stay alive; the Logans clash with Mr. Andersen over the trees; and there is a broader racial conflict at play between the Logans and Mr. Andersen.

Guided Practice: Apply

Ask students if they can identify broader ideas, or themes, addressed in this novella. If students struggle to answer the question, have them revisit the Reading Skills Focus graphic organizer and discuss how the ideas on the organizer relate to the story so far.

Big Ma's soft brown eyes clouded over with fear as she looked first at Mr. Andersen, then at Mama. But Mama clenched her fists and said, "In Mississippi, black men do not have accidents."

"Hush, child, hush," Big Ma said hurriedly. "How many trees for the sixty-five dollars, Mr. Andersen?"

"Enough 'til I figure I got my sixty-five dollars' worth."

"And how many would that be?" Mama persisted.

Mr. Andersen looked haughtily at Mama. "I said I'd be the judge of that, Mary."

"I think not," Mama said.

Mr. Andersen stared at Mama. And Mama stared back at him. I knew Mr. Andersen didn't like that, but Mama did it anyway. Mr. Andersen soon grew uneasy under that piercing gaze, and when his eyes swiftly shifted from Mama to Big Ma, his face was beet red.

"Caroline," he said, his voice low and menacing, "you're the head of this family and you've got a decision to make. Now, I need them trees and I mean to have them. I've offered you a good price for them and I ain't gonna haggle over it. I know y'all can use the money. Doc Thomas tells me that Mary's not well." He hesitated a moment, then hissed venomously, "And if something should happen to David . . ."

> Big Ma's soft brown eyes clouded over with fear.

"All right," Big Ma said, her voice trembling. "All right, Mr. Andersen."

"No, Big Ma!" I cried, leaping onto the porch. "You can't let him cut our trees!"

Mr. Andersen grasped the arms of the rocker, his knuckles chalk white. "You certainly ain't taught none of your younguns how to behave, Caroline," he said curtly.

"You children go on to the back," Mama said, shooing us away.

"No, Mama," Stacey said. "He's gonna cut them all down. Me and Cassie heard him say so in the woods."

"I won't let him cut them," I threatened. "I won't let him! The trees are my friends and ain't no mean ole white man gonna touch my trees—"

Mama's hands went roughly around my body as she carried me off to my room.

"Now, hush," she said, her dark eyes flashing wildly. "I've told you how dangerous it is . . ." She broke off in midsentence. She stared at me a moment, then hugged me tightly and went back to the porch.

Stacey joined me a few seconds later, and we sat there in the heat of the quiet room, listening miserably as the first whack of an ax echoed against the trees.

That night I was awakened by soft sounds outside my window. I reached for Big Ma, but she wasn't there. Hurrying

M **Read and Discuss** The word *venomously* (VEHN uh muhs lee) means "poisonously." What is the author comparing Mr. Andersen to by the use of the phrase *hissed venomously?* How does this make you feel about Mr. Andersen?

Vocabulary **curtly** (KURT lee) *adv.:* rudely; with few words.

Cross-Curricular Connection

HISTORY: The Great Depression

Remind students that *Song of the Trees* takes place during the Great Depression, a devastating time period in American history.

• In October of 1929, the United States' stock market crashed. Stocks that had been worth large amounts of money suddenly became almost worthless, and people watched helplessly as their fortunes disappeared before their eyes. The stock market continued to fall until 1932.

• By that time, almost a quarter of Americans eligible for work were unemployed, and workers' salaries had fallen drastically. Many people did not have enough food to eat, and some were homeless.

• President Franklin Roosevelt introduced several economic programs in an attempt to restore the economy, but it was not until 1939, during the early days of World War II, that the United States was finally freed from the grasp of the Great Depression.

HSS Analysis Skills: HR 1, 2

to the window, I saw Mama and Big Ma standing in the yard in their nightclothes and Stacey, fully dressed, sitting atop Lady, our golden mare. By the time I got outside, Stacey was gone.

"Mama, where's Stacey?" I cried.

"Be quiet, Cassie. You'll wake Christopher-John and Little Man."

"But where's he going?"

"He's going to get Papa," Mama said. "Now be quiet."

"Go on, Stacey, boy," I whispered. "Ride for me, too." **N**

As the dust billowed after him, Mama said, "I should've gone myself. He's so young."

Big Ma put her arm around Mama. "Now, Mary, you know you couldn't've gone. Mr. Andersen would miss you if he come by and see you ain't here. You done right, now. Don't worry, that boy'll be just fine."

Three days passed, hot and windless.

Mama forbade any of us to go into the forest, so Christopher-John, Little Man, and I spent the slow, restless days hovering as close to the dusty road as we dared, listening to the foreign sounds of steel against the trees and the thunderous roar of those ancient loved ones as they crashed upon the earth. Sometimes Mama would scold us and tell us to come back to the house, but even she could not ignore the continuous pounding of the axes against the trees. Or the sight of the loaded lumber wagons rolling out of the forest. In the middle of washing or ironing or hoeing, she would look up sorrowfully and listen, then turn toward the road, searching for some sign of Papa and Stacey.

On the fourth day, before the sun had risen, bringing its cloak of miserable heat, I saw her walking alone toward the woods. I ran after her.

She did not send me back.

"Mama," I said. "How sick are you?"

Mama took my hand. "Remember when you had the flu and felt so sick?"

"Yes'm."

"And when I gave you some medicine, you got well soon afterward?"

"Yes'm."

"Well, that's how sick I am. As soon as I get my medicine, I'll be all well again. And that'll be soon, now that Papa's coming home," she said, giving my hand a gentle little squeeze.

The quiet surrounded us as we entered the forest. Mama clicked on the flashlight, and we walked silently along the cow path to the pond. There, just beyond the pond, pockets of open space loomed before us.

"Mama!"

"I know, baby, I know."

On the ground lay countless trees. Trees that had once been such strong, tall things. So strong that I could fling my arms partially around one of them and feel safe and secure. So tall and leafy green that their boughs had formed a forest temple.

And old.

So old that Indians had once built fires at their feet and had sung happy songs of happy days. So old they had hidden fleeing black men in the night and listened to their sad tales of a foreign land.

In the cold of winter, when the ground lay frozen, they had sung their frosty

---

N | Read and Discuss | What is happening now?

Universal Access

Struggling Readers
Strategic Students To help students understand the racial undertones of the conflict between Mr. Andersen, Mama, and Big Ma, guide them in activating prior knowledge about the time and place in which the story events happen. Draw a simple time line on the board by drawing a horizontal line and including vertical hash marks only for the events that follow. Remind students that the story takes place in Mississippi in the 1930s. Draw a mark in the middle of the time line and write, "1930s: Song of the Trees." Then, point out that in the South, nearly all African Americans were enslaved until the 1860s. Draw a mark to the left of 1930s and write, "1860s: slavery is outlawed in the South." Finally, tell students that the Civil Rights movement, in which African Americans fought for and won equal rights, happened in the 1960s. Draw a mark to the right of the 1930s and write, "1960s: African Americans gain equal rights." Point out to students that "Song of the Trees" takes place in a middle ground, between the end of slavery and the Civil Rights movement. Discuss as a group what sort of treatment African Americans received during this time, and how the story conflict reflects racial tensions of the time.

Think About/Talk About

▶ Comprehension
M Read and Discuss
Possible response: The author compares Mr. Andersen to a poisonous snake. This lets us know that Mr. Andersen is the villain of the story and that his words cannot be trusted.

N Read and Discuss
Possible response: Stacey is sent to bring Papa home.

▶ Extend the Discussion
Theme In the first paragraph on p. 546, Mama says, "In Mississippi, black men do not have accidents." How does this comment relate to one of the themes of the novella?
Possible response: One of the story's themes is that interracial tension can be dangerous and destructive. Mama's comment illustrates this theme because she's suggesting that black men in Mississippi are often purposefully hurt by white people.

Symbolism Reread the last three full paragraphs on p. 547. What might the cutting of the trees symbolize?
Possible response: Their cutting could symbolize the destruction of safety and strength by people who want to harm Cassie's family.

Setting How are descriptions of the setting on p. 547 different from those at the beginning of the story? Why do you think this is?
Possible response: The setting is different because the sights, sounds, and weather have changed. It is very hot and dry now, which makes the family feel especially miserable about the cutting of the trees. There are loud noises of crashing trees and axes chopping, and the family constantly sees lumber wagons carrying away their forest.

Vocabulary: Own the Word
curtly: Demonstrate a person's voice who is speaking *curtly*. Ask one or two students to stand at their desks and demonstrate.

- Remind students that the **setting** is the time and place in which story events occur. The setting directly impacts the plot, or story events.

- Review with students how to identify setting details. At this point in the story, the author has already established that this family lives on the edge of a forest in the Deep South during the Great Depression. The setting is critical because the family owns and is fond of the forest, but has been forced to sell their trees to a white man who wants to cut the trees down. Another element of the setting—race relations in that time and place—precipitated the sale as the family was bullied by the white man.

- Have students read the first three full paragraphs of p. 548. Ask them to identify the setting details. *Students should recognize that the images of the ruined forest and of the ghostly sunrise clarify the setting in these paragraphs.*

Guided Practice: Apply

Turn-and-Talk Have students read pp. 548–549 in groups, starting at the top of column 2 on p. 548. Ask them to observe and discuss how the forest setting contributes to the action on these pages.

ballads of years gone by. Or on a muggy, sweat-drenched day, their leaves had rippled softly, lazily, like restless green fingers strumming at a guitar, echoing their epic tales.

But now they would sing no more. They lay forever silent upon the ground.

Those trees that remained standing were like defeated warriors mourning their fallen dead. But soon they, too, would fall, for the white *X*'s had been placed on nearly every one. **O**

"Oh, dear, dear trees," I cried as the gray light of the rising sun fell in ghostly shadows over the land. The tears rolled hot down my cheeks. Mama held me close, and when I felt her body tremble, I knew she was crying too.

When our tears eased, we turned sadly toward the house. As we emerged from the forest, we could see two small figures waiting impatiently on the other side of the road. As soon as they spied us, they hurried across to meet us.

"Mama! You and Cassie was in the forest," Little Man accused. "Big Ma told us!"

"How was it?" asked Christopher-John, rubbing the sleep from his eyes. "Was it spooky?"

"Spooky and empty," I said listlessly.

"Mama, me and Christopher-John wanna see too," Little Man declared.

"No, baby," Mama said softly as we crossed the road. "The men'll be done there soon, and I don't want y'all underfoot."

"But, Mama—" Little Man started to protest.

"When Papa comes home and the men are gone, then you can go. But until then, you stay out of there. You hear me, Little Man Logan?"

"Yes'm," Little Man reluctantly replied.

But the sun had been up only an hour when Little Man decided that he could not wait for Papa to return.

"Mama said we wasn't to go down there," Christopher-John warned.

"Cassie did," Little Man cried.

"But she was with Mama. Wasn't you, Cassie?"

"Well, I'm going too," said Little Man. "Everybody's always going someplace 'cepting me." And off he went. **P**

Christopher-John and I ran after him. Down the narrow cow path and around the pond we chased. But neither of us was fast enough to overtake Little Man before he reached the lumbermen.

"Hey, you kids, get away from here," Mr. Andersen shouted when he saw us. "Now, y'all go on back home," he said, stopping in front of Little Man.

"We are home," I said. "You're the one who's on our land."

"Claude," Mr. Andersen said to one of the black lumbermen, "take these kids home." Then he pushed Little Man out of his way. Little Man pushed back. Mr. Andersen looked down, startled that a little black boy would do such a thing. He shoved Little Man a second time, and Little Man fell into the dirt.

Little Man looked down at his clothing covered with sawdust and dirt and wailed,

---

O Read and Discuss How is the forest now different from the way it used to be?

P Literary Focus Novella How does the event of Little Man running off help to develop his character?

Developing Oral Fluency

Use the exchange between Mama and the Logan children on p. 548 to give students practice in reading dialogue. Explain to students that in this scene, Cassie, Little Man, and Christopher-John are upset about the trees' being cut down, and Mama is trying to calm them down. Remind students that punctuation marks within lines of dialogue give readers clues about when to pause, when to stress certain words or phrases, and when to make changes in intonation.

Group Activity Put students into groups of five, making sure that there is at least one fluent reader in each group.

- Model reading a few lines of dialogue from the scene, making sure to look for signal words in the text about tone and volume. For example, in the ninth full paragraph, the author indicates that Mama speaks softly. This line should be read in a soft voice.

- Next, have each group read the scene aloud. They should begin reading at the fifth full paragraph in column 1 ("Mama! You and Cassie..."), and stop read-

Analyzing Visuals   **Connecting to the Text**   How does this photograph help you visualize the setting?

"You got my clothes dirty!"

I rushed toward Mr. Andersen, my fist in a mighty hammer, shouting, "You ain't got no right to push on Little Man. Why don't you push on somebody your own size—like me, you ole—"

The man called Claude put his hand over my mouth and carried me away. Christopher-John trailed behind us, tugging on the man's shirt.

"Put her down. Hey, mister, put Cassie down."

The man carried me all the way to the pond. "Now," he said, "you and your brothers get on home before y'all get hurt. Go on, get!"

As the man walked away, I looked around. "Where's Little Man?"

Christopher-John looked around too.

"I don't know," he said. "I thought he was behind me."

Back we ran toward the lumbermen.

We found Little Man's clothing first, folded neatly by a tree. Then we saw Little Man, dragging a huge stick and headed straight for Mr. Andersen.

"Little Man, come back here," I called.

But Little Man did not stop.

Mr. Andersen stood alone, barking orders, unaware of the oncoming Little Man.

"Little Man! Oh, Little Man, don't!"

It was too late.

Little Man swung the stick as hard as he could against Mr. Andersen's leg.

---

ing at the end of the second paragraph in column 2 ("...Little Man reluctantly replied."). Have a fluent reader in each group play the role of the "narrator" by reading the parts of the passage that are not written in dialogue. Each of the remaining students in the group may choose to read the role of Cassie, Little Man, Christopher-John, or Mama.

- Remind students to look for signal words in the text that indicate how each line should be spoken, such as "listlessly" or "reluctantly."

Analyzing Visuals

Connecting to the Text: *This illustration gives me a visual image of the forest on the Logans' land.*

▶ ## Comprehension

ⓘ ### Read and Discuss

Possible response: *It's decimated, and the trees that are left are portrayed as souls mourning the loss of relatives.*

Follow up Knowing what we do about Cassie, what will she think of what she sees? ***Possible response:*** *She'll be devastated and angry that part of her life has been destroyed by an awful man.*

▶ ## Analysis

ⓟ ### Literary Focus

Possible responses: *Little Man's decision to run off develops his character by revealing to readers his frustration with being the youngest sibling and never being allowed to do what he wants.*

▶ ## Extend the Discussion

Conflict In the second column on p. 548, how do two of the story's conflicts interact with each other? ***Possible response:*** *The conflict between Little Man and his siblings causes Little Man to confront the lumbermen, making the Logan family's conflict with Mr. Andersen worse.*

Tone Toward the end of p. 549, the author uses short sentences and paragraphs, such as "But Little Man did not stop" and "It was too late," to describe the action. How does this sentence structure affect the story's tone? ***Possible response:*** *The short sentences on this page give extra emphasis to Little Man's actions. These sentences don't contain extra words to slow or confuse readers, and they all build toward a single event, creating a fast-paced, climactic tone.*

Model the Skill

- Check that students have copies of the Reading Skills Focus graphic organizer and have responded to item 3 on the organizer before reading pp. 550–551.

- Model checking **prior knowledge** to confirm what you know or have learned from a text. Direct students' attention to item three of the Reading Skills Focus graphic organizer. You might say, "I know that Papa is willing to die and even kill other people to protect his forest. He talks about 'dying right.' If his plan to die to keep the white lumbermen from cutting down his forest is 'dying right,' that means that he is standing up for something he feels very strongly about. Papa doesn't have much of a forest left to save, and he will have no forest left if he blows it up. By challenging Mr. Andersen, the only thing he has left to gain is self-respect. From my experience, people who stand up for what they feel is right gain or keep self-respect. So my answer, yes, will not change."

Guided Practice: Apply

Have students revisit their responses to item three. Ask them if Papa's stand against Mr. Andersen confirms or changes what they know from experience about people's gaining self-respect. Have students revise their answers and rationales as applicable.

Mr. Andersen let out a howl and reached to where he thought Little Man's collar was. But, of course, Little Man had no collar.

"Run, Man!" Christopher-John and I shouted. "Run!"

"Why, you little . . ." Mr. Andersen cried, grabbing at Little Man. But Little Man was too quick for him. He slid right through Mr. Andersen's legs. Tom stood nearby, his face crinkling into an amused grin.

"Hey, y'all!" Mr. Andersen yelled to the lumbermen. "Claude! Get that kid!"

But sure-footed Little Man dodged the groping hands of the lumbermen as easily as if he were skirting mud puddles. Over tree stumps, around legs, and through legs he dashed. But in the end, there were too many lumbermen for him, and he was handed over to Mr. Andersen.

For the second time, Christopher-John and I went to Little Man's rescue.

"Put him down!" we ordered, charging the lumbermen.

I was captured much too quickly, though not before I had landed several stinging blows. But Christopher-John, furious at seeing Little Man handled so roughly by Mr. Andersen, managed to elude the clutches of the lumbermen until he was fully upon Mr. Andersen. Then, with his mightiest thrust, he kicked Mr. Andersen solidly in the shins, not once, but twice, before the lumbermen pulled him away.

Mr. Andersen was fuming. He slowly took off his wide leather belt. Christopher-John, Little Man, and I looked woefully at the belt, then at each other. Little Man and Christopher-John fought to escape, but I closed my eyes and awaited the whining of the heavy belt and its painful bite against my skin.

What was he waiting for? I started to open my eyes, but then the zinging whirl of the belt began and I tensed, awaiting its fearful sting. But just as the leather tip lashed into my leg, a deep, familiar voice said, "Put the belt down, Andersen."

I opened my eyes.

"Papa!"

"Let the children go," Papa said. He was standing on a nearby ridge with a strange black box in his hands. Stacey was behind him, holding the reins to Lady.

The chopping stopped as all eyes turned to Papa.

"They been right meddlesome," Mr. Andersen said. "They need teaching how to act."

"Any teaching, I'll do it. Now, let them go."

Mr. Andersen looked down at Little Man struggling to get away. Smiling broadly, he motioned our release. "Okay, David," he said.

As we ran up the ridge to Papa, Mr. Andersen said, "It's good to have you home, boy."

Papa said nothing until we were safely behind him. "Take them home, Stacey."

"But, Papa—"

"Do like I say, son."

Stacey herded us away from the men. When we were far enough away so Papa

Q Read and Discuss How have things ended up for the children?

Vocabulary elude (ih LOOD) *v.*: avoid; cleverly escape.

Universal Access

EL English Learners

To help students understand the conflict between Papa and Mr. Andersen, have them skim the scene of their confrontation on pp. 550–551. Then have students list important words or phrases associated with these two characters. Encourage them to include academic words like *bluffing* and *cunningly* on their lists.

Struggling Readers

Use p. 551 to discuss how students' responses to the Reading Skills Focus graphic organizer have changed.

- First, review the statements with students. Draw attention to the statement, "Nobody owns the earth."

- You might say, "Before I read the story, I did not understand how this could be true. People own property, which is land, which is also earth. On p. 551, it seems like Papa is trying to protect his land from being destroyed by people who do not own it. Is he making a statement about owning the earth? Do you think he is defending the trees, or his own property?"

- Discuss with students how Papa's actions on p. 551 are connected to the idea of nature and ownership. Point couldn't see us, Stacey stopped and handed me Lady's reins.

"Y'all go on home now," he said. "I gotta go help Papa."

"Papa don't need no help," I said. "He told you to come with us."

"But you don't know what he's gonna do."

"What?" I asked.

"He's gonna blow up the forest if they don't get out of here. So go on home where y'all be safe."

"How's he gonna do that?" asked Little Man.

"We been setting sticks of dynamite since the middle of the night. We ain't even been up to the house cause Papa wanted the sticks planted and covered over before the men came. Now, Cassie, take them on back to the house. Do like I tell you for once, will ya?" Then, without waiting for another word, he was gone.

"I wanna see," Little Man announced.

"I don't," protested Christopher-John.

"Come on," I said.

We tied the mare to a tree, then belly-crawled back to where we could see Papa and joined Stacey in the brush.

"Cassie, I told you . . ."

"What's Papa doing?"

The black box was now set upon a sawed-off tree stump, and Papa's hands were tightly grasping a T-shaped instrument which went into it.

"What's that thing?" asked Little Man.

> "I mean what I say," Papa said. "Ask anyone."

"It's a plunger," Stacey whispered. "If Papa presses down on it, the whole forest will go *pfffff!*"   **R**

Our mouths went dry and our eyes went wide. Mr. Andersen's eyes were wide, too.

"You're bluffing, David," he said. "You ain't gonna push that plunger."

"One thing you can't seem to understand, Andersen," Papa said, "is that a black man's always gotta be ready to die. And it don't make me any difference if I die today or tomorrow. Just as long as I die right."

Mr. Andersen laughed uneasily. The lumbermen moved nervously away.

"I mean what I say," Papa said. "Ask anyone. I always mean what I say."

"He sure do, Mr. Andersen," Claude said, eyeing the black box. "He always do."

"Shut up!" Mr. Andersen snapped. "And the rest of y'all stay put." Then turning back to Papa, he smiled cunningly. "I'm sure you and me can work something out, David."

"Ain't nothing to be worked out," said Papa.

"Now, look here, David, your mama and me, we got us a contract . . . "

"There ain't no more contract," Papa replied coldly. "Now, either you get out or I blow it up. That's it."

"He means it, Mr. Andersen," another frightened lumberman ventured. "He's crazy and he sure 'nough means it."

"You know what could happen to you, boy?" Mr. Andersen exploded, his face

---

R Read and Discuss | What does Papa's plan tell you about his view of Mr. Andersen's actions?

---

out details that suggest Papa is standing up for the land, such as the sentence, "Just as long as I die right" at the top of the second column. Explain to students that Papa's idea of "dying right" might be dying for a worthy cause, such as dying to prevent the destruction of the trees.

AAVE Students Who Use African American Vernacular English

English for Academic Success Some students may struggle with the formal English rules of subject-verb agreement. Explain that in formal English, the subject and verb must always agree in number. A plural subject must always have a plural verb, and a singular subject must always have a singular verb. The characters in "Song of the Trees" often use informal English, which does not follow the same rules of subject-verb agreement. On p. 549, Claude the lumberman says, "He sure do, Mr. Andersen." *He* is a singular subject, and *do* is a plural verb; the singular verb would be *does*. In formal English this sentence would read, "He sure does, Mr. Andersen." Have students identify the verb form that matches each of the following subjects: *He [to run], We [to scream], I [to walk], They [to laugh].*

Think About/Talk About

▶ **Comprehension**

Q Read and Discuss

Possible response: Thanks to Papa, Mr. Andersen has let the children go.

R Read and Discuss

Possible response: Papa is willing to die, lose the entire forest, and put himself and others in danger in order to protect his family. He views Mr. Andersen's actions as a threat to his family and to his self-respect.

Follow up How does Papa's plan connect to the way in which the Logan children stood up for themselves earlier? *Possible response: The kids were determined to save their trees even though the act of trying was dangerous. They've learned from Papa that sometimes it's more important to do the right thing than to be safe.*

▶ **Extend the Discussion**

Motivation Re-read the exchange between Papa and Mr. Andersen in the second column of p. 550. How do Mr. Andersen's actions reflect his feelings toward Papa? *Possible response: Though Mr. Andersen is acting nice, he is not respecting Papa's authority. He also calls Papa "boy," which is condescending and rude.*

Theme On p. 551, Papa talks about his desire to "die right." How does this concept connect to one of the novella's themes? *Possible response: "Dying right" seems to be dying bravely and with self-respect. One of the themes of the story is that it's important to maintain dignity and self-respect when you stand up for your beliefs, and you shouldn't let other people take advantage of you.*

Vocabulary: Own the Word

elude: Explain that *elude* means "avoid;" an antonym is *confront.* Use both words in a sentence. You might say, "William tried to *elude* Carla after he lost her textbook, but Carla soon confronted him about it."

▶ **Comprehension**

⑤ Read and Discuss

Possible response: The plan was successful; the men left without any trees.

Follow up How do Papa's words to the trees in the second to last paragraph of the story connect to what we know about Cassie? ***Possible response:*** *Cassie must have gotten her inclination to talk and listen to the trees from Papa. They're both devastated by their loss.*

ⓣ Reading Focus

Possible response: If Papa didn't have self-respect, people like Mr. Andersen would be able to take advantage of him and hurt him and his family.

▶ **Extend the Discussion**

Conflict Do you think the Logans have successfully resolved their conflict against Mr. Andersen? What evidence from the last page of the story supports your answer? ***Possible response:*** *They are successful for now because they got Mr. Andersen to leave. However, he has already cut down a lot of trees. And when he says, "You won't always have that black box, David," he is warning Papa that there might be more trouble later.*

Vocabulary: Own the Word

incredulously: Point out to students that *incredulously* is related to the word *incredible*, which means "hard to believe." When you react *incredulously*, you act as if you don't believe what you've seen.

Monitor Students' Comprehension

To check students' understanding of the selection, ask them what the trees' transformation throughout the story might symbolize. [*The trees' inability to sing might symbolize Cassie's growing realization that the world is not always a cheerful, magical place.*]

---

beet red again. "Threatening a white man like this?"

Papa said nothing. He just stood there, his hands firmly on the plunger, staring down at Mr. Andersen.

Mr. Andersen could not bear the stare. He turned away, cursing Papa. "You're a fool, David. A crazy fool." Then he looked around at the lumbermen. They shifted their eyes and would not look at him.

"Maybe we better leave, Mr. Andersen," Tom said quietly.

Mr. Andersen glanced at Tom, then turned back to Papa and said as lightly as he could, "All right, David, all right. It's your land. We'll just take the logs we got cut and get out." He motioned to the men. "Hey, let's get moving and get these logs out of here before this crazy fool gets us all killed." **⑤**

"No," Papa said.

Mr. Andersen stopped, knowing that he could not have heard correctly. "What you say?"

"You ain't taking one more stick out of this forest."

"Now, look here—"

"You heard me."

"But you can't sell all these logs, David," Mr. Andersen exclaimed incredulously.

Papa said nothing. Just cast that piercing look on Mr. Andersen.

> Papa said nothing. Just cast that piercing look on Mr. Andersen.

"Look, I'm a fair man. I tell you what I'll do. I'll give you another thirty-five dollars. An even hundred dollars. Now, that's fair, ain't it?"

"I'll see them rot first."

"But—"

"That's my last word," Papa said, tightening his grip on the plunger.

Mr. Andersen swallowed hard. "You won't always have that black box, David," he warned. "You know that, don't you?"

"That may be. But it won't matter none. Cause I'll always have my self-respect." **ⓣ**

Mr. Andersen opened his mouth to speak, but no sound came. Tom and the lumbermen were quietly moving away, putting their gear in the empty lumber wagons. Mr. Andersen looked again at the black box. Finally, his face ashen, he too walked away.

Papa stood unmoving until the wagons and the men were gone. Then, when the sound of the last wagon rolling over the dry leaves could no longer be heard and a hollow silence filled the air, he slowly removed his hands from the plunger and looked up at the remaining trees standing like lonely sentries in the morning.

"Dear, dear old trees," I heard him call softly, "will you ever sing again?"

I waited. But the trees gave no answer.

---

⑤ ☐ **Read and Discuss** How has Papa's plan worked out so far?

ⓣ ☐ **Reading Focus** **Prior Knowledge** Why is having self-respect so important to Mr. Logan? Base your response on your own knowledge and experience as well as evidence in the text.

Vocabulary **incredulously** (ihn KREHJ uh luhs lee) *adv.:* unbelievingly.

 California Standards, pp. 553–555

■ **Reading Standard 3.1** Articulate the expressed purposes and characteristics of different forms of prose (e.g., short story, novel, novella, essay).

Applying Your Skills

Reading Standard 3.1 Articulate the expressed purposes and characteristics of different forms of prose (e.g., short story, novel, **novella**, essay).

Song of the Trees
Literary Response and Analysis

Reading Skills Focus
Quick Check

1. Why does Mr. Andersen want to cut down the trees?
2. How do the Logans stop him?

Read with a Purpose

3. How do the Logans work together to overcome a difficult situation?

Reading Skills: Activating Prior Knowledge

4. After reading *Song of the Trees,* fill out the "After Reading" column of the chart. Have your answers changed? Why or why not?

Before Reading   *After Reading*

____ 1. Given the chance, most people won't take advantage of another person. ____
____ 2. Nobody owns the earth. ____
____ 3. People gain self-respect by standing up for their beliefs. ____

Literary Skills Focus
Literary Analysis

5. **Analyze** A novella allows writers to develop characters a bit more than a short story does. What methods of characterization does Taylor use to bring her various characters to life? Why is characterization so important in this particular story?
6. **Literary Perspectives** What impact does the time period of the Great Depression have on the characters in the story? How does the historical context affect the plot?

Literary Skills: Novella

7. **Evaluate** What characteristics of the **novella** form did you see in this story? How might this narrative have been told differently if it were a **short story**? What might the author have added if it were a **novel**?

Literary Skills Review: Theme

Theme is the meaning of a story: not what happens, but what the story is really *about.* Theme relates to what the main characters in a story learn as well as to the insights that you, the reader, gain as you share the characters' experiences.

8. **Analyze** A novella will sometimes have more than one theme, but one theme will stand out as most important. Articulate the main theme this story expresses. How does the author develop this theme with specific incidents, such as plot complications? How does the title *Song of the Trees* relate to the theme?

Writing Skills Focus
Think as a Reader/Writer

Use It in Your Writing Look back at the list you made of Cassie's descriptions of the trees acting as people. These are examples of **personification**—a figure of speech in which something nonhuman is given human characteristics. Write a brief paragraph in which you describe something nonhuman—cars, clouds, or sports equipment, for example—as though it were human.

 What Do You Think Now How has reading *Song of the Trees* affected your ideas about how people support one another during difficult times?

Vocabulary Development

Your Turn

1. A fight *might be physical, but a dis-pute is usually verbal.*

2. Curtly *has a suggestion of rudeness;* matter-of-factly *doesn't.*

3. Elude *means "getting away from someone who is looking for you," and* avoiding *someone means not wanting to be around them.*

4. Incredulously *is more extreme than* doubtfully. *If you're doubtful, you're not sure you believe; if you're incredulous, you don't believe.*

English for Academic Success
Language Coach

Tell students that a word's meaning may change when its part of speech changes. For example, the verb *mark* has a different meaning from the noun *mark.*

Possible responses:

• *The dessert tasted sweet and **rich**.*

• *The successful novelist became **rich**.*

• *I wore a brown **belt** yesterday.*

• *Sharon liked to **belt** out songs.*

• *The new coach left her **mark** on the soccer team.*

• *I **marked** the page in my book.*

English for Academic Success
Academic Vocabulary

Possible response: The trees repre-sented happiness and safety. Their destruction would have an <u>impact</u> on the Logans because it would destroy their sense of security. I learned that people can have strong connections to their environments.

 WordSharp: An Interactive Vocabulary Tutor

Learn It Online

Holt's **WordSharp: An Interactive Vocabulary Tutor** provides additional support for vocabulary development. Multimedia tutorials show stu-dents how to apply vocabulary skills to unfamiliar words—and how to make those words their own.

go.hrw.com   H7-554   **Go**

Applying Your Skills

Song of the Trees

Vocabulary Development
Choosing the Right Synonym

Synonyms are words that have nearly the same meaning, but synonyms are not necessarily inter-changeable. In fact, choosing the wrong synonym can be downright embarrassing in some cases. Imagine telling someone, "You're really *nosy* about everything" when what you really meant was "You're really *curious* about everything." In the first case, the person would be insulted; in the second case, he or she would probably feel com-plimented. *Curious* and *nosy* have similar diction-ary meanings, or **denotations,** but very different **connotations,** or feelings and associations that have come to be attached to them. *Curious* sug-gests that you are interested in the world around you and want to learn about it. To be called *nosy,* though, has negative connotations: It suggests that you are someone who aggressively puts your nose into other people's business. When you're choosing synonyms, always keep their connota-tions in mind.

Your Turn

Test your skill at recognizing shades of meaning in synonyms. What are the differences between the following words? Re-reading the Vocabulary words in the context of the story may help you contrast each pair of synonyms.

> dispute
> curtly
> elude
> incredulously

1. fight and **dispute**

2. matter-of-factly and **curtly**

3. avoid and **elude**

4. doubtfully and **incredulously**

Language Coach
Multiple-Meaning Words Many words have more than one meaning. For example, the word *soft* can mean

• not hard

• gentle

• quiet

• weak

Work with a partner to find the various meanings of the following words from the story. Then, write a sentence for each different meaning. Share your sentences with the class.

> rich   belt   mark

Which meanings of these familiar words were new or a surprise to you?

Academic Vocabulary

Talk About . . .
Explain the significance of the trees for Cassie and her family. What <u>impact</u> would the destruction of the trees have on the whole family? Explain what <u>insights</u> about the relationship between people and their environment you gained from reading this novella.

 Learn It Online
Take another look at synonyms using *WordSharp:*

go.hrw.com   H7-554   **Go**

Universal Access: Vocabulary Development

EL English Learners/ Struggling Readers

English for Academic Success English learners and struggling readers may have difficulty grasping shades of meaning among synonym sets. Divide students into mixed-ability groups with at least one fluent speaker

in each group. Have students work together, using a dictionary or thesaurus if necessary, to describe the variations in meaning among the following related terms: *incredible, unbelievable, amazing, remarkable, huge.* Then, discuss the shades of meaning as a class.

Grammar Link
Subject-Verb Agreement

A common error people make in writing and speaking involves **subject-verb agreement.** The rule is simple: Subjects and their verbs must always agree. A singular subject takes a singular verb, and a plural subject takes a plural verb. The problem arises when identifying the subject and deciding whether it is singular or plural. Be careful when a sentence contains *neither/nor* or *either/or* and when a subject is separated from its verb by a prepositional phrase.

> **Neither Mama nor Big Ma** *[wants, want]* **Cassie to hear their conversation.** [Singular subjects joined by *or* or *nor* take a singular verb. The correct verb is *wants*.]

> **Neither Cassie nor her brothers** *[wants, want]* **Mr. Andersen to cut down the trees.** [When a singular subject and a plural subject are joined by *or* or *nor*, the verb agrees with the subject closer to the verb. Since *brothers* is plural, the correct verb is *want*.]

> **The clothes of the six-year-old** *[is, are]* **very important to him.** [The number of a subject is not affected by a prepositional phrase following the subject. The correct verb is *are*.]

Your Turn

Rewrite these sentences to correct errors in subject-verb agreement.

Neither I nor my brothers wants the forest cut down. The thud of the axes was a terrifying sound. Neither Christopher-John nor Little Man were allowed to go to the forest.

CHOICES

As you respond to the Choices, use these **Academic Vocabulary** words as appropriate: <u>articulate</u>, <u>characteristics</u>, <u>impact</u>, <u>insight</u>.

REVIEW
Reflect on Forms of Prose

Timed **Writing** *Song of the Trees* was inspired by an experience Taylor's father had when he was young. Why do you think Taylor chose to tell the story as fiction rather than nonfiction? Reflect on the differences between fiction and nonfiction prose. Then, in a paragraph, explain why you think Taylor tells the story as fiction.

CONNECT
Describe an Experience

Cassie and her family reach a goal together that one of them could not have reached alone. Recall a time when you worked with others to accomplish something. Write a brief essay about the experience in which you describe why you came together, what you achieved, and what <u>insights</u> you gained.

EXTEND
Debate an Issue

Listening and Speaking Do you think old forests should be cut down? First, consider your own **prior knowledge** of trees and forests. Next, in a library or on the Internet, research the <u>impact</u> of the lumber industry on both the economy and the environment. Then, form two teams to debate the pros and cons of cutting old-growth forests.

✳ **Learn It Online**
Learn more with the Internet links at:
go.hrw.com H7-555 **Go**

Independent Practice
Grammar Link
Your Turn _____

Neither I nor my brothers want the forest cut down. The thud of the axes was a terrifying sound. Neither Christopher-John nor Little Man was allowed to go to the forest.

Choices:
Evaluation Criteria
Review: Timed Writing
40-50 Minutes

The paragraph explains differences between fiction and nonfiction and explains why the author chose to write *Song of the Trees* as fiction.

Connect: Homework
Describe an Experience

The essay describes an experience with collaboration and explains how it contributed to success.

Extend: Homework
Debate an Issue

Students present a clear argument for or against cutting old-growth trees, using factual evidence.

Assess

📝 **Chapter 5 Resources,** Selection Standards Check, p. 21

ThinkCentral Online Assessment, Selection Standards Check

Teacher One Stop™, editable Selection Standards Check

Reteach

ThinkCentral Online Remediation

✳ **Learn It Online**
The **Digital Storytelling** mini-site shows students how to take a personal experience and craft it into a short film—complete with music, images, and special effects.

go.hrw.com H7-555 **Go**

Universal Access: Grammar Link

 English Learners
Struggling Writers
English for Academic Success Help students identify subject-verb agreement with a prepositional phrase.

- Write the following sentences on the board:

  This book about bugs are interesting.

  This book about bugs is interesting.

- Tell students that one of these sentences uses the correct verb form; the other does not.

- Tell students that an effective way to determine the correct verb form is to remove the prepositional phrase. In this case, the prepositional phrase is *about bugs*. Write the following sentences on the board:

  This book are interesting.

  This book is interesting.

- Ask students which sentence uses the correct verb form. [*This book is interesting.*] Therefore, the correct sentence is *This book about bugs is interesting*.

- Repeat this exercise with a few more sentences with prepositional phrases.

Standards Focus

Objectives

Students will

- understand the tone and structure of an essay
- set a purpose for reading
- understand adjectives and shades of meaning

Motivate

What Do You Think?/QuickWrite

Have students discuss different ways in which they could show loyalty to a friend in need. Suggest that students record their thoughts in their **Reader/Writer Notebook.**

English for Academic Success

Academic Vocabulary

Look for opportunities to use the Academic Vocabulary words in this chapter.

- **articulate, v.:** express clearly and specifically
- **characteristics, n. pl.:** distinguishing qualities or features
- **significance, n.:** importance; meaning
- **insight, n.:** power to understand

California Standards, pp. 556–567

- **Reading Standard 3.1** Articulate the expressed purposes and characteristics of different forms of prose (e.g., short story, novel, novella, essay).

PERSONAL NARRATIVE

Preparing to Read

A Mason-Dixon Memory

by Clifton Davis

What Do You Think What does it mean to be a loyal friend to someone?

QuickWrite What would you do to support a friend who needs your help?

Selection Readability	
Easily Accessible **Accessible** Challenging	familiar syntax; familiar theme; selection provides background information

Selection Plot Summary

In this essay, Clifton Davis describes a childhood experience with racism. He recalls how his classmates rallied to support him after an amusement park denied him entry because of his skin color. Davis connects his experience with that of Dondré Green, a golf team member who was forbidden to play on a whites-only course.

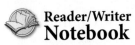

Reader/Writer Notebook

Use your **RWN** to complete the activities for this selection.

Reading Standard 3.1 Articulate the expressed purposes and characteristics of different forms of prose (e.g., short story, novel, novella, **essay**).

Literary Skills Focus

Forms of Prose: Essay / Personal Narrative One form of nonfiction that you'll often be asked to read—and write—is the **essay,** a short piece of nonfiction prose that focuses on a single topic. An essay can be formal or informal, and it can be about anything from "Why I Don't Like Horror Films" to "What I've Learned from My Parakeet."

An essay's tone and structure will depend on its purpose. Does the writer want to inform you? persuade you? entertain you? Not all essays tell a story, but the kind of essay called a **personal narrative** or **personal essay** does. These kinds of essays usually focus on a particular event in a person's life and often use that event to demonstrate a point.

Personal narratives are often told in **chronological order,** or the order in which events occurred. "A Mason-Dixon Memory" is structured around **flashbacks:** The narrator twice goes back in time, breaking out of chronological order to tell a story that relates to his main story.

Reading Skills Focus

Setting a Purpose When you **set a purpose** for reading, you focus on *why* you are reading the text in front of you. Preview the title, text, and illustrations before you read.

Into Action Use a chart like the one below to set an initial purpose and to list any new ones you may discover while reading. Check them off as you accomplish them.

What's Your Purpose?

Purpose 1:	to learn what the title means	☐
Purpose 2:	to determine the reason why Davis wrote the essay	☐
Purpose 3:		☐

Writing Skills Focus

Think as a Reader/Writer

Find It in Your Reading As you read, record three details from Davis's childhood experience that he connects to the way he looks at life today.

Vocabulary

predominantly (prih DAHM uh nuhnt lee) *adv.:* mainly. *The story is predominantly about friendship.*

forfeit (FAWR fiht) *v.:* lose the right to something. *The team would forfeit the tournament.*

resolve (rih ZAHLV) *v.:* decide. *People can resolve to do the right thing.*

ominous (AHM uh nuhs): *adj.:* threatening. *The look on the chaperone's face was ominous.*

bigotry (BIHG uh tree): *n.:* prejudice; intolerance. *Whites-only policies were based on bigotry.*

Language Coach

Synonyms Words with the same or almost the same meanings are called **synonyms.** For instance, *mainly* is a synonym of the Vocabulary word *predominantly.* Which other Vocabulary words above are defined by a synonym?

 Learn It Online
Use Word Watch to strengthen your vocabulary at:
go.hrw.com [H7-557] **Go**

Introducing Vocabulary

Read aloud the Vocabulary words and sample sentences. Then, have students complete each sentence with the correct Vocabulary word.

1. The sky looked _____ before the storm. [*ominous*]

2. The rock fans were _____ young. [*predominantly*]

3. People who treat others badly might show _____. [*bigotry*]

4. We had to _____ the game when only two players showed up. [*forfeit*]

5. I _____ to help people in need. [*resolve*]

English for Academic Success
Language Coach

Tell students that they might think of synonyms as brief definitions for other words. For example, *prejudice* is a one-word definition for *bigotry.* [*bigotry, ominous, resolve*]

Literary Skills Focus

As you read and discuss the selection with students, have them pay close attention to the essay's structure.

Reading Skills Focus

Give students a copy of the Reading Skills Focus graphic organizer. Tell them to use their responses to answer the questions on the Applying Your Skills page.

Writing Skills Focus

Have students record details of Davis's childhood experience from the text in their **Reader/Writer Notebook.** Students may use their notes to complete the Writing Skills Focus activity.

 Learn It Online
Send students to **WordWatch** for audio pronunciations, synonyms, and antonyms, and brief histories of word origins.

go.hrw.com [H7-557] **Go**

Selection Resources

Chapter 5 Resources, on-level practice and assessment, p. 24

PowerNotes, interactive lesson presentation with activities

Teacher One Stop™, on-level lesson plans and all print resources

Holt Audio Library

Holt Audio Library: Selections and Summaries in Spanish

UA: Holt Interactive Reader, p. 140

Holt Interactive Reader for ELD, p. 158

Holt Audio Tutor for ELD

UA: Differentiating Instruction, modified lesson plans and leveled assessment, p. 127

UA: Resources for Teaching Advanced Students, lesson plans, p. 124

UA: Supporting Instruction in Five Languages, selection summary

ThinkCentral Online Assessment, Selection Standards Check

ThinkCentral Online Remediation

More About the Writer

During his movie career, **Clifton Davis** portrayed Leroy "Satchel" Paige, an all-star pitcher who started playing in the Negro baseball leagues and went on to play major league baseball beginning in 1948.

Think About the Writer

Tell students to consider different aspects of their life, such as school, hobbies, and relationships, to answer the question. Ask how these parts of their lives allow them to take on or "perform" different roles.

For Independent Reading

■ Students interested in life below the Mason-Dixon Line around the time of the Civil Rights movement might enjoy reading Christopher Paul Curtis' *The Watsons Go to Birmingham–1963,* in which a young African American boy comes face-to-face with violent opposition to equality.

■ If students are interested in further examination of the injustices faced by African Americans prior to the civil rights movement, recommend Mildred D. Taylor's *Roll of Thunder, Hear My Cry,* in which a nine-year-old girl comes face to face with racism in the 1930s South.

MEET THE WRITER

Clifton Davis
(1946–   )

A Man of Many Talents

Clifton Davis is probably better known for his songs than for his essays. He wrote the hit song "Never Can Say Goodbye," which sold two million records, and he has recorded several gospel albums as well. Davis is also an actor. He has appeared on Broadway, in movies, and on TV shows. He is perhaps best known for his role as Reverend Reuben Gregory on the television series *Amen,* which aired from 1986 to 1991.

A Spiritual Journey

After a time of personal struggles, Davis temporarily withdrew from the limelight in the early 1980s to study theology and become a minister. Davis believes it's important to do what's right, even while making a living amid the glitz and glamour of Hollywood.

"I had to go down the path to see my calling."

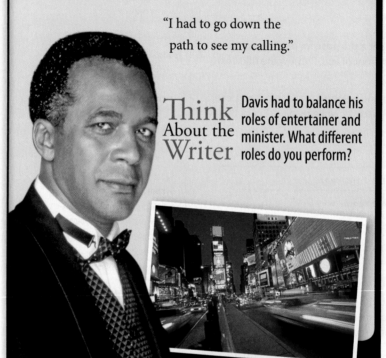

Think About the Writer Davis had to balance his roles of entertainer and minister. What different roles do you perform?

Build Background

The Mason-Dixon line forms part of the borders of four states. It was considered a dividing line between free and slave states before slavery was abolished, but its creation had nothing to do with slavery. Charles Mason and Jeremiah Dixon surveyed the line in the 1760s to settle a border dispute between the British colonies of Maryland and Pennsylvania.

Preview the Selection

In 1991, **Dondré Green,** an African American high school golfer in Louisiana, experienced racial discrimination. He was asked to speak about his experience. **Clifton Davis** was on hand and recounts the speech and the childhood memories it brought back to him. Davis interrupts Dondré's story with a flashback that takes you back to earlier times and events in his own life.

Universal Access

EL English Learners

Students may be unfamiliar with the significance of the Mason-Dixon line. Read aloud the Build Background paragraph, and point out that the title of this essay is "A Mason-Dixon Memory." Help students set a purpose for reading by having them determine how the Mason-Dixon line relates to the people, places, and events in the essay.

✔ See **UA: Differentiating Instruction** for lesson plans and strategies for teaching English learners.

Struggling Readers

Tell students that they can use the essay's title, text, and other information to set a purpose for reading. Point out that the reader learns in the first paragraph that a young man named Dondré Green is an honored guest at a banquet. A purpose for reading the essay might be to learn more about Green. Work with students to develop two other class purposes for reading.

✔ See **UA: Differentiating Instruction** for lesson plans and strategies for teaching struggling readers.

A Mason-Dixon Memory

by Clifton Davis

Dondré Green glanced uneasily at the civic leaders and sports figures filling the hotel ballroom in Cleveland. They had come from across the nation to attend a fundraiser for the National Minority College Golf Scholarship Foundation. I was the banquet's featured entertainer. Dondré, an eighteen-year-old high school senior from Monroe, Louisiana, was the evening's honored guest.

"Nervous?" I asked the handsome young man in his starched white shirt and rented tuxedo.

"A little," he whispered, grinning.

One month earlier, Dondré had been just one more black student attending a predominantly white Southern school. Although most of his friends and classmates were white, Dondré's race had never been an issue. Then, on April 17, 1991, Dondré's black skin provoked an incident that made nationwide news.

"Ladies and gentlemen," the emcee[1] said, "our special guest, Dondré Green."

As the audience stood applauding, Dondré walked to the microphone and began his story. "I love golf," he said quietly. "For the past two years, I've been a member of the St. Frederick High School golf team. And though I was the only black member, I've always felt at home playing at the mostly white country clubs across Louisiana."

The audience leaned forward; even the waiters and busboys stopped to listen. As I listened, a memory buried in my heart since childhood began fighting its way to life.

"Our team had driven from Monroe," Dondré continued. "When we arrived at the Caldwell Parish Country Club in Columbia, we walked to the putting green."

Dondré and his teammates were too absorbed to notice the conversation

---

1. **emcee** (EHM SEE): master of ceremonies.

A **Literary Focus** Personal Narrative From your knowledge of Dondré Green, what do you think this essay's topic will be?

Vocabulary **predominantly** (prih DAHM uh nuhnt lee) *adv.*: mainly.

Advanced Learners

Enrichment Have students analyze the essay's tone.

- First, tell students to read from the beginning of the essay to the beginning of the flashback on p. 560. Have students discuss their overall impression of the tone.
- Then, have students perform a close reading of the paragraph on p. 560 that begins, "In 1959 I was thirteen years old." Have students discuss the paragraph's tone.
- Finally, have students compare and contrast this paragraph's tone with the tone of the essay's introduction. Ask what the author's purpose might be.

✔ See **UA: Resources for Teaching Advanced Learners** for strategies for teaching advanced learners.

Students with Disabilities

Before students read the essay, explain that this essay contains two stories: the "frame" story about Dondré Green and the story within a story about Clifton Davis. Help students identify the transitions between the two stories.

✔ See **UA: Differentiating Instruction** for lesson plans and strategies for teaching students with disabilities.

Model the Skill

■ Tell students that just as every text is written for a reason, every text is read for a reason. Readers should think about why they are reading a text before, during, and after reading. This is **setting a purpose.**

■ Provide students with copies of the Reading Skills Focus graphic organizer. (See **Chapter 5 Resources.**) Point out the purposes for reading. Explain that revisiting these purposes as they read will help them evaluate what they are learning from the text. For example, one of their purposes for reading might be to find out what the title had to do with the essay.

■ Point out that on p. 561, we learn that the Mason-Dixon Line is a line that divides Pennsylvania and Maryland, but it is also the border between the North and the South. Glen Echo Park is in the South, and the laws of the South keep Clifton, an African American, out of the park.

■ Tell students that the Mason-Dixon Line is a big part of Clifton's memory of experiencing racism. Since the line is so important to the memory, he chose to include it in the title. Now that they understand the connection, they can check the box on their charts.

What's Your Purpose?

Purpose 1:	to learn what the title means	✓
Purpose 2:	to determine the reason why Davis wrote the essay	☐
Purpose 3:		☐

Guided Practice: Apply

Have students independently assess the purposes they set for reading and determine whether they learned what they set out to learn.

---

between a man and St. Frederick athletic director James Murphy. After disappearing into the clubhouse, Murphy returned to his players.

"I want to see the seniors," he said. "On the double!" His face seemed strained as he gathered the four students, including Dondré.

"I don't know how to tell you this," he said, "but the Caldwell Parish Country Club is reserved for whites only." Murphy paused and looked at Dondré. His teammates glanced at each other in disbelief. "I want you seniors to decide what our response should be," Murphy continued. "If we leave, we forfeit this tournament. If we stay, Dondré can't play."　　**B**

As I listened, my own childhood memory from thirty-two years ago broke free.　**C**

I n 1959 I was thirteen years old, a poor black kid living with my mother and stepfather in a small black ghetto on Long Island, New York. My mother worked nights in a hospital, and my stepfather drove a coal truck. Needless to say, our standard of living was somewhat short of the American dream.

Nevertheless, when my eighth-grade teacher announced a graduation trip to Washington, D.C., it never crossed my mind that I would be left behind. Besides a complete tour of the nation's capital, we would visit Glen Echo Amusement Park in Maryland. In my imagination, Glen Echo

B **Read and Discuss** What is happening with the team?

C **Literary Focus** Personal Narrative The writer adds extra space here. What else indicates a flashback? What year is he describing?

Golf team photograph from the 1991 *Warrior* yearbook.

was Disneyland, Knott's Berry Farm, and Magic Mountain rolled into one.

My heart beating wildly, I raced home to deliver the mimeographed letter describing the journey. But when my mother saw how much the trip would cost, she just shook her head. We couldn't afford it.

After feeling sad for ten seconds, I decided to try to fund the trip myself. For the next eight weeks, I sold candy bars door-to-door, delivered newspapers, and mowed lawns. Three days before the deadline, I'd made just barely enough. I was going!　　**D**

The day of the trip, trembling with excitement, I climbed onto the train. I was the only nonwhite in our section.

Our hotel was not far from the White House. My roommate was Frank Miller, the son of a businessman. Leaning together out of our window and dropping water balloons on passing tourists quickly cemented our new friendship.

D **Read and Discuss** What is the author telling you about himself?

Vocabulary　**forfeit** (FAWR fiht) *v.:* lose the right to something.

Developing Oral Fluency

Use Clifton Davis's autobiographical account on p. 560 to have students practice adjusting their pacing as they read aloud. Remind students that pacing is important when reading aloud. Punctuation marks such as commas, periods, exclamation points, and question marks indicate where students should slow down or stop.

Paired Activity Put students into groups that contain fluent speakers and struggling readers if possible.

• Ask a fluent student to model reading the fourth full paragraph aloud to the group (beginning with "In

1959 I was thirteen years old . . .").

• Have the remaining members of each group read that same paragraph aloud, mimicking the pacing of the fluent reader.

• Then, have a different group member in each group read the next paragraph aloud.

• Have group members take turns reading paragraphs aloud until the end of p. 560.

✔ See **UA: Differentiating Instruction** for practice passages for developing oral fluency.

Every morning, almost a hundred of us loaded noisily onto our bus for another adventure. We sang our school fight song dozens of times—en route[2] to Arlington National Cemetery and even on an afternoon cruise down the Potomac River.

We visited the Lincoln Memorial twice, once in daylight, the second time at dusk. My classmates and I fell silent as we walked in the shadows of those thirty-six marble columns, one for every state in the Union that Lincoln labored to preserve. I stood next to Frank at the base of the nineteen-foot seated statue. Spotlights made the white Georgian marble seem to glow. Together, we read those famous words from Lincoln's speech at Gettysburg, remembering the most bloody battle in the War Between the States: "We here highly resolve that these dead shall not have died in vain—that this nation, under God, shall have a new birth of freedom. . . ."

As Frank motioned me into place to take my picture, I took one last look at Lincoln's face. He seemed alive and so terribly sad.

The next morning I understood a little better why he wasn't smiling. "Clifton," a chaperone said, "could I see you for a moment?"

The other guys at my table, especially Frank, turned pale. We had been joking about the previous night's direct water-balloon hit on a fat lady and her poodle. It was a stupid, dangerous act, but luckily

nobody got hurt. We were celebrating our escape from punishment when the chaperone asked to see me.

"Clifton," she began, "do you know about the Mason-Dixon line?"

"No," I said, wondering what this had to do with drenching fat ladies.

"Before the Civil War," she explained, "the Mason-Dixon line was originally the boundary between Maryland and Pennsylvania—the dividing line between the slave and free states." Having escaped one disaster, I could feel another brewing. I noticed that her eyes were damp and her hands shaking.

"Today," she continued, "the Mason-Dixon line is a kind of invisible border between the North and the South. When you cross that invisible line out of Washington, D.C., into Maryland, things change."

There was an ominous drift to this conversation, but I wasn't following it. Why did she look and sound so nervous?

"Glen Echo Amusement Park is in Maryland," she said at last, "and the management doesn't allow Negroes inside." She stared at me in silence.

I was still grinning and nodding when the meaning finally sank in. "You mean I can't go to the park," I stuttered, "because I'm a Negro?"

She nodded slowly. "I'm sorry, Clifton," she said, taking my hand. "You'll have to stay in the hotel tonight. Why don't you and I watch a movie on television?"

---

2. **en route** (ahn ROOT): on the way.

E **Reading Focus** **Setting a Purpose** How does this information about the Mason-Dixon line help clarify the essay's title?

Vocabulary **resolve** (rih ZAHLV) *v.*: decide.
ominous (AHM uh nuhs): *adj.*: threatening.

- Explain to students that **essays** are pieces of prose written about one topic: anything from ancient history to the history of bubble gum. Being able to identify a piece of writing as an essay helps readers know how to approach it.

- Tell students that "A Mason-Dixon Memory," is a personal essay that the essay is focuses on a specific event from the writer's life.

- Remind students that this essay is structured around a a flashback. The essay starts by telling the story of Dondré Green, who was ordered off a golf course because of his race. Then the author flashes back to a moment in his own life when he dealt with being excluded because of racism. On p. 563, we return to Green's story to find out that his experience ended like the author's—friends defended him.

Guided Practice: Apply

- Ask students to think about a topic that Green's story and the author's story have in common. Students may suggest racism or friendship.

- **Think-Pair-Share** Have students discuss with their partners the topics that both stories have in common. Then, have partners organize their ideas into one topic statement before sharing with the class.

Think as a Reader/Writer

Find It in Your Reading On the top of p. 563, Davis writes that he "was filled with pride." His pride in his friends and in their battle against racism has affected his adult views on the subject.

Use It in Your Writing Have students write a few sentences about an event that affected the way in which they view the world.

I walked to the elevators feeling confusion, disbelief, anger, and a deep sadness. "What happened, Clifton?" Frank said when I got back to the room. "Did the fat lady tell on us?"

Without saying a word, I walked over to my bed, lay down, and began to cry. Frank was stunned into silence. Junior-high boys didn't cry, at least not in front of each other.

It wasn't just missing the class adventure that made me feel so sad. For the first time in my life, I was learning what it felt like to be a "nigger." Of course there was discrimination in the North, but the color of my skin had never officially kept me out of a coffee shop, a church—or an amusement park.

"Clifton," Frank whispered, "what is the matter?"

"They won't let me go to Glen Echo Park tonight," I sobbed.

"Because of the water balloon?" he asked.

"No," I answered, "because I'm a Negro."

"Well, that's a relief!" Frank said, and then he laughed, obviously relieved to have escaped punishment for our caper with the balloons. "I thought it was serious!"

Wiping away the tears with my sleeve, I stared at him. "It *is* serious. They don't let Negroes into the park. I can't go with you!" I shouted. "That's pretty serious to me."

I was about to wipe the silly grin off Frank's face with a blow to his jaw when I heard him say, "Then I won't go either."

For an instant we just froze. Then Frank grinned. I will never forget that moment. Frank was just a kid. He wanted to go to that amusement park as much as I did, but there was something even more important

The Alpine Hi-Ride at Glen Echo Park, Maryland.
Photo by U.S. National Park Service. Courtesy of Richard A. Cook.

than the class night out. Still, he didn't explain or expand.

The next thing I knew, the room was filled with kids listening to Frank. "They don't allow Negroes in the park," he said, "so I'm staying with Clifton."

"Me too," a second boy said.

"Those jerks," a third muttered. "I'm with you, Clifton." My heart began to race. Suddenly, I was not alone. A pint-sized revolution had been born. The "water-balloon brigade," eleven white boys from Long Island, had made its decision: "We won't go." And as I

Universal Access

Struggling Readers

Benchmark Students Help students understand the structure of the essay by helping them connect Davis's autobiographical tale with Dondré Green's experience. Work with students to create a Venn diagram in which they can compare and contrast Davis's experience with Green's as they read. To highlight the similarities between the two men's experiences, have students read the first full paragraph on p. 563 and discuss what they've learned before recording that information in the Venn diagram.

AAVE Students Who Use African American Vernacular English

English for Academic Success Help students identify the proper use of *a* and *an* in formal English. Tell students that to determine which to use, they should look at the next word. If it begins with a vowel or a vowel sound, the correct word is an. If it begins with a consonant sound, the correct word is a. Point out "a word" in the second paragraph of p. 562 and "an amusement park" in the third paragraph as examples of this rule.

sat on my bed in the center of it all, I felt grateful. But above all, I was filled with pride. **F**

Dondré Green's story brought that childhood memory back to life. His golfing teammates, like my childhood friends, had an important decision to make. Standing by their friend would cost them dearly. But when it came time to decide, no one hesitated. "Let's get out of here," one of them whispered.

"They just turned and walked toward the van," Dondré told us. "They didn't debate it.

And the younger players joined us without looking back."

Dondré was astounded by the response of his friends—and the people of Louisiana. The whole state was outraged and tried to make it right. The Louisiana House of Representatives proclaimed a Dondré Green Day and passed legislation permitting lawsuits for damages, attorneys' fees, and court costs against any private facility that invites a team, then bars any member because of race.

As Dondré concluded, his eyes glistened with tears. "I love my coach and my

F **Read and Discuss** Davis says, "A pint-sized revolution had been born." What does he mean? What impact did it have on Davis?

Reaching Reluctant Readers

To help students become engaged with the text, lead a discussion about examples of discrimination or unfair treatment that students have witnessed, experienced, heard about, or seen in books or movies.

• Ask students to form small discussion groups to talk about these instances of discrimination or prejudice. What happened? How did they feel? Discuss the ways in which people can respond to such a situation.

• Have students work together to write an open letter to people who might face such a situation, suggesting courageous, ethical steps that they might take.

Analyzing Visuals

Extension Activity Ask students to analyze the photograph and discuss whether Glen Echo Park looks similar to the way that Davis imagined it would look. *Possible response: It doesn't look quite as wonderful as Davis thought it would be. It looks like a normal amusement park rather than the magical, perfect place that Davis expected.*

Think About/Talk About

▶ **Comprehension**

F Read and Discuss
Possible response: He means that a small number of young people gave up an exciting park trip for justice's sake. It wasn't a big social change, but it was important, and touched Davis.

▶ **Extend the Discussion**

Making Generalizations Do you think the experiences of Green and Davis are common among people who experience racism? Why or why not? *Possible response: Based on my experiences, I think that people will defend their friends against racism, but most people do not stand up for total strangers who are treated unfairly.*

Tone Reread the paragraphs beginning with "I was about to wipe the silly grin . . ." and "For an instant . . .." How does the author's tone shift between the two paragraphs? *Possible response: At first, the author's tone is frustrated and angry, because he has been discriminated against and Frank is laughing about it. But when Frank offers to stay behind with Clifton, the author's tone becomes more positive and appreciative of Frank's gesture.*

Character In the third full paragraph on p. 563, Dondré is "astounded by the response of his friends." What has he learned about their characters? *Possible response: Dondré was surprised and grateful that his teammates forfeited the tournament just to support him. Even though they likely worked very hard to get to the tournament, they showed loyalty to their friend above everything else.*

▶ Comprehension

❶ Read and Discuss

Possible response: One of the chaperones bought baseball tickets for the boys who stuck by Clifton, and they all went to a ballgame.

▶ Analysis

❻ Literary Focus

Possible response: I know the author has flashed back again because the next paragraph starts with "my."

❼ Literary Focus

Possible response: "…the most effective weapon is a simple act of love and courage."

▶ Extend the Discussion

Theme How does Dondré's quotation in the final paragraph connect to the theme of the essay? *Possible response: The theme is that while discrimination may exist, many people are willing to fight it.*

Vocabulary: Own the Word

bigotry: Write *bigotry* on the board and circle it. Have students brainstorm words, phrases, or situations that they associate with the word *bigotry*. Have volunteers write their ideas on the board, linking them to the circle by drawing a spider leg from the idea to the circle.

Monitor Students' Comprehension

Guide the class in answering these comprehension questions.

1. How did Davis feel when Frank Miller said he would stay with him? [*Davis was touched that Frank would give up a chance to go to an amusement park to support him.*]

2. How did the state of Louisiana rally around Dondré? [*The government made it easier to file lawsuits against discriminatory clubs.*]

---

teammates for sticking by me," he said. "It goes to show that there are always good people who will not give in to bigotry. The kind of love they showed me that day will conquer hatred every time."

Suddenly, the banquet crowd was standing, applauding Dondré Green. **❻**

My friends, too, had shown that kind of love. As we sat in the hotel, a chaperone came in waving an envelope. "Boys!" he shouted. "I've just bought thirteen tickets to the Senators-Tigers game. Anybody want to go?"

The room erupted in cheers. Not one of us had ever been to a professional baseball game in a real baseball park.

On the way to the stadium, we grew silent as our driver paused before the Lincoln Memorial. For one long moment, I stared through the marble pillars at Mr. Lincoln, bathed in that warm yellow light. There was still no smile and no sign of hope in his sad and tired eyes.

"We here highly resolve . . . that this nation, under God, shall have a new birth of freedom . . ."

In his words and in his life, Lincoln had made it clear that freedom is not free. Every time the color of a person's skin keeps him out of an amusement park or off a country-club fairway, the war for freedom begins again. Sometimes the battle is fought with fists and guns, but more often the most effective weapon is a simple act of love and courage. **❼**

Whenever I hear those words from Lincoln's speech at Gettysburg, I remember my eleven white friends, and I feel hope once again. I like to imagine that when we paused that night at the foot of his great monument, Mr. Lincoln smiled at last. As Dondré said, "The kind of love they showed me that day will conquer hatred every time." **❶**

(inset) Tiger Woods (2004) and his Stanford University golf team (1994).

Analyzing Visuals

Connecting to the Text
How have conditions for aspiring golfers of all backgrounds changed from the time of Dondré Green's experience?

---

❻ Literary Focus **Personal Narrative** How do you know the writer is using a flashback again?

❼ Literary Focus **Personal Narrative** A key characteristic of nonfiction prose is the main idea, the most important point a writer makes. What main idea does Davis make in this paragraph?

❶ Read and Discuss How did things work out for Davis?

Vocabulary **bigotry** (BIHG uh tree): *n.:* prejudice; intolerance.

Analyzing Visuals

Connecting to the Text: *Conditions have improved. Golf is becoming open to people of all backgrounds.*

🐻 California Standards, pp. 564–567

■ **Reading Standard 3.1** Articulate the expressed purposes and characteristics of different forms of prose (e.g., short story, novel, novella, essay).

Applying Your Skills

Reading Standard 3.1 Articulate the expressed purposes and characteristics of different forms of prose (e.g., short story, novel, novella, **essay**).

A Mason-Dixon Memory
Literary Response and Analysis

Reading Skills Focus
Quick Check

1. What experiences did Green and Davis share? Fill in a chart like the one below to compare their experiences.

	Experience	Friends' Responses
Green		
Davis		

Read with a Purpose

2. How do Green's teammates and Davis's classmates stand up to injustice? Why does Davis think their actions are significant?

Reading Skills: Setting a Purpose

3. Review the purposes you set for reading this personal narrative. Explain how focusing your reading added to your understanding of it.

Literary Skills Focus
Literary Analysis

4. **Analyze** Davis says, "Sometimes the battle is fought with fists and guns, but more often the most effective weapon is a simple act of love and courage." What does he mean by this statement?

5. **Interpret** Davis and Green both refer to love as a weapon in the "war for freedom." How can love be a weapon? Include examples from the essay in your answer.

6. **Connect** Have you or a friend ever felt unwelcome someplace? How did your experience compare with Green's or Davis's?

Literary Skills: Essay / Personal Narrative

7. **Analyze** Explain what <u>characteristics</u> make this essay a **personal narrative.**

8. **Interpret** <u>Articulate</u> the purpose of this essay. Why do you think Davis wrote it?

Literary Skills Review: Recurring Themes

The **theme** is what a piece of literature reveals about people and life. It is the meaning you take away from the story.

9. **Compare and Contrast** How does the theme of "A Mason-Dixon Memory" compare with the theme of *Song of the Trees*? Do you see any similarities? How do the themes differ?

Writing Skills Focus
Think as a Reader/Writer

Use It in Your Writing The childhood experience Davis recalls in "A Mason-Dixon Memory" gave him important <u>insights</u> about friendship and courage. Write a brief personal essay about the significance of an experience of yours and what you learned from it. Tell why it was important and what you remember from the experience today.

What Do You Think Now

How do the actions of Green's and Davis's friends reflect your idea of what it means to be loyal?

Universal Access

Struggling Writers

Some students may have difficulty writing an essay about the significance of an experience. To help them organize their thoughts, encourage them to fill out a three-column chart. In the first column, have them write what the experience was. In the second column, have them describe why it was important. In the third column, have them explain what they learned from the experience. Have students use this information to help them write their essays.

Experience	Why Important	What I Learned

Check for Understanding

Independent Practice
Reading Skills Focus
Answers:

1. *Green: kept from golf course because of his race; friends refused to play on course. Davis: kept from amusement park because of his race; friends refused to go.*

2. *They refuse to go to places that discriminate. Davis thinks their actions are significant because they stand up for what is right.*

3. *By focusing my reading on particular topics, I better understood the events and ideas of the story.*

Literary Skills Focus
Possible Responses:

4. *This means that people can make more of a statement by peacefully protesting discrimination than by using violence.*

5. *Love is a "weapon" because it overcomes hatred. Davis and Green's friends use love to strike back against racism.*

6. *When I try to hang out with my older brother and his friends, they don't want me around. It is upsetting, but it is not as serious a situation as Green and Davis faced.*

7. *It describes a real-life experience, but it is not as long as an autobiography.*

8. *Davis wanted to inspire other young people to fight injustice.*

9. *Both texts advocate taking a stand against injustice, and suggest that strength and unity are stronger than hatred. The themes are not quite the same, though, because strength of family is important in Song of the Trees, but is not mentioned in "A Mason-Dixon Memory."*

What Do You Think Now?

Ask students to discuss the sacrifices made by Green's and Davis's friends. What other sacrifices or gestures might people make to show loyalty to their friends? Encourage students to cite examples from their own experience if they can.

Independent Practice

Vocabulary Development

Your Turn _____
Possible responses:

- **predominantly:** *largely. Lara spent her night predominantly on her report.*

- **forfeit:** *give up. Because he was ill, Jim forfeited his trip to the beach.*

- **resolve:** *the will or spirit. I have the resolve to run a marathon.*

- **ominous:** *scary. The film's ominous music raised the tension.*

- **bigotry:** *prejudice. He was mistreated because of bigotry.*

English for Academic Success

Language Coach

Possible responses:

- **predominantly:** *mostly. Dondré Green went to a mostly white school.*

- **forfeit:** *abandon. Dondré's team could choose to abandon the tournament.*

- **resolve:** *determined. In his speech, Abraham Lincoln was determined to honor those who died.*

- **ominous:** *gloomy. The chaperone's gloomy tone worried Clifton.*

- **bigotry:** *intolerance. Dondré's friends hated prejudice.*

English for Academic Success

Academic Vocabulary

Possible response: I agree with this <u>insight</u> because I've found that when you treat people with love and respect, they will treat you well in return. I notice this when I smile at a neighbor and get a smile in return.

 WordSharp: An Interactive Vocabulary Tutor

 Learn It Online

Holt's **WordSharp Interactive Vocabulary Tutor** provides additional support for vocabulary development. Multimedia tutorials show students how to apply vocabulary skills to unfamiliar words—and how to make those words their own.

go.hrw.com   H7-566   **Go**

Applying Your Skills

A Mason-Dixon Memory

Vocabulary Development

Synonyms: Shades of Meaning

Words with the same or almost the same meaning are called **synonyms.** Synonyms usually have different shades of meaning. *Rigid* and *firm* are synonyms, but most people would rather be called *firm* than *rigid*. *Firm* suggests steadiness, and *rigid* suggests stiffness or inflexibility. A dictionary or thesaurus, a book of synonyms, can help you pick exactly the word you need.

Your Turn _____

Synonyms Make a word map like the following one for the rest of the Vocabulary words. Find at least one synonym for each word, and put it in the word map. Then, write at least one sentence using each Vocabulary word. Discuss the synonyms and their shades of meaning, if any.

Language Coach

Thesaurus A book of synonyms is called a **thesaurus.** You use one when you're looking for a word that expresses a specific meaning. You can find a thesaurus in print or online.

predominantly
forfeit
resolve
ominous
bigotry

1. Find each Vocabulary word in the essay. Then, use a thesaurus to look for synonyms. For each word, choose the synonym that best conveys the writer's meaning.

2. Now, use the synonyms to paraphrase the sentences from the essay where the Vocabulary words appear. (Paraphrasing a sentence means putting it in your own words without changing the meaning.) In each of your paraphrased sentences, include the synonym you chose.

Academic Vocabulary

Write About . . .

Dondré Green says that love "will conquer hatred every time." Explain why you agree or disagree with this <u>insight</u>. Write down three examples of behavior that you've seen or read about that support Green's statement.

 Learn It Online

Examine synonyms with *WordSharp* and take your vocabulary to a new level:

go.hrw.com   H7-566   **Go**

Universal Access: Vocabulary Development

 English Learners

English for Academic Success Some students may be unfamiliar with the thesaurus and its practical use. Explain to students that students and writers typically refer to a thesaurus when they want to replace a word they have used many times in a paragraph or essay, when they would like to find a synonym with a slightly different shade of meaning, or when they want to enhance a descriptive phrase. Pair students with fluent English speakers, and have them use a thesaurus to complete the following activity. Ask volunteers to share their findings with the class.

- Find a synonym for *angry* in the following sentence: "Kayla's sister was angry when the boys knocked over her sandcastle."

- Find a more vivid descriptive word than *big* in the following phrase: "my neighbor's dog is big."

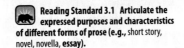

Reading Standard 3.1 Articulate the expressed purposes and characteristics of different forms of prose (e.g., short story, novel, novella, **essay**).

Grammar Link

Problems in Agreement: Phrases Between Subjects and Verbs

Sometimes, you might be confused about the number of a subject and a verb because the writer has included a phrase between the subject and the verb. In such cases, the number of a subject is not changed by the phrase that follows the subject.

INCORRECT **Dondré Green,** along with civic leaders and sports figures, **have come** to the hotel ballroom in Cleveland. [*Dondré Green* and *have* do not agree.]

CORRECT **Dondré Green,** along with civic leaders and sports figures, **has come** to the hotel ballroom in Cleveland. [*Dondré Green* and *has* agree.]

Your Turn _____

Identify which form of the verb in parentheses agrees with its subject.

1. I, the banquet's featured entertainer, (*was, were*) also there.

2. His teammates, as well as Dondré, (*does, do*) not accept intolerance.

3. Frank, not to mention the other eleven boys, (*is, are*) standing up for justice.

CHOICES

As you respond to the Choices, use these **Academic Vocabulary** words as appropriate: articulate, characteristics, impact, insight.

REVIEW
Discuss Forms of Prose

Group Discussion "A Mason-Dixon Memory" is a moving personal essay. Suppose you read about Davis's experiences in a newspaper article. How would the article be different? Would you gain as much insight about Davis's feelings from a news article? As a group, discuss other differences between a personal essay and a news article.

CONNECT
Support a Position

Timed **Writing** Many people devote their lives to fighting for important causes, such as civil rights. Write a brief persuasive essay on an issue *you* really care about. Try to write about an issue that matters to other people, too. Write a sentence that identifies the issue and articulates your opinion on it. Then, provide one or two reasons that support your opinion.

EXTEND
Shoot a Scene

TechFocus In a group, create a video showing one "scene" from the essay. Write the script based on details in the essay. Finally, with your classmates, participate in acting and filming.

 Learn It Online
There's more to this story than meets the eye. Expand your view at:

 go.hrw.com | H7-567 | **Go**

Independent Practice

Grammar Link

Your Turn _____

1. *was*

2. *do*

3. *is*

Choices:
Evaluation Criteria

Review: **Homework**
Discuss Forms of Prose

- The students differentiate newspaper articles and personal essays.

- The students reflect on what readers learn from the essay.

Connect: Timed Writing
40–50 Minutes

The essay offers strong reasons that support the student's position.

Extend: **Homework**
Shoot a Scene

- The video presents one scene from the essay with dialogue.

- The video script contains identifiable details from the essay.

Assess

 Chapter 5 Resources, Selection Standards Check, p. 27

ThinkCentral Online Assessment, Selection Standards Check

Teacher One Stop™, editable Selection Standards Check

Reteach

To reteach **forms of prose,** see **Reteaching Lessons,** p. 842A.

ThinkCentral Online Remediation

Learn It Online
Literature Links direct students to prescreened Web sites offering more information related to a selection.

go.hrw.com | H7-567 | **Go**

Universal Access: Grammar Link

EL English Learners

English for Academic Success If students struggle to determine subject-verb agreement when a phrase separates the subject and verb, suggest that they cover up the phrase or even rewrite the sentence without the phrase so they can place the subject and verb directly next to one another. This will help them determine whether the subject is truly singular or truly plural, and therefore determine which verb form they should use in the sentence. For example, students might rewrite the example

sentence as "Dondré Green has come to the hotel ballroom in Cleveland." Remind students to be certain that they are removing a phrase and not part of the subject. "Dondré Green, civic leaders, and sports figures" is a complete subject, and that sentence would be written as, "Dondré Green, civic leaders, and sports figures have come to the hotel ballroom in Cleveland."

Literary Skills Focus

Objectives

Students will
- understand and analyze forms of poetry
- understand and analyze characteristics of poetry

Build Background Encourage students to approach poetry with a positive, confident attitude. Compare poems to music, and state that the objective of a poem is to create emotions or tell a message through its words, sounds, and lines.

Forms of Poetry

Tell students that the forms of poetry reflect the genre's history and great diversity. Lyric poems date back to the Ancient Greeks, while sonnets were popular during the Renaissance. Many modern poems take the free verse form.

The Structure of a Poem

Direct students to the excerpt from "Harlem Night" on p. 568. Have the class discuss what they find interesting or noteworthy about the poem's form.

LITERARY RESPONSE AND ANALYSIS

Literary Skills Focus

by **Linda Rief**

What Are the Forms and Characteristics of Poetry?

Most poets will tell you that a poem should be read aloud at least twice before you talk about it. When you read poetry aloud, listen to the cadence, the rhythm, and the tone. What's the feeling you get from the sounds, the words, and the way the lines are shaped? What does the poem bring to mind for you? Don't be afraid of poetry. With each reading, let the words wash over you the way they do when you listen again and again to songs you love.

Forms of Poetry

Poetry is a kind of musical and focused writing designed to appeal to emotion and imagination. There are many types of poems:

- A **narrative poem**, such as a ballad or an epic, tells a story.
- A **lyric** poem expresses the speaker's feelings.
- An **ode** is a type of lyric poem that celebrates something, such as a person, event, or thing.
- A **sonnet** is a lyric poem with a very specific structure and rhyme scheme.
- A **elegy** mourns the loss of something important to the poet, such as a person or a time.
- **Free verse** has no regular rhythm or rhyme.
- A **catalog poem** is free verse that lists the poet's thoughts or feelings on a subject.

Use the word web above to think about the various forms of poetry. In this chapter, you will read examples of some of these forms.

The Structure of a Poem

Like sculptors, poets are concerned with **structure**, or form. When they write and revise, poets are chiseling their words to create the shapes you see on the page. Poets think about how long their lines should be and whether they should group lines into units, called **stanzas**. Some poets use forms based on strict rules, while others experiment with new forms. The poet's purpose is to give the words a pleasing shape and help them convey meaning.

> Come,
> Let us roam the night together
> Singing.
>
> I love you.
>
> from "Harlem Night Song"
> by Langston Hughes

Universal Access

 English Learners/Struggling Readers
- Tell students that the word *lyric* comes from a Latin word meaning "of the lyre" (a musical instrument). Today, the words to songs are referred to as lyrics. As a form of poetry, lyric poems express a writer's emotions and are often very songlike or musical.
- Explain that *elegy* comes from the word *elegos,* meaning "a poem or song of lament." Elegies are poems that mourn, or regret the loss of, something or someone.

Tone

Poets choose every word with great care to reflect a specific **tone,** or attitude toward the subject. If a poet thinks that a scene is happy and carefree, the details in the lines will reflect that attitude.

Imagery

Think of a poet as an artist who is creating a picture with words. Like painters, poets want to share a special, personal vision of the world. To do this, poets use **imagery,** or word pictures, that put your imagination to work. Such images can make you see things in new and unexpected ways. Read the following description from "The Highwayman," a poem in Chapter 3. What do you see?

> He'd a French cocked hat on his forehead,
> a bunch of lace at his chin,
> A coat of the claret velvet, and breeches of
> brown doeskin.
> They fitted with never a wrinkle. His boots
> were up to the thigh.
> > from "The Highwayman"
> > by Alfred Noyes

Images in poetry focus on all of the senses. Here are some not-so-pleasant images that appeal to touch, smell, and taste:

> Cellophane from green baloney,
> Rubbery blubbery macaroni,
> Peanut butter, caked and dry,
> Curdled milk and crusts of pie,
> > from "Sarah Cynthia Sylvia Stout
> > Would Not Take the Garbage Out"
> > by Shel Silverstein

Figurative Language

Along with images, poets use figures of speech to share their special, personal visions of the world. **Figures of speech** are comparisons that point out startling connections between dissimilar things. A **simile** is a comparison of two unlike things using the word *like, as, than,* or *resembles.* This simile compares a horse in a snowstorm to a shadow:

> And we saw him, or thought we saw him,
> dim and gray,
> Like a shadow against the curtain of
> falling flakes.
> > from "The Runaway"
> > by Robert Frost

A **metaphor** compares two unlike things, but it does so without using *like* or other such words.

> Stars are great drops
> Of golden dew.
> > from "Harlem Night Song"
> > by Langston Hughes

Your Turn Analyze Forms and Characteristics of Poetry

1. What makes poetry different from prose? Include specific characteristics as examples.

2. Identify a form or characteristic of poetry that you would like to understand better, and explain why.

Learn It Online
Use *PowerNotes* to reinforce your learning at:
go.hrw.com   H7-569   **Go**

Tone

Tell students to pay attention to a poem's words, form, and sounds. All of these elements contribute to a poem's tone.

Imagery

- Tell students that poetry, like prose selections they have read, uses images to allow the reader to picture its content. Unlike prose, however, the images in poetry can be brief and fragmented, requiring the reader to piece them together to understand the poet's meaning.

- Ask students to describe in their own words the images in the excerpts from "The Highwayman" and "Sarah Cynthia Sylvia Stout Would Not Take the Garbage Out."

Figurative Language

Have students read the definitions of simile and metaphor. Provide additional examples of each form, such as *the stars shone like diamonds* or *hope is a bird.*

Check for Understanding

Your Turn

Possible responses:

1. *Poetry uses images in a different way than prose, it can take a wider variety of forms than prose, and it uses figurative language.*

2. *I would like to learn about extended metaphors, because I want to know how a metaphor can be extended across many lines or an entire poem.*

Reteach

 ThinkCentral Online Remediation

Learn It Online
For a multimedia version of the instruction found on this page, use the **PowerNotes** Literary Skills Focus presentation.

go.hrw.com   H7-569   **Go**

- Compare a *catalog poem* to a *catalog,* a text or manuscript that lists items, especially items for sale. A *catalog poem* contains a poet's thoughts or feelings in a list format.

Advanced Learners

Extension Have students discuss what the tone of the various forms of poetry might be. For instance, an elegy will most likely have a mournful tone, while an ode might have a celebratory tone. Have students determine which form might be best for writing a funny poem, a nostalgic poem, or a serious poem.

Literary Skills Focus

by **Linda Rief**

What Are the Sounds of Poetry?

Like musicians, poets are concerned with sounds—perhaps the most noticeable characteristics of poetry. Imagine a composer of music trying various patterns of notes on a piano in order to create a pleasing melody. Poets do likewise with words, choosing them with great care. They revise their poems repeatedly, trying to find the combination of words that produces just the right sound—perhaps a harsh sound, a beautiful sound, or a sound that matches the gallop of a horse. A poet's goal is to match sound with the feelings and ideas that the poem is meant to convey.

Rhythm

Rhythm refers to the rise and fall of our voices as we stress, or emphasize, some sounds more strongly than others. As in music, rhythm in a poem can be fast or slow, light or solemn. It can even sound like everyday speech.

Poetry that is written in **meter** has a regular pattern of stressed and unstressed syllables. When poets write in meter, they count out the number of stressed syllables (or strong beats) and unstressed syllables (weaker beats) in each line. Then, they repeat the pattern throughout the poem. To avoid a singsong effect, poets usually vary the basic pattern from time to time. Read these lines aloud to listen for the meter:

> "You are old, Father William," the young
> man said,
> "And your hair has become
> very white;
> > from "Father William"
> > by Lewis Carroll

Scanning Rhythm

A poem's rhythm can be shown by using accent marks: (ˊ) for stressed syllables and (˘) for unstressed syllables. This marking is called **scanning.**

> ˘ ˘ ˊ ˊ ˘ ˊ ˘ ˊ ˘
> "You are old, Father William," the young
>
> ˘ ˊ
> man said,
> > from "Father William"
> > by Lewis Carroll

Poetry that is written in **free verse** does not have a regular pattern of stressed and unstressed syllables. Free verse sounds like ordinary speech:

> Generation on generation, your neck
> rubbed the window sill
> of the stall, smoothing the wood as the sea
> smooths glass.
> > from "Names of Horses"
> > by Donald Hall

Rhyme

Rhyme is the repetition of a stressed syllable and any unstressed syllables that follow. You can hear the rhymes in the lines from "Father William": *said* and *head*; *white* and *right*.

Poets use a variety of rhyming patterns. **End rhymes** are found at the end of two lines. **Internal rhymes** occur within lines, as shown below:

> Candy the *yams* and spice the *hams*, . . .
> Soggy *beans* and *tangerines*, . . .
> from "Sarah Cynthia Sylvia Stout
> Would Not Take the Garbage Out"
> by Shel Silverstein

Words such as *yams* and *hams* are **exact rhymes.** For variation, poets may use **slant rhymes,** which are sounds that almost rhyme, such as the words *sun* and *soon*.

Poets may use a **rhyme scheme,** or a pattern of rhymes. To describe a rhyme scheme, assign a new letter of the alphabet to each new end rhyme. For "Father William," it is *abab*.

> "You are old, Father William," the young
>   man said,   *a*
> "And your hair has become
>   very white;   *b*
> And yet you incessantly stand
>   on your head—   *a*
> Do you think, at your age, it is right?   *b*
> from "Father William"
> by Lewis Carroll

Repetition

Like musicians, poets use **repetition** to create an effect. The recurring use of a sound, a word, a phrase, or a line creates music, appeals to our emotions, and emphasizes important ideas.

Alliteration

Another way poets create sound effects is through **alliteration,** which is the repetition of consonant sounds in words that are close together. Listen for the *l* and *r* sounds in the following lines:

> But I *love* to hear it sung;
> how the water*lillies* fi*ll* with *r*ain unti*l*
> they ove*r*turn . . .
> from "I Ask My Mother to Sing"
> by Li-Young Lee

Onomatopoeia

Onomatopoeia (ahn uh mat uh PEE uh) is the use of words whose sounds echo their meaning. *Buzz, hiss, crash* are examples of onomatopoeia. Read these lines aloud to hear the sound of "The Highwayman":

> Over the cobbles he *clattered* and *clashed*
>   in the dark inn yard.
> And he *tapped* with his whip on the
>   shutters, but all was locked and barred.
> from "The Highwayman"
> by Alfred Noyes

Your Turn   Analyze Sound Effects in Poetry

Identify the sound effects that you enjoy most in songs or poetry, and explain why you like them.

Objectives

Students will
- learn skills for reading and re-reading poetry
- use questioning to understand a poem

Preteach

Build Background Tell students that when you have an "Ah-ha!" experience, you make a sudden realization or understand something clearly for the first time. Then, explain that many readers have "Ah-ha!" experiences when they read poetry. A poem's meaning may not be clear at first, but discovering the meaning can be fun and satisfying.

Direct Teach

How to Read a Poem

Suggest that students keep a list of unfamiliar words in their **Reader/ Writer Notebook** as they read. After they finish reading the poem once, they can look up the words before reading it.

Re-reading a Poem

Suggest that each time students read a poem, they look for something different in the text. For example, students may read for the first time focusing on literal meaning. As they re-read, they may choose to focus on rhythm, rhyme, or tone.

Reading Skills Focus

by **Kylene Beers**

How Do I Read and Analyze Poetry?

Robert Frost once said that poetry begins in delight and ends in wisdom. In other words, poetry should be enjoyable to read, and it should leave us with an "Ah-ha!" feeling. That "Ah-ha!" moment should not be a "Huh?" question. If you follow the suggestions for reading a poem and remember to re-read and ask questions, you will have more "Ah-ha!" moments than "Huh?" questions!

© The New Yorker Collection 1989 David Pascal from cartoonbank.com. All Rights Reserved.

How to Read a Poem

Follow these guidelines when you read poetry:

1. Read the poem aloud. The sense, or meaning, of a poem is linked to its sound.

2. Pay attention to punctuation. Pause at commas. Stop briefly at semicolons or after periods. Look for shifts in thought after dashes. If a line does not end in punctuation, do not make a full stop; pause briefly and continue to the end of the sentence.

3. Always read a poem in a normal voice, as if you were speaking to a friend. If the poem has a steady beat, let it emerge naturally.

4. Look up unfamiliar words. Poets choose words carefully, so sometimes words in a poem mean more than one thing. Each word adds to the poem's meaning.

5. Remember that poets use **similes** and **metaphors** to describe one thing in terms of another. For example, a poet might describe snowflakes as if they were insects.

6. Remember that many of the reading strategies that you use to understand prose will also help you understand poetry.

Re-reading a Poem

You might read a story only once, but a poem is meant to be read again and again. After the first reading, stop and think about the poem. Especially think about its images and sounds and the flow of its emotions and ideas. Then, read the poem a second time. You may read it through three times or more. With each re-reading, you will discover something new about the poem.

As you re-read a poem and become more comfortable with the images and sound effects, think about the poem's meaning. What message is the poet sending to you? What ideas occur to you, or what lessons come to mind as you read? You'll find that your response to some poems will be, "It tells me something I always knew but never thought about that way before."

Have you ever felt this way about fame?

How dreary to be Somebody!
How public—like a Frog—
To tell your name the livelong June
To an admiring Bog!
        from "I'm Nobody"
        by Emily Dickinson

Resources

Chapter 5 Resources, Reading Skills Focus Skill Builder, p. 33
PowerNotes, interactive lesson presentation with activities
Teacher One Stop™, on-level lesson plans and all print resources

Universal Access

EL English Learners/Struggling Readers

To help students better appreciate poetry, make sure they understand the terms *simile, metaphor,* and *imagery.*

- Explain that similes and metaphors are frequently used in poetry or descriptive writing to compare two things. A simile uses *like* or *as* to compare one thing to another. Explain that the sentence "Jon was as cold as ice" uses a simile to describe Jon's coldness.

- A metaphor says that something has literally become the object to which it is being compared. Tell students that an example would be "Jon was a giant block of ice."

Questioning

When you read a poem—especially the first time through—record questions about it. There may be an image you don't understand or a word you need to check before you re-read the poem. You can use a chart like this one to organize your questions and record your answers as you read or after you have finished reading:

"The Runaway"

Questions	Answers
Is the colt lost?	
What's a Morgan?	
What does "winter-broken" mean?	

You can also use specific questioning techniques to help you understand the imaginative comparisons poets make through similes and metaphors. Use a chart like the one below to identify your ideas and to guide you in recognizing the poet's images:

How Is One Thing like Another?

Characteristics	Object 1	Object 2
How does it look?		
How does it sound?		
What does it do?		

You can use a similar chart for any two objects that a poet compares in a figure of speech. List characteristics, such as appearance and sounds.

As you read, also record the thoughts and associations that come to mind from a poem's images. Try it. Think about your own family photos:

> This is the pond, and these are my feet.
> This is the rooster, and this is more
>   of my feet.
>
> *Mamá was never good at pictures.*
>   from "Ode to Family Photographs"
>   by Gary Soto

Your Turn Apply Reading Skills

1. What can you do to unlock a poem's meaning?

2. What reading strategies associated with prose will also be useful for reading poetry?

3. If you were reading a poem about the moon, what thoughts or associations would come to mind?

Now go to the Skills in Action: Reading Model

Learn It Online
Learn to read a poem with the *PowerNotes* version of this lesson on:

go.hrw.com   H7-573   Go

Questioning

■ Draw a two-column chart on the board. Label one column "Questions" and one column "Answers."

■ Use the excerpt on p. 572 to model the reading skill of questioning. You might say, "As I read the excerpt, I don't understand why *Somebody* is capitalized. It is not a person's name or a place. Why is *Somebody* capitalized?" Write the question.

■ Then, model finding the answer. You might say, "If I read a little further, I see that the author is talking about fame. She mentions being public and having everyone know your name. *Somebody* refers to a type of somebody—a famous somebody. It must be capitalized to draw attention to this." Write this answer in the chart.

Check for Understanding

Your Turn
Possible responses:

1. *look up unfamiliar words, pay attention to similes and metaphors, write down questions*

2. *re-reading, questioning, looking up unfamiliar words, looking for similes and metaphors*

3. *light, nighttime, astronauts, mystery*

Reteach

ThinkCentral Online Remediation

Learn It Online
For a multimedia version of the instruction found on this page, use the **PowerNotes** Reading Skills Focus presentation.

go.hrw.com   H7-573   Go

• Explain to students that imagery is a vivid description of something using the five senses that allows them to picture in their heads the object or concept that is being descibed.

Advanced Learners

Acceleration Pair students with partners. Have each pair choose a poem from this collection or from an outside source. Then, have each student read the poem silently, writing down questions as they read. After students have finished reading, have them compare questions with their partners. Have partners work together to try to answer every question.

Reading Model

Objectives

Students will

- understand rhythm, rhyme, alliteration, and onomatopoeia
- question for comprehension

Preteach

Read with a Purpose Direct students to the Read with a Purpose statement. Ask them to jot down in their **Reader/Writer Notebook** words and phrases that indicate how Longfellow views the blacksmith and what lesson the blacksmith teaches.

Direct Teach

Model the Skill

Use the Reading Model to demonstrate the application of the Literary and Reading skills in a poem. As you or students read the model aloud, stop to discuss the side annotations and highlighting, which are aids to comprehension and analysis.

▶ **Literary Focus**

Imagery What images does Longfellow use in the first stanza of the poem? *Possible response: Longfellow describes the blacksmith as a "mighty man" with "large and sinewy hands" and "brawny arms."*

▶ **Reading Focus**

Reading Poetry Read the first two lines of the third stanza of the poem. Where should readers pause, and for how long? *Possible response: Readers should pause briefly after "Week in," "week out," and "night," and take a longer pause after "bellows blow."*

Build Background

A blacksmith makes and repairs iron objects by hammering them against an anvil, which is a heavy iron block. Blacksmiths would heat the iron and shape it into objects, including hinges, household tools, and horseshoes. Because of improvements in the production of such objects, blacksmiths are rare today.

Read with a Purpose Read this poem to discover how Longfellow views the blacksmith and learn what lesson the blacksmith teaches.

The Village Blacksmith

by Henry Wadsworth Longfellow

Literary Focus

Imagery Longfellow uses **imagery** to create a picture of the blacksmith's powerful hands and arms. The next stanza presents more visual details to help you see the blacksmith at work.

> Under a spreading chestnut tree
>   The village smithy° stands;
> The smith, a mighty man is he,
>   With large and sinewy hands;
> 5 And the muscles of his brawny arms
>   Are strong as iron bands.
>
> His hair is crisp,° and black, and long,
>   His face is like the tan;
> His brow is wet with honest sweat,
> 10 He earns whate'er he can,
> And looks the whole world in the face,
>   For he owes not any man.

Reading Focus

Reading Poetry Pay attention to punctuation as you read. Pause briefly at a comma and longer at a semicolon. Don't stop at the end of a line that has no punctuation: The poet wants you to keep reading. (This is called a run-on line.)

> Week in, week out, from morn till night,
>   You can hear his bellows° blow;
> 15 You can hear him swing his heavy sledge,°
>   With measured beat and slow,
> Like a sexton ringing the village bell,
>   When the evening sun is low.

---

2. **smithy:** workshop of a blacksmith.
7. **crisp:** closely curled and wiry.
14. **bellows:** device for quickening the fire by blowing air in it.
15. **sledge:** sledgehammer; a long, heavy hammer, usually held with both hands.

Selection Readability	
Easily Accessible **Accessible** Challenging	familiar vocabulary; accessible theme

Selection Summary

The high quality of the blacksmith's work materializes in his physical strength and honest appearance. On Sundays he and his sons listen to his daughter as she sings in the church choir, and he thinks longingly of his deceased wife. Through his work, his faith, and his pain, his life serves as an example. Each night's rest is earned through the completion of a hard day's work.

Analyzing Visuals

Connecting to the Text
How does the painting help you visualize what a blacksmith does?

Shoeing
by Sir Edwin Henry Landseer (1802–1873).

And children coming home from school
20   Look in at the open door;
They love to see the flaming forge,
    And hear the bellows roar,
And catch the burning sparks that fly
    Like chaff from a threshing floor.

25 He goes on Sunday to the church,
    And sits among his boys;
He hears the parson pray and preach,
    He hears his daughter's voice,
Singing in the village choir,
30   And it makes his heart rejoice.

It sounds to him like her mother's voice,
    Singing in Paradise!
He needs must think of her once more,
    How in the grave she lies;
35 And with his hard, rough hand he wipes
    A tear out of his eyes.

Reading Focus

Questioning If you don't understand all of the images in these lines, write down a question before you continue reading. Be sure to answer the question before you re-read the poem.

Literary Focus

Rhyme and Rhythm
Longfellow uses sound effects such as **rhyming words** (*voice* and *rejoice*) and a metered **rhythm** to convey meaning.

Literary Focus

Imagery The poet's choice of words creates images that connect to all of the senses. This image appeals to the sense of touch.

Model the Skill

▶ Reading Focus

Questioning What is Longfellow describing in the first stanza of p. 575? ***Possible response:*** *Schoolchildren are coming to watch the blacksmith work.*

▶ Literary Focus

Rhyme and Rhythm What rhyme scheme does the author use in the fifth stanza? ***Possible response:*** *In the fifth stanza, the rhyme scheme is abcbdb.*

Imagery What specific words in line 35 appeal to the sense of touch, and how do they contribute to the reader's image of the blacksmith?

Possible response: *The words "hard" and "rough" appeal to the sense of touch, and emphasize the strong, work-worn body of the blacksmith.*

Analyzing Visuals

British artist **Sir Edwin Henry Landseer** was particularly well known for his visual representations of animals. Landseer designed the famous bronze sculptures of lions that appear at the base of Nelson's Column in Trafalgar Square, London. ***Connecting to the Text:*** *The picture shows a blacksmith working with his hands to make iron horseshoes.*

Universal Access

EL English Learners/ Struggling Readers

To help students understand the selection, introduce them to the following vocabulary words:

- **sinewy**—muscled, strong, or powerful. *The speaker notices how sinewy the blacksmith is.*
- **morn**—morning. *The blacksmith wakes early each morn.*
- **forge**—a furnace where metal is heated. *The children are amazed by the hot, fiery forge.*
- **toiling**—working hard. *The blacksmith spends most of his time toiling at the smithy.*
- **sorrowing**—mourning, feeling sad. *Thinking of his mother causes the blacksmith to begin sorrowing.*
- **repose**—rest. *Each night, the blacksmith enjoys repose.*

Then, give students this statement that explains how the words relate to the meaning of the poem:

The blacksmith is a sinewy man who is used to toiling from morn until night at the forge. By the time he goes to bed, he has earned his repose. Sometimes he is sorrowing and sometimes he feels happy, but he always works hard.

Reading Focus

Re-reading What new revelations has re-reading helped you discover? *Possible response:* Re-reading helped me understand that the poem is about recognizing the value of hard work.

Check for Understanding

Read with a Purpose Ask students to identify words and images that convey Longfellow's admiration for the blacksmith. Also, ask them what lesson the blacksmith teaches. *Possible response:* Words and images that convey Longfellow's admiration include "mighty man" and "my worthy friend." The speaker learns that life forces shape in the same way that the blacksmith shapes metal.

More About the Writer

Along with John Greenleaf Whittier, Oliver Wendell Holmes, James Russell Lowell, and William Cullen Bryant, **Henry Wadsworth Longfellow** was part of a group of New England poets known as the "Fireside Poets."

Think About the Writer

Ask students to think about memorable moments in American history. Then, have students discuss what might be poetic about these moments. Ask students what kind of message a poet might be sending by using historical information as background for a work of art.

 For Independent Reading

Recommend "A Jar of Tiny Stars: Poems by NCTE Award-Winning Poets," a volume of poems chosen by young people, to introduce students to the pleasure of reading poetry.

Reading Model

> Toiling—rejoicing—sorrowing,
>   Onward through life he goes;
> Each morning sees some task begin;
> 40   Each evening sees it close;
> Something attempted, something done,
>   Has earned a night's repose.
>
> Thanks, thanks to thee, my worthy friend,
>   For the lesson thou hast taught!
> 45 Thus at the flaming forge of life
>   Our fortunes must be wrought;
> Thus on its sounding anvil shaped
>   Each burning deed and thought.

Reading Focus

Re-reading Re-read the poem at least once. It will help you answer your questions and discover more about the poem's meaning.

Read with a Purpose What words and images convey Longfellow's admiration for the blacksmith? What lesson does the blacksmith teach?

MEET THE WRITER

Henry Wadsworth Longfellow

(1807–1882)

The Most Popular Poet

During his lifetime, Henry Wadsworth Longfellow was America's most popular poet. He was inspired by American history, which he often used as background material. Before the American Revolution and for the first few decades thereafter, most literature that was considered important came from England and Europe. Longfellow helped American poets become recognized and respected. His works have been translated into twenty-four languages.

Think About the Writer Why do you think Longfellow chose to write about moments in American history?

Resources

Chapter 5 Resources, Literary and Academic Vocabulary Skill Builder, p. 34

UA: Academic and Selection Vocabulary Skill Builder, p. 148

Teacher One Stop™, on-level lesson plans and all print resources

WordSharp: An Interactive Vocabulary Tutor, more practice with academic language

Academic Vocabulary

Writing About Forms of Poetry

Write the following questions on the board. Tell students these are the kinds of questions they will encounter on standardized tests. Discuss the meaning of the words, then have students use "The Village Blacksmith" to answer the questions.

- What is the **structure** of "The Village Blacksmith"? *Possible response:* The poem is broken into eight stanzas of six lines each. In each stanza, the second, fourth, and sixth lines rhyme.

Into Action: Questioning to Understand the Poem

Use questioning to help you understand the form, characteristics, and message of "The Village Blacksmith." Complete a chart like the one below with your questions. Two questions are provided that help you think about a simile used in the poem. Then, re-read the poem and identify what's clearer to you this time.

"The Village Blacksmith"

Questions	Answers
What is chaff?	It's the hard coating around a grain of wheat.
Why are burning sparks like chaff?	When grain is processed, chaff flies into the air like sparks.

Talk About . . .

How does the line "our fortunes must be wrought" connect to the blacksmith's work? How does it connect to our lives? Discuss your ideas with a partner. Try to use each Academic Vocabulary word listed on the right at least once in your discussion.

Write About . . .

Using the Academic Vocabulary words on the right, generate at least three questions about "The Village Blacksmith." Be sure to use the Academic Vocabulary words in ways that demonstrate that you know what they mean.

Writing Skills Focus
Think as a Reader/Writer

The Writing Skills Focus activities with the poetry in Chapter 5 explain each poet's style and use of literary elements. You'll have a chance to write about these elements and to use them yourself.

Academic Vocabulary for Chapter 5

Talking and Writing About Forms and Characteristics of Poetry

Academic Vocabulary is the language you use to write and talk about literature. Use these words to discuss the poetry you read in this chapter. The words are underlined throughout the rest of the chapter.

comment (KAHM ehnt) *v.*: make a remark or observation on. *Poets often comment on the relationship between society and nature.*

structure (STRUHK chuhr) *n.*: the way in which a set of parts is put together to form a whole. *To understand the structure of the poem, you must examine its parts.*

tradition (truh DIHSH uhn) *n.*: a set of beliefs or customs that have been handed down for generations. *Poetic traditions stretch back to the ancient world.*

vision (VIHZH uhn) *n.*: force or power of imagination. *The theme of the poem reflects the poet's vision.*

Your Turn

Copy the Academic Vocabulary words into your *Reader/Writer Notebook*. Use each word in a sentence that describes a feeling or idea you have about poetry.

Guided Practice: Apply
Into Action: Questioning to Understand the Poem

Some students may wish to work with a partner as they attempt to answer their questions. Have pairs of students discuss each question and arrive at an answer together.

Talk About...

Model for students how to incorporate the Academic Vocabulary words into a conversation. You might say, "The line suggests that the tradition of the blacksmith's work is similar to the way in which people build their own destinies."

Write About...
Possible responses:

1. *What details from the poem describe the traditions of village blacksmiths?*

2. *How does the structure of the poem influence its tone?*

3. *How does the speaker comment about the blacksmith's work?*

Writing Skills Focus

The Think as a Reader/Writer activities in the chapter focus on the reading-writing relationship. Use the activities to help students explore the writer's craft in a text and to practice this aspect of craft in their own writing.

Independent Practice

Chapter 5 Resources, Skill Builders, pp. 32-34

UA: Differentiating Instruction, Academic and Vocabulary Skill Builder, p. 148

- What **vision** do you think Longfellow had for this poem? Explain. ***Possible response:*** *I think Longfellow probably envisioned a poem that showed readers how an average person's everyday experiences can serve as an artistic metaphor for life's successes and failures.*

- What **comment** can you make about Longfellow's willingness to follow the **traditional** rules of poetry? ***Possible response:*** *Longfellow seems to enjoy incorporating traditional poetic elements such as rhyme and rhythm into his poetry. "The Village Blacksmith" contains many of the features that I associate with poetry.*

Objectives

Students will

- understand extended metaphors and other figures of speech
- apply the strategy of questioning before and during reading

Motivate

What Do You Think?/QuickWrite

Have students recall experiences that inspired them to act or create something. Then, have students use their **Reader/Writer Notebook** to record specific reasons why an experience might inspire a poet to write a poem.

English for Academic Success

Academic Vocabulary

Look for opportunities to use the Academic Vocabulary words in this chapter.

- **vision, n.:** force of imagination
- **structure, n.:** the way in which a set of parts is put together to form a whole
- **comment, v.:** explain or interpret something
- **tradition, n.:** a set of beliefs or customs that have been handed down for generations

Analyzing Visuals

Extension Activity Ask students how the word magnets in the image might relate to elements of poetry. **Possible response:** Words are a poet's building blocks. One important element of a poem is word choice.

Forms and Characteristics of Poetry

CONTENTS

 What Do You Think Why might people feel the need to write poetry?

QuickWrite Think of an experience that had a profound <u>impact</u> on you. How might writing about it in a poem help you better understand the experience?

Selection Readability	
Easily Accessible **Accessible** Challenging	familiar vocabulary; figurative language; familiar situations; unfamiliar form

Selection Summary

In "I'm Nobody!," Emily Dickinson explores her identity.

Preparing to Read

I'm Nobody!

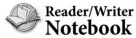

Reader/Writer Notebook

Use your **RWN** to complete the activities for this selection.

Literary Skills Focus

Figures of Speech In "I'm Nobody!" poet Emily Dickinson highlights her ideas by using figures of speech. **Figures of speech** compare things that at first glance seem very different. Thinking about these unusual comparisons helps you see familiar things in a new light. The comparisons in figures of speech are imaginative and are not meant to be understood as literally true.

Reading Skills Focus

Questioning the Text To prepare to read a poem and to stay engaged while you're reading it, ask yourself questions about the text. After reading, review your questions to see if all of them have been answered. Where in the text did you find your answers?

Into Action In your *Reader/Writer Notebook,* make a chart like the one below. Answer any questions you can before you read. Leave space to add questions you may have as you read.

Questions	Answers	More Questions
What does "Nobody" mean to me?	A nobody is unimportant. I wouldn't want to be nobody.	
What does "Nobody" mean to Dickinson?		
What do a public person and a frog have in common?		

Writing Skills Focus

Think as a Reader/Writer

Find It in Your Reading As you read, record Dickinson's figures of speech in your *Reader/Writer Notebook.* Then, explain how the figures of speech help you see things in a new way.

Learn It Online
See a good reader in action, and practice your own skills, at:

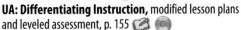

go.hrw.com   H7-579   **Go**

Preteach

Language Coach
Tell students that similes and metaphors offer complex descriptions in very few words by comparing or associating two unlike things. Have students consider what they are describing about the animal they admire as they write their own similes and metaphors.

Literary Skills Focus
As you read and discuss the selection with students, have them compare the literary readings of figures of speech to their figurative meanings.

Reading Skills Focus
Give students a copy of the Reading Skills Focus graphic organizer before they read. (See **Chapter 5 Resources.**) Tell them to use their responses to answer the questions on the Applying Your Skills page.

Writing Skills Focus
Have students record the figures of speech that Dickinson uses to help them see things in a new way in their **Reader/Writer Notebook.** Students can use their notes to complete the Writing Skills Focus activity.

Selection Resources

Chapter 5 Resources, on-level practice and assessment, p. 35

PowerNotes, interactive lesson presentation with activities

Teacher One Stop™, on-level lesson plans and all print resources

Holt Audio Library

Holt Audio Library: Selections and Summaries in Spanish

UA: Holt Interactive Reader, p. 152

Holt Interactive Reader for ELD, p. 172

Holt Audio Tutor for ELD

UA: Differentiating Instruction, modified lesson plans and leveled assessment, p. 155

UA: Resources for Teaching Advanced Students, lesson plans

UA: Supporting Instruction in Five Languages, selection summary

ThinkCentral Online Assessment, Selection Standards Check

ThinkCentral Online Remediation

Learn It Online
Online reading support for this selection includes audio segments that model the thought processes of a good reader. These Think-Aloud models are followed by prompts that let the student to record their own thoughts about the selection.

go.hrw.com   H7-579   **Go**

Learn It Online
Learn more about the author at:
go.hrw.com H7-580 Go

Selection Introduction

More About the Writer

At certain points in her life, **Emily Dickinson** wrote a poem a day on average. At her death she left behind 1,775 poems. Dickinson's poems have appealed to a variety of audiences, and there is little dispute over her high place among American writers.

Think About the Writer

Discuss how American literature was still in its early stages during the time that Emily Dickinson wrote most of her poetry. Furthermore, Dickinson was a female writer in a time when writing was dominated by males, and she also wrote in a unique style.

For Independent Reading

- Students interested in what daily life was like during Emily Dickinson's lifetime might enjoy the historical fiction text *A Gathering of Days: A New England Girl's Journal* by Joan Blos.

- Students interested in "American originals" might enjoy *Celebrating America: A Collection of Poems and Images of the American Spirit,* a collection of poetry and images compiled by Laura Whipple.

Learn It Online

Additional high-interest information about the author, including maps, timelines, and activities, is available at **go.hrw.com**.

go.hrw.com H7-580 Go

MEET THE WRITER

Emily Dickinson
(1830–1886)

An American Original

Today, Emily Dickinson is regarded as one of America's greatest poets. During her lifetime, however, she was anything but famous. Only seven of her poems were published while she was alive—and she refused to have her name put on any of them. After a sociable childhood and adolescence, Dickinson seemed to retreat from the world. By the time she was forty, she rarely left her family's house in Amherst, Massachusetts.

After Emily Dickinson died, her sister discovered in a locked box seven or eight hundred poems written on envelopes, paper bags, and scraps of paper, many neatly sewn into little packets. It looked as if the poet had been hoping someone would find the poems and publish them. In her lifetime, however, no one had really understood what poetry meant to Emily Dickinson. The quote below reveals her vision of poetry.

"If I read a book, and it makes my whole body so cold no fire can ever warm me, I know that is poetry. If I feel physically as if the top of my head were taken off, I know that is poetry. These are the only ways I know it. Is there any other way?"

© The Granger Collection, New York.

Think About the Writer What makes Dickinson an "American original"?

Build Background

The American artist Andy Warhol once said, "In the future everyone will be world-famous for fifteen minutes." Think about the benefits and drawbacks of being famous. Keep them in mind as you read "I'm Nobody!"

Preview the Selection

Unlike many nineteenth-century poets, Emily Dickinson experimented with the structure of poetry and did not use regular rhymes and rhythms. She is famous for using the dash—and for choosing strong images to express her bold ideas.

Real Issues, Real Experts

Holt author **Linda Rief** offers strategies for teaching poetry.

Poetry is so unique in its connections to a reader. In order to show kids that we all don't like the same poems, or take the same things to and from a poem (yet there are things we can admire or learn or take from different poets), I choose five to seven different poems (including "I'm Nobody"), all with different styles of writing. I type up the poems with the same font and same size printing. Depending on the number of students in the class, I cut the poems up into the same number of students—twenty-five kids, twenty-five chunks of poems. I put all the pieces of all the different poems together in one envelope and have the kids each choose one piece.

After they have each chosen a piece, they must walk around the room to find the people who have all the remaining parts of their poem. They have to use topic, style, and voice to try and find the remaining stanzas to their poem. Once they think they have all the parts, they sit together, figure out the organization for the poem, practice reading it—with a sense of voice for the

Senecio (1922) by Paul Klee. Oil on gauze on cardboard (40.5 cm × 38 cm).

Oeffentliche Kunstsammlung Basel, Kunstmuseum. Accession no. 1569. ©2003 Artists Rights Society (ARS), New York/VG Bild-Kunst, Bonn.

I'm Nobody!

by **Emily Dickinson**

I'm Nobody! Who are you?
Are you Nobody too?
Then there's a pair of us!
Don't tell! they'd banish us, you know!   **A**

How dreary to be Somebody!
How public—like a Frog—
To tell your name the livelong June
To an admiring Bog!   **B**

A Read and Discuss What has the poet told you so far?

B Literary Focus Figures of Speech To what does the speaker compare a "Somebody"?

Analyzing Visuals

Connecting to the Text
Explain whether you think this painting depicts a "Somebody" or a "Nobody."

speaker or narrator, and figuring out words they don't know—and plan a way to read/present their poem to the class.

After each group reads its poem, I talk about what I know about each poet. We talk about questions the readers have, what they liked or didn't like, what surprised them, or reading the poems and figuring them out helped them think about different poets, including Emily Dickinson.

Independent Practice

Reading Skills Focus

Answers:

1. *The speaker feels glad to be someone who is not famous.*

2. *To Dickinson, being a "Nobody" meant being a unique person who could thrive in private. Does this suggest she chose to remain a Nobody during her lifetime?*

Literary Skills Focus

Possible responses:

3. *A Nobody is a quiet, unassuming individual who does not seek attention or conform to society. A Somebody is a noisy, self-promoting celebrity with many fans.*

4. *"They," the "Somebodies," would banish the speaker because they feel the "Nobodies" are inferior.*

5. *In line 5, the speaker comments on how awful it must be to be a "Somebody," which supports the idea that she'd rather be a "Nobody."*

6. *The speaker is talking to another Nobody, or another unassuming individual. This Nobody might be another poet, artist, or shy person.*

7. *A frog can be similar to a celebrity because there are many of them and both make a lot of noise. This isn't flattering; it suggests that celebrities are noisy, annoying, and not very important.*

8. *The poet has an unfavorable view of people who idolize celebrities. Many creatures in marshes are generally thought of as slimy, ordinary pests, suggesting that celebrity-worshippers are no better.*

9. *Dickinson is suggesting that anonymity is preferable to fame, and that people who are not famous are more true to themselves.*

What Do You Think Now?

Ask students to compare Dickinson's portrayal of a Nobody to the lifestyle she chose for herself. What might she have feared about becoming a Somebody?

I'm Nobody!

Literary Response and Analysis

Reading Skills Focus

Read with a Purpose

1. How does the speaker feel about fame?

Reading Skills: Questioning the Text

2. Review the questions you had about "I'm Nobody!" Expand on any of your answers, and write additional questions on the chart you made in your *Reader/Writer Notebook* before reading the poem.

Questions	Answers	More Questions
What does "Nobody" mean to me?	A nobody is unimportant. I wouldn't want to be nobody. Maybe the desire to be famous, though, is superficial.	If the desire for fame is superficial, why do so many of us desire it?

Literary Skills Focus

Literary Analysis

3. **Interpret** What does "Nobody" mean in this poem? What does "Somebody" mean?

4. **Interpret** Who are "they" in line 4 of the poem? Why would "they" banish the speaker?

5. **Interpret** Dickinson talks about what it is like to be "Nobody" and what it is like to be "Somebody." What <u>comment</u> does she make on which she would rather be?

6. **Make Judgments** To whom might the speaker be talking? Explain your opinion.

Literary Skills: Figures of Speech

7. **Analyze** The simile in the second stanza of "I'm Nobody" compares a celebrity to a frog. How can a frog and a celebrity be similar? Explain whether or not this comparison is meant to be flattering.

8. **Draw Conclusions** In the metaphor in the last line, admirers of famous people are compared to creatures in a bog (a marshy place) that admire a croaking frog. What does this tell you about how the poet views people who idolize celebrities?

Literary Skills Review: Theme

9. **Make Judgments** The **theme** of a work is the idea that the writer wishes to convey about a particular subject. What might Dickinson want to convey about the subject of anonymity (an uh NIHM uh tee)—the state of being unknown or unrecognized?

Writing Skills Focus

Think as a Reader/Writer

Use It in Your Writing Review the figures of speech Dickinson uses to express her views on fame precisely and efficiently. Now, create a simile and a metaphor of your own that convey your feelings about celebrities and their admirers.

What Do **You Think Now** In what ways might Dickinson's poem reflect her solitary, reclusive nature?

Struggling Writers

To complete the Writing Skills Focus, provide additional scaffolding for students by having them create semantic maps. In the middle of the map, students should write "celebrities and their admirers." Then, they should write words that they associate with celebrities and their admirers on the lines around the center circle. Tell students to use these ideas to write a simile and a metaphor.

celebrities and their admirers

Preparing to Read

Madam and the Rent Man / Harlem Night Song / Winter Moon

Literary Skills Focus

Tone Has anyone ever said to you, "Don't use that tone of voice with me"? Your tone can change the meaning of what you say. Tone can turn a statement such as "You're a big help" into a genuine compliment or a remark full of sarcasm (SAHR kaz uhm). (Sarcasm is a way of speaking or writing in which your tone expresses the opposite of what you actually mean.)

In poems and stories, writers convey their **tone,** or attitude toward a subject, by their choice of words and details. As you read "Madam and the Rent Man," think about the writer's attitude toward his no-nonsense speaker. Use a chart like the one below to explain how the same comment can take on different tones. The first example has been completed for you.

Comment	Tone 1	Tone 2
"Thanks a lot!"	genuine compliment	sarcastic remark when someone is not helpful

Imagery Language that appeals to the senses is called **imagery.** When you read about a rose, you may *smell* its pleasing scent and *see* its bright color. You might *feel* its thorn prick you. Poets hope their imagery will unlock storehouses of memory and stir our imaginations. They hope their poetic <u>vision</u> will make us say, "Oh yes, I see what you mean."

Writing Skills Focus
Think as a Reader/Writer

Find It in Your Reading Look for sensory images in "Madam and the Rent Man," "Harlem Night Song," and "Winter Moon." Explain to which of your senses—sight, hearing, touch, taste, smell—the images appeal. Find one image for each of the five senses.

Reader/Writer Notebook

Use your **RWN** to complete the activities for these selections.

Language Coach

Idioms Some expressions don't make sense even when you know the meaning of each individual word. For example, "pass the buck" may not be easy for you to understand even though you know the words *pass, the,* and *buck.* "Pass the buck" is an **idiom,** a commonly used expression that is not literally true. It means "to pass responsibility to someone else." You encounter idioms frequently when you read, and you probably use them yourself. For example, if you say you're going to pass your math test "with flying colors," what do you really mean?

Learn It Online
To hear a professional actor read these poems, visit the selections online at:

go.hrw.com   H7-583   **Go**

English for Academic Success
Language Coach
Tell students that idioms are examples of figurative language and are not meant literally. However, it is important to understand the literal meaning of the phrase in order to understand the idiom. [*To pass a test "with flying colors" means that you did very well.*]

Literary Skills Focus
As you read and discuss the selection with students, have them translate the poet's imagery into a visual form, such as a sketch or collage. Give students a copy of the graphic organizer before they read. (See **Chapter 5 Resources.**) Tell them to use their responses to answer the questions on the Applying Your Skills page.

Writing Skills Focus
Have students record sensory images in their **Reader/Writer Notebook.** Students can use their notes to complete the Writing Skills Focus activity.

Learn It Online
The online version of this selection includes audio support to engage all students and to help struggling readers with reading comprehension and vocabulary.

go.hrw.com   H7-583   **Go**

Selection Introduction

More About the Writer

Langston Hughes was more than a poet; he was also a playwright, essayist, novelist, and columnist. His writing showed a strong sense of racial pride and spoke out against racial discrimination and other forms of injustice.

Think About the Writer

Remind students that in the 1920s, African Americans did not have equal rights or opportunities in the United States. Also note that Hughes worked many jobs in various cities. Because a writer often writes about what he or she has seen and experienced in life, ask students to think about what Hughes might have seen or experienced that influenced his work.

For Independent Reading

- Students interested in reading more about Langston Hughes might enjoy Jack Rummel's biography, "Langston Hughes: Poet of the Harlem Renaissance."

- For students interested in poetry by African Americans, recommend Angela Johnson's childhood recollections in "The Other Side: Shorter Poems."

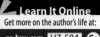
Langston Hughes
(1902–1967)

Singing the Music of Poetry

Langston Hughes was one of the first African American writers to win worldwide favor. Still, he never lost his popularity with the people he wrote about. Hughes once said:

"I knew only the people I had grown up with, and they weren't people whose shoes were always shined, who had been to Harvard, or who had heard of Bach."

Hughes was born in Joplin, Missouri. He wrote his first poem in elementary school *after* he was elected class poet. The position inspired him to write and to reveal his gift as a poet.

As an adult, Hughes worked many different jobs in various cities while writing poetry in his spare time. For two years he worked as a busboy at a hotel in Washington, D.C. During this time he wrote many poems, among them blues poems, which he would make up in his head and sing on his way to work.

Hughes became a major literary figure in what is now known as the Harlem Renaissance of the 1920s. His poems often echo the rhythms of blues and jazz music.

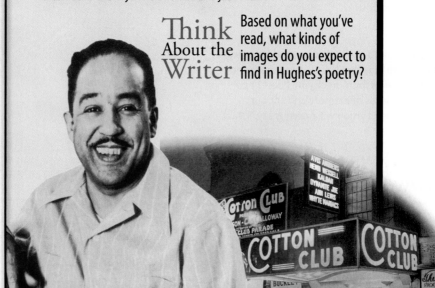

Think About the Writer Based on what you've read, what kinds of images do you expect to find in Hughes's poetry?

Build Background

"Madam and the Rent Man" is set in Harlem, a section of New York City where many people live in rented apartments.

Preview the Selections

In "Madam and the Rent Man," the speaker is **the renter,** a woman who has reason to be angry with **her landlord** and with the landlord's **agent,** an employee who has come to collect the rent.

"Harlem Night Song" and "Winter Moon" paint pictures of a night in the city with a loved one and of a beautiful winter moon.

Selection Readability

Easily Accessible **Accessible** Challenging	These poems include familiar vocabulary; figurative language; familiar situations; unfamiliar form

Selection Summary

"Madam and the Rent Man" presents an antagonistic conversation between a tenant and a rent collector. "Harlem Night Song" and "Winter Moon" both give views of the night and the moon.

Read with a Purpose Read this poem to discover what happens when an angry tenant confronts the landlord's rent collector.

MADAM AND THE RENT MAN

by
Langston Hughes

The Apartment by Jacob Lawrence (1917–2000).

Hunter Museum of American Art, Chattanooga, Tennessee. Museum purchased with funds provided by the Benwood Foundation and the 1982 Collectors Group. HMA 1982.10. ©2005 Gwendolyn Knight Lawrence/Artists Rights Society (ARS), New York.

The rent man knocked.
He said, Howdy-do?
I said, What
Can I do for you?
5 He said, You know
Your rent is due.

I said, Listen,
Before I'd pay
I'd go to Hades°
10 And rot away! **A**

The sink is broke,
The water don't run,
And you ain't done a thing
You promised to've done.

15 Back window's cracked,
Kitchen floor squeaks,
There's rats in the cellar,
And the attic leaks.

He said, Madam,
20 It's not up to me.
I'm just the agent,
Don't you see?

I said, Naturally,
You pass the buck.
25 If it's money you want
You're out of luck. **B**

He said, Madam,
I ain't pleased!
I said, Neither am I.

30 So we agrees!

---

9. Hades (HAY deez): in Greek mythology, the underworld, or world of the dead.

A What has the speaker told you so far?

B **Literary Focus** Tone What tone does the poet convey through Madam's comment in lines 25–26?

Model the Skill

■ Tell students that poets rely on **imagery,** or sensory details created with words, to help readers understand the meaning they are trying to create. Imagery often seeks to create a visual, but it may appeal to any of the reader's five sentences.

■ Have a volunteer read aloud lines 5–10 of "Harlem Night Song." Point out that most of the stanza focuses on creating a sense of place: nighttime in Harlem. The writer uses detail words, particularly colors, to help the reader visualize the night sky. Model translating these details into a mental picture of the night sky. You might say, "I am picturing a dark blue sky with a big, bright moon surrounded by large, golden stars. I think that is the picture Hughes wants to create with his description."

Guided Practice: Apply

Have students listen as you read aloud "Winter Moon." Then, read it a second time and ask students to focus on the details Hughes uses to try to see the moon as he wants us to see it. Have volunteers describe how they picture the moon.

Think as a Reader/Writer

Find It in Your Reading Point out that Hughes uses imagery to describe two different moons in the two poems here.

Use It in Your Writing Have students write two sentences, using imagery to describe two different suns that they have seen.

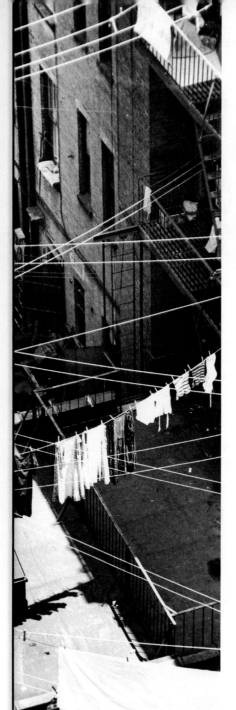

HARLEM NIGHT SONG

by **Langston Hughes**

Come,
Let us roam° the night together
Singing.

I love you.

5   Across
The Harlem roof-tops
Moon is shining.
Night sky is blue.
Stars are great drops
10 Of golden dew.   Ⓐ

Down the street
A band is playing.

I love you.

Come,
15 Let us roam the night together
Singing.   Ⓑ

---

2. roam (rohm): wander.

Ⓐ **Literary Focus** **Imagery** What picture of the night sky and the moon do you get from these words?

Ⓑ **Read and Discuss** What is the importance of the word *singing*?

Universal Access

AAVE Students Who Use African American Vernacular English

English for Academic Success Some students may not voice the *th* consonant pairing as /th/ in their everyday speech. Explain to students that although informal English allows for diverse pronunciations, it will benefit them to practice the formal English pronunciation of the *th* consonant setting for academic use. Model the formal English voicing of *th* by reading aloud "Harlem Night Song" for students, emphasizing the /th/ sound.

Then, have students choral read the poem, taking care to pronounce all /th/ sounds using formal English. Provide feedback as needed.

✔ For additional instruction and strategies, see **Holt Pronunciation DVD-Rom** and **ThinkCentral, Teacher Access**.

Winter Moon

by Langston Hughes

How thin and sharp is the moon tonight!
How thin and sharp and ghostly white   **A**
Is the slim curved crook of the moon tonight!   **B**

A **Literary Focus** Imagery How do you picture this moon?
B **Read and Discuss** What mood does the poet create with this poem?

SOCIAL STUDIES LINK

The Harlem Renaissance

Langston Hughes is among the African American writers, musicians, artists, and performers who were part of the Harlem Renaissance. A "renaissance" is a rebirth or revival of culture. The Harlem Renaissance was a blossoming of African American culture that developed in New York City's Harlem neighborhood in the 1920s and early 1930s. It was primarily a literary movement, but it also encompassed music, art, and theater. Other well-known contributors to the Harlem Renaissance include the novelist Zora Neale Hurston and jazz musician Duke Ellington.

Ask Yourself

Why do you think Hughes is an important figure in the Harlem Renaissance? What aspects of the movement do you find in his poetry?

Think About/Talk About

Read with a Purpose Have students read the Read with a Purpose statement. Have students brainstorm ways in which their senses interact with the night and the moon.

▶ Comprehension
"Harlem Night Song"
B Read and Discuss
Possible response: It seems as though the speaker is so in love that he has to sing.

"Winter Moon"
B Read and Discuss
Possible response: The words sharp, ghostly white, *and* crook *all evoke a harsh, chilly mood.*

▶ Analysis
"Harlem Night Song"
A Literary Focus
Possible response: There is a cloudless, deep blue sky, and the stars and moon are shining. The moon looks almost full and very bright.

"Winter Moon"
A Literary Focus
Possible response: I imagine it as a pale moon with only a sliver showing.

▶ Extend the Discussion
Tone How do the punctuation marks in "Winter Moon" contribute to the poem's tone? *Possible response: The only punctuation marks are two exclamation points. The poem has an excited, breathless tone because it only lets the reader pause at exclamations.*

Social Studies Link
Ask Yourself _____
Possible response: Hughes gave voice to the African American experience and became one of the first African American writers to be taken seriously by the rest of the nation. He was influenced by other artists like jazz musicians, and condemned racial injustice with his writing, both of which were important aspects of the movement.

 HSS Analysis Skills, HR 1, 3

Independent Practice

Reading Skills Focus

Answers:

1. *The rent man and Madam both agree that they are displeased.*

2. *In "Harlem Night Song," the night and moon are clear and bright, but in "Winter Moon" the moon is thin and barely visible.*

Literary Skills Focus

Possible responses:

3. *If a landlord expects the rent to be paid, he needs to take care of the property.*

4. *In "Madam and the Rent Man," Hughes portrays the rougher side of life in Harlem, but in "Harlem Night Song" he celebrates the good things about life in Harlem.*

5. *Hughes uses only a few words, but is still able to convey clear imagery and a chilly, somber mood.*

6. *The tone of frustration is lightened somewhat by sarcastic humor from the tenant.*

7. *The sentences "Come, let us roam the night singing" and "I love you" are repeated. There is a tone of celebration and joy.*

8. *The author appeals to the sense of sight by describing how the night looks and the sense of hearing by describing the band playing.*

9. *The images of roaming the night and singing reveal that the speaker is happy and in love.*

10. *I would describe it as a crescent moon, because the poet calls it "a curved crook."*

11. *The poem is in first-person from the tenant's point of view. It is subjective, because the reader's reactions are guided by what she presents and how she presents it.*

12. *The Rent Man and Madam agree that obligations must be filled, and that neither of them is responsible for the problems. They disagree on her refusal to pay the rent.*

Applying Your Skills

Madam and the Rent Man / Harlem Night Song / Winter Moon

Literary Response and Analysis

Reading Skills Focus
Read with a Purpose

1. The rent man and Madam seem to disagree throughout the poem. The last line, however, is "So we agrees!" How can that be?

2. How do the descriptions of the night and the moon in "Harlem Night Song" differ from the descriptions in "Winter Moon"?

Literary Skills Focus
Literary Analysis

3. **Infer** What do you think is the message of "Madam and the Rent Man"?

4. **Compare and Contrast** What different views of life in Harlem does Hughes present in "Madam and the Rent Man" and "Harlem Night Song"?

5. **Analyze** How does "Winter Moon" demonstrate the power of poetry to express emotions in only a few words?

Literary Skills: Tone and Imagery

6. **Analyze** How does the author's use of playful language and dialogue affect the tone of "Madam and the Rent Man"?

7. **Analyze** Poems, like songs, often repeat lines, stanzas, or words. What sentences are repeated in "Harlem Night Song"? Describe the tone you hear in these lines.

8. **Interpret** Explain the sensory images in "Harlem Night Song."

9. **Infer** What do the images in "Harlem Night Song" reveal about the speaker?

10. **Connect** Visualize the moon in "Winter Moon." What words in particular help you visualize the moon?

Literary Skills Review: Point of View

11. **Analyze** From whose point of view is "Madam and the Rent Man" told? Is the speaker's point of view subjective or objective? Explain.

12. **Compare and Contrast** How is the Rent Man's perspective on the apartment situation different from Madam's? How is it similar?

Writing Skills Focus
Think as a Reader/Writer

Use It in Your Writing Write two paragraphs that compare and contrast the images in "Harlem Night Song" and "Winter Moon." Which images are most powerful? To which senses do the images appeal? Be sure to include examples to support your analysis.

What Do You Think Now?

What kinds of personal experiences might have led Hughes to <u>comment</u> on Harlem in these poems?

What Do You Think Now?

Remind students that writers often draw on familiar subjects and experiences for inspiration. Discuss how the subject matter of each poem is related to Hughes's daily life.

Preparing to Read

I Ask My Mother to Sing /
Ode to Family Photographs

Reader/Writer
Notebook
Use your **RWN** to complete the activities for these selections.

Literary Skills Focus

Forms of Poetry: Lyric Poem There are two basic types of poems: A **narrative poem** tells a story. Like a short story, a narrative poem has characters, a setting, and a plot with conflict and complications. A **lyric poem** is a poetic form used to express personal thoughts and feelings. In ancient Greece, lyric poems were sung to the music of a stringed instrument called a *lyre* (lyr), from which the word *lyric* comes. Lyric poems come in many shapes and sizes and express a wide range of tones and emotions.

Sonnet Li-Young Lee's "I Ask My Mother to Sing" is a sonnet. A **sonnet** is a lyric poem of fourteen lines. There are several types of sonnets. In the type of sonnet that Lee wrote, the lines are divided into three **quatrains** (a quatrain is four lines of verse). Each quatrain focuses on one aspect of a subject. The sonnet ends with a **couplet** (two lines that usually rhyme). As you will see, Lee varies this <u>structure</u> somewhat.

Ode An **ode** is a poem that pays tribute to someone or something of great importance to the poet. The first odes, written in honor of famous people, were long, complex, and elegant. Over the centuries, odes have been written in a formal style to praise lofty subjects, such as beauty, joy, and freedom. Today's odes tend to be more informal. Some are even humorous. Many have been written about everyday objects, such as tomatoes, frogs, and socks. Gary Soto's ode celebrates something most people have in their homes—family photos.

Writing Skills Focus

Think as a Reader/Writer

Find It in Your Reading As you read "Ode to Family Photographs," note that the speaker's important memories are inspired by everyday items and events.

Language Coach

Sensory Language Writing that creates a clear image and appeals to the senses of touch, sight, smell, taste, or hearing is called **sensory language.** Writers use sensory language to help you imagine characters, places, and events. You encounter sensory language in all forms of fiction, nonfiction, and poetry.

As you read "I Ask My Mother to Sing" and "Ode to Family Photographs," notice that the poets use images that appeal to several senses at once. In these poems, sensory language also reveals how the writers feel about their subjects.

 Learn It Online
To hear a professional actor read these poems, visit the selections online at:

go.hrw.com   H7-589   **Go**

 Preteach

English for Academic Success

Language Coach

Ask students to brainstorm a list of sensory words that may help them understand which sense the writer is appealing to by relating the types of sensory words. [*touch—rough, slippery, warm; sight—handsome, massive, wrinkled; smell—fragrant, pungent, stale; taste—bitter, salty, sweet; hearing—booming, chuckles, sings*]

Literary Skills Focus

As you read and discuss the selection with students, have them identify and record the features of lyric poems, sonnets, and odes.

Writing Skills Focus

Have students record notes on the poem's plot in their **Reader/Writer Notebook.** Students can use their notes to complete the Writing Skills Focus activity.

 Learn It Online
The online version of this selection includes audio support to engage all students and to help struggling readers with reading comprehension and vocabulary.

go.hrw.com   H7-589   **Go**

Selection Introduction

More About the Writer

- **Li-Young Lee** has won several awards for his poetry. He also has taught poetry at several universities.

- **Gary Soto** does not teach, but his poems are used in many classrooms. Soto says his highest honor was finding out a teacher in Georgia named her dog after him.

Think About the Writer

Point out that both Soto and Lee are American poets, but come from distinct cultural backgrounds. Discuss how both poets' backgrounds may affect their poetry.

 For Independent Reading

- If students enjoy Soto's and Lee's poetic reflections on childhood, recommend Cynthia Rylant's *Waiting to Waltz, a Childhood: Poems.*

- Students interested in the power of photographic images might also enjoy *Stolen Dreams: Portraits of Working Children,* by David L. Parker.

Learn It Online
Get more on Soto's life at:
go.hrw.com H7-590 Go

Li-Young Lee
(1957–   )

Li-Young Lee once made the following comment:

"I think immigrants have beautiful stories to tell. But the problem is to make art out of it."

Lee succeeded in using art to tell his family's story in the award-winning memoir *The Winged Seed: A Remembrance.* An important part of the narrative is based in Jakarta, Indonesia, Lee's birthplace. His family had moved to Indonesia from China, where Lee's father had been a physician to the Communist leader Mao Tse-tung. The family was forced to flee Indonesia in 1959. After spending time in Hong Kong and Japan, the family settled in the United Statesin 1964.

Gary Soto
(1952–   )

Gary Soto first discovered poetry in college, where he had originally planned to major in geography:

"I know the day the change began, because it was when I discovered in the library a collection of poems . . . called *The New American Poetry.* . . . I discovered this poetry and thought, 'This is terrific: I'd like to do something like this.' So I proceeded to write my own poetry, first alone, and then moving on to take classes."

Soto's award-winning fiction and poetry are loved by readers of all ages.

Think About the Writers

Lee and Soto both write poems about their families. Why do you think each writer might have made such a choice?

Build Background

Li-Young Lee's mother was a member of the Chinese royal family. His family fled China when the Communists took control of the country. The Summer Palace is the compound to which the royal family would go to escape the heat. The palace is located in the hills outside the capital city of Peking (now called Beijing) and consists of many beautiful buildings situated around Kuen Ming Lake. One of these buildings is a large teahouse made of stone in the shape of a boat. When an emperor ruled China, the palace was visited only by the royal family and its attendants. Today it is a museum, open to tourists from around the world.

Preview the Selections

In "I Ask My Mother to Sing," you will meet the speaker's **mother** and **grandmother.** Note the mixture of sweet and melancholy images in the poem.

In "Ode to Family Photographs," you will meet a **speaker** reminiscing about his family, particularly his **mother,** as he looks at photographs from his childhood.

Selection Readability	
Easily Accessible **Accessible** Challenging	familiar vocabulary and language; familiar situations; unfamiliar form

Selection Summary

In both selections, the poets recall memories of their families. In "I Ask My Mother to Sing," Lee explains how his mother's and grandmother's singing brings back memories. In "Ode to Family Photographs," Soto explains the memories captured in images.

Read with a Purpose Read this poem to discover how faraway places can seem close to home.

I Ask My Mother to Sing

by **Li-Young Lee**

She begins, and my grandmother joins her.
Mother and daughter sing like young girls.
If my father were alive, he would play
his accordion and sway like a boat.

5 I've never been in Peking, or the Summer Palace,
nor stood on the great Stone Boat to watch
the rain begin on Kuen Ming Lake, the picnickers
running away in the grass.

But I love to hear it sung;
10 how the waterlilies fill with rain until
they overturn, spilling water into water,
then rock back, and fill with more.

Both women have begun to cry.
But neither stops her song. **B**

A | **Literary Focus** | Lyric Poem/Sonnet How can you tell from this stanza that this poem may be a sonnet?

B | **Read and Discuss** | What can you infer from the actions of the women?

Summer Palace, Beijing, China.

Direct Teach

Think About/Talk About
Read with a Purpose Have students read the Read with a Purpose statement. Ask students to share some of the stories that their families tell about their family's history and heritage.

▶ Comprehension
B Read and Discuss
Possible response: The speaker loves the music, but it brings back sad memories for the mother and grandmother.

▶ Analysis
A Literary Focus
Possible response: The first stanza is four lines, so it may be a sonnet that is written in three quatrains and a pair of lines (a couplet).

▶ Extend the Discussion
Analyzing What is the effect of the poem's final couplet? Does it change your interpretation of the poem's topic or mood? Explain. *Possible response:* The final couplet brings the focus of the poem away from the speaker's memories and back to his relatives. It changes the poem's mood from wistful to sad.

Universal Access

EL English Learners
Read the second and third quatrain of "I Ask My Mother to Sing" to students. Explain to students that the speaker of the poem is talking about a place his family has been to that they love enough to sing about in a special song. Ask students to describe other ways in which people and families keep track of important names, dates, people, and places, and how this information is shared.

Struggling Readers
Have a volunteer restate the definitions of narrative and lyric poems. Then, guide students in comparing and contrasting narrative poems and lyric poems. Start by pointing out the most significant similarity: both types of poems focus on communicating themes, feelings, or ideas that the poets want to share with readers. Have students suggest other similarities, such as length of the poems and senses of place, and differences, such as the purpose of telling a story versus the purpose of expressing emotion. Make a list of the similarities and differences, and have students reference it as they read the selection.

Think About/Talk About

Read with a Purpose Have students read the Read with a Purpose statement. Then, ask students to make a list of some of the things that they like to do with their family, and ways that they can have a laugh together. Tell students to observe if any of the items on their lists are mentioned in the poem.

▶ Comprehension

Ⓐ Read and Discuss

Possible response: The family has had a few adventures, but the mother cannot seem to take very good pictures of them.

▶ Analysis

Ⓑ Literary Focus

Possible response: The speaker is expressing amusement at the photos and joy at the time he has spent with his family.

▶ Extend the Discussion

Intepreting How do the italicized lines differ from the rest of the poem? Why might the author have chosen to italicize these lines?
Possible response: The italicized lines describe the speaker's loving thoughts about his Mamá, while the rest of the stanzas describe the photographs in a more straightforward, less emotional way. The author might have italicized these lines to emphasize the connection between the photographs and the speaker's emotions and memories.

Read with a Purpose Read to find out what makes the speaker in this poem laugh.

Ode to Family Photographs

by **Gary Soto**

This is the pond, and these are my feet.
This is the rooster, and this is more of my feet.

Mamá was never good at pictures.

This is a statue of a famous general who lost an arm,
5   And this is me with my head cut off.

This is a trash can chained to a gate,
This is my father with his eyes half-closed.

This is a photograph of my sister
And a giraffe looking over her shoulder.   Ⓐ

10   This is our car's front bumper.
This is a bird with a pretzel in its beak.
This is my brother Pedro standing on one leg on a rock,
With a smear of chocolate on his face.

Mamá sneezed when she looked
15   *Behind the camera: the snapshots are blurry,*
The angles dizzy as a spin on a merry-go-round.

But we had fun when Mamá picked up the camera.
How can I tell?
Each of us laughing hard.
20   Can you see? I have candy in my mouth.   Ⓑ

Ⓐ **Read and Discuss** What have you learned about the speaker's family so far?
Ⓑ **Literary Focus** Lyric Poem/Ode You know that lyric poems express emotions. What emotion is the author expressing in this poem?

Applying Your Skills

I Ask My Mother to Sing /
Ode to Family Photographs

Literary Response and Analysis

Reading Skills Focus
Read with a Purpose

1. List at least three details that make China seem close to home in "I Ask My Mother to Sing."

2. List two examples of humor in "Ode to Family Photographs." What do these humorous touches reveal about the speaker?

Literary Skills Focus
Literary Analysis

3. **Infer** In "I Ask My Mother to Sing," the speaker tells about the songs of his mother's and grandmother's Chinese heritage. What is left unsaid?

4. **Interpret** How does the speaker of "Ode to Family Photographs" feel about his family? Support your response with textual evidence.

Literary Skills:
Lyric Poem, Sonnet, Ode

5. **Interpret** A **lyric poem** expresses the speaker's thoughts and feelings. How does the speaker in "I Ask My Mother to Sing" react to the song his mother and grandmother sing?

6. **Summarize** Look at how Li-Young Lee fits his thoughts into the <u>structure</u> of a sonnet. What is the topic of each of the first three quatrains? How do the last two lines convey the poem's message?

7. **Interpret Odes** are written in praise of something. What do you think "Ode to Family Photographs" is praising? (Hint: It's not just family photographs.)

Literary Skills Review: Imagery

8. **Interpret** List at least five sensory images from "I Ask My Mother to Sing," and explain to which senses each of the images appeals.

9. **Visualize** Explain whether you imagined yourself or anyone you know in Soto's pictures as you read "Ode to Family Photographs." <u>Comment</u> on which images in this ode made you smile or reminded you of familiar people or experiences.

Writing Skills Focus
Think as a Reader/Writer

Use It in Your Writing Write an ode celebrating something special to you. Try to convey your feelings for all aspects of your subject. For example, if you write "An Ode to a Baseball Bat," you might praise the bat's weight, balance, and power; the way it swings through the air; and how it helped you win a game. In your ode, you can either talk directly to the reader or you can talk to the object you are celebrating ("Bat, you are . . .").

What Do **You Think Now** Why might people find inspiration or comfort in poems about <u>tradition</u> or family?

What Do You Think Now?
Review with students the inspirations for some of the poems they have read so far, such as a city neighborhood, photographs, and the moon. What aspects of these subjects appeal to readers?

Check for Understanding

Independent Practice
Reading Skills Focus
Answers:

1. *the familiar song, the images the song evokes, and the memories of the father playing the accordion*

2. *a bird holding a pretzel, a giraffe looking over the speaker's sister's shoulder; These images reveal the speaker's amusement at his family.*

Literary Skills Focus
Possible responses:

3. *That the speaker is talking about how the song makes him feel.*

4. *The speaker enjoys being with his family. They have fun together.*

5. *The speaker loves to hear the song, but it makes him wonder about his father and a place he's never been.*

6. *The first three stanzas describe the song and details of place; the last couplet shows that it is an emotional song for the family.*

7. *The poem is praising the speaker's happy, loving family.*

8. *Rain on a lake; picnickers running; waterlilies filling with rain; women crying; the Stone Boat. They appeal to sight and sound because they are visual and musical.*

9. *The photos of body parts made me laugh. I pictured my family as I read.*

- exaggeration
- understand rhythm and rhyme
- understand alliteration and onomatopoeia
- understand free verse and elegy

Motivate

What Do You Think?/QuickTalk

Ask students to name a song that makes them happy and a song that makes them sad. What is it about the sound of the music that makes them feel this way?

English for Academic Success

Academic Vocabulary

Look for opportunities to use the Academic Vocabulary words in this chapter.

- **comment, *v.:*** explain or interpret something
- **structure, *n.:*** a set of parts put together to form a whole
- **vision, *n.:*** force of imagination

Analyzing Visuals

Extension Activity Ask students where they would expect to see an image like this. Have them discuss how it might relate to sounds of poetry. ***Possible response:*** *I'd expect to see it in a comic book. It could connect to poetry because poets use certain "sound effects" in their writing.*

CONTENTS

 What Do **You Think** Why is sound (or its absence) useful in expressing feeling?

 QuickTalk
Think of your favorite song. How does it affect you? Share your thoughts in a discussion.

Preparing to Read

Reader/Writer Notebook
Use your **RWN** to complete the activities for these selections.

Father William / Sarah Cynthia Sylvia Stout Would Not Take the Garbage Out

Literary Skills Focus

Humorous Poems Many poems are written to make you laugh—or at least smile. That doesn't mean they don't have a point to make. They just make their point with humor. One element that many humorous poems share is **exaggeration**—that is, describing something as bigger or smaller or better or worse than it really is. There's a name for this kind of exaggeration in literature: **hyperbole** (hy PUR buh lee). As you read the two poems that follow, notice what they exaggerate. Then ask yourself, "Were the poems written to make a serious point, or were they written just for fun?"

Rhythm In English and other languages, **rhythm** is a musical quality produced by the repetition of stressed and unstressed syllables or by the repetition of words, phrases, or even whole lines or sentences. When the stressed and unstressed syllables are arranged in a regular pattern, we call the pattern **meter.**

You can discover the meter of a line by reading it aloud and exaggerating the stressed syllables. For example, in the line *The girl is walking to the store,* you can sound out the meter like this: The GIRL is WALKing TO the STORE. You can also show the poem's meter by using accent marks—(´) over stressed syllables and (˘) over unstressed syllables. This marking is called **scanning.**

˘ ´ ˘ ´ ˘ ´ ˘ ´
The girl is walking to the store.

Notice that a regular beat is often found in ordinary speech as well as in poetry. In a poem written in meter, the meter supplies the underlying beat. Just as you wouldn't want to exaggerate the stressed syllables when you talk to your friends, you also don't want to overemphasize them when you read a poem.

Writing Skills Focus

Think as a Reader/Writer

Find It in Your Reading Find and record at least eight examples of exaggeration as you read "Father William" and "Sarah Cynthia Sylvia Stout Would Not Take the Garbage Out."

Vocabulary

Father William

incessantly (ihn SEHS uhnt lee) *adv.:* without ceasing; continually. *A chatty person talks incessantly.*

supple (SUHP uhl) *adj.:* easily bent; flexible. *Father William can bend his supple body to do a somersault.*

Sarah Cynthia Sylvia Stout Would Not Take the Garbage Out

withered (WIHTH uhrd) *v.* used as *adj.:* dried up. *Withered lettuce is not crunchy.*

rancid (RAN sihd) *adj.:* spoiled; rotten. *Rancid meat looks and smells awful.*

Language Coach

Adverbs Adverbs, such as *incessantly,* are used to describe verbs and adjectives. List some of the descriptive words in each of these poems.

Learn It Online
Improve your vocabulary with Word Watch:

go.hrw.com   H7-595   **Go**

Introducing Vocabulary

■ Review the Vocabulary words, definitions, and sentences with students.

■ To reinforce the Vocabulary words, tell students that these words help develop the humor within the poems. In "Father William," the youth *incessantly* asks his father questions, leading to ridiculous assertions, such as the claim his father is *supple* enough to somersault out the back door. In "Sarah Cynthia Sylvia Stout," the words *withered* and *rancid* vividly illustrate the piles of filth that develop from not taking out the garbage.

English for Academic Success
Language Coach

As you read and discuss the selection with students, have them record examples of adverbs. Ask students to remove the suffix *–ly* from the adverbs. Ask students if removing the suffix changes the meaning of the word.

Literary Skills Focus

As you read and discuss the selection with students, have them identify the meter of each poem by scanning lines.

Writing Skills Focus

Have students record examples of exaggeration from each poem in their **Reader/Writer Notebook.** Students can use their notes to complete the Writing Skills Focus activity.

Selection Resources

Chapter 5 Resources, on-level practice and assessment, p. 45

Teacher One Stop™, on-level lesson plans and all print resources

UA: Differentiating Instruction, graphic organizers, p. 135

UA: Supporting Instruction in Five Languages, selection summary

ThinkCentral Online Assessment, Selection Standards Check

ThinkCentral Online Remediation

Learn It Online
Send students to **Word Watch** for audio pronunciations, synonyms and antonyms, and brief histories of word origins.

go.hrw.com   H7-595   **Go**

Selection Introduction

More About the Writers

- Along with his mathematical and writing skills, **Lewis Carroll** was also quite musical and sang often in public. His understanding of music may have helped him create rhythm in his writings.

- **Shel Silverstein** was also a musician. He wrote the songs "A Boy Named Sue" and "The Cover of the Rollin' Stone," and composed the music for several movies.

Think About the Writers

Ask students if they have ever tried to make up a joke or riddle. Did they find it easy or difficult? Have students consider the complexities of wordplay when writing humorous stories or poems.

 For Independent Reading

- If students want to read more humorous poems by Shel Silverstein, recommend *Where the Sidewalk Ends*.

- Recommend *Hist-Wist and Other Poems for Children* to students interested in whimsical poetry.

Learn It Online
Get more on the authors' lives at:
go.hrw.com   H7-596   Go

Lewis Carroll
(1832–1898)

"He Was One of Us"

Lewis Carroll had two separate careers. Under the pen name Lewis Carroll, he was the author of *Alice's Adventures in Wonderland* and its sequel, *Through the Looking Glass*. Under his real name, he was Reverend Charles Lutwidge Dodgson, a teacher of mathematics and a clergyman in England. In both roles, Carroll spent many days in the company of children and enjoyed writing nonsense verse and creating puzzles for them. As one of his young friends said:

> "He was one of us, and never a grown-up pretending to be a child in order to preach at us. . . ."

Shel Silverstein
(1932–1999)

"A Personal Sense of Discovery"

Shel Silverstein began drawing and writing when he was a boy growing up in Chicago. He said he "didn't have anyone to copy, be impressed by," so he developed his own unique style. Silverstein created children's books, poems, songs, and cartoons. He said:

> "I would hope that people, no matter what age, would find something to identify with in my books, pick one up and experience a personal sense of discovery."

Think About the Writers Carroll and Silverstein are both known for their lively, humorous verse. How easy do you think it is to be funny?

Build Background

Once Lewis Carroll went on a picnic with three young girls, one of whom was named Alice. He told them a story about a girl named Alice, who went down a rabbit hole into a fabulous wonderland. That was the beginning of *Alice's Adventures in Wonderland,* from which "Father William" is taken. "Sarah Cynthia Sylvia Stout Would Not Take the Garbage Out" is from *Where the Sidewalk Ends,* Shel Silverstein's first collection of poetry for children. In the poem, "Golden Gate" refers to the Golden Gate Bridge in San Francisco, California.

Preview the Selections

"Father William" is a conversation between **Father William** and his **son.** The son has questions for his father, and Father William is ready with answers.

In "Sarah Cynthia Sylvia Stout Would Not Take the Garbage Out," **Sarah Cynthia Sylvia Stout** learns why it's important to *always* take the garbage out!

Selection Readability

Selection Readability	
Easily Accessible **Accessible** Challenging	accessible vocabulary; figurative language; familiar situations; unfamiliar form

Selection Summary

In "Father William" by Lewis Carroll, a son asks his father to explain his behavior, which is more suited for a young person. In "Sarah Cynthia Sylvia Stout Would Not Take the Garbage Out" by Shel Silverstein, the garbage piles higher and higher, but Sarah Cynthia Sylvia Stout still refuses to take it out.

 Learn It Online
The enhanced author biography offers more information on the life of the author as well as Holt's interactive resources pertaining to the author.

go.hrw.com   H7-596   Go

Read with a Purpose Read this poem to discover what Father William's son wants to know.

FATHER WILLIAM

by **Lewis Carroll**

Illustrations on pages 597–598 by John Tenniel (1820–1914), the original illustrator of Carroll's *Alice's Adventures in Wonderland*.

"You are old, Father William," the young man said,
    "And your hair has become very white;
And yet you incessantly stand on your head—
    Do you think, at your age, it is right?" Ⓐ

5 "In my youth," Father William replied to his son,
    "I feared it might injure the brain;
But now that I'm perfectly sure I have none,
    Why, I do it again and again."

 Literary Focus Rhythm Which words are stressed in this sentence? Listen for the poem's meter as you continue reading.

Vocabulary incessantly (ihn SEHS uhnt lee) *adv.*: without ceasing; continually.

Model the Skill

- Tell students that poets often make use of **rhythm,** or the arrangement of stressed and unstressed syllables, in their writing to give it a musical quality. Rhythm is based on the natural pronunciation of the words in the poem. The pattern of the stressed and unstressed syllables in the poem is called **meter**.

- Tell students that meter is identified by scanning the line and using pronunciation clues to figure out the pattern of stressed (or emphasized), and unstressed syllables. Scan the first line on p. 598 for students as an example. Point out that the strongest emphasis is on *old*, *youth*, the first syllable of *mentioned*, and the last syllable of *before*. Those are the stressed syllables, and the others are unstressed. This pattern indicates that the meter is two unstressed syllables, then a stressed syllable.

Guided Practice: Apply

Numbered Heads Together Divide the class into four groups and have each group scan one line of the stanza ending at point B. Have a member of each group share the meter they identified with the class. Combine the findings into a meter for the entire stanza.

Analyzing Visuals **Connecting to the Text** What details from the poem are illustrated in this drawing?

"You are old," said the youth, "as I mentioned before,
10   And have grown most uncommonly fat;
      Yet you turned a back somersault in at the door—
         Pray, what is the reason of that?"

Developing Oral Fluency

Use the first five stanzas of "Father William" to give students experience with reading a poem that has a strong underlying meter. Explain to students that while meter is an important quality in poems like "Father William," readers should not ignore natural speech patterns when they read such poems aloud. Encourage students to make their reading sound as natural and conversational as possible without neglecting the poem's meter.

Paired Activity Put students into pairs.
- Model reading the first stanza aloud. Tell students to

pay attention to your expression of the poem's meter. Have a fluent volunteer read the second stanza aloud.

- Then, have students read the remaining stanzas of the poem aloud with their partners. Have one student read Father William's stanzas and the other student read the young man's stanzas. Encourage students to help each other identify the most natural way of reading each stanza while still following its meter.

✔ See **UA: Differentiating Instruction** for practice passages for developing oral fluency.

"In my youth," said the sage,° as he shook his gray locks,
  "I kept all my limbs very supple
15 By the use of this ointment—one shilling the box—
  Allow me to sell you a couple." **B**

"You are old," said the youth, "and your jaws are too weak
  For anything tougher than suet;°
Yet you finished the goose, with the bones and the beak;
20 Pray, how did you manage to do it?"

"In my youth," said his father, "I took to the law,
  And argued each case with my wife;
And the muscular strength which it gave to my jaw,
  Has lasted the rest of my life."

25 "You are old," said the youth; "one would hardly suppose
  That your eye was as steady as ever;
Yet you balanced an eel on the end of your nose—
  What made you so awfully clever?" **C**

"I've answered three questions, and that is enough,"
30 Said his father; "don't give yourself airs!
Do you think I can listen all day to such stuff?
  Be off, or I'll kick you downstairs!"

---

13. sage (sayj): an old, wise person.
18. suet (SOO iht): a kind of fat.

B Read and Discuss What is going on between Father William and his son?
C Literary Focus Humorous Poems What is exaggerated in this stanza?

Vocabulary **supple** (SUHP uhl) *adj.:* easily bent; flexible.

▶ **Comprehension**

B **Read and Discuss**

Possible response: The young man is amazed that his father can stand on his head and turn somersaults. He asks him how he's able to do such things at his age. Father William gives his son responses that don't really answer his questions.

▶ **Analysis**

C **Literary Focus**

Possible response: Father William probably didn't balance an eel on the end of his nose.

▶ **Extend the Discussion**

Rhythm Describe the poem's rhythm. How does this rhythm contribute to the poem's tone? *Possible response:* The rhythm is consistent, catchy, and strong. Because the rhythm is so powerful and unlike normal speech, it adds to the poem's over-the-top, humorous tone.

Humor What is humorous about Father William's response in the third line of the final stanza? *Possible response:* Father Williams implies that it is his son who is talking nonsense when it is he who has been giving nonsensical replies.

Vocabulary: Own the Word

supple: Provide students with the following analogies to help them understand the meaning of *supple.* Gymnasts are *supple.* Most plastic straws are *supple.* Then, ask students to provide antonyms of the word *supple.* Have them provide an similar analogy using one of the antonyms. *Possible response: stiff, inflexible, rigid; Rocks are rigid. Robots are stiff.*

Universal Access

Students With Disabilities

Read the poem aloud one time for students and answer any questions they may have about the old-fashioned language or events that take place in the poem. Then, have students perform the poem as a Readers' Theater. Divide students into pairs, with one partner taking the role of Father William, and the other taking the role of the youth. Assign one pair to each stanza (have students choral-read roles if there are more than eight pairs), and allow them 10 minutes to practice their lines before performing the poem.

Analyzing Visuals

Artist **John Tenniel** (1820–1914) is best known as the illustrator of Lewis Carroll's *Alice's Adventures in Wonderland.* He also drew many cartoons for the British humor magazine *Punch.*

Connecting to the Text: The drawing shows the young man asking Father William how he managed how to eat an entire goose.

Model the Skill

- Remind students that **hyperbole** is a literary device. A hyperbole is an exaggeration and is used to emphasize a point.

- Use this example from the poem to help students understand hyperbole: "And so it piled up to the ceilings." Point out to students that it is nearly impossible for garbage to be piled up to the ceiling, so the reader knows that this is an exaggeration. The author uses hyperbole here to emphasize to the reader that the pile of garbage is unusually large. The same effect could not have been achieved if the author had simply written, "And so the pile grew very large."

Guided Practice: Apply

Think-Pair-Share Have students read the rest of the poem independently and find another example of exaggeration. Have them discuss their findings with a partner to determine if it is a hyperbole. Then, have pairs discuss why the author chose to use hyperbole is their examples. Have pairs report their findings to the class.

Think as a Reader/Writer

Find It in Your Reading Reread this example of exaggeration, from line 7, aloud for students: "And so it piled up to the ceilings." Remind students that this example emphasizes how big the pile of garbage had grown.

Use It in Your Writing Have students write a few lines of exaggeration to describe a big mess.

Sarah Cynthia Sylvia Stout Would Not Take the Garbage Out

by **Shel Silverstein**

Sarah Cynthia Sylvia Stout
Would not take the garbage out!
She'd scour the pots and scrape the pans,
Candy the yams and spice the hams,
5   And though her daddy would scream and shout,
She simply would not take the garbage out.   **A**
And so it piled up to the ceilings:
Coffee grounds, potato peelings,
Brown bananas, rotten peas,
10   Chunks of sour cottage cheese.
It filled the can, it covered the floor,
It cracked the window and blocked the door
With bacon rinds and chicken bones,
Drippy ends of ice cream cones,
15   Prune pits, peach pits, orange peel,
Gloppy glumps of old oatmeal,
Pizza crusts and withered greens,

A **Literary Focus** Rhythm Which words and syllables are stressed in these lines? Listen for the rhythm of the poem as you continue reading.

Vocabulary **withered** (WIHTH uhrd) v. used as *adj.:* dried up.

Word-Attack Skills Mini-Lesson

Point out to students that "Sarah Cynthia Sylvia Stout" contains a large number of plural words. Point out that the ending -s, the most common suffix for plurals, is used over and over again, as in *pots* and *pans* from line 3. In the case of *pots*, *pans*, and most other words, -s or -es is simply added to the end of the word. Plurals follow a more complex rule in the word *fries* in line 31. In this case, the word *fry*, as with many other words ending in a consonant and y, changes its ending from -y to -ie before adding the -s to become plural. Clarify that

this rule does not apply to words ending with a vowel and y, such as *day*, which simply becomes *days* when pluralized.

Activity Have students work in pairs to determine the proper plural of the following words.

1. plate [*plates*]
2. neighborhood [*neighborhoods*]
3. reply [*replies*]
4. notebook [*notebooks*]
5. wish [*wishes*]

Soggy beans and tangerines,
Crusts of black burned buttered toast,
20   Gristly bits of beefy roasts . . .
The garbage rolled on down the hall,
It raised the roof, it broke the wall . . .
Greasy napkins, cookie crumbs,
Globs of gooey bubble gum,
25   Cellophane from green baloney,
Rubbery blubbery macaroni,
Peanut butter, caked and dry,
Curdled milk and crusts of pie,
Moldy melons, dried-up mustard,
30   Eggshells mixed with lemon custard,
Cold french fries and rancid meat,
Yellow lumps of Cream of Wheat.
At last the garbage reached so high
That finally it touched the sky.
35   And all the neighbors moved away,
And none of her friends would come to play. **B**
And finally Sarah Cynthia Stout said,
"OK, I'll take the garbage out!"
By then, of course, it was too late . . .
40   The garbage reached across the state,
From New York to the Golden Gate. **C**
And there, in the garbage she did hate,
Poor Sarah met an awful fate,
That I cannot right now relate
45   Because the hour is much too late.
But children, remember Sarah Stout
And always take the garbage out!

B Read and Discuss What has the speaker told you about the people in Sarah's life?

C Literary Focus Humorous Poems What is exaggerated in the poem, and what makes it funny?

Vocabulary   **rancid** (RAN sihd) *adj.:* spoiled; rotten.

---

6. sky [*skies*]
7. play [*plays*]
8. sandwich [*sandwiches*]
9. toy [*toys*]
10. pony [*ponies*]

✔ For additional instruction, see **ThinkCentral, Teacher Access**.

Universal Access

AAVE Students Who Use African American Vernacular English

English for Academic Success   Some students may not voice the *s* consonant that appears at the end of a plural word. Explain to students that in formal English, the /s/ on the end of a plural word is always clearly voiced. Have students read through the poem in pairs and choose their four favorite descriptors that are pluralized (such as "chunks of sour cottage cheese"). Then, read aloud the poem, instructing students to "shout out" their chosen descriptors, emphasizing the /s/ sound, with you as you read.

Think About/Talk About

Read with a Purpose   Ask students to read the Read with a Purpose statement. Ask them to predict what might happen to someone who doesn't take out the garbage.

▶ Comprehension

B Read and Discuss

Possible response: The neighbors have moved away and not even Sarah's friends will visit.

▶ Analysis

A Literary Focus

Possible response: "Would," "take," and "garbage" are stressed.

C Literary Focus

Possible response: The poet is saying that the garbage from Sarah's house stretched all across the country. It's funny because she cannot possibly have accumulated that much garbage.

▶ Extend the Discussion

Alliteration   Which sound is repeated in line 15? How does this alliteration affect the meter of the poem? *Possible response: The "p" sound at the beginning of the words is repeated. Alliteration makes the words trip off the tongue, which increases the speed of reading and makes the list of trash items sound even longer.*

Vocabulary: Own the Word

- **withered:** Tell students that plants and flowers that are dead and dried up are often described as *withered*. Have students describe a withered flower. [*wrinkly, brown, smelly*]

- **rancid:** Explain to students that food can become *rancid* if it gets old or is not refrigerated properly. Ask students if they have ever smelled or tasted something *rancid*. Have them describe how the rancid food smelled or tasted. *Possible response: Rancid eggs smell like sulfer. Rancid fruit tastes bitter.*

Independent Practice

Reading Skills Focus
Answers:

1. *The young man in "Father William" is nosy. Sarah Cynthia Sylvia Stout is stubborn and messy.*

Vocabulary Check
Answers:

2. *withered*
3. *incessantly*
4. *rancid*
5. *supple*

Literary Skills Focus
Possible responses:

6. *He is being disrespectful because elsewhere in the poem he tells his father that he has grown "uncommonly fat."*

7. *Sarah was buried under a pile of garbage and died.*

8. *In "Father William," the son says that his father can do impossible tasks, such as balancing an eel on his nose. In "Sarah Cynthia Sylvia Stout," Sarah leaves her garbage for so long that it stretches across the country.*

9. *From "Father William:" "Do you THINK, at your AGE, it is RIGHT?" From "Sarah Cynthia Sylvia Stout": "She'd SCOUR the POTS and SCRAPE the PANS"*

10. *Potato peelings; prune pits; peach pits. The consonant "p" is repeated.*

11. *The theme of "Father William" is father-son relationships. The theme of "Sarah Cynthia Sylvia Stout" is completing chores. Both poets are having fun with their messages. They use hyperbole rather than realistic consequences.*

What Do You Think Now?

Ask volunteers to share their overall impressions of each poem. Then, have students discuss what each poem might be like without rhythm or meter. Ask students how rhythm might make a poem humorous.

Applying Your Skills

Father William / Sarah Cynthia Sylvia Stout
Would Not Take the Garbage Out

Literary Response and Analysis

Reading Skills Focus
Read with a Purpose

1. How would you describe the children in these poems?

> ✅ **Vocabulary Check**
>
> incessantly
> supple
> withered
> rancid
>
> Complete each sentence with the correct Vocabulary word.
>
> 2. The _____ flowers had limp petals.
> 3. The noisy dog barked _____.
> 4. The _____ cheese attracted flies.
> 5. The young tree was _____ and bent in the wind.

Literary Skills Focus
Literary Analysis

6. **Infer** When his son tells Father William, "You are old," is he being disrespectful, or does he admire his father? Use examples from the poem to explain your answer.

7. **Interpret** In "Sarah Cynthia Sylvia Stout Would Not Take the Garbage Out," the poet says, "Poor Sarah met an awful fate, / That I cannot right now relate." What do you think that fate might be?

Literary Skills: Humor and Rhythm

8. **Evaluate** How do both poets use exaggeration to create humor? Use examples of the poets' hyperbole in your explanations.

9. **Identify** Identify the meter of "Father William." Write out a line of the poem, and use the scanning method explained on page 595. Do the same to show the meter in line 3 of "Sarah Cynthia Sylvia Stout Would Not Take the Garbage Out."

10. **Analyze** "Sarah Cynthia Sylvia Stout Would Not Take the Garbage Out" is full of **alliteration**—the repetition of similar consonant sounds in nearby words, as in *"gloppy glumps."* Find three examples of alliteration, and identify the repeated sounds. What effect does alliteration have on the poem?

Literary Skills Review: Theme

11. **Extend** State the theme of each poem. Are these poets being serious in their messages, or are they just having fun? Support your response with textual examples.

Writing Skills Focus
Think as a Reader/Writer

Use It in Your Writing Write a humorous description of a person or an object from everyday life. Review the examples of exaggeration in the poems, and include exaggeration in your writing. Structure your description however you wish—as prose or poetry.

 What Do You Think Now

How did you respond to each poem? Explain how rhythm and humor contributed to your response.

Universal Access

Struggling Writers

To complete the Writing Skills Focus, provide additional scaffolding for students by having them create T-charts. On the left side, have them write desriptions of an oridinary person or thing. On the right side, have them exaggerate that description.

Description	Exaggeration
A pair of smelly sneakers	A pair of sneakers whose stench casued my canary to drop dead

Preparing to Read

The Runaway

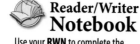

Reader/Writer Notebook

Use your **RWN** to complete the activities for this selection.

Literary Skills Focus

Rhyme and Rhyme Scheme What words rhyme with each of the following words?

- *star*
- *mice*
- *peaches*
- *stopping*

Your answers probably came quickly and automatically. There's something about rhyme that just comes naturally to people.

Rhyme is a common characteristic in many forms of poetry. When a poem's <u>structure</u> includes rhyme, the rhyming words often come at the ends of lines. These **end rhymes** determine the **rhyme scheme,** or pattern of rhymes. Assigning a different letter to each new end rhyme identifies the rhyme scheme. In "The Runaway," the rhyme scheme begins with *abacbc*.

> ### Language Coach
>
> **Dialogue** A conversation between two or more characters in a work of literature is called **dialogue**. In prose and poetry, dialogue is enclosed in quotation marks. While dialogue is common in prose, it is unusual to find a conversation between two characters in poetry. As you read "The Runaway," notice that dialogue is used to express the opinions of human characters.

Reading Skills Focus

Reading a Poem Robert Frost writes in a conversational tone. Use a similar tone as you read his poems aloud. Here is a tip to help you read poems: *Pay attention to punctuation.*

Into Action Follow the advice in the list below as you read Frost's poems.

- Don't stop reading at the end of a line of poetry unless you see punctuation.
- Make a full stop at a period.
- Pause briefly at a comma, colon, semicolon, or dash.
- If a poem has no punctuation, do your best to figure out where to pause based on the thought groups in the poem.

Writing Skills Focus

Think as a Reader/Writer

Find It in Your Reading Look for ways that Frost celebrates nature in his poetry. Write down your favorite nature images and rhymes in the poem.

Learn It Online
See a good reader in action, and practice your own skills, at:

go.hrw.com   H7-603   **Go**

Resources

Chapter 5 Resources, on-level practice and assessment, p. 50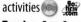

PowerNotes, interactive lesson presentation with activities

Teacher One Stop™, on-level lesson plans and all print resources

Holt Audio Library

Holt Audio Library: Selections and Summaries in Spanish

UA: Holt Interactive Reader, p. 156

Holt Interactive Reader for ELD, p. 176

Holt Audio Reader Tutor for ELD

UA: Differentiating Instruction, modified lesson plans and leveled assessment, p. 136

UA: Resources for Teaching Advanced Students, lesson plans

UA: Supporting Instruction in Five Languages, selection summary

ThinkCentral Online Assessment, Selection Standards Check

ThinkCentral Online Remediation

Preteach

English for Academic Success

Language Coach
Tell students that dialogue is usually marked with quotation marks in prose and poetry, but some authors may choose not to use quotation marks to punctuate dialogue. Remind students to use the natural rhythms of everyday speech when reading dialogue in poetry or prose.

Literary Skills Focus
As you read and discuss the selection with students, have them write out the rhyme scheme of the poem.

Reading Skills Focus
Tell students to follow the tips in the Reading Skills Focus guidelines to help them pay attention to punctuation as they read.

Writing Skills Focus
Have students record their favorite nature images from the poems in their **Reader/Writer Notebook.** Students can use their notes to complete the Writing Skills Focus activity.

Learn It Online
The online version of this selection includes audio support to engage all readers and to help struggling readers with reading comprehension and vocabulary.

go.hrw.com   H7-603   **Go**

Selection Introduction

More About the Writer

While Robert Frost was employed at times as a teacher, cobbler, farmer, and editor of the Lawrence, Massachusetts, *Sentinel*, poetry was always close to his heart. His first poem to be published, in 1894, was titled "My Butterfly." Frost passed away in 1963, and his tombstone reads, "I had a lover's quarrel with the world."

Think About the Writer

Direct a class discussion on how poetry can reach a reader's emotional core. Tell students that poems can cover a wide range of emotions, and that writers often try to translate their own emotion into their poetry.

 For Independent Reading

■ Recommend Jan Greenberg's collection *Heart to Heart: New Poems Inspired by Twentieth-Century American Art* to students interested in reading additional poetry from the twentieth century.

■ Students who enjoy Frost's depictions of the natural world might also enjoy *Old Elm Speaks: Tree Poems,* by Kristine O'Connell George.

Robert Frost
(1874–1963)

Pulitzer Prize WINNER

"The Thought Finds the Words"

While in high school in Lawrence, Massachusetts, Robert Frost decided to become a poet. Not only did he succeed, but he was for a time America's most celebrated living poet.

He was the first poet ever to read a poem for a presidential inauguration, that of John F. Kennedy in 1961. On his seventy-fifth birthday, the U.S. Senate passed a resolution in his honor, stating, "His poems have helped to guide American thought and humor and wisdom, setting forth to our minds a reliable representation of ourselves and of all men."

"Rob" Frost lived most of his life on farms in Vermont and New Hampshire. There he grew corn, taught, and raised a family. Frost filled his poems with images of the people of New England and their barns, farmhouses, pastures, apple orchards, and woods. His work speaks to people everywhere because it springs from intense feelings.

Frost says this about poetry:

> "A poem . . . begins as a lump in the throat, a sense of wrong, a homesickness, a lovesickness. . . . It finds the thought and the thought finds the words."

Think About the Writer What kinds of emotions do you think inspired Robert Frost's poetry?

Build Background

The subject of "The Runaway" is a Morgan colt. Morgans are a breed of swift, strong horses named for Justin Morgan (1747–1798), a Vermont schoolteacher who owned the stallion that founded the line. Morgans are small, sturdy horses that excel at weight-pulling contests. Today they are used mostly for riding and pulling carts.

Preview the Selection

"The Runaway" is a good example of how Robert Frost included farm life and nature in his poetry. The poem describes a **young colt** experiencing snow for the first time.

Selection Readability	
Easily Accessible **Accessible** Challenging	accessible vocabulary; figurative language; familiar situations; unfamiliar form

Selection Summary

In "The Runaway," the speaker encounters a colt who has been separated from his mother on a snowy day.

The Runaway

by **Robert Frost**

Once when the snow of the year was beginning to fall,
We stopped by a mountain pasture to say, "Whose colt?"
A little Morgan had one forefoot on the wall,
The other curled at his breast. He dipped his head
5   And snorted at us. And then he had to bolt.
We heard the miniature thunder where he fled,   **Ⓐ**
And we saw him, or thought we saw him, dim and gray,
Like a shadow against the curtain of falling flakes.
"I think the little fellow's afraid of the snow.
10 He isn't winter-broken.° It isn't play
With the little fellow at all. He's running away.
I doubt if even his mother could tell him, 'Sakes,
It's only weather.' He'd think she didn't know!
Where is his mother? He can't be out alone."
15 And now he comes again with clatter of stone,
And mounts the wall again with whited eyes
And all his tail that isn't hair up straight.
He shudders his coat as if to throw off flies.
"Whoever it is that leaves him out so late,
20 When other creatures have gone to stall and bin,
Ought to be told to come and take him in."   **Ⓑ**

---

10. **winter-broken:** used to winter; to break a colt is to get a young
     horse used to being ridden.

Ⓐ **Literary Focus** Rhyme and Rhyme Scheme   Where are the end rhymes?
Identify whether the rhyme scheme is consistent throughout the poem.

Ⓑ **Read and Discuss**   What happens at the end of the poem?

Real Issues, Real Experts

*Holt author **Deborah Appleman** offers strategies for helping students compare and contrast information.*

This poem can help students learn that poetry, even a short poem such as this one, can tell a story. To demonstrate the narrative element of poetry, I ask students to retell the story of the poem in prose form.

"The Runaway" also breathtakingly demonstrates the vivid imagery of poetic language. When I read this poem with students, we focus on phrases such as "miniature thunder" and "dim and grey, / Like a shadow against the curtain of falling flakes." We discuss how the comparisons

that form the basis of figurative language, such as similes and metaphor, help paint a vivid word picture of the runaway colt. We also focus on the rhyme scheme in this particular poem, which is notable for its intricacy as well as its seeming invisibility.

Finally, we consider that the significance of a poem like this is that while it is clearly about one thing—a colt who has gotten away and is unprepared for the harsh realities of the winter he encounters—it is also about something else. Discovering what that something else is will be at the heart of your class discussion.

Check for Understanding

Independent Practice
Reading Skills Focus
Possible responses:

1. *He is afraid of the snow.*
2. *The weather makes him sympathetic towards the colt.*
3. *the colt's owner*
4. *The title reflects the owner's sympathy for the colt that ran away and is now frightened. It points to the larger idea of the fear that can result when a person runs away and is put into a situation that he or she is not prepared for.*
5. *I would not pause, because there is no punctuation.*
6. *Students should read fluently with attention to punctuation.*

Literary Skills Focus
Possible responses:

7. *The speaker realizes the horse is young. This supports the idea that the colt might represent a lost or runaway child.*
8. *Yes, I saw a stray cat wandering around in the rain. I felt sorry for the cat and angry at whoever put the cat out in the rain.*
9. *I agree. The colt is young and childlike, and has run away to an experience he is not prepared for.*
10. *fall/wall; colt/bolt; head/fled; gray/play/away; flakes/'Sakes; snow/know; alone/stone; eyes/flies; straight/late; bin/in; aabbacbcdefddefgghihijj*
11. *It reflects the speaker's belief that the colt is a lost child that needs to be cared for.*
12. *"The Runaway" is told by a first-person narrator; "The Highwayman" is told by a third-person omniscient narrator.*

What Do You Think Now?
As they answer the questions, ask students to consider how various sounds convey different emotions. For example, soft sounds like the letter "s" in *sleep* often suggest a feeling of peace.

The Runaway
Literary Response and Analysis

Reading Skills Focus
Quick Check

1. Why is the colt in the poem afraid?
2. How does the weather affect the speaker's feelings about the colt?
3. With whom is the speaker angry at the end of the poem?

Read with a Purpose

4. How might the poem's title relate to the speaker's feelings? How might the title and the poem point to some larger meaning?

Reading Skills: Reading a Poem

5. How would you read lines 10 and 11 based on their punctuation? Explain whether you would pause at the end of line 10 and why.

> "He isn't winter-broken. It isn't play
> With the little fellow at all. He's running
> away."

6. Practice reading "The Runaway" aloud. As you practice, pay attention to the punctuation. When you have practiced enough to read the poem smoothly, perform it for the class.

Literary Skills Focus
Literary Analysis

7. **Interpret** In line 14, the speaker says, "Where is his mother? He can't be out alone." Why would the speaker ask a question like this about a horse? What might this tell you about the poem's meaning?
8. **Connect** Have you ever seen someone who seemed lost or in need of shelter? How did your experience compare with the speaker's in "The Runaway"?

9. **Evaluate** Some readers think the colt in "The Runaway" symbolizes a lost child or someone too young to understand his or her experiences. Do you agree with this interpretation, or do you have another one? Support your interpretation with details from the poem.

Literary Skills: Rhyme and Rhyme Scheme

10. **Analyze** Make a list of the rhyming words in "The Runaway." What is its rhyme scheme?
11. **Interpret** <u>Comment</u> on how the final rhyme reveals the speaker's concern for the colt.

Literary Skills Review: Point of View

The speaker in a poem with a **first-person point of view** uses first-person pronouns to relate his or her experiences or thoughts. A poem with a **third-person omniscient point of view** has an all-knowing speaker.

12. **Compare and Contrast** Compare the speaker of "The Runaway" with that of "The Highwayman" on page 255. What is the main difference you notice?

Writing Skills Focus
Think as a Reader/Writer
Use It in Your Writing Write a paragraph describing Frost's references to nature in "The Runaway." In your analysis, include images from the poem that reveal Frost's <u>vision</u>.

What Do **You Think Now** What feeling did you get from this poem? How did sound contribute to creating that feeling?

Universal Access

Struggling Writers
To complete the Writing Skills Focus, provide additional scaffolding for students by having them write down the references to nature in "The Runaway." Tell students that descriptions of the young horse should be considered references to nature because the horse is part of the wild landscape. Then, have students brainstorm what vision these references suggest before writing their paragraphs. Ask students to think about whether Frost likes or dislikes nature. How can they tell?

Preparing to Read

Names of Horses

Reader/Writer
Notebook
Use your **RWN** to complete the activities for this selection.

Literary Skills Focus

Free Verse "Names of Horses" is written in free verse. **Free verse** does not follow a regular rhyme scheme or meter; instead, it reproduces the natural rhythms of everyday speech. Free verse does not have a set structure, but it does make use of many other <u>traditional</u> elements of poetry, including

- **imagery**—language that appeals to any of the five senses; most often sight, but also hearing, touch, taste, and smell. Imagery allows the reader to share in the writer's perceptions. It also helps build the setting and mood of a poem.
- **alliteration** (uh liht uh RAY shuhn)—the repetition of consonant sounds in words close to each other *(marvelous memories of mangoes and melons)*. Alliteration is often pleasing to the ear and can be used for emphasis.
- **onomatopoeia** (ahn oh maht oh PEE uh)—the use of words that sound like what they mean (the goose's *honk*). Onomatopoeia adds a musical element to poetry and can be clever or humorous.
- **rhythm**—a musical quality produced by repetition. Rhythm can imitate action (think of a galloping horse) and emphasize key words and ideas.

Elegy "Names of Horses" is an **elegy** (EHL uh jee), a poem that mourns the passing of something—a person, an animal, a way of life, a season of the year—that is important to the writer. There are many important elegies in literature. Walt Whitman wrote a heartfelt elegy mourning the death of Abraham Lincoln. Oliver Goldsmith wrote a comic elegy about a cat who was drowned in a goldfish bowl. The most famous elegy is probably Thomas Gray's "Elegy Written in a Country Churchyard," in which Gray mourns the anonymous people buried in a rural graveyard.

Writing Skills Focus
Think as a Reader/Writer

Find It in Your Reading As you read "Names of Horses," write down images that help you picture the lives of the horses in the poem.

Language Coach

Word Study in Poetry "Names of Horses," like many free verse poems, contains imagery, alliteration, and onomatopoeia. Here is an image from "Names of Horses" that appeals to your sense of touch: "your neck rubbed the window sill / of the stall, smoothing the wood as the sea smooths glass." You can also hear the alliteration of the *s* and *sm* sounds, which suggest smoothness. The poem also features other examples of alliteration, such as the repeated /m/ sound in "*made your monument.*" Onomatopoeia is present in words such as *clacketing.*

As you read "Names of Horses," look for imagery, alliteration, and onomatopoeia.

English for Academic Success
Language Coach

Elicit that the onomatopoeic words *clacketing* and *shuddering* have the suffix *-ing* and are used as verbs. Have students identify examples of alliterative words that represent different parts of speech, such as *made* [verb] and *monument* [noun].

Literary Skills Focus

As you read and discuss the selection with students, have them identify examples of rhythm and figurative language in free verse and discuss how they differ from those in rhymed poetry.

Writing Skills Focus

Have students record images that help them picture the horses in the poem in their **Reader/Writer Notebook.** Students can use their notes to complete the Writing Skills Focus activity.

Learn It Online
Listen to this free-verse poem online at:
go.hrw.com H7-607 **Go**

Resources

Chapter 5 Resources, on-level practice and assessment, p. 53

Teacher One Stop™, on-level lesson plans and all print resources

Holt Audio Library

Holt Audio Library: Selections and Summaries in Spanish

UA: Supporting Instruction in Five Languages

ThinkCentral Online Assessment, Selection Standards Check

ThinkCentral Online Remediation

Learn It Online
The online version of this selection includes audio support to engage all students and to help struggling readers with reading comprehension and vocabulary.

go.hrw.com H7-607 **Go**

Selection Introduction

More About the Writer

Billy Collins said of **Donald Hall,** "[He] has long been placed in the Frostian tradition of the plain-spoken rural poet. His reliance on simple, concrete diction . . . imbues [his poems] with a tone of sincere authority. It is a kind of simplicity that succeeds in engaging the reader in the first few lines."

Think About the Writer

Discuss Hall's biography with students. Then tell them that poets often write about subjects that hold personal significance for them. Ask them why horses are important to farming communities and what significance they may have had in Hall's life.

For Independent Reading

- If students want to read more works by a well-known American poet, suggest *Rainbows Are Made*, a collection of Carl Sandburg poems.
- Recommend Sharon Creech's novel told in free verse, *Heartbeat*, to students who find free verse poetry appealing.

Donald Hall
(1928–   )

Donald Hall started writing at a young age. When he was only sixteen years old, he was accepted to one of the oldest writers' conferences in the United States. Hall's work was also first published that year. About his early fascination with poetry, Hall has said:

> "When I was twelve I started writing poetry; when I was fourteen I got serious. I began to work a couple of hours every day on my poems. And when I finished working on a poem, I would go back to the beginning and start writing it over again. . . . When I was fourteen I really wanted to do in my life what I in fact have . . . ended up doing, which is astounding."

Growing Up with Poetry

Born in New Haven, Connecticut, Hall spent a childhood full of poetry. His mother read poems to him, and during Hall's summers at his grandfather's New Hampshire farm, his grandfather recited poems "all day long without repeating himself."

For many years Hall was an instructor at the University of Michigan at Ann Arbor. In 1975, he moved to the family farm in New Hampshire, where he currently devotes his time to writing. From 1984 to 1989, Hall served as poet laureate of New Hampshire. He was the poet laureate of the United States from 2006 to 2007.

Think About the Writer What in Hall's background prepared him to write about horses?

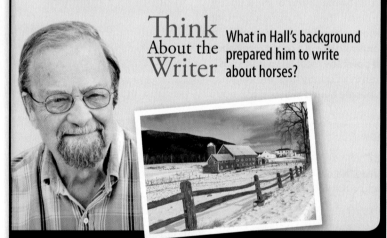

Build Background

"Names of Horses" describes farm life and the life of a farm horse in the days before machinery took over the work. Horses were important to American agriculture and were used extensively to pull plows on farms. By 1945, however, the amount of tractor power on American farms finally became greater than the amount of horsepower, and tractors became the norm for farming.

Preview the Selection

In this poem, Donald Hall writes about the **horses** that labored through the seasons and years for their **owner.** By giving us a glimpse of these horses' lives, Hall helps us to appreciate all of the horses that have contributed to family farms across hundreds of years.

Selection Readability	
Easily Accessible **Accessible** **Challenging**	accessible vocabulary; figurative language; familiar situations; unfamiliar form

Selection Summary

"Names of Horses" is an elegy describing the life of a farm horse. The speaker speaks with respect of farm horses' laborious lives and mourns their deaths, naming seven specific horses who toiled on a farm in the final line of the poem.

NAMES *of* HORSES

by **Donald Hall**

All winter your brute shoulders strained against collars, padding
and steerhide over the ash hames,° to haul
sledges of cordwood for drying through spring and summer,
for the Glenwood stove next winter, and for the simmering range.

5 In April you pulled cartloads of manure to spread on the fields,
dark manure of Holsteins,° and knobs of your own clustered with oats.
All summer you mowed the grass in meadow and hayfield, the mowing machine
clacketing beside you, while the sun walked high in the morning;

---

2. **hames** (haymz): rigid pieces along a horse's collar,
to which lines connecting the collar to a wagon are
attached.
6. **Holsteins** (HOHL steenz): a breed of large, black-
and-white dairy cattle.

Think About/Talk About

▶ Comprehension

Ⓐ Read and Discuss
Possible response: The horse has an incredibly hard life working on a farm.

▶ Analysis

Ⓑ Literary Focus
Possible response: He is mourning the loss of the work horses. He also misses a time before machinery when horses were important to farming.

▶ Extend the Discussion

Tone What happens to the horses once they are old and lame? What tone does the poet use in lines 17–24 when he is describing this procedure? *Possible response: The horses are taken out and shot once they are old and lame. The poet describes this in a very matter-of-fact tone, which expresses the idea that this is part of the circle of life on the farm.*

and after noon's heat, you pulled a clawed rake through the same acres,
10 gathering stacks, and dragged the wagon from stack to stack,
and the built hayrack back, uphill to the chaffy° barn,
three loads of hay a day, hanging wide from the hayrack.   Ⓐ

Sundays you trotted the two miles to church with the light load
of a leather quartertop buggy, and grazed in the sound of hymns.
15 Generation on generation, your neck rubbed the window sill
of the stall, smoothing the wood as the sea smooths glass.

When you were old and lame, when your shoulders hurt bending to graze,
one October the man who fed you and kept you, and harnessed you every morning,
led you through corn stubble to sandy ground above Eagle Pond,
20 and dug a hole beside you where you stood shuddering in your skin,

and lay the shotgun's muzzle in the boneless hollow behind your ear,
and fired the slug into your brain, and felled you into your grave,
shoveling sand to cover you, setting goldenrod upright above you,
where by next summer a dent in the ground made your monument.

25 For a hundred and fifty years, in the pasture of dead horses,
roots of pine trees pushed through the pale curves of your ribs,
yellow blossoms flourished above you in autumn, and in winter
frost heaved your bones in the ground—old toilers, soil makers: Ⓑ

O Roger, Mackerel, Riley, Ned, Nellie, Chester, Lady Ghost.

---

11. chaffy (CHAF ee): full of chaff (hay or straw).

Ⓐ **Read and Discuss** What is the poet showing you about this horse?

Ⓑ **Literary Focus** **Elegy** What is the poet mourning? Why?

Applying Your Skills

Names of Horses
Literary Response and Analysis

Reading Skills Focus
Read with a Purpose

1. In what ways do these horses contribute to life on the farm?

Literary Skills Focus
Literary Analysis

2. **Interpret** How does the last line of the poem reflect the title?

3. **Interpret** Discuss the lives of the seven horses. How would you characterize the way the horses are used by their owner?

4. **Infer** Why do you think the speaker calls the horses "old toilers, soil makers" in line 28?

5. **Interpret** How does the speaker feel about the horses he names in line 29? Support your response with examples from the poem.

6. **Extend** Read this comment from a reader:

> "When someone asks me why I love poetry, I read 'Names of Horses' to them, and they always say, 'Oh, I didn't know poetry could be like that.' And then they, too, say they love poetry."

Explain what characteristics of "Names of Horses" could make a person love poetry. How did the poem affect you?

Literary Skills: Free Verse and Elegy

7. **Extend** This free verse poem is rich in imagery. Take your favorite image, and draw or describe what it helps you visualize.

8. **Analyze** What personal pronouns are repeated throughout the poem? To whom is the speaker addressing this elegy?

9. **Analyze** Study lines 7 and 8. Find and explain one example of each of these devices: imagery, alliteration, onomatopoeia.

10. **Interpret** This poem is an **elegy,** a lyric poem that mourns the passing of something. Do you think Hall is mourning anything besides the horses he names? If so, what?

11. **Analyze Tone** is the writer's overall feeling for his or her subject, expressed through the writer's choice of words and details. What words would you use to describe the tone of "Names of Horses"?

Literary Skills Review: Theme

12. **Infer** A poem or story can convey more than one **theme,** or truth about life. What ideas might Hall be conveying about the relationship between humans and animals in "Names of Horses"? What might the poem be saying about the passing of time? about natural cycles? Choose the theme that you think is most important in this poem and state it in the form of a complete sentence.

Writing Skills Focus
Think as a Reader/Writer

Use It in Your Writing Think about an animal you once knew, or something else that is no longer in your life, and write an elegy for it. You may want to try writing in free verse. Include precise imagery and try to include some of the other poetic elements you learned about on page 607.

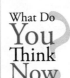
What Do You Think Now Why is it important to both mourn and celebrate something or someone no longer with us?

What Do You Think Now?

Have students find evidence in the poem to support the idea that mourning and celebrating might sometimes be very similar.

Independent Practice
Reading Skills Focus
Answer:

1. *The horses contribute to life on the farm by plowing, mowing, and spreading manure on the fields.*

Literary Skills Focus
Possible responses:

2. *It gives the names of the seven horses who worked on the farm.*

3. *The horses are constantly working. When they are no longer useful, their owner shoots them.*

4. *The speaker calls the horses "old toilers" because of the amount of work they have to do. They are "soil makers" because when they die, their bodies become part of the earth they plowed.*

5. *He respects them and sympathizes with them, describing the difficult work they did each season.*

6. *"Names of Horses" provides an example of how poetry can convey beauty and speak to a reader's emotions. The poem enabled me to picture the horses vividly and made me feel sorry for them.*

7. *The image of pine trees pushing though the horses' ribs enables me to visualize the recycling of nature.*

8. *The poet uses the pronouns "you" and "your," as if he is speaking directly to one of the horses.*

9. *Imagery: "the sun walked high in the morning" (allows the reader to picture the sun); alliteration: "mowing machine" (repeats the letter m); onomatopoeia: "clacketing" (the sound of the machine).*

10. *He is mourning a time when the lives of human beings and animals were intricately connected.*

11. *The tone is reverent and respectful.*

12. *I think the most important theme is: "People and animals are interconnected and subject to the cycles of the natural world."*

Standards Focus

Objectives
Students will
- interpret a writer's message by reading and analyzing several of her works
- make generalizations from a text

Motivate

What Do You Think?/QuickWrite
Use the QuickWrite to discuss people in the community that interest the students. Then, have students use their **Reader/Writer Notebook** to explain what they would want to write about these people and why.

English for Academic Success

Academic Vocabulary
Look for opportunities to use the Academic Vocabulary words in this chapter.

- **articulate, v.:** express clearly
- **characteristics, n.:** qualities
- **insight, n.:** power to understand
- **structure, n.:** a set of parts put together to form a whole

Analyzing Visuals
Extension Activity Point out that this is a photograph of author Sandra Cisneros at her home. Ask students what they think Cisneros might be like based on the details in the photograph. ***Possible response:*** *She appears friendly and thoughtful. Her clothing, the color of her house, and the garden suggest that she is creative.*

California Standards, pp. 612–627

- **Reading Standard 3.1** Articulate the expressed purposes and characteristics of different forms of prose (e.g., short story, novel, novella, essay).

Author Study: Sandra Cisneros

CONTENTS

Sandra Cisneros at her home in San Antonio, Texas.

 Why do people write about painful memories? about pleasant ones?

QuickWrite
Think about the people you've met in life. Which of them stimulate you to write about them? What makes you want to write about these people?

Comparing Texts Resources

Chapter 5 Resources, on-level practice and assessment, p. 56

Teacher One Stop™, on-level lesson plans and all print resources

Holt Audio Library

Holt Audio Library: Selections and Summaries in Spanish

UA: Differentiating Instruction, graphic organizer, p. 139

Preparing to Read

An Interview with Sandra Cisneros / Salvador Late or Early / Chanclas / Abuelito Who / The Place Where Dreams Come From

Reading Standard 3.1 Articulate the expressed purposes and characteristics of different forms of prose (e.g., short story, novel, novella, **essay**).

Literary Skills Focus

A Writer's Messages Sandra Cisneros writes about feelings we can all understand. She writes with humor about life's joys and frustrations and about being lonely and afraid. She writes about wanting what we can't have. She describes the fear of not fitting in—as well as the feeling of perhaps not really wanting to fit in.

These feelings are close to Cisneros's heart and often come from her own experiences. Many of her works celebrate her memories of her Mexican American childhood. Thus, her writing often focuses on the lives of people who belong to two cultures and speak two languages. Cisneros explores these topics in different forms of prose as well as poetry.

Reading Skills Focus

Making Generalizations A **generalization** is a broad statement about something. When you make a generalization, you combine evidence in the text with what you already know. After you read the following prose and poetry selections, you will be able to make generalizations about Cisneros's work. To make a generalization, ask yourself these questions:

- What is the work's **conflict,** or problem?
- What **message,** or insight about life, do the combined pieces of evidence reveal?
- What do I know from my own experience?

Writing Skills Focus

Think as a Reader/Writer

Find It in Your Reading Sandra Cisneros is famous for using **figurative language** such as similes and metaphors. As you read Cisneros's works, pay attention to the similes and metaphors she uses. Make a list of them in your *Reader/Writer Notebook*.

Reader/Writer Notebook

Use your **RWN** to complete the activities for these selections.

Vocabulary

Interview

intimately (IHN tuh muht lee) *adv.:* in a very familiar way. *We know the people in our families intimately.*

The Place Where Dreams Come From

literally (LIHT uhr uh lee) *adv.:* according to the basic meaning of the word. *The grandfather's term for allowance translated literally as "Sunday," the day on which he distributed it.*

ritual (RIHCH oo uhl) *n.:* an established routine. *Abuelito had a ritual he performed every Sunday.*

mistranslate (mihs TRANS layt) *v.:* change from one language to another incorrectly. *Abuelito would mistranslate into English the Spanish word for "heaven."*

Language Coach

Prefixes *Mis*– is a prefix that means "bad" or "badly." How does this prefix affect the meaning of the word *misbehave*? How does it affect the meaning of *mistranslate*?

 Learn It Online

Use Word Watch to master vocabulary words at:

go.hrw.com H7-613 **Go**

Preteach

Introducing Vocabulary

Read aloud the Vocabulary words and sample sentences. Then, have students complete each analogy with a Vocabulary word.

1. *beautiful* is to *ugly* as *figuratively* is to [*literally*]
2. *smile* is to *grin* as *closely* is to [*intimately*]
3. *earth* is to *land* as *tradition* is to [*ritual*]
4. *speech* is to *misspeak* as *translation* is to [*mistranslate*]

English for Academic Success

Language Coach

Tell students that if they remove the prefix from *mistranslate*, they will be left with the root word *translate*. Thus, *mistranslate* means "to translate badly or incorrectly." Provide students with other examples of words with the prefix *mis-*, such as *misfortune* and *misread*.

Literary Skills Focus

As you read and discuss the selection with students, have them discuss in pairs the messages that Sandra Cisneros conveys through her writing.

Reading Skills Focus

Remind students to make generalizations as they read the selections.

Writing Skills Focus

Have students record examples of figurative language in their **Reader/Writer Notebook.** Students can use their notes to complete the Writing Skills Focus activity.

 Learn It Online

Send students to **Word Watch** for audio pronunciations, synonyms and antonyms, and brief histories of word origins.

go.hrw.com H7-613 **Go**

Selection Introduction

More About the Writer

- **Sandra Cisneros** was the only daughter among seven children, and her brothers often tried to make her assume a traditional female role in the household. This led to her writing novels that explored women searching for their own independence.

- Her family frequently moved back and forth between the United States and Mexico because of her father's homesickness, which made Cisneros feel homeless and lonely. This is when she began to read to seek comfort and think about other children like herself.

Think About the Writer

To help students answer the question, suggest that they discuss how they write their own stories. Then, have students use their own questions and difficulties with the writing process to formulate questions for Cisneros.

🕐 For Independent Reading

- Recommend Patricia Beatty's *Lupita Mañana* to students interested in stories with Latina heroines.

- Students interested in reading additional poetry might enjoy Carl Sandburg's *Grassroots: Poems by Carl Sandburg*.

Sandra Cisneros

(1954–   )

Sandra Cisneros was born and raised in Chicago, the only daughter in a working-class family with six sons. The harshness of life in her neighborhood made Cisneros shy as a child, and she escaped into a world of books. By the age of ten, she was writing her own poetry.

Cisneros grew up speaking Spanish with her Mexican-born father, but she didn't explore her heritage until she attended the Writers' Workshop at the University of Iowa. There she began a series of sketches about her old Spanish-speaking neighborhood in Chicago. These sketches grew into her first book, *The House on Mango Street* (1984), which includes the story "Chanclas."

"I wanted to write a series of stories that you would open up at any point. . . . You would understand each story like a little pearl, or you could look at the whole thing like a necklace."

Think About the Writer

What questions would you ask Cisneros about the way she writes?

Key Elements of Cisneros's Writing

Everyday language, including slang and sentence fragments, gives the feeling of people speaking aloud.

Strong images and **figures of speech** bring the work alive.

Spanish words mixed with English words reflect the heritage of the characters and of the writer.

Messages often focus on family relationships and learning how to fit into the world.

A Cisneros Time Line

In **1966**, Cisneros's parents buy a house on Campbell Avenue in Chicago.

Teaches at the Latino Youth Alternative High School in Chicago, **1978–1980**.

Publishes *Woman Hollering Creek* (**1991**), a collection of short stories. Buys a house of her own in San Antonio, Texas, which she later paints purple.

1950	1960	1970	1980	1990	2000

Born on December 20, **1954**, in Chicago, Illinois.

Attends Loyola University from **1972** to **1976**. Takes a creative writing class in which she begins to write seriously.

Begins a series of sketches about her family and childhood while at the University of Iowa Writers' Workshop program in **1977**.

Receives several artist grants in **1983** that allow her to travel and live in France.

Publishes *The House on Mango Street* (**1984**), based on sketches she began writing in Iowa.

In **1995**, receives a MacArthur Foundation genius grant. *The House on Mango Street* is translated into Spanish.

Her long-awaited second novel, *Caramelo* (**2002**), is published.

An Interview with

Sandra Cisneros

from The Infinite Mind

Read with a Purpose
Read this interview to discover the connection Cisneros feels with Salvador in the short story "Salvador Late or Early."

Build Background
Lichtenstein Creative Media's Marit Haahr interviewed Sandra Cisneros on the public radio program *The Infinite Mind*. During the broadcast she asks Cisneros to read her short story "Salvador Late or Early" to the listeners. The two then talk about the story and the way it relates to Cisneros's life. From their conversation we learn something about how writers draw from their own experiences to create literature.

Marit Haahr. Writer Sandra Cisneros was born in Chicago in the 1950s, the third child and only daughter of seven. Her books include *The House on Mango Street* and *Woman Hollering Creek*. She's won numerous awards, including the MacArthur Foundation Fellowship, which is often called the genius grant. Her latest novel, *Caramelo*, [was] published in September [2002].

Haahr. You were recently published in an anthology entitled *Growing Up Poor*. With

that in mind, I'd actually like to begin with a reading from your short story collection *Woman Hollering Creek*. Can you describe this story, "Salvador Late or Early," for our listeners?

Sandra Cisneros. I didn't intend it to be a story. I thought perhaps it'd be a poem. I was remembering a classmate of mine I couldn't forget. So it began from that place of not being able to forget.

Cisneros now reads the story.

A | **Read and Discuss** | What do you learn about Cisneros from these introductory comments?

Selection Readability	
Easily Accessible	familiar theme; familiar genre; complex syntax
Accessible	
Challenging	

Selection Plot Summary
Sandra Cisneros is interviewed by Marit Haahr. During the interview, Cisneros reads a short story called "Salvador Late or Early." Haahr and Cisneros then discuss the story and how it relates to Cisneros's own experience growing up poor and the lessons she learned as a result.

Salvador Late or Early

Salvador with eyes the color of caterpillar, Salvador of the crooked hair and crooked teeth, Salvador whose name the teacher cannot remember, is a boy who is no one's friend, runs along somewhere in that vague direction where homes are the color of bad weather, lives behind a raw wood doorway, shakes the sleepy brothers awake, ties their shoes, combs their hair with water, feeds them milk and cornflakes from a tin cup in the dim dark of the morning. **Ⓑ**

Salvador, late or early, sooner or later arrives with the string of younger brothers ready. Helps his mama, who is busy with the business of the baby. Tugs the arms of Cecilio, Arturito, makes them hurry, because today, like yesterday, Arturito has dropped the cigar box of crayons, has let go the hundred little fingers of red, green, yellow, blue, and nub of black sticks that tumble and spill over and beyond the asphalt puddles until the crossing-guard lady holds back the blur of traffic for Salvador to collect them again. **Ⓒ**

Salvador inside that wrinkled shirt, inside the throat that must clear itself and apologize each time it speaks, inside that forty-pound body of boy with its geography of scars, its history of hurt, limbs stuffed with feathers and rags, in what part of the eyes, in what part of the heart, in that cage of the chest where something throbs with both fists and knows only what Salvador knows, inside that body too small to contain the hundred balloons of happiness, the single guitar of grief, is a boy like any other disappearing out the door, beside the schoolyard gate, where he has told his brothers they must wait. Collects the hands of Cecilio and Arturito, scuttles off dodging the many schoolyard colors, the elbows and wrists crisscrossing, the several shoes running. Grows small and smaller to the eye, dissolves into the bright horizon, flutters in the air before disappearing like a memory of kites. **Ⓓ**

Ⓑ Literary Focus Writer's Message Which images in this paragraph create the mood of the story?

Ⓒ Literary Focus Writer's Message Why does Cisneros include this detail about the crayon spill? What does it reveal to you about Salvador?

Ⓓ Read and Discuss Cisneros uses precise images to describe Salvador. What point is she trying to make?

Analyzing Visuals   Connecting to the Text   How do you think Salvador feels as he hurries through his busy day?

Think About/Talk About

▶ **Comprehension**

Ⓓ **Read and Discuss**

Possible response: Salvador is a boy who doesn't have a lot going for him— he appears to be poor, he has an unkempt appearance, and he has to take care of his siblings.

▶ **Analysis**

Ⓑ **Literary Focus**

Possible response: Images like "homes . . . the color of bad weather" and "the dim dark of morning" create a gloomy mood that makes me feel sorry for Salvador.

Ⓒ **Literary Focus**

Possible response: It reveals that Salvador is responsible for looking out for his brothers and picking up things that they drop.

▶ **Extend the Discussion**

Metaphor   In the third paragraph on p. 616, Cisneros says that Salvador has "limbs stuffed with feathers and rags." What do you think this metaphor might mean? ***Possible response:** Perhaps Salvador is not very muscular because he does not get enough to eat.*

Analyzing Visuals

***Connecting to the Text:** Salvador probably feels exhausted and lonely with all of his worries and responsibilities, but he is probably too preoccupied to really be upset or depressed.*

Advanced Learners

Enrichment   Point out to students that while "Salvador Late or Early" is a work of fiction, the main character's background is very similar to the author's. Ask students to discuss in small groups why writers might prefer to describe their personal experiences and feelings in fiction rather than as an autobiographical account.

Students with Disabilities

"Salvador Late or Early" may be challenging for students to comprehend due to its unusual pace and sentence structure. Read the story aloud at a slow pace, pausing after every few sentences to ensure that students comprehend what is being read. Make sure students understand the framework of the story's placement within Cisneros's interview with Marit Haahr.

Think About/Talk About

▶ **Comprehension**

E Read and Discuss

Possible response: Because she grew up poor, she learned to value money. She also was protective of her family because she knew they were at a different place in society from her peers.

F Reading Focus

Possible response: She means that she learned to value and appreciate the things that she had, and she didn't always want more things. She thinks she wouldn't have learned that lesson by going to an expensive school.

Vocabulary: Own the Word

intimately: Explain to students that the adverb *intimately* comes from the Latin word *intimus*, which means "innermost." To know a subject *intimately* is to be familiar with its every aspect of its content, including ideas known by very few. Ask students to describe subjects or activities that they know *intimately*.

Monitor Students' Comprehension

Guide the class in answering these comprehension questions.

1. Why is Salvador often late? [*He has to help take care of his younger brothers.*]

2. How did Cisneros grow up? [*She was the only daughter in a large family that did not have much money.*]

3. How did Cisneros come up with the character of Salvador? [*She based him on a classmate she could not forget.*]

Haahr. Thank you. It's certainly clear that the image that Salvador left in your mind was very strong. Why do you think that was?

Cisneros. Because he sat in front of me and his shirts were always wrinkled and the collars were dirty. I thought, "Doesn't his mama love him?" I thought about him a lot, and I remembered him so clearly. I remember walking down streets visiting my aunt and thinking, "Now that kind of building must be the kind that Salvador lives in." I knew him intimately, perhaps more than he knew himself, and he stayed with me all the years. I realized when I finished writing the story that he was me. That's why I could know what he did and what kind of a house he lived in and who his younger brothers were and who he had to wait for—all the things that a tiny being like that knew and the remarkable things that perhaps he had to take care of that he never thought of as remarkable.

Haahr. I know that one of the defining features of your childhood was growing up without much money. What were the physical circumstances of your childhood like?

> *I realized when I finished writing the story that he was me.*

Cisneros. Well, you know, it came [to me] at a very young age that we just didn't have money for everything. My older brother was the one that would always pull me aside and say, "Don't ask for anything. Papa doesn't have any money," or "Don't shame him by asking for something that he can't give you or that he'll give you and that'll hurt us later in the week." So there was the sense of being responsible for the others. I was very conscious of it when I went to Catholic school, because there was a class difference between myself and the majority of the students in the school that I went to. **E**

Haahr. How did being conscious of that affect you?

Cisneros. It made you responsible. It made you want to be protective of your mother and father and not ask for too many things. It made you, sometimes, I think, value money in a way that perhaps your classmates did not, because you had to save for the things that you really wanted. When my father died, he was sad and cried and said he wished he could have given us more. And I said he gave us just enough, because we valued what we had, and we worked for what we had. That was a lesson you can't learn in Harvard. **F**

E Read and Discuss How does this new information connect with what you already know about Cisneros?

F Reading Focus Making Generalizations What does Cisneros mean when she says, "That was a lesson you can't learn in Harvard"? What lesson is she talking about?

Vocabulary intimately (IHN tuh muht lee) *adv.*: in a very familiar way.

California Standards, p. 619

■ **Reading Standard 3.1** Articulate the expressed purposes and characteristics of different forms of prose (e.g., short story, novel, novella, essay)

Applying Your Skills

Reading Standard 3.1 Articulate the expressed purposes and characteristics of different forms of prose (e.g., short story, novel, novella, essay).

An Interview with Sandra Cisneros / Salvador Late or Early

Literary Response and Analysis

Reading Skills Focus
Quick Check

1. Describe your reaction to "Salvador Late or Early." Include support from the story and interview.

Read with a Purpose

2. What does Cisneros mean when she says Salvador "was me"?

Reading Skills: Making Generalizations

3. Think of what Cisneros reveals about her childhood in the interview. Then, make a generalization about the lesson she learns from her family.

✔ Vocabulary Check

4. If you know a subject **intimately,** how well do you understand it?

Literary Skills Focus
Literary Analysis

5. **Interpret** Precise imagery is a poetic element in "Salvador Late or Early." Draw or describe one of the visual images that especially appeals to you.

6. **Interpret** What is the mood of the story? What does the mood tell you about Cisneros's attitude toward Salvador?

7. **Interpret** Do you agree with Cisneros that Salvador is "a boy like any other"? Cite details in the story to support your interpretation.

Literary Skills: A Writer's Messages

8. **Compare and Contrast** Explain how Cisneros is able to communicate similar messages in two different forms of prose—the short story and the interview.

9. **Analyze** Think about Cisneros's purpose in writing "Salvador Late or Early." Use her responses in the interview to help you decide on the story's message. Some possible messages are:
   - Remarkable people come from all walks of life.
   - Life without much money can still be rich.
   - It's important to make sacrifices for others.

Choose one of these messages, or think of one of your own. Write the message in a chart like the one below, and then <u>articulate</u> why you chose it and what you think about it.

Cisneros's message in "Salvador Late or Early" is

_____

My response to the message is

_____

Writing Skills Focus
Think as a Reader/Writer

Use It in Your Writing Powerful **metaphors**—comparisons of unlike things—are a prominent characteristic of "Salvador Late or Early." Choose one metaphor from each paragraph, and explain what it helps you understand about Salvador and about life.

Universal Access

Struggling Writers

Allow students to work with a partner to identify the metaphor within each paragraph of "Salvador Late or Early." Show them how to use a graphic organizer to record each metaphor and how it helps them understand something about Salvador or about life.

Then, have students choose their favorite metaphor from the graphic organizer and write a paragraph elaborating on what it helps them understand about Salvador or life.

Metaphor	What it helps you understand
where homes are the color of bad weather	Salvador lived in a gray-colored, gloomy house.

Check for Understanding

Independent Practice
Reading Skills Focus
Answers:

1. *"Salvador Late or Early" made me think about how difficult it is to have lots of responsibility when you are young. Salvador has to take care of his brothers, which makes his life more difficult.*

2. *Salvador has much in common with Cisneros's childhood, including loneliness, importance of family, and poverty.*

3. *Growing up without much money is extremely difficult, but it does give you a better appreciation of the things you have.*

Vocabulary Check
Possible response:

4. *If you understand a subject intimately, you know it extremely well; it is very familiar to you.*

Literary Skills Focus
Possible responses:

5. *I particularly liked the image of Salvador's eyes being "the color of a caterpillar." I imagine his eyes as greenish brown and lively.*

6. *The mood of the story is wistful and a little sad. It seems like Cisneros is remembering Salvador and feeling sorry for all of the problems he has to face.*

7. *Though Salvador is unique, he does have things in common with every boy—he seems to love his family, and he goes to school.*

8. *Cisneros can communicate the same message in both forms because the experience that generated the message is so much a part of her that she can express it in more than one way.*

9. *Cisneros's message is that life without much money can still be rich. I chose this because both Salvador and Cisneros form a rich life from little material wealth. I know what it's like to work hard for your money, and I believe that you can have a full life without being rich.*

Chanclas[1]

by Sandra Cisneros

Read with a Purpose
Read this story to discover what embarrasses the narrator and what happens to that feeling by the end of the story.

Preparing to Read for this selection is on page 613.

Build Background
"Chanclas" is a story from Cisneros's well-loved book *The House on Mango Street.* Her novel takes the form of a series of very short stories linked by the voice of a narrator, a girl named Esperanza, who is growing up in a Latino neighborhood in Chicago. In this particular story, Cisneros writes about a feeling we've probably all experienced—the embarrassment of not having the right clothes or not looking good enough.

It's me—Mama, Mama said. I open up and she's there with bags and big boxes, the new clothes and, yes, she's got the socks and a new slip with a little rose on it and a pink-and-white striped dress. What about the shoes? I forgot. Too late now. I'm tired. Whew!

Six-thirty already and my little cousin's baptism is over. All day waiting, the door locked, don't open up for nobody, and I don't till Mama gets back and buys everything except the shoes. **Ⓐ**

Now Uncle Nacho is coming in his car, and we have to hurry to get to Precious Blood Church quick because that's where the baptism party is, in the basement rented for today for dancing and tamales and everyone's kids running all over the place.

Mama dances, laughs, dances. All of a sudden, Mama is sick. I fan her hot face with a paper plate. Too many tamales, but Uncle Nacho says too many this and tilts his thumb to his lips.

Everybody laughing except me, because I'm wearing the new dress, pink and white with stripes, and new underclothes and new socks and the old saddle shoes I wear to school, brown and white, the kind I get every September because they last long and they do. My feet scuffed and round, and the heels all crooked that look dumb with this dress, so I just sit.

Meanwhile that boy who is my cousin by first communion or something asks me to dance and I can't. Just stuff my feet

---

1. **chanclas:** (CHAHNG klahs): Spanish slang for "old, worn-out shoes."

Ⓐ Read and Discuss What has the narrator told you so far?

Connecting to the Text What moment in the story might this photograph illustrate?

under the metal folding chair stamped Precious Blood and pick on a wad of brown gum that's stuck beneath the seat. I shake my head no. My feet growing bigger and bigger.

Then Uncle Nacho is pulling and pulling my arm and it doesn't matter how new the dress Mama bought is because my feet are ugly until my uncle who is a liar says, You are the prettiest girl here, will you dance, but I believe him, and yes, we are dancing, my Uncle Nacho and me, only I don't want to at first. My feet swell big and heavy like plungers, but I drag them across the linoleum floor straight center where Uncle wants to show off the new dance

we learned. And Uncle spins me, and my skinny arms bend the way he taught me, and my mother watches, and my little cousins watch, and the boy who is my cousin by first communion watches, and everyone says, wow, who are those two who dance like in the movies, until I forget that I am wearing only ordinary shoes, brown and white, the kind my mother buys each year for school.   **B**

And all I hear is the clapping when the music stops. My uncle and me bow and he walks me back in my thick shoes to my mother who is proud to be my mother. All night the boy who is a man watches me dance. He watched me dance.   **C**

B | Read and Discuss | What has changed for the narrator?

C | Literary Focus | Writer's Message Does the evening end the way the narrator expected it to? What truth about life does this short story illustrate?

Universal Access

EL English Learners

- Have students copy sentences that they are struggling with, underline words that are familiar or seem important, and connect those words to find meaning.
- Demonstrate by writing the following sentence from the story on the board: "My feet swell big and heavy like plungers, but I drag them across the linoleum floor straight center where Uncle wants to show off the new dance we learned." Underline *feet, heavy, plungers, Uncle, linoleum,* and *dance.*

- Connect the words into a sentence: "Her feet felt big and heavy like plungers when her Uncle dragged her across the linoleum to dance." Model the strategy as many times as needed, providing less assistance with each new sentence.
- Provide students with access to a dictionary or thesaurus so that they can look up unfamiliar words from the story.

Applying Your Skills

Reading Standard 3.1 Articulate the expressed purposes and characteristics of different forms of prose (e.g., short story, novel, novella, essay).

Independent Practice

Reading Skills Focus

Answers:

1. *The narrator is torn between wanting to dance and being embarrassed about her shoes.*

2. *By the end of the story, she has forgotten about her shoes and is happily dancing with her uncle.*

3. *Sometimes we get wrapped up in material possessions, but spending time with the people we love is what's most important.*

Literary Skills Focus

Possible responses:

4. *They joke with one another and compliment one another. Everyone claps after the narrator and her uncle dance.*

5. *"It's me—Mama," "What about the shoes, I forgot. Too late now. I'm tired. Whew," "You are the prettiest girl here," and "wow, who are those two who dance like in the movies" represent dialogue.*

6. *I picked pretty, clapping, and dance. When the narrator dances, her family claps for her and she finally feels like the pretty girl that she probably is.*

7. *Cisneros's message in "Chanclas" is that there are more important things in life than clothes. The narrator is so preoccupied with looking good that she almost misses the fun of dancing and being with her family and friends.*

8. *This form of prose is ideal for sharing the author's message because it is a message best revealed through experience, which the author is able to describe in fiction.*

Chanclas

Literary Response and Analysis

Reading Skills Focus

Quick Check

1. What is the narrator's main conflict?

Read with a Purpose

2. What has happened to the narrator's embarrassment by the end of the story?

Reading Skills: Making Generalizations

3. Think about the plot events in "Chanclas" and how they affect the narrator's feelings and attitude. Make a generalization about what teenagers could learn from this story and why that lesson is important for them.

Literary Skills Focus

Literary Analysis

4. **Interpret** How do you know that the people in this family are close and affectionate?

5. **Analyze** In this story the **dialogue** runs into the text instead of being set off with quotation marks. Re-read the story, and identify the passages that represent actual conversations. If you want, read the dialogue aloud.

6. **Analyze** Cisneros uses precise words to make her images come alive. Pick out a noun, a verb, and an adjective that you think are particularly powerful. Explain why you chose them.

Literary Skills: A Writer's Messages

7. **Connect** Choose a message you think is significant from "Chanclas." Write it in a chart like the one below, and record your responses to the message. Here are some possibilities. You may have your own ideas.

   • There are more important things in life than clothes.

   • Certain kinds of beauty lie beneath the surface.

   • You may find pleasure in a situation when you least expect to.

   Cisneros's message in "Chanclas" is

   _____

   My response to the message is

   _____

8. **Evaluate** Explain why a short story is a good form of prose to reveal the message you identified. What specific <u>characteristics</u> make it so?

Writing Skills Focus

Think as a Reader/Writer

Use It in Your Writing Cisneros uses a very effective **simile** to tell how the narrator's feet feel as she starts dancing with her uncle: "My feet swell big and heavy like plungers." Recall a time when you felt awkward or embarrassed about something. Write a description of the experience. Use at least one simile in your description.

Universal Access

Struggling Writers

Students may need additional scaffolding to complete the Writing Skills Focus activity. Have them brainstorm a list of words that describe how they felt during an awkward or embarrassing experience. Tell students to refer to this list and to incorporate these feelings when describing the experience. You may also suggest that students refer to the list when creating a simile to include in their description. Remind them to use "like" or "as" in their simile.

California Standards, p. 622

■ **Reading Standard 3.1** Articulate the expressed purposes and characteristics of different forms of prose (e.g., short story, novel, novella, essay).

Abuelito Who

by **Sandra Cisneros**

Read with a Purpose
Read this poem to find out how the speaker feels about her grandfather.

Preparing to Read for this selection is on page 613.

Build Background
"Abuelito Who" is a collection of memories about a grandfather. *Abuelito* (ah bweh LEE toh) is Spanish for "granddaddy."

Abuelito who throws coins like rain
and asks who loves him
who is dough and feathers
who is a watch and glass of water
5 whose hair is made of fur
is too sad to come downstairs today
who tells me in Spanish you are
          my diamond
who tells me in English you are my sky
whose little eyes are string
10 can't come out to play
sleeps in his little room all night and day
who used to laugh like the letter *k*
is sick
is a doorknob tied to a sour stick
15 is tired shut the door
doesn't live here anymore
is hiding underneath the bed   **Ⓐ**
who talks to me inside my head

is blankets and spoons and big
          brown shoes
20 who snores up and down up and
          down up and down again
is the rain on the roof that falls
          like coins
asking who loves him
who loves him who?   **Ⓑ**

Ⓐ | Read and Discuss | What is the speaker letting you know about her *abuelito*?

Ⓑ | Literary Focus | Writer's Message The speaker repeats the phrase "who loves him" three times. What message is she trying to convey through this repetition?

Selection Readability

Easily Accessible	familiar theme; familiar genre;
Accessible	complex syntax
Challenging	

Selection Summary
"Abuelito Who" is a poem about the author's grandfather. She recalls how her grandfather used to act and compares it to the way he is behaving now, when he is sick.

The Place Where Dreams Come From

by **Sandra Cisneros**

When I was little, my grandpa—my Abuelito, that is, which is sort of like Granddaddy, only sweeter—my Abuelito used to love to give all his grandchildren their *domingo* (literally "Sunday," because that's the day children receive it), that is, their allowance. But my Abuelito loved the ritual of asking in a loud voice, "Who loves Grandpa?" and we would answer, also in a loud voice, "We do!" Then he would take a handful of change he'd been saving all week for this purpose, Mexican coins which are thick and heavy, and toss them up in the air so that they'd fall like rain, like a *piñata*,[1] and we'd scramble all over each other picking up as many coins as we could. To me it was much more fun to get our *domingo* this way instead of having it placed in our hands. **A**

Well, it's this fun grandpa that this poem is about. And about the coins falling like rain, and rain falling like coins, that at times makes me think of him and miss him. I recall he became rather sick and cranky in his last years. I suppose that's what some of the images refer to, but I was grown and gone already, and my Abuelito in faraway Mexico City. **B**

I'm not sure what exactly all the images refer to, and I'm not sure I ever knew. But that's what's so wonderful about poetry. It comes from some deep and true place inside you, the place where dreams come from. We don't always know what dreams mean, do we, and we don't have to always know to enjoy and experience them. That's how it is with poetry, too. When I write, I don't question where

---

1. **piñata:** (pee NYAH tah): papier-mâché container filled with toys and candy, which is hung above the heads of blindfolded children, who hit it with a stick to release its contents.

A **Literary Focus** Writer's Message Look back at "Abuelito Who." Which lines in the poem does this paragraph explain?

B **Read and Discuss** What do these two paragraphs show you about the poet and her grandfather?

Vocabulary **literally** (LIHT uhr uh lee) *adv.:* according to the basic meaning of the word.
ritual (RIHCH oo uhl) *n.:* an established routine.

images are coming from. I write dictated by sound and directed by my heart. And these images—"dough and feathers," "little eyes are string," and "doorknob tied to a sour stick"— felt right then and still feel right as I read them now. "Dough and feathers" I suppose has to do with how he felt when I held him and he held me. He was soft and squishy as dough or feathers. But it could also mean the color of his skin and hair. The texture of his skin. The silliness of his being. They're all "right."

"Little eyes are string" is harder to pinpoint. Did I mean like a spiral of string, like when we are sick? Maybe. But then again, perhaps it's the way he looked at me when he was sick. And "doorknob tied to a sour stick." I recall a cane he had and how he changed when he was very old and cranky and waved it when he wanted to make a point. So I suppose he had "soured." Why tied to a door-knob? Who knows?

A few biographical tidbits. My grandfather *did* laugh like the letter *k*. A kind of "kkkk" sound when he chuckled, which, surprisingly, I've inherited.

And. He was very proud that he could speak English, even though he lived in Mexico City most of his life. And so he liked to show off his English to his grandchildren from the United States when they came to visit. "You are my diamond," my grandpa would say in typical Mexican fashion. But then he would mistranslate "You're my heaven" and instead come out with "You're my sky," because "sky" and "heaven" are the same word in Spanish. I remember thinking even as a child that it

Wagon Crossing the Tracks: The Hat (1934–1938) by Jackson Pollock (1912–1956). Gouache on paper.
Artist Rights Society (ARS), New York.

sounded wonderful—"You're my sky." How much better than *heaven*. All, all of that! Imagine. I've always been much more partial to sky and clouds, and am even now.

Finally, the older we grow, the younger we become as well, don't you think? That is, our Abuelito had to take naps, and he liked to play games, like the one with the coins, and he talked to us in a way that other adults didn't, and he couldn't climb the stairs very well, like my baby brothers. So in a way he was getting younger and younger and younger until he wasn't anymore. **C**

C Literary Focus **Writer's Message** What does Cisneros mean when she says, "the older we grow, the younger we become"?

Vocabulary **mistranslate** (mihs TRANS layt) *v.*: change from one language to another incorrectly.

▶ **Comprehension**

B **Read and Discuss**
Possible response: The poet has fond memories of her grandfather.

▶ **Analysis**

A **Literary Focus**
Possible response: It explains the lines "who throws coins like rain/and asks who loves him".

C **Literary Focus**
Possible response: Once people get past a certain age, their behavior starts to become more like a child's behavior.

Vocabulary: Own the Word

- **literally:** Warn students that some speakers use the word *literally* incorrectly, as a modifier like *really* instead of a word meaning "actually." The sentence "My head is literally killing me" does not use the word properly unless the speaker is dying because of her head.

- **ritual:** Tell students that *rituals* can also be traditions. Ask students to name any holiday rituals that take place in their homes.

- **mistranslate:** Tell students that *mistranslation* can create many problems, but that in this selection, a mistranslation is a little mistake with no negative consequences. Ask students what may be the consequence of a mistranslation in a business transaction. [*losing money*]

Monitor Students' Comprehension

Guide the class in answering these comprehension questions.

1. Why is the children's allowance called "domingo"? [*They received it on Sunday.*]

2. What was Abuelito like in the last years of his life? [*sick and cranky*]

Universal Access

Struggling Readers

Benchmark Students Work with students to compare the poem "Abuelito Who" with the essay "The Place Where Dreams Come From." Re-read the poem aloud with students, pausing after each line to find the corresponding explanation in the essay. Point out that Sandra Cisneros herself is not entirely sure of the origin of some of the words and phrases in the poem. Invite students to offer alternative explanations for such phrases as "little eyes are string" and "doorknob tied to a sour stick." Students may also discuss the meanings of lines for which Cisneros does not offer an explanation, such as "who is a watch and glass of water" in line 4 of the poem. Discuss with the class why it is possible for many people to have different interpretations of the same poem and why poets may not be entirely sure of the meaning of certain lines themselves.

Independent Practice

Reading Skills Focus

Answers:

1. *Both grandfathers are kind and loving, though the grandfather in the personal narrative seems sicker and sadder.*

2. *She loves her grandfather and still misses him. The essay gave examples of how she came up with some of the images in the poem.*

3. *Readers should enjoy the poetry, but not try to figure out exactly what everything means.*

Vocabulary Check

Possible responses:

4. *Yes; we always go to the movies and out to dinner on Saturday.*

5. *No; cats and dogs will never actually fall out of the sky.*

6. *Yes; I translated "Buenas tardes" as "Good morning," but it means "Good afternoon."*

Literary Skills Focus

Possible responses:

7. *I like the poem and understand it more, especially the part about the coins falling like rain.*

8. *The poem jumps from one idea to another. This is like a dream because dreams can be erratic too.*

9. *Images include "is sick," "is tired shut the door," "can't come out to play," and "doesn't live here anymore."*

10. *Cisneros's message in "Abuelito Who" is, "Memories of everyday life offer lasting inspiration." I think this is very true—I will always remember the fun I had with my grandparents.*

11. *Cisneros wanted to share how she felt about her grandfather.*

Applying Your Skills

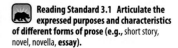

Reading Standard 3.1 Articulate the expressed purposes and characteristics of different forms of prose (e.g., short story, novel, novella, **essay**).

Abuelito Who / The Place Where Dreams Come From

Literary Response and Analysis

Reading Skills Focus

Quick Check

1. List the similarities and differences between the grandfather in the poem and the grandfather described in the personal narrative.

Read with a Purpose

2. How does Cisneros feel about her *abuelito*? How did the personal narrative help you better understand the poem?

Reading Skills: Making Generalizations

3. Recall what Cisneros says in the personal narrative about poetry. Use this information to make a generalization about what readers should do when they read poetry.

✔ **Vocabulary Check**

4. Does your family have a weekend **ritual**?
5. Is the phrase "It's raining cats and dogs" ever **literally** true?
6. Do you ever **mistranslate** words in your foreign-language class?

Literary Skills Focus

Literary Analysis

7. **Interpret** In her personal essay, or personal narrative, Cisneros describes her inspiration for the poem. How do you feel about the poem now? Do you understand it better? Explain.

8. **Compare** Cisneros says that poetry and dreams both come from the same "deep and true place inside you." Think about the structure of "Abuelito Who," and explain how else poetry can be similar to dreams.

9. **Analyze** In her personal narrative, Cisneros says that her grandfather became "sick and cranky in his last years." Identify four images in the poem that might refer to that time.

Literary Skills: A Writer's Messages

10. **Analyze** State the message of "Abuelito Who" in a chart like the one below, and then record your response to that message. Think of your own message, or use one of these possibilities: "People change with the passing of time." "Memories of everyday life offer lasting inspiration." "Family ties strengthen over the years."

   Cisneros's message in "Abuelito Who" is

   My response to the message is

11. **Infer** What purposes might Cisneros have had for writing "Abuelito Who"? for writing "The Place Where Dreams Come From"?

Writing Skills Focus

Think as a Reader/Writer

Use It in Your Writing In the poem, Cisneros uses many **metaphors** to describe her grandfather. Review the metaphors, and think about what they mean. Then, write your own description of someone who is special to you. Use at least three metaphors to describe that person.

Universal Access

Struggling Writers

Some students may need additional scaffolding to complete the Writing Skills Focus activity. Tell students to write down details that describe a person that is special to them. Then, have them relate those details to other objects. Remind students to rely on their senses when creating metaphors. For example, they may think of sounds that remind them of the sounds that the person makes or objects that move like the person moves.

California Standards, pp. 626–627

- **Reading Standard 3.1** Articulate the expressed purposes and characteristics of different forms of prose (e.g., short story, novel, novella, essay)

Reading Standard 3.1 Articulate the expressed purposes and characteristics of different forms of prose (e.g., short story, novel, novella, **essay**).

Author Study: Sandra Cisneros

Writing Skills Focus
Think as a Reader/Writer

Analyzing a Writer's Language Look back at the similes and metaphors you recorded as you read Cisneros's works. Which ones did you think were most effective? Do you recall any other images from these texts?

Use It in Your Writing Write an essay in which you <u>articulate</u> how Cisneros uses everyday language, strong images, metaphors, and Spanish words in "Salvador Late or Early," "Chanclas," and "Abuelito Who." After writing an introductory paragraph, you can organize your essay in one of two ways:

1. You can write a paragraph about each of the three works and give examples of the four elements.

2. You can write a paragraph about each element and describe how it is used in the three works.

Write a final paragraph describing your responses to Cisneros's writing.

What Do You Think Now How has reading Cisneros's works influenced your thinking about writing and reading poetry versus writing and reading prose?

CHOICES

As you respond to the Choices, use the **Academic Vocabulary** words as appropriate: <u>articulate</u>, <u>characteristic</u>, <u>comment</u>, <u>impact</u>, <u>insight</u>, <u>structure</u>, <u>tradition</u>, <u>vision</u>.

REVIEW
Interpret a Writer's Messages

Timed Writing In an essay, discuss Cisneros's messages in these selections. First, review the charts you filled in after you read the selections. Then, write three paragraphs. In the first paragraph, make a generalization about Cisneros's writing based on the message of each work and the <u>insight</u> about her writing that she shares in the interview and the personal narrative. In the second, state the messages in the texts. In the third, describe your responses to the selections and their messages. Use quotations from the texts to support your interpretations.

CONNECT
Write a Short Story

Using "Chanclas" as your model, write a brief story about an embarrassing situation. Begin by conveying what happened. Then, use precise words and images to describe the setting, characters, and events.

EXTEND
Write a Poem

Cisneros turns her experiences into stories by describing the details that make people and situations unique. Write a poem about a relative or a good friend. You may want to use the basic <u>structure</u> of "Abuelito Who" as your model. Begin with the person's name. Then, add descriptive details, beginning each line with *who*.

Independent Practice
Choices:
Evaluation Criteria
Review: Timed Writing
40–50 minutes
- The essay provides a generalization about Cisneros's writing.
- The essay discusses the messages in Cisneros's stories and poem.
- The essay includes the student's response to the selections and their messages.

Connect: Homework
Write a Short Story
- The story discusses an embarrassing event or situation.
- The story uses vivid words and imagery to describe the event, setting, and characters.

Extend: Homework
Write a Poem
- The poem imitates the structure of "Abuelito Who."
- The poem uses vivid examples to describe a friend or relative.

What Do You Think Now?
Ask students to think about the differences between poetry and prose as well as how readers should approach the two forms. Does poetry use the same language as prose? Can poets always identify the meaning behind their language?

Universal Access

Struggling Writers
To complete the Writing Skills Focus, provide students with additional scaffolding. Show students how to create three four-column charts with the headings *everyday language, strong images, metaphors,* and *Spanish words* in their notes. Allow students to list examples of each element for the three selections as a prewriting exercise.

"Salvador Late or Early"

strong images	everyday language
eyes the color of caterpillar	
metaphors	Spanish words
where homes are the color of bad weather	

Standards Focus

Objectives
Students will
- write fictional narratives that include elements of plot, setting, character, and dialogue
- use dialogue to develop characters

Preteach

Write with a Purpose Read aloud the essentials of a good fictional narrative to guide students' understanding of this type of writing. Also refer students to the rubric on p. 636 for more information on fictional narrative that they can use throughout this workshop.

Direct Teach

Model the Skill

Think as a Reader/Writer Use the professional model on this page and others in the chapter to provide examples of the elements of a good fictional narrative. Point out in the model how the writer uses dialogue and action to make the characters come to life.

Think About the Model
Possible responses:

1. *Sensory details help readers to imagine the sights and sounds of the setting, such as the sounds of the boys yelling.*

2. *The mood is introspective and wistful.*

California Standards, pp. 628–637

- **Writing Standard 1.7** Revise writing to improve organization and word choice after checking the logic of the ideas and the precision of the vocabulary.
- **Writing Standard 2.1** Write fictional or autobiographical narratives. **a.** Develop a standard plot line (having a beginning, conflict, rising action, climax, and denouement) and point of view. **b.** Develop complex major and minor characters and a definite setting. **c.** Use a range of appropriate strategies (e.g., dialogue; suspense; naming of specific narrative action, including movement, gestures, and expressions).

Fictional Narrative

Write with a Purpose

Write a **fictional narrative** that includes the elements of plot, setting, and character you've learned about in this chapter. The **purpose** is to entertain the people who will read it—your **audience.**

A Good Fictional Narrative
- develops a plot with a beginning, conflict, rising action, climax, and resolution
- uses dialogue and actions, including movements and gestures, to develop characters
- gives a detailed description of the setting
- ends with a resolution to the conflict the characters faced

See page 636 for complete rubric.

Reader/Writer Notebook
Use your **RWN** to complete the activities for this workshop.

Think as a Reader/Writer
In this chapter, you've seen the techniques writers use to write fictional narratives. Before you begin to write your own fictional narrative, take a few minutes to read the beginning of "The Dive" (page 53), a short story by René Saldaña, Jr.

"Look at them, Papi," said Melly to her father.

Mr. Otero cast his line into the water again and looked up and to his right. "Tan locos, mi'ja. It's a crazy thing to do."

From upriver, Melly and her father could see five or six boys fixing to jump from Jensen's Bridge. They pounded their chests, inched their way to the edge, then dove in all at once, some headfirst, others feet first, and one balled up. The boys disappeared underwater, leaving behind them different-sized splashes, then Melly heard the echoes of their jumping screams a full second or two after they'd gone under. By then, they were shooting up out of the water, their arms raised in the air. They'd done it. Most of the boys in Three Oaks had to dive from the bridge at one time or other to prove themselves real men. Today was their day.

Melly saw the boys crawl from the river and turn over on their backs, stretched out like lizards sunning themselves on the bank. Reeling in her line, she thought, *So what if they can dive off the bridge! I could do it too if I wanted. Who said it was just for the guys to do?*

"You'll do nothing of the kind," said Mr. Otero.

"Huh?"

"You said you could dive too if you wanted?"

"I didn't say anything. You must be hearing things."

← Realistic **dialogue** is used to introduce major and minor characters.

← Specific **details,** such as the boys "pounded their chests" and "shooting up out of the water," describe the setting and characters' actions.

← The story's **conflict** is introduced through realistic dialogue.

Think About the Professional Model
With a partner, discuss the following questions about the model.

1. How do sensory details help you picture the setting?

2. What is the mood of the narrative?

Writing Workshop Resources

UA: Holt Interactive Writer and Speaker, practice and assessment, p. 94

UA: Differentiating Instruction, modified lesson plans, p. 140

WritingNotes, interactive lesson presentations with activities

GrammarNotes, interactive lesson presentations with activities

Writing Standard 1.7 Revise writing to improve organization and word choice after checking the logic of the ideas and the precision of the vocabulary. **2.1 Write fictional** or autobiographical **narratives: a. Develop a** standard plot line (having a beginning, conflict, rising action, climax, and denouement) **and point of view. b. Develop complex major and minor characters and a definite setting. c. Use a range of appropriate** strategies (e.g., dialogue; suspense; naming of specific narrative action, including movement, gestures, and expressions).

Prewriting

Choose a Story Idea

What keeps a reader turning pages? A good narrative needs a complex character facing a conflict. Here are two ways to choose a story idea.

- **Start with a Character** You might build your story around an interesting or unusual person. You don't have to write about a real person—you can make up a character.

- **Start with a Conflict** You might begin with a problem or conflict that you have heard about or actually experienced. You might also enjoy writing about a completely imaginary situation. In either case, the narrative should include a **conflict**—a problem the major character faces.

Plan Characters and Setting

Characters The star of your story will be a complex **major character,** or **protagonist,** who is developed enough to seem like a real person. The supporting roles will be played by **minor characters.** Ask yourself:

- What do your readers need to know about the characters?

- What is the major character's personality? What does he or she like or dislike? How does he or she act toward family and friends?

- How will the minor characters interact with the major character?

Setting You also will develop a definite **setting**—where and when the story takes place. Your setting gives information about your characters (a clean desk indicates neatness), creates a mood (an abandoned house suggests mystery), and creates conflict (a blizzard could bring trouble). Ask yourself:

- Where and when will the story take place?

- What places, weather, or times of day could be important?

- What concrete sensory details describe the setting?

Think About Purpose and Audience

As you think about your story, keep your **purpose** and **audience** in mind. Your **purpose** in writing a fictional narrative is to entertain your readers, who are your audience. Your **audience** is probably your classmates and your teacher. What will keep them so interested that they'll want to read to the end of your narrative?

Idea Starters
- people with unusual jobs
- people with special talents
- people with unique challenges
- dangerous adventures
- someone overcoming a problem
- scary happenings
- unexpected events

Types of Conflict

External: a character's struggle with outside forces

- The boys jump off the bridge into the water below.
- The boys jump to prove themselves to each other.

Internal: a character's struggle within his or her own mind

- Melly asks herself why she can't also dive off the bridge.

Your Turn _____

Get Started Making notes in your **RWN,** decide on the **major and minor characters** and **conflict,** considering **purpose** and **audience.** Then, answer the questions about the **characters** and **setting** on this page. Your notes will help you plan your fictional narrative.

✳ **Learn It Online**
An interactive graphic organizer can help you generate and organize ideas. Try one at:

| go.hrw.com | H7-629 | Go |

Guided Practice: Apply

Choose a Story Idea

- Have students use the idea starters or their own ideas to decide on either a character or a conflict that they want to write about.

- Have students use webs to brainstorm ways to connect their chosen conflicts and characters. Draw two adjacent circles on the board, and write "elephant trainer" in one and "must save an injured elephant" in the other. Have students suggest words or phrases that relate to elephant trainers and helping wounded elephants. Write each word or phrase in a circle extending out from the main circle. If a word or phrase is common to both, only write it once, and draw lines connecting it to both circles.

- Encourage students to think of combinations that will be entertaining or unexpected.

Think About Purpose and Audience

Have students think about books, movies, or plays that they find interesting. Ask them how these stories keep their attention. Have students brainstorm and list ways that they can keep their audience interested in their stories. ***Possible responses:*** *suspense, humor, sentiment, action*

Your Turn _____

Get Started Allow students time to decide on the character, setting, and conflict for their fictional narrative. Then, have students independently answer the questions on this page about character and setting.

✳ **Learn It Online**
ThinkCentral, Student Access includes more than thirty **Interactive Graphic Organizers.** Your students can use them to generate and organize ideas, compare and contrast, evaluate a decision, support a position, and much more.

| go.hrw.com | H7-629 | Go |

Guided Practice: Apply

Plan Your Plot

- Tell students that a plot that is suspenseful will be organized according to climactic order—that is, each event builds on the last to intensify the conflict until it reaches a climax.

- Explain that the Narrative Action Plan on this page shows one student's plan for her story. Point out how the events keep the reader engaged by creating suspense. Encourage students to compare the plan with the actual student draft that appears on pp. 633–634 of this workshop.

Your Turn

Plan Your Plot Have students complete the **Your Turn** activity as independent practice. As they work, monitor their progress by making sure their plot includes a beginning, conflict, rising action, climax, and denouement.

Plan Your Plot

What will happen to the characters in your story? The **plot** is the series of events in a story. A **narrative action plan** organizes the parts of a story's plot. A plot includes the following:

- **Beginning** A good beginning introduces the characters, setting, and conflict and grabs readers' attention so that they keep reading.
- **Rising action** Conflict builds as the major character faces obstacles to solving his or her problem. Each new obstacle complicates the conflict, creates suspense, and helps build to the story's climax.
- **Climax (high point) and suspense** Your story needs a suspenseful moment—one of hight impact—when the conflict reaches a turning point and the problem will be settled, one way or another. Make your reader wonder, "How is this going to turn out?"
- **Denouement, or outcome** After reaching its climax, the conflict is resolved, usually leaving the major character changed in some way.

Narrative Action Plan

Here's one writer's narrative action plan. Use this model to help you create your own plan.

Your Turn

Plan Your Plot To help you build your plot, make a **narrative action plan** for your fictional narrative in your **RWN.** Share your plan with a peer. Think about the feedback and insight your peer provides. Revise your plan as needed, keeping in mind your **purpose** and **audience.**

> ### Narrative Action Plan
>
> **Characters: major**—a girl walking by herself
> **minor**—someone following her
> **Setting:** the woods, near a campsite
> **Conflict:** the girl vs. her fear
> **Beginning:**
> 1. The girl is walking alone in the woods, separated from her friends.
> 2. She realizes she is lost and searches her pocket for something to help her.
> **Rising action:**
> 3. She hears crunching and footsteps and sees a shadow behind her.
> **Climax:**
> 4. The person following the girl finally reaches her.
> **Denouement, or outcome:**
> 5. The person hands the girl her cell phone and leaves. She realizes the person wasn't going to harm her.

Fictional Narrative Writing Prompts

Students can choose their own ideas or use one of the following prompts to write a fictional narrative.

Workplace Write a story whose main character has a career that you find exciting or works in a place that you are interested in learning more about. Write in the first person to show the viewpoint of the main character.

History Select a historical event that you have studied in history class, and write a story about a character who is involved in or is affected by the event. Be as accurate as possible when using historical facts.

Science Science fiction is a popular subgenre of fiction. Write a story based on something that you have learned or discussed in science class. For example, you could write about an experiment that causes an unexpected chain reaction.

Drafting

Determine Point of View

Who will tell, or narrate, your story? A story will be very different if it is told by someone involved in the events rather than by someone not involved. **Point of view** is the vantage point from which a story is told. The chart to the right explains the different points of view.

Use Dialogue

Dialogue, conversations between characters, has many purposes in narratives. It is often used to introduce the setting, characters, and conflict. From dialogue in "The Dive," we learn that the boys are diving from a high bridge and that Melly envies them. This reveals Melly's character traits, and we begin to guess what will happen next. Dialogue can also

- move the action of the plot forward
- create suspense
- explain complications
- explain the denouement

The dialogue in your narrative should be natural and imitate conversations you hear every day. For this reason, dialogue often includes fragments, contractions, and unique expressions.

Point of View		
First person		The narrator is a character in the story and can tell the reader only what he or she is thinking or feeling. The narrator uses the pronoun *I*.
Third-person limited		The narrator is not a character in the story. This narrator tells what *one* character—referred to as *he* or *she*—thinks and feels.
Third-person omniscient		The narrator is not a character in the story but knows what *every* character is thinking and feeling. This narrator can tell things that none of the characters could know.

Grammar Link Punctuating Dialogue

Study the following dialogue from "The Dive." Be sure to follow the punctuation rules when you write dialogue for your narrative.

> "You'll do nothing of the kind," said Mr. Otero.
>
> "Huh?"
>
> "You said you could dive too if you wanted?"
>
> "I didn't say anything. You must be hearing things."

- Begin a new paragraph every time a speaker changes.
- Use quotation marks to enclose what is being said. Punctuation marks for the dialogue—such as a comma, question mark, or period—appear inside the quotation marks.
- Use dialogue tags, such as *said Mr. Otero* to indicate the speaker. Not every line will have one. Use a dialogue tag to make it clear who is speaking.
- Place a period after the dialogue tag when the tag appears at the end of a sentence.

● Writing Tip

In fictional narratives, the main character usually wants something. Conflict occurs when the main character faces plot complications, obstacles that prevent the character from getting what he or she wants. As you develop your fictional narrative, be sure to include plot complications that will increase suspense.

Your Turn _____

Draft Your Narrative

Following your narrative action plan, write a draft of your story. First, think about

- who will tell your story (your narrator). Decide on the **point of view** in your narrative.
- how to use **dialogue** to bring characters to life.

Universal Access

EL English Learners

Tell students that it is important to include transitions such as *next, later,* and *finally* in a narrative to show the order of events and actions. Provide a list of transitional words and phrases for students which they can use in their narratives, such as *initially, then, suddenly,* and *to everyone's surprise.*

✔ See **UA: Differentiating Instruction** for strategies for English learners.

Struggling Writers

If students are having trouble finding a story idea, suggest that they develop a story in which they are the main character but the conflict is fictional. Or, suggest that they use the characters and conflicts in the stories of Chapter 5 for inspiration.

✔ See **UA: Differentiating Instruction** for strategies for struggling writers.

Guided Practice: Apply

Determine Point of View

Tell students that changing point of view within a narrative will confuse readers. It should only be done occasionally, such as to mark the climax of a complex story.

Use Dialogue

Have students re-read the dialogue in the excerpt from "The Dive." Then, ask them to explain how the writer uses realistic dialogue to move the action of the plot forward and to set up the conflict in the story.

Grammar Link

For practice, have students punctuate the dialogue in each of the following sentences.

1. It's too bad that snowboarding can be expensive said Henry. [*"It's too bad that snowboarding can be expensive," said Henry.*]

2. When you think about it Isabel sighed everything can be expensive. [*"When you think about it," Isabel sighed, "everything can be expensive."*]

3. Naomi wondered Do you think individual lessons are less expensive? [*Naomi wondered, "Do you think individual lessons are less expensive?"*]

✎ **Warriner's Handbook,** First Course

Your Turn _____

Draft Your Narrative Ask students to complete the **Your Turn** activity as independent practice. Remind students to use their completed Narrative Action Plan as they begin to draft their narrative. Suggest that students use every other line as they write so that revisions can be made more easily later.

Model the Skill

■ Using a student draft on a transparency, model how to use the questions, tips, and revision techniques suggested in the chart. You might use a student's draft or a draft of your own creation to evaluate and revise using the steps in the chart.

■ Ask volunteers to demonstrate using each of the steps on their own stories.

Peer Review

Before students meet with their partners, have them make a list of the questions they want answers for about their drafts, such as "Do you think I have enough details about my character?" or "How do you think I can improve my opening sentence?"

 Holt Six Traits for Writing, rubrics, prompts, and sample papers

Peer Review

Working with a peer, review the chart at right. Then, review your drafts. Answer each question in this chart to determine how the drafts could be improved. Positive comments about what works well in the drafts are also helpful. Be sure to note on the drafts what you and your partner discuss. You can refer to your notes as you revise your draft.

Evaluating and Revising

The chart below will help you identify how to revise your draft.

Fictional Narrative: Guidelines for Content and Organization

Evaluation Question	Tip	Revision Technique
1. Does the story have an interesting plot with an effective beginning, a conflict, complications, a suspenseful climax, and a clear denouement?	**Place a check mark** next to each of the following elements: beginning, conflict, complications, climax, and denouement.	**Add** or **elaborate** on elements of the plot as necessary. **Delete** any information that ruins the suspense by giving too much away.
2. Is the point of view consistent throughout the story?	**Identify** pronouns (*I, he,* or *she*) that identify the point of view. **Label** the story's point of view; then, **circle** any information not given from that point of view.	If any sentences are circled, **delete** them. If necessary, **add** the same information but tell it from the narrator's point of view.
3. Are the characters complex and realistic?	**Underline** specific details about each of the characters.	If necessary, **add** details about a character's appearance, personality, or background. **Add** dialogue and narrative actions that reveal more about a character.
4. Does the story have a definite setting?	With a colored marker, **highlight** details of the setting.	If there are few highlighted words, **elaborate** on the setting by adding sensory, or descriptive, details.
5. Is the story well organized and coherent? Are transitions used effectively?	**Number** the major events in the story. **Put a star** next to transitional words and phrases such as *next* and *later that day.*	**Rearrange** any events that are out of order. If there are few or no stars, **add** transitional words and phrases to show the order of events.
6. Does the story use precise nouns and adjectives to describe the characters and setting?	**Draw a wavy line** under each precise noun and adjective in the story.	If you see few wavy lines, **replace** any dull or vague nouns or adjectives with precise ones.

Real Issues, Real Experts

Holt Professional Learning for Language Arts

To watch videos on teaching **revision, grammar,** and **on-demand writing skills** featuring Linda Rief, Amy Benjamin, and Leila Christenbury, go to this page at **ThinkCentral, Teacher Access.**

Universal Access

Struggling Writers

Strategic Students Provide the following word bank of dialogue tags for students to use as they add dialogue to their drafts: *exclaimed, said, sighed, shouted, shrieked, laughed, giggled, hesitated, whispered, whimpered, suggested, wondered, asked, questioned, replied, snapped,* and *mumbled.*

Read this student draft and notice comments on its structure and suggestions for how it could be made even stronger.

A Stranger in the Woods
by Ashley Hildebrandt, Abiding Word Lutheran School

I was walking in the forest. I was all alone walking back to my tent. All of my friends had gone ahead of me because I was too slow. I'd been walking for about an hour now, and I knew I was lost now, which isn't very unusual for me. I was instantly sure of what I needed to do. I reached into my pocket and realized it was empty. I frantically searched the ground around myself and walked with panic in my movements. I remembered then where I'd left it. I had left my only hope out by the lake. I then heard a soft crunching of leaves. It continued rhythmically edging closer and closer. As I listened carefully, I hesitantly decided to run to the left.

The beginning of Ashley's fictional narrative establishes the major **character**, the **setting**, and the **conflict**.

Ashley further develops the **conflict** and begins to build **suspense**. Notice the excellent use of sensory details as she hears noises in the woods.

MINI-LESSON **How to Use Dialogue for an Effective Beginning**

Ashley might use dialogue for a more effective beginning. Dialogue will add both interest and needed information to the beginning of her narrative.

Ashley's Draft of Paragraph One

I was walking in the forest. I was all alone walking back to my tent. All of my friends had gone ahead of me because I was too slow. I'd been . . .

Notice that these sentences are repetitive in structure and don't have that "hook" of interest that a good beginning needs. Ashley can improve it by adding dialogue.

Ashley's Revision of Paragraph One

"Hey, Turtle! We'll never get back to camp walking this slow!"

"Yeah," giggled Nina, "I need to change this wet swimming suit. I'm running back to camp."

"Me, too," agreed the rest of my friends. They disappeared, leaving me trudging alone—all alone.

I'd been . . .

Your Turn _____

Use Dialogue Read your draft, and then ask yourself:

- What dialogue would make the narrative more interesting or would provide background information?
- What precise nouns, adjectives, and adverbs would give the dialogue more impact?
- What sensory details or images would make my narrative more vivid?

Guided Practice: Apply
Student Draft
Explain that the Student Draft on this page is the first half of a story written by the student whose Narrative Action Plan appeared on p. 630. Model reading the draft and the annotations in blue, and explain that the yellow highlighting illustrates the student's language choices. Explain that a mini-lesson follows with helpful information about ways to improve this draft as well as their own.

▶ Mini-Lesson
How to Use Dialogue for an Effective Beginning

- Explain that the student writer has revised her opening by using dialogue. Read the student's first draft and the revision aloud. Ask students to comment on the differences.

- Remind students to use dialogue tags, such as "she wondered" and "he exclaimed," to differentiate among speakers and to show expression and personality.

Your Turn _____

Use Dialogue As students complete the **Your Turn** activity, tell them to find two places in their draft where dialogue could naturally be added. The dialogue might be used to convey character motivation, advance the plot, or provide information or suspense. Remind students to use the **Grammar Link** on p. 631 to help them punctuate dialogue correctly.

Advanced Learners
Acceleration Challenge students to use more advanced narrative techniques in their fictional narratives such as flashbacks, flash forwards, intriguing points of view, symbolism, and figures of speech.

Students with Disabilities
The concepts of character, setting, and conflict may be difficult for some students to comprehend. Put students in groups of three, and have each select a story from Chapter 5. Have groups work together to determine the main character, setting, and conflict of the story. Have students share their findings with the class along with any information that helped them find these elements in other stories.

Guided Practice: Apply

Student Draft

■ Explain that the student draft is continued and completed on this page. Again the draft is annotated and highlighted for the students.

■ Read the draft and annotations aloud and discuss. Refer students to the model Narrative Action Plan on p. 630. Ask students to comment on whether the student writer followed her plan.

▶ Mini-Lesson

How to Add Concrete, Sensory Details

■ Tell students that concrete sensory details can convey important details to their readers about the characters, setting, and plot action of their stories as if the readers were in the narrative themselves. Sensory details are any details that appeal to the senses—taste, touch, hearing, sight, and smell.

■ Explain that the writer has revised her draft to include concrete, sensory details. Read the student's first draft and then compare it with her revised version. Ask students to compare the impressions they get of the mysterious man from the two versions. Ask them which is more effective and why.

Your Turn —————

Add Concrete, Sensory Details Tell students to mark with a star two places in their narrative where sensory details or images can be added to the text. Then, direct them to add the additional text.

Student Draft *continues*

> I ran as fast as my legs could carry me until the only sound audible was my hard breathing and my feet gently destroying the leaves beneath me. I breathed a sigh of relief. An owl hoot-hooted. I caught a glimpse of the bright full moon. The soft crunching began again. A jolt of panic shot up my spine as I saw an approaching shadow. My heart and breathing paused, and I couldn't get my legs to move.
>
> The man, now visible, moved closer, with death written all over his face. As I was building up the courage to scream, the man stopped only an arm's length away from me.
>
> The man stared at me for what seemed like a lifetime and finally asked, "This yours?"
>
> "Yes," I whispered.
>
> He handed me the phone and walked off into the darkness of the woods and I stood staring after him. I walked right after him in order to thank him and after walking for a minute, I stood in front of five tents surrounded by my friends. I never thanked the stranger in the woods.

The **suspense** builds as the man gets closer. →

Ashley uses two lines of **dialogue** to show how the conflict is resolved. →

The **denouement,** or **resolution,** shows the main character safely back with her friends, regretting that she did not thank the stranger. →

Your Turn —————

Add Concrete, Sensory Details With a partner, find sentences in your draft where you can add sensory details that show the setting, situation, or characters instead of simply telling the reader about them. Share your revisions with your partner.

MINI-LESSON ▶ How to Add Concrete, Sensory Details

In her draft, Ashley tells the reader that the man following her has "death written all over his face." She does not use sensory details to describe him, and the reader cannot visualize the characteristics of his face from her words. Since the man is simply returning her cell phone, the words do not fit the context of the narrative. How can Ashley create suspense but not mislead the reader? Concrete, sensory details will help her describe the stranger.

Ashley revised the sentence referring to the man by using concrete, sensory details.

Ashley's Draft of Paragraph Three

The man, now visible, moved closer, with death written all over his face.

Ashley's Revision of Paragraph Three

 (in the moonlight)   *perspiration dripping from his red, puffy face.*
The man, now visible, moved closer, with ~~death written all over his face.~~

Universal Access

ⓔⓛ English Learners

Help students think of words they can use to add sensory details to their narratives. List the headings *sight,* *sound, smell, touch,* and *taste* on the board. Then, under each heading, list words that appeal to each sense. Pronounce each word aloud, and make sure students understand its meaning. Then, have students suggest their own words that fall under the headings.

Advanced Learners

Acceleration Challenge students to make their sensory details more vivid by using figurative language such as similes, metaphors, personification, and hyperbole. Have students review the definitions of these terms in small groups before applying them to their draft.

Proofreading and Publishing

Proofreading

Now that you have evaluated and revised your fictional narrative, it is time to polish and present your short story. Edit your narrative to correct any misspellings, punctuation errors, and problems in sentence structure.

Proofreading Partners Ask two classmates to help you edit. For example, one student can read your paper, looking only for misspellings. Another can read for punctuation errors. By specializing, your editing experts will find errors you may have overlooked.

Grammar Link Eliminating Repetition

Be careful to avoid repeating conjunctions, such as *and*, *but*, and *so*. In the last paragraph of her draft, Ashley uses the word *and* three times. To eliminate repetition, Ashley first circled the repeated word and wrote new, more varied sentences.

He handed me the phone and walked off into the darkness of the woods and I stood staring after him. I walked right after him in order to thank him and after walking for a

suddenly

minute, I stood in front of five tents surrounded by my friends.

Notice how Ashley kept the first *and* that separated verbs and also deleted the two *and*'s that separated complete sentences. These changes make her conclusion more effective.

Publishing

Now it is time to publish your narrative to a wider audience. Here are some ways to share your story:

- Illustrate your story, bind it, and give it as a gift to a friend or family member.
- Have a story event in your class. You and your classmates can form small groups and read your stories aloud to each other.

Reflect on the Process
Thinking about how you wrote your fictional narrative will help you with other writing that you'll do. In your **RWN,** write a short response to each of the following questions.

1. What was the most challenging aspect of writing a fictional narrative?
2. What techniques helped you develop your characters, setting, and plot?
3. How did using a narrative action plan help you? Explain.
4. What have you learned from this workshop that might help you with other types of writing?

🔵 Proofreading Tip

One way to catch errors in grammar, usage, and mechanics is to get some help from a peer. Ask a peer to read your draft for repetition in sentence structure and in the use of words like *and, but,* or *very*. Where should you combine sentences or eliminate overuse of some words?

Submission Ideas

- school newspaper
- school literary magazine
- short story contests
- online literary magazine
- your personal Web page
- class or school Web page

Your Turn _____

Proofread and Publish If you are using a computer grammar-checking program, keep in mind that such programs do not check the correct use and placement of quotation marks. Closely re-read the dialogue in your narrative, and check the placement not only of the quotation marks but also of any punctuation marks that adjoin the quotation marks.

Guided Practice: Apply

Proofreading

Integrating with Grammar, Usage, and Mechanics If students make errors in usage, modifiers, pronouns, or capitalization as they proofread, send them to the Using Pronouns Correctly, Using Modifiers Correctly, Glossary of Usage, and Capital Letters chapters in **Warriner's Handbook**.

Publishing

Brainstorm with students additional ways to publish their narratives.

Reflect on the Process

Have students reflect on the entire writing process as well as their final product. Challenge them to reflect metacognitively about how they can improve and apply what they have learned.

Your Turn _____

Proofread and Publish Have students highlight or underline the revisions and submit their drafts with their final narrative so that you can check to make sure they are following the revision guidelines on p. 632.

🏅 Students Who Use African American Vernacular English

Tell students that in informal English, the present tense form or the past participle form of a verb is used in sentences that express an action that happened in the past. Explain to students that in formal English, the past tense form must be used to signal an action that happened in the past. Show students how to use a dictionary to look up the past tense of the verb *go*. Then, have students use the past tense of go to write the following sentences in formal English:

- The boy go to school yesterday morning. [*The boy went to school yesterday morning.*]
- The school bus gone past the bus stop without stopping to pick me up. [*The school bus went past the bus stop without stopping to pick me up.*]

Guided Practice: Apply

Scoring Rubric

- Tell students that the best way to understand rubrics is to use them to score actual writing.

- Have students work with a partner to evaluate the narratives that they wrote in the Writing Workshop. Ask students to score each other's narratives. Have them include a brief paragraph using the language of the rubric to explain the reasons for the score they gave.

✍ **Holt Six Traits for Writing,** rubrics, prompts, and sample papers

Assess

✍ **UA: Interactive Writer and Speaker,** Fictional Narrative analytical scales and rubric, p. 176

ThinkCentral Online Assessment, Writing Workshop Test

💿 **Teacher One-Stop™,** editable Writing Workshop Test

Reteach

ThinkCentral Online Remediation

🐻 **California Standards, pp. 636–637**

- **Writing Standards 2.1** Write fictional or autobiographical narratives.

Scoring Rubric

You can use the rubric below to evaluate your fictional narrative from the Writing Workshop or your response to the prompt on the next page.

	Narrative Writing	Organization and Focus	Sentence Structure	Conventions
4	• Provides a thoroughly developed plot line, including major and minor characters and a definite setting. • Includes appropriate strategies (e.g., dialogue; suspense; narrative action).	• Clearly addresses all parts of the writing task. • Demonstrates a clear understanding of purpose and audience. • Maintains a consistent point of view, focus, and organizational structure, including the effective use of transitions. • Includes a clearly presented central idea with relevant facts, details, and/or explanations.	• Includes a variety of sentence types.	• Contains few, if any, errors in the conventions of the English language (grammar, punctuation, capitalization, spelling). These errors do not interfere with the reader's understanding of the writing.
3	• Provides an adequately developed plot line, including major and minor characters and a definite setting. • Includes appropriate strategies (e.g., dialogue; suspense; narrative action).	• Addresses all parts of the writing task. • Demonstrates a general understanding of purpose and audience. • Maintains a mostly consistent point of view, focus, and organizational structure, including the effective use of some transitions. • Presents a central idea with mostly relevant facts, details, and/or explanations.	• Includes a variety of sentence types.	• Contains some errors in the conventions of the English language (grammar, punctuation, capitalization, spelling). These errors do not interfere with the reader's understanding of the writing.
2	• Provides a minimally developed plot line, including characters and a setting. • Attempts to use strategies but with minimal effectiveness (e.g., dialogue; suspense; narrative action).	• Addresses only parts of the writing task. • Demonstrates little understanding of purpose and audience. • Maintains an inconsistent point of view, focus, and/or organizational structure, which may include ineffective or awkward transitions that do not unify important ideas. • Suggests a central idea with limited facts, details, and/or explanations.	• Includes little variety in sentence types.	• Contains several errors in the conventions of the English language (grammar, punctuation, capitalization, spelling). These errors may interfere with the reader's understanding of the writing.
1	• Lacks a developed plot line. • Fails to use strategies (e.g., dialogue; suspense; narrative action).	• Addresses only one part of the writing task. • Demonstrates no understanding of purpose and audience. • Lacks a point of view, focus, organizational structure, and transitions that unify important ideas. • Lacks a central idea but may contain marginally related facts, details, and/or explanations.	• Includes no sentence variety.	• Contains serious errors in the conventions of the English language (grammar, punctuation, capitalization, spelling). These errors interfere with the reader's understanding of the writing.

Fictional Narrative Writing Prompts

Students can use the writing prompt on p. 637 in the Student Edition or one of the following prompts.

- Write a fictional narrative that takes place in your school. Remember to include characters and a conflict that is resolved by the end of the story.

- Be the star of your story. Write a narrative in which you are the main character. Introduce a fictional setting and characters for you to interact with.

- Imagine what life will be like in twenty-five years. Now, write a narrative about the future. Include a setting, character, or conflict that you would never expect to find in the present day.

- Conflict does not always have to be between two characters. Write a fictional narrative in which the main character must overcome an internal conflict—a conflict within the character.

Fictional Narrative

When responding to an on-demand fictional narrative prompt, use the models you have read, what you've learned from writing your own fictional narrative, the rubric on page 636, and the steps below.

Writing Standard 2.1 Write **fictional** or autobiographical narratives: **a. Develop a standard plot line** (having a beginning, conflict, rising action, climax, and denouement) **and point of view. b. Develop complex major and minor characters and a definite setting. c. Use a range of appropriate strategies** (e.g., dialogue; suspense; naming of specific narrative action, including movement, gestures, and expressions).

Writing Prompt

Conflict is a part of life and an important element of any story. Think about the kinds of problems or conflicts that sometimes arise between good friends. Perhaps you even remember working through a conflict with your own friend. Write a fictional narrative about two best friends in conflict. Create believable characters and place them in a definite setting. Give specific details about events that lead to a resolution of the conflict.

Study the Prompt

Begin by reading the prompt carefully. Note what is required in your narrative: a conflict, believable characters, and a definite setting. **Tip:** Spend about five minutes studying the prompt.

Plan Your Response

Think of an experience (real or imagined), characters, or a place on which you could base a fictional narrative. Which of these do you know well enough to write about in detail? Once you have settled on your story idea,

- write down the conflict the characters will face, along with events that will lead to a resolution
- write vivid descriptions of each character
- list details about the setting

Tip: Spend about fifteen minutes planning your response.

Respond to the Prompt

Using your notes about conflict, characters, and setting, draft your fictional narrative. Follow these guidelines:

- Start writing, even if you're unsure about how to begin. You can always go back and rewrite the beginning of the story later.
- Write from the same point of view throughout your narrative. Will one of the characters tell the story, or will an all-knowing narrator tell the story?
- Use realistic dialogue to bring your characters to life.

As you are writing, remember to use words that are best for your audience—not too formal. Write as neatly as you can. If your fictional narrative can't be read easily, it may not be scored. **Tip:** Spend about twenty minutes writing your draft.

Improve Your Response

Revising Go back over the key aspects of the prompt. Does your fictional narrative explain the conflict? Have you described the setting? Are your characters believable?

Proofreading Take a few minutes to proofread your story to correct errors in grammar, spelling, punctuation, capitalization, and sentence structure. Make sure all your edits are neat, and erase any stray marks.

Checking Your Final Copy Before you turn in your story, read it one more time to catch any errors you may have missed. You will be glad that you took the extra time for one final review. **Tip:** Save five to ten minutes to improve your paper.

Standards Focus

Objectives

Students will

• present fictional narratives
• use verbal and nonverbal techniques while speaking

Preteach

Speak with a Purpose Remind students that an oral narrative is a story told to someone else. Their oral narratives should have the same literary elements as a written narrative—a plot, setting, characters, and conflict.

Direct Teach

Model the Skill

Plan Your Short Story

Model for students how to analyze and adapt the words in their written narratives so that they sound like natural speech. For example, students may want to change the formal structure of the phrase *I am* to the more informal contraction, *I'm.* Tell students that they can use natural speech while still using the rules and conventions of formal English.

Guided Practice: Apply

Suggest that students read their written narratives aloud to themselves to identify any awkward or stilted phrasing. Remind students to use formal English as they revise their narratives.

 California Standards, pp. 638–639

■ **Listening and Speaking Standard 2.1** Deliver narrative presentations: **a.** Establish a context, standard plot line (having a beginning, conflict, rising action, climax, and denouement), and point of view. **b.** Describe complex major and minor characters and a definite setting. **c.** Use a range of appropriate strategies, including dialogue, suspense, and naming of specific narrative action (e.g., movement, gestures, expressions).

Presenting a Fictional Narrative

> ### Speak with a Purpose
>
> Present a short story as an oral fictional narrative. Practice delivering your short story orally, and then present it to your class.

Think as a Reader/Writer When you prepare a fictional narrative, such as a short story, for oral presentation, you still need to think like a writer. You'll want to hook your listeners with an interesting introduction and give them a clear understanding of the story's plot.

Storytelling is a universal human experience. Ancient epics credited to the Greek writer Homer were undoubtedly shared orally long before he wrote them down. You may remember being told stories as a child, or maybe you've even told some yourself to a younger relative.

Plan Your Story

Story Idea

You may want to adapt your written fictional narrative for oral presentation. However, if you decide to prepare a new story for your presentation, you may again want to start with an idea from personal experience. Also, try to think of a story that will appeal to your classmates.

Plot

As with your written fictional narrative, you'll need to consider the conflict your characters face. You may decide that a physical danger or challenge is more fun to present orally than a conflict that involves a character's internal emotions or struggles.

Characters and Setting

Describing characters and reading their dialogue can be a lot of fun. Try to use the most colorful descriptions you can think of, and prepare believable dialogue that will also be interesting to read and hear aloud. Remember to tell the story from the same point of view throughout. If you start the story from the point of view of a character (first person), don't start telling listeners what other characters are thinking.

You can describe setting much as you did in your written fictional narrative, with the added benefit of using nonverbal language for effect. Try to sprinkle descriptions of setting throughout your story, including in dialogue. You will learn more about using nonverbal language on the next page.

 Reader/Writer Notebook

Use your **RWN** to complete the activities for this workshop.

Resources

UA: Holt Interactive Writer and Speaker, practice and assessment, p. 172

UA: Differentiating Instruction, modified lesson plans, p. 142

Teacher One Stop™, on-level lesson plans and all print resources

Universal Access

EL English Learners

English learners may wish to incorporate words or phrases from their native languages in their fictional narratives. If students choose to do this, remind them that because their audience may not understand the meanings of non-English words, students should include definitions for those words in their narratives. For example, students might write, "In the summer, I loved to go to *la playa*, the beach, with my family."

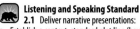
Deliver Your Short Story

Be an Entertainer

In your written story, your only way to describe characters and setting was with written words. In oral storytelling, however, you are free to use some acting techniques. Use the verbal and nonverbal techniques below to liven up your presentation and entertain your audience.

Verbal Technique	Example
Pitch	Change the pitch (rise and fall) of your voice when reading dialogue between different characters or to add emphasis.
Rate	Speak more slowly or more quickly to show excitement in a story or to portray a character's personality.
Volume	Speak loudly enough for listeners in the back to hear you.
Tone	The tone you use will be determined by your story. Is your story serious, humorous, mysterious, or exciting?

Nonverbal Technique	Example
Eye contact	Use eye contact to involve your readers or for humorous effect.
Facial expressions	Show meaning with squints, raised eyebrows, smiles, or frowns.
Gestures	Use gestures, such as shrugs, nods, or hand movements, to show a character's behavior.
Posture	Slouch or stand upright to help portray a character's attitude.

Use Note Cards

You may be allowed to read your fictional narrative directly from your paper. If not, note cards are a useful way to keep your story on track. Write a basic plot outline on your note cards, listing the conflict, main events, and resolution. You might also want to write down specific lines of dialogue, with notes on which nonverbal techniques to use. Practice your verbal and nonverbal techniques in front of a mirror. Finally, rehearse your presentation over and over, using a tape recorder or video camera,

---

A Good Fictional Narrative Presentation

- presents a clear conflict
- uses colorful character descriptions and dialogue
- gives listeners specific details about setting
- uses verbal and nonverbal techniques effectively

🔵 *Speaking Tip*

You may want to alter your voice to respresent different characters, but always speak clearly enough for your listeners to understand you. Standard English is not essential when using dialogue, but avoid using words and phrases that might be unclear to some listeners.

Learn It Online
Pictures can help bring your narrative to life. See how in *MediaScope*, on:

go.hrw.com | H7-639 | Go

Model the Skill

Deliver Your Short Story

Model delivering a fictional narrative using note cards. Model looking down at the note cards for cues and looking up and making eye contact with the audience while speaking.

Guided Practice: Apply

- Remind students to use short prompts on their note cards instead of writing out the whole presentation.
- Advise students to put reminders on their note cards about gestures, tone of voice and keeping eye contact with the audience.

Teaching Tip

Bring the Experience to Life If students struggle to make eye contact with the audience, have them practice their narratives in small groups. Tell students to divide their narratives into a beginning, middle and conclusion. They should try to make eye contact with a different member of the group during each part of their narrative.

English for Academic Success

Remind students to use standard English when telling their story. They should use informal English, such as slang, only when a character is speaking.

Assess

UA: **Holt Interactive Writer and Speaker,** Fictional Narrative Evaluation Guide, p. 176

Learn It Online
The **Digital Storytelling Mini-Site** shows students how to take a personal experience and craft it into a short film-complete with music, images, and special effects.

go.hrw.com | H7-639 | Go

Struggling Readers

Benchmark Students Explain to students that as they organize their narrative and adapt it for a spoken performance, they may want to leave out some of the events that they included in their written narrative.

- Tell students that they may choose to leave out the least important events or any events that do not directly contribute to the audience's understanding of the narrative.
- Model organizing a narrative by writing a few sentences about an autobiographical experience on the board.

- Then, review each sentence with students, and have them determine which sentences are interesting and important, as well as which sentences can be removed from the narrative for the sake of length or clarity.
- For example, you might write, *My family and I went to the lake. We had a great time going for a ride in my brother's sailboat. My brother is 16 years old. At night, we sang songs around the campfire.*
- Explain to students that the third sentence in this paragraph can be left out.

Standards Focus

Objectives

Students will

- review forms of prose
- clarify word meanings
- review fictional and autobiographical narratives and their components

Literary Skills Review

Review

Guided Practice

If necessary, use the following questions to guide students in their reading before they answer the questions at the end of the review.

▶ **Forms of Prose**

Which of the books on the list might you enjoy reading if you were interested in factual events that happened in the past? Explain. ***Possible response:*** *I'd read* The Renaissance and the New World *because it is nonfiction and takes place in the 1700s.*

How is *Boy* similar to *Long Walk to Freedom?* ***Possible response:*** *They are both autobiographies.*

Test-Taking Tip

Suggest that students attempt to answer multiple-choice questions before they read the answer choices. After they formulate a response, they should look at the answer choices to find the one that best matches their answer.

California Standards, pp. 640–641

- **Reading Standard 3.1** Articulate the expressed purposes and characteristics of different forms of prose (e.g., short story, novel, novella, essay).

Literary Skills Review

Forms of Prose **Directions:** Read the Key to Abbreviations and the following list of prose works. Then choose the best answer to each question.

A Prose Reading List

Key to Abbreviations				
E = Easy	A = Average	C = Challenging	F = Fiction	NF = Nonfiction

Anderson, Laurie Halse. *Fever 1793.* **A, F** Sixteen-year-old Matilda Cook confronts a citywide outbreak of yellow fever in this accurately detailed novel set in late-eighteenth-century Philadelphia.

Brooks, Polly Schoyer. *Queen Eleanor: Independent Spirit of the Medieval World.* **A, NF** This biography presents an engaging portrait of Eleanor of Aquitaine, one of the most influential figures of the Middle Ages.

Caselli, Giovanni. *The Renaissance and the New World.* **C, NF** The author looks at Renaissance advancements in commerce and technology that became the foundation of eighteenth-century life in England and America.

Dahl, Roald. *Boy.* **C, NF** With a humorous touch, the renowned author tells about his childhood years in England.

Mandela, Nelson. *Long Walk to Freedom.* **A, NF** Mandela reflects on a lifetime of commitment to overturning apartheid in South Africa.

Saint-Exupéry, Antoine de. *The Little Prince.* **E, F** In this fable, a stranded pilot meets a little boy who recounts his fantastic adventures on various planets.

Soto, Gary. *Baseball in April.* **E, F** In this collection of short stories, one story tells how Michael and Jesse fail to make the Little League team but still find a way to play the game they love.

Taylor, Mildred D. *Song of the Trees.* **A, F** In this novella, the Logan family must prevent a businessman from destroying the forest that has brought joy to their lives.

Yep, Laurence. "Puzzle Pieces." **A, NF** In this essay, Laurence Yep tells about how he became a writer.

Zindel, Paul. *The Pigman.* **C, F** In this prize-winning novel, John and Lorraine are dissatisfied with their lives until they meet Mr. Pignati, who teaches them to cherish every moment.

Resources for Skills and Standards Review

Chapter 5 Resources, Chapter Standards Mastery, Chapter Vocabulary Review, p. 62

UA: Differentiating Instruction, below-level Chapter Standards Mastery

Teacher One Stop™, editable Chapter Standards Mastery

Focus on Standards

ThinkCentral Online Assessment, Chapter Standards Mastery

ThinkCentral Online Remediation

Holt Online Essay Scoring

Assess

Answers and Explanations

1. **C** *Both A and D are true of fiction but not nonfiction. B is not true of either form of prose.*

2. **A** *Fever 1793 is set in the past, but the characters and details are fictional. The Little Prince is a fable (B). The Pigman is not set in the past (C), and "Puzzle Pieces" is an autobiography (D).*

3. **D** *Boy is different because it is an autobiography. Both texts relate facts about real people and events (A), are about events of the past (C), and are nonfiction (B).*

4. **A** *An autobiography is a nonfiction account of the author's life. A biography is a nonfiction account of someone else's life (C).*

5. **A** *Song of the Trees is a made-up story. Both texts include a conflict (C) and have a theme (D). Neither of them is written as an essay (B).*

Timed Writing

6. *The two selections are both about the life of a real person. Boy contains stories about the author's life, so it is an autobiography. The book about Queen Eleanor is a biography written by someone else.*

7. *They differ in length. A novella is longer than a short story, and a novel is longer than a novella.*

Reteach

 ThinkCentral Online Remediation

---

1. Which one of the following statements is true of both fiction and nonfiction?
   - **A** They are not based on actual events.
   - **B** They are not longer than 100 pages.
   - **C** They often reveal important truths.
   - **D** They must have a conflict.

2. If *Queen Eleanor: Independent Spirit of the Medieval World* were rewritten as fiction, it would be *most* like
   - **A** *Fever 1793.*
   - **B** *The Little Prince.*
   - **C** *The Pigman.*
   - **D** "Puzzle Pieces."

3. Roald Dahl's *Boy* is similar to *The Renaissance and the New World* except that *Boy*
   - **A** relates facts about real people and events.
   - **B** is written as nonfiction.
   - **C** is about events of the past.
   - **D** is about the life of the author.

4. *Long Walk to Freedom* is an autobiography, the story of a person's life written
   - **A** by that person.
   - **B** in a fictional manner.
   - **C** by someone else.
   - **D** to teach history.

5. *Song of the Trees* is different from *Long Walk to Freedom* because *Song of the Trees*
   - **A** is a made-up story.
   - **B** is written as an essay.
   - **C** includes a conflict.
   - **D** has a theme, or message.

Timed Writing

6. How are *Boy* and *Queen Eleanor: Independent Spirit of the Medieval World* similar? How are they different? Be sure to mention in your response which form of prose each book represents.

7. Describe what makes a short story, a novel, and a novella different from one another.

Word-Attack Skills Mini-Lesson

Review Use the activity below to check students' grasp of the word-attack skills taught in this collection.

Activity Display these lists of words containing the vowel digraphs *ai* and *ea*. Have students decide whether the word contains a long vowel sound or a short vowel sound.

1. remain [*long*]
2. against [*short*]
3. exclaim [*long*]
4. waist [*long*]
5. threat [*short*]
6. defeat [*long*]
7. bread [*short*]
8. clean [*long*]

✔ For additional instruction and strategies, see **ThinkCentral, Teacher Access**.

Vocabulary Skills Review

Vocabulary Skills Review

Reading Standard 1.3 Clarify word meanings through the use of definition, example, restatement, or contrast.

Context Clues
Directions: Use context clues to help you determine the correct meaning of the italicized words. Then, choose the best answer.

Assess

Answers and Explanations

1. **C** *The word* wild *suggests that the fighters' punches were fast and frenzied.*

2. **D** *If something is* ominous, *it warns that something bad is going to happen.* Foretold *gives the idea of a warning, and* frightened *implies something bad happened.*

3. **C** Shelter *is the only option usually associated with protection from the elements.*

4. **A** *None of the other options are a synonym for* dispute.

5. **B** *The words* gymnasts *and amazing feats* suggest flexibility.

6. **C** Ripe *and* tasty *suggest that something is good enough to eat, and* solid *is unrelated.*

7. **A** Regimented *means followed a routine, which is related to* ritual.

Academic Vocabulary

8. **A** *The two stories combined have a stronger effect on the reader.*

9. **B** Structure *refers to how something is arranged.*

Reteach

 ThinkCentral Online Remediation

California Standards, p. 642

- **Reading Standard 1.3** Clarify word meanings through the use of definition, example, restatement, or contrast.

---

1. The crowd's reaction was as *frenzied* as the flurry of punches thrown by the fighters.
   - A sloppy
   - B ridiculous
   - C wild
   - D dangerous

2. The *ominous* sky foretold a stormy night, frightening the children.
   - A hectic
   - B dark
   - C long
   - D threatening

3. The jungle's lack of protection made it a poor *refuge*.
   - A happiness
   - B clothing
   - C shelter
   - D food

4. They didn't agree on much, but this *dispute* promised to drive them even farther apart.
   - A argument
   - B difficulty
   - C separation
   - D idea

5. Gymnasts' bodies are *supple*, a necessity for performing such amazing feats.
   - A brittle
   - B flexible
   - C abnormal
   - D breakable

6. Ian could not eat his cereal because the milk in the refrigerator had become *rancid*.
   - A ripe
   - B tasty
   - C rotten
   - D solid

7. Thiago is normally very regimented, but this morning he chose to sleep in rather than adhere to his usual morning *ritual*.
   - A routine
   - B instructions
   - C agreement
   - D business

Academic Vocabulary

Directions: Answer the following questions about Academic Vocabulary words from this chapter:

8. Taken alone, Davis's and Green's stories are each touching. Combined, the stories had greater *impact*. Here, *impact* means
   - A effect.
   - B importance.
   - C fearlessness.
   - D interest.

9. When you study the *structure* of a poem, you look at how the poem's elements are
   - A commented upon.
   - B arranged.
   - C interpreted.
   - D imagined.

Vocabulary Review

Use this activity to assess whether students have retained the collection Vocabulary. Ask students to choose the word from the box that fits the context of each sentence.

incessantly	withered	pensively
incredulously	dispute	

1. When I told my sister that aliens had invaded our classroom, she looked at me _____. and I couldn't make her believe me. [*incredulously*]

2. Andrea talked _____, about her new puppy the day after she got him. [*incessantly*]

3. When my brother ruined my favorite CD, we had a _____ over when he would replace it. [*dispute*]

4. I looked at the blank piece of paper _____ as I thought about how to start my essay. [*pensively*]

5. The entire garden _____ and died in the summer heat. [*withered*]

Writing Skills Review

Fictional Narrative **Directions:** Read the following paragraph from a short story. Then, answer each question that follows.

Writing Standard 2.1 Write fictional or autobiographical **narratives:** **a.** Develop a standard plot line (having a beginning, conflict, rising action, climax, and denouement) and point of view. **b.** Develop complex major and minor characters and a definite setting. **c.** Use a range of appropriate strategies (e.g., dialogue; suspense; naming of specific narrative action, including movement, gestures, and expressions).

---

(1) Breannah stood in the goal, shifting her weight from one foot to the other, as a swarm of red jerseys nudged the soccer ball toward her. (2) A lone blue-clad defender tried and failed to cut off the attack. (3) Now no one stood between her and the lanky star forward of the Red Hots. (4) The forward kicked the ball, and Breannah leaped to her right. (5) The ball whooshed past her left ear and into the net. (6) She rose slowly and brushed herself off, ignoring the cheers from the Red Hots' bleachers. (7) Next time, Breannah thought, she would be ready.

---

1. What strategy does the writer use to develop the main character?

  A dialogue spoken by the character

  B description of the character's appearance

  C description of the character's thoughts and actions

  D explanation of how other people respond to the character

2. What details does the writer use to show point of view in this passage?

  A The words *she* and *her* and the main character's thoughts are used to show third-person-limited point of view.

  B The word *I* is used to show first-person point of view.

  C The word *you* is used to show second-person point of view.

  D Information about other characters' thoughts is used to show third-person-omniscient point of view.

3. If this passage occurs near the story's beginning, what might the writer do in later passages to build toward the climax?

  A summarize previous events in the story

  B describe additional problems that add to the story's conflict

  C change the point of view to include other characters' views of events

  D describe the setting in detail

4. If a speaker were telling this story out loud, why might she begin by explaining that the story is based on a friend's experience playing soccer?

  A to point out the story's climax

  B to create a mood of suspense

  C to establish a context for the story

  D to include realistic dialogue

Writing Skills Review

Assess

Answers and Explanations

1. *C* *The writer develops Breannah's character by describing her thoughts about the game and her actions as goalie. There is no dialogue (A) in the passage. The writer does not focus on Breannah's appearance (B), nor does she focus on how others respond to her (D).*

2. *A* *The writer uses the words she and her and tells only Breannah's thoughts. The words I (B) and you (C) are not used, and we do not learn others' thoughts (D).*

3. *B* *Problems that add to a story's conflict build toward its climax. A summary of events (A), change in point of view (C), or additional setting description (D) have nothing to do with the climax of a story.*

4. *C* *Explaining what this story was based on would establish a context for it. This fact says nothing about the story's climax (A) and does not necessarily create a suspenseful mood (B). Likewise, it does not add dialogue to the story (D).*

Reteach

 ThinkCentral Online Remediation

California Standards, p. 643

■ **Writing Standard 2.1** Write fictional or autobiographical narratives: **a.** Develop a standard plot line (having a beginning, conflict, rising action, climax, and denouement) and point of view. **b.** Develop complex major and minor characters and a definite setting. **c.** Use a range of appropriate strategies (e.g., dialogue; suspense; naming of specific narrative action, including movement, gestures, and expressions).

Application **Homework**
Illustrate a Fictional Narrative

For homework, have interested students create one or more visuals or illustrations to go with the fictional narratives they wrote in the Writing Workshop. Allow them to use any medium they choose, including paint, pencil, or colored pencil. Tell students that their visuals should provide insight into character traits or convey aspects of the story's plot.

Extension
Create a Comic Strip

Tell students that comic strips have similar features to short stories, including dialogue, characterization, conflict, and resolution. However, they are shorter and have much less writing than stories, and they tell much of the story through the use of visuals. Assist interested students in converting their short stories into comic strips. Provide materials such as markers and colored pencils for students to illustrate their comics.

If students enjoyed the themes and topics explored in this collection, you might recommend the following books for independent reading.

Assessment Options

The following projects can help you evaluate and assess your students' outside work. Videotapes or audiotapes of completed projects may be included in students' portfolios.

Explore a Poet's Process

If students are inspired by *A Writing Kind of Day,* they may want to put Fletcher's descriptions of a poet's writing process to work in their own writing. Suggest that students take notes on Fletcher's book in their Reader/Writer Notebook, as well as practicing writing their own lines or full poems.

Create a Character Study

■ The fiction selection *Somewhere in the Darkness* contains some complex characters. Have students work independently to create a character study of their favorite character from books.

■ Discuss different elements that can go into a character study, such as the character's name, occupation, unique characteristics, conflicts, and motivations.

■ Suggest that students create an image of their character to accompany their character study.

Read On

For Independent Reading

Fiction

Somewhere in the Darkness

While suffering from a kidney disease and confined to a prison hospital, Cephus "Crab" Little decides to make up for lost time with his son Jimmy in *Somewhere in the Darkness* by Walter Dean Myers. After Crab is released from prison, he and his son journey together to Crab's hometown in Arkansas, where Jimmy's growing understanding of his father's past helps him come to terms with his father and himself.

A Writing Kind of Day: Poems for Young Poets

Ralph Fletcher steps into the mind of a young writer—one who is thinking imaginatively about metaphors and plagiarism, writer's block, and subject matter. From this point of view, Fletcher looks closely at the writing process and describes how a young person can work magic with images and words. *A Writing Kind of Day* is your invitation to pick up a pen and paper and take the playfulness and power of poetry into your own hands.

Brian's Song

The 1971 television movie *Brian's Song* is still considered by many to be one of the best TV movies ever made. The movie tells the story of the real-life relationship between Chicago Bears teammates Brian Piccolo and Gale Sayers. Despite the fact that Sayers is black and Piccolo is white, they become roommates on the road and eventually close friends, especially when Sayers is injured and Piccolo helps him recover. The screenplay by William Blinn conveys the moving story so well that you'll feel as if you've seen the movie even if you haven't.

A Fury of Motion: Poems for Boys

Forty-six poems, all written by Charles Ghigna, explore scrimmage, playground showdowns, and loneliness, among other themes. Ghigna has provided a balance of humorous and serious works, using both free verse and rhymes. And even though the title says "Poems for Boys," girls will find that *A Fury of Motion* is also for them—and for adults as well.

Selection Readability

Estimated Word Counts and Readabilities of Read On Books

Fiction	Estimated Word Counts	Readability
Somewhere in the Darkness	45,500	Accessible
Brian's Song	18,445	Accessible
A Writing Kind of Day	1,600	Accessible
A Fury of Motion	2,754	Accessible

Nonfiction

Carl Sandburg: Adventures of a Poet

Besides being a great twentieth-century American poet, Carl Sandburg was a hobo, a soldier, a reporter, a musician, a historian, a husband, and a father. All of his experiences influenced his writing, especially his admiration for President Abraham Lincoln and the poet Walt Whitman. The biographer Penelope Niven has written eleven short essays on various aspects of Sandburg's life and has paired each essay with his poetry or prose. *Carl Sandburg: Adventures of a Poet* will give you a well-rounded introduction to the beloved man of letters.

Long Road to Freedom: Journey of the Hmong

In *Long Road to Freedom*, Linda Barr recounts the escape of the Hmong people from their Southeast Asian homeland to life in the United States and other countries. In this book, you'll learn about the Hmong people's unique cultural traditions as well as their strength of spirit.

Muhammad Ali: Legends in Sports

Matt Christopher's book *Muhammad Ali: Legends in Sports* introduces you to a true legend. It discusses the impact the former heavyweight champion has had inside and outside the ring. In the 1960s, Ali proved himself to be a strong supporter of civil rights and a devoutly religious person. Today, he works for charitable causes, one of which is the search for a cure for Parkinson's disease.

Jim Thorpe: Original All-American

Written from his subject's point of view, Joseph Bruchac's book tells the life story of Jim Thorpe, Olympic gold medalist, football star, and American Indian hero. In the 1912 Olympics, he set long-standing world records in the pentathlon and decathlon. This biography is not a typical sports-hero tale—it also delves into such issues as racism and money's effect on sports.

Learn It Online
Explore other novels and find tips for choosing, reading, and studying books at:

go.hrw.com | H7-645 | **Go**

Estimated Word Counts and Readabilities Scores of Read On Books

Nonfiction	Estimated Word Counts	Readability
Long Road to Freedom: Journey of the Hmong	4,424	Easily Accessible
Jim Thorpe: An American Original	62,786	Challenging
Carl Sandburg: Adventures of a Poet	4,953	Accessible
Muhammad Ali: Legends in Sports	21,726	Accessible

Learn It Online
The **NovelWise** mini-site includes instruction on choosing, reading, and analyzing novels; it also contains a catalogue of book summaries, study guides, teaching guides, and PowerPoint presentations.

go.hrw.com | H7-645 | **Go**

Features highlighted in **yellow** constitute a suggested minimum course of study.

Introducing The Skills

Selection or Feature	Grade–Level Standards
Informational Text Focus: What Is Reading for Life?	**Reading Standard 2.2:** Consumer, workplace, and public documents
Reading Skills Focus: How Do I Locate Information in Documents?	**Reading Standard 2.2:** Consumer, workplace, and public documents
Reading Model: So You Want to Start a Club… Tips from the Association of School Clubs (Accessible, Lexile N/A) **Skills in Action:** Wrap Up	**Reading Standard 2.2:** Consumer, workplace, and public documents

Applying The Skills

Selection or Feature	Grade–Level Standards
Informational Text Focus: **Public Documents**	**Reading Standard 2.2:** Consumer, workplace, and public documents
• **Casting Call** (Accessible, Lexile N/A)	
• **Hollywood Beat** (Accessible, Lexile 920) • **Application for Permission to Work** (Accessible, Lexile N/A)	
Informational Text Focus: **Workplace Documents**	**Reading Standard 2.2:** Consumer, workplace, and public documents
• **Letter from Casting Director** (Accessible; Lexile 1030)	
• **Talent Instructions** (Accessible, Lexile 650) • **Work Emails** (Accessible, Lexile N/A)	
Informational Text Focus: **Consumer Documents**	**Reading Standard 2.2:** Consumer, workplace, and public documents
• **BART System Map** (Accessible, Lexile N/A)	
• **BART Bicycle Rules** (Accessible, Lexile 1030) • **BART Ticket Guide** (Accessible, Lexile N/A) • **BART Schedule** (Accessible, Lexile N/A)	
Informational Text Focus: **Technical Directions**	**Reading Standard 2.5:** Follow technical directions
• **How to Change a Flat Tire** (Accessible, Lexile 1100)	

6 Reading for Life

Mastering The Skills

Selection or Feature	Grade–Level Standards
Writing Workshop: Multimedia Presentation: Public Service Announcement	**Writing Standard 1.2:** Support statements and claims. **Writing Standard 1.3:** Note taking, outlining, and summarizing **Writing Standard 1.4:** Inquire, investigate, and research **Writing Standard 1.6:** Word-processing skills and publishing programs; databases and spreadsheets **Writing Standard 1.7:** Revise **Writing Standard 2.4:** Support a proposition or proposal.
Standards Practice: Informational Skills Review	**Reading Standard 2.2:** Consumer, workplace, and public documents

Daily and Weekly Support

- **Reader/Writer Notebook**
- **Reading and Writing Transparencies**
- **Weekly Standards Review Transparencies**
- **Family Involvement Activities in Five Languages**
- **Language Handbook Worksheets**
- **Holt Virtual File Cabinet for Language Arts**
- **Spelling Lessons and Activities**

Assessment Resources

- **Chapter 6 Resources**, Chapter Diagnostic Test; Selection Standards Checks, Chapter Standards Mastery
- **Universal Access: Differentiating Instruction**, leveled assessment
- **Formal Assessment**, Progress Monitoring Test 5
- **English-Language Conventions Progress-Monitoring Test**, Chapters 1–15
- **ThinkCentral Online Assessment**

Print Resources for Universal Access

	On-Level Learners	English Learners	Struggling Readers/Writers	Students Who Use African American Vernacular Engish	Advanced Learners	Students with Disabilities
Chapter 6 Resources practice and assessment for all selections and features	✔				✔	
Universal Access: Holt Interactive Reader interactive readings for Minimum-Course-of-Study Selections		✔	✔	✔		✔
Holt Interactive Reader for English Language Development adaptations of Minimum-Course-of-Study Selections		✔				
Universal Access: Differentiating Instruction modified lesson plans, graphic organizers, and leveled assessment		✔	✔	✔		✔
Universal Access: Resources for Teaching Advanced Students lesson plans for Minimum-Course-of-Study Selections					✔	
Universal Access: Supporting Instruction in Five Languages translations of selection summaries and key terms		✔				
Universal Access: Holt Interactive Writer and Speaker practice and assessment	✔	✔	✔	✔	✔	✔
Language and Sentence Skills Practice for Warriner's Handbook Chapters 1–15	✔				✔	
Universal Access: Developmental Language and Sentence Skills Practice for Warriner's Handbook Chapters 1–15		✔	✔	✔		✔

Technology Resources

Assessment Resources

Teacher Management Resources

Student Edition Extension Activities

Student Edition Support

Find all of Holt's technology resources at go.hrw.com. Technology resources are also listed as point-of-use in the wrap; below are our featured components for Chapter 6.

Teacher Management Resources

ThinkCentral, Teacher Access
Teacher One Stop™
Holt Professional Learning for Language Arts

Spotlight on Teacher One Stop™

The Teacher One Stop™ contains all of the print resources that you will need when using *Holt Literature and Language Arts.* Online suggestions:
- Use the Exam View Assessment Suite to access editable banks of questions; create customized tests for your classes.

Student Edition Support

PowerNotes
ThinkCentral, Student Access
Student One Stop™
Interactive Reading Workshops
Interactive Graphic Organizers
Writers' Lives
Holt Audio Library
Holt Audio Library: Selections and Summaries in Spanish

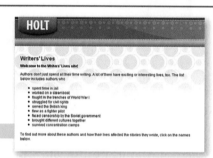

Spotlight on Writers' Lives

Find out more about the writers that appear in *Holt Literature and Language Arts* with the Writers' Lives site!

Student Edition Extension Activities

Digital Storytelling Mini-Site
NovelWise Mini-Site
MediaScope Mini-Site
WordSharp: An Interactive Vocabulary Tutor
Writing and Research in a Digital Age
GrammarNotes
WritingNotes
Literature Links
Holt Audio Tutor for English Language Development

Spotlight on Writing and Research in a Digital Age

These interactive lessons will take your students through the research process, and address the use of technology in research and publication.
- Use these presentations to help your students to research with and cite online resources.

Assessment Resources

ThinkCentral Online Assessment
Holt Online Essay Scoring
ThinkCentral Online Remediation

5. When a writer uses a **first-person narrator**, the story —

○ A does not contain dialogue between the characters
→ ○ B is told by one of the characters
○ C does not contain a main character
○ D has only one character

Correct Answer: B

7.1.5
point of view

Spotlight on ThinkCentral Online Assessment

Find the Chapter 6 Diagnostic and Summative tests here, correlated to standards covered in this chapter. The individual diagnostic reporting will let you see the concepts in this chapter for which each student might need extra help.

Reading for Life

6

The wrap for these selections includes specific ideas and strategies from *Holt Literature and Language Arts* authors.

From the Author

For Writing Workshop: Multimedia Presentation, p. 687
Students should learn that images and sounds used in presentations should be limited to those that are directly connected to the presentation. Having students construct storyboards that map out the multimedia elements of their presentations can help them determine which elements are essential and which can be discarded.

Sarah Kajder

Teacher to Teacher

Preteach When introducing students to consumer documents, I bring in the instruction manual from a new "toy" of mine (for example, my MP3 player). I make an overhead, or scan the pages, so that every student can read the selected pages. I begin with the table of contents and help the students become familiar with the structure of documents.

Direct teach Once I feel each student is familiar with the document's structure, I use specific pages and make a game out of analyzing the content. For instance, using the table of contents, I ask, "In what section would I find . . . ?", "On what page can I learn more about . . . ?" or perhaps, "Where can I go if I am having trouble with . . . . ?"

Assess I ask students to bring in their own instruction manual, along with five questions (with their answers) for a classmate to answer. If some cannot locate a manual, I model how to find these documents online. I also have photocopied samples available for students to borrow. After students exchange documents and questions, I have them work in pairs to analyze how these documents differ from other nonfiction pieces (for example, an encyclopedia entry or magazine article) and what kind of questions proved most difficult.

Diane Tyson
Tustin, California

Holt Professional Learning

Visit the ThinkCentral, Teacher Access to link to Holt's Professional Learning site for English/Language Arts teachers. This site features:

- Videos that share the insights of *Holt Literature and Language Arts* program authors and consultants and demonstrate proven classroom strategies with master teachers
- Study guides for publications by our authors and consultants
- Informative articles and useful Web links
- Help in planning your department's professional learning sessions
- A handbook for new teachers

Becoming a Tech-Savvy Teacher
with Sara Kajder

VIDEO PRODUCTS

Strategies for Helping Struggling Readers
with Kylene Beers

Effective Vocabulary Instruction
with Carol Jago and Kylene Beers

Developing Critical Thinking About Literature
with Carol Jago and Deborah Appleman

Teaching Students to Revise, Not Recopy
with Linda Rief

Teaching English Learners
with Robin Scarcella

Using Literature Circles
with Harvey Daniels

Teaching On-Demand Writing Skills
with Leila Christenbury

Managing the Heterogeneous Classroom
with Leila Christenbury and Patrick Schwarz

Teaching Narrative and Expository Texts
with Judith Irvin and Deborah Appleman

Becoming a Tech-Savvy Teacher
with Sara Kajder

Re-engaging the Disengaged Student
with Alfred Tatum

Teaching Grammar in Context
with Amy Benjamin

CHAPTER 6

California Standards

Reading Comprehension
(Focus on Informational Materials)

- **2.2** Locate information by using a variety of consumer, workplace, and public documents.
- **2.5** Understand and explain the use of a simple mechanical device by following technical directions.

Analyzing Visuals

Extension Activity Ask students to look at these photographs and determine what they all have in common. As a group, what message might these photographs send?

Possible response: All the students in these photos are reading something, whether it is in a book, in a newspaper, on a bulletin board, or on a computer screen. This shows how reading comes in many different forms and is important to everyday life.

Chapter Resources

On Course: Mapping Instruction

Chapter 6 Resources

Warriner's Handbook
- Chapter 14, Punctuation
- Chapter 15, Punctuation

PowerNotes

Teacher One Stop™

Formal Assessment, Progress Monitoring Test 5

English-Language Conventions
Progress-Monitoring Tests

Holt Virtual File Cabinet for Language Arts, grammar, reading, and vocabulary resources

Holt Pronunciation Resources
- Phoneme Sounds and Spellings
- Support for Speakers of African American Vernacular English

ThinkCentral Online Assessment

ThinkCentral Online Remediation

CHAPTER 6

Reading for Life

INFORMATIONAL TEXT FOCUS
Consumer, Workplace, and Public Documents/ Following Technical Directions

California Standards
Here are the Grade 7 standards you will work toward mastering in Chapter 6.

Reading Comprehension (Focus on Informational Materials)
2.2 Locate information by using a variety of consumer, workplace, and public documents.

2.5 Understand and explain the use of a simple mechanical device by following technical directions.

Writing Applications (Genres and Their Characteristics)
2.4 Write persuasive compositions:

a. State a clear position or perspective in support of a proposition or proposal.
b. Describe the points in support of the proposition, employing well-articulated evidence.
c. Anticipate and address reader concerns and counterarguments.

"There is an art of reading, as well as an art of thinking, and an art of writing."

—Benjamin Disraeli

What Do **You** Think
How can reading help you to make decisions or solve problems?

* **Learn It Online**
Let *PowerNotes* show you the information in this collection in a whole new way at:

go.hrw.com H7-647 **Go**

Objectives

Students will learn how to read and interpret consumer, workplace, and public documents.

Build Background Have students think about an everyday process such as applying for volunteer work or planning a trip. Then, ask students to make a list of all of the different types of documents they might have to read or fill out during the process. Explain that these are examples of reading for life.

Consumer Documents

■ Divide students into four groups. Have one group discuss advertisements, one discuss schedules, one discuss labels, and one discuss technical directions. Have groups consider why their type of document might be important and what consequences could arise from not reading the document.

■ Point out that ads may contain information that is subjective or biased, but schedules and manuals contain objective information.

California Standards, pp. 648–649

■ **Reading Standard 2.2** Locate information by using a variety of consumer, workplace, and public documents.

Informational Text Focus

by **Linda Rief** and **Sheri Henderson**

What Is Reading for Life?

Your sister is studying the manual for getting a driver's license. Your dad is filling out the healthcare renewal form at work. You are reading aloud the manufacturer's directions to help your mom assemble a bookcase. These are all examples of reading for life. Analyzing this kind of everyday writing helps you understand how to locate and interpret information that's often crucial to your daily life.

The purpose of **consumer, workplace, and public documents** is to provide information. These documents are everywhere, and that is a good thing. Without them, a society as complex as ours would not be able to function well. Because these documents contain information that is essential for all of us, they deserve—and require—our close attention and careful reading. The information they contain can be as simple as an advertisement for a new movie or as complex as a warning about a prescription medication.

Consumer Documents

On most days, you probably use **consumer documents** to locate a variety of information.

- **Advertisements** tell you what is available for purchase and how much it costs, what movie just came out on DVD, and when your favorite store is having a sale.
- Service providers publish **schedules** of movie showtimes; school lunch menus; TV programs; and bus, train, or plane timetables.
- **Labels** on the goods you buy give you information about what you are buying. Labels on packaged food list the food's ingredients and nutritional value. Labels on shoes declare which parts are synthetic and which parts are not. Labels on clothing tell you what fabric the article is made of and how to care for it.
- Mechanical and electronic equipment comes with **warranties, contracts, instruction manuals,** and **technical directions.** These guide you in the safe and proper use of products. Whenever you encounter consumer information, especially technical directions, it is a good idea to read them through slowly and carefully. A manufacturer is required only to include the information. It's up to you to read and understand it. Informed consumers know that it's better to read consumer documents *before* they use a product.

Workplace Documents

As their name suggests, **workplace documents** are informational texts you encounter in a job. Your first communication with a possible employer may be through a **business letter,** in which you state your qualifications and request a job interview. A business letter isn't always necessary, however. Sometimes, you may be asked to

Resources

Chapter 6 Resources, Informational Text Skill Builder, p. 3

PowerNotes, interactive lesson presentations with activities

Teacher One Stop™, on-level lesson plans and all print resources

Universal Access

English Learners/Struggling Readers
English for Academic Success Help students learn unfamiliar terms in the Informational Text Focus by explaining each term's definition and using it in context.

- Explain to students that *consume* means "use up." A *consumer* is someone who uses goods or services. You might say: "Tracy loves to buy comic books. She is a *consumer* of comic books."

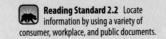

Reading Standard 2.2 Locate information by using a variety of consumer, workplace, and public documents.

simply complete an **application.** When you are hired, you may be asked to sign an **employment contract,** which spells out what is expected of you as an employee and what you can expect in return from your employer. You may need to provide a Social Security number, a **work permit** showing that you are allowed to work, and a **tax form** for your employer to use when calculating taxes to deduct from your wages. You may also be given **insurance forms** to fill out and sign. To help you succeed in your new job, your employer may provide an **employee manual,** a set of rules and instructions related to the job.

When one employee needs to communicate information to another employee, he or she will usually do so through a **memorandum,** often called a *memo* for short. Businesses frequently use **e-mail memos** to communicate because e-mail is fast, convenient, and easily retrieved.

The number and types of workplace documents you encounter will depend on the kind of work you do. One thing is certain, though: Whatever kind of work you do, workplace documents will play an important role in helping you succeed.

Public Documents

If you wanted to learn about sports programs at local parks, is there a way to find out? If you wanted to know the salary of the mayor of your community, could you obtain that information? The answer to both of these questions is *yes.* You can locate the answers in **public documents.**

Public documents supply citizens with information that may be of interest to them. Public documents are issued by schools, churches, government agencies, the courts, libraries, and fire and police departments, to name just a few.

Typically, most citizens do not read the public

documents put out by the government, the military, and nonprofit agencies or groups. Instead, they read newspaper articles that report on or summarize the documents. Whether you read a document itself or a newspaper account of its contents, public documents exist to help you form a clear picture of a situation.

The Readings Ahead . . .

The following pages will give you some practice reading various kinds of consumer, workplace, and public documents. You'll also get a chance to follow some technical directions. Challenge yourself as you read to see how well you can locate the major information in all of the documents.

Your Turn Analyze Documents

1. Keep track of all of the reading you do in a twenty-four-hour period that is neither schoolwork nor pleasure reading. Each time you read an informational text, write a list of **what** you read and **why** in your *Reader/ Writer Notebook.* Put a *P* next to the public documents, a *W* next to the workplace documents, and a *C* next to the consumer documents.

2. What type of document would you use to learn how to install software on a computer?

3. What type of document would explain what you should wear to a certain job?

✳ Learn It Online
Try the *PowerNotes* version of this lesson on:

go.hrw.com   H7-649   **Go**

Workplace Documents

- Explain that some jobs may not require employees to use business letters or memos, but nearly every job uses tax forms, employee handbooks, and contracts.

- Tell students that most workplace documents will contain only objective information, or facts.

Public Documents

- Identify any public documents that appear in your classroom or school building. Point out to students that school newsletters, lists of school rules, and information about classes and activities are all public documents.

- Have small groups of students list the types of public documents that might be distributed by a school, a library, a police department, or a government agency. Then, have groups compare their results and discuss any differences and similarities they see between public documents from different sources.

Check for Understanding

Your Turn _____
Possible responses:

1. *I read a flier about the hours of operation of my local library (P). I read my sister's summer job application (W). I read a brochure from the sporting goods store that advertised discounts (C).*

2. *a consumer document (technical direction)*

3. *a workplace document (employee manual)*

Reteach

ThinkCentral Online Remediation

✳ Learn It Online
For a multimedia version of the instruction found on this page, use the **PowerNotes** Informational Text Focus presentation.

go.hrw.com   H7-649   **Go**

- Tell students that a *warranty* is a document that makes a guarantee or promise about an item that a consumer has purchased. You might say, "The *warranty* that came with my computer says that if my computer breaks, the company will fix it for free."

- Explain that *memorandums* are short, usually informal notes or written messages from one person to another. You might say, "Carlos sent his team a *memorandum* that explained the next day's schedule of events."

Advanced Learners

Acceleration Have students review the types of informational documents and consider whether each type of document should always be considered trustworthy and credible. Remind students that the document's author might have reasons for writing that he or she does not reveal to the reader of the document. Then, have students discuss what these reasons might be.

Objectives

Students will

- skim and scan informational texts
- preview texts prior to reading
- interpret and use graphic aids
- use strategies to clarify meaning

Preteach

Build Skills Ask students to name strategies they use to read fictional texts, such as re-reading or making predictions. Discuss whether these strategies would be useful for reading informational texts.

Direct Teach

Previewing the Text

Model previewing an informational text by conducting a step-by-step preview of the Reading Skills Focus essay. First, read the essay's title and subtitle aloud. Then, identify the essay's subheadings and explain what these pieces of text reveal about the essay's purpose and structure. Note the boldface terms in the essay and discuss with students what the presence of these boldface terms might mean. Finally, point out the essay's charts and images, and explain what they might have to do with the text of the essay.

 California Standards, pp. 650–651

- **Reading Standard 2.2** Locate information by using a variety of consumer, workplace, and public documents.

Reading Skills Focus

by **Kylene Beers**

How Do I Locate Information in Documents?

When you go someplace new, you look around quickly to get a basic understanding of your surroundings (skimming and scanning); then you focus on visual cues like signs, posters, and diagrams (noting graphics). These same skills can help you read informational texts.

"Now, this policy will cover your home for fire, theft, flood and huffing and puffing."

Reprinted from *The Saturday Evening Post* © 1993.

Previewing the Text

Before you read an informational document, **preview the text** for clues about its content. When you preview, you look over the text without reading every word. The organization of the text can often give you clues. Elements such as **titles, subheadings,** and **boldface terms** tell you the text will present a lot of information in an organized way so that you can locate it easily. You can also get an idea of what the document will be about by looking at the **illustrations** and **photos** that have been provided.

A Model for Previewing the Text Preview the text below to get an idea of what it's about.

> Replacing Your Cell Phone Battery
>
> 1. **Turn off** your telephone. ← This is boldface, so it must be important.
>
> 2. Depress the latch button on the rear of the battery . . . ← I'll need to follow these steps in order.

Skimming and Scanning

Skimming and scanning can help you save time when you are reading. They can help you figure out whether a text contains the information you are seeking.

When you **skim,** you glance through a text quickly to get a general idea of what it's about. You read the title, the subheadings, and the first line or two of each paragraph.

When you **scan,** you look for information that is closely related to what you want to learn. You glance at the text quickly, looking for key words or phrases that relate to your topic.

Term	Purpose	Examples
Skimming	Reading for main points	Glancing at newspaper headlines; reviewing charts and headings in your science textbook before a test
Scanning	Looking for specific details	Looking for an author's name in a table of contents; looking in a geography book for the name of the highest mountain in the United States

Resources

Chapter 6 Resources, Reading Focus Skill Builder, p. 4

PowerNotes, interactive lesson presentations with activities

Teacher One Stop™, on-level lesson plans and all print resources

Understanding Graphic Aids

When you're looking at consumer documents to find information, you're likely to come across **graphic aids,** such as maps, graphs, tables, and illustrations. Read the titles of these graphics to see if they're likely to contain the information for which you are looking.

Maps are drawings of areas of land. They can show natural features, such as mountains and rivers; political features, such as the boundaries between nations; and human-made features, such as public transportation systems.

title identifies subject or main idea   **labels** explain what you're looking at

legend, or key, explains symbols and colors

Graphs show you how things relate to each other. Two common types are line graphs and bar graphs. You might see a bar graph in your school that shows the number of cans each class has donated to the food drive.

Tables organize numbers or facts in categories, making it easier for you to find information and make comparisons. Facts are put into horizontal rows and vertical columns. To use a table, find the column that has the information you need. Then, read down the rows until you find the specific information for which you are searching.

Depart	Time	Arrive	Time	Bikes
WCRK	5:05a	EMBR	5:39a	Yes
WCRK	5:20a	EMBR	5:54a	Yes
WCRK	5:35a	EMBR	6:09a	Yes

Your Turn Apply Reading Skills

1. Preview the list below. Then, explain what you think the text will be about.

> **Talent Instructions: On Location**
> 1. No horseplay is permitted.
> 2. When you arrive, sign in with Jim and pick up a call pager.
> 3. Report *immediately* to makeup, hair, and wardrobe.

2. What strategy would you use if you were reading directions but weren't sure of the meanings of unfamiliar words?

3. What graphic aids might help you if you had to take a train to a place you've never been?

Now go to the Skills in Action: Reading Model

 Learn It Online
Need help with informational text? Go to the interactive Reading Workshops on:

go.hrw.com   H7-651   **Go**

Skimming and Scanning

Tell students that some informational documents begin with a table of contents or end with an index. Remind students that both of these features tell readers where specific information is located in the text. If a document is particularly long, these features can help readers save time by reducing the number of pages they need to scan in order to find information about a certain topic.

Understanding Graphic Aids

After reviewing each type of graphic aid with students, use the Think-Pair-Share routine to have students determine which graphic aids might appear in the following consumer and public documents: a movie schedule, a bus timetable, an instruction manual, a public salary report, a park brochure, and a document that contains facts about a town or city.

Check for Understanding

Your Turn

Possible responses:

1. *The text will probably be about rules for contestants in a talent show, since it says "talent" and talks about hair and makeup.*

2. *If you were reading directions but weren't sure of the meanings of unfamiliar words, you could use context clues to determine them.*

3. *a map of the train route; a table that lists the times of the train's arrivals and departures*

Reteach

ThinkCentral Online Remediation

 Learn It Online
Reading Workshops are interactive versions of real-world informational texts; students exercise their reading skills by responding to polls and answering questions in an engaging online format.

go.hrw.com   H7-651   **Go**

Universal Access

English Learners/ Struggling Readers

English for Academic Success Explain to students that the word *graphic* is used as both an adjective and a noun to refer to a visual representation of something. Maps, art, photos, tables, charts, and graphs are all types of graphics. A *graphic aid* is a graphic that helps readers better understand the text they are reading. In a brochure, for example, a reader might see a list of bulleted text and a map beside it. The map is the graphic aid that clarifies the text by organizing key information visually.

Advanced Learners

Acceleration Have students create a graphic aid to accompany a piece of their own writing. Remind students that graphic aids include pictures, charts, graphs, maps, and diagrams. Have students consider which type of graphic aid will best complement their writing. For example, a bar graph might best illustrate results of a poll, while a line graph might better illustrate changes in the student population over time.

Objectives

Students will

- analyze public documents
- analyze graphic aids
- use strategies such as skimming and scanning to read informational text

Preteach

Read with a Purpose Direct students to read the Read with a Purpose statement. Have students read the titles of the documents and discuss what specific information they expect to learn from each section or document. Ask them to describe what they learned from the titles in their **Reader/Writer Notebook.**

Direct Teach

Model the Skill

Use the Reading Model to demonstrate the application of the Informational Text and Reading skills in a short selection. As you or your students read the model aloud, stop to discuss the side annotations and highlighting, which are aids to comprehension and analysis.

▶ Informational Focus

Public Documents What information in the title identifies this text as a public document? *Possible response: The word "tips" and the "Association of School Clubs" indicate the document was created by a specific group to give general information of public interest.*

☀ California Standards, pp. 652–654

- **Reading Standard 2.2** Locate information by using a variety of consumer, workplace, and public documents.

Read with a Purpose Read the following documents to learn how to plan and create a new club at your school.

Association of School Clubs	**Newsletter** *Volume 1 • Spring 2009*

So You Want to Start a Club . . .

Informational Focus

Public Documents The purpose of this document is to provide information. The **title** and **subtitle** are clues that the document contains advice—things to think about if you are interested in starting a club.

Tips from the Association of School Clubs

Have you ever considered starting a school club? Perhaps you've thought about starting a club that celebrates your culture or that is devoted to a hobby you and your friends share. Clubs can be a lot of fun, but they can be a lot of work as well. That's why it's important to consider a number of things before you launch your club.

1 **Do you have what it takes?**

Starting and running a club take **commitment.** You often need to devote more time and effort than you anticipate to attracting interest in and support for a club and making sure it runs smoothly. You'll need to maintain a positive attitude and listen carefully to others' views. Think about what it will take to see the project through, and ask others for their help.

Selection Readability	
Easily Accessible **Accessible** **Challenging**	clear, concise language; familiar subject

Selection Summary

The public documents in this selection provide students with advice on starting a club, a sample plan for the club's development, and a sample advertisement for attracting new members.

2 Will people want to join your club?

Is there enough student interest in your club? Be sure your club isn't similar to ones that already exist. If your club offers something unique, students will be more likely to join it. Talk to other students about your ideas. They can offer useful suggestions that will help you refine your ideas to make your club more appealing. With commitment and careful planning, you can make your new club a **success.**

3 Do you have a plan?

In order to persuade your school to approve your club and to attract members, you need a **detailed plan.** Creating a Spanish-speakers' club, for example, is a good idea to start with, but you need to consider the following issues:

- the club's purpose
- a time and place to meet
- how often you plan to meet
- how people will find out about the club

A well-thought-out plan inspires confidence. If your plan is vague, people won't support it.

Plan for the Spanish-Speakers' Club

Purpose:
The club will be open to all students—
1. to give fluent speakers the chance to speak Spanish with their classmates on a regular basis
2. to give other students the chance to improve their Spanish
3. to encourage an appreciation for the language and the cultures of Spanish-speaking countries

When: Lunch, every Wednesday at noon (plus special events)
Where: The cafeteria (Permission will be requested to reserve a table and post a sign.)
Getting Members: Post fliers. Make announcements in Spanish classes.

Reading Focus

Previewing the Text The creator of this document used a variety of text features, such as large **headings** in the form of questions, **numbered lists,** a **bulleted list,** and **boldface type** to highlight important words. Previewing elements such as these before you read the entire document can help you learn more about the types of information the document will cover.

Reading Focus

Skimming and Scanning Look at the **headings** in the document. They break up the document into its main parts and give you clues to its organizational structure. **Skimming** the text—including each heading and the first line or two after it—can tell you if the document is likely to contain the information you need.

Reading Focus

Understanding Graphic Aids This plan is included as a **graphic element,** appearing as if a student hand-wrote it on notebook paper. It is an example of a plan meeting the conditions outlined in the main document.

Model the Skill

 Reading Focus

Previewing the Text What does the bulleted list under the heading "Do You Have a Plan?" suggest about the content of the entire document? *Possible response: It tells the reader that the article is about clubs and planning for clubs, which is the purpose of the document as a whole.*

▶ **Reading Focus**

Skimming and Scanning Based on a quick scan of the text, what information would you expect to find under heading 3 ("Do You Have a Plan?")? *Possible response: I would expect to find details on how to plan for a new club.*

▶ **Reading Focus**

Understanding Graphic Aids How might the sample plan benefit students who are attempting to start new clubs? *Possible response: It provides them with a visual representation of the work they must do to establish the club.*

Universal Access: Vocabulary

EL English Learners/ Struggling Readers

 English for Academic Success Help students understand the selection by introducing them to the following vocabulary words.

- **commitment**—dedication and responsibility to a task. *Sheila's commitment to her club led her to spend every weekend planning meetings and events.*
- **vague**—unclear. *Andy's e-mail was so vague that we could not figure out when his club meetings would start.*
- **sponsor**—to organize and support. *All new clubs must have a teacher to sponsor them.*
- **heritage**—the cultural, ethnic, or religious background that a person is born into. *The International Club was created to support the heritage of students.*

Then, give students this statement that explains how the words relate to the meaning of the selection:
Starting a new club requires a strong commitment from the founder. The information given to new members cannot be vague. Some clubs sponsor events to raise money, to help others, or to celebrate the heritage of a particular group.

Model the Skill

Public Documents Scan the information in large type on the poster. What information did you gain from the scan, and how is it useful to a student reading the poster? ***Possible response:*** *I learned the name of the club, its purpose, and when and where it meets. This basic information helps students reading the poster to determine whether they might be interested in the club and therefore whether they should read the poster more closely.*

Check for Understanding

Read with a Purpose Ask students to restate, in their own words, what is required to start a new club. ***Possible response:*** *A clear purpose and plan, dedication to the club's success, and good communication within and about the club.*

Reading Model

Informational Focus

Public Documents This **flier** contains all of the information about the club that members of the public (students in the school) need to know. The title of the flier grabs the reader's interest, as well as quickly conveying the flier's purpose. **Key information**—the time and place of club meetings —is restated near the end of the flier for students who scan it.

¡Participa en el club de hispanohablantes!
(Join the Spanish-Speakers' Club!)

Do you speak Spanish?
Are you trying to learn?

Come converse en Español with your classmates as a member of the school's new Spanish-Speakers' Club. The club will meet every Wednesday at noon in the cafeteria. Both fluent and beginning speakers are welcome. The club will also sponsor occasional special events, such as screenings of Spanish-language movies and celebrations of Latino heritage. The only condition for membership is a desire to speak and appreciate the Spanish language.

Meeting Location: The school cafeteria

Meeting Time: Every Wednesday at noon
(plus special-event times TBA)

¡Nos vemos el miércoles!
(See you Wednesday!)

Read with a Purpose From reading these documents, what specific information did you learn about creating a new club at school?

🐻 **California Standards, p. 655**

■ **Reading Standard 2.2** Locate information by using a variety of consumer, workplace, and public documents.

Resources

Chapter 6 Resources, , Literary and Academic Vocabulary Skill Builder, p. 5 📝 💿

UA: Differentiating Instruction, Vocabulary Skill Builder, p. 183. 📝 💿

Teacher One Stop™, on-level lesson plans and all print resources 💿

WordSharp: An Interactive Vocabulary Tutor, more practice with academic language 💿 🌐

Academic Vocabulary

Writing and Talking About Informational Texts

Write the following questions on the board. Tell students these are the kinds of questions they will encounter on standardized tests. Discuss the meaning of the words, then have students use "So You Want to Start a Club..." to answer the questions.

• Describe the **sequence** of steps involved in planning a club.
Possible response: *The first step is considering whether you and your classmates have a strong enough interest in creating the club. Next, you have to create a clear plan for the club. Finally, you share information about your club with others and begin meeting.*

Reading Standard 2.2 Locate information by using a variety of consumer, workplace, and public documents.

Into Action: Reading for Information

In a chart like the one below, give examples and explain how you were able to use each text feature to help you locate information in "So You Want to Start a Club. . . ."

Informational Text Feature	Examples and Explanations
Headings	
Lists	
Graphics	

Talk About . . .

1. With a partner, discuss the main points of "So You Want to Start a Club. . . ." Challenge yourself to use each Academic Vocabulary word listed on the right at least once in your discussion.

Write About . . .

Answer the following questions about "So You Want to Start a Club. . . ." For definitions of the underlined Academic Vocabulary words, see the column on the right.

2. What information is the creator of this document trying to communicate?

3. What function does the flier serve?

4. What technique did the creator of the document use to organize the information?

Writing Skills Focus
Think as a Reader/Writer

In this chapter the Writing Skills Focus activities on the Preparing to Read pages will help you understand how each type of document delivers information. On the Applying Your Skills pages, you'll check your understanding of these document types.

Academic Vocabulary for Chapter 6

Talking and Writing About Consumer, Workplace, and Public Documents

Academic Vocabulary is the language you will encounter when reading informational texts. Use these words to discuss the documents you read in this chapter. They are underlined throughout the chapter.

communicate (kuh MYOO nuh kayt) v.: share information or ideas. *Most informational texts are written to communicate information to readers.*

function (FUHNGK shuhn) n.: purpose of a specific person or thing. *Public documents inform people of the function of various government organizations.*

sequence (SEE kwuhns) n.: specific order in which things follow one another. *Technical directions arrange the steps you must follow in the correct sequence.*

technique (tehk NEEK) n.: method of doing a particular task. *The technique for performing a task is taught in an instruction manual.*

Your Turn

Copy the Academic Vocabulary words into your *Reader/Writer Notebook*. Then, use each word in a sentence about a public, consumer, or workplace document you've seen.

Guided Practice: Apply
Into Action: Reading for Information

Make sure students' charts include one example and explanation for each item. *Possible response: Headings: The heading "Do You Have What It Takes?" gave me useful information about the time and effort required to start a club; Lists: the bulleted list under heading 3 gives key information about planning a club; Graphics: the poster on p. 654 helped me find out the club's name, purpose, and meeting times and locations.*

Talk About...

1. Model for students how to incorporate the academic vocabulary words into a discussion of public documents. For example, you might say, "There is a clear sequence of steps a person must take to create a new club. . ."

Write About...
Possible responses:

2. *The creator of the document wants to* communicate *the process of creating a new club.*

3. *The flier's* function *is to inform students of the nature of the club and its meeting time and place.*

4. *The document's creator used* techniques *such as eye-catching headings to organize the information.*

Independent Practice

Chapter 6 Resources, Skill Builders, pp. 3—5

UA: Differentiating Instruction, Academic and Selection Vocabulary Skills Builder, p. 183

- What **techniques** does the creator of the documents use to guide readers through them? ***Possible response:*** *The creator of the documents uses headings, questions, and lists to help the reader find information.*

- What is the **function** of the Spanish phrases on the poster? ***Possible response:*** *The phrases catch the interest of a person viewing the poster, who may wonder what the phrases mean. They also reveal the club's purpose.*

- In what ways would you **communicate** the existence and purpose of a new club? ***Possible response:*** *Information about a new club might be communicated through fliers, school announcements, e-mails, posters, or word-of-mouth.*

Objectives

Students will

- learn how to analyze information found in public documents
- learn to skim and scan documents

Motivate

What Do You Think?/QuickTalk

Ask volunteers to describe some of the types of documents they have seen or used in their everyday lives. Then, have students discuss whether or not these documents are public documents.

English for Academic Success

Academic Vocabulary

Look for opportunities to use the Academic Vocabulary words in this chapter.

- **technique, *n.:*** method of doing a particular task
- **function, *n.:*** purpose of a specific person or thing

Analyzing Visuals

Use ThinkCentral Teacher Access to project this image for viewing.

Extension Activity Ask students to describe the kinds of informational texts that are shown on the bulletin board. ***Possible response:*** *flyers, advertisements, announcements*

California Standards, pp. 656–663

- **Reading Standard 2.2** Locate information by using a variety of consumer, workplace, and public documents.

INFORMATIONAL TEXT FOCUS

Public Documents

CONTENTS

 What Do You Think Where would you look for information if you were interested in starting a career?

QuickTalk Think about documents that teachers post in the hallways in your school. Are these public documents? Discuss why or why not.

Selection Readability	
Easily Accessible **Accessible** Challenging	relevant to real-life situations; background information provided in the text

Selection Summary

Sam reads in a magazine and in an online article that a film will be casting in her area for someone who is an expert BMX-type bike rider. Since she is under eighteen years old, she needs to find out if she is qualified to obtain a work permit and thus audition for the film.

Preparing to Read

Public Documents

Informational Text Focus

Public Documents All **public documents** have one thing in common: They inform you of things you might need or want to know. Most people read public documents because they are looking for specific information. On the following pages, you'll follow one person's experience in locating the information she needs by using various public documents.

Reading Skills Focus

Skimming and Scanning Use these <u>techniques</u> to locate information in public documents. **Skim** a document, or read it quickly, to see what it's about. Then **scan** it to find the specific information you want to learn.

Into Action Skim the documents that follow in this section before you read them closely. Then, after you have skimmed the documents, list one piece of information you want to locate in each text.

Title	Information to Locate
Casting Call	
Hollywood Beat	
Permission to Work	

Writing Skills Focus

Preparing for **Timed Writing** When information is crucial, writers take care to call attention to it. As you read "Casting Call," look for ways the writer emphasizes major information.

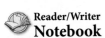
Reader/Writer Notebook
Use your **RWN** to complete the activities for these selections.

Learn It Online
Read more about analyzing public documents, including those found on the Web, with MediaScope at:

go.hrw.com | H7-657 | **Go**

Vocabulary

charismatic (kair ihz MAT ihk) *adj.*: possessing energy, charm, or appeal. *The producers were looking for charismatic teens to play roles in the movie.*

version (VUHR zhuhn) *n.*: a retelling from a certain point of view. *In the modern version of the movie, the hobbits oppose evil characters who ride bicycles.*

Language Coach

Jargon Words that have special meanings among a group of people are called **jargon**. Journalism is a profession with lots of jargon. Words such as *call* and *beat* are good examples. Unlike the *beat* you hear in music, a journalistic *beat* is a group of regularly covered news sources. What are some other examples of jargon from journalism? (Think about television and radio news and the newspaper.)

Model the Skill

■ Tell students that **public documents** are written to give the public information that they may want or need to know about. Public documents, such as fliers or job listings, are posted in public forums, such as on bulletin boards or the Internet.

■ Have students read the description of Sam on p. 658. Explain that Sam, just like them, is a member of the public. Every member of the public has different wants, needs, and goals. When a person like Sam encounters a public document, she is going to look for information relevant to her own wants, needs, and goals.

Guided Practice: Apply

QuickWrite Have students read the Casting Call notice on p. 659. Ask students to spend five minutes explaining in their **Reader/Writer Notebook** what information from this public document appeals to Sam, and why the writers of the document would want a reader like Sam to come across their document. *Students should recognize that Sam, an avid bike rider, would be interested in the chance to use her biking skills in a different forum; the writers of the document are looking for people with Sam's skill set and of her age for their film. (See p. T28)*

Public Documents

Read with a Purpose Read these public documents to find out how a girl named Sam uses the information in them to get a part in a movie.

Casting Call

Meet Sam (Miss Samantha Sallyann Lancaster, and don't you even think about calling her anything but Sam, thank you very much). Anyone who meets Sam for five minutes knows two things about her: She's smart, and she can beat anyone, anytime, anywhere on her BMX bike. So imagine Sam's excitement when she comes across the Casting Call **announcement** in her favorite biking magazine.

Universal Access

 English Learners

English for Academic Success Echo-read the page with students: Read the passage aloud, stopping after each line to allow students to repeat after you. After reading, clarify words in each sentence that are important to their understanding of that section, such as *casting* or *requirements*.

✔ See **UA: Differentiating Instruction** for strategies for teaching English learners.

Struggling Readers

Guide students through the process of skimming a text.

• Explain to students that skimming is more than simply reading faster. Readers should look at each page to identify key information. Skimming can be a prereading process: Readers can look through a passage quickly before reading it more carefully.

• Explain that in the "Casting Call" piece, a reader skimming the text should note that the title is "Casting Call" and the words *audition, talent,* and *movies*

✳ CASTING CALL ✳

If you've been looking for the right break to get into motion pictures, this may be your chance. StreetWheelie Productions is casting fresh talent for an upcoming action movie. **Ⓐ**

Ⓑ

To audition, you must

* ✳ be a charismatic, awesome, off-the-wall male or female individualist
* ✳ be an expert at making your BMX-type bike do whatever you want it to do
* ✳ have your own bike
* ✳ look like you're between the ages of twelve and fifteen
* ✳ meet the requirements for a permit to work in the entertainment industry if you are under age eighteen
* ✳ be living in or near San Francisco during July and August 2009

AUDITIONS WILL BE HELD IN

Golden Gate Park, San Francisco

Saturday, May 23, 2009

10:00 A.M. to 5:00 P.M.

Bring your bike.

See you in the movies!

Ⓐ Informational Focus Public Documents What is the function of this announcement?

Ⓑ Reading Focus Skimming Skim the bulleted list. From what you know about Sam, why might she be interested in this ad?

Vocabulary charismatic (kair ihz MAT ihk) *adj.*: possessing energy, charm, or appeal.

Think About/Talk About

Read with a Purpose Have students read the Read with a Purpose statement. Point out that a key word in the statement is "information." Ask students what information Sam might need from a magazine announcement to try out for a role in a movie.

▶ Comprehension

Ⓐ Informational Focus

Possible response: *The function of this announcement is to find suitable people to audition for an upcoming action movie.*

Ⓑ Reading Focus

Possible response: *Sam owns a BMX bike and is very good at riding it.*

▶ Extend the Discussion

Drawing Conclusions Why does the information about the location of the casting call appear in a different color and larger font than the bulleted list? ***Possible response:*** *This information is more important; it needs to stand out on the page.*

Analyzing Read the first paragraph of the announcement. In what way is this public document similar to a consumer document such as an advertisement? ***Possible response:*** *Like an ad, this announcement attempts to persuade people to try out for the movie. It contains factual information for the general public, but it is also a type of advertisement for the casting call.*

Vocabulary: Own the Word

charismatic: Create a semantic web. Write *charismatic* and its definition in a center circle. Then draw "spider legs" from the circle and have students name any related words they can think of. ***Possible responses:*** *fascinating, exciting, magnetic*

---

appear throughout the text. This suggests that the announcement is about an audition for a new movie.

• Have students practice skimming using "Hollywood Beat." Ask students what stood out as they skimmed.

✔ See **UA: Differentiating Instruction** for strategies for teaching struggling readers.

Advanced Learners

Acceleration Challenge students to skim a chapter of a book they are reading. Students should be given a time limit to skim their chapter and then explain to a partner the most important points in that chapter.

See **UA: Resources for Teaching Advanced Students** for strategies for teaching advanced learners.

Students with Disabilities

Invite students to read "Casting Call" in interactive format in **UA: Holt Interactive Reader** and to use the sidenotes as aids to understanding the selection. The interactive version provides additional instruction, practice, and assessment of the skills taught in the Student Edition.

Model the Skill

- Provide students with copies of the Reading Skills Focus graphic organizer (See **Chapter 6 Resources**) or ask them to use a piece of their own paper.

- Explain that readers **skim** texts to get a general idea of what they contain. Readers may also choose to **scan** texts, either after skimming or without skimming, to locate specific information that they want to find out.

- Show students how to use the graphic organizer to keep track of information they want to find out by scanning the article. You might say, "One piece of information I would like to learn from the Internet article is what the film is going to be about. So I will write that in my chart and look for it as I read."

Title	Information to Locate
Casting Call	
Hollywood Beat	What the film is going to be about

Guided Practice: Apply

Think-Pair-Share Prior to reading the article, have students think about something that they would like to find out from this article, aside from what the film is about. Have students discuss their ideas with a partner to determine whether they would find that information in this article. Then, have students share the ideas they want to scan for with the class. (See p. T28.)

Locating Information: An Article

Sam wants more information. An **Internet search** using the keywords *StreetWheelie Productions* and *San Francisco* yields this **article** from *Hollywood Beat*:

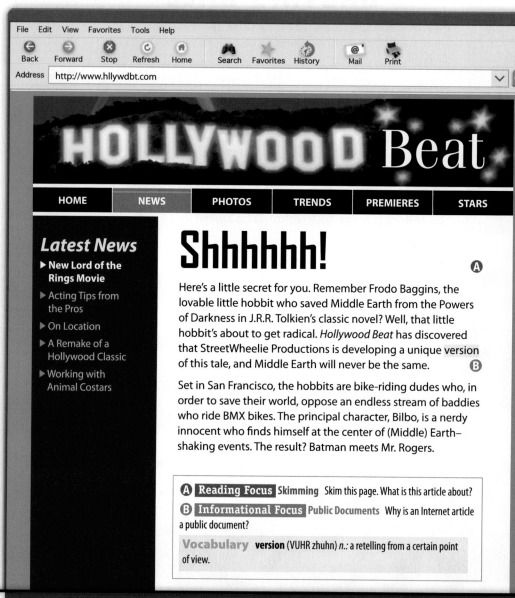

> File   Edit   View   Favorites   Tools   Help
>
> Back   Forward   Stop   Refresh   Home   Search   Favorites   History   Mail   Print
>
> Address   http://www.hllywdbt.com
>
> # HOLLYWOOD Beat
>
> HOME | NEWS | PHOTOS | TRENDS | PREMIERES | STARS
>
> **Latest News**
> - ▶ New Lord of the Rings Movie
> - ▶ Acting Tips from the Pros
> - ▶ On Location
> - ▶ A Remake of a Hollywood Classic
> - ▶ Working with Animal Costars
>
> # Shhhhhh!   Ⓐ
>
> Here's a little secret for you. Remember Frodo Baggins, the lovable little hobbit who saved Middle Earth from the Powers of Darkness in J.R.R. Tolkien's classic novel? Well, that little hobbit's about to get radical. *Hollywood Beat* has discovered that StreetWheelie Productions is developing a unique version of this tale, and Middle Earth will never be the same.   Ⓑ
>
> Set in San Francisco, the hobbits are bike-riding dudes who, in order to save their world, oppose an endless stream of baddies who ride BMX bikes. The principal character, Bilbo, is a nerdy innocent who finds himself at the center of (Middle) Earth–shaking events. The result? Batman meets Mr. Rogers.
>
> Ⓐ **Reading Focus** Skimming   Skim this page. What is this article about?
> Ⓑ **Informational Focus** Public Documents   Why is an Internet article a public document?
> **Vocabulary** **version** (VUHR zhuhn) *n.*: a retelling from a certain point of view.

Developing Oral Fluency

Use the article from *Hollywood Beat* to give students practice in reading with expression. Explain to students that in this passage, the author is trying to get people excited about the upcoming movie. Tell them that fluent readers express emotions in their voices as they read. Remind students that punctuation marks within lines of dialogue give readers clues about when to pause, when to stress certain words or phrases, and when to make changes in intonation.

Provide assistance if some students do not understand the slang used in the passage, so they will know what intonation to use. For example, the word *radical* in the first paragraph is a positive expression that could be read with the same intonation as *wild, awesome,* or *crazy*.

Paired Activity Put students into pairs, with one fluent student in each pair, if possible.

- Model reading the first three sentences of the article, making sure to emphasize expression as you read. For example, the line "Well, that little hobbit's about to get radical" should be read in an excited voice.

Don't quote us yet, but we know whose shooting schedule is open!

Rumor has it LOVE will find Bilbo and a bike girl—in the movie!

Sources close to the production say that there is some big talent interested in the project. As of yet, nobody's talking, but remember . . . you'll hear all about it first on *Hollywood Beat*. **C**

C | **Read and Discuss** | What new information does Sam find?

🌐 Internet

- Next, have students in each pair read the article out loud to each other, pretending as though they are promoting the movie on a news show. Each student should focus on conveying the right emotions to the "audience."
- Conclude the activity by discussing how punctuation and slang enabled the students to read expressively and also to understand the article.

✔ See **UA: Differentiating Instruction** for practice passages for developing oral fluency.

Think About/Talk About

▶ **Comprehension**

A **Reading Focus**

Possible response: It is about a new action movie inspired by the novel The Lord of the Rings.

B **Informational Focus**

Possible response: It is available online for anyone to look at.

C **Read and Discuss**

Possible response: Sam discovers that the movie will be based on a novel by J.R.R. Tolkien and that the hobbits will all ride bikes.

▶ **Extend the Discussion**

Speculating Why might Sam start her search for more information on the Internet? *Possible response: It is probably the cheapest and easiest way of finding out what she wants to know. The Internet is also a good place to look for up-to-date information.*

Point of View Read the Internet article's second paragraph. Is this article written from an objective point of view or a subjective point of view? Explain. *Possible response: This article is fairly subjective. It describes the movie as "an out-of-sight version" of a classic tale and calls the main character a "nerdy innocent." Both of these statements reflect the author's opinion and are not objective facts.*

Vocabulary: Own the Word

version: Ask students to complete the idea: The StreetWheelie Productions film is a *version* of J.R.R. Tolkien's novel because. . .

Comprehension

A Reading Focus

Possible response: The first section requires basic personal information about the applicant, such as name, address, date of birth, and physical appearance. The second section requires information about the applicant's school record, and the third section requires information about the applicant's health.

B Read and Discuss

Possible response: The work permit application requires a lot of personal information. Eligibility for a work permit is determined by an applicant's age, school record, health, and parental permission.

▶ **Extend the Discussion**

Synthesizing Refer to the section titled "Procedures for Obtaining Work Permit." If Sam waits until May 5 to mail her application, will she have her work permit before the audition?
Possible response: Yes. According to the form, work permits are processed in three days. She'll have her permit on May 8, and the audition isn't until May 25.

Monitor Students' Comprehension

Use the Read with a Purpose follow-up question to assess students' understanding. *Possible response:* I know when and where the audition is being held. I also know about the movie that she is auditioning for. I'm not sure what role she is auditioning for or what the audition process will be like.

Locating Information: An Application

Sam is only twelve years old. Can she qualify for a work permit? She doesn't want to audition if she isn't eligible to take the part. All of the information she needs is in this **application.**

APPLICATION

STATE OF CALIFORNIA Division of Labor Standards Enforcement

THIS IS NOT A PERMIT   ☐ NEW ☐ RENEWAL **A**

APPLICATION FOR PERMISSION TO WORK IN THE ENTERTAINMENT INDUSTRY

PROCEDURES FOR OBTAINING WORK PERMIT
1. Complete the information required below.
2. School authorities must complete the "School Record" section below.
3. For minors 15 days through kindergarten, please attach a certified copy of the minor's birth certificate. See reverse side for other documents that may be accepted.
4. Mail or present the completed application to any office of the Division of Labor Standards Enforcement for issuance of your work permit. Work permits will be issued within 3 business days and mailed to you.
5. Please provide a preaddressed, stamped envelope.

Name of Child		Professional Name (if applicable)		

Permanent Address Number Street	City	State	Zip Code	Home Phone Number

School Attending				Grade

Date of Birth	Age	Height	Weight	Hair Color	Eye Color	Gender ☐ Male ☐ Female

STATEMENT OF PARENT OR GUARDIAN: It is my desire that an Entertainment Work Permit be issued to the above named child. I will read the rules governing such employment and will cooperate to the best of my ability in safeguarding his or her educational, moral, and physical interest. I hereby certify, under penalty of perjury, that the foregoing statements are true and correct.

Name of Parent or Guardian (print or type)	Signature	Daytime Phone Number

SCHOOL RECORD
State whether "SATISFACTORY" or "UNSATISFACTORY" for each

Attendance	Scholarship (Grades)	Health

I CERTIFY THAT THE ABOVE-NAMED MINOR:
☐ Meets the school district's requirements with respect to age, school record, attendance and health.
☐ Does not meet the district's requirements and permit should not be issued.

Authorized School Official	Date	
School Address	School Phone Number	[School Seal]

HEALTH RECORD
Complete this Section if instructed to do so or if infant is under One Month of Age

Name of Doctor	Address	Phone Number

I certify that I am a licensed physician and surgeon who is Board Certified in pediatrics, and have carefully examined _____.

In my opinion, (please circle) **he/she is/is not** physically fit to be employed in the production of motion pictures and television. If less than one month, infant **is/ is not** at least 15 days old, **was/was not** carried to full term, and **is/is not** physically able to perform.

Signature _____ M.D. Date _____

DLSE 277 (Rev. 012/08)   **B**

A **Reading Focus** **Scanning** Scan the document before you read. What does each major section require?

B **Read and Discuss** What have you learned about the work permit application?

Read with a Purpose Sam's happy. She knows she'll qualify for a work permit, and she decides to go to the audition. Before she goes, test yourself. In reading these documents, have you been able to find all of the information Sam needs?

Universal Access

AAVE Students Who Use African American Vernacular English

English for Academic Success Some students may have difficulty with forming and using possessives in formal English. Explain to students that possessives for a singular subject or name are formed by adding an apostrophe and an s to the end of the subject or name, as in *district's requirements* under "School Record" on p. 662. The use of the apostrophe and s indicates that the requirements are the possession of the district. Plural possessives, such as *you, we,* and *they,* do not use the apostrophe s, but change to *your, our,* and *their* respectively. Note that *you* can be a singular or plural subject, but it always takes the plural form *your.* Another exception is *I,* which has the possessive form *my.* Have students practice in small groups forming formal English possessives with the following examples: *Dominic/bike, you/birthday, Elizabeth/cousin, they/concert.*

✔ For additional instruction and strategies, see **Think-Central, Teacher Access.**

Applying Your Skills

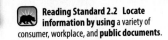
Public Documents
Standards Review

Informational Text and Vocabulary

1. The casting directors put the casting **announcement** in a biking magazine because they want kids who are especially interested in

   A reading well.

   B acting in movies.

   C following directions.

   D riding bikes well.

2. Sam thinks she qualifies for a **work permit.** To do so, she needs all of the following *except*

   A the full support and help of her parent or guardian.

   B a statement of good health from a doctor.

   C a statement from her school that she has met the district's requirements for her grade level.

   D permission from her school to be absent.

3. If Sam wanted to find out more about StreetWheelie Productions, her *best* choice would be to

   A search the Internet using the keywords *StreetWheelie Productions.*

   B look in an encyclopedia under "Film."

   C read *The Hobbit* again.

   D post a question on her school's electronic bulletin board.

4. If Sam is hired to play a part, she will be working during

   A May and June.

   B June and July.

   C July and August.

   D August and September.

5. A *charismatic* person has

   A an attractive personality.

   B athletic ability.

   C good manners.

   D acting talent.

6. A *version* of a story is similar to a

   A review.

   B retelling.

   C criticism.

   D production.

Writing Skills Focus

Timed ⌐Writing How do you locate essential information in public documents? Do you rely on graphic features or your own judgment? Respond in a paragraph.

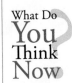 What Do **You** **Think** **Now** What kind of public documents would you review if you were looking for a job?

 California Standards, p. 663

■ **Reading Standard 2.2** Locate information by using a variety of consumer, workplace, and public documents.

Check for Understanding

Independent Practice
Answers and Explanations

1. *D* *The advertisement is in a magazine specifically read by kids who can ride bikes. The casting call does not mention items A, B, or C.*

2. *D* *Sam needs all the items listed except permission from her school to be absent.*

3. *A* *Sam could probably find the most relevant information from an Internet search. None of the other resources are likely to contain information specific to the company.*

4. *C* *The casting call says filming will take place in July and August.*

5. *A* *A charismatic person is attractive to others.*

6. *B* *A version of a story is similar to a retelling of it. No other answer choices have similar meanings.*

 ### Assess

📝 **Chapter 6 Resources,** Selection Standards Check, p. 9.

🖥 **ThinkCentral Online Assessment,** Selection Standards Check

💿 **Teacher One Stop™,** editable Selection Standards Check

Reteach

🖥 **ThinkCentral Online Remediation**

Writing Skills Focus

Possible response: *I use a combination of graphic features and my own judgment. Some authors don't include many graphic features in their documents, so I can't always rely on them.*

What Do You Think Now?

Ask students to explain how looking at public documents might help someone find a job.

Objectives
Students will
- learn how to analyze information found in workplace documents
- preview documents prior to reading

Motivate

What Do You Think?/QuickWrite
Ask volunteers to describe some job descriptions they might have seen. Then, have students use their **Reader/Writer Notebook** to write about where they might expect to find information about starting a new job.

Analyzing Visuals
Extension Activity Ask students what some of the workplace documents pictured in the image might be. *Possible response:* *calendars, letters, memos*

INFORMATIONAL TEXT FOCUS
Workplace Documents

CONTENTS

What Do You Think Where would you look for information about your responsibilities in a new job?

QuickWrite Think about the information you might need if you got a part-time job. Where would you locate the information you need?

California Standards, pp. 664–669

- **Reading Standard 2.2** Locate information by using a variety of consumer, workplace, and public documents.

Selection Readability	
Easily Accessible **Accessible** Challenging	relevant to real-life situations; background information provided in the text

Selection Summary
Having passed her audition, Sam is given a detailed contract. On her first day at work, she is given a list of instructions to guide her behavior on the set. As time passes, Sam learns to check her e-mail often for her constantly changing schedule.

Preparing to Read

Workplace Documents

Informational Text Focus

Workplace Documents Whether you work in a small company with only one other person or in a huge corporation with offices all over the world, your working life will depend on many types of **workplace documents.** Businesses put important information in writing so that agreements, decisions, and requirements are clear to everyone involved. Let's look at some of the workplace documents that Sam encounters after her audition.

Reading Skills Focus

Previewing the Text Before you read an informational document, **preview the text** for clues to its content. Your purpose for reading documents is usually to locate information, and previewing them can help you narrow your search. When you preview, you look over the text without reading every word. Elements such as titles, lists, and tables can give you an idea of what the document contains.

Into Action Preview the business letter on the next page to locate the following information:

- When should Sam check her e-mail?
- When does she report to wardrobe?
- What are her wages?

Writing Skills Focus

Preparing for Timed └Writing As you read the following documents, notice the ways the business letter and the e-mail memo are different in structure.

 Reader/Writer
Notebook
Use your **RWN** to complete the activities for these selections.

Vocabulary

punctuality (puhngk choo AL uh tee) *n.*: quality of being on time. *The actors' punctuality will help keep the production on schedule.*

supervision (soo puhr VIHZH uhn) *n.*: function of overseeing. *The young actors require adult supervision while on the set.*

tentative (TEHN tuh tihv) *adj.*: not fixed. *The schedule is tentative, so check it often to look for changes.*

Language Coach

Prefixes A prefix is a word part that is added to the beginning of a word to change the word's meaning. The prefix *super–* comes from the Latin word *super,* meaning "over; above; in addition." The word *supervise* comes from that word plus the Latin verb meaning "to see." How does the English word reflect the meaning of its Latin roots? Name and provide a definition for two other words with the prefix *super–*. Use a dictionary if necessary.

Selection Resources

Chapter 6 Resources, on-level practice and assessment, p. 12

PowerNotes, interactive lesson presentation with activities

Teacher One Stop™, on-level lesson plans and all print resources

Holt Audio Library: Selections and Summaries in Spanish

UA: Holt Interactive Reader, p. 170

Holt Interactive Reader for ELD, p. 192

Holt Audio Tutor for ELD

UA: Differentiating Instruction, modified lesson plans and leveled assessment, p. 164

UA: Resources for Teaching Advanced Students, lesson plans

UA: Supporting Instruction in Five Languages, selection summary

ThinkCentral Online Assessment, Selection Standards Check

ThinkCentral Online Remediation

Model the Skill

- Tell students that **workplace documents** contain information that is useful to employers and employees. Some workplace documents clarify rules for a workplace; others might establish agreements between two companies regarding work to be done. Understanding workplace documents helps employees understand what is expected of them, as well as helping employers communicate goals and rules.

- Tell students that the documents on pp. 666–667 represent two types of workplace documents: a letter outlining the content of Sam's employment contract and a list of rules for the movie set on which Sam will work. Point out that issues such as knowing one's work schedule and safety instructions are included in the document.

- Ask students how Sam will find out about her work schedule, and note where they found the information. *Students should note that the letter contains a directive to check e-mail twice a day to find out about scheduling information, and to call if her e-mail isn't working.*

Guided Practice: Apply

Read/Talk/Write Have students read over the list of talent instructions carefully. Then, have them discuss with a partner what information might be included in a similar list for a different job they are familiar with, such as delivering newspapers. Have students jot down a list of expectations for the job of their choice.

BUSINESS LETTER

Locating Information: A Business Letter

The audition has gone very well. Everyone is as nice as he or she can be. Someone takes a photograph of Sam and writes down all of her information. Soon Sam receives the business letter shown at the right.

Workplace Documents

Read with a Purpose Read these workplace documents to locate the information Sam needs to know during filming.

StreetWheelie Productions
2323 South Robertson Boulevard, Beverly Hills, CA 90210

June 7, 2009
Miss Samantha Lancaster
1920 Ygnacio Valley Road
Walnut Creek, CA 94598

Dear Sam:

It is my pleasure to offer you a part in our production. Attached is your contract. The items in the contract spell out the issues we discussed last Saturday, as follows: **A**

- You are responsible for your own transportation to and from filming.
- Check your e-mail first thing each morning and last thing each night.
- Report to makeup, hair, and wardrobe two hours before your first call.
- Report with your bike for all calls. You may not wash or otherwise clean the grunge off your bike.
- Because you are not yet age sixteen, a parent or guardian must be present whenever you are working. As we discussed with your mother, your grandfather will be an appropriate guardian.
- Nonprofessional actors are paid a minimum hourly wage. Your eight-hour-maximum workday will begin when you arrive each day and end when you leave each day. By law you may not work more than eight hours a day. One paid hour of rest will be part of your eight-hour workday, but the thirty-minute lunch, also paid, will *not* be part of the workday. You will always have twelve hours or more between the end of one workday and the makeup call for the next.
- You will receive a bonus at the end of your filming schedule. This bonus will be paid on your last day of work, on the condition that you have fulfilled all aspects of your contract with regard to attendance, punctuality, and appearance. This bonus will equal the total of all your previous hourly checks.

If you have any questions, call Juanita Diaz, our lawyer. Her phone number is on the contract. We look forward to having you on the project. **B**

Sincerely,

Cassandra Rice

Cassandra Rice, Casting Director

Responsibility 1: transportation

Responsibility 2: work schedule

Responsibility 3: arrival time

Responsibility 4: appearance

Responsibility 5: equipment

Responsibility 6: parental supervision

wages

A **Informational Focus** **Workplace Documents** Why is it important to understand the contract before signing it?

B **Read and Discuss** What is the purpose of this letter?

Vocabulary **punctuality** (puhngk choo AL uh tee) *n.:* quality of being on time.
supervision (soo puhr VIHZH uhn) *n.:* function of overseeing.

Universal Access

EL English Learners

English for Academic Success Before students read the selection, explain the following terms and their meanings:

- **contract**—an agreement between two parties that is legally binding.
- **schedule**—a plan or guideline for when things should be completed.
- **production**—a piece of work for stage, television, film, or radio.
- **guardian**—an adult who is in charge of a minor when there is no parent present.

✔ See **UA: Differentiating Instruction** for strategies for teaching English learners.

Struggling Readers

Explain to students that when readers preview a text, they look at key elements of the text to get an idea of what the text will be about. Tell students that when readers preview a document, they should look for elements such as lists or tables that provide basic information in an

Locating Information: Workplace Instructions

When Sam gets to the location, the crew is nice, but they all make it clear that everyone is there to work. They also expect Sam to understand that fun movies are just as hard to make as serious ones. Sam's job doesn't require an employee manual, but she does receive a list of **workplace instructions.**

TALENT INSTRUCTIONS: ON LOCATION

1. No horseplay is permitted.

2. When you arrive, sign in with Jim and pick up a call pager.

3. Report *immediately* to makeup, hair, and wardrobe.

4. Movies require a lot of waiting. Bring something that you can do *quietly* while you wait. Music players are fine if the headphones do not interfere with makeup, hair, or costume. Electronic games are popular; their sound effects *must* be turned off. You *could* even read a book. People do. **Ⓐ**

5. When you are ready, report to the call area, and stay there. *Always* keep your call pager with you.

6. Personal cell phones, pagers, etc., may be used only in the call or food areas and only if they do not interfere with filming. Ringers must be set to "off" or "silent alert."

7. Leave all personal belongings in your assigned locker when on the shooting site.

8. You may talk in nonfilming areas, but there is *no talking* on the shooting site.

Ⓐ Informational Focus Workplace Documents Why is it important to have these rules and guidelines?

easy-to-read format. These elements, along with highlighted text and text features, help the reader quickly find out the subject of and information included in the text.

✔ See **UA: Differentiating Instruction** for strategies for teaching struggling readers.

Advanced Learners

Enrichment Have students preview the business letter independently. Then, have students discuss in groups of three what they would expect to find in Sam's contract, based on what was stated in the letter.

✔ See **UA: Resources for Teaching Advanced Students** for strategies for teaching advanced learners.

Students with Disabilities

Invite students to read "Letter from Casting Director" in interactive format in **UA: Holt Interactive Reader** and to use the sidenotes as aids to understanding the selection. The interactive version provides additional instruction, practice, and assessment of the skills taught in the Student Edition.

Think About/Talk About

Read with a Purpose Have students read the Read with a Purpose statement. Ask students what kind of information Sam might need to know to succeed at her new job.

▶ Comprehension

Letter from Casting Director

Ⓐ Informational Focus

Possible response: The contract is legally binding, which means Sam must do everything she agrees to in the contract, and cannot challenge any of the terms it sets forth.

Ⓑ Read and Discuss

Possible response: The purpose of the letter is to inform Sam of her responsibilities during filming and to deliver her contract.

Talent Instructions

Ⓐ Informational Focus

Possible response: These rules and guidelines ensure that filming goes smoothly and that Sam and other employees know what behavior is permitted on the set.

▶ Extend the Discussion

Analyzing Read the second bullet point in the business letter. Why do you think it is important that Sam check her e-mail twice every day? *Possible response: The schedule probably changes often, and Sam needs to be aware of those changes.*

Vocabulary: Own the Word

- **punctuality:** Ask students hypothetical questions: How might you improve your punctuality? When might punctuality be important?

- **supervision:** Remind students that supervision is related to the words *supervise* and *supervisor*, which refer to overseeing. The suffix *–ion* means "of or relating to" and turns *supervise* into a noun, so *supervision* means "of or relating to overseeing."

Think About/Talk About

▶ **Comprehension**

Ⓐ **Informational Focus**

Possible response: The most recent schedule was sent on 07/15/09.

Ⓑ **Read and Discuss**

Possible response: It is very important for her to check her e-mail because she is provided with the shooting schedule via e-mail and if there is a change, it will be posted there.

▶ **Extend the Discussion**

Making Generalizations Based on what you have learned from skimming the list of e-mails that Sam has received, who do you think will send an e-mail to Sam to announce that filming is all complete? *Possible response:* The director, whose e-mail address is GeorgeL@StreetWheelie .com, will most likely send Sam an e-mail announcing that production has wrapped because he sent her an e-mail when filming started.

Vocabulary: Own the Word

tentative: Explain that tentative means not fixed; the antonym is *definite*. Explain that the weather for outdoor events is not definite so event planners usually schedule *tentative* rain dates.

Monitor Students' Comprehension

Use the Read with a Purpose follow-up question to assess students' understanding. *Possible response: I was surprised to learn that Sam would get a bonus just for doing her job efficiently. I have never heard of someone being rewarded for that!*

Locating Information: E-mail Memos and Directories

As time goes on, Sam understands why she is required to check her e-mail every morning and night. It's hard to remember which schedule is the most recent. Luckily, Sam can always look it up in her directory of saved mail. Read one of Sam's e-mail memos at the right.

Change in Schedule, Group C——8/8/09 ONLY

Send Address Attach Spelling Print

From: <AlonsaP@StreetWheelie.com> on 07/25/09 04:52:55 PM
To: SamL@samanthamail.com
Cc:
Subject: Change in Schedule, Group C—8/8/09 ONLY

On 08/08/09, your call will be for 1:00 P.M. instead of the listed 8:00 A.M. Refer to the latest revised schedule for all other calls.

Received Mail

Send Address Attach Spelling Print

Sender	Subject	Date Ⓐ
GeorgeL@StreetWheelie.com	Director's Welcome	06/15/09
AlonsaP@StreetWheelie.com	Tentative Schedule, Group C	06/15/09
MayL@StreetWheelie.com	Important Names and Numbers	06/15/09
AlonsaP@StreetWheelie.com	Revised Schedule, Group C	06/17/09
AlonsaP@StreetWheelie.com	Reminder: EARLY call tomorrow	07/07/09
GeorgeL@StreetWheelie.com	GREAT JOB TODAY!	07/08/09
PhamN@StreetWheelie.com	Promo Stills	07/10/09
GeorgeL@StreetWheelie.com	Ahead of Schedule	07/15/09
AlonsaP@StreetWheelie.com	Revised Schedule, Group C	07/15/09
PhamN@StreetWheelie.com	Press Interviews	07/20/09

Ⓑ

Ⓐ **Informational Focus** **Workplace Documents** What is the date of the most recent schedule?

Ⓑ **Read and Discuss** What has Sam learned about checking her e-mail?

Vocabulary **tentative** (TEHN tuh tihv) *adj.:* not fixed.

Read with a Purpose What surprised you about the information presented in these documents?

California Standards, p. 669

■ **Reading Standard 2.2** Locate information by using a variety of consumer, workplace, and public documents.

Applying Your Skills

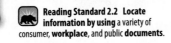
Workplace Documents
Standards Review

Informational Text and Vocabulary

1. The **business letter** discusses *mainly* Sam's

   A audition.

   B contract.

   C ability to act.

   D ability to ride a bike.

2. The **business letter** points out that with the bonus, Sam will

   A be paid only if she fulfills all conditions of her contract.

   B not be paid if she fails to fulfill any conditions of her contract.

   C be paid double if she fulfills all conditions of her contract.

   D earn minimum wage for the project.

3. Sam's **workplace instructions** make it clear that while waiting, actors are expected to be all of the following *except*

   A patient.

   B responsible.

   C self-controlled.

   D loud.

4. Sam's July 25 **e-mail memo** tells her about a change in

   A date.

   B time.

   C part.

   D costume.

5. The word that means the opposite of *punctuality* is

   A promptness.

   B cleanliness.

   C lateness.

   D merriment.

6. A *tentative* schedule is one that

   A may change.

   B is firm.

   C is inaccurate.

   D makes sense.

7. *Interfere* means

   A to authorize.

   B to start filming.

   C to create noise.

   D to get in the way.

Writing Skills Focus

Timed ⌁Writing List the **workplace documents** that Sam has received. Then, give a few examples of the information she can locate in each one.

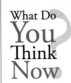 What Do You Think Now How have these documents helped Sam make decisions? Explain.

Writing Skills Focus

Possible response: *Sam has encountered a business letter, an instruction memo, and business-related e-mails. Using the business letter, Sam can find basic information on her employment by StreetWheelie. Using the instruction memo, Sam can locate the rules she must abide by on the set. Using the e-mails, Sam can find information about scheduling of filming and of other events.*

What Do You Think Now?

Have students explain what Sam learned from each document. Then, have students think about what large and small decisions Sam might have used this information to make. If students struggle to identify such decisions, explain that a schedule would help her decide when to leave the house each day, and the bonus information might help her maintain her good behavior on the set.

Objectives

Students will

- understand and analyze information in consumer documents
- learn to use and understand graphic aids

Motivate

What Do You Think?/QuickTalk

Use the QuickTalk to have students talk about their experiences with public transportation. Then, have students reflect on the pros and cons of public transportation in their **Reader/ Writer Notebook.**

English for Academic Success

Academic Vocabulary

Look for opportunities to use the Academic Vocabulary words in this chapter.

- **communicate, v.:** share information or ideas.

- **function, n.:** purpose of a specific person or thing.

Analyzing Visuals

Extension Activity Ask students to identify the location shown in the image and discuss the sorts of documents they might find there.
Possible response: *It's a train station, so it might have train schedules and maps there.*

![California bear logo] **California Standards, pp. 670–677**

- **Reading Standard 2.2** Locate information by using a variety of consumer, workplace, and public documents.

INFORMATIONAL TEXT FOCUS

Consumer Documents

The Millbrae BART Station, San Mateo County, California.

CONTENTS

What Do **You Think** What information would you need to get to a new job?

🕑 **QuickTalk**
Have you ever ridden on a bus, train, or subway system? How did you find out about routes, fares, transfers, and schedules in advance? Discuss your experience with the class.

Selection Readability	
Easily Accessible **Accessible** **Challenging**	unfamiliar format and syntax

Selection Summary

Sam has to travel to work from a suburb of San Francisco into the city. The following documents show how Sam and her grandfather can use the Bay Area Rapid Transit System (BART) to get to their destination.

Preparing to Read

Reading Standard 2.2 Locate information by using a variety of consumer, workplace, and public **documents**.

Consumer Documents

Informational Text Focus

Consumer Documents A consumer uses what someone else sells. Consumers buy things (goods) for their own use and for use by their family and friends. Have you ever treated a friend to an ice cream cone? If so, you and your friend are consumers. Even your pets can be considered consumers—of the foods and toys you buy for them. Consumers need information about the products and services they buy, such as packaged-food ingredients, movie ratings, and airline schedules. **Consumer documents** communicate that information. Text features such as headings, boldface type, bulleted lists, color printing, and other elements are often used in consumer documents to help you locate information.

Reading Skills Focus

Understanding Graphic Aids When you look at consumer documents, you're likely to come across **graphic aids,** such as maps, graphs, tables, and illustrations. Always read the titles of graphics to see if they might contain the information you need.

Maps are drawings of land areas. They can show natural features, political features, or human-made features, such as transportation systems. The function of a **key** is to explain the symbols used on the map.

Tables organize facts in categories put into horizontal rows and vertical columns.

Writing Skills Focus

Preparing for Timed ⏱ Writing Preview the following documents before you begin reading the text. Note the text features that help guide you to the information you need.

Vocabulary

accommodate (uh KAHM uh dayt) *v.*: hold comfortably. *A crowded train cannot accommodate bicycles.*

evacuation (ih vak yoo AY shuhn) *n.*: process of removing people from a potentially dangerous situation. *If an evacuation is required, leave your bike on the train.*

deducted (dih DUHKT ihd) *v.*: taken away. *The cost of the trip will be deducted from your prepaid debit card.*

Language Coach

Suffixes A word part added to the end of a word is called a **suffix.** The word *evacuation* has the suffix –*ation*, which means "the act of." Adding this suffix to *evacuate* creates a new word: *evacuation.* What word is formed when you add this suffix to the word *accommodate*? What does the new word mean?

Reader/Writer Notebook
Use your **RWN** to complete the activities for these selections.

✳ **Learn It Online**
Practice your vocabulary skills with Word Watch online at:
go.hrw.com [H7-671] **Go**

Preteach

Introducing Vocabulary
Have student pairs test one another on the Vocabulary words by having one partner read the definitions and the other identify the words.

English for Academic Success
Language Coach
After students have completed the activity, have them identify the root word of *deducted*. [*deduct*] Then challenge them to add a suffix to *deduct* to form a new word. [*-ion; deduction*] [*accommodation, which means "the act of holding comfortably."*]

Informational Text Focus
As you read and discuss the selection with students, have them think about how the documents benefit consumers.

Reading Skills Focus
Have students study graphic aids, such as maps and tables, in the selection. Tell them to use their findings to answer the questions on the Applying Your Skills page.

Writing Skills Focus
Have students record examples of text features from consumer documents in their **Reader/Writer Notebook.** Students can use their notes to complete the Writing Skills Focus activity.

✳ **Learn It Online**
Send students to **Word Watch** for audio pronunciations of words, synonyms and antonyms, and brief histories of word origins.
go.hrw.com [H7-671] **Go**

Selection Resources

Chapter 6 Resources, on-level practice and assessment, p. 18

PowerNotes, interactive lesson presentation with activities

Teacher One Stop™, on-level lesson plans and all print resources

Holt Audio Library: Selections and Summaries in Spanish

UA: Holt Interactive Reader, p. 174

Holt Interactive Reader for ELD, p. 196

Holt Audio Tutor for ELD

UA: Differentiating Instruction, modified lesson plans and leveled assessment, p. 168

UA: Resources for Teaching Advanced Students, lesson plans

UA: Supporting Instruction in Five Languages, selection summary

Analyzing Visuals Transparencies, p. 37

ThinkCentral Online Assessment, Selection Standards Check

ThinkCentral Online Remediation

Model the Skill

- Tell students that **graphic aids** are supplements, not substitutes, for a text that enhance a reader's understanding of the information being presented.

- You might say, "On the BART system map, I see that all the routes are in different colors. In order to understand what each color represents, I need to consult the key at the bottom of the page. It tells me, for example, that the route marked in red represents the Richmond-Daly City/Colma line." Explain that seeing the routes laid out on a map and in color gives the reader a better idea of how the BART system works and where it goes.

Guided Practice: Apply

Read/Talk/Write Have students study the BART maps in the selection. Then, have them work in groups of three to plan two different routes they could use to travel from San Francisco Airport to Downtown Berkeley. Have each student describe the process of traveling each route in their **Reader/Writer Notebook**. *Students should identify the following routes: take the Dublin/Pleasanton-Daly City line and transfer to the Richmond-Daly City/Colma line at Balboa Park; take the Dublin/Pleasanton-Daly City line and transfer to the Fremont-Richmond line at Bay Fair*

Consumer Documents

Read with a Purpose Read these **consumer documents** to learn how Sam locates the information she needs to get to work.

Locating Information: Transit Map

Sam has to travel from Walnut Creek to the movie set location and back with her bike, and her grandfather has to go with her. The two decide to take the Bay Area Rapid Transit System, better known as BART. BART is a network of trains that can take you just about anywhere in the San Francisco Bay Area. First, Sam and her grandfather log on to the Internet to look at the **BART system map.** They want to be sure they can get from their home in Walnut Creek to the Embarcadero Station, where the StreetWheelie production van will be waiting. They find the map that is shown on the next page.

Universal Access

(EL) English Learners

Although these consumer documents involve only place names, numerals for times, and basic vocabulary, many students may find the small print and unfamiliar formats daunting. Help students by showing them how to follow color-coded lines on the system map and how to look for the color-coded ticket information on the ticket guide.

✔ See **UA: Differentiating Instruction** for strategies for teaching English learners.

Struggling Readers

Have students look over the various documents before they begin reading the text. Point out the main headings, boldface type, bulleted lists, color printing, and other features that help guide readers to the important information they need. After students have spent time familiarizing themselves with the documents, they can read the text and answer the questions.

✔ See **UA: Differentiating Instruction** for strategies for teaching struggling readers.

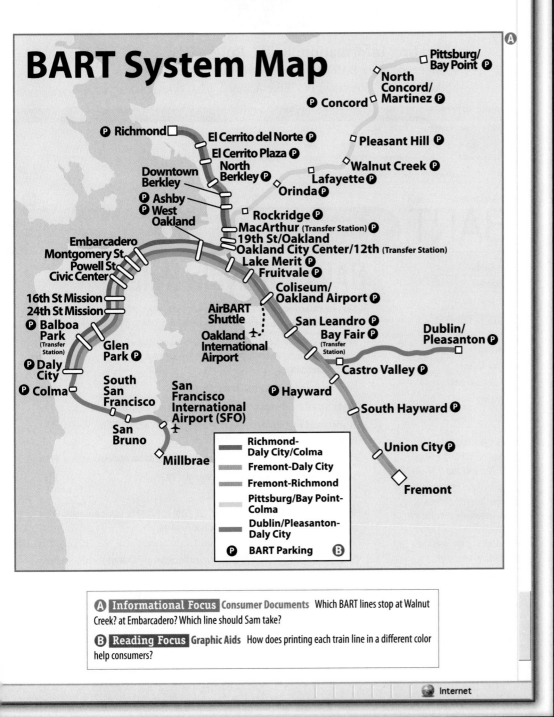

BART System Map

Richmond Ⓟ

El Cerrito del Norte Ⓟ

El Cerrito Plaza Ⓟ

North Berkley

Downtown Berkley

Ashby Ⓟ

West Oakland Ⓟ

Embarcadero

Montgomery St

Powell St

Civic Center

16th St Mission

24th St Mission

Balboa Park Ⓟ **(Transfer Station)**

Daly City Ⓟ

Colma Ⓟ

Glen Park Ⓟ

South San Francisco

San Bruno

San Francisco International Airport (SFO) ✈

Millbrae

Pittsburg/Bay Point Ⓟ

North Concord/Martinez Ⓟ

Concord Ⓟ

Pleasant Hill Ⓟ

Walnut Creek Ⓟ

Lafayette Ⓟ

Orinda Ⓟ

Rockridge Ⓟ

MacArthur (Transfer Station) Ⓟ

19th St/Oakland

Oakland City Center/12th (Transfer Station)

Lake Merit Ⓟ

Fruitvale Ⓟ

Coliseum/Oakland Airport Ⓟ

AirBART Shuttle

Oakland International Airport ✈

San Leandro Ⓟ

Bay Fair Ⓟ **(Transfer Station)**

Castro Valley Ⓟ

Dublin/Pleasanton Ⓟ

Hayward Ⓟ

South Hayward Ⓟ

Union City Ⓟ

Fremont

Legend:

- ▬ Richmond-Daly City/Colma
- ▬ Fremont-Daly City
- ▬ Fremont-Richmond
- ▬ Pittsburg/Bay Point-Colma
- ▬ Dublin/Pleasanton-Daly City
- Ⓟ BART Parking Ⓑ

Ⓐ **Informational Focus** **Consumer Documents** Which BART lines stop at Walnut Creek? at Embarcadero? Which line should Sam take?

Ⓑ **Reading Focus** **Graphic Aids** How does printing each train line in a different color help consumers?

🌐 Internet

Model the Skill

■ Tell students that **consumer documents** are created for people who are looking to obtain goods or services. Some consumer documents are more objective than others. Transportation Web sites, such as the BART site on this page, tend to present factual information. Advertisements, on the other hand, often include persuasive statements or information meant to convince readers to buy a product or service.

■ Demonstrate for students how to interpret a consumer document. You might say, "I can see on this site that certain information is placed on the sidebar, underneath the contents listing for the site. Parts of it are in boldface text or capital letters. I remember that important information is usually in large or boldfaced text. These stations must be larger or more important than the others."

Guided Practice: Apply

Have students form teams of three and go on a scavenger hunt through the BART consumer documents for the following information: the best tickets for two teenage girls, the morning commute hours for San Francisco, and locations for parking bikes. [*Students should recogize that middle and secondary school students receive a discounted fare with the BART orange ticket; morning commute hours are 7:05 to 8:50 A.M. on weekdays; bikes may be parked in racks or lockers.*]

Locating Information: BART Rules

Sam needs more BART information: Is she allowed to bring a bike with her? She clicks on "Bike Access." What does she learn?

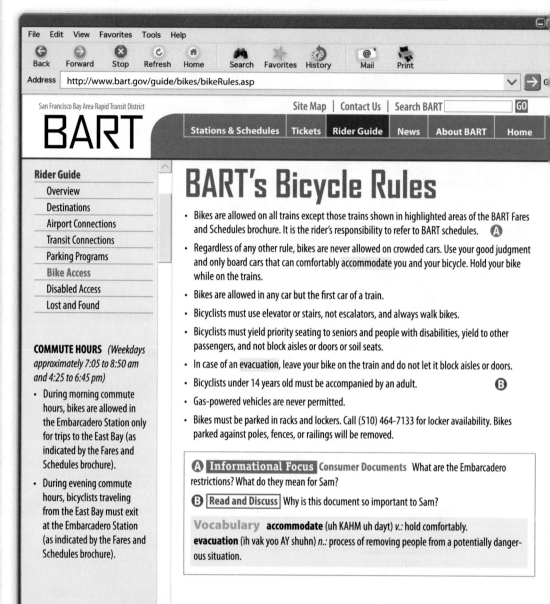

BART's Bicycle Rules

- Bikes are allowed on all trains except those trains shown in highlighted areas of the BART Fares and Schedules brochure. It is the rider's responsibility to refer to BART schedules. **A**
- Regardless of any other rule, bikes are never allowed on crowded cars. Use your good judgment and only board cars that can comfortably accommodate you and your bicycle. Hold your bike while on the trains.
- Bikes are allowed in any car but the first car of a train.
- Bicyclists must use elevator or stairs, not escalators, and always walk bikes.
- Bicyclists must yield priority seating to seniors and people with disabilities, yield to other passengers, and not block aisles or doors or soil seats.
- In case of an evacuation, leave your bike on the train and do not let it block aisles or doors.
- Bicyclists under 14 years old must be accompanied by an adult. **B**
- Gas-powered vehicles are never permitted.
- Bikes must be parked in racks and lockers. Call (510) 464-7133 for locker availability. Bikes parked against poles, fences, or railings will be removed.

A **Informational Focus** **Consumer Documents** What are the Embarcadero restrictions? What do they mean for Sam?

B **Read and Discuss** Why is this document so important to Sam?

Vocabulary **accommodate** (uh KAHM uh dayt) *v.*: hold comfortably.
evacuation (ih vak yoo AY shuhn) *n.*: process of removing people from a potentially dangerous situation.

Universal Access

Struggling Readers

Benchmark Students   To help students understand the practical applications of consumer documents, have them work in small groups to plan a trip using the BART documents. Provide them with the scenario below. Explain to students that they should determine the cost to travel to their destination for each person, taking into account any discounted fares. Next, they should determine what time they must leave in order to reach their destination and return by the appointed time. Finally, groups should note any restrictions that affect their group. Circulate the room and provide guidance as necessary. Have groups compile all the information they gathered into a time line that explains the journey and costs, noting which documents provided each piece of information. Have each group share their work.
Paul Jackson and his daughter Quiana are visiting Quiana's grandmother, aunt, and two young cousins in South Hayward. They want to take a day trip to Berkeley, but they would prefer to avoid morning and evening commute hours. Paul is 45, Quiana is 13, her aunt is 32, her cousins are 3 and 7, and her grandmother is 68.

Locating Information: BART Ticket Guide

Sam wants to know how much it will cost. Grandpa is over sixty-five, and Sam is twelve. Can they get any discount fares?

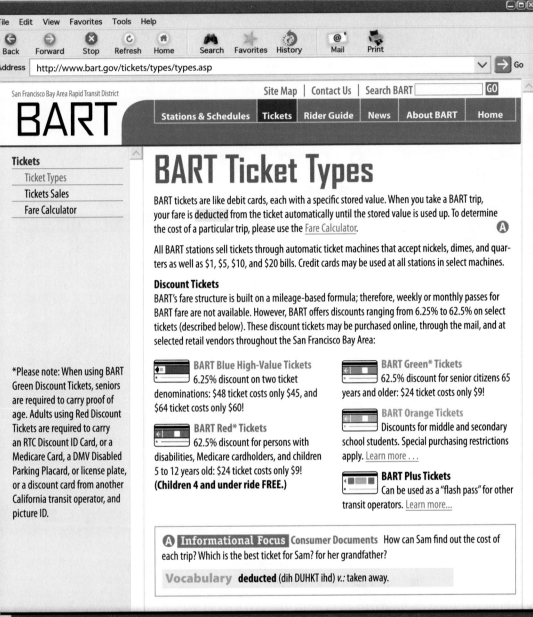

▶ Comprehension

BART's Bicycle Rules

Ⓐ Informational Focus

Possible response: Bikes aren't allowed in the Embarcadero Station during the morning and evening commute hours. Sam must plan her trip around these hours.

Ⓑ Read and Discuss

Possible response: Since Sam is bringing her bike on the trip, it is necessary for her to be aware of the rules ahead of time.

BART Ticket Guide

Ⓐ Informational Focus

Possible response: She can click on the Fare Calculator. Sam's best choice is the Red Ticket, because it is discounted for 12-year-olds. Her grandfather's best choice is the Green Ticket; it is discounted for senior citizens.

▶ Extend the Discussion

Drawing Conclusions Why do you think there are special bike restrictions for commute hours? *Possible response:* Trains are most crowded and there is less room for bikes.

Vocabulary: Own the Word

- **accommodate:** Have students discuss ways that buildings are equipped to *accomodate* people who use wheelchairs. *Possible response:* Doors open automatically; buildings have ramps and elevators.

- **evacuation:** Ask students what might cause an *evacuation*. *Possible response:* an approaching hurricane

- **deducted:** Explain that *deducted* includes the Latin root word *deductus*, which means "bring away." Ask students: How does the meaning of *deducted* relate to *bringing away*? *Possible response:* Deducted refers to taking away something, or subtracting it.

Universal Access

🔵 English Learners

English for Academic Success Read aloud the list of BART's Bicycle Rules while students listen carefully. Ask them to raise their hands when they hear a rule that applies specifically to Sam, and have a volunteer explain why the rule applies to Sam's situation. Then, pair English learners with fluent speakers and have them read the BART ticket types together. Have pairs discuss how knowing about different ticket types is useful to consumers.

🔴 Students Who Use African American Vernacular English

English for Academic Success Some students may not fully voice r-controlled vowels in their everyday speech. Explain that while this is appropriate for informal English, it is important to voice these sounds when speaking formal English. Model pronouncing r-controlled vowels by pronouncing *therefore, fare,* and *determine* for students. Then, have them say the following words as a class, until students have mastered the formal English pronunciations: *card, quarter, formula, purchased, vendors.*

Think About/Talk About

▶ Comprehension

Ⓐ Reading Focus

Possible responses: *They are allowed between 5:05 and 7:04 A.M. and between 8:00 and 8:54 A.M.*

Ⓑ Read and Discuss

Possible responses: *The schedule answers her remaining questions about the cost of tickets and discounts, and most importantly, whether she is allowed to bring her bike on BART.*

▶ Extend the Discussion

Analyzing According to the schedule, which train should Sam and her grandfather take if they want to arrive at the Embarcadero station at 7:04 A.M.? *Possible response: They should take the 6:30 A.M. train.*

Monitor Students' Comprehension

Use the Read with a Purpose follow-up question to assess students' understanding. *Possible response: Sam might need to know when she will be finished filming so that she can plan which train to take on her return trip.*

Locating Information: BART Schedule

Sam goes to the Stations and Schedules page and enters the stations they'll be leaving from and going to. Here's what she finds.

BART Schedule

Extended Schedule   Fare: $4.25
Depart: Walnut Creek   Arrive: Embarcadero   Departing Around: 5:00 AM

Depart	Time	Arrive	Time	Bikes Ⓐ	Depart	Time	Arrive	Time	Bikes
WCRK	5:05a	EMBR	5:39a	Yes	WCRK	7:11a	EMBR	7:45a	No
WCRK	5:20a	EMBR	5:54a	Yes	WCRK	7:15a	EMBR	7:49a	No
WCRK	5:35a	EMBR	6:09a	Yes	WCRK	7:20a	EMBR	7:54a	No
WCRK	5:50a	EMBR	6:24a	Yes	WCRK	7:26a	EMBR	8:00a	No
WCRK	6:05a	EMBR	6:39a	Yes	WCRK	7:30a	EMBR	8:04a	No
WCRK	6:15a	EMBR	6:49a	Yes	WCRK	7:35a	EMBR	8:09a	No
WCRK	6:20a	EMBR	6:54a	Yes	WCRK	7:41a	EMBR	8:15a	No
WCRK	6:30a	EMBR	7:04a	Yes	WCRK	7:45a	EMBR	8:19a	No
WCRK	6:35a	EMBR	7:09a	No	WCRK	7:50a	EMBR	8:24a	No
WCRK	6:45a	EMBR	7:19a	No	WCRK	8:00a	EMBR	8:34a	Yes
WCRK	6:50a	EMBR	7:24a	No	WCRK	8:05a	EMBR	8:39a	Yes
WCRK	7:00a	EMBR	7:34a	No	WCRK	8:15a	EMBR	8:49a	Yes
WCRK	7:05a	EMBR	7:39a	No	WCRK	8:20a	EMBR	8:54a	Yes

Copyright 2007, BART   Your Privacy   Text-Only/Printable Page   Ⓑ

Ⓐ **Reading Focus** Graphic Aids When are bikes allowed on BART trains?

Ⓑ **Read and Discuss** What does Sam learn from the BART schedule?

Read with a Purpose What other information might Sam need before going to the movie set?

Cross-Curricular Connection

HISTORY: The Streets of San Francisco

- During the mid-nineteenth century, horsecars—large passenger vehicles pulled by horses—were the only form of mass transit in cities. Horses had to work especially hard in San Francisco because it was built on a series of steep hills. This may be the reason that San Francisco was the first city in the world to build a cable-powered street railway.

- San Francisco had no railway system until local voters agreed in 1961 to pay taxes to fund the construction.

Today, BART has one hundred and four miles of track.

- Like much of California, San Francisco is prone to earthquakes. Designers and builders worked hard to be sure that BART could withstand earthquakes. When a 1989 earthquake destroyed bridges and expressways and halted the Oakland–San Francisco World Series just before the third game, BART was undamaged and continued to run on schedule.

 HSS Analysis Skills: HI 2

Applying Your Skills

Consumer Documents
Standards Review

Informational Text and Vocabulary

1. Which type of **consumer document** would you consult to learn what BART line to take to get from one place to another?

  A System Map

  B Bicycle Rules

  C Ticket Guide

  D BART Schedule

2. According to the **bicycle rules,** in which cars of the train can you ride with a bike?

  A any car at all

  B any car but the first

  C any car but the last

  D only the first three cars

3. According to the **ticket guide,** Sam (age 12) and Sam's grandfather (age 75) should buy

  A one blue and one red ticket.

  B one red and one green ticket.

  C one orange and one blue ticket.

  D two orange tickets.

4. On the BART Stations and Schedules Web page, you can locate all of the following information *except*

  A the base cost of the trip.

  B the schedule of departures and arrivals.

  C when bicycles are allowed.

  D the discounts available.

5. *Accommodate* means

  A dislike.

  B transport.

  C fit.

  D ride.

6. An *evacuation* would most likely be required

  A after purchasing a ticket.

  B before arriving at the Embarcadero station.

  C on the Fremont-Richmond line.

  D during an emergency.

7. Something *deducted* has been

  A subtracted.

  B monitored.

  C recorded.

  D added.

Writing Skills Focus

Timed ⌐Writing Sam found all the information about the BART system on the Internet. Explain how she might have located this same information if she did not have access to a computer.

 What Do **You Think Now** Which of the BART documents has the most helpful information? Explain.

California Standards, p. 677

■ **Reading Standard 2.2** Locate information by using a variety of consumer, workplace, and public documents.

What Do You Think Now?

Review with students the four documents they looked at in this selection. Discuss what Sam learned from each document to determine its purpose.

Check for Understanding

Independent Practice
Answers and Explanations

1. A The system map shows where each train goes. B, C, and D provide additional information about riding the BART.

2. B This is stated in the third bullet under "BART's Bicycle Rules."

3. B Students can find this information in the ticket guide. Red tickets are for kids; green tickets for seniors.

4. D This document does not tell about available discounts.

5. C Accommodate *means fit, not* dislike (A), *transport* (B), *or ride* (D).

6. D An evacuation *is when people leave an area due to an emergency.*

7. A Deducted *means subtracted, not* monitored (B), *recorded* (C), *or added* (D).

Writing Focus

Possible response: *Sam could have located the same information by phone or by visiting a BART station to obtain printed copies of the documents she found online.*

Assess

Chapter 6 Resources, Selection Standards Check, p. 21

 ThinkCentral Online Assessment, Selection Standards Check

Teacher One Stop™, editable Selection Standards Check

Reteach

ThinkCentral Online Remediation

Technical Directions

Standards Focus

Objectives
Students will
• follow technical directions
• preview the text to find information

Motivate

What Do You Think?/QuickTalk
Have students describe a time they had to follow directions. Good examples may be making a recipe or using a manual to build something. Then, have them use their **Reader/Writer Notebook** to write down as many steps as they can remember.

English for Academic Success

Academic Vocabulary
Look for opportunities to use the Academic Vocabulary words in this chapter.

• **function,** *n.:* purpose of a specific person or thing.

• **sequence,** *n.:* specific order in which things follow one another.

• **technique,** *n.:* method of doing a particular task.

Analyzing Visuals
Extension Activity Ask students to discuss what directions people might need to follow when driving a car. *Possible response: You need to follow directions from road signs and stop lights. You might follow directions to get to a certain destination.*

CONTENTS

 What Do **You** Think

Where can you find instructions on completing a mechanical task?

 QuickTalk
What makes written directions easy or hard to follow?

🐻 **California Standards, pp. 678–683**

■ **Reading Standard 2.5** Understand and explain the use of a simple mechanical device by following technical directions.

Selection Readability	
Easily Accessible **Accessible** **Challenging**	familiar syntax; unfamiliar vocabulary

Selection Summary
The selection gives a point-by-point set of instructions for changing a flat tire. The selection describes the activity for a driver who has never had to change a flat tire before.

Preparing to Read

Reading Standard 2.5 Understand and explain the use of a simple mechanical device by following technical directions.

Technical Directions

Informational Text Focus

Technical Directions **Technical directions** are step-by-step instructions that explain how to accomplish mechanical tasks. You follow technical directions when you assemble the video game system you bought, when you build a bookcase or other furniture item that came in sections, or when you clean the sprockets on your bicycle. You can understand and explain the use of a simple mechanical device by following technical directions.

You're probably too young to drive a car, but you're certainly not too young to be thinking about it. Driving can give you a new feeling of independence, but it also gives you new responsibilities. Any number of things can go wrong with your car, and it's up to you to fix them—or to get them fixed. A flat tire is something every driver will face someday—possibly on a lonely country road, without a person in sight. To be prepared for that, study the directions on the next page.

Reading Skills Focus

Previewing the Text You may come across technical directions that seem overwhelming because they contain so much information. **Previewing the text** by looking at headings, lists, and tables can help you find the specific information you need—the <u>function</u> of a button on your cell phone or the proper <u>technique</u> for removing lug nuts.

Writing Skills Focus

Preparing for Timed ⏱ Writing As you read the following document, notice the way the technical directions are organized in <u>sequence</u>. This organization helps ensure that you perform the tasks in order, step by step.

Reader/Writer Notebook
Use your **RWN** to complete the activities for this selection.

> **Vocabulary**
>
> **procedures** (pruh SEE juhrz) *n.*: methods of doing things. *The proper procedures for changing a flat tire are given in the directions that follow.*
>
> **standard** (STAN duhrd) *adj.*: usual; regularly used or produced. *If you have a standard transmission, put your car in gear.*

> **Language Coach**
>
> **Multiple Meanings** If you see the word *fall* all by itself, you can't tell if it's a noun referring to the season, a verb that means "to drop," or a verb that means "to lose position." In a sentence, though, you can usually tell which definition of the word is meant. Which word above has multiple meanings?

 Learn It Online
For examples of analyzing technical directions, use the interactive Reading Workshops on:

go.hrw.com | H7-679 | **Go**

> **Preteach**

Introducing Vocabulary

Read aloud the Vocabulary words and sample sentences. Then, have students complete each sentence with the correct Vocabulary word.

1. In the event of an emergency, the government follows a specific set of _____. [*procedures*]

2. The _____ sizes for t-shirts are small, medium, and large. [*standard*]

English for Academic Success
Language Coach

Help students complete the Language Coach activity by telling them that *standard* can also be used as a noun. Guide them to understand that *standard* can also mean "a measurement of quality."

Informational Text Focus

As you read and discuss the selection with students, have them restate each step in their own words to check for understanding.

Reading Skills Focus

Have students preview the technical directions before they read. Tell them to use the information gathered during their preview to answer the questions on the Applying Your Skills page.

Writing Skills Focus

Have students record examples of sequence in their **Reader/Writer Notebook.** Students can use their notes to complete the Writing Skills Focus activity.

 Learn It Online
Reading Workshops are interactive versions of real-world informational texts; students exercise their reading skills by responding to polls and answering questions in an engaging online format.

go.hrw.com | H7-679 | **Go**

Direct Teach

Model the Skill

- Tell students that **technical directions** are used in real life as well as school. If a person has to put together a chair, for example, he needs to know in what order to put things together so that the chair does not end up with the legs on the top. Following directions step-by-step is important for the successful completion of a task.

- Read aloud the first two steps of the procedure for changing a flat tire. Point out that the first step tells the driver where to park the car in order to change the tire, and how to set up a safe work area. This step would not make sense anywhere else in the order; it must go first because a driver would not look for a safe work area after the process of changing a tire has already begun.

Guided Practice: Apply

- Direct students' attention to step 2, in which a labeled diagram shows all of the tools needed for the job and what they are called. Ask students why it is important to have this list of tools at step 2, and why this diagram does not appear at step 1. [*Students should note that a driver needs to know what tools are necessary for the job so he or she does not have to stop working and look for tools; students should also note that setting up a safe work area logically must be done before getting out tools or working.*]

How to Change a Flat Tire

Read with a Purpose
Read these technical directions to learn how to change a flat tire.

Before you can change a flat tire on your car, you first have to realize that the tire is flat. You might come out of your house in the morning and see the wheel rim resting on the road with the tire spread around it. You will know right away that the tire's flat. How can you tell, though, if it goes flat while you are driving? A first clue is that your car starts to pull to the right or the left even though you aren't turning the steering wheel. Another clue is that passing motorists honk and point as they drive by. Yet another clue is that the car starts bouncing up and down and making a loud *thumpity-thump-thump* sound.

When you suspect you have a flat tire, follow these procedures:

Park the car as far off the road as possible. Put the car in park (if you have an automatic transmission) or in gear (if you have a standard transmission), turn off the engine, and put on the emergency brake. Turn on your car's flashing lights. Now, get out and look at your tires. If you have a flat, put out emergency triangles or, at night, flares. (It's a good idea to carry warning triangles and flares in your trunk at all times in case of an emergency.) **A**

A **Informational Focus** Technical Directions Why can't you leave out the step of setting the brake?

Vocabulary **procedures** (pruh SEE juhrz) *n.*: methods of doing things.
standard (STAN duhrd) *adj.*: usual; regularly used or produced.

Universal Access

EL English Learners
English for Academic Success Have students read through the directions independently, looking only at the illustrations. Discuss with students what is happening in the series of pictures. Then, have students read the entire selection in mixed-ability groups, with fluent readers clarifying technical terms or complex sentences.

✔ See **UA: Differentiating Instruction** for strategies for teaching English learners.

Struggling Readers
Tell students that technical directions are instructions for carrying out a process on a technical device, such as changing a battery or changing a car's flat tire. Point out that most technical directions consist of written steps and visuals that clarify what is to be done.

Encourage students as they read to ask themselves, "What is happening at this step? What materials do I need, and what do I have to do?"

✔ See **UA: Differentiating Instruction** for strategies for teaching struggling readers.

STEP 2

Remove the spare tire from the trunk. Also take out the jack, the lug wrench, and related tools.

lug nuts

spare tire

lug wrench

jack

screwdriver

STEP 3

Remove the wheel cover from the flat tire, using a screwdriver or the end of the jack handle.

STEP 4

Loosen the lug nuts with the lug wrench, but do not remove them. Most lug nuts turn counterclockwise.

Ⓑ

STEP 5

Position your jack. Different makes of cars come with different types of jacks, so check your owner's manual to learn how to use your jack. Make sure the jack is sitting on a solid, flat surface.

STEP 6

Lift the car with the jack until your flat tire is two or three inches off the ground. *(Never lie under the car when it is on the jack!)*

Ⓑ **Read and Discuss** What do the steps illustrating the way to change a tire show you about the process?

Think About/Talk About

Read with a Purpose Have students read the Read with a Purpose statement. Ask them to discuss whether or not they usually read the instructions before completing a task.

▶ Comprehension

Ⓐ Informational Focus

Possible response: It is important to put the brake on so the car does not move while you change the tire.

Ⓑ Read and Discuss

Possible response: You can't do one step without doing the one before it, but overall it doesn't seem too complicated.

▶ Extend the Discussion

Cause and Effect What are some reasons your tire might go flat? *Possible response: If you drive over something sharp or if a tire is old, the tire might go flat.*

Analyzing In step 5, why does the jack need to rest on a solid, flat surface? *Possible response: Placing the jack on a solid, flat surface will prevent the car from shifting and hurting someone.*

Vocabulary: Own the Word

- **procedures:** Review the vocabulary word and its definition. Ask students: How are *rules* different from *procedures*? *Possible response: Procedures are steps doing things; rules explain how things must be done.*

- **standard:** Demonstrate *standard* by drawing a smiley face on the board. Explain that the smiley face is *standard* because it can be regularly used or produced. Demonstrate a non-standard face by drawing a complex smiley face on the board. Ask students what they think the narrator meant by referring to a *standard* transmission. *Possible response: A transmission with gears is regularly used or produced.*

Think About/Talk About

▶ **Comprehension**

C Informational Focus

Possible response: If the lug nuts are on very tight, you would have to use a good deal of force to loosen and remove them; this motion could cause the car to slip off the jack and hurt you.

▶ **Extend the Discussion**

Analyzing Look at step 10. Why would you want to go directly to a place that can fix your tire even though you've already changed it? *Possible response:* An experienced repair person can check if anything is wrong with the other tires, and give you a replacement spare tire.

Comparing and Contrasting How are these directions similar to or different from other directions you've followed? *Possible response:* These directions require many tools and deal with a larger piece of equipment than I've ever used, but the organization and detail reminds me of the instructions I followed to put together my model airplane.

Monitor Students' Comprehension

Use the Read with a Purpose follow-up question to assess students' understanding. *Possible response:* The written directions are most effective because they tell exactly what to do. The pictures are good supplements, but they do not provide enough information on their own.

STEP 7 Now, finish unscrewing the lug nuts. Put them inside the wheel cover so you don't lose them. **C**

STEP 8 Remove the flat tire, and replace it with the spare tire. Replace the lug nuts, and tighten them by hand.

STEP 9 Lower the jack until the spare tire is firmly on the ground. Remove the jack. Firmly tighten the lug nuts with the lug wrench. Work diagonally—tighten one on the top, then one on the bottom; one on the left, then one on the right; and so on.

STEP 10 Place the flat tire, the wheel cover, and all of your tools in the trunk. As soon as you can, drive to a garage or a tire repair shop to get the tire fixed or replaced. You never want to be without a spare, because you never know when you'll get another flat!

C Informational Focus Technical Directions Why do you think you should loosen the lug nuts, then jack up the car, then take off the lug nuts, instead of jacking up the car first and removing the lug nuts in one step?

Read with a Purpose

What part of the technical directions was most effective in teaching you how to change a flat tire?

Word-Attack Skills Mini-Lesson

Remind students that the digraph *ch* most often stands for the sound /ch/ as in *change*. Then, point out that the digraph *ch* can also stand for the sound /k/. The letter-sound relationship commonly occurs in words that have Greek roots—for example, *technical* or *mechanical*. Display these sets of words. Have volunteers tell which word has the same *ch* sound as the first word.

1. chronic   chirp   chronicle
2. chorus   chores   choreography
[*Answers: chronicle, choreography*]

Applying Your Skills

Reading Standard 2.5 Understand and explain the use of a simple mechanical device by following technical directions.

Technical Directions
Standards Review

Informational Text and Vocabulary

1. If you think you have a flat tire, what should you do first?

   A Drive the car to your family's garage.

   B Call your parents to pick you up.

   C Park the car as far off the road as possible.

   D Look out the window to see if the tire is flat.

2. According to the passage, the *best* tool for loosening the lug nuts is

   A a screwdriver.

   B a lug wrench.

   C a jack.

   D a wheel cover.

3. You should lift the car with the jack until

   A you can fit comfortably underneath the car.

   B the car is two to three feet in the air.

   C the flat tire is two to three inches off the ground.

   D the flat tire comes off the wheel.

4. According to the passage, what should you do as soon as possible after you have changed a flat tire?

   A Call your parents to let them know what happened.

   B Drive to a garage to get the flat tire fixed.

   C Continue traveling to wherever you were going before you got the flat.

   D Throw away the flat tire.

5. What is the main purpose of this passage?

   A to persuade you to learn to change a flat tire

   B to instruct you how to change a flat tire safely

   C to show you the parts needed to change a flat tire

   D to remind you to use caution when changing a flat tire

6. *Procedures* are all of the following *except*

   A processes.

   B steps.

   C plans.

   D passageways.

7. Which word is most closely related to *standard*?

   A normal

   B necessary

   C automatic

   D gear

Writing Skills Focus

Timed └Writing Write a list of instructions explaining how to operate a simple technical device, such as a DVD player, microwave oven, or MP3 player. Be sure to include all of the necessary steps in your directions.

 What Do You Think Now

After reading the technical directions, could you change a flat tire? Explain.

 California Standards, p. 683

■ **Reading Standard 2.5** Understand and explain the use of a simple mechanical device by following technical directions.

What Do You Think Now?

Ask students if they feel prepared to tell someone else how to change a tire. Would they be able to help a friend or family member who was stranded with a flat tire?

Check for Understanding

Independent Practice
Answers and Explanations

1. C *Students should recognize that they should stop driving and park off the road for safety reasons.*

2. B *Students can find this answer in step 4.*

3. C *Students can find this answer in step 6.*

4. B *Students can find this answer in step 10.*

5. B *The main purpose of the passage is to instruct you how to safely change a tire. The other items are important components of safe tire-changing, but they are not the main purpose of the passage.*

6. D *Procedures can be processes (A), steps (B), or plans (C).*

7. A *Something standard, or usual, often is considered normal (A).*

Writing Skills Focus

Possible response: *To use a microwave to warm up my dinner, I have to: 1) open the door, 2) put the food in the microwave, 3) shut the door, 4) enter the cooking time, 5) press start, 6) take the food out when it's done.*

Assess

📝 **Chapter 6 Resources,** Selection Standards Check, p. 27

go. hrw .com **ThinkCentral Online Assessment,** Selection Standards Check

💿 **Teacher One Stop™,** editable Selection Standards Check

Reteach

💿 **ThinkCentral Online Remediation**

Standard Focus

Objectives

Students will

- create public service announcement in the form of a multimedia presentation
- support a message with evidence

Preteach

Write with a Purpose Read aloud the essentials of a good public service announcement to guide students' understanding of this type of writing.

Direct Teach

Model the Skill

Think as a Reader/Writer Use the professional model on this page and others in the chapter to provide examples of the elements of a public service announcement. Point out that the model focuses on a topic of public concern—children's futures.

Think About the Professional Model

Possible responses:

1. The purpose is to urge the audience to help provide computers for kids.

2. The PSA appeals to parents by showing a young man in distress.

3. Anecdotal evidence is used in the form of a story about a specific person being unprepared for the future. This evidence is effective because it appeals to the audience's emotions.

California Standards, pp. 684–691

- **Writing Standard 1.2** Support all statements and claims with anecdotes, descriptions, facts and statistics, and specific examples.
- **Writing Standard 1.4** Identify topics; ask and evaluate questions; and develop ideas leading to inquiry, investigation, and research.
- **Writing Standard 1.7** Revise writing to improve organization and word choice after checking the logic of the ideas and the precision of the vocabulary.
- **Writing Standard 2.4 a.** State a clear position or perspective in support of a proposition or proposal. **b.** Describe the points in support of the proposition, employing well-articulated evidence.

Multimedia Presentation: Public Service Announcement

Write with a Purpose

Write a public service announcement that presents persuasive information about a topic of public concern. Your **purpose** is to convince your audience that they too should be concerned about this issue. Your **audience** consists of the teachers and students at your school.

A Good Public Service Announcement

- focuses on a topic of public concern
- targets its audience
- appeals to its audience emotionally as well as logically
- supports its message with facts, examples, expert opinions, statistics, and other evidence
- may use print, visuals, and/or sound to deliver its message
- wraps up its conclusion by clearly restating the purpose of the message

Reader/Writer Notebook

Use your **RWN** to complete the activities for this workshop.

Think as a Reader/Writer

It is time for you to think beyond just words. Now you can use voice-overs, moving images, photos, graphics, music, and other elements to convince an audience of your idea. Before you create your own public service announcement (PSA), read the following excerpt from the PSA script to be shot for TV for "Media for Kids," an organization that donates computers to schools.

VIDEO	AUDIO	
CLOSEUP ("CU") OF NEWS-PAPER WANT AD, SHOW-ING FINGER ON TEXT.	VOICEOVER ("V/O") OF YOUNG MAN: Good spelling and grammar. OK. Basics of bookkeeping. OK.	← The beginning draws in members of the **audience** with a **topic** they can relate to. The focus is job hunting.
PULL BACK TO SHOW MAN READING.	YOUNG MAN: Computer experience. None.	← Information is revealed through video and audio.
ANGLE ON MAN AND FATHER AT TABLE.	YOUNG MAN: How am I supposed to get any computer experience. . .	← PSA uses **audio, video,** and visuals to deliver **message.**
CU OF YOUNG MAN.	. . . when we didn't have computers at my school?	
STILL OF "MEDIA FOR KIDS" 12 Curie St. New Orleans, LA 70122 1-800-555-KIDS	V/O NARRATOR: Help our children compete . . . . For information, write . . . Or call 1-800-555-KIDS	← The **conclusion** clearly wraps up the message.
FADE TO STILL OF CRUMPLED AD.	MUSIC UP. MUSIC OUT	← The final shot is an **emotional appeal.**

Think About the Professional Model

With a partner, discuss the following questions about the model.

1. What is the purpose of this public service announcement?
2. How does the announcement try to appeal to its target audience?
3. What type of evidence does the announcement use? Do you think it is effective? Why, or why not?

Writing Workshop Resources

UA: Holt Interactive Writer and Speaker, on-level practice and assessment, p. 112

UA: Differentiating Instruction, modified lesson plans, p. 175

WritingNotes, interactive lesson presentations with activities

GrammarNotes, interactive lesson presentations with activities

Writing and Research in a Digital Age, interactive lesson presentations with activities

Writing Standards 1.2 Support all statements and claims with anecdotes, descriptions, facts and statistics, and specific examples. **1.4** Identify topics; ask and evaluate questions; and develop ideas leading to inquiry, investigation, and research. **1.6 Create documents by using** word-processing skills and publishing programs; develop **simple databases and spreadsheets to manage information** and prepare reports. **1.7** Revise writing to improve organization and word choice after checking the logic of the ideas and the precision of the vocabulary. **2.4a. State a clear position or perspective in support of a proposition or proposal. b. Describe the points in support of the proposition,** employing well-articulated **evidence. c. Anticipate and address reader concerns** and counterarguments.

Prewriting

Choose a Topic

A public service announcement, often called a PSA, communicates a persuasive or informative message that is in the community's interest. In terms of technical and artistic requirements, there is little difference between a PSA and an advertisement or commercial. To get ideas for your own PSA,

- read your school and local newspapers
- check out school bulletin boards
- listen to the news on the radio or television
- explore electronic databases on the Internet

Think About Purpose and Audience

As you plan your PSA, be clear about what your **purpose** is. You want to inform your audience about an issue of concern to you. What else do you hope to do? Do you hope to educate your audience about a topic they may not know? Do you want your audience to take action on this issue? If so, what action are you hoping they'll take? Now, make sure you are clear about who your **audience** is.

- Will your audience be limited to students in your class or your grade, or are you hoping to reach a wider audience?
- What is a typical member of your audience like? What do you think he or she knows about this issue?
- Should your language be formal or casual?
- What types of evidence would be most persuasive to this audience?

Know Your Attitude

Tone refers to a writer's attitude toward a subject. Tone can be serious, critical, comic, sarcastic, romantic, admiring, and so on. When you have the topic for your PSA, decide what will be the best tone to use to "sell" your idea. The tone will help you determine the choice of visuals and audio.

Idea Starters

- promoting media literacy
- saving energy at school by "going green"
- eating healthful foods
- giving tips about communicating online
- eliminating littering in your school's neighborhood

🔵 Writing Tip

For topic ideas and for presentation elements, take a look at your local public television channel to see PSAs there. Also, look through different national and local newspapers and magazines to find print PSAs.

Your Turn _____

Get Started Making notes in your **RWN**, explore different topics for your **PSA**. Narrow your choices until you have decided on the two or three issues you want to tackle. Then, think about your **purpose** and your **audience.** Which topic are you most interested in addressing with this audience?

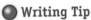
Learn It Online
To see how one writer met all the assignment criteria, visit:

go.hrw.com | H7-685 | Go

Guided Practice: Apply
Choose a Topic

Guided Practice: Apply

Choose a Topic

- As students generate ideas, encourage them to choose topics that affect them and their peers. Choosing a topic that they feel strongly about will help them stay motivated and involved.

- Suggest that students use the web on p. 685 while planning their topics and target audiences as a natural progression into identifying suitable tones for their pieces.

Think About Purpose and Audience

Warn students that the people affected by the issues mentioned in a PSA will not always be the target audience. For example, a PSA about helping the hungry does not target the people who are hungry. Rather, the PSA will have a target audience of people who are not hungry because they have the means to help others. As they think about audience, tell students to consider who can do the most to help their cause.

Your Turn _____

Get Started Have students complete the **Your Turn** activity as independent practice. To help students choose a topic, have them consider which issues are likely to generate the strongest appeals. This should help them eliminate weak topics from their list of ideas.

Learn It Online
The **Interactive Writer's Models** at **ThinkCentral, Student Access** provide annotated sample essays along with writing tips and strategies.

go.hrw.com | H7-685 | Go

Teacher One Stop™, on-level lesson plans and all print resources 🔘

Holt Six Traits for Writing, rubrics, prompts, and sample papers 📝 🔘

Language and Sentence Skills Practice 📝 🔘

UA: Developmental Language and Sentence Skills Practice 📝 🔘

Language Handbook Worksheets, p. 130 📝 🔘

Formal Assessment, Progress Monitoring Test 5 📝 🔘

ThinkCentral Online Assessment, Writing Workshop Test

ThinkCentral Online Remediation

Holt Online Essay Scoring

Guided Practice: Apply

Select Your Media

■ Point out to students that the nature of their public service announcement may determine the medium they choose to present it. For example, a PSA about music education would probably be most effective if it included sound. In this case, a print presentation may not be the best choice.

■ Explain to students that there are advantages and disadvantages to using each medium. Print and audio presentations are ideal for presenting lists of information, whereas a visual presentation that displays lists of words may be considered boring. Charts and graphs displaying information can only be used in visual and print presentations, but in an audio presentation, simple sound effects can simulate almost any location or scenario. Have students use the checklist in the Student Edition to help them determine which medium they will use to present their PSA.

Your Turn _____

Plan Your Presentation Have students complete the **Your Turn** activity as independent practice. As students map out their plans, tell them to write their ideas on index cards. They can arrange the cards on their desk to work out the most effective order for their PSA.

⬤ Writing Tip

How will you deliver your message? Here are some options:
Audio: narration; music; sound effects
Visual: video; photos; Web site; animation
Print: pamphlet; poster; graphics

Make a list of the equipment you'll need for your PSA, and be sure you'll have access to all the necessary materials before you commit to using a particular medium.

⬤ Writing Tip

You are going to need to locate accurate evidence to support your message. Most libraries have **online catalogs,** where you can find and borrow the library's media materials. These materials are good sources to use for presentation ideas and items of evidence.

Your Turn _____

Plan Your Presentation Make notes in your **RWN** as you figure out how you are going to deliver your PSA. Then, work on your plan. As you plan, make sure you have mapped out what you want to say, how you want to say it, and the order in which you will lay it out.

Multimedia Presentation: Public Service Announcement

Gathering and Managing Information: Databases and Spreadsheets

To gather and organize the information and evidence you will need for a convincing and powerful PSA, consider creating and using simple databases and spreadsheets. For example, if you want to create a PSA on recycling, you could create a **database** that collects and sorts the information you have researched. You could, for example, sort recycling information into categories such as *glass*, *paper*, and *plastic*, and then input the information you have found about each. Then, as you work on drafting your PSA, you can search your database for specific information by typing in a word like *glass* to bring up all the collected data about that aspect of your topic.

You can also use simple **spreadsheets** to create tables of information that display statistics, percentages, poll results, and other numerical information that can be useful in your PSA. Spreadsheet programs can also create professional-looking charts and graphs that can provide strong, persuasive visual support for your PSA.

Map Out a Plan

Before you start writing your PSA, map out what you are going to say and how you are going to present it. You can chart on a plot, or story map, what you want to say in the beginning, the middle, and the end.

- If you're going to write a script for a video, you may want to use a storyboard, like the ones used for television commercials, shows, or movies. A storyboard looks like a comic strip in which each panel represents a basic sketch of what each camera shot will look like. You'll also have to plan how the audio on your video will complement the visual.

- For an audio PSA, you'll need to write an audio script. What music or sound effects will attract your audience's attention, as well as strengthen your message? How many speakers will you need to be convincing and interesting?

- For a print PSA, plan how your text and any images will work together to convey your persuasive message. What photographs or drawings should you include?

Public Service Announcement Prompts

Students can choose their own ideas or use one of the following prompts to create a public service announcement.

World Languages Learning multiple languages is increasingly important in today's society. Make a PSA campaigning for better language instruction at your school.

Physical Education Staying in shape, making friends, and building self-esteem: there are many benefits to playing sports as a kid. Make a PSA for kids your age about the importance of being part of a team.

Science Some people think it's important to protect animal habitats and rain forests. Other people think that people should not interfere in the natural balance of the Earth. Make a PSA that supports one of these opinions.

Drafting

Follow the Writer's Framework

To reach your audience, you need to express your purpose and then provide persuasive and convincing specifics. Use the Framework shown at the right to help you proceed with your draft.

Appeal to Your Audience

To be convincing, you have to appeal to your audience's hearts and minds. You can use these two kinds of appeals in your PSA:

- **logical appeal:** What solid evidence can you provide to support your message?
- **emotional appeal:** How can you move your audience to action by touching their feelings?

Format Your Announcement

Depending on the materials available to you, your PSA can involve visuals and sound, as well as text. Decide on the best format for your announcement. Formats include

- a small brochure that can be distributed
- an audiotape that can be aired on radio
- a video that can be shot with a camera and shown on school TV
- an interactive Web page

Regardless of your format, be sure your audience knows how to contact you.

Framework for a Multimedia Presentation

Introduction
- Express the purpose of your message.
- Decide what the audio portion will do and what the video portion will do.
- Use language and media that will appeal to your target audience emotionally and logically.

Body
- Use facts, examples, anecdotes, statistics, and expert opinions that will get your point across.
- Use different forms of media so that they complement each other and make your message convincing.

Conclusion
- Wrap up your announcement, restating the purpose of the message.
- Try to end with an emotional appeal.
- Include contact information.

Grammar Link Punctuation in Addresses and Phone Numbers

If you use addresses in your PSA, use commas to separate place names, cities, and states.

CONFUSING	12 Curie St. New Orleans LA 70122
CLEAR	12 Curie St., New Orleans, LA 70122

If you use phone numbers in your PSA, use hyphens to separate groups of digits and/or letters.

CONFUSING	1800555KIDS
CLEAR	1-800-555-KIDS

● Writing Tip

As you write your draft, stop from time to time to read aloud what you have written so far. Ask yourself these questions: "Is my point clear and concise?" "Will the language and media help me reach my target audience?"

Your Turn _____

Write Your Draft Following your plan, write a draft of your PSA. As you write your draft, think about these points:

- What **language** is your **audience** most likely to respond to?
- What **media** will most **effectively** get your message across?
- What **message** do you want your audience to take away?

Real Issues, Real Experts

*Holt author **Sara Kajder** offers strategies for creating a multimedia presentation.*

Teaching economy in technology-based presentations is essential. Each image, piece of text, or sound needs to do narrative work. This is essential in a PSA as it is concise and tight. Without attention to economy, students lose instructional time adding effects "because they are there."

In the classroom:
- Require that students storyboard their work prior to constructing the presentation. The storyboard should re-quire placement of images (by sketching onto a piece of paper), alignment with any audio text (spoken or music), and the placement of any motion or effects. With a peer, students workshop the storyboard, using highlighters to mark those aspects of the layered text that are essential and which are "bells and whistles."

- Establish a set time period in which students may work on the "bells and whistles" components of their projects. Set a timer in the class lab (or workspace) which sounds at the designated time. Outside of that time, have students focus on the "raw content" of the work.

Model the Skill

■ Using a student draft on a transparency, model how to use the questions, tips, and revision techniques suggested in the chart. You might use a student's draft or a draft of your own creation to evaluate and revise using the steps in the chart.

■ Ask volunteers to demonstrate using each of the steps on their own drafts.

Peer Review

As students work with a peer, have them offer support as well as criticism. Tell students that when they respond to a peer's paper, they should start by telling the writer what he or she did well, then ask any questions they have about the paper, and finally, offer any suggestions for improving the paper.

Holt Six Traits for Writing, rubrics, prompts, and sample papers

Peer Review

Working with a peer, review your drafts. Answer each question in this chart to locate where and how your drafts could be improved. As you discuss your drafts, be sure to take notes about each other's suggestions. You can refer to your notes as you revise your drafts.

Multimedia Presentation: Public Service Announcement

Evaluating and Revising

Read the questions in the left column of the chart. Then, use the tips in the middle column to help you make revisions to your announcement. The right column suggests techniques you can use to revise your draft.

Public Service Announcement: Guidelines for Content and Organization

Evaluation Question	Tip	Revision Technique
1. Does your introduction express the purpose of your message? Does it draw in your audience's attention?	**Underline** the information that shows the purpose of your message. **Circle** the words or visuals that attract your audience.	**Add** a sentence or visual that identifies the purpose of your message. **Add** a short sentence or a visual that will draw in your audience's interest.
2. Have you targeted your audience?	**Bracket** words or visuals that identify your audience.	If appropriate, **name** or **identify** the people being targeted.
3. Does your message appeal to your audience emotionally as well as logically?	**Highlight** information that is an emotional appeal. **Draw a wavy line** under a logical appeal.	**Include** visuals and audio that will add emotional importance to your message.
4. Have you supplied evidence, such as facts and examples, to support your message?	**Put a star** next to evidence that supports your message.	**Add** facts, examples, and other details that support your main points.
5. Did you use different forms of media in your presentation?	**Put a check mark** next to each different form of media used in your presentation.	When possible, **replace** print with another form of media, such as a sound effect, a video clip, or an image.
6. Did you wrap up your message and restate it in your conclusion?	**Underline** the statement, visual, or audio that provides a conclusion to your message.	**Add** a sentence, an audio, or visual that restates your message.

Real Issues, Real Experts

Holt Professional Learning for Language Arts

To watch videos on teaching **revision, grammar,** and **on-demand writing skills** featuring Linda Rief, Amy Benjamin, and Leila Christenbury, go to this page in **ThinkCentral, Teacher Access.**

Universal Access

English Learners

English for Academic Success Review the definitions of any academic vocabulary words from the workshop that students may be unfamiliar with, such as *audio, visual, print, pamphlet,* and *persuasive.* Explain how each word relates to creating a public service announcement. If possible, provide samples.

Read this draft of a pamphlet and the comments about it as a model for revising your own PSA.

Online-Course Netiquette
by Wendy Starr, Willett Street Middle School

Netiquette = Network Etiquette

[Photo of regular classroom full of students at top right corner. Photo of single student at library computer at top left corner.]

When taking an online class, use common courtesy and good manners.

- **Don't** use acronyms (ROFL, MBF, and so on). Not everyone knows the meaning of these.
- **Do** be clear and concise. Explain your ideas entirely but get quickly to the point.
- **Don't** lurk in a class chat. This means you're reading online and not participating. [Cartoon of student in back of regular classroom, hiding behind palm tree.]

← The **pamphlet** format introduces the **topic** and **purpose** with its title, subheading, and photographs.

← The writer expresses the **purpose** of the PSA in the introduction.

← The writer uses **specific details** and **examples** to get the **message** across. She includes graphics.

← The writer uses a **clear method** for stating her points, although she could give her message more "audience appeal" through the use of **different media.**

MINI-LESSON ▶ How to Target Your Audience

Will your audience be interested in your message? Do you need to add visuals to make your point? Would adding audio, such as a voice-over or music, help make your message more effective or memorable? The writer of "Netiquette" changed her mind about making a pamphlet and decided to deliver her PSA as a video posted online. Her target audience— students and a teacher of a Web-only course—are people who are comfortable and interested in working online.

Wendy's Revision

VIDEO	AUDIO
OPEN ON CU OF COMPUTER SCREEN, TITLE BEING TYPED OUT O-n-l-i-n-e-C-o-u-r-s-e N-e-t-i-q-u-e-t-t-e	V/O YOUNG WOMAN #1: "Welcome to Online-Course Netiquette, or How to Behave Yourself in Web Class."
WIDE ANGLE OF FULL REGULAR CLASSROOM WAVING HELLO.	V/O YOUNG MAN #1: "When taking an online class, do use common courtesy and good manners."

Your Turn _____

Get Your Message Across

- Read your draft. Have you stated your topic clearly at the beginning?
- Have you used specific details and examples to get your point across?
- Is there anything you could do to make your delivery more appealing to your audience?

Guided Practice: Apply

Student Draft
Explain that the Student Draft on this page is the first half of a Public Service Announcement written by a student. Model reading the draft and the annotations in blue, and explain that the yellow highlighting illustrates the student's language choices. Explain that a mini-lesson follows with helpful information about ways to improve this draft as well as their own.

▶ Mini-Lesson
How to Target Your Audience

- Explain that the student writer has revised her draft by presenting her PSA as an online video instead of a poster to target her audience of Web users. Instruct students to read the student's first draft and the revision. Ask students to comment on the differences.

- Remind students to consider whether their audience uses the medium in which they are drafting their PSA as they revise their draft. If students neglect their audience, their message may not receive the attention it deserves.

Your Turn _____

Get Your Message Across As students complete the **Your Turn** activity, tell them to circle two places in their PSA where they use details or examples to support their topic. Have students add examples if they are lacking specific support for their topic. Remind students to use the **Grammar Link** on p. 687 if they have included addresses or phone numbers in their announcement.

Struggling Writers
To help students successfully target their audience, have them construct an audience analysis. In the analysis, students should list all of the details that they know about their audience, including age, occupation, gender, and views on relevant topics. Students should also determine when and where they expect their audience will see their public service announcement. Knowing these details should help students revise their draft to appeal to their specific audience.

Advanced Learners
Acceleration Challenge students to remake an existing public service announcement in a new format or medium. Have students include new information, such as an alternative statistic or anecdote, to make their version stronger than the original.

Multimedia Presentation:
Public Service Announcement

Guided Practice: Apply
Student Draft

- Explain that the Student Draft is continued and completed on this page. Again the draft is annotated and highlighted for the students.
- Read the draft and annotations aloud and discuss.

▶ Mini-Lesson
How to Conclude Strongly

- Tell students that the conclusion of their announcement should leave a lasting impression with the audience. If students are requesting their audience to act in response to the issue they raise in the PSA, the conclusion should motivate the audience to do so.
- Point out that the first draft ends rather abruptly and on a negative note. Explain that the student writer has revised her announcement by restating the PSA's purpose in the conclusion and ending with a more positive tone.

Your Turn

Using Different Media Tell students to work in pairs and evaluate the effectiveness of their partner's PSA. Have students highlight areas in their partner's PSA where an audio or visual aid could be added to improve the clarity or impact of the message.

Student Draft *continues*

The writer has identified her **audience** as an online class and is writing her PSA with them in mind. →

The writer is supplying different forms of **evidence** to support her message. Here is an **example** to the right. →

The form of evidence here is a **fact** because it can be proven. →

The writer has used **video** and **audio** (voices, music, sound effects)—all popular with her audience. →

Here is a negative **emotional appeal** saying not to plagiarize. →

VIDEO	AUDIO
CU OF TEACHER'S FACE WITH QUIZZICAL LOOK, SHAKING HEAD.	V/O TEACHER: "Don't use acronyms (ROFL, MBF, and so on). Not everyone (ahem, such as your teacher) knows what these mean."
EXTREME CU OF COMPUTER SCREEN: Don't type in all CAPITAL letters. It looks as if you're SCREAMING.	COMPUTER-SOUNDING VOICE, "SCREAMING" ON CAPPED WORDS: "Don't type in all CAPITAL letters. It looks as if you're SCREAMING."
OVER-THE-SHOULDER SHOT OF STUDENT TYPING SCREEN FULL OF EMOTICONS AND ACRONYMS.	V/O YOUNG MAN #2: "Do use proper grammar, complete words, and correct spelling. Their usage will affect your grade."
WIDE-ANGLE OF STUDENT HIDING IN BACK OF CLASS, BEHIND PALM TREE.	V/O YOUNG WOMAN #2: "Don't lurk in a class chat. This means you're reading online and not participating."
MEDIUM ANGLE OF PRINCIPAL'S DOOR; OPENS; UNHAPPY PRINCIPAL MOTIONS, "COME IN."	V/O PRINCIPAL: "Don't present work or ideas of others as your own (otherwise known as plagiarism)."

● Presentation Tip
Remember: If you don't have access to video and audio equipment at the present time, you can still prepare a script and make a live presentation.

Your Turn
Using Different Media Review your PSA draft. Have you used media effectively? Is there any way you could make your PSA more visually appealing? Do you need to add any audio to get your message across?

MINI-LESSON How to Conclude Strongly

Wendy has a strong script but has left her message dangling at the end. Remember that the **conclusion** is the last idea an audience takes away from your PSA. Wendy needs to revise in order to use the end as an opportunity to wrap up the PSA's main message and restate its purpose.

Wendy's Revision of the Script

VIDEO	AUDIO
SLIDE SHOW CUTS TO DIFFERENT STUDENTS AT INDIVIDUAL COMPUTERS AND LAPTOPS IN VARIOUS LOCATIONS, SUCH AS AT SCHOOL, AT THE LIBRARY, AND AT HOME.	V/O YOUNG WOMAN #1: "Remember, when you're in class online, behave as if you're in class in person. We know the rules. Let's all follow them. See you this semester on the Web."
STILL SHOT ON POSTERBOARD: Netiquette = Network Etiquette FADE OUT.	MUSIC UP. MUSIC OUT.

Universal Access

English Learners
English for Academic Success Help students think of words they can add to their imperative sentences to express urgency and severity to strengthen a conclusion. Have students brainstorm words as you list them on the board. To stimulate discussion, suggest the following words: *now, urgent, necessary, vital, pressing, critical, please,* and *dire.* After generating a list of words that suggest urgency, have students discuss how these words can persuade people to care about their cause and act.

Students with Disabilities
Provide students with a variety of materials they can use as models to create an effective conclusion for their PSA. Examples might include newspaper or magazine advertisements, and TV , Internet, or radio campaigns. Have students discuss in groups what makes each of these campaigns effective.

Proofreading and Publishing

Proofreading

Even if you are the only one reading the PSA for your final presentation, you should still fix any errors in your writing. Check your final version to make sure it is free of any errors in spelling, punctuation, and sentence structure. Proofread your writing carefully, using proofreading marks to make the necessary corrections.

Grammar Link Using Imperative Sentences

Because a persuasive PSA often asks someone to do or change something, imperative sentences should be used in the PSA. An imperative sentence gives a command or makes a request. Most end with a period; however, a strong command may end with an exclamation point.

EXAMPLES	Don't use acronyms. [command]
	Please be courteous. [request]
	Don't type in all CAPITALS! [strong command]

The subject of a command or request is always *you,* even if *you* doesn't appear in the sentence. In such cases, *you* is called the **understood** subject.

| EXAMPLE | (You) Don't lurk in a class chat. |

The word *you* is the understood subject even when the person spoken to is addressed by name.

| EXAMPLE | Sam, (you) please don't plagiarize. |

Publishing

Now it is time to share your PSA with a wider audience. Here are some ways to "publish" your PSA:

- Deliver it through the school's public address system or present it as part of a public service school assembly.
- Share it online.
- Post it on a bulletin board for others to read.

Reflect on the Process In your **RWN,** write a short response to the following questions.

1. Which forms of media did you use? Which was the most effective?
2. Do you think you got your message across? Why or why not? What feedback did you receive from your target audience?

● Proofreading Tip

There are three main areas to focus on when proofreading: spelling, punctuation, and sentence structure. It makes sense to focus on just one area at a time while proofreading. Ask two peers to help you, assigning each person just one area to check.

Your Turn _____

Proofread and Publish

Proofread your PSA, making sure you have used imperative sentences correctly. Think about the best way to share your message and to make sure that you will be able to follow through with your plan. Is there anyone you need to get permission from? Do you need any special materials?

Analyzing Electronic Journalism

Listen with a Purpose

Analyze a television or online news broadcast, focusing on the uses and effects of images, text, and sound.

Think as a Reader/Writer Electronic journalism, such as a TV or online news broadcast, uses specific techniques to present images, words, and sounds for a specific purpose. In this workshop you will learn about these techniques, their purposes, and their possible effects.

Analyze the Uses and Effects of Images

Photojournalists, people who record, edit, and present **images** in news broadcasts, make important decisions that determine how their images will look on your TV or computer monitor. In order to better interpret the stories you receive through electronic media, you must understand how camera techniques can affect your perception of reality.

Camera Shots

- **Long shot** A long shot shows a scene from far away, such as a large crowd or a landscape. Long shots help provide context for the viewer and are a relatively reliable portrayal of reality.
- **Close-up** A close-up, a shot taken very close to the subject, is useful for showing fine details, such as the emotion in a person's face, and for emphasis in a news story. Close-ups, however, have the potential to exaggerate a subject, creating ugly or menacing features.
- **High-angle** A high-angle shot is taken from above, with the camera looking down on the subject. High-angle shots provide an overview of the scene, but they can also make a subject look small, unimportant, and vulnerable.
- **Low-angle** A low-angle shot is taken from below, with the camera looking up at the subject. It has the opposite effect of a high-angle shot; it can be used to distort reality, making subjects look much larger than they are.

Framing and Props

Framing is the process by which the photojournalist decides which details to include in a shot. Unfortunately, framing can leave out important information. For example, in a news story on price increases for food products, framing could be used to show only the highest priced eggs even though less expensive eggs might be just out of the camera frame.

Viewing Tip

News broadcasts, especially national news broadcasts, often include the **newsroom** in the broadcast set. The viewer may see a room full of computers with people hustling to and fro behind the news anchor. Why might the news producers want viewers to see the newsroom during a broadcast?

Reader/Writer Notebook

Use your **RWN** to complete the activities for this workshop.

The objects, or **props,** that appear in a camera shot can also add meaning to a story. They can distract a viewer and, depending on the story, can even bias the viewer for or against the object—or brand of object—itself.

Analyze the Uses and Effects of Text and Audio

The words you hear and sometimes see in a TV or online news broadcast are simply called **text.** News reporters and producers write text to achieve specific purposes—to capture the viewer's attention, engage the viewer's mind and emotions, and provide information. Background **audio,** such as sirens, automobile traffic, or the chants of a crowd, adds depth to the text of a story.

News broadcasts are typically no more than a half-hour long, so individual news stories are limited to two or three minutes. A news anchor or reporter reads the text of a news story either from a desk in a news studio or in a **live shot** from the scene of the story. The text of a news story generally follows a simple **structure,** as shown in the list below.

Broadcast News Text Structure

1. **Lead-in:** In the studio, the anchor introduces the story.
2. **Setup:** The reporter, often at the scene of the story, gets the viewer's attention and introduces the images that are about to be shown.
3. **Sound bites:** Short audio pieces of interviews are mixed in with video clips.
4. **Voice-overs:** The reporter talks while the video is playing. Usually, the reporter explains the images being shown.
5. **Back announcing:** After the video clips, the reporter briefly sums up the main points of the story.
6. **Stand-up:** The reporter addresses the camera and the anchor with closing commentary.

Because broadcast news stories are short, they are not able to present a great deal of **context,** or background information, for a story. The **content** of a broadcast news story is therefore often limited to a brief, repetitive structure that can affect a viewer's understanding of the situation. As with images, text can distort reality either intentionally or unintentionally. Electronic journalists must choose both text and images very carefully in order to present the most accurate and balanced view of reality possible.

An Analysis of Electronic Journalism

- describes the news segment, identifying text, image, or sound techniques used in the segment
- explains the purposes of each major technique (*why* the technique may have been used)
- explains the effects of each major technique on viewers (*how* the technique makes you feel)

 Listening Tip

The goal of mainstream journalism is to report the news in a fair, objective manner. Nevertheless, **bias**—a slanted point of view for or against a subject—can find its way into the most careful journalist's story. Watch out for signs of bias in text, such as personal opinions and loaded language that has a strong positive or negative emotional effect. Try to base your opinion of a news story on objective information rather than on emotional interviews or text that includes bias or loaded language.

✳ Learn It Online
For more tips on analyzing electronic media, visit Media Scope:

| go.hrw.com | H7-693 | **Go** |

Model the Skill

Analyze the Uses and Effects of Text and Audio

If students struggle with analyzing the effects of audio components of broadcasts, have them consider each audio element separately before thinking about how they function in combination. Suggest organizing information in a two-column chart with separate entries for "announcer says," "background noise," "sound effects," and "interview comments."

Guided Practice: Apply

Have students outline their analyses and trade outlines with a partner. Partners should check to see that audio and visual elements of the broadcast are analyzed, and that the analysis logically interprets the broadcast described.

Teaching Tip

Organize Suggest that students begin their analysis by describing their chosen broadcast in detail and as a whole, so their listeners can easily follow the analysis of components such as images and audio.

English for Academic Success

Remind students to use formal English in their discussions. They should use informal English, such as slang, only if it came from the news broadcast they are describing.

Assess

UA: Holt Interactive Writer and Speaker, Analysis of Electronic Journalism analytical scales and rubrics, p. 179

Universal Access

EL English Learners

Have students begin their analysis by sketching what they remember of the broadcast in storyboard form. Suggest that students note sound effects or music in the image frame, and write the announcer's comments below the frame. Then, review with them the journalistic terms from pp. 692–693, and have them work in pairs to label elements of each frame with the terms as appropriate. Students should use their storyboards to think critically about the effect each labeled element had on them as they watched.

Advanced Learners

Enrichment Challenge students to analyze a broadcast to determine the opposite perspective from that presented by the broadcast. Have students work in small groups to create and present their own broadcast, showing the opposite perspective and incorporating as many multimedia elements as they are able. After the broadcast, have students explain what the original perspective was and how they determined it.

✳ Learn It Online
On the **MediaScope** mini-site, students can analyze other types of media, such as a Web page, a TV news story, a political TV ad, and a print advertisement.

| go.hrw.com | H7-693 | **Go** |

Standards Focus

Objectives

Students will analyze a variety of informational texts.

Informational Skills Review

 Review

If necessary, use the following questions to guide students in their reading before they answer the questions at the end of the review.

▶ **Informational Texts**

What type of informational document is the memo, and how do you know? ***Possible response:*** *The memo is a workplace document; it provides information to employees of GreatBUYS Stores. I know because it is addressed to "All Floor Managers."*

What clues on the web site suggest that this is a consumer document? ***Possible response:*** *The URL references shipping, payment, place order, and gift wrap, which suggest a purchase. The side text also says an item has been purchased and has free shipping.*

Test-Taking Tip

Tell students to look for key words in the instructions and questions such as *choose, describe, explain, compare, identify,* or *similar.*

 California Standards, pp. 694–695

- **Reading Standard 2.2** Locate information by using a variety of consumer, workplace, and public documents.

Informational Skills Review

Informational Texts **Directions:** Read the following texts. Then, read and answer the questions that follow.

MEMO

GreatBUYS Stores, Inc.

Date: January 22, 2009

To: All Floor Managers

From: Casey Cross

Our public relations team has built a campaign for the new and exciting sci-fi video game Forest World, which will take place at all stores the week of March 1. To prepare your staff, see the attached instructions and agenda. Make sure all are familiar with the product and on hand during peak hours. Send your concerns forward. Let's make this a fun week for all!

Casey Cross

Casey Cross
GreatBUYS General Manager

MAGAZINE ARTICLE

Saving the Forest, One Level at a Time

New Games Pit Players Against Pollution
by **Mario Mann**

Not all game missions are created equal. First came games aimed at getting people off their couches. Players could rev up heart rates while matching their dance moves to those on-screen. Now there's the ambitious "green" lineup, including Forest World, which is attracting plenty of market interest. Players fight to save their world from destruction.

9 PLAYTIME: GAMES

WEB SITE

File   Edit   View   Favorites   Tools   Help

Back   Forward   Stop   Refresh   Home   Search   Favorites   History   Mail   Print

Address http://www.TECHnicalities.com/signin/shipping and payment/giftwrap/place order   Go

You have selected the item **Forest World.** *This feature item comes with **FREE** second-day shipping.*

Make sure the address is entered correctly. If not, your package may be returned as undeliverable.

FULL NAME:
ADDRESS LINE 1:
ADDRESS LINE 2:
CITY: STATE/PROVINCE/REGION:
ZIP/POSTAL CODE: COUNTRY:
PHONE NUMBER:

Internet

Resources for Skills and Standards Review

Chapter 1 Resources, Chapter Standards Mastery, Chapter Vocabulary Review, p. 30

UA: Differentiating Instruction, below-level Chapter Standards Mastery

Teacher One Stop™, editable Chapter Standards Mastery

Focus on Standards

ThinkCentral Online Assessment, Chapter Standards Mastery

ThinkCentral Online Remediation

Holt Online Essay Scoring

1. The *main* point of the memo is that
   A an agenda of activities is attached.
   B a video campaign needs preparation.
   C floor managers should schedule extra staff.
   D Casey Cross will answer questions.

2. What is the *main* purpose of the magazine article?
   A to give information about a new video game
   B to sell a new video game in GreatBUYS stores
   C to explain the change in focus of video games over time
   D to teach people how to buy good video games

3. According to the magazine article, the video game Forest World
   A helps get people off their couches.
   B is a new and exciting sci-fi game.
   C has players battle the evils of pollution.
   D plays music to on-screen dance moves.

4. The article most likely appears in a magazine called *Playtime* because
   A the magazine editor thinks readers will be interested in the topic.
   B the readers of the article will likely buy the game.
   C the writer of the article has strong feelings about the game.
   D stores are planning to sell many copies of the game.

5. According to the Web site, people should
   A have their order gift-wrapped.
   B pay for the game with a credit card.
   C double-check their address for mistakes.
   D choose the method of shipping they want.

6. If you bought the Forest World game and wanted directions for playing it, where would you look first?
   A the employee manual at GreatBUYS
   B the Web site of the store from which you bought the game
   C an article in *Playtime* magazine
   D the included instructions booklet

Timed Writing

7. List the kind of information you can locate in each of the following types of documents: workplace, consumer, and public. Then, give an example of each type of document.

Word-Attack Skills Mini-Lesson

Review Use the activities below to check students' grasp of the word-attack skills taught in this Chapter.

Activity Display these sets of words. Have students identify the two words in each set in which the digraph *ch* stands for the sound /ch/.

1. <u>charity</u>   chrome   <u>charge</u>
2. <u>clench</u>   school   <u>witch</u>
3. echo   <u>chief</u>   <u>bench</u>
4. orchid   <u>chime</u>   <u>churn</u>
5. <u>breach</u>   <u>grouch</u>   scholar

Activity Display these pairs of related words. Have students determine if the digraph /ch/ is pronounced the same way in both words.

1. chemist   architect   [*same*]
2. stomach   quench   [*different*]
3. preach   wrench   [*same*]
4. trench   chaos   [*different*]
5. scorch   mulch   [*same*]

Answers and Explanations

1. **B** A video game is being released. Although the memo states an agenda is attached (A), this is not its central idea, nor is it that managers should schedule extra staff (C) or that Casey Cross will answer questions (D).

2. **A** The article explains a new video game with a "green" focus. Although it discusses changes over time (C), this is not its main focus. GreatBUYS (B) is never mentioned, and the article is not trying to teach people how to buy video games (D).

3. **C** The article describes nontraditional video games, some of which get people off the couch (A) or play music with dance moves (D), but Forest World is described as "green," or an environmental awareness game. The article does not describe Forest World as a sci fi game (B).

4. **A** The editor probably thinks readers will be interested in the article's topic because people who read *Playtime* are probably interested in playing new games.

5. **C** The site asks customers to ensure their address is correct.

6. **D** Video games usually include instruction manuals. You would not go to an article (C) for instructions. An employee manual (A) or the store's site (B) would not contain the instructions.

Timed Writing

7. *A workplace document, such as a job application, provides information for employees and employers. A consumer document, such as a food label, provides information about products. A public document, like a newsletter, gives information to citizens.*

Reteach

 ThinkCentral Online Remediation

Read On

If students enjoyed the various types of informational texts in this Chapter, you might recommend the following magazines and Web sites for independent reading and investigation.

A Note on Web Sites

Web sites and online materials change continually and without notice. Holt cannot ensure the accuracy or appropriateness of these materials. Students, teachers, and guardians should assume responsibility for checking all online materials. The sites described on these Read On pages are well established and have been developed for—and in some cases, by—students.

Assessment Options

The following projects can help you evaluate and assess your students' outside work. Videotapes or audiotapes of completed projects may be included in students' portfolios.

Explore Sports Journalism

■ Students who enjoy *Sports Illustrated KIDS* magazine may want to write their own sports-themed article.

■ Suggest they write about an athlete they are interested in or review a sporting event they have gone to in a few brief paragraphs. Remind them to use the articles in the magazine as a guide for style and formatting.

Read On

Reading for Life: Magazines

Sports Illustrated KIDS

Stories about star athletes, performance tips from professionals, sports cards, comics, and articles on exercise and healthful eating—*Sports Illustrated KIDS* has it all for girls and boys who love sports. Filled with action photos, this award-winning magazine will encourage you to read it from start to finish—and then go out and join in the activities.

Calliope

Have you ever daydreamed about living in another century, in another country? Do you wonder about the lives of famous people from the past: Muhammad, Charlemagne, and other great leaders, artists, and scientists? Pick up a copy of the magazine *Calliope,* and check out who and what are being featured from the past. In addition to fantastic features, *Calliope* includes maps, time lines, and activities to enhance your enjoyment of history.

Stone Soup: The Magazine by Young Writers and Artists

If you like writing, reading, and drawing, look for *Stone Soup*. In it you'll find short stories and poems written by kids from all around the world. You may even decide to submit your own work for publication. Go to its Web site, www.stonesoup.com, for links to more sites for young writers, such as ZuZu, Young Girl Writers, and Just Write.

Archaeology's dig

Do you dig Egyptian mummies? If you do, unearth a copy of the magazine *Archaeology's dig*. Learn about the latest discoveries in the field of archaeology, from fossils to Vikings. The magazine also features games and experiments and invites you to ask Dr. Dig all the questions you have about archaeology.

Word Counts and Readabilities of Read On Books

Magazines	Estimated Word Counts	Readability
Sports Illustrated KIDS Magazine	Magazine	Accessible
Calliope	Magazine	Accessible
Stone Soup: The Magazine by Young Writers and Artists	Magazine	Accessible
Archaeology's Dig	Magazine	Accessible

Web Sites

Earth from Space: Astronauts' Views of the Home Planet

Photographs from NASA's Space Shuttle Earth Observations database are a national treasure. Each image comes with an explanatory caption. The database, located at earth.jsc.nasa.gov/sseop/efs/, illustrates some of Earth's most fascinating features, including cities as seen from space. Type in the name of the largest city near you to see it from an astronaut's point of view.

Kids.gov: The Official Kid's Portal for the U.S. Government

Check out www.kids.gov, a collection of links to the kid-friendly sites of various government agencies, along with links to other groups' sites for children. Click on one of the subjects—such as Fighting Crime, Computers, Health, or Fun Stuff—to find links to hundreds of sites of interest.

Jazz in the Schools

Sponsored by the National Endowment for the Arts, this Web site is a study guide and tool kit that explores jazz not only as a unique American art form but also as a special way of looking at American life. You can follow an interactive time line to see jazz's place in history as you listen to the music of famous jazz artists like Louis Armstrong, Sarah Vaughan, and Wynton Marsalis. Included is a file of biographies of these and many other major artists. Visit neajazzintheschools.org, produced by Jazz at Lincoln Center, for sounds that have influenced American music since the 1800s.

Exhibits from The Tech Museum of Innovation

Online interactive exhibits created by the Tech will grab your attention. Some are about robotics and energy-efficient cars—you get to design and race your own. If you can't get to the actual museum in San Jose, California, go to www.thetech.org/exhibits/online/ for a virtual visit.

Learn It Online
Learn how to analyze a Web site online with MediaScope:

go.hrw.com | H7-697 | **Go**

Assessment Options
Submit Your Writing or Artwork to a Magazine
- Students who enjoy writing or drawing may want to submit their own work to *Stone Soup*.
- Suggest submitting a poem, story, or essay written for class, or on their own time. Invite students who submit works to share them with the class.

Research a Topic
- Have students choose a topic of interest from *Kids.gov,* such as health or computers, on which to conduct further research.
- Tell students to use additional print or electronic resources to perform their research, and have them share their findings with the class in a brief presentation.

Create Your Own Hybrid
- Suggest that students interested in the online exhibits from the Tech Museum of Innovation create and design their own hybrid car using the program found on the web site.
- Then, have them present the information they learned about hybrid vehicles to the class.

Learn It Online
For an in-depth look at media literacy, direct students to the **MediaScope** mini-site, which shows students how to create, analyze, and critique media.

go.hrw.com | H7-697 | **Go**

Web Sites	Estimated Word Counts	Readability
Earth from Space: Astronauts' Views of the Home Planet	Web Site	Accessible
Kids.gov: The Official Kid's Portal for the U.S. Government	Web Site	Accessible
Jazz in the Schools	Web Site	Accessible
Exhibits from The Tech Museum of Innovation	Web Site	Accessible

Expository Critique

Informational Text Focus: Assessing Author's Evidence

Features highlighted in **yellow** constitute a suggested minimum course of study.

Introducing The Skills

Selection or Feature	Grade–Level Standards
Literary Skills Focus: How Do I Know If I Can Trust the Information in a Text?	**Reading Standard 2.6:** Evaluate author's evidence
Reading Skills Focus: What Skills Can Help Me Critique Expository Texts?	**Reading Standard 2.6:** Evaluate author's evidence
Reading Model: Music Makers: Musicians Help Keep Music Alive in Schools by World Almanac (Accessible, Lexile 1040) **Skills in Action:** Wrap Up	**Reading Standard 2.6:** Evaluate author's evidence

Applying The Skills

Selection or Feature	Grade–Level Standards
Informational Text Focus: Claims and Assertions **Borders of Baseball: U.S. and Cuban Play** by World Almanac (Accessible, Lexile 990)	**Reading Standard 2.6:** Evaluate author's evidence
Informational Text Focus: Author's Evidence **Hungry Here? For Millions of Americans, the Answer is "Yes"** by World Almanac (Accessible, Lexile 1000)	**Reading Standard 2.6:** Evaluate author's evidence
Informational Text Focus: Assessing Evidence • **Virtual Sticks and Stones** (Accessible, Lexile 1010) • **Debate on Bullying** (Accessible, Lexile 980) • **Sound Off to the Editor** (Accessible, Lexile 710)	**Reading Standard 2.6:** Evaluate author's evidence

Mastering The Skills

Selection or Feature	Grade–Level Standards
Writing Workshop: Research Report	**Writing Standard 1.4:** Develop topics for research. **Writing Standard 1.5:** Cite sources. **Writing Standard 2.3:** Write research reports.
Listening and Speaking Workshop: Presenting a Research Report	**Listening and Speaking Standard 1.4:** Organize information. **Listening and Speaking Standard 1.6:** Use speaking techniques. **Listening and Speaking Standard 2.3:** Deliver research presentations.
Standards Practice: Informational Skills Review Vocabulary Skills Review Writing Skills Review	**Reading Standard 2.6:** Evaluate author's evidence. **Writing Standard 2.3:** Write research reports.

Daily and Weekly Support

- Reader/Writer Notebook
- Reading and Writing Transparencies
- Weekly Standards Review Transparencies
- Family Involvement Activities in Five Languages
- Language Handbook Worksheets
- Holt Virtual File Cabinet for Language Arts
- Spelling Lessons and Activities

Assessment Resources

- **Chapter 7 Resources**, Chapter Diagnostic Test; Selection Standards Checks, Chapter Standards Mastery
- **Universal Access: Differentiating Instruction**, leveled assessment
- **English-Language Conventions Progress-Monitoring Test**, Chapters 1–13, 16–17
- ThinkCentral Online Assessment

Print Resources for Universal Access

	On-Level Learners	English Learners	Struggling Readers/Writers	Students Who Use African American Vernacular Engish	Advanced Learners	Students with Disabilities
Chapter 7 Resources practice and assessment for all selections and features	✔				✔	
Universal Access: Holt Interactive Reader interactive readings for Minimum-Course-of-Study Selections		✔	✔	✔		✔
Holt Interactive Reader for English Language Development adaptations of Minimum-Course-of-Study Selections		✔				
Universal Access: Differentiating Instruction modified lesson plans, graphic organizers, and leveled assessment		✔	✔	✔		✔
Universal Access: Resources for Teaching Advanced Students lesson plans for Minimum-Course-of-Study Selections					✔	
Universal Access: Supporting Instruction in Five Languages translations of selection summaries and key terms		✔				
Universal Access: Holt Interactive Writer and Speaker practice and assessment	✔	✔	✔	✔	✔	✔
Language and Sentence Skills Practice for Warriner's Handbook Chapters 1–13, 16–17	✔				✔	
Universal Access: Developmental Language and Sentence Skills Practice for Warriner's Handbook Chapters 1–13, 16–17		✔	✔	✔		✔

Assessment
Resources

Teacher Management
Resources

go.
hrw.
com

Student Edition
Extension Activities

Student Edition
Support

Technology Resources

Find all of Holt's technology resources at go.hrw.com. Technology resources are also listed as point-of-use in the wrap; below are our featured components for Chapter 7.

Teacher Management Resources

ThinkCentral, Teacher Access
Teacher One Stop™
Holt Professional Learning for Language Arts

Master Frog

Vietnamese, retold by

Lynette Dyer Vuong

Except for his strange appearance, Master Frog was really quite a

Giang Dung[1] was a plain girl, so plain in fact that all the townspeople parents finally found her a husband. Then they nodded their heads know to one another that the young man must have been after her father's m of it, it was true, and Giang Dung was his only child. The day of the wed passed, and the people found more interesting things to gossip about u later, when Giang Dung's husband died.

Spotlight on ThinkCentral, Teacher Access

All of the chapter's resources are available on ThinkCentral, Teacher Access. Online suggestions:
• Play the point-of-use audio version of "Borders of Baseball: U.S. and Cuban Play" while projecting the text, so your students can read along.

Student Edition Support

ThinkCentral, Student Access
PowerNotes
Student One Stop™
Interactive Reading Workshops
Interactive Graphic Organizers
Writers' Lives
Holt Audio Library
Holt Audio Library: Selections and Summaries in Spanish

Orpheus, the Great Musician by Olivia Coolidge

Feature Menu
Video — Introducing the Myth
Quickwrite — Literary Focus: The Underworld of Myth
Background — Reading Focus: Summarizing
Meet the Writer — Writing Focus

Spotlight on PowerNotes

Introduce "Virtual Sticks and Stones" and provide your students with instruction in an alternative, interactive format through these editable PowerPoint presentations.

Universal Access: English learners in particular may benefit from the intensive vocabulary instruction in these presentations.

Supported Strands: Literature, Reading, Writing ,Vocabulary
Available on DVD-ROM as well as on go.hrw.com.

Student Edition Extension Activities

Writing and Research in a Digital Age
Digital Storytelling Mini-site
NovelWise Mini-Site
MediaScope Mini-Site
WordSharp: An Interactive Vocabulary Tutor
GrammarNotes
WritingNotes
Literature Links
Holt Audio Tutor for English Language Development

HOLT

Writers' Lives
Welcome to the Writers' Lives site!
Authors don't just spend all their time writing. A lot of them have exciting or interesting lives, too. T below includes authors who
• spent time in jail
• worked on a steamboat
• fought in the trenches of World War I
• struggled for civil rights
• served the British king
• flew as a fighter pilot
• faced censorship by the Soviet government
• brought different cultures together
• survived concentration camps

Spotlight on Writing and Research in a Digital Age

These interactive lessons will take your students through the research process, and address the use of technology in research and publication.
• Use these presentations to help your students prepare to research with and cite online sources.

Assessment Resources

ThinkCentral Online Assessment
Holt Online Essay Scoring
ThinkCentral Online Remediation

5. When a writer uses a **first-person narrator**, the story —
○ A does not contain dialogue between the characters
→ ○ B is told by one of the characters
○ C does not contain a main character
○ D has only one character

Correct Answer: B

7.1.5
point of view

Spotlight on ThinkCentral Online Assessment

Preview and assign the Chapter 7 Diagnostic Test and Chapter Standards Mastery here.

Real Issues, Real Experts

The wrap for these selections includes specific ideas and strategies from *Holt Literature and Language Arts* authors.

From the Author

For Writing Workshop: Research Report, p. 743

Academic research reports can often be presented using a variety of technologies. Some possibilities include short videos, podcasts, and wikis. These allow students to strengthen their ability to communicate using a variety of methods.

Sara Kajder

Teacher to Teacher

Preteach To introduce the idea of analyzing expository text, I have students do two quick writes. First, I ask them to respond to the chapter quotation, "Readers are plentiful; thinkers are rare." Second, I ask them to answer the question, "How do I know if I can trust the information in a text or Web site?" Students share their responses with their partner before we have a class discussion. I display the chapter quotation and question on my doorway while we study this chapter.

Direct Teach In addition to the articles in the textbook, I bring in various newspapers and magazines to show students the way both are organized and how the sources in each are readily available. This is a huge contrast to information on the Web. Most students are unaware of the public nature of the Internet and the fact that it is unregulated and unmonitored. I emphasize the idea that it is a great treasure chest filled with traps and they need to question everything.

Maria Veronica La Frossia
Santa Ana, California

Assess Students evaluate articles from the textbook by answering the following questions: Who is responsible for the article? What is the articles purpose—to inform, explain or sell? What sources are cited? How are quotations and data used?

Holt Professional Learning

Teaching English Learners
with Robin Scarcella

Visit the ThinkCentral, Teacher Access to link to Holt's Professional Learning site for English/Language Arts teachers. This site features:

- Videos that share the insights of *Holt Literature and Language Arts* program authors and consultants and demonstrate proven classroom strategies with master teachers
- Study guides for publications by our authors and consultants
- Informative articles and useful Web links
- Help in planning your department's professional learning sessions
- A handbook for new teachers

VIDEO PRODUCTS

Strategies for Helping Struggling Readers
with Kylene Beers

Effective Vocabulary Instruction
with Carol Jago and Kylene Beers

Developing Critical Thinking About Literature
with Carol Jago and Deborah Appleman

Teaching Students to Revise, Not Recopy
with Linda Rief

Teaching English Learners
with Robin Scarcella

Using Literature Circles
with Harvey Daniels

Teaching On-Demand Writing Skills
with Leila Christenbury

Managing the Heterogeneous Classroom
with Leila Christenbury and Patrick Schwarz

Teaching Narrative and Expository Texts
with Judith Irvin and Deborah Appleman

Becoming a Tech-Savvy Teacher
with Sara Kajder

Re-engagin the Disengaged Student
with Alfred Tatum

Teaching Grammar in Context
with Amy Benjamin

California Standards

**Reading Comprehension
(Focus on Informational Materials)**

■ **2.6** Assess the adequacy, accuracy, and appropriateness of the author's evidence to support claims and assertions, noting instances of bias and stereotyping.

**Writing Applications
(Genres and Their Characteristics)**

■ **2.3** Write research reports:
  a. Pose relevant and tightly drawn questions about the topic.
  b. Convey clear and accurate perspectives on the subject.
  c. Include evidence compiled through the formal research process (e.g., use of a card catalog, *Reader's Guide to Periodical Literature*, a computer catalog, magazines, newspapers, dictionaries).
  d. Document reference sources by means of footnotes and a bibliography.

Analyzing Visuals

Extension Activity Ask students to consider what the illustration suggests about making decisions and judgments while reading.

Possible response: The illustration shows two different paths, so it might be saying that there are usually multiple ways to interpret a text, and that readers must think carefully in order to make the best judgments.

Chapter Resources

On Course: Mapping Instruction

Chapter 7 Resources

Warriner's Handbook
  • Chapter 16, Spelling
  • Chapter 17, Correcting Common Errors

PowerNotes

Teacher One Stop™

English-Language Conventions
Progress-Monitoring Tests

Holt Virtual File Cabinet for Language Arts,
grammar, reading, and vocabulary resources

Holt Pronunciation Resources
  • Phoneme Sounds and Spellings
  • Support for Speakers of African American Vernacular English

ThinkCentral Online Assessment

ThinkCentral Online Remediation

CHAPTER **7**

Expository Critique

INFORMATIONAL TEXT FOCUS
Assessing Author's Evidence

California Standards
Here are the Grade 7 standards you will work toward mastering in Chapter 7.

Reading Comprehension (Focus on Informational Materials)
2.6 Assess the adequacy, accuracy, and appropriateness of the author's evidence to support claims and assertions, noting instances of bias and stereotyping.

Writing Applications (Genres and Their Characteristics)
2.3 Write research reports:
a. Pose relevant and tightly drawn questions about the topic.
b. Convey clear and accurate perspectives on the subject.
c. Include evidence compiled through the formal research process (e.g., use of a card catalog, *Reader's Guide to Periodical Literature,* a computer catalog, magazines, newspapers, dictionaries).
d. Document reference sources by means of footnotes and a bibliography.

"Readers are plentiful; thinkers are rare."
—**Harriet Martineau**

What Do
You?
Think

How do you decide whether to believe what you read?

Learn It Online
Can you read pictures? Let *PowerNotes* show you how at:

go.hrw.com | H7-699 | **Go**

Chapter Objectives
■ Students will learn to examine an author's claims and assertions, in conjunction with the evidence supporting them, to determine whether such support is adequate, accurate, and appropriate.

■ Students will learn to identify bias and stereotyping in texts.

■ At the end of the chapter, students will write a research report and present an oral report on their research.

Routines for California Classrooms

For ideas on classroom practices and approaches to grouping, see the discussion of routines on pages T34–T37 of this Teacher's Edition.

What Do You Think?
How do you decide whether to believe what you read?
Read the quotation aloud. Explain that Martineau suggests that anyone who learns to read and write may read or create text, but that reliable text requires careful thought and adequate support of assertions made in the text. Ask students to brainstorm ways in which an author might support a claim made in his or her writing.

Learn It Online
For a multimedia version of the instruction found on this page, use the **PowerNotes** presentation.

go.hrw.com | H7-699 | **Go**

Informational Text Focus

Objectives

Students will
- identify and analyze an author's assertions and supporting evidence
- learn to identify stereotyping and bias, and understand their effect on a text's validity

Preteach

Build Background Ask students to describe types of informational texts they have read. Have them explain whether they felt these texts were trustworthy and why.

Direct Teach

Claims and Assertions

Explain that a claim in a piece of writing may be likened to a main idea statement, a thesis, or an opinion. A claim or assertion in an informational text is likely to be influenced by the author's beliefs, but it will important to the text and will be proven with details and other evidence in the text.

The "Triple A's" of Evidence

Tell students to think of the evidence for a claim as a lawyer's argument of a trial. A lawyer cannot expect a jury simply to believe him when he says, "my client is innocent"; the lawyer has to produce adequate amounts of reliable (or accurate) witnesses and other appropriate factual material to support his client's innocence.

California Standards, pp. 700–701

■ **Reading Standard 2.6** Assess the adequacy, accuracy, and appropriateness of the author's evidence to support claims and assertions, noting instances of bias and stereotyping.

Informational Text Focus

by **Carol Jago**

How Do I Know If I Can Trust the Information in a Text?

You may turn to reference books, articles, or Web sites when you want to learn something, solve a problem, or make a purchase. The information you find in print or on the Web is not always trustworthy, however. To determine the value of the information you find, you must be able to **critique** (krih TEEK) it—to assess it in order to determine if it is accurate, well-supported, and not slanted, or biased.

Claims and Assertions

Writers of expository texts make **claims** and **assertions**—statements of either fact or opinion (or a little of both) that present a position or idea. Even though it's easy to simply accept these claims and assertions without thinking, it's unwise to accept all information as credible, or reliable. Any claim or assertion a writer makes must be supported with evidence. Here's an example of an assertion from an editorial on Internet bullying:

> Bullying is all around us—you just have to deal with it.
>
> from "Debate on Bullying"

You'll have to read the editorial to see how well the author supports this assertion.

The "Triple *A*'s" of Evidence

You should expect a writer to support his or her claims and assertions with evidence that is adequate, accurate, and appropriate.

Adequate Evidence How much evidence is **adequate,** or enough, to support a writer's claims? It depends. A writer may need to provide several facts, statistics, or quotations by experts to adequately support a claim that's controversial (something that people argue about). A writer may need to provide only a single statistic or quotation to support other claims.

Accurate Evidence You can determine if evidence is **accurate,** or free from mistakes, by asking these questions: Is the writer an expert in the field about which he or she is making the claim? If not, are the sources he or she has referred to, or cited, factual and reliable? Can the writer's claims be verified, or checked, in an authoritative source, such as an up-to-date encyclopedia or other reference work? Here is an example of evidence whose accuracy can be easily verified:

> Baseball became an Olympic sport in 1992. Cuba has won three of four gold medals: 1992, 1996, and 2004.
>
> from "Borders of Baseball: U.S. and Cuban Play"

Resources

Chapter 7 Resources, Informational Text Focus Skill Builder, p. 3

PowerNotes, interactive lesson presentation with activities

Teacher One Stop™, on-level lesson plans and all print resources

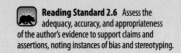

Reading Standard 2.6 Assess the adequacy, accuracy, and appropriateness of the author's evidence to support claims and assertions, noting instances of bias and stereotyping.

Appropriate Evidence **Appropriate** evidence applies directly to the subject; it is fitting and to the point. Although it may involve some opinion, appropriate evidence cannot rely solely on emotional appeal; it has to be anchored in fact. It also cannot be overly biased, or slanted in a particular direction. Look at this example of appropriate evidence from an article on hunger in the United States:

> We like to think of America as a land of plenty. Yet about one in ten Americans uses a food bank or soup kitchen on a regular basis in order to get food.
>
> from "Hungry Here? For Millions of Americans, the Answer Is 'Yes'"

Bias: Favoring One Side

Bias is made up of all the attitudes and beliefs that shape a person's thinking—often in spite of the facts. No one is immune to bias—we all have tendencies to favor certain things over others. Some expository texts include obvious examples of bias that suggest the writer has already made up his or her mind about a person, group of people, idea, or situation. Not all bias is bad; the important thing is to be able to recognize when a writer is presenting information in a one-sided way, from his or her own values and perspective. This response to a debate about bullying shows one student's bias toward being strong and uncompromising:

> You can't change people—you can't get rid of bullies. You have to stand up and not be a wimp. Be strong for yourself and your friends.
>
> from "Sound Off to the Editor"

In its most extreme form, bias can become prejudice—a sweeping, negative judgment of a person or entire group.

Stereotypes: Dangerous Generalizations

"Teenagers all have such bad taste in clothes." "Kids today don't read." "Rich people only care about their investments." These are all examples of **stereotypes**—unfair, fixed ideas about a group of people. Stereotypes are lazy generalizations; they brand every member of a group with the same characteristics and don't allow for individual differences. Stereotypes are harmful, and they are often used to persuade us to think in a certain way. When a writer uses stereotypes to support his or her claims, it's a warning that you should be wary of that writer's information.

> Let's face it—smart kids are geeky.
>
> from "Sound Off to the Editor"

Your Turn Evaluate Claims and Evidence

1. Give an example of a claim that can be supported by evidence.
2. What makes evidence adequate, accurate, and appropriate?
3. Define the terms *bias* and *stereotype*. How might the writer of an editorial use both when writing about a politician he or she wants to see lose an election?

Learn It Online
Try the *PowerNotes* version of this lesson on:
go.hrw.com [H7-701] **Go**

Bias: Favoring One Side

Remind students that no person or text is truly objective, or free from opinion. When this opinion heavily influences the way a text is created, and leads a writer to ignore other views on a subject, the opinion becomes bias. Bias, in turn, makes a text unreliable.

Stereotypes: Dangerous Generalizations

Explain that stereotyping is an extreme form of bias. It does not simply present a limited perspective on an issue, it actually encourages prejudicial views. Texts that rely on stereotypes to prove a claim are in no way reliable.

Check for Understanding

Your Turn _____

Possible responses:

1. *The claim "the online music industry is growing rapidly" could be supported by sales statistics.*
2. *Adequate evidence is sufficient in quantity, accurate evidence is factually correct, and appropriate evidence is related to the subject and free from bias or stereotyping.*
3. *Bias is attitudes that lead a writer to present a limited perspective on a subject. Stereotypes are general statements about a group that are generally negative and fail to acknowledge individual differences. An editorial writer might present a biased perspective on the politician, and present his or her views as a stereotype.*

Reteach

ThinkCentral Online Remediation

Learn It Online
For a multimedia version of the instruction found on this page, use the **PowerNotes** Informational Text Focus presentation.

go.hrw.com [H7-701] **Go**

Universal Access

English Learners/ Struggling Readers

English for Academic Success Help students learn the academic terms in the Informational Text Focus by providing these words and their student-friendly definitions:

- **claim**—statement claiming something is true
- **assertion**—statement strongly claiming something is true

- **verify**—to prove that something is accurate or true
- **bias**—a strong opinion in favor of or against something

Advanced Learners

Acceleration Have students discuss in pairs a text they have read recently and evaluate the text for adequate, accurate, and appropriate evidence.

Reading Skills Focus

Objectives

Students will
- determine an author's purpose for writing
- evaluate an author's claims and evidence
- identify bias and stereotyping in a text
- re-read for understanding

Preteach

Build Background Read the title and introductory paragraph of this essay with students. Discuss how the title and introduction reveal the author's motivation for writing the essay.

Direct Teach

Determining the Author's Purpose

Explain to students that writers may write with more than one of the purposes defined in the text; for example, they may write to inform and persuade, or to describe and explain. Being able to identify the author's purpose or purposes for writing is important to determining whether the author has presented information honestly and accurately.

Evaluating Evidence

Read aloud for students the Tips for Evaluating Evidence. Then, ask volunteers to give examples of adequate/inadequate, accurate/inaccurate, and appropriate/inappropriate evidence.

Reading Skills Focus

by **Carol Jago**

What Skills Can Help Me Critique Expository Texts?

Expository texts don't come with warning labels, but if you want to be a successful reader you need to be careful and alert when you sit down to read an informational text. You need to determine the author's purpose, evaluate the evidence that is presented, and notice when the writer ignores the facts and tries to slip something by you, such as a biased opinion or a stereotype.

Determining the Author's Purpose

It's important to be able to stand back and judge whether or not you trust the author and the information in an expository text. Start by asking this important question: "Why did the author write this?" There are many different reasons, or **purposes,** why an author might write an expository text: to inform, to define, to describe, or to explain something. Some expository texts might have a secondary purpose of entertaining you. Other expository texts don't just present information but also try to persuade you to think or do something—and this underlying persuasive purpose is not always obvious.

To determine an author's purpose, pay attention to these characteristics of the writing:

1. The author's point of view and attitude toward the subject	1. Look for examples of bias—a tendency to favor one side. Identify the tone. Is it neutral, serious, sarcastic?
2. The context within which the article or information appears	2. Note whether the writer is reflecting the goals and viewpoints of a particular publication or organization.
3. The language the author uses to explain the material	3. Look for words with positive or negative connotations.

Evaluating Evidence

Writers use different kinds of evidence to support their claims and assertions: facts, quotations, statistics, expert opinions, case studies, anecdotes, and examples. Each type of evidence can strengthen an author's assertions. It's not enough for a writer to provide evidence, though; you need to **assess,** or evaluate, the evidence for yourself.

Tips for Evaluating Evidence When you evaluate evidence, you check to make sure that it is adequate, accurate, and appropriate.

Evidence is **adequate** when: There are plenty of facts that can be verified. More than one reliable source is cited.

Evidence is **inadequate** when: Most claims are unsupported, or are supported only by the writer's feelings. You're left with questions about details that have been left out.

Evidence is **accurate** when: The author cites quotations, statistics, case studies, and other forms of fact-based evidence, using reliable sources.

Evidence is **inaccurate** when: The writer uses vague language and does not cite sources. Many generalizations use words such as *all*, *every*, and *everyone*.

California Standards, pp. 702–703

- **Reading Standard 2.6** Assess the adequacy, accuracy, and appropriateness of the author's evidence to support claims and assertions, noting instances of bias and stereotyping.

Reading Standard 2.6 Assess the adequacy, accuracy, and appropriateness of the author's evidence to support claims and assertions, noting instances of bias and stereotyping.

Evidence is **appropriate** when: The author chooses only relevant evidence—facts and valid opinions (judgments backed up by facts) that support his or her points. The evidence is not based on emotional appeal and does not favor one side over another. The author considers different points of view and is respectful of the audience.

Evidence is **inappropriate** when: The author has included irrelevant information that makes you think, "What does that have to do with anything?" You feel misled and find many examples of evidence based only on emotional appeal. The author clearly shows bias.

Recognizing Bias and Stereotyping

To critique an expository text, be sure to check for signs of bias and stereotyping. A **bias** can be *for* or *against* something; generally, bias refers to a tendency to favor one person or issue over another. Sometimes a writer's bias is obvious, but often you will have to read between the lines to recognize it. **Stereotyping** occurs when a writer expresses a fixed, oversimplified, or preconceived picture of an individual or group, making sweeping generalizations, as in "Young people are only interested in themselves" and "Unemployed people are lazy." The use of stereotypes indicates unreliable information and simplistic thinking.

Tips for Recognizing Bias and Stereotyping A writer who is biased or uses stereotyping—

- makes sweeping claims and assertions that are not supported by logic and facts.
- frequently uses words like *all, nothing, no one, every, only, never, always, everyone* to make unsupported generalizations.
- ignores, hides, or distorts any information that contradicts, or opposes, his or her viewpoint.

- uses words with strong positive or negative connotations, like *beautiful/ugly, good/evil, strong/weak, right/wrong.*
- does not acknowledge opposing viewpoints.
- conveys a tone that suggests a strongly positive or negative impression of the subject.

Re-reading

Some expository texts can be challenging to read, especially if you are unfamiliar with the subject. An expository text with a complicated assertion and a great deal of evidence can be especially challenging to read. You may have to re-read passages—or even the entire text—in order to follow the writer's thoughts. You may have to read through the material first simply to get a sense of what the writer is trying to explain, then re-read it in order to understand the details. Re-reading may slow you down, but it will pay off in helping you comprehend and retain information.

Your Turn Critique Expository Texts

1. Name two ways to determine an author's purpose.

2. Why would a writer's use of words like *always, never, everyone,* and *all* make you suspicious of an expository text?

> **Now go to the Skills in Action: Reading Model**

※ **Learn It Online**
For more practice critiquing media, visit MediaScope:
go.hrw.com   H7-703   **Go**

Reading Model

Objectives

Students will

• determine an author's purpose for writing

• evaluate evidence

• use strategies such as skimming and scanning to read informational text

Preteach

Read with a Purpose Direct students to read the Read with a Purpose statement. Have students consider the reasons that a writer might choose to write about the impact of a music program on students. Ask them to brainstorm in their **Reader/Writer Notebook** the types of evidence the author might use to support a claim regarding students and music.

Direct Teach

Model the Skill

Use the Reading Model to demonstrate the application of the Informational Text and Reading skills in a short selection. As you or your students read the model aloud, stop to discuss the side annotations and highlighting, which are aids to comprehension and analysis.

California Standards, pp. 704–709

■ **Reading Standard 2.6** Assess the adequacy, accuracy, and appropriateness of the author's evidence to support claims and assertions, noting instances of bias and stereotyping.

Read with a Purpose Read this selection to discover the ways a music program affects students in Nashville.

Music Makers

Musicians Help Keep Music Alive in Schools

by WORLD ALMANAC

Selection Readability	
Easily Accessible **Accessible** Challenging	accessible language; situation familiar to students

Selection Summary

This article explores the funding crisis facing the music program of a Nashville school.

▶ **Informational Text Focus**

Claims and Assertions What claim does the author make about the quality of the instruments at Hume-Fogg Academic Magnet High School? **_Possible response: The author claims that many of the instruments owned by the band were old and worn-out._**

▶ **Informational Text Focus**

Evidence How do the descriptions of the instruments serve as evidence for the author's claim? Is this evidence appropriate, accurate, and adequate? Explain. **_Possible response: The descriptions of the instruments prove that the band had many old, worn-out instruments by providing clear examples of the poor quality of the instruments. The evidence is completely appropriate, and seems to be based on observations of the instruments, so it is also accurate and adequate._**

NASHVILLE'S
FIRST PUBLIC SCHOOL
Nashville's first public school, Hume School, opened here Feb. 26, 1855. A three story brick building, the school employed 12 teachers and served all grades. In 1874 high school classes were moved to Fogg School built on adjoining corner lot. Named for educators, Alfred E. Hume & Francis B. Fogg, the schools were replaced by Hume-Fogg in 1912.

Hume-Fogg Academic Magnet High School, Nashville, Tennessee.

Old, worn-out instruments were common in the band hall at Nashville's Hume-Fogg Academic Magnet High School. Trombone slides weren't working right. Saxophones made breathy sounds as air leaked from them. Parts fell off the ancient bass clarinet. And then there were the two hulking metal tubas that had played their first notes before World War II.

Then one day in May 2006, Hume-Fogg music students were greeted with boxes full of brand-new equipment. "We just opened them like it was Christmas," says music director Rich Ripani. "Every-body was ripping open boxes and saying things like, 'Look, a brand-

Informational Focus

Claims and Assertions This article begins with an **asser-tion,** or **claim**—a direct statement about the quality of the musical instruments at a Nashville high school.

Informational Focus

Evidence These sentences are included as **evidence** for the author's initial assertion. They give examples of the age and condition of certain instruments at the school.

Model the Skill

▶ **Reading Focus**

Determining Author's Purpose Does the author have an additional purpose for writing, besides informing the reader? Explain. **Possible response:** *The author may also want to persuade the reader of the importance of arts education programs to students. The inclusion of the comparison of new instruments to Christmas suggests that music is important to them and should be supported in the schools.*

Reading Focus

Determining Author's Purpose This sentence is a clue to the **author's purpose** for writing the article: to inform readers about the state of Nashville's school music programs and what some organizations are doing to help the situation.

---

new oboe,' and 'Look, a brand-new Fox bassoon.'"

Santa Claus, in this case, was the Nashville Alliance for Public Education. The nonprofit group recently teamed up with professional musicians from the Country Music Association (CMA). They aim to raise the $8 million that "Music City" music programs need to get back on their feet.

"We set a goal to provide musical instruments for all Nashville public schools," says the Nashville Alliance's executive director, Kay Simmons.

Reaching Reluctant Readers

Use the following options to nurture students' varied responses to "Music Makers."

- Have students imagine that they are students at a Nashville public school who have the opportunity to address the school board and request their support for music education in the schools. Have students work in small groups to develop a three-minute speech that they would give to the school board, using claims and evidence from "Music Makers" as a basis for their presentation. Invite groups to deliver their presentations to the class.

Programs on Their Last Notes

Nashville may be America's capital of country music, but like many other cities, its cash-strapped school district spends very little on music education. For decades, area music teachers like Ripani have had to beg, borrow, or buy with their own money whatever equipment they could get. That's tough when one new baritone horn can cost $3,500. The expense of outfitting an entire school band with instruments can easily reach $200,000.

Such steep costs worry school officials nationwide. Many have chosen to cut back on music education or shut down programs altogether. Michael Blakeslee of MENC: The National Association for Music Education says that poor school districts in inner cities and rural areas tend to be hit the hardest. For example, in 2007, budget cuts shut down the music program at Nashville's Dalewood Middle School. "It's [common] across the country," Blakeslee says.

Part of the problem is that people view arts courses as merely add-ons to "core" classes in reading and math. In order to improve test scores in core areas, some schools have begun chipping away at the time allotted each day for music and other arts. But there's plenty of evidence to suggest that this is short-sighted. Recent studies showed that students involved in the arts earn higher grades and have fewer discipline problems. MENC recently conducted a poll of school principals. Most of them agreed that a strong music program boosts attendance and graduation rates.

Hearing the Call

To Nashville's country western stars, helping public school music programs through the CMA just makes sense. The group donated about $360,000 in 2007 and plans to give more in years to come. In many cases, the children of musicians are the ones sitting in public school classrooms. For instance, the Nashville School of the Arts has a unique guitar program whose recent graduates include the son of singer Crystal Gayle. "Many of us live here," says Troy Gentry, half of the singing duo Montgomery Gentry. "Our businesses are here. We are invested in the community."

Together, the Nashville Alliance and the CMA have raised $1.5 million of the $8 million needed, and more is to come. At Hume-Fogg, senior Kyle Burgess says the new instruments have boosted students' confidence and improved the sound of bands there.

Model the Skill

▶ **Reading Focus**

Evaluating Evidence What accurate, adequate, and appropriate evidence could the author present to demonstrate that cutting funds to music programs is "common across the country"? ***Possible response:*** *The author could quote music teachers from other areas in the country, or include statistics showing a decline in funding for music programs or a decline in time allotted to arts education.*

▶ **Informational Text Focus**

Bias and Stereotyping What specific words or phrases in this sentence alert the reader to potential bias? Explain. ***Possible response:*** *The phrases "part of the problem," and "merely add-ons" alerted me to potential bias. They suggest that not believing in the importance of arts courses, or not thinking of them as equal to academics, is a problem, which is an opinion.*

▶ **Reading Focus**

Evaluating Evidence Why would studies and polls constitute accurate, adequate, and appropriate evidence? ***Possible response:*** *Polls and studies are accurate because they are conducted by experts. They are adequate because statistics are a form of strong evidence, and they are appropriate because they are unbiased and relevant to the subject.*

- Have students create a written, audio, or visual response to the selection that explains their own involvement with arts education (you may wish to expand this to include electives such as physical education), and how this education affects them. Invite students to share their responses with classmates and their arts or elective instructors.

- Have students consider the "other side" of one or more of the author's assertions about music and arts education. Ask students to construct an outline of their claim that includes reasons they disagree with the author, and the types of evidence they have or would use to support their own claim.

Model the Skill

► Reading Focus

Re-reading Ask students to identify one assertion that became clearer to them on a second reading. Possible response: For me, the re-reading clarified exactly how much music programs suffer from a lack of funding.

Check for Understanding

Read with a Purpose Ask students to explain what the author claimed as the effects of music programs on students in Nashville, and how this claim was supported. ***Possible response:*** *The author claimed that music is extremely important to the students in Nashville. The evidence of this claim included anecdotes and quotations from the students and band director regarding the excitement over receiving new instruments, and the effect of the gift on the band members.*

 California Standards, p. 709

■ **Reading Standard 2.6** Assess the adequacy, accuracy, and appropriateness of the author's evidence to support claims and assertions, noting instances of bias and stereotyping.

Reading Model

Reading Focus

Re-reading **Re-reading** is a good strategy to help you understand informational texts. Now that you've read "Music Makers" once, re-read it a second time to make sure that you understand the assertions in the text and the evidence the author uses to support them.

"It's just kind of fun to play something new like that, when everything on it works," says Kyle, who plays a new baritone saxophone. "A new horn makes everyone feel better."

Read with a Purpose What points did the writer make in this article that most convinced you of the value of a strong music program?

Troy Gentry of Montgomery Gentry performs at Farm Aid 2007 at Randall's Island in New York City.

Resources

Chapter 7 Resources, Literary and Academic Vocabulary Skill Builder, p. 5

UA: Differentiating Intruction, graphic organizer, p. 193

Teacher One Stop™, on-level lesson plans and all print resources

WordSharp: An Interactive Vocabulary Tutor, more practice with academic language

Academic Vocabulary

Writing About Expository Critique

English for Academic Success Write the following questions on the board. Tell students these are the kinds of questions they will encounter on standardized tests. Discuss the meaning of the words, then have students use "Music Makers" to answer the questions.

• **Assess** the overall validity of the author's assertions in "Music Makers." ***Possible response:*** *Overall, the author of "Music Makers" raises valuable points regarding music and arts education in schools. The author demonstrates the value of arts education to students and the benefits that apply the entire school system.*

Reading Standard 2.6 Assess the adequacy, accuracy, and appropriateness of the author's evidence to support claims and assertions, noting instances of bias and stereotyping.

Into Action: Evaluating an Author's Evidence

Complete the following chart on a separate sheet of paper or in your *Reader/Writer Notebook*. List assertions from "Music Makers" in the first column, and give the evidence in support of each assertion in the second column. Then, explain whether you find the author's evidence to be adequate, accurate, and appropriate—and why.

Author's Assertion	Evidence Supporting It
"Old, worn-out instruments were common in the band hall at Nashville's Hume-Fogg Academic Magnet High School."	

Talk About . . .

1. With a partner, share your thoughts on what makes evidence adequate, accurate, and appropriate. Try to use each Academic Vocabulary word listed on the right at least once in your discussion.

Write About . . .

Answer the following questions about "Music Makers." For definitions of the underlined Academic Vocabulary words, see the column on the right.

2. What specific benefits of school music programs does the author cite?

3. What does the author conclude about why country musicians are contributing to this cause?

4. After reading the article, how would you assess the value of school music programs? Explain your thoughts.

Writing Skills Focus
Think as a Reader/Writer

The Writing Skills Focus activities in Chapter 7 will give you opportunities to examine and critique authors' explorations of a variety of topics.

Academic Vocabulary for Chapter 7

Writing and Talking About Expository Critique

Academic Vocabulary is the language you use to write and talk about texts. Use these words to discuss the informational texts you read in this chapter. The words are underlined throughout the chapter.

assess (uh SEHS) *v.*: examine and judge the value of something; evaluate. *To assess the strength of an author's argument, look carefully at the evidence he or she provides.*

conclude (kuhn KLOOD) *v.*: decide by reasoning. *Re-reading a text can help you conclude whether the assertions in it are well supported.*

instance (IHN stuhns) *n.*: occurrence or example. *An instance of stereotyping can make an author's argument seem less credible.*

specific (spih SIHF ihk) *adj.*: definite and particular. *"Music Makers" includes information from specific experts on the topic of music education.*

Your Turn

Copy the Academic Vocabulary words into your *Reader/Writer Notebook*. Then, use a dictionary or thesaurus to find and list synonyms for each one.

Guided Practice: Apply

Into Action: Evaluating an Author's Evidence

Make sure students' charts include several assertions and one piece of evidence for each assertion. *Possible response: Evidence: descriptions of instruments squeaking, breaking, and having poor sound quality. Additional assertion: "there's plenty of evidence to suggest that this [cutting arts programs] is short-sighted. Evidence: studies that show students involved in the arts get better grades and have fewer discipline problems than those who do not.*

Talk About. . .

1. Model for students how to incorporate the academic vocabulary words into a discussion of expository critique. For example, you might say, "The instance of the Hume-Fogg band demonstrates the importance of music because. . ."

Write About. . .
Possible responses:

2. *The author cites the specific benefits of higher attendance, higher graduation rates, greater academic achievement, and fewer behavior problems.*

3. *The author concludes that musicians are passionate about keeping music alive in part because their own children are affected by cuts to arts education funding.*

4. *I assess the value of school music programs to be quite high, for the benefits cited by the author.*

Independent Practice

Chapter 7 Resources, Skill Builders, p. 3–5

UA: Differentiating Intruction, graphic organizer, p. 193

- What does the author **conclude** about the efforts of the Nashville Alliance and the CMA? *Possible response: The author concludes that they are doing great work that is benefitting students greatly.*

- Identify an **instance** of how the Nashville Alliance directly benefitted Hume-Fogg students. *Possible response: One such instance is the self-esteem boost that new instruments gave the band students, as explained by senior Kyle Burgess.*

- What **specific** evidence does the author use to support the claim that high costs of instruments are contributing to the decline in music education? *Possible response: The author uses a quotation from an expert source, Michael Blakeslee of the National Association of Music Education. The author also uses the factual example of the shutdown of Dalewood Middle School's music program.*

INFORMATIONAL TEXT FOCUS
Claims and Assertions

CONTENTS

What Do **You?** Think

What can you learn from reading about a sport? from playing it?

QuickWrite

Think about a sport, hobby, or other activity that you engage in with a group. How has participating in this activity affected you as a person?

MAGAZINE ARTICLE
Preparing to Read

Reading Standard 2.6 Assess the adequacy, accuracy, and appropriateness of **the author's evidence to support claims and assertions,** noting instances of bias and stereotyping.

Borders of Baseball: U.S. and Cuban Play

Informational Text Focus

Claims and Assertions An **assertion,** or **claim,** is a positive statement that an author makes. An assertion can be either a fact or an opinion—but if it is an opinion, it needs to be supported. The writer of "Borders of Baseball: U.S. and Cuban Play" makes many assertions about the differences between baseball in the United States and baseball in Cuba. For example, the writer claims that there are fewer opportunities to play different sports in Cuba than in the United States. The writer is careful to support such claims with **evidence.** Solid evidence makes assertions more believable. Identifying claims and assertions in a text will help you understand what the author of a text wants you to believe.

Reading Skills Focus

Determining Author's Purpose As with other forms of writing, nonfiction prose is written with a <u>specific</u> purpose in mind. An author may have multiple purposes, but one will usually stand out as the main purpose. Sometimes, the author's purpose can affect *how* you read. If the author is trying to persuade you to believe something, for <u>instance</u>, you may read more slowly and carefully to identify the author's assertions and the evidence he or she offers in support of them. The following are common examples of author's purpose:

- to inform
- to explain
- to persuade
- to entertain
- to reveal a truth about life
- to share an experience

Re-reading If you are reading a text for pleasure, once might be enough. If you are reading for information or analyzing assertions, however, you will probably need to read the text a second or third time.

Writing Skills Focus

Preparing for **Timed ⎿Writing** As you read "Borders of Baseball," list the similarities and differences between baseball in the two nations. You'll use that information to respond to a timed-writing prompt later.

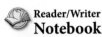 **Reader/Writer**
Notebook
Use your **RWN** to complete the activities for this selection.

 Vocabulary

traditions (truh DIHSH uhnz) *n.:* accepted social attitudes and customs. *The United States and Cuba have different baseball traditions because the game means different things in each country.*

identity (y DEHN tuh tee) *n.:* distinguishing characteristics that determine who or what a person or thing is. *Having good baseball players is part of Cuba's national identity.*

intense (ihn TEHNS) *adj.:* showing strong feelings and seriousness. *Baseball fans have intense admiration for the players.*

Language Coach

Pronouncing –*tion* In the English language, certain letter patterns are always pronounced the same way. One of those letter patterns is *–tion,* as in *tradition.* This pattern always comes at the end of a word, and it is pronounced *shuhn.* What are three other words that end with this same pattern?

 Learn It Online
To increase your knowledge of comparison and contrast, visit the interactive Reading Workshops on:
go.hrw.com | H7-711 | Go

Preteach

Introducing Vocabulary
Read the Vocabulary words and sample sentences aloud. Then, have students complete each analogy with the correct Vocabulary word.

1. *rules* are to *games* as *customs* are to [*traditions*]
2. *title* is to *book* as *name* is to [*identity*]
3. *weak* is to *strong* as *mild* is to [*intense*]

English for Academic Success
Language Coach
Provide examples of other words that end in the suffix *–tion,* such as *solution, notion, caution,* and *action.* Read the words aloud with students. Then, have students think of and pronounce other words that end in *–tion* [*description, animation, completion*].

Informational Text Focus
As you read and discuss the article with students, suggest that students organize their notes on Cuban and American baseball in outline form with assertions as main entries and details beneath.

Reading Skills Focus
As you read and discuss the text with students, encourage them to make notes about the author's purpose as they read. Is the article informative, persuasive, or entertaining? What is the author's purpose?

Writing Skills Focus
Tell students to note in their **Reader/ Writer Notebook** how Cuban and American baseball are similar and different. Students can use their notes to complete the Writing Skills Focus activity.

Learn It Online
Reading Workshops are interactive versions of real-world informational texts; students exercise their reading skills by responding to polls and answering questions in an engaging online format.

go.hrw.com | H7-711 | Go

Selection Resources

Chapter 7 Resources, on-level practice and assessment, p. 6

PowerNotes, interactive lesson presentation with activities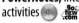

Teacher One Stop™, on-level lesson plans and all print resources

Holt Audio Library

Holt Audio Library: Selections and Summaries in Spanish

UA: Holt Interactive Reader, p. 188

Holt Interactive Reader for ELD, p. 217

Holt Audio Tutor for ELD

UA: Differentiating Instruction, modified lesson plans and leveled assessment, p. 194

UA: Supporting Instruction in Five Languages, selection summary

UA: Resources for Teaching Advanced Students, lesson plans, p. 152

ThinkCentral Online Assessment, Selection Standards Check

ThinkCentral Online Remediation

Model the Skill

■ Explain to students that an **assertion**, if it is an individual author's claim of truth, cannot be considered factual and true unless there is **evidence** to prove it. When an author makes assertions, he or she must provide such evidence for readers to evaluate and determine that the assertion should be taken seriously.

■ Read aloud the section titled "Diamonds in the Rough." Point out that in this section, the author is asserting that, although both Cuban and American children play baseball, baseball is much more important in Cuba than in America. The evidence he offers is that baseball is only one of many sports in the United States that the children can play. It is also one of many that all Americans can take an interest in. Baseball is the only widely popular sport in Cuba, and children grow up with a focus on baseball over any other sport.

■ Discuss with students how this evidence supports or does not support the author's assertion. Ask volunteers to suggest additional evidence the author might have used to support the assertion.

Guided Practice: Apply

Have students read the selection in small groups, pausing after they read each section to discuss what assertions the author made and what evidence was provided to support the assertions. Ask students to consider whether they are persuaded by the evidence.

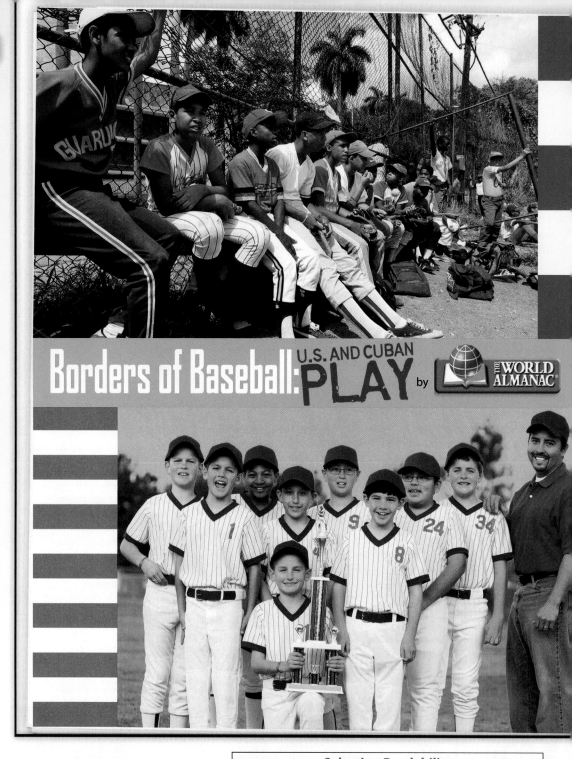

Borders of Baseball: U.S. AND CUBAN PLAY by THE WORLD ALMANAC

Selection Readability	
Easily Accessible **Accessible** Challenging	historical context; familiar subject matter; accessible vocabulary; informational tone

Selection Summary

This article compares and contrasts baseball in the United States and Cuba. The text describes how players are paid, how fans treat players, and how each country's teams have fared in international competitions.

Read with a Purpose
Read to discover the biggest differences between baseball in the United States and baseball in Cuba.

After the U.S. World Series ends, you won't see many Americans paying attention to baseball until the spring. However, that's when Cuban baseball players step up to bat and begin their season. Organized baseball started being played in both the United States and Cuba at roughly the same time—at the end of the 1800s. The basics of play are similar in both countries. The differences between the two traditions, however, are major. **Ⓐ**

Diamonds in the Rough
Baseball is called "America's pastime," but it competes at the professional level with the National Football League, the National Basketball Association, and other organizations. In a similar fashion, children in the United States can sign up for Little League Baseball and similar programs, but they can also participate in organized hockey, ice skating, dancing lessons, and more.

The opportunities to play different sports are slimmer in Cuba. For example, when World Cup soccer was televised in 2006, the Associated Press reported, Cuban kids caught soccer fever. But children were rolling up paper to make balls, because soccer balls are rare on the island. Baseballs, however, are widely available. Cubans are raised on stickball. "Kids learn to throw baseballs and hit them with a stick," says Roberto González Echevarría, the author of *The Pride of Havana: A History of Cuban Baseball* and a professor of Hispanic and comparative literature at Yale University. "There is more competition [in the United States] from football, basketball, and so on." **Ⓑ**

Pay for Play
Young, talented U.S. baseball players can decide to go professional. Scouts might discover them, or their parents and coaches might push them to attend colleges with strong baseball programs. But becoming a success is mostly a private matter. Not so in Cuba: Boys with talent are identified as early as age ten. The government moves gifted players into boarding academies, where they are trained in the sport.

Cuban baseball is under government control. Therefore, Cubans play for the nation, not for a team owner. "Baseball is more important to national identity in Cuba," says González Echevarría. Playing

Ⓐ Read and Discuss What is the author setting up for you?

Ⓑ Reading Focus Determining Author's Purpose Why does the author mention other sports?

Vocabulary **traditions** (truh DIHSH uhnz) *n.*: accepted social attitudes and customs.
identity (y DEHN tuh tee) *n.*: distinguishing characteristics that determine who or what a person or thing is.

Universal Access

English Learners
English for Academic Success Point out words and text features that identify an author's use of evidence to support an assertion. Words and phrases such as *for example* and *in this case* may signal the introduction of evidence to support an assertion. Evidence may also be identified with quotation marks to signal an expert's opinion, or with capitalization or acronyms to identify a reputable source. Have students read in the selection in mixed-ability groups, using these words and text features to identify evidence supporting assertions.

✔ See **UA: Differentiating Instruction** for lesson plans and strategies for teaching English learners.

Struggling Readers
Tell students that magazine articles often contain headings that separate the article into many smaller sections. Point out the article's headings to students. Then, discuss with students whether the headings indicate use of the block method or the point-by-point method.

✔ See **UA: Differentiating Instruction** for lesson plans and strategies for teaching struggling readers.

Think About/Talk About

▶ Comprehension

ⓒ Read and Discuss
Possible response: In America, individuals play for themselves. In Cuba, good players are expected to play for their country.

ⓔ Reading Focus
Possible response: The author might have included this information to support the assertion that Cuban baseball focuses more on the game itself, which brings them success.

▶ Analysis

ⓓ Informational Focus
Possible response: In Cuba, the stadiums are plainer, and the game is the main focus.

▶ Extend the Discussion

Determining Author's Purpose Based on the tone of the article and the evidence cited, what seems to be the opinion of the author in regard to Cuban versus American baseball? *Possible response: The author seems to prefer Cuban baseball and respects the fact that Cubans focus on the game rather than on the commercial side of the sport.*

Vocabulary: Own the Word

intense: Ask students to applaud in order to indicate whether they would like to be described as *intense*. *Possible response: Some students may applaud if they feel seriousness and strong feelings are desirable; other students may not care to be called intense.*

Monitor Students' Comprehension

Use the Read with a Purpose follow-up question to assess students' understanding. *Possible response: I was most surprised to learn how much cheaper a ticket to a Cuban baseball game is than a ticket to a U.S. baseball game.*

and coaching baseball are duties, not options, for Cubans with the required skills. Players are state workers who receive state salaries and assignments. Better players are paid about the same as lesser ones. Some are given gifts, such as expense accounts at restaurants. But individuals are not rewarded in the way U.S. baseball stars are.

Major League Baseball players can argue for contracts worth millions of dollars. They work for privately owned teams, and better players earn much more money than weaker players. That is a big reason U.S. scouts were able to lure several Cuban players from their home country in recent decades. Some of Cuba's top talent left the island forever for the chance to play professional baseball and earn millions. ⓒ

In the Ballpark

Ballpark visitors say they feel a difference between the fans at U.S. and Cuban games. Baseball fans in both countries can be intense. But it is common for U.S. fans to be fenced off from their idols, while Cubans have greater access to their players. After batting practice, U.S. stadium walls are rushed by people handing items to the players to be autographed. In Cuba, fans show their admiration differently. "The people stare at them, respect them, adore them, attend to them,

---

ⓒ **Read and Discuss** How does Echevarría's comment on national identity connect to what you know about baseball in the United States?

ⓓ **Informational Focus Claims and Assertions** What assertion does the author make about Cuban ballparks here?

help them," says Carlos Rodriguez Acosta, the commissioner of Cuban baseball, in the PBS Web series *Stealing Home.* U.S. ballparks, too, are different from Cuban ones. Fans pass souvenir and food stands while going to and from their seats. Team logos are plastered on everything from cups to T-shirts. Cuban ballparks, by contrast, are not very commercialized. In Cuba, baseball is a source of national pride, not a way to push people to buy certain products. ⓓ

U.S. players are better paid than their counterparts in Cuba, partly because it costs much more for U.S. fans to go to the ballpark. In 2005, the cost of an opening-day ticket in the United States ranged from around $14 to $45. The Cuban league also charges admission, but a seat costs mere pennies. So while the players in both countries play the same game, the culture surrounding that game is very different in the two nations.

Score Board

Baseball became an Olympic sport in 1992. Cuba has won three of four gold medals: 1992, 1996, and 2004. The United States won in 2000. By 2006, Cuba had taken 25 of 36 World Cups in baseball; the United States, 2. ⓔ

Read with a Purpose

Explain which difference between baseball in the United States and baseball in Cuba most surprised you.

ⓔ **Reading Focus Determining Author's Purpose** Why might the author have included the information in this section?

Vocabulary intense (ihn TEHNS) *adj.:* showing strong feelings and seriousness.

Universal Access

Advanced Learners

Enrichment After students read "Borders of Baseball," have them develop their own assertions regarding Cuban and American baseball by researching each sport and gathering evidence to support their claims. Allow students to work in groups, if they wish, and have them present their assertions and evidence to the class.

✔ See **UA: Resources for Teaching Advanced Students** for lesson plans and strategies for teaching advanced learners.

Students with Disabilities

Invite students to read "Borders of Baseball" in interactive format in **Holt Interactive Reader for ELD** and to use the sidenotes as aids to understanding the selection. The interactive version provides additional instruction, practice, and assessment of the skills taught in the Student Edition.

Reading Standard 2.6 **Assess** the adequacy, accuracy, and appropriateness of **the author's evidence to support claims and assertions,** noting instances of bias and stereotyping.

Check for Understanding

Independent Practice
Answers and Explanations

Borders of Baseball: U.S. and Cuban Play

Standards Review

Informational Text and Vocabulary

1. Which of the following **assertions** does the author *not* make in the article?

A Cuban baseball players are better than American baseball players.

B U.S. baseball players make more money than Cuban baseball players.

C Cuban baseball players play for their country rather than team owners.

D There are major differences between the baseball traditions in Cuba and the United States.

2. Which statement *best* supports the author's **claim** that there are more opportunities to play different sports in the United States than in Cuba?

A Baseball is "America's pastime."

B Cuban baseball is controlled by the government.

C In 2006, soccer became very popular in Cuba.

D U.S. children can participate in organized baseball, hockey, ice skating, dancing, and other activities.

3. There is enough information in this article to show that the author believes that

A American baseball is more entertaining than Cuban baseball.

B Cuban baseball should not be controlled by the government.

C American baseball is heavily influenced by money and business.

D Cuban baseball is not very successful in international competition.

4. Another word for *traditions* is

A leagues.

B academies.

C autographs.

D customs.

5. A nation's *identity* is determined by its

A essential characteristics.

B type of government.

C unique language.

D national sport.

Writing Skills Focus

Timed Writing In a paragraph, explain the major similarities and differences between the baseball traditions in the United States and in Cuba. A Venn diagram can help you sort out and analyze the similarities and differences. In each circle, note differences. In the center, where the circles overlap, note similarities.

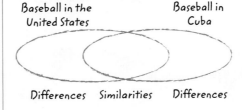

Baseball in the United States — Baseball in Cuba

Differences   Similarities   Differences

What Do **You Think Now**

Why might playing a sport for your country, rather than for a team, make you play harder?

1. A *The author makes no claim about the skills of the players in each country, but notes differences between the two styles of baseball (D), of which (B) and (C) are examples.*

2. D *The variety of sports available to American children is the best evidence of the opportunities they have over their Cuban counterparts.*

3. C *The author acknowledges Cuba's baseball success (D), and makes no comment on points (A) and (B).*

4. D *Customs is a synonym for traditions.*

5. A *A country's identity is determined by its essential characteristics. Items B, C, and D might be included in these characteristics.*

Writing Skills Focus

Possible response: *Baseball is a popular sport in both countries. However, Americans have more opportunities to play baseball than Cubans do. The author of the article claims that American baseball revolves around money and commercialism, while in Cuba, players and fans alike care more about the patriotic spirit of the game.*

Assess

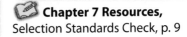 **Chapter 7 Resources,** Selection Standards Check, p. 9

 ThinkCentral Online Assessment, Selection Standards Check

Reteach

ThinkCentral Online Remediation

 California Standards, p. 715

■ **Reading Standard 2.6** Assess the adequacy, accuracy, and appropriateness of the author's evidence to support claims and assertions, noting instances of bias and stereotyping.

What Do You Think Now?

Have students consider the differences between loyalty to a team and patriotic feelings for a country.

Objectives

Students will

- identify evidence used to support an author's assertions
- evaluate evidence to determine its accuracy and support of the argument

Motivate

What Do You Think?/QuickWrite

Use the QuickWrite to have students to consider the effects of poverty on individuals and families. Then have students discuss in their **Reader/Writer Notebook** the value of having correct information about poverty, hunger, and how to prevent them.

English for Academic Success

Academic Vocabulary

Look for opportunities to use the Academic Vocabulary words in this chapter.

- **assess**, *v.*: examine and judge the value of something; evaluate.
- **conclude**, *v.*: decide by reasoning.
- **specific**, *adj.*: definite and particular.

Analyzing Visuals

Extension Activity How are the people in this image working to combat hunger? *Possible response: They seem to be volunteering at a soup kitchen, working to feed others.*

California Standards, pp. 716–721

- **Reading Standard 2.6** Assess the adequacy, accuracy, and appropriateness of the author's evidence to support claims and assertions, noting instances of bias and stereotyping.

INFORMATIONAL TEXT·FOCUS
Author's Evidence

CONTENTS

What Do **You** Think Why do we need accurate information about the realities of poverty and hunger?

⊙ QuickWrite
Often poverty and hunger in our society go unnoticed. What can happen when these problems are not addressed?

Preparing to Read

Reading Standard 2.6 Assess the adequacy, accuracy, and appropriateness of the author's evidence to support claims and assertions, noting instances of bias and stereotyping.

Hungry Here?

Informational Text Focus

Author's Evidence Writers of persuasive texts use **evidence**—information that supports an argument—to back up their claims and conclusions. Types of evidence include **facts, examples, statistics** (number facts), **expert opinions,** and **quotations.**

Reading Skills Focus

Evaluating Evidence When you **evaluate evidence,** you think about whether it is **accurate,** or correct; **appropriate,** or related to the topic; and **adequate,** or sufficient to prove the conclusion and persuade you that it is valid. Don't take for granted that an author's evidence meets these criteria. **Assess,** or judge, it for yourself. If you read a statement and think to yourself that it really doesn't have much to do with the topic, you may be looking at **inappropriate** evidence. If a writer states an opinion using words such as *all, each,* and *every,* you're probably looking at **inaccurate** evidence. If you have to trust the writer's feelings instead of relying on facts, the evidence is most likely **inadequate.**

Into Action As you read, record and <u>assess</u> the evidence you think is important in this article. Identify its type and note whether it supports the writer's claims and conclusions.

Evidence	Type	Accurate	Appropriate	Adequate

Writing Skills Focus

Preparing for Timed **Writing** As you read, note the evidence that best supports the author's claims and assertions. You will use these notes to complete a timed writing assignment later.

 Reader/Writer Notebook
Use your **RWN** to complete the activities for this selection.

Learn It Online
Discover the power of an increased vocabulary at:
go.hrw.com H7-717 Go

Vocabulary

deprivation (dehp ruh VAY shuhn) *n.:* hardship resulting from a lack of something. *Some people living in Cayce's county experience food deprivation on a regular basis.*

malnutrition (mal noo TRIHSH uhn) *n.:* ill health caused by a lack of food or by a lack of healthy foods. *Malnutrition is a medical problem that causes weakness and slows growth.*

prolonged (pruh LAWNGD) *adj.:* continuing for a long time. *The prolonged lack of food will result in a serious condition called malnutrition.*

Language Coach

Prefixes Prefixes are word parts added to the beginnings of words to change their meaning. In both Spanish and English, the prefix *mal–* is used to indicate that something is bad or abnormal. *Mal–* comes from the Latin word *malus,* which means "bad." How does knowing the meaning of *mal–* help you understand the meaning of *malnutrition*? Name three other words with the same prefix. What do they mean?

Preteach

Introducing Vocabulary

Have students complete each sentence with the correct Vocabulary word.

1. The cast of the play received a _____ round of enthusiastic applause. [*prolonged*]

2. Lee suffered from sleep _____. [*deprivation*]

3. Food banks help prevent _____ . [*malnutrition*]

English for Academic Success

Language Coach

Discuss the parts of the word *malnutrition*. Show students that if they remove the prefix, they are left with the word *nutrition*. Then, ask them to reconstruct the word, combining the meanings of the base word and the prefix. [*malnourished, malpractice, malcontent; badly fed, bad practice, someone who's not happy*]

Informational Text Focus

As you read and discuss the selection with students, have them track each piece of evidence used to support the author's assertion, and indicate its accuracy, adequacy, and appropriateness.

Reading Skills Focus

Give students a copy of the Reading Skills Focus graphic organizer before they read. (See **Chapter 7 Resources.**) Tell them to use their responses to answer the questions on the Applying Your Skills page.

Writing Skills Focus

Have students jot down notes about the author's arguments and evidence in their **Reader/Writer Notebook.**

Learn It Online
Send students to **Word Watch** for audio pronunciations, synonyms and antonyms, and brief histories of word origins.

go.hrw.com H7-717   Go

Direct Teach

Model the Skill

■ Provide students with the Reading Skills Focus graphic organizer for "Hungry Here?" (See **Chapter 7 Resources**).

■ Tell students that **evidence**, or proof, makes an assertion stronger. That is why writers of persuasive texts back up their claims with evidence, such as statistics, facts, examples, expert opinions, or quotations. Readers of persuasive texts should assess every piece of evidence they encounter to determine what type of evidence it is, and whether it is accurate and appropriate to the assertions.

■ Point out the second paragraph on p. 718. This is where the author states the assertion: that hunger is a growing problem in America. Immediately following this assertion, the author cites the U.S. Department of Agriculture's data about the number of homes in which people sometimes or often go hungry. A reader of this persuasive article should identify this piece of evidence as a statistic, and understand that it is very appropriate to the author's claim and likely accurate, as it comes from the government, and certainly adequate.

Evidence	38 million food insecure households
Type	statistic
Accurate	probably
Appropriate	yes
Adequate	yes

Guided Practice: Apply

Have students continue reading the article in pairs, pausing as they read to note in their graphic organizers types of evidence, their accuracy, and how appropriate they are.

HUNGRY HERE?

For Millions of Americans, the Answer Is "Yes"

by THE WORLD ALMANAC

Read with a Purpose
Read this article to learn how a teen is helping to combat hunger in his hometown.

When you think of starving people, how do you picture them? Do you imagine people living in the past? Or do you think of people living far away—in huts in Africa or on city streets in India? Does it ever cross your mind that right now, in your own state and probably in your own city or town, somebody is suffering from hunger? Ⓐ

Many of us like to think of hunger as something long ago and far away. But the reality is that hunger is a huge problem here and now. And even with ongoing government initiatives such as the Food Stamp Program, it's a problem that's getting worse. In 2005, the U.S. Department of Agriculture estimated that more than 38 million Americans live in "hungry or food insecure" households. (*Food insecure* is a government term that means "not knowing where your next meal is coming from.") That's an

Ⓐ **Informational Focus** Author's Evidence At this point in the article, can you guess the author's position on the topic?

Selection Readability	
Easily Accessible **Accessible** Challenging	familiar sentence structure; some complex vocabulary; statistical information

Selection Summary

The number of Americans struggling to find food increased by 5 million between 2000 and 2005. At the same time, food banks saw a 9 percent increase in regular food recipients. One Arkansas teenager has formed a program to supplement the free lunches provided to hungry students through the Federal School Lunch Program.

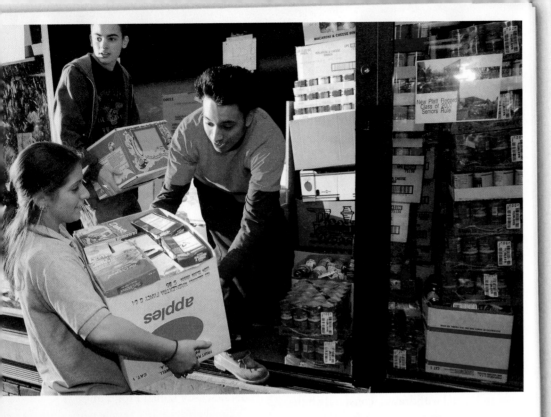

Think About/Talk About

Read with a Purpose Have students read the Read with a Purpose statement. Ask students what teens might be able to do to fight hunger.

▶ Analysis

Ⓐ Informational Focus

Possible response: *The author's position is that hunger is a big problem in America.*

Ⓑ Informational Focus

Possible response: *The author is using statistical evidence.*

▶ Extend the Discussion

Making Predictions The article's section heading on p. 871 is "Faces of Hunger." Based on this heading, what information do you predict the author will present in this section? ***Possible response:*** *I predict that the author will describe the different types of people who are suffering from hunger. The author might introduce readers to one or two specific people who are hungry in America.*

Identifying Evidence In paragraphs 2 and 3, how does the author attempt to prove that the problem of hunger in the United States is increasing? ***Possible response:*** *The author cites a 5 million-person increase in number of "hungry or food insecure" homes and a 9 percent increase in the number of those who use food banks.*

increase of 5 million people since 2000.

In 2005, America's Second Harvest, the country's largest charitable food distribution network, surveyed the people using its food banks. The survey showed that 25 million people use them on a regular basis. That's 9 percent more people than had been using the food banks in 2000. **Ⓑ**

Faces of Hunger

We like to think of America as a land of plenty. Yet about one in ten Americans uses a food bank or soup kitchen on a regular basis in order to get food. And such charitable services do not reach everyone. Many people live in constant hunger, and some are literally starving to death.

Who are America's hungry? You might be surprised. Second Harvest found that 36 percent of its food bank users come from homes with at least one working adult. For these families, a regular wage does not guarantee regular meals. When expenses—such as rent, heat, electric, and medical bills—run higher than

Ⓑ Informational Focus **Author's Evidence** What type of evidence is the writer using here to back up these assertions?

Universal Access

 English Learners

English for Academic Success Some students may struggle with the use of rhetorical questions in the article. Explain that writers will sometimes ask questions in order to make the reader think about the answers as they read. Point out that often, writers will answer their own questions soon after they pose them. For example, in the second column on p. 719, the author asks, "Who are America's hungry?" The author uses this question as a device to make readers think about what its answer might be. The author gives the answer to this question later in the paragraph: "Second Harvest found that 36 percent of its food bank users come from homes with at least one working adult."

Struggling Readers

Strategic Students Before students read, review with them the differences among the types of evidence discussed in the selection. Distribute sticky notes, and have students flag and identify types of evidence in two different colors as they read.

▶ Comprehension

◉ Read and Discuss

Possible response: It shows us that many of the people going hungry are kids just like us.

ⓓ Reading Focus

Possible response: The author does not cite the source of her evidence. This makes it less believable and effective, and inappropriate.

▶ Extend the Discussion

Analyzing Evidence What effect does the author's use of an ancedote under "Helping Those Left Behind" have on the reader? *Possible response: The anecdote puts a human face on the issue of hunger. It becomes solution-oriented. It shows how one person can make a difference.*

Vocabulary: Own the Word

• **deprivation:** Ask students to list ways that *deprivation* affects many Americans today.

• **prolonged:** A *prolonged* experience is one that lasts for a long time or an extended period. Ask students to list some *prolonged* experiences.

• **malnutrition:** Remind students that the prefix *mal–* means bad or wrong. In the word *malnutrition*, the prefix shows that *malnutrition* is the opposite of good nutrition. Ask students for examples of *malnutrition*.

Monitor Students' Comprehension

Use the Read with a Purpose follow-up question to assess students' understanding. *Possible response: The program that Daniel founded supplies more than 250 students with food that they wouldn't otherwise be able to afford.*

---

family income, little may be left over for food.

Sadly, millions of those who go hungry in America are senior citizens. An even greater number—around 13.9 million—are children. Because of their lack of mobility, these people may not have access to the food available through charitable organizations. ◉

Growing Up Hungry

Hunger takes a horrible and often permanent toll on growing children. If a young child is underfed during the first two years of his or her life, brain growth can be stunted, and mental retardation can result. In older children, food deprivation causes weakness, stunts growth, affects intelligence, and cripples the immune system. If hunger goes on and on, it becomes malnutrition, which is eventually fatal.

Because prolonged hunger causes drowsiness and social withdrawal, constantly hungry children have a hard time functioning in school. To put it simply, little learning can occur when a child is starving. ⓓ

Helping Those Left Behind

High school student Daniel Cayce lives in Arkansas, in one of the poorest counties in the country. Cayce started a program at his school called No Child Left Behind in Nutrition. He obtained donations of food and backpacks from church and community

Daniel Cayce working at the annual Thanksgiving food and blanket giveaway.

groups and from the Arkansas State Food Bank. With the help of his Boy Scout troop, he sorts and bags the food, which is given to needy students at the end of the school day. Through his program, more than 250 students receive food for weeknight and weekend meals. These free meals supplement the lunches the children receive through the Federal School Lunch Program.

Daniel grew up in a family with a history of helping the needy. He has been working side-by-side with his grandmother, the founder of the Jo Ann Cayce Charities, since age three. It was obvious to Daniel that hunger was not something long ago and far away. Perhaps it is time for the rest of us to realize this same truth and to take action in our own communities and as a nation.

Read with a Purpose How does Daniel's work help his community?

◉ **Read and Discuss** What can you conclude from this information about who is going hungry in America?

ⓓ **Reading Focus** Evaluating Evidence Is the specific evidence the author presents here appropriate?

Vocabulary **deprivation** (dehp ruh VAY shuhn) *n.*: hardship resulting from a lack of something.
malnutrition: (mal noo TRIHSH uhn) *n.*: ill health caused by a lack of food or by a lack of healthy foods.
prolonged (pruh LAWNGD) *adj.*: continuing for a long time.

Universal Access

Advanced Learners

Acceleration Have students research the reliability of the author's sources. When you discuss the accuracy and appropriateness of the evidence as a class, rely on advanced learners to report on whether sources such as the U.S. Department of Agriculture and Second Harvest are reputable.

Students with Disabilities

Help students comprehend some of the statistics in the article by drawing a pie chart or bar graph on the board to illustrate them. For example, to help students visualize the information in paragraph 2 of the selection, you might draw a bar graph to illustrate the fact that in the year 2000, more than 33 million Americans lived in food insecure households, while in 2005, more than 38 million Americans lived in food insecure households.

Reading Standard 2.6 Assess the adequacy, accuracy, and appropriateness of the author's evidence to support claims and assertions, noting instances of bias and stereotyping.

Hungry Here? For Millions of Americans, the Answer Is "Yes"

Standards Review

Informational Text and Vocabulary

1. There is enough **evidence** in the article to show that the author believes

  A food banks serve all of the people who need their services.

  B only in foreign countries do people experience hunger on a regular basis.

  C charitable organizations cannot help elderly people.

  D the problem of hunger in the United States gets worse each year.

2. Which of the following pieces of **evidence** would *not* be appropriate to use in an article about hunger?

  A the variety of food available at a food pantry

  B the number of U.S. children whose development has been stunted by malnutrition

  C a list of all of the causes that Jo Ann Cayce Charities supports

  D the average amount of money people who use food pantries spend on rent per month

3. Which of the following effects of hunger is *not* addressed by the author?

  A stunted brain growth

  B death

  C decreased ability to learn

  D crippled immune system

4. The section of the article titled "Helping Those Left Behind" is an example of

  A an anecdote.

  B a quote from an expert.

  C inaccurate evidence.

  D bias and stereotyping.

5. The opposite of *prolonged* is

  A universal.

  B dynamic.

  C irritable.

  D momentary.

6. Another word for *deprivation* is

  A liquidation.

  B neediness.

  C misstatement.

  D delusion.

Writing Skills Focus

Timed ⃝ L Writing Review your notes about author's evidence. In a paragraph, explain why this author's use of evidence was effective. First, give a short description of the author's main claims and assertions. Then, list the type of evidence used to support each claim or assertion. Finally, comment on the adequacy, accuracy, or appropriateness of each example.

What Do **You** Think Now**?** In what ways has this article made a powerful point about the issue of hunger?

California Standards, p. 721

■ **Reading Standard 2.6** Assess the adequacy, accuracy, and appropriateness of the author's evidence to support claims and assertions, noting instances of bias and stereotyping.

What Do You Think Now?

Ask students for their reactions after reading the article. Were they surprised by the information they read?

Assessing Evidence

Standards Focus

Objectives

Students will

- identify an author's assertions
- analyze and evaluate evidence
- identify stereotypes and bias

Motivate

What Do You Think?/QuickTalk

Ask students to discuss signs that might indicate someone or something is a threat. Continue the discussion to include their experiences with online bullying.

English for Academic Success

Academic Vocabulary

- **conclude**, *v.*: decide by reasoning.
- **instance**, *n.:* occurrence or example
- **specific**, *adj.:* definite and particular

Analyzing Visuals

Extension Activity Ask students what effect the camera angle has on the image. ***Possible response:*** *Since this photo is taken from the ground looking up at the boys, it makes the boys seem powerful and menacing.*

CONTENTS

What Do **You** Think How can you tell if something or someone is a threat?

QuickTalk
Discuss what you know about the problem of online bullying—the reasons for it, effects of it, and ways to combat it.

California Standards,
pp. 722–735

- **Reading Standard 2.6** Assess the adequacy, accuracy, and appropriateness of the author's evidence to support claims and assertions, noting instances of bias and stereotyping.

NEWSPAPER ARTICLE
Preparing to Read

Reading Standard 2.6 Assess the adequacy, accuracy, and appropriateness of the **author's evidence to support claims and assertions,** noting instances of bias and stereotyping.

Virtual Sticks and Stones

Informational Text Focus

Claims and Assertions Writers who present an **argument** want to persuade you to think or behave in a certain way. They express **claims and assertions**—their ideas or opinions on a topic—but merely making these claims should not be enough to convince you. Writers who are skillful at presenting arguments often start with an **anecdote,** a brief story used to make a point. They go on to present solid, <u>specific</u> **evidence** to back up their claims and assertions. They cite **facts** (statements that can be proved true), include **statistics** (number facts), or quote **experts** so that you will <u>conclude</u> that their argument is sound.

Reading Skills Focus

Determining Author's Purpose Authors write for a number of reasons. For <u>instance</u>, an **author's purpose** may be to inform, to describe, to entertain, or to persuade. Determining an author's purpose is an important skill. You may find that a text that at first seems written to inform or entertain may actually be written to persuade or convince you of something.

Into Action Understanding an author's argument will help you determine the author's purpose. After you read a text that presents an argument, ask yourself these questions (leave space within each box for your answers):

What is the topic, or subject, of this text?	What is the writer's point of view on the subject? What kind of language does he or she use?	What evidence (facts, statistics, expert opinions) supports the writer's assertions?

Writing Skills Focus

Preparing for **Timed Writing** Take notes on the evidence the author uses in this article on cyberbullying, or online harassment. You'll use the notes later in a timed writing exercise.

Reader/Writer Notebook
Use your **RWN** to complete the activities for this selection.

Learn It Online
Do pictures and animation help you learn? Try the *PowerNotes* lesson at:
go.hrw.com   H7-723   Go

Vocabulary

misrepresentations (mihs rehp rih zehn TAY shuhnz) *n.:* false ideas given for the purpose of deceiving someone. *Some bullies make up misrepresentations about their targets.*

consequences (KAHN suh kwehns ihz) *n.:* results caused by a set of conditions. *People sometimes bully others over the Internet to avoid the consequences of challenging them in person.*

Language Coach

Prefixes The prefix *mis-*, which goes back to Old English, means "not," "bad or wrong," "false," "the opposite of," "the lack of." Words that begin with *mis-* include *misunderstand*, *mistake*, and the Vocabulary word *misrepresentations*. What other *mis-* words can you think of?

Preteach

Introducing Vocabulary
Read aloud the Vocabulary words and sample sentences. Then, use this activity to check students' understanding.

1. Explain why **misrepresentations** of people might be dangerous. [*They lead to unfair treatment.*]

2. Illustrate the **consequences** of standing too close to the edge of a pool. [*You may fall into the pool.*]

English for Academic Success
Language Coach
Draw students' attention to the connotations of *mis-* using the examples in the Student Edition. For instance, *mistake* suggests an accidental error, while *misrepresentation* suggests a deliberate intent to deceive. [*misjudge, mistrust, miscarry, mislead, misuse*]

Informational Text Focus
As you read and discuss the selection with students, have them locate examples of different types of evidence, including facts, statistics, and quotations from experts and explain how they support the author's argument.

Reading Skills Focus
As you read and discuss the article with students, have them add information to the Reading Skills Focus graphic organizer.

Writing Skills Focus
Have students record notes on the authors' evidence in their **Reader/Writer Notebook.** Students can use their notes to complete the Writing Skills Focus activity.

Learn It Online
For a multimedia version of the instruction found on this page, use the **PowerNotes** introduction to this selection.
go.hrw.com   H7-723   Go

Selection Resources

Chapter 7 Resources, on-level practice and assessment, p. 18

PowerNotes, interactive lesson presentation with activities

Teacher One Stop™, on-level lesson plans and all print resources

Holt Audio Library

Holt Audio Library: Selections and Summaries in Spanish

UA: Holt Interactive Reader, p. 194

Holt Interactive Reader for ELD, p. 221

Holt Audio Tutor for ELD

UA: Differentiating Instruction, modified lesson plans and leveled assessment, p. 198

UA: Resources for Teaching Advanced Students, lesson plans, p.155

UA: Supporting Instruction in Five Languages, selection summary

ThinkCentral Online Assessment, Selection Standards Check

ThinkCentral Online Remediation

Direct Teach

Model the Skill

■ Provide students with the Reading Skills Focus graphic organizer for "Virtual Sticks and Stones" (See **Chapter 7 Resources**).

■ Tell students that authors may write a piece of nonfiction, such as an article, to persuade readers to adopt a certain belief or perspective. To convince readers to accept their perspectives, authors create an **argument** using evidence to give readers reasons to believe assertions made. Evidence takes many forms, including facts, figures, real-life stories, and information from experts on a topic.

■ Model using the graphic organizer to track a writer's argument and use of evidence. In the first box, note the topic as cyberbullying. In the second box, note that the author believes cyberbullying to be both harmful and prevalent.

■ Tell students that the third box will help organize the evidence the author uses to support the claim. Have a volunteer read the types of evidence from the Preparing to Read Page. Identify one type of evidence in the text for students, such as, "Because Iris Salters is president of an educational organization and is knowledgeable about what goes on in schools, she can give her expert opinion as evidence."

Guided Practice: Apply

Have students read the rest of the article and identify as many pieces of supporting evidence as they can for the claim that cyberbullying is prevalent but harmful. Tell them to note all evidence in the graphic organizer.

Student Forum

Virtual Sticks and Stones

Bullying is as threatening online as it is in person.

by

Read with a Purpose

Read this article to examine positive and negative aspects of using the Internet.

Selection Readability	
Easily Accessible **Accessible** Challenging	relevant topic; familiar situations; clear message

Selection Summary

The Internet allows us to communicate with people around the world, but it also makes us vulnerable to cyberbullying. Some people do not realize that their online remarks may be insulting, while others intentionally post comments intended to hurt others. One good rule to follow when posting online is to limit your comments to those you would also make in person.

CHICAGO, OCT. 11 — My first time sending a message on the Internet, I made mistakes and had to hit the Delete key. Still, those first clicks and blips made me feel powerful. I felt as if I could reach out to the world as I never had before. Did you feel that your world became larger when you began using the Internet? Suddenly, you didn't have to see friends in person or call people to communicate. It was all very exciting. Ⓐ

> *"Cyberbullying is the fastest-growing trend in bullying among teens."*

Maybe you, too, were like Katie: "I was thrilled with the idea that I now had access to all aspects of the Internet," writes Katie, fourteen, for Teen Angels, a youth group that works to combat Internet abuse. "The promising new window the Internet opened up for me seemed too good to be true, and in fact, it was."

Online Threats

Katie was nine when she first started to message people. She was home alone when she received an unforgettable note. The words *You wait. I'm coming after you* popped up from an unknown screen name. She was new to the Internet and didn't know that she shouldn't open a message from a stranger. She does now.

The threat scared Katie, and she hid in her room until her mom came home. She kept the incident to herself for a while, afraid that her parents would take away her Internet privileges. Now she shares her experience as a way to get kids to talk about cyberbullies. Ⓑ

Cyberbullying Statistics

A threat like this is extreme, but we all probably know of someone who's been burned on the Internet. In May 2006, two professors of criminal justice, one at Florida Atlantic University and one at the University of Wisconsin, Eau Claire, released results of a study of 1,388 youths. One third of those surveyed said they had been victims of cyberbullying. Another survey, from i-Safe America, said 60 percent of middle school kids have been sent hurtful messages. Ⓒ

"Little-noticed cyberbullying is the fastest-growing trend in bullying among teens," wrote Iris Salters, Michigan Education Association president, in a recent editorial.

Hidden Personalities

Some Web sites encourage people to create a Web personality, which can be very different from a person's real personality. Once invisible behind a new personality, cyberbullies can write misrepresentations on buddy profiles,

---

Ⓐ **Reading Focus** Determining Author's Purpose What type of evidence does the writer use to begin the article?

Ⓑ **Read and Discuss** What has the author set up for you?

Ⓒ **Informational Focus** Claims and Assertions How does the writer support an assertion in this paragraph?

Vocabulary **misrepresentations** (mihs rehp rih zehn TAY shuhnz) *n.:* false ideas given for the purpose of deceiving someone.

Think About/Talk About

Read with a Purpose Have students read the Read with a Purpose statement. Remind students to look for both positive and negative aspects of using the Internet.

▶ Comprehension

Ⓐ **Reading Focus**

Possible response: The writer uses an anecdote. The lead is meant to draw the reader in with a bit of humor and also a bit of fear.

Ⓑ **Read and Discuss**

Possible response: The author gave two examples of using computers and the Internet. The description of the author's own experience illustrates some positives of Internet use, while Katie's experience is frightening and negative.

▶ Analysis

Ⓒ **Informational Focus**

Possible response: The writer includes statistics to demonstrate how widespread the problem is.

▶ Extend the Discussion

Identifying an Argument What assertion does the author make by relating Katie's story in paragraphs 2-4? *Possible response: The author claims that scary and dangerous things can happen to people when they're on the Internet, even when they're not doing anything wrong.*

Vocabulary: Own the Word

misrepresentations: Ask students to describe *misrepresentations* that they are familiar with. *Possible response: one sibling framing another for breaking a vase, making a task seem easier than it really is*

Universal Access

EL English Learners

English for Academic Success To help students understand the topic of the author's argument, explain that cyberbullying is a term for using the Internet to treat people badly. Tell students that the prefix *cyber–*, which means "virtual or computer-generated" is often added to words that are related to computers or the Internet. For example, *cyberspace* is another term for the Internet.

✔See **UA: Differentiating Instruction** for lesson plans and strategies for teaching English learners.

Struggling Readers

Tell students that they can use this newspaper article's features to determine the topic of the author's argument before they read the article. Point out the article's subhead, "Bullying is as threatening online as it is in person." Then, direct students' attention to the pull quote on p. 725. Have students use these two pieces of evidence to predict what the author's argument will be. Tell students to evaluate the accuracy of their predictions as they read the article.

✔See **UA: Differentiating Instruction** for lesson plans and strategies for teaching struggling readers.

▶ **Comprehension**

D Read and Discuss

Possible response: The author means that when people deal with others in person rather than over the Internet, they remember more easily that their words and actions can be hurtful.

E Reading Focus

Possible response: The writer wants the readers to think about how they treat others on the Internet. The writer believes people should not accept cyberbullying.

▶ **Extend the Discussion**

Identifying Evidence What evidence does the author provide to support the claims that the Internet helps bullies commit harmful acts without accepting the consequences? *Possible response: The author presents the fact that bullies can conceal their identities and alternate identities using avatars. If a bully is anonymous, no one can punish the bully for his or her behavior.*

Vocabulary: Own the Word

consequences: Ask students to list potential *consequences* for victims of cyberbullying. *Possible response: Victims of cyberbullying may be ostracized, live in fear of the bullies, and suffer from low self-esteem as a result of the bullying.*

Monitor Students' Comprehension

Use the Read with a Purpose follow-up question to assess students' understanding. *Possible response: The author asserts that cyberbullies are a serious threat and teaches readers how to behave responsibly online. Although the author doesn't cite many hard facts, the author's argument is fairly strong because the anecdotes in the article are relevant and convincing.*

spill personal secrets about former friends, and join combative cliques that can attack under an assumed name. Because those who bully online are physically distant from their targets, they can feel more confident.

One seventh-grader I know was in a band that had a page on a social networking site. A kid hacked in and wrote violent threats that sounded as if band members had written them on the page. This hacker hid behind his victims' personalities. When Web personalities act in ways that real ones never would, they become a way to hide from truth, from consequences, and mostly from themselves.

Think about the people on the receiving end of your messages.

Interpreting Web Behavior

Because cyberbullying appears in words, many people discount the damage it does. Sure, a good portion of online comments are meant in jest, so many people think, "What's the big deal?" Cyberbullying, however, doesn't come across as harmless to the target or to those who read the attack. Comments

D Read and Discuss What does the author mean by "being face to face reflects reality, keeping intent in perspective"?

E Reading Focus Determining Author's Purpose Why does the writer end with a question? What can you conclude about the purpose of his article from his word choice and tone?

online may be written to be funny or to be cruel. It's hard to sense attempts at humor in a computer message. If someone passes by you in the school hallway and calls you a name, you can turn to him or her. Maybe the kid smiles to show it was meant in fun. Maybe not. Being face to face reflects reality, keeping intent in perspective. **D**

Online Responsibility

The First Amendment to the U.S. Constitution guarantees freedom of speech, but there are laws to protect people from verbal and written abuse. Many schools already have in place policies regarding cyberabuse and punishments for students who attack others through e-mails, Web posts, and text messages.

If you are being bullied online, don't just take it. Tell an adult—a teacher, a parent, or a coach. Don't let a friend be cyberbullied. Urge them to get help.

Handle yourself responsibly online: Think about the people on the receiving end of your messages. Would you like the virtual sticks and stones of lies about you or your friends or family circulating throughout the Internet? **E**

Read with a Purpose

Restate and assess the author's argument.

Vocabulary consequences (KAHN suh kwehns ihz) *n.*: results caused by a set of conditions.

Universal Access

Advanced Learners

Acceleration After students read the article, have them analyze the article's evidence to determine whether cyberbullying is a more or less serious threat than real-life bullying. Ask students to write a paragraph making an assertion of their own on this issue. Remind students to back up their claim with appropriate evidence.

✔ See **UA: Resources for Teaching Advanced Students** for lesson plans and strategies for teaching advanced learners.

Students with Disabilities

Invite students to read "Virtual Sticks and Stones" in interactive format in **Holt Interactive Reader for ELD** and to use the sidenotes as aids to understanding the selection. The interactive version provides additional instruction, practice, and assessment of the skills taught in the Student Edition.

Applying Your Skills

Reading Standard 2.6 Assess the adequacy, accuracy, and appropriateness of the author's evidence to support claims and assertions, noting instances of bias and stereotyping.

Virtual Sticks and Stones
Standards Review

Informational Text and Vocabulary

1. There is enough information in the article to show that the author believes that

  A the First Amendment should allow for on-line bullying.

  B the Internet has reduced the number of victims of bullying.

  C adults actually suffer more from cyberbullying than teens do.

  D communicating face to face is clearer than communicating online.

2. Information from the article supports the claim that cyberbullying

  A is less vicious than bullying in person.

  B stops happening in college.

  C can be well hidden by a Web personality.

  D appears mostly in e-mail messages.

3. Which quotation *best* shows that some think cyberbullying is not dangerous?

  A "The First Amendment to the U.S. Constitution guarantees freedom of speech."

  B "A kid hacked in and wrote violent threats . . . on the page."

  C "Because cyberbullying appears in words, many people discount the damage it does."

  D "We all probably know of someone who's been burned on the Internet."

4. Read this sentence from the article:

> Think about the people on the receiving end of your messages.

  The **author's purpose** for this sentence is to remind readers that

  A they must take responsibility for what they write online.

  B our Web personalities write angry comments, even to friends.

  C it is harder to tell a joke in e-mails than to tell a joke face to face.

  D schools can catch and punish cyberbullies.

5. The author makes the **assertion** that a bully's Web personality

  A can allow him or her to avoid facing the truth.

  B has the right to be completely free to write anything.

  C makes tracking and catching the bully easy.

  D helps make vicious attacks on Web sites.

Writing Skills Focus

Timed ⏱ Writing Choose two paragraphs from the article that include poorly supported **assertions**. For each paragraph, describe evidence that you think would strenghten the author's argument.

What Do **You Think Now** How did this article affect your thinking about online threats?

1. **D** *The writer clearly does not believe A and B, while there is no mention of C in the text.*

2. **C** *The article states that Web personalities become "wall[s] to hide from the truth." A, B, and D are not supported by textual evidence.*

3. **C** *A does not directly address bullying, while B and D suggest cyberbullying is dangerous.*

4. **A** *The author talks directly to readers to remind them of their personal responsibility. While the other statements are supported by the article, they do not relate to this sentence.*

5. **A** *B is the opposite of what the writer believes, while C is factually incorrect. D is not completely true because Web personalities on their own do not make vicious attacks.*

Writing Skills Focus

Possible response: Paragraph 7 would be improved if it cited statistics about the percentage of cyberbullies who hide behind anonymity or fake personalities. Paragraphs 3 and 8 include anecdotes, but expert opinions might make the anecdotes even stronger.

Assess

 Chapter 7 Resources, Selection Standards Check, p. 25

ThinkCentral Online Assessment, Selection Standards Check

Teacher One Stop™, editable Selection Standards Check

California Standards, p. 727

■ **Reading Standard 2.6** Assess the adequacy, accuracy, and appropriateness of the author's evidence to support claims and assertions, noting instances of bias and stereotyping.

What Do You Think Now?

Ask students to refer to the notes they made in their **Reader-Writer Notebook** before reading the article. Has this article changed their ideas about cyberbullying?.

Reteach

To reteach **author's argument,** see **Reteaching Lessons,** p. 842A.

ThinkCentral Online Remediation

Preparing to Read

Reading Standard 2.6 Assess the adequacy, accuracy, and appropriateness of the author's evidence to support claims and assertions, noting instances of bias and stereotyping.

Introducing Vocabulary

Read aloud the Vocabulary words and sample sentences. Then, use this activity to check students' understanding.

1. Why would cyberbullies want to be **anonymous**? *[so they cannot be identified and punished]*

2. Why does bullying **alienate** other people? *[It makes people feel badly about themselves.]*

3. How would having a legal **conviction** affect someone's life? *[It may be difficult to find a job.]*

English for Academic Success
Language Coach

Have students look up the Vocabulary words in a dictionary in order to determine which word has multiple meanings, which *[Conviction also means "strong belief."]*

Informational Text Focus

As you read and discuss the selection with students, have them pause after each article and discuss whether the article's evidence is adequate, accurate, and appropriate.

Reading Skills Focus

As you read and discuss the article with students, have them consider the convincing nature and quality of the evidence presented.

Writing Skills Focus

Have students use a two-column chart to keep track of the most persuasive evidence in their **Reader/Writer Notebook**. Students can use their notes to complete the Writing Skills Focus activity.

Learn It Online
Send students to **Word Watch** for audio pronunciations, synonyms and antonyms, and brief histories of word origins.

go.hrw.com   H7-728   **Go**

Debate on Bullying

Informational Text Focus

Author's Evidence To form an effective persuasive argument, writers or speakers must back up their opinions with **evidence**. Evidence can take the form of **anecdotes, facts, statistics, expert opinions, quotations,** or **examples.** Your job as a reader or listener is to decide whether the author's evidence supports his or her claims and assertions.

Reading Skills Focus

Evaluating Evidence You turn on a TV courtroom drama, and here's what the prosecutor presents as evidence against the accused: a dog's bark in the night, a chewed piece of gum, a bag found in the trash. A defense attorney holds up a baseball cap, too small for the accused, found at the crime scene, as evidence to free her client. It is up to the jury to decide if the evidence against the accused is **adequate**—that is, they have to decide if there is enough evidence to prove the defendant guilty. *Adequate* means "enough for what is needed; sufficient."

Experts are brought in to testify whether the DNA in the chewed gum matches the defendant's DNA. The jury determines whether the expert's opinions are **accurate**. *Accurate* means "free from mistakes or errors."

The evidence of a dog's barking on the night of the crime may or may not be **appropriate** evidence for the case. *Appropriate* means "relevant; right for the purpose."

As you read the following perspectives on bullying, evaluate the evidence that you feel is inappropriate, inaccurate, and/or inadequate.

Writing Skills Focus

Preparing for **Timed** **Writing** As you read each side of this debate, write down examples of evidence that you find persuasive. Next to each piece of evidence, explain why you find it convincing. Which writer do you find more persuasive?

Reader/Writer Notebook
Use your **RWN** to complete the activities for this selection.

Learn It Online
Sharpen your vocabulary skills with Word Watch:

go.hrw.com   H7-728   **Go**

Selection Resources

Chapter 7 Resources, on-level practice and assessment, p. 21

Teacher One Stop™, on-level lesson plans and all print resources

Holt Audio Library

Holt Audio Library: Selections and Summaries in Spanish

UA: Supporting Instruction in Five Languages, selection summary

ThinkCentral Online Assessment, Selection Standards Check

ThinkCentral Online Remediation

Student Forum
Debate on Bullying

by THE WORLD ALMANAC

Read with a Purpose
Read to compare two different perspectives on bullying.

Question: What can or should be done about bullying?

Just Deal with It
by Jared Hoffman

Bullying is all around us—you just have to deal with it. In one study, nearly 60 percent of U.S. fourth- through eighth-graders said others had said hurtful things to them online (*Teaching Tolerance*). Almost 160,000 students stay home from school out of fear of bullies there (*Education World*). **A**

Cyberbullying is making the situation worse. "Now you don't have to confront someone to bully them in person," said Mark Chapell of Rowan University about his new study on Internet bullying. "You can do it electronically and remain anonymous."

The world never has been and never will be without bullies. It is part of life. There's no way to avoid it. The playground isn't the only place bullying occurs. Adults face it in the workplace. Just look at politicians, who push each other around, insult each other, and even lie just to get one more vote. **B**

Because bullying can't be stopped, people need to learn to handle it. You probably don't want to tell on a bully, but you must tell an adult if you think you or a friend is in danger. Talk to the friend being bullied and let him or her know that they have a shoulder to lean on. It is essential to help your friend regain self-esteem so life can go on.

Some people suggest finding ways to reduce bullying, like ignoring the abuse, using humor to deflect it, and never resorting to violence (*Teens Health*). However, these methods will never stop it completely. You'd be a fool to think they would. Learn to deal with it, because there's no way around it. **C**

A **Informational Focus** Author's Evidence Why does Jared cite *Teaching Tolerance* and *Education World*?

B **Read and Discuss** What is Jared telling you here?

C **Informational Focus** Author's Evidence What is Jared's argument about bullying?

Vocabulary **anonymous** (uh NAHN uh muhs) *adj.*: not identified by name.

Selection Readability	
Easily Accessible	relevant topic; familiar situations
Accessible	
Challenging	

Selection Summary
Two writers take slightly different approaches to bullying. The first writes that we can all count on experiencing a bully. Since bullying affects almost everyone, we should all learn how to react in ways that minimize the behavior. The second writer argues that bullying can be avoided altogether if victims and observers discourage it. Elimination of the problem is critical since both bullies and their victims are at risk for long-term psychological problems.

Think About/Talk About

▶ Comprehension

Ⓓ Reading Focus

Possible response: *These statistics show the danger and negative impact of bullying.*

Ⓔ Read and Discuss

Possible response: *Marissa offers substantial information regarding bullying, its victims, and its immediate and long-term consequences. Her argument seems a lot stronger than Jared's.*

▶ Extend the Discussion

Evaluating an Argument What would make paragraph 3 more effective? ***Possible response:*** *Marissa is general in her references to sources and studies. Being more specific would improve her argument.*

Vocabulary: Own the Word

- **alienate:** To **alienate** is to cause feelings of isolation; to accept is to make a person feel welcome. When people **alienate** others, they cause pain; when they accept others, they cause happiness.

- **conviction:** **Conviction** means being found guilty of a crime; acquittal means being found innocent. Prosecutors go to trial hoping for a **conviction;** defense attorneys hope for acquittal.

Monitor Students's Comprehension

Use the Read with a Purpose follow-up question to assess students' understanding. ***Possible response:*** *Jared's argument that bullies are everywhere is supported by the fact that almost 60 percent of fourth- through eighth-graders have been bullied. Marissa's argument that bullying is too dangerous to be acceptable is supported by the fact that people who are bullied are more likely to be depressed and anxious.*

Get Serious
by Marissa Barbaro

There is no excuse for bullying. Almost 30 percent of U.S. youth (more than 5.7 million students) are involved as a bully, a target of bullying, or both. Bullying has a negative effect on all involved, and more steps must be taken to prevent it. Ⓓ

Bullies usually target people they consider to be different from themselves. . . .

Bullies usually target people they consider to be different from themselves, based on such things as appearance, status, behavior, or religion. Bullying often leads to other forms of prejudice, including racism and gender bias. Seeing bullying all the time leads kids to believe that it is okay to disrespect and alienate others because of their differences.

Kids subjected to threats and violence are often fearful and have difficulty concentrating, so their health and schoolwork suffer. Studies show a higher rate of depression and anxiety in adults who were bullied as children.

Bullying also has a negative impact on the bullies themselves, who tend to grow into violent and hateful teenagers and adults. They perform poorly academically and can't form healthy relationships. Sixty percent of bullies in grades 6 through 9 have at least one criminal conviction by age twenty-four (SafeYouth.org). Dropouts probably account for most criminals. Ⓔ

Parents and teachers must encourage kids to be accepting of others. Adults have to educate kids about the effects of prejudice on bullies, as well as on their targets. Without education, this abuse will continue.

Remember: Bullying can and must be stopped. Bullies are not the only ones responsible for their behavior; everyone who allows it to happen is just as guilty as the bully. There is no excuse for bullying.

> *What do you think? Send your letters to the editor for publication in next month's issue.*

Read with a Purpose
What evidence did you find to support the authors' points?

Ⓓ **Reading Focus** **Evaluating Evidence** Why does Marissa include these statistics in her argument? How do the statistics support her claim in this paragraph?

Ⓔ **Read and Discuss** How has Marissa approached her argument?

Vocabulary **alienate** (AYL yuh nayt) *v.:* cause to feel isolated or unaccepted.
conviction (kuhn VIHK shuhn) *n:* instance of being declared guilty of a criminal offense.

Universal Access

ⓔⓛ English Learners

English for Academic Success Remind students that *anonymous* means "unknown or nameless." Then, write this sentence starter on the board: "Bullies like to stay anonymous because . . . " Have students write three endings to the sentence.

Advanced Learners

Acceleration Ask students to debate the assertion that Jared makes in the article. Divide students into two teams, and assign one team to agree with Jared's assertion that bullying is an inevitable part of life and one team to disagree. Have teams discuss their position in small groups and identify evidence from the article or from other sources that supports their claim. As students debate, ask them to address the assumptions that are inherent in Jared's argument.

Reading Standard 2.6 Assess the adequacy, accuracy, and appropriateness of the author's evidence to support claims and assertions, noting instances of bias and stereotyping.

Debate on Bullying
Standards Review

Informational Text and Vocabulary

1. Which claim from Marissa's argument is *least* supported by factual evidence?

  A School-age bullies often break the law as they get older.

  B The targets of bullying can suffer from emotional problems.

  C Criminals may have started their lives as bullies.

  D Bullies often attack people who are different from them.

2. Which phrase from Jared's argument is contradicted by an assertion from Marissa's argument?

  A "Learn to deal with [bullying] because there's no way around it."

  B "The playground isn't the only place bullying occurs."

  C "Just look at politicians, who push each other around."

  D "However, these methods will never stop [bullying] completely."

3. Jared supports his argument that there is no way to avoid bullying by stating that

  A bullying exists even among adults at work.

  B cyberbullying is better than face-to-face bullying.

  C grown-ups can protect kids who are targets.

  D targets of bullying should fight back.

4. It is appropriate for Marissa to discuss prejudice in paragraph 2 because she believes that

  A students from different backgrounds should be separated.

  B bullies stop being prejudiced when they're older.

  C bullying makes people enemies because of their differences.

  D watching bullying protects others from becoming bullies.

5. Read the first and final sentence of Marissa's argument:

> There is no excuse for bullying.

In this sentence, it is clear that Marissa wants student readers to

  A encourage targeted kids to form discussion groups.

  B work together with adults until there is no more bullying.

  C realize that parents don't understand the sources of bullying.

  D expect adults to assist in resolving prejudice among kids.

Writing Skills Focus

Timed **Writing** Review the notes you took while reading this debate. Briefly explain which argument against bullying you found to be more effective, and why.

 California Standards, p. 731

■ **Reading Standard 2.6** Assess the adequacy, accuracy, and appropriateness of the author's evidence to support claims and assertions, noting instances of bias and stereotyping.

Writing Skills Focus

Possible response: *I found Marissa's argument to be much more effective than Jared's. Jared doesn't provide any evidence to convince me that "just dealing with" bullying is safe or healthy, while Marissa provides evidence to support her argument that bullying is dangerous and destructive both to those being bullied and to the bullies themselves.*

Check for Understanding

Independent Practice
Answers and Explanations

1. ***D*** *A, B, and C seem to be backed by research, while D is a possible interpretation of the facts.*

2. ***A*** *Marissa does not contradict B, C, or D.*

3. ***A*** *B is mentioned but Jared does not say that cyberbullying is better than being face-to-face. He doesn't believe people should fight back (D) or that adults can prevent bullying (C).*

4. ***C*** *Marissa does not believe people should be separated (A) and believes that bullies do not improve with age (B). She contradicts D by saying that seeing bullying makes kids think that it is OK.*

5. ***B*** *Marissa does not mention discussion groups (A) or tell kids to expect adults to help them (D). She does not claim that adults can't understand the reasons for bullying (C). She wants everyone to work together to reduce bullying.*

Assess

✎ **Chapter 7 Resources,** Selection Standards Check, p. 25

ThinkCentral Online Assessment, Selection Standards Check

Reteach

To reteach **author's argument,** see **Reteaching Lessons,** p. 842A.

ThinkCentral Online Remediation

Preteach

Introducing Vocabulary

Read aloud the Vocabulary word and sample sentence. Then, ask students to explain why a school might **expel** someone. [*A student might be expelled for repeatedly breaking school rules.*]

English for Academic Success

Language Coach

Tell students that they can remember the meaning of the suffixes *–ible* and *–able* by noticing that they look and sound similar to the word *able*. [Accessible *might mean "able to be accessed."*]

Informational Text Focus

As you read and discuss the selection with students, have them flag examples of bias and stereotyping with sticky notes.

Reading Skills Focus

As you read and discuss the letter to the editor, ask students to identify possible sources of the bias and stereotypes used by students.

Writing Skills Focus

Have students record biased statements and stereotypes in their **Reader/Writer Notebook.** Students can use their notes to complete the Writing Skills Focus activity.

732 Chapter 7

WEB SITE
Preparing to Read

Sound Off to the Editor

Informational Text Focus

Bias and Stereotyping Imagine you're sitting on a bench outside a shopping mall, waiting for your ride to arrive. You begin hearing bits of conversations from shoppers as they walk by:

"People who drive sportscars like that are insecure showoffs."

"What do you expect? All politicians are dishonest."

"Football players don't care about schoolwork."

You've just heard people express generalizations about others using **stereotypes.** That means they are using unfair, fixed ideas about groups of people. Stereotypes don't take individuality into account. They brand every member of a group with the same characteristics. Stereotypes can be hurtful and are often used to persuade you to do or believe something.

If you've ever watched your favorite sports team on the opposing team's host TV channel, you've probably noticed that the broadcasters favor the home team with their comments and calls. What you're really noticing is called **bias**—attitudes and beliefs that can shape a person's thinking in spite of the facts. Of course, your bias is evident as well—you want your favorite team to win!

Reading Skills Focus

Recognizing Bias and Stereotyping As you read editorials or any kind of political or social commentary, be on the lookout for expressions that suggest the writer has already made up his or her mind about someone or something. Think of bias as an inclination to think a certain way. In its worst form, bias becomes prejudice. To spot <u>instances</u> of stereotyping, look for generalizations about "types" of people. Common stereotypes include those based on gender, age, job, and social status, but any group with some common characteristics can be stereotyped.

Writing Skills Focus

Preparing for **Timed** **Writing** As you read the letters that follow, take note of the biased statements and stereotypes in them. You'll use your notes to respond to a writing prompt later.

Reader/Writer Notebook

Use your **RWN** to complete the activities for this selection.

Vocabulary

expelled (ehk SPEHLD) *v.*: forced to leave. *The principal expelled the students responsible for bullying.*

Language Coach

Suffixes Suffixes can help you recognize the meaning of a word that might otherwise be unfamiliar to you. For instance, you probably know the meaning of *access.* You might also know that the suffix *–ible* or *–able* often means "capable of." Based on these clues, what do you think *accessible* might mean?

Selection Resources

Chapter 7 Resources, on-level practice and assessment, p. 22

Teacher One Stop™, on-level lesson plans and all print resources

Holt Audio Library

Holt Audio Library: Selections and Summaries in Spanish

UA: Differentiating Instruction, graphic organizer, p. 201

UA: Supporting Instruction in Five Languages, selection summary

ThinkCentral Online Assessment, Selection Standards Check

ThinkCentral Online Remediation

Read with a Purpose

Read these online responses to the preceding editorial debate to identify and assess more opinions about bullying.

Student Forum

SEARCH | HOME | ABOUT | BLOG | SITE MAP | CONTACT

Sound Off to the Editor

by THE WORLD ALMANAC

In the last issue of *Student Forum,* the editorial debate focused on ways to deal with bullying. (See two opinions on pages 729–730.) Many responses were sent to the editors. Here are just a few.

from	comment
Candace Branch "All bullies should be expelled."	Those studies about bullying are disturbing because they prove that most kids get bullied. Adults think bullies are just little troublemakers. They don't even try to stop the bullying. All bullies should be expelled because, like Jared says, they will never change.

Vocabulary expelled (ehk SPEHLD) *v.:* forced to leave.

Selection Readability	
Easily Accessible **Accessible** Challenging	familiar Internet format; relevant topic; conversational tone; accessible vocabulary

Selection Summary

In response to an editorial debate in the school newspaper, students write to the editor expressing their thoughts on bullying. One believes that bullies should be expelled from school. Another agrees that people must learn to defend themselves. And a basketball player represents the bullies' perspective by complaining of students who are happy to yell for his team at games but balk at doing the players' homework.

▶ Comprehension

ⓑ Read and Discuss

Possible response: *Not all students agree that bullying is harmful, and each student has a different reason for his or her opinion.*

▶ Analysis

Ⓐ Informational Focus

Possible response: *She presents the stereotype that all bullies become criminals.*

▶ Extend the Discussion

Evaluating an Argument What problems do you see with Timothy Mann's suggestion that students "stand up" and "be strong"? **Possible response:** *Some students' self-esteem may not allow them to stand up and be strong. Some students need advocates and support.*

Monitor Students' Comprehension

Use the Read with a Purpose follow-up question to assess students' understanding. **Possible response:** *Some of the writers used anecdotes or stereotypes, some used facts, and one used an expert source: The Constitution.*

Timothy Mann "You just have to deal with bullying."	I agree with Jared that you just have to deal with bullying. You can't change people—you can't get rid of bullies. You have to stand up and not be a wimp. Be strong for yourself and for your friends.
Jonathan Roper "We ought to do what we want to do!"	I'm on the basketball team, and I don't understand what all the fuss is about. We work hard on the team, and the rest of the students just watch the games and then pretend like they've won. We're like school heroes so we ought to do what we want to do! So what if we want somebody to do our homework. Let's face it—smart kids are geeky.
Tamara Holmes "Teachers and parents need to teach kids how to act."	Nobody bullies me because I don't pay attention to stupid people's stupid comments. They know I'd get them back if they did. Anyway, Marissa is right. Teachers and parents need to teach kids how to act. This is an important subject, just like math and English. If you don't learn how to act right, you will never know how to act properly. Look at that study about criminals in Marissa's argument—that's what happens to bullies and dropouts when they grow up. Ⓐ
Calista Tallman "Protect our right to free speech!"	No attempt should be made to stop cyberbullying because that would be a challenge to our right to free speech. The U.S. Constitution protects our right to say what we want. Let's keep it that way. If you don't want to be attacked online, turn off your computer. We have the right to protect our free speech! Ⓑ

> Ⓐ **Informational Focus** Bias and Stereotyping What stereotype does Tamara present in her letter?
>
> Ⓑ **Read and Discuss** What do all these responses show you?

Read with a Purpose
How do these writers support their opinions?

 Internet

Universal Access

Advanced Learners
Acceleration Have students evaluate the effects of stereotyping and bias in an argument through a class discussion. Have students point out the bias and stereotypes present in these responses and in other media. How do bias and stereotyping affect an author's assertions? Can bias or stereotyping be used to help an author's argument?

Students with Disabilities
Tell students that the comments in this selection represent a variety of different students' assertions and opinions. To emphasize this fact, have small groups of students read this selection together. Tell each group member to read one or two of the comments aloud. After each comment is read, have group members pause to discuss what claims each comment made and how the author of the comment feels about bullying.

Reading Standard 2.6 Assess the adequacy, accuracy, and appropriateness of the author's evidence to support claims and assertions, noting **instances of bias and stereotyping.**

Sound Off to the Editor
Standards Review

Informational Text and Vocabulary

1. To which stereotyped idea does Timothy Mann refer?

A Bullying must be stopped.

B Bullies should be expelled.

C Bullies will always be bullies.

D Adults don't understand bullying.

2. Jonathan Roper's letter is written from the point of view of a

A conceited athlete.

B professional jock.

C lazy player.

D failing student.

3. Whose letter expresses bias against targets of Internet bullying?

A Tamara Holmes's

B Jonathan Roper's

C Candace Branch's

D Calista Tallman's

4. The target of Candace's bias is

A free speech.

B adults.

C fellow classmates.

D parents of bullies.

5. Tamara Holmes reveals bias against

A performing research.

B Marissa's writing.

C parents' teaching.

D students' dropping out.

6. If an object is *expelled*, it is

A forced out.

B falling.

C accessible.

D broken open.

Writing Skills Focus

Timed ⌐Writing Refer to the notes you took while you were reading the responses. Then, write a paragraph explaining how biases and stereotypes can weaken an argument.

What Do You Think Now   How do you think bullying should be handled, whether it occurs online or in person?

What Do You Think Now?

To help students respond to the question, ask them to think about their own personal experiences with bullying.

Check for Understanding

Independent Practice
Answers and Explanations

1. C *He believes bullying just has to be dealt with; he does not believe it can be stopped.*

2. A *Jonathan Roper is on the basketball team, and we can tell that he is conceited because he says that he and his teammates are "heroes."*

3. B *Jonathan Roper expresses bias when he says "smart kids are geeky."*

4. B *She says that all school employees and other adults think kids are just troublemakers.*

5. D *Tamara says that bullies and dropouts will become criminals.*

6. A *Expelled means "forced out." Someone who let her breath out forcefully forced it to leave her body.*

Writing Skills Focus

Possible response: *Biases and stereotypes can weaken a person's argument by demonstrating that the person is not able to think clearly and logically about a topic. Arguments are strongest when they are based on facts rather than on opinions, and biases and stereotypes are opinions, not facts.*

Assess

📝 **Chapter 7 Resources,** Selection Standards Check, p. 25

🔵 **ThinkCentral Online Assessment,** Selection Standards Check

💿 **Teacher One Stop™,** editable Selection Standards Check

Reteach

🔵 **ThinkCentral Online Remediation**

Preteach

Write with a Purpose Read aloud the essentials of a good research report to guide students' understanding of this type of writing. Also refer students to the rubric on p. 744 for more information on research reports that they can use throughout this workshop.

Direct Teach

Model the Skill

Think as a Reader/Writer Use the professional model on this page and others in the chapter to provide examples of the elements of a good research report. Note that the excerpt from "Flying High—Again" uses several types of evidence and states its main idea clearly.

Think About the Model
Possible responses:

1. *The report gives evidence about how the eagles' situation has improved.*

2. *The writer restates the main idea after supporting it with evidence.*

3. *The writer uses statistics as evidence to support the thesis.*

Research Report

Write with a Purpose

Write a research report on a topic of your choice. Your **purpose** is to find, organize, and present evidence that supports your thesis. Think about how to write clearly so that your **audience** can easily gain more knowledge about the topic.

A Good Research Paper

• focuses on a thesis, or main idea, supported by evidence
• includes accurately documented information from several sources
• uses different types of evidence, including facts, examples, statistics, and direct quotations
• organizes information in a logical way
• ends by summarizing ideas or drawing an overall conclusion

See page 744 for complete rubric.

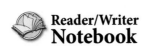

Reader/Writer Notebook

Use your **RWN** to complete the activities for this workshop.

Think as a Reader/Writer
You take in information all the time. In this collection, you've read some articles about contemporary issues. Now it's time to use your research skills to find and present factual information in a research report. First read this excerpt from the end of an article titled "Flying High—Again." The first paragraph of the article (not seen here) states the thesis: "Although bald eagles were in danger of becoming extinct in the 1950s, the efforts of many groups over the last ten years have helped them make an amazing comeback."

> With the help of many people all over the United States, eagles are slowly recovering. From a low point of fewer than 500 nesting pairs in the 1960s, the numbers have grown to an estimated 4,500 nesting pairs in the continental United States. If you count eagles and young adults there are about 55,000 bald eagles in the United States today. In 1998, Secretary of the Interior Bruce Babbitt took steps to remove the bald eagle from the endangered species list. In an interview, Babbitt said, "The eagle is doing splendidly. It's making a wonderful comeback everywhere."
>
> The bald eagle is not completely out of danger yet, but its future looks better every day. If eagles keep making a comeback, our national symbol should be around for a long time to come.

← Different types of **evidence** are used throughout the article. Here, we see statistics and a direct quotation.

← The **thesis** is restated effectively, both in this quote by Babbitt and in the concluding paragraph.

Think About the Professional Model
With a partner, discuss the following questions about the model.

1. How does the information here support the main idea of the article?

2. What has the writer done to present the information clearly?

3. Why does the writer use statistics to support the article's thesis?

Writing Standards 1.4 Identify topics; ask and evaluate questions; and develop ideas leading to inquiry, investigation, and research. 1.5 Give credit for both quoted and paraphrased information in a bibliography by using a consistent and sanctioned format and methodology for citations. 2.3 Write research reports: a. Pose relevant and tightly drawn questions about the topic. b. Convey clear and accurate perspectives on the subject. c. Include evidence compiled through the formal research process (e.g., use of a card catalog, Reader's Guide to Periodical Literature, a computer catalog, magazines, newspapers, dictionaries). d. Document reference sources by means of footnotes and a bibliography.

Prewriting

Choose a Subject

Choose a research subject that interests you and that you think will interest your readers. For help in brainstorming a subject, use the Idea Starters in the margin. Since you will be depending on research to find the information you need, check to see if you will be able to find information about a topic before you choose it. Next, you need to limit your focus. Try to keep your subject manageable. Use an organizer like the one below to narrow your topic.

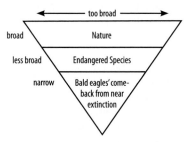

Find Sources

Your report should be based on a minimum of three reliable sources. Reliable sources are authored by qualified people. They are written to inform, not to express opinions or persuade people. Whenever possible, use **primary sources,** such as diaries, letters, and interviews. You can also use **secondary sources,** such as magazine and newspaper articles, encyclopedia entries, and media documentaries. Search your library catalog, the Reader's Guide to Periodical Literature, various reference works, and the Internet for the best sources. Be sure that the information is trustworthy and current.

Take Notes

Use note cards to record the information you find. Each note card should contain one main idea. You can **paraphrase** the information (rewrite it in your own words) or place the writer's exact words inside quotation marks to show that it is an exact **quotation.** Remember to write the title, author, and page number of the source on the card. You will have to give proper credit for both quoted and paraphrased information in your report, both in a bibliography and in footnotes (or parenthetical citations, if your teacher prefers).

Idea Starters

- scientific discoveries
- historical events
- hobbies
- current news events
- predictions
- interesting careers

⬤ Writing Tip

Evaluate sources, particularly those from the Web, by asking these questions:

- Who is the author? What is the author's background?
- How trustworthy is the information? What are the author's sources?
- Is the information up-to-date? If you use a Web site, check when the site was developed or last revised.

Your Turn _____

Get Started Choose a narrow subject and begin to research it. As you find good sources, list them in your **RWN,** using the style of citation selected by your teacher. This way, when it comes time to credit your sources, you will have all the information in one place.

✳ Learn It Online
Use an interactive graphic organizer to help focus your ideas. Try one at:
go.hrw.com   H7-737   **Go**

Guided Practice: Apply

Choose a Subject

- To help students narrow their focus, model using the graphic organizer on this page. Have a volunteer suggest a topic that interests him or her, such as science. Write the word *science* in the broadest row of the triangle. Then, ask specific questions to fill out the rest of the triangle. Examples might include: "What branch of science are you interested in?" followed by: "What was an important biological discovery?"

- Tell students their topic should not be so specific that they are unable to find enough information about it to write a paper on.

Find Sources

- Remind students that primary sources are often the places they would naturally think of looking. For instance, if they are writing about a particular career, they might interview a person who has a job in that field.

- Tell students that Web sites ending with *.gov* or *.org* are often the most accurate sources of information on the Internet. Any other Web sites should be used with caution.

Your Turn _____

Get Started Tell students to include complete information about sources. For a Web site, this will include the Web site's address and the date that the student accessed the Web page.

Writing and Research in a Digital Age, interactive lesson presentations with activities 📀

Teacher One Stop™, on-level lesson plans and all print resources 📀

Holt Six Traits for Writing, rubrics, prompts, and sample papers 📀

Language and Sentence Skills Practice 📀

UA: Developmental Language and Sentence Skills Practice 📀

Language Handbook Worksheets, pp. 57, 122 📀

ThinkCentral Online Assessment, Writing Workshop Test

ThinkCentral Online Remediation

Holt Online Essay Scoring

✳ Learn It Online
The **ThinkCentral, Student Access** includes more than thirty **Interactive Graphic Organizers.** Your students can use them to generate and organize ideas, compare and contrast, evaluate a decision, support a position, and much more.

go.hrw.com   H7-737   **Go**

Guided Practice: Apply

Think About Purpose and Audience

Suggest students work in pairs to ask each other questions about their respective topics. If they are unable to answer the questions with the information they have so far, then their audience will probably have similar difficulties. Explain to students that they must then conduct further research to answer the questions.

Organize Your Report

Tell students that the way they organize their information is determined by the type of information they are presenting. If the information is explaining a process, such as a scientific experiment, the report should be organized in chronological order. If the information is focused on convincing the reader of a particular idea, organizing by order of importance would be more effective.

Your Turn _____

State Your Main Idea Have students complete the **Your Turn** activity as independent practice. As they work, monitor students' progress by making sure the main idea sentence is supported by details in their outline and paper.

⦿ Writing Tip

Your audience may have varying degrees of knowledge about your topic, so make sure that you give them enough information to explain the important ideas but not so much information that they could lose interest.

Your Turn _____

State Your Thesis Write your thesis statement in your **RWN.** Refer to it constantly as you plan and write your report, since this statement should guide the choices you make regarding what information to include or leave out. Also develop your outline, which will guide your writing.

Think About Purpose and Audience

Remember that the **purpose** of a research report is to find information and share it with other people. Your **audience** will probably include your teacher and classmates, but anyone who is interested in your topic could be your audience. As you review your notes, think about your readers and what they need to know. If you think readers might have questions that your notes do not answer, you should continue your research.

Organize Your Report

Decide how you will organize the information in your report—by **order of importance** or **chronological** (time) **order.** Then, you can sort your note cards to reflect this pattern. Once you are happy with the order of your note cards, you can create an outline. Use a framework like the one below to outline your research report.

State Your Thesis

Now that you have done your research, taken notes, and organized your thoughts, you must be sure that you are clear about your thesis and can state it clearly for others. The **thesis statement** appears in the introductory paragraph of your report and tells what you will say about your topic. Your thesis is then supported by the paragraphs in the body of your report. Each paragraph should have a main idea, supported by evidence. A good thesis statement will enable you to convey a clear, accurate perspective on your subject.

Your outline should include your thesis statement, which will then be an umbrella for your outline's main headings.

```
                              Outline
Focused Topic: _____
Organization: _____
Thesis:
1. Main idea of paragraph 1:
   A. Supporting fact, example, or quotation: _____
   B. Supporting fact, example, or quotation: _____
2. Main idea of paragraph 2:
   A. Supporting fact, example, or quotation: _____
   B. Supporting fact, example, or quotation: _____
```

Research Report Writing Prompts

Students can choose their own topics or use one of the following prompts to write a research report.

Social Studies Research a building or tradition in your town. Write a report explaining how it began and how it has changed over the years, as well as why it is important to the community.

Science Research a simple experiment you have already tried or would like to try. Explain how to conduct the experiment and why it produces important results.

Workplace Research a career that seems interesting to you. Report on how someone begins the career and what the job involves. Remember to explain why you find this to be an interesting career.

Language Arts Research the life and work of your favorite author. How have the author's experiences influenced his or her writing? What impact has his or her work had on the literary world? Remember to develop a thesis statement about the author, and to support it with facts, examples, or quotations from scholars.

Drafting

Follow the Writer's Framework

Draft your report, using your framework to guide you. Remember that in your first paragraph you should capture your readers' attention and include your thesis statement.

Write the body paragraphs so that each one addresses a main heading in your outline. Sometimes, you might need more than one paragraph to explain an idea. Make sure that the main point in each paragraph is supported by **evidence.** Remember that evidence should include a variety of facts, examples, statistics, and direct quotations. If you find that your evidence is not adequate, go back to your sources, this time looking for specific information.

Bring your report to a close by restating your thesis and tying the information together. Draw a conclusion about your research or reflect on the information, and consider leaving readers with a memorable image.

List Your Sources

At the end of your paper, document your sources of information in a bibliography, under the heading *Works Cited.* Refer to a style guide such as the Modern Language Association (MLA) handbook for guidelines on formatting your source citations.

Grammar Link Writing Titles Correctly

When you list your sources, remember the rules for writing the titles of different genres.

- <u>Underline</u> (or use *italics* on a computer) the titles of books, Web sites, encyclopedias, magazines or newspapers, movies or video recordings, and television or radio programs.
- Place quotation marks around the titles of documents on a Web site, encyclopedia articles, and magazine or newspaper articles.

Here's an example of a complete citation, following the MLA Handbook, for an online source that could possibly have been used to research and write the professional model on page 736.

> Martell, Mark, and MaryBeth Garrigan. "Bald Eagle." *The Raptor* Sept. 1994. U of Minnesota. 18 Nov. 1998 <http://www.raptor.cvm.umn.edu/>.

A Framework for a Research Report

Introduction
- Grabs readers' interest
- Identifies topic

Body
- Discusses each main idea in one or more paragraphs
- Supports each main idea with facts, examples, or quotations

Conclusion
- Summarizes or restates main idea
- Draws conclusions

Writing Tip

Effective "hooks," or attention-grabbing beginnings, for a research report include interesting facts, quotations, or questions.

Writing Tip

To see a complete version of a research paper, log on to the Interactive Student Edition at go.hrw.com, and go to page 739.

Your Turn _____

Write Your Draft Following your plan, write a draft of your research report. Be sure to think about

- putting information you gathered from sources in your own words
- organizing each paragraph around one important idea
- supporting each paragraph with details, such as facts and statistics
- citing sources correctly

Model the Skill

■ Using a student draft on a transparency, model how to use the questions, tips, and revision techniques suggested in the chart. You might use a student's report or a report of your own creation to evaluate and revise using the steps in the chart.

■ Ask volunteers to demonstrate using each of the steps on their own reports.

Peer Review

When students share their draft with their partner, have them read the draft aloud. This will help keep both students focused and may even help the writer realize some of his or her own writing errors.

Holt Six Traits for Writing, rubrics, prompts, and sample papers

Peer Review

Working with a peer, review your drafts and take notes about each other's questions. Answering each question in this chart can help you identify where and how your drafts could be improved.

Evaluating and Revising

Read the questions in the left column of the chart, and then use the tips in the middle column to help you make revisions to your report. The right column suggests techniques you can use to revise your draft.

Research Report: Guidelines for Content and Organization

Evaluation Question	Tip	Revision Technique
1. Does your introduction include a thesis statement? Does it grab the readers' attention?	**Underline** the thesis statement. **Put brackets** around the "hook" you used.	**Add** a thesis statement. **Add** an attention-grabber.
2. Does each paragraph in the body of the paper develop one important topic or main idea?	In the margin, **label** each paragraph with the topic it develops.	**Cut** unrelated ideas. **Rearrange** information into specific paragraphs where necessary.
3. Does each body paragraph contain supporting evidence, such as facts, examples, statistics, and direct quotations?	**Highlight** the facts, examples, statistics, and quotations that support each paragraph.	**Add** supporting details from your notes, if necessary.
4. Is the information in each paragraph properly summarized or quoted?	**Circle** sentences that sound as if someone else wrote them. **Draw a wavy line** under quoted information.	**Replace** with your own words, or **add** quotation marks.
5. Does your conclusion restate your thesis and sum up your findings?	**Put a check mark** next to the restatement. **Put an asterisk** next to the summary.	**Add** a restatement. **Elaborate** on your findings.
6. Have you included at least three sources in the *Works Cited* list?	**Number** the sources listed.	**Add** sources to the *Works Cited* list, if needed. **Add** information from these sources to your report.

Real Issues, Real Experts

Holt Professional Learning for Language Arts

To watch videos on teaching **revision, grammar,** and **on-demand writing skills** featuring Linda Rief, Amy Benjamin, and Leila Christenbury, go to this page in **ThinkCentral, Teacher Access**.

Universal Access

 English Learners

English for Academic Success Help students understand the differences among types of evidence. Explain that *quotations* are statements made about a topic, usually by someone regarded as an expert in the field. Explain that *statistics* are numeric data, such as the number of people who have seen a particular movie. *Facts* are basic pieces of information that can be proven, such as the year an event took place. *Examples* are specific samples of something. A paragraph about famous nineteenth century English authors would name specific authors.

Read this student's draft of a research report (your own report may be much longer) and the comments about it as a model for revising your own report.

Greek Afterlife

by Kaitlin Heikes, Bailey Middle School

What happens when you die? The Ancient Greeks answered that question by developing a complex mythology of the afterlife.

Burial preparations usually involved placing a coin in the dead person's mouth. The coin would later be used as payment to cross the River Styx in the Underworld. Most people were also buried with something of personal significance, such as weapons or jewelry.

According to Greek mythology, souls of the dead were guided into the Underworld by Hermes, the Messenger of the Gods. After Hermes led these souls to the River Styx, Charon would then ferry them across the river into the Underworld. At that time the coin that had been placed in the dead person's mouth was taken. It was the price of passage across the river.

← The opening paragraph grabs the reader's attention with a **thought-provoking question** and then states the report's **thesis.**

← **Examples** provide details while also supporting the thesis statement.

← The writer has used **chronological order** to present the information about passing into the Underworld.

MINI-LESSON ▶ **How to Focus Paragraphs**

Kaitlin's second paragraph develops the topic of ancient Greek burial preparation by focusing on the kinds of items buried with the dead. Mentioning coins, weapons, and jewelry is pertinent to the topic of the second paragraph. However, her explanation of the purpose of the coin is discussed in the third paragraph; therefore, it is unnecessary and redundant in the second. Kaitlin decides to omit this information from the second paragraph and add an introductory transitional statement to better focus the purpose of the second paragraph.

Kaitlin's Revision of Paragraph Two

When an ancient Greek died, burial preparations included careful consideration of what the person might need in the afterlife. Usually a coin was placed in the dead person's mouth. ~~The coin would later be used as payment to cross the River Styx in the Underworld. Most people were also buried with something of personal significance, such as weapons or jewelry.~~

Your Turn _____

Focus Your Paragraphs

Read your draft, paragraph by paragraph, asking yourself these questions:

- Do I stick to one topic in this paragraph?
- Do I need to delete unnecessary details or add more support to this paragraph?

Guided Practice: Apply

Student Draft

Explain that the Student Draft on this page is the first half of a research report written by a student. Model reading the draft and the annotations in blue, and explain that the yellow highlighting illustrates the student's language choices. Explain that a mini-lesson follows with helpful information about ways to improve this draft as well as their own.

▶ Mini-Lesson
How to Focus Paragraphs

■ Point out to students how the student writer revises her draft by rearranging the placement of certain sentences. By moving the sentence about the meaning of the burial coin from the second to the third paragraph, the writer ensures that each paragraph contains its own topic.

■ Remind students to keep related ideas in the same paragraph and take unrelated ideas or redundancies out of a paragraph as they revise their draft.

Your Turn _____

Focus Your Paragraphs As students complete the **Your Turn,** tell them to underline the main idea of each paragraph. Have students place brackets around sentences that need to be moved to another paragraph or deleted so that each paragraph contains its own topic.

Struggling Writers

Benchmark Students Have students work in pairs to give partners a "tour" of their topic. Students should draw a box, or "room," to represent each paragraph. In each room, they should jot down points that will go in the paragraph. Then, have students orally give their partner a tour through the rooms.

Students with Disabilities

Have students choose whether they will write in chronological order or order of importance. Then, work with students who choose chronological order to make a time line using their note cards. Work with students writing in order of importance to draw a staircase and to arrange their note cards in descending order.

Guided Practice: Apply

Student Draft

- Explain that the Student Draft is continued and completed on this page. Again the draft is annotated and highlighted for the students.

- Read the draft and annotations aloud and discuss. Refer students to the Writer's Framework on p. 739. Ask students to comment on whether the student writer followed her framework.

▶ Mini-Lesson
How to Provide Supporting Evidence

- Point out to students that the student writer revises her draft to add supporting details and evidence. She then gives a specific example to back up her point.

- Tell students that any time they make a statement, they should imagine someone saying, "Prove it." Students should make sure that any claims they make are followed by information to prove them.

Your Turn _____

Provide Supporting Evidence Ask students to complete the **Your Turn** activity as independent practice. Have students mark with a star sections of their report that should be supported by facts, examples, and quotations. Then, direct them to add the additional text.

Student Draft *continues*

This body paragraph fully explores one idea—what happens once the dead reach the Asphodel Fields. →

> Once across the river, the souls would go to the Asphodel Fields, where they would wander aimlessly with no memory of their earthly existence. Some souls would be called beyond the Asphodel Fields to a Place of Judgment. Those who had led exceptional lives would go to Elysium, whereas those who had committed crimes were sent to Tartarus. Those somewhere in the middle would return to Asphodel Fields. Greek myths indicate that those who reached Elysium had the option of returning to earth and starting a new life.

The closing paragraph summarizes and restates the **thesis.** →

> The Ancient Greeks used these highly inventive and complex myths to answer a central question of human existence. Many of the Greeks' wide array of mythological gods played important roles in the afterlife myths.

MINI-LESSON ▶ How to Provide Supporting Evidence

Remember that each paragraph in a research report is focused on an important idea, and that this idea needs to be supported by a variety of evidence. Kaitlin does a great job of keeping the focus clear in the paragraph about what happens once the dead reach Asphodel Fields. However, some of her explanations do not include supporting evidence. For example, readers might wonder what kind of crimes merited the punishment of being sent to Tartarus. Kaitlin can go back to her sources to try to find some specific information about this.

Kaitlin's Revision of Paragraph Four

> . Those who deserved punishment were sent to Tartarus. The punishment might be for committing horrible crimes such as murder, or it might come from a god's unhappiness with the dead. For example, the god Zeus sent all Titans to Tartarus for daring to fight against him in a war. The dead souls who had been neither bad nor good on earth
>
> ... Those who had led exceptional lives would go to Elysium, ~~whereas those who had committed crimes were sent to Tartarus. Those somewhere in the middle~~ would return to Asphodel Fields. Greek myths indicate that those who reached Elysium had the option of returning to earth and starting a new life. Thus, the ultimate goal for leading an exemplary life was to reach Elysium and begin anew.

Your Turn _____

Provide Supporting Evidence
Read through your research report, specifically checking for your use of supporting evidence in each paragraph. How could statistics, facts, examples, or direct quotations support your main ideas and make them clearer to readers? Return to your sources to find supporting evidence to add to paragraphs that need it.

Universal Access

Struggling Writers

Discuss with students how the supporting evidence makes it easier to understand the main ideas in the revised essay. Point out that the student writer could also have chosen to quote an expert on Greek mythology to support her paragraph. Then, work with students to write possible supporting evidence for the following claims: *Summer vacation is enjoyable; Being on a sports team is hard work; Seventh grade is different from sixth grade.*

Have students think about what type of supporting evidence would best fit each claim. Write their ideas on the board so they can refer to them when revising their own report.

Advanced Learners

Enrichment Challenge students to use at least one example each of a statistic, fact, example, and quotation to support their evidence. Challenge students to support the main point of at least one paragraph with more than one kind of evidence.

Proofreading and Publishing

Proofreading

You have carefully revised your research report to be sure that every paragraph is clear and well-developed. Now it's time to look at the report in a different way, focusing more narrowly to find and eliminate any errors. Mistakes in spelling, punctuation, and sentence structure can interfere with the readers' ability to focus on the new information they will learn from your paper. When you edit for errors and polish the report, you make it even easier to read and understand.

● **Proofreading Tip**

Ask a partner to help you proofread your report. In turn, you will proofread your partner's report. Gather good proofreading tools to use: a dictionary (to check spelling), a style guide or handbook (to check citations), and your favorite text for looking up grammar questions.

Grammar Link **Introductory Prepositional Phrases**

Introductory prepositional phrases can be excellent transitions to use when you show the order of events. Kaitlin uses introductory prepositional phrases in her report:

> **At that time** the coin that had been placed in the dead person's mouth was taken.

> **Once across the river,** the souls would go to the Asphodel Fields, where they would wander aimlessly with no memory of their earthly existence.

Note that the second phrase is followed by a comma, whereas the first one is not. Kaitlin has used a comma to avoid confusing the reader. Even though the words "the souls" is not capitalized, without the comma it is possible that someone might read the phrase "Once across the river the souls . . ." to mean that "the souls" was the name of the river. This is even more likely if the sentence were read aloud without the comma reminding the reader to pause after the word *river*.

Publishing

Now it is time to publish your research report to a wider audience. Begin by giving your report to your teacher and fellow classmates. Then, you might want to publish it on a personal or school Web page.

Reflect on the Process
In your **RWN,** write a short response to each of these questions.

1. How did you determine if your sources were reliable?
2. Which piece of evidence in your report do you think is most powerful? Why?

Your Turn _____

Proofread and Publish

Proofread your report several times. Each time, look for errors in one area. For example, focus first on spelling. Then look closely at punctuation—for example, are introductory prepositional phrases punctuated correctly? During a third editing pass look at sentence structure. Then make the corrections and publish your polished report so that others can learn from your work.

Guided Practice: Apply

Proofreading

Integrating with Grammar, Usage, and Mechanics If students make common errors, or errors in spelling as they are proofreading, send them to the Spelling and Correcting Common Errors chapters in **Warriner's Handbook.**

Grammar Link

- Point out that the examples of prepositional phrases used in the Student Draft help establish that the report is organized in chronological order. Words and phrases such as *after* and *at that time* help to explain exactly when things occurred and in what order.

- Challenge students to add at least two introductory prepositional phrases to their report. Point out to students who have organized their information in order of importance that they can still use prepositional phrases to show the order of events within paragraphs.

Publishing

Brainstorm with students additional ways to publish their research reports.

Reflect on the Process

Have students reflect on the entire writing process as well as their final product. Challenge them to reflect metacognitively about how they can improve and apply what they have learned.

Your Turn _____

Proofread and Publish Have students check their final draft against the Evaluating and Revising Guidelines on p. 740. Have them go through each item on the list and make sure that their draft meets all the requirements.

Real Issues, Real Experts

*Holt author **Sara Kajder** offers strategies for presenting research in different forms.*

When I ask students to write an academic research paper, I usually pair it with the opportunity to present findings in a multimodal or multigenre form. I do this largely in an attempt to provide students with an opportunity to enter into the work through a different mode. By opening up what counts as valued communication, we bridge students from writing in one form (e.g., multimedia presentation) to another (e.g., research report).

Some prompts for providing students with a means for sharing, packaging, or presenting their findings follow:

- Present your findings through a 3–4 minute digital video which models the "In Search of. . ." television show.
- Create a "This I believe. . ." podcast which addresses what you've learned from your research work.
- Use a wiki to create a multimodal resource on your topic.

Guided Practice: Apply
Scoring Rubric

■ Tell students that the best way to understand rubrics is to use them to score actual writing.

■ Have students work independently to score their research report using the rubric. Have them include a brief paragraph using the language of the rubric to explain the reasons for their score. Have students reflect on their strengths and weaknesses in the paragraph.

✎ **Holt Six Traits for Writing,** rubrics, prompts, and sample papers

Bibliography

You must provide a **bibliography,** or Works Cited list, at the end of every research report. There are various approved, or sanctioned, bibliographic formats; the important thing is to follow consistently the format your teacher directs you to use.

For most language arts and literature classes, the preferred format for bibliographies is the Modern Language Association (MLA) style. The chart below shows the MLA style for documenting some common kinds of sources. For an example of how to document an online source (such as a Web site), see page 739.

MLA GUIDE FOR LISTING SOURCES

Book	Author/editor. <u>Title</u>. City (and state, if city is unfamiliar): Publisher, year.
	Grambo, Rebecca L., ed. <u>Eagles: Masters of the Sky</u>. Stillwater, OK: Voyageur, 1997.
Magazine or Newspaper Article	Author. "Title of Article." <u>Publication Name</u> Date: page number(s).
	Gerstenzang, James. "Eagle May Fly from Nest of Endangered." <u>Los Angeles Times</u> 6 May 1998: A1.
Encyclopedia Article	Author (if known). "Title of Article." <u>Name of Encyclopedia</u>. Edition (if known) and year.
	Grier, James W. "Eagle." <u>The World Book Encyclopedia</u>. 1998.
Interview	Speaker. The words *Personal interview, Guest speaker,* or *Telephone interview.* Date.
	Sullivan, Vanessa. Personal interview. 17 Nov. 2003.
Television or Radio Program	<u>Title of Program.</u> Name of Host (if any). Network. Station Call Letters, City. Date of Broadcast.
	<u>The Amazing Eagle</u>. Discovery Channel. DISC, Austin. 26 Nov. 2003.

Footnotes and Parenthetical Citations

You must give credit any time you directly quote from, summarize, or paraphrase someone else's work. Two ways of documenting sources within the body of a research report are footnotes and parenthetical citations. Your teacher will tell you which kind of citation to use.

Footnotes appear at the bottom of each page on which information from bibliographic sources is used. Place the footnote number in the text just after, and slightly above, the period at the end of the sentence(s) in which you are citing source material. At the bottom of the page, repeat the footnote number and write the source information. The first time you cite a particular source, give full information for it. Later footnotes to the

same source can be in a shortened form—just the author's last name and page number.

First footnote:
[1] Karen Dudley, <u>Bald Eagles</u> (Austin: Raintree Steck-Vaughn, 1998) 54-55.

Later footnote:
[7] Dudley 52.

Parenthetical citations are placed in parentheses in the text of the report, before the period at the end of the sentence(s) in which you are citing the source material. Usually you will need to list only the author's last name and the page number(s) where you found the information: just enough information for readers to be able to find the correct source in your bibliography.

(Dudley 54-55).

Universal Access

Struggling Writers

As students prepare their bibliographies, you may need reinforce the concept of authority: An authoritative source is a reliable source from which to take notes and cite in a bibliography. Its author has credentials, such as a degree in the field about which he or she writes. The author may also have published the article in a magazine or newspaper that has a good reputations. Explain that reputable magazines, newspapers, and publishers act as a filter for unreliable writing. Libraries act as a second filter; therefore, most books,

magazines, and newspapers found in the school library can be considered fairly reliable. Anyone can publish on the World Wide Web, so it is important to evaluate carefully the authority of Web sites.

Have students work in groups of three to evaluate one another's source lists and make sure that each source is authoritative, according to the above description of authority. If a non-authoritative source is identified, have students meet with you one-on-one to discuss how to ensure that their reports contain only information from authoritative sources.

🐻 **California Standards, pp. 744–745**

■ **Writing Standard 1.5** Give credit for both quoted and paraphrased information in a bibliography by using a consistent and sanctioned format and methodology for citations.

■ **Writing Standard 2.3** Write research reports: **a.** Pose relevant and tightly drawn questions about the topic. **b.** Convey clear and accurate perspectives on the subject. **c.** Include evidence compiled through the formal research process (e.g., use of a card catalog, Reader's Guide to Periodical Literature, a computer catalog, magazines, newspapers, dictionaries). **d.** Document reference sources by means of footnotes and a bibliography.

Scoring Rubric

You can use the rubric below to evaluate your research report.

	Research Report	Organization and Focus	Sentence Structure	Conventions
4	• Includes a clearly and fully developed main idea statement. • Provides relevant supporting evidence in the form of facts, examples, statistics, and direct quotations. • Restates the main idea and summarizes findings in a fully developed conclusion. • Documents reference sources by means of footnotes and a bibliography.	• Clearly addresses all parts of the writing task. • Demonstrates a clear understanding of purpose and audience. • Maintains a consistent point of view, focus, and organizational structure, including the effective use of transitions. • Includes a clearly presented central idea with relevant facts, details, and/or explanations.	• Includes a variety of sentence types.	• Contains few, if any, errors in the conventions of the English language (grammar, punctuation, capitalization, spelling). These errors do not interfere with the reader's understanding of the writing.
3	• Includes a fully developed main idea statement. • Provides mostly relevant supporting evidence in the form of facts, examples, statistics, and direct quotations. • Restates the main idea and summarizes findings in the conclusion. • Documents reference sources by means of footnotes or a bibliography.	• Addresses all parts of the writing task. • Demonstrates a general understanding of purpose and audience. • Maintains a mostly consistent point of view, focus, and organizational structure, including the effective use of some transitions. • Presents a central idea with mostly relevant facts, details, and/or explanations.	• Includes a variety of sentence types.	• Contains some errors in the conventions of the English language (grammar, punctuation, capitalization, spelling). These errors do not interfere with the reader's understanding of the writing.
2	• Includes only a partially developed main idea statement. • Provides little supporting evidence. • Makes only a general reference to the main idea in the conclusion. • Documents some reference sources, with obvious omissions.	• Addresses only parts of the writing task. • Demonstrates little understanding of purpose and audience. • Maintains an inconsistent point of view, focus, and/or organizational structure, which may include ineffective or awkward transitions that do not unify important ideas. • Suggests a central idea with limited facts, details, and/or explanations.	• Includes little variety in sentence types.	• Contains several errors in the conventions of the English language (grammar, punctuation, capitalization, spelling). These errors may interfere with the reader's understanding of the writing.
1	• Lacks a main idea statement or provides an obscure or irrelevant statement. • Provides little or no evidence, and evidence provided may be irrelevant. • Lacks a clear conclusion. • Lacks documentation of reference sources.	• Addresses only one part of the writing task. • Demonstrates no understanding of purpose and audience. • Lacks a point of view, focus, organizational structure, and transitions that unify important ideas. • Lacks a central idea but may contain marginally related facts, details, and/or explanations.	• Includes no sentence variety.	• Contains serious errors in the conventions of the English language (grammar, punctuation, capitalization, spelling). These errors interfere with the reader's understanding of the writing.

English Learners

English for Academic Success Some students may have difficulty keeping track of the information needed to cite each type of source. Suggest that they restrict sources to books, if possible, and provide them with the following "frame" for citing books:

Last Name, First Name [,ed. if editor]. Title. City, State: Publisher, Year.

Advanced Learners

Have students work in pairs and exchange papers to check source lists against the chart, *MLA Guide for Listing Sources*. Suggest that partners highlight parts of citations they feel are incorrect. Then you can monitor progress by quickly checking the highlighted errors. Discuss common errors with the class.

Guided Practice: Apply

Documenting Reference Sources

■ Have students consult the most recent version of the MLA Handbook for more detailed source citation information on a broader range of sources that might be used by students in developing research reports.

■ Students may be confused about whether to add a period when a sentence ends with an Internet address. Explain that a period *should* be added. The final period in such a sentence is the punctuation for the sentence; it is not part of the Internet address. One way to avoid confusion is to put the entire address within angle brackets, or < >, with the end punctuation following.

Teaching Tip

Using and Citing Electronic Sources Students may find sources more efficiently if if they begin their electronic source research by using a single CD-ROM database in the school's library. Later they might attempt to use a search engine that can find multiple sources. Remind students to keep track of all articles or Web sites that they review during the research process, and to include them in their bibliography.

Assess

UA: Interactive Writer and Speaker, research report analytical scales and rubric

ThinkCentral Online Assessment, Writing Workshop Test

Teacher One Stop™, editable Writing Workshop Test

Reteach

ThinkCentral Online Remediation

Standards Focus

Objectives

Students will
- present research reports orally
- use verbal and nonverbal techniques

Preteach

Speak with a Purpose Remind students that when they deliver an oral research report, their goal is to tell their listeners what they learned. Tell students to imagine what questions other students might have about the topic, and be prepared to answer them.

Direct Teach

Model the Skill

Adapt Your Report

- Remind students that they do not need to start their research over; they simply need to turn their report into a format that is more appropriate for a speech. They should review their written reports and identify key information to reorganize into a speech.

- Guide students in adapting the text structure and phrasing from their written research report to make it sound more natural when spoken aloud. Caution students not to use slang or colloquial speech,.

California Standards, pp. 746–747

- **Listening and Speaking Standard 1.4** Organize information to achieve particular purposes and to appeal to the background and interests of the audience.
- **Listening and Speaking Standard 1.6** Use speaking techniques, including voice modulation, inflection, tempo, enunciation, and eye contact, for effective presentations.
- **Listening and Speaking Standard 2.3** Deliver research presentations: **a.** Pose relevant and concise questions about the topic. **b.** Convey clear and accurate perspectives on the subject.

Presenting a Research Report

Speak with a Purpose

Give your research report as an oral presentation. Practice your speech, and then present it to your class.

Speaking Tip

To credit your sources in a speech, work in references smoothly, saying, for example, "As Author X notes in her article _____"; "In his book _____, Author Y says that. . . "; "A quote from Critic Y in a recent review says. . .," and so on.

Listening Tip

Listen carefully for the speaker's purpose and attitude toward the subject. Does the speaker include enough convincing evidence to support his or her claims and conclusions? If you are not completely convinced, jot down questions and wait for an opportunity to politely question the speaker's claims and conclusions.

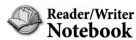
Reader/Writer Notebook

Use your **RWN** to complete the activities for this workshop.

Think as a Reader/Writer Delivering a speech can be a nerve-racking experience. If you prepare well, however, it can also be fun. A research presentation tells an audience the important points a researcher has discovered. You will do the same as you present your own research findings as a speech.

Adapt Your Report

Giving your research report as a speech does not mean simply reading it aloud. You will need to make changes to turn your report into an effective speech.

Tighten the Focus

Be sure to tighten the focus of your topic to keep the oral presentation down to a manageable length. Ask yourself which points are most **relevant,** or closely tied to the topic. Ask yourself, "What do I want my audience to gain from my speech?" Then, stick with the information that best helps you achieve this goal.

Hit the Perfect Note from Start to Finish

Your **introduction** gives the audience its first impression of you *and* your topic. Consider using one of the following methods to catch your listeners' attention:

- Begin with a question.
- Begin with a personal anecdote.
- Begin with an interesting or unusual fact.

For the **body** of the speech, choose an organizational pattern that will help your audience best understand your ideas. Finally, keep your **conclusion** short. Use it to reemphasize your main idea in a memorable way.

Credit Your Sources

Just as you listed your sources of information in your written research report, you will also need to give your sources credit in your speech. Credit each source by mentioning its author, title, or both.

c. Include evidence generated through the formal research process (e.g., use of a card catalog, *Reader's Guide to Periodical Literature,* computer databases, magazines, newspapers, dictionaries).
d. Cite reference sources appropriately.

Resources

UA: Holt Interactive Writer and Speaker, on-level practice and assessment, p. 122

UA: Differentiating Instruction, modified lesson plans, p. 205

Teacher One Stop™, on-level lesson plans and all print resources

Listening and Speaking Standards
1.4 Organize information to achieve particular purposes and to appeal to the background and interests of the audience. 1.6 Use speaking techniques, including voice modulation, inflection, tempo, enunciation, and eye contact, for effective presentations. 2.3 Deliver research presentations: a. Pose relevant and concise questions about the topic. b. Convey clear and accurate perspectives on the subject. c. Include evidence generated through the formal research process (e.g., use of a card catalog, *Reader's Guide to Periodical Literature,* computer databases, magazines, newspapers, dictionaries). d. Cite reference sources appropriately.

Deliver Your Research Report

To turn your ideas and outline into an effective speech, create **note cards** listing the main points you want to cover. Using note cards to jog your memory allows you to sound natural and make eye contact with your listeners.

Your speech will need one more ingredient: **coherence.** Use **transitional words and phrases** to connect ideas. Transitions can compare and contrast, indicate cause and effect, and show time, place, and supporting details.

Use Effective Verbal and Nonverbal Techniques

Using your note cards, practice your speech until you can get through it comfortably without stopping. Try rehearsing in front of a few friends or family members. As you practice, pay attention to the way you use your hands, eyes, and voice. Use natural **gestures,** and make **eye contact** with your listeners. Practice using these speaking techniques effectively:

- **Enunciation**—Speak clearly and carefully.
- **Tempo**—Talk at a slower rate than you normally would. This will help your listeners follow your ideas.
- **Voice modulation**—Stay calm to control your pitch.
- **Inflection**—Stress, or emphasize, important words and phrases.

Use Multimedia Tools for Support

Consider including audio and visual materials, such as charts, graphs, illustrations, and audio or video recordings, in your speech. Audiovisual materials can make your ideas clearer and easier to remember for listeners and can provide additional information to your speech.

Be sure that your materials can be heard and seen by all the members of your audience. Always explain to your audience what the audiovisual material means, and continue to face the audience. Be sure to cue any audiotape or videotape before you begin. This will help avoid wasting time rewinding or fast-forwarding during your speech. If you are using a computer to show any graphics or illustrations, be sure to set up the computer in advance so it is working properly. Being well-prepared with any multimedia tools will create a good impression on your listeners.

A Good Oral Presentation of a Research Report:

- includes a clear thesis statement in the introduction and restates it in a memorable way in the conclusion
- organizes and presents main ideas clearly so that the audience follows and understands them easily
- adequately supports every main idea with a variety of evidence from different sources
- reveals that the speaker fully understands the topic
- effectively communicates ideas both verbally and nonverbally

---

 Speaking Tip

When you choose the words you will use in your speech, be sure to use only **standard,** or formal, **American English,** the kind of English you hear in newscasts. For example, do not use contractions, slang, or other forms of informal language.

Model the Skill

Use Effective Verbal and Nonverbal Techniques

To teach the concept of using effective verbal techniques, model public speaking for students, asking them every minute or two to focus on a different aspect of your delivery. Ask questions like, "How quickly am I speaking? When do I emphasize words?"

Guided Practice: Apply

Have students practice their presentations in small groups. After each student has presented, have groupmates rate the performances and offer thoughtful, constructive comments, using "A Good Oral Presentation of a Research Report" as criteria.

Teaching Tip

Multimedia Tools Have students work in pairs to identify multimedia elements that might be appropriate in their research presentations. When students have independently developed these elements and inserted them into their presentation, have them practice the presentation with multimedia for their partner. Ask partners to provide feedback on how the multimedia worked with their presentation.

English for Academic Success

Remind students to use formal English when presenting their research report. They should use informal English, such as slang, only when quoting a source that uses it.

Assess

UA: Holt Interactive Writer and Speaker, Giving A Research Presentation Evaluation Guide

---

Universal Access

English Learners

English learners may struggle with the pronunciations of words. Before they begin creating their speeches, have them look through their research reports and circle words they are not sure how to pronounce. Go over the pronunciation of the words, or ask a fluent English speaker in the class to go over them. Students should repeat words as they hear them.

Struggling Learners

Before students create their presentations, pair them up and have them tell their partners about their topics, and share some of the information they plan to include in their oral presentations. Partners should tell each other what sounds interesting about each other's topics and what seems confusing. Allow students to work with their partners as they revise their presentations.

Standards Focus

Objectives

- analyze an author's argument
- identify and evaluate evidence
- identify synonyms
- develop a research report

Informational Skills Review

Review

If necessary, use the following questions to guide students in their reading before they answer the questions at the end of the review.

▶ **Evaluating Arguments**

After reading the paragraphs under the heading "Precious Underwater Habitats," identify one statistic that Ritu Upadhyay uses in her argument. **Possible responses:** *More than one quarter of the world's coral reefs have been destroyed; some coral reefs are 2.5 million years old; though coral reefs take up less than one percent of the ocean floor, they are home to 25 percent of all underwater species.*

Read paragraph 3. What expert does Upadhyay cite to support her argument? **Possible response:** *Clive Wilson of the Coral Reef Monitoring Network*

Test-Taking Tip

Encourage students to maintain their focus throughout the test. Tell students to keep their minds on the task at hand until they have answered each question.

 California Standards, p. 749

- **Reading Standard 2.6** Assess the adequacy, accuracy, and appropriateness of the author's evidence to support claims and assertions, noting instances of bias and stereotyping.

Informational Skills Review

Evaluating Arguments   **Directions:** Read the following selection. Then, read and respond to the questions that follow.

Can We Rescue the Reefs?

by **Ritu Upadhyay**
from *Time for Kids*

Time is running out to stop the destruction of coral reefs.

Under the clear blue sea, bustling communities of ocean creatures live together in brightly colored, wildly stacked structures called coral reefs. These silent, majestic underwater cities are home to four thousand different species of fish and thousands of plants and animals. For millions of years, marine creatures have lived together in reefs, going about their business in their own little water worlds.

But danger looms. At an international meeting on coral reefs in October 2000, scientists issued a harsh warning. More than one quarter of the world's reefs have been destroyed. . . . Unless drastic measures are taken, the remaining reefs may be dead in twenty years. "We are about to lose them," says Clive Wilkinson of the Coral Reef Monitoring Network.

Precious Underwater Habitats

The destruction of coral reefs, some of which are 2.5 million years old, would have a very serious impact on our oceans. Though coral reefs take up less than 1 percent of the ocean floor, they are home to 25 percent of all underwater species. Wiping them out would put thousands of creatures at risk of extinction. It would also destroy one of our planet's most beautiful living treasures.

Though it's often mistaken for rock because of its stony texture, coral is actually made up of tiny clear animals called coral polyps. Millions stick together in colonies and form a hard outer shell. When coral die, their skeletons are left behind, and new coral build on top. The colonies eventually grow together, creating large reefs. Reefs grow into complex mazelike structures with different rooms, hallways, holes, and crevices for their inhabitants to live in. Over the years the ancient Great Barrier Reef off Australia's coast has grown to be 1,240 miles long!

To the Editor:

My response to Ritu Upadhyay's article "Can We Rescue the Reefs?" is who cares! The environment is doing just fine without all these troublemakers making us pay attention to issues that have no relevance to us. Not only are coral reefs under the sea but they make up less than 1 percent of the ocean floor. Why should I worry

---

Resources for Skills and Standards Review

Chapter 7 Resources, Chapter Standards Mastery, Chapter Vocabulary Review

UA: Differentiating Instruction, below-level Chapter Standards Mastery

Teacher One Stop™, editable Chapter Standards Mastery

Focus on Standards

ThinkCentral Online Assessment, Chapter Standards Mastery

ThinkCentral Online Remediation

Holt Online Essay Scoring

about such a small percentage of something I can't see (especially in Australia, which is, like, 100,000 miles away), when I have three hours of homework each night and all sorts of boring chores to do at home. Let Ritu Upadhyay hug her tree, but leave me out of it! When the fish start helping me with my homework, then we'll talk. Till then, I'll be surfing the Internet.

Sincerely,

Matt Bruno

1. There is enough information in the article to show that the author believes coral reefs

   A must be saved immediately.

   B are being killed by pollution.

   C eventually turn into rocks.

   D will be dead in twenty years.

2. Evidence in the article supports the assertion that coral reefs

   A are magnificent cities of marine creatures.

   B can be replaced by man-made structures.

   C aren't important to young people.

   D may possibly die off within twenty years.

3. Which of the following statements *best* summarizes the article?

   A The outlook for the future of coral reefs is hopeless.

   B Coral reefs are important undersea little worlds.

   C Efforts to save endangered coral reefs must start now.

   D Global warming is a threat to oceans as well as to land.

4. Read this sentence from the article:

   > "It would also destroy one of our planet's most beautiful living treasures."

   The author *most likely* uses this sentence as

   A an attack on polluters.

   B an emotional appeal.

   C statistical evidence.

   D an appropriate description.

5. The writer of the letter to the editor uses the stereotyped idea that

   A all nature lovers are tree huggers.

   B students are too young to change the world.

   C doing chores around the house is not important.

   D environmental problems can be solved without human interference.

Timed Writing

6. Do you think the evidence in the article is adequate to support its assertion? Write a paragraph explaining why or why not.

Assess

Answers and Explanations

1. *A* Item B is not mentioned, C is negated by information, and D is stated by an authority—not the author.

2. *D* Item A states the author's opinion about reefs, while B and C are not mentioned. The quotation from Clive Wilkinson supports Item D.

3. *C* The article suggests that time may be running out but the situation is not hopeless (A). B is a reason for saving coral reefs, while D is not directly mentioned.

4. *B* The statement does not directly attack polluters (A) or cite statistics (C). It is an opinion, so it may or may not be an appropriate description (D).

5. *A* Matt Bruno stereotypes Upadhyay as a tree-hugger. Items B and D are not mentioned, while Bruno believes that chores are important (C).

Timed Writing

6. *The evidence in the article is adequate to support its assertion because the author uses several statistics, a quotation from an expert, and additional factual evidence to make a point about saving coral reefs.*

Reteach

ThinkCentral Online Remediation

Chapter Review

Review Informational Text Focus

1. Have students look back through the chapter to find the meanings of the terms listed below.

2. Ask students to cite passages from the chapter that illustrate the meanings of those terms.

Assertion, Claim, Evidence, Expert Opinions, Quotations, Facts, Examples, Statistics, Argument, Anecdote, Bias, Stereotyping

Review Reading Skills Focus

1. Have students look back through the chapter to find the meanings of the terms listed below.

2. Ask students to cite passages from the chapter that illustrate the meanings of those terms.

Author's Purpose, Re-reading, Evaluate Evidence, Accurate, Appropriate, Adequate, Assess, Inappropriate, Inaccurate, Inadequate

Assess

Answers and Explanations

1. B Deprivation *means lacking in something, which is the opposite of A, C, and D. The closest synonym is* loss.

2. C Consequences *are the results that stem from an action, behavior, or circumstance.*

3. C Intense *describes strong feelings or seriousness.*

4. D *A prolonged* experience lasts a long time.

5. A Expelled *means* forced out, *not* destroyed *(B),* purchased *(C), or* dried up *(D).*

6. B *Although* alienation *can be harmful, it does not necessarily involve injury. People who are alienated do not feel free (C) or promoted (D).*

7. C Traditions *may have advantages (D) or involve* speeches *(B) or gifts (A), but are best described as customs.*

8. A Anonymous *means nameless, or* unidentified.

Academic Vocabulary

9. A *Talking about a* specific *movie means a* particular *movie.*

10. A *The act of assessing is best described as judging.*

 WordSharp: An Interactive Vocabulary Tutor

Vocabulary Skills Review

Synonyms   **Directions:** Choose the word that means the same, or about the same, as the italicized word.

1. *Deprivation* is most like
   A abundance.
   B loss.
   C privilege.
   D growth.

2. *Consequences* are most similar to
   A actions.
   B truths.
   C results.
   D benefits.

3. An *intense* person is very
   A lighthearted.
   B loud.
   C serious.
   D confused.

4. Something that is *prolonged*
   A gets canceled.
   B falls apart.
   C is repaid.
   D continues.

5. *Expelled* means
   A forced out.
   B destroyed.
   C purchased.
   D dried up.

6. To *alienate* someone means to
   A injure them.
   B isolate them.
   C free them.
   D promote them.

7. *Traditions* are most similar to
   A gifts.
   B speeches.
   C customs.
   D advantages.

8. An *anonymous* author is
   A unidentified.
   B widely read.
   C discredited.
   D remembered fondly.

Academic Vocabulary

Directions: Choose the best synonym for the italicized Academic Vocabulary word.

9. *Specific* means
   A particular.
   B undersized.
   C significant.
   D outdated.

10. *Assess* is most similar to
    A judge.
    B complete.
    C erase.
    D begin.

Vocabulary Review

Use this activity to assess whether students have retained the chapter Vocabulary. Ask students to give a synonym of the underlined word in each sentence from the chapter vocabulary.

1. Children around the world suffer from <u>not getting enough nutrients</u>. [*malnutrition*]

2. When you go online, you can adopt a completely different <u>personality</u>. [*identity*]

3. Errors happen, but <u>manipulation of facts</u> in a paper is against the rules. [*misrepresentation*]

4. The student <u>was required to leave school</u> after she was caught cheating. [*expelled*]

5. A <u>guilty verdict</u> can be overturned on appeal. [*conviction*]

Writing Skills Review

Research Report **Directions:** Read the following passage from a research report. Then, answer the questions that follow.

Writing Standard 2.3 Write research reports. a. Pose relevant and tightly drawn questions about the topic. b. Convey clear and accurate perspectives on the subject. c. Include evidence compiled through the formal research process (e.g., use of a card catalog, Reader's Guide to Periodical Literature, a computer catalog, magazines, newspapers, dictionaries). d. Document reference sources by means of footnotes and a bibliography.

Answers and Explanations

1. **C** *All evidence, quotations, and statistics in the passage refer to the endangerment of bald eagles.*

2. **D** *All of the sources would be appropriate because they would provide reliable, valuable information about bald eagles.*

3. **C** *The writer states that the Bald Eagle Protection Act was a good start to protecting bald eagles, but this law alone could not save the eagles. The closest equivalent to "but" on the list is "however."*

4. **C** *Combining sentences 4 and 5, which describe the Endangered Species Act, would eliminate two shorter sentences and improve the flow of the passage.*

5. **A** *Sentence 10 states the main idea of the passage, and would provide a solid introduction to the passage.*

(1) Under the Bald Eagle Protection Act of 1940, people who killed eagles could be punished by a fine and time in jail. (2) This act was a good beginning; it was not enough to halt the danger to the eagles. (3) Protection of habitat and restrictions on harmful pesticides were also needed. (4) The bald eagle was helped further by the Endangered Species Act of 1973. (5) It protected millions of acres where bald eagles could live without being threatened by hunting or construction. (6) The passage of these laws, along with the banning of the pesticide DDT in 1972, provided much-needed protection for the bald eagle. (7) Scientists also helped bald eagles by developing a captive breeding program. (8) In this program injured eagles that could not survive in the wild laid eggs in a laboratory. (9) After hatching, the eaglets were returned to the wild. (10) Government regulations and conservation efforts have brought eagles back from the brink of extinction.

1. This is an excerpt from a research paper. What is the *most likely* topic of the complete paper?
   A physical characteristics of bald eagles
   B habitat of bald eagles
   C history of the endangerment of bald eagles
   D bald eagles as symbols

2. Which of the following Web sites would be appropriate to consult when writing this research report?
   A U.S. Fish and Wildlife Service Web site
   B an encyclopedia Web site
   C American Museum of Natural History Web site
   D all of the above

3. Which of the following words could *best* be used to connect the ideas in sentence 2?
   A and
   B so
   C however
   D therefore

4. Which two sentences could *best* be combined to improve the flow of the passage?
   A sentences 1 and 2
   B sentences 3 and 4
   C sentences 4 and 5
   D sentences 8 and 9

5. Where could sentence 10 be moved to improve the logical flow of the passage?
   A before sentence 1
   B before sentence 4
   C before sentence 7
   D before sentence 9

ThinkCentral Online Remediation

California Standards, p. 751
■ **Writing Standard 2.3** Write research reports.

Application **Homework**

Have students brainstorm a list of resources that could be used to create the entire research report on the history of the endangerment of bald eagles. Tell students to include a primary source, a secondary source, and an electronic source. Remind them that all sources must be credible.

Extension

Have students research another endangered species and efforts to preserve its habitat. Have them organize their findings into a paragraph that describes the species and relates it to the efforts to save the bald eagle from extinction. Remind students to include names, dates, locations, and other important information in the paragraph.

If students enjoyed the topics explored in this collection, you might recommend these titles for independent reading.

Assessment Options

The following projects can help you evaluate and assess your students' outside work. Videotapes or audiotapes of completed projects may be included in students' portfolios.

Write a Response

■ After students read *911: The Book of Help*, suggest that they create their own textual or artistic response to what they know or read about the events of September 11, 2001.

■ Allow students to work independently, with a partner, or in groups to create their response. Suggest that students review the stories, essays, and poems in the book for inspiration.

■ Display student artwork and written responses in the classroom or on a bulletin board.

Explore a Profession

If students find *Fire in Their Eyes* intriguing, have them research the profession of firefighting and prepare brief presentations on their findings to the rest of the class.

Read On
For Independent Reading

Nonfiction

911: The Book of Help

More than twenty authors of different ages and backgrounds, some famous, some not, wrote their remembrances of the horrific events of September 11, 2001. Some memories take the form of a short story, some an essay, others a poem. As you read *911: The Book of Help*, you will come to understand a moment in time that shook the world and continues to affect it today.

Fire in Their Eyes: Wildfires and the People Who Fight Them

What drives some people to stand in the path of a wall of flame? Who are these brave and visionary firefighters? *Fire in Their Eyes* explores the trials, tragedies, and triumphs of these courageous few. Karen Magnuson Beil takes you into the heart of one of nature's most destructive and unpredictable forces—fire—and the heroes who battle it.

The Acorn People

The Acorn People is more than just a story about children overcoming the difficulties of living with a disability. Ron Jones's memoir tracks his growth and spirit, which were influenced by the determination and friendship of a group of campers called the Acorn People.

At Her Majesty's Request: An African Princess in Victorian England

In *At Her Majesty's Request*, Walter Dean Myers tells the story of Sarah Forbes Bonetta, an African princess who was saved from a ritual killing at the age of seven by a British sea captain. As a result, the orphaned girl spent most of her life in England, receiving an upbringing under the eye of Queen Victoria. Myers includes newspaper articles and portraits to add to the reality of Bonetta's compelling story.

Word Counts and Readabilities of Read On Books

Fiction	Estimated Word Counts	Readability
911: The Book of Help	40,595	Challenging
Fire in Their Eyes: Wildfires and the People Who Fight Them	7,746	Easily
The Acorn People	12,575	Accessible
At Her Majesty's Request: An African Princess in Victorian England	20,000	Accessible

Nonfiction

Machu Picchu: Story of the Amazing Inkas and Their City in the Clouds

High in the remote mountains of the Andes, the great Inka city of Machu Picchu remained hidden from the Spanish conquistadors despite their years-long search. Elizabeth Mann describes the city's construction and grand architecture, plus the exciting adventures of the Inka people. Along with realistic illustrations, *Machu Picchu* will reveal the ancient city's mysteries to you.

A Walk Through the Heavens

When you look into the night sky, you are looking at the same sky your distant ancestors enjoyed. Besides enjoying the stars for their beauty, people from long ago used them for navigating the seas, predicting changes in the seasons, and explaining the mysteries of life. In this easy-to-use guide for beginner sky watchers, Milton D. Heifetz and Wil Tirion have provided a good introduction to stargazing as well as retellings of ancient myths and legends that early peoples used to interpret their nighttime sky.

How Would You Survive in the Middle Ages?

Fiona MacDonald and David Salariya get you as close as possible to the Middle Ages without using a time machine. With illustrations and descriptions of the lives of royals, soldier-knights, and everyday workers, this book will help you answer the question "How would I survive in the Middle Ages?"

Facing the Lion: Growing Up Maasai on the African Savannah

This memoir recounts the life of Joseph Lemasolai Lekuton, a member of the Maasai people of Kenya. From years learning the ways of a Maasai warrior to a journey on a cattle truck to a college interview in the United States, *Facing the Lion* offers both the unique and the universal experiences of a maturing boy.

Explore other novels—and find tips for choosing, reading, and studying books—at:

go.hrw.com   H7-753   **Go**

Nonfiction	Estimated Word Counts	Readability
A Walk Through the Heavens	27,100	Accessible
Machu Picchu: Story of the Amazing Inkas and Their City in the Clouds	4,814	Easily Accessible
Facing the Lion: Growing Up Maasai on the African Savannah	23,247	Accessible
How Would You Survive in the Middle Ages?	9,239	Easily Accessible

Features highlighted in **yellow** constitute a suggested minimum course of study.

Introducing The Skills

Selection or Feature	For Independent Reading	Grade–Level Standards
Literary Skills Focus: What Is Literary Criticism?		**Reading Standard 3.6:** Analyze responses to literature.
Reading Skills Focus: How Do I Analyze Literary Criticism?		**Reading Standard 3.6:** Analyze responses to literature.
Reading Model: The Listeners/A Critical Response to "The Listeners" by Walter De La Mare (Challenging) **Skills in Action:** Wrap Up	• **The Westing Game** by Ellen Raskin	**Reading Standard 3.6:** Analyze responses to literature.

Applying The Skills

Selection or Feature	For Independent Reading	Grade–Level Standards
King Arthur: The Sword in the Stone by Hudson Talbott (Accessible Lexile 860)	• **Passager** by Jane Yolen • **The Lady of Guadalupe** by Tomie dePaola	**Reading Standard 3.6:** Analyze responses to literature. **Reading Standard 1.2:** Greek, Latin, and Anglo-Saxon roots and affixes
Three Responses to Literature (Accessible Lexile 860)		**Reading Standard 3.6:** Analyze responses to literature.
Merlin and the Dragons by Jane Yolen (Accessible Lexile 730)	• **Parzival: The Quest of the Grail Knight** by Katherine Paterson • **Eragon** by Christopher Paolini	**Reading Standard 3.6:** Analyze responses to literature. **Reading Standard 1.2:** Greek, Latin, and Anglo-Saxon roots and affixes
Sir Gawain and the Loathly Lady by Betsy Hearne (Accessible Lexile 870)	• **Book of the Lion** by Michael Cadnum • **Crispin: The Cross of Lead** by Avi	**Reading Standard 3.6:** Analyze responses to literature.

Selection or Feature	Grade–Level Standards
Writing Workshop: Response to Literature	**Writing Standard 2.2:** Write responses to literature.
Preparing for Timed Writing	**Writing Standard 2.2:** Write responses to literature.
Listening and Speaking Workshop: Presenting a Response to Literature	**Listening and Speaking Standard 1.4:** Organize information. **Listening and Speaking Standard 1.5:** Arrange supporting details. **Listening and Speaking Standard 1.6:** Use speaking techniques.
Standards Practice: Literary Skills Review Vocabulary Skills Review Writing Skills Review	**Reading Standard 3.6:** Analyze responses to literature. **Writing Standard 2.2:** Write responses to literature.

Daily and Weekly Support

- **Reader/Writer Notebook**
- **Reading and Writing Transparencies**
- **Weekly Standards Review Transparencies**
- **Family Involvement Activities in Five Languages**
- **Language Handbook Worksheets**
- **Holt Virtual File Cabinet for Language Arts**
- **Spelling Lessons and Activities**

Assessment Resources

- **Chapter 8 Resources**, Chapter Diagnostic Test; Selection Standards Check, Chapter Standards Mastery
- **Universal Access: Differentiating Instruction**, leveled assessment
- **Formal Assessment**, Progress Monitoring Test 6, End-of-Year Summative Test
- **English-Language Conventions Progress-Monitoring Test**, Chapters 1–18
- **ThinkCentral Online Assessment**

Print Resources for Universal Access

	On-Level Learners	English Learners	Struggling Readers/Writers	Students Who Use African American Vernacular Engish	Advanced Learners	Students with Disabilities
Chapter 8 Resources practice and assessment for all selections and features	✔				✔	
Universal Access: Holt Interactive Reader interactive readings for Minimum-Course-of-Study Selections		✔	✔	✔		✔
Holt Interactive Reader for English Language Development adaptations of Minimum-Course-of-Study Selections		✔				
Universal Access: Differentiating Instruction modified lesson plans, graphic organizers, and leveled assessment		✔	✔	✔		✔
Universal Access: Resources for Teaching Advanced Students lesson plans for Minimum-Course-of-Study Selections					✔	
Universal Access: Supporting Instruction in Five Languages translations of selection summaries and key terms		✔				
Universal Access: Holt Interactive Writer and Speaker practice and assessment	✔	✔	✔	✔	✔	✔
Language and Sentence Skills Practice for Warriner's Handbook Chapters 1–18	✔				✔	
Universal Access: Developmental Language and Sentence Skills Practice for Warriner's Handbook Chapters 1–18		✔	✔	✔		✔

Technology Resources

Assessment Resources

Teacher Management Resources

go.hrw.com

Student Edition Extension Activities

Student Edition Support

Find all of Holt's technology resources at go.hrw.com. Technology resources are also listed as point-of-use in the wrap; bBelow are our featured components for Chapter 8.

Teacher Management Resources

ThinkCentral, Teacher Access
Teacher One Stop™
Holt Professional Learning for Language Arts

Spotlight on Teacher One Stop™

The Teacher One Stop™ contains all of the print resources that you will need when using *Holt Literature and Language Arts*. Find resources to help reach advanced students, struggling readers, and English learners.

- Student Readers that give students different opportunities to master the standards
- Diagnostic, formative, and summative assessment
- Resources to help students master important grammatical concepts

Student Edition Support

ThinkCentral, Student Access
PowerNotes
Student One Stop™
Interactive Reading Workshops
Interactive Graphic Organizers
Writers' Lives
Holt Audio Library
Holt Audio Library: Selections and Summaries in Spanish

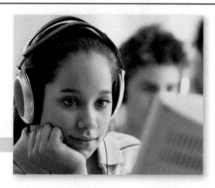

Spotlight on Holt Audio Library

Bring the adventures of King Arthur to life with the audio recording of the selection available on this CD. You may want to play the recording as the entire class follows along in the text, pausing the CD for discussion where appropriate.

Student Edition Extension Activities

Digital Storytelling Mini-Site
Literature Links
NovelWise Mini-Site
MediaScope Mini-Site
WordSharp: An Interactive Vocabulary Tutor
GrammarNotes
WritingNotes
Writing and Research in a Digital Age
Holt Audio Tutor for English Language Development

The Monsters Are Due on Maple Street
Rod Serling

Literature Links

Holt Resources

Literary Elements: Elements of the Short Story

More About the Writer

A Face for Television
By the late 1960s, just about every American knew Rod Serling's face. You say you wouldn't recognize him? Step into the Rod Serling Memorial Foundation's photo gallery. Discover why Serling's face appeared on everything from TV screens to posters, buttons, and comic strips.

Spotlight on Literature Links

Take your students farther with Literature Links that connect to interesting sites across the Internet.

Universal Access: Struggling readers may be motivated by this opportunity to connect the texts they read to science, history, and geography in a twenty-first century way.

Supported Strands: Literature, Reading

Assessment Resources

ThinkCentral Online Assessment
Holt Online Essay Scoring
ThinkCentral Online Remediation

5. When a writer uses a **first-person narrator**, the story —

○ A does not contain dialogue between the characters
→ ○ B is told by one of the characters
○ C does not contain a main character
○ D has only one character

Correct Answer: B

7.1.5
point of view

Spotlight on ThinkCentral Online Assessment

Preview and assign the Chapter 8 Diagnostic Test and Chapter Standards Mastery here.

The wrap for these selections includes specific ideas and strategies from *Holt Literature and Language Arts* authors.

From the Author

For "King Arthur: The Sword in the Stone," p. 768
To help students find their way through difficult texts, I have them use the Say Something strategy as they read. This strategy keeps them focused on major comprehension processes: predicting, connecting, questioning, summarizing, visualizing, and inferring. As they read, students occasionally stop and with a reading partner, say something about the text in the form of a prediction, connection, question, summary, visualization, or inference. The partner responds and then students continue reading.

Kylene Beers

Teacher to Teacher

Preteach To introduce students to "Sir Gawain and the Loathly Lady," I describe a woman who is hunchbacked, has one tooth, smells bad, and makes obscene noises. I tell students that we are about to read a story in which the main character marries a woman that fits this description. Students make predictions about the type of man that would marry a woman such as this.

Direct Teach I inform students that the man who marries the repulsive lady is Sir Gawain, the most honorable and noble night of the round table. As they read, students are instructed to create a list of things that Sir Gawain says, does, or others say about him that show that he is both honorable and noble.

Assess After reading the story, students share their notes. I make a master list on the board and we discuss it as a whole group.

Ann-Marie Krenik
Costa Mesa, California

Holt Professional Learning

Developing Critical Thinking About Literature
with Carol Jago and Deborah Appleman

Visit the ThinkCentral, Teacher Access to link to Holt's Professional Learning site for English/Language Arts teachers. This site features:

- Videos that share the insights of *Holt Literature and Language Arts* program authors and consultants and demonstrate proven classroom strategies with master teachers
- Study guides for publications by our authors and consultants
- Informative articles and useful Web links
- Help in planning your department's professional learning sessions
- A handbook for new teachers

VIDEO PRODUCTS

Strategies for Helping Struggling Readers
with Kylene Beers

Effective Vocabulary Instruction
with Carol Jago and Kylene Beers

Developing Critical Thinking About Literature
with Carol Jago and Deborah Appleman

Teaching Students to Revise, Not Recopy
with Linda Rief

Teaching English Learners
with Robin Scarcella

Using Literature Circles
with Harvey Daniels

Teaching On-Demand Writing Skills
with Leila Christenbury

Managing the Heterogeneous Classroom
with Leila Christenbury and Patrick Schwarz

Teaching Narrative and Expository Texts
with Judith Irvin and Deborah Appleman

Becoming a Tech-Savvy Teacher
with Sara Kajder

Re-engaging the Disnegaged Student
with Alfred Tatum

Teaching Grammar in Context
with Amy Benjamin

CHAPTER 8

 California Standards

Word Analysis, Fluency, and Systematic Vocabulary Development

- **1.2** Use knowledge of Greek, Latin, and Anglo-Saxon roots and affixes to understand content-area vocabulary.

Literary Response and Analysis

- **3.6** Analyze a range of responses to a literary work and determine the extent to which the literary elements in the work shaped those responses.

Writing Applications (Genres and Their Characteristics)

- **2.2** Write responses to literature:
  - **a.** Develop interpretations exhibiting careful reading, understanding, and insight.
  - **b.** Organize interpretations around several clear ideas, premises, or images from the literary work.
  - **c.** Justify interpretations through sustained use of examples and textual evidence.

Analyzing Visuals

Use ThinkCentral, Teacher Access to project this image for viewing.

Extension Activity Ask students to describe the story they expect would go along with this image. Where is the figure in the image going? ***Possible response:*** *The image shows a knight, a horse, and a castle, so I would expect a story about fantasy and chivalry. The knight is probably on his way to battle or to save someone from danger.*

Chapter Resources

On Course: Mapping Instruction

Chapter 8 Resources

Warriner's Handbook
- Chapter 18, Writing Effective Sentences
- Chapter 19, Sentence Diagramming

PowerNotes

Teacher One Stop™,

Formal Assessment, Progress Monitoring Test 6

English-Language Conventions Progress-Monitoring Tests

Holt Virtual File Cabinet for Language Arts, grammar, reading, and vocabulary resources

Holt Pronunciation Resources
- Phoneme Sounds and Spellings
- Support for Speakers of African American Vernacular English

ThinkCentral Online Assessment

ThinkCentral Online Remediation

CHAPTER 8

Literary Criticism: Analyzing Responses to Literature

California Standards

Here are the Grade 7 standards you will work toward mastering in Chapter 8.

Word Analysis, Fluency, and Systematic Vocabulary Development
1.2 Use knowledge of Greek, Latin, and Anglo-Saxon roots and affixes to understand content-area vocabulary.

Literary Response and Analysis
3.6 Analyze a range of responses to a literary work and determine the extent to which the literary elements in the work shaped those responses.

Writing Applications (Genres and Their Characteristics)
2.2 Write responses to literature:
  a. Develop interpretations exhibiting careful reading, understanding, and insight.
  b. Organize interpretations around several clear ideas, premises, or images from the literary work.
  c. Justify interpretations through sustained use of examples and textual evidence.

"The hero is one who kindles a great light in the world, who sets up blazing torches in the dark streets of life for men to see by."

—Felix Adler

What Do You Think?

What truths about life can we learn from tales about great heroes?

Learn It Online
Can you read pictures? Let *PowerNotes* show you how at:

go.hrw.com | H7-755 | Go

Chapter Objectives

■ Students will learn how to the elements of a literary work shape their reaction and response.

■ Students will learn skills and strategies to help analyze and critique literature.

■ At the end of the collection, students will write a character analysis as a response to a literary work.

Routines for California Classrooms

For ideas on classroom practices and approaches to grouping, see the discussion of routines on pages T34–T37 of this Teacher's Edition.

What Do You Think?
What truths about life can we learn from tales about great heroes?

Tell students that the heroes in stories that they read face challenges that may be similar to the challenges in their own lives. Ask students what they can learn from reading about how kings, wizards, and knights overcome difficulties. How can they apply this to their own lives?

Real Issues, Real Experts: Professional Learning

Spotlight on . . .
Effective Vocabulary Instruction

Are you looking for ways to keep all of your students engaged in reading assignments?

In *Responding to Literature*, **Leila Christenbury**, **Deborah Appleman**, and **Harvey Daniels**, showcase methods for inviting student responses to literature—through writing, whole-class discussion, and student-run literature circles.

In *Thinking Critically About Text*, **Carol Jago** explains how to implement close-reading strategies in any classroom level, and **Deborah Appleman** discusses teaching students to consider multiple perspectives on a selection. Each of these videos is accompanied by article, handouts for students, Web links for further exploration, a training guide for supervisors. For these resources and more, visit **Holt Professional Learning** by going to this page in **ThinkCentral, Teacher Access.**

Learn It Online
For a multimedia version of the instruction found on this page, use the **PowerNotes** Literary Skills Focus presentation.

go.hrw.com | H7-755 | Go

Literary Skills Focus

Objectives
Students will
- understand literary criticism
- consider the influence of literary elements when responding to literature

---

Preteach

Build Background Ask students if they have ever asked someone to recommend a book. What did they learn about the book that helped them decide whether or not to read it? What did they learn that was not helpful?

Direct Teach

Literary Criticism

- Tell students that a literary criticism conveys an opinion, but the opinion is supported by facts or examples from the literature.

- Tell students that, unlike the use of the word *criticism* that they may be familiar with, a literary criticism does not always point out the weaknesses of a piece of literature. A literary criticism can be positive as well.

Criticism of a Short Story: Literary Elements

Tell students that plot, character, and theme can be examined individually or they can be combined to convey an opinion about a literary work.

California Standards, pp. 756–757

- **Reading Standard 3.6** Analyze a range of responses to a literary work and determine the extent to which the literary elements in the work shaped those responses.

LITERARY RESPONSE AND ANALYSIS
Literary Skills Focus

by **Carol Jago**

What Is Literary Criticism?

Suppose your friend asks you if you liked a story you have both read for homework. You might answer, "It was great!" or "It was OK. I've read better." On their own, these answers don't say much about the story. Yet each of these answers could be the beginnings of literary criticism if they were expanded and supported with explanations of the literary elements that shaped your response.

Literary Criticism

What Is "Literary Criticism"? *Criticism* can mean "the act of finding fault with something," as in this statement: *The coach's criticism of my playing really hurt.* The word *criticism* can also refer to **literary criticism**—the analysis and evaluation of a piece of literature. The worst kind of literary criticism consists of simple, unsupported responses like "I really liked it" or "I hated that poem." The best kind of literary criticism includes an explanation of how a literary element shaped your response: *The plot of "The Highwayman" was so suspenseful I could not stop reading, and the poet really surprised and shocked me at the end.*

Criticism of a Short Story: Literary Elements

When you write literary criticism of a short story, think about how the various elements of the work shaped your responses. Was the story successful because of the eerie mood created by its setting, or were you most affected by the skillful characterization? Any literary element, from setting to point of view, may contribute to your response to a work. Three central elements, however, are often at the core of literary criticism of a short story: **plot, character,** and **theme.**

Plot **Plot** refers to what happens in a story. When you write a criticism of a story and you want to talk about how the plot shaped your response, focus on these questions:

1. Is the plot believable?
2. Is the plot clear—do you understand the sequence of causes and effects?

Character **Characters** are the actors in a story. When you write a criticism of a story and want to talk about how the characterization shaped your responses, focus on these questions:

1. Are the characters believable?
2. What motivates the characters?
3. How do you feel about the characters? How did the author bring them to life?

Theme **Theme** is the truth about life that a story reveals. When you write a criticism of a story and you want to talk about how theme shaped your response, focus on these questions:

1. What truth did the story reveal to you?
2. Does the theme seem old and tired, or does the writer say something fresh and interesting—or even timeless—about life?
3. Does the theme reflect a view of life that you share or at least understand?

Resources

Chapter 8 Resources, Literary Focus Skill Builder, p. 3

PowerNotes, interactive lesson presentation with activities

Teacher One Stop™, on-level lesson plans and all print resources

---

Universal Access

 English Learners/Struggling Readers

To help students write literary criticisms, provide them with the following sentence starters and examples.

- After reading [title], I feel that the [literary element] is _____. [*After reading "Hum," I feel that the theme is timeless and important.*]
- The [literary element] of [title] contributes to the _____. [*The timeless theme and modern plot of "Hum" contribute to the important lesson that we can all learn from the story.*]

Criticism of a Poem: Literary Elements

When you write literary criticism of a poem, you should think about how the elements of poetry shaped your response. Three important elements of poetry are **sound, figures of speech,** and **imagery.** Focus on these questions:

1. Is the poem written with a strict rhyme scheme and meter? Did the sounds make your reading pleasurable or difficult?

2. What figures of speech are in the poem? Are they fresh and original, or are they old clichés? Which figures of speech were easy or difficult to understand?

3. What major images are in the poem? Are the images fresh and new? How did they help you understand the poet's message?

Examples of Literary Criticism

A Good Literary Criticism Here is a brief criticism of "Rikki-tikki-tavi" (page 15):

> "Rikki-tikki-tavi" is brilliant because of its exciting plot and because of its animal characters. The plot of the story creates suspense, as the mongoose tries one strategy after another to get rid of the snakes that could kill the family. The final encounter, when Teddy is frozen in fear because the cobra is ready to kill him, made my hair stand on end. The characters in the story are memorable and seem like humans. The mongoose is so sweet, but he is a fierce fighter and very loyal to his family. He is willing to die to save Teddy. The other animal characters are also memorable, especially the evil snakes and the funny birds and featherbrained Darzee. I loved reading this story, mostly because of the plot and characters.

Why Is This Good? This criticism is good because the writer specifically tells us how the literary elements of plot and character shaped her enthusiastic response to the story.

A Poor Literary Criticism Here is another brief criticism of the same story. Notice how this writer fails to explain how literary elements shaped her response to the story:

> "Rikki-tikki-tavi" is about a mongoose who lives with a family in India. One day the family is threatened by cobras. Rikki saves the family by fighting the cobras, and by the end everyone lives happily ever after. All the animals are safe and the family is too.

Why Is This Poor? This writer merely summarizes the plot of the story and fails to explain the extent to which any literary elements shaped her response to the work.

Your Turn Analyze Literary Elements

Choose one story or poem you have read in class. Then, divide into three groups and discuss the story or poem for five minutes, focusing on one of the numbered questions from these two pages. When you finish, report on your discussions. Did concentrating on a particular literary element help focus the discussion? What did group members learn from the discussion?

Learn It Online
Reinforce your learning with *PowerNotes* at:
go.hrw.com **H7-757** **Go**

Criticism of a Poem: Literary Elements

- Remind students that *sound* can refer to the rhyme scheme, alliteration, onomatopoeia, and stressed and unstressed syllables of a poem.

- Remind students that some common figures of speech are simile, metaphor, hyperbole, and personification.

Examples of Literary Criticism

Point out to students that the example of a poor literary criticism does not express an opinion about the story. Ask students to suggest ways that they could improve this literary criticism. ***Possible response:*** *The literary responses could be improved with the addition of the writer's opinion about whether this plot is or is not realistic, using details from the story as support.*

Check for Understanding

Independent Practice
Your Turn _____
Possible response:
Focusing on one literary element helped me express my response to the story "Seventh Grade." By examining what motivated the characters, I was able to articulate my opinion that the story realistically portrayed what kids in middle school worry about.

Reteach

ThinkCentral Online Remediation

Learn It Online
For a multimedia version of the instruction found on this page, use the **PowerNotes** Literary Skills Focus presentation.

go.hrw.com **H7-757** **Go**

- [title] is _____ because of [literary element]. [*"Hum" is an intriguing story with an important lesson because of its timeless theme and modern plot.*]

Advanced Learners
Acceleration Adjust the Your Turn activity for advanced students. Have students focus on two literary elements instead of one. Instruct students to draw a conclusion about the story or poem they have chosen based on these two literary elements.

In addition to plot, character, and theme, students may choose to focus on the following literary elements: setting, conflict, climax, point of view, foreshadowing, tone, mood, irony, and symbolism. ***Possible response:*** *The realistic characters and modern-day plot of "Seventh Grade" made the story realistic and easy for me to relate to.*

Reading Skills Focus

Objectives
Students will
- learn techniques for thinking critically about responses to literature
- analyze a response to literature

Preteach

Build Background Ask students to think about what makes a critic credible. Ask students what they would expect to find in a credible literary criticism.

Direct Teach

Analyzing a Response to a Literary Work

Work with students to create a list of words and phrases that signal that a critic has a positive opinion of the literature he or she is critiquing. Then, create a list of words and phrases that signal a negative opinion. *Possible responses: Positive: enjoyable, believable, exciting, interesting, compelling, well-organized, imaginative. Negative: boring, unrealistic, dull, simple, confusing, erratic.*

California Standards, pp. 758–759
- **Reading Standard 3.6** Analyze a range of responses to a literary work and determine the extent to which the literary elements in the work shaped those responses.

Reading Skills Focus

by **Carol Jago**

How Do I Analyze Literary Criticism?

You analyze responses to creative works all the time. Before you go to see a new movie, you may read reviews to see if the film is a "bomb" or if it sounds like something you'd want to see. Before you decide what new music to buy, you may check out reviewers you trust whose responses are thoughtful and match your own taste. This is the same kind of critical thinking you want to apply to analyzing responses to literature, or literary criticism.

Analyzing a Response to a Literary Work

When you analyze a **response to a literary work,** you read what a critic says about a story, novel, poem, or play. You then analyze the critic's remarks, taking the response apart to see what it says and how it supports its main points.

Tips for Analyzing a Response to a Literary Work If you are asked to analyze a response to a literary work, here is what you do:

- First, read the response closely to see what the critic says. In general, what does the critic think of the work? Is the critic's response positive or negative—or a bit of both?

- Second, examine the critic's analysis of the elements of the work. On what specific elements in the text does the critic focus? How did those elements shape the critic's response? For example, does the critic think the plot is suspenseful, or that the plot is contrived? Does the critic think the characters are believable or not believable? Does the critic think the writer's characters are weak but the plot is strong, or that the story has too many descriptions and not enough action?

- Third, look to see if the critic offers specific examples from the text to support the literary response. If the critic says the plot and characters are unbelievable, how does he or she support this opinion?

Literary Response: Models and Analysis

Below is one critical response to the novel *Hatchet* by Gary Paulsen. (Another is on the next page.)

A Response to the Novel *Hatchet* by Gary Paulsen Notice that this critic focuses on the element of characterization:

> In this heart-stopping novel, Gary Paulsen uses many realistic details to bring the main character, Brian, to life. The boy's terror when he realizes the pilot has died and that he is on his own makes him not only believable but also sympathetic. The boy's grief over the divorce of his parents and his distress about a disturbing secret make him like many young people today. In the first chapter, the details describing Brian's reaction to the pilot's heart attack add realism to the story: He smells the gas emitted by the dying pilot, for example, and when he lands, he vomits. Many writers of books for young adults would steer away from such realistic details.

Resources

Chapter 8 Resources, Reading Focus Skill Builder, p. 4

PowerNotes, interactive lesson presentation with activities

Teacher One Stop™, on-level lesson plans and all print resources

Universal Access

EL English Learners/Struggling Readers
English for Academic Success Help students learn the academic terms in the Reading Skills Focus by linking the terms with their root words.

- Explain that the word *analysis* is from a Greek word meaning "to break up." *Analysis* is the noun form of the verb *analyze*. An analysis is an examination or a statement that summarizes the finding of such an examination. When you analyze, you break up something complex into its parts so that you can study it.

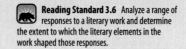

Reading Standard 3.6 Analyze a range of responses to a literary work and determine the extent to which the literary elements in the work shaped those responses.

Analysis of the Response This critic has a positive response to *Hatchet*. The critic focuses on the realistic portrayal of the main character. He supports his analysis by citing the boy's feelings about his parents' divorce and his profound upset over a "disturbing secret." The critic also mentions the realistic detail about the boy vomiting and his horror at the death of the pilot.

Another Response to *Hatchet* Another, longer response to the novel *Hatchet* follows. Notice that this response focuses on plot. Even though this critic's response to the novel is more negative than the first review, this review is well-supported and convincing. The writer finds fault with the book but still finds it entertaining.

Gary Paulsen's novel *Hatchet*, though entertaining and very exciting, contains some plot details that are not believable. One example is that the boy, Brian, lands a Cessna 406 airplane in the wilderness without ever having flown a plane before. A Cessna has sophisticated controls, and I did not believe for a minute that a terrified 13-year-old boy, with a dead pilot at the controls, could land the plane and survive. In addition, Brian has to land on water, and it seems contrived that a lake should suddenly appear just as the plane is running out of fuel.

The next unbelievable element in the plot is Brian's survival. He has never been in the Canadian wilderness before; he is a boy from the suburbs. Yet, with only a hatchet, he manages to survive hunger, sickness, injuries, wild animals, a tornado, insects, and psychological terror and loneliness for 54 days. How many real kids—or even adults— could do that?

The third unbelievable element of the plot is the rescue, which comes just before winter sets in. This is extremely fortunate timing, since Brian could not have survived winter in the wilderness. I thought the writer was being lazy and unimaginative with this "in the nick of time" plot device.

Despite these details, the novel is spellbinding, and it is difficult to put down. After all, most action movies today also contain unrealistic plot details—it seems to be something we expect in our entertainment.

Your Turn Analyze a Critical Response to Literature

Try your hand at analyzing a critical response to literature. Re-read the second response to *Hatchet*. As you read, fill out a chart like the one below to help you organize your thoughts. Then, write a short analysis (one or two paragraphs) of the response.

Analyzing a Critical Response to a Literary Work		
Elements on Which the Critic Focuses	Critic's Evaluation of the Elements	Textual Evidence for Critic's Response
1.	1.	1.
2.	2.	2.
3.	3.	3.

✳ **Learn It Online**
For more information on Gary Paulsen's *Hatchet*, visit *NovelWise*:
go.hrw.com H7-759 **Go**

Literary Response: Models and Analysis

Point out to students that the Analysis of the Response on p. 759 follows the Tips for Analyzing a Response to a Literary Work on p. 758. The first sentence states how the critic responds to the work, positively. The second sentence examines the critic's evaluation of an element of the work, characterization. The last two sentences point out the specific examples from the text that the critic provides to support his or her response.

Check for Understanding

Your Turn

Possible response: *The critic has a mixed response to the novel, claiming it to be unrealistic yet entertaining. The critic focuses on the unrealistic plot. He or she offers the examples of Brian's landing an airplane all by himself, Brian's ability to survive in the Canadian wilderness, and Brian's timely rescue before conditions worsened as support.*

Reteach

ThinkCentral Online Remediation

- Tell students that the word *critical* is the adjective form of the word *critic*. *Critic* comes from the Latin word *criticus*, which means "able to discern or judge." A critical response is a response that judges or evaluates. Explain that *critical* also carries a negative connotation: a critical person is someone who judges unfavorably. *Critical* is used in the Reading Skills Focus to mean "something that has been constructed by a critic" and remains a neutral word.

Students with Disabilities

To help students complete the Your Turn activity, have them assign one of three highlighter colors to each heading on the "Analyzing a Response to a Literary Work" (elements, evaluation, and evidence). Then, as students read and reread the second response to *Hatchet*, instruct them to highlight words and phrases that are connected to one of these three categories. This will help students recognize that there are three separate pieces of information that they are looking for as they analyze a response to literature.

✳ **Learn It Online**
The **NovelWise** mini-site includes instruction on choosing, reading, and analyzing novels; it also contains a catalogue of book summaries, study guides, teaching guides, and PowerPoint presentations.
go.hrw.com H7-759 **Go**

Reading Model

Objectives

Students will

- analyze a response to literature
- consider the influence of literary elements when responding to literature

Preteach

Read with a Purpose Direct students to the Read with a Purpose statement. Ask them to think about a situation in which a traveler knocks on a door but does not get a response from those inside. Ask them to record in their **Reader/Writer Notebooks** their thoughts about the listeners' and the Traveler's identities.

Direct Teach

Model the Skill

Use the Reading Model to demonstrate the application of the Literary and Reading skills in a short selection. As you or students read the model aloud, stop to discuss the side annotations and highlighting, which are aids to comprehension and analysis.

▶ Literary Focus

Plot and Setting How does the image in line 5 contribute to your interpretation of the setting of the poem? *Possible response: The bird makes me think of an eerie, still place where the only movement is a single bird.*

California Standards, pp. 760–764

- **Reading Standard 3.6** Analyze a range of responses to a literary work and determine the extent to which the literary elements in the work shaped those responses.

Build Background

The poet gives this poem the flavor of a fairy tale through his word choice. The word *turret* refers to a small tower on a castle. *Smote* is the past tense of *smite*, which means "to pound hard." *Hearkening* means "listening with attention." *Spake* is an old form of *spoke*.

According to one account, de la Mare was inspired to write "The Listeners" after he attended a class reunion to which no one else came. The empty school building inspired the eerie house in the poem.

Literary Focus

Plot and Setting Critical readers will see that the opening lines of the poem reveal the basic situation of a **plot**: A Traveler is knocking on a door at night. Various details of setting—the "moonlit door," the horse eating grass "in the silence" on the "forest's ferny floor"—establish a nighttime forest setting that is isolated and mysterious.

Read with a Purpose Read to see if you can come up with any answers to the mystery of the listeners and the reason for the Traveler's visit.

The Listeners

by **Walter de la Mare**

"Is there anybody there?" said the Traveler,
  Knocking on the moonlit door;
And his horse in the silence champed the grasses
  Of the forest's ferny floor;
5 And a bird flew up out of the turret,
  Above the Traveler's head:
And he smote upon the door again a second time;
  "Is there anybody there?" he said.
But no one descended to the Traveler;

Selection Readability	
Easily Accessible **Accessible** **Challenging**	unfamiliar characters; sophisticated language, abstract ideas

Selection Summary

The Listeners is a poem about a Traveler who fulfills his promise at a lonely, quiet house as mysterious "listeners" take note, but do not respond. A critical response to the poem follows.

Model the Skill

 Literary Focus

Point of View What images does the author use to characterize the "listeners" on the other side of the door? How do they influence your ideas about who the "listeners" may be? ***Possible response:*** *The author refers to these characters as "phantom listeners," which makes their presence eerie and uncertain. That they are alone in a dark and empty house adds to the sense of mystery. The author describes them listening "to that voice from the world of men," which makes me think that the "listeners" may be ghosts.*

10   No head from the leaf-fringed sill
     Leaned over and looked into his grey eyes,
       Where he stood perplexed and still.
       But only a host of phantom listeners
         That dwelt in the lone house then
15   Stood listening in the quiet of the moonlight
       To that voice from the world of men:
     Stood thronging the faint moonbeams on the dark stair
       That goes down to the empty hall,
     Hearkening in an air stirred and shaken
20   By the lonely Traveler's call.

Literary Focus

Point of View Critical readers will appreciate that, by using an **omniscient,** or "all-knowing," point of view, the poet is able to show us what lies on *both* sides of the door. By revealing that there are unseen "phantom listeners" in the quiet house, the poet increases the effect of eeriness and mystery.

Universal Access

EL English Learners/ Struggling Readers

English for Academic Success To help students understand the poem, introduce them to the following vocabulary words.

- champed—bit or gnashed. *The horse champed the grass as it waited for its rider to return.*

- descended—came nearer to the ground. *No one inside the house descended from the stairs to answer the Traveler's knocks.*

- host—large group. *The Traveler was aware that a host of beings listened from the other side of the door.*

- thronging—crowded into or filled a place. *The phantom listeners were thronging the quiet house as the Traveler knocked on the door.*

- aye—an affirmative vote; yes. *If asked if he had fulfilled his promise, the Traveler could confidently reply, "aye."*

- stirrup—a metal ring that hangs from a horse's saddle and supports the rider's foot. *The Traveler climbed into the horse's saddle and slid his foot into the stirrup.*

Literary Focus

Imagery and Mood In lines 21-24, does the Traveler know that the "listeners" are behind the door? How can you tell? ***Possible response:*** *The author suggests that the traveler knows that the listeners are there and can feel their presence.*

Literary Focus

Sound Effects What is the rhyme scheme of this poem? What technique does the author use when repeating the s sound in line 35? ***Possible response:*** *The rhyme scheme is ABCB. The author uses alliteration in line 35 with the repetition of the beginning consonant sound s.*

Check for Understanding

Read with a Purpose Ask students to use details from the poem to speculate on the identities of the "listeners" and the Traveler. ***Possible response:*** *I think the "listeners" are ghosts, or memories, because they are not able to respond to the Traveler. I think the Traveler is fulfilling his promise to not forget the ghosts by returning to the house where they reside. The poem is most effective when these questions are not answered because it can be interpreted by the reader to suit his or her imagination.*

Reading Model

Literary Focus

Imagery and Mood Critical readers will notice that the **images** in this poem—such as "the dark turf" and "starred and leafy sky"—are important in creating a lonely, otherworldly **mood** (the overall feeling of the work). Words like "strangeness" and "stillness" add to the eerie mood.

Literary Focus

Sound Effects Critical readers will appreciate one of the poem's strongest elements: its use of sound. **Rhyme, rhythm,** and **repetition** give the poem a hypnotic, dreamlike quality that is well-suited to the subject. The frequent repetition of ghostly, softly hissing s sounds, as in these concluding lines, echoes the eerie quiet of the phantom listeners. The sounds the horse and rider make in the final lines—"iron on stone" and "plunging hoofs"— contrast sharply with the silence, which once again takes over after the Traveler has gone.

And he felt in his heart their strangeness,
    Their stillness answering his cry,
While his horse moved, cropping the dark turf,
    'Neath the starred and leafy sky;
25 For he suddenly smote on the door, even
    Louder, and lifted his head—
"Tell them I came, and no one answered,
    That I kept my word," he said.
Never the least stir made the listeners,
30   Though every word he spake
Fell echoing through the shadowiness of the still house
    From the one man left awake:
Aye, they heard his foot upon the stirrup,
    And the sound of iron on stone,
35 And how the silence surged softly backward,
    When the plunging hoofs were gone.

Read with a Purpose Who do you think the "listeners" are? What do you think the Traveler's purpose was in visiting them? Explain whether you think the poem would have been more effective or less effective if the poet had told you these things outright.

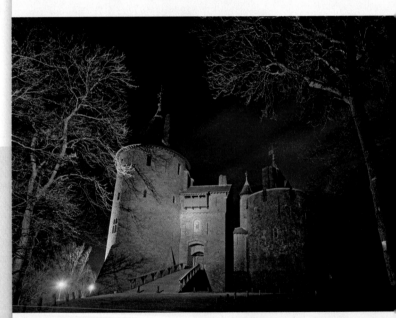

Cross-Curricular Connection

FINE ARTS: Film Criticism
Tell students that film criticism is the analysis and evaluation of films or motion pictures. Film critics work for newspapers, magazines, television shows, radio programs, and Web sites. Their reviews have the capability to influence people to see or not see movies.
Explain to students that film critics use many of the same criteria to judge films as literary critics use to judge literature. Movies have plots, characters, and themes, and some may also have imagery. Some other factors that film critics consider are cinematography, music and sound effects, and costuming.

Activity Have students work in groups to analyze a critical response to a film. They may use the library or the Internet to find a movie review. Then, instruct students to use the tips for analyzing a response to a literary work that they learned in the Reading Skills Focus on p. 758 to analyze the review.

A Critical Response to "The Listeners"

The bare-bones plot of the poem "The Listeners" is easy to describe: A man knocks three times at the door of a house in a forest at night. There are "listeners" inside, but they do not respond. After receiving no answer, the traveler mounts his horse and rides away. From these simple events Walter de la Mare created a poem of eerie mystery and haunting sounds that deserves its reputation as a classic.

The events described in the poem are related from two different perspectives: that of the Traveler and that of the "phantom listeners." The poet's use of an omniscient point of view allows us to see what happens on either side of the unopened door. The fact that the listeners not only hear the Traveler but are standing and "hearkening" suggests that they have been waiting for the Traveler. Like the Traveler, we are "perplexed" by their lack of response, and this mystery creates a sense of suspense. All we know for certain is that the Traveler is keeping a promise—and is therefore likely to be an honorable man—and that the listeners hear his call but do not (or cannot, or will not) offer a response.

The setting—a moonlit and starry night, a "leaf-fringed" house with dark stairs and an empty hall—contributes to the mystery. Imagery that would not be out of place in a ghost story—a "lone house" in which a "host of phantom listeners" stand "thronging the faint moonbeams"—creates a sense of otherworldly loneliness, sadness, and dread. Yet the imagery the poet creates is not limited to the visual. Sounds—and the contrast of sounds with silence—are especially important in creating the poem's atmosphere of supernatural mystery.

Throughout the poem, the poet's use of soft s sounds imitate the whispering and subtly sinister silence of the haunting setting. The Traveler's knocks and calls—his "voice from the world of men"—are the only things that break the increasingly eerie silence. The Traveler, "feeling in his heart their strangeness," tries one last time to get the listeners' attention with a loud knock, but then he gives up his quest: "Tell them I came, and no one answered,/That I kept my word." He has done what he said he would do and is eager, it seems, to depart. When he leaves, his mission unaccomplished, silence returns.

Reading Focus

Analyzing a Response to a Literary Work When reading literary criticism, look for evidence of the writer's overall response to the work. In the first paragraph, the critic reveals a favorable, or positive, response to "The Listeners." You should expect to find solid support for this positive response throughout the review.

Reading Focus

Analyzing a Response to a Literary Work The reviewer finds the poet's use of point of view important to an appreciation of the poem and explains why.

Reading Focus

Analyzing a Response to a Literary Work A good literary criticism will include textual evidence to support the critic's views. This reviewer cites specific lines from the poem to support points made about literary elements.

Reading Focus

Analyzing a Response to a Literary Work How does the critic react to the poems unanswered questions? **Possible response:** *The critic views them positively, referring to the author as cunning.*

Read with a Purpose Have students compare their response to the poem with the critic's response they have just read.

More about the Writer

Walter de la Mare's first book of poems, which he wrote under the pen name Walter Ramal, was published in 1902. The book, *Songs of Childhood*, was not very successful. He wrote two more overlooked books before he found acclaim with the publication of *The Listeners*, a collection that included the poem "The Listeners."

Think about the Writer

Ask students how their favorite authors are able to capture the feeling of being a child. What advice would they give to an adult writer who wanted to write a book for children about being a child?

For Independent Reading

If students are interested in mystery, recommend Ellen Raskin's *The Westing Game*. In this award-winning novel, a group of people must solve the mystery of a rich man's death.

 California Standards, p. 765

- **Reading Standard 3.6** Analyze a range of responses to a literary work and determine the extent to which the literary elements in the work shaped those responses.

Reading Focus

Analyzing a Response to a Literary Work In the last paragraph, the reviewer concludes with a positive response to the poem that acknowledges the poem's unanswered questions.

Like the Traveler, the reader is eventually overcome by the uneasy atmosphere of this place and the "strangeness" of the silent and unseen beings in the "still house." The poem begins and ends in mystery. What was the promise the Traveler made, and to whom? Why didn't the listeners answer? Who are the listeners? Cunningly, Walter de la Mare, like the listeners themselves, never answers.

Read with a Purpose Explain whether you and the reviewer agree on which elements most affected your responses to "The Listeners."

MEET THE WRITER

Walter de la Mare
(1873–1956)

Outwardly Ordinary, Inwardly Magical

Walter de la Mare, who created magical worlds in his poems, stories, and novels, did not outwardly live a magical life. He came from a well-off family and attended St. Paul's Cathedral Choir School in London. He left school when he was 16 and spent nearly twenty years working as a bookkeeper in the London office of an oil company.

During his working life, Walter de la Mare always took time to write, something he had done since his teens. He often read his new poems to his four children at bedtime. In 1908, a government pension enabled him to quit his job, move to the country, and write full time. For over forty years he published works for both adults and children that showed the high value he placed on the imagination.

"Whatever precisely a child may be, it is very unusual indeed for those who have become men to remember precisely what it was to be one; to become . . . in imagination, the children they actually once were."

Think About the Writer How might the ability to remember what one was like as a child show up in a writer's work?

Resources

Chapter 8 Resources, Literary and Academic Vocabulary Skill Builder, p. 5

UA: Differentiating Instruction, graphic organizer, p. 218

Teacher One Stop™, on-level lesson plans and all print resources

WordSharp: An Interactive Vocabulary Tutor, more practice with academic language

Academic Vocabulary

Writing About Analyzing Responses to Literature

English for Academic Success Write the following questions on the board. Tell students these are the kinds of questions they will encounter on standardized tests. Discuss the meaning of the words, then have students use "The Listeners" and *A Critical Response to "The Listeners"* to answer the questions.

- Which **element** of the poem does the critic analyze in the fourth paragraph of the critical response on p. 763? ***Possible***

Wrap Up

Reading Standard 3.6 Analyze a range of responses to a literary work and determine the extent to which the literary elements in the work shaped those responses.

Into Action: Analyzing Literary Criticism

Complete a chart like the one below to analyze "A Critical Response to 'The Listeners.'" Using a scale of 1 to 4 (1 = *not at all* and 4 = *very much*), rate the effect that each literary element had on the critical response. Then, explain your ratings, using details from the response to support your explanation.

Literary Element	Effect on Response (1–4)	Explanation of Rating
plot		
setting		
point of view		
imagery		
mood		
sound effects		

Talk About . . .

1. Discuss with your classmates what you might have included in a response to "The Listeners" that wasn't in the response you read. Try to use each Academic Vocabulary word listed on the right at least once in your discussion.

Write About . . .

Answer the following questions about "The Listeners" and the response. For definitions of the underlined words, see the column on the right.

2. How do you <u>interpret</u> the listeners' failure to answer the Traveler?

3. What <u>circumstances</u> might have led to the scene in the poem?

4. To what <u>extent</u> did <u>elements</u> in the poem shape the response?

Writing Focus
Think as a Reader/Writer

The Writing Skills Focus activities in Chapter 8 will guide you to examine the literary elements in several legends, create your own responses to the literature, and analyze other responses.

Academic Vocabulary for Chapter 8

Talking and Writing About Literary Criticism

Academic Vocabulary is the language you use to write and talk about literature. Use these words to discuss the literary works you read in this chapter. The words are underlined throughout the chapter.

circumstance (SUHR kuhm stans) *n.:* condition or fact. *Every circumstance of the character's life seemed unbelievable.*

element (EHL uh muhnt) *n.:* essential part of something. *The plot is a key element of any story.*

extent (ehk STEHNT) *n.:* degree to which something extends. *To the extent that a theme touches us, we can find deep truth in literature.*

interpret (ihn TUHR priht) *v.:* explain the meaning of. *Close, careful reading is essential when you interpret a poem.*

Your Turn

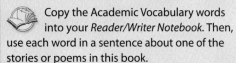 Copy the Academic Vocabulary words into your *Reader/Writer Notebook.* Then, use each word in a sentence about one of the stories or poems in this book.

Guided Practice: Apply
Into Action: Analyzing Literary Criticism

Model filling in the chart by rating the effect of plot on the response to the poem. You might say: "In the first sentence, the critic states that the plot is bare-bones, but does not elaborate on how this affects the poem. I will rate its effect as 1. The critic focuses on other elements."

Talk About . . .

1. Model for students how to use the academic vocabulary words. You might say: "The <u>element</u> of character contributes to the mystery of the poem. The lack of descriptions forces the reader to <u>interpret</u> the <u>circumstances</u> of the Traveler's arrival."

Write About . . .
Possible responses:

1. *I <u>interpret</u> that the listeners are unable to answer the Traveler because they are ghosts.*

2. *One possible <u>circumstance</u> is that the Traveler is responsible for the listeners becoming ghosts and is doomed to revisit them.*

3. *The <u>elements</u> of point of view, setting, and sounds influenced the response to a great <u>extent</u>.*

Writing Skills Focus

The Think as a Reader/Writer activities in the chapter focus on the reading-writing relationship. Use the activities to help students explore the writer's craft in a text and to practice this aspect of craft in their own writing.

Independent Practice

 Chapter 8 Resources, Skill Builders, pp. 3–5

UA: Differentiating Instruction, Academic and Selection Vocabulary Skill Builder, p. 235

UA: Differentiating Instruction, graphic organizer, p. 218

---

response: In the fourth paragraph, the critic analyzes the sounds of the poem, such as the repeated s, the knock on the door, and the silence surrounding the house.

• To what **extent** does the Traveler try to keep his promise in the poem? ***Possible response:*** *The Traveler knocks three times on the door, claiming that it is enough to fulfill his promise.*

• To what **circumstance** in the poem does the critic attribute his or her conclusion that the listeners are wait-

ing for the Traveler? ***Possible response:*** *The critic claims that the listeners are waiting for the Traveler based on the description of them standing and "harkening" in the poem.*

• How does the critic **interpret** the motivation for the Traveler's journey and the listeners' failure to respond in the poem? ***Possible response:*** *The critic suggests that the meeting has an "otherworldly" element, but does not offer a thorough interpretation of the characters' actions.*

LEGEND
Preparing to Read

KING ARTHUR
THE SWORD IN THE STONE

Retold by **Hudson Talbott**

What Do You Think What qualities should a modern-day hero have?

⏱ **QuickWrite**
A few people from recent history might become so famous that stories about them will be told for years to come. Record the names and deeds of some people who could be legends a hundred years from now. Why should their deeds be remembered?

King Arthur, 1903 by Charles Ernest Butler.

Selection Readability	
Easily Accessible **Accessible** Challenging	accessible vocabulary; selection provides background information; accessible theme

Selection Plot Summary

In this version of the legend of King Arthur, Merlin devises a plan to reveal the true heir to the British crown, who is not aware that he was adopted at a young age.

Reading Standard 3.6 Analyze a range of responses to a literary work and **determine the extent to which the literary elements in the work shaped** those **responses**.

Literary Skills Focus

Legend A **legend** is a very old story passed down from one generation to the next. Legends, unlike myths, usually have some connection to a real historical person or event. In a legend, historical facts are combined with imaginary, often fantastic, events. One of the most famous heroes of legend in Western literature is King Arthur, whose adventures have given rise to numerous tales called Arthurian legends. Arthur and his knights are the subject of many traditional stories, songs, and poems. Their exploits have also been recorded in plays, musicals, and operas; in numerous film adaptations; in dozens of modern novels, stories, and comic books; and even in stage and film spoofs.

Literary Perspectives Use the Analyzing Archetypes perspective described on page 769 as you read this story.

Reading Skills Focus

Tracking the Sequence of Events A **narrative** relates a sequence of connected events. When you read a narrative, such as this legend, it is most important that you remember its **sequence of events**. For example, if you were reading a detective story, you would want to remember that the suspect was seen buying a mask the day *after* the bank was robbed by three masked men.

Into Action As you read a narrative, track its main events in a chart like this one:

Merlin helps the king win Lady Igraine. → → → →

Writing Skills Focus
Think as a Reader/Writer

Find It in Your Reading As you read this legend, keep a critical eye out for how the author uses literary elements—such as plot, character, and setting—to make the legend engaging. Consider which literary elements most affect or shape your response to the work.

Vocabulary

turbulent (TUHR byuh luhnt) *adj.*: wild; disorderly. *King Arthur restored peace to a turbulent land.*

integrity (ihn TEHG ruh tee) *n.*: honesty; uprightness. *Sir Ector told his son to pursue his goals with integrity.*

composure (kuhm POH zhuhr) *n.*: calmness of mind. *Sir Ector took some deep breaths in order to regain his composure.*

revered (rih VIHRD) *v.*: regarded with deep respect and affection. *Merlin was revered by the entire kingdom.*

tumult (TOO muhlt) *n.*: uproar; noisy confusion, as in a crowd. *In the midst of the tumult, Arthur whispered thanks to his father.*

Language Coach

Word Families When you come across an unfamiliar word, look at the word closely to see if you can spot a familiar word within it. What verb, for example, can you find in the noun *composure*?

 Learn It Online
To hear a professional actor read this story, visit the selection online at:
go.hrw.com [H7-767] **Go**

Selection Resources

Chapter 8 Resources, on-level practice and assessment, p. 6

PowerNotes, interactive lesson presentation with activities

Teacher One Stop™, on-level lesson plans and all print resources

Holt Audio Library

Holt Audio Library: Selections and Summaries in Spanish

UA: Holt Interactive Reader, p. 204

Holt Interactive Reader for ELD, p. 237

Holt Audio Tutor for ELD

UA: Differentiating Instruction, modified lesson plans and leveled assessment, p. 219

UA: Resources for Teaching Advanced Students, lesson plans, p. 163

UA: Supporting Instruction in Five Languages, selection summary

ThinkCentral Online Assessment, Selection Standards Check

ThinkCentral Online Remediation

Preteach

Introducing Vocabulary
Have students match each vocabulary word to its antonym below.

1. agitation [*composure*]
2. dishonesty [*integrity*]
3. orderly [*turbulent*]
4. peace [*tumult*]
5. disliked [*revered*]

English for Academic Success
Language Coach
After students have determined that *composure* and *compose* are related, ask them about the relationship between the two words. [*Compose means "to put together." A person with composure has his or her thoughts put together.*]

Literary Skills Focus
As you read and discuss the selection with students, have them note the characteristics of legends.

Reading Skills Focus
Give students a copy of the Reading Skills Focus graphic organizer before they read. Tell them to use their responses to answer the questions on the Applying Your Skills page.

Writing Skills Focus
Have students record examples of literary elements that make the legend engaging in their **Reader/Writer Notebook.** Students can use their notes to complete the Writing Skills Focus activity.

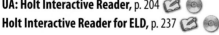 **Learn It Online**
The online version of this selection includes audio support to engage all students and to help struggling readers with reading comprehension and vocabulary.

go.hrw.com [H7-767] **Go**

Selection Introduction

More About the Writer

Hudson Talbott was raised in Louisville, Kentucky, but he has traveled and lived all over the world. Talbott went to art school in Rome, spent time in Amsterdam, and worked in the fashion industry in Hong Kong. Talbott considers his undertaking of compiling and illustrating a series of books that covers the extent of Arthurian legend to be his biggest and most challenging project. He has said that the process of researching Arthurian legend has been a journey of self-discovery.

Think About the Writer

Have students consider what lessons they can learn from stories about knights, kings, and other heroes. How can these lessons have a "lifetime effect" on the people who read them?

For Independent Reading

■ If students are interested in reading more stories about Merlin, suggest they read *Passager* by Jane Yolen. *Passager* is the first of three books by Yolen about the young Merlin.

■ Students may be interested in legends from other cultures. *The Lady of Guadalupe,* written and illustrated by Tomie dePaola, is a retelling of the legend of the patron saint of Mexico.

MEET THE WRITER

Hudson Talbott
(1949–   )

Time Traveler

The first successful series of books written and illustrated by Hudson Talbott featured a gang of time-traveling dinosaurs. *We're Back: A Dinosaur's Story,* the first of Talbott's dinosaur tales, was later adapted into a movie. Some of Talbott's readers, expecting more dinosaurs, may have been surprised by his next subject: King Arthur. Talbott says his travels through England and Wales inspired a love of history and legends:

> "Seemingly random occurrences in my own past— from collecting knights and horses as a child to my years in Europe wandering through castles and cathedrals—all began to make sense . . . and helped inspire this work."

A Lifetime Effect

Writing and illustrating books is Talbott's second career. He supported himself first as an artist and designer. He says that creating books for children is "more rewarding, more permanent" than anything else he has done. "After all, a good children's book can have a lifetime effect on people."

Think About the Writer — What kind of "lifetime effect" might the stories of King Arthur and his knights have had on Talbott?

Build Background

Although there is no proof that there was ever a "real" Arthur, some historians believe that the legendary figure may have been based on an actual military leader of a Celtic people called the Britons, somewhere around A.D. 500.

In the first century B.C., the Romans invaded Britain, and they ruled for about four hundred years. After the armies of Rome pulled out of Britain in A.D. 410, several peoples tried to seize control. According to legend, a leader named Arthur united the Britons and led them to victory against one of the invading European peoples, the Saxons.

After Arthur's death, the Saxons and the Angles, another European people, conquered the Britons, but stories about the warrior king's courage and goodness lived on.

For hundreds of years, minstrels traveled throughout Europe, singing stories about Arthur and his Knights of the Round Table. The legend became a series of stories about noble knights who rode out to do battle with evil wherever they found it.

Preview the Selection

Though there are many characters in this story, the two major players are **Merlin** the magician and **Arthur,** the boy who would become king. Arthur travels to London—and toward his destiny— with his adoptive father, **Sir Ector,** and brother, **Sir Kay.**

Real Issues, Real Experts

Holt author Kylene Beers offers strategies for helping students read strategically.

To help students find their way through difficult texts, I have them use the Say Something strategy. As they read, students occasionally stop and, with a reading partner, say something about the text in the form of a prediction, connection, question, summary, visualization, or inference. The partner responds and then students continue reading.

KING ARTHUR
THE SWORD IN THE STONE

Retold by **Hudson Talbott**

In ancient times, when Britain was still a wild and restless place, there lived a noble king named Uther. After many years of turmoil, Uther defeated the invading barbarians and drove them from the land. For this triumph, his fellow British lords proclaimed him their high king, or Pendragon, meaning "Dragon's Head."

Soon after his coronation, Uther Pendragon met and fell in love with the beautiful Lady Igraine,[1] a widow whose husband Uther had killed in battle. Uther married Igraine and adopted her two young daughters, Margaise and Morgan le Fay. The price for this love was a high one, however. In his passion, the king had asked for the help of his sorcerer, Merlin, in winning the hand of Lady Igraine. In return Uther had agreed to give up their firstborn son. Merlin had foreseen great evil descending upon the king and felt that he alone could protect a young heir in the dangerous times ahead.

Before long, a beautiful boy child was born. But the joy surrounding the birth was brief, for Merlin soon appeared to take the child away.

---

1. **Igraine** (ih GRAYN).

Literary Perspectives

The following perspective will help you think about literary elements in "King Arthur: The Sword in the Stone."

Analyzing Archetypes The word *archetype* (AHR kuh typ) means "original model." Story plots and structures as well as character types and themes can all be archetypes. Archetypes are found in a wide variety of works of art and literature from all periods, from children's stories to adult novels, from classical epics to contemporary movies, and even in computer games. Examples of archetypes include (1) the quest, in which a hero goes on a perilous journey in search of something of great value; (2) the coming-of-age story, in which a young person undergoes some trial in order to leave childhood and enter the adult world; (3) the loss-of-innocence story, in which a young person is changed through encounters with ignorance, evil, or loss; (4) the search-for-a-parent story; (5) the "lost paradise" story, in which something happens to bring about the end of a Golden Age; and (6) the story of death and rebirth. Archetypes evoke powerful responses from readers, perhaps because archetypal images are deeply rooted in our most basic wishes and fears. As you read, be sure to notice the questions in the text, which will guide you in using this perspective.

Direct Teach

Think About/Talk About

Read with a Purpose Have students read the Read with a Purpose statement. Have them predict which qualities will help Arthur become a hero and record these predictions in their **Reader/Writer Notebooks**.

▶ Extend the Discussion

Legend Which characteristics of a legend can you identify in the first paragraph of the selection? *Possible response: The selection is set in ancient times, which shows that it may be a very old story. The first paragraph also establishes a connection to historical fact through British history.*

Making Predictions Margaise and Morgan Le Fay will appear again later in the story. Will they be protagonists or antagonists? What support do you have for your prediction? *Possible response: I think that they will be antagonists. I have read other stories in which the stepsisters were antagonists, so I believe this may be a literary trend.*

Literary Perspectives

Before students read the selection, have them read the **Literary Perspectives** about Analyzing Archetypes. Tell students that the archetypes that appear in "King Arthur: The Sword in the Stone" appear in art and literature that they encounter every day. They may not even realize that they have encountered an archetype because they are so common that they do not stand out.

Have students work in small groups to find examples of the six archetypes listed in the Literary Perspectives. They may look at stories, music, movies, television shows, novels, comic books, and video games.

To extend or accelerate the activity, have students consider what character archetypes they have encountered. They probably expect to read about a hero in this story. Tell students that the hero is one character archetype, but that there are many more. In their groups, have students identify another character archetype and one work of art or literature in which this character archetype has emerged.

Model the Skill

■ Provide students with copies of the Reading Skills Focus graphic organizer for "King Arthur: The Sword in the Stone." (See **Chapter 8 Resources.**)

■ Tell students that this **narrative** transitions from the time surrounding the birth of King Uther's son and a period that begins sixteen years later. This transition occurs at the bottom of the first column on p. 770. Explain to students that keeping track of the **sequence of events** before and after this transition will help them make connections between characters and events.

■ Model filling in the graphic organizer with the events that occur before the transition in the story. You might say: "Because Merlin helped the king, the king promised to give up his first-born son. After this child is born, Merlin takes him away. I will write this event in the second space in my chart."

| "Merlin helps the King win Lady Igraine." | → | "Merlin takes the king's firstborn shortly after his birth." |

Guided Practice: Apply

Have students continue to fill in their charts with the sequence of events leading up to Merlin's plan to reveal the heir to the throne.

"But the child was just born!" exclaimed Uther. "How did you find out so quickly?"

Silently, the old sorcerer led the king to a balcony and pointed upward. There overhead was a great dragon formed by the stars. Its vast wings arched over the countryside, and its tail swept north beyond the horizon. "You see by this sign, my lord, that it is not I who calls for your son, but destiny." Ⓐ

Sadly, the king gave up his son, for Merlin convinced him that the child's great future was threatened. Indeed, Uther Pendragon died within a year from a traitor's poison and Britain was once again plunged into darkness. Ⓑ

After the death of the high king, the struggle for leadership tore Britain to pieces. The great alliance King Uther had forged was shattered into dozens of quarreling, petty kingdoms—leaving no united force to oppose foreign invasion. Barbarians swept in once again and order gave way to chaos. Marauding knights roamed the countryside, taking what they wanted and burning the rest. No one was safe at home, and travel was even more dangerous, with outlaws ruling the roads. Fear was a constant companion of those who managed to stay alive.

After sixteen **turbulent** years, the arch-bishop of Canterbury[2] summoned Merlin to help restore order. Although the two men were of different faiths, they had great respect for each other and shared much wisdom between them. Ⓒ

"I am at a loss, Sir Wizard!" confided the archbishop. "I don't know how to help the people, and they are suffering more each day. If only Uther Pendragon were here!"

"I share your concerns, my lord, but I have good news," said Merlin. "Although the end of King Uther's reign left us in the dark for many years, it is at last time for the sun to return to Britain. A brilliant sun, my lord. Perhaps the brightest that Britain will ever know."

"But the sun was out this morning, sire," said the archbishop. "What has the weather to do with this?"

"I speak of the son of Uther Pendragon, the true heir of royal blood who lives in a distant land and must now be summoned forth to keep his date with destiny." Ⓓ

"His date with who?" asked the archbishop. "But the king had no heirs! Alas, that is our problem!"

"I wish to prove otherwise, my lord," replied Merlin. "If I have your leave to use

---

2. **archbishop of Canterbury:** even today, the highest-ranking bishop of the Church of England.

Ⓐ **Literary Perspective** Analyzing Archetypes One archetype of hero stories is the appearance of a sign or omen, often a sign in the heavens indicating that the hero is favored by higher powers. What is the sign of Arthur's destiny in this story?

Ⓑ **Literary Focus** Legend What events so far could have really happened? Which details are clearly made up?

Vocabulary **turbulent** (TUHR byuh luhnt) *adj*: wild; disorderly.

Ⓒ **Literary Focus** Legend This paragraph mentions two men "of different faiths." Which of these men could have been a real person? Which one is likely to be entirely legendary?

Ⓓ **Read and Discuss** What two words that sound exactly alike have caused the archbishop's confusion? In what ways could the "son" also be the "sun"?

Universal Access

🄴🄻 English Learners

English for Academic Success Point to the second column on p. 770 in which the archbishop confuses the words *sun* and *son*. Tell students that these two words are homophones. Homophones are words that are pronounced the same but differ in meaning. Clarify for students common homophones (*their, they're, there; to, too, two; right, write; it's, its; your, you're; where, wear*) that may present challenges in reading comprehension and writing.

✔ See the English Language Skill Builder in **UA: Differentiating Instruction.**

my magic, I shall create an event to bring forth this young heir and prove to the world that he is the true and rightful high king of Britain."

The delighted archbishop agreed immediately, and Merlin withdrew to devise his scheme.

On a Sunday morning in late November the great cathedral of London was filled to capacity. As Mass was being said, a sudden murmur rippled through the crowd on the cathedral steps. Turning to see the cause of the commotion, the archbishop stopped in midprayer and walked toward the door. In the churchyard he discovered a block of white marble with an anvil[3] sitting on top. Driven into the anvil, gleaming in the pale winter sun, was a sword. Its blade was of flawless blue-white steel, and the hilt was of highly wrought gold, inlaid with rubies, sapphires, and emeralds. Engraved in the marble block were these words:

WHOSO PULLETH OUT THIS SWORD FROM THIS STONE AND ANVIL IS RIGHTWISE KING BORN OF ENGLAND.

Ah, so this is Merlin's plan! thought the archbishop, smiling to himself. A group of barons and knights suddenly pushed their way through the crowd, each stating loudly that he should be the first to try. A few managed to leap onto the stone and give the sword an unsuccessful yank before the archbishop stopped them.

"Order! Order!" he shouted, raising

Morgan le Fay: Queen of Avalon (detail) by Anthony Frederick Augustus Sandys (1829-1904).

---

3. **anvil** (AN vuhl): iron or steel block on which metal objects are hammered into shape.

E **Reading Focus** Tracking the Sequence of Events
What key events explain Merlin's words?

Think About/Talk About

▶ **Comprehension**

D **Read and Discuss**
Possible response: *The archbishop confuses son and sun. The son that Merlin speaks of could save Britain, which has been "plunged into darkness", much like the sun chases away darkness by bringing light.*

E **Reading Focus**
Possible response: *Merlin took the king's son in order to protect him. Now, Merlin has pledged to find him and bring him back to save Britain.*

▶ **Analysis**

A **Literary Perspectives**
Possible response: *The appearance of a dragon formed by the stars after his birth is a sign of Arthur's destiny.*

B **Literary Focus**
Possible response: *The king's marriage to Igraine and death by poison could have happened. His deal with Merlin and Merlin's prediction were made up.*

C **Literary Focus**
Possible response: *The archbishop is probably real. Merlin is legendary because he is a magical character.*

Vocabulary: Own the Word
turbulent: Explain that *turbulence* is the noun form of *turbulent*. Turbulence causes erratic movement and jolting. Have students demonstrate a *turbulent* ride while sitting at their desks.

Struggling Readers
Strategic Students To help students read "King Arthur: The Sword in the Stone," model tracking the sequence of events. You might say, "When I fill in my graphic organizer, I do not want to fill in more information than I need to see the sequence of events. In the paragraph that begins 'After the death of the high king,' I see that an important event is revealed. When I include this event in my chart, I will not include extraneous details such as the quarreling kingdoms. The important event that I will include in my chart is that Britain has fallen into darkness and turmoil."

✔ See **UA: Differentiating Instruction** for strategies for teaching struggling readers.

Advanced Learners
Enrichment Have small groups of students discuss the character of the archbishop. What character traits does the author reveal through the archbishop's conversation with Merlin? What archetype might the archbishop embody?

✔ See **UA: Resources for Teaching Advanced Students** for strategies for teaching advanced learners.

Model the Skill

- Tell students that words that are part of the same **word family** often vary in part of speech. Recognizing which suffixes mark certain parts of speech will help them understand which words are related to each other.

- Point to the last paragraph on p. 773. Write the selection word *congregation* on the board. Underline the ending *–ion*. Tell students that this ending is attached to verbs to turn them into nouns. *Congregation* is a noun, but removing the ending, *–ion*, reveals that it is a form of the verb *congregate*. Knowing this will help students identify the meaning of this unfamiliar word.

Guided Practice: Apply

Have students identify other nouns that end in *–ion*. Then, have them decipher the meanings of these words by identifying which verbs they were formed from. ***Possible responses:*** Action *comes from the verb* act; Satisfaction *comes from the verb* satisfy; Concentration *comes from the verb* concentrate.

Think as a Reader/Writer

Find It in Your Reading Point out that in the last paragraph on p. 773, the author describes the setting of the stadium where the tournament will take place. The author has combined historical facts about real stadiums of the past with ficticious elements to make the legend engaging.

Use It in Your Writing Have students write a description of a historic place, such as a theatre or home of the past. Then, have them incorporate fictitious elements to make the setting come alive.

---

his hands to quiet the crowd. "I hereby proclaim that on Christmas morning, one month from today, all those who consider themselves worthy of attempting to pull this sword from the stone and anvil will be given the opportunity. He who wins the sword, thereby wins the kingdom." **F**

A mighty roar of approval rose from the crowd. Some even danced and stomped their feet. Noticing how pleased they were, the archbishop went further. "And to celebrate this momentous occasion, a tournament shall be held on Christmas Eve."

With this, the delighted parishioners swept the flustered archbishop onto their shoulders and carried him jubilantly around the stone several times before setting him down. They hadn't had such cause for celebration in a long, long time.

To all parts of the kingdom, messengers rushed out, carrying the archbishop's proclamation. Every castle and village was alerted, from Sussex to Cornwall and, finally, to the dark forest of Wales. There lived a certain gentle knight by the name of Sir Ector Bonmaison[4] with his two sons. The elder was a handsome, robust youth, recently knighted and now known

---

4. **Bonmaison** (bohn may ZOHN): French for "good house."

F **Literary Perspective** Analyzing Archetypes Often, the archetypal hero must perform a fantastic deed to prove himself. What deed will Arthur have to perform to prove he is the rightful king?

"PURSUING ONE'S GOALS WITH INTEGRITY IS ALL THAT MATTERS."

---

as Sir Kay. The younger was a gentle blond lad of about sixteen whom Sir Ector and his wife had adopted as an infant. His name was Arthur. Although Arthur was not of his blood, Sir Ector loved both sons equally and devoted himself to their upbringing. **G**

Sir Kay was the first to hear the news of the great events in London, for as usual, he was in the courtyard polishing his helmet when the messenger arrived.

"A tournament! At last, a tournament!" he shouted. "We must set out for London at once! Father, you know what this means to me."

"Yes, son, I do," said Sir Ector, bringing the weary messenger a bowl of food. "I was young and hotblooded once, too, and eager to show the world my worthiness of knighthood. But this sword-pulling contest—do you wish to be king, as well?" he asked Kay with a smile.

"I make no pretense about that, sir. To prove myself on the field of battle is my dream."

"Please remember that, my son," said Sir Ector. "Pursuing one's goals with integrity is all that matters. Now go find Arthur so that we may prepare to leave. London is a long way off."

G **Reading Focus** Tracking the Sequence of Events What prior details explain the circumstances in Sir Ector's home in the dark forest of Wales?

Vocabulary **integrity** (ihn TEHG ruh tee) *n.:* honesty; uprightness.

Cross-Curricular Connection

HISTORY: The Medieval Tourney

Enrichment The Medieval tournament began as a brutal battle between knights in Europe. Those participating faced the possibility of losing their lives. Around the thirteenth century, a set of rules was created that dictated that the events abandon needless bloodshed and embrace sportsmanship and honor. Chivalry became an important part of the tournaments, where knights met to compete in such events as jousting. Often, the winner of an event was awarded with a valuable prize along with a kiss from a fair maiden.

Whole-Group Activity Have students research and report on one aspect of medieval tournaments. Some areas that students may focus on include the road to knighthood, a knight's attire, medieval tournaments, the ring tournament, the mock battle, the rules of jousting, and the occurrence of the sport of jousting today. Students may present their findings as a presentation to the class.

 HSS Analysis Skills: REP1, 4

Arthur had wandered off alone, as he often did after finishing his chores. He was as devoted as ever to being a good squire for his brother. But, after all, Kay was *Sir* Kay now, and he rarely had anything to say to his younger brother except to bark orders at him. Arthur didn't mind, though. He was happy just to watch Kay practice his jousting and to dream of someday riding beside him in battle. In the meantime, he had to content himself with his other companions—Lionel and Jasper, his dogs; Cosmo, his falcon; the orphaned fox cubs he kept hidden in the hollow log; and the deer that came to the edge of the woods when he whistled. He was in the woods now, patiently holding out a handful of oats for the deer, when Kay came bounding through the meadows to find him.

"Arthur, come quickly!" he shouted. "We're leaving for London at once! There's a big tournament. Here's your chance to show me what a good squire you can be! Hurry!"

Arthur stood silently for a moment. He had never been more than a few miles from his home. Was he daydreaming? Or was he really going to London to help Sir Kay bring honor and glory to their family as the whole world looked on? He ran back home, doubting his own ears until he reached the courtyard and saw Sir Ector preparing their horses for the journey.

All of Britain seemed to be making its way to London Town that Christmas. Kings and dukes, earls and barons, counts and countesses funneled into the city gates for the great contest. Sir Ector was pleased to see old friends and fellow knights. Sir Kay was eager to register for the jousting. And Arthur was simply dazzled by it all.

As Sir Ector and his sons made their way through the city streets, a glint of sunlight on steel caught Arthur's eye. How odd, he thought. A sword thrust point first into an anvil on top of a block of marble, sitting in a churchyard—surrounded by guards! London is so full of wonders!

Dawn arrived with a blare of trumpets, calling all contestants to the tournament. In Sir Ector's tent, Arthur buckled the chain mail[5] onto Sir Kay and slipped the tunic of the Bonmaison colors over his brother's head. Sir Ector stood and watched until the preparation was complete and his son stood before him in all his knightly glory. Silently they embraced, mounted their horses, and headed for the tournament grounds.

The stadium for the event was the grandest ever built. Never had there been such a huge congregation of lords and ladies in the history of England. The stands surrounded a great meadow, swept clean of all snow, with the combatants' tents at either end. In the central place of honor sat the archbishop. Patiently, he greeted each king and noble as they came forth to kiss his hand. "I should do this more often," he chuckled to himself.

---

5. **chain mail:** flexible armor made of thousands of tiny metal links.

H **Literary Perspective** Analyzing Archetypes The hero is often contrasted with another person, often an unworthy older brother. The hero may be an outsider, unaware of who his real parents are. How do Arthur and Sir Kay fit these archetypes?

I **Reading Focus** Tracking the Sequence of Events Does Arthur know the <u>circumstances</u> behind the sword's placement? Does he know about the writing on the marble? What earlier details answer these questions?

▶ **Comprehension**

G **Reading Focus**
Possible response: Merlin took Arthur away from his father, the king, and brought him to live with Sir Ector.

I **Reading Focus**
Possible response: Arthur marvels at the sword in the stone, but does not understand why it is there. He does not know the circumstances behind its placement or what is written upon the stone because he had wandered away prior to the messenger's arrival at his home.

▶ **Analysis**

F **Literary Perspectives**
Possible response: Arthur will have to pull a sword from an anvil and stone to prove that he is the rightful king.

H **Literary Perspectives**
Possible response: Arthur fits the archetype of the hero who does not know who his real parents are. He is also an outsider: his only friends are animals. Sir Kay is the unworthy older brother who thinks that he is better than Arthur because he has an important-sounding title.

Vocabulary: Own the Word
integrity: Ask students to think of personal examples of *integrity* that they have witnessed. *Possible response:* Returning money to a cashier who has given you too much change; refusing to cheat on a test.

Model the Skill

■ Tell students that Arthur is not the only character in this legend to appear in several stories. Some of the other characters make appearances in other legends. As is the case with many legends, these characters appear in several intertwined stories and situations, but retain the same characteristics and associations.

■ Tell students that Sir Kay appears later on in the Arthur legend as a knight serving King Arthur, one of the Knights of the Round Table. In later versions of the King Arthur legend, Kay develops a reputation for having a short temper and for manipulating the king to benefit himself. In one retelling of the King Arthur tale, Sir Kay joins Robin Hood, another legendary hero, on a special quest.

Guided Practice: Apply

■ **Think-Pair-Share** Explain to students that Sir Kay is not necessarily portrayed as a hot-head manipulator in this selection. Have students think about the qualities that Sir Kay does possess in this tale and whether they see any potential for him to become a manipulating, short-tempered knight.

■ Then, have students share their ideas with a partner. Partner groups should then share what they have discussed with the class.

The first event was the mock battle, or *mêlée*. The contestants were divided into two teams—the Reds and the Greens. Sir Kay was with the Reds, who gathered at the southern end of the field, while their opponents took the north. They all readied their lances and brought down their helmet visors in anticipation of combat. Everyone looked to the archbishop for a signal. Slowly, he raised his handkerchief, paused, and let it flutter to the ground. From either end of the field, the thunder of thousands of horse hooves rolled forward, shaking the earth, rattling the stands—louder and louder until a terrifying crash of metal split the air. A shower of splintered lances rained down in all directions. The audience gasped, and a few ladies fainted. Nothing had prepared them for this scale of violence.

Sir Kay performed admirably, for he charged ahead of his teammates and unseated two of the Greens. He was already winning accolades[6] as he wheeled his charger around to aid a fellow Red.

6. **accolades** (ak uh LAYDZ): words of praise.

Universal Access

 English Learners

English for Academic Success Review the definitions of the following selection words with students.

• visor: a hinged, metal part at the front of a helmet. Its purpose is to shield the eyes.

• lance: a long pointed spear with a metal point. Lances were used almost like swords, only they were longer and heavy than swords.

• ominously: threateningly.

Students with Disabilities

If students have trouble understanding the description of the mock

Richard II, King of England, presiding at a tournament, 1377–1379.

Think About/Talk About

▶ **Analysis**

ⓙ **Literary Focus**

Possible response: The description of the brutality of the event and the audience's reaction probably reflect what these tournaments were really like.

▶ **Extend the Discussion**

Motivation Read the description of the mock battle up to point J. What might have motivated these men to participate in such a violent sport?
Possible response: The men who participated in this sport might have been trying to prove that they were tough enough for real battle and to win the respect of their neighbors.

Sequence of Events What event follows Sir Kay's outstanding performance in the mock battle starting in the second column on p. 775?
Possible response: Sir Kay returns to his tent and asks Arthur to hand him his sword.

As the teams withdrew, they revealed a battleground strewn with fallen warriors, some struggling to rise under the weight of their armor, others lying ominously still. Bits and pieces of armor and broken lances littered the field. ⓙ

The next charge was to be undertaken with swords. Sir Kay was appointed captain of his team for having done so well in the first round. He trotted over to Arthur and handed down his lance.

"Kay! You were magnificent!" gushed Arthur, wiping down the steaming war horse. "You've brought great honor to our house this day!"

"I need my sword, Arthur," said Sir Kay, struggling to take his helmet off.

"Your sword, of course!" said Arthur brightly. He turned to get it, but then stopped suddenly. Where was the sword?

ⓙ **Literary Focus** **Legend** Which details probably reflect what tournaments were really like in the old days in Britain?

battle on pp. 774–775, have them work in groups to pantomime the action. As one student reads the description up until point J, the other students should carefully mime the knight's actions and the crowd's reactions.

✔ See **UA: Differentiating Instruction** for strategies for teaching students with disabilities.

AAVE **Students Who Use African American Vernacular English**

English for Academic Success Students may need extra practice pronouncing the consonant /r/ in consonant clusters. One of the characteristics of AAVE is an elision or omission of the /r/ sound in the words *through*, *throw*, and *brought*, as well as similar words. Write the following words on the board. Then, pronounce each word according to the conventions of formal English for students and have them repeat: *through, string, throw, strain, brought, price, broken, spray, thrive, strength.*

✔ For additional instruction and strategies, see **Holt Pronunciation Resources** and **ThinkCentral, Teacher Access**.

Model the Skill

- Tell students that keeping track of the **sequence of events** in a story will help them see which events in the story are connected and significant. The sequence of events is sometimes called the chain of events because the events are intertwined, like the links of a metal chain.

- Read aloud the paragraph on p. 776 that begins, "Hey, it's looser than I thought." Tell students that this event is connected to an earlier event in the story. Arthur has removed the sword from the stone that Merlin enchanted. An observant reader will realize that this means that Arthur is the true king of Britain. Failure to register this connection may have led to confusion or even dismissal of this event as unimportant.

Guided Practice: Apply

Guide students' attention to the second column on p. 777. Have students identify which event from earlier in the story is connected to Sir Ector's response to Arthur's achievement. *Possible response: Sir Ector knows that Arthur was not his natural son, and now he knows who Arthur's real parents are.*

AAVE Students Who Use African American Vernacular English

English for Academic Success Point out and write on the board the selection words *dropped* and *climbed*. Tell students that in informal English, many speakers often leave off the inflected ending *-ed*. Some speakers may also pronounce the ending *-ed* as /t/. Have students watch and listen as you demonstrate pronouncing the words *dropped* and *climbed*. Then, have them imitate you as they practice pronouncing *-ed*.

His eyes scanned the little tent with its collection of weaponry. Spear, halberd, mace, bludgeon[7]... but no sword.

"Excuse me, Kay," said Arthur, "could you use a battle axe?"

"Arthur, please! My sword!" said Sir Kay. "We haven't much time."

"Of course, Kay! But just a moment—I'll finish polishing it," said Arthur, slipping out through the slit in their tent. With one great leap, he landed on his pony's back and galloped madly through the deserted streets, rushing back to their camp.

"Sword. Sword. Where did I put that *sword*?" he muttered, desperately searching through the chests and bags. But to no avail.

How could this happen? he thought. Kay without a sword... and the whole world watching!

He paced back and forth, and then a thought struck him: Kay will not be without a sword today. I know where I can get one! **K**

A few minutes later, he trotted into the churchyard where the sword in the anvil stood on the marble block. There wasn't a guard in sight—even they had gone to the tourney. Quietly, he brought his pony up to the stone and tugged on the reins.

"OK, Blaze.... We'll just see if this sword can be unstuck," he whispered. He stretched out his arm until his fingers touched the hilt.

"Hey, it's looser than I thought.... Steady, Blaze! Steady, boy!" As the pony

---

7. **halberd** (HAL buhrd), **mace** (mays), **bludgeon** (BLUHJ uhn): weapons.

K Read and Discuss What is Arthur thinking here? What character traits is he demonstrating?

---

stepped back a few paces, the sword glided out of the anvil's grip, unbalancing Arthur. He regained his seat and looked down in wonder at the mighty blade in his hand. **L**

"This isn't just *any* sword.... Perhaps it's something the church provides for needy strangers. Yes, that must be it! Well, I'll return it after the tournament. Someone else may need it. Thank you, sword, for saving me," he said, pressing its cross to his lips. "Wait until Kay sees this!"

He flung his cloak around the great sword and drove his little horse back to the tournament with lightning speed.

By now, Sir Kay had dismounted and was rather chafed.[8]

"Arthur, where have you been?" he shouted. "You..."

He caught himself as Arthur dropped to one knee and opened the cloak.

"Your sword, my lord," Arthur said confidently. But his smile quickly disappeared when he saw Sir Kay's reaction. Frozen in place, his face white as milk, Sir Kay stared at the sword. Finally, he spoke.

"Where did you get this?" he asked Arthur, although he knew the answer.

Arthur confessed that he had searched in vain for Sir Kay's sword and had borrowed this one instead.

"Get Father at once, and tell no one of this!" said Sir Kay sternly.

Arthur thought he must be in terrible trouble. Surely he could return the sword without his father knowing. Why did Father

---

8. **chafed** (chayft): annoyed.

L Read and Discuss Remember Merlin's test. Interpret the significance of what has just happened.

Developing Oral Fluency

Use the second column on p. 776 and the first column on p. 777 to help students practice reading with appropriate inflection within complex text structures. Remind students to pause, emphasize words, or change their intonation based on punctuation.

Paired Activity Divide students into mixed ability teams of two. Model reading the first full paragraph of the second column on p. 776 using the punctuation to show proper intonation. For example, sentences that end with an exclamation point should have the connect intonation.

- Have one student read the first paragraph while his/her partner notes any words that are not read fluently. Have partners alternate this procedure until they complete all of the paragraphs.

- Have students share notes to review the terms they had difficulty reading fluently. Have students identify any patterns they experience, such as not using the proper inflection in sentences ending with question marks. Provide time for students to practice their recitations independently before allowing them a final opportunity to read with fluency.

have to be told? Nevertheless, he obeyed his brother and returned quickly with Sir Ector.

Sir Kay closed the curtains of the tent and opened the cloak, revealing the sword to his father.

Sir Ector gasped when he saw it. "How can this be?"

"Father, I am in possession of this sword," said Sir Kay nervously. "That is what matters. Therefore, I must be king of all Britain."

"But how came you by it, son?" asked Sir Ector.

"Well, sire, I needed a sword . . . and we couldn't find mine . . . so, I decided to use this one!" said Sir Kay. Beads of sweat formed on his brow.

"Very well, lad. You drew it out of the stone. I want to see you put it back. Let's go," said Sir Ector.

"But *I have the sword*!" said Sir Kay. "Isn't that enough?"

"No," replied Sir Ector, as he mounted his horse and headed toward the cathedral. Arthur rode close behind and, ever so slowly, Sir Kay mounted and followed.

The churchyard was still deserted when the three arrived. "Put the sword back in the anvil," said Sir Ector bluntly. "I must see it."

"Father, I . . ."

"Just do it, Kay, and you shall be king. If that's what you want." Sir Kay climbed onto the block. Sweat was now pouring off him. He raised the mighty sword over his head and plunged it downward. But the sharp point skidded across the surface of the anvil, causing Sir Kay to fall headfirst off the block.

"Now, son, tell me. How came you by this sword?" asked Sir Ector again.

"Arthur brought it to me," said Sir Kay, dusting himself off. "He *lost* my other one."

Suddenly a fear gripped Sir Ector's heart. "Arthur, my boy," he said quietly, "will you try it for us?"

"Certainly, Father," said Arthur, "but do we have to tell anyone about this? Can't we just . . ."

"Son, please," said Sir Ector solemnly. "If you can put the sword in that anvil, please do so now."

With a pounding heart, the lad took the sword from Sir Kay's hand and climbed slowly onto the block of marble. Raising it with both hands over his head, he thrust it downward, through the anvil, burying the point deep within the stone. Effortlessly he pulled it out again, glanced at his stunned father, and shoved the sword into the stone, even deeper this time.

Sir Ector shrieked and sank to his knees. His mouth moved, but no words came out. He put his hands together as in prayer. Silently, Sir Kay knelt and did the same.

"Father! What are you doing?" cried Arthur, leaping down from the stone.

"SIR ECTOR SHRIEKED AND SANK TO HIS KNEES."

M | Read and Discuss | What is Kay trying to do? How would you read aloud this scene with Sir Kay and his father?

Think About/Talk About

▶ **Comprehension**

K Read and Discuss

Possible response: Arthur is remembering the sword he saw in the anvil near the church. He is showing that he is a resourceful problem solver.

L Read and Discuss

Possible response: Arthur has easily pulled the sword out of the stone. This must mean that he is the rightful heir to the throne.

M Read and Discuss

Possible response: Kay is trying to argue that he is the rightful king because he was in possession of the sword. I would read Sir Kay's dialogue in a whiny voice. I would read his father's voice in a stern, calm voice.

▶ **Extend the Discussion**

Comparing and Contrasting Characters Compare how Arthur, the hero, and Sir Kay, the unworthy older brother, react to the sword.

Possible response: Arthur is humble and naïve about pulling the sword form the stone. Sir Kay grows greedy when he learns that Arthur has acquired the sword and attempts to reap the rewards of Arthur's actions.

Model the Skill

■ Tell students that a common error that people make in writing and in speaking is providing **unclear pronoun references**, especially when using the pronoun *it*.

■ Remind students that a pronoun is a word that stands in for a noun. *He, she, it, we,* and *they* are pronouns, and there are several more.

■ Read aloud the paragraph on p. 778 that begins "At this, Arthur broke into tears." Then, model identifying the word that the pronoun *it* refers to. You might say: "Here, *it* refers to an idea in the previous sentences, Arthur being king. If I rewrite the last sentence, replacing *it*, I would get a clear sentence: 'Not if being king means losing my father!' he sobbed.'"

■ Warn students to be careful when using pronouns in their own writing. If they suspect that they have made an unclear pronoun reference, they can use the replacement method you have just demonstrated to check that the pronoun reference is clear.

Guided Practice: Apply

Have students determine to what word the pronoun *it* refers in the following paragraph.

"You have a great destiny before you, Arthur. There's no use avoiding it," said Sir Ector.

Possible response: *It refers to Arthur's destiny.*

"Please! Get up! Get up! I don't understand!"

"Now I know!" sputtered Sir Ector, choking back tears. "Now I know who you are!"

"I'm your son, Father!" said the bewildered lad, crouching down by his father and putting his head to Sir Ector's chest.

After a few deep breaths, Sir Ector regained his composure. He smiled sadly down at Arthur and stroked his head.

"Fate would have it otherwise, my boy. Look there behind you." He pointed to the gold lettering on the marble block, which stated the purpose of the sword and the anvil.

Arthur sat in silence and stared at the words in the marble.

"Although you were adopted, I've loved you like my own child, Arthur," said Sir Ector softly. "But now I realize you have the blood of kings in you. To discover your birthright is the true reason we came to London. You are now our king and we your faithful servants."

At this, Arthur broke into tears. "I don't want to be king. Not if it means losing my father!" he sobbed.

"You have a great destiny before you, Arthur. There's no use avoiding it," said Sir Ector.

Arthur wiped his eyes with his sleeve. He straightened up so he could look Sir Ector in the eyes. A few minutes passed.

"Very well," Arthur finally said slowly.

"Whatever my destiny may be, I am willing to accept it. But I still need you with me." Ⓝ

"Then so it shall be, lad. So it shall be," said Sir Ector.

They sat quietly for a time, comforting each other, until they felt another presence. From across the yard a hooded figure quietly floated into the fading light of the winter afternoon and knelt down beside them.

"Merlin," said Sir Ector, bowing his head to the famous enchanter.

"I've been waiting for you, Arthur," said the wizard.

"You know me, my lord?" asked Arthur.

"I put you in this good man's care many years ago and have kept an eye on you ever since."

"How did you do that, sire? We live far from here."

"Oh, I have my ways," replied Merlin. "But you still managed to surprise me. The sword-pulling contest isn't until tomorrow, and you pulled it out today!" he said with a chuckle.

"But what is to become of me now?" asked Arthur.

"Well, let us start with tomorrow," replied the old sorcerer. "We must still have the contest to prove to the world that you are the rightful heir. I will come for you when the time is right."

"But after that, sire, what is my future?" asked the boy.

Merlin weighed this question carefully. He wasn't at all sure whether the boy was

Ⓝ **Literary Focus** Legend The great heroes of legend are often reluctant to accept their fate. Often they are modest and humble. How does Arthur show that he is not ambitious to be king? How is this unlike Sir Kay?

Vocabulary **composure** (kuhm POH zhuhr) *adj.:* calmness of mind.

Universal Access

Struggling Readers

Strategic Learners To help students identify the heroic qualities that Arthur possesses, have them contrast Arthur with a non-heroic character. You could ask: "How does Arthur react when he learns that he is king? What characteristic does his reaction show? How do you think Sir Kay would have reacted to the news of learning that he was king? What characteristic would his reaction show?" **Possible responses:** *Arthur reacts with hesitance, which shows that he is modest and humble. Sir Kay would react with pride because he is vain.*

Advanced Learners

Acceleration Tell students that Merlin represents a character archetype: the wise mentor. Have students create a web to which they add traits that they attribute to Merlin and the archetype that he fulfills. Then, have students use this web to think of two other characters in literature that also fulfill this archetype. **Possible responses:** *Merlin protects Arthur, has wisdom, and knows what the future holds.* Dumbledore from the Harry Potter *series,* Charlotte *in* Charlotte's Web, Gandalf *in the* Lord of the Rings *series.*

Analyzing Visuals

Connecting to the Text
How closely does this illustration match your image of Arthur as he pulls the sword from the stone?

Arthur draws the sword. Illustration by Walter Crane.

prepared for his answer. Finally, he spoke. "I can tell you only what my powers suggest—and they point to greatness. Greatness surrounds you like a golden cloak. Your achievements could inspire humankind for centuries to come. But you alone can fulfill this destiny and then only if you wish it. You own your future. You alone."

Arthur breathed deeply and cast his eyes downward. He thought of all the goodbyes he would have to say. He thought of his fishing hole, and the birds that ate seeds from his hand. He thought of the deer that came when he called them.

"What time tomorrow, sire?" he asked.

After all have tried and failed, whenever that may be," replied Merlin.

"I will be ready, sire," said Arthur. Then he rose, bade Merlin farewell, and silently returned to his tent.

On Christmas morning, the archbishop said Mass for the largest gathering he had seen in years. The grounds surrounding the cathedral were also filled—with those seek-

Think About/Talk About

▶ Analysis

 Literary Focus
Possible response: *Arthur accepts that his destiny is to serve as the king of Britain, and asks his father to stay by his side. Sir Kay tried to take the title dishonestly.*

▶ Extend the Discussion

Characterization Arthur is a modest and humble character, but he does have some negative character traits. Read paragraph 7 on p. 778 and identify one negative trait that Arthur possesses. ***Possible response:*** *Arthur is young and afraid to accept his destiny as king. He may also be afraid to leave his father.*

Vocabulary: Own the Word

composure: Demonstrate for students how a person who has *composure* looks and acts [*calmly, serenely*]. Select one or two students to also demonstrate from their seats. Then, ask students to demonstrate the opposite of *composure* from their seats. [*Students should appear stressed, upset, or angry.*]

Analyzing Visuals

Connecting to the Text: *The illustration matches my image of Arthur because he looks like he is in a state of deep concentration as he pulls the sword from the stone.*

Model the Skill

■ Tell students that one archetype that appears in this legend is that of an ordinary person suddenly coming into immense power. Like other archetypes, this one spans the literary tradition, popping up in novels, short stories, legends, and plays, and more recently, films, music, and video games.

■ Point out that in this legend, Arthur comes into power by finding out that he is the true heir to the throne of Britain. In the scene described on p. 781, Arthur discloses his newly acquired title to the townspeople. This event will change his life; he will no longer be a simple squire to his brother. In other stories, this great turn of power can come about through the discovery of a great treasure or the revelation of an unknown identity.

Guided Practice: Apply

■ Archetypes survive and reappear because they evoke a powerful response in readers. Have students discuss in small groups why the archetype of suddenly coming into power and being transformed from a nobody into a somebody is so popular with readers. Why would someone want to read about a person who experiences this transformation?

■ Have students make a llist of other examples of transformation from literature or popular media.

ing to make history or watch it being made. As soon as the service ended, those who wished to try for the throne formed a line next to the marble block.

Leading the line was King Urien of Gore, husband to Margaise, Uther Pendragon's adoptive daughter. Ever since the high king's death, Urien had claimed loudly that he was the rightful heir. Indeed, he took his position on the marble block with a great sense of authority and gave the sword a confident tug, then another, and another. Urien was sweating and yanking furiously when finally asked to step down.

Next came King Lot of Orkney, husband to Morgan le Fay. King Lot felt certain that his wife's magical powers would assure his victory. But pull and tug as he might, he couldn't move the sword. After that, King Mark of Cornwall, King Leodegrance of Cameliard, and King Ryence of North Wales all took their place on the stone—and failed. The dukes of Winchester, Colchester, Worcester, and Hamcester did not fare any better. Some thought the longer they waited, the looser the sword would become, thereby improving their chances. But this wasn't the case, for the sword never budged, not even slightly. Kings, dukes, earls, counts, and knights all left that marble block empty-handed. Finally, as the day waned and the line neared its end, the

> THE BLADE FLASHED LIKE LIGHTNING AS HE SWUNG IT AROUND HIS HEAD FOR ALL TO SEE.

Ⓞ **Read and Discuss** Describe what you visualize happening in this famous scene, when the ambitious nobles try their hands at the sword.

crowd grew impatient for a winner. Merlin went for Arthur. **Ⓞ**

Sir Ector and Sir Kay opened the curtains of their tent when they saw Merlin approaching.

"Your hour has come, my lord," said the old wizard to Arthur, who was standing alone in the center of the tent. Silently, the boy walked forth as one in a dream.

The crowd made way for them as they entered, for Merlin was still revered by all. But who could these other people be? Especially that young blond lad dressed all in red. What was he doing here?

Merlin brought Arthur before the archbishop and bowed deeply. Arthur dropped to one knee.

"My lord," said Merlin, "I present to you a most worthy candidate for this contest. Has he your permission to attempt to pull yonder sword from the stone?"

The archbishop gazed down at the handsome lad. "Merlin, we are not familiar with this youth, nor with his credentials. By what right does he come to this place?"

"By the greatest right, my lord," said Merlin. "For this is the trueborn son of King Uther Pendragon and Queen Igraine."

The crowd broke into a loud clamor at hearing this. The startled archbishop raised his hands, but order was not easily restored.

"Merlin, have you proof of this?" asked

Vocabulary **revered** (rih VIHRD) *v.:* regarded with deep respect and affection.

Word-Attack Skills Mini-Lesson

Stressed syllables and the suffix *–tion*

Write the selection word *population* and the base word *populate* on the chalkboard. Compare the pronunciations of the two words. Help students recognize that the stress pattern changes when the suffix *–tion* is added to *populate*. The third syllable, which is unstressed in *populate*, becomes a stressed syllable in *population*. The first syllable, meanwhile, is less stressed in *population* than it is in *populate*.

Tell students that stress also shifts when the suffix *–tion* is added to the base word *prepare*. In *prepare*, the second syllable is stressed, but in *preparation*, it is unstressed.

the archbishop.

"With your permission, sire," blurted Arthur suddenly, "perhaps I can prove it by handling yonder sword in the anvil."

"Very well then, lad," said the archbishop, admiring Arthur's youthful boldness. "You have my permission. If what Merlin says is true, may God be with you."

Arthur rose and stepped up onto the marble block. He grabbed hold of the mighty golden hilt with both hands. A surge of sparkling warmth traveled up his arms, across his shoulders, and throughout his body. With one mighty tug, he freed the sword from the anvil and lifted it heavenward. The blade flashed like lightning as he swung it around his head for all to see. Then, turning the point downward again, he drove it back into the anvil with equal ease.

The entire gathering stood dumbstruck for a long moment, trying to comprehend what they had just seen. Arthur looked about for reassurance. He looked to Sir Ector, then Merlin, and then the archbishop. They all simply stared at him, with eyes wide in amazement. A child giggled and clapped his hands in glee, then so did another, and another. Cheers began to ring out as people found their voices again. Suddenly, a thunder of shouting and clapping rose up around Arthur. Amidst the tumult, he closed his eyes and whispered, "Thank you, Father." **P**

Then he grabbed the sword's hilt for a second time and withdrew it. As he brought it above his head, a thousand swords throughout the crowd were raised in solidarity. Arthur drove the sword back into the anvil and pulled it out once again. This time, as he lifted the great blade to the sky, more swords and halberds were raised, along with brooms, rakes, and walking sticks, as counts and common folk alike saluted their newfound king.

Not everyone was overjoyed at this turn of events, however. Although all had seen the miracle performed, several kings and dukes were unwilling to recognize Arthur's right to the throne. Loudest among the grumblers were King Lot and King Urien, Arthur's brothers-in-law. "How dare this beardless, unknown country boy think he can be made high king to rule over us!" they said. "Obviously, Merlin is using the boy to promote himself!"

But these malcontents[9] gained no support from those around them and were quickly shouted down. So they gathered themselves together and stormed away in a huff of indignation.

To everyone else, the day belonged to Arthur. All the other kings and nobles rushed forth to show their acceptance, for they trusted Merlin and were grateful to

---

9. **malcontents** (MAL kuhn tehnts): discontented or unhappy people.

P **Literary Focus** Legend Often, heroes of legend are very young and seem too ordinary to be real heroes. How does Arthur fit this pattern? How does Arthur continue to show his humility even though he has just done something amazing?

Q **Literary Perspective** Analyzing Archetypes Ambitious, power-hungry rivals to the hero are common in legends. How do King Lot and King Urien fit this archetype? In what ways is Arthur different from them?

Vocabulary **tumult** (TOO muhlt) *n.*: uproar; noisy confusion.

Repeat the procedure with *attraction* and *attract*. Help students recognize that the stress pattern does not change in these words. The second syllable has the greatest stress in both words.

Activity Have volunteers read these pairs of words and tell if the stress shifts when the suffix is added. Using these words, encourage students to make a generalization about when stress shifts and when it doesn't.

1. explore — exploration [*shift*]
2. exhaust — exhaustion
3. complete — completion
4. invite — invitation [*shift*]
5. inspire — inspiration [*shift*]
6. combine — combination [*shift*]
7. pollute — pollution
8. reserve — reservation [*shift*]

Think About/Talk About

▶ Comprehension

Q **Read and Discuss**

Possible response: *I visualize many strong, important-looking men trying with all of their strength to pull a sword out of an anvil and all of them failing.*

▶ Analysis

P **Literary Focus**

Possible response: *Arthur is a young boy and the crowd is stunned to see that he is able to pull the sword from the stone. Arthur shows that he is still humble despite his amazing feat by offering his gratitude.*

Q **Literary Perspectives**

Possible response: *King Lot and King Urien object to Arthur's right to the throne. Arthur is different from them because he accepts fate instead of questioning it.*

Vocabulary: Own the Word

- **revered:** Ask students to identify one person that they *revere*. Why do they *revere* this person? ***Possible response:*** *I revere my coach because she inspires me to push myself farther without making me feel disappointed about my athletic ability.*

- **tumult:** Tell students that a synonym for *tumult* is *commotion*. An antonym is *peace*. Then, use both words in a sentence. You might say: "*Tumult* in the classroom makes learning difficult; an environment of *peace* is the best setting for optimal learning." Invite students to construct their own sentences.

Think About/Talk About

▶ **Comprehension**

Ⓡ Read and Discuss

Possible response: *The king is crowned in the church by the archbishop, which shows that the king and the Church are closely tied. Historical documents or images that recorded the coronation ceremony would support or dismiss the historical accuracy of this practice.*

▶ **Extend the Discussion**

Analyzing Symbols In the first full paragraph of column 2 on p. 782, the author shares that Arthur's coronation took place on May Day. What symbolic meaning may the timing of the coronation signal? **Possible response:** *Arthur's coronation takes place in the spring, which is a time of rebirth. This signals that Arthur's reign will be a time of rejuvenation for Britain.*

Monitor Students' Comprehension

Guide students in answering these comprehension questions.

1. Who is the hero of this legend? [*Arthur, the true heir to the British crown, is the hero of this legend.*]

2. Why does Arthur pull the sword from the stone the first time? [*Arthur tries to borrow the sword to give to Sir Kay after he cannot find Sir Kay's sword.*]

3. Why is Merlin worried about King Lot and King Urien? [*These two men are the husbands of Uther's daughters. They believe that they should be king and do not accept Arthur as their king.*]

---

have a leader at last. They hoisted the young king-to-be above their heads to parade him through the streets of London.

As the noisy procession flowed out of the churchyard, the archbishop hobbled over to Merlin to offer congratulations for a successful plan.

"Thank you, my lord, but I think we are not yet finished," said the wizard.

The archbishop looked puzzled.

"I fear that King Lot and King Urien and those other discontented souls will leave us no peace until they have another chance at the sword," continued Merlin. "We must offer them a new trial on New Year's Day."

And so they did. But again, no one could budge the sword but Arthur. These same troublesome kings and dukes still refused to acknowledge his victory, though. So another trial took place on Candlemas,[10] and yet another on Easter.

By now, the people had grown impatient, for they had believed in Arthur all along and had grown to love him. The idea of having a fresh young king inspired hope and optimism. The world suddenly felt young again.

Finally, after the trial held on Pentecost,[11] they cried out, "Enough! Arthur has proven himself five times now!

---

10. **Candlemas** (KAN duhl muhs): Christian feast celebrated on February 2, on which candles are blessed for the year.

11. **Pentecost** (PEHN tuh kawst): Christian feast held on the seventh Sunday after Easter, traditionally thought of as the "birthday" of the Christian Church.

Ⓡ Read and Discuss What details in the story show a close relationship between the Church and the king? How would you check to see if this is historically accurate?

We will have him for our king—and no other!"

The archbishop and Merlin agreed. There was proof beyond dispute at this point. So the coronation was set for May Day in the great cathedral of London.

Upon arriving that morning, Arthur stepped up on the block and pulled the sword from the anvil for the last time. With the blade pointing heavenward, he entered the church, walked solemnly down the central aisle, and laid the sword upon the altar. The archbishop administered the holy sacraments[12] and finally placed the crown upon Arthur's head.   Ⓡ

Ten thousand cheers burst forth as the young king emerged from the cathedral. At Merlin's suggestion, Arthur stepped up on the marble block to speak to the people. A hush fell over the masses as he raised his hands to address them.

"People of Britain, we are now one. And so shall we remain as long as there is a breath in my body. My faith in your courage and wisdom is boundless. I ask now for your faith in me. In your trust I shall find my strength. For your good I dedicate my life. May this sword lead us to our destiny."

---

12. **sacraments:** here, Holy Communion.

🐻 **California Standards, pp. 783–785**

■ **Reading Standard 3.6** Analyze a range of responses to a literary work and determine the extent to which the literary elements in the work shaped those responses.

■ **Reading Standard 1.2** Use knowledge of Greek, Latin, and Anglo-Saxon roots and affixes to understand content-area vocabulary.

Universal Access

Struggling Writers

To complete the Writing Skills Focus, provide additional scaffolding to students by having them complete the following sentence starters.

• I enjoyed/ did not enjoy the story because _____.

• I felt that the plot was _____.

• I felt that the characters were _____.

• I felt that the theme was _____.

• I felt that the literary element was/were _____.

Applying Your Skills

Reading Standard 3.6 Analyze a range of responses to a literary work and **determine the extent to which the literary elements in the work shaped** those **responses**.

King Arthur: The Sword in the Stone
Literary Response and Analysis

Reading Skills Focus
Quick Check

1. Why does Uther give the baby to Merlin?
2. Why does Merlin want the baby?
3. How does Arthur prove he is the rightful king?

Read with a Purpose

4. What heroic qualities does Arthur display? Support your answer with examples from the text.

Reading Skills: Tracking the Sequence of Events

5. With a group, compare the charts you made as you tracked the sequence of events in the legend. Is your sequence correct? Now, circle events that you think are most important in the plot. Compare your key events with those identified by others.

Literary Skills Focus
Literary Analysis

6. **Interpret** How does Arthur change during the story?

7. **Analyze** What evidence suggests that Arthur will be a great king? How does Sir Kay, Arthur's foster brother, show that he doesn't have what it takes to be king?

8. **Literary Perspective** The chart in the next column shows the pattern of an archetypal hero tale. How closely does Arthur's story fit this pattern? Fill out the chart and see.

Archetypal Hero's Story	Arthur's Story
Threatened as an infant or child	
Raised in obscurity	
Parentage unknown or mysterious	
Unlikely person to be hero	
Passes test to prove greatness	
Will save a people in danger	

Literary Skills: Legend

9. **Identify** Identify two events in this legend that could have happened in real life, and two fantastic events that could not.

10. **Analyze** To what extent does the setting of "King Arthur: The Sword in the Stone" affect your response to the legend? Explain.

Literary Skills Review: Foreshadowing

11. **Predict** What details in the story foreshadow trouble ahead for Arthur? What kind of troubles might he face?

Writing Skills Focus
Think as a Reader/Writer

Use It in Your Writing Which literary elements in this story most affected your response to the story—the plot, the characters, the theme, or something else? Choose one element and briefly explain how it helped to shape your response to the legend.

What Do You Think Now How are modern-day heroes similar to Arthur? How are they different? Review your Quick-Write response for ideas.

Then, have students determine which literary element most affected whether they did or did not enjoy the story and why.

Model this process for students by providing them with the following complete sentences and analysis.

- I enjoyed the story because the message was universal and positive.
- I felt that the plot was too complicated.

- I felt that the characters were unrealistic because they one of them was magical.
- I felt that the theme was timeless and applied to my own life.
- I felt that the setting was very realistic.

The theme most affected my enjoyment of the story because I felt that it was timeless and universal.

Independent Practice
Reading Skills Focus
Answers:

1. *Uther promised to give up his first-born son in exchange for Merlin's help winning Igraine's heart.*
2. *Merlin foresees danger and wants to protect him.*
3. *Arthur proves he is the rightful king by pulling the sword from the stone.*
4. *Arthur is loyal; he pledges to keep Sir Ector by his side after he discovers that he is king. Arthur is humble; he hesitates to accept that he is the true heir to the throne.*
5. *The key events are Merlin placing Arthur with Sir Ector, Merlin designing the contest to find the true heir, and Arthur pulling the sword from the stone.*

Literary Skills Focus
Possible responses:

6. *Arthur changes from an ordinary boy to a king.*
7. *Arthur's modesty and loyalty show that he will make a great king. Sir Kay is greedy and conniving, which are not the traits of a great king.*
8. *There are events that match each of the steps in the pattern, except for the last one, "Will save a people in danger." Arthur has yet to save his people.*
9. *A king could have been raised in obscurity and a king of Britain could have been poisoned. Merlin's power to foresee the future and Arthur's ability to pull a sword out of an anvil are fantasy.*
10. *The realistic setting makes the story believable.*
11. *King Lot and King Urien's reluctance to accept Arthur as their king foreshadows trouble for Arthur. They may turn against him and force him into battle.*

What Do You Think Now?
Remind students that modern-day heroes may exhibit the qualities of a king without being royalty.

Independent Practice
Vocabulary Development
Your Turn _____

1. **turbulent** from Middle French *turbulent* (12c.)

2. **integrity** from Old French *integrité*

3. **composure** from Old French *composer* "put together, arrange" (12c.)

4. **revere** from Latin *revereri* "to revere"

5. **tumult** from Old French *tumulte* (12c.)

English for Academic Success
Language Coach

Tell students that each of the nouns ends in *–ion*. This should signal to them that dropping the *–ion* from the words will help them find the verb on which the noun is built.

1. congregation, congregate

2. celebration, celebrate

3. proclamation, proclaim

4. dedication, dedicate

English for Academic Success
Academic Vocabulary

Possible response: <u>*Circumstances*</u> *such as being raised as a commoner and not knowing that he was heir to the throne have prepared Arthur to be king. As a result of these* <u>*circumstances*</u>*, Arthur is humble and grateful, which are noble traits.*

Applying Your Skills

Reading Standard 1.2 Use knowledge of Greek, Latin, and Anglo-Saxon roots and affixes to understand content-area vocabulary.

King Arthur: The Sword in the Stone

Vocabulary Development
Word Origins

Anglo-Saxon: Plain Words You've learned that after Arthur's death, the Angles and Saxons conquered the Britons, or Celts. At that point, Anglo-Saxon words began coming into the language we now call English. English words derived from Anglo-Saxon tend to be short, one-syllable words, many of them having to do with rural life and farming:

    sheep   pig   cow   earth   dog   work

Think of Anglo-Saxon as being the source of "salt of the earth" words: simple, humble vocabulary.

The French Influence: Fancy Words In 1066, long after Arthur's time, the Norman-French conquered Britain. Some of the longer, "fancier" words in the English that we speak today are words that were once French. In the opening sentence of "King Arthur: The Sword in the Stone," you read the word *ancient*, which comes from the French word *ancien*. The root of *ancient* comes from the Latin *ante*, meaning "before." The Anglo-Saxon word meaning the same thing is a very different word, short and simple: *old*.

French words that were absorbed into English often referred to court life, the law, or the church, because in the past the French controlled all these institutions. *Attorney, nobility, religion,* and *government* are all from the French language.

Your Turn _____

Use a dictionary to look up the origin and history, or **etymology** (eht uh MAHL uh jee), of each of the Vocabulary words from the word list. In most dictionaries you

| turbulent |
| integrity |
| composure |
| revere |
| tumult |

will find brackets that contain information about the word's etymology. For words from Anglo-Saxon, you'll find the abbreviations [ME], [AS], or [OE], standing for Middle English, Anglo-Saxon, and Old English. For words from Latin or French, you'll find the abbreviations [L] and [Fr].

Language Coach

Word Families When you come across a difficult word, look to see if a more familiar form of the word is found within the longer word. In each of the nouns at right, you can find a verb. On what verb is each noun built?

| congregation |
| celebration |
| proclamation |
| dedication |

Academic Vocabulary

Talk About . . .

What literary <u>elements</u> most affected your response to this tale of Arthur's beginnings? Discuss with a partner.

Universal Access: Vocabulary Development

English Learners

English for Academic Success Some students may have difficulty with using word families to determine the meaning of unfamiliar words. Model for students determining the meaning of the word *emancipation*. You might say: "The word emancipation ends in *–ion*. Adding *–ion* to some verbs turns the verb into a noun. The ending *–ion* means "act or process." So, if this word ends in *–ion*, it may be a verb turned into a noun. If I take off the *–ion* ending, I have *emancipat*. This isn't a

word, but it does look like the word *emancipate*. *Emancipate* is a verb that means 'set free.' The noun form of this would be 'the act of setting free.' So, *emancipation* most likely means 'The act of setting free.'"

Give students additional practice by having them determine the meanings of the following words by identifying the verb within the noun: *hydration, regulation, exclamation,* and *validation*.

Grammar Link
Unclear Pronoun References

When you use pronouns in your writing, you must be sure that they clearly refer to a particular word or word group. The word that a pronoun refers to is called its **antecedent.** Suppose you found this sentence in the story:

> **Gleaming in the pale winter sun was a sword driven into an anvil. It was made of flawless blue-white steel.**

"It" was made of "flawless blue-white steel," but what is "it"—the sword or the anvil? You cannot be sure because the antecedent of the pronoun *it* is not clear. The following sentences express the same idea but don't contain unclear pronoun references:

> **Gleaming in the pale winter sun was a sword driven into an anvil. The sword was made of flawless blue-white steel.**

> **Gleaming in the pale winter sun was a sword, made of flawless blue-white steel, driven into an anvil.**

Your Turn

Revise each of the following sentences, correcting each unclear pronoun reference.

1. The archbishop and Merlin agreed, and he departed to work on his scheme.
2. As Sir Ector, Arthur, and Sir Kay went through the streets, a glint of sunlight caught his eye.
3. Sir Kay was riding with Arthur when he saw the sword.
4. When Merlin showed Uther the sign in the sky, he gave up his son.

CHOICES

As you respond to the Choices, use the **Academic Vocabulary** words as appropriate: circumstance, element, extent, interpret.

REVIEW
A Graphic Legend
Partner Work Working with a partner, tell the story of Arthur's childhood up to his coronation as king in graphic novel form. Consider literary elements in Talbott's version of the legend as you decide which key plot events and characters to include. Write your dialogue in word balloons over the characters' heads.

CONNECT
A Letter About the Past
Imagine that you are Arthur and you've just been crowned king. Write a letter to Merlin as if you were Arthur. What questions do you want to ask? How do you feel about the fact you were never told who your biological father is? End your letter by telling Merlin how you feel about being king. What about your old life will you most miss?

EXTEND
A Modern Hero's Story
Timed **Writing** Think of a person whom you consider heroic. In a short essay, explain why he or she is a hero to you. Your hero's life may not fit the archetypal hero story exactly, but be sure to explain whether this person overcame difficult circumstances, survived threats or challenges, or was an unlikely person to become a hero.

Independent Practice
Grammar Link
Your Turn _____

1. The archbishop and Merlin agreed, and Merlin departed to work on his scheme.
2. As Sir Ector, Arthur, and Sir Kay went through the streets, a glint of sunlight caught Arthur's eye.
3. Sir Kay was riding with Arthur when Arthur saw the sword.
4. When Merlin showed Uther the sign in the sky, Uther gave up his son.

Choices: Evaluation Criteria
Review: (Homework)
A Graphic Legend
- Graphic novels include key plot details and characters.
- Students should follow the format of a graphic novel.

Connect: (Homework)
A Letter About the Past
Letters infer Arthur's feelings about being king and living with a foster father.

Extend: Timed Writing
40-50 Minutes
- Essays describe a modern hero and tell why that person is a hero.
- Students should relate their hero to the hero archetype.

Assess

Chapter 8 Resources, Selection Standards Check, p. 9

ThinkCentral Online Assessment, Selection Standards Check

Teacher One Stop™, editable Selection Standards Check

Reteach

ThinkCentral Online Remediation

Universal Access: Grammar Link

(EL) English Learners/ Struggling Writers
English for Academic Success Give students extra practice in correcting unclear pronoun references. Tell students to first identify the pronoun. Then, determine if the pronoun could refer to two or more nouns. If so, they should then determine which noun the pronoun refers to and correct the sentence to make this connection clear. Have students practice with the following sentences.

1. The sword and the stone stood before him, its steel glinting in the sun. [*The sword and the stone stood before him, the sword's steel glinting in the sun.*]

2. "I have never ventured outside of the village before," he thought as Sir Ector, Sir Kay, and Arthur set off for London. [*"I have never ventured outside of the village before," Arthur thought as Sir Ector, Sir Kay, and Arthur set off for London.*]

✔ For more practice with clear pronoun reference, see **Warriner's Handbook, Language Handbook Worksheets**, and **GrammarNotes**.

Motivate
What Do You Think?/QuickWrite
Have students write for 3-5 minutes in their **Reader/Writer Notebook** about what qualities might help someone be successful in life. Then, have them discuss whether these qualities must be learned as a child or whether they can be learned later in life.

English for Academic Success
Academic Vocabulary
Look for opportunities to use the Academic Vocabulary words in this chapter.

- **element, *n.*:** essential part of something
- **extent, *n.*:** degree to which something extends

Analyzing Visuals
Extension Activity Ask students to discuss the portrayal of Arthur in this image. What qualities does he have? ***Possible response:*** *Arthur appears determined and heroic.*

**California Standards,
pp. 786–793**

- **Reading Standard 3.6** Analyze a range of responses to a literary work and determine the extent to which the literary elements in the work shaped those responses.

ESSAYS
Preparing to Read

Three Responses to Literature

Young Arthur drawing the sword from the stone block. Illustration by Ford.

What Do **You** **Think** What can a young person's qualities foreshadow about his or her future self?

⏱ **QuickWrite**
With a partner, discuss whether you think a person's childhood or teen years give an indication of what he or she will be like as an adult. Explain whether you think people's personalities stay basically the same or change as they age.

Reader/Writer Notebook

Use your **RWN** to complete the activities for these selections.

Reading Standard 3.6 Analyze a range of responses to a literary work and determine the extent to which the literary elements in the work shaped those responses.

Literary Skills Focus

Literary Criticism Through **literary criticism**—the analysis and evaluation of a literary work—readers can delve deeper into a piece of literature. In this lesson you will read and evaluate several **responses to a literary work.** You will read three essays that answer a question about the character of Arthur in *King Arthur: The Sword in the Stone*. It will be your job to evaluate each response. How well has each writer answered the question? How well are the ideas about Arthur supported?

Reading Skills Focus

Analyzing a Response to a Literary Work Keep the following items in mind as you evaluate a response to literature:

- **A response should be focused.** A focused response stays on topic. In this case the question asks whether or not Arthur has the potential for greatness. You must determine whether the essay answers that question and does so convincingly. Decide too if the response stays on the topic of Arthur's character.

- **A response must provide textual support.** A supported response will offer details from the text—or from the writer's own experience—to support major ideas. In this case the writer should clearly define the qualities necessary for greatness and then prove or disprove that Arthur has them.

The most successful responses will offer specific, concrete examples from the text to support each main idea. An analysis of the literary <u>element</u> of character should focus on the character's actions and words and on how other characters respond to that character.

The following three essays all answer the same question about Arthur's character. The side notes with the first essay show you how well the writer responds to the question. Read the other two essays carefully to see to what <u>extent</u> they do the same.

Writing Skills Focus

Think as a Reader/Writer

Find It in Your Reading As you read the following three responses to *King Arthur: The Sword in the Stone*, write down what each writer notices about Arthur's character.

Vocabulary

potential (puh TEHN shuhl) *n.*: ability to develop into something or become something. *The literary work tells of Arthur as a boy and his potential to become a great leader.*

capable (KAY puh buhl) *adj.*: having ability or traits required to do something. *You must select and examine aspects of Arthur's character that show he is capable of greatness.*

sacrifices (SAK ruh fys ihz) *n.*: acts of giving up something of value to gain something else. *Arthur's recognizing the sacrifices a king must make for his people is a sign of greatness.*

Language Coach

Words in Context Review the definition of the word *sacrifices* above. *Sacrifice* can be used in many different contexts. Complete each sentence stem below, giving examples of different types of sacrifices.

- People make financial sacrifices in order to . . .
- To help their children, parents make personal sacrifices such as . . .
- An ultimate sacrifice that someone can offer is . . .

 Learn It Online
Listen to a professional actor read these essays at:

go.hrw.com H7-787 **Go**

Introducing Vocabulary

Read aloud the words and sample sentences. Then, have students fill in each sentence below with the correct Vocabulary word.

1. Ed did not think he was _____ of delivering a speech to the class, but he surprised himself by doing well. [capable]

2. Diana has the _____ to be a good basketball player if she practices more. [potential]

3. I made _____ in order to study harder for school—for instance, I stopped watching television. [sacrifices]

English for Academic Success
Language Coach

Point out that the word *capable* can be used in a different context to mean "prone to." For example, a person can be described as "capable" of violence or greed. As students read the selection, encourage them to consider how each Vocabulary word is used in context.

Literary Skills Focus

As students read the selection, have them note in their **Reader/Writer Notebook** how well the writer expresses ideas about Arthur.

Reading Skills Focus

Remind students that a successful response to literature uses evidence from the text to get a point across.

Writing Skills Focus

Have students record details about Arthur's character in their **Reader/Writer Notebook**.

 Learn It Online
The online version of this selection includes audio support to engage all students and to help struggling readers with reading comprehension and vocabulary.

go.hrw.com H7-787 **Go**

Selection Resources

Chapter 8 Resources, on-level practice and assessment, p. 12

PowerNotes, interactive lesson presentation with activities

Teacher One Stop™, on-level lesson plans and all print resources

Holt Audio Library

Holt Audio Library: Selections and Summaries in Spanish

UA: Holt Interactive Reader, p. 225

Holt Interactive Reader for ELD, p. 263

Holt Audio Tutor for ELD

UA: Differentiating Instruction, modified lesson plans and leveled assessment, p. 223

UA: Resources for Teaching Advanced Students, lesson plans, p. 163

UA: Supporting Instruction in Five Languages, selection summary

ThinkCentral Online Assessment, Selection Standards Check

ThinkCentral Online Remediation

- To help students understand a **response to a literary work,** guide them through the side notes included with Essay 1.

- Point out that, in the first paragraph, the writer directly answers the question of whether Arthur is capable of greatness. This immediately tells the reader what the essay will be about.

- In the second paragraph, the writer begins to support this position using evidence from the text. The writer describes Arthur's actions (caring for wild animals) and explains how this contributes to Arthur's greatness (by showing he is generous and patient).

Guided Practice: Apply

Turn and Talk Point out that in the third paragraph, the writer again uses evidence from the text to support the writer's position. With partners, have students discuss the main idea the writer is trying to get across in this paragraph. How does the writer use evidence from the text to express this idea? **Possible response:** *The writer is expressing the point that Arthur is humble and is willing to do what is asked of him, no matter what. The writer explains that Arthur was forced to put aside his own dreams to become king, but he accepted his destiny.*

Read with a Purpose Read the following essays to examine some ways that Arthur, as depicted in *King Arthur: The Sword in the Stone,* shows that he has the potential for greatness.

Three Responses to Literature

Question: Does Arthur have the potential for greatness? Analyze Arthur's character as depicted in the excerpt from *King Arthur: The Sword in the Stone.*

Essay 1

In *King Arthur: The Sword in the Stone,* writer Hudson Talbott contrasts Sir Kay and Arthur to show how Arthur is different from most youths his age. In the choices he makes and in the way he lives, Arthur shows that he is capable of greatness.

Answers the question directly.

To fulfill his destiny of greatness, Arthur has to have wisdom. Although nobody sixteen years old has lived long enough to have a lot of wisdom, the writer shows us that Arthur is already gaining it. Arthur has found and protected orphaned fox cubs. He has tamed birds and deer. This requires patience and the ability to look and listen. In contrast, Kay, a more typical boy, spends most of his time polishing his helmet. Today, it would be a car, but we get the idea. How many teens today would choose to tame wild creatures for the joy of it? Arthur is unusual in a good way, a way that will bring wisdom to him.

States first main idea.

Supports main idea with examples from the text.
Sums up main idea.

There is a more important contrast between Arthur and Kay. Kay ignores the truth and forgets his dream when he sees a chance to be king. Before they leave for London, Kay tells his father, "To prove myself on the field of battle is my dream." Yet, when the sword falls into Kay's hand the next day, Kay forgets all of that. He sees a chance to be the king, and he tries to claim it even though he knows he didn't earn it. In contrast to Kay, Arthur thinks of others. He goes

States second main idea.
Supports second main idea with examples from the text.

A **Read and Discuss** What information does the writer give to show you that Arthur is different both from other teens of his time and from teens of your time?

Vocabulary **potential** (puh TEHN shuhl) *n.:* ability to develop into something or become something.
capable (KAY puh buhl) *adj.:* having ability or traits required to do something.

Universal Access

EL English Learners
English for Academic Success Explain to students that these essays use idioms with which they might not be familiar. In the second paragraph of Essay 2, the writer expresses that Kay is "full of himself." Point out that this means Kay is arrogant and self-centered. Encourage students to seek clarification for any other idioms or expressions with which they are unfamiliar.

✔ See the English Language Skill Builder in **UA: Differentiating Instruction**.

Struggling Readers
Help students analyze the first response to literature essay using the Model the Skill activity. Encourage students to apply what they learn in the instruction as they analyze Essays 2 and 3.

✔ See **UA: Differentiating Instruction** for strategies for teaching struggling readers.

to London hoping to "help bring honor and glory to his family." He takes the sword only to meet Kay's need. He says nothing while Kay claims the kingship as his own. When he is forced to admit that he took the sword, he sees right away that being king will force him to say goodbye to many things he loves: the deer, his birds, fishing. This shows how Arthur is different from most youths. Most would see only the glory of being a king; Arthur sees past that to the sacrifices kingship will require. He realizes that he will never be able to live for himself only. It is a future he does not want. It is his destiny, though, and he has the courage to see that too. "Very well, whatever my destiny may be, I am willing to accept it." This combination of insight and courage also shows his potential for greatness.

When Arthur asks Merlin what his future will be, Merlin replies, "Greatness surrounds you like a golden cloak. Your achievements could inspire humankind for centuries to come. But you alone can fulfill this destiny and then only if you wish it. You own your future. You alone." How many of us are told that, if we fail ourselves, we will fail humankind? Arthur gives it all he has. He faces the archbishop, the crowds, the jealous kings who will now be his enemies. When Arthur tells the people at his coronation, "For your good I dedicate my life," somehow, we know he will not fail them . . . or himself.

Uses a direct quote to support third main idea.

Ends with a key quote from Arthur himself.

B **Literary Focus** Literary Criticism What details from the text does the writer use to support the idea that Arthur is willing to make sacrifices for others?

Vocabulary **sacrifices** (SAK ruh fys ihz) *n*: acts of giving up something of value for the purpose of gaining something else.

Think About/Talk About

Read with a Purpose Have students read the Read with a Purpose statement. Ask students what it means to have a "potential for greatness." Have students recall details from *King Arthur: The Sword in the Stone* as they read these responses to literature.

▶ Comprehension

Ⓐ Read and Discuss

Possible response: *The writer explains that Arthur takes care of orphaned wild animals, which is something that neither Kay nor modern teens tend to do.*

▶ Analysis

Ⓑ Literary Focus

Possible response: *The writer includes a quote from the text in which Arthur says he is willing to do whatever destiny has in store.*

Vocabulary: Own the Word

- **potential:** Tell students that *potential* includes the root word *potent*, which refers to power. Ask students how *potential* is related to power. ***Possible response:*** *When you have potential, you have the power to do something.*

- **capable:** Explain that *capable* means "able;" an antonym is *unable*. Use both words in a sentence. You might say, "Phil was *unable* to complete the puzzle, but his sister was more *capable* and finished it quickly."

- **sacrifices:** Ask students: Have you ever made any *sacrifices* in your life? What did you give up, and why? Have volunteers discuss their answers. ***Possible response:*** *I sacrificed my summer vacation and got a part-time job to save up money.*

Advanced Learners

Acceleration Direct students to the prompt question on p. 788. Have students discuss how they might answer this question if they were writing this response. Which of Arthur's character traits would they focus on? What evidence from the text would they use? As students read the responses to literature, have them think about how well the writer answers the prompt question.

✔ See **UA: Resources for Teaching Advanced Students** for strategies for teaching advanced learners.

Students with Disabilities

Explain to students that in this selection, they will read three different responses to the same literary work: *King Arthur: The Sword in the Stone*. Point out to students that Essay 1 provides the most complete response to the prompt question, Essay 2 provides a somewhat complete response, and Essay 3 provides the least complete response.

✔ See **UA: Differentiating Instruction** for strategies for teaching students with disabilities.

Model the Skill

- Remind students that an effective response to literature should use **textual support,** or information from the text, to support the writer's ideas.

- Direct students to the final paragraph of Essay 1 on p. 790. Point out that the author uses direct quotes from characters in the selection, such as Merlin and Arthur. Using the characters' own words to express an idea is a good way of providing textual support.

- Explain to students that other ways to provide textual support include recounting important plot events and describing characters' actions.

Guided Practice: Apply

Turn and Talk Have students read the first two paragraphs of Essay 2. How does the writer use textual support to prove that Arthur is kind? Have students discuss with their partners. *Possible response: The writer describes Arthur's actions in the text in which he rescues wild animals and lets his brother have the crown.*

Think as a Reader/Writer

Find It in Your Reading Have students read the first paragraph of Essay 2. Point out that the writer describes Arthur as kind, honest, good-hearted, and courageous.

Use It in Your Writing Tell students to write two or three sentences giving their own descriptions of Arthur. Remind students to think about the story *King Arthur: The Sword in the Stone* as they write.

Essay 2

Arthur possesses the potential to be a great king. Throughout the story, Arthur shows kindness, honesty, a good heart, and courage. These are qualities any great person should have.

First, Arthur is kind. He rescues and tames wild animals. If he were not kind, would he do that? He is also nice to his brother, Sir Kay, even when his brother is full of himself. He is also willing to let Kay have the crown, but this might not be a kindness, since Arthur doesn't really want it. A great king must be kind to others in order to keep the love of the people. Arthur will succeed in this way.

Second, Arthur is honest. He does not lie to his father about pulling out the sword. At that point he thinks he is in trouble for it, so that is a courageous thing for him to do. Arthur is also truthful when he says he doesn't want to be a king but will do it if he has to. Arthur would rather stay at home with his animals in the woods and his family. A great person must be honest, and Arthur will succeed in this way, too.

Third, Arthur has a good heart. He tries his hardest in everything he does. He might mess things up, as when he loses Kay's sword, but he still tries his best. A great person cannot ever give up.

Fourth, Arthur is courageous. He stands up and faces all those people to pull out the sword. He is just sixteen years old, and now he will have to be a king of a country that many people want to take over. All in all, Arthur will fulfill his destiny by showing kindness, honesty, a good heart, and courage. **C**

Essay 3

Arthur is the son of King Uther Pendragon and Queen Igraine. On the night he is born, the stars form the shape of a dragon to foreshadow Arthur's greatness. Merlin takes him away to keep him safe. Arthur's father is poisoned a year later, so it is a good decision to take the baby away. When Arthur is sixteen, his country needs him. The years while he has been growing up were lawless and dark. Merlin devises a way to make the people accept Arthur. He puts a

---

C **Reading Focus** Analyzing a Response to a Literary Work   Did this essay convince you that Arthur has the potential for greatness? Which idea or detail did you find the most convincing?

Developing Oral Fluency

Give students practice in reading with appropriate pacing. Remind students that punctuation helps guide their reading. A comma indicates that the reader should take a short pause, and a period indicates that the reader should take a longer pause.

Read the first paragraph of Essay 2 aloud. Have students note that you take a short pause when you reach a comma and a longer pause when you reach a period.

Paired Activity Pair students with a partner. Have partners read paragraphs 2-5 of Essay 2, switching readers for each paragraph. Remind them to focus on their pacing by paying attention to appropriate punctuation.

▶ **Comprehension**

🅒 **Reading Focus**

Possible response: *Yes, this essay convinced me that Arthur has the potential for greatness. The most convincing detail is that Arthur bravely took over as king at just 16 years old.*

▶ **Extend the Discussion**

Summarizing In one or two sentences, summarize the main idea of Essay 2. ***Possible response:*** *King Arthur's actions in the story prove that he is kind, honest, good-hearted, and courageous. He has the potential to be a great king.*

Making Inferences In the last paragraph of Essay 1, what does Merlin's quote mean? Why does the writer include it in the essay? ***Possible response:*** *Merlin's quote means that Arthur has the potential to be a great king and improve many people's lives, but only if Arthur chooses to do so. The writer includes it to show how important Arthur was and how dedicated he was to helping others.*

Analysis

ⒹLiterary Focus

Possible response: This essay focuses mainly on plot. The prompt asked the writer to focus on character, specifically Arthur's character.

▶ **Extend the Discussion**

Drawing Conclusions Why does the writer of Essay 3 believe that Kay is an "annoying character"? ***Possible response:*** *The writer notes that Kay is bossy and orders Arthur around.*

Making Judgments Does this essay effectively explain whether Arthur has the potential for greatness? Why or why not? ***Possible response:*** *No, I don't think this essay is effective. It only gives a plot summary of the story instead of focusing on Arthur and his character traits.*

Monitor Students' Comprehension

Guide students in answering these True-False questions.

1. According to Essay 1, Arthur is unwilling to make sacrifices to become king. [F]

2. The writer of Essay 2 believes that Arthur has the potential to be a great king. [T]

3. The writer of Essay 3 praises Arthur for rescuing and caring for wild animals. [F]

---

sword in an anvil outside the church, with a note that says that whoever could pull out the sword is the rightful king of England. The archbishop declares a contest on Christmas morning to see who is the rightful king, and a tournament on Christmas Eve. Arthur goes along to London to be squire for his bossy brother, Sir Kay. Kay is an annoying character, but Arthur doesn't mind being bossed around by Kay. He spends the time on the way to the tournament thinking of how to be a good squire and bring honor to his family. When they get to London, Arthur is amazed to see a sword in an anvil on a large block of marble with soldiers standing around it. He thinks London is full of wonders. Kay does a really good job in the first part of the tournament. He has just enough time to rest and change before the next event, and he asks Arthur for his sword. Arthur can't find it! He leaps on his pony to go back to their tent, but it isn't there. Arthur decides to borrow the one he saw from the anvil, and he goes to see about getting it. It comes out pretty easily, and Arthur takes it to Sir Kay. Kay tells Arthur to get their father. Then Kay wants to claim he's king. Their father makes him prove it. Of course, Kay cannot put the sword back, but Arthur can. Their father, Sir Ector, is overcome when he realizes who Arthur really is. He tells Arthur he can't avoid his destiny. Merlin comes along and tells Arthur he is going to be a great king, but he will have to fulfill his destiny. It will be Arthur's choice. He has to want it. Arthur is sad to give up the life he loves, but he says he will accept whatever his destiny is. Then he pulls the sword out on five different occasions to prove his worth. The people love him, and he is crowned King of England. **Ⓓ**

Ⓓ Literary Focus Literary Criticism On what literary <u>element</u> does this essay focus? On what literary <u>element</u> did the question prompt ask the writer to focus?

 California Standards, p. 793

■ **Reading Standard 3.6** Analyze a range of responses to a literary work and determine the extent to which the literary elements in the work shaped those responses.

Reading Standard 3.6 Analyze a range of responses to a literary work and determine the extent to which the literary elements in the work shaped those responses.

Three Responses to Literature

Literary Response and Analysis

Reading Skills Focus
Quick Check

1. Which essay states the answer to the question about Arthur in the opening sentence?
2. Which essay uses direct quotations from the text to support its main ideas?
3. Which essay contains a plot summary rather than a character analysis?

Read with a Purpose

4. Of all the points mentioned in the essays, which do you think most strongly shows that Arthur is destined for greatness?

Reading Skills: Analyzing a Response to a Literary Work

5. Evaluate the essays: On a scale of 0 to 5, how would you rate each essay? Base your evaluation on the points mentioned on page 787. Use the chart below to organize your information. Back up any yes/no answers with examples from the essays. Then, discuss your ratings with a partner.

	Character-focused? Convincing answer?	Examples of Strong Textual Support	Other Strengths or Weaknesses	Rating
Essay 1				
Essay 2				
Essay 3				

✓ Vocabulary Check

Match each Vocabulary word with its definition.

6. **potential**   a. things given up; losses
7. **capable**   b. future ability; possibility
8. **sacrifices**   c. able to do something

Literary Skills Focus
Literary Analysis

9. **Infer** How do you think each writer felt about the character of Arthur? Explain.
10. **Evaluate** Is comparison and contrast (as in Essay 1) an effective way to answer the question about Arthur's character? Explain.
11. **Make Judgments** Which of the four qualities of Arthur's greatness listed in Essay 2 is *not* clearly supported in the story?

Literary Skills: Literary Criticism

12. **Analyze** Which of the following criticisms of Essay 3 is valid? Explain your choice.
    - The writer should have summarized the plot.
    - The essay doesn't answer the question.
    - The essay has no paragraph indentions.

Literary Skills Review: Plot

13. **Analyze** If the essay question had asked about plot, which events in Essay 3 would you have chosen to write about? Which plot events point most strongly to Arthur's potential for greatness?

Writing Skills Focus
Think as a Reader/Writer

Use It in Your Writing Write a paragraph comparing what you noticed about Arthur's character to what the writers of the essays noticed.

What Do You Think Now?

Judging by his personality as a young person, what kind of king do you think Arthur will make? Explain.

What Do You Think Now?
To help students respond to the question, have them recall what they read in *King Arthur: The Sword in the Stone* and in the three responses to literature in this chapter. Have students think about what characteristics Arthur possesses and what clues might foretell his future.

Check for Understanding

Independent Practice
Reading Skills Focus
Answers:

1. *Essay 2 opens with the sentence, "Arthur possesses the potential to be a great king."*
2. *Essay 1 uses quotations.*
3. *Essay 3 contains a plot summary.*
4. *I think the quote from Merlin, about Arthur inspiring humankind for centuries to come, indicates that Arthur is destined for greatness.*
5. *Essay 1 ranks a 5. It answers the question completely and gives a lot of textual support. Essay 2 ranks a 3. It answers the question with less textual support. Essay 3 ranks a 0. It does not address the question at all and is unfocused.*

Vocabulary Check
6. *b*
7. *c*
8. *a*

Literary Skills Focus
9. *All three writers seem to respect Arthur's kindness and bravery.*
10. *Yes. Contrasting Arthur with other characters shows how he is exceptional.*
11. *The writer provides little evidence from the story that Arthur has a good heart.*
12. *The essay doesn't answer the question. The question asks whether Arthur has the potential for greatness, but the essay only gives a summary of the plot.*
13. *I would have focused on Arthur's pulling the sword out of the stone and his being named king. These point most strongly to Arthur's potential for greatness.*

Standards Focus

Objectives

Students will

- understand the literary archetypes of hero and quest
- make and revise predictions
- analyze shades of meaning in synonym sets

Motivate

What Do You Think?/QuickWrite

Use the QuickWrite to have students reflect on their experiences with scapegoating. Then have students discuss in their **Reader/Writer Notebook** which behaviors and characteristics represent evil and which represent good in literature.

English for Academic Success

Academic Vocabulary

Look for opportunities to use the Academic Vocabulary words in this chapter.

- **circumstance, *n.:*** condition or fact.
- **element, *n.:*** essential part of something.
- **extent, *n.:*** degree to which something extends.
- **interpret, *v.:*** explain the meaning of.

Analyzing Visuals

Extension Activity What characteristics of King Arthur does this image represent? ***Possible response:*** *He is portrayed as a soldier in full armor, holding a shield and wearing a helmet.*

![California] **California Standards, pp. 794–809**

- **Reading Standard 3.6** Analyze a range of responses to a literary work and determine the extent to which the literary elements in the work shaped those responses.
- **Reading Standard 1.2** Use knowledge of Greek, Latin, and Anglo-Saxon roots and affixes to understand content-area vocabulary.

MERLIN AND THE DRAGONS

by **Jane Yolen**

 What Do You Think What makes one character "good" and another one "evil"?

⏱ QuickWrite

There is a "scapegoat" in this story—someone who is falsely accused of a crime or problem. Scapegoats are innocent, but some scapegoats pay with their lives. What experience have you had with the concept of "scapegoats"?

King Arthur and the Holy Grail. Stained-glass window.

KING ARTH

Selection Readability

Easily Accessible **Accessible** Challenging	familiar theme; familiar genre; complex syntax

Selection Plot Summary

Young King Arthur has difficulty sleeping and goes to Merlin, who tells him a story about a young boy with a talent for predicting the future in his dreams. At the end of the story, the boy is revealed to be Merlin himself and Arthur finds out that his father was actually a king.

Reader/Writer Notebook

Use your **RWN** to complete the activities for this selection.

Reading Standard 3.6 Analyze a range of responses to a literary work and **determine the extent to which the literary elements in the work shaped** those **responses**.

Literary Skills Focus

The Hero's Story Literature from around the world includes stories of heroes, and these stories often follow an archetypal, or typical, pattern. The **hero** is often born in an unusual <u>circumstance</u>, perhaps in secret. Sometimes the identity of the hero's father is unknown; sometimes the hero is an orphan and neither parent is known. As a young boy (the heroes in the old stories are almost always male), the hero is trained by a wise old man. Often the hero receives magic powers or weapons. When he is ready, the hero sets off on his quest, usually to rid the world of some evil. It is the **quest**—the perilous journey to do what must be done—that shows what the hero is really made of.

TechFocus Imagine how today's computer imagery might be used to bring this story to life as an interactive game.

Reading Skills Focus

Making Predictions When you read, you automatically make **predictions** about what is going to happen next. Here are some tips to help you make good predictions.

- Notice clues that foreshadow, or hint at, what will happen next.
- Revise your predictions as you read.
- Make predictions based on your own experiences—including other reading experiences and what you know about how people behave in real life.

Into Action As you read, use a chart like the one below to track your predictions. Pay special attention to the dreams in this story.

Story Events	Predictions

Writing Skills Focus

Think as a Reader/Writer

Find It in Your Reading Take notes on how the words and actions of Merlin, Arthur, Emrys, and Vortigern reveal their true characters.

Vocabulary

ruthless (ROOTH lihs) *adj.:* without pity. *Vortigern was a cruel and ruthless man.*

impudence (IHM pyuh duhns) *n.:* disrespect; insulting rudeness. *The villagers gasped at Emrys's impudence when he accused them of listening to frightened children.*

insolence (IHN suh luhns) *n.:* rudeness. *Vortigern was angry at the boy's insolence when he predicted an attack.*

recognition (rehk uhg NIHSH uhn) *n.:* act of recognizing; realization of something. *A sudden wave of recognition passed over Arthur as he realized who the boy was.*

Language Coach

Synonyms Different words that have more or less the same meaning are called **synonyms**. Which two words in the list above have similar meanings? What word in the list means more or less the same thing as the word *pitiless*?

Learn It Online
Broaden your word power with *Word Watch* at:

go.hrw.com   H7-795   Go

More About the Writer

Jane Yolen began her writing career before she started junior high school. Her first children's book, *Pirates in Petticoats*, was sold on her 22nd birthday, and she has written close to 300 books since.

Think About the Writer

Ask students whether they have ever wanted to explore another time or place. What appealed to them about that particular, different reality? Discuss how such appeal might inspire a writer.

 For Independent Reading

- If students are interested in the Arthurian legends from a young person's point of view, recommend Katherine Paterson's *Parzival: The Quest of the Grail Knight*.

- To provide students with a modern writer's view on the hero and the quest, recommend Christopher Paolini's *Eragon*.

Jane Yolen
(1939–   )

"Empress of Thieves"

Jane Yolen is inspired by legends, tales, and myths told by people from all over the world:

> "As a writer I am the empress of thieves, taking characters like gargoyles off Parisian churches, the *ki-lin* (or unicorn) from China, swords in stones from the Celts, landscapes from the Taino people. I have pulled threads from magic tapestries to weave my own new cloth."

Raised on King Arthur

Yolen was raised on the tales of King Arthur, so it is not surprising that the King Arthur legend is one of her favorites. In fact, she is considered an expert in the study and research of Arthurian legends. The character of Merlin, the magician, especially fascinates her. She has written several books about the mysterious wizard in her *Young Merlin* series of novels.

Fascinated by Dragons

Storytelling was important in Yolen's family. Both of her parents were writers, and one of her great-grandfathers was a storyteller in a Russian village. From the story included here, you'll see that Yolen is fascinated not only by Merlin but also by dragons, those fearsome dinosaur-like creatures that have captured the human imagination for centuries.

Think About the Writer: Why do you think myths and legends set in other worlds hold such fascination for some writers?

Build Background

The Character of Merlin Some versions of the King Arthur legend say that after Arthur pulled the sword from the stone, he was sent to live with the wise man and magician Merlin, who taught Arthur how to be a good ruler. As this story begins, Arthur (who is already living with Merlin) knows he is the rightful king, but he doesn't yet know that his father was the old king, Uther Pendragon.

As many versions of the Arthur story reveal, it was Merlin who engineered Arthur's birth in the first place. At Uther's request, Merlin arranged for the king to father a child with his enemy's wife, Igraine. Merlin disguised Uther as Igraine's husband in order to deceive her. Merlin then had Igraine's husband killed. Thus, deceit and betrayal are at the very heart of the Arthurian legends.

Merlin is probably the most fascinating and mysterious character in the Arthurian legends. In T.H. White's *The Once and Future King*, Merlin lives backward in time, giving him the ability to foretell the future.

Preview the Selection

In "Merlin and the Dragons," you will read how the young **Arthur** finally learns his true parentage from his teacher **Merlin,** after Merlin tells him a story about an unusual boy named **Emrys** and an evil man named **Vortigern.**

Read with a Purpose This is a frame story—that is, one story is contained within another story. Read to learn why Merlin tells a story to young Arthur.

MERLIN
AND THE DRAGONS

by **Jane Yolen**

The night was dark and storm clouds marched along the sky. Rain beat against the gray castle walls. Inside, in a bedroom hung with tapestries, the young King Arthur had trouble sleeping. Awake, he was frightened. Asleep, he had disturbing dreams.

At last he climbed out of bed, took a candle to light his way, and started out the door. Suddenly remembering his crown, he turned back and found it under the bed where he'd tossed it angrily hours before. It felt too heavy for his head, so he carried it, letting it swing from his fingers.

As he walked along the hall, strange shadows danced before him. But none were as frightening as the shadows in his dreams.

He climbed the tower stairs slowly, biting his lip. When he reached the top, he pushed open the wooden door. The old magician

Think About/Talk About

Read with a Purpose Have students read the Read with a Purpose statement. Have students predict the identity of Arthur's father.

▶ **Extend the Discussion**

Summarizing How would you summarize the first three paragraphs of the story? *Possible response: King Arthur, a young boy in this story, can't sleep because he's been having nightmares. He climbs out of bed and walks down the shadowy hallway.*

Character Read the first paragraph. What is unusual about the way in which the author introduces the hero? *Possible response: King Arthur is not doing something brave or heroic. Instead, he is nervous and afraid.*

Symbolism In the second paragraph, the author says that Arthur's crown is "too heavy" for him. How might this statement be symbolic? *Possible response: Arthur feels that the pressure and responsibility of being king is too much for him.*

Model the Skill

■ Provide students with copies of the Reading Skills Focus graphic organizer (See **Chapter 8 Resources**) or ask them to use a piece of their own paper.

■ Read aloud the first three pages of the story or ask a volunteer to read them. Then, discuss with students the events that have happened so far in both the frame story and the story-within-a-story. *Possible response: Students should recognize that Arthur cannot sleep because of nightmares, so he comes to Merlin's room, where Merlin tells him a story. In the story, a young, fatherless boy named Emrys is troubled by strange dreams of towers and dragons. He is educated by an old man of the village. One day, a cruel man claiming to be a king comes to the village and decides to build a tower on the mountain.*

■ Model **making predictions** based on the events that have happened so far in the story. You might say, "I know that Emrys has troubling dreams, specifically, dreams about fighting dragons and a shaking tower. I think the dreams are foreshadowing what will happen later in the story. Maybe Emrys foresees what will happen when Vortigern builds his tower. I will note this as a prediction and revise it, if needed, as I read."

Story Events	Predictions
Emrys dreams of a shaking tower and of dragons	Emry's dreams foreshadow the building of the tower

Guided Practice: Apply

Have students continue reading independently, pausing after every page to make a prediction using their graphic organizer. If students struggle to make predictions, pair them with a student who has been able to make a prediction. Ask the pair to discuss the story events, other reading experiences, and what they know about how people behave to make predictions.

---

was asleep in his chair, but woke at once, his eyes quick as a hawk's.

"What is it, boy?" the old man asked. "What brings you here at this hour?"

"I am the king," Arthur said, but softly as if he were not really sure. "I go where I will." He put the crown on Merlin's desk.

"You are a boy," Merlin replied, "and boys should be in their beds asleep."

Arthur sighed. "I could not sleep," he said. "I had bad dreams."

"Ah . . ." Merlin nodded knowingly. "Dreams." He held out a hand to the boy, but Arthur didn't dare touch those long, gnarled fingers. "Let me read your dreams."

"It is one dream, actually," Arthur said. "And always the same: a fatherless boy who becomes king simply by pulling a sword from a stone."

"Ah . . ." Merlin said again, withdrawing his fingers. "I know the very child. But if you cannot tell me more of your dream, I shall have to tell you one of mine. After all, a dream told is a story. What better than a story on a rainy night?"

Arthur settled onto a low stool and gazed up at the wizard. A story! He hadn't known he wanted a story. He'd come seeking comfort and companionship. A story was better than both.

He listened as Merlin began.

In a small village high up in the rugged mountains of Wales lived a lonely, fatherless boy named Emrys. Dark-haired he was, and small, with sharp bright eyes, and a mouth that rarely smiled. He was troubled by dreams, sleeping and waking. Dreams of dragons, dreams of stone.

His mother was the daughter of the local king and tried to be both mother and father to him. But a princess is only taught lute songs and needlework and prayers. She'd never once climbed a tree after a bird's egg or skinned her knee pursuing a lizard, or caught a butterfly in a net. Emrys had to invent that part of growing up himself. And a lonely inventing it turned out to be.

The other boys in the village teased him for not knowing who his father was. "Mother's babe," they cried, chasing him from their games.

So Emrys went after birds' eggs and lizards, butterflies and frogs by himself, giving them names both odd and admiring, like "flutterby" and "wriggletail," and making up stories of their creation. And he chanted strange-sounding spells because he liked the sounds, spells that sometimes seemed to work, most times did not. **B**

But he never told his dreams aloud. Dreams of dragons, dreams of stone.

Now in the village lived an old man who knew all sorts of things, from reading and writing to how birds speak and why leaves turn brown in autumn. And because Emrys was the son of a princess, the grandson of a king, the old man taught him all he knew. **C**

It was this learning that brought the village boys to him, not in friendship but in curiosity. They would ask Emrys to show them some

A Read and Discuss How do you interpret Arthur's actions so far? Does he seem confident in his role as king?

B Reading Focus Making Predictions Whom do you think Merlin's story might be about? What clues does the writer give you?

C Literary Focus The Hero's Story What similarities in characterization do you see between Emrys and Arthur?

Universal Access

EL English Learners

To help students understand the idea of a hero story, explain to students that King Arthur is a legendary British hero. Many old stories from the United Kingdom and France tell about the great accomplishments of Arthur and his followers. Ask students whether they are familiar with similar heroes from other countries and cultures. Have volunteers share stories of heroes from their own backgrounds with the class.

Struggling Readers

Before reading, point out to students that in "Merlin and the Dragons," the hero in both the frame story and the story within a story are young boys who are uncertain of their own abilities. Explain that this is an unusual scenario for many heroic tales, in which heroes are often depicted as fearless. Tell students that the characters in this selection show us that even heroes can be afraid and lacking in confidence. As students read, have them look for ways in which Arthur and Emrys overcome their fears and prove themselves to be heroic figures.

trick with the birds, or to tell them stories. Glad for the company, Emrys always obliged. He even took to making up harmless predictions to amuse them.

"The rain will soon fall," he would say. And often it did.

"The first spring robin will arrive." And soon after, it came.

Now any farmer's son could have made the same right guesses and after awhile the village boys were no longer impressed. However, one day Emrys found a book of seasons and planetary movements in the old man's cottage and read it cover to cover. Then he went out and announced to the astonished boys: "Tomorrow the sun will disappear."

The next day at noon, just as the calendar had foretold, an eclipse plunged the countryside into darkness. The boys and their parents were equally horrified and blamed Emrys. From then on he was called "demon's son" and avoided altogether. **D**

Years went by and Emrys grew up, terribly alone, dreaming dreams he did not understand: dreams of a shaking tower, dreams of fighting dragons.

One day when Emrys was twelve, a cruel and ruthless man named Vortigern came to the valley. Vortigern had unjustly declared himself High King over all Britain. But the country was

at last in revolt against him and he had been forced to flee, riding ever farther north and west. At last he had arrived at the foot of Dinys Emrys, the mountain which towered above the village, with a bedraggled army on tired horses, bearing tattered banners emblazoned with red dragons. A handful of court magicians rode with them.

Vortigern pointed to the jagged mountain peak. "There," he said in a voice hard and determined. "There I will build my battle tower, so that I may see my enemies when they approach."

D [Read and Discuss] Why might the boys and their parents have been horrified by the eclipse?

Vocabulary **ruthless** (ROOTH lihs) *adj.*: without pity.

Think About/Talk About

▶ **Comprehension**

A **Read and Discuss**
Possible response: I interpret his actions to be those of a frightened, insecure boy. He is extremely unsure about his role as king.

B **Reading Focus**
Possible response: I think Merlin may be talking about himself, based on the author's inclusion of Emrys' experiments with magic. Merlin, as an adult, is a magician.

D **Read and Discuss**
Possible response: The boys and their parents were probably horrified by the eclipse because it seemed like an evil act, and also because it suggested Emrys had great power.

▶ **Analysis**

C **Literary Focus**
Possible response: Emrys, like Arthur, does not know his father. Both are troubled by disturbing dreams.

▶ **Extend the Discussion**

Character Based on the description of Vortigern in the last two paragraphs of p. 799, what can you conclude about his character? *Possible response:* Vortigern is hungry for power and does not care whom he has to hurt in order to get it.

Vocabulary: Own the Word
ruthless: Ask students to applaud to indicate how much they would want to be described as *ruthless*. *Possible response:* Students do not respond, because to be ruthless is to be cruel and lacking in pity.

- Tell students that archetypal heroes of literature are not unlike the heroes or superheroes of the modern day. An **archetypal hero** would likely have extraordinary abilities, such as magic powers. An archetypal hero is not always born of great circumstances; he might be orphaned or have lost a parent, and been trained by a wise older man. Perhaps the most important similarity between modern and archetypal heroes is that they are considered good, and fight against evil in their worlds.

- Explain, point-by-point, how Arthur's characteristics relate to those of an archetypal hero, referring students to the Preparing to Read page if needed. You might say, "Arthur does not know the circumstances of his birth, and he does not know his father. Archetypal heroes may not know one or both parents. Arthur is living with the wise magician Merlin, presumably learning from him; archetypal heroes are often trained by wise older men. Arthur has pulled a sword from a stone, which suggests that he has the magic powers of an archetypal hero. He is also the king, which could present him with a quest against evil when he is older." Tell students that you can conclude from Arthur's similarities to the archetype of a hero, that he is a heroic character.

- Guide students through a parallel comparison of Emrys to the archetype of a hero.

Guided Practice: Apply

Have students work to identify Emrys' quest as they continue reading, and keep track of the events of the quest in a time line.

He turned to his soldiers. "Gather the people of this village and bring them to me, for they will be the hackers and haulers. They will make me a tower of stone."

Young Emrys looked on in amazement. Banners sewn with red dragons? A tower of stone? Such things had been in his dreams. What could it all mean? **E**

The Welsh stonecutters began their work under the watchful eyes of the soldiers. For many days they mined the stone, cutting huge pieces from the sides of Dinys Emrys. They swore they could hear the cries of the mountain at each cut.

Next they hauled the stones with ropes, their little Welsh ponies groaning with the effort. Finally, came the day when they built the tower up on the mountainside, stone upon stone, until it rose high above the valley.

That night Emrys went to bed and dreamed once again his strange dreams. He dreamed that the tower—the very one built by Vortigern—shook and swayed and tumbled to the ground. And he dreamed that beneath the tower slept two dragons, one red as Vortigern's banners, and one white.

That very night the High King's tower

Vortigern's rage could not be contained.

began to shudder and shake and, with a mighty crash, came tumbling down. In the morning, when he saw what had happened, Vortigern was furious, convinced the villagers had done it on purpose.

"Your work is worthless," he bellowed at the Welshmen. "You will be whipped, and then you will get to work all over again."

So the Welshmen had to go back to their stonework, great welts on their backs. They hacked and hauled, and once again the tower rose high above the valley. But the night they were finished, it was the same. The tower shook and tumbled to the ground. By morning there was only a jumble of stones.

Vortigern drove the villagers even harder, and by the following week the tower was once again rebuilt. But a third time, in the night, a great shudder went through the mountain and the work once again lay in ruins. Vortigern's rage could not be contained. He called for his magicians. "There is some dark Welsh magic here. Find out the cause. My tower must stand."

Now these magicians had neither knowledge nor skill, but in their fear of

E **Reading Focus** Making Predictions What do *you* think it means?

Cross-Curricular Connection

LITERATURE: Merlin

The wizard Merlin is one of the most recognizable characters in the Arthurian legends. Students may be interested to learn more about this mysterious magician and mentor to Arthur.

- Some versions of the legend depict the magician in a negative fashion, while others give Merlin a religious or spiritual dimension and link him with the legendary Holy Grail. Depictions of Merlin changed from story to story as popular attitudes towards sorcery shifted between acceptance and suspicion.

- Merlin has sometimes been depicted as being an advisor to Arthur's father Uther Pendragon, while other actions frequently attributed to him include suggesting the creation of the group known as the Knights of the Round Table. He has also been identified as the figure who predicted the next king of Britain would remove a sword from a stone, a feat performed by a young Arthur.

- Merlin's death is sometimes said to involve the mysterious Lady of the Lake, who is said to have provided Excalibur, the sword Arthur pulled from the stone.

Vortigern they put on a good show. They consulted the trees, both bark and root; they threw the magic sticks of prophecy; they played with the sacred stones of fate. At last they reported their findings.

"You must find a fatherless child," they said. "A child spawned by a demon. You must sprinkle his blood on the stones. Only then will the gods of this land let the stones stand." They smiled at one another and at Vortigern, smiles of those sure that what they ask cannot be done. **F**

Vortigern did not notice their smiles. "Go find me such a child."

The magicians stopped smiling and looked nervous. "We do not know if any such child exists," they said. "We do not know if your tower can stand."

Furious, Vortigern turned to his soldiers. "Gold to whomever brings me such a child," he roared.

Before the soldiers could move, a small voice cried out. "Please, sir, we of the village know such a boy." The speaker was a spindly lad named Gwillam.

"Come here, child," said Vortigern. "Name him."

Gwillam did not dare get too close to the High King. "His name is Emrys, sir. He was spawned by a demon. He can cry the sun from the sky."

Vortigern turned to the captain of his guards. "Bring this demon's son to me."

At that very moment, Emrys was on the mountain with the old man, absorbed in a very strange dream. Under the ruins of the tower he saw two huge stone eggs breathing in and out. Just as he emerged from his dream, he was set upon by Vortigern's soldiers. "What shall I do?" he cried.

The old man put a hand on his shoulder. "Trust your dreams."

The soldiers quickly bound Emrys and carried him to the High King, but Emrys refused to show any fear. "You are the boy without a father, the boy spawned by a devil?" Vortigern asked.

"I am a boy without a father, true," Emrys said. "But I am no demon's son. You have been listening to the words of frightened children."

The villagers and soldiers gasped at his impudence, but Vortigern said, "I will have your blood either way." **G**

"Better that you have my dream," Emrys said. "Only my dream can guide you so that your tower will stand."

The boy spoke with such conviction, Vortigern hesitated.

"I have dreamed that beneath your tower lies a pool of water that must be drained. In the mud you will find two hollow stones. In each stone is a sleeping dragon. It is the breath of each sleeping dragon that shakes the earth and makes the tower fall. Kill the dragons and your tower will stand."

Vortigern turned to his chief magician. "Can this be true?"

F Read and Discuss How do the magicians' findings match Emrys's circumstance?

G Literary Focus The Hero's Story How is Emrys's life threatened?

Vocabulary **impudence** (IHM pyuh duhns) *n.*: disrespect; insulting rudeness.

Reaching Reluctant Readers

Help students make a personal connection to the text by asking them to name their favorite action hero from a book or film.

- Choose one of the better known heroes from students' suggestions and write the name in the middle of the board. Have students suggest heroic qualities or characteristics that the character possesses and write these in a word web around the name of the character.

- Ask students to compare the heroic qualities of the action hero on the board with Arthur or Emrys. Are there any similarities? Ask students whether they think Arthur and Emrys are typical literary heroes. Why or why not?

- Have students draw their own word web for the action hero they initially chose. As they read the rest of the text, tell them to compare the qualities of their hero with the characteristics of Arthur and Emrys.

▶ **Comprehension**

E **Reading Focus**

Possible response: His dreams contain elements of what's happening in the village—the dragons, flags, and tumbling tower. I think he can predict the future.

F **Read and Discuss**

Possible response: The magicians' findings match Emrys' circumstance because he is fatherless, and the villagers believe him to be spawned from a demon.

▶ **Analysis**

G **Literary Focus**

Possible response: Emrys' life is threatened because the king thinks he needs to sprinkle the boy's blood on the stones of his castle to make it stand.

▶ **Extend the Discussion**

Comparing and Contrasting How is the relationship between Emrys and the old man similar to that between Arthur and Merlin? *Possible response: King Arthur and Emrys are both young boys who are unsure what to do with their great power. Merlin and the old man give them wise advice to help them find their way.*

Vocabulary: Own the Word

impudence: Explain to students that *impudent* comes from the Latin prefix *im-*, meaning *not*, and verb *pudēre*, meaning *to feel ashamed*. Someone who is *impudent* is not ashamed, and is often overly bold or rude. Have students describe examples of *impudence* that they have seen or heard about.

Model the Skill

■ Explain to students that few **synonyms** have the exact same meaning; usually, there are slight variations among words that can be used as synonyms, though they are close enough to be used in place of one another.

■ Point out the words *great, vast,* and *giant* on pp. 802–803. All three words are used in the story to mean "very big": "great stones," "a vast pool or water," "giant eggs." Their exact definitions, however, differ slightly from one another. *Great* is defined as impressive in largeness of size. *Vast* is defined as extremely great in size. *Giant* is defined as quite large. Although the words do not have precisely the same meaning, they all describe largeness of size, and in most situations can be used in place of one another.

Guided Practice: Apply

Have students work in small groups to identify two synonyms for each of the following story words, also from pp. 802–803: *trembled, removed, scrambled, astonished.*

Think as a Reader/Writer

Find It in Your Reading Point out how Vortigern's words on p. 803 reveal his true nature: "Kill them! Kill the dragons!"

Use It in Your Writing Have students write another line of dialogue for Vortigern that reveals his true nature.

Analyzing Visuals

Connecting to the Text How do these dragons compare with the ones described in the legend?

The chief magician stroked his chin. "Dreams *can* come true. . . ."

Vortigern hesitated no longer. "Untie the boy, but watch him," he said to his soldiers. "And you—Welshmen—do as the boy says. Dig beneath the rubble."

So the Welshmen removed the stones and dug down until they came to a vast pool of water. Then the soldiers drained the pool. And just as Emrys had prophesied, at the pool's bottom lay two great stones. The stones seemed to be breathing in and out, and at each breath the mud around them trembled.

"Stonecutters," cried Vortigern, "break open the stones!"

Two men with mighty hammers descended into the pit and began to pound upon the stones.

Once, twice, three times their hammers rang out. On the third try, like jets of lightning, cracks ran around each stone and they

---

Word-Attack Skills Mini-Lesson

Review these sounds represented by the letter *y*:
- *y* stands for the consonant sound /y/ in *young* and *you*
- *y* stands for /i/ in *sky* and *fry*
- final *y* stands for /e/ in words like *story* and *country* and in words with the suffix *–ly*

Use the word *myth* to introduce another use for the letter *y*. Point out that in *myth* the letter *y* stands for short *i*.

Activity Have students categorize the following words into four groups according to the sound represented by the letter *y*:

crystal	society	dye
tying	yesterday	suddenly
worthy	symbol	trophy
pry	abyss	yellow

[Consonant sound /y/—*yesterday, yellow.* Long *i*—*dye, tying, pry.* Short *i*—*crystal, symbol, abyss.* Long *e*—*society, suddenly, worthy, trophy.*]

broke apart as if they had been giant eggs. Out of one emerged a dragon white as new milk. Out of the other a dragon red as old wine.

Astonished at the power of his dreaming, Emrys opened and closed his mouth, but could not speak. The men in the pit scrambled for safety. **(H)**

The High King Vortigern looked pleased. "Kill them! Kill the dragons!"

But even as he spoke, the dragons shook out their wings and leapt into the sky.

"They are leaving!" cried the chief magician.

"They are away!" cried the soldiers.

"They will not go quite yet," whispered Emrys.

No sooner had he spoken than the dragons wheeled about in the sky to face one another, claws out, belching flame. Their battle cries like nails on slate echoed in the air.

Advancing on one another, the dragons clashed, breast to breast, raining teeth and scales on the ground. For hour after hour they fought, filling the air with smoke.

First the red dragon seemed to be winning, then the white. First one drew blood, then the other. At last, with a furious slash of its jaws, the white dragon caught the

---

(H) **Literary Focus** The Hero's Story What fantastic feat has Emrys performed?

Think About/Talk About

▶ **Comprehension**

(H) Literary Focus
Possible response: Emrys has made a prophecy based on his dream, and it has come true.

▶ **Extend the Discussion**

Making Predictions In the first column of p. 803, Vortigern orders his men to kill the dragons. What impact do you think the dragons will have on the resolution of the story? *Possible response: Vortigern is obviously afraid that the dragons are preventing his rise to power. I think they will eventually cause his downfall.*

Speculating In the first paragraph on p. 802, Emrys learns that his dream about the breathing stones is accurate. What do you think would have happened if Emrys's dream had not come true? *Possible response: Emrys would probably have been killed so that Vortigern could sprinkle his blood on the stones that would be used to build the next tower. This probably would not have helped the tower stand, and Vortigern's magicians would have to come up with something else for Vortigern to do.*

Analyzing Visuals
Connecting to the Text: The dragons appear to be just as fierce as they are in the selection, apparently breathing fire and battling each other. The image also shows a white dragon and a red dragon, as described in the story.

Model the Skill

- Tell students that, although Emrys did not leave his own village, he still went through a **quest**, as an **archetypal hero** must.

- Have a volunteer share his or her time line of the events in Emrys' quest by recreating it on the board and orally reviewing the events. Supplement the time line as needed, and then review the elements of Emrys' quest with students.

- Remind students that Emrys has magic powers of his own, and gains additional knowledge from the wise old man of his village. Point out that the evil Emrys must rid the world of is the cruel Vortigern, who would destroy the earth and treat his fellow men as poorly as he did the Welshmen. Emrys' perilous journey takes the form of using his dreams to guide Vortigern into his own defeat; the boy faces danger from the soldiers and from Vortigern himself. Ultimately, Emrys is able to use the power of his dreams to "do what must be done:" protecting his land and people from a wicked would-be king.

Guided Practice: Apply

- **Three-Minute Review** Have students spend three minutes reviewing the hero and quest information they noted as they read, and consider how the parallel lives of Arthur and Emrys represent two variations of the archetypal hero.

- When the review period is over, ask students to discuss in groups of three how the characters fit the archetype yet remained unique and interesting to readers.

red by the throat. There was a moment of silence, and then the red dragon tumbled end over end until it hit the ground.

The white dragon followed it down, straddling its fallen foe and screaming victory into the air with a voice like thunder.

"Kill it! Kill the white now!" shouted Vortigern.

As if freed from a spell, his soldiers readied their weapons. But before a single arrow could fly, the white dragon leapt back into the air and was gone, winging over the highest peak.

"Just so the red dragon of Vortigern shall be defeated," Emrys said, but not so loud the High King could hear.

Cursing the fleeing dragon, Vortigern ordered the tower to be built again. Then he turned to Emrys. "If the tower does not stand this time, I *will* have your blood."

That night young Emrys stared out his window, past the newly built tower. A hawk circled lazily in the sky. Suddenly the hawk swooped down, landing on his window ledge. There was a moment of silent communion between them, as if Emrys could read the hawk's thoughts, as if the hawk could read his. Then away the hawk flew.

Mountains, valleys, hillsides, forests gave way beneath the hawk's wings until, far off in the distance, it spied thousands of flickering lights coming up from the south. As if in a dream, Emrys saw these things, too. **❶**

Emerging from his vision, Emrys turned

❶ **Literary Focus** **The Hero's Story** Often heroes of legend have special powers, including communion with animals. What has the hawk shown Emrys?

The Komodo Dragon: Namesake of a Legend

Dragons have appeared in the folklore of many cultures, so some people theorize that extinct animals—discovered as fossils—contributed to the widespread dragon legends of long ago. Whatever the origin of dragon beliefs, real creatures have been compared to and even named after the mythical dragon in modern times. The most fearsome real-world "dragon" is the Komodo dragon (*Varanus komodoensis*) of Indonesia. Growing longer than ten feet and weighing as much as 365 pounds, these dragons don't breathe fire, but their saliva contains deadly bacteria. Wounded Komodo prey can die from infection several days after being bitten.

Ask Yourself
How is the Komodo dragon pictured here similar to the dragons in this legend? How is it different?

Universal Access

EL English Learners

English for Academic Success Students may struggle with some of the archaic language used on these pages. Provide them with the following definitions:

became of—happened to

just so—in the same way

a moment of silent communion—brief, nonverbal communication

spied—saw, or noticed

chiefest—best, or most important

was fit—was good enough

AAVE Students Who Use African American Vernacular English

English for Academic Success Some students may transpose, or switch around, adjacent consonants. Explain to students that this is acceptable when using informal English, but in situations that require formal English, students should take care to pronounce consonant sounds in the order in which they appear in a word. For instance, if reading aloud from p. 805, students should take care to say "Arthur asked," instead from the window and went downstairs. He found King Vortigern by the foot of the tower.

"I have seen in a vision that your fate is linked with the red dragon's," Emrys cried. "You will be attacked by thousands of soldiers under the white dragon's flag—attacked and slain."

Vortigern drew his sword, angry enough to kill the boy for such insolence. But at that very moment, a lookout atop the tower shouted: "Soldiers, my lord! Thousands of them!"

Vortigern raced to the top of the tower stairs and stared across the valley. It was true. And as he watched further, one of the knights leading the army urged his horse forward and raced along to the tower foot, shouting: "Come and meet your fate, murderous Vortigern!"

Vortigern turned to his own men. "Defend me! Defend my tower!"

But when they saw the numbers against them, the men all deserted.

"Surrender, Vortigern!" cried a thousand voices.

"Never!" he called back. "Never!"

The old wizard stopped speaking.

"Well?" Arthur asked. "What happened

"A king should forgive his enemies and make them his chiefest friends. You taught me that, Merlin."

to Vortigern? You cannot end a story there."

Merlin looked at him carefully. "What do *you* think happened?"

"Vortigern was slain, just as Emrys said."

"Is that the boy speaking?" asked the wizard. "Or the king?"

"The boy," admitted Arthur. "A king should forgive his enemies and make them his chiefest friends. You taught me that, Merlin. But what did happen?" **J**

"The men of the white dragon defeated Vortigern all right. Burned him up in his own tower."

"And that knight, the one who rode up to the tower first. What became of him?"

"His name was Uther Pendragon and he eventually became the High King," Merlin said.

"Uther," mused Arthur. "He was the last High King before me. But then he was a hero. He was fit to rule. Perhaps one of his sons will come to claim my throne."

"Uther had only one son," Merlin said softly, "though only I knew of it." He looked steadily at the boy. "That son was you, Arthur."

"Me?" For a moment Arthur's voice squeaked. "Uther was my father? Then I

J Read and Discuss What do you think of this statement about kings?

Vocabulary **insolence** (IHN suh luhns) *n.*: rudeness.

---

of "Arthur aksed." Have students pair up and practice using the correct pronunciation.

Struggling Readers

Benchmark Students Lead students in a discussion of the predictions they made and revised during the story. Ask volunteers to share one of their predictions, their reason for making the prediction, revisions to the prediction, and the reason for revising the prediction.

Science Link

Ask Yourself _____

Possible response: The Komodo dragon is similar to the dragons in the legend because both kinds of dragon have scaly, thick skin and sharp claws. Both are dangerous to humans. The dragons in the legend, however, can fly and breathe fire. The Komodo dragon has poisonous saliva.

Think About/Talk About

Comprehension

J Read and Discuss

Possible response: It might not be a good idea for Arthur to trust his enemies, but it is smart to keep them where he can see them.

Analysis

I Literary Focus

Possible response: The hawk has shown Emrys that soldiers are coming to attack Vortigern.

Extend the Discussion

Comparing and Contrasting How does Merlin's advice to Arthur in the second column of p. 805 contrast with the way the men of the white dragon treated Vortigern? *Possible response: Merlin advises Arthur to forgive his enemies and make them his friends, but the men of the white dragon did not. They burned Vortigern in his own tower.*

Conflict At the end of p. 805, Arthur learns that his father was High King. How might this knowledge affect Arthur's internal conflict? *Possible response: Arthur felt conflicted because he didn't believe that he was supposed to be king, but now that he knows he was born to the role, he might feel more confident about his kingship.*

Vocabulary: Own the Word

insolence: Why does Vortigern want to punish Emrys's *insolence*? *Possible response: Emrys has just predicted Vortigern's downfall and death, which Vortigern does not believe and thinks it is a rude trick by Emrys.*

▶ Comprehension

Ⓚ Read and Discuss

Possible response: Merlin's story has reassured Arthur a great deal. Arthur now feels that he is the rightful king, as his father was the last High King.

Ⓛ Reading Focus

Possible response: I predict that Merlin is having another prophetic dream, and he will be the one who helps Arthur create the Knights of the Round Table.

Vocabulary: Own the Word

recognition: Tell students that *recognition* is the noun form of a verb they may be familiar with: *recognize*. *Recognition* is the act of identifying someone or something from memory. Ask students how they will reveal *recognition* of a friend or family member they haven't seen in a long time.

Monitor Students' Comprehension

Guide the class in answering these comprehension questions.

1. How does Emrys play a heroic role? [*His dreams foretell Vortigern's defeat.*]

2. Why does Vortigern's tower keep collapsing? [*It is built on top of a pool of water and mud.*]

3. Who is Arthur's father? [*Uther Pendragon, the last High King*]

am not fatherless? Then I am king by right and not just because I pulled a sword from a stone."

Merlin shook his head. "Don't underestimate your real strength in pulling that sword," Merlin cautioned. "It took a true and worthy king to do what you did."

Arthur gave a deep sigh. "Why did you not tell me this before?"

The old wizard's hawk eyes opened wide. "I could not tell you until you were ready. There are rules for prophets, just as there are rules for kings."

"So now I am king in truth."

Merlin smiled. "You were always king Ⓚ

in truth. Only you doubted it. So you can thank your dreams for waking you up."

"What of Emrys?" Arthur asked. "What happened to him?"

"Oh—he's still around," replied the wizard. "Went on dreaming. Made a career of it." He rummaged around in some old boxes and crates by the desk until he found what he was looking for. "I still have this. Saved it all this time." He tossed a large yellowed dragon's tooth across to Arthur.

Sudden recognition dawned on Arthur's face. "You? You saved this? Then you were the boy named Emrys!"

"Surely you guessed that before," Merlin teased. "But now perhaps we can both go back to sleep."

"Thank you, Merlin," Arthur said. "I don't think I shall dream any more bad dreams."

Merlin's gnarled fingers caged the boy's hand for a moment. "But you shall dream," he said quietly. "Great men dream great dreams, and I have dreamed your greatness." He plucked the crown from the desktop. "Don't forget this, my lord king."

Arthur took the crown and placed it carefully on his head. Then he turned, went out the door, and down the tower stairs.

Merlin watched for a moment more, then sank back down in his chair. Closing his eyes, he fell immediately to sleep, dreaming of knights and a Round Table. Ⓛ

Ⓚ **Read and Discuss** How and to what <u>extent</u> has Merlin's story reassured Arthur?

Ⓛ **Reading Focus** **Making Predictions** What do you predict this last sentence means?

Vocabulary **recognition** (rehk uhg NIHSH uhn) *n.:* act of recognizing; realization of something.

🐻 **California Standards, pp. 807–809**

■ **Reading Standard 3.6** Analyze a range of responses to a literary work and determine the extent to which the literary elements in the work shaped those responses.

■ **Reading Standard 1.2** Use knowledge of Greek, Latin, and Anglo-Saxon roots and affixes to understand content-area vocabulary.

Applying Your Skills

Reading Standard 3.6 Analyze a range of responses to a literary work and **determine the extent to which the literary elements in the work shaped** those **responses**.

Merlin and the Dragons
Literary Response and Analysis

Reading Skills Focus
Quick Check

1. What happens in the **frame story**—the story that starts at the beginning and picks up again at the end?

2. Where does the story-*within*-the-story start and end? Who is telling this story?

Read with a Purpose

3. What is the purpose of the story-within-the-story? What does Arthur learn from it?

Reading Skills: Making Predictions

4. Review the Predictions Chart you filled in as you read the story. How correct (or incorrect) were your predictions? Did anything in the story surprise you?

Story events	Predictions	What actually happens

Literary Skills Focus
Literary Analysis

5. **Analyze** To what <u>extent</u> is Emrys like Arthur? What qualities do they share?

6. **Analyze** What makes Emrys an outsider in his society? How do the boys make Emrys a scapegoat—that is, what do they blame him for, and why?

7. **Identify** Who leads the attack against Vortigern? Were you surprised when Merlin revealed who this knight is? Explain.

8. **Evaluate** The oldest recorded tales of King Arthur say little about Arthur's childhood and even less about Merlin's. Do you agree with the way the author <u>interprets</u> the characters?

9. **Connect** Does the boys' treatment of Emrys remind you of anything in your experience? Explain.

Literary Skills: The Hero's Story

10. **Compare and Contrast** Review your answers to the Literary Focus questions throughout this selection. What <u>circumstances</u> in this story reflect the patterns of other hero stories? Do you know of any hero stories—old or modern—like this one? Include novels, comics, and movies in your answer.

Literary Skills Review: Imagery

11. **Analyze** Yolen uses vivid imagery to help us participate in her story. What images in the story help you visualize the <u>elements</u> of setting and character? What image helps you hear the dragons' battle cries?

Writing Skills Focus
Think as a Reader/Writer

Use It in Your Writing Review the notes you took on how Yolen makes her characters come to life. How did the characterizations of Emrys and Vortigern—and others—help shape your response to this story?

 What Do **You Think Now**

How do the evil characters behave in this story? What do the good characters stand up for?

Universal Access

Struggling Writers

To help students organize their thoughts prior to writing a response, have them create the graphic organizer below to organize visually the presentation of the characters in the selection and the students' response to them. Have students fill in the first row for each character with the characters' statements, thoughts, and behaviors that stood out to them. Then, have them fill in the second row with their personal reactions to the statements, thoughts, and behaviors noted in the first row for each character. Have

students discuss in pairs their reactions—particularly which characters they sympathized with, found inspiring, or despised—prior to writing.

	Emrys	Vortigern	Arthur	Merlin
Statements, Thoughts, Behaviors				
My Response				

Independent Practice
Vocabulary Development

Your Turn _____

1. -less: without; hopeless, harmless, loveless

2. im-: toward, on; impress, imprint

3. in-: not; insufficient, insane

4. re-: again; repeat, rewrite

English for Academic Success
Language Coach
Possible responses:

1. *(a) knotted*

2. *(b) holy*

3. *(a) killed*

English for Academic Success
Academic Vocabulary

Possible response: I interpret Merlin's motivation for telling the story as having two parts: he wants to comfort Arthur, whom he cares for, but he also realizes that Arthur is ready to know the truth about his background, and the story is a good way to reveal the information. Merlin's story relates to Arthur's dream to a good extent. Merlin's story revolves around recurring dreams that were actually prophecies, and Arthur's dream seems to be as well.

Applying Your Skills

Reading Standard 1.2 Use knowledge of Greek, Latin, and Anglo-Saxon roots and affixes to understand content-area vocabulary.

Merlin and the Dragons

Vocabulary Development
Prefixes and Suffixes: Useful Additions

A **prefix** is a word part added to the front of a word to change its meaning. For example, the word *recognition*, meaning "knowing again," contains the prefix *re–* meaning "again."

A **suffix** is a word part added to the end of a word to change its meaning or to give it a different grammatical function. The word *ruthless* is built from the old-fashioned word *ruth*, meaning "pity," and the suffix *–less*, meaning "without."

Here is a word map showing the meaning of the prefix *non–* and words formed with *non–*:

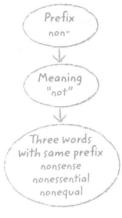

Prefix
non-

↓

Meaning
"not"

↓

Three words
with same prefix
nonsense
nonessential
nonequal

Your Turn _____

Using a dictionary and the model word map above, make word maps for the prefixes and suffixes at right. Then, use your word maps to clarify the meanings of your vocabulary words.

–less
im–
in–
re–

Language Coach

Synonyms Use a thesaurus or dictionary, if necessary, to identify these synonyms.

1. Merlin's fingers are described as *gnarled*. You could also say they were (a) knotted (b) dirty.

2. The magicians call the stones *sacred*. You could also say they were (a) heavy (b) holy.

3. Vortigern was *slain*. You could also say he was (a) killed (b) crippled.

Academic Vocabulary

Talk About ...

Near the beginning of "Merlin and the Dragons," Merlin says: "What better than a story on a rainy night?" How do you interpret Merlin's motivation for telling the story to Arthur? To what extent is the plot of Merlin's story related to Arthur's recurring dream?

Learn It Online
Sharpen your word skills at:
go.hrw.com   H7-808   **Go**

Universal Access: Vocabulary Development

EL English Learners

English for Academic Success Students may have difficulty recognizing the slight variations in meaning among synonyms. Have students work in pairs to look up one of the following words in a thesaurus: *nice, mean, night, gentle*. Have students choose three to five synonyms from the list and look up each in a dictionary.

Have students copy the definitions of the original word and synonyms into their **Reader/Writer Notebook,** and discuss the differences in meaning with a fluent English speaker.

Grammar Link
Punctuating Dialogue

This story's dramatic punch comes in part from its use of **dialogue**—the characters' exact words set in quotation marks. The dialogue in the story also serves to delineate, or define, the characters' personalities. Here are two important rules for punctuating dialogue.

- When using dialogue, begin a new paragraph every time the speaker changes, and enclose each speaker's words in quotation marks.

   "What is it, boy?" the old man asked. "What brings you here at this hour?"

   "I am the king," Arthur said, but softly as if he were not really sure.

- When dialogue is interrupted by a speaker tag—an expression or description that identifies the speaker—the dialogue following the speaker tag begins with a lowercase letter.

   "Stonecutter," cried Vortigern, "break open the stones!"

Your Turn

Punctuate the dialogue in these sentences correctly.

1. Slay the dragons, Vortigern commanded. We cannot, replied his soldiers, because they are already away!

2. Rebuild the tower, Vortigern cried. Emrys, however, knew it would never stand.

CHOICES

As you respond to the Choices, use the **Academic Vocabulary** words as appropriate: <u>circumstance</u>, <u>element</u>, <u>extent</u>, <u>interpret</u>.

REVIEW
Respond to the Literature

Group Discussion Different readers will <u>interpret</u> this story differently. Form a group with three or four classmates, and take turns sharing your interpretations of this story. Include an explanation of which literary <u>element</u> you felt most shaped your response. Present your critique of the story, focusing on that element. Support your choice with textual evidence. As a group, take turns analyzing the various responses to the story and determining the extent to which specific literary elements helped to shape classmates' responses to the work.

CONNECT
Who Are Today's Heroes?

Timed ⏱ Writing Some people think true heroes have been replaced by media celebrities who dominate magazines, TV, and the Internet. Write a brief **character analysis** of someone real or imagined whom you consider to be a *true* hero. First, define what a hero is. Then use real-life examples to support your analysis.

EXTEND
Merlin and the Dragons Game

TechFocus With a group, write a proposal for a video game based on "Merlin and the Dragons." Include an explanation of how your interactive game might be played. Sketch the action figures who would play parts in the game. Think of roles for the two dragons in the story, and determine how the game might be won or lost. Present your proposal to the class.

Independent Practice
Grammar Link
Your Turn _____

1. "Slay the dragons," Vortigern commanded. "We cannot," replied his soldiers, "because they are already away!"

2. "Rebuild the tower," Vortigern cried. Emrys, however, knew it would never stand.

Choices: Evaluation Criteria
Review: **Homework**
Respond to the Literature

- Students present critiques clearly supported with text details.

- Students listen respectfully to one another and offer constructive feedback.

Connect: Timed Writing
45-50 Minutes

- Students develop a character analysis of their hero.

- Students support their analysis with evidence.

Extend: **Homework**
Merlin and the Dragons Game

- Students develop clear proposals answering the questions posed.

- Students explain in detail how the story would translate into a game.

 Assess

✏ **Chapter 8 Resources,** Selection Standards Check, p. 21

💿 **Teacher One Stop™,** editable Selection Standards Check

 ThinkCentral Online Assessment, Selection Standards Check

 Reteach

ThinkCentral Online Remediation

Universal Access: Grammar Link

EL **English Learners/ Struggling Writers**

English for Academic Success Help students understand the function of quotation marks and their use in dialogue.

- Remind students that quotation marks are used in writing to identify only the exact words that a character speaks aloud, whether to himself or to another character. Speaker tags are not enclosed in quotation marks, nor are a character's unspoken thoughts, which generally are identified using italics.

- Work through the following examples as a class to strengthen students' understanding of quotation marks.

   1. *Come back soon, Annie cried.*
   2. *How, asked Donny, did I lose my basketball?*
   3. *Let's see a movie, suggested Xavier, like* Spider-Man. *He hoped his family would agree.*

✔ For more practice with using pronouns, see **Warriner's Handbook, Language Handbook Worksheets,** and **GrammarNotes.**

Objectives

Students will

- understand the elements of a quest, including the use of riddles
- identify and analyze cause-and-effect relationships in a text
- recognize word relationships and parts of speech

Motivate

What Do You Think?/QuickWrite

Use the QuickWrite to have students speculate on the concerns and wishes of men and of women. Then have students discuss in their **Reader/Writer Notebook** the ways in which a hero might improve life for both genders.

English for Academic Success

Academic Vocabulary

Look for opportunities to use the Academic Vocabulary words in this chapter.

- **circumstance, *n.:*** condition or fact.
- **element, *n.:*** essential part of something.
- **extent, *n.:*** degree to which something extends.

Analyzing Visuals

Extension Activity In what ways does this image relate to the idea of the quest? ***Possible response:*** *The knight in the image appears to be on a quest. He is riding a horse, dressed in armor, and carrying his banner.*

 California Standards, pp. 810–823

- **Reading Standard 3.6** Analyze a range of responses to a literary work and determine the extent to which the literary elements in the work shaped those responses.

LEGEND
Preparing to Read

SIR GAWAIN
AND THE LOATHLY LADY

retold by **Betsy Hearne**

What Do You Think How can a hero's choices improve the world?

QuickWrite

What do men want most in the world? What do women want more than anything else? Think carefully about these two questions, which have been asked by modern psychologists as well as by the teller of this legend. Write one or more responses to each question.

Gothic tapestry of knight in full armor.

Selection Readability	
Easily Accessible **Accessible** Challenging	familiar main character; archaic language

Selection Plot Summary

A mysterious knight challenges King Arthur to discover what women desire most. An unattractive lady agrees to tell Arthur the answer as long as she is allowed to marry Sir Gawain. Gawain accepts this offer, and the lady reveals that women desire control of their own lives. When Gawain grants his new wife this control, she turns into a beautiful woman.

Reader/Writer Notebook

Use your **RWN** to complete the activities for this selection.

 Reading Standard 3.6 Analyze a range of responses to a literary work and **determine the extent to which the literary elements in the work shaped** those **responses.**

Literary Skills Focus

The Quest A **quest** is a long and perilous journey taken in search of something of great value: a treasure, a kingdom, the hand of one's beloved, or the answer to an important question. During the quest, the hero faces temptations and difficult tasks—the need to overcome and kill the monstrous guardian of a treasure, for example.

Centuries ago, **riddles**—puzzling questions or problems—were often used in stories as a test for heroes. The hero usually had to answer or solve a riddle correctly before going on with the quest. Riddles were important in real life, too. A riddle contest could become a battle of wits with great rewards for the winner and exile or even death for the loser.

Reading Skills Focus

Identifying Cause and Effect Tightly plotted stories like "Sir Gawain and the Loathly Lady" are made up of a series of causes and their effects. A **cause** is an event that makes something happen. An **effect** is what happens as a result of the cause. As you read, track the series of causes and their effects, using a chart like the one below. Two boxes have been filled in for you. Add as many other boxes as you need.

Arthur goes into the wood to hunt.

↓

Meets a strange knight who wants to kill him because of a grievance.

↓

[ ]

↓

[ ]

Writing Skills Focus

Think as a Reader/Writer

Find It in Your Reading As you read, notice how the writer describes the loathly lady. What descriptive <u>elements</u> help you picture her? How do the descriptions shape your response to the story?

Vocabulary

chivalry (SHIHV uhl ree) *n.*: code that governs knightly behavior, requiring courage, honor, and readiness to help the weak. *Chivalry requires knights to help those in need.*

countenance (KOWN tuh nuhns) *n.*: face; appearance. *King Arthur's countenance revealed fear.*

loathsome (LOHTH suhm) *adj.*: disgusting. *The loathsome appearance of Dame Ragnell contrasts with her sweet voice.*

sovereignty (SAHV ruhn tee) *n.*: control; authority. *King Arthur had sovereignty over all of Britain.*

Language Coach

Parts of Speech Many words have forms that are different parts of speech. For example, look at *chivalry* and *chivalrous*. What is the part of speech of each word? Refer to a dictionary if you need help.

- What verb is found in *loathsome*?
- What adjective is found in *sovereignty*?

✳ **Learn It Online**
Hear a professional actor read this legend. Visit the selection at:

go.hrw.com   H7-811   **Go**

Preteach

Introducing Vocabulary

After students read the definitions of the Vocabulary words, have partners play "Guess My Word!" The first player chooses a word and gives synonyms until the second player guesses the word. When all four words have been used, players switch roles and play again.

English for Academic Success

Language Coach

Explain to students that *chivalry* is the code of knightly behavior, and a *chivalrous* person practices *chivalry*. *Chivalrous*, an adjective, is a form of the noun *chivalry*. [*The verb* loath *is found in* loathsome; *the adjective* sovereign *is found in* sovereignty]

Literary Skills Focus

As you read and discuss the selection with students, have them identify the dangers and the difficult tasks faced on the hero's quest.

Reading Skills Focus

Give students a copy of the Reading Skills Focus graphic organizer before they read. Tell them to use their responses to answer the questions on the Applying Your Skills page.

Writing Skills Focus

Have students use their **Reader/Writer Notebook** to record words and phrases describing the loathly lady. Students can use their notes to complete the Writing Skills Focus activity.

✳ **Learn It Online**
The online version of this selection includes audio support to engage all students and to help struggling readers with reading comprehension and vocabulary.

go.hrw.com   H7-811   **Go**

Selection Introduction

More About the Writer

■ Though **Betsy Hearne** studied history in college, she always had a strong interest in books and writing.

■ After she finished school, she began working at a library as a children's storyteller. Her stories were so popular that over a hundred children came to hear her stories every week.

Think About the Writer

Ask students to describe the differences between an authority figure who shows kindness and concern, as opposed to an authority figure who is unkind and bossy. Which would make the better ruler, and why?

 For Independent Reading

■ Students interested in knights and their adventures might enjoy Michael Cadnum's *Book of the Lion*, the story of a young blacksmith's apprentice turned knight of the Crusades.

■ For students interested in quests and riddles, recommend Avi's *Crispin: The Cross of Lead*, the story of a young man seeking to solve the riddle of his identity.

MEET THE WRITER

Betsy Hearne
(1942–)

Transforming the Beast

Betsy Hearne has collected twenty-seven Beauty and the Beast folk tales from storytellers around the world. She writes that the story of Beauty and the Beast, in all its variations, "is striking in its emphasis on the importance of a woman's power to control her own choices."

Hearne's work in collecting and connecting various types of Beauty and the Beast tales began with her studies in graduate school. She believes that:

> "All of the stories . . . are about journeys in which the heroine or hero is transformed not through winning battles but through love for another being. . . . Beauty and the Beast tales suggest . . . that love is as powerful as force in coming to terms with what we fear."

Folklorist and Storyteller

Hearne, a respected critic and scholar of children's literature, teaches folklore and storytelling at the University of Illinois at Urbana-Champaign. Her love of story is enriched by the summers she spends in the village of Kilcrohane in County Cork, Ireland.

Think About the Writer Think about Hearne's idea about the power of love versus the power of force. What do you think of her idea?

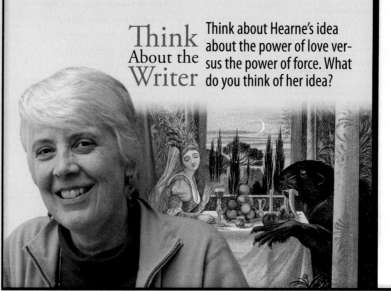

Build Background

Sir Gawain is a perfect model of chivalry (SHIHV uhl ree)—the code that strictly governs the behavior of an ideal knight. Here are some of the rules of chivalry:

- Defend the church.
- Be loyal to your king.
- Defend the poor and weak.
- Maintain your honor in all circumstances.
- Fight against injustice and evil.
- Protect the innocent.
- Respect women.
- Never abandon an ally.

Loathly (LOHTH lee) is an old word for "loathsome," which means "hideous, disgusting, or repulsive." The character of the loathly lady and the question "What do women most desire?" are popular story elements in medieval (mee dee EE vuhl) literature—literature from the Middle Ages (the fifth through fifteenth centuries in Europe).

Preview the Selection

The major figure in this story is **Gawain,** a perfect knight of King Arthur's court. The character who presents him with a serious dilemma, testing his chivalry, is **Dame Ragnell,** the loathly lady.

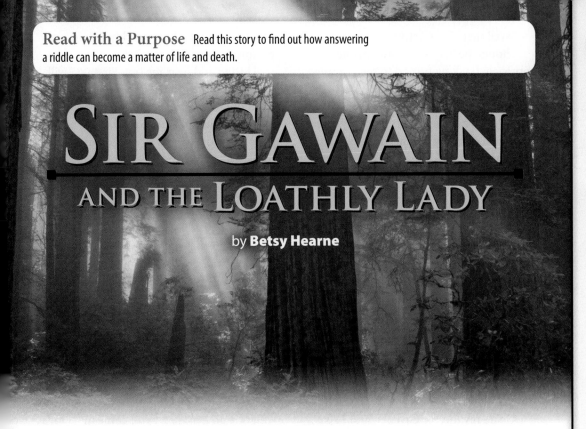

Read with a Purpose Read this story to find out how answering a riddle can become a matter of life and death.

SIR GAWAIN
AND THE LOATHLY LADY

by **Betsy Hearne**

N ow if you listen awhile I will tell you a tale of Arthur the King and how an adventure once befell him. Of all kings and all knights, King Arthur bore away the honor wherever he went. In all his country there was nothing but chivalry, and knights were loved by the people.

One day in spring King Arthur was hunting in Ingleswood with all his lords beside him. Suddenly a deer ran by in the distance and the king took up chase, calling back to his knights, "Hold you still every man, I will chase this one myself!" He took his arrows and bow and stooped low like a woodsman to stalk the deer. But every time he came near the animal, it leapt away into the forest. So King Arthur went a while after the deer, and no knight went with him, until at last he let fly an arrow and killed the deer. He had raised a bugle to his lips to summon the knights when he heard a voice behind him.

Vocabulary **chivalry** (SHIHV uhl ree) *n.*: code that governs knightly behavior, requiring courage, honor, and readiness to help the weak.

- Explain to students that **quests** undertaken by archetypal heroes are more complicated than most journeys, and that the stakes are often higher. On a quest, the hero faces challenges from the difficult tasks posed to him, such as complex **riddles,** and from temptations faced along the way. The hero must find the strength to overcome these obstacles and win the prize that he seeks through successful completion of the quest.

- Have students read to point C. Explain that the bargain Sir Gromer makes with King Arthur gives the king one year to solve a riddle or else he must allow Sir Gromer to kill him. Point out that, although riddles are often incorporated into a quest, this riddle will drive the quest described in this story. It is a test of intelligence and resourcefulness for Arthur, with a reward or consequence of his own life.

Guided Practice: Apply

Listen-Talk-Write Read aloud pp. 814–816 for students. Then, have them discuss in small groups what tasks or temptations King Arthur has faced on his quest. Then, have students reflect briefly in their **Reader/Writer Notebook** on whether or not they think he will succeed.

Think as a Reader/Writer

Find It in Your Reading Point out the description of the loathly lady in the second column on p. 815. Explain that the author compares her face to "that of an animal" "with a pushed-in nose and a few yellowing tusks for teeth."

Use It in Your Writing Have students craft their own sentence describing the loathly lady with vivid adjectives and/or comparisons.

"Well met, King Arthur!"

Though he had not heard anyone approach, the king turned to see a strange knight, fully armed, standing only a few yards away.

"You have done me wrong many a year and given away my northern lands," said the strange knight. "I have your life in my hands—what will you do now, King Alone?"

"Sir Knight, what is your name?" asked the king.

"My name is Gromer Somer Joure."[1]

"Sir Gromer, think carefully," said the king. "To slay me here, unarmed as I am, will get you no honor. All knights will refuse you wherever you go. Calm yourself—come to Carlyle and I shall mend all that is amiss."

"Nay," said Sir Gromer, "by heaven, King! You shall not escape when I have you at advantage. If I let you go with only a warning, later you'll defy me, of that I'm sure." **A**

"Spare my life, Sir Gromer, and I shall grant you whatever is in my power to give. It is shameful to slay me here, with nothing but my hunting gear, and you armed for battle." **B**

"All your talking will not help you, King, for I want neither land nor gold, truly." Sir Gromer smiled. "Still . . . if you will promise to meet me here, in the same fashion, on a day I will choose . . ."

---

1. **Gromer Somer Joure** (groh MEHR soh MEHR zhoor).

A Reading Focus **Identifying Cause and Effect** What has caused Gromer to want to kill Arthur?

B Read and Discuss From King Arthur's appeal, what do you learn about the behavior expected of a knight?

"Yes," said the king quickly. "Here is my promise."

"Listen and hear me out. First you will swear upon my sword to meet me here without fail, on this day one year from now. Of all your knights none shall come with you. You must tell me at your coming what thing women most desire—and if you do not bring the answer to my riddle, you will lose your head. What say you, King?" **C**

"I agree, though it is a hateful bargain," said the king. "Now let me go. I promise you as I am the true king, to come again at this day one year from now and bring you your answer."

The knight laughed, "Now go your way, King Arthur. You do not yet know your sorrow. Yet stay a moment—do not think of playing false—for by Mary[2] I think you would betray me."

"Nay," said King Arthur. "You will never find me an untrue knight. Farewell, Sir Knight, and evil met. I will come in a year's time, though I may not escape." The king began to blow his bugle for his knights to find him. Sir Gromer turned his horse and was gone as quickly as he had come, so that the lords found their king alone with the slain deer.

"We will return to Carlyle," said the king. "I do not like this hunting."

The lords knew by his countenance that the king met with some disturbance,

---

2. **by Mary:** a mild oath.

C Literary Focus **The Quest** How will Sir Gromer test Arthur?

Vocabulary **countenance** (KOWN tuh nuhns) *n.:* face; appearance.

Cross-Curricular Connection

LITERATURE: Arthur and Gawain

King Arthur and Sir Gawain, two of the main characters in "Sir Gawain and the Loathly Lady," are featured in many Arthurian legends. Provide students with additional information to help them appreciate the characters' rich mythological background.

- Legends name Arthur's parents as King Uther Pendragon and Ygerna (sometimes Igraine) of Cornwall. Historians

have long debated whether Arthur was an actual historical figure. Today it is generally accepted that the legend of Arthur has some historical basis, albeit greatly embellished and romanticized. Other important figures in the tales include Arthur's wife Guinevere and Lancelot, one of the most famous of Arthur's knights. Some tales tell of the collapse of Arthur's kingdom following a romance between Guinevere and Lancelot.

but no one knew of his encounter. They wondered at the king's heavy step and sad look, until at last Sir Gawain[3] said to the king, "Sire, I marvel at you. What thing do you sorrow for?"

"I'll tell you, gentle Gawain," said Arthur. "In the forest as I pursued the deer, I met with a knight in full armor, and he charged me I should not escape him. I must keep my word to him or else I am foresworn."[4]

"Fear not my lord. I am not a man that would dishonor you."

"He threatened me, and would have slain me with great heat, but I spoke with him since I had no weapons."

"What happened then?" said Gawain.

"He made me swear to meet him there in one year's time, alone and unarmed. On that day I must tell him what women desire most, or I shall lose my life. If I fail in my answer, I know that I will be slain without mercy."

"Sire, make good cheer," said Gawain. "Make your horse ready to ride into strange country, and everywhere you meet either man or woman, ask of them the answer to the riddle. I will ride another way, and every man and woman's answer I will write in a book." **D**

"That is well advised, Gawain," said the king. They made preparations to leave immediately, and when both were ready, Gawain rode one way and the king another—each one asked every man and woman they found what women most desire.

Some said they loved beautiful clothes; some said they loved to be praised; some said they loved a handsome man; some said one, some said another. Gawain had so many answers that he made a great book to hold them, and after many months of traveling he came back to court again. The king was there already with his book, and each looked over the other's work. But no answer seemed right.

"By God," said the king, "I am afraid. I will seek a little more in Ingleswood Forest. I have but one month to my set day, and I may find some good tidings."

"Do as you think best," said Gawain, "but whatever you do, remember that it is good to have spring again."

King Arthur rode forth on that day, into Ingleswood, and there he met with a lady. King Arthur marveled at her, for she was the ugliest creature that he had ever seen. Her face seemed almost like that of an animal, with a pushed-in nose and a few yellowing tusks for teeth. Her figure was twisted and deformed, with a hunched back and shoulders a yard broad. No tongue could tell the foulness of that lady. But she rode gaily on a palfrey[5] set with gold and precious stones, and when she spoke her voice was sweet and soft.

"I am glad that I have met with you, King Arthur," she said. "Speak with me, for your life is in my hand. I know of your situation, and I warn you that you will not find your answer if I do not tell you."

---

3. **Gawain** (GAH wihn).
4. **foresworn:** untrue to one's word; shown to be a liar.

5. **palfrey** (PAWL free): gentle riding horse.

D Literary Focus **The Quest** What is the purpose of the quest? What are its perils?

- Gawain is the nephew of Arthur and one of the king's most loyal and devoted knights. Other close relations are his brothers Aggravain, Gaheris, and Gareth. He is also said to be a half-brother of Mordred, the traitorous knight who causes Arthur's downfall in some stories. Gawain is the hero of many Arthurian tales, one of the most famous being "Sir Gawain and the Green Knight."

▶ Comprehension

A Reading Focus

Possible response: Sir Gromer believes King Arthur has done him wrong, and has given away his lands.

B Read and Discuss

Possible response: Knights consider honor and chivalry extremely important, and they should not attack a defenseless enemy.

▶ Analysis

C Literary Focus

Possible response: Sir Gromer will test King Arthur by having him find the answer to an extremely difficult riddle.

D Literary Focus

Possible response: The purpose of the quest is to find the right answer to the riddle that will save King Arthur's life. The biggest peril of the quest is failure, but they may also face hostility in strange countries, or danger from bad weather or accidents.

Vocabulary: Own the Word

countenance: King Arthur's lords could tell from the king's *countenance* that he was upset. What do you think his face looked like when he returned from talking with Sir Gromer? *Possible response: He might have been pale, or frowning, or looking otherwise anxious*

Model the Skill

- Explain to students that the forms of a word will be related in structure and meaning, but may be different **parts of speech.** Variations of a word may exist as a noun, a verb, an adjective, or an adverb. Understanding parts of speech is useful to understanding the exact application of a word in context.

- Point out the words *choose* and *choice* in the paragraphs above and below point E. Read aloud the sentence containing each word. Explain that choice is a form of choose, but that they are not the same part of speech. *Choice* is a noun meaning *that which is decided upon,* while *choose* is a verb meaning *to decide on something.* Though they are forms of the same word, they are different parts of speech and are used differently in context.

Guided Practice: Apply

Think-Pair-Share Have students scan the story independently and identify one or more sets of related words. Then, have students discuss their chosen words with a partner, identifying the meanings and parts of speech for each of the sets. Ask volunteers to share their words, meanings, and parts of speech with the class.

Analyzing Visuals   Connecting to the Text

To what extent does this image match your idea of the horror of Dame Ragnell's appearance?

"What do you want with me, lady?" said the king, taken aback by the lady's boldness.

"Sir, I would like to speak with you. You will die if I do not save you, I know it very well."

"What do you mean, my lady, tell me," stammered the king. "What is your desire, why is my life in your hand? Tell me, and I shall give you all you ask."

"You must grant me a knight to wed," said the lady slowly. "His name is Sir Gawain. I will make this bargain: If your life is saved another way, you need not grant my desire. If my answer saves your life, grant me Sir Gawain as my husband. Choose now, for you must soon meet your enemy." **E**

"By Mary," said the king, "I cannot grant you Sir Gawain. That lies with him alone— he is not mine to give. I can only take the choice to Sir Gawain."

"Well," she said. "Then go home again and speak to Sir Gawain. For though I am foul, yet am I merry, and through me he may save your life or ensure your death."

"Alas!" cried the king. "That I should cause Gawain to wed you, for he will not say no. I know not what I should do."

"Sir King, you will get no more from me. When you come again with your answer I will meet you here."

"What is your name, I pray you tell me?"

"Sir King, I am the Dame Ragnell, that never yet betrayed a man."

"Then farewell, Dame Ragnell," said the king.

Thus they departed, and the king returned to Carlyle again with a heavy heart. The first man he met was Sir Gawain. "Sire, how did you fare?" asked the knight.

E **Literary Focus** The Quest What bargain does the lady strike with King Arthur?

Analyzing Visuals

Connecting to the Text: *This distorted image only gives a hint of Dame Ragnell's appearance. The woman appears elderly and strange-looking, but she does not seem as remarkably hideous as the story suggests.*

"Never so ill," said the king. "I fear I will die at Sir Gromer's hand."

"Nay," said Gawain. "I would rather die myself I love you so."

"Gawain, I met today with the foulest lady that I ever saw. She said she would save my life, but first she would have you for her husband."

"Is this all?" asked Gawain. "Then I shall wed her and wed her again! Though she were a fiend, though she were as foul as Beelzebub,[6] her I shall marry. For you are my king and I am your friend—it is my part to save your life, or else I am a false knight and a great coward. If she were the most loathsome woman that ever a man might see, for your love I would spare nothing."

"Thank you, Gawain," said King Arthur then. "Of all knights that I have found, you are the finest. You have saved my life, and my love will not stray from you, as I am king in this land."

The day soon came when the king was to meet the Dame Ragnell and bear his answer to Sir Gromer. Gawain rode with him to the edge of Ingleswood Forest, but there the king said, "Sir Gawain, farewell. I must go west, and you must go no further."

"God speed you on your journey. I wish I rode your way," said Gawain.

The king had ridden but a mile or so more when he met the Dame Ragnell. "Ah, Sir King, you are welcome here bearing your answer."

"Now," said the king, "since it can be no other way, tell me your answer, save my life, and Gawain shall you wed; so he has promised. Tell me in all haste. Have done, I may not tarry."[7]

"Sire," said the Dame Ragnell, "now you will know what women desire most, high and low. Some men say we desire to be fair, or to wed, or to remain fresh and young, or to have flattery from men. But there is one thing that is every woman's fantasy: We desire of men, above all other things, to have sovereignty, for then all is ours. Therefore go on your way, Sir King, and tell that knight what I have said to you. He will be angry and curse the woman who told you, for his labor is lost. Go forth—you will not be harmed."

The king rode forth in great haste until he came to the set place and met with Sir Gromer.

"Come, come, Sir King," said the knight sternly. "Now let me have your answer, for I am ready."

The king pulled out the two books for Sir Gromer to see. "Sir, I dare say the right one is there."

Sir Gromer looked over them, every one, and said at last, "Nay, nay, Sir King, you are a dead man."

"Wait, Sir Gromer," said the king. "I have one more answer to give."

---

6. **Beelzebub** (bee EHL zuh buhb): devil; Satan.

7. **tarry**: linger; delay.

F **Read and Discuss** What does this exchange tell you about the feelings between King Arthur and Sir Gawain?

G **Literary Focus** **The Quest** Explain how Arthur has accomplished his quest.

Vocabulary **loathsome** (LOHTH suhm) *adj.*: disgusting.
sovereignty (SAHV ruhn tee) *n.*: control; authority.

▶ **Comprehension**
F **Read and Discuss**

Possible response: The king gives Sir Gawain the chance to duck out of this marriage, so the king must value Sir Gawain's happiness more than his own life. Sir Gawain is unselfish, saying he'd die for his king, and so, of course he's willing to marry the woman to save the king. Both are willing to sacrifice for each other, which shows the strength of their friendship.

▶ **Analysis**
E **Literary Focus**

Possible response: The lady agrees to tell Arthur the correct answer to Sir Gromer's riddle. In exchange for saving his life, she wants to marry Sir Gawain.

G **Literary Focus**

Possible response: Sir Gawain has accomplished his quest by helping the king find the answer to the riddle that will save his life. He secured the answer by agreeing to marry Dame Ragnell.

▶ **Extend the Discussion**

Conflict What internal conflict does Arthur face because of his meeting with Dame Ragnell? *Possible response:* Arthur does not want to be killed by Sir Gromer, but he doesn't want Gawain to have to marry an incredibly ugly lady, either. He's torn between his desire to solve the riddle and his concern for his friend.

Vocabulary: Own the Word

- **loathsome:** Ask students: Have you ever encountered something *loathsome*? Explain what it was, and what made it so awful.

- **sovereignty:** *Sovereignty* means supreme authority and is usually associated with a country or state. The ruler of a country that gives power to one individual is called a *sovereign.* An individual can also have personal *sovereignty* or power over themselves.

Developing Oral Fluency

Provide students with practice reading dialogue using the conversation between Gawain and King Arthur on p. 817. Divide the class in half, assigning one half the role of Sir Gawain, and the other half the role of Arthur.

Whole-Class Activity Model reading with a fluent reader. Assign the role of Gawain to the student, starting with the line "Sire, how did you fare?" in the second paragraph of p. 817.

- After modeling, cue students speaking the role of Sir Gawain to begin saying the dialogue as a casual inquiry into Arthur's search for the answer to the riddle, but speaking with growing concern for the king in each line. Instruct the group speaking Arthur's role to begin by sounding anxious and desperate, then softening into gratitude at Gawain's generosity. Allowing pauses between each character's speech, cue groups in turn to say their lines.

- After reading the dialogue through once, slowly, have students begin again, this time more quickly and with shorter pauses between speakers. Continue until students are able to read at a natural pace.

Model the Skill

- Tell students that many stories, particularly those describing a hero's quest, are driven by a series of causes and effects. On a quest, for example, difficult tasks and temptations cause the hero to use every ounce of his strength and intelligence to bring about the effect of succeeding at his quest.

- Model identifying causes and effects from pp. 818–819. Point out that in the first column of p. 818, King Arthur has to use Dame Ragnell's answer. This causes him to have to honor his promise—that Dame Ragnell would marry Sir Gawain. The effect of honoring the promise means that King Arthur must bring Dame Ragnell back to his castle, a journey on which everyone in the countryside will see him riding with the loathsome lady.

- Have volunteers identify other causes and effects from pp. 818–819. Write each cause and effect on the board, and discuss connections among the various cause and effect pairs from these pages.

Guided Practice: Apply

Three-Minute Review Have students spend three minutes reviewing the text and their notes regarding Arthur's and Gawain's quests. When the review period is over, have students form groups of three to create cause-and-effect charts describing the relationship of the events from the quests. Display the charts in the classroom, and allow students time to discuss with one another any differences among the charts.

"Say it," said Sir Gromer, "or so God help me you shall bleed."

"Now," said the king, "here is my answer and that is all—above all things, women desire sovereignty, for that is their liking and their greatest desire; to rule over any man. This they told me."

Sir Gromer was silent a moment with rage, but then he cried out, "And she that told you, Sir Arthur, I pray to God I might see her burn in a fire, for that was my sister, Dame Ragnell. God give her shame—I have lost much labor. Go where you like, King Arthur, for you are spared. Alas that I ever saw this day, for I know that you will be my enemy and hunt me down."

"No," said King Arthur, "you will never find me an attacker. Farewell." King Arthur turned his horse into the forest again. Soon he met with the Dame Ragnell, in the same place as before. "Sir King," she said. "I am glad you have sped well. I told you how it would be, and now since I and none other have saved your life, Gawain must wed me."

"I will not fail in my promise," said the king. "If you will be ruled by my council, you shall have your will."

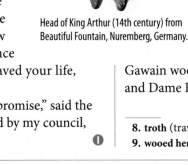

Head of King Arthur (14th century) from Beautiful Fountain, Nuremberg, Germany.

"No, Sir King, I will not be ruled," said the lady. "I know what you are thinking. Ride before, and I will follow to your court. Think how I have saved your life and do not disagree with me, for if you do you will be shamed."

The king was ashamed to bring the loathly lady openly to the court, but forth she rode till they came to Carlyle. All the country wondered when she came, for they had never seen so foul a creature, but she would spare no one the sight of her. Into the hall she went, saying, "Arthur, King, fetch in Sir Gawain, before all the knights, so that you may troth[8] us together. Set forth Gawain my love, for I will not wait."

Sir Gawain stepped forward then, and said, "Sir, I am ready to fulfill the promise I made to you."

"God have mercy," said the Dame Ragnell when she saw Gawain. "For your sake I wish I were a fair woman, for you are of such goodwill." Then Sir Gawain wooed her[9] as he was a true knight, and Dame Ragnell was happy.

---

8. troth (trawth): engaged to marry.
9. wooed her: said romantic things; spoke of love.

H Read and Discuss Why do you think King Arthur gives Sir Gromer all the other answers before giving him Dame Ragnell's?

I Literary Focus The Quest How does the king show his honor?

Universal Access

Struggling Readers

Point out to students that, in the second column of p. 818, Sir Gawain states to King Arthur that he is ready to fulfill the promise he made: to marry Dame Ragnell. Though marrying the loathly lady sounds like a straightforward event, the events leading up to and immediately following the marriage follow the archetype of the quest. Sir Gawain must make his new bride feel loved, in spite of her hideous appearance; he must marry her in public, in front of many people; he must choose whether to have her beautiful by day and ugly by night, or vice versa. The first two challenges are much like the difficult tasks of a quest, and the third is much like the complex riddle that King Arthur had to solve. Ask students to identify the item of great value sought in this mini-quest, and whether they consider Sir Gawain successful.

Students with Disabilities

Help students create a "Promises" chart to record the instances in which a promise is made and kept in the selection. Ask students to note:

"Alas!" said the Queen Guinevere, and all the ladies in her bower.[10] "Alas!" said both king and knights, that the beautiful Gawain should wed such a foul and horrible woman.

She would be wedded in no other way than this—openly, with announcements in every town and village, and she had all the ladies of the land come to Carlyle for the feast. The queen begged Dame Ragnell to be married in the early morning, as privately as possible. "Nay," said the lady. "By heaven I will not no matter what you say. I will be wedded openly, as the king promised. I will not go to the church until High Mass time,[11] and I will dine in the open hall, in the midst of all the court." **J**

At the wedding feast there were lords and ladies from all estates, and Dame Ragnell was arrayed in the richest manner—richer even than Queen Guinevere. But all her rich clothes could not hide her foulness. When the feasting began, only Dame Ragnell ate heartily, while the knights and squires sat like stones. After the wedding feast, Sir Gawain and the Lady Ragnell retired to the wedding chamber that had been prepared for them.

"Ah, Gawain," said the lady. "Since we are wed, show me your courtesy and come to bed. If I were fair you would be joyous— yet for Arthur's sake, kiss me at least."

---

10. **bower** (BOW uhr): old-fashioned word for a private room.
11. **High Mass time:** main mass of Sunday morning. People of the highest class would attend High Mass.

J **Literary Focus** The Quest What further trials and tests does the lady put on Gawain?

Sir Gawain turned to the lady, but in her place was the loveliest woman that he had ever seen. **K**

"By God, what are you?" cried Gawain.

"Sir, I am your wife, surely. Why are you so unkind?"

"Lady, I am sorry," said Gawain. "I beg your pardon, my fair madam. For now you are a beautiful lady, and today you were the foulest woman that ever I saw. It is well, my lady, to have you thus." And he took her in his arms and kissed her with great joy.

"Sir," she said, "you have half-broken the spell on me. Thus shall you have me, but my beauty will not hold. You may have me fair by night and foul by day, or else have me fair by day, and by night ugly once again. You must choose." **L**

"Alas!" said Gawain. "The choice is too hard—to have you fair on nights and no more, that would grieve my heart and shame me. Yet if I desire to have you fair by day and foul by night, I could not rest. I know not in the world what I should say, but do as you wish. The choice is in your hands."

"Thank you, courteous Gawain," said the lady. "Of all earthly knights you are blessed, for now I am truly loved. You shall have me fair both day and night, and ever while I live as fair. For I was shaped by witchcraft by my stepmother, God have mercy on her. By enchantment I was to be the foulest creature, till the best knight of England had wedded me and had given me the sovereignty of all his body and goods. Kiss me,

K **Reading Focus** Identifying Cause and Effect What has caused this transformation?

L **Reading Focus** Identifying Cause and Effect Why does the lady put Gawain to yet another test?

Think About/Talk About

▶ **Comprehension**

H **Read and Discuss**

Possible response: *If Arthur can come across the answer to the riddle without Dame Ragnell's help, Sir Gawain will not have to marry her.*

K **Reading Focus**

Possible response: *The marriage to Sir Gawain most likely caused Dame Ragnell's transformation.*

L **Reading Focus**

Possible response: *The lady is testing Sir Gawain's willingness to give her the sovereignty that all women desire.*

▶ **Analysis**

I **Literary Focus**

Possible response: *The king shows his honor by keeping the promise he made to Dame Ragnell in exchange for saving his life.*

J **Literary Focus**

Possible response: *She tests his willingness to love her and marry her; she also tests whether he will dishonor the promise by marrying in secret or hiding her in shame, instead of marrying her openly as she desires.*

▶ **Extend the Discussion**

Theme This story's theme is connected to the concepts of honor and chivalry. How does Sir Gromer's behavior in column 1 of p. 818 relate to these concepts? ***Possible response:*** *Sir Gromer shows honor by letting King Arthur go. Even though he hates Arthur, Gromer keeps his promise to spare his life.*

Universal Access

What causes the promises to be made and kept? Explain to students that keeping a promise and maintaining honor was extremely important to knights in medieval times. Point out that this is a common theme in many stories set during this time period.

AAVE **Students Who Use African American Vernacular English**

English for Academic Success Some students may form the future tenses of verbs without including *will.* Read aloud the paragraph ending at point J, taking care to

emphasize the instances of future tense in the paragraph: *will be, will not, will dine,* and *will not.* Explain to students that using *will* to form future tenses is necessary in situations that require formal English. Have students work in pairs to practice forming formal English future tenses in sentences with the following examples: *we/go to the store, Marco/ride the bus to school; Amir/go to swim practice tomorrow.*

Think About/Talk About

▶ **Comprehension**

M Read and Discuss

Possible response: Dame Ragnell is transformed into a beautiful lady as a result of Sir Gawain's chivalrous response to the choice she asks him to make. This breaks the spell that was cast on his bride by her evil step-mother.

▶ **Extend the Discussion**

Making Judgments Gawain allows his wife to choose when she will be fair and when she will be foul. Do you think that Gawain did the right thing by responding this way? *Possible response: Yes, because he remembered what his wife told him. Her greatest wish was to have the freedom to make her own choices, so he allowed her to do so.*

Monitor Students' Comprehension

Guide the class in answering these comprehension questions.

1. What is King Arthur's quest? [*He must discover what women most desire.*]

2. How does Gawain give his wife her "sovereignty"? [*He allows her to choose her appearance for herself.*]

Sir Gawain on the magic bed. Miniature from manuscript of Arthurian romances (13th century). © The Granger Collection, New York.

Sir Gawain—be glad and make good cheer, for we are well." The two rejoiced together and thanked God for their fortune. **M**

King Arthur came himself to call them to breakfast the next day, wondering why Gawain stayed so late with his loathly bride. Sir Gawain rose, taking the hand of his lady, and opened the door to greet the king.

The Dame Ragnell stood by the fire, with her pale lovely skin and red hair spilling down to her knees. "Lo," said Gawain to the king, "this is my wife the Dame Ragnell,

who once saved your life." And Gawain told the king the story of the lady's enchantment.

"My love shall she have, for she has been so kind," said the king. And the queen said, "You will have my love forever, Lady, for you have saved my Lord Arthur." And from then on, at every great feast, that lady was the fairest, and all his life Gawain loved the Lady Ragnell.

Thus ends the adventure of King Arthur and of the wedding of Sir Gawain.

 M **Read and Discuss** How do things end? How does Sir Gawain break the spell?

California Standards, pp. 821–823

■ **Reading Standard 3.6** Analyze a range of responses to a literary work and determine the extent to which the literary elements in the work shaped those responses.

Applying Your Skills

Reading Standard 3.6 Analyze a range of responses to a literary work and **determine the extent to which the literary elements in the work shaped** those **responses**.

Sir Gawain and the Loathly Lady

Literary Response and Analysis

Reading Skills Focus
Quick Check

1. Myths, legends, and folk tales are full of **metamorphoses** (meht uh MAWR fuh seez)—marvelous changes from one shape or form to another one. (For example, a frog might be transformed into a prince.) A metamorphosis can be a punishment or reward. Why has Lady Ragnell been transformed into the loathly lady? What other metamorphosis occurs later in the story?

2. What ultimately frees Lady Ragnell from her enchantment?

Read with a Purpose

3. What if you had been given choices like the ones presented to Gawain? What decisions would you have made? What values would have guided you?

Reading Skills: Identifying Cause and Effect

4. Compare the cause-and-effect chart you filled in as you read the story with charts filled in by your classmates. Do your lists of key events match? Would you make any changes to your list? Is the chain of causes and effects clear? Explain.

Literary Skills Focus
Literary Analysis

5. **Analyze** Gawain is presented with a troubling choice on his wedding night. He makes the correct choice and is rewarded for it. How does Gawain's clever answer prove that the answer to the riddle is true?

6. **Interpret** Dame Ragnell says that women want "sovereignty." What does she mean by this? How might sovereignty remain a factor in her future life? What effect might her sovereignty have on Sir Gawain?

Literary Skills: The Quest

7. **Analyze** King Arthur and Gawain each undertake a quest: Arthur wants to save his life, and Gawain wants to be true to his code of honor. Find three places on the quest when either Arthur or Gawain could have made big mistakes—yet managed to stay on the right path. How did the code of chivalry help each of them make the right choices?

Literary Skills Review: Theme

8. **Interpret** **Theme** is the truth about life revealed to us in a literary work of fiction. What truth about life and values do you think is revealed in this story of a man presented with a terrible choice? Explain.

Writing Skills Focus
Think as a Reader/Writer

Use It in Your Writing How did the vivid descriptions of the loathly lady affect your response to this quest story? Write about the effects the writer's descriptions had on you, and cite specific examples of descriptions you found especially powerful or memorable.

What Do **You Think Now** How does Gawain's choice to marry the loathly lady serve to improve the world?

What Do You Think Now?
Have students consider how women of the time might have benefitted from Sir Gawain's choice. What values or ideals would he have promoted with his marriage, and later, his choice to grant sovereignty to his wife?

Check for Understanding

Independent Practice
Reading Skills Focus
Answers:

1. *Lady Ragnell was transformed into the loathly lady by her stepmother's witchcraft. The second metamorphosis is her transformation into a beautiful lady.*

2. *Sir Gawain gives Lady Ragnell sovereignty, which was the condition required by her stepmother to break the enchantment.*

3. *I would have made the same choice as Sir Gawain because I believe that people should be free to be who they choose to be.*

4. *I would add to my chart Queen Guinevere's request to Dame Ragnell that she marry in secrecy because it is important to understanding her transformation. The causes and effects are clear because the author lays out the chain of events for readers to follow.*

Literary Skills Focus
Possible responses:

5. *It proves the answer to the riddle is true because Dame Ragnell was cursed if she did not get what all women wanted: sovereignty.*

6. *Dame Ragnell means women want to be equal to men. I think Sir Gawain understands this and will value her. Others may not understand his choice, but I think he will benefit from an equal partner.*

7. *Arthur could have broken his vow to Sir Gromer, he could have ignored Dame Ragnell, and Gawain could have refused to consider marrying her. Chivalry helped the men value honor over saving one's own life, by insisting on fair treatment for all, and for demanding loyalty over personal interest.*

8. *The truth revealed in the story is that valuing others is its own reward. Sir Gawain respects and values Dame Ragnell, loathsome as she is, and he is rewarded for his kind treatment by having a beautiful wife.*

Independent Practice

Vocabulary Development

Your Turn

1. *Loathsome* is an English word, and originally meant *evil*. *Chivalry* is from French, and meant *knight*. *Countenance* came from French and meant *restraint* or *composure*. *Sovereignty* is French and referred to a *sovereign*, or leader.

2. **a.** King Arthur's knights were good men, and people loved them.

   b. The lords could tell by his face that something bad had happened.

   c. For you, I'd even marry the ugliest woman in the world.

   d. More than anything, we want power over men, because then we have everything.

English for Academic Success

Language Coach

Possible responses:

announcement: announce, announcer

beautiful: beauty, beautifully

preparation: prepare, preparatory

enchantment: enchanted, enchanter, enchantress

wedding: wed, wedded, unwed

disturbance: disturb, disturbing

English for Academic Success

Academic Vocabulary

Possible response: The story encourages people not to judge by looks to the <u>extent</u> of suggesting that appearances are deceiving. Dame Ragnell's transformation and Gawain's combination of looks and kindness equate good looks with personal goodness. Stories about appearances can be harmful if they suggest that only beautiful people are good.

Sir Gawain and the Loathly Lady

Vocabulary Development
French Word Origins

In 1066, the Normans, who lived in France, invaded England, led by William the Conqueror. As you may have guessed from his name, William and his Normans conquered England. Within a few years the language spoken by important people in England started to be French. Words used in government, by the church, and by people at court were French.

In fact, the stories about King Arthur and his knights include many stories from France. You can spot some French influence in this story of the loathly lady:

- The angry knight's name is *Gromer Somer Joure,* a French name.
- *Palfrey,* meaning "gentle horse," is from the French language.
- The word *chivalry* itself is from the French word *chevaler,* meaning "knight."

Your Turn

chivalry
countenance
loathsome
sovereignty

1. Use a dictionary to look up the Vocabulary words listed at right. Most dictionaries tell you in brackets the history of a word, followed by the word's definition. Which words are from the French language? Which word is English? What was the word's original meaning in French or English?

2. The reteller of this King Arthur legend has tried to give the story an old-fashioned flavor. Translate the following sentences into the kind of English you and your friends speak today.

   a. In his country **chivalry** was followed faithfully, and knights were loved by the people.

   b. The lords knew by his **countenance** that the king met with some disturbance.

   c. "If she were the most **loathsome** woman that ever a man might see, for your love I would spare nothing."

   d. "We desire of men, above all other things, to have **sovereignty,** for then all is ours."

Language Coach

Parts of Speech Many words in the English language can be made into other words or other parts of speech by respelling them slightly. Look at the words at right from the story. How many related words can you list for each?

announcement
beautiful
preparation
enchantment
wedding
disturbance

Academic Vocabulary

Talk About . . .

Discuss what this legend has to say about ugliness. To what <u>extent</u> does the story encourage people *not* to judge someone by his or her looks? What <u>elements</u> of the story *do* seem to equate good looks with favorable personal qualities? Under what <u>circumstances</u> can stories about appearances be harmful?

Universal Access: Vocabulary Development

 English Learners

English for Academic Success Students may have difficulty differentiating and using the forms and parts of speech of words. Have English learners work with fluent speakers to use each word from the sets of related words created in the Language Coach activity in discussion. For example, students might discuss the announcement that the announcer will announce over the loudspeaker the following morning. Circulate the room and guide the discussions as needed.

Grammar Link

Words Often Confused

The words *its/it's* and *your/you're* give writers a lot of trouble. The words in each pair sound alike, but they have different uses.

Its and *your* are personal possessive pronouns that show ownership. Possessive pronouns do not have apostrophes.

"Sir Knight, what is *your* name?" [The name belongs to the knight.]

The horse was gentle; *its* halters were jeweled. [The halters belong to the horse.]

It's and *you're* are both shortened combinations of a personal pronoun and the verb *is, has, was, are,* or *were.* A contraction needs an apostrophe to show where letters are omitted.

If you are unsure which word is correct, try substituting *it is* or *you are* in the sentence. If the sentence makes sense, you need an apostrophe.

***It's* easy to make a bad choice.** [*It is* easy to make a bad choice.]

***You're* welcome to try it out.** [*You are* welcome to try it out.]

Your Turn _____

Choose the correct form of the boldface words.

1. **Its/it's** clear the writer likes old-fashioned words.
2. Hearne makes you feel as if **your/you're** reading the original.
3. Arthur set up the Round Table; **its/it's** purpose was to make every knight equal.
4. For **your/you're** research paper, look up the Grail.

CHOICES

As you respond to the Choices, use these **Academic Vocabulary** words as appropriate: circumstance, element, extent, interpret.

REVIEW
Write a Literary Response

Timed └Writing Write a personal response to this story, exploring one or more elements that most helped shape your response. Maybe you felt that the characters did not act believably. Perhaps you agreed with the theme of the story. Support the reasons for your opinion with textual references. Then, with two other classmates, share your responses. Discuss the extent to which your responses were shaped by specific elements in the work that you each identified.

CONNECT
Update the Legend

TechFocus Film or perform a short, modern-day version of this legend. The riddle that must be answered should remain the same. What quest does the hero or heroine undertake to find the answer to the riddle? If the riddle is not answered, or is answered incorrectly, what will happen? Is there a loathly lady (or gentleman)? If possible, post your film on a class Web site.

EXTEND
Research Riddle Stories

Research Activity Research riddle stories down through the ages. Consider the story of Oedipus from ancient Greece; the German fairy tale "Rumpelstiltskin"; Gollum's riddles in J.R.R. Tolkien's *The Hobbit;* the evil Riddler in Batman comics. What is the riddle in each story? What is at stake? What is the correct solution to the riddle, and how does the hero come up with it?

Independent Practice

Grammar Link
Your Turn _____

1. It's clear the writer likes old-fashioned words.
2. Hearne makes you feel as if you're reading the original.
3. Arthur set up the Round Table; its purpose was to make every knight equal.
4. For your research paper, look up the Grail.

Choices:
Evaulation Criteria
Review: Timed Writing
45-50 Minutes
- Students explain their responses to the legend.
- Students support their responses with details from the text.

Connect: (Homework)
Update the Legend
- Students adapt the legend to modernize characters, setting, and plot.
- Students build their adaptations around the original riddle.

Extend: (Homework)
Research Riddle Stories
- Students identify riddle stories from the past and present.
- Students explain the function of riddles in each story.

Assess

Chapter 8 Resources, Selection Standards Check, p. 27

Teacher One Stop™, editable Selection Standards Check

ThinkCentral Online Assessment, Selection Standards Check

Reteach

ThinkCentral Online Remediation

Universal Access: Grammar Link

EL English Learners/Struggling Writers
English for Academic Success Help students understand the function of *it's/its* and *you're/your* and their formal English usage.

- Explain that homonyms, or words that have the same pronunciation, can be difficult to translate from speech to print. *It's/its* and *you're/your* are commonly reversed for this reason. Tell students that another good way to determine which form is appropriate is to consider whether they are describing how, where, or what something is (*it's, you're*) or describing possession of one thing

by another (*its, your*).

- Ask students to identify which form of *it's/its* and *you're/your* would best fit each of the uses below.
  1. the feather toy belonging to the cat
  2. you being happy with a birthday gift
  3. a day of good weather
  4. the pair of shoes you like best

✔ For more practice with using pronouns, see **Warriner's Handbook, Language Handbook Worksheets,** and **GrammarNotes.**

Standards Focus

Objectives
Students will
- write a response to literature
- support their interpretations with examples and textual evidence

Preteach

Write with a Purpose Read aloud the essentials of a good character analysis to guide students' understanding of this type of writing. Also refer students to the rubric on p. 828 for more information on character analysis that they can use throughout this workshop.

Direct Teach

Model the Skill

Think as a Reader/Writer Use the professional model on this page and others in the collection to provide examples of the elements of a good character analysis. Note that the excerpt presents a clear thesis in the first paragraph of the analysis. The paragraphs that follow offer support for the thesis statement.

Think About the Model
Possible responses:

1. *The writer includes this to help the audience understand the conditions of Gawain's sacrifice.*

2. *The quotation helps prove the thesis by showing Gawain's commitment to love and friendship.*

California Standards, pp. 824–830

- **Writing Standard 2.2** Write responses to literature: a. Develop interpretations exhibiting careful reading, understanding, and insight. b. Organize interpretations around several clear ideas, premises, or images from the literary work. c. Justify interpretations through sustained use of examples and textual evidence.
- **Writing Standard 1.1** Create an organizational structure that balances all aspects of the composition and uses effective transitions between sentences to unify important ideas.
- **Writing Standard 1.2** Support all statements and claims with anecdotes, descriptions, facts and statistics, and specific examples.

Response to Literature

Write with a Purpose

Write a **response to literature** in which you analyze a character from a short story or novel. Your **purpose** in writing a character analysis is to help you and your readers better understand the character and the story. Your **audience** includes your teacher and classmates.

A Good Character Analysis

- includes a thesis and summary statement that provides the story's title, author, main character, setting, and conflict
- includes several character traits that are supported by details from the story
- is logically organized, presenting only one character trait in each body paragraph
- includes a summary of the character traits discussed and restates the main idea of the analysis

See page 832 for complete rubric.

Reader/Writer Notebook

Use your **RWN** to complete the activities for this workshop.

Think as a Reader/Writer
When you go to a store or a movie, do you ever watch people around you and try to learn something about them from what they say and do? You can use those same skills of observation to learn about the characters in a short story or novel. By reading stories, you get to know all kinds of people—some just like you and others as different from you as they can be. In this workshop, you will write a character analysis using details from the story to tell your readers what the character is really like. Before you think about writing your own character analysis, study this analysis of the character Sir Gawain from the story "Sir Gawain and the Loathly Lady," on page 813.

> Sir Gawain, one of the knightly heroes of Arthurian legend, is the embodiment of love and friendship. In "Sir Gawain and the Loathly Lady," as retold by Betsy Hearne, Gawain gladly agrees to marry the "ugliest creature that [King Arthur] had ever seen" in order to save Arthur from a rival knight.
>
> The rival, Sir Gromer, catches Arthur off guard and threatens to kill him. Gromer agrees to spare Arthur only if he can answer the riddle of "what thing women most desire." Arthur finds the woman with the answer in the foul Dame Ragnell. Unfortunately, Dame Ragnell also has her price. She will give Arthur the answer to Gromer's riddle only if Gawain will marry her.
>
> Arthur fears he must die, but Gawain's unfailing love and friendship vanquish those fears. "I would rather die myself I love you so. . . . I shall wed her and wed her again! Though she were a fiend, though she were as foul as Beelzebub, her I shall marry. For you are my king and I am your friend. . . ."

← The analysis begins with a clear **thesis statement.**

← The thesis is followed by a thorough **summary statement** that provides context for the character analysis.

← Textual **details,** in the form of a long **quotation,** support the character traits introduced in the thesis.

Think About the Professional Model
With a partner, discuss the following questions about the model.

1. Why might the writer have included more background information in the second paragraph?

2. Does the quotation in the third paragraph help prove the thesis? Explain.

Writing Workshop Resources

UA: Holt Interactive Writer and Speaker, on-level practice and assessment, p. 139

UA: Differentiating Instruction, modified lesson plans and leveled assessment, p. 227

WritingNotes, interactive lesson presentations with activities

GrammarNotes, interactive lesson presentations with activities

Writing and Research in a Digital Age, interactive lesson presentations with activities

Writing Standard 1.1 Create an organizational structure that balances all aspects of the composition and uses effective transitions between sentences to unify important ideas. **1.2 Support all statements and claims** with anecdotes, descriptions, facts and statistics, and **specific examples**. **1.3** Use strategies of notetaking, outlining, and summarizing to impose structure on composition drafts. **2.2** Write responses to literature: a. Develop interpretations exhibiting careful reading, understanding, and insight. b. Organize interpretations around several clear ideas, premises, or images from the literary work. c. Justify interpretations through sustained use of examples and textual evidence.

Prewriting

Choose a Character

For this workshop, you need to choose an interesting character that faces a clear conflict. You can write about a character in a short story or novel that you have already read, or you can choose a new story. To help you choose a suitable character, complete these sentences:

(Character's name) in (author's name and title of story) is interesting because (two or three of the character's feelings or actions that make him or her seem like a real person). The conflict (character's name) faces is (description of conflict).

Notetaking: Study a Character

Carefully read or re-read your story, focusing on the character you have chosen to analyze. Take notes on that character. Start by looking for clues that tell you what the character is like. The chart below shows what kinds of clues to look for in the story.

Clues to Characterization

Details	Questions to Ask
Character's thoughts	Does the character have any recurring thoughts?
Character's words	What does the character say? Do the character's words agree with his or her thoughts and feelings?
Character's actions	How does the character behave? Does he or she avoid the conflict? ignore it? take action to resolve it?
Character's appearance	What does the character look like? What does this appearance tell you about the character?
Other characters' reactions	What do other characters think and say about the character?

Make categories of notes for each of the details listed in the chart above. You will want several notes for each category (Character's thoughts, Character's words, and so on). If you use the writer's exact words, enclose them in quotation marks. You will use these **examples** as **evidence** for your analysis. Beside each detail, write your **interpretation,** or what you think the detail shows about the character.

Idea Starters

- a character like you and your friends
- a character from another country, or even another "world"
- a character who overcomes a great obstacle
- a character who learns an important lesson about life

Your Turn _____

Get Started In your **RWN,** list some stories with characters that interest you. Think about the characters, and choose the story that is best suited for your analysis. Then, carefully re-read the story, and write down clues that tell you what the character is like.

An interactive graphic organizer can help you generate and organize ideas. Try one at:

go.hrw.com [H7-825] **Go**

Guided Practice: Apply

Choose a Character

- Tell students that choosing a character that they relate to or admire will make writing about the character more enjoyable. Choosing a character from a story that they find dull or frustrating may harm their ability to focus and enjoy the writing process.

- Have students brainstorm a list of potential characters to analyze. Then, have them complete the sentence starters for each of their potential characters. This process should help them narrow down their options.

Study a Character

Tell students that they may need to investigate some of the answers to these questions. If a story is told in limited third person point of view, the reader may not know the character's thoughts. But, interpreting the character's expressions, reactions, and words will help students determine how the character feels.

Your Turn _____

Get Started Once students have carefully re-read the story that they have chosen, have them work independently to fill in the chart on p. 825. Remind students to use the notes that they made while reading to help them answer the questions.

Teacher One Stop™, on-level lesson plans and all print resources

Holt Six Traits for Writing, rubrics, prompts, and sample papers

Language and Sentence Skills Practice

UA: Developmental Language and Sentence Skills Practice

Formal Assessment, Progress Monitoring Test 6, End-of-Year Summative

ThinkCentral Online Assessment, Writing Workshop Test

ThinkCentral Online Remediation

Holt Online Essay Scoring

Learn It Online

The **Interactive Student Edition** includes more than thirty Interactive Graphic Organizers. Your students can use them to generate and organize ideas, compare and contrast, evaluate a decision, support a position and much more.

go.hrw.com [H7-825] **Go**

Guided Practice: Apply

Write a Summary Statement

Tell students that they should assume that their audience has read the story that they are summarizing, but to write as if the audience needs to be reminded of what happens in the story. This may help them include only the most important details in their summary.

State Your Thesis

Tell students that a thesis statement expresses an opinion or interpretation of a literary work. It should a statement that someone could argue for or against.

Organize Your Information

If students are unsure which method to use to organize their analysis, have them complete two different outlines following each method of organization. If the clear choice does not stand out at that point, have students discuss their options with a partner.

Think About Purpose and Audience

Point out to students that their audience will appreciate reading a thoughtful, well-organized analysis. They should try to incorporate original ideas into their analysis and make it easy to understand by following a clear organizational pattern.

Your Turn _____

Make an Outline Have students complete the Your Turn activity as independent practice. Remind students to use the chart that they completed on p. 825 for support that they can include in their outline.

● Writing Tip

You can fill in the blanks below to develop a general outline for your own summary statement:

> The main character in (author's name) story (title of story) is (name of main character), who lives in (setting). The problem the main character faces is (conflict). During the course of the story, the main character (what the character does to try to solve his or her problem).

Your Turn _____

Make an Outline To organize the information for your analysis, list your character's major traits in the order that you will present them. Then, under each trait, list several examples or story details that you will use to support your discussion of the trait.

Write a Summary Statement

Introduce your audience to your story by writing a **summary statement**—two or three sentences that clearly restate several **key ideas** of the story without including all the details. The summary statement provides a context for your character analysis. It should include the story's title, author, main character, setting, and conflict.

State Your Thesis

How would you describe your best friend? You might focus on one or two of your friend's major traits, such as cheerfulness, intelligence, or humor. Traits like these will also be the focus of your character analysis. Focus on two or three of the character's major traits that are most important to the story's plot. Then, write a **thesis statement,** or main idea statement, that introduces your character's major traits and tells how those traits shape the story's events. Here are three ways you can use the character's traits to write a thesis.

- Focus on how the character's traits drive the plot.
- Focus on how the character changes.
- Focus on how the character is similar to or different from real people.

Organize Your Information

You will want to organize your analysis by either **order of importance** or **chronological order.** If your character has one dominant trait, you may want to organize your ideas in order of importance. The dominant trait would be described either first or last. Saving the most important trait for last is a good way of leaving the reader with a strong impression of the character. If, however, you want to show how the character changes during the story, you may want to use chronological order, in which the character's traits are discussed in the same order that they appear in the story.

Think About Purpose and Audience

The **purpose** of a character analysis is to learn as much as possible about a character and share that information with your readers. Learning about the character will help you and your readers understand the story better and maybe even understand yourselves and others better.

The **audience** for a character analysis is usually your teacher and classmates. Be sure to consider what might interest your audience when you choose details to support the character traits that you discuss.

Response to Literature Writing Prompts

Students can choose their own characters to analyze or use one of the following suggestions to help them write a character analysis.

History Write about a real person who appears in a work of historical fiction. Analyze whether the character that is based on this real person is an accurate portrayal and why.

Personal Experience Write about a character who faces a conflict that you have experienced in real life. Then, analyze whether the character reacts realistically to the conflict, calling upon your first-hand knowledge and experience for support.

Science Find a character from a science fiction novel or short story with an out-of-this-world setting. Think about whether the character could exist in a more realistic setting and why or why not.

Drafting

Follow the Writer's Framework

To help your readers thoroughly understand the insights you have gained about a character, you must present information in a clear, logical, and interesting manner. The **Writer's Framework** at right will help you plan your character analysis.

Present Ideas Clearly

In order to present your ideas as clearly as possible, each paragraph should discuss only one character trait and its supporting evidence, including examples and descriptions. Another way to make sure your ideas are understood is to use **transitional words and phrases** within and between sentences and paragraphs to show how ideas are related. Along with the logical organization of your ideas, these transitions will help create coherence, or connectedness.

A Writer's Framework
Introduction
• Attention-getting opener
• Thesis and summary statement
Body
• First character trait and supporting evidence
• Second character trait and supporting evidence
• Third character trait (if needed) and supporting evidence
Conclusion
• Summary of traits
• Restatement of thesis

Grammar Link Using Transitions

Transitions are words and phrases that show how ideas are related to one another. There are three types of transitions: words showing order of importance, words showing chronological order, and words showing spatial organization. The two types of transitions that are most useful when writing a character analysis are order of importance transitions and chronological transitions.

Order of importance transitions answer the question *Which?*	**Chronological transitions** answer the question *When?*
Examples: *mainly, most important, first of all, furthermore, finally, least important*	**Examples:** *first, next, then, after, while, during*

● Writing Tip

When you write a response to literature, use present-tense verbs to describe characters' thoughts, words, actions, and appearance. Note the use of present-tense verbs in the model on page 824: "Arthur *fears* he must die, but Gawain's unfailing love and friendship *vanquish* those fears."

Your Turn _____

Write Your Draft Follow your plan and the framework to write a draft of your character analysis. Be sure to consider the following:

- Have you presented your character traits clearly and in a logical order?
- Have you used appropriate transitional words and phrases to connect ideas?

Model the Skill

■ Using a student draft on a transparency, model how to use the questions, tips, and revision techniques suggested in the chart. You might use a student's essay or an essay of your own creation to evaluate and revise using the steps in the chart.

■ Ask volunteers to demonstrate using each of the steps on their own essays.

Peer Review

As students work with their partner, encourage them to offer praise as well as criticism. Pointing out what their partner did well can help them see what techniques or methods are effective. Also, offering positive feedback can boost morale and help students stay confident.

Peer Review

Working with a classmate, review each other's drafts and trade revision suggestions. Answer each question in the chart to identify where and how your drafts can be improved. As you discuss your papers, be sure to write down your classmate's suggestions. You can refer to your notes as you revise your draft.

Evaluating and Revising

After completing your draft, it's time to go back through and smooth out the rough spots. You can improve your draft by using the evaluation questions and revision techniques shown below.

Character Analysis: Guidelines for Content and Organization

Evaluation Question	Tip	Revision Technique
1. Does the introduction summarize the story and identify key information about it? Does the thesis statement identify the traits to be discussed?	**Bracket** the summary, and **underline** the story's title, author, main character, setting, and conflict. **Circle** each trait listed in the thesis.	**Add** a summary if needed, and **add** any key elements missing from the introduction. If necessary, **add** traits to the thesis statement.
2. Is each character trait supported by details from the story?	**Highlight** the story details that support each character trait.	**Add** story details or **elaborate** on the details included.
3. Is the analysis logically organized?	**Write** the trait discussed in each body paragraph in the margin next to the paragraph. Make sure each paragraph discusses only one character trait.	**Rearrange** information, moving any misplaced examples or descriptions of a trait into the paragraph where that trait is discussed.
4. Are the ideas and details connected with appropriate transitions?	**Draw a box** around each transitional word or phrase.	**Add** transitions where they are needed to connect ideas.
5. Does the conclusion sum up the character traits discussed and restate the thesis?	**Circle** each trait in the conclusion, and **draw a wavy line** under the restated thesis.	**Add** any missing traits. **Add** a restatement of the thesis, if necessary.

Real Issues, Real Experts

Holt Professional Learning for Language Arts

To watch videos on teaching **revision, grammar,** and **on-demand writing skills** featuring Linda Rief, Amy Benjamin, and Leila Christenbury, go to this page in **ThinkCentral, Teacher Access.**

Read this student's draft along with the comments on its structure and how it could be made even better.

Character Analysis of "Rikki-tikki-tavi"

by Daryl Williams, Colonel Mitchell Paige Middle School

The short story "Rikki-tikki-tavi," by Rudyard Kipling, is a suspenseful tale about a clever, curious, and brave mongoose who saves his owners from two deadly snakes. The story, set in India, involves a conflict between Rikki-tikki and two cobras, which plan to kill them so they can have the family's garden to themselves. In the end, good triumphs over evil as Rikki-tikki saves his owners' lives while ending the snakes'!

← Daryl begins her analysis with a clear **thesis** and **summary statement.**

Rikki-tikki is a very clever character. He predicts what the snakes will do before they even do it. He also contemplates the best location for fighting the snakes. Rikki-tikki thinks, "Now, if I kill him here, Nagaina will know; and if I fight him on the open floor, the odds are in his favor." Rikki also spends hours thinking about where he should bite Nag to kill him quickly.

← Daryl uses textual **evidence,** including a direct quotation, to support her discussion of the first **character trait.**

Rikki-tikki's curiosity is another prominent trait. He spends a day exploring the house and almost gets in over his head. "He nearly drowned himself in the bathtubs, put his nose into the ink on a writing table, and burnt it on the end of the big man's cigar. . . ." Rikki-tikki is also fascinated by watching the family light kerosene lamps.

← Daryl's analysis is clearly and **logically organized,** with only one character trait discussed in each paragraph.

MINI-LESSON ▶ **Mini-lesson: How to Write an Attention-Getting Opener**

Daryl's introductory paragraph includes a clear, well-written thesis and summary statement. It could be improved, however, by adding an attention-getting opener. Daryl revised her introduction to include a more appealing opening sentence.

Daryl's Revision of Paragraph One

You've probably heard stories about heroic animals that rescued their owners, but can you imagine being saved from certain death by something that looks like a weasel? ∧ The short story "Rikki-tikki-tavi," by Rudyard Kipling, is a suspenseful tale about a clever, curious, and brave mongoose who saves his owners from two deadly snakes. . . .

Your Turn _____

Grab Your Reader's Attention
Read your draft and ask yourself the following questions:

- Have I included an attention-getting opener to draw the reader into my analysis?
- Will my opener appeal to my audience?

Guided Practice: Apply

Student Draft

- Explain that the Student Draft is continued and completed on this page. Again the draft is annotated and highlighted for the students.

- Read the draft and annotations aloud and discuss.

▶ Mini-Lesson

How to Write a Strong Conclusion

- Tell students that the conclusion is the last thing that their audience will read, so it should leave a lasting impression.

- Explain that the student writer has revised her draft by restating the thesis. The revised draft is stronger because it restates all important information and leaves a lasting impression on the reader.

Your Turn _____

Strengthen Your Conclusion Have students highlight the character traits that they have chosen to analyze and the thesis statement in the first paragraph of their draft. Then, have them highlight the same information in the conclusion. If they are unable to highlight any of the character traits or the thesis in the conclusion, they need to revise the conclusion to include this information.

Student Draft *continues*

> Finally, Rikki-tikki is very brave. He fights snakes that are at least three times his size, risking his life for Teddy by killing a dusty brown snakeling named Karait. Rikki-tikki's courage is most evident when he follows Nagaina into her hole to kill her: ". . . Very few mongooses, however wise and old they may be, care to follow a cobra into its hole."
>
> In the end, Rikki-tikki and his owners are safe and can once again walk in their garden without fearing snakes. Rikki-tikki's characteristics led to this happy outcome, and they make him an interesting character to read about.

Daryl organizes her analysis by **order of importance,** *ending with the most important character trait. By saving the most important trait for last, Daryl leaves the reader with a memorable impression of the character.*

MINI-LESSON ▶ **Mini-Lesson: How to Write a Strong Conclusion**

As you write your conclusion, make sure you sum up the character traits you discussed in your analysis and restate the thesis.

Daryl's Draft of Paragraph Five

> In the end, Rikki-tikki and his owners are safe and can once again walk in their garden without fearing snakes. Rikki-tikki's characteristics led to this happy outcome, and they make him an interesting character to read about.

When Daryl re-read her draft, she noticed that her conclusion merely told readers how the story ends, making only a general reference to the character traits. Daryl revised her conclusion to better sum up the character traits and to more clearly restate the thesis.

Daryl's Revision of Paragraph Five

> In the end, ∧*Nag and Nagaina are no match for Rikki-tikki's clever-ness, curiosity, and bravery. After* **Rikki-tikki** ∧*kills the cobras,* ~~and his~~ owners are safe and can once again walk in their garden without fearing snakes. ~~Rikki-tikki's characteristics led to this happy outcome, and they make him an interesting character to read about.~~

Your Turn _____

Strengthen Your Conclusion
With a partner, review the conclusion to your character analysis. If it doesn't sum up the specific character traits you have discussed, add a sentence that sums them up. Your partner can help you evaluate your conclusion and suggest ways to restate your thesis.

Universal Access

🔵 EL English Learners

English for Academic Success To help students ease the transition into the conclusion of their essay, give them the following sentence starters:

In the end. . .

In conclusion. . .

After all. . .

Overall. . .

To sum up. . .

🔵 AAVE Students Who Use African American Vernacular English

English for Academic Success Point out the revised last paragraph of the student model. Tell students that there are two negative statements, "Nag and Nagaina are no match for Rikki-tikki" and "can once again walk in their garden without fearing snakes." In informal English, these statements may be written, "Nag and Nagaina aren't no match for Rikki-tikki" and "can once gain walk in their garden without fearing no snakes."

Proofreading and Publishing

Proofreading

After you have revised your character analysis, it's time to go back through it one more time to correct any errors in grammar, usage, or mechanics. It's easy to overlook you own errors, so try to have your paper read by at least one other classmate.

> **Grammar Link** Avoiding Unclear Pronoun References
>
> When you use a pronoun, such as *he, she, his, hers, they, them, their,* and *theirs,* you need to make sure the reader will understand *to whom* or *to what* the pronoun refers. The word the pronoun refers to is called the antecedent. In the first sentence below, there are no clear antecedents to the pronouns **them** and **they.**
>
> **Confusing** The story, set in India, involves a conflict between Rikki-tikki and two cobras, which plan to kill **them** so **they** can have the family's garden to themselves.
>
> **Clear** The story, set in India, involves a conflict between Rikki-tikki and two cobras, which plan to kill **him and his owners** so **the snakes** can have the family's garden to themselves.

Publishing

Now it is time to publish your character analysis, sharing it with a wider audience. Here are some ways to share your paper:

- E-mail your character analysis to a friend or family member who might be interested in reading the story.
- Ask your librarian if you and your classmates can keep all of your character analyses in a library file. The papers can be used by other students as a preview of the books and stories.

Reflect on the Process
In your **RWN,** write a short response to the following questions as you think about how you wrote your character analysis.

1. Did you have any trouble identifying your character's traits? Explain.
2. Did studying the character help you understand the story better? If so, how?

Proofreading Tip
Ask two or three classmates to help you proofread your analysis. Have each one focus on a different aspect of your writing, such as misspellings, punctuation errors, and problems in sentence structure.

Your Turn _____
Make Pronoun References Clear Proofread your character analysis, paying special attention to your use of pronouns. Correct any unclear pronoun references as well as other errors, including errors in grammar, usage, or punctuation.

Guided Practice: Apply

Proofreading
Integrating with Grammar, Usage, and Mechanics If students make errors in subject-antecedent agreement and tense errors as they are proofreading, send them to the Agreement and Using Verbs Correctly chapters in the **Warriner's Handbook.**

Grammar Link
- Tell students to read their final draft for pronouns. Have students underline each pronoun, including *them* and *they.*
- Have students determine whether the pronouns clearly reference their antecedents. Have them revise any sentences with unclear pronoun references.

Publishing
Brainstorm with students additional ways to publish their summaries.

Reflect on the Process
Have students reflect on the entire writing process as well as their final product. Challenge them to reflect metacognitively about how they can improve and apply what they have learned.

Your Turn _____
Making Pronoun References Clear Have students check their final drafts against the Evaluating and Revising guidelines on p. 828. Ask students to particularly look for pronouns to make sure that they clearly reference their antecedents. Also remind students to include transitions in their drafts as shown in the **Grammar Link** on p. 827.

Remind students that in formal English, only one negative word is used to signal a negation. The use of two negative words would result in a double negative, which is used in informal English but should be avoided in formal English. Have students read over their draft to look for any instances of double negation.

✔ See **UA: Differentiating Instruction** for strategies for teaching students who use African American Vernacular English.

Advanced Learners
Acceleration Challenge students to further strengthen their conclusions by using one of the following techniques.
- Relate the subject of the essay to your own life.
- Raise a question to keep your audience thinking.
- Include a quotation that sums up the essay.

Guided Practice: Apply

Scoring Rubric

- Tell students that the best way to understand rubrics is to use them to score actual writing. Review the rubric on p. 832 with students.

- Have students work with a partner. Tell them to use the rubric to evaluate their partner's final copy of the summary they wrote in the Writing Workshop. Ask students to score their partner's summary, then write a brief paragraph using the language of the rubric to explain the reasons for their partner's score.

Holt Six Traits for Writing, rubrics, prompts, and sample papers

Assess

UA: Interactive Writer and Speaker, summary analytical scales and rubric

ThinkCentral Online Assessment, Writing Workshop Test

Teacher One Stop™, editable Writing Workshop Test

Reteach

ThinkCentral Online Remediation

California Standards, pp. 832–833

- **Writing Standard 2.2** Write responses to literature: a. Develop interpretations exhibiting careful reading, understanding, and insight. b. Organize interpretations around several clear ideas, premises, or images from the literary work. c. Justify interpretations through sustained use of examples and textual evidence.

Scoring Rubric

You can use the rubric below to evaluate your character analysis from the Writing Workshop or your response to the prompt on the next page.

	Response to Literature	Organization and Focus	Sentence Structure	Conventions
4	• Develops interpretations that demonstrate a thoughtful, comprehensive grasp of the text. • Organizes accurate and coherent interpretations around clear ideas, premises, or images from the literary work. • Provides specific textual examples and details to support the interpretations.	• Clearly addresses all parts of the writing task. • Demonstrates a clear understanding of purpose and audience. • Maintains a consistent point of view, focus, and organizational structure, including the effective use of transitions. • Includes a clearly presented central idea with relevant facts, details, and/or explanations.	• Includes a variety of sentence types.	• Contains few, if any, errors in the conventions of the English language (grammar, punctuation, capitalization, spelling). These errors do not interfere with the reader's understanding of the writing.
3	• Develops interpretations that demonstrate a comprehensive grasp of the text. • Organizes accurate and reasonably coherent interpretations around clear ideas, premises, or images from the literary work. • Provides textual examples and details to support the interpretations and prior knowledge.	• Addresses all parts of the writing task. • Demonstrates a general understanding of purpose and audience. • Maintains a mostly consistent point of view, focus, and organizational structure, including the effective use of some transitions. • Presents a central idea with mostly relevant facts, details, and/or explanations.	• Includes a variety of sentence types.	• Contains some errors in the conventions of the English language (grammar, punctuation, capitalization, spelling). These errors do not interfere with the reader's understanding of the writing.
2	• Develops interpretations that demonstrate a limited grasp of the text. • Includes interpretations that lack accuracy or coherence as related to ideas, premises, or images from the literary work. • Provides few, if any, textual examples and details to support the interpretations.	• Addresses only parts of the writing task. • Demonstrates little understanding of purpose and audience. • Maintains an inconsistent point of view, focus, and/or organizational structure, which may include ineffective or awkward transitions that do not unify important ideas. • Suggests a central idea with limited facts, details, and/or explanations.	• Includes little variety in sentence types.	• Contains several errors in the conventions of the English language (grammar, punctuation, capitalization, spelling). These errors may interfere with the reader's understanding of the writing.
1	• Demonstrates little grasp of the text. • Lacks an interpretation or may be a simple retelling of the passage. • Lacks textual examples and details.	• Addresses only one part of the writing task. • Demonstrates no understanding of purpose and audience. • Lacks a point of view, focus, organizational structure, and transitions that unify important ideas. • Lacks a central idea but may contain marginally related facts, details, and/or explanations.	• Includes no sentence variety.	• Contains serious errors in the conventions of the English language (grammar, punctuation, capitalization, spelling). These errors interfere with the reader's understanding of the writing.

Response to Literature Writing Prompts

Students can use the writing prompt on p. 833 in the Student Edition or one of the following prompts.

- Think of a character from a novel or short story that you felt was unrealistic. Write a character analysis for the author of the novel or short story explaining why you think the character was not believable.

- Think of a memorable fictional character that made an impact on your life. Write a character analysis for your classmates to help them understand why and how this character affected you so much.

- Think of a character from a novel or short story that changed. Write a character analysis for your classmates to help them understand how the character changed throughout the novel or story.

- Think of a character from a novel or short story that did not change. Write a character analysis for your classmates to help them understand how the character remained the same throughout the novel or story and whether this lack of change impacted another literary element of the novel or story.

Preparing for Timed Writing

Response to Literature

When responding to a prompt that requires a response to literature, use the models you read in this collection, what you learned writing your character analysis, the rubric on page 832, and the steps below to help you respond quickly to the on-demand task.

Writing Standard 2.2 Write responses to literature. a. Develop interpretations exhibiting careful reading, understanding and insight. b. Organize interpretations around several clear ideas, premises, or images from the literary work. c. Justify interpretations through sustained use of examples and textual evidence.

Writing Prompt

Think of a memorable fictional character from a story or novel that you enjoyed. Write a character analysis for your classmates to help them understand what the character and story are like. Discuss several of the character's main traits, and support the traits with textual evidence.

Study the Prompt

Read the prompt carefully. You probably read stories frequently for English class, so choose a character that is fresh in your memory. The prompt tells you that your **audience** is your classmates and your **purpose** is to help them understand the character and story. Finally, you are reminded to present the character's main traits and the textual evidence that reflects those traits.

Tip: Spend about five minutes studying the prompt.

Plan Your Response

Writing a character analysis requires you to briefly **summarize** the story and discuss how the character's main **traits** affect the story. Try to summarize the story in only a few sentences. Then, take notes on the following as you plan your response.

- Title, author, setting, plot, conflict, and character to be analyzed
- Thesis statement
- Two or three main character traits, with supporting evidence
- Summary of traits and restatement of thesis

Tip: Spend about ten minutes planning your response.

Respond to the Prompt

Using the notes you've just made, draft your character analysis. Begin your analysis with a **thesis statement** and **summary statement** that include the story's title, author, main character, setting, plot, and conflict. Then, present one **character trait** in each paragraph that follows. For each trait, provide important details from the text as supporting **evidence.** Organize the traits by either **order of importance** or **chronological order.** Write as neatly as you can. If your analysis can't be read easily, it won't be scored. **Tip:** Spend about twenty minutes writing your draft.

Improve Your Response

Revising Go back over the key aspects of the prompt, and add any missing information.

- Did you include a clear thesis and summary statement?
- Did you include sufficient evidence (textual examples) to support the character traits?

Proofreading Take a few minutes to edit your response to correct errors in grammar, spelling, punctuation, and capitalization. Make sure your edits are neat and the character analysis is legible. **Checking Your Final Copy** Before you turn in your analysis, read it one more time to catch any errors you may have missed and to make any finishing touches. This final read will help ensure that you are presenting your best writing. **Tip:** Save five or ten minutes to read and improve your draft.

Standard Focus

Objectives
Students will
- write a character analysis
- revise and edit using a rubric

Direct Teach

Study the Prompt
Before students begin writing, encourage them to answer the following questions:

1. What is my time limit?
2. What are the key skills assessed in the scoring rubric?
3. Who is my audience?
4. What is my purpose?

Plan Your Response
Remind students that the scoring rubric emphasizes the importance of addressing all aspects of the writing task. Tell students that they should carefully read the writing prompt and follow all instructions presented.

Improve Your Response
Point out that the scoring rubric emphasizes the consistent use of an organizational method. Encourage students to check that they have use transitional words that support one method of organization. Advise students to add transitional words if the analysis does not flow easily from one idea to another.

Assess

 Use the rubric on p. 832 to assess student's essays.

Universal Access

EL English Learners
Explain to students that *evidence* is any piece of information that proves or supports something. They should look for details or quotes from the text to use as evidence. They will need evidence to support each trait that they claim the character they are analyzing possesses.

Struggling Writers
Strategic Students Model for students how to choose a character to analyze. Tell them that the best options are characters who have many strong, obvious character traits, since they will need to analyze these traits in the essay. They should avoid analyzing secondary or minor characters. The main character of a story is best because he or she is the focus of the story.

Standards Focus

Objectives
Students will
- organize information to appeal to an audience
- arrange details, reasons, and examples effectively
- use speaking techniques for effective presentations

Preteach

Speak with a Purpose Ask students: "Do you ever talk about a character from a story, movie, or TV show with your friends? What features of these characters make them interesting?" Have students write a list of features that appeal to them in a character.

Direct Teach

Model the Skill

Adapt Your Character Analysis

Model for students how to take notes about their character. Choose a character from a selection in Chapter 8 or a previous chapter. Then, work with the class to fill in information about the character in five categories: Thinks, Says, Behaves, Looks, Is Reacted To. Remind students that this information is essential for completing a character analysis.

Guided Practice: Apply

Have students make notes about their characters using the same five categories above: Thinks, Says, Behaves, Looks, Is Reacted To. Explain that these notes will help students decide the most important information to include in their character analysis.

Presenting a Response to Literature

Speak with a Purpose

Deliver an oral response to literature in which you analyze a character from a short story or novel. Discuss several of the character's major traits, using details from the text to support your discussion. Also include a brief summary of the story.

🔵 Speaking Tip

Your listeners won't have the benefit of seeing how character traits and details are organized on a written page, so be very clear when introducing a new trait or detail. Don't be afraid to use introductory phrases such as "The second major trait is..." or "Another example of this trait is..." You may also want to pause briefly between details or traits to give your audience an oral cue that you are about to introduce a new idea.

Reader/Writer Notebook
Use your **RWN** to complete the activities for this workshop.

Think as a Reader/Writer Now is your chance to give an oral presentation of a character analysis. You will consider which of your character's traits to discuss, practice presenting them orally, and then share the information with your teacher and classmates.

Adapt Your Character Analysis

Choose a Character
You may adapt your character analysis from the Writing Workshop, or you may want to select a different character to analyze for your oral presentation. If you choose to adapt your written character analysis, make sure you don't merely read it word for word. Reconsider the traits and evidence you used in your written analysis. Is all of the evidence appropriate or necessary in your oral presentation? Remember, you can use your voice and body movements to help "show" what the character is like.

Take Notes and Organize Your Presentation
Carefully review the novel or story, and take notes on the following:
- What the character thinks
- What the character says
- How the character behaves
- How the character looks
- How other characters react to him or her

When you present your response to literature, you will need to give a brief **summary** of the story as context for the character analysis. Remember that your **purpose** is to tell your audience what the character is like. Note any details that will appeal to your audience and help keep their attention, such as gestures or exclamations your character uses.

Once you have chosen a few major traits to discuss and have decided which textual details to use as supporting evidence, think about how to organize your presentation.

- **Introduction:** Get your audience's attention, summarize the story, and explain how the character's main traits affect the story.
- **Body:** Discuss two or three major character traits one at a time, and provide examples from the text to support your discussion.
- **Conclusion:** Summarize the traits and restate your main idea.

Listening and Speaking Standards
1.1 Ask probing questions to elicit information, including evidence to support the speaker's claims and conclusions. **1.4** Organize information to achieve particular purposes and to appeal to the background and interests of the audience. **1.5** Arrange supporting details, reasons, descriptions, and examples effectively and persuasively in relation to the audience. **1.6** Use speaking techniques, including voice modulation, inflection, tempo, enunciation, and eye contact, for effective presentations. **1.7** Provide constructive feedback to speakers concerning the coherence and logic of a speech's content and delivery and its overall impact upon the listener.

Deliver Your Character Analysis

Once you know *what* you will say, you need to think about *how* you will say it and then practice it until you can present it effortlessly. You can practice your presentation in a variety of ways: you might try standing in front of a full-length mirror so you can see your facial expressions and gestures; you can record your presentation so you can analyze your voice modulation, inflection, tempo, and enunciation; and you can practice in front of family and friends to concentrate on making eye contact and staying calm in front of a live audience. As you practice your presentation, concentrate on the speaking techniques below. The tips may help you decide how to work the techniques into your presentation.

Speaking Techniques

Technique	Explanation	Tips
Voice Modulation	The stress you place on certain words and phrases through the volume of your voice	To stress certain points, speak more loudly or softly. Ask a partner if your volume is varied enough and if you can be heard clearly no matter what your volume.
Inflection	The high and low tones of your voice (your voice may go up at the end of a question and down at the end of a statement)	Avoid speaking in a monotone. Emphasize important ideas by making your inflection higher or lower. Ask a partner if you sound convincing and reasonable. The sound of your voice should fit your audience and suit your purpose.
Tempo	The speed and rhythm of your speech	Speak slowly enough for your audience to keep up. Use pauses to emphasize major points; a pause shows your audience that the idea was important, and it gives people time to think about your point. Remember to stop and catch your breath if necessary.
Enunciation	Words pronounced carefully and clearly	Practice your speech with a partner. Ask your partner to note any words that he or she does not understand. Look up in a dictionary or ask your teacher how to pronounce words that are unfamiliar to you.
Eye contact	A way of keeping the audience involved by looking at them	Practice glancing at your note cards, if needed, and then making eye contact with your partner again. Also, look at different places in the room so you can practice engaging as much of the audience as possible.

An Effective Presentation of a Character Analysis

- grabs the audience's attention with a brief summary of the story. The summary provides the story's title, author, character to be analyzed, setting, and conflict.
- includes a discussion of several character traits that are supported by details from the story
- is organized in a way that is easy for listeners to follow
- uses effective speaking techniques

 Listening Tip

As a listener, you should be aware of whether or not the speaker is including sufficient specific details and evidence to convince you of his or her claims and conclusions. Be attentive to the overall impact the speech is having on you and try to analyze why the speaker's content, organization, and delivery are having that effect. Be prepared to provide constructive feedback to the speaker and help him or her to see where the coherence and logic of the speech might be improved.

Universal Access

EL English Learners/ Struggling Learners

English for Academic Success Remind students that an *analysis* is a study of something's features. When students create a character analysis, they consider all the features of that character, from how they look to how they act to how they think and feel. Tell students that it may be helpful to visualize the character in their mind before they begin to write their descriptions.

Advanced Learners

Enrichment Have students imagine that they were to meet and talk to their character in real life. Challenge students to write a brief dialogue between themselves and their character. Encourage them to make the dialogue as true to their character's personality as possible, using the information they have gathered in their character analyses.

Model the Skill
Deliver Your Character Analysis
Model each technique on the Speaking Techniques list for students. Give an example of the correct way and the incorrect way to use each technique (for instance, making eye contact with students versus staring at your feet) and discuss with the class why certain techniques are more effective than others.

Guided Practice: Apply
Have students practice using the speaking techniques listed on the chart. Select an excerpt from a selection in Chapter 8 and have each student read two sentences aloud to the class. Remind them to use correct voice modulation, inflection, tempo, and enunciation as they speak.

Teaching Tip
Rehearse Have students create a checklist with the categories "Voice Modulation," "Inflection," "Tempo," "Enunciation," and "Eye Contact." Then have students pair up with a partner and present their character analyses to each other. As one student reads, his or her partner should mark a check in each category in which the student does well and leave a blank in each category that is not effective.

English for Academic Success
Remind students to use formal English in their discussions. They should use informal English, such as slang, only when a character is speaking.

Assess

UA: **Holt Interactive Writer and Speaker,** response to literature analytical scale and rubric

Standards Focus

Objectives

Students will

• analyze responses to a literary work

• decode multiple-meaning words

Literary Skills Review

Review

If necessary, use the following questions to guide students in their reading before they answer the questions at the end of the review.

▶ Literary Criticism

In Essay 1, does the writer approve of the decisions made by Arthur and Gawain? Why or why not? **Possible response:** *Yes. Arthur and Gawain gave their word and they followed through on it.*

In Essay 2, why does the writer mention *Harriet the Spy*? **Possible response:** *The writer is giving an example of a story that has a female main character, as opposed to the Arthur legends.*

Test-Taking Tip

Remind students not to get stalled on one question of the test. They should work through the entire test at a fairly steady pace. They can always go back to more difficult questions later if there is enough time.

California Standards, pp. 836–837

■ **Reading Standard 3.6** Analyze a range of responses to a literary work and determine the extent to which the literary elements in the work shaped those responses.

Literary Skills Review

Literary Criticism

Directions: Read the essays. Then, answer each question that follows.

Essay 1

Themes in Arthurian Legends

There are many themes in the stories of King Arthur and his knights. The themes all speak to our deepest wishes: We all wish for a leader who will come and save us in our hour of need; we all wish that might will be used for right; we all wish that goodness will always be rewarded. The Arthur stories are also about doing the right thing, even when the cost of such action is great.

In *King Arthur: The Sword in the Stone*, Arthur is only sixteen when he is faced with a destiny that fills him with unhappiness: to be king of England. Yet he shoulders the burden because it is his fate. It is the right thing to do.

"Sir Gawain and the Loathly Lady" is the best story built around the theme of doing the right thing. Arthur and Gawain must make horrible choices, and they both choose to do the right thing. Sir Gromer makes Arthur promise to return unarmed one year from that day. Arthur will not break his word to save his life, even when the bargain he was forced to make is most unfair. Sir Gawain must make a truly horrifying choice. He weds the loathly lady because, for him, it is the right thing to do. He gave his word.

The end of each story shows that characters are rewarded for choosing to do the right thing. We wish that were always true in real life.

Essay 2

Women Characters in the King Arthur Stories

The three selections *King Arthur: The Sword in the Stone*, "Merlin and the Dragons," and "Sir Gawain and the Loathly Lady" all reveal the way women are portrayed in the King Arthur stories. In *King Arthur: The Sword in the Stone* and "Merlin and the Dragons," there are no women characters at all. All of the characters are male, and all of them are heroic because they are strong and brave. They earn the reader's approval by pulling swords out of stones and stabbing people in battle. In "Sir Gawain and the Loathly Lady," one of the main characters is a lady changed by magic into a beast. She is doomed to stay in this state until a man loves her for herself alone. She is freed from her enchantment when a man agrees to marry her, although the truth is that Sir Gawain marries her only because he has agreed to in order to save King Arthur.

None of these stories show women or girls in active roles. I prefer to read *Harriet the Spy*. At least there is a character girls can identify with.

Resources for Skills and Standards Review

Chapter 8 Resources, Chapter Standards Mastery, Chapter Vocabulary Review, p. 30

UA: Differentiating Instruction, below-level Chapter Standards Mastery

Teacher One Stop™, editable Chapter Standards Mastery

Focus on Standards

ThinkCentral Online Assessment, Chapter Standards Mastery

ThinkCentral Online Remediation

Holt Online Essay Scoring

1. What literary element is the focus of Essay 1?
   A plot
   B character
   C setting
   D theme

2. What literary element is the focus of Essay 2?
   A plot
   B character
   C setting
   D theme

3. Which of these generalizations is supported by details in the essays?
   A The writer of Essay 1 wishes that people were rewarded for doing the right thing in real life.
   B The writer of Essay 1 hates the King Arthur stories.
   C The writer of Essay 2 dislikes male characters.
   D The writer of Essay 2 likes the women characters in the King Arthur stories.

4. Which criticism would you apply to Essay 1?
   A The writer does not mention *King Arthur: The Sword in the Stone.*
   B The writer does not mention "Merlin and the Dragons."
   C The writer does not supply any details to support the main idea.
   D The writer talks about too many literary elements.

5. Which criticism would you apply to Essay 2?
   A The literary elements discussed do not support the main idea.
   B The writer focuses too much on women characters in "Merlin and the Dragon."
   C The writer relies too heavily on direct quotations as evidence to support the main idea.
   D The end of the essay reveals that the response may be shaped more by personal opinion than by literary elements.

Timed Writing

6. What is the main idea in Essay 1?

7. What is the main idea in Essay 2?

Assess

Answers and Explanations

1. **D** The first sentence shows that the essay will focus on theme. Plot (A) and character (B) are not the main focus, and setting (C) is not discussed.

2. **B** The essay points out that nearly all the characters are male. Plot (A) is mentioned in passing, and setting (C) and theme (D) are not discussed.

3. **A** Answer A is stated in the last paragraph of Essay 1. The writer does not dislike the King Arthur stories (B). The writer of Essay 2 does not dislike the male characters (C), but wishes there were women characters (D).

4. **B** The writer mentions King Arthur: The Sword in the Stone (A) and "Sir Gawain and the Loathly Lady," but does not mention "Merlin and the Dragons" (B).

5. **D** The writer includes his or her preference for reading stories with women in active roles in the last paragraph.

Timed Writing

6. The main idea of Essay 1 is that the King Arthur legends all have a similar theme: that doing the right thing will be rewarded in the end.

7. The main idea of Essay 2 is that the King Arthur stories lack strong women characters.

Reteach

ThinkCentral Online Remediation

Chapter Review

Review Literary Skills Focus
1. Have students look back through the chapter to find the meanings of the terms listed below.
2. Ask students to cite passages from the chapter that illustrate the meanings of those terms.

Literary Criticism; Plot; Character; Theme; Sound; Figures of Speech; Imagery; Legend; Responses to a Literary Work; Hero; Quest; Riddles

Review Reading Skills Focus
1. Have students look back through the chapter to find the meanings of the terms listed below.
2. Ask students to cite passages from the chapter that illustrate the meanings of those terms.

Response to a Literary Work; Narrative; Sequence of Events; Predictions; Cause; Effect

Vocabulary Skills Review

Multiple Meaning Words **Directions:** Choose the answer in which the italicized word is used in the same way it is used in the quotation from *King Arthur: The Sword in the Stone*.

1. "In the churchyard he discovered a *block* of white marble with an anvil sitting on top."
   - **A** The football player tried to *block* his opponent's kick.
   - **B** They walked one *block* to the bus stop.
   - **C** The statue was placed on a large wooden *block*.
   - **D** Our class bought a *block* of tickets for the performance.

2. "Nothing had prepared them for this *scale* of violence."
   - **A** Weigh yourself on the *scale* in the bathroom.
   - **B** The pianist practiced each *scale* twenty times.
   - **C** The *scale* of talent at this year's gymnastic competition was quite impressive.
   - **D** On this *scale* model, one inch represents three feet.

3. "As soon as the service ended, those who wished to try for the throne formed a *line* next to the marble block."
   - **A** The *line* to buy tickets was longer than we expected.
   - **B** The fisherman attached the hook to his *line*.
   - **C** The actor had only one *line* to memorize.
   - **D** The truck crossed the state *line* at six o'clock.

4. "'My lord,' said Merlin, 'I *present* to you a most worthy candidate for this contest.'"
   - **A** When the teacher called my name, I said, "*Present*."
   - **B** For my birthday I was given the *present* of my dreams.
   - **C** Don't dwell on the past; focus on the *present*.
   - **D** The emcee at the wedding reception finally said, "I now *present* the bride and groom."

5. "Then, turning the *point* downward again, he drove it back into the anvil with equal ease."
   - **A** It's not polite to *point*.
   - **B** At a certain *point* in the discussion, the group felt it was time to take a break.
   - **C** The warrior sharpened the *point* of his spear before going into battle.
   - **D** "Get to the *point*," she said impatiently.

Academic Vocabulary

Directions: Which phrase correctly completes the introductory phrase containing the italicized Academic Vocabulary word?

6. If you analyze an *element* of a short story,
   - **A** you study one of its basic parts.
   - **B** you look at its chemical makeup.
   - **C** you examine the history of the story.
   - **D** you determine in which language it was originally written.

Vocabulary Review

Use this activity to assess whether students have retained the chapter Vocabulary. Ask students to choose the word from the box that fits the context of each sentence.

turbulent	capable	impudence
composure	loathsome	

1. Gary's _____ toward his teacher earned him a week in detention. [*impudence*]

2. I knew I would do well on the exam as long as I stayed calm and kept my _____ . [*composure*]

3. Lu proved to be a very _____ chess player, and she easily beat all her friends. [*capable*]

4. The _____ storm knocked down the power lines in our neighborhood. [*turbulent*]

5. I find spiders to be _____ , and I run the other way whenever I see one. [*loathsome*]

Writing Skills Review

Writing Standard 2.2 Write responses to literature. a. Develop interpretations exhibiting careful reading, understanding and insight. b. Organize interpretations around several clear ideas, premises, or images from the literary work. c. Justify interpretations through sustained use of examples and textual evidence.

Response to Literature **Directions:** Read the following paragraphs. Then, read the questions below, and choose the best answer to each question.

(1) Beauty, we are told, is only skin deep. (2) However, the female character in Betsy Hearne's retelling of "Sir Gawain and the Loathly Lady" turns that saying on its head. (3) Dame Ragnell, an ugly lady whom King Arthur meets in Ingleswood Forest, exhibits an inner beauty that toward the end of the story is reflected even in her outward appearance. (4) Dame Ragnell has agreed to give Arthur the answer to a riddle that will save him from a knight called Sir Gromer, but in return she wants Arthur's most loyal knight, Sir Gawain, to marry her. (5) Although Dame Ragnell is described as having a face "almost like that of an animal," we are given clues to her inner beauty early in the story: "But she rode gaily on a palfrey set with gold and precious stones, and when she spoke her voice was sweet and soft." (6) Dame Ragnell's character is further revealed when she meets Gawain and learns how willing he is to marry her. (7) She wishes, for Gawain's sake, that she were beautiful. (8) By marrying Dame Ragnell, Gawain breaks an enchantment placed on her by her stepmother. (9) She was to remain ugly until England's best knight married her. (10) After Gawain marries her, Dame Ragnell becomes as beautiful outwardly as inwardly. (11) "And from then on, at every great feast, that lady was the fairest, and all his life Gawain loved the Lady Ragnell."

1. Sentence 1 is an example of
   A a thesis.
   B an attention-getting opener.
   C a summary statement.
   D a summary of traits.

2. The thesis of this passage is in
   A sentence 1.
   B sentence 2.
   C sentence 3.
   D sentence 4.

3. On which character trait does this passage focus?
   A inner beauty
   B outward beauty
   C ugliness
   D loyalty

4. Which two sentences provide the best supporting evidence for the thesis?
   A sentences 2 and 4
   B sentences 3 and 9
   C sentences 5 and 7
   D sentences 8 and 10

5. The title and author are provided in sentence 2, but the summary statement is in
   A 3.
   B 4.
   C 5.
   D 6.

6. The thesis is restated in
   A sentence 8.
   B sentence 9.
   C sentence 10.
   D sentence 11.

Writing Skills Review

Assess

Answers and Explanations

1. **B** *Sentence 1 gets the reader's attention (B) by expressing a well-known saying. It does not provide a thesis statement (A) or a summary (C, D).*

2. **C** *Sentence 3 expresses the thesis that Dame Ragnell has inner beauty (C). Sentences 1 and 2 are an opener (A, B), and sentence 4 describes the plot (D).*

3. **A** *The passage mainly focuses on Dame Ragnell's inner beauty (A), not on outward beauty (B), ugliness (C), or loyalty (D).*

4. **C** *Sentences 5 and 7 provide the best evidence of Dame Ragnell's inner beauty (C).*

5. **B** *Sentence 4 gives the most complete summary of the plot (B). Sentence 3 provides the thesis statement (A), and sentences 5 and 6 describe Dame Ragnell (C, D).*

6. **C** *Sentence 10 mentions Dame Ragnell's inner beauty (C). Sentences 8, 9, and 11 provide details about the plot (A, B, D).*

Reteach

 ThinkCentral Online Remdiation

Application Homework
Research a Character

Have students research another character who is connected to the Arthurian legend. Have them organize their findings into a paragraph that describes the character and his or her connection to the legend. Remind students to include important information about the character in their paragraphs.

Extension
Write an Ode

Tell students that an ode is a poem that praises a particular person. Have students reorganize the information from their character analyses to create a 10-line ode describing their character. Remind students that their odes should explain what they enjoy about the character.

California Standards, p. 839
■ **Writing Standard 2.2** Write responses to literature: a. Develop interpretations exhibiting careful reading, understanding, and insight; b. Organize interpretations around several clear ideas, premises, or images from the literary work; c. Justify interpretations through sustained use of examples and textual evidence.

If students enjoyed the themes and topics explored in this chapter, you might recommend these titles for independent reading.

Assessment Options

The following projects can help you evaluate and assess your students' outside work. Videotapes or audiotapes of completed projects may be included in students' portfolios.

Create Character Cards

If students enjoy *Sir Gawain and the Green Knight, Pearl, and Sir Orfeo*, have them create "character cards," similar to baseball cards, showing the traits of each character. One side of the card should have a drawing of the character, while the other side should list the character's "statistics," such as his or her age, location, and important characteristics.

Draw a Motif Mural

■ Have students who read *The Nightingale that Shrieked* choose a motif that is common to more than one of the stories.

■ Students should create a mural showing an artistic representation of the motif in the stories. For instance, if bravery is a motif, students might draw a superhero battling an enemy.

Read On

For Independent Reading

Fiction

Sir Gawain and the Green Knight, Pearl, and Sir Orfeo

The legends in this book are masterpieces of the distant past—the age of chivalry and knights and holy quests. This translation of fourteenth-century narrative poems by J.R.R. Tolkien, the author of the *Lord of the Rings* series, sparkles with his unique imagination and artistry.

The Lightning Thief

Percy Jackson is a good kid whose world is turned upside down when, on a museum field trip, he discovers that he is the son of a Greek god. To educate Percy about his ancestry and protect him from angry forces, his mother sends him to a summer camp with other children of mixed mortal and Olympian heritage. A warning is printed at the beginning of Rick Riordan's novel—*Close the book right away and go back to your uninformed life.* It is up to you to make the decision: Dare to read this book, or continue to live your safe, boring life.

The Nightingale that Shrieked

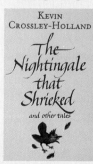

Kevin Crossley-Holland, the author of an award-winning trilogy about the life of the young King Arthur, has collected tales from a variety of cultures and traditions—European, African, and Near and Middle Eastern—each of which is bound by its myths and legends. This collection celebrates the similarities and differences between the stories of peoples around the world.

Sword of the Rightful King

The newly crowned King Arthur has yet to win the support of his people. So Merlin, his teacher, creates a trick: a sword magically placed into a slab of rock that can only be withdrawn by Arthur. Merlin then announces that whoever removes the blade will rule all of England and invites any man who dares to try to pull out the sword. Jane Yolen has written more than two hundred books for children and adults and has won several of the most prestigious awards in children's literature.

Word Counts and Readablilites of Read On Books

Estimated Word Counts and Readabilities of Read On Books

Fiction	Estimated Word Counts	Readability
Sir Gawain and the Green Knight, Pearl, and Sir Orfeo	59,377	Challenging
The Nightingale that Shrieked	40,341	Accessible
The Lightning Thief	87,133	Easily Accessible
Sword of the Rightful King	89,100	Accessible

Fiction

Tuck Everlasting

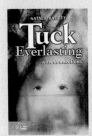

Have you ever wished you could live forever? In Natalie Babbitt's *Tuck Everlasting*, members of the Tuck family are granted eternal life when they drink from a hidden stream. Then they learn that the dream of living forever can also be a nightmare. This memorable, much-loved novel has had quite an impact on readers since its publication, and it has been filmed twice, most recently as a major motion picture. It is published in Spanish as *Tuck para siempre*.

Where the Red Fern Grows

In Wilson Rawl's *Where the Red Fern Grows*, set in the Ozark Mountains, Billy Colman works tirelessly through two years of the Great Depression to save money to purchase two hunting dogs. Billy trains the dogs to become the finest raccoon-hunting team in the valley. Persistent, hard-working, and loyal, Billy experiences sadness along with his glory.

Sundiata—An Epic of Old Mali

Sundiata: An Epic of Old Mali, by D. T. Niane, is a retelling of a Malian epic. Part man and part legend, Sundiata joined the kingdoms of Mali into an empire. This edition features background information on the era as well as a glossary that will enhance your reading experience.

Esperanza Rising

Twelve-year-old Esperanza enjoys a privileged life on her family's Mexican ranch until she is forced to flee with her mother and three servants to California. Esperanza experiences hard labor for the first time when she begins her new life as a migrant farm worker. In *Esperanza Rising*, by Pam Muñoz Ryan, readers witness the transformation of a rich, sheltered girl into a mature young woman.

Learn It Online
Explore other novels—and find tips for choosing, reading, and studying works—at:

go.hrw.com | H7-841 | **Go**

Estimated Word Counts and Readabilities of Read On Books

Fiction	Estimated Word Counts	Readability
Tuck Everlasting	28,000	Accessible
Sundiata—An Epic of Old Mali	35,520	Accessible
Where the Red Fern Grows	75,528	Accessible
Esperanza Rising	41,905	Accessible

Learn It Online
The **Novel Wise** mini-site includes instruction on choosing, reading, and analyzing novels; it also includes a catalogue of book summaries, study guides, teaching guides, and PowerPoint presentations.

go.hrw.com | H7-841 |

Reteaching Lessons

Plot

Objective: To analyze elements of plot, including conflict, complications, climax, and resolution.

Direct Teaching: Introduce the lesson to the students with the following information:

> Every story or narrative is made up of a series of related events, called the plot. The plot answers the question "What happened?" When creating a plot, a writer involves characters in a conflict, challenges them with complications, pushes events to a climax, or peak of suspense, and finally wraps up the characters' story in a resolution. Together, this structure of related events makes up a narrative's plot.

Guided Practice: Have students re-read the first two and a half pages of "Rikki-tikki-tavi" (p. 15). Explain that in this section of the story, Rikki faces a minor obstacle, or conflict, that he quickly overcomes. Then, draw the following plot chain on the chalkboard:

Conflict	Complication 1	Complication 2	Resolution
Flood carries Rikki off.	Teddy thinks he's dead.		Family adopts Rikki.

Have volunteers complete this chain by describing the acts that revive Rikki and result in his adoption. Let students add more complication boxes and a climax box. Have them use time-order words, such as *first*, *next*, *then*, and *after*, to make transitions between events. Make sure that all the events students record relate to the conflict at hand—Rikki's near drowning and his rescue by the family.

Independent Practice: Have students fill in a second chain based on the main conflict of the story—Rikki's fight with the cobras—using as many boxes as necessary. When students come to class with their completed plot chains, have them put the two chains together to reveal the entire plot of the story.

Possible chain:

Conflict	Complication 1	Complication 2	Complication 3
First Rikki meets Nag and is almost killed by Nagaina. He knows he must fight the cobras.	Then Teddy is threatened by another snake, Karait, but Rikki kills him and saves the boy.	Next Rikki learns through Chuchundra that the cobras have eggs and plan to kill the family and take over the house.	Knowing this, Rikki finds Nag in the bathroom and kills him, saving Teddy's father.

Complication 4	Complication 5	Climax	Resolution
In order to defeat Nagaina, Rikki gets Darzee's wife to distract the cobra while Rikki destroys her eggs.	Meanwhile, however, Nagaina threatens Teddy and his family on the veranda.	Finally, using her last egg, Rikki lures Nagaina away from Teddy and then pursues and kills her in her den.	Rikki has made the family and the garden safe, so Darzee sings a song of praise to the mongoose.

Forms of Prose

Objective: To analyze the purposes and characteristics of different forms of prose (for example, short story, novel, novella, essay).

Reteaching Lessons

Direct Teaching: Share the following ideas with the class:

Different forms of literature, such as short stories, novels, poems, articles, and essays, don't just have different forms and characteristics; they also have different purposes. A short story may be written to entertain, enlighten, inspire, or frighten its readers, while an article is more often written to inform or educate its readers or to capture a particular place, person, or event. An essay is often written to convince the reader of something or to explain a particular perspective. As you read, you should think about the author's purpose in writing the text. If you decide the author's purpose is to convince you of something, does he or she provide a logical argument to convince you, supported by credible evidence? If the author's purpose is to inspire or entertain you, does she or he challenge you with new ideas; striking imagery; eloquent, original language; and well-structured form? If the author's purpose is to frighten or create suspense, does the plot build tension and surprise you with unexpected twists and turns, or is the story predictable?

Guided Practice: Genre and purpose. Direct students to the Table of Contents in their Student Editions. Arrange students in pairs, and have them select three texts: one short story, one novella, and one essay. For each selection, partners should devise a statement of purpose. For instance, for the short story "Three Skeleton Key," students might write, "The purpose of the short story 'Three Skeleton Key' by George G. Toudouze is to frighten and entertain the reader using a suspenseful plot, foreshadowing, and precise details." Make sure students also express an opinion about how well the author fulfills his or her purpose.

Independent Practice: Genre and purpose. After partners have written their statements of purpose, they must decide whether or not the selection succeeds in accomplishing this purpose. For each selection, students should choose four passages or examples from the text (with page numbers) that help to fulfill or fail to fulfill the author's purpose. For instance, with "Three Skeleton Key," students might note that the story of the island's name on p. 35 works because it foreshadows the lighthouse keepers' fates and builds suspense. When partners have finished collecting support for their conclusions about how well the author achieved his or her purpose, have each pair share their findings with the rest of the class.

Interrelated Plot Events

Reading Standard 3.2 Identify events that advance the plot and determine how each event explains past or present action(s) or foreshadows future action(s).

Objective: To identify events that advance the plot, and determine how each event explains past or present action(s) or foreshadows future action(s).

Direct Teaching: Share the following information with students:

> The plot of a narrative or story is more than just a list of what happens. It is a tightly structured web of related events. The plot usually begins with the introduction or exposition, which sets the scene. The exposition is followed by complications, which build to a climax. Good readers notice that some events move the plot forward, while other events may serve to clarify past or present actions in the story. Still other events may hint at, or foreshadow, future actions in the narrative. When you read, you should be thinking about how each event relates to what happens before and after it.

Guided Practice: Function of plot events. Have students read "Bargain" (p. 393) by A. B. Guthrie. Then, divide the class into groups of four or five. First, have the groups review "Bargain", using a reader's theater format. (Have one student assume the role of the narrator, another the role of Mr. Baumer, another Freighter Slade, and so on.) When students have finished re-reading the story, have each group select four events that are crucial to the advancement of the plot. Have the group summarize each event in writing, in a few sentences. Then, have students identify each event as part of the introduction or exposition, the complications or problems, the climax, or the resolution of the story. Students should then identify the function of each event in the plot. Does it clarify an earlier incident, hint, allusion, or description? Does it foreshadow what happens later in the plot? Does it contribute to the mounting tension before the story's climax?

Independent Practice: Interrelated time line. Have students take home a piece of poster paper and create an illustrated time line for "Bargain." For each event that students include, they should identify which part of the plot it belongs to and what function it serves in the story. Students should draw arrows that connect some events to the events they foreshadow and other arrows from later incidents to prior events they clarify.

[Possible time line:

1. Slade crumples the bill and twists Mr. Baumer's nose—*complication*. This event foreshadows future trouble between the two men.

2. Mr. Baumer complains about Slade's stealing whisky—*exposition*. This event contributes background information about Slade and other freighters and foreshadows the means of Slade's death.

3. Moore announces that Slade is dead—*climax*. This event heightens the mystery of Mr. Baumer's changed attitude toward Slade and marks the turning point in the conflict between the two men.

4. The narrator notices the barrel from Slade's wagon containing poisonous wood alcohol—*resolution*. This event explains Mr. Baumer's different approach to Slade—he was simply waiting for Slade's evil temperament to cause his own inevitable downfall. It also resolves the conflict between the two men as a story of completed revenge.]

Reteaching Lessons

Characterization

Reading Standard 3.3 Analyze characterization as delineated through a character's thoughts, words, speech patterns, and actions; the narrator's description; and the thoughts, words, and actions of other characters.

Objective: To analyze the methods writers use to reveal character.

Direct Teaching: Share the following thoughts with the class:

> We learn about the people around us in many different ways. We hear about them from their friends and family, we read their biographies or their own writings, we see their artwork, or we talk to them directly. Every detail we hear, see, or experience in relation to that person adds to our overall portrait of that person's character. In the same way, authors characterize the people in their stories through a wide range of techniques. While sometimes the narrator of a story will describe a character directly, like "good King Arthur," more often characterization is accomplished *indirectly*, through the character's thoughts, words, speech patterns, and actions or the thoughts, words, and actions of other characters. As you read, you should think about how even small details in a story contribute to characterization.

Guided Practice: Details of characterization. Have students re-read the short story "After Twenty Years" (p. 383). Assign each student a major character in the story to focus on as they complete their second reading—either Silky Bob or Jimmy Wells. As they read, students should take notes on the character traits of their assigned character. Tell students that they will be required to cite examples from the text that support each trait. When the reading is completed, ask for volunteers to share character traits of their character with the whole class. Construct a character web like the one pictured here with three traits and evidence about Patrolman Jimmy Wells from " After Twenty Years."

Independent Practice: Characterization web. Pair students up, and have each team construct a characterization web for a character in a story the class has already read. In the center of each web, students should write the name of the selected character. Then students should choose three important characteristics of that character and arrange them around the center of the web. These characteristics should be described with a phrase or short sentence. For each characteristic, students should provide three details that communicate that characteristic to the reader. Remind students to choose a range of details from what the narrator, the character in question, and other characters say and do. Have the partners combine their webs to make a giant web for the story.

Characteristic 1:
Impressive Figure

"Stalwart form and slight swagger"

"Fine picture of a guardian of the peace"

Natural and "habitual" manner

Characteristic 2:
Reliable

"truest, staunchest old chap"

"I was at the appointed place on time"

Jimmy Wells

Characteristic 3:
Law-abiding

Recognizes his old friend as a man wanted in Chicago

Sends another officer to arrest Silky Bob

Doesn't let friendship sway his duty

Reteaching Lessons

Recurring Themes

Reading Standard 3.4 Identify and analyze recurring themes across works (e.g., the value of bravery, loyalty, and friendship; the effects of loneliness).

Objective: To identify the theme of a work and analyze recurring themes across works.

Direct Teaching: Share the following information with the class:

> Part of what makes a literary theme or message powerful is that it doesn't apply just to the characters in a story or the speaker of a poem. Themes often have universal qualities that make them relevant to the lives of readers. Since a theme is often a general idea or statement about life, it may appear in a number of different contexts and genres. The importance of bravery, independence, and chivalry is emphasized in the medieval tales about King Arthur, but it is also emphasized in the *Star Wars* movie series. As good readers, you should be thinking not only about what general message or theme is being conveyed by a work but also about how it relates to similar themes in other works. By comparing and contrasting themes across works, you will have a better appreciation of what each writer is trying to say.

Guided Practice: Finding the theme. Have the class review the teleplay "The Monsters Are Due on Maple Street" (p. 67) and "The War of the Wall" (p. 173) by reading their notes and retelling the two selections. When students finish the review, divide the class in half. One groups will focus on the story; the other half will concentrate on the teleplay. Choose a student moderator for each group, and have the group discuss the overall theme of the selection. What does it say about human nature? Remind each mod-

erator to focus on the big questions that each selection raises about fear, distrust and judgment on appearances. Is it human nature to fear the unknown? Does that make us stronger or weaker? How do people react when they are afraid or distrustful of others? What is the best way to fight fear, mistrust and quick judgment? When each group has finished brainstorming, have each student in each group write a statement about the theme or main idea of the work the group focused on. Remind students that this statement should express the general observation or statement about life that the work communicates. Then, have students in each group exchange their statements with someone from the other group. These partners should compare and contrast their statements about the teleplay and about the story, taking notes on the thematic overlap between the two works. Finally, partners should write a general thesis statement that applies to both works and present it to the class.

Independent Practice: Themes across genres. Have the class discuss the ideas about fear and judging others that are expressed by "The Monsters Are Due on Maple Street" and "The War of the Wall." At home, have students select a poem, play, movie, or TV show that they think makes a strong statement about the nature of friendship. Students should present their selections in class, reading a passage (or describing a scene in detail) that they think illustrates the theme of the work.

Point of View

Reading Standard 3.5 Contrast points of view (e.g., first and third person, limited and omniscient, subjective and objective) in narrative text and explain how they affect the overall theme of the work.

Objective: To analyze point of view (for example, first and third person, limited and omniscient, subjective and objective) in narrative text and explain how point of view affects the overall theme of the work.

Reteaching Lessons

Direct Teaching: Introduce the lesson to the students with the following information:

> One of the most important things about any story is the point of view, or perspective, from which it is told. A story's point of view can affect not only the tone and style but also the message, or theme, that the author wants to communicate to the reader. Just as a detective story isn't as mysterious if it is told by the villain who committed the crime, so almost any story will say something different depending on who is telling it.

Guided Practice: Listening and speaking. Help students to recall the selection "Rikki-tikki-tavi" (p. 15) by Rudyard Kipling. Then, display on the chalkboard the following paragraph from the selection:

> Darzee was a featherbrained little fellow who could never hold more than one idea at a time in his head, and just because he knew that Nagaina's children were born in eggs like his own, he didn't think at first that it was fair to kill them. But his wife was a sensible bird, and she knew that cobra's eggs meant young cobras later on; so she flew off from the nest and left Darzee to keep the babies warm and continue his song about the death of Nag. Darzee was very like a man in some ways.

Have a volunteer read the passage aloud. Have students listen carefully and then discuss whether the passage is told from a first- or third-person point of view. Ask students how they could tell that the passage is in the third person. [The narrator is not in the story but stands above it, describing all the events and people from a distance.] Remind students that an omniscient point of view reflects an all-knowing perspective, which allows us to hear the thoughts of different characters, while a limited point of view lets us hear only one character's perspective on the world. Have another student read the passage aloud again, and ask students whether they think this passage is told from an omniscient or a limited point of view. Ask them to support their answers with evidence from the text. [We hear what different characters, Darzee and his wife, are thinking, and Darzee's behavior is compared with that of men in general. The perspective is all-knowing and omniscient.] Next, have students discuss the difference between an objective story and a subjective one. Ask students to decide whether the narrator's description of the birds is scientific, clinical, and detached (objective) or opinionated and full of feeling (subjective). [It is subjective.]

Independent Practice: Writing application. Have students take out a piece of paper. Read the passage aloud, and ask students to jot down a list of words and phrases from the passage that they think show the narrator's perspective on Darzee, his wife, and their behavior. [Possible responses: *featherbrained, could never hold more than one idea at a time, sensible, like a man in some ways.*] Have students share their lists with the class and discuss how the narrator seems to admire the sensible, brave actions of Darzee's wife and to criticize the foolish attitude of Darzee. Discuss how this passage might capture the overall theme of the story. Have students write down a statement using the form "Rudyard Kipling's 'Rikki-tikki-tavi' conveys the message that. . . ." [Responses will vary. Students might emphasize the idea that a sensible response to danger and evil requires taking precautions and having courage and that people often forget this because they are foolish or softhearted.]

Ask students to look at the passage on the chalkboard again, this time considering it from a different point of view. Have students use the other side of their paper to rewrite the passage from one of the following points of view:

1. **A subjective first-person point of view.** Remind students that this point of view might include the thoughts of Darzee and his unique "featherbrained" perspective on the cobra's eggs. Remind students to use first-person pronouns, like *I, me, mine, we, us,* and *ours*.

2. **An objective third-person point of view.** Point out that this point of view must describe the birds, the snakes, the eggs, and the forest from a completely *external* perspective. No thoughts or other subjective elements can be included in this point of view.

Whichever option students choose, remind them to try to capture the same message or theme of the original passage. When students have finished writing, have them share their rewrites with the class. Have them discuss how the different points of view affected the theme of the story.

Response to Literature

Reading Standard 3.6 Analyze a range of responses to a literary work and determine the extent to which the literary elements in the work shaped those responses.

Objective: To analyze a range of responses to a literary work, and to determine how the literary elements in the work shaped those responses.

Reteaching Lessons

Direct Teaching: Share the following thoughts with your students:

> In reading any story you shape your criticism in part by the literary elements of plot, character, setting, point of view, theme, and figurative language and in part by your life experiences. The author's artistry with words evokes certain images, associations, and ideas in your mind. These personal associations help to determine the way you respond to the work. For example, your response to Mildred D. Taylor's characters depends in part on your previous experience with people who talk in a black southern dialect and in part on what the characters say and do. If the characters you've met before were plain, honest folk, you'll probably assume these characters are too—until they prove otherwise. Because everyone's experiences are different, people respond to the same story in different ways.

Guided Practice: Rating three responses. Read the following three responses to *Song of the Trees* (p. 539). Consider to what extent each response is affected by the literary elements in the novella. Then, rate these responses from 1 (not affected much) to 3 (affected deeply).

> **Response 1.** This was a wonderful story about the way a family fights to defend what it owns. I cried when I read it because here in Russia my family has to fight to keep a tiny room in a cramped apartment. Please read this book. It is great. [2—affected by theme]

> **Response 2.** I didn't like this story because in the end the Logans actually lose most of the trees they are trying to protect. Although I was glad when Cassie's father forces Mr. Andersen to back off, the trees remaining at the close of the story stand "like lonely sentries" and are silent. This ending left me with a feeling of defeat. [3—affected by the resolution of the plot, simile, and personification]

> **Response 3.** I really liked this story. It was awesome. I recommend it to other students my age. It was easy to read and short. [1—not affected much by literary elements, only by length and readability of work]

Help students to see that response 3 does not discuss any literary elements. Response 1 focuses on theme and how the theme relates to the writer's own experience. Response 2 discusses the resolution of the plot and the author's use of simile and personification at the end of the novella. Therefore, this response is most strongly affected by the literary elements in the work.

Independent Practice: Literary Criticism. Challenge students to choose another work from this text and write a criticism to it that is shaped by various literary elements.

Cause and Effect

Reading Standard 2.3 Analyze text that uses the cause-and-effect organizational pattern.

Objective: To analyze the cause-and-effect organizational pattern.

Direct Teaching: Introduce the lesson to the students with the following information:

> Causes are reasons that things happen. *Effects* are results. When writers show why something happens, they're writing about causes; when they show what something leads to, they're writing about effects. Exploring causes and effects is one way to analyze an event or an issue. You can tell that a writer is exploring causes and effects when you notice signal words and phrases such as *why, because, since, resulted in,* and *so.*

Guided Practice: Cause-and-effect chain. Have students re-read "A Mason-Dixon Memory" (p. 559). Point out the following sentences:

- "Why did she look and sound so nervous?"

- "'You mean I can't go to the park,' I stuttered, 'because I'm a Negro?'"

- "'They don't allow Negroes in the park,' he said, 'so I'm staying with Clifton.'"

Have volunteers identify the cause-and-effect signal words [underlined] in each excerpt. Next, put the following cause-and-effect chain on the chalkboard:

| Amusement park has racist policy. | → | Clifton is barred from park. | → | Frank says he won't go either. | → |
| Ten other boys decide not to go. | | Chaperone gets baseball tickets for them all. | → | Clifton sees how love and courage can conquer bigotry. | |

Independent Practice: Cause-and-effect chain. Assign students to make a second cause-and-effect chain for the experiences of Dondré Green. Tell them to write "Country club has racist admission policy" in the first box and to add as many boxes as they need to show how the policy affected Dondré, what actions his teammates took as a result, and what other effects the incident had. When students bring their completed cause-and-effect chains to class, have them use both chains to compare the causes and effects of both incidents.

> [Possible answers: Country club has racist admission policy. → Dondré is barred from playing. → Coach asks team to decide what to do. → Team walks out and forfeits tournament. → Louisiana citizens are outraged at the injustice. → Legislature proclaims Dondré Green Day. → Law is passed prohibiting racist policies for sports events at private clubs. → Dondré learns that love can conquer hatred and bigotry.]

Reteaching Lessons

Author's Argument

Objective: To analyze the development of an author's argument in informational texts.

Direct Teaching: Share the following explanation with students:

> In informational texts, perspective and point of view refer to the way the writer feels about a subject. On the subject of school vouchers, for example, there are many perspectives, or points of view. Some people think vouchers will help schools in poor-performing areas. Others think the threat of vouchers will make public schools try harder to improve their own instruction. Others think vouchers will spell the end of public education. Some like vouchers because they think vouchers will help their own private schools. These are all perspectives on the controversial topic of school vouchers.
>
> An argument is a kind of writing that uses evidence to try to persuade us to think or act in a certain way. We find many arguments in the editorial pages of newspapers. We could say that anyone who presents an argument has a point of view, or perspective, on a subject. If you present an argument in favor of school vouchers, it means your perspective on school vouchers is favorable.

Guided Practice: Analyzing an argument. In this exercise, students will trace the details of a writer's argument on a topic. Have students read the following brief letter about roads in wilderness areas. Tell them that as they read the letter, they are searching for the following three things:

1. the topic of the letter

2. evidence showing how the writer feels—and wants us to feel—about the topic

3. evidence "Concerned Hiker" uses to support position

Finally, they are evaluating the evidence; they are separating opinion from facts.

Roads Can Hurt Us

Just before the end of his presidency, President Clinton ordered that 60 million acres of our national forests be kept off limits to new roads. This ruling is very important and should not be overturned, for several reasons. First, roadless areas are sources of clean water. Second, they are vital to preserving endangered species. Opponents of roadless areas say that the ruling would have an adverse economic impact on the logging and mining industries; but this is not so, because more than half of the 192 million acres would be available for industry. Some people argue that new roads are needed for access to our national parks, but 360,000 miles of roads already exist in the national parks, and most of them are in great need of repair. Some argue that a ban on roads will put people nearby at greater risk of fire, but the rule permits the building of roads where there is a threat of fire. The public overwhelmingly supports a ban on roads in the national parks. It is heartbreaking to think of these wilderness areas defaced by ugly roads, the trees felled and hacked up. I believe that the president should save the rule to protect our wilderness.

—Signed,

Concerned Hiker

Independent Practice: Analyzing an argument. After students have read the letter, have them fill out a chart like this one:

Topic	
How the writer feels about the topic (the writer's perspective)	
Main point of the letter	
Key supporting details	

When the chart is filled out, have the students divide the supporting details into **facts** and **opinions**. (Facts carry much more weight than opinions in a serious argument.) Finally, have them **evaluate** the argument: Is it a convincing argument? Did Concerned Hiker fail to answer some objections to the ban on roads in wilderness areas?

[Possible answers for chart:

Topic—the ruling to prohibit road building in wilderness areas.

How the writer feels about the topic—The writer feels that it would be heartbreaking to build new roads in wilderness areas.

Main point of the letter—The arguments supporting new roads in wilderness areas are not supported by the facts; the writer feels that new road building should be banned.

Key supporting details—Roadless areas are sources of water; they support endangered species; half the wilderness acres are still available for industry; many roads in national parks are in bad repair and should be fixed before new ones are built; provisions have been made for protection from fire; there is overwhelming public support.]

[Possible answers to questions:

Facts versus opinions—All of the above are facts except for the opinion that the building of roads would be heartbreaking. Ask students: Did the writer provide any factual support (statistics, for example) for the statement that the public overwhelmingly supports a ban on new roads in wilderness areas? (No)

Evaluation—In general this is a good argument, although the writer seems unable to resist the emotional appeal at the end. Ask students, however, how that appeal affected them. Did it influence them more or less than the factual evidence did?]

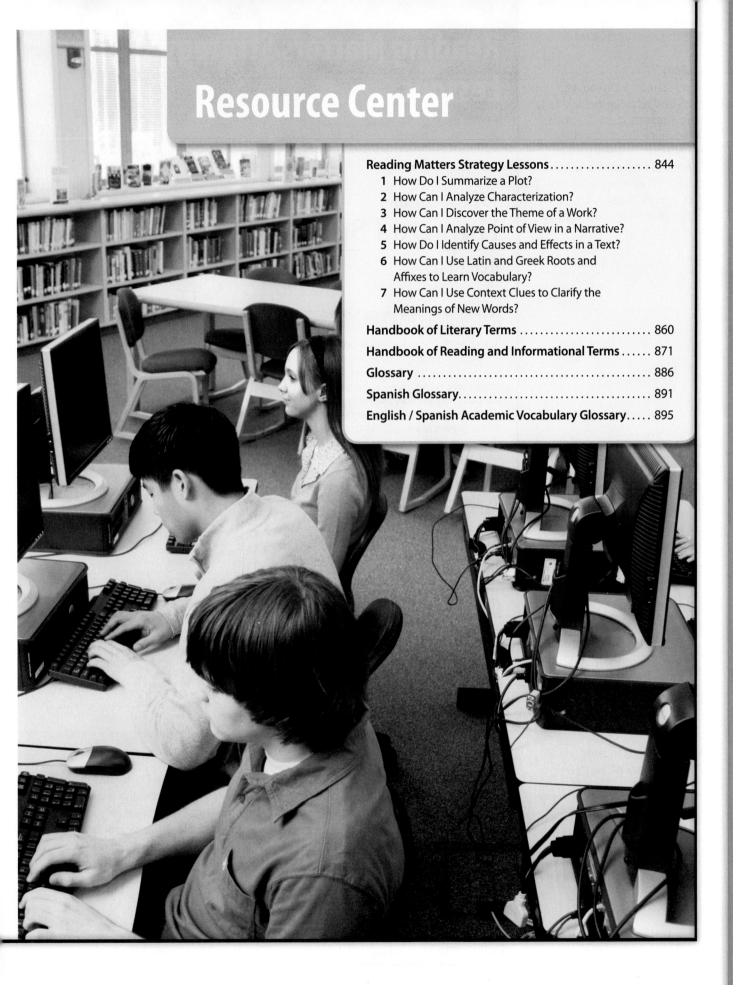

Resource Center

Reading Strategies

Lesson 1

Use this Strategy Lesson with the stories and teleplay in Chapter 1, where students identify events that advance the plot and explain how the events relate to past and future actions. This strategy will also be useful with "After Twenty Years" in Chapter 4, and "Sir Gawain and the Loathly Lady" in Chapter 8.

Reading Matters Strategy Lessons by Kylene Beers

 Reading Standard 3.2 Identify events that advance the plot and determine how each event explains past or present action(s) or foreshadows future action(s).

Strategy Lesson 1

How Do I Summarize a Plot?

Retelling

Identifying a Plot

"Is this the plot?" Josh asked as he pointed to the first paragraph of a story. He didn't understand that plot isn't a single thing he can point to. **Plot** is the "what happens" in a story—all the related events that occur from the story's beginning to its end.

The first part of a plot, usually revealed at the very beginning of a story, is the **basic situation.** Here you meet the characters, learn what they want, and discover their **conflicts**—the problems they face getting what they want. The major part of the plot involves a series of events in which **complications,** or obstacles, develop as the characters struggle to resolve their conflicts. The plot then moves to a **climax**—the most suspenseful part of the story, when the main character's problem is solved. In the **resolution** all the loose ends of the plot are tied up, and the story is over.

Using the Retelling Strategy

Keeping up with all the information in a story can be difficult. A strategy called **retelling** can help you identify the elements of a plot and help you keep all the information straight in your mind. With this strategy, you practice telling a story using an organizer called a **Retelling Summary Sheet,** a tool that will

help you remember to include all the events in the story's plot. Study the sample Retelling Summary Sheet, with annotations, on the next page.

> **Your Turn** Retell a Short Story
>
> Retell a short story, movie, or TV show plot. Use a Retelling Summary Sheet to help you remember and organize the key events of the plot. Score your own retelling. (*Zero* means you didn't tell about an event at all, and *3* means you did a good job covering the plot.) The sample opposite gives you tips on how to fill out a summary sheet.
>
> ### Retelling Summary Sheet
> #### Rating of Coverage
>
> | 0 | 1 | 2 | 3 |
> |---|---|---|---|
> | No coverage | A little | Some | A lot |
>
> 1. Introduction
> 2. Characters
> 3. Conflict
> 4. Complications
> 5. Climax
> 6. Resolution

Using Reading Matters

Reading Matters is a handbook of seven Strategy Lessons designed to help students master various Grade 7 reading standards for informational and literary text. The strategies presented in each lesson can be used with many selections in *Holt Literature and Language Arts*. As you plan your instruction for each standard, examine the corresponding Reading Matters Strategy Lesson to see if the strategy can be used as *preteaching* instruction? If you prefer, save the Strategy Lesson to use as *reteaching* instruction for students who need remediation.

As you look through Reading Matters, note that each lesson is addressed directly to students. Preview Reading Matters with students early in the year. Tell them that they should use the information here much as they would use the information in a handbook: Information in handbooks can be accessed at any point, read in any order, and revisited as many times as needed. That's the underlying philosophy of Reading Matters.

Retelling Summary Sheet
Rating of Coverage

0	1	2	3
No coverage	A little	Some	A lot

1. Introduction
Begin with the **title** and **author** of the story. Then, tell where and when the story is **set**—if that's important.

2. Characters
Tell the **characters'** names, and explain how the characters are related or connected to one another. Tell what the main character **wants.**

Strategy Tip The terms **protagonist** (the hero) and **antagonist** (the character who opposes the hero) are often used. The character Harry Potter is a protagonist; Voldemort is his antagonist.

3. Conflict
What is the main character's problem, or **conflict**—that is, who or what is keeping the main character from getting what he or she wants?

Strategy Tip If it's hard to keep events in **chronological order**, consider how each event caused another event to occur. Use **cause-effect words** such as *because of, since, as a result of.*

4. Complications
Tell the **main events**—what happens as the character tries to solve the conflict.

5. Climax
Describe the **climax,** the most suspenseful moment in the story, when you discover at last how the conflict ends.

Strategy Tip This is the moment when you know you are finally about to find out how the protagonist will overcome the conflict—or be defeated.

Strategy Tip Avoid linking the events with a string of *and's.* Here are some good **time-order words** to use: *first, second, third, next, eventually, later, afterward, finally, in conclusion.*

6. Resolution
Finally, tell what happens after the **climax.** How does the story end?

Your Turn
Possible responses:
1. "Rikki-tikki-tavi," by Rudyard Kipling, is set in India in the 1800s.

2. The main characters are Rikki-tikki-tavi, a mongoose; Teddy and his family, who take in Rikki-tikki-tavi after he is caught in a flood; Nag and Nagaina, the cobras living in the garden; and Darzee, the tailorbird, who also lives in the garden. Rikki-tikki-tavi wants to live with his human family and protect them, if need be, against snakes.

3. Nag and Nagaina want Rikki-tikki-tavi and the family to leave the bungalow so they can rule the garden; they plan to kill the family to get rid of them. This goes against what Rikki-tikki-tavi wants, putting him in conflict with the snakes.

4. Rikki-tikki-tavi and Teddy's father kill Nag, which makes Nagaina angry and prompts her to attack the family. Rikki-tikki-tavi destroys all but one of Nagaina's eggs and uses it to bargain with her when she threatens the family. They fight.

5. Rikki-tikki-tavi ultimately kills Nagaina and destroys the last egg.

6. The snakes are gone, and Rikki-tikki-tavi remains with the family and keeps the garden free of snakes.

Reading Strategies

Lesson 2

Use this strategy with the stories in Chapter 2, where students analyze a character based on the character's words and actions, the narrator's description of the character, and the words, thoughts, and actions of other characters. You can also refer students to this strategy when they read "The Highwayman" and "Echo and Narcissus," both in Chapter 3.

Reading Standard 3.3 Analyze characterization as delineated through a character's thoughts, words, speech patterns, and actions; the narrator's description; and the thoughts, words, and actions of other characters.

Strategy Lesson 2

How Can I Analyze Characterization?

If . . . Then . . .

Characters Affect Plot

What would happen in *Star Wars* if Anakin Skywalker successfully resisted the temptation of the dark side? How would the cartoon *Scooby Doo* be different if Scooby were brave? What would happen in a Super-man comic or movie if Superman decided he no longer wanted to use his powers for good?

In each of those situations, the outcome of the plot would certainly change if the characters changed. In other words, if a character acts one way, then the plot proceeds in a certain way. If a character acts in a different way, the outcome of the plot changes also.

Imagine what would have happened in "Cinderella" if Cinderella had not been kind and gentle. The fairy godmother probably would never have shown up to help a Cinderella who was as nasty and selfish as the stepsisters. Think about what would have happened in "Sleeping Beauty" if the princess hadn't been curious. Most likely she wouldn't have wandered into the one room that had the spinning wheel that was to put her and the whole kingdom to sleep for one hundred years.

We All Have Character Traits

To understand how character affects plot, you must first identify the main character's qualities, or **traits**. We all have character traits. We may be ambitious, shy, generous, fearless, kind—you name it.

You discover the traits of a character you meet in a story the same way you discover the qualities of a real person: You observe the character. You see how other characters respond to him or her (or it!). You pay attention to all the ways writers delineate a character's traits: through the character's thoughts, words, and actions; through the narrator's descrip-tions and comments; and through the thoughts, words, and actions of the other characters.

Here are some adjectives you can use to describe character traits:

Character Traits

strong/weak	wise/foolish	truthful/sneaky
kind/mean	selfish/unselfish	dependable/unreliable
brave/cowardly	adventurous/timid	generous/stingy
honest/dishonest	clever/silly	open/guarded
bold/shy	modern/old-fashioned	gloomy/optimistic

If . . . Then . . .

When you're trying to analyze a character or figure out how that character's traits affect the plot, think of what would happen if the character acted differently—or were a different kind of person. Think **If . . . Then . . .** : *If* the character is like this, *then* what would happen in the story? On the other hand, *if* the character is like *that*, *then* what would happen?

Your Turn Changing Character Traits

1. When you read "Rikki-Tikki-Tavi" (page 15), decide which word in each of the following pairs describes Rikki-Tikki.

   a. brave/fearful   b. confident/insecure   c. strong/weak

   Next, decide how the story would change if you were to choose the other word in each pair. If you think Rikki-Tikki is brave, then how would the story change if he were timid? Would he fight the cobras? Would he save the lives of Teddy and his family? If you think he is strong, then what would happen if he were weak? Would he lose the battle? Would he somehow betray his human family?

2. When you read "A Day's Wait" (page 187), think about Schatz. Decide which word in each of the following pairs best describes him.

   a. uncomplaining/whiny   b. brave/cowardly   c. controlled/emotional

   Now, choose the other word in the pair to describe Schatz. Explain how the plot and its resolution would likely change if Schatz had this trait.

3. In "The Dive" (page 53), think about Melly. Decide which word in each of the following pairs best describes Melly.

   a. brave/timid   b. strong/weak   c. hopeful/defeated

   Predict how the story would progress and how it would end if Melly were the opposite of whichever word you chose.

Your Turn

Possible responses:

1. **a.** brave
   b. confident
   c. strong

If Rikki-Tikki were fearful, insecure, or weak, the story would be dramatically different. He would likely not be able or willing to fight the cobras and to save Teddy and his family. He might even be frightened into taking the side of the cobras over that of his human family.

2. **a.** uncomplaining
   b. brave
   c. controlled

If Schatz were whiny, cowardly, or emotional, he would have revealed his worries at the beginning of the story and the misunderstanding that advances the plot would be resolved early. The plot might focus on a breakdown caused by his fear of dying.

3. **a.** brave
   b. strong
   c. hopeful

If Melly were timid, weak, or defeated, the plot might change in one of two ways: Melly's conflict might involve finding the courage to make the jump, as she would be too frightened to believe she could do it; if she were easily defeated, she might have given in to her father's order instead of considering defying it.

Reading Strategies

Lesson 3

Use this strategy with the poems, story, myth, and personal narrative in Chapter 3, where students identify recurring themes across works. Ask students to think about one or two words that relate to each of these selections. You will be surprised at how quickly students make the connections. Theme is one of the most difficult concepts for students to master. This lesson graphically distinguishes theme from topic and gives students a very specific strategy—Most Important Word—to use to discover theme.

California Standards

- **Reading Standard 3.4** Identify and analyze recurring themes across works (e.g., the value of bravery, loyalty, and friendship; the effects of loneliness.

Reading Standard 3.4 Identify and analyze recurring themes across works (e.g., the value of bravery, loyalty, and friendship; the effects of loneliness).

Strategy Lesson 3

How Can I Discover the Theme of a Work?

Most Important Word

Where Do You Find the Theme?

Has your teacher ever asked you that dreaded theme question—the one that begins "What is the theme of . . . ?" What do you do when you hear that question? A group of seventh-graders all immediately started turning the pages of their books when their teacher asked them to identify the theme of a story. "Why are you doing that?" she asked. "I'm looking for the theme," one student replied. "Yeah," another said, "I sure hope the writer remembered to include it."

What Is Theme?

The writer *did* include a theme, but not in the way the students were hoping. Writers don't end (or begin) their stories with a note to the reader that says, "And the theme of this story is . . ." No, instead writers let their readers meet the characters and share an experience with them. At the end of the experience, the reader, along with the characters, has discovered something about human experience. It might be something the reader already knows but rediscovers under new circumstances. It might be something new. The **theme,** then, is a truth about life or people that we discover as we share the characters' experiences. When you write or state a theme, remember that a theme isn't a word or a phrase—it's at least one sentence!

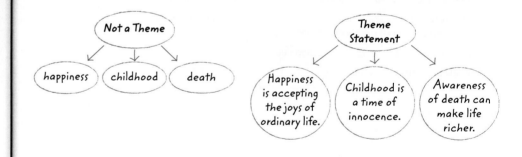

Most Important Word

To come up with a theme statement, try the strategy **Most Important Word.** After you've read a selection, skim through it again looking for the word that you think is most important to the meaning of the work. Three students made the following comments after reading a poem called "The Secret Heart" by Robert P. Tristram Coffin. In this poem, a father checks on his son, who is sleeping.

"I say **heart** is the most important word, because it's used a lot and is in the title and because the boy thinks his dad's hands look like they are making a heart, and that's the image the boy always remembers."

"I think the most important word is **father**, because it is the father who is checking on his son when he is sleeping at night."

"I think the most important word is **love**, because if the father didn't love his son, he wouldn't have been checking on him at night, wanting to protect him."

What's the most important word and why?

After deciding on the most important word and coming up with reasons for your choice, think about how that word could be related to the theme. Since different readers can pull different themes from the same selection, statements of themes usually differ from reader to reader. Look at the following three themes, and match them to the comments above.

1. A parent's love for a child is never-ending—it goes on day and night.
2. Children remember their parents' simple acts of love.
3. A father is his child's protector.

Your Turn Find the Most Important Word

Read this short, short poem by Langston Hughes, and select what you think is the most important word (or words—there could be more than one). Write down the reasons for your choice. Then, think of how that word could point to the theme of the poem. Try stating, in a sentence, the theme that you have discovered. Be sure to compare your themes in class.

O God of dust and rainbows help us see

That without dust the rainbows would not be.

—Langston Hughes

Your Turn _____

Possible response:

The most important word is _without_. I chose _without_ because the most important idea in the poem is that rainbows cannot exist _without_ dust. I would state the theme as: there can be no positive circumstances _without_ negative circumstances to make the good seem greater.

Reading Strategies

Lesson 4

Use this strategy with the fiction and nonfiction selections in Chapter 4, where students practice identifying a variety of points of view. This strategy helps students think about a story from various characters' perspectives. You might also want to introduce this strategy when students work on the Your Turn activity that accompanies Carol Jago's essay on point of view (pp. 372–373).

California Standards

■ **Reading Standard 3.5** Contrast points of view (e.g., first and third person, limited and omniscient, subjective and objective) in narrative text and explain how they affect the overall theme of the work.

Reading Standard 3.5 Contrast points of view (e.g., first and third person, limited and omniscient, subjective and objective) in narrative text and explain how they affect the overall theme of the work.

Strategy Lesson 4

How Can I Analyze Point of View in a Narrative?

Somebody Wanted But So

Who Tells the Story?

Is this glass half empty or half full? The very thirsty child would complain that it's half empty. The mom, who doesn't want the child drinking so much soda anyway, would say it's half full. What you're seeing in this situation is the effect of point of view.

When we talk about **point of view** in stories, we are talking about who is telling the story. Here are the three main points of view:

- **First-person point of view.** The story is told by "I," a character in the story.

- **Omniscient point of view.** The story is told by an all-knowing narrator who is not a character in the story. This narrator can tell everything about everyone in the story. This narrator can even tell the future.

- **Third-person limited point of view.** The story is told by a narrator who is not in the story. This narrator zooms in on one character and tells the story through that character's eyes and emotions.

Writers are especially aware of point of view, and they experiment with it all the time. Skilled readers also think about how a story would be changed if it were told from a different viewpoint. Often, not only the events of a story but also the story's theme can be completely altered by changes in the point of view. Think, for example, what would happen in a Spider-Man story if we saw everything through the eyes of the villain, a petty criminal who robs people. Spider-Man might be portrayed as a bullying, superpowered "guy who has everything" who prevents a poor, weaker "ordinary Joe" from getting the money he needs to feed his family.

Somebody Wanted But So

Try experimenting with point of view by using a strategy called **Somebody Wanted But So.** This simple strategy helps you summarize a story; it can also help you think about the story from various characters' perspectives—or points of view. Read the next page to find out how this strategy works.

On a sheet of paper, jot down the words *Somebody Wanted But So*. Now, think about a story you've just read. For right now, let's think about "Cinderella," a fairy tale you probably know. First, decide which character in the story you want to think about. Here are some choices: Cinderella, the stepmother, the stepsisters, the prince, maybe even the fairy godmother. Now, write your choice under the heading "Somebody," like this:

Somebody	Wanted	But	So
The prince			

With a focus on the prince, next think about what the prince wanted. "But" means he faced a problem getting what he wanted. "So" tells what the outcome is. Once you think through all of this, you have an SWBS chart that looks like this:

Somebody	Wanted	But	So
The prince	to find the young woman he met at the ball,	she left the ball without telling him who she was,	he traveled far and wide until he found her and married her.

You've just thought about the story from the prince's point of view. Now, try thinking about it from Cinderella's point of view. You might come up with a statement like this:

Somebody	Wanted	But	So
Cinderella	to escape the kitchen and a cruel family; she also wanted to go to the prince's ball,	her cruel stepmother would not let her get a dress for the ball,	a fairy godmother visited Cinderella and magically granted her wish.

Notice that as you change the character under the "Somebody" heading, you are shifting focus. If the prince tells the story or if a storyteller tells the story zooming in on the prince, you will not hear about Cinderella and her sad, ragged state until later. You will hear the prince telling you that he has fallen in love with a mysterious, beautiful young woman wearing the most fantastic gown, who left a tiny glass slipper on the palace steps.

Your Turn Changing the Point of View

Look back at "After Twenty Years" (page 383). Create SWBS charts for Jimmy, Bob, and the plainclothes policeman. How would the story's events change if the point of view were narrowed to what only one of these characters knows and sees? How would the theme of the story change?

Your Turn _____

Possible responses:

Jimmy wanted to meet his old friend Bob, as promised, but Bob turned out to be a wanted criminal, and Jimmy, a police officer, felt horrible about having to turn him in. So, he got the plainclothes officer to pose as him and arrest Bob.

Bob, a criminal, wanted to meet his old friend Jimmy, as promised, but Jimmy deceived Bob by having a police officer pose as Jimmy and arrest Bob. So, Bob was shaken but went along to prison.

The plainclothes policeman wanted to arrest Bob, but did not want him to be suspicious or escape, so he posed as Jimmy to make the arrest, only revealing the deception when Bob was in custody.

If the point of view were limited to any one of the three men, the element of surprise would be lost.

Reading Standard 2.3 Analyze text that uses the cause-and-effect organizational pattern.

Reading Strategies

Lesson 5

Use this strategy with the informational texts in Chapter 4, where students identify techniques of cause and effect. See in particular two selections that follow a cause-effect structure, "Tilting at Windmills," and "Saving the Earth: Teens Fish for Answers."

Strategy Lesson 5

How Do I Identify Causes and Effects in a Text?

Cause/Effect Tips and Signal Words

First a Cause, Then an Effect

Here are three situations:

- You press the right button on your stereo, and music starts to play.
- Someone tells you your clothes are cool, and you feel good about yourself.
- Your brother barges into your room without knocking, and you get angry.

In each of those situations, something has happened (an **effect**) because of something else (a **cause**). Look at this chart, and you can see which part of each sentence is the cause and which is the effect:

Cause	Effect
pressing the stereo's right button	music starting to play
hearing your clothes are cool	feeling good about yourself
brother barging into your room	getting angry

Finding the Cause and Its Effect

If writers showed us cause-and-effect relationships (sometimes called **causal relationships**) by using charts like the one above, then finding causes and effects would be easy. Most of the time, information isn't delivered in chart format, so you've got to find causes and effects on your own. Here are some tips for doing that:

1. **Change the words.** Think of cause as "source" or "reason" and effect as "result" or "outcome."
2. **Check out the question.** If a question in your history book or science book (even in this book!) asks you to identify causes and effects, look carefully at the question. The question itself often lets you know if you are hunting for the cause or the effect.

 California Standards

- **Reading Standard 2.3** Analyze text that uses the cause-and-effect organizational pattern.

- **What are three causes of the Civil War?**
  In this question you see that you are looking for the causes of (reasons for) the Civil War (outcome or effect).

- **What are three effects of poor nutrition?**
  This time you've got the cause (poor nutrition), and you're looking for its effects or results.

- **Why is George Washington called the father of our country?**
  With this question you are given the effect, or outcome: Washington came to be called the father of our country. Now you've got to find the reason or reasons why, so you are looking for the causes.

3. **Be on the lookout for signal words.** Certain words can signal that a reason for something or a cause of something is about to be mentioned. Other words can signal that a result or an effect is being described.

Words That Signal Causes		Words That Signal Effects	
because	since	therefore	thus
due to	were caused by	consequently	so
given that	results from	as a result	for that reason
as		then	

Your Turn   Identifying Causes and Effects

Read the sentences that follow, and make a cause-and-effect chart like the one on the opposite page. Decide which part of each sentence goes under the "Cause" heading and which part goes under the "Effect" heading. Look for signal words that help you spot causes and effects.

1. The California population grew from about 114,000 in 1848 to about 750,000 in 1852 as people moved to California in search of gold.

2. People rushing to California to find gold were called forty-niners because most of them arrived in 1849, the height of the gold rush.

3. Many of the mining towns that sprang up quickly were unsafe because they had no sheriffs.

4. Because so many people came so quickly to California looking for gold, by 1850, much of the easily found surface gold was already gone.

5. Although most people who went to California did not become rich from mining gold, many thousands decided to stay because of the wonderful climate and good farmland.

Your Turn _____

1. **Cause:** people moved to California in search of gold; **Effect:** the California population grew from about 114,000 in 1848 to about 750,000 in 1852

2. **Cause:** most of them arrived in 1849, the height of the gold rush; **Effect:** people rushing to California to find gold were called forty-niners

3. **Cause:** they had no sheriffs; **Effect:** many of the mining towns that sprang up quickly were unsafe

4. **Cause:** so many people came so quickly to California looking for gold; **Effect:** by 1850, much of the easily found surface gold was already gone

5. **Cause:** because of the wonderful climate and good farmland; **Effect:** many thousands decided to stay

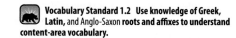
Reading Strategies

Lesson 6

Use this key lesson on Latin and Greek roots and affixes with the Vocabulary Development activities in Chapters 2 and 8.

Strategy Lesson 6

How Can I Use Latin and Greek Roots and Affixes to Learn Vocabulary?

Becoming Word-Wise

Figuring Out Word Meanings

Can you read the following sentence?

Ifay ouyay ancay eadray isthay, enthay ouyay ancay eadray igpay atinlay.

Well, how did you do? If you know Pig Latin, then you probably did just fine. Pig Latin—not at all related to the Latin the ancient Romans spoke—requires you to take off the first letter (or sometimes letters) of a word, put that letter at the end of the word, and then add the long *a* sound (ā). So, *pig* becomes *igpay*. Once you figure out how words work in Pig Latin *(owhay ordsway orkway inay igpay atinlay),* then you can speak it, write it, read it, and understand it.

Latin and Greek: The Key to Understanding Words in English

Figuring out the meaning of words and how they work to make meaning is the key to mastering any language. Mastering English vocabulary is especially difficult because English has borrowed words from many different languages, and it continues to do so. A large number of English words can be traced back to ancient Latin and Greek. If you can learn to see Latin or Greek roots and affixes in some English words and understand what those roots and affixes mean, then you have a key to understanding many English words.

For instance, if you know that the Latin prefix *dis–* means "not" or "the opposite," you can figure out that the word *dislocate* means "put out of place" or "locate in a different place" (as in "dislocate a shoulder"). You'll then be able to figure out what words like *disbelief, dissimilar,* and *distrust* mean.

If you know that the Latin root *–aud–* means "hear," then you can guess that *audio* has something to do with hearing, as do the related words *audible, auditory, auditorium,* and *audience.*

On the next pages are lists of some common roots and affixes from Latin and Greek. Note their meanings. Note examples of how these roots and affixes are used to build English words. (*L* in the chart stands for "Latin"; *G* stands for "Greek.") If you can learn to recognize even a portion of these roots and affixes, you'll have an advantage in figuring out the meanings of new words you encounter.

> *Remember...*
>
> Roots are the fundamental parts of a word.
> *-Loc-* is a Latin root for "place." *Locate* is based on the Latin root *-loc-*.
>
> Affixes are word parts added to a root to alter its meaning.
>
> Prefixes are affixes added to the front of a word (*dislocate*).
>
> Suffixes are affixes added to the end of a word (*location*).

 California Standards

■ **Vocabulary Standard 1.2** Use knowledge of Greek, Latin, and Anglo-Saxon roots and affixes to understand content-area vocabulary.

Commonly Used Roots

Root	Meanings	Examples
–act– (L)	act	action, actor, react, transact, enact
–aud– (L)	hear	audience, auditorium, audible, audition
–bio– (G)	life	biology, biography, biofeedback, bionics
–cred– (L)	believe; trust	credit, discredit, credible, credulous
–dem– (G)	people	democracy, Democrat, demographics
–dic– (L)	speak; say	dictate, predict, contradict, verdict, diction
–geo– (G)	earth	geography, geology
–graph– (G)	write; draw; record	autograph, paragraph, phonograph, photograph, telegraph
–loc– (L)	place	allocate, locate, location
–man– (L)	hand	manual, manufacture, manuscript, manipulate
–ped– (L)	foot	pedal, pedestrian, pedestal
–pop– (L)	people; nation	population, popular, populace
–port– (L)	carry	import, export, portable, porter, transport
–sig– (L)	mark; sign	insignia, signal, significant, signature
–spec– (L)	see; look at	inspect, respect, spectacle, spectator, suspect
–tract– (L)	pull; drag	attract, detract, contract, subtract, traction, tractor
–vid– (L)	see; look	evidence, video, provide, providence
–volv– (L)	roll	evolve, involve, revolve, revolver, revolution

Commonly Used Prefixes

Prefix	Meanings	Examples
anti– (G)	against; opposing	antiwar, anticlimax
bi– (L)	two	bisect, bimonthly
co– (L)	with; together	coexist, codependent
de– (L)	away from; off; down	debrief, debug
dia– (G)	through; across; between	diameter, diagonal
in–, *im–* (L)	in; into; within	introduce, imprison
inter– (L)	between; among	interpersonal, intersect
non– (L)	not	nonprofit, nonfat
post– (L)	after; following	postnasal, postgraduate
pre– (L)	before	prepayment, preview
re– (L)	back; backward; again	reverse, return, recur
sub– (L)	under; beneath	submarine, substandard
syl–, *sym–*, *syn–*, *sys–* (G)	together; with / with	syllable, symmetric, synthesis, system
trans– (L)	across	transplant, translate

Commonly Used Suffixes

Suffix	Meanings	Examples
–able (L)	able; likely	readable, lovable
–ance, *–ancy* (L)	act; quality	admittance, constancy
–ate (L)	to become; to cause; to be	captivate, activate
–fy (L)	to make; to cause; to be	liquefy, simplify
–ible (L)	able; likely	flexible, digestible
–ity (L)	state; condition	reality, sincerity
–ize (L)	to make; to cause; to be	socialize, motorize
–ment (L)	result; act of; state of being	judgment, fulfillment
–ous (L)	characterized by	dangerous, malicious
–tion (L)	action; condition	rotation, election

Your Turn Build a Vocabulary Tree

You can increase your vocabulary by building "vocabulary trees" from the root up. For an example of a vocabulary tree, look below at the tree a student made using the root *–cred–*. Here are the steps you can follow to create your own vocabulary tree:

1. On a piece of paper, draw a tree like the one below, and put a word root from the list on page 855 in the root section of the tree.

2. In the trunk, put one word from the "Examples" column that uses that root, and define the word.

3. In the branches, put other words that you hear or read or use in your own writing that come from that root. You'll find that many words consist of the root combined with a prefix or suffix.

4. On the twigs of the branches, explain how you used that word or where you read it.

5. Add as many branches as possible to your vocabulary tree.

Remember: The more you use a word, the more likely you are to remember what it means.

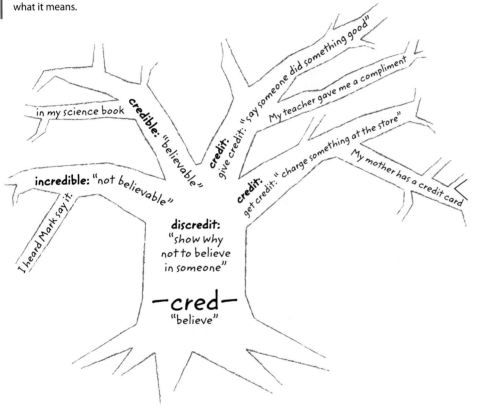

Your Turn _____

Possible response:

Trunk:

–spec– (L) see; look at

Branch: *inspect*—to look closely at something. **Twig:** a sticker in my coat said that someone inspected it

Branch: *respect*—to see another person in a positive light. **Twig:** our teachers talk about it

Branch: *spectacle*—something exciting or unusual to see. **Twig:** my grandma called the circus a spectacle

Branch: *spectator*—someone who watches an event. **Twig:** I was one at a baseball game

Branch: *suspect*—a person being looked at as guilty of a crime. **Twig:** detective stories and movies

Reading Strategies

Lesson 7

Use this lesson on context clues with Chapters 1, 4, and 5, which focus on Vocabulary Development Standard 1.3: Clarify word meanings through the use of definition, example, restatement, or contrast.

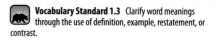

Vocabulary Standard 1.3 Clarify word meanings through the use of definition, example, restatement, or contrast.

Strategy Lesson 7

How Can I Use Context Clues to Clarify the Meanings of New Words?

Becoming Word-Wise

Finding the Meanings of Unknown Words

See if you can complete the following sentences:

- When you get in a car, be sure to buckle your seat _____.
- I really like to pour _____ over my pancakes.
- Most people turn on a _____ when they walk into a dark room.

You probably quickly figured out that the missing words were *belt, syrup,* and *light*. You could supply the missing words because you used the **context**— the other words in the sentence.

Using context clues is only one way of figuring out the meaning of an unknown word. You can also use a dictionary; you can study the word's root and its affixes, if there are any; and you can look for familiar words within the word.

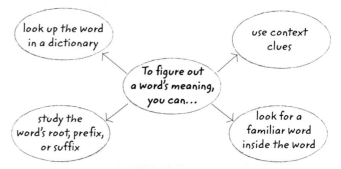

Types of Context Clues

If you don't have a dictionary handy, if knowing word parts isn't helping, and if no familiar words seem to be within the word you don't know, turn to **context clues.** Context clues are often found in the surrounding words, sentences, or paragraphs that include the word you don't know. There are a variety of types of context clues, but the four on the next page are particularly helpful.

California Standards

■ **Vocabulary Standard 1.3** Clarify word meanings through the use of definition, example, restatement, or contrast.

1. **Definition clues** define or explain the unfamiliar word in the same sentence in which the word appears.

Symbols, <u>things that stand for something else</u>, are often found in the poems of Robert Frost.

definition clue

2. **Restatement clues** explain the unfamiliar word in the text by restating it in simpler terms or by using a synonym. The restatement might be in the same sentence or in another sentence close by—so be sure to read on!

The food was so bland, or <u>tasteless</u>, that everyone stopped eating.

restatement clue

The food was bland. Everyone stopped eating because <u>the food had no taste.</u>

restatement clue

3. **Example clues** provide an example of the unfamiliar word.

José wants some sort of rodent for a pet, either a <u>mouse</u> or a <u>squirrel</u>.

example clue

4. **Contrast clues** offer an opposite meaning of the unfamiliar word. Again, the contrast might be in the same sentence or in a nearby sentence.

Chad is <u>calm</u> and <u>quiet</u>, but his brother is usually boisterous.

contrast clues

Your Turn — Using and Identifying Context Clues

Define the following underlined words by using context clues. Identify the type of context clue you find in each sentence.

1. His logic was <u>fallacious</u>, or faulty, so everyone reached the wrong conclusions.
   Clue _____
   Meaning _____

2. Most snakes are meat eaters, or <u>carnivores</u>.
   Clue _____
   Meaning _____

3. A <u>mendicant</u> is a beggar.
   Clue _____
   Meaning _____

4. I like <u>conifers</u>, such as pine trees or cypress trees.
   Clue _____
   Meaning _____

5. His <u>conjecture</u>, or guess, was wrong.
   Clue _____
   Meaning _____

6. The thief ran out the <u>postern</u> while the police ran in the front door.
   Clue _____
   Meaning _____

7. The rider merely tapped the <u>quirt</u>. This small whip is used to make the racehorse run faster.
   Clue _____
   Meaning _____

8. <u>Subterranean</u> temperatures can be higher than temperatures above the earth's surface.
   Clue _____
   Meaning _____

9. That girl is <u>narcissistic</u>. The other girl, however, really isn't overly interested in herself.
   Clue _____
   Meaning _____

10. I was so happy while on vacation that my <u>elation</u> lasted for weeks afterward.
   Clue _____
   Meaning _____

Your Turn
Answers:

1. **Clue:** restatement, **Meaning:** faulty

2. **Clue:** restatement, **Meaning:** meat eaters

3. **Clue:** definition, **Meaning:** beggar

4. **Clue:** example, **Meaning:** type of tree

5. **Clue:** restatement, **Meaning:** guess

6. **Clue:** contrast, **Meaning:** rear exit

7. **Clue:** definition, **Meaning:** small whip

8. **Clue:** contrast, **Meaning:** underground

9. **Clue:** contrast, **Meaning:** self-absorbed

10. **Clue:** example, **Meaning:** very happy

Handbook of Literary Terms

For more information about a topic, turn to the page(s) in this book indicated on a separate line at the end of the entries. To learn more about *Alliteration,* for example, turn to pages 571 and 607.

On another line are cross-references to entries in this handbook that provide closely related information. For instance, at the end of *Autobiography* is a cross-reference to *Biography.*

ALLITERATION **The repetition of the same or very similar consonant sounds in words that are close together.** Though alliteration usually occurs at the beginning of words, it can also occur within or at the end of words. Among other things, alliteration can help establish a mood, emphasize words, and serve as a memory aid. In the following example the *s* sound is repeated at the beginning of the words silken and *sad* and within the words *uncertain* and *rustling*:

> And the silken sad uncertain rustling of each
> purple curtain
>
> —Edgar Allan Poe, from "The
> Raven"

See pages 571, 607.

ALLUSION **A reference to a statement, a person, a place, or an event from literature, history, religion, mythology, politics, sports, or science.** Allusions enrich the reading experience. Writers expect readers to recognize an allusion and to think, almost at the same time, about the literary work and the person, place, or event that it refers to. The following lines, describing a tunnel in the snow, contain an allusion to Aladdin, a character in *The Thousand and One Nights:*

> With mittened hands, and caps drawn low,
> To guard our necks and ears from snow,
> We cut the solid whiteness through.
> And, where the drift was deepest, made
> A tunnel walled and overlaid
> With dazzling crystal: we had read
> Of rare Aladdin's wondrous cave,
> And to our own his name we gave.
>
> —John Greenleaf Whittier,
> from "Snow-Bound"

The cave in the tale contains a magic lamp that helps Aladdin discover vast riches. By alluding to Aladdin's cave, Whittier makes us see the icy tunnel in the snow as a magical, fairy-tale place.

The cartoon below makes an allusion to a popular fairy tale.

"Now, this policy will cover your home for fire, theft, flood and huffing and puffing."

ATMOSPHERE   **The overall mood or emotion of a work of literature.** A work's atmosphere can often be described with one or two adjectives, such as *scary, dreamy, happy, sad, or nostalgic.* A writer creates atmosphere by using images, sounds, and descriptions that convey a particular feeling.

See also *Mood.*

AUTOBIOGRAPHY   **The story of a person's life, written or told by that person.** Maijue Xiong wrote an autobiography called "An Unforgettable Journey" (page 527) about her escape from war-torn Laos as a child. Another well-known autobiographical work is Amy Tan's *Fish Cheeks.*

See pages 435, 501, 523.
See also *Biography.*

BIOGRAPHY   **The story of a real person's life, written or told by another person.** Milton Meltzer has written a number of biographies of historical figures, such as George Washington and Mark Twain. "Elizabeth I" (page 423) is his biography of the remarkable queen of England who reigned in the sixteenth century. Frequent subjects of biographies are movie stars, television personalities, politicians, sports figures, self-made millionaires, even underworld figures. Biographies are among the most popular forms of contemporary literature.

See pages 419, 501, 523.
See also *Autobiography.*

CHARACTER   **A person or animal who takes part in the action of a story, play, or other literary work.** In some works, such as Aesop's fables, a character is an animal. In myths and legends a character may be a god or a superhero. Most often a character is an ordinary human being, such as Kevin in "User Friendly" (page 267).

The process of revealing the personality of a character in a story is called **characterization.** A writer can reveal a character in the following ways:

1. by letting you hear the character speak
2. by describing how the character looks and dresses

3. by letting you listen to the character's inner thoughts and feelings
4. by revealing what other people in the story think or say about the character
5. by showing you what the character does—how he or she acts
6. by telling you directly what the character's personality is like (cruel, kind, sneaky, brave, and so on)

When a writer uses the first five ways to reveal a character, you must make an inference, based on the evidence the writer provides, to decide what the character is like. When a writer uses the sixth method, however, you don't make a decision but are told directly what kind of person the character is.

Characters can be classified as static or dynamic. A **static character** is one who does not change much in the course of a work. Mr. Andersen in *Song of the Trees* (page 539) is a static character. By contrast, a **dynamic** character changes as a result of the story's events.

A character's **motivation** is any force that drives or moves the character to behave in a particular way. Many characters are motivated by the force of fear or love or ambition.

See pages 136–137, 147, 159, 185.

CONFLICT   **A struggle or clash between opposing characters or opposing forces.** In an external conflict a character struggles against some outside force. This outside force may be another character or society as a whole or a storm or a grizzly bear or even a machine. In "Three Skeleton Key" (page 35), the characters have an external conflict with a swarm of sea rats. An **internal conflict,** on the other hand, takes place within a character's mind. It is a struggle between opposing needs, desires, or emotions. In "After Twenty Years" (page 383), Officer Wells must resolve an internal conflict: Should he arrest an old friend or let him go?

See pages 4, 13, 51, 500, 509.

CONNOTATION **The feelings and associations that a word suggests.** For example, *tiny, cramped,* and *compact* all have about the same dictionary definition, or **denotation,** but they have different connotations. A manufacturer of small cars would not describe its product as tiny or cramped.

Instead, the company might say that its cars are compact. To grasp a writer's full meaning, you must pay attention not only to the literal definitions of words but also to their connotations. Connotations can be especially important in poetry.

See pages 147, 156, 159, 168.

DENOTATION **The literal, dictionary definition of a word.**

See pages 147, 156, 159, 168.
See also *Connotation.*

DESCRIPTION **The kind of writing that creates a clear image of something, usually by using details that appeal to one or more of the senses: sight, hearing, smell, taste, and touch.** Writers use description in all forms of fiction, nonfiction, and poetry. In "Fish Cheeks" (page 504), Amy Tan vividly describes the colors, sounds, and tastes of her family's Christmas celebration.

See page 223.

DIALECT **A way of speaking that is characteristic of a particular region or group of people.** A dialect may have a distinct vocabulary, pronunciation system, and grammar. In a sense, we all speak a dialect. One dialect usually becomes dominant in a country or culture and is accepted as the standard way of speaking. In the United States, for example, the formal written language is known as standard English. This is the dialect used in most newspapers and magazines.

Writers often reproduce regional dialects, or speech that reveals a character's economic or social

class, in order to give a story local color. Mr. Baumer in "Bargain" (page 393) speaks in a dialect that reveals that his first language is German. The poem "Madam and the Rent Man" (page 585) is written in a dialect spoken in some urban African American communities in the northeastern United States.

DIALOGUE **A conversation between two or more characters.** Most stage dramas consist of dialogue together with stage directions. (Screenplays and teleplays sometimes include an unseen narrator.) The dialogue in a drama, such as *The Monsters Are Due on Maple Street* (page 67), must move the plot along and reveal its characters almost single-handedly. Dialogue is also an important element in most stories and novels as well as in some poems and nonfiction. It is one of the most effective ways for a writer to show what a character is like. It can also add realism and humor.

In the written form of a play, dialogue appears without quotation marks. In prose or poetry, however, dialogue is usually enclosed in quotation marks.

A **monologue** is a part of a drama in which one character speaks alone.

See pages 222, 631.

DRAMA **A story written to be acted for an audience.** (A drama can also be appreciated and enjoyed in written form.) In a drama, such as *The Monsters Are Due on Maple Street* (page 67), the action is usually driven by characters who want something very much and take steps to get it. The related events that take place within a drama are often separated into **acts.** Each act is often made up of shorter sections, or **scenes.** Most plays have three acts, but there are many, many variations. The elements of a drama are often described as **introduction** or **exposition, complications, conflict, climax,** and **resolution.**

ESSAY **A short piece of nonfiction prose that examines a single subject.** Most essays can be categorized as either personal or formal.

The **personal essay** generally reveals a great deal about the writer's personality and tastes. Its tone is often conversational, sometimes even humorous. In a personal essay the focus is the writer's feelings and response to an experience.

The **formal essay** is usually serious, objective, and impersonal in tone. Its purpose is to inform readers about a topic or to persuade them to accept the writer's views.

See pages 501, 557.

FABLE **A brief story in prose or verse that teaches a moral or gives a practical lesson about how to get along in life.** The characters of most fables are animals that behave and speak like human beings. Some of the most popular fables are attributed to Aesop, who is thought to have been a slave in ancient Greece.

See also *Folk Tale, Myth*.

FICTION **A prose account that is made up rather than true.** The term *fiction* usually refers to novels and short stories. Fiction may be based on a writer's experiences or on historical events, but characters, events, and other details are altered or added by the writer to create a desired effect.

See page 500.
See also *Nonfiction*.

FIGURE OF SPEECH **A word or phrase that describes one thing in terms of something else and is not literally true.** Figures of speech always involve some sort of imaginative comparison between seemingly unlike things. The most common forms are **simile** ("The stars were like diamonds"), **metaphor** ("My soul is an enchanted boat"), and **personification** ("The sun smiled down on the emerald-green fields").

See pages 569, 579.
See also *Metaphor, Personification, Simile*.

FLASHBACK **An interruption in the action of a plot to tell what happened at an earlier time.** A flashback breaks the usual movement of the narrative by going back in time. It usually gives background information that helps the reader understand the present situation. "A Mason-Dixon Memory" (page 559) contains a long flashback.

A break in the unfolding of a plot to an episode in the future is known as a **flash-forward.**

See pages 198, 557.

FOLK TALE **A story with no known author that originally was passed on from one generation to another by word of mouth.** Folk tales tend to travel, so similar plots and characters are found in several cultures. For example, "Yeh-Shen" (page 458) is a Chinese folk tale that is very similar to the European story of Cinderella. Folk tales often contain **fantastic** elements, or events that could not happen in the world as we know it.

See pages 447, 498.
See also *Fable, Myth*.

FORESHADOWING **The use of clues to suggest events that will happen later in the plot.** Foreshadowing is used to build suspense or create anxiety. In a drama a gun found in a bureau drawer in Act One is likely to foreshadow violence later in the play. In "Three Skeleton Key" (page 35), the story of three convicts who perished on the key foreshadows the danger the three lighthouse keepers will face.

See pages 5, 33.
See also *Suspense*.

FREE VERSE **Poetry without a regular meter or a rhyme scheme.** Poets writing in free verse try to capture the natural rhythms of ordinary speech. To create their music, poets writing in free verse may use internal rhyme, repetition, alliteration, and onomatopoeia. Free verse also frequently makes use of vivid imagery. The following poem in free verse effectively uses images and the repetition of words to describe the effects of a family's eviction for not paying rent:

> **Eviction**
> what i remember about that day
> is boxes stacked across the walk
> and couch springs curling through the air
> and drawers and tables balanced on the curb
> and us, hollering,
> leaping up and around
> happy to have a playground;
>
> nothing about the emptied rooms
> nothing about the emptied family
>
> —Lucille Clifton

See pages 570, 607.
See also *Poetry, Rhyme, Rhythm.*

IMAGERY **Language that appeals to the senses.** Most images are visual—that is, they create pictures in your mind by appealing to the sense of sight. Images can also appeal to the sense of hearing, touch, taste, or smell or to several senses at once. The sensory images in "The Highwayman" (page 255) add greatly to the enjoyment of the poem. Though imagery is an element in all types of writing, it is especially important in poetry.

See pages 569, 583, 607.
See also *Poetry.*

IRONY **In general, a contrast between expectation and reality.** Irony can create powerful effects, from humor to strong emotion. Here are three common types of irony:

1. **Verbal irony** involves a contrast between what is said or written and what is meant. If you were to call someone who failed a math test Einstein, you would be using verbal irony.
2. **Situational irony** occurs when what happens is very different from what is expected to happen. The surprise ending of "After Twenty Years" (page 383) involves situational irony.
3. **Dramatic irony** occurs when the audience or the reader knows something a character does not know. In Part 2 of "The Highwayman" (page 255), the reader feels an anxious sense of irony when King George's soldiers have Bess tied up. Although the highwayman doesn't yet know it, we know that a trap is set for him.

See page 102.

MAIN IDEA **The most important idea expressed in a paragraph or in an entire essay.** The main idea may be directly stated in a **topic sentence,** or you may have to look at all the details in the paragraph and make an **inference,** or educated guess, about its main idea.

See pages 13, 110, 201, 407.

METAMORPHOSIS **A marvelous change from one shape or form to another one.** In myths the change is usually from human to animal, from animal to human, or from human to plant. Greek and Roman myths contain many examples of metamorphosis. The myth of Echo and Narcissus (page 289) tells how the vain youth Narcissus pines away for love of his own reflection until he is changed into a flower.

See page 821.
See also *Myth*

METAPHOR **An imaginative comparison between two unlike things in which one thing is said to be another thing.** A metaphor is an important type of figurative language. Metaphors are used in all forms of writing and are common in ordinary speech. If you were to say someone has a heart of gold, you would not mean that the person's heart is actually made of metal. You would mean, instead, that the person is warm and caring. You would be speaking metaphorically.

PEANUTS reprinted with permission of the United Feature Syndicate, Inc.

Metaphors differ from similes, which use specific words (notably *like, as, than,* and *resembles*) to state comparisons. William Wordsworth's famous comparison "I wandered lonely as a cloud" is a simile because it uses *as.* If Wordsworth had written "I was a lonely, wandering cloud," he would have been using a metaphor.

An **extended metaphor** is a metaphor that is developed, or extended, through several lines of writing or even throughout an entire poem. For example, Emily Dickinson wrote a short poem called "I Like to See It Lap the Miles" in which she used an extended metaphor to compare a train to a horse.

See pages 263, 569.
See also *Figure of Speech, Personification, Simile.*

MOOD **The overall emotion created by a work of literature.** A work of literature can often be described with one or more adjectives: *sad, scary, hopeful, exciting,* and so on. These are descriptions of the work's mood—its emotional atmosphere. For example, the mood of "Annabel Lee" (page 283) could be described as haunting or romantic. That mood has a lingering effect on its readers.

See also *Atmosphere.*

MOTIVATION **See Character.**

See page 171.

MYTH **A story that explains something about the world and typically involves gods or other superhuman beings.** Myths, which at one time were believed to be true, reflect the traditions of the culture that produced them. Almost every culture has **origin myths** (or **creation myths**), stories that explain how something in the world (perhaps the world itself) came to be. Myths may also explain many other aspects of nature. The ancient Greek myth of Echo and Narcissus (page 289), for example, explains the origins of a flower. Most myths are very old and were handed down orally long before being put in written form. In some of the world's greatest myths, a hero or even a god embarks on a **quest,** a perilous journey taken in pursuit of something of great value.

See also *Fable, Folk Tale.*

NONFICTION **Prose writing that deals with real people, events, and places without changing any facts.** Popular forms of nonfiction are the **autobiography,** the **biography,** and the essay. Other examples of nonfiction include newspaper stories, magazine articles, historical writing, scientific reports, and even personal diaries and letters.

Nonfiction writing can be subjective or objective. **Subjective writing** expresses the feelings and opinions of the writer. **Objective** writing conveys the facts without introducing any emotion or personal bias.

See pages 297, 501.
See also *Autobiography, Biography, Fiction.*

NOVEL **A fictional story that is usually more than one hundred book pages long.** A novel uses all the elements of storytelling—**plot, character, setting, theme,** and **point of view.** A novel, because of its length, usually has more characters, settings, and themes and a more complex plot than a short story. Modern writers sometimes do not pay much attention to one or more of the novel's traditional elements. Some novels today are basically character studies that include only the barest story lines. Other novels don't look much beyond the surface of their characters and concentrate instead on plot and setting. A novel can deal with almost any topic. Many of the books recommended in the Read On sections of this text are novels. A **novella** is shorter than a novel and longer than a short story.

See page 500.

ONOMATOPOEIA **The use of words whose sounds echo their sense.** Onomatopoeia (ahn uh mat uh PEE uh) is so natural to us that we use it at a very early age. *Buzz, rustle, boom, ticktock, tweet,* and *bark* are all examples of onomatopoeia. Onomatopoeia is an important element in creating the music of poetry. In the following lines the poet creates a frenzied mood by choosing words that imitate the sound of alarm bells:

> Oh, the bells, bells, bells!
> What a tale their terror tells
> Of Despair!
> How they clang, and clash, and roar!
> What a horror they outpour
> On the bosom of the palpitating air!
> Yet the ear, it fully knows
> By the twanging
> And the clanging
> How the danger ebbs and flows.
>
> —Edgar Allan Poe,
> from "The Bells"

See pages 571, 607.
See also *Alliteration.*

PERSONIFICATION **A figure of speech in which a nonhuman or nonliving thing or quality is talked about as if it were human or alive.**

See page 537.
See also *Figure of Speech, Metaphor, Simile.*

PLOT **The series of related events that make up a story.** Plot is what happens in a short story, novel, play, or narrative poem. Most plots are built on these bare bones: An **introduction,** or **exposition,** tells us who the characters are and what their **conflict** is. **Complications** arise as the characters take steps to resolve the conflict. The plot reaches a **climax,** the most emotional or suspenseful moment in the story, when the outcome is decided one way or another. The last part of a story is the **resolution,** when the characters' problems are solved and the story ends.

Not all works of fiction or drama have this traditional plot structure. Some modern writers experiment, often eliminating parts of a traditional plot in order to focus on elements such as character, point of view, or mood.

See pages 4–5, 51, 55, 91, 756.
See also *Conflict.*

POETRY **A kind of rhythmic, compressed language that uses figures of speech and imagery designed to appeal to emotion and imagination.** We know poetry when we see it because it is usually arranged in a particular way on the page. Traditional poetry often has a regular pattern of rhythm (**meter**) and may have a regular **rhyme scheme.**

Free verse is poetry that has no regular rhythm or rhyme. "Names of Horses" (page 609) is a free-verse poem that is also an **elegy,** a poem that mourns the passing of something that is important to the writer. A special kind of free-verse poem is the **catalog poem,** a poem that lists the poet's thoughts or feelings about a subject. Another major form of poetry is the **narrative poem,** which tells a story, such as "The Highwayman" (page 255). Two popular narrative forms are the **epic** and the **ballad.** Another major form of poetry is the **lyric poem,** which expresses a speaker's feelings. "I Ask My Mother to Sing" (page 591) is a lyric poem that is also a **sonnet**—a poem of fourteen lines that follows a strict form. The **ode** is a type of lyric poem that celebrates something. A lighthearted example is "Ode to Family Photographs" (page 592).

See pages 568–572.
See also *Figure of Speech, Free Verse, Imagery, Refrain, Rhyme, Rhythm, Speaker, Stanza.*

POINT OF VIEW The vantage point from which a story is told. The most common points of view are the **omniscient,** the **third-person limited,** and the **first person.**

1. In the **omniscient** (ahm NIHSH uhnt), or all-knowing, **point of view** the narrator knows everything about the characters and their problems. This all-knowing narrator can tell about the characters' past, present, and future. This kind of narrator can even tell what the characters are thinking or what is happening in other places. This narrator is not in the story. Instead, he or she stands above the action, like a god. The omniscient is a very familiar point of view; we have heard it in fairy tales since we were very young. "Yeh-Shen" (page 458), a Chinese Cinderella story, is told from the omniscient point of view.

> Her loveliness made her seem a heavenly being, and the king suddenly knew in his heart that he had found his true love.

2. In the **third-person limited point of view,** the narrator focuses on the thoughts and feelings of only one character. From this point of view, you observe the action through the eyes and feelings of only one character in the story. "Hum" (page 314) is told from the third-person limited point of view of an Arab student after the United States was attacked on September 11, 2001.

> A counselor came to take Sami out of class. She had a worried expression. "You realize that you are the only Arab student in this school at a very difficult time. If anyone gives you any trouble . . ."
> Sami didn't think he could tell her what had already happened.
> It would make him seem weak.
> If anyone found out he told, they would hate him even more.

3. In the **first-person point of view,** one of the characters, using the personal pronoun I, is telling the story. You become very familiar with this narrator but can know only what he or she knows and can observe only what he or she observes. All information about the story must come from this character. In some cases the information is incorrect. "User Friendly" (page 267) is told from the first-person point of view of the boy whose computer starts acting funny.

> As I walked by the corner of my room, where my computer table was set up, I pressed the on button, slid a diskette into the floppy drive, then went to brush my teeth. By the time I got back, the computer's screen was glowing greenly, displaying the message: *Good morning, Kevin.*

See pages 372–373, 381, 391, 407, 435.

REFRAIN **A group of words repeated at intervals in a poem, song, or speech.** Refrains are usually associated with songs and poems, but they are also used in speeches and other forms of literature. Refrains are most often used to create rhythm, but they may also provide emphasis or commentary, create suspense, or help hold a work together. Refrains may be repeated with small variations in a work in order to fit a particular context or to create a special effect.

RHYME **The repetition of accented vowel sounds and all sounds following them in words close together in a poem.** *Mean* and *screen* are rhymes, as are *crumble* and *tumble*. Rhyme has many purposes in poetry: It creates rhythm, lends a songlike quality, emphasizes ideas, organizes the poem (for instance, into stanzas or couplets), provides humor or delight, and makes the poem memorable.

Many poems—for example, "The Runaway" (page 605)—use **end rhymes,** rhymes at the end of a line. In the following stanza, *walls/calls/falls* form end rhymes, as do *hands/sands*. The pattern of end rhymes in a poem is called a **rhyme scheme.** To indicate the rhyme scheme of a poem, use a separate letter of the alphabet for each rhyme. For example, the rhyme scheme below is *aabba.*

> Darkness settles on roofs and walls,
> But the sea, the sea in the darkness calls;
> The little waves, with their soft,
>   white hands,
> Efface the footprints in the sands,
> And the tide rises, the tide falls.
>
> —Henry Wadsworth Longfellow,
>   from "The Tide Rises, the Tide Falls"

Internal rhymes are rhymes within lines. The following line has an internal rhyme (*turning/burning*):

> Back into the chamber turning, all my soul within me burning
>
> —Edgar Allan Poe,
>   from "The Raven"

Rhyming sounds need not be spelled the same way; for instance, *gear/here* forms a rhyme. Rhymes can involve more than one syllable or more than one word; *poet/know it* is an example. Rhymes involving sounds that are similar but not exactly the same are called **slant rhymes** (or **near rhymes** or **approximate rhymes**). *Leave/live* is an example of a slant rhyme. Poets writing in English often use slant rhymes because English is not a very rhymable language. It has many words that rhyme with no other word (*orange*) or with only one other word (*mountain/fountain*). Poets interested in how a poem looks on the printed page sometimes use **eye rhymes,** or **visual rhymes**—rhymes involving words that are spelled similarly but are pronounced differently. *Tough/cough* is an eye rhyme. (*Tough/rough* is a "real" rhyme.)

See pages 571, 603.
See also *Free Verse, Poetry, Rhythm.*

RHYTHM **A musical quality produced by the repetition of stressed and unstressed syllables or by the repetition of certain other sound patterns.** Rhythm occurs in all language—written and spoken—but is particularly important in poetry.

The most obvious kind of rhythm is the regular pattern of stressed and unstressed syllables that is found in some poetry. This pattern is called **meter.**

In the following lines describing a cavalry charge, the rhythm echoes the galloping of the attackers' horses:

> ⌣ ⌣ ′⌣ ⌣ ⌣ ′ ⌣ ⌣ ′ ⌣ ⌣
> The Assyrian came down like the wolf on the
> ′
> fold,
> ⌣ ⌣ ′ ⌣ ⌣ ′ ⌣ ⌣ ′ ⌣ ⌣
> And his cohorts were gleaming in purple and
> ′
> gold;
> ⌣ ⌣ ′ ⌣ ⌣ ′ ⌣ ⌣ ′ ⌣
> And the sheen of their spears was like stars on
> ⌣ ′
> the sea,
> ⌣ ⌣ ′ ⌣ ⌣ ′ ⌣ ⌣ ′
> When the blue wave rolls nightly on deep
> ⌣ ⌣ ′
> Galilee.
>
> —George Gordon, Lord Byron,
> from "The Destruction
> of Sennacherib"

Marking the stressed (′) and unstressed (˘) syllables in a line is called **scanning** the line. Lord Byron's scanned lines show a rhythmic pattern in which two unstressed syllables are followed by a stressed syllable. Read the lines aloud and listen to this rhythmic pattern. Also, notice how the poem's end rhymes help create the rhythm.

Writers can also create rhythm by repeating words and phrases or even by repeating whole lines and sentences.

See pages 570, 595, 607.
See also *Free Verse, Poetry, Rhyme.*

SETTING The time and place in which the events of a work of literature take place. Most often the setting of a narrative is described early in the story. Setting often contributes to a story's emotional effect. In *Song of the Trees* (page 539), the forest setting helps create a soothing (yet mysterious) mood. Setting frequently plays an important role in a story's plot, especially one that centers on a conflict between a character and nature. In "Three Skeleton Key" (page 35), the characters must fight elements of a deadly setting to survive—they are threatened by a vast army of rats. Some stories are closely tied to particular settings, and it is difficult to imagine them taking place elsewhere. By contrast, other stories could easily take place in a variety of settings.

See pages 91, 499.

SHORT STORY A fictional prose narrative that is usually ten to twenty book pages long. Short stories were first written in the nineteenth century. Early short story writers include Sir Walter Scott and Edgar Allan Poe. Short stories are usually built on a plot that consists of at least these bare bones: the **introduction** or **exposition, conflict, complications, climax,** and **resolution.** Short stories are more limited than novels. They usually have only one or two major characters and one important setting.

See pages 500, 509, 756–757.
See also *Conflict, Fiction, Plot.*

SIMILE A comparison between two unlike things, using a word such as *like, as, than,* or *resembles.* The simile is an important type of figure of speech. In the following lines a simile creates a clear image of moths in the evening air:

> When the last bus leaves, moths stream
> toward lights like litter in wind.
>
> —Roberta Hill,
> from "Depot in Rapid City"

This example shows that similes can generate a strong emotional impact. By choosing to compare the moths to litter, the poet not only creates a picture in the reader's mind but also establishes a lonely, dreary mood.

See page 569.
See also *Figure of Speech, Metaphor.*

SPEAKER **The voice talking in a poem.** Sometimes the speaker is identical to the poet, but often the speaker and the poet are not the same. The poet may be speaking as a child, a woman, a man, an animal, or even an object.

See also *Poetry.*

STANZA **In a poem a group of consecutive lines that forms a single unit.** A stanza in a poem is something like a paragraph in prose; it often expresses a unit of thought. A stanza may consist of any number of lines. "I'm Nobody!" (page 581) consists of two four-line stanzas, each expressing a separate idea. In some poems each stanza has the same rhyme scheme.

See page 568.
See also *Poetry, Rhyme.*

SUSPENSE **The uncertainty or anxiety you feel about what will happen next in a story.** In "Three Skeleton Key" (page 35), the narrator hooks your curiosity in the first sentences when he says he is about to describe his "most terrifying experience."

See pages 5, 33, 167.
See also *Foreshadowing.*

SYMBOL **A person, a place, a thing, or an event that has its own meaning and stands for something beyond itself as well.** Examples of symbols are all around us—in music, on television, and in everyday conversation. The skull and crossbones, for example, is a symbol of danger; the dove is a symbol of peace; and the red rose stands for true love. In literature, symbols are often more personal. For example, in "Names/Nombres" (page 411), Julia Alvarez's name is a symbol of her cultural identity.

See page 87.

THEME **The truth about life revealed in a work of literature.** A theme is not the same as a subject. The subject of a work can usually be expressed in a word or two: *love, childhood, death.* The theme is the idea that the writer wishes to convey about a particular subject. The theme must be expressed in at least one sentence. For example, the subject of *The Monsters Are Due on Maple Street* (page 67) is alien invasion. The play's theme might be this: Prejudice is the fearful, unseen enemy within each of us.

A story can have several themes, but one will often stand out from the others. A work's themes are usually not stated directly. You have to think about all the elements of the work and use them to make an **inference,** or educated guess, about what the themes are.

It is not likely that two readers will ever state a theme in exactly the same way. Sometimes readers even differ greatly in their interpretations of theme. A work of literature can mean different things to different people.

See pages 242–243, 265, 281, 287, 307.

TONE **The attitude that a writer takes toward the audience, a subject, or a character.** Tone is conveyed through the writer's choice of words and details. The poem "Sarah Cynthia Sylvia Stout" (page 600) is light and playful in tone. By contrast, the poem "Annabel Lee" (page 283) is serious in tone.

See pages 569, 583.

Handbook of Reading and Informational Terms

For more information about a topic, turn to the page(s) in this book indicated on a separate line at the end of the entry. To learn more about *Cause and Effect*, for example, turn to pages 469 and 474.

On another line are cross-references to entries in this handbook that provide closely related information. For instance, the entry *Chronological Order* contains a cross-reference to *Text Structures*.

ANALOGY

1. An **analogy** is a point-by-point comparison made between two things to show how they are alike. An analogy shows how something unfamiliar is like something well-known.

2. Another kind of analogy is a **verbal analogy.** A verbal analogy is a word puzzle. It gives you two words and asks you to identify another pair of words with a similar relationship. In an analogy the symbol ":" means "is to." The symbol "::" means "as."

> Select the pair of words that best completes the analogy.
>
> Toe : foot :: _____
>
> A   house : barn
> B   finger : hand
> C   road : path
> D   light : darkness
>
> The correct answer is B: Toe : foot :: finger : hand, or "Toe is to foot as finger is to hand." The relationship is that of part to whole. A toe is part of the foot; a finger is part of the hand.

Another relationship often represented in verbal analogies is that of opposites:

> clear : cloudy :: bright : dark

Both sets of words are opposites. Clear is the opposite of cloudy, and bright is the opposite of dark.

Verbal analogies are often found in tests, where they are used to check vocabulary and thinking skills.

See pages 305, 406.

ARGUMENT   An **argument** is a position supported by evidence. Arguments are used to persuade us to accept or reject an opinion on a subject. Arguments are also used to persuade us to act in a certain way.

Supporting evidence can take the form of facts, statistics, anecdotes (brief stories that illustrate a point), and expert opinions. Not all arguments are logical. **Emotional appeals** find their way into most arguments, and you should learn to recognize them. Details that appeal to your feelings make an argument more interesting and memorable—but you should not accept an argument that is based only on an emotional appeal.

> Athletes should not charge kids for autographs. The most popular players are the ones that fans ask for autographs. These players don't need extra money. They already earn millions of dollars. Kids are much poorer than star athletes. I had to spend six weeks of my allowance and borrow twenty dollars from my brother to attend a game. After the game I started waiting in line to get an autograph. The line broke up quickly when we heard that the player was charging fifty dollars for each autograph. We were all disgusted. After all, the athletes' fans make them famous. My soccer coach says players should see that an autograph is a way of saying "thank you" to a loyal fan. Signing a name isn't hard. It takes less than a minute. To be asked to pay for an autograph is an insult.

Position

Opinion
Fact

Anecdote

Emotional appeal

Expert opinion

Fact
Emotional appeal

See pages 344, 723, 748–749.
See also *Evidence*.

BIAS A leaning in favor of or against a person or issue is called a **bias** (BY uhs). Sometimes a writer's bias is obvious. For instance, Rudyard Kipling in "Rikki-tikki-tavi" (page 15) reveals his bias against snakes. In the conflict between the cobras and a mongoose, Kipling is clearly biased in favor of the mongoose. People are often not upfront about their biases. You should look for bias whenever writers or speakers make claims and assertions that they don't (or can't) support with logical reasons and facts. When people ignore, distort, or hide the facts that oppose their bias, they may be guilty of prejudice.

See pages 701, 732.

CAUSE AND EFFECT A **cause** is the event that makes something happen. An **effect** is what happens as a result of the cause. Storytellers use the cause-and-effect organizational pattern to develop their plots. Writers of historical texts use this organizational pattern to explain things like the causes and effects of war. Scientific writers use this organizational pattern to explain things like the causes and effects of an epidemic. Some of the words and phrases that point to causes and effects are *because, since, therefore, so that,* and *if . . . then.* Notice the cause-and-effect chain in the following summary of the Midas myth:

> Because he did a favor for a god, Midas was granted the golden touch. Since everything he touched turned to gold, his daughter also turned to gold. Because of that, he asked to be released from the golden touch. Since gold had brought him such trouble, he then turned to nature and rejected riches.

See pages 245, 265, 297, 469, 474, 811.
See also *Text Structures*.

CHRONOLOGICAL ORDER Most narrative texts, true or fictional, are written in **chronological order.** Writers use chronological order when they put events in the sequence, or order, in which they happened in time, one after the other. Recipes and technical directions are usually written in chronological order. When you read a narrative, look for words and phrases like *next, then,* and *finally.* Writers use such words as transitions to signal the order in which events or steps occur.

See page 557.
See also *Text Structures*.

COMPARE-AND-CONTRAST PATTERN When you **compare,** you look for similarities, or likenesses. When you **contrast,** you look for differences. You've used comparison and contrast many times. For instance, you might compare and contrast the features of several dogs when you choose a puppy that is like the dog you used to have. When writers compare and contrast, they organize the text to help readers understand the **points of comparison,** the features that they're looking at.

A Venn diagram can help you tell similarities from differences. The one below compares and contrasts two stories: "Yeh-Shen" (page 458) and the "Cinderella" folk tale. Where the circles overlap, note how the stories are alike. Where there is no overlap, note differences.

Venn Diagram

"Cinderella"   "Yeh-Shen"

- helped by fairy godmother
- meets prince at ball

- has wicked step mother
- wants to go to ball
- has wish granted
- has rags changed to beautiful clothes
- obeys one rule
- loses shoe
- is found by royalty

- helped by fish
- meets king when he is searching for owner of shoe

Differences   *Similarities*   *Differences*

An effective comparison-and-contrast text may be organized in the block pattern or the point-by-point pattern.

Block pattern. A writer using the block pattern first discusses all the points of subject 1, then goes on to discuss all the points of subject 2.

> **Subject 1—"Yeh-Shen":** In the Chinese folk tale "Yeh-Shen" a magic fish dies, but its spirit gives Yeh-Shen, a kind orphan, advice and help. It changes her rags into beautiful clothes. Her wicked stepmother treats Yeh-Shen badly. [*And so on*]
>
> **Subject 2—"Cinderella":** American children probably know best the Cinderella story in which a fairy godmother changes Cinderella's rags into beautiful clothes. Cinderella also has a wicked stepmother. [*And so on*]

Point-by-point pattern. A writer who uses the point-by-point pattern goes back and forth between the two things being compared and contrasted.

> In "Yeh-Shen" a magic fish helps the orphan girl. In "Cinderella," however, a fairy god-mother helps the girl. In both stories, there is a wicked stepmother. [*And so on*]

Some of the words that signal comparison and contrast are *although, but, either . . . or, however,* and *yet.*

See pages 502, 509.
See also *Text Structures.*

CONCLUSIONS   A **conclusion** is a general summing up of the specific details in a text. The text below is from "Borders of Baseball: U.S. and Cuban Play" (page 712). One reader's conclusion based on these details follows the text.

> U.S. ballparks are different from Cuban ones. Fans pass souvenir and food stands while going to and from their seats. Team logos are plastered on everything from cups to T-shirts. Cuban ballparks, by contrast, are not very commercialized. In Cuba, baseball is a source of national pride, not a way to push people to buy certain products.
> **Conclusion:** In Cuba, baseball is less affected by economic considerations.

See pages 690, 830.
See also *Evidence.*

CONNOTATION AND DENOTATION The **connotation** of a word is all the feelings and associations that have come to be attached to the word. The **denotation** of a word is its strict dictionary definition. Not all words have connotations. Words like *the, writer,* and *paper* do not have connotations. Words like *Democrat, Republican, conservative,* and *liberal* are loaded with associations and feelings.

The words *skinny, slender, gaunt,* and *lean* have approximately the same denotation. They all mean "thin; having little fat." There are important shades of meaning among those words, however. If a relative said you were skinny or gaunt, you'd probably feel hurt or angry. *Skinny* and *gaunt* have negative connotations. They suggest that the thin person may have been sick and is now unattractive. *Slender* and *lean,* on the other hand, have positive connotations. They suggest a healthy, athletic body.

See pages 147, 156, 168.

CONTEXT CLUES When you don't know the meaning of a word, look for a clue to its meaning in the **context,** the words and sentences surrounding the unfamiliar word. Here are some common types of context clues. In each sentence, the unfamiliar word appears in boldface type; the clue is underlined.

Definition clue. Look for a familiar word that defines the meaning of the unfamiliar word.

> Sarah was seldom <u>bothered</u> by competition, but today she was **perturbed** to see that Maya had been chosen for the swim team.

The word *bothered* tells you that *perturbed* also means "something like bothered."

Example clue. Look for examples of the unfamiliar word. In the context of the sentence, the examples reveal the meaning of the unfamiliar word.

> **Tugs** and <u>other boats</u> were washed ashore by the tidal wave.

The words *other boats* tell you that a tug is a kind of boat.

Restatement clue. Look for words that restate the meaning of the unfamiliar word.

> We **delved** into the criminal's past—we <u>searched through</u> hundreds of pieces of evidence.

The restatement clue that helps you guess the meaning of *delved* is *searched through.* (*Delved* means "dug into; searched; investigated.")

Contrast clue. Look for words that contrast the unfamiliar word with a word or phrase in the sentence that you know.

> Although Helen wanted to **detain** the visitors, she had to <u>let</u> them <u>go.</u>

This sentence tells you that *detain* means the opposite of "let go."

See pages 294, 406, 418.

EVIDENCE When you read informational and persuasive texts, you need to **assess,** or judge, the **evidence** that a writer uses to support a position. That means you need to read carefully, looking critically at the writer's claims and assertions. You need to evaluate the writer's sources. You also need to look at the writer's own background and expertise. One way to assess evidence is to give it the **3As test**. The *As* stand for *adequate, appropriate,* and *accurate.*

Adequate means "sufficient" or "enough." You have to see if the writer has provided enough evidence to support his or her position. For some positions, one or two supporting facts may be adequate. For others a writer may need to provide many facts, maybe even statistics. Sometimes a direct quotation from a well-respected expert, an authority on the subject, will be convincing.

You must make sure that the writer's evidence is **appropriate,** that it has direct bearing on the conclusion. Sometimes a writer presents a lot of flashy evidence, such as details loaded with emotional appeals. When you look at this kind of evidence closely, you realize that it doesn't have much, if anything, to do with the writer's conclusions.

To make sure that the evidence is **accurate,** or correct, check to see that it comes from a source you can trust. Don't assume that everything (or anything) you see online or even printed in a newspaper or book is accurate. If a fact, example, or quotation doesn't sound accurate, check it out. Look for the title of the magazine or book that the quotation comes from. Is it a reliable source? Look up the writer's background. Does the writer have the background and education to qualify him or her as an expert on the subject? Is the writer biased in some way?

See pages 480, 700, 701–703, 709, 717, 723, 728.
See also *Argument*.

FACT AND OPINION A **fact** is a statement that can be proved true. Some facts are easy to prove by **observation.** For instance, *Cats make different vocal sounds* is a fact you can prove by listening to cats meow and purr. Other facts can be *verified,* or proved, if you look them up in a reliable source. You need to be sure that the source is **authoritative**—an official source that can be trusted, such as an encyclopedia. In fields where new discoveries are being made, you need to check facts in a *recently* published source.

An **opinion** expresses a personal belief or feeling. Sometimes strongly held opinions look and sound like facts. Dog lovers would never question the statement *Dogs are smarter than cats*. Cat lovers, however, would express the opposite opinion, *Cats*

are smarter than dogs, and believe it just as strongly. Even if a statement sounds as if it's true, it's not a fact unless it can be proved. Here are some opinions:

> Travel to other planets will happen in my lifetime.
> We have the best football team in the United States.
> Every teenager should receive an allowance.

A **valid opinion** is a personal belief that is supported by facts. An **invalid opinion** is a belief that is either not supported by facts or is supported by illogical and wishful thinking.

Remember that what you see in print or on the Internet may or may not be true. If a statement looks like a fact but you suspect it's an opinion, check it out in a reliable source. Ask: Can this be proved true?

See pages 717, 723.

FALLACIOUS REASONING
Fallacious (fuh LAY shuhs) means "false." **Fallacious reasoning** is false reasoning. Here are four major types of false reasoning:

1. **Hasty generalizations** are reached without considering enough facts. A **generalization** is a conclusion drawn after considering as much of the evidence as possible. If there is even one exception to the conclusion, your generalization is not true or valid.

> **Fact:** "User Friendly" is a story with a surprise ending.
> **Fact:** "After Twenty Years" is a story with a surprise ending.
> **Hasty generalization:** All stories have surprise endings.

That conclusion is a hasty generalization. You could name many stories that do not have a surprise ending. Sometimes hasty generalizations can be corrected by using a qualifying word such as *most, usually, some, many,* or *often.* It is especially important to watch out for hasty generalizations when you're reading a persuasive text.

2. With **circular reasoning** a writer tries to fool you by restating the opinion in different words.

> Hungry students can't study because they haven't had enough to eat.
> Jean is the best candidate for student-council president because she's better than all the other candidates.

3. **Cause-and-effect fallacies.** One common **cause-and-effect fallacy** assumes that if something happens right before another event, the first event caused the next event.

> I wasn't wearing my lucky shirt, so I failed my history test.

Another **cause-and-effect fallacy** names a single cause for a complicated situation that has many causes.

> Popularity in middle school depends on wearing the right clothes.

4. The **either-or fallacy** suggests that there are only two sides to an issue.

> Either you get a summer job, or you waste the whole summer.

See also *Argument, Evidence, Persuasion.*

5W-HOW? The first paragraph of a news story, called the **lead** (leed) paragraph, usually answers the questions *who? what? when? where? why?* and *how?* Look for the answers to these *5W-How?* questions when you read a newspaper story or any eyewitness account.

GENERALIZATION A **generalization** is a broad statement that covers several particular situations. Scientists and detectives, for instance, begin their investigations by amassing many specific facts. Then they put the facts together and draw a conclusion about what all this evidence tells them, what it adds up to.

> **Fact:** Cobras are poisonous.
> **Fact:** Rattlesnakes are poisonous.
> **Fact:** Garter snakes are not poisonous.
> **Generalization:** Some snakes are poisonous.

The generalization *Most snakes are poisonous* would have been incorrect. Only three species out of a population of more than 2,500 species of snakes were considered. About four fifths of all snakes are not poisonous. To be valid, a generalization must be based on all the evidence (the facts) that can be gathered.

See page 701.
See also *Stereotyping.*

GRAPHIC FEATURES **Graphic features** are design elements in a text. They include things like headings, maps, charts, graphs, and illustrations. Graphic features are visual ways of communicating information.

Some design elements you may find in a text are **boldface** and *italic* type; type in different styles (called fonts), sizes, and colors; bullets (dots that set off items in a list); and logos (like computer icons).

For example, the Quickwrite heading in this book always appears with the stopwatch. Design elements make a text look more attractive. They also steer your eyes to different types of information and make the text easier to read.

A **heading** serves as a title for the information that follows it. Size and color set off from the rest of the text the type used for a heading. A repeated heading, like "Reading Skills" in this textbook, is always followed by the same type of material. Skimming the headings is one way to preview a text.

Graphic features such as **maps, charts,** and **graphs** display and sometimes explain complex information with lines, drawings, and symbols. Graphic features usually include these elements:

1. A **title** identifies the subject or main idea of the graphic.
2. **Labels** identify specific information.
3. A **caption** is text (usually under an illustration) that explains what you're looking at.
4. A **legend,** or **key,** helps you interpret symbols and colors, usually on a map. Look for a **scale,** which relates the size or distance of something on a map to the real-life size and distance.
5. The source tells where the information in the graphic comes from. Knowing the source helps you evaluate the accuracy.

Different types of **maps** present special information. **Physical maps** show the natural landscape of an area. Shading may be used to show features like mountains and valleys. Different shades of color are often used to show different elevations (heights above sea level). **Political maps** show political units, such as states, nations, and capitals. The map of Canada, the United States, and Mexico shown here is a political map. **Special-purpose maps** present information such as the routes of explorers or the location of earthquake fault lines.

A **flowchart** shows a sequence of events or the steps in a process. Flowcharts are often used to show cause-and-effect relationships. See page 265 for an example of a flowchart. **Pie charts,** also called **circle graphs,** show how parts of a whole are related. A pie chart is a circle divided into different-sized sections, like slices of a pie. The emphasis in a pie chart is always on the proportions of the sections, not on the specific amounts of each section.

Pie Chart

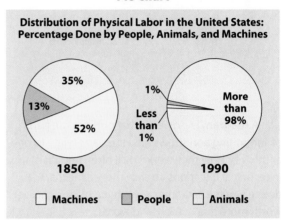

Distribution of Physical Labor in the United States: Percentage Done by People, Animals, and Machines

Bar Graph

Line Graph

A **diagram** is a graphic that outlines the parts of something and shows how the parts relate to one another or how they work. You'll often find diagrams in technical directions, to show how a mechanical device works. Diagrams prove that a picture can be worth more than a thousand words.

A **time line** identifies events that take place over the course of time. In a time line, events are organized in chronological order, the order in which they happened.

Graphs usually show changes or trends over time. In line graphs, dots showing the quantity at different times are connected to create a line. **Bar graphs** generally compare various quantities.

A **table** presents information arranged in rows and columns. There are many different types of tables. See page 610 for an example of a table showing a train schedule.

Tips for Understanding Graphic Aids

1. Read the title, labels, and legend before you try to analyze the information.
2. Read numbers carefully. Note increases or decreases in sequences. Look for the direction or order of events and for trends and relationships.
3. Draw your own conclusions from the graphic. Then, compare your conclusions with the writer's conclusions.

See pages 651, 671.

Time Line

IMAGES Descriptive writing appeals to the senses to create **mental images,** pictures in the reader's mind. Most description appeals to the sense of sight, but description can also appeal to one or more of the other senses. When you read a description, use the details to *visualize,* or form mental pictures of, the characters, settings, and events. Forming mental images is especially important when you read descriptions in scientific texts.

See page 51.

INFERENCE An **inference** is an educated guess, a conclusion that makes sense because it's supported by evidence. The evidence may be a collection of **facts,** information that can be proved, or it may come from experiences in your own life. However, the evidence must provide some reason for believing that the conclusion is true if the inference is to be valid, or based on sound, logical thought. Nevertheless, people may draw different conclusions from the same evidence—especially if there isn't much evidence to go on.

> Bobby has recently transferred to your school. You ask Bobby to join you and a couple of other friends, Sam and Ali, at your house after school on Thursday. Bobby says, "Sorry. I have to go home right after school." Inferences: Sam infers that Bobby's parents are really strict. Ali infers that Bobby is stuck-up. You infer that Bobby doesn't like you.

As you read, you make inferences based on clues that the writer provides. For example, when you read a narrative, you **infer,** or guess, what will happen next based on what the writer has told you and on your own knowledge and experience. Sometimes a writer deliberately gives clues that lead you to different—and incorrect—inferences. That's part of the fun of reading. Until you get to the end of a suspenseful story, you can never be completely sure about what will happen next.

In O. Henry's short story "After Twenty Years" (page 383), a policeman speaks to a well-dressed man waiting in a doorway in New York City. The man is waiting for his boyhood friend, Jimmy. He hasn't seen Jimmy for more than twenty years. Read the following dialogue, and the inferences that follow it.

> "Did pretty well out West, didn't you?" asked the policeman.
>
> "You bet! I hope Jimmy has done half as well. He was a kind of plodder, though, good fellow as he was. I've had to compete with some of the sharpest wits going to get my pile. A man gets in a groove in New York. It takes the West to put a razor edge on him."
> Inferences: The policeman seems to be impressed by the man in the doorway. The well-dressed man thinks a lot of himself and looks down on his old friend Jimmy, who may have been too "good" to be successful.

See pages 138, 147.
See also *Evidence, Fact and Opinion.*

INSTRUCTIONAL MANUALS **Instructional manuals** tell you how to operate a specific device, such as a DVR or a car. Instructional manuals contain detailed directions, usually organized in chronological steps. Drawings and diagrams, such as flowcharts, might be included to help you understand the different parts of the device.

See pages 211, 648.

KWL CHART Using a **KWL** chart is a way to focus your reading and record what you learn. KWL means "What I **k**now, what I **w**ant to know, and what I **l**earned." When you use a KWL strategy, you first skim the text, looking at headings, subtitles, and illustrations. You decide what the topic of the text is. Then, on a blank sheet of paper, you draw a KWL chart. In the K column you note what you already know about the subject. In the W column you write down what you'd like to find out. After you finish reading the text, you write the answers under the L column to the questions you asked in the W column. Here is the beginning of a KWL chart based on "Sir Gawain and the Loathly Lady" (page 813).

K	W	L
What I **K**now	What I **W**ant to Know	What I **L**earned
Sir Gawain was a knight.	Why was the lady loathly?	It was a spell that made her ugly.

MAIN IDEA The most important point or focus of a passage is its **main idea.** Writers of essays, nonfiction narratives, and informational articles have one or more **main ideas** in mind as they write a text. The writer may state the main idea directly. More often the main idea is suggested, or implied. Then it's up to you, the reader, to infer, or guess at, what it is. To infer the main idea, look at the key details in the text. See if you can create a statement that expresses a general idea that covers all these important details. When you are deciding on the main idea, look especially for a key passage at the beginning or end of the text. That's where a writer often refers to a key idea.

See pages 13, 110, 201, 407.

NEWSPAPERS **Newspapers** are informational texts that present facts about current events. Newspapers may also contain feature articles that aim to entertain as well as inform. Newspapers often contain editorials that support a *position* for or against an issue. **Headlines** at the top of each story indicate the topic of the story. They are worded to catch your attention. The writer of a **news story** usually organizes the details in order of importance. If the article is running too long, the less important details can easily be cut from the end of the story.

See page 201.

OBJECTIVE WRITING **Objective writing** sticks to the facts. It does not reveal the writer's feelings, beliefs, or point of view about the subject. In a newspaper, news articles are usually written objectively. Readers of news articles want to get a true and accurate account of what happened. If they want to know a writer's point of view or perspective on the news, they turn to the **editorial page.** Editorials and letters to the editor are usually *not* written objectively. They are examples of **subjective writing.** See page 789 for an example of a letter to the editor.

See also *Subjective Writing.*

OUTLINING **Outlining** an informational text can help you identify main ideas and understand how they are related to one another. Outlining also shows you the important details that support each main idea. When you have an outline, you have a visual summary of the text.

Many readers start an outline by taking notes. Note taking is an especially good idea if you're reading a text with many facts, such as names and dates, that you want to remember.

Tips for Taking Notes

1. You can jot down notes in a notebook or on note cards. Put your notes in your own words, writing each main idea on its own note card or page.
2. As you continue to read, add details that relate to the important idea you have on each card.
3. Whenever you copy the writer's exact words, put quotation marks around them. Write down the page number for the source of each note.

After you have your notes on the text, you're ready to make an outline. Many outlines label the main ideas with Roman numerals. You need to have at least two headings at each level. This is how an outline might begin:

I. Main idea
  A. Detail supporting main idea I
    1. Detail supporting A
      a. Detail supporting 1
      b. Detail supporting 1
    2. Detail supporting A
  B. Detail supporting main idea I
II. Main idea

See page 105, 738.

PERSUASION **Persuasion** is the use of language or pictures to convince us to think or act in a certain way. Recognizing **persuasive techniques** will help you evaluate the persuasion that you read, hear, and see all around you today. Here are some persuasive techniques to watch for:

1. **Logical appeals** are based on correct reasoning. Logic appeals to reason with opinions supported by strong factual evidence, such as facts, statistics, or statements by experts on the issue being considered.

2. **Emotional appeals** get your feelings involved in the argument. Some writers use vivid language and supporting evidence that arouse basic feelings, such as pity, anger, and fear. Persuasion tends to be most effective when it appeals to both your head and your heart. However, it's important to be able to recognize emotional appeals—and to be suspicious of how they can sway you.
3. **Logical fallacies** (FAL uh seez) are mistakes in reasoning. If you're reading a text quickly, fuzzy or dishonest reasoning may look as if it makes sense. See the entry for *Fallacious Reasoning* for examples of specific logical fallacies.

See also *Argument*.

PREDICTIONS Guessing what will happen next in a narrative text is a reading skill called **making predictions.** To make predictions, you look for clues that **foreshadow,** or hint at, future actions. You try to connect those clues with past and present actions in the story. You quickly check your memory for other things you've read that are in any way like the story you're reading. You recall your real-life experiences. Then you make your predictions. As you read, you'll continuously revise your guesses, adjusting your predictions as new clues crop up.

See pages 6, 65, 375, 381, 391, 795.

PROPAGANDA Propaganda is an organized attempt to influence a large audience of readers, listeners, or TV watchers. Propaganda techniques are used in all kinds of persuasive texts. You see them especially in advertisements, speeches, and editorials. Some writers use propaganda to advance good causes—for instance, to persuade people to recycle, to exercise, or to join together to fight a terrible disease. However, many writers of propaganda use emotional appeals to confuse readers and to convince them that the writer's biased opinions are the only ones worth considering.

Common propaganda techniques include the following:

- The **bandwagon** appeal urges you to do or believe something because everyone else does.

> "Shop where the action is! Join the parade to Teen-Town Mall."

- The **testimonial** uses a famous person, such as an actor or an athlete, to testify that he or she supports the issue or uses the product.

> "I'm professional basketball player Hank Smith, and I drink Starade every day for quick and long-lasting energy."

- **Snob appeal** suggests that by using this product you can be superior to others—more powerful, wealthy, or beautiful.

> "You deserve this car. Don't settle for less than the best."

- **Stereotyping.** Writers who use stereotyping refer to members of a group as if they were all the same.

> Teenagers are bad drivers.
> Didn't I tell you that Martians can't
>   be trusted?

- Writers using **name-calling** avoid giving reasons and logical evidence for or against an issue. Instead, they attack people who disagree with them by giving those people negative labels.

> That's just what I'd expect a nerd like you
>   to say.
> I won't waste time listening to a puppet-
>   politician whose strings are controlled by
>   ill-informed special-interest groups.

PURPOSES OF TEXTS Texts are written for different **purposes:** to inform, to persuade, to express feelings, or to entertain. The purpose of a text, or the reason why a text is written, determines its **structure,** the way the writer organizes and presents the material.

See pages 201, 205, 211, 375, 409, 421, 723.

READING RATE The speed at which you read a text is your **reading rate.** How quickly or slowly you should read depends on the type of text you are reading and your purpose for reading it.

Reading Rates According to Purpose		
Reading Rate	Purpose	Example
Skimming	Reading for main points	Glancing at newspaper headlines; reviewing charts and headings in your science textbook before a test
Scanning	Looking for specific details	Looking for an author's name in a table of contents; looking in a geography book for the name of the highest mountain in North America
Reading for mastery	Reading to understand and remember	Taking notes on a chapter in your science textbook to study for a test; reading a story or poem for understanding.

See pages 650, 657.

RETELLING The reading strategy called **retelling** helps you identify and remember events that advance the plot of a story. Retelling is also useful when you read informational texts, such as science or history texts. From time to time in your reading, stop for a moment. Review what's gone on before you go ahead. Focus on the important events or key details. Think about them, and retell them briefly in your own words. When you read history or science texts, you should stop after each section of the text and see if you can retell the key details to yourself.

SQ3R The abbreviation **SQ3R** stands for a reading and study strategy that takes place in five steps: **s**urvey, **q**uestion, **r**ead, **r**etell, **r**eview. The SQ3R process takes time, but it helps you focus on the text—and it works.

- S—*Survey.* Glance through the text. Skim the headings, titles, charts, illustrations, and vocabulary words in boldface type. Read the first and last sentences of the major sections of the text, if they are indicated by headings.
- Q—*Question.* List the questions that you have. These may be questions that came out of your survey, or they may be general questions about the subject. Ask the questions that you hope to find answers to in the text.
- R—*Read.* Read the text carefully, keeping your questions in mind. As you read, look for answers. Take brief notes on the answers you find.
- R—*Retell.* Use your notes to write down the main ideas and important details in the text. Before you write, say your answers out loud. Listen to your answers to hear if they make sense.
- R—*Review.* Look back over the text. See if you can answer your questions without using the notes and answers you wrote down. Write a brief summary of the text so you'll be able to remember it later.

STEREOTYPING Referring to all members of a group as if they were all the same is called stereotyping. **Stereotyping** (STEHR ee uh typ ihng) ignores the facts about individuals. The most important fact about members of a group is that each individual person is *different* from all the others. Stereotyping does not allow for individual differences. Whenever you assess a writer's evidence, be on the lookout for stereotyping. When a writer makes a claim about an individual or a group and supports the assertion with a stereotype, you know that the writer is guilty of faulty reasoning. Here are some examples of stereotyping:

> All teenagers are lazy.
> Senior citizens have more money than
>   they need.
> All lawyers are dishonest.
> All football players are dumb.

See pages 701, 732.
See also *Propaganda.*

SUBJECTIVE WRITING Writing that reveals and emphasizes the writer's personal feelings and opinions is called **subjective.** Subjective and objective writing are opposites. *Subjective* means "personal; resulting from feelings; existing only in the mind." *Objective means* "real; actual; factual; without bias." Writers may combine subjective and objective details in the same text. As a reader you must figure out which statements are based on subjective impressions and which are based on factual, objective evidence.

We expect subjectivity in some writing. We would expect an autobiography to reveal the writer's personal feelings. In a historical text, however, we expect objectivity—we want facts, not the writer's personal feelings.

See also *Objective Writing.*

SUMMARIZING Restating the main ideas or major events in a text is called **summarizing.** A summary of text is much shorter than the original. To summarize an informational text, you must include the main ideas and the important details that support those main ideas. To summarize a narrative, you must include the main events and be certain you have indicated cause and effect. In a summary, except for direct quotations from the text, you put the writer's ideas into your own words. (Every time you jot down a direct quotation, be sure to put quotation marks around it and write down the source.) Here is a summary of the selection from *Barrio Boy* by Ernesto Galarza (page 439):

> Ernesto's family had recently moved to Sacramento from Mazatlán, Mexico. This true account begins with Ernesto's mother taking him to school. The new school seems strange to Ernesto, who speaks no English. Ernesto finds out that many of his first-grade classmates are from other countries or have different ethnic backgrounds. Several of them, along with Ernesto, receive private English lessons from their teacher. The teachers at the school help Ernesto learn that he can be proud of being American while still feeling proud of his Mexican roots.

See pages 7, 13, 110, 114–121.
See also *Main Idea.*

TEXT STRUCTURES There are some basic ways in which writers structure informational texts: **cause and effect, chronological order,** and **comparison-and-contrast.** Sometimes a writer will use one pattern throughout a text. Many writers will combine two or more patterns. These guidelines can help you analyze text structure:

1. Search the text for the main idea. Look for words that signal a specific pattern of organization.
2. Study the text for other important ideas. Think about how the ideas are connected to one another. Look for an obvious pattern.
3. Draw a graphic organizer that shows how the text seems to be structured. Your graphic organizer may look like one of the common text structures shown below.

The **cause-and-effect pattern** presents a series of causes and their effects. This example shows the effect of an earthquake, which led to another effect, which became the cause of another effect, and so on:

Causal Chain

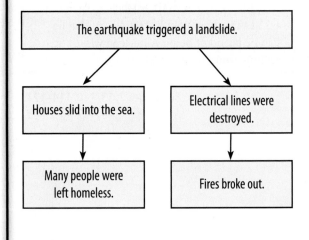

Chronological-order pattern shows events or ideas happening in time sequence. The example below gives directions for getting from school to a student's home:

Sequence Chain

The **comparison-and-contrast pattern** points out similarities and differences. A Venn diagram can help you see how two subjects are alike and how they are different. Similarities are listed where the two circles overlap. Differences are shown where the circles don't overlap. This example compares a middle school with a high school.

Venn Diagram

Middle School   **High School**

- smaller— 500 students
- students from four K–5 schools
- everyone knows everyone else

- classes same length
- many electives
- three foreign languages to choose from

- big school— 2000 students
- students from four middle schools
- more cliques; hard to get to

Differences   *Similarities*   *Differences*

Another kind of graphic organizer focuses on points of comparison (the features being compared).

Comparing and Contrasting		
	Middle School	**High School**
Size of school		
Length of school day		
Sports program		

See pages 234–235.
See also *Cause and Effect, Chronological Order, Compare-and-Contrast Pattern*.

TEXTBOOKS **Textbooks** are informational texts written to help students learn about a subject. This textbook is quite different in structure from a geography textbook. Nonetheless, both kinds of textbooks have certain elements in common. For example, they have the same general purpose. In addition, most textbooks present information followed by questions that help students determine whether they have learned the material. Finally, most textbooks contain a table of contents, an index, illustrations, charts, and other graphic features.

See page 205.

WRITER'S PERSPECTIVE **Perspective** is the way a person looks at a subject. Some people have a negative perspective, for instance, on violent computer games. They believe that such games may influence children to become violent. Other people have a positive perspective on violent computer games. They say that when children play such games, they may rid themselves of some of their aggressive feelings. Figuring out a writer's perspective can help you understand and evaluate what you are reading. The following paragraph is from Clifton Davis's "A Mason-Dixon Memory" (page 559). A statement describing Davis's perspective follows:

> In his words and in his life, Lincoln had made it clear that freedom is not free. Every time the color of a person's skin keeps him out of an amusement park or off a country-club fairway, the war for freedom begins again. Sometimes the battle is fought with fists and guns, but more often the most effective weapon is a simple act of love and courage.
>
> **Writer's perspective:** Prejudice still exists today, and it can be fought best with simple, nonviolent actions.

See page 337.

Glossary

The glossary that follows is an alphabetical list of words found in the selections in this book. Use this glossary just as you would use a dictionary—to find out the meaning of unfamiliar words. (Some technical, foreign, and more obscure words in this book are not listed here but instead are defined for you in the footnotes that accompany many of the selections.)

Many words in the English language have more than one meaning. This glossary gives the meanings that apply to the words as they are used in the selections in this book. Words closely related in form and meaning are usually listed together in one entry (for instance, *cower* and *cowered*), and the definition is given for the first form.

The following abbreviations are used:

adj.	adjective
adv.	adverb
n.	noun
v.	verb

Each word's pronunciation is given in parentheses. For more information about the words in this glossary or for information about words not listed here, consult a dictionary.

A

absently (AB suhnt lee) *adv.* in a way that shows one is not thinking about what is happening.

accommodate (uh KAHM uh dayt) *v.* hold comfortably.

alienate (AYL yuh nayt) *v.* cause to feel isolated or unaccepted.

alliance (uh LY uhns) *n.* pact between nations, families, or individuals that shows a common cause.

altitude (AL tuh tood) *n.* height; high level.

anonymous (uh NAHN uh muhs) *adj.* not identified by name.

apparent (uh PAR uhnt) *adj.* seeming.

arduous (AHR joo uhs) *adj.* difficult.

arrogant (AR uh guhnt) *adj.* overly convinced of one's own importance.

assured (uh SHURD) *v.* guaranteed; promised confidently.

awe (aw) *n.* feeling of fear and amazement.

B

barbarian (bahr BAIR ee uhn) *adj.* referring to a group considered uncivilized and inferior by another nation or group.

bigotry (BIHG uh tree): *n.* prejudice; intolerance.

boasting (BOHST ihng) *v.* speaking too highly about oneself; bragging.

bouts (bowts) *n.* matches; contests.

C

capable (KAY puh buhl) *adj.* having ability or traits required to do something.

caressed (kuh REHST) *v.* touched gently.

charismatic (kar ihz MAT ihk) *adj.* possessing charm or appeal.

chivalry (SHIHV uhl ree) *n.* code that governed knightly behavior, requiring courage, honor, and readiness to help the weak.

commenced (kuh MEHNST) *v.* began.

composure (kuhm POH zhuhr) *n.* calmness of mind.

concentration (kahn suhn TRAY shuhn) *n.* act of thinking carefully about something one is doing.

consequences (KAHN suh kwehns ihz) *n.* results caused by a set of conditions.

consolation (KAHN suh LAY shuhn) *n.* comfort.

contemplate (KAHN tuhm playt) *v.* consider; look at or think about carefully.

contraption (kuhn TRAP shuhn) *n.* strange machine or gadget.

converging (kuhn VUR jihng) *v.* used as *adj.* coming together.

conviction (kuhn VIHK shuhn) *n.* certainty; belief; instance of being declared guilty of a criminal offense.

convinced (kuhn VIHNST) *v.* made to feel sure; persuaded firmly.

convoluted (KAHN vuh loo tihd) *v.* used as *adj.* complicated.

countenance (KOWN tuh nuhns) *n.* face; appearance.

crinkling (KRIHNG klihng) *v.* used as *adj.* wrinkling.

curtly (KURT lee) *adv.* rudely; with few words.

D

dedicate (DEHD uh kayt) *v.* do or make something in honor of another person.

deducted (dih DUHKT ihd) *v.* taken away.

defiant (dih FY uhnt) *adj.* boldly resisting authority.

deflation (dih FLAY shuhn) *n.* loss of confidence or high spirits.

deprivation (dehp ruh VAY shuhn) *n.* condition of not having something essential; hardship resulting from a lack of something.

detached (dih TACHT) *adj.* not involved emotionally; indifferent.

detain (dih TAYN) *v.* delay.

dismally (DIHZ muh lee) *adv.* miserably; gloomily.

dispelled (dihs PEHLD) *v.* driven away.

dispute (dihs PYOOT) *n.* argument.

E

edible (EHD uh buhl) *adj.* fit to be eaten.

egotism (EE guh tihz uhm) *n.* conceit; talking about oneself too much.

elective (ih LEHK tihv) *n.* course that is not required.

elude (ih LOOD) *v.* avoid; cleverly escape.

encounter (ehn KOWN tuhr) *n.* face-to-face meeting.

entranced (ehn TRANST) *v.* used as *adj.* cast a spell on; enchanted.

ethnicity (ehth NIHS uh tee) *n.* common culture or nationality.

evacuation (ih vak yoo AY shuhn) *n.* process of removing people from a potentially dangerous situation.

evaporation (ih vap uh RAY shuhn) *n.* process by which a liquid changes into a gas.

exotic (ehg ZAHT ihk) *adj.* not native.

expelled (ehk SPEHLD) *v.* forced to leave.

F

facilitate (fuh SIHL uh tayt) *v.* ease; aid.

fidelity (fuh DEHL uh tee) *n.* faithfulness.

flourishing (FLUR ihsh ihng) *adj.* thriving.

forbade (fuhr BAD) *v.* ordered not to; outlawed.

forfeit (FAWR fiht) *v.* lose the right to something.

formidable (FAWR muh duh buhl) *adj.* awe inspiring; impressive.

frenzied (FREHN zeed) *adj.* wild; out of control.

furiously (FYUR ee uhs lee) *adv.* rapidly, with intensity.

G

glistening (GLIHS uhn ihng) *adj.* sparkling; reflecting light.

H

habitat (HAB uh tat) *n.* used as *adj.* place where an animal or plant naturally lives.

habitual (huh BIHCH oo uhl) *adj.* done or fixed by habit.

hazards (HAZ uhrdz) *n.* dangers.

heritage (HEHR uh tihj) *n.* traditions that are passed along.

hordes (hawrdz) *n.* densely packed crowds that move as groups.

I

identity (y DEHN tuh tee) *n.* distinguishing characteristics that determine who or what a person or thing is.

idiosyncrasy (ihd ee uh SIHNG kruh see) *n.* peculiarity.

illegal (ih LEE guhl) *adj.* unlawful; against official regulations.

immensely (ih MEHNS lee) *adv.* enormously.

impudence (IHM pyuh duhns) *n.* disrespect; insulting rudeness.

incessantly (ihn SEHS uhnt lee) *adv.* without ceasing; continually.

incident (IHN suh duhnt) *n.* happening; occurrence.

incredulously (ihn KREHJ uh luhs lee) *adv.* unbelievingly.

inscription (ihn SKRIHP shuhn) *n.* words written on something.

insolence (IHN suh luhns) *n.* disrespect.

integration (ihn tuh GRAY shuhn) *n.* process of bringing together people of all races in schools and neighborhoods.

integrity (ihn TEHG ruh tee) *n.* honesty; uprightness.

intense (ihn TEHNS) *adj.* showing strong feelings and seriousness.

intently (ihn TEHNT lee) *adv.* with great focus.

interplanetary (ihn tuhr PLAN uh tehr ee) *adj.* between or among planets.

intimately (IHN tuh muht lee) *adv.* in a very familiar way.

intimidated (ihn TIHM uh day tihd) *v.* frightened with threats.

intolerable (ihn TAHL uhr uh buhl) *adj.* unbearable.

intricate (IHN truh kiht) *adj.* complicated; full of detail.

L

liberation (lihb uh RAY shuhn) *n.* release from slavery, prison, or other limitation.

lingered (LIHNG guhrd) *v.* stayed on.

literally (LIHT uhr uh lee) *adv.* according to the basic meaning of the word.

loathsome (LOHTH suhm) *adj.* disgusting.

M

malice (MAL ihs) *n.* meanness; hatred.

malnutrition (mal noo TRIHSH uhn) *n.* ill health caused by a lack of food or by a lack of healthy foods.

maneuver (muh NOO vuhr) *v.* move or manipulate skillfully.

menace (MEHN ihs) *n.* danger, threat.

merchandise (MUR chuhn dys) *n.* items that are for sale in stores.

misrepresentations (mihs rehp rih zehn TAY shuhnz) *n.* false ideas given for the purpose of deceiving someone.

mistranslate (mihs TRANS layt) *v.* change from one language to another incorrectly.

modifications (mod uh fuh KAY shuhnz) *n.* slight changes.

monarch (MAHN ahrk) *n.* sole and absolute ruler.

monopoly (muh NAHP uh lee) *n.* exclusive control of a market.

mounts (mownts) *v.* gets up on; climbs up.

O

ominous (AHM uh nuhs): *adj.* threatening.

opponents (uh POH nuhnts) *n.* people on opposite sides in a fight or a game.

P

pensively (PEHN sihv lee) *adv.* thoughtfully.

persecution (pur suh KYOO shuhn) *n.* act of attacking others because of their beliefs or their ethnic background.

persisted (puhr SIHS tihd) *v.* refused to give up.

potential (puh TEHN shuhl) *n.* ability to develop into something or become something.

predominantly (prih DAHM uh nuhnt lee) *adv.* mainly.

procedures (pruh SEE juhrz) *n.* methods of doing things.

prodded (PRAHD id) *v.* urged on, here by poking with a stick.

profession (pruh FEHSH uhn) *n.* paid occupation.

profound (pruh FOWND) *adj.* very deep; felt strongly.

prolonged (pruh LAWNGD) *adj.* continuing for a long time.

propelled (pruh PEHLD) *v.* moved or pushed forward.

proposal (pruh POH zuhl) *n.* suggestion.

punctuality (puhngk choo AL uh tee) *n.* quality of being on time.

Q

quizzical (KWIHZ ih kuhl) *adj.* puzzled; baffled.

R

rancid (RAN sihd) *adj.* spoiled; rotten.

reassuring (ree uh SHUR ihng) *v.* used as *adj.* comforting.

receding (rih SEED ihng) *v.* used as *adj.* moving back.

recognition (rehk uhg NIHSH uhn) *n.* act of recognizing; realization of something.

recourse (REE kawrs) *n.* help in a difficult situation.

refuge (REHF yooj) *n.* place of safety.

renewable (rih NOO uh buhl) *adj.* able to be replaced by a new thing of the same sort.

renovation (rehn uh VAY shuhn) *n.* restoration of something to a better condition.

reservoir (REHZ uhr vwahr) *n.* large supply.

resolve (rih ZAHLV) *v.* decide.

revered (rih VIHRD) *v.* regarded with deep respect and affection.

ritual (RIHCH oo uhl) *n.* an established routine.

ruthless (ROOTH lihs) *adj.* cruel; without pity.

S

sacrifices (SAK ruh fys ihz) *n.* acts of giving up something of value to gain something else.

sheepishly (SHEEP ihsh lee) *adv.* awkwardly; with embarrassment.

shortages (SHAWR tihj ihz) *n.* situations in which needed things cannot be gotten in sufficient amounts.

simultaneously (sy muhl TAY nee uhs lee) *adv.* at the same time.

slack (slak) *adj.* loose.

solemn (SAHL uhm) *adj.* gloomy; serious.

solitude (SAHL uh tood) *n.* state of being alone.

spectators (SPEHK tay tuhrz) *n.* people who watch at an event.

splendor (SPLEHN duhr) *adj.* magnificence.

standard (STAN duhrd) *adj.* usual; regularly used or produced.

sterile (STEHR uhl) *adj.* barren; lacking in interest or vitality.

stubble (STUHB uhl) *n.* short, bristly growth.

supervision (soo puhr VIHZH uhn) *n.* function of overseeing.

supple (SUHP uhl) *adj.* easily bent; flexible.

suppressing (suh PREHS ihng) *v.* holding back.

survey (suhr VAY) *v.* look carefully in order to make a decision or gather information.

T

tentative (TEHN tuh tihv) *adj.* not fixed.

thermometer (thuhr MAHM uh tuhr) *n.* instrument that measures temperature.

torrent (TAWR uhnt) *n.* flood; rush.

traditions (truh DIHSH uhnz) *n.* accepted social attitudes and customs.

transfixed (trans FIHKST) *v.* used as *adj.* very still, as if nailed to the spot.

transition (tran ZIHSH uhn) *n.* change; passing from one condition to another.

treacherous (TREHCH uhr uhs) *adj.* unfaithful.

treacherously (TREHCH uhr uhs lee) *adv.* deceptively; unreliably.

tumult (TOO muhlt) *n.* uproar; noisy confusion, as in a crowd.

turbulent (TUHR byuh luhnt) *adj.* wild; disorderly.

U

unrequited (uhn rih KWY tihd) *adj.* not returned.

V

vainly (VAYN lee) *adv.* uselessly.

valiant (VAL yuhnt) *adj.* brave and determined.

version (VUHR zhuhn) *n.* a retelling from a certain point of view.

vigil (VIHJ uhl) *n.* overnight watch.

W

wafting (WAHFT ihng) *v.* used as *adj.* floating in the wind.

withered (WIHTH uhrd) *v.* used as *adj.* dried up.

wriggled (RIHG uhld) *v.* wiggled; squirmed.

Spanish Glossary

A

a traición *loc. adv.* de manera engañosa.

acariciar *v.* tocar suavemente.

agazaparse *v.* agacharse para ocultarse o protegerse de algo.

aislar *v.* provocar que alguien se sienta solo o no aceptado.

alardear *v.* hablar demasiado bien de uno mismo; fanfarronear.

alianza *sust.* pacto entre naciones, familias o individuos que tienen una causa común.

altitud *sust.* altura.

amenaza *sust.* peligro.

anónimo *adj.* que no está identificado con un nombre.

aparente *adj.* que parece y no es.

apocadamente *adv.* con vergüenza.

apremiar *v.* apresurar a alguien para que haga algo.

arduo *adj.* difícil.

arrogante *adj.* excesivamente convencido de la propia importancia.

arrugado *adj.* rugoso.

artilugio *sust.* aparato o máquina extraña.

atentamente *adv.* con gran concentración.

B

bárbaros *adj.* se dice de un grupo de personas consideradas incivilizadas e inferiores por otro grupo de personas u otra nación.

bruscamente *adv.* de manera descortés; con pocas palabras.

C

caballerosidad *sust.* código que regía el comportamiento de los caballeros en el que se exigía coraje, honor y disposición para brindar ayuda a los que la necesitaran.

capaz *adv.* que tiene la aptitud o características necesarias para hacer algo.

cargar *v.* transportar.

carismático *adj.* que posee energía, encanto o atractivo.

coacción *sust.* fuerza irresistible que obliga a hacer algo.

combate *sust.* asalto; partido.

comestible *adj.* que se puede comer.

compostura *sust.* calma; serenidad.

concentración *sust.* acción de pensar detenidamente en algo que uno está haciendo.

condena *sust.* acción de ser declarado culpable de un delito.

consecuencia *sust.* resultado de una serie de acciones.

consuelo *sust.* alivio.

contemplar *v.* considerar; mirar o pensar en algo con atención.

convencer *v.* asegurar que algo es verdad; persuadir.

converger *v.* acercarse a un punto.

convicción *sust.* certeza; creencia.

D

dedicar *v.* hacer algo en honor de otra persona.

deducir *v.* descontar; inferir.

desafiante *adj.* que se resiste a la autoridad.

desesperadamente *adv.* con gran agitación.

desilusión *sust.* desengaño; decepción.

desnutrición *n.* mala salud provocada por la falta de comida o la falta de comida sana.

despiadado *adj.* cruel; sin compasión.

detestable *adj.* desagradable.

disipar *v.* hacer que algo se evapore; hacer que algo desaparezca.

disputa *sust.* discusión.

distante *adj.* que no se implica emocionalmente; indiferente.

distorsión *sust.* acción de dar información falsa con el objeto de engañar a alguien.

distraídamente *adv.* de manera que muestra que no se está pensando en lo que está ocurriendo.

E

egocentrismo *sust.* amor propio excesivo que se caracteriza por hablar mucho de uno mismo.

eludir *v.* esquivar; evitar con astucia.

emprender *v.* empezar.

encuentro *sust.* acción de reunirse personalmente con alguien.

enrevesado *adj.* complicado.

escasez *sust.* situación en la que no se consiguen cantidades suficientes de las cosas que se necesitan.

escaso *adj.* en poca cantidad.

espectador *sust.* persona que observa un acontecimiento.

esplendor *sust.* magnificencia.

estándar *adj.* habitual; producido o usado normalmente.

estéril *adj.* que no da frutos; que no aporta nada.

etnia *sust.* cultura o nacionalidad común.

evacuación *sust.* proceso de sacar a las personas de una situación peligrosa.

evaporación *sust.* proceso por el cual un líquido se convierte en gas.

examinar *v.* observar algo con atención para tomar una decisión o para reunir información.

exótico *adj.* extraño; que viene de otro lugar.

expulsar *v.* obligar a abandonar un lugar.

F

facilitar *v.* hacer más sencillo; ayudar.

familiarmente *adv.* con mucha confianza.

fanatismo *sust.* prejuicio o intolerancia desmedida en defensa de algo.

fidelidad *sust.* lealtad.

flexible *adj.* que se dobla fácilmente; ágil.

flojo *adj.* suelto.

floreciente *adj.* próspero.

flotar *v.* moverse en el aire.

formidable *adj.* que provoca asombro; impresionante.

frenético *adj.* desenfrenado; fuera de control.

G

garantizar *v.* asegurar; prometer con seguridad.

H

hábitat *sust.* lugar donde vive una planta o un animal naturalmente.

habitual *adj.* que se hace por costumbre.

hechizar *v.* usar poderes mágicos; encantar.

horda *sust.* multitud de personas que se mueven en grupo.

hosco *adj.* malhumorado, huraño.

hospedar *v.* brindar alojamiento.

I

identidad *sust.* rasgos propios que caracterizan a una persona o una cosa.

idiosincrasia *sust.* particularidad.

ilegal *adj.* en contra de las normas oficiales.

impertinente *adj.* demasiado atrevido; arrogante.

impulsar *v.* mover o empujar hacia delante.

incesantemente *adv.* sin parar; de forma continuada.

incidente *sust.* acontecimiento.

inconsolable *adj.* que no puede ser tranquilizado; destrozado.

incrédulamente *adv.* de manera difícil de creer.

inmensamente *adv.* enormemente.

inquietante *adj.* amenazante.

inscripción *sust.* palabras escritas en algo.

insolencia *sust.* descaro; falta de respeto.

integración *sust.* proceso de reunir a personas de distintas razas en las escuelas y los vecindarios.

integridad *sust.* honestidad; honradez; rectitud.

intenso *adj.* que muestra sentimientos fuertes.

interplanetario *adj.* entre dos o más planetas.

intimidar *v.* asustar, por ejemplo, con amenazas o violencia.

intolerable *adj.* insoportable.

intrincado *adj.* complicado; con muchos detalles.

inútilmente *adv.* en vano.

L

legado *sust.* tradiciones que se transmiten.

liberación *sust.* acción de librar a alguien de la esclavitud, la cárcel u otras limitaciones.

literalmente *adv.* según el significado básico de la palabra.

M

malicia *sust.* maldad; crueldad.

maniobrar *v.* mover o manipular con habilidad.

marchitarse *v.* secarse.

meditadamente *adv.* de manera pensada.

mercadería *sust.* artículos que están a la venta en una tienda.

modificación *sust.* pequeño cambio.

monarca *sust.* gobernante único y absoluto.

monopolio *sust.* control exclusivo de un mercado.

O

oponentes *sust.* personas que están en lados opuestos en una pelea o un juego.

optativa *adj.* materia escolar que no es obligatoria.

P

paralizarse *v.* quedarse muy quieto, como clavado en el lugar.

penalizar *v.* quitar el derecho a algo.

permanecer *v.* quedarse.

perplejo *adj.* desconcertado; confundido.

persecución *sust.* acción de acosar a otros por sus creencias religiosas o su origen étnico.

persistir *v.* negarse a dejar de hacer algo.

potencial *sust.* que puede suceder o existir.

predominantemente *adv.* principalmente.

privación *sust.* carencia o falta de algo que se necesita; dificultad que resulta de la falta de algo.

procedimiento *sust.* método para hacer algo.

profesión *sust.* ocupación por la que una persona recibe un pago.

profundo *adj.* hondo; intenso.

prohibir *v.* no permitir hacer algo; no autorizar la ley.

prolongar *v.* continuar por un período largo.

propuesta *sust.* sugerencia.

provisional *adj.* experimental.

puntualidad *sust.* cualidad de llegar a tiempo.

R

rancio *adj.* estropeado, podrido.

rastrojo *sust.* residuo que queda en la tierra después de segar.

realzar *v.* mejorar.

reconfortante *adj.* tranquilizador.

reconocimiento *sust.* acto de reconocer; apreciación.

recurso *sust.* fuente de ayuda.

refugio *sust.* lugar que brinda protección.

renovable *adj.* una cosa vieja que se pude cambiar por otra nueva del mismo tipo.

renovación *sust.* acción de mejorar el estado de algo.

reprimir *v.* contener.

resarcimiento *sust.* algo que se hace para compensar un daño.

reserva *sust.* grandes existencias de algo.

resolver *v.* decidir.

resplandeciente *adj.* brillante.

retener *v.* retrasar, demorar.

retorcerse *v.* hacer movimientos serpenteantes.

retroceder *v.* moverse hacia atrás.

reverencia *sust.* acto mediante el que se muestra gran respeto y veneración.

riesgo *sust.* peligro.

ritual *sust.* rutina establecida.

S

sacrificio *sust.* acto de dar algo de valor para obtener alguna cosa.

semblante *sust.* rostro; apariencia.

simultáneamente *adv.* al mismo tiempo.

sobrecogimiento *sust.* sentimiento de temor y asombro.

soledad *sust.* falta de compañía.

solemne *adj.* serio; formal.

sombríamente *adv.* con desaliento; con tristeza.

soveranía *sust.* control; autoridad.

supervisión *sust.* acción de controlar que algo se haga o suceda de una determinada manera.

T

taciturno *adj.* desalentado, triste.

termómetro *sust.* instrumento que sirve para medir la temperatura.

torrente *sust.* riada; corriente.

tradiciones *sust.* actitudes y costumbres aceptadas.

traducir (mal) *v.* pasar algo de un idioma a otro (de manera incorrecta).

traicionero *adj.* engañoso; desleal.

transición *sust.* cambio; paso de un estado o condición a otro.

tumulto *sust.* confusión agitada y ruidosa; alboroto.

turbulento *adj.* confuso; desordenado.

U

unilateral *adj.* no correspondido, que solo viene de una parte.

V

valiente *adj.* que tiene coraje y resolución.

veloz *adj.* que se mueve rápidamente.

versión *sust.* interpretación que se da de algo desde otro punto de vista.

veteado *adj.* que tiene manchas de color o de luz.

vigilia *sust.* acción de estar despierto toda la noche.

Academic Vocabulary Glossary

The Academic Vocabulary Glossary is an alphabetical list of the Academic Vocabulary words found in this textbook. Use this glossary just as you would use a dictionary—to find out the meanings of words used in your literature class to talk about and write about literary and informational texts and to talk about and write about concepts and topics in your other academic classes.

For each word, the glossary includes the pronunciation, part of speech, and meaning. A Spanish version of the glossary immediately follows the English version. For more information about the words in the Academic Vocabulary Glossary, please consult a dictionary.

English

A

advance (ad VANS) *v.* move forward.

analyze (AN uh lyz) *v.* examine in detail.

articulate (ahr TIHK yuh layt) *v.* express clearly and specifically.

assess (uh SEHS) *v.* examine and judge the value of something; evaluate.

attribute (AT ruh byoot) *n.* quality or trait of someone or something.

C

characteristics (kar ihk tuh RIHS tihks) *n. pl.* distinguishing qualities or features.

circumstance (SUHR kuhm stans) *n.* condition or fact.

comment (KAHM ehnt) *v.* make a remark or observation on.

communicate (kuh MYOO nuh kayt) *v.* share information or ideas.

conclude (kuhn KLOOD) *v.* decide by reasoning.

D

delineate (duh LIHN ee ayt) *v.* describe in detail; portray.

E

element (EHL uh muhnt) *n.* essential part of something.

explain (ehk SPLAYN) *v.* give reasons for; make understandable.

extent (ehk STEHNT) *n.* degree to which something extends.

F

function (FUHNGK shuhn) *n.* purpose of a specific person or thing.

I

identify (y DEHN tuh fy) *v.* recognize and be able to say what someone or something is.

impact (IHM pakt) *n.* powerful effect.

implicit (ihm PLIHS iht) *adj.* suggested or understood but not stated directly.

insight (IHN syt) *n.* power to understand.

instance (IHN stuhns) *n.* occurrence or example.

interpret (ihn TUR priht) *v.* explain the meaning of.

N

narrative (NAR uh tihv) *adj.* that narrates or recounts; being in story form.

O

organizational (AWR guh nuh ZAY shuh nuhl) *adj.* pertaining to organization or structure.

P

perceive (puhr SEEV) *v.* be aware of through the senses; observe.

R

recur (rih KUR) *v.* occur again.

relevant (REHL uh vuhnt) *adj.* directly relating to the subject.

respond (rih SPAHND) *v.* say or write something as a reply.

reveal (rih VEEL) *v.* show something that was previously hidden.

S

sequence (SEE kwuhns) *n.* specific order in which things follow one another.

significant (sihg NIHF uh kuhnt) *adj.* important.

similar (SIHM uh luhr) *adj.* almost the same.

specific (spih SIHF ihk) *adj.* definite and particular.

structure (STRUHK chuhr) *n.* the way in which a set of parts is put together to form a whole.

T

technique (tehk NEEK) *n.* method of doing a particular task.

tradition (truh DIHSH uhn) *n.* a set of beliefs or customs that have been handed down for generations.

V

vision (VIHZH uhn) *n.* force or power of imagination.

Spanish

A

adelantar *v.* mover o llevar hacia adelante.

alcance *sust.* efecto o trascendencia de algo.

analizar *v.* examinar con detalle.

articular *v.* expresar de manera clara y concisa.

atributo *sust.* cualidad o propiedad de una cosa o una persona.

C

calcular *v.* examinar y juzgar el valor de una cosa; evaluar.

característica *sust.* cualidad o rasgo distintivo.

circunstancia *sust.* situación o hecho.

comentar *v.* explicar o interpretar algo.

comunicar *v.* compartir información o ideas.

D

decidir *v.* tomar una determinación.

delinear *v.* trazar; describir.

E

elemento *sust.* parte esencial de una cosa.

específico *adj.* definido y particular.

estructura *sust.* modo en que un conjunto de partes se ubican para formar un todo.

explicar *v.* hacer comprender una cosa; aclarar; clarificar.

F

función *sust.* tarea que cumple alguien o algo.

identificar *v.* reconocer y poder decir qué es algo o quién es alguien.

impacto *sust.* efecto fuerte.

implícito *adj.* sugerido o entendido pero no dicho directamente.

interpretar *v.* explicar el significado de una cosa.

N

narrativo *adj.* que narra o cuenta algo; estilo literario.

O

occasión *sust.* ejemplo; caso; acontecimiento.

organizativo *adj.* perteneciente a la organización o estructura.

P

percivir *v.* advertir; observar; comprender algo.

perspicacia *sust.* capacidad de comprensión.

R

relevancia *sust.* importancia.

relevante *adj.* que se relaciona directamente con el tema.

repetir *v.* ocurrir de nuevo.

replicar *v.* decir o escribir algo como respuesta.

revelar *v.* descubrir o manifestar algo que estaba oculto.

S

secuencia *sust.* orden específico en el que suceden las cosas.

significativo *adj.* importante.

similar *adj.* casi igual.

T

técnica *sust.* método para hacer una tarea en particular.

tradición *sust.* conjunto de creencias o costumbres que se transmiten de generación en generación.

V

visión *sust.* fuerza o poder de la imaginación.

ACKNOWLEDGMENTS

Quote by Shaquille O'Neal from "Officer Shaq? Online Education Scores with Sports Pros" by Dawn Papandrea from *msn.encarta*® Web site, accessed September 5, 2007, at http://encarta.msn.com/encnet/departments/elearning/?article=officershaq. Copyright © by Shaquille O'Neal. Reproduced by permission of **Alliance Sports Management & Agassi Enterprises.**

Quote by Mildred D. Taylor from Newbery Award Acceptance Speech, 1977. Copyright © 1977 by Mildred D. Taylor. Reproduced by permission of **American Library Association.**

From "Mongoose on the Loose" by Larry Luxner from *Américas,* vol. 45, no. 4, p. 3, July/August 1993. Copyright © 1993 by Américas. Reproduced by permission of *Américas,* bimonthly magazine published by the General Secretariat of the Organization of American States in English and Spanish.

From *Great Books for Girls* by Kathleen Odean. Copyright © 1997 by Kathleen Odean. Reproduced by permission of **Ballantine Books, a division of Random House, Inc.** and electronic format by permission of **The Spieler Agency/East.**

BART Bicycle Rules from *BART* Web site, accessed September 5, 2007, at http://www.bart.gov/guide/bikes/bikeRules.asp. Copyright © 2007 by Bay Area Rapid Transit. Reproduced by permission of **BART.**

BART Stations and Schedules from *BART* Web site, accessed September 5, 2007, at http://www.bart.gov/stations/quickplanner/extended.asp?o=WCRK&d=EMBAR&dm=6&dd=18&dt=2%3A00+PM&tm=departs. Copyright © 2007 by Bay Area Rapid Transit. Reproduced by permission of **BART.**

BART System Map from *BART* Web site, accessed September 5, 2007, at http://www.bart.gov/images/map500.gif. Copyright © 2007 by Bay Area Rapid Transit. Reproduced by permission of **BART.**

BART Ticket Guide from *BART* Web site, accessed September 5, 2007, at http://www.bart.gov/tickets/types/types.asp. Copyright © 2007 by Bay Area Rapid Transit. Reproduced by permission of **BART.**

"Names/Nombres" by Julia Alvarez. Copyright © 1985 by Julia Alvarez. First published in *Nuestro,* March 1985. All rights reserved. Reproduced by permission of **Susan Bergholz Literary Services, New York.**

"Chanclas" from *The House on Mango Street* by Sandra Cisneros. Copyright © 1984 by Sandra Cisneros. Published by Vintage Books, a division of Random House, Inc., and in hardcover by Alfred A. Knopf in 1994. All rights reserved. Reproduced by permission of **Susan Bergholz Literary Services, New York.**

"The Place Where Dreams Come From" by Sandra Cisneros. Copyright © 2003 by Sandra Cisneros. All rights reserved. Reproduced by permission of **Susan Bergholz Literary Service, New York.**

"Salvador Late or Early" from *Woman Hollering Creek* by Sandra Cisneros. Copyright © 1991 by Sandra Cisneros. Published by Vintage Books, a division of Random House, Inc., and originally in hardcover by Random House, Inc. All rights reserved. Reproduced by permission of **Susan Bergholz Literary Services, New York.**

"User Friendly" by **T. Ernesto Bethancourt** from *Connections: Short Stories,* edited by Donald R. Gallo. Copyright © 1989 by Ernesto Bethancourt. Reproduced by permission of the author.

"I Ask My Mother to Sing" from *Rose: Poems by Li-Young Lee.* Copyright © 1986 by Li-Young Lee. Reproduced by permission of **BOA Editions, Ltd.**

"Home" from *Maud Martha* by Gwendolyn Brooks. Copyright © 1993 by Gwendolyn Brooks. Published by Third World Press, Chicago. Reproduced by permission of **Brooks Permissions.**

Essay by Pat Mora. Copyright © 2007 by Pat Mora. Reproduced by permission of **Curtis Brown, Ltd.**

"Gold" by Pat Mora, www.patmora.com. Copyright © 1998 by Pat Mora. All rights reserved. Reproduced by permission of **Curtis Brown, Ltd.**

"Looking Beneath the Surface" by Jane Yolen. Copyright © 2007 by Jane Yolen. Reproduced by permission of **Curtis Brown, Ltd.**

"The Twelve Tasks of Heracles" from *Greek Myths for Young Children* by Marcia Williams. Copyright © 1991 by Marcia Williams. Reproduced by permission of **Candlewick Press, Inc., Cambridge, MA, on behalf of Walker Books Ltd., London.**

From *Merlin and the Dragons* by Jane Yolen, illustrated by Li Ming. Copyright © 1995 by Lightyear Entertainment, L.P. Reproduced by permission of **Cobblehill Books, an affiliate of Dutton Children's Books, a Division of Penguin Young Readers Group, A Member of Penguin Group (USA) Inc., www.penguingroup.com.**

"The Monsters Are Due on Maple Street" by Rod Serling. Copyright © 1960 by Rod Serling. Reproduced by permission of **Code Entertainment.**

Quote by Rod Serling. Copyright © by Rod Serling. Reproduced by permission of **Code Entertainment.**

Excerpt from *Brian's Song* by William Blinn. Copyright © 1971 by Screen Gems, a division of Columbia Pictures. Reproduced by permission of **CPT Holdings, Inc.**

"The Flight of Icarus" from *Stories of the Gods and Heroes* by Sally Benson. Copyright 1940 and renewed © 1968 by Sally Benson. All rights reserved. Reproduced by permission of **Dial Books for Young Readers, a Division of Penguin Young Readers Group, A Member of Penguin Group (USA) Inc., www.penguingroup.com.**

Song of the Trees by Mildred D. Taylor. Copyright © 1975 by Mildred Taylor. Reproduced by permission of **Dial Books for Young Readers, a Division of Penguin Young Readers Group, A Member of Penguin Group (USA) Inc.,** www.penguingroup.com.

Excerpt (retitled "The Only Girl in the World for Me") from *Love & Marriage* by Bill Cosby. Copyright © 1989 by Bill Cosby. Reproduced by permission of **Doubleday, a division of Random House.**

From "Elizabeth I" from *Ten Queens: Portraits of Women of Power* by Milton Meltzer. Copyright © 1998 by Milton Meltzer. Reproduced by permission of **Dutton Children's Books, A Division of Penguin Young Readers Group, A Member of Penguin Group (USA) Inc.**

From "Three Skeleton Key" by George G. Toudouze from *Esquire Magazine,* January 1937. Copyright 1937 by **Esquire Magazine / Hearst Communications, Inc.** All rights reserved. Esquire is a trademark of Hearst Magazines Property, Inc. Reproduced by permission of the publisher.

Excerpt (retitled "The Red Girl") from *Annie John* by Jamaica Kincaid. Copyright © 1985 by Jamaica Kincaid. Reproduced by permission of **Farrar, Straus and Giroux, LLC** and electronic format by permission of **The Wiley Agency, Inc.**

"That October" by D.H. Figueredo. Copyright © 2003 by D.H. Figueredo. Reproduced by permission of **Danilo Figueredo.**

Essay by Gary Paulsen. Copyright © 2007 by Gary Paulsen. Reproduced by permission of **Flannery Literary Agency.**

"The Dream of Good Fortune: Arabian Nights" from *More from Story Theatre* by Paul Sills. Copyright © 1981 by Paul Sills. CAUTION: Professionals and amateurs are hereby warned that "The Dream of Good Fortune" being fully protected under the copyright laws of the United States of America, the British Commonwealth countries, including Canada, and the other countries of the Copyright Union, is subject to a royalty. All rights, including professional, amateur, motion picture, recitation, public reading, radio, television and cable broadcasting, and the rights of translation into foreign languages, are strictly reserved. Any inquiry regarding the availability of performance rights, or the purchase of individual copies of the authorized acting edition, must be directed to Samuel French, Inc., 45 West 25th Street, NY, NY 10010 with other locations in Hollywood and Toronto, Canada. Reproduced by permission of **Samuel French, Inc.**

"The Dinner Party" by Mona Gardner from *The Saturday Review of Literature,* vol. 25, no. 5, January 31, 1941. Copyright © 1979 by **General Media International, Inc.** Reproduced by permission of the copyright holder.

"Sir Gawain and the Loathly Lady" from *The Oryx Multicultural Folktale Series: Beauties and Beasts* by Betsy Hearne. Copyright © 1993 by The Oryx Press. Reproduced by permission of **Greenwood Publishing Group, Inc., Westport, CT.**

Quote by Donald Hall. Copyright © by **Donald Hall.** Reproduced by permission of the author.

Quote by Virginia Hamilton from *In the Beginning.* Copyright © 1988 by Virginia Hamilton. Reproduced by permission of **Harcourt, Inc.**

Excerpt from "Arithmetic" from *The Complete Poems of Carl Sandburg.* Copyright © 1969, 1970 by Lilian Steichen Sandburg, Trustee. Reproduced by permission of **Harcourt, Inc.**

From "Tentative (First Model) Definitions of Poetry" from *Good Morning, America.* Copyright 1928 and renewed © 1956 by Carl Sandburg. Reproduced by permission of **Harcourt, Inc.**

"Ode to Family Photographs" from *Neighborhood Odes* by Gary Soto. Copyright © 1992 by Gary Soto. Reproduced by permission of **Harcourt, Inc.**

"Seventh Grade" from *Baseball in April and Other Stories* by Gary Soto. Copyright © 1990 by Gary Soto. Reproduced by permission of **Harcourt, Inc.**

From *The Crane Wife* retold by S. Yagawa, translated by Katherine Paterson. English translation from Japanese copyright © 1981 by Katherine Paterson. Reproduced by permission of **HarperCollins Children's Books, a division of HarperCollins Publishers, Inc.**

Excerpt from *You Learn by Living: Eleven Keys for a More Fulfilling Life* by Eleanor Roosevelt. Copyright © 1960 by Eleanor Roosevelt; copyright renewed © 1988 by Franklin A. Roosevelt. Reproduced by permission of **HarperCollins Publishers, Inc.**

"Master Frog" from *The Brocaded Slipper and Other Vietnamese Tales* by Lynette Dyer Vuong. Text copyright © 1982 by Lynette Dyer Vuong. Reproduced by permission of **HarperCollins Publishers, Inc.**

From *On the Banks of Plum Creek* by Laura Ingalls Wilder. Copyright © 1937 by Laura Ingalls Wilder; copyright renewed © 1965, 1993 by Roger Lea MacBride. Illustration copyright © 1953 and renewed © 1981 by Garth Williams. Reproduced by permission of **HarperCollins Publishers, Inc.**

From *King Arthur: The Sword in the Stone* by Hudson Talbott. Reproduced by permission of **HarperCollins Publishers, Inc.**

"288: I'm Nobody! Who are you?" from *The Poems of Emily Dickinson,* edited by Thomas H. Johnson. Copyright © 1951, 1955, 1979, 1983 by the President and Fellows of Harvard College. Published by The Belknap Press of Harvard University Press, Cambridge, Mass. Reproduced by permission of **Harvard University Press and the Trustees of Amherst College.**

"585: I Like to See It Lap the Miles" from *The Poems of Emily Dickinson,* edited by Thomas H. Johnson. Copyright © 1951, 1955, 1979, 1983 by the President and Fellows of Harvard University Press. Published by The Belknap Press of Harvard University Press, Cambridge, Mass. Reproduced by permission of **Harvard University Press and the Trustees of Amherst College.**

"Zoo" by Edward D. Hoch. Copyright © 1958 by King-Size Publications, Inc.; copyright renewed © 1986 by **Edward D. Hoch.** Reproduced by permission of the author.

"A Minor Bird" from *The Poetry of Robert Frost,* edited by Edward Connery Lathem. Copyright 1956 by Robert Frost; copyright 1928 and © 1969 by Henry Holt and Company, Inc. Reproduced by permission of **Henry Holt and Company, LLC.**

Quote by Langston Hughes from *The Big Sea*. Copyright 1940 by Langston Hughes and renewed © 1968 by Arna Bontemps and George Houston Bass. Reproduced by permission of **Hill and Wang, a division of Farrar, Straus and Giroux, LLC.**

"The War of the Wall" from *Deep Sightings and Rescue Missions* by Toni Cade Bambara. Copyright © 1996 by The Estate of Toni Cade Bambara. Reproduced by permission of **Pantheon Books, a division of Random House, Inc.**

"Who is Your Reader?" from *The Effects of Knut Hamsun on a Fresno Boy: Recollections and Short Essays* by Gary Soto. Copyright © 1983, 2001 by Gary Soto. Reproduced by permission of **Persea Books, Inc. (New York).**

From *Yeh-Shen: A Cinderella Story from China*, retold by Ai-Ling Louie. Text copyright © 1982 by Ai-Ling Louie. All rights reserved. Reproduced by permission of **Philomel Books, a division of Penguin Young Readers Group, a Member of Penguin Group (USA) Inc.** and electronic format by permission of **McIntosh and Otis, Inc.**

"Girls, and the Circle of Death" (retitled "Girls") from *How Angel Peterson Got His Name and Other Outrageous Tales about Extreme Sports* by Gary Paulson. Copyright © 2003 by Gary Paulsen. Reproduced by permission of **Random House Children's Books, a division of Random House, Inc., www.randomhouse.com** and CD-ROM format by permission of **Flannery Literary Agency.**

"The Dive" from *Stories: Finding Our Way* by René Saldaña, Jr. Copyright © 2003 by René Saldaña, Jr. Reproduced by permission of **Random House Children's Books, a division of Random House, Inc., www.randomhouse.com.**

"Narcissus" (retitled "Echo and Narcissus") from *Tales the Muses Told* by Roger Lancelyn Green. Copyright © 1965 by Don Bolognese. Published by The Bodley Head. Reproduced by permission of **The Random House Group Ltd.**

From "Overture" (retitled "The Power of Music") from *Nadja on My Way* by Nadja Salerno-Sonnenberg. Copyright © 1989 by **Nadja Salerno-Sonnenberg.** Reproduced by permission of the author.

From "Comic Relief" by Emily Costello, published in *Scholastic Action*, vol. 29, issue 10, February 20, 2006. Copyright © 2006 by **Scholastic Inc.** Reproduced by permission of the publisher.

"A Day's Wait" from *The Short Stories of Ernest Hemingway*. Copyright 1933 by Charles Scribner's Sons; copyright renewed © 1961 by Mary Hemingway. Reproduced by permission of **Scribner, an imprint of Simon & Schuster Adult Publishing Group.**

"Sarah Cynthia Sylvia Stout Would Not Take the Garbage Out" from *Where the Sidewalk Ends* by Shel Silverstein. Copyright © 2004 by Evil Eye Music, Inc. Reproduced by permission of the **Estate of Shel Silverstein and HarperCollins Children's Books.**

"Comments on the Short Story" by **Gary Soto.** Copyright © 2007 by Gary Soto. Reproduced by permission of the author and **BookStop Literary Agency.**

"Fish Cheeks" by Amy Tan. Copyright © 1987 by Amy Tan. Originally appeared in *Seventeen Magazine*, December 1987. Reproduced by permission of **Amy Tan and Sandra Dijkstra Literary Agency.**

From "An Unforgettable Journey" by Maijue Xiong from *Hmong Means Free: Life in Laos and America*, edited by Sucheng Chan. Copyright © 1994 by Temple University. All Rights Reserved. Reproduced by permission of **Temple University Press.**

"Abuelito Who" from *My Wicked, Wicked Ways* by Sandra Cisneros. Copyright © 1987 by Sandra Cisneros. Published by Third Woman Press and in hardcover by Alfred A. Knopf. All rights reserved. Reproduced by permission of **Third Woman Press and Susan Bergholz Literary Services, New York.**

"Amigo Brothers" from *Stories from El Barrio* by Piri Thomas. Copyright © 1978 by **Piri Thomas.** Reproduced by permission of the author.

"Can We Rescue the Reefs?" by Ritu Upadhyay from *Time for Kids*, vol. 6, no. 9, November 10, 2000. Copyright © 2000 by **Time for Kids, a division of Time, Inc.** Reproduced by permission of the publisher.

"Interview" by Sara Henderson Hay from *Story Hour*, University of Arkansas Press, 1982. Copyright © 1982, 1998 by Sara Henderson Hay. Reproduced by permission of **The University of Arkansas Press, c/o The Permissions Company.**

From *Barrio Boy* by Ernesto Galarza. Copyright © 1971 by **University of Notre Dame Press.** Reproduced by permission of the publisher.

Interview with Sandra Cisneros from *Interviews with Writers of the Post-Colonial World* by Reed Dasenbrock and Feroza Jussawalla. Copyright © 1992 by Reed Dasenbrock and Feroza Jussawalla. Reproduced by permission of **University Press of Mississippi.**

Quote by Marcia Williams from *Walker Books* Web site: http://www.walkerbooks.co.uk/Marcia-Williams. Copyright © 2005 by Marcia Williams. Reproduced by permission of **Walker Books.**

"A Mason-Dixon Memory" by Clifton Davis, slightly adapted from *Reader's Digest*, March 1993. Copyright © 1993 by **Mel White.** Reproduced by permission of the copyright holder.

"Pronunciation Key" from *World Book Online Reference Center* at www.worldbook.com. Reproduced by permission of **World Book, Inc.** "For Poets" by Al Young. Copyright © 1968 and 1992 by **Al Young.** Reproduced by permission of the author.

Sources Cited:

Quote by Olivia Coolidge from *Something About the Author*, vol. 1, edited by Anne Commire. Published by Gale Research Inc., Detroit, MI, 1971.

From *The Letters of Robert Frost to Louis Untermeyer*. Published by Holt, Rinehart and Winston, New York, 1963.

Quote by Carl Sandburg from *Contemporary Authors*, vol. 53, edited by James G. Lesniak. Published by Gale Research Group Inc., Farmington Hills, MI, 1992.

PICTURE CREDITS

The illustrations and photographs on the Contents pages are picked up from pages in the textbook. Credits for those can be found either on the textbook page on which they appear or in the listing below.

Picture Credits: Page iii (all), Sam Dudgeon/HRW Photo; **iv** (tl,tr), Sam Dudgeon/HRW Photo; (cr), Courtesy of Mabel Rivera; (bl), Courtesy of Hector Rivera; (br), Sam Dudgeon/HRW Photo; **v** (tr), Courtesy of Margaret McKeown; (cr, bl), Sam Dudgeon/ HRW Photo; vi (tl), Courtesy of Eric Cooper; (tr, cl, bl br), Sam Dudgeon/HRW Photo; **A4,** © Images.com/Corbis; **A5** (t),© Mira / Alamy; (b), (c) Corbis; **A6,** 20TH CENTURY FOX / THE KOBAL COLLECTION; **A7** (t), © E. Pollard/PhotoLink/Getty Images; (br), © blickwinkel/Alamy; **A8, A9** (bl), Private Collection/The Bridgeman Art Library;(b), Salim Madjd; **A10,** Kenneth Morris/ Covered Images via Getty Images; **A11** (l), Diana Ong/ SuperStock; (br), Polygram Filmed Entertainment/PhotoFest; **A12,** New Line/Saul Zaentz/Wing Nut Films/The Kobal Collection; **A13,** Private Collection/The Bridgeman Art Library; **A14,** Patrick Clark/Getty Images; **A15,** Blend Images/ SuperStock; **A16** (t), © Images.com/CORBIS; (b), Myrleen Ferguson Cate/PhotoEdit; **A17,** © Jeff Topping/Reuters/CORBIS; **A18,** © Barry Mead/Alamy; **A25,** © Dynamic Graphics Group/ Creatas/Alamy; **A26,** Macduff Everton/Getty Images; **A28,** Steve Hamblin/Alamy; **A29,** Luca DiCecco/Alamy; **A36,** © Masterfile; **A37,** © Jose Luis Pelaez Inc/Alamy; **2–3** © Images.com/Corbis; **3,** (bkgd), © Bob Barbout/Getty Images; **9,** The De Morgan Centre, London/ Bridgeman Art Library; **10,** Ron Stroud/Masterfile; **12,** © Mira / Alamy; **14** (bl), © Lebrecht Music and Arts Photo Library/Alamy; (br), © Mary Evans Picture Library/Alamy; **15,** © Siede Preis/Getty Images; **16,** © Siede Preis/Getty Images; **17,** © Dinodia/Omni-Photo Communications; **19,** © age fotostock/ Superstock; **20,** © Siede Preis/Getty Images; **21,** © Purestock/ Getty Images; **22,** © blickwinkel/Alamy; **24,** © Medio Images/ Getty Images; **25,** © Siede Preis/Getty Images; **26,** © Siede Preis/ Getty Images; **27,** Tony Sinclair/Nature Picture Library; **28,** K. Senani/OSF/Animals Animals/Earth Scenes; **31,** Comstock; **32,** © Stephen Dalton/Photo Researchers, Inc.; **34,** © Andrew Stweart/ Alamy; **35,** © Tim Flach/Getty Images; **39,** © Tim Flach/Getty Images; **40,** Kim Taylor/naturepl.com; **42,** David Kjaer/Naure Picture Library; **43,** © Chad Ehlers/Getty Images; **45,** J. Downer/ OSF/Animals Animals/Earth Scenes; **46,** © Tim Flach/Getty Images; **50,** © Images.com/CORBIS; **52,** (cr), Scott B. Rosen/HRW; (bl, br), Courtesy of Rene Saldana, Jr.; **54–55,** © A. Belov/CORBIS; **59,** Private Collection/The Bridgeman Art Library; **64,** Michael Grimm/Getty Images; **66,** (bl), © Bettman/Corbis; (br), Warner Bros. / The Kobal Collection; **68–69,** © Corbis; **71,** © Louis K. Meisel Gallery, Inc./CORBIS; **75,** Paul Burns/Getty Images; **78,** Image Source Black/Getty Images; **79,** © Bettman/Corbis; **83,** Hans Neleman/Getty Images; **86,** © Mc Pherson Colin/Corbis Sygma; **90,** DACS/The Bridgeman Art Library; **95,** ©Forrest J. Ackerman Collection/CORBIS; **98,** © Dale O'Dell/ Alamy; **101,** (tl), © Thomas Northcut/Getty Images; (r), © Jeff Spielman/Getty Images; **104,** S. Vitale, Ravenna, Italy Scala/Art Resource, New York ; **106,** © Archivo Iconografico, S.A/CORBIS; **108,** © Gianna Dagil Orti/CORBIS; **111,** (inset), Vanni/Art Resource, NY; (border) Dorling Kindersley; (cr), Vanni/Art Resource, NY; **112,** Copyright Dorling Kindersley; **118,** HRW Photo; **132,** (br), Cover image from *Visit to a Small Planet* by Gore Vidal. Copyright © 1956 and renewed © 1984 by Gore Vidal. Reproduced by permission of Dramatists Play Service, Inc.; **133,** (tl), Cover image from *City: A Story of Roman Planning and Construction* by David Macaulay. Copyright © 1974 by David Macaulay. Reproduced by permission

of Houghton Mifflin Company; (tr), Cover image from *Final Frontier: Voyages into Outer Space* by David Owen. Copyright © 2003 by Firefly Books Ltd. Reproduced by permission of NASA; (bl), Cover image from *Snakes* by John Bonnett Wexo. Copyright © 2006 by Wildlife Education, Ltd. Reproduced by permission of the publisher; (br), Cover image from *Inventing the Television* by Joanne Richter. Copyright © 2006 by Crabtree Publishing Company. Reproduced by permission of the publisher; **134–135** (all), 20TH CENTURY FOX / THE KOBAL COLLECTION; **134–135** (bkgd), Digital Vision/Getty Images; **135** (bkgd), © KitStock/ Getty Images; **141,** ©Purestock/Superstock; **142,** ©Diana Ong/ SuperStock; **144** (bkgd), © Bill Heinsohn/Alamy; (bl), © Tim Keating; **146,** © Gayle Ray/SuperStock; **148** (bl), John Medina/ NewsCom; (br), © Lake County Museum/CORBIS; **158,** © Juan Carlos Ulate/Reuters/Corbis; **160** (bl), Daniel A. Figuerdo; (br), Jupiter Images/Comstock/Alamy Images; **161,** Siede Preis/ Photodisc/Getty Images; **162** (l), © Siede Preis/Photodisc/Getty Images; (r), Siede Preis/Photodisc/Getty Images; **163,** Bettmann/ CORBIS; **164,** © blickwinkel/Alamy; **166,** Siede Preis/Photodisc/ Getty Images; **170,** Private Collection/The Bridgeman Art Library; **172,** (bkgd), Jupiter Images/Comstock/Alamy Images; (inset), Corey Wise/Alamy; **176,** © Pam Ingalls/CORBIS; **179,** © Morton Beebe/Corbis; **184,** ©Todd Davidson/Illustration Works/ Corbis; **186,** © Bettmann/CORBIS; **192,** © Comstock Images/ Alamy; **193,** Private Collection/The Bridgeman Art Library; **200,** © Karen Kasmauski/CORBIS; **202,** © E. Pollard/PhotoLink/Getty Images; **212,** © Ted Streshinsky/CORBIS; **213** (t), © Dr. Tony Brain/Photo Researchers, Inc.; (b), © Nicole Duplaix/CORBIS; **214,** © Robert Fried/Alamy; **224,** HRW photo; **238,** (bl), Cover image from Fever 1793 by Laurie Halse Anderson. Copyright © 2002 by Simon & Schuster Books for Young Readers. Reproduced by permission of the copyright holder; (br), Cover image from *Tangerine* by Edwards Bloor. Copyright © 1997 by Edward Bloor. Reproduced by permission of Harcourt, Inc; **239** (tl), Cover image from *Murals: Walls That Sing* by George Ancona. Copyright © 2003 by Cavendish Children's Books. Reproduced by permission of the publisher; (tr), Cover image from *Bill Nye the Science Guy's Great Big Book of Science featuring Oceans and Dinosaurs.* Copyright © 2005 by Bill Nye. Reproduced by permission of Hyperion Books for Children; (bl), Cover image from *Pride of Puerto Rico: The Life of Roberto Clemente* by Paul Robert Walker. Copyright © 1988 by Harcourt, Brace & Company. Reproduced by permission of Harcourt, Inc; **240–241,** Private Collection/The Bridgeman Art Library; **241** (bkgd), © Ian Mckinnell/Getty Images; **247,** Réunion des Musées Nationaux/ Art Resource, NY; **248,** H. Armstrong Roberst/Classic Stock; **250,** Farrell Grehan/CORBIS; **252,** Hulton Archive/Getty Images; **254,** Peter Matthews/Alamy; **255,** Galleria Sabuada, Turin, Italy Scala/ Art Resource, NY; **256–261** (border), Joe Cornish/Getty Images; **256** (inset), SuperStock, Inc.; **258** (inset), Private Collection, © Christopher Wood Gallery, London, UK; **260** (inset), Tate Gallery, London/Art Resouce, NY; **264,** Peter Maltz/Images.com/Corbis; **266** (t), Stockbyte/Getty Images; (b), © Randy Duchaine; **269,** James Porto/Getty Images; **274,** Benjamin Shearm/Getty Images; **276,** Akira Inoue/amana images/Getty Images; **280,** Private Collection/Snark/Art Resource, NY; **282** (bl), © Print Collector/HIP/The Image Works; (br), Byran Smith/Newscom; **283,** Adam Crowley/Getty Images; **284** (border), Adam Crowley/ Getty Images; (inset), Picture Collection, The Branch Libraries, The New York Public Library, Astor, Lenox and Tilden Foundations; **286,** Alinari Archives/The Image Works; **288** (bl), courtesy R. Lancelyn Green; (br), © Richard T. Nowitz/CORBIS; **289,** Digital Vision/Punchstock; **290,** photodisc/Punchstock; **291,** © Stapleton Collection/CORBIS; (border)Zen Shui/

Punchstock; **296,** © Tom & Dee Ann McCarthy/CORBIS; **298,** © NBC/courtesy Everett Collection; **301,** Private Collection/The Bridgeman Art Library; **302,** ©Richard H.Fox/SuperStock; **306,** © Hyacinth Manning/SuperStock; **308** (t), Nancy Kaszerman/Newscom; (b), Associated Press; **310–311,** Andre Jenny/Alamy; **315,** ©Gari Wyn Williams/Alamy; **316,** ©Andrew Holt/Alamy; **321,** ©Dynamic Graphics Group/Creatas/Alamy; **326–333** (border), ©Angelo Cavalli/Getty Images; **326,** FogStock,LLC/Index Stock Imagery; **329,** Private Collection/Bridgeman Art Library; **336,** Blickwinkel/Alamy; **338,** Associated Press; **339,** Andrea Booher/FEMA/Getty Images; **340, 341, 342, 345,** Associated Press; **346,** Lawrence Migdale Photography; **352,** Sam Dudgeon/HRW; **368** (tr), Cover image from *The Flag of Childhood* by Naomi Shihab Nye. Copyright © 1998 by Aladdin Paperbacks, an imprint of Simon & Schuster, Inc. Reproduced by permission of the publisher.; (br), Cover image from *User Unfriendly* by Vivian Vande Velde. Copyright ©1991 by Vivian Vande Velde, illustration copyright © 1991 by Gary Lippincott. Reproduced by permission of Harcourt, Inc.; **369** (tl), Cover image from *Second-Hand Dog: How to Turn Yours Into a First-Rate Pet* by Carol Lea Benjamin. Copyright © 1998 by Carol Lea Benjamin. Reproduced by permission of John Wiley & Sons, Inc.; (bl), Cover image from *Sylvia Stark: A Pioneer* by Victoria Scott and Ernest Jones. Copyright © 1991 by Victoria Scott. Reproduced by permission of Open Hand Publishing, Inc., photo by Victoria Smith/HRW; **370–371,** Kenneth Morris/Covered Images via Getty Images; **371** (br), Ron Chapple/Getty Images; **377,** Victor Baldizon/NBAE via Getty Images; **378** (bl), Allstar Picture Library /Alamy; (br), Photodisc/Getty Images; (bkgd), Hitoshi Nishimura/Getty Images; **382,** Bettmann/CORBIS; **385** (r), © Carrie Boretz/CORBIS; (bl), Ron Stroud/Masterfile; **390,** Darren Greenwood/Design Pics/CORBIS; **392** (inset), Comstock Images/Alamy; (bl), Bettmann/CORBIS; **397,** Americana Images/Super Stock; **398–399,** Salim Madjd; **403,** Bettmann/Corbis; **410** (bl), copyright Bill Eichner. Reprinted with permission of Susan Bergholz; Literary Services, New York, NY and Lamy, NM. All rights reserved.; (br), Jeremy Walker/Getty Images; **416,** © Neville Elder/CORBIS; **420,** Polygram/The Kobal Collection; **422** (bl), Courtesy of Catherine Noren; (br), © Visions of America/Alamy; **425,** Private Collection/The Bridgeman Art Library; **426,** Victoria & Albert Museum, London/Art Resource, NY; **429,** Polygram FilmedEntertainment/PhotoFest; **430,** Polygram/The Kobal Collection/Alex Bailey; **436,** Diana Ong/SuperStock; **438** (bl), University of Notre Dame Press; (br), Tony Savino/The Image Works; **440,** Polka Dot Images/Jupiter Images; **446,** © Oleksiy Maksymenkl/Alamy; **448** (t), Bildarchiv Preussischer Kulturbesitz/Art Resource, NY; (c), Reprinted by Permission of McIntosh and Otis, Inc.; (b), The Pittsburgh Press/Carnegie Mellon University Library of Special, Collections; **450,** Private Collection, Photo © Christie's Images/The Bridgeman Art Library; **453,** © Christie's Images/CORBIS; **454,** Private Collection/The Bridgeman Art Library; **461,** Victoria & Albert Museum, London/Art Resource, NY; **464,** © Twentieth Century Fox Film Corp./Photofest; **468,** Gary Braasch/CORBIS; **470,** Adrian Buck/Alamy; **472,** Steve Hamblin/Alamy; **476,** Courtesy of Save Our Stream; **482,** Victoria Smith/HRW; **497** (tl), Cover image from *Children of the Wild West* by Russell Freedman. Copyright © 1983 by Russell Freedman. All rights reserved. Reproduced by permission of Clarion Books, an imprint of Houghton Mifflin Company. Photo Victoria Smith/HRW; (tr), Cover image from *The Circuit* by Francisco Jimenez. Copyright © 1997 by Francisco Jimenez. Reproduced by permission of University of New Mexico Press.; (bl), Cover image from *Chinese Cinderella* by Adeline Yen Mah. Copyright © 1999 by Adeline Yen Mah. Reproduced by permission of Random House Children's

Books, a division of random House, Inc., www.randomhouse.com.; (br), Cover image from *Elizabeth I and the Spanish Armada* by Colin Hynson. Copyright © 2006 by School Specialty Publishing. Reproduced by permission of the publisher.; **498–499,** New Line/Saul Zaentz/Wing Nut Films/The Kobal Collection; **505,** © Purestock/SuperStock; **506** (t), © Fridmar Damm/zefa/CORBIS; (b), © Gregory Pace/CORBIS; **508** (l, r), Scott B. Rosen/HRW; (bkgd), © Thinkstock/CORBIS; **510** (bl), Chris Lawrence; (br), Vintage front cover from *DOWN THESE MEAN STREETS* by Piri Thomas. Used by permission of Alfred A. Knopf, a division of Random House, Inc.; **511** (l, r), Scott B. Rosen/HRW; **513,** © Popperfoto/Alamy; **515** (l, r), **516, 517,** Scott B. Rosen/HRW Photo; **519,** ©Superstock/Alamy; **520** (l, r), Scott B. Rosen/HRW Photo; **526** (bkgd), © G P Bowater/ALAMY; **532,** © Sharon Dominick/IstockPhoto; **536,** Museum of Art, Serpukhov, Russia/The Bridgeman Art Library; **538** (bkgd), © David Muench/CORBIS; (bl), reprinted by permission of Penguin Young Readers Group; **541** (tr), Private Collection/The Bridgeman Art Library; **543,** © Eran Yardeni/Alamy; **544** (inset), © SuperStock, Inc.; (l), © Eran Yardeni/Alamy; **546,** © Eran Yardeni/Alamy; **549, 551, 552,** © Renee Morris/Alamy; 556, Saint Frederick High School Yearbook; **558** (bl), © Warner Bros./PhotoFest; (br), © Ian Shaw/Alamy; **560,** Saint Frederick High School Yearbook; **564** (bkgd), © David Madison/Newsport/CORBIS; (inset), © Mike Blake/Reuters/CORBIS; **574,** davies & starr/Getty Images; **575,** Tate, London/Art Resource, NY; **578,** Elly Godfroy/Alamy; **580** (br), Associated Press; **584** (bl), Hulton Archive/Getty Images; (br), Frank Driggs Colletion/Getty Images; **586,** SuperStock, Inc.; **587** (tr), Craig Aurness/CORBIS; (bl), Robert W. Kelley/Time & Life Pictures/Getty Images; **590** (t), ©Andrew Downes; (b), Courtesy Gary Soto; **591,** Macduff Everton/Getty Images; **592** (b), Ronnie Kaufman/CORBIS; (bkgd), James Randklev/Getty Images; **594,** Images.com/Corbis; **596** (tl), Bettmann/Corbis; (cr), ©iStockphoto.com/stasvolik; (bl), Alice Ochs/Michael Ochs Archives/Getty Images; **604** (bl), E.O. Hoppe/CORBIS; (br), © Dave G. Houser/CORBIS; **605,** Bruce Dale/Getty Images; **608** (bl), Courtesy of Donald Hall; (br), Paul Rezendes; **609–610,** Jerry Driendl Photography/Panoramic Images; **612,** Bryce Harper; **614,** Associated Press; **615,** Corbis/Punchstock; **616–617,** Sami Sarkis Lifestyles/Alamy; **620,** Grace Davies; **621,** © Grace/zefa/CORBIS; **623** (t), PhotoDisc/PunchStock; (b), Digital Vision, Ltd. /SuperStock; **632,** Victoria Smith/HRW **644** (bl), Cover image from *Brian's Song* by Blinn William. Copyright © 1971 by Screen Gems, a division of Columbia Pictures. Reproduced by permission of Bantam Books, a division of Random House, Inc., www.randomhouse.com; (br), Cover image from *A Fury of Motion: Poems for Boys* by Charles Ghigna. Copyright © 2003 by Boyds Mills Press, Inc. Reproduced by permission of the publisher; **645** (tr), Cover image from *Long Road to Freedom: Journey of the Hmong* by Linda Barr. Copyright © 2005 by Red Brick Learning. Reproduced by permission of the copyright holder; (bl), Cover image from *Legends in Sports: Muhammad Ali* by Matt Christopher. Copyright © 2005 by Matt Christopher Royalties, Inc. Reproduced by permission of Little, Brown and Company; (br), Cover image from *Jim Thorpe: Original All-American* by Joseph Bruchac. Copyright © 2006 by Joseph Bruchac. All rights reserved. Reproduced by permission of Dial Books for Young Readers, a Division of Penguin Books for Young Readers, a Division of Penguin Group (USA) Inc., 345 Hudson Street, New York, NY 10014, www.penguin.com; **646** (tl), Adam Gault/Digital Vision.Getty Images; (bl), Creatas/Punchstock; **647** (tr), Patrick Clark/Getty Images; (br), Bryan Mullenix/Iconica/Getty Images; (bkgd), © JUPITERIMAGES/ Brand X / Alamy; **652,** © Michael Newman; **656,** Blend Images/SuperStock; **658,** Johannes

Kroemer/Getty Images; **659,** Don Farrall/Photodisc/Getty Images; **660,** Reza Estakhrian/Getty Images; **661** (t), Kevin Hatt/ Photonica/Getty Images; (b), Darryl Leniuk/Digital Vision/Getty Images; **664,** Luca DiCecco/Alamy; **666,** 2007 Jupiter Images; **667** (inset), Peter Dazeley/Getty Images; (bkgd), Peter Dazeley/ Getty Images; **670,** Ei Katsumata/Alamy; **672** (c), Stockbyte Platimun/Alamy; (b), Visions of America, LLC/Alamy; **678,** JG Photography/Alamy; **686,** © HRW Photo; **696** (tl), Cover image from *Sports Illustrated for Kids,* July 2007. Copyright © 2007. Reproduced by permission of Time, Inc.; **697** (bl), © Image Source/Corbis; (br), Suza Scalora/PhotoDisc/Getty Images; **698– 699,** © Images.com/CORBIS; **704,** Myrleen Ferguson Cate/ PhotoEdit; **705** (both), M Stock/Alamy; **706,** Design Pics/Corbis; **708,** ©John Davisson/CORBIS; **710,** © Jeff Topping/Reuters/ CORBIS; **712** (t), © Juan Carlos Ulate/Reuters/CORBIS; (b), Brand X Pcitures/Alamy; **716,** © Myrleen Ferguson Cate/PhotoEdit, Inc.; **719,** Enigma/Alamy; **720,** Courtesy of Daniel Cayce; **722,** ©Don Hammond/Design Pics/Corbis; **724** (inset), ©George Doyle/ Stockbyte/Getty Images; (c), ©Ryan McVay/Getty Images; **729,** Wire Image Stock/Masterfile; **730** (inset), Christina Kennedy/ Getty Images; **740,** HRW Photo; **752** (tl), Cover image from *911: The Book of Help* by Marianne Carus and Marc Aronson, edited by Michael Cart. Copyright © 2002 by Marianne Carus and Marc Aronson. Reproduced by permission of Cricket Books/Marcato. photo, Victoria Smith/HRW; (bl), Cover image from *The Acorn People* by Ron Jones. Copyright © 1976 by Ron Jones, cover art copyright © 1990 by Ben Stahl. Reproduced by permission of Random House Children's Books, a division of Random House, Inc., www.randomhouse.com, photo,Victoria Smith/HRW; **753** (tl), Cover image from *Machu Picchu* by Elizabeth Mann. Copyright © 2000 by Mikaya Press, Inc. Reproduced by permis- sion of the publisher; (tr), Cover image from *A Walk Through the Heavens: A Guide to Stars and Constellations and their Legends* by Milton D. Heifetz and Wil Tirion. Copyright © 1996 by Cambridge University Press. Reproduced by permission of the publisher; (bl), Cover image from *How would you Survive in the Middle Ages* by Fiona Macdonald. Copyright © 1995 by The Salariya Book Co, Ltd. Reproduced by permission of Franklin Watts, a division of Scholastic, Inc.; (br), Cover image from *Facing the Lion: Growing*

Up Masai on the African Savanna by Joseph Lemasolai Lekuton and Herman Viola. Copyright © 2003 by National Geographic Society. Reproduced by permission of the copyright holder.; **754–755,** © Barry Mead/Alamy; **755** (br), © Barry Mead/Alamy; **760,** Edmund Nägele/photolibrary; **761,** © Dave Wheeler/ Trevillion Images; **762,** TonyHowell/photolibrary; **764** (t), R. Strange/PhotoLink/Getty Images; (b), © Hulton-Deutsch Collection/CORBIS; **766,** Private Collection/Bridgeman Art Library; **768** (l), Courtesy of Hudson Talbott; (r), © Massimo Listri/CORBIS; **771,** © Birmingham Museums and Art Gallery/The Bridgeman Art Library; **772,** © Richard T. Nowitz/CORBIS; **774– 775,** © Franz-Marc Frei/CORBIS; **775** (r), ©Art Media-Lambeth Palace Library/Heritage-Images/The Image Works; **777,** © Richard T. Nowitz/CORBIS; **779,** Mary Evans Picture Library/ EDWIN WALLACE/Everett Collection; **780,** © Richard T. Nowitz/ CORBIS; **786,** ©2004 Charles Walker/TopFoto/The Image Works; **789,** ©Alex Kouprianoff/AA World Travel/TopFoto/The Image Works; **794,** Lightworks Media/Alamy; **796** (l), Jason Stemple; (r), © Adam Woolfitt/Robert Harding World Imagery/CORBIS; **804,** Theo Allofs/Getty Images; **810,** Time Life Pictures/Stringer/Getty Images; **812** (bl), Courtesy Betsy Hearne; (br), © Historical Picture Archive/CORBIS; **813,** Robert Glusic/Getty Images; **816,** tompiodesign.com/Alamy; **818** (bkgd), Robert Glusic/Getty Images; (c), Scala / Art Resource, NY; **828,** RK Studio/Blend Images/Getty Images; **840** (tl), Cover image from *Sir Gawain and the Green Knight, Pearl,* and *Sir Orfeo* by J.R.R. Tolkien. Copyright © 1975 by J.R.R. Tolkien. Reproduced by permission of Random House, Inc., www.randomhouse.com; (tr), Cover image from *The Lightning Thief* by Rick Riordan. Copyright © 2005 by Hyperion Books for Children. Reproduced by permission of the publisher; (bl), Cover image for *The Nightingale that Shrieked* by Kevin Crossley-Holland. Copyright © 1998. Reproduced by permission of Oxford University Press; (br), Cover image from *Sword of the Rightful King* by Jane Yolen. Copyright © 2004 by Harcourt, Inc. Reproduced by permission of the publisher; **841** (bl), Cover image from *Sundiata: An Epic of Old Mali* by D.T. Niane. Copyright © 2003. Reproduced by permission of Pearson Education, Ltd.

INDEX OF SKILLS

The boldface page numbers indicate an extensive treatment of the topic.

WRITING STRATEGIES AND APPLICATIONS

READ ON: FOR INDEPENDENT READING

INDEX OF AUTHORS AND TITLES

ACKNOWLEDGMENTS:

Sources Cited:

Quote by Kathleen Krull from *Kathleen Crull, Children's Book Author* Web site, accessed November 15, 2007 at http://www.kathleenkrull.com/author.html.

Quote by Allan Knee from *Word: The Official Blog of READ and WRITE magazines* Web site, accessed November 15, 2007 at http://www.weeklyreader.com/readandwriting/PermaLink,guid,f9b4c893-fa94-480e-9ba5-b24ed84e899b.aspx.